THE
CAMBRIDGE
MEDIEVAL HISTORY

VOLUME V

THE CAMBRIDGE
MEDIEVAL HISTORY

PLANNED BY
J.B.BURY

EDITED BY
J.R.TANNER
C.W.PRÉVITE-ORTON
Z.N.BROOKE

VOLUME V
CONTEST OF EMPIRE AND
PAPACY

CAMBRIDGE
AT THE UNIVERSITY PRESS
1968

Published by the Syndics of the Cambridge University Press
Bentley House, 200 Euston Road, London, N.W. 1
American Branch: 32 East 57th Street, New York, N.Y. 10022

Standard Book Number: 521 04537 1

First Edition 1926
Reprinted with corrections 1929
Reprinted 1943 1948 1957 1964
1968

Printed in Great Britain
at the University Printing House, Cambridge
(Brooke Crutchley, University Printer)

PREFACE.

IN the Preface to Volume IV the Editors referred to the loss which the enterprise had sustained by the death of Sir Edwin Pears before he saw his chapter in type, and of M. Ferdinand Chalandon when he had only seen the first proofs of his chapters, although in this case they were able to obtain a second revision by Madame Chalandon of her husband's proofs. They are also indebted to her for a similar revision in the present volume. But another misfortune has befallen Volume V, for Count Ugo Balzani died before he could revise his chapters, and this duty has been discharged by the Editors themselves. They were obliged to abbreviate them to a certain extent, but except in one instance, duly indicated in a foot-note, they made no real change in the author's statement of his conclusions.

They wish to express their gratitude to Mrs Stenton for undertaking the chapter on Henry II of England at short notice, and for the promptitude with which she completed the work; to Mr C. J. B. Gaskoin of Jesus College for preparing the maps; and to Mr C. C. Scott, Sub-Librarian of St John's College, for indispensable assistance in preparing the bibliographies for the press. The index has been compiled by Mr E. H. F. Mills of St John's College, the Librarian of the University of Birmingham.

For the Corrigenda to Volume IV, the Editors are mainly indebted to the kindness of Mr E. W. Brooks.

Since this Preface was in type, the Cambridge History School has suffered a grievous loss by the death of Mr W. J. Corbett of King's College, whose original researches in English history have already lent distinction to Volumes II and III, and whose last work appears in the present volume. Even if his researches on Domesday should never now be published, his main conclusions will be found in the *Cambridge Medieval History*.

J. R. T.
C. W. P.-O.
Z. N. B.

January, 1926.

INTRODUCTION.

THE century and a half, roughly from 1050 to 1200, with which this volume is concerned, follows on a period when the disorganisation and anarchy of the ninth century had barely been made good. Order had been to some extent restored; the desire for order and for peace was at any rate widespread. The opportunity for fruitful development, both in the sphere of ecclesiastical and of secular government, and also in those pursuits which especially needed peace for their prosecution, such as culture and commerce, had now arrived. We have to deal, then, with a period, on the one hand, of new movements and new ideas—the appearance of new monastic orders, a renaissance of thought and learning, the rise of towns and the expansion of commerce; on the other, of consolidation and centralisation—the organisation of the monarchical government of the Church, the development of monarchical institutions in the various countries of Europe, and, to give direction and solidity to the whole, the revived study of Civil and Canon Law. Finally, and most novel of all, we see Europe at once divided by the great conflict of Empire and Papacy and united by the Crusades in the holy war against the infidel. The former as well as the latter implies a conception of the unity of Western Christendom, a unity which found expression in the universal Church. For the Church alone was universal, European, international; and, as its institutions begin to take more definite form, the more deeply is this character impressed upon them.

The volume opens with a chapter on the Reform of the Church, which was not merely a prelude to, but also a principal cause of, the striking events that followed; for in the pursuit of the work of reform the Papacy both developed its own organisation and was brought into conflict with the secular power. In the first half of the eleventh century, it had been entirely dominated by the secular interests of the local nobles. It had been rescued by the Emperor Henry III, and Pope Leo IX had immediately taken his natural place as leader of the reform movement. When he undertook personally, in France, Germany, and Italy, the promulgation and enforcement of the principles of reform, he made the universality of papal power a reality; the bishops might mutter, but the people adored. The Papacy was content to take a subordinate place while Henry III was alive; Henry IV's minority worked a complete change. The first great step was the Papal Election Decree of Nicholas II, and, though the attempt of the Roman nobles to recover their influence was perhaps the immediate cause, the Papacy took the opportunity to shake off imperial control as well. An opening for interference still remained in the case of a disputed election, as was clearly shewn in the contest of Innocent II and Anacletus II, and especially in that of Alexander III and Victor IV. This gap was closed by the Third Lateran Council in 1179, which decreed that whoever obtained the votes of two-thirds of the cardinals should be declared Pope.

The Papal Election Decree had a further result. By giving to the cardinals the decision at an election, and reducing other interests to a merely nominal right of assent, it raised the College of Cardinals to a position of the highest importance. There were normally at this time 7 (later 6) cardinal-bishops, 28 cardinal-priests, and 18 cardinal-deacons, and, unless they were employed on papal business, their functions were confined to Rome. Leo IX had surrounded himself with cardinals who were reformers like himself; they composed the chief element in the Pope's Council, or, as it came to be called, the Curia. But he could not find them in Rome, and had to recruit them from the chief reforming centres, especially north of the Alps. As they were, and continued to be, drawn from different countries, so in them was displayed the international character of the Roman Church; and from their number, in almost every case, was the Pope elected. A further development came when Alexander III instituted the practice of including bishops from different parts of Europe among the cardinals; for the regular duties and residence of such cardinals were no longer in Rome itself.

The freedom of episcopal elections in general was in the forefront of the reform programme. The papal policy was to restore canonical election "by clergy and people," a vague phrase which received its definition at Rome in the Election Decree. During the twelfth century a similar definition was arrived at for other sees. The cathedral chapter, helped by its corporate unity, and especially by the fact that it constituted the permanent portion of the bishop's *concilium* and that its consent was necessary in any disposition of the property of the see, established itself as the electoral body. To the clergy of the diocese and the lay vassals of the see was left, as at Rome, only the right of assent and acclamation. The chapter thus became the local counterpart of the College of Cardinals. The Papacy was principally concerned with the freedom of elections, and did not yet claim the right of appointment for itself, except in cases of dispute. The Third Lateran Council, which gave the decision at a papal election to a majority vote, expressly decreed that elsewhere the old rule of the "maior et sanior pars" was to hold good; for, with the exception of Rome, there was a higher authority which could decide in cases of dispute.

Leo IX had initiated the campaign of reform at Councils in France and Germany. The Councils over which the Popes presided passed decrees which were to be universally binding. Usually they were held in Rome, and regularly in Lent by Gregory VII. In them, besides the Curia, any leading ecclesiastic who happened to be at the papal court, whether on a visit or in obedience to a personal summons, took part, just as the nobles did in a king's Council. A further development occurred in the twelfth century. Hitherto all the Councils recognised by the Western Church as Ecumenical had taken place in the East. The schism of 1054 had cut off the Greek Church from communion with Rome, and in the twelfth century three Councils were held, each of them at Rome in the Lateran basilica, which, owing to the importance of their business and the general rather than particular summonses which were issued, were included later among the Ecumenical Councils. The First Lateran Council in 1123 ratified the Concordat of Worms, the Second in 1139 solemnised the end of a schism, and the Third in 1179 the end of another and a greater one.

The next step was the local enforcement of the papal decrees. The Church had its local officials—archbishops, bishops etc.—and they were expected both to promulgate the decrees at local synods and to enforce their execution. It soon became clear that the bishops regarded themselves as anything but the docile officials of the central government, and the Papacy had to establish its authority and to work out a coordinated system of government by which its policy could be carried into effect. First of all, for the Pope could no longer do everything in person like Leo IX, legates were sent to act in his name, travelling about, like the Carolingian *missi*, with overriding authority, to investigate the local churches and put into force the papal decrees. The appointment of legates for this general work tends more and more to take a permanent form, and soon the post of permanent legate—a position of high honour and at the same time of personal responsibility to the Pope—becomes the prerogative of the leading ecclesiastics in each country. But the Pope still continued to send legates from Rome, both as ambassadors to temporal sovereigns and as functionaries with special commissions; these legates *a latere* as direct papal agents again had overriding powers. It was not sufficient, however, for the Pope to control the local officials through his representatives. He insisted on their personal contact with himself. Visits *ad limina* were first of all encouraged and then directly ordered, and archbishops were expected to receive the *pallium* from the Pope in person.

It is impossible to say how far at any time this development of papal authority was deliberate, and how far it arose out of the practical exigencies of the moment. It became conscious at any rate with Gregory VII, though even with him the moving cause at first was to enforce the principles of reform. Opposition, whether from the local officials or from the lay power, led to a definition of the bases on which this authority rested and the sphere within which it could be exercised. The decretals, especially the Forged Decretals, provided a solid foundation, and to build upon this came opportunely the revived study of the Canon Law. It is not a question of a finished legal system, but of a continuous process of construction, in which the legal training of Popes like Urban II and Alexander III was of great value. Collections of decretals and opinions, of which Gratian's was the most complete, were continually being added to by the decrees of Roman Councils and the decisions of Popes given in their letters. This led to uniformity in ritual also, to the victory of the Roman use over local customs; for here again it was the Roman that was to be universal.

In the papal government, even on its ecclesiastical side, there is a general resemblance to the secular governments of the day. Like a lay monarch, the Pope was concerned with the organisation of central and local government, with the formation of a legal system, and with the recognition of his overriding jurisdiction. When we come to the secular side of papal government, the resemblance is still more close. Both as landlord and overlord the Pope acted as any secular ruler, though payments in money and kind are the usual services rendered to him, rather than military service; for this he was really dependent on external assistance. The problem of finance faced him, as it faced every secular ruler. The work of government, both ecclesiastical and secular, involved the expenses of government, and, though in ordinary times the revenue from the Papal States might be sufficient, a period of conflict, by increasing expenditure or by preventing the Pope from obtaining his ordinary revenues, would create serious financial difficulties. This was especially the case with Urban II, and still more with Alexander III, in the crisis of the conflict with the Empire; and, in the interval of peace, the Pope was seriously embarrassed by the sustained effort of the Roman people to obtain self-government.

We have a detailed account of various sources of papal revenue at the end of our period in the *Liber Censuum* drawn up under the direction of the *camerarius* Cencius, afterwards Pope Honorius III, in the year 1192. Besides the revenue from the papal domain proper, a *census* was received: (1) from monasteries who had placed themselves under the papal "protection," and who in the course of the twelfth century gained exemption from the spiritual as well as the temporal control of their diocesans ; (2) from some lay rulers and nobles, who put themselves under papal "protection" or, like the kings of Aragon and the Norman rulers of South Italy and Sicily, recognised papal overlordship; (3) in the form of Peter's Pence, from England since Anglo-Saxon times, and, in the twelfth century, from Norway, Sweden, and some other countries as well. But the *census* provided only a relatively small revenue, and this was difficult to collect; there were frequent complaints of arrears of payment, especially with regard to Peter's Pence. On the other hand, the papal expenditure was often heavy. Alexander III had frequently to have recourse to borrowing; and his complaints about some of his creditors seem to have an echo in the decree against usury at the Third Lateran Council. In its difficulties the Papacy had to depend upon the voluntary offerings of the faithful, especially from France, on subsidies from the Normans, or on the support of a wealthy Roman family ; thus the Pierleoni constantly supplied the Popes with money, until one member of the family, Anacletus II, was defeated in his attempt to ascend the papal throne. We are still in the early days of papal financial history. Not yet were the visitation offerings from bishops made compulsory, and the *servitia* taxes and annates had not yet been introduced. Nor did the Popes claim the right to tax the clergy, though perhaps the first step to this was taken in the second half of the twelfth century, when prohibitions were issued against the taxation of the clergy by lay rulers without papal consent. At any rate the desire to finance the Crusades soon led them to assert the right.

As the Reform Movement had led directly to the creation of a centralised government of the Church, so too it led, almost inevitably, to the contest for supremacy between the Papacy and its counterpart on the secular side, the Empire. Those ecclesiastics whom the Pope expected to be his obedient officials in the local government of the Church were already the obedient officials of the Empire both in its central and its local government. The Pope was on strong ground in insisting that the spiritual duties of the bishop were his primary consideration. But the Emperor was on strong ground too. The ecclesiastical nobles were an essential part of the economic framework and the political machinery of the Empire, and to justify his authority over them the Emperor could point to an almost unbroken tradition. The relative importance of spiritual and temporal considerations in the medieval mind gave an initial advantage to the Pope, and in the end the victory. On the other hand, the Emperor could appeal not only to the iron law of necessity, but to the medieval reverence for custom and precedent. Henry IV, moreover, could not forget that the Papacy had itself been subject to his father, and it was his object to recover what he considered to be his lawful authority. With this aim he deliberately provoked the contest. The details of the struggle are described in several chapters in this volume, and need only be briefly alluded to here. Henry's challenge was taken up by his greater opponent, Pope Gregory VII, who in his turn claimed the supreme power for the Papacy; there could be no real peace until the question of supremacy was settled. Though on this issue the first contest was indecisive, the Papacy registered a striking advance. The Concordat of Worms marked a definite limitation of imperial authority over the ecclesiastical nobility, and it was followed by the reigns of Lothar III and Conrad III, when the German ruler was too complaisant or too weak to press his claims. The Pope was emboldened to take the offensive, and Hadrian IV threw down the challenge that was taken up by Frederick Barbarossa. The positions were reversed, but again the challenger found himself faced by a greater opponent, who again defended himself by asserting his own supremacy. Once more the result was indecisive. The Pope had a single cause to maintain, the Emperor a dual one. Henry IV was defeated by revolt in Germany, Frederick Barbarossa by revolt in Italy, and both alike had been forced to recognise the impossibility of maintaining a subservient anti-Pope. But the greatness of Frederick was never so conspicuous as in his recovery after defeat, and his son Henry VI seemed to be on the point of making the Empire once more supreme when death intervened to ruin the imperial cause. Herein was revealed the second great asset of the Papacy. Built on the rock of spiritual power, the weakness or death of its head was of little permanent moment. The Empire, however, depended on the personality of each of its rulers, and the transference of authority on the deaths of Henry III and Henry VI was on each occasion disastrous. During the minority of Henry IV, the Papacy had built up its power; in the minority of Frederick II, Innocent III was Pope.

In this struggle of Empire and Papacy no insignificant part was played by the Norman rulers of South Italy and Sicily, whose history falls exactly within the compass of this volume. Frequently did they come to the help of the Papacy in its extremity, and skilfully did they make use of papal exigencies to improve their own position. Only once did the Pope whom they supported fail to maintain himself; and the victory of Innocent II over Anacletus II, chosen by a majority of the cardinals and backed by Norman arms, was in many respects unique. Then, and then only, did Pope and Emperor combine against the Normans, but there was no stability in an alliance so unusual. In the Sicilian kingdom were displayed the peculiar characteristics of the Norman race—its military prowess and ferocity, its genius for administration, its adaptability and eclecticism. They brought from Normandy the feudal customs they had there acquired, but they maintained and converted to their use the officials and institutions, the arts and sciences, of the races they conquered—Italian, Greek, and Arab—each of which was tolerated in the use of its own language, religion, and customs. The court of Roger II at Palermo presented an appearance unlike anything else in the West; and the essential product of this extraordinary environment was "the wonder of the world," Frederick II. The Normans pieced together a most remarkable mosaic, but they never made a nation of their subjects; the elements were too discordant, and they themselves too few. They remained a ruling caste, and then, as the royal house, once so prolific, gradually became sterile, Frederick Barbarossa seized the opportunity to marry his son Henry VI to the heiress Constance and to unite the crowns of Germany and Sicily. But, though the Norman rulers had disappeared, their deeds survived; for their own purposes they had recognised papal overlordship and received from the Pope their titles as dukes and kings. By so doing they added materially to the temporal authority of the Papacy, and created the situation which made so bitter the conflict of Empire and Papacy in the thirteenth century.

As the Normans exercised an important influence on the great struggle which divided the unity of Europe, so did they also have a decisive effect upon the other great struggle, in which Europe was united against the infidel. The story of the Crusades is described in this volume from the Western point of view, and it has already been told from the Eastern standpoint in Volume IV. Its importance in world-history, and also in the more limited field of European history, need not be stressed here; but it is worth while to characterise the different interests involved, and to regard the Crusading movement in its proper setting, as an episode in the general history of the relations of East and West. It was not merely a Holy War between Christian and Muslim. The Seljūqs, already in decline and hampered by internal divisions, were concerned with the effort to maintain what they had won. The Eastern Empire was concerned firstly with the defence of its existence, secondly with the recovery of Asia Minor. The Latins, to whom they appealed for help, were interested rather in Syria and Palestine, to which they were equally attracted by religious enthusiasm and by the prospects of territory or trade. Europe also had its own injuries to avenge. It too had suffered from Saracen invaders, against whom it was now beginning to react—in the advance of the Christian kingdoms in Spain, in the Norman conquest of Sicily, in the capture of Mahdīyah by Genoa and Pisa in 1087. The Crusades were, in one aspect, an extension Eastwards of this reaction, a change from the defensive to the offensive. Against a common foe Eastern and Western Christians had a common cause, but the concord went no further. In the first place, seventeen years before the fatal battle of Manzikert, which had caused the Eastern Empire to turn to the West for aid, the great Schism between the Eastern and Western Churches had already occurred. One of the results hoped for from the First Crusade was the healing of that schism, and to the Western mind the obstinate perversity of the Greek Church made it as dangerous an enemy of the faith as Mohammedanism itself. And, secondly, the Normans in South Italy had conquered Greeks as well as Saracens, and their first advance eastwards was against Greeks not against Saracens. Robert Guiscard by his attack on the Eastern Empire in 1081 began the policy, which was continued by his successors and was adopted by the Emperor Henry VI as part of his Norman inheritance. In other quarters, too, the experiences of the first two Crusades created a body of opinion in favour of the conquest of the Eastern Empire as a necessary part of the whole movement; this opinion gathered strength when the Eastern Emperor came to terms with Saladin to oppose the Western advance which was now a menace to both. Finally, Venice was alienated by the ambition of Manuel Comnenus and the folly of Andronicus, and from being the chief obstacle to the Norman policy became its chief supporter. It was now the aim of the Crusaders to conquer the whole of the Near East, Christian and Muslim alike, and their first objective was Constantinople.

In the internal history of Europe this volume deals, outside Italy, with the three leading countries of Germany, France, and England; the history of the outlying and more backward countries—Spain, Scandinavia, Poland, Bohemia, Hungary—is reserved for the next volume. In these three countries there was much that was similar, for the underlying ideas inherent in feudal society were common to them all. But similar conceptions produced widely differing results. On the one hand, feudal society with its deep reverence for custom and tradition was much affected by local conditions and lapse of time. On the other hand, it was peculiarly sensitive to the workings of human nature, to the ambition of individuals who stressed the privileges and minimised the obligations arising from the idea of contract on which the feudal system was essentially based; it was poised on a delicate balance which the accident of death might immediately upset. In the secular governments, as in the ecclesiastical government of the Church, the trend is in favour of monarchy, and the rulers make, with varying success, a continual effort towards centralisation; but they were all at an initial disadvantage compared with the Pope. The success of the electoral principle might be fatal to monarchical authority; and the hereditary principle had its dangers too, in the event of a minority or the failure of a direct heir. The hereditary principle could not be applied to the Papacy, for which the electoral system worked as a means of continual development; for the cardinals, having no opportunity of obtaining an independent position apart from the Pope, had everything to gain as individuals and nothing to lose by electing the ablest of their number as Pope.

Monarchy was in the most favourable position in England, and here it was therefore the most successful. William I started with the initial advantage that the whole land was his by conquest, and to be dealt with as he chose. The Normans, here as in Sicily, displayed their genius in administration, their adaptability and eclecticism. The political feudalism they brought from Normandy placed the king in England in the strong position that, as duke, he had held in Normandy; and he adopted what he found suitable to his purpose already existing—the manorial system, the shire and hundred courts, Danegeld. As it had been won by conquest, the whole land was royal domain. Wisely the king kept a large share for himself, though feudal dues and the precedent of general taxation made him less dependent on his own estates for revenue than were his French and German contemporaries. The lands he granted out were held directly from him, as fiefs on military tenure, liable to forfeiture and not transferable at will. No individual baron could match himself with the king or hope to establish an independent position. The king was not dependent upon the barons in the central government, nor were they, as on the Continent, all-powerful in local government. They were not officials but tenants-in-chief, and the strength of the Crown in local affairs is clearly displayed in that the king not only appointed and dismissed the sheriffs at will, but also insisted on their attendance at his Court and a rendering of their stewardship at his Exchequer—just as the Pope insisted on the visits *ad limina* of his local officials, the archbishops and bishops. So too did royal justice penetrate through the country, with the system of inquests, writs, and itinerant judges; the local courts were maintained under royal control, and it was the baronial jurisdiction that suffered. Not that it was directly attacked; the kings were careful not to transgress the letter of the feudal contract. But they preserved their supremacy, and in Church as well as in State; moreover, in spite of

Henry I's dispute with Anselm and Henry II's long contest with Becket, they avoided any serious conflict with the Papacy. They were, from the English point of view, too much absorbed in their continental possessions, which involved long absences of the king and too heavy a burden on English resources. Yet still, at the end of our period, the monarchy is at the height of its power, both in England and on the Continent. A rapid decline set in with John, who not only lost most of his continental possessions but, by making the mistakes which the wisdom of his predecessors had avoided, entered into a serious conflict both with the Pope and with the united baronage.

France presents a complete contrast. In the eleventh century the French monarchy was almost helpless. The great nobles had become practically independent, and, unlike the nobles in Germany, had ceased to be even in theory royal officials. The king had to start *de novo*, and perhaps in the long run this was an advantage. He was not fettered by all those traditions of the past which hampered royal initiative in Germany, and the strongest of the fetters had rusted from disuse. The Capetians had enjoyed the supreme fortune of an uninterrupted succession; the custom of two centuries hardened into a right; and the electoral privileges of the nobles gave way to the hereditary right of the eldest son. In this volume we deal only with the reigns of Louis VI and VII, during which the monarchy recovered from the weakness of the eleventh century and prepared the way for the great period which begins with Philip Augustus. The king had two assets: a domain, which though small was compact, and the potentialities inherent in the kingly office. Louis VI, by his wisdom in concentrating almost entirely on the former, was able eventually to make use of the latter. After a long series of petty wars, he overcame the brigand-nobles of the domain, and so established peace and order within it, made the roads safe for merchants and travellers, and made royal justice attractive. He had his reward in the appeals for his intervention that came from other quarters. So sure was his building that even Louis VII managed to add a few bricks to the edifice. The great vassals absorbed in their own domains ignored the central government, and the king, much to his advantage, was able to create a body of officials directly dependent upon himself. In local government he was confined almost entirely to the royal domain, but soon, by escheat and conquest, this was to become the larger part of France; the king reaped the advantage from the over-aggrandisement of his greatest vassal. Finally, one source of strength had grown out of past weakness. The Papacy in the eleventh century had succeeded in carrying out its reform policy more completely in France than elsewhere, because of the weakness of royal opposition. On France, therefore, it could rely for welcome and a refuge, whatever the king's attitude, and frequently the Popes availed themselves of this. The result was that they came to depend, Alexander III in particular, on French support; this, as the king became powerful, meant the support of the French king, who soon attained a unique position among lay rulers in his relations with the Papacy.

In Germany the situation is much harder to assess; monarchy was firmly established, with a long tradition of power, but the king was handicapped by tradition as well, and still more by his imperial position. His Italian kingdom prevented him from concentrating upon Germany, while the long struggle with the Papacy gave the opportunity for the anti-monarchical forces in both countries to defeat his aims at centralisation. Another weakness was the lack of continuity. More than once already the king had left no son to succeed him, and twice again this happened within our period. So the hereditary principle was never established, and the grip of the electors tightened with each vacancy. The royal resources were distinctly inferior to those of the English kings, for a large part of the land was not held directly from the king and he had no power of instituting general taxation. The royal domain, in which in a sense must be included the ecclesiastical territories held from the king, was widely scattered, and the king was unable to concentrate on one area, as Louis VI did in France. Henry IV attempted this in Saxony, and was defeated by the Saxon revolt; Henry V's attempt in the Rhine district was cut short by his death; Lothar III started with an extensive Saxon domain, but again a change of dynasty upset his plans; Frederick Barbarossa, who added his Swabian domain to the Salian inheritance, was the most favourably placed of all, and he was the most powerful. He it was too who solved the problem of the duchies.

The German kings, while very powerful compared with their French contemporaries, were still hampered by the conditions to which the weakness of the ninth century had given rise, and from which they had never been able to shake themselves free. Germany had been saved from the fate of France in the ninth century by the tribal feeling, which prevented her from breaking up into small units. But the very cohesion of the tribal duchies was a handicap to the central authority. In the first place, tribal institutions and tribal customs were too strong to be overridden, and tended to make of Germany a federation rather than a nation; and, secondly, the dukes, as leaders of the tribes, were a constant embarrassment to the king. Various expedients had been adopted, from Otto I onwards, to control them, but once again in the twelfth century they had risen, in Swabia, Bavaria, and Saxony, to a position little inferior to that of their predecessors in the ninth century. The fall of Henry the Lion at last gave Frederick Barbarossa the opportunity, by partitioning the duchies, to destroy the old tribal units. The smaller units he could more easily control, but he did nothing to replace the tribal bond by a national bond, and so Germany became a federation of many small states in place of a few large ones.

What stood in his way particularly was the status of the German nobility. Dukes, margraves, and counts remained in theory what they had once been in fact—royal officials, entrusted with local government and jurisdiction. These functions they now exercised by hereditary right, and themselves reaped the financial advantages. So, while the nobles could often interfere in the central government, the king, where he was not present, could not control the local government. One important change he did make, by which a landed status tended to supersede the official status. The first rank of German nobles, the *principes*, had included all holders of official titles, lay and ecclesiastical. After 1180, only those who held directly from the king were ranked as "princes." So, while the bishops and the abbots of royal abbeys retained princely rank (and were often, in a real sense, royal officials), only some sixteen lay nobles remained in the highest grade. The princes of Germany had the right of choosing the king; this right was now confined to a much smaller number, and already it was recognised that with a privileged few the real decision lay. The elective system was becoming crystallised, and both Frederick Barbarossa and Henry VI vainly attempted to combat it. Frederick was a great ruler himself, a great respecter of law, a great guardian of order. But, though he was successful in preserving order in Germany, he had to be present himself to enforce it. The local magnates, though with a landed rather than an official status, continued like the princes to exercise local control. No attempt was made by Frederick to imitate the English kings, to create a bureaucracy directly responsible to himself and by a system of itinerant justices to enforce locally the king's law and to make the king's justice universal. He was so scrupulous in his administration of feudal custom that it was hardly possible that he should contemplate such a change. It was the nobles who instituted the process against Henry the Lion, and it was they, and not the king, who reaped the results of his fall. In fact, there was no real effort at centralisation in Germany, and this was fatal to German unity and so to monarchy in Germany.

Hitherto the political side of feudalism had been displayed in arrangements or conflicts between the king on the one side and the nobles on the other. But now, as the more settled state of things gave opportunity for the development of more peaceful pursuits, a third factor enters in with the rise of the towns. In this volume we are concerned with the political importance of these urban communities, and the economic history of the development and organisation of trade and industry, as well as of agricultural conditions, is reserved for later volumes. The king was naturally interested in keeping control of the towns, which provided useful sources of revenue: in England the leading boroughs were retained as royal boroughs by William I and were heavily taxed by Henry I; in Germany there were many royal towns, and, as most towns were under a bishop, royal control was usually maintained. The towns, for their part, were anxious to hold directly from the king, and were willing to pay the price. For the king alone could legally grant the privileges they coveted, and a strong monarchy was the best guarantee of the peace which was so necessary a condition for the expansion of trade and industry. They were, therefore, naturally on the side of the king against the nobles, and often rendered him valuable support. The work of Louis VI in the royal domain was so much to their interest that we find the towns a constant ally of monarchy in France, though the kings until Philip Augustus were slow to recognise the advantage this gave them. In England, the support of London was one of Stephen's chief assets. In Germany, the assistance of the Rhine towns turned the tide in favour of Henry IV when his fortunes were at their lowest ebb, and he never lost their support. Henry V, depending at first on the nobles, had to throw over the towns, but he tried energetically, though not altogether successfully, to regain their support later on. The twelfth century was the great flowering period of corporate town-life in Germany, aided by royal grants of self-government. Frederick II in the thirteenth century handed the towns over to the nobles; they were forced to depend upon themselves, and adopted the plan of leagues for mutual support and the furtherance of trade.

In the towns of northern and central Italy, for different reasons, this stage had already been reached in the twelfth century; the motives governing their actions, though the same as elsewhere, led to contrary results. The Italian towns had been accustomed to city-organisation from Roman times, and their geographical situation caused an earlier development of trade and greater prosperity than elsewhere in Europe. Some of them had already acquired charters and liberties in the eleventh century, and they found their opportunity when they were practically left to themselves by Lothar III and Conrad III. During this period they suppressed the local feudal nobility, who made peaceful trading impossible, and, getting rid of their episcopal lords, established themselves as self-governing communities. The royal power had not assisted them, and was now the only bar to complete independence. They had violated the sovereign rights of the Emperor, and such a breach with feudal law could only be made good by revolution. Frederick Barbarossa was entirely within his rights in enforcing at Roncaglia the recovery of the *regalia*, so important a source of revenue, which they had usurped. The towns justified themselves by success, and, though they consented to an outward recognition of imperial overlordship, the tie was too slender to affect their independence. But the league of Italian cities, its defensive purpose achieved, did not continue, as the later leagues in Germany, for the preservation of order and the mutual furtherance of trade. City rivalries and trade jealousies counterbalanced the bond of common interest, and the cities suffered from constant internal as well as external strife; the rise of oligarchies of wealth led to class struggles, and the competition of different crafts to conflicts between the gilds.

In an age when monarchical government, secular and ecclesiastical, was not only regarded as divinely instituted but was also the best guarantee of peace and order, the capacity of the ruler was of the first importance and attention is focussed upon individuals. The second half of the eleventh century is dominated by the personality of Pope Gregory VII, the second half of the twelfth by that of the Emperor Frederick Barbarossa. In the middle period it is neither lay ruler nor ecclesiastical ruler, but a Cistercian abbot, St Bernard, who fills the centre of the stage; and that this could be so is a sign of the effect on medieval life of spiritual considerations. It was the admiration felt for the holiness of his life, and his reputation as a great and fearless preacher, that gave St Bernard his extraordinary influence over his generation. He figures in several chapters in this volume, and his life-story provides an epitome of most of the leading features of contemporary human endeavour. It was an age of new monastic experiments, which were of great importance in the life of the Church; for monastic reform had preluded, and constantly recurred to reinvigorate, the Reform of the Church as a whole. Not only did St Bernard's outstanding personality make Cistercianism the most popular Order of the day; his ardent zeal put new life into the older Benedictine monasteries and materially assisted the beginnings of the other new Orders— Carthusians, Templars, Premonstratensians, Augustinian canons; particularly did he encourage the substitution of regular for secular canons in cathedral chapters. The twelfth century witnessed also a new wave of intellectual endeavour, and St Bernard was the arbiter on some of the leading questions of the day, including the condemnation of Abelard and Arnold of Brescia in 1140, and the less successful trial of Gilbert de la

Porrée in 1147. In this way he exercised an unfortunate influence; his rigid orthodoxy made him immediately suspicious of a critical mind, and was more in place in combating the heresy which was already beginning to spread in the south of France.

In a larger sphere he also predominated. It was his decision in favour of Innocent II that settled the issue of the papal schism following the death of Honorius II in 1130. It was his preaching that kindled the Second Crusade, and his influence that caused the Kings of France and Germany to participate in it; its disastrous failure reacted on his popularity but did not deter him from attempting to assemble a new crusade. He not only laid down rules of life for bishops, monks, secular clergy, and laity, but he dispatched admonitions and censures, in the plainest of language, to Popes, cardinals, and kings. Most interesting of all is the long lecture he addressed to Eugenius III on the duties of the papal office—the *De Consideratione*. In this he develops a view of the extent of spiritual authority that did not fall short of the extreme conception of Gregory VII; he speaks of the *plenitudo potestatis* of the Pope and of the two swords, material as well as spiritual, belonging to the Church. But, on the other hand, he was quite emphatic that this power must be used for spiritual purposes only, and the idea of the Pope as a ruler is abhorrent to him. The Pope has a *ministerium* not a *dominatio*; the Roman Church is the *mater* not the *domina* of all the churches; the Pope's power is "in criminibus non in possessionibus." He is especially vehement against the increasing absorption of the Pope in the pomps and secular cares of his office, and though his treatise does not supply a very practical solution of the difficulties with which the Pope was faced, it does convey a timely warning, and in a sense a prophecy of the fate that was soon to overtake the Papacy.

CORRIGENDA.

Vol. III.

p. 121, l. 19. *For* Courci-sur-Dive *read* Courci-sur-Dives.
p. 250, l. 6. *For* St Vanne's *read* St Vannes.

Index.

p. 663, col. 2. *For* Courci-sur-Dive *read* Courci-sur-Dives.

Vol. IV.

p. xvi, Chap. I, l. 2. *Delete* late.
p. 119, l. 11. *For* Hubaira *read* Hubairah.
p. 120, ll. 6–7. *For* still 7000 men *read* 7000 men to meet the advancing enemy.
p. 120, l. 36, p. 124, l. 10, p. 126, ll. 33, 38, p. 128, l. 23, p. 133, l. 5. *For* Semaluos *read* Semalus.
p. 120, n. 2. *For* 'Taiba' *read* 'Ṭaibah.'
p. 123, *passim* and p. 124, l. 6. *For* Thumāma *read* Thumāmah.
p. 123, ll. 18 and 16 from bottom and p. 124, l. 7. *For* 'Isa *read* 'Īsà.
p. 126, l. 9. *For* Vardan *read* Bardanes.
p. 127, ll. 11 and 13–14. *For* Harthama *read* Harthamah.
p. 133, l. 4. *For* Bugha *read* Bughā.
p. 135, ll. 3 and 8. *For* Balāṭa *read* Balāṭah.
p. 138, headline and l. 15. *For* Khafāja *read* Khafājah.
p. 193, l. 7 from bottom. *For* Ibn Haukal *read* Ibn Hauqal.
p. 234, l. 5. *For* a thousand *read* eleven hundred.
p. 316, last line. *For* Kerbogha *read* Karbōghā.
p. 359, l. 7 from bottom. *For* Bizā'a *read* Buzā'ah.
p. 367, l. 22. *For* abandoned the Crusade *read* quitted the army.
p. 375, l. 7 from bottom. *For* Bukaia *read* Buqai'ah.
p. 711, l. 10 from bottom. *For* 911 *read* 912.
p. 899, an. 757. *For* Paul IV *read* Paul I.

Index.

p. 913, col 1. *Insert entry* Andrasus, p. 125 n.
p. 918, col. 1. *For* Balāṭa *read* Balāṭah.
p. 920, col. 2. *Delete entry* Bizā'a.
p. 922, col. 1. *For* Bugha *read* Bughā.
      ,,   ,,   *Delete entry* Bukaia.
p. 922, col. 2. *Insert entry* Buqai'ah, the, battle of, 375.
p. 923, col. 1. *Insert entry* Buzā'ah, in Syria, 359.
p. 929, col. 1. *Under existing entry* Constantine, the patrician, *delete* defeated and slain, 135.
p. 929, col. 1. *Insert new entry* Constantine, patrician, defeated and slain in Sicily, 134 sq.
p. 930, col. 2. *In entry* Corum, *for* 128, 130 *read* 128; 130.
p. 936, col. 1. *Read* Enna (Castrogiovanni), in Sicily, besieged by Saracens, 135 sq.; finally captured, 46, 137; 138.

p. 940, col. 1.   *Read* Ghamr, Arab prince, 121.
                 Ghamr, Arab general, 128.

p. 942, col. 2.   *For* Harthama *read* Harthamah.

p. 944, col. 1.   *For* Hubaira *read* Hubairah.

p. 945, col. 1.   *For* Ibn Haukal *read* Ibn Hauqal.
      ,,   ,,   *Under entry* Ibrāhīm ibn al-Aghlab *delete* 141;
      ,,   ,,   *Insert entry* Ibrāhīm II, Aghlabid emir of Africa, 141.

p. 950, col. 2.   *Insert entry* Karbōghā (Qawwām-ad-Daulah Karbuqā), prince of Mosul, at Antioch, 316, 339

p. 951, col. 1.   *Delete entry* Kerbogha.
      ,,   ,,   *For* Khafāja *read* Khafājah.

p. 957, col. 2.   Manuel, the strategus, and Manuel, the Magister, are the same person.

p. 958, col. 2.   *Under entry* Maslamah *delete* sq.
      ,,   ,,   *Insert entry* Maslamah ibn Hishām, 121.

p. 959, col. 1.   *Read* Melas, river in Cappadocia, Byzantine defeat on, 122.
                 Melas, river in Bithynia, 131 *note*.

p. 966, col. 1.   *Read* Omar ibn Hubairah.

p. 973, col. 2.   *Read* Ragusa, in Sicily, raided by Saracens, 137; 138 sq.
                 Ragusa, in Dalmatia, Robert Guiscard and, 325; *etc.*

p. 976, col. 1.   *Under entry* Ṣafṣāf *read* 125 sq.

p. 979, col. 1.   *Under entry* Seleucia, theme of, *delete* pillaged by Byzantine fleet, 130.
      ,,   ,,   *Insert entry* Seleucia, Syrian town, pillaged by Byzantine fleet, 130.
      ,,   ,,   *For* Semaluos *read* Semalus.

p. 984, col. 2.   *Under entry* Tarsus *add to list of emirs* ʿAḥmad, Naṣr.

p. 985, col. 1.   *Under entry* Theoctistus, the Logothete, *delete* uncle and.

p. 988, col. 2.   *Under entry* Turcus, Bardanes, *add* , 126.

p. 990, col. 1.   *Delete entry* Vardan, Armenian rebel.

TABLE OF CONTENTS.

INTRODUCTION.

CHAPTER I.

THE REFORM OF THE CHURCH.

By the late J. P. Whitney, D.D., Dixie Professor of Ecclesiastical
History, Cambridge.

CHAPTER II.

GREGORY VII AND THE FIRST CONTEST BETWEEN EMPIRE AND PAPACY.

By Z. N. Brooke, Litt.D., F.B.A.

CHAPTER III.

GERMANY UNDER HENRY IV AND HENRY V.

By Z. N. Brooke, Litt.D., F.B.A.

CHAPTER IV.

(A)

THE CONQUEST OF SOUTH ITALY AND SICILY BY THE NORMANS.

By the late FERDINAND CHALANDON, Archiviste Paléographe.

(B)

THE NORMAN KINGDOM OF SICILY.

By the late FERDINAND CHALANDON.

CHAPTER V.

THE ITALIAN CITIES TILL *c.* 1200.

By C. W. Previté-Orton, Litt.D., F.B.A., Professor of Medieval
History and Fellow of St John's College, Cambridge.

CHAPTER VI.

ISLĀM IN SYRIA AND EGYPT, 750—1100.

By WILLIAM B. STEVENSON, D.Litt., Professor of Semitic
Languages in the University of Glasgow.

CHAPTER VII.

THE FIRST CRUSADE.

By Professor WILLIAM B. STEVENSON, D.Litt.

CHAPTER VIII.

THE KINGDOM OF JERUSALEM, 1099—1291.

By the late CHARLES LETHBRIDGE KINGSFORD, M.A., F.B.A., sometime
Scholar of St John's College, Oxford.

CHAPTER IX.

THE EFFECTS OF THE CRUSADES UPON WESTERN EUROPE.

By E. J. PASSANT, M.A., Fellow of Sidney Sussex College,
Cambridge.

CHAPTER X.

GERMANY, 1125—1152.

By AUSTIN LANE POOLE, M.A., Fellow of St John's College,
Oxford, late Lecturer of Selwyn College, Cambridge.

CHAPTER XI.

ITALY, 1125—1152.

By the late COUNT UGO BALZANI, Member of the R. Accademia
dei Lincei.

CHAPTER XII.

FREDERICK BARBAROSSA AND GERMANY.

By Austin Lane Poole, M.A.

CHAPTER XIII.

FREDERICK BARBAROSSA AND THE LOMBARD LEAGUE.

By the late COUNT UGO BALZANI.

CHAPTER XIV.

THE EMPEROR HENRY VI.

By Austin Lane Poole, M.A.

CHAPTER XV.

THE DEVELOPMENT OF THE DUCHY OF NORMANDY AND THE NORMAN CONQUEST OF ENGLAND.

By the late William John Corbett, M.A., Fellow of King's College, Cambridge.

CHAPTER XVI.

ENGLAND, 1087—1154.

By the late WILLIAM JOHN CORBETT, M.A.

CHAPTER XVII.

ENGLAND: HENRY II.

By Mrs Doris M. Stenton, Lecturer in History at University College, Reading.

CHAPTER XVIII.

FRANCE: LOUIS VI AND LOUIS VII (1108—1180).

By Louis Halphen, Professor in the University of Paris.

CHAPTER XIX.

THE COMMUNAL MOVEMENT, ESPECIALLY IN FRANCE.

By the late Miss ELEANOR CONSTANCE LODGE, D.Litt., Lady Margaret Hall, Oxford, Principal of Westfield College in the University of London.

CHAPTER XX.

THE MONASTIC ORDERS.

By ALEXANDER HAMILTON THOMPSON, M.A., Hon. D.Litt., F.B.A.,
F.S.A., Hon. Fellow of St John's College, Cambridge, Professor
of History in the University of Leeds.

CHAPTER XXI.

ROMAN AND CANON LAW IN THE MIDDLE AGES.

By HAROLD DEXTER HAZELTINE, Litt.D., F.B.A., Downing
Professor of the Laws of England, Cambridge.

CHAPTER XXII.

MEDIEVAL SCHOOLS TO *c.* 1300.

By Miss MARGARET DEANESLY, M.A., Bishop Fraser Lecturer in
History in the University of Manchester, late Mary Bateson
Fellow, Newnham College, Cambridge.

CHAPTER XXIII.

PHILOSOPHY IN THE MIDDLE AGES.

By W. H. V. READE, M.A., Sub-Warden and Tutor of
Keble College, Oxford.

Contents

LIST OF BIBLIOGRAPHIES.

LIST OF MAPS.

(See separate portfolio.)

CHAPTER I.

THE REFORM OF THE CHURCH.

THE early part of the eleventh, as well as the tenth, century is often and rightly called a dark age for the Western Church. Everywhere we find deep corruptions and varied abuses, which can easily be summed up in broad generalisations and illustrated by striking examples. And they seem, on a first survey, almost unrelieved by any gleams of spiritual light. The comparative security of the Carolingian Age, which gave free scope to individual enthusiasm and personal activity, had been followed by wide and deep disunion, under which religion suffered no less than learning and government. Beginning with the central imperial and monarchical power, the social nerves and limbs fell slack; outside dangers, Northmen and Saracens, furthered the inner decay. Communities and men alike lost their sense of wider brotherhood, along with their former feeling of security and strength. Hence came the decay in Church life. If it was to be arrested, it could only be, not by isolated attacks upon varied abuses, but by a general campaign waged upon principles and directed by experience.

Yet condemnations of a particular age, like most historical generalisations, are often overdone[1]. This is the case here, too. There were to be found, in regions far apart, many men of piety and self-devotion. Among such reformers was Nilus (*ob.* 1005), who founded some monasteries in Italy. Greek by descent, born at Rossano in Calabria, he was inspired even in his early years by the Life of St Anthony (which so deeply touched St Augustine) and so turned to a life of piety, penitence, and self-sacrifice. His visions gained him followers, but his humble service to others carried him into the world of human sympathy. Even when he was a feeble man of eighty-eight he took the long journey to Rome to offer himself as humble companion to Philagathus of Piacenza, whom Otto III had imprisoned after cutting out his tongue and blinding him (998); his brave and courageous reproof moved the youthful ruler, and this accidental association has given Nilus a reputation which his whole less dramatic life deserved. Through him and Romuald of Ravenna, who did much in a small sphere for ascetic life, a fresh stream of Greek influence was brought to strengthen Western monachism, which was growing into an almost independent strength of its own. More widely influential was

---

[1] Many of the worst and unnameable evils belonged more to society at large than to the Church alone. And, as they existed before the monastic reform, they cannot be ascribed to it.

William of Dijon (*ob.* 1031), a German born in Italy, commended by his father to the favour of Otto I, and by his mother to the care of the Blessed Virgin. He was brought up in a cloister near Vercelli, but soon came to look towards Cluny as his spiritual home, and in its abbot, Odilo, he found a religious guide who sent him to the task of reform at Dijon, whence his monastic reform spread in Burgundy, France, and Lorraine. Everywhere his name, William *supra regulam*, was revered, and at St Arnulf at Gorze, and St Aper at Toul, the spirit of Cluny was diffused through him.

Richard of St Vannes near Verdun (*ob.* 1046) specially affected Lorraine, and his name, Richard of the Grace of God, shews the impression he made in his day. Poppo, Abbot of Stablo in the diocese of Liège (1020–1048), was a pupil of his, and through him the movement, favoured by kings and utilised by bishops, reached Germany. In some cases, such men had not to work in fields untilled. Gerard of Brogne, near Namur, (*ob.* 959) and the earlier history of monastic reform must not be forgotten. But while the earlier monastic revival was independent of the episcopate, in the later part of the eleventh century monasticism and the episcopate worked, on the whole, together. Better men among the bishops, and through royal influence there were many such, rightly saw in the monastic revival a force which made for righteousness. It was so at Liège, Cambrai, Toul, and at Cologne, where a friend of Poppo, Pilgrim (1021–1036), favoured Cluniacs and their followers. Thus in Germany, more perhaps than elsewhere, reform gained strength.

The life and wandering of Ratherius (*c.* 887–974), no less than his writings, illustrate the turmoil and degradation of the day; born near Liège, with a sound monastic training and in close touch with Bruno, the excellent Archbishop of Cologne (953–965), his spiritual home was Lorraine while his troubles arose mainly in Italy. From Lorraine he followed Hilduin, afterwards Archbishop of Milan (931), to Italy (for the revival in Lorraine threw its tendrils afar), and became Bishop of Verona (931–939). Italian learning he found solely pagan in its scholarship; ignorance abounded (his clergy reproached him for being ready to study books all day); clerks did not even know their creed; at Vicenza many of them were barely believers in the Christian God; morals were even worse, clerks differed little from laity except in dress, the smiles or the tears of courtesans ruled everything. The strife of politics prevented reform and intensified disorder. The Italian wars of Otto I, Hugh, and Berengar affected the fate of Ratherius; his episcopal rule was only intermittent (931–939; 946–948; 961–968), and when for a time Bruno of Cologne made him Bishop of Liège (953–955), he was faced through the Count of Hainault by a rival, as at Verona, and found refuge at Lobbes. He was specially anxious to force celibacy upon his Veronese clergy, some married and many licentious; not all would come to a synod, and even those who came defied him; some he cast into prison, a fate which once at least befell himself. With the ambition of a reformer, he lacked the needed patience and wisdom; he toiled overmuch in the spirit of his death-bed saying: "Trample under foot the salt which has lost its savour." "He had not," says Fleury, "the gift of making himself loved," and it is doubtful if he desired it. The vivid and tangled experiences of his life, political and ecclesiastical, are depicted for us in his works and give us the best, if the darkest, picture of his times.

Nor should it be forgotten that some ecclesiastics did much for the arts which their Church had so often fostered. Bernward of Hildesheim (Bishop 992–1022), for instance, was not only a patron of Art, but, like our English Dunstan, himself a skilled workman; in his personal piety and generosity he was followed by his successor Godehard. Later monks condemned this secular activity, and Peter Damian held Richard of St Vannes, who like Poppo of Stablo was a great builder and adorner of churches, condemned to a lengthy Purgatory for this offence. In France, however, activity was shewn rather in the realm of thought, where Gerbert's pupil, Fulbert Bishop of Chartres (*ob.* 1028), and Odo of Tournai (*ob.* 1113) were pre-eminent; out of this activity, reviving older discussions, arose the Berengarian controversy, in which not only Berengar himself, but Lanfranc, of Bec and Canterbury, and Durand of Troarn (*ob.* 1088) took part. The age was not wholly dead.

One foremost line of German growth was that of Canon Law, which gave, as it were, a constitutional background to the attempts at reform, drawn from the past and destined to mould the future. Here Burchard, Bishop of Worms (1000–1025), was renowned, combining as he did respect for authority systematised by the past with regard to the circumstances of his day. Wazo, Bishop of Liège (1041–1048), the faithful servant of Henry III, had much the same reputation, and his *obiter dicta* were held as oracles.

Some reformers were bishops, but more of them were monastics—for reform took mainly the monastic turn. Here and there, now and then, could be found really religious houses, and their influence often spread near and far. Yet it was difficult for such individuals or communities to impress a world which was disorderly and insecure. But soon, as so often, reforms, which were first to check and then to overcome the varied evils, began to shape themselves. Sometimes the impulse came from single personalities, sometimes from a school with kindred thoughts; sometimes general resemblances are common, sometimes local peculiarities overpower them. The tangled history only becomes a little easier to trace when it is grouped around the simony which Sylvester II held to be the central sin of the day. It must not be forgotten that Christian missions although at work had only partly conquered many lands; abuses in the older churches paralysed their growth, and the semi-paganism which was left even percolated into the mother-lands.

Bohemian history illustrates something of this process. A bishopric had been founded at Prague (*c.* 975) in which the Popes took special interest, and indeed the Latin rite was used there from the outset. So Bohemia looked towards the Papacy. But Willigis of Mayence had consecrated St Adalbert to Prague (983), and so to claims of overlordship by the German kings was now added a German claim to ecclesiastical control over Christians who, as we are told, live much as barbarians. Then Vratislav II of Bohemia, largely for political reasons, founded or restored a lapsed Moravian see at Olmütz, over which he placed John, a monk from near Prague, Severus of Prague being promised compensation in Moravia. In 1068 Vratislav, for family and political reasons, made his troublesome brother Jaromir Bishop of Prague, in the hope of rendering him more amenable. But the only change in the disorderly prince was that of taking the name of Gebhard. He, like Severus, strove for the delayed compensation but took to more drastic means: he visited (1071) his brother-bishop at Olmütz, and after a drunken revel mishandled his slumbering host. John complained to Vratislav, who shed tears over his brother's doings, and sent to Rome to place the burden of the unsavoury quarrel upon Alexander II. His messenger spent a night at Ratisbon on his road with a burgher friendly to Gebhard. Then, strangely enough, he was stopped and robbed on his farther way and came back to tell his tale. A second and larger embassy, headed by the Provost of St George at Prague, an ecclesiastic so gifted as to speak both Latin and German, was then sent, and reached Rome early in 1073. A letter from Vratislav, weighted with two hundred marks, was presented to the Pope, and probably read at the Lenten Synod. Legates were sent who, at Ratisbon, were to investigate the case, but its settlement remained for Gregory VII. It is a sordid story of evil ecclesiastics on a background of equally sordid social and dynastic interests. And there were many like it.

The common corruption is better told us and easier to depict for regulars than for seculars. In the districts most open to incursions, many monasteries were harried or sorely afflicted. If the monks walled their houses as protection against pirates or raiders, they only caused neighbouring lords to desire them for fortresses. The spirit of the ascetic life, already weakened by the civil employment of monks, seemed lost. The synod of Trosly, near Soissons, called by Hervé of Rheims in 909, ascribed the decay of regular life mainly to abbots, laymen, for the most part unlearned, and also married, and so eager to alienate property for their families. Lay lords and laymen generally were said to lack respect for Church laws and even for morality itself; debauchery and sensuality were common; patrons made heavy charges on appointments to their parish churches. This legislation was a vigorous protest against the sins of the day, and it is well to note that the very next year saw the foundation of Cluny. The Rule was kept hardly anywhere; enclosure was forgotten, and any attempt to enforce episcopal control over monasteries was useless when bishops were so often themselves of careless or evil life. Attempts at improvement sometimes caused bloodshed: when the Abbot Erluin of Lobbes, trying to enforce the Rule, expelled some malcontents, three of them fell upon him, cut out his tongue, and blinded him.

The story of the great Italian monastery of Farfa is typical. It had been favoured by Emperors and was scarcely excelled for splendour. Then it was seized by the Saracens (before 915) and afterwards burnt by Christian robbers. Its members were scattered to Rome, Rieti, and Fermo; its lands were lost or wasted; there was no recognised abbot, and after Abbot Peter died his successor Rimo lived with the Farfa colony at Rome and there was poisoned. Then as the great nobles strove eagerly for so useful a fortress, King Hugh supported a new abbot, Rafred, who began to restore it: he settled in the neighbourhood 100 families from Fermo and rebuilt the cloister. As far as was possible, the monks were recalled and the monastic treasures restored. But there was little pretence of theology or even piety; only the study of medicine was kept up, and that included the useful knowledge of poisons, as abbot after abbot was to learn. When Rafred was disposed of, one of his poisoners maintained himself in the monastery by military force; the so-called monks lived openly with concubines; worship on Sundays was the sole relic of older habits, and at length even that was given up. One Campo, to whom King Hugh had given the monastery in fief, enriched his seven daughters and three sons out of its property. When some monks were sent from Rome to restore religion, he sent them back. Then Alberic drove Campo out by force, and installed as abbot one Dagobert, who maintained himself for five tumultuous years until he, too, fell before the local skill in poison. Adam of Lucca, who followed with the support of Alberic and John XII, led much the life of Campo. Then Theobald of Spoleto made his own brother Hubert abbot, but he was removed by John XII, and succeeded by Leo, Abbot of Sant' Andrea at Soracte. But the task of ruling was too hard for any man, and only force heavily applied could procure even decency of life. If this was the sad state and tumultuous history of monasteries, once homes of piety and peace, it can be guessed how, with less to support them, parishes suffered and missions languished. Priests succumbed and forgot their holy task. Their bishops, often worse than themselves, neither cared nor attempted to rule or restrain them. For the episcopate was ineffective and corrupt.

The primitive rule for election of bishops had been that it should be made by clergy and people. To choose a fit person was essential, but the mode of choice was not defined. Soon the clergy of the cathedral, first to learn of the vacancy and specially concerned about it, began to take a leading part. They, the clergy of the neighbouring country, and the laity, were separate bodies with different interests, and tended to draw together and to act as groups. But the forces, which made for centralisation of all kinds in civil politics, worked in the ecclesiastical sphere as well, and the cathedral clergy gained the leading part in elections, other clerks dropping off, and later on leading abbots appearing. Among laymen a like process took place, and the populace, more particularly, almost ceased to appear in the election. Thus, in place of election by clergy and laity, we have a process in which the cathedral clergy, the lay vassals of the see, and the leading nobles of the diocese, alone appear. We can trace a varied growth, in which the elements most concerned and most insistent eventually gained fixed and customary rights[1].

But the more or less customary rights gained in this process were soon encroached upon by the crown. The king had a special interest in the bishops: they were his spiritual advisers, a function more or less important. But they were largely used by him for other purposes. In Germany they were given civil duties, which did not seem so alien to their office when the general conception was that of one general Christian society inside which churchman and layman worked for common Christian ends. To gain their help and to raise them in comparison with the lay nobility, it was worth while, quite apart from piety and religious reasons, to enrich their sees, and even to heap secular offices upon them. Ecclesiastical nobles were always a useful counterpoise to secular nobles; as a rule they were better trained for official duties, the Church had reason to remember gratefully past services rendered to it by kings, and it had always stood for social unity and larger fields of administration. In France, where the authority of the king did not cover a large territory[2], the greater vassals gained the same power for their own lands. Popular election, even its weakened form, tended to disappear. Ancient and repeated canons might assert election by clergy and laity, but those of them who kept their voice did so rather as surviving representatives of smaller classes than as individuals. More and more the chapters alone appeared for the clergy and the Church; more and more the king or a great feudal lord came to appoint. By the middle of the eleventh century the old style of election had disappeared in France, and the bishopric was treated as a fief.

In Germany the bishops, although for the most part men of high character, were often supporters of the crown and the mainstay of its administration; when a bishop or a great abbot died, the chapter and the great laymen of the diocese sent deputies to the court, and after a consultation with them, in which they might or might not suggest a choice, the king filled up the office. For England such evidence as we have points to selection by the king, although his choice was declared in

---

[1] The lapse of popular election was furthered by canon 13 of Laodicea (364?), which forbade election by a mob. The canon, which was sometimes held to forbid any voice to the populace, was copied into Gallican codes and the Forged Decretals, and had much effect. Leo I said: *electio clericorum: expetitio plebis*; Stephen VI: *sacerdotum quippe est electio, et fidelis populi consensus.*

[2] The Capetians only disposed of Rheims, Sens, Tours, Bourges, and, until it passed to Germany, Lyons.

the Witan, where both laymen and churchmen were present. In all these lands, the decisive voice, indeed the real appointment itself, lay with the king; the part played by others was small and varying. To the Church remained, however, the safeguard of consecration by the metropolitan and bishops; to the diocese itself the local ceremony of enthronement.

For parochial clergy and parishes the history is much the same. In the central countries of Europe the missionary stage of the Church had long passed away, although in newer lands varying traces, or more than traces, of it remained. In most cases the cathedral church had been the mission centre, and from it the Church had spread. Of the early stages we know but little, but there were many churches, serving a parish, which the landowner had built, and in such cases he usually appointed the parish priest. The right of approval lay with the bishop, who gave the spiritual charge. But more and more the office came to be treated as private property, and in some cases was even bought and sold. The patron—for here we come to the origin of patronage, a field tangled and not yet fully worked—was the landowner, who looked on the parish priest as a vassal, and on the church as a possession. For the parish as for the diocese distinct and even hostile conceptions were thus at work. A fit person for the spiritual work was needed; to see to this was the duty and indeed the purpose of the Church. It could be best safeguarded by a choice from above, and in early days a missionary bishop had seen to it. But when a parish church was held to be private property, a totally new conception came into conflict with the ecclesiastical conception. We have a history which can be traced, although with some unsettled controversy[1].

The legislation of the Eastern Empire, following that of Constantine the Great, allowed churches to be private property, and forbade their alienation, but it also safeguarded the claims of the Church to secure the proper use of the building, and adequate provision for the priest attached to it. Justinian (543) gave the founder of a church and his successors the right to present a candidate for due examination by the bishop.

In the West this was also recognised by a law of A.D. 398, and the priest serving the church was, at least sometimes, chosen by the parishioners. It was well to encourage private generosity, but it soon became necessary to safeguard the control of the bishop, and Gelasius I (492–496), an active legislator, restricted the rights of the founders of

---

[1] In the early Christian Roman Empire, although private property in churches was admitted, the restrictive rights of the bishop prevented any evil arising. For the West the existing evidence is scantier than for the East. The origin of the "private churches" (Eigenkirchen) and of appropriation is regarded by Stutz as based on early Teutonic custom, by Imbart de la Tour as due to a process of encroachment.

churches and attempted[1] to make papal consent necessary for consecration; in this way the Pope might make sure of ample provision for the maintenance of the Church. This clearly recognised the two opposed rights, those of the Church and of the lay founder, but became a dead letter. Legislation under Charles the Great also recognised the private ownership: the Council of Frankfort (794) allowed churches built by freemen to be given away or sold, but only on condition that they were not destroyed and that worship was performed. The Council at Rome in A.D. 826 had to deal as no uncommon case with churches which the patrons had let fall into ruin; priests were to be placed there and maintained. The Synod of Trosly (909) condemned the charges levied by laymen upon priests they appointed; tithes were to be exempted from such rapacity. The elaboration with which (canon 5) relations of patrons and parish priests are prescribed shews that great difficulties and abuses had arisen. But the steady growth of feudalism, and the growing inefficiency of bishops, intensified all these evils. From the ninth century onward the leading principles become blurred. Prudentius of Troyes (*ob.* 861) and Hincmar of Laon led a movement against these private churches, insisting that at consecration they should be handed over to the Church. Charles the Bald and the great canonist Hincmar of Rheims took a different view; the latter wished to remove the abuses but to allow the principle of private churches. Patronage in its later sense (the term itself dates from the eighth century) was in an early stage of growth; abuses were so rife that principles seemed likely to be lost. Simony grew to an astonishing height, and it was only after a long struggle was over that Alexander III (1159–1181) established a clear and coherent system, which is the basis of Church law to-day.

When we come to the eleventh century, we find that in parish churches, built by a landowner, the priest was usually appointed by him; thus the right of property and local interests were recognised. But the actual power of laymen combined with the carelessness of many bishops to make encroachment easy; there was a tendency to treat all churches as on the same footing, and the right of approving the appointment which belonged to the bishop, and which was meant to secure spiritual efficiency, tended to disappear. More and more parish churches were treated as merely private property, and in many cases were bought and sold. The patron treated the priest as his vassal and often levied charges upon him. Moreover, open violence, not cloaked by any claim to right, was common. There were parishes in which a bishop had built a church, either as part of the original mission machinery of the Church or on lands belonging to the see. But sees were extensively robbed and some of these churches too fell into lay hands. There were probably also cases in which the parishioners themselves had elected their priest, but, with the growth

---

[1] Writing to the Bishops of Lucania, Brutii, and Sicily. Jaffé-Löwenfeld, *Regesta*, No. 636.

of feudal uniformity, here too the lay landowner came to nominate. The tenth and eleventh centuries give us the final stage—of usurpation or corruption—in which the principle of private ownership was supreme, and the spiritual considerations, typified by episcopal control, were lost, almost or even utterly; and with lay ownership in a feudal age, simony, the sale of property which was no longer regarded as belonging to a religious administration, became almost the rule.

Where the king had the power to fill vacant bishoprics, simony was easy and in a feudal age natural. Kings were in constant need of money, and poverty was a hard task-master. Some of the German kings had really cared for the Church, and saw to the appointment of fit men, but others like Conrad II made gain of the transaction; it was only too easy to pass from the ordinary gift, although some conscientious bishops refused even that, to unblushing purchase. In France simony was especially rife. Philip I (1060–1108) dismissed one candidate for a see because his power was smaller than a rival's, but he gave the disappointed clerk some words of cheer: "Let me make my profit out of him; then you can try to get him degraded for simony, and afterwards we can see about satisfying you." Purchase of sees became a recognised thing: a tainted bishop infected his flock and often sold ordinations; so the disease spread until, as saddened reformers said, Simon Magus possessed the Church.

It must not be supposed that this result was reached without protest. Old Church laws though forgotten could be appealed to, and councils were the fitting place for protest, as bishops were the proper people to make it. Unhappily, councils were becoming rarer and many bishops were careless of their office. Nevertheless, at Ingelheim (948) laymen were forbidden to instal a parish priest or to expel him without the bishop's leave; at Augsburg (952) laymen were forbidden to expel a priest from a church canonically committed to him or to replace him by another. At the important Synod of Seligenstadt (1023) it was decreed that no layman should give his church to any priest without the consent of the bishop, to whom the candidate was to be sent for proof of age, knowledge, and piety sufficient to qualify him for the charge of God's people. The equally important Synod of Bourges (1031) decreed that no layman should hold the land (*feudum*) of a priest in place of a priest, and no layman ought to place a priest in a church, since the bishop alone could bestow the cure of souls in every parish. The same synod, it may be noted, forbade a bishop to receive fees for ordination, and also forbade priests to charge fees for baptism, penance, or burial, although free gifts were allowed[1]. In England laws betray the same evils: a fine was to be

---

[1] Earlier councils also spoke of the same evil of lay encroachments: at Trosly near Rheims (909), laymen were forbidden to use the tithes of their churches for their dogs or concubines. The earlier and reforming Council of Mayence (888) decreed that the founder of a church should entrust its possessions to the bishop. So, too, at Pavia (1018).

levied for making merchandise of a church[1], and again no man was to bring a church into servitude nor unrighteously make merchandise of it, nor turn out a church-thegn without the bishop's leave[2].

It was significant that against abuses appeal was thus being made to older decrees reiterated or enlarged by sporadic councils. And the growth of religious revival in time resulted in a feeling of deeper obligation to Canon Law, and a stronger sense of corporate life. But it was the duty of the bishops to enforce upon their subjects the duty of obedience. In doing this, they had often in the past been helped by righteous kings and courageous Popes. But now for the needed reforms to be effectively enforced it needed a sound episcopate, backed up by conscientious kings and Popes. Only so could the inspiration of religion, which was breathing in many quarters, become coherent in constitutional action. When king and Pope in fellowship turned to reform, an episcopate, aroused to a sense of duty, might become effective.

But the episcopate itself was corrupt, bad in itself, moving in a bad social atmosphere, and largely used for regal politics. Two of the great Lorraine reformers, William of Dijon (962–1031) and Richard of St Vannes (*ob.* 1046), sharply criticised the prelates of their day: "They were preachers who did not preach; they were shepherds who lived as hirelings." Everywhere one could see glaring infamies. Guifred of Cerdagne became Archbishop of Narbonne (1016–1079) when only ten years old, 100,000 *solidi* being paid on his behalf. His episcopate was disastrous: he sold nearly everything belonging to his cathedral and his see; he oppressed his clergy but he provided for his family; for a brother he bought the see of Urgel through the sale of the holy vessels and plate throughout his diocese. In the Midi such abuses were specially prevalent. In 1038 two viscounts sold the see of Albi, while it was occupied, and confirmed the sale by a written contract. But even over the Midi the reforming zeal of Halinard of Lyons had much effect; Lyons belonged to Burgundy, and Burgundy under Conrad II became German. Halinard had been Abbot of St Rémy at Dijon, and was a reformer of the Cluniac type; at Rome, whither he made many pilgrimages, he was well known and so popular that the Romans sought him as Pope on the death of Damasus II. One bishop, of the ducal house of Gascony, is said to have held eight sees which he disposed of by will. The tables of the money-changers were not only brought into the temple, but grouped round the altar itself. Gerbert (Sylvester II), who had seen many lands and knew something of the past, spoke strongly against the many-headed and elusive simony. A bishop might say, "I gave gold and I received the episcopate; but yet I do not fear to receive it back if I behave as I should.

---

[1] *Laws of Northumbrian priests,* chap. 20 (?950). Johnson, *English Canons,* p. 375.

[2] *Synod of Eanham* (1009), chap. 9. Johnson, p. 485. The thriving of a ceorl includes his possession of a church. Stubbs, *Select Charters* (ed. Davis), p. 88.

I ordain a priest and I receive gold; I make a deacon and I receive a heap of silver....Behold the gold which I gave I have once more unlessened in my purse."[1]

Sylvester II held simony to be the greatest evil in the Church. Most reformers, however, attacked the evil morals of the clergy, and their attack was justified. But strict morality and asceticism went hand in hand, and the complicated evils of the day gave fresh strength to the zeal for monasticism and the demand for clerical celibacy. The spirit of asceticism had in the past done much to deepen piety and the sense of personal responsibility, even if teaching by strong example has its dangers as well as successes. In the West more than in the East the conversion of new races had been due to monks, and now the strength of reformation lay in monasticism. The enforcement of clerical celibacy seemed an easy, if not the only, remedy for the diseases of the day. In primitive times married priests were common, even if we do not find cases of marriage after ordination, but the reverence for virginity, enhanced by monasticism, turned the stream of opinion against them. At Nicaea the assembled Fathers, while forbidding a priest to have a woman, other than wife or sister, living in his house, had refrained, largely because of the protest of Paphnutius, from enforcing celibacy. But the Councils of Ancyra and Neocaesarea (both in 314) had legislated on the point, although with some reserve. The former allowed deacons, who at ordination affirmed their intention to marry, to do so, but otherwise they were degraded. The latter decreed that a priest marrying after ordination should be degraded, while a fornicator or adulterer should be more severely punished. The Council of Elvira (*c.* 305), which dealt so generally and largely with sexual sins, shut out from communion an adulterous bishop, priest, or deacon; it ordered all bishops, priests, deacons, and other clerks, to abstain from conjugal intercourse. This was the first general enactment of the kind and it was Western. As time went on, the divergence between the more conservative East and the newer West, with its changing conditions and rules, became more marked. In the East things moved towards its present rule, which allows priests, deacons, and sub-deacons, married before ordination, to live freely with their wives (*Quintisext in Trullo*, held 680, promulgated 691); bishops, however, were to live in separation from their wives. Second marriages, which were always treated as a different matter, were forbidden. The present rule is for parish priests to be married, while bishops, chosen from regulars, are unmarried. The West, on the other hand, moved, to begin with, first by legislation and then, more slowly, by practice, towards uniform celibacy.

Councils at Carthage (390, 398, and 419), at Agde (506), Toledo (531), and Orleans (538), enjoined strict continency upon married clerks

---

[1] See Saltet, *Les Réordinations*, Paris, 1907—an excellent work—for the nature and content of simony in the tenth and eleventh centuries, pp. 173 sqq.; he quotes Gerbert, *De informatione episcoporum*, MPL, cxxxix, col. 174; Olleris, *Op. Gerberti*, p. 275.

from sub-deacons upwards. Siricius (384–398), by what is commonly reckoned the first Decretal (385), and Innocent I (402–419) pronounced strongly against clerical marriage. Henceforth succeeding Popes plainly enunciated the Roman law. There was so much clerical immorality in Africa, in spite of the great name and strict teaching of St Augustine, and elsewhere, that the populace generally preferred a celibate clergy. Ecclesiastical authorities took the same line, and Leo I extended the strict law to sub-deacons. The Theodosian Code pronounced the children of clergy illegitimate, and so the reformers of the tenth and eleventh centuries could appeal to much support. Nevertheless, there were both districts and periods in which custom accorded badly with the declared law, and the confusion made by reformers between marriages they did not accept and concubinage which opinion, no less than law, condemned makes the evidence sometimes hard to interpret. St Boniface dealt firmly with incontinent priests, and on the whole, although here popular feeling was not with him, he was successful both in Austrasia and Neustria. The eighth and ninth centuries saw the struggle between law and custom continuing with varying fortune. Custom became laxer under the later Carolingians than under Charlemagne, who had set for others a standard he never dreamt of for himself; Hincmar, who was an advocate of strictness, gives elaborate directions for proper procedure against offending clerks, and it is clear that the clergy proved hard either to convince or to rule. By the end of the ninth century, amid prevalent disorder, clerical celibacy became less general, and the laws in its favour were frequently and openly ignored. It was easy, as Pelagius II (578–590), in giving dispensation for a special case, had confessed, to find excuse in the laxity of the age. So too St Boniface had found it necessary to restore offenders after penance, for otherwise there would be none to say mass. Italy was the most difficult country to deal with, and Ratherius of Verona says (966) that the enforcement of the laws, which he not only accepted but strongly approved, would have left only boys in the Church. It was, he held, a war of canons against custom. By about the beginning of the eleventh century celibacy was uncommon, and the laws enforcing it almost obsolete. But they began to gain greater force as churchmen turned more to legal studies and as the pressure of abuses grew stronger.

The tenth and eleventh centuries had special reason for enforcing celibacy and disliking clerical families. Married priests, like laymen, wished to enrich their children and strove to hand on their benefices to them. Hereditary bishops, hereditary priests, were a danger[1]: there was much alienation of clerical property; thus the arguments urged so repeatedly in favour of celibacy were reinforced. Bishops, and not only

---

[1] Atto of Vercelli (from 945) links clerical marriage and alienation of church property together, putting the latter as a cause of abuse. The case is well put by Neander, vi, 187 (Eng. trans.) and Fleury, Bk. lv, c. 55.

those who held secular jurisdiction, thought and acted as laymen, and like laymen strove to found dynasties, firmly seated and richly endowed. Parish priests copied them on a humbler scale. Hence the denial of ordination to sons of clerks is frequent in conciliar legislation.

One attempt at reform of the secular clergy, which had special importance in England, needs notice. This was the institution of canons, which has a long and varied history. The germ of the later chapter appears at a very early date in cathedrals, certainly in the sixth century; a staff of clergy was needed both for ordinary mission work and for distribution of alms. But poverty often, as with monasteries later on, led to careless and disordered life. Chrodegang of Metz (*ob.* 766), the pious founder of Gorze, near his city, and of Lorsch, set up, after a Benedictine model, a rule for his cathedral clergy: there was to be a common life, although private property was permitted; a synod under Louis the Pious at Aix-la-Chapelle (817) elaborated it and it was widely applied. The ideal was high, and although inspired by the asceticism which produced monasticism, it paid regard to the special tasks of seculars; it infused a new moral and intellectual life into the clergy at the centre of the diocese, and education was specially cared for. So excellent an example was soon copied by other large churches, and the system spread widely. In its original form it was not destined to live long: decay began at Cologne with the surrender of the common administration of funds; Gunther, the archbishop, yielded to the wish for more individual freedom, and his successor Willibert in a synod (873) confirmed his changes[1]. After this the institution of prebends (benefices assigned to a canon) grew, and each canon held a prebend and lived apart. This private control of their income, and their surrender of a common life, began a long process of decay. But variations of the original form, which itself had utilised much older growths, appeared largely and widely in history. Brotherhood and the sympathy of a common life furthered diligence and devotion.

In councils of the tenth and eleventh centuries, clerical celibacy and simony are repeatedly spoken of. With few exceptions[2], all well-wishers of reform, whether lay or clerical, desired to enforce celibacy, although

---

[1] At the Roman Council of 1059 Hildebrand spoke against the laxity of the system, especially its permission of private property and its liberality as to fare (Mabillon, ASB, and Hefele-Leclercq, pp. 1177–8, with references there). In 1074 Hildebrand, as Gregory VII, put out a Rule for canons (Hefele-Leclercq, v, p. 94 n. Duchesne, *Lib. Pont.* I, CLXVIIII); it was wrongly ascribed to Gregory IV. See Dom Morin, R.Ben. 1901, XVIII, pp. 177–183. Hildebrand's Rule breaks off short in the MS., and the abbreviation *can.* for *canonicorum* led to its being attributed to musical history (*canendi*).

[2] Ulrich (Udalrich) of Augsburg (923–973) is sometimes said to be an exception, but his letter *De continentia clericorum* is now held to be a forgery. So, later on, was Cunibert of Turin, himself a celibate whose clerks reached a high standard of life: he permitted them to marry, for which Peter Damian reproved him. Both these prelates were earnest reformers. Damian tried to get Adelaide, regent of Piedmont and Savoy, to enforce his policy against Cunibert.

some thought circumstances compelled laxity in applying the law. Thus in France the Council of Poitiers (1000) forbade priests and deacons to live with women, under pain of degradation and excommunication. The Council of Bourges (1031), while making the same decrees (repeated at Limoges the same year), went further by ordering all sub-deacons to promise at ordination to keep neither wife nor mistress. This promise resembles the attempt of Guarino of Modena[1] a little earlier to refuse benefices to any clerk who would not swear to observe celibacy. In Germany the largely-attended Council of Augsburg (952) forbade marriage to ecclesiastics, including sub-deacons; the reason assigned was their handling the divine mysteries, and with German respect for Canon Law appeal was made to the decrees of many councils in the past. Under Henry III the prohibitions were better observed, not only through the support of the Emperor, but because collections of Canons, especially that by Burchard of Worms (*Decretum*, between 1008 and 1012), were becoming known and gaining authority[2]. The statement of principles, especially from the past, as against the practice of the day was becoming coherent. But the Papacy, which had so repeatedly declared for celibacy, was not in a state to interfere authoritatively. Thus we come to the question of reform at Rome. The movement for reform needed authority and coherence, which were to be supplied from Rome. But first of all Reform had to capture Rome itself.

At Rome a bad ecclesiastical atmosphere was darkened by political troubles and not lightened by religious enthusiasm. There as elsewhere local families were striving for local power; the nobility, with seats outside, was very disorderly and made the city itself tumultuous and unsafe. The Crescentii, so long and so darkly connected with papal history, had lands in the Sabina and around Farfa, and although with lessening influence in the city itself they stood for the traditions of civic independence, overshadowed, it is true, by the mostly distant power of the Saxon Emperors. Nearer home they were confronted by the growing power of the Counts of Tusculum[3], to whose family Gregory, the naval prefect under Otto III, had belonged; they naturally, although for their own purposes, followed a German policy. Either of these houses might have founded at Rome a feudal dynasty such as rose elsewhere, and each seemed at times likely to do so. But in a city where Pope and Emperor were just strong enough to check feudal growth, although not strong enough to

---

[1] This tendency to enforce celibacy on seculars by an oath might have led to a general policy, but was not followed. It was an obligation understood to be inherent in the priestly office.

[2] Burchard illustrates, on celibacy and lay interference, the conflict between old canons and later customs. He copies the former, but accepts the latter, and allows for them.

[3] For a discussion of their genealogy see R. L. Poole, *Benedict IX and Gregory VI* (reprinted from *Proceedings of British Academy*, VIII), pp. 31 sqq.

impose continuous order, the disorderly stage, the almost anarchy, of early feudalism lingered long.

When Sergius IV (1009–1012) "Boccaporco," son of a Roman shoemaker and Bishop of Albano, died soon after John Crescentius, the rival houses produced rival Popes: Gregory, supported by the Crescentii, and the Cardinal Theophylact, son of Gregory of Tusculum. Henry II of Germany, hampered by opposition from Lombard nobles and faced by King Arduin, had watched Italian politics from afar, and the disputed election gave him an opening. Rome was divided. Theophylact had seized the Lateran, but could not maintain himself there; Gregory fled, even from Italy, and (Christmas 1012) appeared in Henry's court at Pöhlde as a suppliant in papal robes. Henry cautiously promised enquiry, but significantly took the papal crozier into his own keeping, just as he might have done for a German bishopric. He had, however, partly recognised Theophylact, and had indeed sent to gain from him a confirmation of privileges for his beloved Bamberg[1]: a decision in Theophylact's favour was therefore natural. Henry soon appeared in Italy (February 1013); his arrival put Arduin in the shade. Theophylact, with the help of his family, had established himself, and it was he who, as Benedict VIII, crowned Henry and Cunegunda (14 February 1014). The royal pair were received by a solemn procession, and six bearded and six beardless Senators bearing wands walked "mystically" before them. The pious Emperor dedicated his former kingly crown to St Peter, but the imperial orb bearing a cross was sent to Cluny. Benedict VIII was supported now by the imperial arm, and in Germany his ecclesiastical power was freely used; he and the Emperor worked together on lines of Church reform, even if their motives differed.

Benedict VIII (1012–1024) proved an efficient administrator, faced by the constant Saracen peril, and wisely kept on good terms with Henry II. Although he was first of all a warrior and an administrator[2], he also appears, probably under the influence of the Emperor, as a Church reformer. A Council was held at Pavia (1018)[3], where the Pope made an impressive speech, which, it is suggested, may have been the work of Leo of Vercelli, on the evils of the day, denouncing specially clerical

[1] For the foundation of Bamberg see Hefele-Leclercq, *Les Conciles*, IV, pp. 909 sqq.; Hauck, *op. cit.* III, p. 418; and Giesebrecht, *Deutsche Kaiserzeit*, II, pp. 52 sqq. The missionary importance, as well as the ecclesiastical interest, of the new see and the disputes about it should be noted. For the Church policy of Henry II see *supra*, Vol. III, pp. 231 sqq.

[2] A more favourable view of him is summarised in Hefele-Leclercq, IV, p. 914. So K. W. Nitzsch, *Gesch. des deutschen Volkes*, Leipsic, 1892, I, pp. 392 sqq., in the same sense.

[3] The date of this Council is disputed. 1022 was accepted until Giesebrecht suggested 1018 (*op. cit.* II, p. 188, and note 623–4). Also Hauck (who prefers 1022), *op. cit.* III, p. 528, n. 2. The earlier date seems a little more probable. In Vol. III *supra*, p. 251, the date 1022 is accepted.

concubinage and simony. His starting point was a wish to protect
Church property from alienation to priestly families, a consideration
likely to weigh with a statesmanlike administrator, although Henry II
might have had a more spiritual concern. By the decrees of the Council,
marriage and concubinage were forbidden to priests, deacons, and sub-
deacons, indeed to any clerk. Bishops not enforcing this were to be
deposed. The children of clerks were to be the property of the Church.
In the Council the initiative of the Pope seems to have been strong.
The Emperor gave the decrees the force of law, and a Council at Goslar
(1019) repeated them. Italy and Germany were working as one.

There was little difference between the ecclesiastical powers of Henry
'n Italy and in Germany. He knew his strength and did not shrink
from using it. Before his imperial coronation he held a synod at Ravenna
(January 1014) where he practically decreed by the advice of the bishops;
for Ravenna he had named as archbishop his half-brother Arnold, who
was opposed by a popularly-supported rival Adalbert. This probably
canonical prelate was deposed, and after Henry's coronation a Roman
synod approved the judgment, although it did obtain for the victim the
compensation of a smaller see. Decrees against simonist ordinations and
the alienation through pledges of Church lands were also passed, and
published by the Emperor. A liturgical difference between Roman and
German use in the mass was even decided in favour of the latter. So
far did German influence prevail.

The reforming tendencies of the German Church found full expression
at the Synod of Seligenstadt (12 August 1023). In 1021 a young
imperial chaplain Aribo had been made Archbishop of Mayence; and he
aimed at giving the German Church not only a better spirit but a more
coherent discipline. In the preamble to the canons, Aribo states the aim
of himself and his suffragans, among whom was Burchard of Worms
(Bishop 1000–1025): it was to establish uniformity in worship, discipline,
and ecclesiastical morals. The twenty canons regulated fasting, some
points of clerical observance, observance of marriage, in which the
canonical and not the civil reckoning of degrees of kinship was to hold[1];
lay patrons were forbidden to fill vacancies without the approval and
assent of the bishop; no one was to go to Rome (*i.e.* for judgment)
without leave of his bishop, and no one subjected to penance was to go
to Rome in the hope of a lighter punishment. This legislation was
inspired by the reforming spirit of the German Church, due not only to
the saintly Emperor but to many ecclesiastics of all ranks, with whom
religion was a real thing; and for the furtherance of this the regulations
of the Church were to be obeyed. The Canon Law, now always including
the Forged Decretals, involved respect to papal authority, but Aribo

---

[1] The civil law reckoned brothers and sisters as in the first degree; the canonical
law was now reckoning cousins-german as such.

and his suffragans laid stress also upon the rights of metropolitans and bishops in the national Church, which gave them not only much power for good but the machinery for welding the nation together.

In June 1024 Benedict VIII died and was followed by his brother Romanus the Senator, who became John XIX; his election, which was tainted by bribery and force, was soon followed by the death of the Emperor (13 July 1024). The new monarch, Conrad II, was supported by the German adherents in Italy and especially by the Archbishop Aribert of Milan, a city always important in imperial politics. Both he and John XIX were ready to give Conrad the crowns which it was theirs to bestow. So in 1026 he came to Italy; and he and his wife Gisela were crowned in St Peter's (26 March 1027). Then, after passing to South Italy, he slowly returned home, leaving John XIX to continue a papacy, inglorious and void of reform, until his death in January 1032. Under him old abuses revived, and so the state of things at Rome grew worse, while in Germany, although Conrad II (1024–1039) was very different from Henry II in Church affairs, the party of reform was gaining strength.

With the election of Benedict IX, formerly Theophylact, son of Alberic of Tusculum, brother of a younger Romanus the Consul, and nephew of Benedict VIII and John XIX, papal history reached a crisis, difficult enough in itself, and distorted, even at the time, by varying accounts. According to the ordinary story, Benedict IX was only twelve years old at his election, but as he grew older he grew also in debauchery, until even the Romans, usually patient of papal scandal, became restive, then at length the Emperor Henry III had to come to restore decency and order at the centre of Western Christendom. But there is reason to doubt something of the story. That Benedict was only twelve years old at his accession rests on the confused statement of Rodulf Glaber; there is reason to suppose he was older. The description of his depravity becomes more highly coloured as years go by and the controversies of Pope and Emperor distort the past. But there is enough to shew that as a man he was profligate and bad, as a Pope unworthy and ineffective. It was, however, rather the events of his papacy, singular and significant, than his character, that made the crisis. He was the last of a series of what we may call dynastic Popes, rarely pious and often bad; after him there comes a school of reformed and reformers.

Conrad II differed much in Church matters from Henry II. It is true that he kept the feasts of the Church with fitting regularity and splendour and that he also was a "brother" of some monasteries. But his aims were purely secular, and the former imperial regard for learning and piety was not kept up. Some of his bishops, like Thietmar of Hildesheim, were ignorant; others, like Reginhard of Liège and Ulrich of Basle, had openly bought their sees, and not all of them, like Reginhard, sought absolution at Rome. Upon monasteries the king's hand was heavy: he dealt very freely with their possessions, sometimes forcing them to give lands as fiefs to his friends, sometimes even granting the royal abbeys themselves as such. Thus the royal power worked harmfully or, at any rate, not favourably for the Church[1], and bishops or abbots eager for reform could no longer reckon upon kingly help. It is true that Poppo of Stablo enjoyed royal favour, but other ecclesiastics who, like Aribo of Mayence, had supported Conrad at his accession, received small encouragement. Conrad's marriage with Gisela trespassed on the Church's rule of affinity, and the queen's interest in ecclesiastical appointments, by which her friends and relatives gained, did not take away the reproach; but she favoured reformers, especially the Cluniacs, whose influence in Burgundy was useful.

A change in imperial policy then coincided with a change in Popes. Benedict VIII may have been inspired by Henry II, but John XIX was a tool of Conrad. For instance, he had to reverse a former decision, by which the Patriarch of Grado had been made independent of his brother of Aquileia. Poppo of Aquileia was a German and naturally an adherent of Conrad; everyone knew why the decision was changed[2]. It was even more significant that the Emperor spoke formally of the decree of the faithful of the realm, "of the Pope John, of the venerable patriarch Poppo, and others." It was thus made clear that, whether for reform or otherwise, the Pope was regarded by the Emperor exactly as were the higher German prelates. They were all in his realm and therefore in his hands. Here he anticipated a ruler otherwise very differently-minded, Henry III.

Benedict IX[3] could be treated with even less respect than John XIX. It is true that he held synods (1036 and 1038), that he made the Roman Bishop of Silva Candida *bibliothecarius* (or head of the Chancery) in succession to Pilgrim of Cologne. But in 1038 he excommunicated Aribert of Milan, who was giving trouble to Conrad. To the Emperor he was so far acceptable, but in Rome where faction lingered on he had trouble. Once (at a date uncertain) the citizens tried to assassinate him at the altar itself. Later (1044) a rebellion was more successful: he and his brother were driven from the city, although they were able to hold

---

[1] See *supra*, Vol. III, p. 271.

[2] The later incident, 1042, in which Poppo entered Grado by force, burning and destroying churches and houses, slaughtering and ravaging, illustrates what some bishops of the day were and did. The story of this revived quarrel between Grado and Aquileia is well told by F. C. Hodgson, *Early History of Venice*, London, 1901, pp. 196–206 sqq.; also *supra*, Vol. IV, pp. 407–8. The quarrel, which was old ecclesiastically, had now a twofold connexion with Venetian and German politics.

[3] On the difficult chronology of Benedict's papacy see R. L. Poole, *Benedict IX and Gregory VI* (*Proceedings of the British Academy*, VIII). For the chronology of, and authorities for, the Italian journey of Henry III, Steindorff, *Jahrbücher des deutschen Reiches unter Heinrich III*, I, pp. 456–510.

the Trastevere. Then John, Bishop of Sabina, was elected Pope, taking the name of Sylvester III. Again we hear of bribery, but as John's see was in the territory of the Crescentii, we may suppose that this rival house was concerned in this attack upon the Tusculans; in fifty days the latter, helped by Count Gerard of Galeria, drove out Sylvester's party, and he returned to his former see. Then afterwards Benedict withdrew from the Papacy in favour of his godfather, John Gratian, Archpriest of St John at the Latin Gate, who took the name of Gregory VI. The new Pope belonged to the party of reform; he was a man of high character, but his election had been stained by simony, for Benedict, even if he were weary of his office and of the Romans, and longed, according to Bonizo's curious tale, for marriage, had been bought out by the promise of the income sent from England as Peter's Pence. The change of Popes, however, was welcomed by the reformers, and Peter Damian in particular hailed Gregory as the dove bearing the olive-branch to the ark. Even more significant for the future was Gregory's association with the young Hildebrand; both were probably connected with the wealthy family of Benedict the Christian[1]. There was a simplicity in Gregory's character which, in a bad society calling loudly for reform, led him to do evil that good might come. For nearly two years he remained Pope, but reform still tarried.

Attention has been too often concentrated on the profligacy of Benedict IX, which in its more lurid colours shines so prominently in later accounts. What is remarkable, however, is the corruption, not of a single man, even of a single Pope, but of the whole Roman society. Powerful family interests maintained it; the imperial power might counterbalance them, and, as we have seen, the Papacy had been lately treated much as a German bishopric. In the Empire itself there had been a change; Conrad II had died (4 June 1039), and his son Henry III, a very different man, now held the sceptre.

Whether it be true or not that, as Bonizo tells us, Peter the Archdeacon became discontented and went to ask Henry's interference, it is certain that in 1046 Henry came to Italy; German interests and the state of the Church alike incited him. At Pavia (25 October) he held a Council, and the denunciation of simony made there[2] by him gave the keynote of his policy, now, after Germany, to be applied to Italy and Rome itself.

Henry was now a man of twenty-two, versed in business, trained to responsibilities and weighty decisions since his coronation at eleven.

---

[1] For a very probable genealogy see Poole, *Benedict IX and Gregory VI*, pp. 23 sqq. The connexion explains but avoids Hildebrand's alleged Jewish descent.

[2] Steindorff places here Henry's discourse (given by Rodulf Glaber, ed. Prou, p. 133). See Steindorff, *op. cit.* pp. 309 sqq. and 497 sqq., followed by Hefele-Leclercq, IV, pp. 979 sqq. But see also Hauck, *op. cit.* III, p. 586, n. 3, who rightly holds the words not to be taken as an exact report.

He had been carefully taught, but, while profiting from his teachers, had also learnt to think and decide for himself. He had a high ideal of his kingly office; to a firm belief in righteousness he added a conception of his task and power such as Charlemagne had shewn. He was hailed, indeed, as a second Charlemagne, and like him as a second David, destined to slay the Goliath of simony. But in his private life he far surpassed the one and the other in purity. He saw, as he had declared at Constance and Trèves (1043), the need of his realm for peace, but the peace was to come from his royal sway.

He was every inch a king, but heart and soul a Christian king. Simony he loathed, and at one breath the atmosphere of Court and Church was to be swept clear of it. Inside the Church its laws were to bind not only others but himself as well: no son of a clerk, for instance, could hope for a bishopric under him, because this was a breach of law, and he told Richard of St Vannes that he sought only spiritually-minded men for prelates. His father had been guilty of simony, but, at much loss to himself, he abstained from it; his father had been harsh, but he did not hesitate to reverse his decisions: thus he reinstated Aribert at Milan. But on the other hand, election by chapters, for bishoprics and monasteries, was unknown: he himself made the appointments and made them well; in the ceremony of investiture he gave not only the staff but the ring. Synods he called at his will, and in them played much the part of Constantine at Nicaea. This was for Germany, and in Italy he played, or meant to play, the same part. The case of Widger of Ravenna is significant. This canon of Cologne had been named as Archbishop of Ravenna (1044), but when two years had passed he was still unconsecrated, although he wore episcopal robes at mass. He was summoned to the imperial court, and the German bishops were asked to decide his case. Wazo of Liège asserted that an Italian bishop could not be tried in Germany, but clearly to Henry the distinction meant nothing. Wazo also laid down the principle, of novel sound then although common later, that to the Pope they owed obedience, to the Emperor fealty; secular matters the one was to judge, ecclesiastical matters the other. Widger's case, then, was for the Pope and Italy, not for Henry and Germany. Nevertheless, Henry gained his point and Widger had to return his ring and staff. It was doubly significant that the distinction between ecclesiastical and secular authority should be drawn by Wazo, for the king had no more devoted servant; he said once that if the Emperor put out his right eye he should still serve him with the left, and his acts, notably in defending the imperial rights around Liège even by force, answered to his words. He was the bishop, too, to whom, when he asserted the superiority of his episcopal anointing, Henry answered that he himself was also anointed. Here then, in the principles of Wazo, canonist, bishop, loyalist, and royal servant, but a clear thinker withal, were the signs of future conflict. In Henry's own principles might be seen something of the same unformed conflict, but with him they were reconciled in his own authority and power.

Such was the king whom the scandals of the Papacy called from Germany, where for six years the Church had rapidly improved, to Rome, over which reformers grieved. Of Rome, Desiderius, Abbot of Monte Cassino and afterwards Pope as Victor III (1086–7), could write, although with the exaggeration of a critic: "the Italian priesthood, and among them most conspicuously the Roman pontiffs, were in the habit of defying all law and all authority; thus utterly confounding together things sacred and profane.......Few prelates kept themselves untainted with the vile pollution of simony; few, very few, kept the commandments of God or served him with upright hearts."

After his synod at Pavia, Henry III went on to Piacenza, where Gregory VI, the only Pope actually in power, came to meet him and was received with fitting honour. Then in Roman Tuscany another synod was held at Sutri; at this point later and conflicting accounts, papal and imperial, begin gravely to distort the evidence and the sequence of events[1]. At the synod the story of the payment made by Gregory VI for the Papacy was told; he was most probably deposed, although a later pro-papal account made him resign of himself, as the bishops refused to judge him. Up to their interview at Piacenza Henry had treated him as the legitimate Pope, but afterwards there was certainly a change. The details of his accession were probably now more clearly unfolded; stress may have been laid upon them, and so Henry may have been influenced. It was not an unknown thing for an Emperor to remove a Pope. Another motive may also have influenced him. His second marriage to Agnes of Poitou, sound as a piece of policy, was within the prohibited degrees. It had caused some discussion in Germany[2], but there no bishop, whatever he thought, cared to withstand a king so good. Probably at Rome it would be looked at more suspiciously, and to the eyes of a strict Pope might go against the coronation of the royal pair. We are reminded of the marriage of William the Conqueror; both cases would at a later date have been rightly covered by a dispensation, but the law and its system of dispensations was only beginning to grow into shape. And Henry might naturally wish for a Pope who would support him without reserve, for such was his view of bishops generally. The exile, which Gregory was to pass in Germany up to his death (probably in October 1047), is a strange ending to an almost blameless life; it can only be accounted for

---

[1] Here the reconstruction by R. L. Poole, *Benedict IX and Gregory VI*, a fine piece of criticism, is followed. See also Steindorff's Excursus, noted before, and G. B. Borino, *L'elezione e la deposizione di Gregorio VI* (*Archivio della R. Soc. Rom. di Storia Patria*, xxxix).

[2] See *supra*, Vol. iii, pp. 283–4. The letters of Siegfried of Gorze, who would have had strong measures taken, to Poppo of Stablo and Bruno of Toul, in Giesebrecht, *op. cit.* ii, Dokumente 10 and 11.

by the fear of danger arising from him if he were left in Italy. The doubt about Henry's marriage, and the recognition of Gregory VI as the true Pope, wide-spread in Italy and testified to by Wazo of Liège in Germany, might be used for trouble.

But if Gregory was removed from the papal throne on the ground of an invalid title, either Benedict IX or Sylvester III must be the rightful Pope; the throne could hardly now be treated as vacant. Henry had doubtless made up his mind for a German Pope, who could be better relied on than an Italian; Rome could well be treated as Milan or Ravenna had been, and a German Pope was a good precedent since the days of Gregory V. The claims of Benedict IX and even of Sylvester III were stirred into life, although they may not have been urged; the story that they were considered at Sutri comes from later writers and is unlikely. It was probably in a synod at Rome (23-24 December) that Benedict was deposed; at one time he had certainly been a rightful, if an unrighteous, Pope, and so he must be legally deposed. Sylvester III, whose claims were weaker, disappeared into monastic retirement at Fruttuaria, and was, if dealt with at all, probably deposed in the same synod.

The way was now clear, and Suidger of Bamberg, a worthy bishop, was chosen as Pope (Christmas 1046). Then, as Clement II, he crowned Henry and Agnes. We can judge of the degradation of the papal office, in spite of the enhanced appeal to it through the spread of Canon Law, by the refusal of Adalbert of Bremen to accept it on Henry's offer; his own see, even apart from his special Baltic plans, seemed to be more important. There was a show of election in the appointment, but the real power lay with Henry, who named Suidger with the approval of a large assembly; once again he treated an Italian bishopric, even that of Rome, as he would have done a German. Significant is the renunciation by the Romans of their election rights, which must be taken along with the title of Patrician given to Henry[1].

But the new state of things was not to pass without criticism. From Lower Lorraine came a curious and rather bitter tractate (*De ordinando pontifice auctor Gallicus*) written late in 1047[2]. It betrays some unrevealed discussion, and the writer urges the French bishops, who had not been consulted in the election of Clement, to stand aloof; it was not for the Church to palter with the laws of marriage at the wish of a king. Evidently, therefore, Henry's marriage was held to be of moment in the election. Even in Germany there were some who, like Siegfried of Gorze and like Wazo a little later, were uneasy. Siegfried had disliked the marriage, and Wazo protested to Henry, when he sought a successor to

---

[1] For the title see *supra*, Vol. III, pp. 291, 305.

[2] Ed. by E. Dümmler, MHG, *Libelli de lite*, I, pp. 9 sqq. But it is to be dated, not as by Dümmler in 1048, but late in 1047. See Sackur, *Die Cluniacenser*, II, pp. 305 sqq.; R. L. Poole, *Benedict IX and Gregory VI*, pp. 29-30.

Clement, that no Pope could be made while Gregory VI was still alive[1].

Clement II was worthy of his office, but his papacy was short, and so uneventful; he was overshadowed by the presence of the Emperor, whom he followed to southern Italy, but he held in January 1047 a Council at Rome, where deposition was decreed against all simonists, while those ordained by a simonist bishop were to do forty days' penance. Like preceding Popes he was ready to excommunicate the Emperor's foes, and the Beneventans, who refused admittance to the German army, were sufferers. But, setting a strange example to later Popes, he kept his old bishopric, to which, as "his sweetest bride," he sent an affectionate letter, and where on his unexpected death (9 October 1047) his body was laid to rest (he was the only Pope buried in Germany); a widely-accepted rumour had it that his unexplained illness was due to poison administered in the interests of Benedict IX, and the same was said about his successor. It is certain, at any rate, that on 9 November Benedict returned to Rome, and, supported by the Marquess Boniface of Tuscany, kept his old office until July (1048). Neither Roman families nor Italian nobles would accept imperial control if they could help it. The power of Boniface now threatened to become dangerous: his grandfather Azzo owned Canossa and his father Tedald, favoured by Henry II, had held Mantua, Ferrara, and other towns, and kept them faithful to the Emperors. Boniface at first followed his father's policy and Conrad had given him the March of Tuscany. But his choice of a second wife, Beatrice, daughter of Frederick, Duke of Upper Lorraine, brought him into a wider sphere of politics. Distrust grew between him and the Emperor. At Rome he could injure the Emperor most, and hence his support of Benedict. The Romans, however, did not follow him; a deputation was sent to Henry at Pöhlde seeking a new nomination, and Poppo, Bishop of Brixen, was chosen (Christmas 1047). But Boniface, although Henry's representative in Italy, at first refused to lead the new Pope to Rome, and only renewed orders brought him to obedience; then at length he expelled Benedict IX, and the new Pope was enthroned as Damasus II (17 July 1048). On 9 August he too died at Palestrina, after a pontificate of only twenty-three days; poison was again suspected, although malaria may have been the cause. It was no wonder that the deputation which again visited Germany found the papal throne little desired. They suggested Halinard of Lyons[2], much beloved in Rome, where he had sojourned long. But he did not accept, even if Henry offered it. At Worms the Emperor chose a relative of his own, Bruno of Toul, and so there began a papacy which was to change even the unchanged Rome itself.

[1] Wazo, *Sententia de Gregorio VI*, in Watterich, *Vitae Pontificum*, I, pp. 79–80, quoted from Anselm of Liège.

[2] It seems better, with Hauck and others, to place the suggestion of Halinard here, and not earlier.

Bruno, Bishop of Toul, was son of Hugo, Count of Egisheim, and related to Conrad II, who destined him for rich preferment. Herman of Toul died on 1 April 1026, and the clergy and citizens at once chose for successor Bruno, who was well known to them but was then with the army of Conrad II in Italy. The Emperor hinted at a refusal in hope of better things, but the unanimous election seemed to the young ecclesiastic a call from God; there had been no secular influence at work on his behalf, and so to Toul, a poor bishopric, often disturbed by border wars, he determined to go.

The future Pope had been born 21 June 1002, and, as destined for the Church, was sent to a school at Toul, noted equally for its religious spirit and its aristocratic pupils. His parents were religious and devoted patrons of monasteries in Alsace, and at Toul reforming tendencies, due to William of Dijon, were strong, while an earlier bishop, Gerard (963–994), was revered as a saint; the young man, learned and literary, became a canon of Toul, and although not a monk had a deep regard for St Benedict, to whose power he attributed his recovery from an illness. From Toul he passed to the chapel of the king, and as deputy for Herman led the vassals of the bishopric with Conrad; in military affairs he shewed ability, and was, from his impressive figure, his manners and activity, liked by many besides Conrad and Gisela. His acceptance of Toul seemed to others a self-denial, but even its very poverty and difficulties drew him. He was not consecrated until 9 September 1027, as Poppo of Trèves wished to impose a stricter form of oath upon his suffragan, and not until Conrad's return did the dispute end by the imposition of the older form. This difficulty cleared, Bruno devoted himself to his diocese: monastic reform in a city where monasteries were unusually important was a necessity, and to this he saw; the city lay open to attacks from the Count of Champagne, and Bruno had often occasion to use his military experience, inherited and acquired. Thus, like the best bishops of his day, notably Wazo of Liège, he was a good vassal to the Emperor and a defender of the Empire. On the ecclesiastical side, too, he had that love of the past which gave a compelling power to historic traditions: it was he who urged Widerich, Abbot of St Evré, to write a life of his predecessor, St Gerard; as a pilgrim to the apostolic threshold, he often went to Rome. In diplomacy he was versed and useful: in Burgundian politics he had taken a share; he had helped to negotiate the peace with France in 1032. As a worthy bishop with many-sided interests and activities he was known far beyond his diocese, and even in countries besides his own.

Christmas 1048 Bruno spent at Toul, and then, accompanied by other bishops and by Hildebrand, the follower of Gregory VI, he went to Rome. It was a journey with the details of which clerical and partisan romance afterwards made itself busy. But an election at Rome was usual and, to Leo more than to other men, necessary. As before at Toul, his path must be plain before him. Only when accepted by his future flock could he begin his work, although the real choice had been the Emperor's. Leo moved along a path he had already trodden, and he needed no Hildebrand, with the warning of an older prophet, to guide his steps. Already he knew a bishop's duty and the needs of the Church. He now passed into a larger world, even if he kept his former see up to August 1051: his aims and his spirit were already set, only he was now to work on an international field; reading, travel, diplomacy, and episcopal work had trained him into a strong, enlightened statesman, of fixed principles and piety, clear as to the means he ought to use. Church reform had begun in many places and under many leaders; its various forms had been tending to coherence in principles and supports, removal of abuses, and recognition of Canon Law. Taught by these, many eyes had turned to Rome. But guidance had been lacking thence, and abuses had flourished to excess. Leo IX was to bring to the movement guidance; he was to give it a coherence based on papal leadership and power. We find under him all the former elements of the movement welded together, and re-interpreted by a Pope who knew what the Papacy could do. Hence came its new strength. His papacy is marked by its many Councils, held not only at Rome but also far afield: Rome (after Easter 1049), Pavia (Whitsuntide), Rheims (October), Mayence (October), Rome (Easter 1050), Salerno, Siponto, Vercelli (September 1050), Rome (Easter 1051), Mantua (February 1053), Rome (Easter)[1]. But this itinerary gives little idea of his travels; on his route from place to place he made visits of political importance, such as to Lorraine, and southern Italy, and even to Hungary; everywhere he strove to rouse the Church, and incidentally composed political or ecclesiastical strifes. Details are wanting for some of these councils, but we must assume that in all of them decrees against simony and clerical marriage, often spoken of as concubinage (which was sometimes the truth), were issued. At the Roman Council of 1049 simony was much discussed; guilty bishops were deposed, and one of them, Kilian of Sutri, while trying to clear himself by false witness, fell like another Ananias and died soon afterwards. There was a like incident later at Rheims, when the innocent Archbishop of Besançon, pleading for the guilty and much accused Hugh of Langres, suddenly lost his voice. It was ascribed to a miracle by St Rémy (Remigius), but such details shew how personal responsibility was now being pressed home on the bishops. There was a suggestion that ordinations by simonist bishops should be declared null, and it is sometimes said that Leo decreed they were so[2]. This, as it was urged, would have made almost a clean sweep

---

[1] An account of Leo's councils is given in Hefele-Leclercq, IV, pp. 995 sqq., with a very full bibliography for the reign; points of chronology, etc., are discussed.

[2] For a full discussion see Saltet, *Les Réordinations*, Paris, 1907, pp. 181 sqq. and note, p. 408. The evidence comes from Peter Damian, and the difficulty lies in the translation of his "tanquam noviter ordinavit." I agree with the text of the Abbé Saltet, and am not convinced by his note correcting his views as given there.

of the Roman clergy, for many Popes of late had been simoniacal. Finally it was settled on the lines laid down by Clement II that a penance of forty days met the case. But Leo brought up the matter again in 1050 and 1051, and on the last date he bade the bishops seek light from God. In the Curia there were different views. Peter Damian insisted that the acts of simoniacal bishops were valid, and he supported this by the assertion that some of them had worked miracles; Cardinal Humbert, on the other hand, went strongly on the other side. The two men were foremost in rival schools of thought, divided by opinions on other matters also. Peter Damian, for instance, welcomed the help of pious kings like Henry III, while Humbert held any lay interference in Church affairs an outrage. Strife on this matter was to grow keener, and the fortune of battle is recorded as by an index in the treatment of simonist ordinations. There was a side issue in the question whether simony was not a heresy, as the musician-monk Guido of Arezzo suggested; if it were, simonist ordinations, according to received doctrine, would be automatically void.

The Council of Rheims (3 October 1049) was of special importance. In France local conditions varied: here the king and there a great vassal controlled episcopal appointments, but everywhere simony was rife. It arose, however, not as in Germany from the policy of one central power, based upon a general principle of law or administration; it was a widespread abuse of varied local origin to be attacked in many individual cases. The needed reform was now to be preached on French soil by the Pope himself; it was to be enforced with all the authority given to the Pope by the Canon Law, genuine or forged; it appealed to ancient decisions, such as that of Chalcedon (canon II, repeated at Paris in 829), against simony, whether in ordinations or in ecclesiastical appointments, and such as those enforcing attendance at councils, which were henceforth commoner. The appearance of a Pope with definite claims to obedience was thus emphasised by an appeal to the deficient but reviving sense of corporate life. And, when the synod had done its work, the appeal was driven home by the summons of guilty bishops to Rome, and by the Pope's bold guardianship of free elections against royal interference, as in the case of Sens (1049) and Le Puy (1053), and Henry I shewed himself fairly complaisant.

But a German Pope was by no means welcome in France; national diplomacy rather than a fear of papal authority made Henry I look askance on the assembly at Rheims. The consecration of the new abbey church of St Rémy was the occasion of Leo's visit, but the king, by summoning his episcopal vassals to service in a well-timed campaign, made their attendance at the synod difficult, and so many held aloof. An attack upon simony was the first and main business, and after an allocution the bishops one by one were called upon to declare their innocence of it. To do this was notoriously difficult for Guy, the local Archbishop, and the Bishops of Langres, Nevers, Coutances, and Nantes were in the same plight.

The archbishop promised to clear himself at Rome the next Easter, which he may have done; the much-accused Hugh of Langres fled and was excommunicated; Pudicus of Nantes was deposed; the two others cleared themselves of suspicion. The Archbishop of Sens, and the Bishops of Beauvais and Amiens, were excommunicated for non-attendance with insufficient reason. The canons enjoined election by clergy and people for bishops and abbots, forbade the sale of orders, safeguarded clerical dues but prohibited fees for burials, eucharists, and service to the sick; some canons recalled the objects of the Truce of God, and others dealt with infringements of the marriage law. If the synod had been in itself and in many ways, and above all in its vigorous reforms, an expression of the Church's corporate life, it also drove home with unexpected energy the lesson of individual responsibility. The new Papacy as a means of reform had justified itself in a hitherto disorderly field. Summonses to Rome, attendance at Roman synods, and the visits of Roman legates to France, were to secure for the future the gains that Leo had made possible.

From Rheims the Pope passed by way of Verdun, Metz, and Trèves, to Mayence, where (in October) a large Council was held. Here simony and clerical marriage were sternly condemned. Adalbert of Bremen and other bishops after their return home enforced these decrees with varying strictness, but without much success; Adalbert drove wives of clerics from his city to the country outside. But the unhappy fact that a few of the bishops, and notably Sigebod of Spires, were not above moral reproach gave Bardo of Mayence, who was named legate, a difficult task. On leaving Germany, Leo visited Alsace and Lorraine, having with him Humbert, a monk of Moyenmoutier in the Vosges; he was designed for a new arch-see in Sicily, but that not being created he was named Cardinal-bishop of Silva Candida. It was doubtless meant that he was to help Leo in the plans already forming against the Normans in southern Italy. Then, whether before or after the Easter Council at Rome (1050) it is hard to say, Leo went to southern Italy where matters religious and secular needed attention. At the outset of his reign an embassy, it is said[1], from Benevento had begged for his help; there was another embassy in 1052, and probably an intermediate one. And one of the legates whom Leo sent to report upon the situation was Cardinal Humbert. In his own visit of 1050 Leo held Councils at Salerno and at Siponto, in the Norman territory; here the customary decrees were made and some simoniacal bishops deposed. The Easter Council at Rome (1050) was largely attended, as was becoming usual, fifty-five bishops and thirty-two abbots

---

[1] By his archdeacon and biographer, Wibert of Toul; this is the oldest life of Leo, and is written in the older panegyrical style, but is a sound authority for detailed events; like the other biographies of the time, it shews the influence of the Cluniac spirit. See Giesebrecht, *op. cit* II, p. 566; Wibert's Life of Leo in Muratori, RR.II.SS. Ed. I, III, pp. 282 sqq., and in Watterich, I, pp. 127–170.

being present. Guido of Milan successfully cleared himself from a charge of simony, but his very appearance to do so marked, much as similar trials at Rheims and Mayence, a triumph for papal power. But, unhappily for Guido, the struggle for precedence between him and Humfred of Ravenna ended in his being wounded so severely as to be healed only on his return by the miraculous help of St Ambrose. But Humfred himself offended by words against the Pope, for which he was excommunicated at the Council of Vercelli, and his forgiveness at Augsburg (February 1051) was followed by a somewhat dramatic death. The very stars seemed to fight against Leo's foes, and submissions to his commands became more general.

It is needless to follow the later councils of Leo; they were all part of the policy so strikingly begun. A few fresh matters appear in them, mingled with the old: at Vercelli (1 September 1050) the heresy of Berengar, previously discussed in the Roman Council of the same year, was brought up afresh and was to come up again and again. It was an outcome, almost inevitable, of the varied and growing movements of the day.

From Vercelli Leo went by way of Burgundy and Lorraine to Germany, only coming back to Rome for the Easter Council of 1051. He wished to get the Emperor's support for a Norman campaign, but the advice of Gebhard of Eichstädt (afterwards Victor II) swayed Henry against it. Then later in the year he visited southern Italy, whither he had already sent Cardinal Humbert and the Patriarch of Aquileia as legates. His plans almost reached a Crusade; he wished for help both from Henry and the Emperor Constantine IX (1042–1055); he had visions of a papal supremacy which should extend to the long-severed East. Hence a campaign against the Normans and negotiations with Constantinople were combined. Benevento, whence the citizens had driven the Lombard Princes, and which Leo now visited, was at Worms (autumn 1052) in a later visit to Germany given to the Papacy in exchange for Bamberg. Leo IX therefore, like many a Pope, has been called, though for services further afield, the founder of the Temporal Power. On his return from the south, Councils at Mantua (February 1053), where opposition to the decrees for celibacy raised a Lombard riot, and at Rome (Easter) followed; at the latter, the rights of the Patriarch of Grado over Venice and Istria were confirmed, and to the see of Foroiulium (Udine), where the Patriarch of Aquileia had taken refuge after the destruction of his city by the Lombards, was now left only Lombard territory. These measures are to be taken along with the Pope's Eastern plans, in the general policy and military preparations for which Hildebrand had a share. But the host, like other crusading forces, was strangely composed, and the battle of Civitate, which was to have crowned everything, brought only disaster and disappointment. An honourable captivity with the Normans at Benevento made warfare, against which Peter Damian raised a voice, impossible, but Leo could still carry on correspondence and negotiations. The story of the papal embassy to Constantinople, whence help was expected more hopefully than from Germany, has been told elsewhere[1]. The three legates, Cardinal Humbert, Frederick of Lorraine, Cardinal and Chancellor, and Peter, Bishop of Amalfi, had small success, and the breach between the Churches of the East and of the West only became wider and more lasting. Constantine IX had hoped by conquering the Normans to revive his failing dominion over southern Italy, where the Catapan Argyrus was as anti-Norman as Leo himself. But Michael Cerularius, Patriarch since March 1043, had his own large views, carried into politics with much ability, and a natural dislike of the now more strongly-urged Roman claims. Constantinople for many centuries had jealously maintained its independence of Rome; it knew nothing of the Forged Decretals, while Canon Law, Church customs, and ritual were now taking separate paths in East and West. Eastern Emperor and Eastern Patriarch thus had very different interests and views about Leo's designs. The fortune of war favoured the Patriarch, for Argyrus, like Leo, was routed in Italy (February 1053), and the negotiations at Constantinople came to worse than naught.

But the end of a great papal reign was near. Sick in heart and health, Leo left Benevento (12 March 1054), slowly travelling to the Rome where he had dwelt so little but which he tried to make so great. Before his death he besought the Romans to keep from perjury, forbidden marriages, and robbery of the Church; he absolved all whom he had excommunicated; he prayed for the Church and for the conversion of Benedict IX and his brothers, who had set up simony over nearly all the world. Then (19 April 1054) he died.

There seems to us a contrast between the more political schemes of his later and the reforming work of his earlier years. But to him they were both part of the task to which he had been called. To breathe a new spirit into the Church and to extend its power were both to make it more effective in its duty. Even his warfare for the Church was merely doing as Pope what had been part of his recognised duty as Bishop of Toul. And his papal reign made a new departure. His conciliar and legislative activity had been great, even if, amid the pressure of large events and policies, it slackened, like that of Gregory VII, before the end. He brought bishops more generally into varied touch with Rome. He renewed the papal intercourse and growing control for many lands, such as Hungary and England. He made Adalbert of Bremen (1053) Papal Vicar for his Baltic lands, with power to form new sees, even "regibus invitis." Much that he had begun was carried further by later Popes, and great as it was in itself his pontificate was perhaps even greater as an example and an inspiration. Under the influence of reform in Germany, of his own training, his own piety, and his devotion to the

[1] *Supra*, Vol. IV, pp. 255 sqq.

Church, he had shewn, as Bishop of Toul, a high conception of a bishop's office. He brought the same to Rome, and with wider and more historic responsibilities he formed a like conception for the Papacy. His friend and almost pupil Hildebrand was wont[1], we are told, to dwell upon the life of Leo, and the things which tended to the glory of the Roman Church. One great thing above all he did in raising the College of Cardinals, which succeeding Popes, and notably Stephen IX, carried further. His very travels, and the councils away from Rome at which he presided, brought home to men the place and jurisdiction of the Papacy which was being taught then by the Canon Law. These councils were now attended not only by bishops but also by abbots, in quickly increasing numbers; first by such as those of Cluny and Monte Cassino, and then by others, until at Rheims (1049) about fifty appeared and at Rome (1050) thirty-two. Many abbots were now privileged to wear mitres and to ordain; attendance at councils was thus natural. They formed a solid phalanx of reformers, and the nucleus of a papal majority. Thus his pontificate abounded in beginnings upon which future days were to build. He brought the Papacy, after its time of degradation, and with the best impulses of a new day, into a larger field of work and power.

Leo IX left his mark in many ways upon following reigns. The central direction of the Western Church continues, although with some fluctuations of policy and persons, while the improved organisation enables us to see it in the documents now more carefully preserved. The Chancery, upon which fell much work due to the new and wide-spread activity of the Popes, was re-organised by him after the model of the imperial Chancery[2]. After his time the signatures of witnesses often appear, and so we can see who were the chief advisers of the Pope; this we can connect with the growing importance of the cardinals. Papal activities are seen in the number of privileges to monasteries, and many documents shew a diligent papal guardianship of clerical and monastic property. Rome is kept closely in touch with many lands[3], leading prelates are informed of papal wishes and decrees. A continuity of policy and of care for special districts can also be traced in series of letters, such as those to Rheims.

Leo's reforming policy was carried on. Conciliar decrees upon clerical celibacy were repeated, and simony, sometimes forbidden afresh, like marriage, met with new punishment. The policy is much the same, and it is still more directed by Rome. But one difference between him and

---

[1] So Bruno of Segni, *Vita Leonis IX*, in Watterich, *Vitae Pontificum*, I, p. 97.

[2] Privileges, grants or confirmation of rights to property or jurisdiction, took under him a new form, and are distinguished from letters. See R. L. Poole, *Lectures on the History of the Papal Chancery* and *Imperial Influences on the Forms of Papal Documents* (*Brit. Acad.* VIII). Sovereignty and control thus entered into a new and larger field.

[3] *E.g.* England under Edward the Confessor, Dalmatia, France.

his successors soon appears, and slowly grows. He had worked well with the Emperor, but the new spirit breathed into the Papacy brought, with a new self-consciousness, a wish for independence. This was natural, and harmonised with the new feeling, intensified by Canon Law, that the hierarchy of the Church should not be entangled with that of the State. About the difficult application of this principle, views began to differ. The papal reigns to which we pass shew us the gradual disentanglement of these rival principles amid the clash of politics.

But Leo's successor was long in coming, and the exact course of events is somewhat doubtful. Gebhard of Eichstädt had been a trusted counsellor of Henry, he had thwarted the hopes of Leo for large help against the Normans, and now at length he became Pope. The Emperor might well hesitate to part with such a friend, and the prospect of the impoverished Papacy in difficult Italy was not enticing. Here as in the case of Leo IX the real decision lay with Henry. Gebhard's elevation was settled in the last months of 1054, and he was received and, as Victor II, enthroned " hilariter " at Rome (13 April 1055).

The Norman victory, and another event, had altered affairs in Italy. Boniface of Tuscany, whose power and policy were threatening to Pope and Emperor alike, was assassinated on 6 May 1052, and his widow Beatrice married (1054) the dangerous and ambitious Godfrey the Bearded, the exiled Duke of Lorraine, who had been administering her estates. Hence arose difficulties with Henry[1]. He was needed in Italy; in April he was in Verona, at Easter in Mantua. In spite of her defence he put Beatrice and her only remaining child Matilda in prison. Godfrey fled across the Alps, and his brother Frederick, lately returned from Constantinople, took refuge at the fortress-monastery of Monte Cassino; here (May–June 1057) he became abbot, after a short but fervid monastic career entered upon under the influence of Desiderius. At Whitsuntide (4 June 1055) Pope and Emperor were present at a council in Florence. Before leaving Italy Henry gave to the Pope Spoleto and Camerino, as well as making him Imperial Vicar in Italy. This may throw light on Henry's choice of Gebhard and also his alleged promise to restore papal rights. But on 5 October 1056 the great Emperor died. The removal of a strong hand brought new responsibilities to the Pope, his old adviser and friend.

Victor II, like Leo, dwelt little in Rome; he left it at the end of 1055 and travelled slowly to Germany; he was by Henry's death-bed at Botfeld, and he buried him at Spires. Then at Aix-la-Chapelle he enthroned the young king Henry IV; his presence and experience were valuable to the Empress Agnes, now Regent, and he was able to clear her path and his own by a reconciliation with Godfrey, who was allowed to take the place of Boniface. By Lent 1057 Victor was in Rome to hold the usual council. Then he left the city for Monte Cassino to bring the

[1] See *supra*, Vol. III, pp. 293-9.

stubborn monastery, which had elected an Abbot Peter without consulting Pope or Emperor, into accord with the Papacy. The elevation of the Cardinal-deacon Frederick to be its abbot and also Cardinal-priest of St Chrysogonus (14 June) marked a reconciliation, significant ecclesiastically and politically. In July Monte Cassino was left for a journey towards Rheims, where a great Council was to be held. But Victor's death at Arezzo (28 July 1057) removed from the Empire a pillar of peace, and left the Church without a head. In those days of stress, workers who really faced their task rarely lived long. He was buried, not at Eichstädt as he and his old subjects would have wished, but at Ravenna.

It is not so easy to sketch the character of Victor II as to record his doings. As a young man he had been chosen bishop almost incidentally by Henry III, who may have judged rightly his powers of steady service. The Eichstädt chronicles tell us that as a young man he did nothing puerile; it is also true that as an old man he did nothing great. But neither as German bishop nor as Pope did he ever fail in diligence or duty: his earlier reputation was gained rather as servant of the State than as prelate of the Church; as Imperial Vicar he might have brought peace to Italy as he had to Germany and its infant king. But death prevented his settling the Norman difficulty; there is no reason to think that he had forsaken his former view which had crossed that of Leo IX. His dealings with Monte Cassino, always strongly anti-Norman, had given him a new base upon which he could rely for peace as easily as for war. His work was sound but was not completed. He seems to us an official of many merits, but confidence was the only thing he inspired. He was no leader with policies and phrases ready; he was only a workman who needed not to be ashamed.

On 2 August 1057, the festival of Pope Stephen I, Frederick of Lorraine was elected Pope[1], and took the name of Stephen IX[2]. He was in Rome when the news of Victor's death came, and was asked to suggest a successor; he named Humbert, three Italian bishops, and Hildebrand. Then, when asked to be Pope himself, he unwillingly accepted. He was no imperialist like Victor, and he was, like the monks of his abbey, strongly anti-Norman. Above all he was an ecclesiastic, heart and soul. Moreover, he was freely elected at Rome; not until December was a deputation sent to inform the German Court; there was no whisper of kingly recognition and indeed there was no Emperor; he was elected, as a German chronicler complains, *rege ignorante*, although the circumstances may account for this.

The new Pope had been a canon at Liège. His riches, increased by gifts at Constantinople, made him popular, but he was a monk of deep

---

[1] He kept his abbacy as preceding Popes their sees. Victor II's successor Gunther was only elected to Eichstädt on 20 August 1057.

[2] Sometimes called Stephen X. See R. L. Poole, *The Names and Numbers of medieval Popes*, EHR, xxxii, pp. 465 sqq. For our period, pp. 471-2.

conviction. His short papacy leaves room for conjecture as to what with longer days he might have done. There were rumours that he meant to make Duke Godfrey Emperor, but he differed very widely from his more secular-minded brother. Like his predecessors he did not stay long in Rome; he soon left it for Monte Cassino, which he reached at the end of November; he arranged for Desiderius to be abbot after his death, but meanwhile to be sent on an embassy to Constantinople. The shadow of death was already on the Pope, when in February 1058 he went to Rome. Before this he had sent representatives, of whom Hildebrand was one, to Germany, probably to announce his election. Now he resolved to meet his brother, but before he set out he gathered together the cardinal-bishops and other clergy of Rome with the burghers. He told them he knew that after his death men would arise among them who lived for themselves, who did not follow the canons but, though laymen, wished to reach the papal throne. Then they took an oath not to depart from the canons and not to assent to a breach of them by others. He also bound them in case of his death to take no steps before Hildebrand's arrival. Then he set out for Tuscany, but on 29 March 1058 died at Florence where he was buried. Weakness and sickness had long been his lot; it was needless to attribute his death to poison given by an emissary from Rome.

It is clear that Pope Stephen's thoughts were intent upon the Normans; what support Hildebrand had gained from the Empress-regent we do not know, and the Pope himself was eagerly awaiting his legate's return. What further help and of what kind he was to gain from Duke Godfrey was even more uncertain. A policy of peace, such as Victor II had adopted, had more to recommend it than had one of war; Monte Cassino was under papal control, and all the cards were in the papal hand. The hurried fever of a dying man made for haste, but death was even quicker. Stephen's papacy ended amid great possibilities.

But one thing was certain: any line taken would be towards the continued reform of the Church. Stephen had drawn more closely around him able and determined reformers. Peter Damian he called to be Cardinal-bishop of Ostia, a post from which that thorough monk recoiled. He had been unwilling to pass from his beloved Fonte-Avellana to Ocri where Leo IX had made him prior; the sins of the monks filled him with horror, and now he shrank even more from the open world which did not even profess the monastic rule. The Pope had to appeal to his obedience and even to threaten excommunication. So Damian was consecrated at Rome in November 1057, under pressure which he held to be almost uncanonical. He was called from his diocese in 1059 to enforce the programme of discipline at Ambrosian Milan; with him was to go the active reformer Anselm, Bishop of Lucca. To their embassy we must return later. It is enough to notice here that Milan was thus brought into the papal sphere; Guido, its Archbishop, was ordered on 9 December 1057 to appear at the papal Court to discuss the situation.

At length in 1070 Peter Damian gained his release from Alexander II so that he could return to his beloved penitential desert. But his cardinalate he kept and his influence he never lost. As legate, however, he brought his personal power into fresh fields: he was sent to difficult Milan in 1057; to France in 1063 to settle the dispute between Drogo of Macon and the exempted Cluny; and as an old man of 62 to Germany in 1069 to handle the suggested divorce of Henry IV and Bertha. Each mission was a triumph for his firmness or, as he would have preferred to say, for the laws of the Church. The employment of legates to preside at councils superseded the heroic attempts of Leo IX to do so in person; the reverence owed to the Apostolic See was paid to its legates. So we have Humbert's legateship to Benevento in 1051 and to Ravenna in 1053; that of Hildebrand to France in 1055, when he not only, as Damian tells us, deposed six bishops for simony but, as he himself told Desiderius, saw the simonist Archbishop of Lyons smitten dumb as he strove to finish the Gloria with the words "and to the Holy Ghost." With the same great aim, Victor II named the Archbishops of Arles and Aix his permanent Vicars for southern France. Leo IX solemnly placed a mitre on the head of Eberhard of Trèves to mark him as Primate of Gallia Belgica (12 March 1049), on 29 June 1049 gave Herman of Cologne the pallium[1] and cross, on 6 January 1053 gave the pallium and mitre to Adalbert of Bremen as Papal Vicar for the north, and on 18 October 1052 gave the pallium and the use of a special mitre to the Archbishop of Mayence; on 25 April 1057 Victor confirmed the privileges of Trèves, and gave the mitre and pallium to Ravenna. The papal power was thus made more and more the mainspring of the Church. Metropolitans became the channels of papal power. To the Papacy men looked for authority, and from it they received honours which symbolised authority. Grants of the pallium to other sees extended the process, and other marks of honour, such as the white saddle-cloths of Roman clerics, were given and prized. The eleventh century, like the tenth, was one in which this varied taste for splendour, borrowed from the past, was liberally indulged. The mitre, papal and episcopal, was being more generally used and was altering in shape, and its growth illustrates a curious side of our period[2]. Laymen shared the tastes of

---

[1] The pallium was given from the fifth century to archbishops named as Vicars of the Roman Patriarch. In the eighth century it was given to other metropolitans. Originally it was an honorary decoration given by the Emperor, and then acquired an ecclesiastical meaning. It was an age in which, as all evidence shews, decoration and robes, splendid and symbolic, were valued and sought after; diplomatically bestowed by the Popes they gratified the recipients and enhanced the papal power. See for the eighth century the letters between Pope Zacharias and Boniface in *S. Bonifacii et Lulli Epistolae*, MGH, *Epp. Sel.* I (ed. Tangl), pp. 80–205.

[2] The mitre probably originated in the Phrygian cap, a secular sign of honour supposed to be given to the Popes by the Donation of Constantine and worn *ad imitationem imperii*. About the middle of the eleventh century it was used liturgically and not only in secular processions. The whole development, use, and interpretation are interesting. See Sachsee, *Tiara und Mitra der Päpste*, ZKG, xxxiv, pp. 481 sqq.; Duchesne, *Christian Worship* (Engl. transl.), p. 398.

churchmen; Benzo's vivid picture of "the Roman senate" wearing head-dresses akin to the mitre charmed the pencil of a medieval chronicler.

The death of Stephen IX gave the Roman nobles, restless if submissive under imperial control and papal power, a wished-for chance. Empire and Papacy were now somewhat out of touch, and other powers, Tuscan and Norman, had arisen in Italy. Gerard, Count of Galeria, formed a party with Tusculan and Crescentian help, burst into the city by night, 5 April 1058, and elected John Mincius, Cardinal-bishop of Velletri, as Benedict X[1]; and money played its part in the election. The name was significant, but the Pope himself, more feeble than perverse, had previously been open to no reproach[2]; he had been made cardinal by Leo IX, and on the death of Victor II had been suggested by Stephen himself as a possible Pope. Reform had thus made great strides between Benedict IX and Benedict X. Some of the cardinals were afar, Humbert in Florence, and Hildebrand on his way from Germany[3], whither he had gone, a little late, to announce the election of Stephen. But as a body they were now more coherent, less purely Roman, and more ecclesiastical; they declared against Benedict, threatening him with excommunication, and fled the city. Then they gathered together in Tuscany and consulted at leisure on another choice. In the end they settled on a Burgundian, Gerard Bishop of Florence, a sound and not too self-willed prelate of excellent repute, favoured by Duke Godfrey[4] and not likely to take a line of his own. Besides the help of Godfrey the approval of the Empress Agnes was sought. Even in Rome itself there was a party against Benedict, headed by Leo de Benedicto Christiano[5], a rich citizen, son of a Jewish convert, influential in the Trastevere and in close touch with Hildebrand; they sent a deputation to the Empress Agnes at Augsburg, pleading that the election of Benedict had been due to force. As a result Duke Godfrey was ordered to lead the cardinals' nominee to Rome. Gerard was elected at Siena, probably in December 1058, by the cardinals, together with high ecclesiastics and nobles, and chose the name of Nicholas II[6]. His old see he kept until his death. Then an approach was made towards Rome; a synod was held at Sutri. Leo de Benedicto opened the Trastevere

---

[1] On the election and date see Hefele-Leclercq, IV, pp. 1133 sqq.

[2] The invective of Peter Damian against him judges after the election. For it see Watterich, I, pp. 204–5.

[3] Less probably in Germany itself. But see Hefele-Leclercq, IV, p. 1134, note 2.

[4] In war against Ancona he was helped by a papal excommunication of the opposing citizens. Thus the Papacy was useful to him. Peter Damian did not approve this action of the Pope (*Ep.* I, 7). See Langen, III, pp. 528–9.

[5] From his son Peter his descendants were known as the Pierleoni. On him see Poole, *Benedict IX and Gregory VI*, pp. 23 sqq.; he was probably connected by marriage with Hildebrand's mother.

[6] For an election near 6 December (St Nicholas' Day), the choice of name was natural. Martens wrongly assumes a reference to Nicholas I. A Pope chose his own name, from the time of John XVI (983) whose baptismal name was Peter (see Poole, EHR, XXXII, pp. 459 sqq.).

to them, and Benedict X fled for a few days to Passarano and thence to Galeria, where for three months he was besieged by the Normans under Richard of Aversa. Nicholas was enthroned on 24 January 1059; and the captured Benedict was deposed, stripped of his vestments, and imprisoned in the *hospitium* of the church of Sant' Agnese[1]. His name was long left in the papal lists, and he was not an anti-Pope in the ordinary sense until Nicholas II was elected[2]. The choice of Gerard had removed the election of a Pope from the purely Roman sphere to one of wider importance, and the alliance with the Normans, brought about by the help of Desiderius, Abbot of Monte Cassino, gave the Pope a support independent of the Empire or Rome. In all these negotiations Hildebrand played a great part[3]. In the interval between his enthronement and the Easter Council, Nicholas visited Spoleto, Farfa, and Osimo, and at the last place on 6 March 1059 appointed Desiderius as cardinal. In Italy, after the Easter Council at Rome, he held a Council at Melfi, where decrees on clerical celibacy were repeated stringently, and the famous peace was made with the Normans[4]. Then he returned to Rome, accompanied by a Norman army, and the papal sovereignty was enforced. The Norman alliance, and the celebrated decree on papal elections, worked together, and a new era began.

A great Council of 113 bishops was held on 14 April 1059 at the Lateran[5]. Earlier decrees had broadly regulated the election of a Pope; Stephen III (769) and Stephen IV (862–3) had anathematised anyone contesting an election made by priests, prelates, and the whole clergy of the Roman Church. Otto I had renewed the settlement of Lothar I (824), by which the election was to be made by the whole clergy and nobility of the whole Roman people, canonically and justly, but the elect was not to be consecrated until he had taken the oath to the Emperor. The normal canonical form was prescribed, but disorderly nobles, imperial pressure, civic riots, and simony, had tampered with Rome even more than other churches. The German Popes had brought reform but at the price of ecclesiastical freedom.

The Election Decree of 1059 has come down to us in two forms, known

---

[1] The final scene of his condemnation may belong to the winter of 1059 or the Easter Council of 1060. For details see Meyer von Knonau, I, pp. 177–8 and note 13.

[2] On this point see Poole, *Names and Numbers of Medieval Popes*, EHR, xxxII, pp. 465 and 473–4. Benedict's name has now disappeared from the official list.

[3] Yet the views of Hauck, *op. cit.* III, pp. 680–1 seem to me to go too far.

[4] See *infra*, Chapter IV, pp. 174 sq.

[5] A discussion of the literature with bibliography in Meyer von Knonau, *Jahrbücher*, I, Excursus VII, pp. 678 sqq.; Hefele-Leclercq, IV, p. 1139, note 2; Hauck, *op. cit.* III, p. 683, note 4. Also A. Werminghoff, *Verfassungsgeschichte der deutschen Kirche im Mittelalter* (in Aloys Meister, *Grundriss der Geschichtswissenschaft*); Langen, *Geschichte der römischen Kirche*, III, p. 503, note 3; J. v. Pflugk-Harttung, *Die Papstwahlen und das Kaisertum* (1046–1328), in ZKG, xxvII, pp. 283 sqq.

as imperial and papal respectively. The latter is now generally accepted, and the former is held to have been falsified by Guibert, then Imperial Chancellor for Italy and afterwards Archbishop of Ravenna and anti-Pope as Clement III[1]. The business of election was, in the first place, to be treated of by the cardinal-bishops. Then they were to call in firstly the cardinal-clerics, and secondly the rest of the Roman clergy and the people. To prevent simony, the cardinal-bishops, taking the place of a metropolitan, were to superintend the election, the others falling in after them. The elect should be taken from the Roman Church, if a suitable candidate were found; if not, from another Church. The honour due to Henry, at present king and as it is hoped future Emperor, was reserved as conceded to him, and to such of his successors as should have obtained in person the same right from the apostolic throne. If a pure, sincere, and voluntary election could not be held in Rome, the cardinal-bishops with the clergy and catholic laity, even if few, might hold the election where they were gathered together. If the enthronement had to be postponed by reason of war or other evil, the Pope-elect might exercise his powers as if fully Pope. Anyone elected, consecrated, or enthroned contrary to this decree was to be anathematised.

The imperial form differed from the papal form summarised above in giving the Emperor a place with the cardinals as a body in leading the election; it does not distinguish the cardinal-bishops from the others, and it does not mention the rest of the clergy or the people. If an election were not possible in Rome, it might be held where the electors chose, in agreement with the king. The differences lie rather in the way in which the king is brought into the election than in the reservation of the imperial rights, which is much the same in both forms, and the cardinal-bishops are not given the rights of a metropolitan; and the imperial form mentions the mediation of Guibert, Chancellor of Italy and imperial representative. The changes seem to be made less on general principles than to suit a special case, and if due to Guibert this is what we might expect.

The decree was not strictly kept, but the place given to the cardinals, who were now growing into a College, was significant for the future. Its details had reference to the past election; judged by its standard, the election of Nicholas was correct and that of Benedict was not. But it laid stress on the special place of the Papacy, and in the papal form at

[1] The papal form (from the Vatican MS. 1994) in MGH, *Constitutiones*, I. pp. 539 sqq., Watterich, I, p. 229, and Mirbt, p. 140. The imperial form in MGH, *Constitutiones*, I, pp. 542 sq. and Mirbt, p. 141, note 2. Both forms conveniently in Bernheim, *Quellen zur Geschichte des Investiturstreites*, I, pp. 12 sqq., followed by the announcements to Christendom at large, to the West Franks, and to the Province of Amalfi. These agree more closely with the papal form. The papal form was preserved by the Canonists and in the Conciliar collections. For the later falsification by Guibert see Watterich, I, p. 233, note 1. The papal form agrees with Peter Damian's comment.

any rate it threw aside all imperial influence before assent to the accomplished act. It remained to be seen whether this freedom could be maintained.

Other matters were also dealt with in the Council. Berengar appeared and made a profession of faith dictated by Cardinal Humbert. The regulation of the papal election was announced as a matter of European importance, as indeed it now was, and here the cardinal-bishops are mentioned expressly; the decree on celibacy was strict, and for those clerks who obediently observed chastity the common canonical life was enforced. In this detail we have a trace of the discussion already mentioned[1]. No clerk or priest was to obtain a church either gratis or for money through laymen. No one was to hear a mass said by an unchaste priest: the precedent of this canon was to be followed later under Alexander II and Gregory VII. Laymen were not to judge or expel from their churches clerks of any rank. The boldness of this canon may be compared with a more hesitating grant in 1057 to the clergy of Lucca that none of them should be taken to secular judgment. The fuller treatment of simonist ordinations and simony of all kinds belongs to the synods of 1060 and 1061[2]. The upshot of conciliar activity under Nicholas II was to crystallise the former campaign for celibacy into definite decisions, backed by the whole power of the Papacy and the Curia. What had before been tentative was now fixed. Opinion was consolidated, and policy was centralised, not only about celibacy but also about simonists. If those who had been ordained by simonists in the past were allowed to keep their orders and their offices, thus conforming to the policy of Peter Damian at Milan, it was lest the Church should be left without pastors. But for the future there was to be no hesitation, and the correspondence of the Popes with Gervais of Rheims[3] (a see carefully watched as in previous reigns) illustrates the carrying out of the policy[4].

The Council at Rome (1060) decreed that for the future anyone ordained without payment by a simonist bishop should remain in his order if he was open to no other charge; this decision was made not on principle but from pity, as the number affected was so great. It was not to be taken as precedent by following Popes; for the future, however, anyone ordained by a bishop whom he knew to be a simonist should be deposed, as should the bishop also. Thus a long-standing difficulty was for the time disposed of. Reforming councils in France at Vienne and Tours, held under the legate Cardinal Stephen, made stringent decrees against simony, marriage

---

[1] See *supra*, p. 13 and note 1.

[2] Hefele-Leclercq, iv, p. 1169. See also for canons of 1060 Bernheim, *Quellen*, pp. 22 sq.

[3] Jaffé-Löwenfeld, *Reg.*, *passim* [some 20 letters].

[4] For the views of Nicholas on reordination see Saltet, *Les Réordinations*, pp. 198-9, and A. Fliche, *Les Prégrégoriens*, Paris, 1916, p. 246. Decision on the crucial point was avoided.

of priests, and alienation of church property or tithes under legal form. Abbot Hugh of Cluny did the same at Avignon and Toulouse[1]. But it was now more a matter of enforcing decrees already made than issuing new. In Italy some bishops found it difficult to publish reforming decrees, and in some cases did so with risk of violence.

It has been noted as strange that in such a remarkable reign we hear little about the character of the Pope himself. The predominance of the cardinals partly explains it: Humbert, Peter Damian, and Hildebrand (now archdeacon) were not always in accord, and it was for Nicholas to balance conflicting views and policies. He was the president of the College rather than its director. Like other Popes Nicholas kept his old bishopric, and like them too he was often absent from Rome, which was not without its drawbacks, as the English bishops, robbed by the Count of Galeria, found out. But we breathe an air of greater largeness in his Papacy, and things seem on a larger scale.

Nicholas died suddenly near Florence on 27 July 1061, returning from an expedition in southern Italy. The Election Decree was to be tested.

The Norman alliance, and still more the Election Decree, had affected the delicate relations of Pope and Emperor[2]. During the minority of Henry IV, matters had been allowed to slide, and when attention was at length given to them the barometer registered a change of atmosphere. So great was the irritation in Germany that the name of Nicholas was left out in intercessions at mass; legates from Rome met with bad receptions.

Meanwhile events in Milan[3] had taken a decisive turn for papal and ecclesiastical history. In position, in wealth, in traditions, both political and ecclesiastical, the city of St Ambrose was a rival of Rome, and hitherto it had proudly kept its independence. Aribert's opposition to the Emperor Conrad had shewn the power of the archbishop; and if an enemy to the Empire were to rule there, imperial influence would be weakened. This Henry III understood. On Aribert's death in 1045 Guido was appointed. Class distinctions were strongly marked, and the new archbishop belonged not to the barons but to the vavassors; in strength and in reputation he was undistinguished, and Bonizo with his usual exaggeration calls him "vir illiteratus et concubinatus et symoniacus," but concubinage he was not guilty of. He was not the man for a difficult post, still less the man to lead reform. He valued more the traditions of St Ambrose as a rival of Rome than as a teacher of

[1] For France, Langen, III, pp. 524–5. R. Lehmann, *Forschungen zur Geschichte Abtes Hugo I von Cluny*, Göttingen, 1869, pp. 83–9. Hefele-Leclercq, IV, pp. 1199 sqq. Nicholas was, as Langen has noted, specially interested in France, as a Burgundian might be. It may be mentioned that in later years his enemies spread a rumour that his birth was irregular.

[2] See Meyer von Knonau, *Jahrbücher*, I, Excursus VIII, pp. 684 sqq. Hefele-Leclercq, IV, pp. 1209 sqq. Hauck, *op. cit.* III, pp. 700–1, especially note 5.

[3] For Milan cf *infra*, Chapter V, pp. 217 sqq.

righteousness. In Italy as a whole the poor were more devoted to the Church than the rich (who tended to have their own chapels), and they were keen to criticise the lives of their spiritual teachers; outbursts of violence against unworthy priests had not been rare in Milan. But these had been isolated acts; what mattered more was that the Milanese Church had settled down into a worldly, possibly respectable, but certainly unspiritual life of its own. It was content to breathe the air around it but did nothing to revive or purify it, although the clergy were numerous "as the sands of the sea" and the churches were rich. For the most part the clerks were married, and so the Church was deeply intertwined in the social state. Sale of Church offices was common, and there was a recognised scale of charges for orders and for preferments. It was certain that reformers would find much to complain of; so long had the growth of secularisation gone on that, even with a more placid populace, reform when it came was likely to become revolution.

About 1056 the new streams of thought and new ideals began to flow around the hitherto firm footing of the clergy. The movement was headed by a deacon Ariald, a vavassor by birth and a canonist by training, an idealist, inspired by visions of the primitive Church and the simple teaching of Christ: contrasting these with the example of priests whose life could teach but error. He began his campaign in the villages where he was at home; then, when his hearers pleaded their simplicity and urged him to go to Milan, where he would find men of learning to answer him, he took their advice. In the city he found allies ready to help although starting from a different point—Landulf, who was in minor orders, and (later on) his brother Erlembald, of the Cotta family, both gifted with eloquence, ambitious, and thorough demagogues. The movement soon became political and social as well as religious, owing to the social standing of those they attacked. With these two worked Anselm of Baggio, one of the collegiate priests, whom Guido persuaded the Emperor to appoint to the see of Lucca (1056 or 1057). Guido, appointed by Henry III who had misjudged his character, was himself a simonist, and his arguments that clerical marriage was an ancient custom in Milan, that abuse and violence were evil ways of reproving offenders, that the clergy were not immoral but for the most part respectable married men, and that abstinence was a grace not given to all and was not imposed by divine law, had small effect. In other cities, Pavia and Asti for instance, the populace rose against their bishop, and Milan was moved in the same way. Landulf worked in the city; Ariald carried on the campaign in the surrounding villages whose feudal lords were citizens of the town. And Anselm brought the movement into touch with the wider circle of reformers at Rome and elsewhere. Landulf's eloquence soon filled the poorer citizens with hatred of the clergy, with contempt for their sacraments, and a readiness to enforce reform by violence. The undoubted devotion of the leaders, enforced by their eloquence in sermons

and speeches, soon made them leaders of the populace. The use of nick-
names—Simonians and Nicolaitans—branded the clerical party; that of
Patarines brought in class distinctions, and those to whom it was given
could claim like Lollards in England the special grace of simple men. On
the local festival of the translation of St Nazarius a riot broke out, and
the clergy were forced to sign a written promise to keep celibacy. They
had to choose between their altars and their wives. Their appeal to the
archbishop, who took the movement lightly, brought them no help. The
nobles for some reason or other took as yet no steps to help them. The
bishops of the province when appealed to proved helpless, and in
despair the clerks appealed to Rome, probably to Victor II. His care for
the Empire made the Pope anxious to keep order. He referred the
matter to Guido, and bade him call a provincial synod, which he did at
Fontaneto in the neighbourhood of Novara (1057). Ariald and Landulf
were summoned, but, in their scornful absence, after three days they were
excommunicated. Although this synod had been called, its consequences
fall in the pontificate of Stephen IX, who is said to have removed
the ban from the democratic leaders. The movement had become, as
democratic movements so easily do, a persecution with violence and
injury[1]. Guido's position was difficult and in the autumn (1057) he
went to the German Court.

But the movement now took a new and wider turn; not only clerical
marriage but simony, the prevalent and deeply-rooted evil of the city,
was attacked. A large association, sworn to reach its ends, was formed.
The new programme affected Guido, equally guilty with nearly all his
clergy. It was of small avail that now the higher classes, more sensitive
to attacks on wealth than on ecclesiastical offences, began to support the
clergy; the strife was only intensified. In the absence of Guido, and with
new hopes from the new Pope, Ariald went to Rome and there complained
of the evils prevalent at Milan. It was decided to send a legate, and
Hildebrand on his way to the German Court made a short stay at Milan
(November 1057). He was well received; frequent sermons did something
to control the people already roused. But his visit wrought little change,
and it was not until Damian[2] and Anselm came as legates that anything

[1] The chronology is difficult and doubtful. That adopted by Meyer von Knonau
(*Jahrb.* I, especially Excursus v, pp. 669 sqq.) seems best. It is not certain whether
the Milanese clergy appealed to Victor II or Stephen IX; Arnulf says the latter,
but the former is more probable. For the chronology see also Hefele-Leclercq, IV,
pp. 1126 sqq.

[2] The legateship is best dated early in 1059 before the Easter Synod at Rome.
We have Damian's own account addressed to Hildebrand, Archdeacon. Hence a
difficulty, for Hildebrand was not Archdeacon until autumn 1059. But Damian
speaks of his having been asked by Hildebrand to put together matters bearing on
Roman supremacy; the account was probably meant in that sense as a record of an
important decision. For other arguments in favour of this date see Hefele-Leclercq,
IV, p. 1191, note 2; Meyer von Knonau, I, p. 127, note 17. Hauck, III, p. 696, note
1, holds the date as good as certain.

was done. Damian persuaded Guido to call a synod, and here, at first to the anger of the patriotic Milanese, the legate presided. It seemed a slur upon the patrimony and the traditions of St Ambrose; even the democratic reformers were aghast. It was then that Damian, faced by certain violence and likely death, shewed the courage in which he never failed. With no attempt at compromise, with no flattery to soothe their pride, he spoke of the claims of St Peter and his Roman Church to obedience. Milan was the daughter, the great daughter of Rome, and so he called them to submission. It was a triumph of bold oratory backed by a great personality; Guido and the whole assembly promised obedience to Rome. Then Damian went on with his inquest; one by one the clerics present confessed what they had paid, for Holy Orders, for benefices, and for preferment. All were tainted, from the archbishop to the humblest clerk. Punishment of the guilty, from which Damian was not the man to shrink, would have left the Church in Milan without priests and ministers of any kind. So the legate took the course taken by Nicholas II in his decree against simonists (1059). Those present, beginning with the archbishop, owned their guilt, and promised for the future to give up simony and to enforce clerical celibacy. To this all present took an oath. Milan had fallen into line with the reformers, and in doing so had subjected itself to Rome. Bonizo, agreeing with Arnulf on the other side, is right in taking this embassy as the end of the old and proud independence of Milan. When Guido and his suffragans were summoned to the Easter Council of 1059 at Rome some Milanese resented it. But the archbishop received absolution and for some six years was not out of favour at Rome.

The unexpected death of Nicholas II was followed by a contested election and a long struggle. Both the Roman nobles and the Lombard bishops wished for a change but knew their need of outside help. At Rome Gerard of Galeria, whose talents and diplomacy were typical of his class, was the leader; he and the Abbot of St Gregory on the Caelian were sent to the German Court, and they carried with them the crown and insignia of the Patrician. The Lombard bishops, with whom the Chancellor Guibert worked, met together and demanded a Pope from Lombardy—the paradise of Italy—who would know how to indulge human weakness. Thus civic politics at Rome and a reaction against Pataria and Pope worked together; the young king Henry acted at the impulse of Italians rather than of Germans; the latter had reason for discontent, but the imperial nominee was not their choice and their support was somewhat lukewarm. Henry met the Lombard bishops (some of whom Peter Damian thought better skilled to discuss the beauty of a woman than the election of a Pope) and the Romans at Basle on 28 October 1061, and, wearing the Patrician's crown which they had brought, invested their elect, Cadalus, Bishop of Parma, who chose the name of Honorius II[1], "a man rich in silver, poor in virtue" says Bonizo.

[1] There is some conflict of evidence, especially as to the part played by the

Meanwhile the cardinal-bishops and others had met outside Rome, and, hastening when they knew of the opposition, elected, 30 September 1061, Anselm of Baggio, the Patarine Bishop of Lucca[1]. It was a wise choice and likely to commend itself; there could be no doubt as to the ortho-doxy or policy of this old pupil of Lanfranc at Bec, tested at Milan and versed in Italian matters; at the same time he was in good repute at the German Court and a friend of Duke Godfrey. Desiderius of Monte Cassino carried a request for military help to Richard of Capua, who came and led Alexander II to Rome. Some nobles, especially Leo de Benedicto Christiano ("of the Jewish synagogue," says Benzo), influenced the Trastevere, but there was much fighting and Anselm was only taken into the Lateran at night and by force. He was consecrated on 1 October 1061, and like his predecessors kept his old bishopric.

Cadalus found his way to Rome blocked by Godfrey's forces, but in Parma he gathered his vassals, and could thus march on. But another help was of greater use. Benzo, Bishop of Alba in Piedmont, was sent by the Emperor as his ambassador to Rome; he was a popular speaker with many gifts and few scruples; his happy if vulgar wit was to please the mob and sting his opponents; he was welcomed by the imperialists and lodged in the palace of Octavian. Then he invited the citizens, great and small, and even Alexander with his cardinals, to a popular assembly. The papal solemnity had little chance with the episcopal wit. "Asinan-drellus, the heretic of Lucca," and "his stall-keeper Prandellus," as Benzo calls the Pope and Hildebrand, were worsted in the debate; Cadalus was able to enter Rome on 25 March 1062, and a battle on 14 April in the Neronian Field after much slaughter left him victor. But he could not gain the whole city, and it was divided into hostile camps. Honorius hoped for help from Germany, and he was negotiating with Greek envoys for a joint campaign against the Normans. But after the arrival of Duke Godfrey there came an end to the strife, both claimants were to withdraw to their former sees until they could get their claims settled at the German Court. Honorius was said to have paid heavily for the respite, but Alexander could rest easy as to his final success.

Alexander was not without some literary support. Peter Damian from his hermitage wrote to Cadalus two letters, fierce and prophetic—the second addressed "To Cadalus, false bishop, Peter, monk and sinner, wishes the fate he deserves": he had been condemned by three synods; he had broken the Election Decree; his very name derived from *cado* λαός was sinister, he would die within the year; the old prophet believed

German bishops. A summary of references in Hefele-Leclerq, iv, p. 1217, note 1. The part played by Henry corresponds to the imperial falsification of the Election Decree of 1059 (clause 6).

[1] An election outside Rome was provided for in the Election Decree, and Peter Damian expressly mentions the presence of the cardinal-bishops, a mention which supports the papal form of the Election Decree.

the prophecy fulfilled by the excommunication, the spiritual death, of Honorius within the year. At the same time he was writing treatises on the episcopal and clerical life. At this time, too, he wrote his well-known *Disceptatio Synodalis*, a dialogue between champions of the Papacy and the Empire; it is not, as was once supposed, the record of an actual discussion, but a treatise intended to influence opinion at the assembly called at Augsburg, 27 October 1062, to settle the papal rivalry. But he was an embarrassing ally[1]: his letters to Henry and Anno of Germany, if full of candid advice, laid overmuch stress on the royal rights, and Alexander and Hildebrand were displeased. Damian, perhaps ironically, begged the mercy of his " Holy Satan."

It was the practical politics of the day, and not theories or arguments, which turned the balance at Augsburg and elsewhere in favour of Alexander. The abduction of the twelve-year-old boy at Kaiserswerth (April 1062) and his guardianship by Anno of Cologne, first alone and then with Adalbert, changed affairs. The Empress Agnes, who had taken the veil about the end of 1061, withdrew from politics. The German episcopate, weak, divided, and never whole-hearted for the Lombard Honorius, turned towards Alexander. The Synod of Augsburg, led by Anno, declared for Alexander and so gained commendation from Damian; "he had smitten off the neck of the scaly monster of Parma." Before the end of 1062 Alexander moved towards Rome, and before Easter 1063 Godfrey supported the decision of Augsburg; the inclination of Anno and his position of Imperial Vicar led him to Rome. At the Easter Synod Alexander acted as already and fully Pope. As a matter of course he excommunicated Cadalus, and repeated canons against clerical marriage and simony; the faithful were again forbidden to hear mass said by guilty priests.

But the opposition was not at an end, so the irrepressible Benzo again led Cadalus to Rome in May 1063; they took the Leonine City, Sant' Angelo, and St Peter's, but his seat was insecure. His supporters and his silver dwindled together; the castle was really his prison until he bought freedom from his jailor Cencius with three hundred pounds of silver; with one poor attendant he escaped to the safer Parma.

Then at Whitsuntide, probably in 1064[2], he met the Council at Mantua attended by German and Italian prelates. Anno ("the high-priest" Benzo calls him) stated candidly the charges against Alexander. Alexander on oath denied simony, and on the question of his election without Henry's leave or approval satisfied the assembly. Everyone

---

[1] His letters to Cadalus, *Epp.* i, 20, 21 (MPL, cxliv); to Henry IV, vii, 3; to Anno, iii, 6; to Hildebrand, clearing himself, i, 16.

[2] The year is taken as 1064, 1066, and 1067 by various writers. The arguments are most clearly discussed in Hefele-Leclercq, iv, pp. 1237 sqq. See also Meyer von Knonau, i, p. 375, note 19. Benzo's account with its alternate swoonings of Beatrice and Anno has a touch of drama.

present may not have looked at the Council in the same way, but all were glad to settle the disputed succession. On the second day a mob of Cadalists attacked the gathering. Only the appearance of Beatrice of Tuscany with a small force saved the Pope's life; some bishops fled. Cadalus was excommunicated, and Alexander could safely go to Rome. But his city was still not a pleasant seat. Benzo did not give up hope and in 1065 visited the German Court; even up to 20 April 1069 Honorius signed bulls as Pope.

The remaining years of Alexander's pontificate can be summarised.

The Norman vassals or allies of the Pope soon deserted him; Richard of Capua ravaged Campania and approached Rome, probably anxious to be made Patrician. Duke Godfrey, acting in his own interests and not those of Henry, marched towards Rome with an army of Germans and Tuscans, and a treaty followed. Once more Pope and Normans were at peace, irrespective of imperial plans and hopes. The balance between Duke Godfrey and the Normans was finally kept. Elsewhere too it was a question of balance. As Anno's influence at the German Court lessened he depended more upon Rome, and from the German episcopate, lacking any great national leader like Aribo and now gradually losing its former moral strength, he gained small support. At Rome he was humiliated; in 1068 and again in 1070 he had to clear himself of accusations. The system by which metropolitans were to be channels of papal authority was beginning to work its way[1]. But provincial synods both in France and Germany became commoner, and some, such as that of Mayence (August 1071)[2] where Charles, the intended Bishop of Constance, resigned in order to avoid a trial, acted independently. But there as in other cases legates, the Archbishops of Salzburg and Trèves, were present. Such councils, often repeating decrees from Rome, raised papal power, and at this very synod the Archbishop of Mayence is called for the first time *Primas et Apostolicae sedis legatus*. It was no wonder that not only Anno but Siegfried[3] dreamt of a calm monastic life.

The growth of reform seemed to slacken in Alexander's later years: it may be that Damian was right in contrasting the indulgence shewn to bishops with the severity towards the lower clergy; it may be that the movement was now throwing itself more into constitutional solidification than into spiritual awakening; it may be that the machinery at Rome was not equal to the burden thrown upon it by the vast conception of its work. In England alone, where Alexander had blessed the enterprise of

---

[1] Alexander exercised his power more in matters of discipline than of property. The Thuringian tithes dispute he left for German settlement.

[2] Siegfried's letter to the Pope (see *Mon. Bamb.* ed. Jaffé, p. 77) does not seem to me so subservient as it is often held to be, *e.g.* by Hauck, *op. cit.* III, p. 743.

[3] Siegfried retired to Cluny and made his profession, only returning to his see at the command of Abbot Hugh (1072). He would have resigned in 1070 but for Alexander II.

William of Normandy, was success undiluted. The king was just and conscientious; Lanfranc was a theologian and a reformer, even if of the school of Damian rather than of Humbert. The episcopate was raised, and the standard of clerical life; councils, such as marked the movement, became the rule, as was seen at Winchester and London in 1072. But if England moved parallel to Rome it was yet, as an island, apart. It was also peculiar in its happy co-operation of a just king and a great arch-bishop.

The growth of canonical legislation (1049-1073) is easily traced. It begins with an attempt to regain for the Church a control over the appointment of its officers through reviving canonical election for bishops and episcopal institution for parish priests. But the repetition of such canons, even with increasing frequency and stringency, had failed to gain freedom for the Church in face of royal interests and private patronage. The Synod of Rheims under Leo IX (1049) had led the way: no one was to enter on a bishopric without election by clergy and laity. The spread of Church reform and literary discussion moved towards a clearer definition of the rival principles: the Church's right to choose its own officers, and the customary rights of king or patron in appointments. So the Roman synod of 1059 went further: its sixth canon forbade the acquisition either gratis or by payment by any cleric or priest of a Church office through a layman. The French synods at Vienne and Tours (1060), held under the legate Stephen, affirmed the necessity of episcopal assent for any appointment. Alexander II, with greater chance of success, renewed in his Roman synod of 1063 Pope Nicholas' canon of 1059. Under him the two elements, the cure of souls, which was obviously the Church's care, and the gift of the property annexed to it, about which king and laymen had something to say, were more distinctly separated. It was significant when on 21 March 1070 Alexander gave to Gebhard of Salzburg[1] the power of creating new bishops in his province, and provided that no bishop should be made by investiture as it was accustomed to be called or by any other arrangement, except those whom he or his successors should, of their free will, have elected, ordained, and constituted[2]. So far, and so far only, had things moved when Alexander II died.

The constant use of legates was continued if not increased, and France was as before a field of special care. Thither Damian had gone, returning in October 1063, and Gerard of Ostia (1072) dealt specially and severely with simony. In France, and also elsewhere, the frequency of councils

---

[1] Throughout the Middle Ages the right of confirming his suffragans was left to this archbishop, and the peculiarity was mentioned at the Council of Trent.

[2] Jaffé-Löwenfeld, *Regesta*, no. 4673. The history is clearly summarised in Scharnagl, *Der Begriff der Investitur in den Quellen und der Litteratur des Investitur-streites* (*Kirchenrechtliche Abhandlungen*, ed. U. Stutz, No. 86). Some of the canons mentioned are in Bernheim, *Quellen*. Also at length Hefele-Leclercq (*passim*). The Latin originals in Mansi.

locally called is now noticeable. Not only the ordinary matters but laxity of marriage laws among the laity arising from licence among great and small were legislated upon.

The course of affairs at Milan, however, needs longer and special notice. Alexander II had been for many years concerned in the struggle at Milan; his accession gave encouragement to the Patarines; to the citizens and clergy he wrote announcing his election. When Ariald visited Rome under Stephen IX, Landulf, who was on his way thither, was wounded at Piacenza; his wound was complicated by consumption, and he lost the voice and the energy which he had used so effectively. After his death, the date of which is uncertain, his place was more than filled by his brother Erlembald, a knight fresh from a pilgrimage to the Holy Land, and with, as it was said, private, as well as family, wrongs to avenge upon the clergy. He had a personality and appearance very different from his brother's; striking and handsome as became a patrician, splendidly dressed, gifted with that power of military control and organisation which was destined to reappear so often in medieval Italian States. He fortified his house, he moved about with a bodyguard; he became the Captain of the city; personal power and democratic rule were combined and so he was the real founder of the Italian commune. Ariald was content, as he put it, to use the word while Erlembald wielded the more powerful sword. The new leader visited Rome (1065) when Alexander was settled there; he received from the Pope a white banner with a red cross, and so became the knight of the Roman and the universal Church. The archbishop, with no traditions of family or friendship to uphold him, saw power slipping from his hands, and the Emperor counted for naught. From a second visit to Rome (1066) Erlembald returned with threats of a papal excommunication of Guido, and fresh disturbances began. Married priests and simonists were sharply condemned from Rome, and believers were forbidden to hear their masses. But the Papacy sought after order, and the cathedral clergy, faced by persecution, gathered around the archbishop. More tumult arose when Ariald preached against local customs of long standing. Milan had not only its own Ambrosian Liturgy[1], but various peculiar customs: the ten days between Ascension Day and Pentecost had been kept since the fourth century as fasts; elsewhere only Whitsun Eve was so observed. Ariald, preferring the Roman custom, preached against the local use, and so aroused indignation. Then Guido at Whitsuntide seized his chance, and rebuked the Patarines for their action against him at Rome in

---

[1] It seems best with Duchesne (*Origins of Christian worship*, p. 88) to connect the Ambrosian Rite with the Gallican group. Aquileia and the Danubian districts followed Milan. The Carolingian changes affected the Gallican Church, and through imperial influence reached Rome. But Milan kept its Ambrosian traditions, dating from the days of Auxentius (355–374), a Cappadocian Arian and immediate predecessor of St Ambrose; no doctrines were concerned (Duchesne, *op. cit.* pp. 93 sqq.).

seeking his excommunication; a worse tumult than before arose, and the city was again in uproar. But the day after the riot the mass of citizens took better thought and repented. The archbishop placed the city under an interdict so long as Ariald abode in it. For the sake of peace the threatened preacher left, and (27 June) was mysteriously murdered, at Guido's instigation as his followers said. Ten months later his body was, strangely and it was said miraculously, recovered. He had perished by the sword of violence which he had taken, but the splendid popular ceremonies of his funeral restored his fame, and so in death he served his cause.

Once again two legates came to still the storm (August 1067): Mainard, Cardinal-bishop of Silva Candida, and the Cardinal-priest John[1]. The settlement they made went back to that of Damian, and so recognised the position of Guido, but years of violence had by now changed the city. The legatine settlement attempted to re-establish Church order and Damian's reforms, and the revenue of the Church was to be left untouched. Violence was forbidden, but things had gone too far; revolution had crystallised, and neither side liked the settlement; Guido thought of re-signing.

Erlembald, supported from Rome, thought he could increase his power by enforcing canonical election on the resignation of Guido, setting aside the imperial investiture and gaining the approval of the Pope. But Guido now chose the sub-deacon Godfrey, a man of good family, in his confidence, eloquent, as even his later enemies confessed, and therefore likely to be influential. Guido formally although privately resigned, and Godfrey went to the imperial Court where he was already known through services rendered; he returned with his ring and staff, but was driven away. Alexander II condemned not only Godfrey but also Guido, who had resigned without papal leave; Guido took up his duties again, and remained in power; disorder passed into war. Erlembald, with an army made up of his followers and some nobles, attacked Godfrey. Revolution had become war against a claimant chosen by the Emperor but in defiance of ecclesiastical law and the Papacy. During Lent 1071 part of the city was set on fire, causing great destruction and misery; Guido withdrew to the country and there on 23 August 1071 his life and trouble ended. Not until 6 January 1072 did Erlembald find it possible to elect a successor; by a large assembly from the city, its neighbourhood, and even farther afield, in the presence of a legate Cardinal Bernard, Atto, a young cathedral clerk of good family but little known, was elected. Erlembald, the real ruler of the city, was behind and over all; and many, laymen and ecclesiastics, disliked the choice. The discontented took to arms, the legate escaped with rent robes, and Atto, torn from the intended feast at the palace, was borne to the cathedral, where in mortal fear he was made to swear never to ascend the throne of St Ambrose. But next day Erlembald regained control; he "ruled the

---

[1] The embassy, often slurred over in narratives, is described by Arnulf, Chap. 21.

city as a Pope to judge the priests, as a king to grind down the people, now with steel and now with gold, with sworn leagues and covenants many and varied." It mattered little that at Rome a synod declared Atto rightly elected, and condemned Godfrey and his adherents as enemies of God. Meanwhile the Patarines held the field, and their success at Milan encouraged their fellows in Lombardy as a whole. But the new turn of affairs had involved the Pope; he wrote (*c.* February 1072) to Henry IV, as a father to a son, to cast away hatred of the servants of God and allow the Church of Milan to have a bishop according to God. A local difficulty, amid vested interests, principles of Church reform, and civic revolution, had merged into a struggle between Emperor and Pope. Henry IV sent an embassy to the suffragans of Milan announcing his will that Godfrey, already invested, should be consecrated; they met at Novara where the consecration took place.

At the Easter Synod (1073) the Pope, now failing in strength, excommunicated the counsellors of Henry IV who were, it was said, striving to alienate him from the Church. This was one of Alexander's last acts. Death had already removed many prominent leaders, Duke Godfrey at Christmas 1069, the anti-Pope Cadalus at the end of 1072 (the exact day is not recorded). Peter Damian died on 22 February 1072, and Adalbert of Bremen on 16 March of the same year, both men of the past although of very different pasts. Cardinal Humbert had died long before, on 5 May 1061. Hildebrand was thus left almost alone out of the old circle of Leo IX.

On 21 April 1073 Alexander died, worn out by his work and responsibilities; even as Pope he had never ceased the care of his see of Lucca; by frequent visits, repeated letters, and minute regulations he fulfilled his duty as its bishop[1]. It was so with him also as Pope. The mass of great matters dealt with was equalled by that of smaller things. Even the devolution of duties, notably to cardinals and especially to the archdeacon, did not ease the Pope himself. He seems to us a man intent mainly upon religious issues, always striving (as we should expect from a former leader at Milan) for the ends of clerical reform, able now to work towards them through the Papacy itself. Reform, directed from Rome and based upon papal authority, was the note of his reign. A man of duty more than of disposition or temperament, he gained respect, if not the reverent love which had gathered around Leo IX. His measure of greatness he reached more because he was filled with the leading, probably the best, ideas of his day than because of any individual greatness of conception or power. But he had faced dark days and death itself with devotion and unswerving hope. It was something to have passed from his earlier trials to his later prosperity and firm position, and yet to have shewn himself the same man

---

[1] The history of the Chancery under him is "peculiarly anomalous." And this was because he not only was, but acted as, Bishop of Lucca. See Poole, *The Papal Chancery*, p. 69.

CH. I.

CHAPTER II.

GREGORY VII AND THE FIRST CONTEST BETWEEN EMPIRE AND PAPACY.

I.

On 21 April 1073 Pope Alexander II died. The strained relations between the Papacy and the ruler of the Empire made the occasion more than usually critical; moreover, the Election Decree of Nicholas II, for which so narrow a victory had been won at the previous vacancy, was to be put to a second test. Fortunately for the Papacy, there was no division of opinion within the Curia; the outstanding personality of the Archdeacon Hildebrand made it certain on whom the choice of the cardinals would fall. But their deliberations were anticipated by the impatience of the populace. While the body of Alexander was being laid to rest in the church of St John Lateran on the day following his death, a violent tumult arose. The crowd seized upon the person of Hildebrand, hurried him to the church of St Peter ad Vincula, and enthusiastically acclaimed him as Pope. The formalities of the Election Decree were hastily complied with; the cardinals elected, the clergy and people gave their assent, and Hildebrand was solemnly enthroned as Pope Gregory VII[1]. Popular violence had compromised the election, and provided a handle for the accusations of his enemies. But the main purpose of the Election Decree had been fulfilled. The Pope was the nominee neither of the Emperor nor of the Roman nobles; the choice of the cardinals had been anticipated indeed, but not controlled, by the enthusiasm of the multitude. Hildebrand only held deacon's orders; a month later he was ordained priest, and on 30 June[2] consecrated bishop. In the interval, he seems, in accordance with the Election Decree, to have announced his election to the king and to have obtained the royal assent.

We have little certain information[3] of the origin and early life of this great Pope. He is said to have been the son of one Bonizo and to have been born at Sovana in Tuscany; the date of his birth is uncertain, but he was probably about fifty years old at the time of his accession. The important fact, to which he himself bears emphatic testimony, is that his early days were passed in Rome and that it was there that he received his

---

[1] The choice of name is significant. It seems most probable that he took it in memory of his predecessor and master, Gregory VI.

[2] Or 29 June. But as 30 June was a Sunday, the regular day for episcopal consecrations, it is the more likely date, although 29 June was a great festival.

[3] But see R. L. Poole, *Benedict IX and Gregory VI* (from *Proc. Brit. Acad.* Vol. VIII).

education. So he saw the Papacy in its degradation and was to participate in every stage of its recovery. He received minor orders (reluctantly,
he tells us) and was attached in some capacity to the service of Gregory VI,
the Pope who bought the Papacy in order to reform it. With him he
went into exile in 1047, and spent two impressionable years in the Rhine
district, then the centre of the advanced reform movement of the day, and
probably it was at this time that he received the monastic habit[1]. In
1049 Leo IX, nominated Pope by Henry III, was filling the chief places
in the Papal Curia with leading reformers especially from this district; on
his way to Rome he took with him the young Hildebrand, whose life was
for the future to be devoted entirely to Rome and the Papacy. With
every detail of papal activity he was associated, in every leading incident
he played his part; his share in the papal councils became increasingly
important, until at the last he was the outstanding figure whose qualifications for the papal throne none could contest.

By Leo IX he was made sub-deacon and entrusted with the task of
restoring both the buildings and the discipline of the monastery of St
Paul without the walls. Later he was sent to France to deal with heresy
in the person of Berengar of Tours, whose views he condemned but whose
person he protected. By Victor II he was given the important task of
enforcing the decrees against simony and clerical marriage in France,
where in company with Abbot Hugh of Cluny he held synods at Lyons
and elsewhere. With Bishop Anselm of Lucca he was sent by Pope
Stephen IX to Milan, where the alliance of Pope and Pataria was for the
first time cemented; and from Milan to Germany to obtain the royal
assent to Stephen's election. He had a share in vindicating the independence of papal elections against the turbulence of the Roman nobles at
the election of Nicholas II, and again in the papal Election Decree which
was designed to establish this independence for the future. By Nicholas he
was employed in initiating the negotiations which led to the first alliance
of the Papacy with the Normans in South Italy. In the same year (1059)
his appointment as Archdeacon of the Roman Church gave him an
important administrative position; shortly afterwards occurred the death
of Cardinal Humbert of Silva Candida, and Hildebrand took his place as
the leading figure in the Papal Curia. To his energy and resolution was
due the victory of Alexander II over the rival imperial nominee, and he
held the first place in the Pope's councils during the twelve years of
Alexander's papacy. The extent of his influence has been exaggerated by
the flattery of his admirers and by the abuse of his enemies. He was the
right-hand man, not the master, of the Pope; he influenced, but did not

---

[1] His statement to Archbishop Anno of Cologne (*Reg.* i, 79)—ob recordationem
disciplinae, qua tempore antecessoris vestri in ecclesia Coloniensi enutriti sumus—
seems to bear this interpretation, and can only be referred to this period. In view of
the testimony of friends and enemies alike, I find it impossible to accept the contention of Dr W. Martens that Hildebrand never became a monk.

dominate Alexander. That other counsels often prevailed we know. When he became Pope he revoked more than one privilege granted by his predecessor, suggesting that Alexander was too prone to be led away by evil counsellors. Even when, as in the case of the papal support given to the Norman conquest of England, his policy prevailed, it is clear from his own statement that he had to contend against considerable opposition within the Curia. On all the major issues, however, Pope and archdeacon must have been in complete agreement, especially with regard to Milan, the greatest question of all. They had been associated together in the embassy that inaugurated the new papal policy with regard to the Pataria, and, as Bishop of Lucca, Alexander had been more than once employed as papal legate to Milan. This was the critical issue that led to the breach between Pope and king, and it was the extension of the same policy to Germany that produced the ill-will of the German episcopate which is so noticeable at the beginning of Gregory's papacy. That there is a change of masters when Gregory VII becomes Pope is clear. The policy is the same, but the method of its execution is quite different. Hildebrand must have chafed at the slowness and caution of his predecessor. When he becomes Pope, he is urgent to see the policy carried into immediate effect. The hand on the reins is now a firm one, the controlling mind is ardent and impatient. Soon the issue is joined, and events move rapidly to the catastrophe.

Superficially the new Pope was not attractive. He was small of stature, his voice was weak, his appearance unprepossessing. In learning he fell short of many of his contemporaries; the knowledge of which he gives evidence is limited, though very practical for his purpose. Thus he had a close acquaintance with the collections of Decretals current in his time[1]. Besides them he depended mainly on Gregory the Great, with several of whose works he was obviously familiar. Otherwise there is practically no indication of any first-hand acquaintance with the works of the Fathers or other Church writers. He adduces the authority of a few passages from Ambrose and John Chrysostom in urging on Countess Matilda of Tuscany the importance of frequent communion. Once only does he quote from Augustine[2], and then the reference is to the *De doctrina christiana*; the *Civitas Dei*, quoted so frequently by his supporters and opponents alike, is not mentioned by him at all.

The chief authority with him was naturally the Bible. The words of Scripture, both Old and New Testament, were constantly on his lips.

---

[1] That many of these Decretals were forged is well known, but of course to Gregory, as to all his contemporaries, they were not known to be other than genuine.

[2] It has been shewn by Mirbt, Bernheim, and others that he follows closely the views of Augustine, especially as expressed in the *Civitas Dei*; but when he quotes his authority for these views it is the authority of Gregory the Great that he adduces. It seems to me therefore that it is from Gregory that he absorbs Augustine, not from a selection of Augustine as Mirbt thinks.

But, though quotations from the New Testament are the more numerous, it is the spirit of the Old Testament that prevails. His doctrine is of righteousness as shewn in duty and obedience, rather than as expressed in the gospel of love. The language of the Old Testament came most naturally to him; he was fond of military metaphors, and his language is that of a general engaged in a constant campaign against a vigilant enemy. A favourite quotation was from Jeremiah, "Cursed be the man that keepeth back his sword from blood," though he usually added with Gregory the Great "that is to say, the word of preaching from the rebuking of carnal men." He was, in fact, in temperament not unlike a prophet of the Old Testament—fierce in denunciation of wrong, confident in prophecy, vigorous in action, unshaken in adversity. It is not surprising to find that contemporaries compared him with the prophet Elijah. His enthusiasm and his ardent imagination drew men to him; that he attracted men is well attested. One feature his contemporaries remarked—the brightness and keenness of his glance. This was the outward sign of the fiery spirit within that insignificant frame, which by the flame of its enthusiasm could provoke the unwilling to acquiescence and stimulate even the fickle Roman population to devotion. It was kindled by his conviction of the righteousness of his aims and his determination, in which self-interest did not participate, to carry them into effect.

This had its weak side. He was always too ready to judge of men by their outward acquiescence in his aims, without regarding their motives. It is remarkable that with his experience he could have been deceived by the professions of Cardinal Hugo Candidus, or have failed to realise the insincerity of Henry IV's repentance in 1073. Here he was deceived to his own prejudice. It is not easy, however, to condone his readiness in 1080 to accept the alliance of Robert Guiscard, who had been under excommunication until that date, or of the Saxons, whom he had spoken of as rebels in 1075, and who were actuated by no worthier motives in 1076 and 1080. In the heat of action he grievously compromised his ideal. Another and a more inevitable result of his temperament was the frequent reaction into depression. Like Elijah, again, on Mount Horeb we find him crying out that there is not a righteous man left. Probably these moods were not infrequent, though they could only find expression in his letters to intimate friends such as Countess Matilda of Tuscany and Abbot Hugh of Cluny. And the gentler tone of these letters shews him in a softer light—oppressed by his burden, dependent solely on the helping hand of the "pauper Jesus." It was a genuine reluctance of which he spoke when he emphasised his unwillingness at every stage of his life to have fresh burdens, even of honour, imposed upon him. There is no reason to doubt that he was unwilling to become Pope; the event itself prostrated him, and his first letters, announcing his election and appealing for support, had to be dictated from his bed.

This was a temporary weakness, soon overcome. And it would be a mistake to regard him merely, or even mainly, as an enthusiast and a visionary. He had a strong will and could curb his imagination with an iron self-control. As a result he has been pictured most strangely as cold and inflexible, untouched by human weakness, unmoved by human sympathies. It is not in that light that we should view him at the Lenten Synod of 1076, where he alone remained calm and his will availed to quell the uproar; it was self-control that checked his impatience in the period following Canossa, and that was responsible for his firmness and serenity amid defeat and disappointment, so that he remained unconquered in spirit almost to the end. But there was another influence too, the experience of the years that preceded his papacy. As cardinal-deacon for over twenty years, and Archdeacon of the Roman Church for thirteen, his work had lain particularly among the secular affairs of the Papacy; from this he had acquired great practical knowledge and a keen sense of the actual. It coloured his whole outlook, and produced the contrast between the theories he expressed and the limitation of them that he was willing to accept. He had a clear vision both of what was essential and of what was possible; it was later clouded by the dust of conflict, after he had joined issue with the Emperor.

His early life had been spent in the service of the Church and the Papacy. This service remained his single aim, and he was actuated, as he justly claimed, by no feeling of worldly pride or self-glorification. He naturally had a full sense of the importance of his office, and realised both its potentialities and its responsibilities. To St Peter, who had watched over the training of his youth, he owed his earliest allegiance; as Bishop of Rome he had become the successor and representative of St Peter. It was not the least of his achievements that he realised the logical inferences that could be drawn from the Petrine authority; he was careful to sink his own individuality, and to picture himself as the channel through which the will of the Apostle was expressed to mankind. Every communication addressed to the Pope by letter or by word of mouth is received by St Peter himself; and, while the Pope only reads the words or listens to the message, St Peter can read the heart of the sender. Any injury done, even in thought, to the Pope is thus an injury to the Prince of the Apostles himself. He acts as the mouthpiece of St Peter, his sentences are the sentences of St Peter, and from St Peter has descended to him the supreme power of binding and of loosing in heaven and on earth. So his power of excommunication is unlimited: he can excommunicate, as in the case of six bishops with all their supporters at the Lenten Synod of 1079, *sine spe recuperationis*. Similarly his power of absolution is unlimited, whether it be absolution to the penitent, absolution from all their sins to those who fight the battles of the Church against her enemies, or absolution of the subjects of an excommunicated ruler from the oath of allegiance they had taken to him. These are not the assertions of a claim; they are the simple expression of his absolute belief.

CH. II.

How supreme was his confidence is shewn in his prophecies. The authority descended from St Peter extends over material prosperity in this life; yes, and over life itself. Glory and honour in this life, as well as in the life to come, depend on obedience to him, he assured the magistrates of Sardinia in 1073. In 1078 he proclaimed that all who hindered the holding of a synod in Germany would suffer not only in soul but also in body and property, would win no success in war and no triumph in their lifetime. And at Easter 1080 he pronounced his famous prophecy that Henry, if he did not repent, would be dead or deposed before August. This is the confidence of complete conviction.

But it was a delegated authority that he was exercising, and therefore it must not be exercised arbitrarily. The obedience to God which he enforced on all Christians must be rendered by himself first of all. Obedience to God implies obedience to the Church and to the law of the Church, to the decrees of the Fathers, the canonical tradition. He shews no disposition to over-ride this; in fact he is careful to explain that he is subject to its authority. Frequently he protested that there was nothing new in his decrees. His decree against lay investiture was not new, not of his own invention; in promulgating it he had merely returned to the teaching and decrees of the Early Fathers and followed the prime unique rule of ecclesiastical discipline. He did not make new laws; he issued edicts which interpreted the law or prohibited the illegal practices that had grown up in course of time. The Holy Roman Church, he says, has always had and will always have the right of issuing new decrees to deal with particular abuses as they arise. Its custom has always been to be merciful, to temper the rigour of the law with discretion, to tolerate some things after careful consideration, but never to do anything which conflicts with the harmony of canonical tradition.

Now the prime importance of this consideration of Gregory VII's views is in its bearing on his relations with the temporal authority. He started with the orthodox Gelasian view of the two powers each supreme in its own department, and it is clear that at first he sees no conflict of his ideas with this. In the ecclesiastical department of course he must be absolute master. Archbishops, bishops, and abbots must acknowledge his complete authority, obey his summons to Rome, submit to his over-riding of their actions, and not interfere with direct appeals to Rome. The legates he sends act in his name. Anywhere they can call synods, preside over them, and issue decrees on his behalf. But, as his own office is divinely ordained, so he recognises is the royal office. In 1073 he speaks of the two powers and compares them with the two eyes of the human body; as these give light to the body, so the *sacerdotium* and *imperium* should illumine with spiritual light the body of the Church. They should work together in the harmony of pure religion for the spiritual good of Christianity; the spiritual end is the final object of both, in accordance with the accepted medieval view. Obedience, therefore, is due to kings;

he shews no indulgence with the Saxon revolt in 1073, and congratulates
Henry on his victory over the rebels in 1075. Over churches he continually
repeats that the lay power has a protective not a possessive function, but
he is anxious not to appear to be encroaching on imperial prerogative.
Though he is convinced that the practice of lay investiture is an abuse
that has arisen in the course of time, he recognises that it has come to
be regarded almost as a prescriptive right[1]; he is careful not to promulgate his decree against it in 1075 until he has consulted the king,
upon whose rights, he declares, he is anxious not to encroach. The
language of these early days is markedly different from that of his later
years. The normal contrast between medieval theory and practice is noticeable at the beginning, when he is content to subordinate his theory to
practical considerations; in later years he is striving to bring his practice
up to the level of his theory. The difference lies not so much in a change
in his point of view[2], as in a recognition of its real implications and of its
actual incompatibility with the orthodox Gelasian theory. This recognition was forced upon him by the circumstances of the struggle with the
king, without which he might never have adopted the extreme attitude
of his later years. His methods help to mark the difference. At first he
attempts to promote his aims by mutual agreement and negotiation;
afterwards he acts by decree, issuing his orders and demanding implicit
obedience.

The key to his development is to be found in his insistence on righteousness[3] as the criterion by which he tests his own actions and those of
all with whom he has to deal. Righteousness, with him as with Augustine,
consists in obedience to the commandments of God. Truth, obedience,
humility, are the marks of the righteous man, the servant of God, as
falsehood, disobedience, pride, are the marks of the wicked man, whose
master is the devil. If this is merely medieval commonplace, it becomes
something more in its application. It is when he has to deal with an
unrighteous king that he discovers the logical results of his opinions.
The Pope, as St Peter's successor, has authority over the souls of men;
he has in consequence an awful responsibility as he will have to answer
for them before the tribunal of God. It is incumbent upon him to rebuke
those that err; it is he, in fact, that must be the judge of right and wrong,
and to this judgment all men, even kings, must be subject. Every act of
a king must have the test of right and wrong applied to it, for it is a

---

[1] In a letter to Bishop Anselm of Lucca in 1073 he indirectly recognises the royal
right of investiture.

[2] The recent work of Father Peitz and others has demonstrated that the *Registrum
Gregorii VII* is the actual Register of the Pope's letters kept by the papal Chancery
(which must have done its work rather casually). This establishes the authenticity
of the *Dictatus Papae* of 1075, with its extreme claims, as a genuine expression of
papal theory at that time.

[3] I prefer to translate *iustitia* by "righteousness" rather than "justice," as I
think it conveys a more accurate rendering of Gregory VII's meaning.

king's duty to govern for the spiritual welfare of his subjects. Obedience to God is the sign of the *iustus homo*, how much more of the *iustus rex*! And so, if a king does not act as a *iustus homo* he at once becomes amenable to papal jurisdiction. The head of the spiritual department is entitled accordingly to obedience from secular rulers. "As I have to answer for you at the awful Judgment," he writes to William I of England[1], "in the interests of your own salvation, ought you, can you avoid immediate obedience to me?" The implication is that the obedience which is expected from all Christians is obedience to himself.

When the great question came as to the sentence of a king who was, in his view, manifestly unrighteous, there could be no doubt with him as to the authority he could exercise. The theory of passive obedience to a wicked king could not influence him or his supporters for a moment; a king who aimed at his own glory had ceased to be the servant of God and become the servant of the devil; he was no longer a king but a tyrant. With the Pope, the judge of right and wrong, lay the sentence. Saul, ordained by God for his humility, was deposed by Samuel, the representative of God, for his pride and disobedience. The Pope is through St Peter the representative of God; as he has power to bind and loose in spiritual things, how much more in secular! Henry had not merely been disobedient; his pride had led him to attempt the overthrow of the Pope, a direct outrage on St Peter himself. St Peter, therefore, through the Pope's mouth, pronounces sentence of excommunication and deposition. Gregory has faced the logical outcome of his point of view. The two powers are not equal and independent; the head of the ecclesiastical department is dominant over the head of the temporal. And so, when the enemies of Henry in Germany were contemplating the election of an anti-king to succeed Rudolf, he sends them the wording of the oath that their new choice must take to him—the oath of fealty of a vassal to his overlord.

Gregory found himself faced at his accession with a situation that gave him every cause for anxiety, but much real ground for optimism. In the twenty-four years following his recall to Rome by Pope Leo IX a great advance had been made. The reformed Papacy had assumed its natural position as leader and director of the reform movement. It had vindicated the independence of its own elections against the usurpation of the Roman nobles and the practice of imperial nomination, it was asserting its absolute authority in ecclesiastical matters over all archbishops and bishops, and it was beginning to recover its temporal power in Italy. But its progress was hampered by difficulties and opposition from every

---

[1] *Reg.* VII, 25. This is the letter in which he expresses the relations between the two powers by the simile of the sun and moon. As in 1073 they both give light, but no longer equal light.

quarter. Papal decrees had been promulgated against simony and clerical marriage, but there was more opposition to these decrees than obedience. The absolute authority of the Pope over all metropolitans was not denied in theory, but it had not been maintained in practice, and much resentment was aroused by its exercise. The temporal possessions of the Pope were continually exposed to the encroachments of the Normans, who would acknowledge themselves vassals of the Papacy but paid no heed to its instructions. And all these difficulties were complicated and controlled by the relations of the Pope with the King of Germany, and by the clash of their conflicting interests. The situation would have been easier had Henry III been on the throne. He at any rate was an earnest promoter of ecclesiastical reform. Henry IV was not even in sympathy with the reform movement, and simony in episcopal elections had become frequent once more; while he was as firmly resolved as his father that royal control over all his subjects, lay and ecclesiastical, should be maintained, and this implied royal control of nominations to bishoprics and abbeys both in Germany and North Italy. Hence the crisis that had arisen with regard to Milan just before Alexander II's death. In the establishment of his authority in the ecclesiastical department, Gregory was thus faced by the opposition of the higher clergy (except in Saxony where the bishops as a whole allied themselves with the local opposition to Henry), supported by the king, and also of the lower ranks of the secular clergy, who considered that clerical celibacy was an ideal of perfection to which they ought not to be expected to aspire. He was supported on the whole by the regulars and often by the mass of the common people, who were readily aroused to action, as at Milan, against the laxity of the secular clergy.

It was evident to the Pope that his best chance of success lay in obtaining the king's support. Without it he could not coerce the higher clergy; with it the decrees for Church reform could be made efficacious. He regarded the royal power as the natural supporter of the Papacy, and the protector of its temporal authority in South Italy against Norman aggression. His imagination led him to visualise the magnificent conception of a united Empire and Papacy working together in harmony for the same spiritual objects, and he was sanguine enough to believe that Henry could be induced to take the same view. And so the first task he undertook was to bring about a reconciliation with the king. To effect this he sought assistance from every quarter—the Empress-mother Agnes, Beatrice and Matilda of Tuscany, Dukes Rudolf of Swabia and Godfrey of Lower Lorraine, Bishop Rainald of Como—from anyone in short who might exercise influence over the king, and who might be expected to influence him in the right direction. Henry yielded, but he yielded to necessity, not to persuasion. In August he had with difficulty evaded the Saxons by flight and had made his way south, where he was remaining isolated and almost without support. The situation was in many respects

CH. II.

similar to that at Canossa, and the king's policy was the same on both occasions—as his enemies in Germany had the upper hand, he must propitiate the anger of the Pope, and this could only be done by a complete outward submission. The letter Gregory VII received from the king in September 1073 was as abject as the humiliation of 1077, without the personal degradation of Canossa. The king confesses that he is guilty of all the charges brought against him and asks for papal absolution; he promises obedience to Gregory's bidding in the matter of reform, especially in regard to Milan, and expresses his keen desire for the harmonious co-operation of the spiritual and temporal powers. The delight of Gregory was unbounded when he received this letter, so full, he says, of sweetness and obedience, such as no Pope had ever received from Emperor before. He failed to realise, though he saw it clearly enough later, that the Saxon situation was entirely responsible, and that Henry's humility depended on his position in Germany; he even did his best to bring Henry and the Saxons to terms. To Henry's appeal for absolution he responded with enthusiasm, and early in the following year it was effected by an embassy headed by two cardinal-bishops and accompanied by Henry's mother Agnes.

Assured of royal support, or at any rate relieved from the embarrassment of royal opposition, he now took in hand the important questions of Church reform and the assertion of his ecclesiastical authority. He knew the hostility he had to face. In North Italy, Archbishop Guibert of Ravenna had submitted himself to Alexander II and promised obedience, but little reliance could be placed on his promises; in general, the morals of the clergy were lax, the episcopate was mutinous. In Germany, there was an atmosphere of sullen resentment against the measures already taken by Alexander, and of ill-will towards his successor. It was not until 1074 that the two leading metropolitans—Siegfried of Mayence, the German Arch-Chancellor, and Anno of Cologne (ex-regent of Germany, now living in retirement and devoted to good works)—wrote to congratulate Gregory on his election; and there is no evidence to shew that any of the others were more forward in this respect. Siegfried took the opportunity of expressing his pleasure and congratulations in a letter which he wrote on the subject of the dispute between the Bishops of Prague and Olmütz, Bohemian sees within his province. In this letter he complained of the intervention of the late Pope in a matter which came within his own jurisdiction; particularly that Alexander had allowed the Bishop of Olmütz to appeal direct to Rome, and had sent legates to Bohemia who without reference to Siegfried had suspended the Bishop of Prague from his office. This was a test case, and Gregory replied with great vigour. He rebutted the arguments from Canon Law which Siegfried had urged, and accused him of neglect of his office and of arrogance towards the Apostolic See. Siegfried's timid attempt to assert himself was overwhelmed by the Pope's vehemence, and he made no further effort to interfere with the papal settlement of the question. The Bishop of Prague obeyed the Pope's summons to Rome, and Gregory, by his lenient treatment of him, gave the episcopate a lesson in the value of ready obedience.

This was a signal victory. He passed on to deal with the questions of simony and clerical marriage. In the first synod he held in Rome, in Lent 1074, he repeated the decrees of his predecessors against these abuses, and proceeded to take measures for their enforcement in Germany. The two cardinal-bishops, who had given absolution to the king and to his excommunicated councillors at Easter 1074, had the further task imposed upon them of summoning a synod of German clergy, promulgating the decrees at this synod, and enforcing acquiescence in their execution. This was a difficult task, rendered impossible by the overbearing manner of the papal legates. They addressed themselves first to two of the leading archbishops, Siegfried of Mayence and Liemar of Bremen, with a haughty injunction to them to hold a synod. They met their match in Liemar. A supporter of the reform movement, the methods of the Pope and his legates roused his pride and independence. He refused to do anything without previous consultation with the episcopate as a whole, and sneered at the impracticable suggestion that he should hold a synod to which his suffragans far distant in North Germany or in Denmark would not be able to come[1]. Siegfried deprecated the whole business, but from timidity rather than pride. He temporised for six months and at last called a synod at Erfurt in October. As he expected, he was faced by a violent outburst from the secular clergy, who fortified themselves against the decree enforcing celibacy by the words of St Paul, and the synod broke up in confusion. Another incident that happened at the same time well illustrates the temper of the episcopate. Archbishop Udo of Trèves was ordered by the Pope to investigate the charges brought against the Bishop of Toul by one of his clergy. He held a synod at which more than twenty bishops were present. They commenced by a unanimous protest against the Pope's action in submitting a bishop to the indignity of having to answer before a synod to charges that any of his clergy might please to bring against him. Needless to say, the bishop was unanimously acquitted. In only one quarter, in fact, could the Pope find support—in Saxony. Here the episcopate was allied with the lay nobility in opposition to Henry, and it was part of its policy to keep on good terms with the Pope. It is not surprising, then, to learn that Bishop Burchard of Halberstadt, one of the chief leaders of the Saxons, wrote to Gregory to deplore the unworthy treatment of the papal legates in Germany, and received his reward in a warm letter of commendation from the Pope.

Gregory now began to take vigorous action to enforce his will. Archbishop Liemar, defiant to the legates who had summoned him to appear in Rome in November, was ordered by the Pope himself to come to the

[1] Liemar gives a lively account of his altercation with the legates in a letter to the Bishop of Hildesheim (Sudendorf, *Reg.* 1, 5).

Lenten Synod of 1075. The same summons was sent to Archbishop Siegfried, and to six of his suffragan bishops as well. The Pope further issued circulars appealing especially to prominent laymen to assist him in executing his decrees. Siegfried's answer to Gregory's summons was typical of the timid man striving to extricate himself from the contest between two violently hostile parties. Afraid to oppose the Pope's will, and equally afraid to enforce it, he excused himself from coming to Rome on the ground of ill-health, pleaded lack of time for his inability to examine the conduct of the six suffragans mentioned in Gregory's letter, but declared that he had sent on the Pope's order with instructions to them to obey it. He expressed his compliance with the decrees against simony and clerical marriage, but urged moderation and discretion in their execution.

The synod sat at Rome from 24 to 28 February 1075. At this synod the Pope suspended the absent and disobedient Liemar, and passed the same sentence on the Bishops of Bamberg, Strasbourg, and Spires, three of the six suffragans of Mayence whose attendance he had ordered; the other three seem to have satisfied him, temporarily at any rate, by their appearance or through representatives. Decrees were also passed against simony and clerical marriage, with the special addition, in conformity with Gregory's policy, of a clause calling on the laity to assist by refraining from attending the mass celebrated by an offending priest. In sending the text of these decrees to Archbishop Siegfried[1], he shewed that the moderation urged by Siegfried was not in his mind at all. The decrees are to be issued and enforced in their full rigour. Instructions to the same effect were sent to other metropolitans and bishops, for instance to the Archbishops of Cologne and Magdeburg, with injunctions to hold synods to enforce the decrees. This was again pressed on Siegfried and distressed him still further. He eventually replied to the Pope in July or August, in a letter intended to be tactful and to shift responsibility from his own shoulders. It was no use; Gregory was quite firm. He replied on 3 September, acknowledging the weight of Siegfried's arguments but declaring them of no effect when set in the balance against his pastoral duty. Siegfried was forced to comply, especially as the submission of the Saxons took away from him his chief excuse for delay. He held a synod at Mayence in October, and, as before, it was broken up by the turbulence of the secular clergy. But the whole question was now to be transferred to a larger stage, and the next act in the drama is the Council of Worms.

In this struggle with the German episcopate, in which matters were rapidly coming to a crisis, Gregory had been able to act unhampered by royal interference, and so far his policy of effecting a reconciliation with

---

[1] Jaffé, *Mon. Greg. ep. coll.* 3. The same letter was sent as well to Archbishop Werner of Magdeburg (*ep. coll.* 4) and to Bishop Otto of Constance (*ep. coll.* 5). There seems little doubt that these letters should be dated February 1075 and not, as by Jaffé, March 1074.

Henry had justified itself. But in North Italy, where he required the active co-operation rather than the non-interference of the king, the policy had not been so successful. Little, however, could be expected from Henry when his position in Germany itself was so difficult, and for two years Gregory seems to have persisted in his confidence in the king's sincerity. He did complain, indeed, in December 1074 that Henry had not yet taken any action with regard to Milan, and he administered a gentle warning as to the councillors he had around him. But the more personal letter he wrote at the same time gives expression to his confidence in the king. In this letter he detailed his plan of leading a vast expedition to the East both to protect the Eastern Christians and to bring them back to the orthodox faith; he is careful to seek Henry's advice and assistance in this, because in the event of his going he intends to leave the Roman Church under Henry's care and protection. If he could trust the king to this extent, he was profoundly suspicious of his councillors and of their confederates the Lombard bishops. At the Lenten Synod of 1075, three Italian bishops were suspended for disobedience to his summons, and five of Henry's councillors, promoters of simony, are to be excommunicated if they have not appeared in Rome and given satisfaction by 1 June. At the same synod was passed the first decree against lay investiture.

Against the practice of lay ownership of churches, great and small, the reformed Papacy had already raised its protest, and the necessity of obtaining suitable agents for the work of reform had turned its attention to the method of appointment. While denying the right of the king to control appointments, the Popes allowed him a considerable though undefined rôle, both as head of the laity and as the natural protector of the Church. In this Gregory VII acquiesced, and where the appointments were good from the spiritual point of view, as was the case in England under William I, he was little disposed to question the method. It was the insubordination of the episcopate in Germany and North Italy, and especially the clash of papal and imperial claims at Milan, that led him to take definite action against a royal control that led to bad appointments. The king, for his part, regarded bishoprics as being in his gift, and allowed no bishop to exercise his functions until he had invested him with ring and staff. To the Church party the use of these symbols betokened the conferring by the king of spiritual functions; this was an abuse the removal of which might lead to the restoration of true canonical election. In Gregory VII's eyes it was clearly not an end in itself, but only a step towards the end, which was through free election by clergy and people to obtain a personnel adequate for its spiritual functions and amenable to papal authority.

The importance of lay investiture had been early recognised by Cardinal Humbert in his *Liber adversus Symoniacos*, but Gregory VII was the first Pope to legislate directly on the subject. The first decree prohibiting lay investiture (though not imposing any penalty on laymen who invested) was passed at this synod in 1075. But it was never properly published. Bishops elected and invested in 1075 and 1076 could plead ignorance of its existence and the Pope accepted their plea. No German writer seems to know of it, and we are indebted for its wording solely to a Milanese writer, Arnulf, which gives weight to the suggestion that the Milanese situation was principally responsible for the framing of the decree. The fact was that Gregory knew that he was dealing with a long-established custom, regarded by the king as a prescriptive right, and he knew that he must walk warily. He first of all sent the text of the decree to the king accompanied by a message to explain that it was no new step that he was taking but a restoration of canonical practice, and urging the king, if he felt his rights to be in any way infringed, to communicate with him, so that the matter could be arranged on a just and amicable footing. Gregory attempted to establish his point by negotiation, and he seems to have imagined that the king would recognise the fairness of his claim. Henry made no reply to these overtures, and the Pope does not seem to have been immediately perturbed by this ominous silence. In July he warmly praised the king for his zeal in resisting simony and clerical marriage, which gives him reason, he says, to hope for still higher and better things—acquiescence, doubtless, in the new decree. Just after this, two ambassadors from Henry arrived in Rome with a strictly confidential message to the Pope to be communicated to no one except the king's mother Agnes, or Beatrice and Matilda of Tuscany. This has been conjectured, with great probability, to have had reference to the king's desire to be crowned Emperor by the Pope; if this be so we have a ready explanation of his willingness to keep on good terms with the Pope, even after his great victory over the Saxons in June. Gregory took some time to reply, owing to illness; but, when he did, he warmly congratulated the king on his victory over the rebels, and wrote in a tone of confidence that they were going to work together in harmony.

This was the last time that he expressed any such confidence, and in the meantime the situation in Italy, especially at Milan, had been getting steadily worse. Revolt against the Pope was spreading in North Italy, and Archbishop Guibert of Ravenna once more took the opportunity of proclaiming the independence of his see. In Milan, Erlembald, the leader of the Pataria and practical ruler of the city, had, in accordance with the Pope's appeal to the laity, forbidden the offending clergy to exercise their functions, which were usurped by a priest of his own party, Liutprand. A riot ensued in which Erlembald was killed and Liutprand mutilated. Their enemies in triumph reported the facts to Henry, and asked him to appoint a new archbishop in place of his previous nominee Godfrey, from whom he had practically withdrawn support. That Henry for some time ignored this request may have encouraged the Pope in the confidence that he expressed in August. But, with the situation in Germany be-

coming increasingly favourable, Henry seems to have felt himself strong
enough to follow his own inclinations, and to listen again to those councillors from whom Gregory had been most anxious to separate him. His
two ambassadors, who were still waiting instructions from him in Rome,
suddenly received a message at the beginning of September to make public
what he had previously wished to be a close secret, a discourtesy to the
Pope which the latter rightly felt to be ominous. And at the same time
he sent an embassy into Italy which revealed a complete change in his
policy. It was headed by Count Eberhard of Nellenburg, who was almost
certainly one of the councillors placed under a ban by the Pope. Its first
object was to make an alliance with the Lombard bishops and to attempt
to ally the king with the excommunicated Norman duke, Robert Guiscard.
Further, by royal authority, bishops were appointed to the vacant sees of
Fermo and Spoleto, sees which lay within the *provincia Romana*[1]. But
the main purpose of the embassy was to make a settlement of affairs at
Milan, so as completely to re-establish the old imperial authority.
Acceding to the request of the anti-Patarian party, Henry ignored both
his own nominee Godfrey and also Atto, whom the Pope recognised as
archbishop, and proceeded to invest one Tedald, who was consecrated
archbishop by the suffragans of Milan. As in 1072, Henry so long
compliant deliberately provoked a rupture on the question of Milan. It
was an issue in which imperial and papal interests vitally conflicted, and
now that he was master once more in Germany it was an issue that he
felt himself strong enough to raise. Henry had revealed himself in his
true colours. The Pope's eyes were opened. He realised at last the meaning
of Henry's submission in 1073, and that it was due not to sincerity but
to defeat. It was clear that compliance could be expected from Henry
only when his fortunes were at a low ebb, and that at such times no reliance could be placed on his promises. The Pope's dream is at an end;
he is now awake to the realities of the situation, the bitter frustration of
all his hopes.

His tone to the usurper Tedald and his orders to the suffragan bishops
of Milan were sharp and uncompromising. With the king he tried the
effect of threats to see if they would succeed where persuasion had failed.
By the king's own ambassadors he sent him a letter in which he summed
up the leading offences of Henry—he is reported to be associating with
his excommunicated councillors, and if this be true must do penance and
seek absolution; he is certainly guilty with regard to Fermo and Spoleto
and most culpable of all in his action at Milan, which was a direct breach
of all his promises and a proof of the falseness of his pretended humility
and obedience to Rome. A more mild rebuke follows for Henry's silence
to his overtures regarding the investiture decree; if the king felt himself
aggrieved he ought to have stated his grievances. Until he has given satisfaction on all these points, the king must expect no answer to his previous

---

[1] Hence Gregory's complaint that they were men unknown to him.

enquiry (again, doubtless, on the question of his coronation at Rome). He concludes with a warning to the king to remember the fate of Saul, who, like Henry, had displayed pride and disobedience after his victory; it is the humility of David that a righteous king must imitate. The letter was stern, but not uncompromising; the message given to the ambassadors to deliver by word of mouth was more direct. It amounted to a distinct threat that, failing compliance, Henry must expect the sentence of excommunication, and possibly of deposition also, to be pronounced against him from the papal chair. This verbal message was in effect an ultimatum.

The embassy reached Henry early in January 1076. He could not brook threats of this nature when policy no longer required him to yield to them. He had been humble to the Pope only until he had defeated his other foe; now that he was victorious, the need for humility was past, and he could deal directly with the other enemy that was menacing the imperial rights. His previous humiliation only made his desire for revenge more keen, and his indignation demanded a speedy revenge. The bishops he knew to be as bitter against the Pope as himself; and he summoned them to a Council at Worms on 24 January. The short notice given in the summons must have prevented the attendance of several, such as Archbishop Liemar, who would gladly have been present; even so, two archbishops, Siegfried of Mayence and Udo of Trèves, and twenty-four bishops, subscribed their names to the proceedings. There was no need for persuasion or deliberation. They readily[1] renounced allegiance to the Pope, and concocted a letter addressed to him in which they brought forward various charges (of adultery, perjury, and the like) to blacken his character, but laid their principal stress on the only serious charge they could bring—his treatment of the episcopate. The king composed a letter on his own account, making the bishops' cause his own, and indignantly repudiating Gregory's claim to exercise authority over himself, who as the Lord's anointed was above all earthly judgment, ordered him to descend from the papal throne and yield it to a more worthy occupant. The next step was to obtain the adhesion of the North Italian bishops, which was very readily given at a council at Piacenza, and to Roland of Parma was entrusted the mission of delivering to the Pope the sentence of deposition pronounced by the king and the bishops of the Empire.

At Christmas 1075 had occurred the outrage of Cencius, who laid violent hands on the Pope and hurried him, a prisoner, into a fortress of his own. Gregory was rescued by the Roman populace, and had to intervene to prevent them from tearing his captor in pieces. The horror aroused at this incident gave an added reverence to the person of the Pope, and it was in these circumstances, and while the Lenten Synod was about to commence its deliberations, that Roland of Parma arrived. The message

---

[1] Except Bishop Herman of Metz, who was doubtless coerced into signing.

which he delivered to the assembled synod was an outrage beside which
that of Cencius paled into insignificance. It shocked the general feeling
of the day, which was accordingly prejudiced on the Pope's side at the
commencement of the struggle. At the synod itself there was a scene of
wild disorder and uproar. The Pope, depressed at the final ruin of his
hopes and at the prospect of the struggle before him, alone remained calm;
he intervened to protect Roland from their fury, and succeeded at last in
quieting the assembly and recalling it to its deliberations. The verdict
was assured and he proceeded to pass sentence on his aggressors. Archbishop Siegfried and the other German bishops that subscribed are
sentenced to deposition and separated from communion with the Church;
a proviso is added giving the opportunity to those who had been coerced
into signing to make their peace before 1 August. The same sentence is
passed on the Lombard bishops. Finally he deals with the king in an
impressive utterance addressed to St Peter, in whose name he declares
him deposed and absolves his subjects from their oath of allegiance; and
then he bans him from the communion of the Church, recounting his
various offences—communicating with the excommunicated councillors;
his many iniquities; his contempt of papal warnings; his breach of the
unity of the Church by his attack on the Pope.

The hasty violence and the fantastic charges of the king and the bishops
contrasted very strikingly with the solemn and deliberate sentence of the
Pope. Confident himself in the justice of his action, there were some who
doubted, and for these he wrote a circular letter detailing the events that
led to Henry's excommunication. The facts spoke for themselves, but
there were still some who continued to doubt whether in any circumstances the Pope had the right to excommunicate the king; to convince
these he wrote a letter to Bishop Herman of Metz (who had hastened to
make his peace with the Pope for his enforced signature at Worms), in
which he justifies himself by precedents, by the power given to St Peter,
and by the authority of Scripture and the Fathers. It is rather a hurried
letter, in which he answers briefly and somewhat impatiently several
questions put to him by Herman. He makes it quite clear, however,
that he regards the spiritual power as superior to the temporal, and that
his authority extends over all temporal rulers. Henceforward there is no
sign of his earlier attitude which seemed to imply adherence to the
Gelasian standpoint; he is now the judge who decides whether the king
is doing that which is right (*i.e.* is worthy to be king), and the test of
right-doing is obedience to the papal commands. One point calls for remark. It is only the excommunication that he justifies. The sentence of
deposition plays little part in 1076; it is not a final sentence as in 1080,
and even by Henry's enemies in Germany, who considered this to be a
question rather for them to decide, little attention is paid to this part of
the sentence. Probably in the Pope's eyes it was subsidiary; deposition
and the absolving of the king's subjects from their oath of allegiance was

a necessary consequence of excommunication in order to save from the same penalty the subjects of the excommunicated king. As is clear from his letter to Bishop Herman, he contemplated the absolution of the king as a possibility in the near future, and he did not at present contemplate the appointment of a successor to Henry.

The king received intelligence of the papal sentence at Easter, and immediately summoned a council to meet at Worms on Whitsunday. The crisis had been reached. The king had ordered the Pope to descend from St Peter's chair; the Pope treated the king as contumacious, excommunicated him, and declared him to be no longer king. Which was to prevail? The answer to this was quickly given. The papal ban was seen to be speedily efficacious. It frightened the more timid of Henry's adherents, it impressed moderate men who had been horrified by the king's attack on the Pope. Moreover it gave the excuse for revolt to raise its head in Saxony once more, and to win adherents from among the higher nobility in the rest of Germany, alienated by the high-handed measures of the king in his moment of triumph and resenting their own lack of influence in the affairs of the kingdom. The situation in Germany is dealt with in another chapter. Here it is enough to say that Henry found himself isolated, and faced by a coalition far more dangerous to his power than the revolt of 1073. His summons to councils at Worms and Mayence were ignored, and the bishops of Germany were hastening to make their peace with the Pope, either directly or indirectly through the papal legate, Bishop Altmann of Passau. Only in North Italy were his adherents still faithful, and with them it was not possible for him to join forces. The imperial authority was humiliated between the encroachments of the spiritual power on the one hand, and the decentralising policy of the leading nobles on the other. At the Diet of princes held at Tribur in October these two powers came to terms for mutual action. Two papal legates were present, and the Pope's letter of the previous month, in which for the first time he contemplates the possibility of a successor to Henry, was probably before the diet. He insists in that event on being consulted as to their choice, requiring careful information as to personal character; he claims that the Apostolic See has the right of confirming the election made by the nobles. Such a right was not likely to be conceded by them, but to obtain papal support they were willing to satisfy him essentially. Henry was forced to send a solemn promise of obedience to the Pope and of satisfaction for his offences, and to promulgate his change of mind to all the nobles, lay and ecclesiastical, of the kingdom. The diet then arrived at two important decisions. Accepting the justice of Henry's excommunication, they agreed that if he had not obtained absolution by 22 February they would no longer recognise him as king. Secondly, they summoned a council to be held at Augsburg on 2 February, at which they invited the Pope to be present and to preside; at this council the question of Henry's worthiness to reign was to be decided and, if necessary, the choice of a successor was to be made. These decisions were communicated to the Pope, and also to Henry, who was remaining on the other side of the river at Oppenheim, carefully watched, with only a few attendants, almost a prisoner.

The Pope received the news with delight and accepted the invitation with alacrity. It meant for him the realisation of his aims and the exhibition to the world of the relative importance of the spiritual and temporal powers; Pope Gregory VII sitting in judgment on King Henry IV would efface the unhappy memory of King Henry III sitting in judgment on Pope Gregory VI thirty years before. He left Rome in December and travelled north into Lombardy. But the escort promised him from Germany did not arrive, and the news reached him that Henry had crossed the Alps and was in Italy. Uncertain as to the king's intentions and fully aware of the hostility of the Lombards, he took refuge in Countess Matilda's castle of Canossa.

The king was in a desperate position. He could expect little mercy from the council of his enemies at Augsburg in February. The conjunction of the Pope and the German nobles was above all things to be avoided. The only resource left to him was to obtain absolution, and to obtain it from the Pope in Italy, before he arrived in Germany. To effect this a humiliation even more abject than that of 1073 was necessary: he must appear in person before the Pope not as a king but as a penitent sinner; it would be hard for the Pope to refuse absolution to a humble penitent. His decision arrived at, he acted with singular courage and resolution. He had to elude the close vigilance of the nobles and escape from his present confinement; as they were guarding the other passes into Italy, only the Mont Cenis pass was left to him, which was in the control of his wife's family, the counts of Savoy; but the winter was one of the most severe on record, and the passage of the Mont Cenis pass was an undertaking that might have daunted the hardiest mountaineer. All these difficulties Henry overcame, and with his wife, his infant son, and a few personal attendants he reached the plains of Lombardy. Here he found numerous supporters, militant anti-Papalists, eager to flock to his banner. It was a serious temptation, but his good sense shewed him that it would ultimately have been fatal, and he resisted it. With his meagre retinue he continued his journey until he arrived at the gates of Canossa, where the final difficulty was to be overcome, the obtaining of the papal absolution. To this end he strove to obtain the intercession of his godfather Abbot Hugh of Cluny, of the Countess Matilda, of any of those present whose influence might prevail with the Pope. And he carried out to the full his design of throwing off the king and appearing as the sinner seeking absolution; bare-footed, in the woollen garb of the penitent, for three days he stood humbly in the outer courtyard of Canossa.

There are few moments in history that have impressed later generations so much[1] as this spectacle of the heir to the Empire standing in the courtyard of Canossa, a humble suppliant for papal absolution. But it is within the castle that we must look for the real drama of Canossa. Paradoxical as it sounds, it was the king who had planned and achieved this situation; the plans of the Pope were upset by this sudden appearance, his mind was unprepared for the emergency. The three days of waiting are not so much the measure of Henry's humiliation as of Gregory's irresolution. Could he refuse absolution to one so humble and apparently so penitent? The influence of those on whom he was wont to lean for spiritual help, especially the Abbot of Cluny, urged him to mercy; the appeal of the beloved Countess Matilda moved him in the same direction. But they only saw a king in penitential garb; he had the bitter experience of the last two years to guide him, and what confidence could he feel that the penitence of Henry was more sincere now, when his need was greater, than it had been in 1073? He saw before him too the prospect of the wrecking of all his hopes, the breach of his engagement with the German nobles, which would probably result from an absolution given in circumstances that neither he nor they had contemplated. His long hesitation was due, then, to the conflict in his mind; it was not a deliberate delay designed to increase to the utmost the degradation of the king.

But at last the appeal to the divine mercy prevailed over all other considerations. The doors were opened and Henry admitted to the Pope's presence; the ban was removed, and the king was received once more into communion with the Church. From him the Pope extracted such assurances of his penitence and guarantees for his future conduct as would justify the absolution and at the same time leave the situation as far as possible unaltered from the papal point of view. With his hand on the Gospels the king took an oath to follow the Pope's directions with regard to the charges of the German nobles against him, whichever way they might tend, and further by no act or instigation of his to impede Gregory from coming into Germany or to interfere with his safe-conduct while there. The Pope sent a copy of this oath to the German nobles with a letter[2] describing the events at Canossa. He realised that the absolution of Henry in Italy would appear to them in the light of a betrayal of the compact he had entered into with them. His letter is an explanation, almost an apology of his action; while he points out that

[1] Or contemporary opinion so little. Bismarck's famous words "zu Canossa gehen wir nicht" indicate the aspect of Canossa that impresses the modern mind. But the brief allusions to Canossa in contemporary writers only refer to the king's absolution and its political results; it did not occur to them that the monarchy had been degraded by Henry's action. His seat on the throne had been shaken by the excommunication; he righted himself by his penance at Canossa.

[2] This letter (*Reg.* IV, 12) is our only real authority for the details of Canossa. Lampert of Hersfeld's account is clearly based on the Pope's letter, with characteristic embellishments of his own invention.

the non-appearance of the promised escort had prevented him from reaching Germany, he is careful to insist firstly that it was impossible for him to refuse absolution, secondly that he has entered into no engagement with the king and that his purpose is as before to be present at a council in Germany. He lingered, in fact, for some months in North Italy, waiting for the escort that never came; at last he resigned himself to the inevitable and slowly retraced his steps to Rome, which he reached at the beginning of September.

Henry's plan had been precisely fulfilled. He had counted the cost—a public humiliation—and was prepared to pay the additional price in the form of promises; he had obtained his end—absolution—and the results he had anticipated from this were to prove the success of his policy[1]. In Lombardy he resumed his royal rights, but resisted the clamour of his Italian adherents, whose ardour he most thoroughly disappointed; he must still walk with great discretion, and Germany, not Italy, was his immediate objective. Thither he soon returned, and the effects of his absolution were at once revealed. By the majority of his subjects he was regarded as the lawful sovereign once more. He had endured a grave injury to imperial prestige, but he had administered an important check to the two dangerous rivals of imperial power—the spiritual authority and the feudal nobility.

The news of Henry's absolution came as a shock to his enemies in Germany, upsetting their plans and disappointing their expectations. Nor were they comforted by the Pope's effort to reassure them. They decided, however, to proceed with their original purpose and to hold a diet at Forchheim in March. Their invitation to the Pope to be present at this diet must have contained a reference to their disappointment at his action, for in his reply he finds it necessary to justify himself again, laying stress also on their failure to provide an escort. This was still the difficulty that prevented him from coming to Germany, but he sent two papal legates who were present at Forchheim, and who seem on their own responsibility to have confirmed the decision of the nobles and to have given papal sanction to the election of Duke Rudolf of Swabia as king.

The election of Rudolf created a difficult situation, but one full of possibilities for the Pope which he was not slow to recognise. He refused, indeed, to confirm the action of his legates at Forchheim, but he recognised the existence of two kings and claimed for himself the decision between them. If he could establish this claim and obtain acquiescence in his decision, the predominance of the spiritual power would be revealed as a fact. His decision must not be hurried; it must be given only after clear evidence and on the spiritual and moral grounds which were the justification of the supremacy he claimed. Righteousness must be the supreme test; he will give his decision to the king *cui iustitia favet*.

[1] This is very clearly stated by the writer most favourable to him, *Vita Heinrici imperatoris*, c. 3, SGUS, p. 16.

Again and again he emphasised this, and that the marks of *iustitia* were humility and obedience, obedience to the commandments of God and so to St Peter, and through St Peter to himself. Obedience to the Pope was to be the final test of worthiness to rule, and he gave one practical application of this principle. He still continued for a time to cherish the hope that he would preside in person over a council in Germany; when this was proved impossible, his plan was to send legates to preside in his place. From both kings he expected assistance. The king who was convicted of hindering the holding of the council would be deposed, and judgment given in favour of the other; for as Gregory the Great had said, "even kings lose their thrones if they presume to oppose apostolic decrees." Naturally his attitude gave intense dissatisfaction to both Henry and Rudolf; neither felt strong enough to stand alone, and both expected papal support. Henry urged the Pope to excommunicate the traitor Rudolf, who had presumed to set himself up against God's anointed. The supporters of Rudolf were equally persistent. The Pope had absolved them from their allegiance to Henry. In conformity with this they had made a compact with him for joint action, a compact which they felt he had broken by his absolution of Henry. They had persisted, however, with the scheme and had elected Rudolf, and papal legates had been present and confirmed the election. Moreover, a garbled version of Canossa soon prevailed among them, which made it appear that the king had been granted absolution on conditions (distinct from those in his oath) which he had immediately broken, and was thereby again excommunicate. In this view they were again supported by the papal legates, who continued to embarrass the Pope by exceeding their instructions. Rudolf and his supporters can hardly be blamed for interpreting the action of the legates as performed on behalf of the Pope and by his orders. His continued neutrality and his constant reference to *two* kings only bewildered and irritated them. He persisted, however, in neutrality, undeterred by the complaints of either side, determined to take no action until the righteousness of one party or the absence of it in the other could be made apparent. But there could never have been much doubt as to the final decision. He always shewed complete confidence in Rudolf's rectitude; his previous experience could have given him little confidence in Henry. The three days' hesitation at Canossa had ended when he allowed himself to be assured of Henry's penitence; the hesitation of the three years following Canossa was to be resolved when he could feel complete assurance of Henry's guilt.

From 1077 to 1080 the decision in Germany is naturally the chief object of the Pope's attention. This did not divert his mind from the important questions of Church government and papal authority, but to some extent it hampered and restricted his actions; it would appear that he was careful to avoid any cause of friction with Henry which might compromise the settlement of the great decision. His authority was set at naught by the bishops of North Italy, who refused to execute his decrees and defied his repeated excommunications. In Germany there is hardly a trace of the struggle that had been so bitter in 1074 and 1075; this was mainly due to the confusion arising from the state of civil war. Probably too the German episcopate was not anxious to engage in another trial of strength with the Pope. Their revolt at Worms had resulted in bringing them in submission to the Pope's feet, and their leader, Archbishop Siegfried of Mayence, had given up all further thoughts of revolt against him. He had even abandoned his royal master and had consecrated Rudolf as king; his instinct in every crisis for the losing side remained with him to the end. In Gregory's correspondence during this period there is an almost complete absence of reference to ecclesiastical affairs in Germany. At the same time it is the period of his chief legislative activity. At the Lenten and November Synods of 1078, especially at the latter, he issued a number of decrees dealing with the leading questions of Church discipline, most of which were subsequently incorporated by Gratian into his *Decretum*. The increased stringency of the measures taken to deal with ecclesiastical offenders is the principal feature of these decrees. Bishops are ordered to enforce clerical chastity in their dioceses, under penalty of suspension. The sacraments of married clergy had previously been declared invalid, and the laity ordered not to hear the mass of a married priest; now entry into churches is forbidden to married clergy. All ordinations, simoniacal or otherwise uncanonical, are declared null and void, as are the orders of those ordained by excommunicated bishops. Naturally, then, the ordinations of simoniacal bishops are invalid; an exception is made in the case of those ordained *nescienter et sine pretio* by simoniacal bishops before the papacy of Nicholas II, who, after the laying-on of hands, might be confirmed in their orders[1]. As to the enforcement of these decrees by the Pope we hear nothing; but they raised issues which were to be seriously contested after his death, and his immediate successors were eventually to take less extreme views. Further, the Pope dealt with the unlawful intervention of the laity in ecclesiastical affairs. Not only are the laity sternly prohibited from holding Church property or tithes; a decree is also passed in November 1078 condemning the practice of lay investiture. It is noticeable that it only prohibits investiture with the spiritual office, and that it enforces penalties only on the recipients, not on the laity who invest. Finally, there were a number of decrees connected with points of doctrine, the most important of which was issued after considerable debate at the Lenten Synod of 1079, affirming the substantial change of the elements after consecration. It was an answer to the heresy of Berengar of Tours, who is compelled once more to recant; Gregory as before shewed great leniency in dealing with him, and actually threatened with excommunication anyone who should molest him.

---

[1] *Reg.* vi, 39. Saltet, *Les Réordinations*, pp. 205 sq., fails to notice this important letter, and therefore forms a different conclusion as to Gregory's attitude.

All this legislation, important as it was and fruitful in future controversies, was subsidiary to the question of the German kingdom, which at
every synod took the leading place. Gregory was continually striving to
bring about the council in Germany over which his legates were to preside.
Both kings promised to co-operate and to abide by the decision of the
legates; both promised an escort to ensure the safe-conduct of the legates.
But nothing was done by either; Rudolf was doubtless unable, Henry
was certainly unwilling. There was in consequence a strong feeling at the
Lenten Synod of 1079 that the Pope should immediately decide for Rudolf.
Gregory, however, persevered and contented himself with renewed promises,
guaranteed by oath, from the ambassadors of both kings. Henry was becoming impatient. As his position in Germany grew more secure, his
need to conciliate the Pope became less urgent. At the Lenten Synod of
1080 his ambassadors appeared not with promises but with the demand,
accompanied probably by threats, that the Pope should immediately
excommunicate Rudolf; Rudolf's ambassadors replied with a string of
charges against Henry, to prove his unrighteousness and insincerity. The
Pope could remain neutral no longer. Henry's embassy had provided the
evidence he required to prove the king's breach of faith. Against Henry
the decision was given.

The proceedings of the synod commenced with a renewal of the decree
against lay investiture, accompanied, now that negotiation with Henry
was at an end, by a further decree threatening with excommunication the
lay power that presumed to confer investiture of bishopric or abbey. A
third decree enforced the pure canonical election of bishops, and provided
that, where this was in any way vitiated, the power of election should
devolve on the Pope or the metropolitan. The synod terminated with
the pronouncement of the papal decision on the German kingdom. Again
in the form of a solemn address, this time with added effect to both
St Peter and St Paul, Gregory dwells on his reluctance at every stage in his
advancement to the papal chair, and recounts the history of his relations
with Henry during the three preceding years, marking the insincerity of
the king and his final disobedience in the matter of the council, which, with
the ruin and desolation he had caused in Germany, proved his unrighteousness and unfitness to reign. Then follows the sentence—Henry, for his
pride, disobedience, and falsehood, is excommunicated, deposed from his
kingdom, and his subjects absolved from their oath of allegiance. Rudolf
by his humility, obedience, truthfulness, is revealed as the righteous man;
to him the kingdom, to which he had been elected by the German people,
is entrusted by the Pope acting in the name of the two Apostles, to whom
he appeals for a vindication of his just sentence.

The sentence has a ring of finality in it that was not present in 1076.
Henry is now deposed for ever and a successor appointed in his place. So it
is on the deposition that the main emphasis is laid, as it was on the excommunication in 1076. Gregory's justification of his action is again addressed

to Bishop Herman of Metz, though not written till the following year. Unlike the similar letter of 1076 it shews no sign of haste or impatience; it is a reasoned statement, full of quotations from precedent and authority, and is concerned mainly with emphasising the complete subjection of the secular to the spiritual power, for even the lowest in the ecclesiastical hierarchy have powers which are not given to the greatest Emperors. It is a mighty assertion of the unlimited autocracy of the Pope over all men, even the greatest, on earth. And it was an assertion of authority in the justice of which Gregory had the supremest confidence. In the sentence he had prayed that Henry might acquire no strength in war, no victory in his lifetime. He followed this up on Easter Monday by his famous prophecy that Henry, if he did not repent, would be dead or deposed before St Peter's day. He felt assured that the easy victory of 1076 would be repeated. But the situation was entirely different from that in 1076, as also the issue was to be. Then opinion in Germany had been shocked by the violence and illegality of the king in attempting to expel the Pope. The papal excommunication had been obeyed as a just retribution; to the sentence of deposition little attention had been paid. As soon as the king was absolved he received again the allegiance of all those who were in favour of legitimacy and a strong central authority, and were opposed to the local ambitions of the dukes who set up Rudolf. The Pope's claim to have the deciding voice was not regarded very seriously by them, and still less attention was paid to his assertion of the complete autocracy of the spiritual power. When Henry would do nothing to make possible the council that the Pope so earnestly desired, his action was doubtless approved by them; and when the Pope in consequence excommunicated and deposed the king and appointed Rudolf in his place, he aroused very wide-spread indignation. It is Gregory who is the aggressor now, as Henry was in 1076; it is he that is regarded now as exceeding his powers in attempting to dethrone the temporal head of Western Christendom. The situation is completely reversed, and it is not too much to say that as a result of the papal sentence Henry's power in Germany became stronger than it had been for some years.

Henry was probably more alive than Gregory to the real facts of the situation. Rapidly, but with less precipitancy than he had shewn in 1076, he planned his counter-stroke. A council of German bishops held at Mayence on Whitsunday decreed the deposition of the Pope and arranged another council to be held at Brixen on 25 June, where a successor to Gregory was to be appointed. To this council the bishops of North Italy came in large numbers; the king was present and many nobles both of Germany and Italy. The bishops confirmed the Mayence decree and unanimously declared Gregory deposed; to the royal power was entrusted the task of executing the sentence. They also proceeded to the election of a successor, and their choice fell on Archbishop Guibert of Ravenna, the leader of the Lombard bishops in their revolt against papal authority.

A man of strong determination, resolute in upholding the independence he claimed for his see, he had been repeatedly summoned to Rome by the Pope, and for his absence and contumacy repeatedly excommunicated. Though violently attacked by papalist writers and likened to the beast in the Apocalypse, no charges were made against his personal character; he seems also to have been in sympathy with Church reform, as his decrees shew. A stubborn opponent of Gregory, unmoved by papal excommunications, he was eminently the man for Henry's purpose in the final struggle that had now begun. For it was a struggle that admitted of no compromise—king and anti-Pope *versus* Pope and anti-king. St Peter's day came and Gregory's prophecy was not fulfilled; in October Rudolf was killed in battle. It was now possible for Henry to take in hand the execution of the Brixen decree, and to use the temporal weapon to expel the deposed Pope.

Even before the Council of Brixen met, Gregory had realised the danger that threatened him. Spiritual weapons were of avail no longer; he must have recourse to the aid of temporal power. The Romans, he knew, were loyal to him and would resist the invader. In Tuscany he could rely absolutely on the devotion of Countess Matilda, but against this must be set the hostility of Lombardy. To restore the balance in his favour he was driven to seek assistance from the Normans in South Italy. He knew that they would welcome the alliance if he was willing to pay their price. The issues at stake were so vital to the Papacy and the Church that he felt justified in consenting to the price they demanded, though it involved what in other circumstances he would have regarded as an important breach of principle. To understand this it is necessary to review briefly his relations with the Normans during the past seven years.

The relations of the Pope with the Normans were affected by two considerations—the protection of papal territory, and the possible need for their assistance. Robert Guiscard, Duke of Apulia, Calabria, and Sicily, who was trying to form a centralised Norman state in South Italy, had readily done homage to previous Popes in return for the cession of territory, and had rendered valuable assistance to the Papacy at Alexander II's accession. Gregory was determined to yield no more territory. This and the reconciliation with Henry were the two chief objects of his attention during the first few months of his papacy. He increased the area of papal suzerainty by the addition of the lands belonging to the surviving Lombard rulers in the south, especially Benevento and Salerno; in return for his protection they surrendered them to the Pope and received them back again as fiefs from the Papacy. Richard, Prince of Capua, the only Norman who could rival Robert Guiscard, took the same step, and Gregory was delighted at the success of his policy, which was, as he himself declared, to keep the Normans from uniting to the damage of the Church. Robert Guiscard, desiring to expand his power, could only do so at the expense of papal territory. This, in spite of his oath, he did not scruple to do, and was in consequence excommunicated at the Lenten Synods of 1074 and 1075. But the breach with Henry in 1076 caused the Pope to contemplate the desirability of Norman aid; Robert made the cession of papal territory a necessary condition, and negotiations fell through. Moreover Richard of Capua had in the meantime broken his allegiance and allied himself with Robert Guiscard, and together they made a successful attack on various portions of the papal territory. In Lent 1078 the Pope issued a bull of excommunication against them once more. Richard died soon afterwards and on his death-bed was reconciled with the Church; his son Jordan came to Rome and made his peace with the Pope on the old terms. So once more Gregory had brought about disunion; and a serious revolt of his vassals against Robert Guiscard, which it took the latter two years to quell, saved the Pope from further Norman aggression. The revolt was extinguished by the middle of 1080, at the very moment that the Pope decided to appeal to Robert for aid. They met at Ceprano in June. The ban was removed, Robert did fealty to the Pope, and in return received investiture both of the lands granted him by Popes Nicholas II and Alexander II and of the territory he had himself seized, for which he agreed to pay an annual tribute to the Pope. The Pope thus confirmed what he is careful to call "an unjust tenure," and to gain Robert's aid sacrificed the principle for which he had stood firm in 1076. Whether justifiable or not the sacrifice was ineffectual. Robert Guiscard welcomed the alliance because his ambitions were turned to the East. Instead of obtaining the immediate help he required, the Pope had to give his blessing to Robert's expedition against the Eastern Empire. The duke's absence in Greece gave the opportunity for a renewed outbreak of revolt among his vassals. This forced him to return and he was not successful in crushing the revolt until July 1083; it was not till the following year, when it was as much to his own interest as to the Pope's to check the successful advance of Henry, that he at last moved to Gregory's support. Up to this time the alliance, without bringing any advantage to the Pope, had actually assisted the king. It gained for him two useful allies, both of whom were anxious to hamper the power of Robert Guiscard—Jordan of Capua and the Eastern Emperor Alexius. The latter supplied Henry with large sums of money, intended for use against Robert, but which the king was eventually to employ with success in his negotiations with the Romans.

Robert Guiscard did at any rate, as previously in 1075, reject Henry's proposals for an alliance. But he also disregarded the Pope's appeals, and set sail for the East at the very time that Henry was marching on Rome. The Pope therefore had to rely on his own resources and the assistance of Countess Matilda. This did not weaken his determination; convinced of the righteousness of his cause he was confident of the result. At the Lenten Synod of 1081 he excommunicated Henry and his followers afresh, and from this synod he sent his legates directions with regard to the election of a successor to Rudolf. He must not be hastily chosen; the chief qualifications must be integrity of character and devotion to the Church. The Pope also sent them the wording of the oath he expected from the new king—an oath of fealty, promising obedience to the papal will in all things. This was the practical expression of the theories he enunciated at the same time in his letter to Bishop Herman of Metz justifying the excommunication and deposition of Henry. It is important as marking the culmination of his views, but it was without effect; at the new election it seems to have been completely disregarded.

The weakness of the opposition in Germany made it possible for Henry to undertake his Italian expedition. He came to assert his position, and to obtain imperial coronation at Rome: by negotiation and from Gregory, if possible, but if necessary by force and from his anti-Pope. His first attempt was in May 1081; whether from over-confidence or necessity he brought few troops with him. He announced his arrival in a letter to the Romans, recalling them to the allegiance they had promised to his father. The Romans, however, justified Gregory's confidence in their loyalty, and Henry was forced to retire after a little aimless plundering of the suburbs. The situation was not affected by the election of Count Herman of Salm at the end of 1081 as successor to Rudolf. Henry could not reduce Saxony to submission, but he could safely ignore Herman and resume his Italian design. He reappeared before Rome in February 1082, preceded by a second letter to the Romans; this attempt was as unsuccessful as the former one, and for the rest of the year he was occupied with the resistance of the Countess Matilda in northern Italy. He returned to Rome at the beginning of 1083 and settled down to besiege the Leonine City, which he finally captured in June, thus gaining possession of St Peter's and all the region on the right bank of the Tiber except the castle of Sant' Angelo. This success shewed that the loyalty of the Romans to Gregory was weakening; they were not equal to the strain of a long siege, and the money supplied by the Emperor Alexius was beginning to have its effect. At the same time a moderate party was being formed within the Curia itself, which managed to obtain the papal consent to the holding of a synod in November, at which the questions at issue between Pope and king were to be discussed; Henry's party was approached and promised a safe-conduct to those who attended the synod. Thus in both camps there were influences at work to procure a peaceful settlement. The king himself was not averse to such a settlement. He had moreover come to a private understanding with the leading Romans on the matter of greatest importance to himself. Unknown to the Pope they had taken an oath to Henry to obtain for him imperial coronation at Gregory's hands, or, failing this, to disown Gregory and recognise the anti-Pope.

The attempt at reconciliation came to nothing. The Pope issued his summons to the synod, but the tone of his letters, addressed only to those who were not under excommunication, shewed that he would not compromise his views or negotiate with the impenitent. The king, who had been further irritated by what he regarded as the treachery of certain of the Romans in demolishing some fortifications he had constructed, adopted an attitude equally intransigeant. He deliberately prevented Gregory's chief supporters from coming to the synod, and actually took prisoner a papal legate, the Cardinal-bishop Otto of Ostia. The synod, therefore, was poorly attended and entirely without result. But the secret negotiations of Henry were more successful. He was about to leave Rome, in despair of attaining his object, when a deputation arrived promising him instant possession of the main city. With some hesitation he retraced his steps to find the promise genuine and his highest hopes unexpectedly fulfilled. On 21 March 1084 he entered Rome in triumph with his anti-Pope. A council of his supporters decreed anew the deposition of Pope Gregory VII, and on Palm Sunday Guibert was enthroned[1] as Pope Clement III. On Easter Day the new Pope crowned Henry and Bertha as Emperor and Empress, and Henry's chief object was attained. He had followed in the footsteps of his father—the deposition of Pope Gregory, the appointment of Pope Clement, the imperial coronation—and felt that he had restored the relations of Empire and Papacy as they existed in 1046.

The Emperor proclaimed his triumph far and wide, and his partisans celebrated it in exultant pamphlets. But their rejoicing was premature and short-lived. Gregory VII was still holding the castle of Sant' Angelo and other of the fortified positions in Rome, his determination unmoved by defeat. And at last his appeals to Robert Guiscard were heeded. The Norman duke at the head of a large army advanced on Rome. As he approached, Henry, who was not strong enough to oppose him, retreated, and by slow stages made his way back to Germany, leaving the anti-Pope at Tivoli. His immediate purpose had been achieved, and he had to abandon Rome to its fate. He could not, like his father, take the deposed Pope with him to Germany; the degradation of Gregory VII was to be the work of the man who came to his rescue. The brutal sack of Rome by the Normans lasted for three days, and put in the shade the damage done to the city in former days by Goths and Vandals. When Robert Guiscard returned south he took with him the Pope, whom he could not have left to the mercy of the infuriated populace. Gregory would fain have found a refuge at Monte Cassino; but his rescuer, now his master, hurried him on (as if to display to him the papal territory that had been the price of this deliverance), first to Benevento and then to Salerno. In June they arrived at the latter place, where Gregory was to spend the last year of his life, while the anti-Pope was able quietly to return to Rome and celebrate Christmas there. At Salerno the Pope held his last synod,

---

[1] It added to the weakness of Guibert's position that the functions of the cardinal-bishops at this ceremony were usurped by the Bishops of Modena and Arezzo.

repeated once more his excommunication of Henry and his supporters, and dispatched his final letter of justification and appeal to the Christian world. The bitterness of failure hung heavily upon him. He, who had prayed often that God would release him from this life if he could not be of service to the Church[1], had now no longer any desire to live. He passed away on 25 May 1085, and the anguish of his heart found expression in his dying words: "I have loved righteousness and hated iniquity[2]; therefore I die in exile."

The emphasis was on righteousness to the last. And it was justified. Had he consented to compromise his principles and to come to terms with Henry he could have maintained himself unchallenged on the papal throne. The rough hand of the Norman had made his residence at Rome impossible; but without Norman aid it would have been equally impossible. The Romans had deserted him; the king was master of the city. His end might even have been more terrible, though it could not have been more tragic. What impresses one most of all is not his temporary defeat, but the quenching of his spirit. The old passionate confidence has gone; though still convinced of the righteousness of his cause, he has lost all hope of its victory on earth. "The devil," he wrote, "has won no such victory since the days of the great Constantine; the nearer the day of Anti-Christ approaches, the more vigorous are the efforts he is making." His vision was dimmed by the gloom of the moment, and this gave him a pessimistic outlook that was unnatural to him and was not justified by facts. The Papacy had vindicated its independence, had taken the lead in Church reform, and had established the principles for which the reformers had been fighting. It had also asserted its authority as supreme within the ecclesiastical department, and exercised a control unknown before and not to be relaxed in the future. This was largely the work of Gregory VII. The great struggle too in which he was engaged with Henry IV was to end eventually in a complete victory for the Papacy; his antagonist was to come to an end even more miserable than his own. The great theories which he had evolved in the course of this struggle were not indeed to be followed up in practice by his immediate successors. But he left a great cause behind him, and his claims were repeated and defended in the pamphlet-warfare that followed his death. Later they were to be revived again and to raise the Papacy to its greatest height; but they were to lead to eventual disaster, as the ideal which had inspired them was forgotten. They were with Gregory VII the logical expression of his great ideal—the rule of righteousness upon earth. He had tried to effect this with the aid of the temporal ruler; when that was proved impossible, he tried to enforce it against him. The medieval theory of the two equal and independent powers had proved impracticable; Gregory inaugurated the new papal theory that was to take its place.

---

[1] As he tells Hugh of Cluny in 1075.   [2] Psalm xlv. 8.

The main interest of Gregory VII's papacy is concentrated on the great struggle with the Empire and the theories and claims that arose out of it. If his relations with the other countries of Europe are of minor interest, they are of almost equal importance in completing our understanding of the Pope. He was dealing with similar problems, and he applied the same methods to their solution; the enforcement of his decrees, the recognition of his supreme authority in the ecclesiastical department, co-operation with the secular authority, are his principal objects. Conditions differed widely in each country; he was keenly alive to these differences, shrewd and practical in varying his policy to suit them. He had frequently to face opposition, but in no case was he driven into open conflict with the secular authority. This must be borne in mind in considering the claims which he advanced against the Empire, which were the result of his conflict with the temporal ruler; where no such conflict occurred, these claims did not emerge. Evidently then they must not be taken to represent his normal attitude; they denote rather the extreme position into which he was forced by determined opposition.

Gregory had himself been employed as papal legate to enforce the reform decrees in France, and had thus been able to familiarise himself with the ecclesiastical situation. The king, Philip I, had little real authority in temporal matters, but exercised considerable influence in ecclesiastical, as also did the leading nobles[1]. The alliance of monarchy and episcopate, a legacy to the Capetians from the Carolingians, was of importance to the king, both politically and financially. The rights of *regalia* and *spolia*, and the simoniacal appointments to bishoprics, provided an important source of revenue, which the king would not willingly surrender; he was therefore definitely antagonistic to the reform movement. The simoniacal practices of the king and his plundering of Church property naturally provoked papal intervention. Remonstrance and warning were of no effect, until at the Lenten Synod of 1075 a decree was passed threatening Philip with excommunication if he failed to give satisfaction to the papal legates. The threat was apparently sufficient. Philip was not strong enough openly to defy the Pope and risk excommunication. Co-operation of the kind that Gregory desired was impossible, but Philip was content with a defensive attitude, which hindered the progress of the papal movement but did not finally prevent it. At any rate there is no further reference to papal action against the king, who seems to have made a show of compliance with the Pope's wishes in 1080, when Gregory wrote to him, imputing his former moral and ecclesiastical offences to youthful folly and sending him precepts for his future conduct. The

---

[1] In France, unlike Germany, the lay control complained of was exercised as much by the nobles as by the king. Gregory, who knew the local conditions, recognised that it was often not the king but a noble, such as the Count of Flanders, whose influence had to be counteracted.

episcopate adopted an attitude similar to that of the king. The lay influence at elections, the prevalence of simony and of clerical marriage, had created an atmosphere which made the work of reform peculiarly difficult. The bishops, supporting and supported by the king, were extremely averse to papal control, but owing to the strength of the feudal nobility they lacked the territorial power and independence of the German bishops. They had to be content therefore, like the king, with a shifty and defensive attitude; they resisted continually, but only half-heartedly.

In Gregory VII's correspondence with the French Church there are two striking features. In the first place his letters to France are, at every stage of his papacy, more than twice as numerous as his letters to Germany. These letters reveal the laxity prevailing in the Church, and the general disorder of the country owing to the weakness of the central government; they also shew the timidity of the opposition which made it possible for the Pope to interfere directly, not only in matters affecting the ecclesiastical organisation as a whole but also in questions of detail concerning individual churches and monasteries. Secondly, while the Pope's correspondence with Germany was mainly concerned with the great questions of his reform policy, his far more numerous letters to France have hardly any references to these questions. His methods were the same in both countries: in 1074 he sent papal legates to France, as to Germany, to inaugurate a great campaign against simony and clerical marriage. The legates in Germany had met with determined resistance, but those in France had pursued their work with such ardour and success that the Pope established them eventually as permanent legates in France —Bishop Hugh of Die being mainly concerned with the north and centre, Bishop Amatus of Oloron with Aquitaine and Languedoc. To them he left the task of enforcing compliance with the papal decrees; hence the silence on these matters in his own correspondence. The legates, especially Bishop Hugh, were indefatigable. They held numerous synods[1], publishing the papal decrees and asserting their own authority. Inevitably they provoked opposition, especially from the lower clergy to the enforcement of clerical celibacy, and their lives were sometimes in danger; at the Council of Poictiers in 1078 there was even a popular riot against them. The archbishops were naturally reluctant to submit to their authority, but had to be content with a passive resistance. They refused to appear at the synods, or questioned the legatine authority. The sentence of interdict, which Hugh never failed to employ, usually brought them to a reluctant submission. Only Manasse, Archbishop of Rheims, for whose character no writer has a good word, took a decided stand. He refused to appear at the synods when summoned, and appealed against the Pope's action in giving full legatine authority to non-Romans. As he

---

[1] Hugh of Flavigny (MGH, *Script.* VIII, pp. 412 sqq.) gives an account of several of these synods.

continued obstinate in his refusal to appear before the legates, he was deposed in 1080 and a successor appointed in his place; not even the king's support availed to save him. The action of the papal legates was often violent and ill-considered. Hugh in particular was a man of rigid and narrow outlook whose sentences never erred on the side of leniency. The Pope repeatedly reminded him of the virtues of mercy and discretion, and frequently reversed his sentences. The legate was aggrieved at the Pope's leniency. He complained bitterly that his authority was not being upheld by the Pope; offenders had only to run to Rome to obtain immediate pardon. In the Pope's mind, however, submission to Rome outweighed all else; when that was obtained, he readily dispensed with the penalties of his subordinates. An important step towards the strengthening of the papal authority was taken in 1079, when he made the Archbishop of Lyons primate of the four provinces of Lyons, Rouen, Tours, and Sens, subject of course to the immediate control of the Papacy; and in 1082 the legate Hugh was, practically by the Pope's orders, promoted Archbishop of Lyons. The Pope, in his decree, spoke of the restoration of the ancient constitution, but the Archbishop of Sens had by custom held the primacy, and Lyons was now rather imperial than French in its allegiance. A consideration of this nature was not likely to weigh with the Pope; it was against the idea of national and independent churches, which monarchical control was tending to produce, that he was directing his efforts. If he was not able definitely to prevent lay control of elections in France, he had firmly established papal authority over the French Church. If his decrees were not carefully obeyed, the principles of the reform movement were accepted; in the critical years that followed his death, France was to provide many of the chief supporters of the papal policy.

The situation with regard to England was altogether different. Gregory's friendship with King William I was of long standing. His had been the influence that had induced Alexander II to give the papal blessing to the Norman Duke's conquest of England. William had recognised the obligation and made use of his friendship. On Gregory's accession he wrote expressing his keen satisfaction at the event. William was a ruler of the type of the Emperor Henry III. Determined to be master in Church and State alike, he was resolved to establish good order and justice in ecclesiastical as well as in secular affairs. He was therefore in sympathy with Church reform and the purity of Church discipline and government. He was fortunate in his Archbishop of Canterbury, Lanfranc, whose legal mind shared the same vision of royal autocracy; content to be subject to the king he would admit no ecclesiastical equal, and successfully upheld the primacy of his see against the independent claims of York. The personnel of the episcopate, secularised and ignorant, needed drastic alteration; William was careful to refrain from simony and to make good appointments, but he was equally careful to keep the appointments in his own hands. He took a strong line against the immorality and ignorance of the lower clergy, and promoted reform by the encouragement he gave to regulars. Frequent Church councils were held, notably at Winchester in 1076, where decrees were passed against clerical marriage, simony, and the holding of tithes by laymen; but the decrees were framed by the king, and none could be published without his sanction. The work of Church reform was furthered, as Gregory wished, by the active co-operation of the king; the separation of the ecclesiastical from the civil courts, creating independent Church government, was also a measure after Gregory's heart. The Pope frequently expressed his gratification; the work of purifying the Church, so much impeded elsewhere, was proceeding apace in England without the need of his intervention. Disagreement arose from William's determination to be master in his kingdom, in ecclesiastical affairs as well as in secular; he made this clear by forbidding papal bulls to be published without his permission, and especially by refusing to allow English bishops to go to Rome. The Pope bitterly resented the king's attitude; a novel and formidable obstacle confronted him in the one quarter where he had anticipated none. Matters were not improved by the papal decree of 1079, subjecting the Norman archbishopric of Rouen to the primacy of the Archbishop of Lyons. So for a time relations were much strained, but an embassy from William in 1080 seems to have restored a better understanding, and even to have encouraged Gregory to advance the striking claim that William should do fealty to the Papacy for his kingdom. There is good reason to believe that the claim was made in 1080, and that it took the form of a message entrusted to the legate Hubert with the letter he brought to William in May 1080[1]. The king abruptly dismissed the claim on the ground that there was no precedent to justify it. The Pope yielded to this rebuff and made no further attempt, nor did William's refusal interfere with the restored harmony. Gregory was sensible, as he wrote in 1081, of the many exceptional merits in William, who moreover had refused to listen to the overtures of the Pope's enemies. And in one respect William made a concession. He allowed Lanfranc to visit Rome at the end of 1082, the first visit that is recorded of any English bishop during Gregory's papacy[2]. It was only a small concession. For, while the reform movement was directly furthered by royal authority in England, the Church remained quasi-national under royal control; the introduction of papal authority was definitely resisted.

In the remaining parts of Europe the Pope's efforts were mainly directed towards three objects—missionary work, uniformity of ritual, and the extension of the temporal power of the Papacy. With backward

[1] Cf. EHR, xxvi, pp. 225 sqq.
[2] Ordericus Vitalis says that Lanfranc went to Rome in 1076. The statements in Gregory's letters, *Reg.* vi, 30 (1079) and viii, 43 (1082), are sufficient contradiction of this.

countries such as Norway and Sweden, where the difficulty of the language was an obstacle to the sending of Roman missionaries, he urged that young men should be sent to Rome for instruction, so that they might return to impart it to their fellow-countrymen. In Poland it was the undeveloped ecclesiastical organisation that called for his attention; it possessed no metropolitan and hardly any bishops, and he sent legates to introduce the necessary reforms. The question of uniformity of ritual arose with regard to the territory recently recovered to Christianity from the Saracens, especially in Spain. The acceptance by the Spanish Church of the *Ordo Romanus* was an event of great importance for Catholicism in the future. Over Spain, and on the same grounds over Corsica and Sardinia as well, the Pope claimed authority temporal as well as spiritual. They were all, he declared, in former times under the jurisdiction of St Peter, but the rights of the Papacy had long been in abeyance owing to the negligence of his predecessors or the usurpation of the Saracens. Though he does not state the ground for his assertion, it is doubtless the (forged) Donation of Constantine to Pope Sylvester I that he had in his mind[1]. He was more precise in his claims over Hungary. St Stephen had handed over his kingdom to St Peter, as the Emperor Henry III recognised after his victory over Hungary, when he sent a lance and crown to St Peter. King Salomo, despising St Peter, had received his kingdom as a fief from King Henry IV; later he had been expelled by his cousin Géza. This was God's judgment for his impiety. In these cases Gregory was trying to establish claims based on former grants. He was equally anxious to extend papal dominion by new grants. He readily acceded to the request of Dmitri that the kingdom of Russia might be taken under papal protection and held as a fief from the Papacy; the King of Denmark had made a similar suggestion to his predecessor, which Gregory tried to persuade him to confirm.

His positive success in this policy was slight. The interest lies rather in the fact that he rested all these claims on grants from secular rulers; in no case does he assert that the ruler should do fealty to him in virtue of the overlordship of the spiritual power over all earthly rulers. This was a claim he applied to the Empire alone, his final remedy to cure the sickness of the world, and to prevent a recurrence of the great conflict in which he was engaged. He seems to have been loth to resort to this remedy until open defiance drove him to its use. It is not unlikely, however, that he did contemplate the gradual extension over Western Christendom of papal overlordship; but he conceived of this overlordship as coming into being in the normal feudal manner, established by consent and on a constitutional basis. In this way, when he could compel obedience even from temporal rulers to the dictates of the moral law, his dream of the rule of righteousness would at last be fulfilled.

[1] Urban II in 1091 directly quotes Constantine's Donation as the source of the authority he claims over Corsica and Lipara.

II.

Gregory VII was dead, but his personality continued to dominate the Church, his spirit lived on in the enthusiasm of his followers. The great pamphlet-warfare, already in existence, became fuller and more bitter over his final claims against the Empire. But his immediate successors were concerned with the practical danger that threatened the Papacy. They had to fight not for its supremacy so much as for the continued existence of its independence, once more threatened with imperial control. With Henry, endeavouring to establish a Pope amenable to his wishes, there could be no accommodation. Until his death in 1106 everything had to be subordinated to the immediate necessities of a struggle for existence. But in the rest of Europe the situation is entirely different. Nowhere was Henry's candidate recognised as Pope, and outside imperial territory the extreme claims of Gregory VII had not been put forward. In these countries, therefore, the policy of Gregory VII was continued and developed, and, considering the extent to which the Papacy was hampered by its continual struggle with the Emperor, the advance it was able to make was remarkable, and not without effect on its attitude to the Empire when communion was restored on the succession of Henry V to the throne.

When Gregory VII died, in exile and almost in captivity, the position of his supporters was embarrassing in the extreme, and it was not until a year had passed that a successor to him was elected. Nor was the election of Abbot Desiderius of Monte Cassino as Pope Victor III of hopeful augury for the future. Desiderius was above all things a peace-maker, inclined thereto alike by temperament and by the position of his abbey, which lay in such dangerous proximity to the encroaching Normans. He had acted as peace-maker between Robert Guiscard and Richard of Capua in 1075, and thereby assisted in thwarting the policy of Gregory VII; in 1080 he had made amends by effecting the alliance of Gregory with Robert Guiscard at Ceprano. But in 1082 he had even entered into peace negotiations with Henry IV and assisted the alliance of the latter with Jordan of Capua; hence for a year he was under the papal ban. Possibly his election was a sign that the moderate party, anxious for peace, had won the ascendency. More probably it indicates the continued dominance of Norman influence. Robert Guiscard, indeed, had died shortly after Gregory VII, but his sons Roger and Bohemond in South Italy and his brother Roger in Sicily continued his policy, affording the papal party their protection and in return enforcing their will. And for this purpose Desiderius was an easy tool. The unfortunate Pope knew himself to be unequal to the crisis, and made repeated attempts to resign the office he had so little coveted. It was, therefore, a cruel addition to his misfortunes that he was violently attacked by the more extreme followers of Gregory VII, especially by the papal legates in

France and Spain, Archbishop Hugh of Lyons and Abbot Richard of Marseilles, who accused him of inordinate ambition and an unworthy use of Norman assistance to obtain his election. Perhaps it was this opposition that stiffened his resolution and decided him at last in March 1087 at Capua, fortified by Norman support, to undertake the duties of his office. He went to Rome, and on 9 May was consecrated in St Peter's by the cardinal-bishops, whose action was in itself an answer to his traducers. But his reign was to be of short duration. Unable to maintain himself in Rome, he soon retired to Monte Cassino, his real home, where he died on 16 September. The only noteworthy act of his papacy was the holding of a synod at Benevento in August, at which he issued a decree against lay investiture, passed sentence of anathema on the anti-Pope, and excommunicated Archbishop Hugh and Abbot Richard for the charges they had presumed to bring against him.

For six months the papal throne was again vacant. At last, on 12 March 1088, the cardinals met at Terracina, and unanimously elected Otto, Cardinal-bishop of Ostia, as Pope Urban II. The three years of weakness and confusion were at an end, and a worthy leader had been found. On the day following his election he wrote a letter to his supporters in Germany, stating his determination to follow in the steps of Gregory VII, and affirming solemnly his complete adhesion to all the acts and aspirations of his dead master. To this declaration he consistently adhered; it was in fact the guiding principle of his policy. Yet in other respects he presents a complete antithesis to Gregory VII. He was a Frenchman of noble parentage, born (about 1042) near Rheims, educated at the cathedral school, and rising rapidly in ecclesiastical rank. Suddenly he abandoned these prospects and adopted the monastic profession at Cluny, where about 1076 he was appointed prior. Some two years later, the Abbot Hugh was requested by Pope Gregory VII to send some of his monks to work under him at Rome. Otto was one of those selected, and he was made Cardinal-bishop of Ostia in 1078. From this time he seems to have been attached to the person of the Pope as a confidential adviser, and he was occasionally employed on important missions. He was taken prisoner by Henry IV when on his way to the November synod of 1083. Released the next year, he went as legate to Germany, where he worked untiringly to strengthen the papal party. In 1085 he was present at a conference for peace between the Saxons and Henry's supporters and, after the failure of this conference, at the Synod of Quedlinburg, where the excommunication of Henry, Guibert, and their supporters was again promulgated. On the death of Gregory VII he returned to Italy, and was the candidate of a section of the Curia to succeed Gregory, who had indeed mentioned his name on his death-bed. He loyally supported Victor III, and in 1088 was unanimously elected to succeed him. Tall and handsome, eloquent and learned, his personality was as different from that of Gregory VII as his early career had been. In his case it was the gentleness and moderation of his nature that won admiration; we are told that he refused at the price of men's lives even to recover Rome. His learning, especially his training in Canon Law, was exactly what was required in the successor of Gregory VII. He was well qualified to work out in practice the principles of Church government inherited from his predecessor, and to place the reconstructed Church on a sound constitutional basis. The continual struggle with the Empire, which outlasted his life, robbed him of the opportunity, though much that he did was to be of permanent effect. It was in his native country, France, that his talents were to be employed with the greatest success.

It is mainly in connexion with France, therefore, that we can trace his general ideas of Church government, his view of papal authority and its relations with the lay power. There is no divergence from the standpoint of Gregory VII; he was content to carry on the work of his predecessor, following the same methods and with the same objects in view. Papal control was maintained by the system of permanent legates, and Urban continued to employ Archbishop Hugh of Lyons, and Amatus who now became Archbishop of Bordeaux. The former he had pardoned for his transgression against Victor III and he had confirmed him as legate. Hugh's fellow-offender, Abbot Richard of Marseilles, was also pardoned and was soon promoted to be cardinal (1095) and later archbishop of Narbonne. But he was not employed again as legate in Spain; this function was attached to the archbishopric of Toledo. Germany too was now given a permanent legate in the person of Bishop Gebhard of Constance. These legates were empowered to act with full authority on the Pope's behalf, were kept informed of his wishes, and were made responsible for promoting the papal policy.

Urban's ultimate object was undoubtedly the emancipation of the Church from the lay control that was responsible for its secularisation and loss of spiritual ideals. He had to combat the idea inherent in feudal society that churches, bishoprics, and abbeys were in the private gift of the lord in whose territory they were situated. To this he opposed the papal view that the laity had the duty of protecting the Church but no right of possession or authority over it. Free election by clergy and people had been the programme of the reform party for half a century, and even more than Gregory VII did Urban II pay attention to the circumstances attending appointments to bishoprics and abbeys. At several synods he repeated decrees against lay investiture, and forbade the receiving of any ecclesiastical dignity or benefice from a layman. At the Council of Clermont in 1095 he went further, prohibiting a bishop or priest from doing homage to a layman. According to Bishop Ivo of Chartres, Urban recognised the right of the king to take part in elections "as head of the people," that is to say the right of giving, but not of refusing, assent. He also allowed the king's right to "concede" the regalia—the temporal possessions of the see that had come to it by royal grant; here again the right of refusing "concession" is not implied. Ivo of Chartres was prepared to allow the king a much larger part in elections than the Pope conceded, and his interpretation of Urban's decrees is, from the point of view of the king, the most favourable that could be put upon them. The Pope was undoubtedly advancing in theory towards a condition of complete independence, but his decrees are rather an expression of his ideal than of his practice.

In practice he was, like Gregory VII, much more moderate, and when good appointments were made was not disposed to quarrel with lay influence. His temperament, as well as the political situation, deterred him from drastic action, for instance, in dealing with the Kings of England and France. He tried every means of persuasion before issuing a decree of excommunication against Philip I in the matter of his divorce; and though he took Anselm under his protection, he never actually pronounced sentence against William II. It was a difficult position to maintain. His legates, especially the violent Hugh, followed the exact letter of the decrees, and by their ready use of the penal clauses often caused embarrassment to the Pope. On the other hand, the bishops and secular clergy, as was shewn in France over the royal divorce question, were too complaisant to the king and could not be trusted. On the regular clergy he could place more reliance, and it is to them that he particularly looked for support. It is remarkable how large a proportion of the documents that issued from Urban's Chancery were bulls to monasteries, confirming their privileges and possessions, exempting them sometimes from episcopal control, and taking them under papal protection (always with the proviso that they shall pay an annual census to the papal treasury); the extension of Cluniac influence with Urban's approval naturally had the same effect. Nor was his interest confined to Benedictine monasteries; he gave a ready encouragement to the new orders in process of formation, especially to the regular canons who traced their rule to St Augustine. And so, at the same time that he was trying to secure for the bishops freedom of election and a loosening of the yoke that bound them to the lay power, he was narrowing the range of their spiritual authority. Indirectly too the authority of the metropolitans was diminishing; it was becoming common for bishops to obtain confirmation of their election from the Pope, and in some cases consecration as well, while the practice of direct appeal to Rome was now firmly established. Moreover, the appointment of primates, exalting some archbishops at the expense of others, introduced a further grading into the hierarchy, and at the same time established responsibility for the enforcement of papal decrees. The primacy of Lyons, created by Gregory VII, was confirmed by Urban in spite of the protests of Archbishop Richer of Sens, who refused to recognise the authority of Lyons; his successor Daimbert was for a time equally obstinate, but had to submit in order to obtain consecration. Urban extended the system by creating the Archbishop of Rheims primate of Belgica Secunda[1], the Archbishop of Narbonne primate over Aix, and the Archbishop of Toledo primate of all Spain. The Pope, therefore, was modelling the ecclesiastical constitution so as to make his authority effective throughout. A natural consequence of this was his zeal for uniformity. He was anxious, as he had been as legate, to get rid of local customs and to produce a universal conformity to the practice of the Roman Church. This is evident in many of his decretals, those, for instance, that regulated ordinations and ecclesiastical promotions or that prescribed the dates of the fasts *quattuor temporum*.

While Urban II undoubtedly increased the spiritual authority of the Papacy, he was far less concerned than Gregory VII with its temporal authority. He certainly made use of the Donation of Constantine to assert his authority in Corsica and Lipara, but he did not revive Gregory VII's claims to Hungary, nor did he demand from England anything more than the payment of Peter's Pence. It was not until 1095 that he received the recognition of William II, and his mild treatment of that king, in spite of William's brutality to Archbishop Anselm, has already been mentioned. In Spain and Sicily he was mainly concerned with the congenial task of re-creating bishoprics and rebuilding monasteries in the districts recently won from the infidel; he was careful to make papal authority effective, and to introduce uniformity to Roman practice by the elimination of local uses. One great extension of temporal authority he did not disdain. In 1095 King Peter of Aragon, in return for the payment of an annual tribute, obtained the protection of the Holy See, and acknowledged his subordination to its authority. Papal overlordship was recognised also by the Normans in South Italy, and Roger, Robert Guiscard's son, was invested by Urban with the duchy of Apulia. The Normans, however, were vassals only in name, and never allowed their piety to interfere with their interests. In 1098 Urban was a helpless witness of the siege and capture of Capua, and the same year Count Roger of Sicily obtained for himself and his heirs a remarkable privilege. No papal legate, unless sent *a latere*, was to enter his territory. The count himself was to hold the position of papal legate, and, in the case of a papal summons to a Roman Council, was allowed to decide which of his bishops and abbots should go and which should remain. Urban owed much to Norman protection, but he had to pay the price.

At any rate, at the time of his accession, Urban was safe only in Norman territory. Guibert held Rome, and Urban's adherents in the city were few and powerless. Countess Matilda was loyal as ever, but all her resources were needed for her own security. Lombardy was still strongly anti-papal, while in Germany (apart from Saxony) there were hardly half-a-dozen bishops who upheld the papal cause, and the rebel nobles were absorbed in their own defence. But in North Italy the tide soon

---

[1] The old Roman province. This gave the archbishop the title of primate, but nothing more.

began to turn. Already in 1088 the Archbishop of Milan had renounced allegiance to Henry and had become reconciled with the Pope, who pardoned his offence of having received royal investiture. There followed in 1089 the marriage of the younger Welf with the ageing Countess Matilda of Tuscany, truly (as the chroniclers relate) not prompted by any weakness of the flesh, but a political move which reflected little credit on either party; the Duke of Bavaria, at any rate, was completely outwitted, but the Papacy gained the immediate help it required. It brought Henry into Italy to wage a campaign that was for two years successful, culminating in the capture of Mantua, and a signal victory over Matilda's troops at Tricontai, in 1091, but he was now fighting to maintain his authority in Lombardy, where it had previously been unchallenged. The final blow came with the revolt of his son Conrad in 1093. Conrad, bringing with him stories of fresh crimes to blacken his father's name, was welcomed by the papal party with open arms, and crowned (he had already been crowned King of Germany) with the iron crown of Lombardy. A regular Lombard League sprang into being with Milan at its head. The unfortunate father was in very evil plight, almost isolated at Verona, unable, as his enemies held the passes, even to escape into Germany until 1097.

Success in North Italy reacted on Urban's authority elsewhere. The winter of 1088–1089 he had indeed spent in Rome, but in wretched circumstances, living on the island in the Tiber under the direction of the Pierleoni, and obtaining the necessities of life from the charity of a few poor women. Later in 1089 the expulsion of Guibert from Rome improved the Pope's position, but it was only a temporary improvement. The hostile element (probably the recollection of 1084 was still smarting) was too strong for him, and he had to retire south in the summer of 1090. Though he managed to celebrate Christmas both in 1091 and 1092 in the suburbs, he was not able to enter the city again until Christmas 1093. Refusing to allow bloodshed to secure his position, he adopted the safer method of winning the Romans by gold, instituting collections for this purpose, especially in France. In 1094 Abbot Geoffrey of Vendôme, on a visit to the Pope, found him living in mean state in the house of John Frangipani, and supplied him with money with which he purchased the Lateran from a certain Ferruchius left in charge of it by Guibert. From this time Urban's fortunes began to mend, and only the castle of Sant' Angelo remained in the hands of the Guibertines. But his tenure of Rome was insecure; papal authority within the city was not popular, while outside his enemies made the approaches dangerous for those who came to visit the Pope. It was not surprising, then, that he took the opportunity of the success of his cause in North Italy to commence the northern tour which was to have such important results.

In Germany progress was made with difficulty. The bishops as a whole were too deeply implicated in the schism to withdraw, and the papal legate, Bishop Gebhard of Constance, in spite of his undoubted zeal, could make little headway. The deaths of Bishops Herman of Metz and Adalbero of Würzburg in 1090, and of Abbot William of Hirschau and Bishop Altmann of Passau in 1091, robbed the papal party of its staunchest supporters. But Henry's absence in Italy and the revolt of Conrad gave an opportunity to the two sections of opposition to Henry in South Germany to unite for concerted action. At an assembly held at Ulm in 1093 all present pledged themselves by oath to accept Bishop Gebhard as the spiritual head, and his brother Duke Berthold as the temporal leader, of the party; further, Dukes Berthold and Welf did homage as vassals to the papal legate and thus recognised the overlordship of the Pope. At the same time, the leading bishops in Lorraine renounced obedience to the excommunicated Archbishop of Trèves and brought a welcome reinforcement to the papal party. The improvement in the situation is shewn by the largely-attended synod presided over by Gebhard at Constance in the following Lent. Shortly afterwards Europe was devastated by a pestilence, which was particularly severe in Germany. The fear of death had a considerable effect in withdrawing adherents from an excommunicated king, and the increasing sentiment in favour of the lawful Pope was heightened by the commencement of the crusading movement. The political situation, however, was less satisfactory than the ecclesiastical. Duke Welf, foiled in his expectations of the results of his son's marriage with Matilda, reverted to Henry's allegiance in 1095, and Henry's return to Germany in 1097 prevented the revolt against him from assuming greater proportions.

The reconciliation with the Church of so many that had been in schism before made it urgently necessary to find an answer to the question—in what light were to be regarded the orders of those who received ordination from schismatics or simonists? Ever since the war on simony began, the question of ordinations by simonists had agitated the Church. Peter Damian had argued for their validity. Cardinal Humbert had been emphatic against, and Popes Nicholas II and Gregory VII had practically adopted his opinion. On one thing all alike were agreed—there could be no such thing as reordination. In Humbert's view, simonists were outside the pale of the Church, and could confer nothing sacramental; those who received ordination from them in effect received nothing, and so, unless they afterwards received Catholic ordination, they had no orders at all. Urban was obviously at a loss for some time, and his rulings were of a contradictory nature. He uses the language of Humbert when he says in 1089 that he himself ordained Daimbert, Bishop-elect of Pisa, as deacon, because Daimbert had previously been ordained by Archbishop Werner of Mayence, heretic and excommunicate, and "qui nihil habuit, nil dare potuit"; and again in 1091 when he ruled that Poppo, Bishop-elect of Metz, must be ordained deacon by a Catholic bishop if his previous ordination had been simoniacal, because in that case it would be null[1]. But circumstances were too strong for him, and even in 1089 he gave permission to his legate in Germany to allow the retention of their orders to those who without simony had received ordination from schismatic bishops, provided the latter had themselves received Catholic ordination. It was at the great Council of Piacenza in 1095 that he at last issued authoritative decrees on this subject. Those ordained by schismatic bishops, who had themselves received Catholic ordination, might retain their orders, if and when they returned to the unity of the Church. Also those who had been ordained by schismatics or simonists might retain their orders if they could prove their ignorance of the excommunication or simony of their ordainers. But in all cases where such ignorance was not alleged the orders were declared to be altogether of no effect (*omnino irritae*). The meaning of this is not clear, but evidently the validity of such orders is in fact recognised, as the validity of the sacrament could not depend on the knowledge or ignorance of the ordinand. Some light is thrown by a letter of uncertain date to one Lucius, provost of St Juventius. After having declared the validity of the orders and sacraments of criminous clergy, *provided* they are not schismatics, he goes on to say that the schismatics have the *forma* but not the *virtutis effectus* of the sacraments, unless and until they are received into the Catholic communion by the laying-on of hands. This then was the bridge by which the penitent schismatic might pass into the Catholic fold, and the ceremony of reconciliation, which included the performance of all the rites of ordination save that of unction, was laid down by him in letters written both in 1088 and 1097. Urban's position was neither easy to comprehend nor to maintain, and the anti-Pope Guibert was on firmer ground when he condemned those who refused to recognise the ordinations of his partisans. Urban's successor was able, when the death of Henry IV brought the schism to an end, to assist the restoration of unity by a more generous policy of recognition.

As we have seen, in 1094, when the Pope was at last in possession of the Lateran palace, his cause was victorious throughout Italy and gaining adherents rapidly in Germany. In the autumn he left Rome and commenced his journey, which lasted two years and was not far short of a triumphal progress, through France and Italy. He came first to Tuscany

---

[1] Here in particular I disagree from the interpretation of Urban's attitude given by the Abbé Saltet (*Les Réordinations*, pp. 222 sqq.). He uses these two instances as evidence that, in the case of deacons as distinct from priests, etc., Urban insisted on an entirely new ordination. But the reasons given by the Pope for his decisions in these two cases have a general application and are not influenced by the fact that he is dealing with ordinations to the diaconate only. Clearly none of their orders are valid. Though on various points I cannot accept the Abbé's conclusions, it is only fair to add that, but for the illumination that he has thrown upon this most involved subject, it would have been difficult to find one's way at all.

where he spent the winter, and then proceeded into North Italy which had been persistent, under the lead of the bishops, in its hostility to the Pope, and which, now that the episcopal domination was beginning to wane[1], was looking to the Pope as an ally against imperial authority. Even the bishops, following the example of the Archbishop of Milan, were rapidly becoming reconciled with the Pope. In March 1095 Urban held a Council at Piacenza, which was attended by an immense concourse of ecclesiastics and laymen. The business, some of which has already been mentioned, was as important as the attendance. Praxedis, Henry IV's second wife, was present to shock the assembly with stories of the horrors her husband had forced her to commit. These found a ready credence, and she herself a full pardon and the Pope's protection. The case of King Philip of France, excommunicated for adultery by Archbishop Hugh at Autun the previous year, was debated and postponed for the Pope's decision in France. Finally there appeared the envoys of the Emperor Alexius imploring the help of Western Christendom against the infidel, and the inspiration came to Urban that was to give a great purpose to his journey to France. From Piacenza Urban passed to Cremona, where he met Conrad, who did fealty to him and received in return the promise of imperial coronation. Conrad further linked himself with the papal cause by marrying the daughter of Count Roger of Sicily shortly afterwards at Pisa. It is easy to blame the Pope who welcomed the rebel son; but it is juster to attribute his welcome as given to the penitent seeking absolution and a refuge from an evil and excommunicated father. The fault of Urban was rather that he took up the unfortunate legacy from Gregory VII of attempting to establish an Emperor who would be his vassal, falling thus into the temptation that was to be fatal to the Papacy. Urban in this respect was as unsuccessful as his rival, who attempted to establish a compliant Pope; Conrad lived on for six more years, but without a following, and he and Guibert alike came to their end discredited and alone.

In July the Pope entered France, where judgment was to be passed on the king and the Crusade to be proclaimed. But the Pope's energies were not confined to these two dominant questions. He travelled ceaselessly from place to place, looking into every detail of the ecclesiastical organisation, settling disputes, and consecrating churches. Philip I made no attempt to interfere with the papal progress, and the people everywhere hailed with enthusiasm and devotion the unaccustomed sight of a Pope. The climax was reached at the Council of Clermont in the latter half of November, where both of the important questions were decided. The king was excommunicated and the First Crusade proclaimed. Urban recognised that he was again following in the footsteps of Gregory VII, but his was the higher conception and his the practical ability that realised the ideal. A less disinterested Pope might have roused the enthusiasm of the faithful against his enemy in Germany; personal considerations

[1] Cf. *infra*, Chap. v, pp. 219 sq., 222 sq.

might at least have checked him from sending the great host to fight against the infidel when the Emperor still threatened danger, the King of France was alienated by excommmnication, and the King of England was anything but friendly. His disinterestedness had its reward in the position the Papacy secured in consequence of the success of his appeal, but this reward was not in Urban's mind in issuing the appeal. Clermont was followed by no anti-climax. The papal progress was continued in 1096, the Crusade was preached again at Angers and on the banks of the Loire, synods were held at Tours and Nîmes, and the popular enthusiasm increased in intensity. He had the satisfaction too of obtaining the submission of Philip.

When he returned to Italy in September, and, accompanied by Countess Matilda, made his way to Rome, he was to experience even there a great reception and to feel himself at last master of the papal city. "Honeste tute et alacriter sumus" are the concluding words of his account of his return in a letter to Archbishop Hugh of Lyons. And in 1098 the last stronghold of the Guibertines, the castle of Sant' Angelo, fell into his hands. But his joy was premature. It would seem that the turbulent Roman nobles, who had tasted independence, were not willing to submit for long to papal authority. It was not in the Lateran palace but in the house of the Pierleoni that Urban died on 29 July 1099, and his body was taken by way of Trastevere to its last resting place in the Vatican.

But, on the whole, his last three years were passed in comparative tranquillity and honour. The presence of Archbishop Anselm of Canterbury, in exile from England, added distinction to the papal Court. Received with the veneration that his character merited, Anselm acted as champion of Western orthodoxy against the Greeks at the Council of Bari in 1098. And three months before his death Urban held in St Peter's his last council, at which the decrees of Piacenza and Clermont were solemnly re-affirmed. Anselm returned to England with the decrees against lay investiture and homage as the last memory of his Roman visit. They were to bring him into immediate conflict with his new sovereign.

It was perhaps due to the unsettled state of Rome that the cardinals chose San Clemente for the place of conclave; there on 13 August they unanimously elected Rainer, cardinal-priest of that basilica, as Urban's successor, in spite of his manifest reluctance. The anti-Pope was hovering in the neighbourhood and a surprise from him was feared, but nothing occurred to disturb the election. Rainer, who took the name of Paschal II, was a Tuscan by birth, who had been from early days a monk in some south Italian monastery[1]. Sent to Rome by his abbot while still quite young, he had been retained by Gregory VII and appointed Abbot of San Lorenzo fuori le mura and afterwards cardinal-priest of San Clemente. By Urban II, in whose election he took a leading part, he had been employed

[1] See March, J. M., *Liber Pontificalis* (Barcelona, 1925) p. 154, n. 3.

as papal legate in Spain. Here our knowledge of his antecedents ceases. So general was the agreement at his election that he was conducted at once to take possession of the Lateran palace, and on the following day was solemnly consecrated and enthroned at St Peter's. Guibert was dangerously close, but the arrival of Norman gold enabled the Pope to chase him from Albano to Sutri; soon afterwards he retired to Civita Castellana, and died there in September 1100. Two anti-Popes were set up in succession by his Roman partisans, both cardinal-bishops of his creation—Theodoric of Santa Rufina and Albert of the Sabina—but both were easily disposed of. Paschal, so far fortunate, was soon to experience the same trouble as Urban II from the Roman nobles. The defeat of Peter Colonna (with whom the name Colonna first enters into history) was an easy matter. More dangerous were the Corsi, who, after being expelled from their stronghold on the Capitol, settled in the Marittima and took their revenge by plundering papal territory. Closely connected with this disturbance was the rising of other noble families under the lead of a German, Marquess Werner of Ancona, which resulted in 1105 in the setting-up of a third anti-Pope, the arch-priest Maginulf, who styled himself Pope Sylvester IV. Paschal was for a time forced to take refuge in the island on the Tiber, but the anti-Pope was soon expelled. He remained, however, as a useful pawn for Henry V in his negotiations with the Pope, until the events of 1111 did away with the need for him, and he was then discarded. The nobles had not ceased to harass Paschal, and a serious rising in 1108–1109 hampered him considerably at a time when his relations with Henry were becoming critical. Again in 1116, on the occasion of Henry's second appearance in Italy, Paschal was forced to leave Rome for a time owing to the riots that resulted from his attempt to establish a Pierleone as prefect of the city.

The new Pope was of a peaceful and retiring disposition, and in his attempts to resist election he shewed a just estimate of his own capacity. Lacking the practical gifts of Urban II and Gregory VII, and still more the enlightened imagination of the latter, he was drawn into a struggle which he abhorred and for which he was quite unequal. Timid and unfamiliar with the world, he dreaded the *ferocia gentis* of the Germans, and commiserated with Anselm on being *inter barbaros positus* as archbishop. He was an admirable subordinate in his habit of unquestioning obedience, but he had not the capacity to lead or to initiate. Obedient to his predecessors, he was obstinate in adhering to the text of their decrees, but he was very easily overborne by determined opponents. This weakness of character is strikingly demonstrated throughout the investiture struggle, in which he took the line of rigid obedience to the text of papal decrees. Probably he was not cognisant of all the complicated constitutional issues involved, and the situation required the common sense and understanding of a man like Bishop Ivo of Chartres to handle it with success; Ivo had the true Gregorian standpoint. Paschal devised a solution of the difficulty with Henry V in 1111 which was admirable on paper but impossible to carry into effect; and he shewed no strength of mind when he had to face the storm which his scheme provoked. A short captivity was sufficient to wring from him the concession of lay investiture which his decrees had so emphatically condemned. When this again raised a storm, he yielded at once and revoked his concession; at the same time he refused to face the logic of his revocation and to stand up definitely against the Emperor who had forced the concession from him. The misery of his later years was the fruit of his indecision and lack of courage. The electors are to blame, who overbore his resistance, and it is impossible not to sympathise with this devout, well-meaning, but weak Pope, faced on all sides by strong-minded men insistent that their extreme demands must be carried out and contemptuous of the timid nature that yielded so readily. Eadmer tells us of a characteristic outburst from William Rufus, on being informed that the new Pope was not unlike Anselm in character: "God's Face! Then he isn't much good." The comparison has some truth in it, though it is a little unfair to Anselm. Both were unworldly men, drawn against their will from their monasteries to a prolonged contest with powerful sovereigns; unquestioning obedience to spiritual authority was characteristic of them both, but immeasurably the greater was Anselm, who spoke no ill of his enemies and shielded them from punishment, while he never yielded his principles even to extreme violence. Paschal would have left a great name behind him, had he been possessed of the serene courage of St Anselm.

For seven years the tide flowed strongly in his favour. The death of the anti-Pope Guibert in 1100 was a great event. It seems very probable that if Henry IV had discarded Guibert, as Henry V discarded Maginulf, he might have come to terms with Urban II. But Henry IV was more loyal to his allies than was his son, and he refused to take this treacherous step. It seemed to him that with Guibert's death the chief difficulty was removed, and he certainly gave no countenance to the anti-Popes of a day that were set up in Rome to oppose Paschal. He was indeed quite ready to recognise Paschal, and, in consonance with the universal desire in Germany for the healing of the schism, announced his intention of going to Rome in person to be present at a synod where issues between Empire and Papacy might be amicably settled. It was Paschal, however, who proved irreconcilable. In his letters and decrees he shewed his firm resolve to give no mercy to the king who had been excommunicated and deposed by his predecessors and by himself. Henry was a broken man, very different from the antagonist of Gregory VII, and it was easy for Paschal to be defiant. The final blow for the Emperor came at Christmas 1104, when the young Henry deserted him and joined the rebels. Relying on the nobles and the papal partisans, Henry V was naturally anxious to be reconciled with the Pope. Paschal welcomed the rebel with open arms, as Urban had welcomed Conrad.

CH. II.

The formal reconciliation took place at the beginning of 1106. Born in 1081, when his father was already excommunicated, Henry could only have received baptism from a schismatic bishop. With the ceremony of the laying-on of hands he was received by Catholic bishops into the Church, and by this bridge the mass of the schismatics passed back into the orthodox fold. The Pope made easy the path of reconciliation, and the schism was thus practically brought to an end. The young king, as his position was still insecure, shewed himself extremely compliant to the Church party. He had already expelled the more prominent bishops of his father's party from their sees, and filled their places by men whom the papal legate, Bishop Gebhard of Constance, had no hesitation in consecrating. But he shewed no disposition to give up any of the rights exercised by his father, and Paschal did not take advantage of the opportunity to make conditions or to obtain concessions from him. Towards the old king, who made a special appeal to the apostolic mercy, promising complete submission to the papal will, Paschal shewed himself implacable. There could be no repetition of Canossa, but the Pope renewed the ambition of Gregory VII in announcing his intention to be present at a council in Germany. The temporary recovery of power by Henry IV in 1106 prevented the holding of this council in Germany, and it was summoned to meet in Italy instead. In the interval Henry died, and still the Pope was implacable, refusing to allow the body of the excommunicated king to be laid to rest in consecrated ground. It was a hollow triumph; the Papacy was soon to find that it had exchanged an ageing and beaten foe for a young and resolute one. The death of his father had relieved Henry V from the immediate necessity of submission to the papal will. He soon made clear that he was as resolute a champion of royal rights as his father, and he faced the Pope with Germany united in his support.

III.

With the death of Henry IV and the reconciliation of Henry V with the Church, the schism that had lasted virtually for thirty years was at an end. The desire for peace, rather than any deep conviction of imperial guilt, had been responsible perhaps for Henry V's revolt, certainly for his victory over his father. By the tacit consent of both sides the claims and counter-claims of the years of conflict were ignored; the attempt of each power to be master of the other was abandoned, and in the relations between the *regnum* and *sacerdotium* the *status quo ante* was restored. On the question of lay investiture negotiations had already been started before the schism began; they were resumed as soon as the schism was healed, but papal decrees in the intervening years had increased the difficulty of solution. Universal as was the desire for peace, this issue prevented its consummation for another sixteen years. The contest of Henry V and the Papacy is solely, and can very rightly be named, an Investiture Struggle[1].

Gregory VII's decrees had been directed against the old idea by which churches and bishoprics were regarded as possessions of laymen, and against the practice of investiture by ring and staff which symbolised the donation by the king of spiritual functions. He shewed no disposition to interfere with the feudal obligations which the king demanded from the bishops as from all holders of land and offices within his realm. But his successors were not content merely to repeat his decrees. At the Council of Clermont in 1095 Urban II had prohibited the clergy from doing homage to laymen, and at the Lenten Synod at Rome in 1102 Paschal II also prohibited the clergy from receiving ecclesiastical property at the hands of a layman, that is to say, even investiture with temporalities alone. To Gregory investiture was not important in itself, but only in the lay control of spiritual functions which it typified, and in the results to which this led—bad appointments and simony; the prohibition of investiture was only a means to an end. To Paschal it had become an end in itself. Rigid in his obedience to the letter of the decrees, he was blind to the fact that, in order to get rid of the hated word and ceremony, he was leaving unimpaired the royal control, which was the real evil.

He had already obtained his point in France, and was about to establish it in England also. In France, owing to the weakness of the central government, papal authority had for some time been more effective than elsewhere; Philip I also exposed himself to attack on the moral side, and had only recently received absolution (in 1104) after a second period of excommunication. Relations were not broken off again, as the Pope did not take cognisance of Philip's later lapses. The king, at any rate, was not strong enough to resist the investiture decrees. There was no actual concordat; the king simply ceased to invest, and the nobles followed his example[2]. He, and they, retained control of appointments, and in place of investiture "conceded" the temporalities of the see, usually after consecration and without symbol; the bishops took the oath of fealty, but usually did not do homage.

Paschal was less successful in England, where again political conditions were largely responsible for bringing Henry I into the mood for compromise. Henry and Paschal were equally stubborn, and on Anselm fell the brunt of the struggle and the pain of a second exile. At last Henry was brought to see the wisdom of a reconciliation with Anselm, and the Pope relented so far as to permit Anselm to consecrate bishops even though

---

[1] The controversial literature shews this very clearly. It is, from now onwards, confined to the question of lay investiture. Up to this time it was the greater issues raised by Gregory VII that had been mainly debated.

[2] France was peculiar in this, that not only the king but also nobles invested even to bishoprics. Normandy was in a special position, and what is said with regard to England should be taken as applying to Normandy also.

they had received lay investiture or done homage to the king. This paved the way for the Concordat of August 1107, by which the king gave up the practice of investing with ring and staff and Anselm consented to consecrate bishops who had done homage to the king. Thus what the Pope designed as a temporary concession was turned into a permanent settlement. The subsequent practice is seen from succeeding elections and was embodied in the twelfth chapter of the Constitutions of Clarendon. The king had the controlling voice in the election, the bishop-elect did homage and took the oath of fealty, and only after that did the consecration take place. In effect, the king retained the same control as before. The Pope was satisfied by the abolition of investiture with the ring and staff, but the king, though hating to surrender an old custom[1], had his way on all the essential points.

Paschal II's obsession with the question of investiture is shewn in the letter he wrote to Archbishop Ruthard of Mayence in November 1105, a letter which is a fitting prelude to the new struggle. Investiture, he says, is the cause of the discord between the *regnum* and the *sacerdotium*, but he hopes that the new reign will bring a solution of the difficulty. Actually it was the new reign that created the difficulty. During the schism papal decrees were naturally disregarded in Germany; royal investiture continued uninterruptedly, and Henry V from the beginning of his reign regularly invested with the ring and staff. But when Germany returned to the Catholic fold, papal decrees became operative once more, and the discrepancy between Henry's profession of obedience to Rome and his practice of investiture was immediately apparent. He was as determined as his father that the royal prerogative should remain unimpaired, but he shewed his sense of the direction the controversy was taking and the weakness of the royal position by insisting that he was only investing with the *regalia*[2]. This made no difference to Paschal, who refused all compromise on the exercise of investiture; his assertion of his desire not to interfere with the royal rights, which had some meaning in Gregory VII's mouth, carried no conviction. He must have been sanguine indeed if he expected in Germany a cessation of investiture as in France; there was nothing to induce Henry V even to follow the precedent set by his English namesake. In Germany there was no parallel to the peculiar position in England of St Anselm, the primate who put first his profession of obedience to the Pope. Archbishops and bishops, as well as lay nobles, were at one with the king on this question; even the papal legate, Bishop Gebhard of Constance, who had endured so much in the papal cause, did not object to consecrate bishops appointed and invested by Henry. And the German king had legal documents to set against the papal claims—the

[1] His reluctance is seen in the jealous complaint he made in 1108 through Anselm, that the Pope was still allowing the King of Germany to invest.

[2] This meant the important part, but not the whole, of the temporalities of the see.

privileges of Pope Hadrian I to Charles the Great and of Pope Leo VIII to Otto the Great—forged documents, it is true, but none the less useful. It needed a change in the political atmosphere to induce Henry V to concessions.

The council summoned by Paschal met at Guastalla on 22 October 1106. The Pope was affronted by the scant attention paid by German bishops to his summons. Instead there appeared an embassy from Henry claiming that the Pope should respect the royal rights, and at the same time inviting him again to Germany. To the first message Paschal replied by a decree against lay investiture, to the second by an acceptance of the invitation, promising to be at Mayence at Christmas. He soon repented of his promise, whether persuaded of the futility of the journey or wishing to avoid the personal encounter, and hastily made his way into France, where he could be sure of protection and respect. Here he met with a reception which fell little short of that accorded to Urban; in particular he was welcomed by the two kings, Philip I and his son Louis, who accompanied the Pope to Châlons in May 1107, where he received the German ambassadors with Archbishop Bruno of Trèves at their head. To the reasoned statement they presented of the king's demands Paschal returned a direct refusal, which was pointed by the decree he promulgated against investiture at a council held at Troyes on 23 May. At this council he took action against the German episcopate, especially for their disobedience to his summons to Guastalla: the Archbishops of Mayence and Cologne and their suffragans, with two exceptions, were put under the ban, and his legate Gebhard received a sharp censure. It was of little avail that he invited Henry to be present at a synod in Rome in the following year. Henry did not appear, and Paschal was too much occupied with difficulties in Rome to take any action. But at a synod at Benevento in 1108 he renewed the investiture decrees, adding the penalty of excommunication against the giver as well as the receiver of investiture. Clearly he was meditating a definite step against Henry. The king, however, had a reason for not wishing at this moment to alienate the Pope—his desire for imperial coronation. Accordingly during 1109 and 1110 negotiations were resumed. An embassy from Henry proposing his visit to Rome was well received by Paschal, who welcomed the proposal though remaining firm against the king's demands. At the Lenten Synod of 1110 he repeated the investiture decree, but, perhaps to prevent a breach in the negotiations, abstained from pronouncing excommunication on the giver of investiture. He had reiterated to Henry's embassy his intention not to infringe the royal rights. Had he already conceived his solution of 1111? At any rate he took the precaution of obtaining the promise of Norman support in case of need, a promise which was not fulfilled[1].

[1] Duke Roger of Apulia died on 21 February 1111, and the Normans were too weak to come to the Pope's assistance. In fact they feared an imperial attack upon themselves.

In August 1110 Henry began his march to Rome. From Arezzo, at the end of December, he sent an embassy to the Pope, making it clear that he insisted on investing with the temporalities held from the Empire. Paschal's answer was not satisfactory, but a second embassy (from Acquapendente) was more successful. It was now that Paschal produced his famous solution of the dilemma—the separation of ecclesiastics from all secular interests. If Henry would renounce investiture, the Church would surrender all the *regalia* held by bishops and abbots, who would be content for the future with tithes and offerings. Ideally this was an admirable solution, and it may have appeared to the unworldly monk to be a practical one as well. Henry must have known better. He must have realised that it would be impossible to obtain acquiescence from those who were to be deprived of their privileges and possessions. But he saw that it could be turned to his own advantage. He adroitly managed to lay on the Pope the onus of obtaining acquiescence; this the Pope readily undertook, serenely relying on the competency of ecclesiastical censures to bring the reluctant to obedience. The compact was made by the plenipotentiaries of both sides at the church of Santa Maria in Turri on 4 February 1111, and was confirmed by the king himself at Sutri on 9 February.

On 12 February the king entered St Peter's with the usual preliminary formalities that attended imperial coronations. The ratification of the compact was to precede the ceremony proper. Henry rose and read aloud his renunciation of investiture. The Pope then on behalf of the Church renounced the *regalia*, and forbade the holding of them by any bishops or abbots, present or to come. Immediately burst forth the storm that might have been expected[1]. Not only the ecclesiastics, who saw the loss of their power and possessions, but also the lay nobles, who anticipated the decline in their authority consequent on the liberation of churches from their control, joined in the uproar. All was confusion; the ceremony of coronation could not proceed. Eventually, after futile negotiations, the imperialists laid violent hands on the Pope and cardinals; they were hurried outside the walls to the king's camp, after a bloody conflict with the Romans. A captivity of two months followed, and then the Pope yielded to the pressure and conceded all that Henry wished. Not only was royal investiture permitted; it was to be a necessary preliminary to consecration. They returned together to St Peter's, where on 13 April the Pope handed Henry his privilege and placed the imperial crown upon

---

[1] The accounts published afterwards by both sides are contradictory as to the actual order of events. The imperial manifesto declares that Henry read his privilege and that the uproar arose when he called upon the Pope to fulfil his share of the compact. The papal manifesto implies that neither privilege was actually read aloud. The account that Ekkehard gives in his Chronicle (MGH, *Script.* VI, p. 224 sq.) is that the uproar occurred after the reading of both privileges. Whatever actually happened, it is clear that the contents of the two documents were in some way made public.

his head. Immediately after the ceremony the Pope was released; the Emperor, who had had to barricade the Leonine city against the populace, hastily quitted Rome and returned in triumph to Germany.

The Pope had had his moment of greatness. He had tried to bring the ideal into practice and to recall the Church to its true path; but the time was not ripe, the violence of the change was too great, and the plan failed. The failure was turned into disaster by the weakness of character which caused him to submit to force and make the vital concession of investiture; for the rest of his life he had to pay the penalty. The extreme Church party immediately gave expression to their feelings. Led by the Cardinal-bishops of Tusculum and Ostia in Rome, and in France and Burgundy by the Archbishops of Lyons and Vienne[1], they clamoured for the repudiation of the "concession," reminding Paschal of his own previous decrees and hinting at withdrawal of obedience if the Pope did not retract his oath. In this oath Paschal had sworn, and sixteen cardinals had sworn with him, to take no further action in the matter of investiture, and never to pronounce anathema against the king. Both parts of the oath he was compelled to forswear, helpless as ever in the presence of strong-minded men. At the Lenten Synod of 1112 he retracted his concession of investiture, as having been extracted from him by force and therefore null and void. The same year Archbishop Guy of Vienne held a synod which condemned lay investiture as heresy, anathematised the king, and threatened to withdraw obedience from the Pope if he did not confirm the decrees. Paschal wrote on 20 October, meekly ratifying Guy's actions. But his conscience made his life a burden to him, and led him into various inconsistencies. He felt pledged in faith to Henry, and wrote to Germany that he would not renounce his pact or take action against the Emperor. The unhappy Pope, however, was not man enough to maintain this attitude. Harassed by the vehemence of the extremists, whose scorn for his action was blended with a sort of contemptuous pity, he was forced at the Lenten Synod of 1116 to retract again publicly the concession of 1111 and to condemn it by anathema. Moreover, Cuno, Cardinal-bishop of Palestrina, complained that as papal legate at Jerusalem and elsewhere, he had in the Pope's name excommunicated Henry, and demanded confirmation of his action. The Pope decreed this confirmation, and in a letter to Archbishop Frederick of Cologne the next year, he wrote that hearing of the archbishop's excommunication of Henry he had abstained from intercourse with the king. Paschal had ceased to be Head of the Church in anything but name.

If the events of 1111 brought humiliation to Paschal from all sides, the Emperor was to get little advantage from his successful violence. The

[1] Their efforts in France were, however, to a large extent discounted by the moderate party with Bishop Ivo of Chartres as its spokesman. He deprecated the action of the extremists, especially in their implied rebuke of the Pope, and emphatically denied that lay investiture could rightly be stigmatised as heresy.

revolt that broke out in Germany in 1112 and lasted with variations of fortune for nine years was certainly not unconnected with the incidents of those fateful two months. The Saxons naturally seized the opportunity to rebel, but it is more surprising to find the leading archbishops and many bishops of Germany in revolt against the king. Dissatisfaction with the February compact, indignation at the violence done to the Pope, as well as the ill-feeling caused by the high-handed policy of Henry in Germany, were responsible for the outbreak; if Archbishop Adalbert of Mayence was controlled mainly by motives of personal ambition, Archbishop Conrad of Salzburg was influenced by ecclesiastical considerations only. Henry's enemies hastened to ally themselves with the extreme Church party, and Germany was divided into two camps once more. Even neutrality was dangerous, and Bishop Otto of Bamberg, who had never lost the favour of Pope or Emperor, found himself placed under anathema by Adalbert.

An important event in 1115, the death of Countess Matilda of Tuscany, brought the Emperor again into Italy. He came, early in 1116, to enter into possession not only of the territory and dignities held from the Empire but, as heir, of her allodial possessions as well. Matilda, at some time in the years 1077–1080, had made over these allodial possessions, on both sides of the Alps, to the Roman Church, receiving them back as a fief from the Papacy, but retaining full right of disposition[1]. This donation she had confirmed in a charter of 17 November 1102. Her free right of disposal had been fully exercised, notably on the occasion of Henry's first expedition to Italy. Both on his arrival, and again at his departure, she had shewn a friendliness to him which is most remarkable in view of his dealings with the Pope. Moreover it seems to be proved that at this time she actually made him her heir[2], without prejudice of course to the previous donation to the Papacy. The Pope must have been aware of the bequest, as he made no attempt to interfere with Henry when he came into Italy to take possession. The bequest to Henry at any rate prevented any friction from arising on the question during the Emperor's lifetime, especially as Henry, like Matilda, retained full disposal and entered into no definite vassal-relationship to the Pope. For Henry it was a personal acquisition of the highest value. By a number of charters to Italian towns, which were to be of great importance for the future, he sought to consolidate his authority and to regain the support his father had lost. His general relations with the Pope do not seem to have caused him any uneasiness. It was not until the beginning of 1117 that he proceeded to Rome, where he planned a solemn coronation at Easter and a display of imperial authority in the city proper, in which he had been unable to set foot in 1111.

[1] A. Overmann, *Gräfin Mathilde von Tuscien*, pp. 143–4.

[2] *Ib.* pp. 43 ff. Overmann shews that this was a personal bequest to her relative Henry, and was not made to him as Emperor or King of Germany.

During the previous year Paschal's position in Rome had been endangered by the struggles for the prefecture, in which a boy, son of the late prefect, was set up in defiance of the Pope's efforts on behalf of his constant supporters the Pierleoni. The arrival of Henry brought a new terror. Paschal could not face the prospect of having to retract his retractation; he fled to South Italy. Henry, supported by the prefect, spent Easter in Rome, and was able to find a complaisant archbishop to perform the ceremony of coronation in Maurice Bourdin of Braga, who was immediately excommunicated by the Pope. For the rest of the year Paschal remained under Norman protection in South Italy, where he renewed with certain limitations Urban II's remarkable privilege to Count Roger of Sicily. Finally in January 1118, as Henry had gone, he could venture back to Rome, to find peace at last. On 21 January 1118 he died in the castle of Sant' Angelo.

His successor, John of Gaeta, who took the name of Gelasius II, had been Chancellor under both Urban II and Paschal II, and had distinguished his period of office by the introduction of the *cursus*, which became a special feature of papal letters and was later imitated by other chanceries[1]. His papacy only lasted a year, and throughout he had to endure a continual conflict with his enemies. The Frangipani made residence in Rome impossible for him. The Emperor himself appeared in March, and set up the excommunicated Archbishop of Braga as Pope Gregory VIII. In April at Capua Gelasius excommunicated the Emperor and his anti-Pope, and so took the direct step from which Paschal had shrunk, and a new schism definitely came into being. At last in September Gelasius set sail for Pisa, and from there journeyed to France where he knew he could obtain peace and protection. On 29 January 1119 he died at the monastery of Cluny.

The cardinals who had accompanied Gelasius to France did not hesitate long as to their choice of a successor, and on 2 February Archbishop Guy of Vienne was elected as Pope Calixtus II; the election was ratified without delay by the cardinals who had remained in Rome. There was much to justify their unanimity. Calixtus was of high birth, and was related to the leading rulers in Europe—among others to the sovereigns of Germany, France, and England; he had the advantage, on which he frequently insisted, of being able to address them as their equal in birth. He had also shewn himself to be a man of strong character and inflexible determination. As Archbishop of Vienne he had upheld the claims of his see against the Popes themselves, and apparently had not scrupled to employ forged documents to gain his ends. He had taken the lead in Burgundy in opposing the "concession" of Paschal in 1111, and, as we have seen, had dictated the Pope's recantation. But the characteristics that made him acceptable to the cardinals at this crisis might seem to have

---

[1] On this see R. L. Poole, *The Papal Chancery*, ch. IV.

militated against the prospects of peace. The result proved the contrary however, and it was probably an advantage that the Pope was a strong man and would not be intimidated by violence like his predecessor, whose weakness had encouraged Henry to press his claims to the full. Moreover the revival of the schism caused such consternation in Germany that it was perhaps a blessing in disguise. It allowed the opinions of moderate men, such as Ivo of Chartres and Otto of Bamberg, to make themselves heard and to force a compromise against the wishes of the extremists on both sides.

Calixtus soon shewed that he was anxious for peace, by assisting the promotion of negotiations. These came to a head at Mouzon on 23 October, when the Emperor abandoned investiture to churches, and a settlement seemed to have been arranged. But distrust of Henry was very strong among the Pope's entourage; they were continually on the alert, anticipating an attempt to take the Pope prisoner. So suspicious were they that they decided there must be a flaw in his pledge to abandon investiture; they found it in his not mentioning Church property, investiture with which was equally repudiated by them. On this point no accommodation could be reached, and the conference broke up. Calixtus returned to Rheims to preside over a synod which had been interrupted by his departure to Mouzon. The synod pronounced sentence of excommunication on Henry V and passed a decree against lay investiture; the decree as originally drafted included a condemnation of investiture with Church property, but the opposition of the laity to this clause led to its withdrawal, and the decree simply condemned investiture with bishoprics and abbeys. A little less suspicion and the rupture with Henry might have been avoided.

Investiture was not the only important issue at the Synod of Rheims. During its session the King of France, Louis VI, made a dramatic appeal to the Pope against Henry I of England[1]. On 20 November Calixtus met Henry himself at Gisors, and found him ready enough to make peace with Louis but unyielding on the ecclesiastical questions which he raised himself. They were especially in conflict on the relations between the Archbishops of Canterbury and York. Calixtus had reversed the decision of his predecessors and denied the right of Canterbury to the obedience of York, which Lanfranc had successfully established. Perhaps his own experience led him to suspect the forgeries by which Lanfranc had built up his case, or he may have been anxious to curb the power of Canterbury which had rendered unsuccessful a mission on which he had himself been employed as papal legate to England. He insisted on the non-subordination of York to Canterbury; in return, Pope Honorius II granted to the Archbishop of Canterbury the dignity of permanent papal legate in England. This may have given satisfaction to the king; it also gave a foothold for papal authority in a country which papal legates had not been allowed to enter without royal permission.

[1] See *infra*, Chap. xviii, pp. 603–4.

For more than a year Calixtus remained in France. When he made his way into Italy and arrived at Rome in June 1120, he met with an enthusiastic reception; though he spent many months in South Italy, his residence in Rome was comparatively untroubled. The failure of the negotiations at Mouzon delayed peace for three more years, but the universal desire for it was too strong to be gainsaid. Two events in 1121 prepared the way. Firstly, the capture of the anti-Pope in April by Calixtus removed a serious obstacle; the wretched Gregory VIII had received, as he complained, no support from the Emperor who had exalted him. Secondly, at Michaelmas in the Diet of Würzburg the German nobles restored peace between Henry and his opponents in Germany, and promised by their mediation to effect peace with the Church also. This removed the chief difficulties. Suspicion of the king had ruined negotiations at Mouzon; his pledges were now to be guaranteed by the princes of the Empire. Moreover with Germany united for peace, the Papacy could have little to gain by holding out against it; Calixtus shewed his sense of the changed situation by the conciliatory, though firm, letter which he wrote to Henry on 19 February 1122 and sent by the hand of their common kinsman, Bishop Azzo of Acqui. Henry had as little to gain by obstinacy, and shewed himself prepared to carry out the decisions of the Diet of Würzburg and to promote the re-opening of negotiations. The preliminaries took time. The papal plenipotentiaries fixed on Mayence as the meeting-place for the council, but the Emperor won an important success in obtaining the change of venue from this city, where he had in the archbishop an implacable enemy, to the more loyal Worms; here on 23 September was at last signed the Concordat which brought Empire and Papacy into communion once more.

The Concordat of Worms[1] was a treaty of peace between the two powers, each of whom signed a diploma granting concessions to the other. The Emperor, besides a general guarantee of the security of Church property and the freedom of elections, surrendered for ever investiture with the ring and staff. The Pope in his concessions made an important distinction between bishoprics and abbeys in Germany and those in Italy and Burgundy. In the former he granted that elections should take place in the king's presence and allowed a certain authority to the king in disputed elections; the bishop or abbot elect was to receive the *regalia* from the king by the sceptre, and in return was to do homage and take the oath of fealty, before consecration. In Italy and Burgundy consecration was to follow a free election, and within six months the king might bestow the *regalia* by the sceptre and receive homage in return[2]. This distinction marked a recognition of existing facts. The Emperor had exercised little

---

[1] The original of the imperial diploma is in the Vatican archives. A facsimile of it is given in MIOGF, Vol. vi.

[2] In both cases the words used are: "Sceptrum a te recipiat et quae ex his iure tibi debet faciat."

control over elections in Burgundy, and had been gradually losing
authority in Italy. Two factors had reduced the importance of the Italian
bishoprics: the growing power of the communes, often acquiesced in by
the bishops, had brought about a corresponding decline in episcopal
authority, and the bishops had in general acceded to the papal reform
decrees, so that they were far less amenable to imperial control. As far
as Germany was concerned, it remained of the highest importance to the
king to retain control over the elections, as the temporal authority of the
bishops continued unimpaired. And here, though the abolition of the
obnoxious use of spiritual symbols satisfied the papal scruples, the royal
control of elections remained effective. But it cannot be denied that the
Concordat was a real gain to the Papacy. The Emperor's privilege was
a surrender of an existing practice; the Pope's was only a statement of
how much of the existing procedure he was willing to countenance[1].

On 11 November a diet at Bamberg confirmed the Concordat, which
forthwith became part of the constitutional law of the Empire. In
December the Pope wrote a letter of congratulation to Henry and sent
him his blessing, and at the Lenten Synod of 1123[2] proceeded to ratify
the Concordat on the side of the Church as well. The imperial diploma
was welcomed with enthusiasm by the synod; against the papal concessions
there was some murmuring, but for the sake of peace they were tolerated
for the time. It was recognised that they were not irrevocable, and
their wording rendered possible the claim that, while Henry's privilege
was binding on his successors, the Pope's had been granted to Henry
alone for his lifetime. There were also wide discrepancies of opinion as
to the exact implication of the *praesentia regis* at elections and the
influence he could exercise at disputed elections. By Henry V, and later
by Frederick Barbarossa, these were interpreted in the sense most favourable to the king. Between Henry and Calixtus, however, no friction arose,
despite the efforts of Archbishop Adalbert to provoke the Pope to action
against the Emperor. Calixtus died in December 1124, Henry in the
following summer, without any violation of the peace. The subordination
of Lothar to ecclesiastical interests allowed the Papacy to improve its
position, which was still further enhanced during the weak reign of Conrad.
Frederick I restored royal authority in this direction as in others, and the
version of the Concordat given by Otto of Freising represents his point
of view; the difference between Italian and German bishoprics is ignored,
and the wording of the Concordat is slightly altered to admit of interpretation in the imperial sense. It is clear that the Concordat

[1] See A. Hofmeister, *Das Wormser Konkordat* (*Festschrift Dietrich Schäfer zum
70 Geburtstag*). Hofmeister, following Schäfer against Bernheim and others, insists
also that, though Henry's privilege was to the Papacy in perpetuity, the Pope's
was only to Henry for his lifetime. The Church party certainly adopted this view,
but that it was recognised by the imperialists seems to be disproved by subsequent
history.

[2] The First Lateran Council.

contained within itself difficulties that prevented it from becoming a permanent settlement; its great work was to put on a legal footing the relations of the Emperor with the bishops and abbots of Germany. What might have resulted in connexion with the Papacy we cannot tell. The conflict between Frederick I and the Papacy was again a conflict for mastery, in which lesser subjects of difference were obliterated. Finally Frederick II made a grand renunciation of imperial rights at elections on 12 July 1213, before the last great conflict began.

The first great contest between Empire and Papacy had virtually come to an end with the death of Henry IV. Its results were indecisive. The Concordat of Worms had provided a settlement of a minor issue, but the great question, that of supremacy, remained unsettled. It was tacitly ignored by both sides until it was raised again by the challenging words of Hadrian IV. But the change that had taken place in the relations between the two powers was in itself a great victory for the papal idea. The Papacy, which Henry III had controlled as master from 1046 to 1056, had claimed authority over his son, and had at any rate treated as an equal with his grandson. In the ecclesiastical sphere the Pope had obtained a position which he was never to lose. That he was the spiritual head of the Church would hardly have been questioned before, but his authority had been rather that of a suzerain, who was expected to leave the local archbishops and bishops in independent control of their own districts. In imitation of the policy of the temporal rulers, the Popes had striven, with a large measure of success, to convert this suzerainty into a true sovereignty. This was most fully recognised in France, though it was very widely accepted also in Germany and North Italy. In England, papal authority had made least headway, but even here we find in Anselm an archbishop of Canterbury placing his profession of obedience to the Pope above his duty to his temporal sovereign. The spiritual sovereignty of the Papacy was bound to mean a limitation of the authority of the temporal rulers.

Papal sovereignty found expression in the legislative, executive, and judicial supremacy of the Pope. At general synods, held usually at Rome and during Lent, he promulgated decrees binding on the whole Church; these decrees were repeated and made effective by local synods also, on the holding of which the Popes insisted. The government was centralised in the hands of the Pope, firstly, by means of legates, permanent or temporary, who acted in his name with full powers: secondly, by the frequent summons to Rome of bishops and especially of archbishops, who, moreover, were rarely allowed to receive the pallium except from the hand of the Pope himself. A more elaborate organisation was contemplated in the creation of primacies, begun in France by Gregory VII and extended by his successors; while certain archbishops were thus given authority over others, they were themselves made more directly responsible to Rome.

And as papal authority became more real, the authority of archbishops and bishops tended to decrease. The encouragement of direct appeals to Rome was a cause of this, as was the papal protection given to monasteries, especially by Urban II, with exemption in several cases from episcopal control. Calixtus II, as a former archbishop, was less in sympathy with this policy and guarded episcopal rights over monasteries with some care. But the close connexion of the Papacy with so many houses in all parts tended to exalt its position and to lower the authority of the local bishop; it had a further importance in the financial advantage it brought to the Papacy.

Papal elections were now quite free. The rights that had been preserved to Henry IV in the Election Decree of Nicholas II had lapsed during the schism. Imperial attempts to counteract this by the appointment of subservient anti-Popes had proved a complete failure. In episcopal elections, too, progress had been made towards greater freedom. There was a tendency towards the later system of election by the chapter, but at present clergy outside the chapter and influential laymen had a considerable and a lawful share. In Germany and England the royal will was still the decisive factor. It may be noticed here that the Popes did not attempt to introduce their own control over elections in place of the lay control which they deprecated. They did, however, frequently decide in cases of dispute, or order a new election when they considered the previous one to be uncanonical in form or invalid owing to the character of the person elected; occasionally too, as Gregory VII in the case of Hugh and the archbishopric of Lyons, they suggested to the electors the suitable candidate. But the papal efforts were directed primarily to preserving the purity of canonical election.

The Reform Movement had led to a devastating struggle, but in many respects its results were for good. There was undoubtedly a greater spirituality noticeable among the higher clergy, in Germany as well as in France, at the end of the period. The leading figure among the moderates, Bishop Otto of Bamberg, was to become famous as the apostle of Pomerania, and Archbishop Conrad of Salzburg was to be prominent not only in politics but also for his zeal in removing the clergy from secular pursuits. In the age that followed, St Bernard and St Norbert were able by their personality and spiritual example to exercise a dominance over the rulers of France and Germany denied to the Popes themselves.

There was indeed another side of papal activity which tended to lessen their purely spiritual influence. The temporal power was to some extent a necessity, for spiritual weapons were of only limited avail. Gregory VII had apparently conceived the idea of a Europe owning papal suzerainty, but his immediate successors limited themselves to the Papal States, extended by the whole of South Italy, where the Normans recognised papal overlordship. The alliance with the Normans, so often useful, almost necessary, was dangerous and demoralising. It had led to the fatal results of Gregory's last years and was for some time to give the Normans a considerable influence over papal policy, while the claim of overlordship of the South was to lead to the terrible struggle with the later Hohenstaufen and its aftermath in the contest of Angevins and Aragonese. In Rome itself papal authority, which had been unquestioned during Gregory's archidiaconate and papacy up to 1083, received a severe check from Norman brutality; it was long before it could be recovered in full again.

The great advance of papal authority spiritual and temporal, its rise as a power co-equal with the Empire, was not initiated indeed by Gregory VII, but it was made possible by him and he was the creator of the new Papacy. He had in imagination travelled much farther than his immediate successors were willing to follow. But he made claims and set in motion theories which were debated and championed by writers of greater learning than his own, and though they lay dormant for a time they were not forgotten. St Bernard shewed what spiritual authority could achieve. Gregory VII had contemplated the Papacy exercising this authority, and his claims were to be brought into the light again, foolishly and impetuously at first by Hadrian IV, but with more insight and determination by Innocent III, with whom they were to enter into the region of the practical and in some measure actually to be carried into effect. Gregory VII owed much to Nicholas I and the author of the Forged Decretals; Innocent III owed still more to Gregory VII.

CHAPTER III.

GERMANY UNDER HENRY IV AND HENRY V.

THE death of Henry III on 5 October 1056 was one of the greatest disasters which the medieval Empire experienced. It is true that his power had declined in the latter years of his reign, but the difficulties before him were not so great that he himself, granted good health, could not have successfully surmounted them. Imperial prestige had suffered, especially from Hungary in the south-east; yet even the weak government of the regency was soon able to restore, though it could not retain, its overlordship. It was rather in the internal affairs of Germany and in the Italian kingdom that the death of the great Emperor was fatal. The German princes needed a master to keep them from usurping or claiming independence of action. And in Italy the situation was critical, as Henry III had recognised. Imperial authority was challenged in the north and centre by Duke Godfrey of Lower Lorraine, the husband of Beatrice of Tuscany, while in the south the rise of the Norman power and the prospect of a secular sword on which the now regenerated Papacy could rely put it in a position to shake off its subservience to its former rescuer and protector, the Emperor. The more absolute Henry's authority had been, the greater the loss of imperial prestige should the Papacy become independent.

The heir to the throne was a boy not quite six years of age. Henry III had averted the gravest danger to which monarchy was liable—the danger of a vacancy in the kingdom—as his son Henry had already been recognised and anointed as king. But he could not avert the lesser, though often hardly less grave, evil of a regency. Probably in accordance with the Emperor's own wishes, and certainly following the usual precedent, the Empress-mother Agnes was recognised as regent, a woman distinguished only for her piety. Had she combined with this the firm character of a Blanche of Castile, she might have made of her son a Louis IX, but she failed alike to maintain imperial government and to impress her piety on her son. For the few months that Pope Victor II survived his master and friend, all indeed went well. His counsels brought peace in Germany (especially in Lorraine and Bavaria), his influence it was that caused the change in government to be effected with so little disturbance, and during his lifetime Empire and Papacy were united in the closest harmony. But with his death Agnes was left to depend on the counsel of such of the bishops as enjoyed her favour: in particular Henry of Augsburg, whose influence at court seriously weakened the regency owing to the jealousy to which it gave rise.

The effect of the five years and a half of Agnes' regency was to produce a steady decline in the prestige and power of the central authority. At first, indeed, there was an improvement on the eastern frontiers. The birth of a son, Salomo, to King Andrew of Hungary had disappointed the king's brother Béla in his hopes of the succession. To counteract this danger Andrew made peace with the Empire in 1058, and a marriage-alliance was arranged between Salomo and Agnes' daughter Judith. This alliance, however, only produced disaster. An imperial army sent in 1060 to the assistance of Andrew was severely defeated. Andrew himself was killed in battle, Salomo had to take refuge in Germany, and Béla and his son Géza established themselves as rulers of Hungary. The Duke of Poland, who had given a refuge and assistance to Béla, seized the opportunity to throw off the imperial overlordship, and by his continual alliance with the anti-German party in both Hungary and Bohemia was able to maintain himself in a practically independent position. The Duke of Bohemia, therefore, was on the side of the Empire[1], and his loyalty was to be of the greatest value, placed as he was in direct contact with the duchies both of Saxony and Bavaria. During practically the whole of the eighty years covered by the reigns of Henry IV and Henry V this situation prevailed in the three countries. There was frequent civil war in each of them, and the brothers of the ruler were constantly in revolt against him, but, while the German party maintained itself in Bohemia, the anti-German party was successful in both Hungary and Poland. Towards the end of the period Hungary became more concerned in Eastern than in Western politics, though its contest with Venice for the coast of Dalmatia introduced a further complication into the international situation.

It was not surprising that the frontier-states refused obedience to a government which could not enforce its authority within the kingdom. The majesty of the imperial name was still sufficient to leave the disposition of appointments, both lay and ecclesiastical, in the hands of the Empress-regent. Agnes, too, was fortunate in the patronage that she had to bestow, though singularly unfortunate in its disposal. The duchy of Franconia, as before, remained in royal hands. When Swabia became vacant by the death of Duke Otto in 1057, Agnes bestowed the duchy on the Burgundian Count, Rudolf of Rheinfelden, and his marriage with the king's sister Matilda in 1059 was designed to bind him to the interests of the court; but Matilda died in 1060, and his subsequent marriage with Adelaide, Henry IV's sister-in-law, tended perhaps rather to rivalry than to union with the king. To the leading noble in Swabia, Count Berthold of Zähringen, was given the duchy of Carinthia in 1061; Carinthia, however, remained quite independent of its duke, and the local family of

---

[1] In 1085 Vratislav II as a reward for his loyalty received the title of king, and was crowned by Archbishop Egilbert of Trèves at Prague. The title was for his lifetime only, and did not affect his duties to his overlord.

Eppenstein was predominant in the duchy. In Saxony, Agnes does not seem to have attempted to interfere with the recognised claims of the Saxons to independence within the duchy or with the hereditary right of the Billung family, and on the death of Duke Bernard in 1059 his son Ordulf succeeded without challenge. But it was probably with the aim of obtaining valuable support in Saxony that in 1061 she handed over the duchy of Bavaria, which had been entrusted to her own charge by Henry III, to Count Otto of Nordheim. The dukes so appointed used their new authority solely to further their own ambitious ends, and the mother exalted her son's most determined opponents. The leading ecclesiastics were no more disinterested in their aims than the secular princes. Archbishop Anno of Cologne was entering into relations with the leading nobles in Germany, and with the Papacy and Duke Godfrey in Italy, and was using his influence already in episcopal elections; his nephew Burchard, who became Bishop of Halberstadt, was one of the principals in every Saxon revolt. The Archbishop of Mayence, Siegfried[1], was a man of little resolution, whose weakness of character prevented him from playing the part in German history to which his office entitled him. The most serious rivalry to Anno came from the north, where Archbishop Adalbert of Bremen was establishing a dominant position, partly by taking the lead in missionary work in Scandinavia and among the Slavs, partly by the extension of his secular authority so that even nobles were willing to accept his overlordship in return for his powerful protection. His ambition, however, aroused the hostility of the Billung family, and was directly responsible for the first disturbances in Saxony.

It was in Italy that imperial authority was displayed at its weakest. Here the death of Henry III had enabled Duke Godfrey of Lower Lorraine to establish an influence which the German government was unable to challenge. The election of his brother Frederick as Pope Stephen IX in 1057 was serious in itself, besides the fact that it marked the end of the imperial control of papal elections. The Empress-regent, indeed, ratified this election, as well as that of Nicholas II in 1059, but even her piety took alarm at the Papal Election Decree and the alliance with the Normans. It shews how serious the situation was when Agnes could feel herself bound to oppose the reform party and recognise Cadalus as Pope in 1061, an action which only damaged imperial prestige still further, since she was unable to give him any support. On the other hand, Duke Godfrey intervened, probably in collaboration with Anno, compelling the rival Popes to return to their dioceses to await the decision of the German government.

But it was not the decision of Agnes that was to settle this question. The regency had already been taken out of her hands. Dissatisfaction

---

[1] He was appointed by Agnes in 1060; as he was of high birth, he may have been designed to counter the ambitions of Anno.

with the weak government of a woman and a child had been for some time openly expressed, especially by those princes whose selfish ambition had contributed greatly to this weakness. Archbishop Anno had been intriguing to get control of the government, and the plot that he contrived was probably carried out with the connivance of Duke Godfrey. The plot culminated at Kaiserswerth on the Rhine in April 1062, when Anno, with the assistance of Duke Otto of Bavaria and Count Ekbert of Brunswick, beguiled the young king on board a boat, took possession of his person and of the royal insignia, hurried him by river to Cologne, and there took charge of the government in his name. Agnes made no attempt to recover her lost authority, and retired at once to the life of religion to which indeed she had dedicated herself the previous year.

For two years Anno retained control, and used his authority to enrich his province and to advance his relatives[1]. He thought it politic, indeed, when the court was in Saxony in 1063, to associate Archbishop Adalbert in the government, and in a diploma of 27 June Adalbert is described as *patronus*, Anno as *magister* of the young king. This was the title under which he usually appears; the way in which he performed his tutorship may be inferred from the charges, so constantly repeated afterwards, of the vicious life of Henry's early years. Italian affairs in particular engrossed Anno's attention. In concert with Duke Godfrey he had certainly decided for Alexander II and against Cadalus, but it was important that the German government should formally have the decisive voice. At the diet of Augsburg in 1062, and finally at the synod of Mantua in 1064, Anno dictated a decision in favour of Alexander. But in this he clearly over-reached himself, and the Papacy, which was asserting its independence of imperial authority, did not accept the position that a German archbishop could have the decisive voice in a papal election. Both in 1068 and in 1070 Anno received a lesson at Rome as to who was master and who servant. And his absence at Mantua gave the opportunity to his rival in Germany. Anno returned to find himself superseded by Adalbert.

For another two years the control rested with Adalbert, who had won increased fame by a victory in Hungary which temporarily restored Salomo. The regency, indeed, came to an end when in his fifteenth year the young king came of age and girded on the sword at Worms on 29 March 1065. But the archbishop remained master, and made imperial policy subservient to his own ambitions. He received lavish grants from the royal domain in Saxony, and further impoverished the

---

[1] On 14 July 1063 a royal charter granted one-ninth of the royal revenues to the Archbishop of Cologne to be distributed among the monasteries of his province. On 31 August 1063 Archbishop Engelhard of Magdeburg died, and Anno's brother Werner (Wezil) was appointed to succeed him; he was only second to Anno's nephew Burchard in instigating revolt in Saxony.

crown by a bountiful distribution of royal abbeys, mainly among bishops. The coming-of-age of the king was to have been followed by his imperial coronation at Rome, but this was prevented by Adalbert, who feared that Godfrey and Anno would regain influence over the king in Italy. His ambition brought about his sudden downfall. Anno was able to engineer another *coup d'état* with his old associates, and to unite the leading bishops and nobles on his side. At the diet of Tribur, in the beginning of 1066, Henry was compelled to dismiss Adalbert. Though he had used his authority for merely selfish aims, the principality he had erected might have done great service to the cause of imperial unity in limiting the independence of the Saxons, but it collapsed with his fall. The Billungs, under Duke Ordulf's son Magnus, took advantage of his humiliation to drive him from Bremen, and the collapse of the German missions, which he had done so much to foster, among the Slavs and Scandinavians both completed the ruin of his prestige and diminished the sphere of imperial authority.

From the fall of Adalbert may be dated the commencement of Henry IV's personal government. Anno made a bid for power once more, but the murder of his nephew Conrad, whose appointment to the archbishopric of Trèves he had just secured, combined with a serious illness to force him into the background. Henceforward he devoted himself to his province, using his remaining energies in the foundation of monasteries and the reform of monastic discipline; rather more than a century later his name was enrolled among the saints of the Church. There was no one else ambitious or bold enough to succeed Adalbert. The lay princes could only be roused to take an interest in imperial affairs when their independence of action was threatened or when the actual safety of the kingdom was at stake. A dangerous illness of the king caused alarm as to the succession, and they united to bring about his marriage with Bertha of Turin, to whom he had already been betrothed for ten years. The imperial coronation was again contemplated, and indeed welcomed by the Pope who was desiring imperial assistance against the Normans, but was again prevented, this time by Duke Godfrey. Godfrey, alarmed at the prospect of a revival of imperial authority in Italy, anticipated the imperial expedition by himself marching against the Normans. His lack of success compelled the Pope to come to terms with the Normans once more. By Godfrey's action the German king lost all the advantage he might have obtained from intervening as protector of the Papacy; the attempt to interfere in the papal election had already been unsuccessful, and imperial prestige in Italy was thus completely ruined when Henry took over the reins of power.

The regency of the kingdom, in the hands of a weak woman and of ambitious metropolitans, had had disastrous results for the central authority. Nor was there much change during the early years of Henry IV's direct rule. The accounts of his enemies continually refer to the excesses at any rate of his youth. The exaggeration of these accounts is evident, but there is probably a substratum of truth, and the chief blame must fall on Anno and Adalbert, if not on Agnes as well. The marriage with Bertha, it was hoped, would prove a steadying influence. The king, however, was a reluctant, if not an unfaithful, husband, and visited his dislike of the marriage upon his wife. In 1069 he even attempted to obtain a divorce, but the Papacy intervened, and the papal legate, Peter Damian, who never minced his words, compelled the king to receive back his wife. This seems to have been the turning-point in the reign. From this time he was a constant and an affectionate husband, and from this time he clearly abandoned the path of pleasure and devoted himself assiduously to the task of government.

The history of Germany under Henry IV and Henry V is in the main a record of civil war, producing confusion and disorder throughout the country and involving untold hardships and miseries for the lower classes. The king was faced with formidable opposition even before the Papacy joined the ranks of his foes. To realise this, as well as to note the changes that resulted in Germany as a whole, it is necessary at the outset to survey briefly the political and social structure of Germany. Difficult too as it is to distinguish between the theoretical and the actual, some attempt must be made to do so; particularly as the theoretical derives from the past, and the past ideas, even in this period of change, still have their effect in determining the relations of the various parts of the constitution to one another. In the first place, the king held a unique position, obscured as it often was by the actual weakness of the ruler. In theory he owed his throne to election by the nobles, but in fact the hereditary principle was dominant. Henry IV always insisted on his *ius hereditarium* against the claims of Pope and nobles, and it was not until the death of Henry V that the elective idea, asserted already in 1077 and 1081 at the elections of the anti-kings Rudolf and Herman, won a victory over the hereditary. The king alone held office *dei gratia*, and this was marked by the religious ceremony of unction and coronation. He was supreme liege lord, commander-in-chief, the source of justice, the enforcer of peace; these attributes were symbolised by the royal insignia—crown, lance, sceptre, sword, etc.—the possession of which was so important, as was evidenced in the contest of Henry V with his father in 1105–6 and again in the events which occurred after Henry V's death. Further, there were vested in him the sovereign rights[1]—lordship of towns, offices, jurisdictions, mints, tolls, markets, and the like—all of which were coveted for their financial

---

[1] All that came under the heading of *regalia*. These were defined by Frederick Barbarossa's lawyers at Roncaglia. Cf. also the definition of them in Paschal II's privilege to Henry V of 12 February 1111 (MGH, *Constitutiones*, Vol. I, No. 90, pp. 141 sq.).

advantages, and these could only lawfully be exercised after the grant of a charter from the king.

Such a position carried with it potentialities towards absolutism, and in the case of a strong ruler like Henry III the trend was in that direction. But to this theoretical supremacy were attached definite limitations as well. The king was subject to law, not above it, and as supreme judge it was his duty to do justice; the breach of this obligation, his opponents declared, justified rebellion against him. In great issues affecting the kingdom, or the person and property of a prince of the kingdom, the king had to act by consent, to summon a diet of the princes and in effect to be guided by their decision. These "princes"—dukes, margraves, counts, bishops, abbots of royal abbeys—owed their status originally to their official position. With the office went land, and as the lay nobles ceased in fact to be royal officials their landed position becomes the more important. The period of transition is a long one, but the change is especially rapid during the second half of the eleventh century; naturally public recognition of the change lags behind the fact. One result of this change from an official to a landed status was the decline in rank of those nobles who held their fiefs from duke or bishop and not directly from the king.

Among these lay princes, the dukes held a place apart, differing from the counts not only in priority of rank. They had owed their position originally not to appointment by the king but to election by the people of the tribe, and this origin was still perpetuated in the claim of the nobles of Bavaria to be consulted in the appointment of their duke. At the same time the king was especially concerned to insist on the dependence of these offices upon himself; he did not even feel himself obliged to fill a vacancy in one of them within the year and a day that was customary with other offices. Franconia during this period remained in his hands, except that the Bishops of Würzburg were given ducal rights in the eastern portion; Swabia after Rudolf's deposition for treason in 1077 remained vacant for two years. On the other hand, in Saxony, where the duke indeed had only a limited authority, the hereditary right of the Billung family was not contested.

Of the counts (*grafen*), the margraves (*markgrafen*), important especially for the defence of the eastern frontiers, retained exceptional judicial and military privileges, and in some cases maintained their independence even of the dukes. The counts-palatine (*pfalzgrafen*) too retained their old position. They were four in number, one for each of the tribes that formed the original stem-duchies—Franks, Swabians, Bavarians, Saxons—and they acted in theory as representatives of royal justice within the duchies and as the administrators of the royal domains. Of these the Count-Palatine of the Franks, who had his seat at Aix-la-Chapelle and was known now usually as Count-Palatine of Lorraine, though later as Count-Palatine of the Rhine, was the most important. There was no duke in Franconia to usurp his authority ; he was, beneath the king, supreme judge, and commonly acted during the king's absence as his representative. But there was, on the other hand, a great change in the position of the ordinary counts. There were few whose authority extended over the whole of a *gau* or *pagus*, as had formerly been usual; of these few, some, whose control extended over more than one *gau*, came to be distinguished in the twelfth century, for example the Count of Thuringia, by the new title of landgrave (*landgraf*). In most cases the county had been divided up, often by division among sons, into several districts each of them under a count, often of quite small extent. The family residence, soon converted into a castle, gave the count his name, and, whatever other dignities the counts might acquire, they never lost their connexion with the duchy of their origin[1]. Their political importance, therefore, varied in proportion to the extent of their lands, and in fact there was little distinction between those who had merely the title of count and ordinary freemen with free holdings.

The increasing importance of landed-proprietorship in the status of nobles had its effect in tending to depress the majority of ordinary freemen to a half-free status. In the country districts there was little real distinction between the half-freeman and the freeman who held from a noble in return for services in work and kind, and who had lost the right of bearing arms. On the other hand, the rise of the class of *ministeriales*, especially when they held land by military tenure, forming as they did an essential element in the domain of every lord, lay and ecclesiastical, gave an opening to freemen by joining this class to increase their opportunities at the expense of a lowering of status. It was a particular feature of the period. Conrad II had especially encouraged the formation of this class of royal servant, and on it his successors continued to rely.

As in the countryside, so in the towns there was a tendency to obliterate the distinction between the free and half-free classes, though in the towns this took the form of a levelling-up rather than a levelling-down. The "free air" of the towns, the encouragement to settlers, the development of trade especially in the Rhine district, as well as the protection of the town walls, caused a considerable increase in their population ; they acquired both constitutional and economic importance. Some towns were royal towns, but all were under a lord, usually a bishop, and it was to the bishops that the trading element in the town owed its first privileges. It was to the bishop's interest to obtain for his town from the king special rights such as the holding of a market and exemption from tolls in royal towns, and all charters to towns till the latter part of the eleventh century are granted through the bishops. The first sign of a change is in the charter of Henry IV to Worms in 1074. The privileges

---

[1] The original home of the Welfs was Altdorf in Swabia. So it was to a diet of Swabian nobles that Henry the Lion, Duke of Bavaria and Saxony, was first summoned to answer the charges against him.

granted are of the usual nature—exemption from toll in certain (in this case, specified) royal towns. But for the first time the charter is given not to the bishop but to the townsmen, and they are described, for the first time, not as "negotiatores" or "mercatores" but as "cives." The circumstances attending the grant of this charter[1], including the welcome to the king, the well-equipped military support given to him, the payment by the community of a financial aid, the reception and preservation of the charter, all imply a town-organisation of a more advanced nature than previous charters would have led us to expect. The Jews played an important part in these early trading communities, and they are specially mentioned in the charter to Worms; so too the Bishop of Spires in 1086 for the advantage of his town was careful, as he states, to plant a colony of Jews and to give them special privileges, which were confirmed by the king in 1090[2]. If Worms was the first town which gives evidence of an organisation independent of its bishop, it was soon followed by others where the bishop as at Worms was hostile to the king. The rising of the people at Cologne against Archbishop Anno in 1074, the expulsion of Archbishop Siegfried and the anti-king Rudolf from Mayence in 1077, the expulsion of Bishop Adalbero from Würzburg the same year and the defence of the city against Rudolf, and, above all, the devotion of the Rhine towns to Henry IV during his last years, shew clearly a wide extension of this movement[3].

The townsmen, then, were coming into more direct relations with the king. As far as the nobles were concerned, the change is rather in the contrary direction. The duty of fidelity to the head of the State was still a general conception; even ecclesiastics who scrupled to take an oath of liege-fealty to the king did not disavow this obligation. The oath of fealty was not taken by the people as a whole, but only by the princes of the kingdom, whether to the king or to his representative, and they took the oath in virtue of their official capacity and as representing the whole community[4]. It mattered not whether they held fiefs from the king or from another noble; it was not the fief but the office, through which the royal authority had been, and in theory still was, asserted, that created the responsibility on behalf of the people within their spheres of control. So the relation of the king with the nobles was not yet strictly

---

[1] See H. Wibel, *Die ältesten deutschen Stadtprivilegien* (*Archiv für Urkundenforschung*, 1918, Vol. VI, pp. 234 sqq.).

[2] Altmann and Bernheim, *Ausgewählte Urkunden zur Erläuterung der Verfassungsgeschichte Deutschlands*, pp. 158 sqq.

[3] In Flanders, Cambrai set the example by founding a commune in 1077. Here the movement was also directed against the bishop, but in this case it was, as at Milan, allied with the Church reform movement. See Pirenne, *Histoire de Belgique*, Vol. I, pp. 192 sq. In Germany proper the movement was definitely royalist in character.

[4] Cf. Waitz, *Deutsche Verfassungsgeschichte*, Vol. VI (ed. Seeliger), pp. 487 sqq.; G. von Below, *Der deutsche Staat des Mittelalters*, Vol. I, pp. 232 sqq.

a feudal relation. It was not to become so until the end of the twelfth century, when the status of prince was confined to those nobles who held directly from the king. The *feudum* was not yet the all-important thing, at any rate in theory and law. There were many fiefs without military service, some without service at all; there were vassals too without fiefs. But these became, more and more, exceptional cases, and rapidly the change from the official to the feudal status was being accomplished in practice. Always the grant of a fief had accompanied the bestowal of an office; and, as the fiefs had become hereditary, so too had the offices. In the majority of cases, offices and fiefs had become identified, and the official origin was preserved in little more than the title[1].

In fact, the great nobles were no longer royal officials but territorial magnates with alods and fiefs to which their children (sons if possible, but failing them daughters) succeeded, and their aim was to loosen the tie which bound them to the sovereign and to create an independent position for themselves. Two circumstances combined to assist them in this ambition—the rise of the class of *ministeriales* and the continual civil war. The military fief became the normal type, and every important noble had his band of armed and mounted retainers. He soon had his castle, or castles, as well, built in defiance of the king; for castle-building was a sovereign right, which only the stress of civil war enabled the noble to usurp. Medieval society was based especially on custom and precedent. If the central authority was weak, the nobles began at once to encroach; usurpations were in a few years translated into rights, and it was difficult, if not impossible, for the king to recover what had been lost. Moreover, while the counts had ceased to be royal officers, the system of maintaining the royal control by *missi* had long disappeared. This made a fixed seat of government impossible. The king himself had to progress ceaselessly throughout his dominions to enforce his will on the local magnates. There was no system of itinerant justices, and, except in the royal domains, no official class to relieve the direct burden of the central government. So there was no permanent machinery which could function normally; everything depended on the personality of the ruler.

But from the point of view of the king there were compensations. Each noble played for his own hand, and there was rarely any unity of purpose among them. It was from the dukes that the king had most to fear, and with regard to them he started with many advantages. They had no claim to divine appointment, no royal majesty or insignia, no sovereign rights but such as he had granted. The nobles in each duchy held office in theory from the king, to whom, and not to the duke, they

---

[1] This is true even of the counts-palatine, with the exception of the Count-Palatine of the Rhine who still retained much of his old official position; for instance, when Henry IV went to Italy in 1090, the Count-Palatine of the Rhine was appointed co-regent of the German kingdom with Duke Frederick of Swabia. So too when Henry V went to Italy in 1116.

had sworn liege-fealty[1], and they were far more jealous of the assertion of the ducal, than of the royal, authority over them. Moreover the duke by virtue of his office acquired little, if any, domain in his duchy[2]. Where his family possessions lay, there alone, in most cases, was he really powerful. Agnes in her appointments had at any rate shewn herself wise in this, that she had appointed as dukes nobles whose hereditary lands lay outside the duchies to which they were appointed. Berthold of Zähringen, the most powerful noble in Swabia, was a nonentity as Duke in Carinthia; Otto of Nordheim, one of the leading nobles in Saxony, could not maintain himself in his duchy of Bavaria when he revolted in 1070.

In other words, the noble depended on his domain, and this is equally true of the king. There was no direct taxation[3] as in England, and the king had in a very real sense to live of his own. The royal domain[4] was scattered throughout the kingdom; in each duchy there were royal estates and royal palaces, though the largest and richest portion lay in eastern Saxony, stretching from Goslar to Merseburg, the inheritance of the Saxon kings. In the first place, it supplied the needs of the royal household, and this, as well as the maintenance of royal authority, made necessary the continual journeyings of the king and his court. The domain, too, provided a means whereby the king could make grants of lands whether in reward for faithful service or, more usually, in donations to bishoprics and abbeys. And, finally, in these manors, as also in the manors of nobles and ecclesiastics, there emerged out of the mass of half-free tenants a class of men who played an important and peculiar rôle in Germany. These royal *ministeriales* were employed by the king in administrative posts, as well as in the management of his estates; they were armed and mounted, and provided an important part of the king's army. On them he began to rely, therefore, to counteract the growing independence of the greater nobles, both in his Council and on military expeditions. In return, they were granted fiefs, and rose often to knightly rank[5],

---

[1] A duke or other noble might obtain an oath of fealty from his vassals, but there should, by right, be in it a saving clause, preserving the superior fealty due to the king.

[2] Ct. Waitz, *op. cit.* Vol. VII, pp. 133 sq.

[3] Unless the *bede* comes under this category. But all *nobiles* were exempt from this, and other exemptions had been granted by charter.

[4] Cf. M. Stimming, *Das deutsche Königsgut im 11 und 12 Jahrhundert*; B. Heusinger, *Servitium regis in der deutschen Kaiserzeit* (*Archiv für Urkundenforschung*, Vol. VIII, pp. 26–159). Between the royal and the private domain of the king as a rule little distinction was made. But the issue sometimes arose, notably on the question of the inheritance of the Hohenstaufen from Henry V; see *infra*, p. 336.

[5] Eventually this had its result in the rise of a number of new noble families to take the place in German history of older ones that had become extinct. One leading cause for the disappearance of old noble families—the ecclesiastical career (with its enforced celibacy) which in the abbeys especially had been almost a prerogative of the nobility—is very clearly demonstrated by A. Schulte, *Der Adel und die deutsche Kirche im Mittelalter* (*Kirchenrechtliche Abhandlungen*, ed. U. Stutz, LXIII, LXIV).

sometimes even to episcopal. The same process was occurring in the domains of the nobles. The ecclesiastical nobles had probably set the example[1], which was followed by the secular nobility and by the king. As it provided him with the possibility of making himself self-sufficient and so independent of princely support, it provided them too with a means of furthering their independence of him.

The royal domain, then, plays a central part in the policy of the Salian kings, as it was to do with the Capetians in France. During the regency it had been grievously depleted. But there were many ways in which it could be increased and in which gaps could be made good— by inheritance, by exchange, by conquest, by escheat. There were also other sources of royal revenue, notably the sovereign rights, of justice and the like, which were assumed by the king wherever he might happen to be and which were frequently lucrative. From the towns too, as well as from the domain, he could levy contributions[2], and, as has been indicated above, could look to them for valuable support especially in time of war. The loyalty and devotion of the Rhine towns is most marked, particularly when the episcopal lord of the town was disloyal. But only in a few cases was the bishop himself among the king's enemies, and so a direct alliance with the townsmen, which might have been as useful to the German monarchy as it was to the French, occurred only in isolated cases. It was not to the king's interest to make the bishops antagonistic.

For the alliance with the episcopate had, from the time of Otto I, been a cardinal factor in the policy of the king of Germany. The political importance of the ecclesiastical nobles was evident: on them, as well as on *ministeriales* and lesser nobles, the king relied both for his Council and government[3] and for his military expeditions. They could never make their offices and fiefs hereditary, and they could be depended upon as a counterpoise to the dangerous power of the dukes; while in the continual civil wars of this period the summons to the host was not of much avail, nor could it be made effective without the consent of the nobles. But they were equally valuable to the king from the economic point of view. In the first place, the royal abbeys made annual payments in kind, which began to be converted into money payments or at any rate to

[1] Compare with this the prominent part played by ecclesiastics in the drift towards feudalism in Saxon England (*supra*, Vol. III, pp. 375–7). The great difference is that in Germany it was an unfree class to whom these military fiefs were granted.

[2] The tax known as "bede" (*petitio, precaria*)—originally, as its name shews, a voluntary contribution. On the nature of this tax see G. von Below, *op. cit.* pp. 85 sqq., and generally for the taxation of towns, K. Zeumer, *Die deutsche Städtesteuern* (*Staats- und socialwissenschaftliche Forschungen*, ed. G. Schmoller, Vol. I, No. 2).

[3] The lay nobles would take part only if they happened to be present, or if they were summoned to diets on important issues of state or to judge one of their number. The great offices of the household were held by dukes, but had become merely titular and ceremonial.

be reckoned on a monetary basis early in the twelfth century; from these abbeys, too, when he visited them, he could claim hospitality. There is no evidence that the episcopal services included fixed payments in kind, but the obligation seems to have been imposed upon the bishops of maintaining the king and his retinue during the king's stay in their towns, whether or no these contained a royal palace. It is at any rate noticeable how prominently they figure in the itineraries of the Salian kings[1]. And on the death of a bishop the king exercised his rights of *regalia* and took possession of the revenues of the see during the vacancy, and sometimes of *spolia* as well, seizing the personal effects of the dead bishop. These great ecclesiastical offices were regarded by the king as very distinctly part of his personal possessions[2]. His lavish grants to them of territory were therefore not lost to the Crown, and the ecclesiastical as distinct from the lay nobles remained essentially royal officials. Royal control of appointments to bishoprics and abbeys was a reality and at the same time a necessity; and the royal chapel, which was a natural centre for the training of ecclesiastics, was also a stepping-stone to advancement. From among the royal chaplains, trained under the king's eye and experienced often in the work of his chancery, appointments were commonly made to vacant bishoprics.

This was bound to lead sooner or later to conflict with the reformed Papacy, though the conflict might have been delayed and would certainly have been less fatal in result had not this control of the German king in ecclesiastical matters been extended to Italy and to the Papacy itself. To the crown of Germany were attached the crowns of Burgundy and Italy, and finally the imperial crown as well. These additional dignities brought little real advantage to the German king. In Burgundy, the royal authority was slight and rarely asserted; it was, however, of some importance to the Emperor that his suzerainty and not that of the French king should be recognised. In Italy, the royal domain and episcopal support were sometimes of definite advantage, but usually the interest of the king in his Italian kingdom prejudiced his position in Germany. And the imperial title was a similar handicap[3]. It magnified the importance of his office and gave him increased prestige, but it added enormously to his responsibilities and prevented him from concentrating on his real interests. The imperial title added nothing to the royal authority in Germany. In a sense it added nothing in Italy either. The title " rex Romanorum " was used before imperial coronation occasionally by Henry IV, frequently

---

[1] B. Heusinger, *op. cit.* Cf. especially, p. 70, "Für das 11 Jahrhundert ergibt sich also, dass das deutsche Königtum in stärkstem Masse, vielleicht überwiegend auf den bischöflichen Servitien ruhte."

[2] Cf. U. Stutz, *Die Eigenkirche als Element des mittelalterlich-germanischen Kirchenrechtes*, pp. 32 sqq.

[3] See, for a discussion of this question, and a consideration of opposing views on the revival of the Empire by Otto I, G. von Below, *op. cit.* pp. 353–369.

by Henry V, and as Emperor-designate the king acted with full imperial authority in Italy and with regard to the Pope. But the imperial crown was the right of the German king, to his mind an essential right, and it was by virtue of this right that he claimed the control from which the Papacy was now beginning to free itself, with results fatal to the monarchy in Germany.

The task that Henry IV set before himself was to undo the damage that had been wrought during his minority and to restore imperial authority both in Germany and Italy; he was determined to be master as his father had been at the height of his power. In Germany, he had first of all to build up the royal domain, to force the nobles to a direct subordination to his will, and to break down the independence of Saxony. In Italy, where imperial authority was practically ignored, there were the special problems of Tuscany[1], the Normans, and above all the Papacy. But, determined as he was to revive the authority over the Papacy that his father had exercised from 1046 until his death, the question of Germany had to come first, and so for a time he was willing to make concessions. Control of the Church in Germany and Italy was so essential to him that he could not be in sympathy with the reform policy of the Papacy. This was now beginning to be directed not only against the simony and secularisation that resulted from lay control but against the lay control itself; and it was a definite feature of that policy to demand from the higher clergy an obedience to papal authority which could not fail to be prejudicial to the royal interests. But at present the king was anxious to keep on good terms with the Pope; as he was obedient to his orders on the divorce question in 1069, so in 1070 he allowed Charles, whom he had invested as Bishop of Constance, to be deposed for simony, and in 1072 Abbot Robert of Reichenau to suffer the same penalty[2]. The Papacy was given no indication of his real intentions.

His compliant attitude to the Papacy on this question was in accordance with his general policy. He worked patiently for his ends, and strove to do the task first that lay within his power, careful to separate his adversaries and to placate one while he was overcoming the other. Adversity always displayed him at his best. Again and again he revived his fortunes, shewing a speedy recognition and making a wise use of the

---

[1] The death of Duke Godfrey in 1069 removed one great obstacle from Henry's path. His son Godfrey (Gibbosus) succeeded to the duchy of Lower Lorraine and was already the husband of Countess Matilda. But he quarrelled with his wife and confined his interests to his German duchy, where he remained loyal to Henry.

[2] In these cases, as also in the case of Bishop Herman of Bamberg in 1075, when his attitude to the Pope was dictated by the same motives, he protested his own innocence of simony in the appointments. There is no evidence against him. Probably the offenders had paid money to court-favourites, whose influence had secured the appointments.

possibilities at his disposal, dividing his enemies by concessions and by stimulating causes of ill-feeling between them, biding his time patiently till his opportunity came. Nor was he prevented from following out his plan by considerations of personal humiliation. Not only at Canossa but also in 1073 a personal humiliation was his surest road to success, and he took it. He was not the typically direct and brutal knight of the Middle Ages, and he was not usually successful in battle; he generally avoided a pitched battle, in contrast to his rival Rudolf, to whom he really owed his one great victory in the field—over the Saxons in 1075. He recognised his limitations. His armies were rarely as well-equipped as those of his opponents: they were often composed of *ministeriales*, royal and episcopal, and of levies from the towns, which were not a match for the Saxon knights; also he had more to lose than they had by staking all on the result of a battle. In an unstatesmanlike generation he shewed many statesmanly qualities, which was the more remarkable in that he had received so little training in the duties of his office. His enemies, when they comment with horror on his guile and cunning, are really testifying to these qualities; for it was natural that they should give an evil name to the ability which so often overcame their perfidy and disloyalty.

But, as his greatness is best seen in adversity, so in the moment of victory were the weaknesses of his character revealed. He allowed himself to be overcome by the arrogance of success both in 1072 and 1075. Having decisively defeated his Saxon enemies, he made a vindictive use of his victory, when clemency was the right policy; by his arbitrary actions he alienated the other nobles whose assistance had ensured his success, and they formed a coalition against him to anticipate his too clearly revealed intentions against themselves. His victory gave him so false a sense of security that on both occasions he chose the moment to throw down the challenge to the Pope, entirely miscalculating both the reality of his position in Germany and the strength of his new adversary. He profited by his lesson later, but never again did he have the same opportunity. He certainly shewed a clear sense of the strength of the papal position in the years 1077–1080, and also of the means by which this strength could be discounted. On the whole he was a good judge of the men with whom he had to deal. It may appear short-sighted in him to pardon so readily a man like Otto of Nordheim and to advance him to a position of trust in 1075; but he was faced with treachery on every side and he had to attempt to bind men to his cause by their interests. At any rate he was successful with Otto's sons, and also even in detaching Duke Magnus himself from the party of Rudolf. The only occasions when he was really overwhelmed were when the treachery came from his own sons, and there is no more moving document in this period than his letter to King Philip of France, in which he relates the calculated perfidy and perjury of his son Henry V. For he was naturally of an affectionate and sympathetic disposition, a devoted father and a kind master, especially to the non-noble classes throughout his dominions. Even if we discount the glowing panegyric of the author of the *Vita Heinrici IV*, we cannot ignore the passionate devotion of the people of Liège, who, scorning the wrath of all the powers of Church and kingdom, refused to dissemble their grief or to refrain from the last tokens of respect over the body of their beloved master. That tribute was repeated again at Spires; and, though for five years his body was denied the rites of Christian burial, few kings have had so genuine a mourning.

The reconciliation of Henry with his wife in 1069 marked a definite stage in his career. From this time he devoted himself wholeheartedly to affairs of state, and his policy at once began to take shape. The particularist tendencies of the German princes in general had to be overcome, but the extreme form which particularism took was to be found in Saxony. Saxony, ever since it had ceased to supply the king to Germany, had held itself aloof and independent. In various ways was its distinctive character marked. It held proudly to its own more primitive customs, which it had translated into rights, and the maintenance of which had been guaranteed to it by Conrad II and Henry III; especially was the royal system of justice, with inquest and oath-takers, foreign to Saxon custom[1], which stood as a permanent bar to unity of government. These customary rights formed a link between the classes in Saxony, giving it a homogeneity lacking in the other duchies. Allodial lands were more extensive here than elsewhere, and the nobles accordingly more independent. Among them the duke took the leading place, but only in precedence. Margraves and counts did not recognise his authority over them; on the other hand, the ducal office was hereditary in the Billung family, and so it was not at the free disposal of the king. Finally, beneath the nobles, the proportion of free men was exceptionally high; they were trained to arms, and, though they usually fought on foot, were formidable soldiers in an age when cavalry was regarded as the decisive arm. It was a bold policy for a young king to attempt, at the beginning of his reign, to grasp the Saxon nettle. It was essential that he should obtain assistance from the other duchies, and this he might expect. The Saxons looked with contempt on the other German peoples, who in their turn were jealous of the Saxons and irritated by their aloofness. The ill-feeling between the two was always a factor on which he could count.

But the determination of Henry IV to attack the problem of Saxony had a further and more immediate cause. The effects of his minority had not merely been to give the opportunity to particularism, here as elsewhere. It had been disastrous also to the royal domain, that essential basis of royal power, which had suffered from neglect or deliberate squandering at the hands of the unscrupulous archbishops who had controlled the government for their own advantage. The first task of the

---

[1] K. Hampe, *Deutsche Kaisergeschichte im Zeitalter der Salier und Staufen*, p. 40.

young king was to concentrate on the domain, to fill up gaps and make compact areas where possible, to take effective measures to recover services that had been lost, and finally to protect it against further usurpation. It was natural that his attention should first be directed to eastern Saxony and Thuringia, where lay by far the richest portion of the domain[1], and which afforded the best opportunity for creating a compact royal territory. It was here, moreover, that the domain had suffered most; it had not only been wasted by grants, but also services had been withheld[2], *ministeriales* had usurped their freedom[3], and probably neighbouring lords had made encroachments. One of Henry's first measures was the building of castles on an extensive scale in this region, designed primarily for the recovery and maintenance of the domain and the services attached to it[4], and having at the same time the strategic advantage of being situated so as to divide the duchy and in case of revolt to prevent a coalition of Saxon princes. This was a menace to the independent spirit of the Saxons, and he irritated them still more by appointing royal *ministeriales* from South Germany[5] as officials in the domain-lands and as garrisons in the castles. There were clearly grievances on both sides, which only made the subsequent contest the more bitter. The Saxons had infringed royal rights by neglect and usurpation. The South German *ministeriales* in their turn shewed little respect for Saxon customs, and acted in an oppressive manner in making requisitions and forcing labour. And probably the Saxons were right in their suspicion that the king would take every

---

[1] This is evident from the *Indiculus curiarum ad mensam regis Romanorum pertinentium* (best text in *Neu. Arch.* Vol. XLI, pp. 572–4). A comprehensive survey of this has been made by B. Heusinger, *Servitium regis* (*Archiv für Urkundenforschung*, Vol. VIII, pp. 26–159). M. Stimming, *Das deutsche Königsgut*, pp. 86 sqq., has elaborated the central importance of the domain on Henry's policy in Saxony and on the subsequent Saxon revolt. J. Haller, *Das Verzeichnis der Tafelgüter des römischen Königs* (*Neu. Arch.* Vol. XLV, pp. 48–81), rejects the accepted date (1065) of the *Indiculus* and dates it 1185. His arguments seem to me to be untenable, and to raise more difficulties than they solve. I am convinced that it was drawn up at any rate for one of the last two Salian kings, and that it is a rough draft prepared at a time when an imperial coronation was anticipated. Anyhow, the statement in the text is not really affected by the date of the *Indiculus*.

[2] Lampert of Hersfeld, sub 1066, ed. Holder-Egger, SGUS, p. 100.

[3] Bruno, c. 16, ed. Wattenbach, SGUS, p. 11. Cf. Stimming, *op. cit.* p. 93.

[4] Cf. Stimming (*op. cit.* pp. 98 sqq.), who supports the view that the policy was originated by Archbishop Adalbert of Bremen. He also points out the contiguity of the chief leaders of the Saxon revolt, bishops as well as lay nobles, to the royal domain.

[5] The Saxons especially complained of the low-born "Swabians" employed by the king on official and garrison duty in their duchy. The term Swabian in their mouth seems to be a generic term for the rest of Germany (or, at any rate, for Franconia and Swabia), just as in southern Europe we find Alemannia used for Germany (cf. *Gregorii VII Reg.* III, 15), a use which has been continued to the present day in France. There cannot have been many royal *ministeriales* in the duchy of Swabia.

opportunity of increasing the royal domain at their expense, and that he was anxious to suppress their customary rights which stood in the way of the centralising policy of the monarchy.

It is significant in this connexion, firstly, that the two nobles mentioned as Anno's colleagues in his *coups d'état* at Kaiserswerth in 1062 and at Tribur in 1066 were Otto of Nordheim and Ekbert of Brunswick, whose allodial territories were adjacent to the main portion of the royal domain and were so extensive as to make them, next to the duke, the most powerful nobles in Saxony. Otto was already Duke of Bavaria, and in 1067 Ekbert was appointed Margrave of Meissen; on his death in 1068 his son Ekbert II succeeded to the margravate as well as to Brunswick. Similarly adjacent, and equally concerned in the great revolt of 1073, were Anno's two relatives, Archbishop Werner of Magdeburg and Bishop Burchard of Halberstadt. In the second place, the actual outbreak of civil war, which was to be henceforth almost continuous, had its origin in the downfall of Duke Otto in 1070. Probably Henry rather seized than created the opportunity. Otto's military skill had been of considerable assistance to him on more than one occasion, and there is no actual evidence either to justify the charge of treachery brought against Otto or to convict Henry of a deliberate intention to ruin the duke. A diet at Mayence left the decision to the test of battle between Otto and his low-born accuser. Otto refused to submit to the indignity of such a contest, and was accordingly condemned in his absence by a diet of Saxon[1] nobles at Goslar and deprived of his possessions in Saxony. His duchy was forfeited and, at the special instance of Duke Rudolf of Swabia, was given by Henry to Welf, the first of the new line of that name[2]. The fall of Otto was not viewed with alarm in Upper Germany; the replacement of a Saxon by a Swabian noble was rather a cause for congratulation. The ill-feeling of the rest of Germany towards Saxony was very pronounced, and only identity of interest against the king could lead to common action.

In Saxony, however, where Otto immediately took refuge, he obtained the powerful support of Magnus, son and heir of Duke Ordulf. This brought the king into direct conflict with the Billung family. The rebels were not able to resist for long—revolt was not yet organised—and they had to submit unconditionally to the king in 1071. Otto, after a year's detention, was released, and was allowed to retain his hereditary possessions in Saxony; Magnus was kept in close confinement at the castle of Harzburg. In this can be seen the influence of Archbishop

---

[1] As he was of Saxon origin, his case, in accordance with constitutional practice, had to be decided by Saxons.

[2] The male line had died out with Welf III, whose sister Cuniza (Cunegunda) had married Marquess Azzo of Este. Their son Welf IV, who had become Duke of Bavaria, had acquired his uncle's estates in Germany, which lay in Swabia and on the borders of Bavaria.

Adalbert, who in the last year of his life entered into public affairs again to revenge himself for the humiliations he had suffered from the Billungs in 1066. He brought about a meeting with King Svein of Denmark, and a regular coalition was concerted against the Billungs. The king's interests were all in the same direction. Magnus, by his marriage with the sister of Géza, cousin and rival of Henry's brother-in-law Salomo, had allied himself with the anti-imperial party in Hungary. Moreover, when Duke Ordulf died in 1072, Magnus was recognised as duke throughout Saxony. Henry did not deny Magnus' right of succession, but it was the more necessary to him to retain so important a hostage. The king's policy in Saxony could now be definitely advanced in both directions. The building of the castles was continued and extended, and the king took possession of Lüneburg, the chief town of the Billungs, and placed in its castle a garrison of seventy men under Count Eberhard of Nellenburg.

The victory had been an easy one: too easy, because it deluded him as to the strength of the forces he had to counteract. Saxony was thoroughly alarmed, and in the mood for a more serious revolt than the previous one; with Magnus in his hands, Henry perhaps discounted this danger. But the other German princes were alarmed too. Henry had shewn his hand too plainly, and it was a fatal misjudgment that led him to rely on their further concurrence against the Saxons. To him, however, it seemed that he had recovered his position in Germany, and that the necessity to humour the Pope no longer existed. It can hardly be due to chance that at this very time he threw down a deliberate challenge to the Pope, to whose injunctions he had previously so meekly submitted, over the archbishopric of Milan. Just before his death, at the Lenten synod of 1073, Alexander II replied by excommunicating the counsellors of the king. Henry did not refrain from communion with them, and so, when Alexander died and Gregory VII became Pope, there was a breach between the German king and the Roman Church.

In spite of his commitments in Saxony and Italy, Henry chose the occasion for an emphatic assertion of imperial majesty in another quarter. In 1071 the Dukes of Poland and Bohemia had been summoned to appear before the king at Meissen, and had received the royal command to keep the peace. This was significant of the recovery that Henry had already effected, and, when the Duke of Poland disobeyed the injunction in 1073, it was necessary to take immediate measures to punish him. The king accordingly summoned an expedition against Poland to assemble on 22 August, and came to Goslar himself, probably to ensure obedience to the summons. The expedition was not destined to take place. Under cover of the assembling of troops for the Polish campaign, a formidable conspiracy was organised in eastern Saxony. The bishops, led by Werner of Magdeburg and Burchard of Halberstadt, played a leading part. All the chief nobles were concerned in it, especially Margrave Ekbert of

Meissen and the Margraves of the North and East Marks. Count Otto of Nordheim was soon induced to join. Count Herman, uncle of Magnus and so the acting-head of the Billung family, needed no inducement. Moreover, the Thuringians, equally affected by the building of the castles, with customary rights of their own to defend, and having a private grievance arising out of the claims of the Archbishop of Mayence to the payment of tithes[1], soon threw in their lot with the Saxons. Their plans were concerted to anticipate the date for the expedition, and so to take Henry by surprise before the troops from the rest of Germany were assembled.

The plot was successful. Taken completely by surprise, the king sought refuge in his castle at Harzburg, but the sudden appearance of a large Saxon army made his further stay there impossible. On the night of 9–10 August he made his escape with a few followers, and after four days of hardship and peril arrived at the monastery of Hersfeld. Count Herman had recaptured Lüneburg and taken captive the royal garrison; to effect their release the king on 15 August had to consent to the surrender of Magnus; the castles were now closely besieged, and his hold on Saxony was lost. But the day appointed for the Polish expedition (22 August) was close at hand. The army was assembling, and he determined to use it against the Saxons. He summoned the princes to meet him at the village of Kappel near Hersfeld, to obtain their consent to this change of plan. And now the fundamental insecurity of his position was to be revealed to him. The princes debated, and finally decided to postpone the expedition to October. They were determined to make it clear that on their will was the king dependent, and the royal authority suffered a blow more serious than defeat in battle. Henry had to submit, and he retired to the Rhine district, conscious that the initiative had passed from his hands. There he came to a wise decision. Germany must for the time engage his whole attention; the challenge to the Papacy must be postponed to a more favourable opportunity. He wrote, accordingly, to the Pope a humble letter acknowledging his faults and asking for absolution. The Pope, as anxious as Henry for peace, welcomed this apparent repentance, and the breach was healed. This left the king free to concentrate on Germany. Enlightened at last as to the true state of affairs, he shewed remarkable judgment in appreciating the factors that could be turned to his advantage, and great patience and skill in so making use of them that he was able gradually to build up again the shaken edifice of royal power.

He had, first of all, to endure further humiliation. The princes met in October for the deferred expedition, but having obtained the upper hand they were determined to maintain it; in place of an expedition they

---

[1] A synod at Erfurt at the beginning of 1073 had just decided this question in the archbishop's favour.

instituted negotiations on their own account with the Saxons. Henry had no choice but to acquiesce; he was sovereign in name only. But at this crisis he found assistance in a new quarter. Coming to Worms, whose bishop, Adalbert, was his constant foe for more than thirty years, he met with an enthusiastic reception from the citizens, who expelled their bishop on news of the king's approach. In return he granted them, on 18 January 1074, the first charter given directly to the citizens of a town[1], and in the preamble he expressed his gratitude for the loyalty which set so striking an example amid the disloyalty of all the magnates of the kingdom. The action of Worms was contagious, and from this time he was able to rely on the support of the Rhine towns, whatever the attitude of the bishops. The serious rising of the trading classes at Cologne in 1074, on the occasion of the Easter fair, against Archbishop Anno, was probably inspired by the example of Worms[2]. The towns indeed had everything to gain from royal favour. A strong central authority, able to enforce peace and order throughout the kingdom, was a necessity if trade was to flourish and expand, and from the king alone could the privileges dear to the trading classes be obtained.

The king's circumstances were immediately improved, and he was able, in spite of the aloofness of the leading nobles, to raise an army and march north again; he was accompanied by a number of bishops, who in view of the independent action of the towns found it to their interest to render material support to the king once more. But he was not yet strong enough to meet the Saxons in the field, and was forced to come to terms with them, which were confirmed in an assembly at Gerstungen on 2 February 1074. The castles built by both sides during his reign were to be destroyed, a general amnesty was to be proclaimed, and the Saxons returned to his allegiance on condition that in matters concerning their duchy the king should be advised by Saxons only. He had to pardon the rebels, but the peace was a sign of recovered authority. The South German dukes had no part in it, and did not readily forgive the Saxons[3] for thus depriving them of their control of the king's actions. Henry by this peace divided his enemies in Germany.

The peace had an immediate result in the changed attitude of the dukes, who were reconciled with Henry just after Easter, at the same time that he made his formal reconciliation with the Pope. In the meantime, an outrage had occurred which he was able to turn to his own advantage. In accordance with the peace terms at Gerstungen, the fortifications of Harzburg had been destroyed; but the church and other ecclesiastical buildings remained intact. The local peasantry, indignant

---

[1] See *supra*, pp. 119–120.

[2] Lampert of Hersfeld, ed. Holder-Egger, SGUS, p. 187. In this case, as with Adalbert at Worms, the loyalty of Anno was certainly suspect. It was his friends and relatives who were primarily responsible for the Saxon revolt.

[3] Bruno, cc. 31 and 44, ed. Wattenbach, SGUS, pp. 20, 29.

that a stone of this obnoxious place should be left standing, took the law into their own hands and violently demolished the sacred buildings, even in their passion going so far as to scatter to the winds the bones of Henry's son and brother who had died there in infancy. The Saxon nobles protested that the crime was the work of a few ignorant peasants (though indeed they took no steps to punish them), but Henry was determined to fasten the guilt of it on the whole people, and proclaimed far and wide that the Saxons had broken the peace. He was able to use this argument with effect upon the South German princes, who were already irritated against the Saxons on their own account. Before the year was out he had succeeded in obtaining their agreement to an expedition against the Saxons in the following spring.

Hungary had, meanwhile, occupied Henry's attention. The rivalry between King Salomo, Henry's brother-in-law, and his cousin Géza had resulted eventually in the success of Géza. Salomo with his wife took refuge in Germany, placed his kingdom under Henry's overlordship, and appealed to him for help. Henry led an expedition into Hungary in the autumn, but without success, and imperial authority was not recovered. The Pope tried to avail himself of the opportunity, giving his support to Géza and declaring Salomo's deposition a judgment of God upon him for handing over to the Empire a kingdom which was subject to St Peter. But Géza, though he had sought papal aid while his position was still insecure, was determined to be free of Pope and Emperor alike and to break every link which bound Hungary to the West; and in the following year he had himself crowned king with a crown which he received from the Eastern Emperor, Michael VII.

The opening months of 1075 were occupied with preparations for the reduction of Saxony. The Saxons in alarm endeavoured to appease the king; they further claimed to be judged by a diet of all the nobles, and appealed to the South German princes, trying to establish direct negotiations with them as in 1073. Their efforts were wholly unavailing: the king was determined to be revenged, the nobles could not forgive the peace made without their concurrence. Henry issued his summons to the host, which assembled at Bredingen on 8 June; never again was he to be at the head of so powerful and representative an army. The Dukes of Swabia, Bavaria, Carinthia, Upper and Lower Lorraine, and Bohemia were all present with strong contingents, and all the other leading nobles, lay and spiritual[1]. On 9 June, the day after the army had assembled, the king by a forced march surprised the Saxons encamped by the river Unstrut. Duke Rudolf, claiming the Swabian privilege of fighting in the van of the royal host, led the charge, supported by Duke Welf with the Bavarians. It was a battle of knights, and, when the superior numbers of the king's army had finally decided the issue, the Saxon foot-soldiers

---

[1] Except of course Archbishop Anno, who pleaded age and infirmity. He died the following December.

CH. III.

suffered severely. The losses indeed were heavy on both sides, but the king won a decisive victory and advanced to the invasion of Saxony. Lack of provisions caused him to disband his troops in July, and another expedition was arranged for October. On 22 October the army assembled at Gerstungen, but this time the Dukes of Swabia, Bavaria, and Carinthia were absent, on the insufficient plea of their losses in June. The king, however, was strong enough without them, and was probably not sorry to be independent of them. The Saxons had lost their cohesion; the common soldiers in particular felt that they had been selfishly sacrificed on the Unstrut. The nobles, therefore, made an unconditional surrender, throwing themselves on the king's mercy. Contrary to expectation, but in accordance with his fixed determination, he treated them with great severity: all the leaders, both laymen and ecclesiastics, were imprisoned in different parts of Germany, entrusted to the custody of South German nobles. Much of their territory was confiscated and given to his supporters or added to the royal domain, and the building of the castles was taken in hand once more. When the king disbanded his army in November, he seemed to have won a complete triumph.

The situation was remarkably similar to that in 1072. The Saxon rebels had been forced to an unconditional surrender and their leaders were in captivity. Now, as then, the situation at Milan gave the opportunity to the king, at what seemed a particularly favourable moment, to re-assert imperial authority in Italy by a direct challenge to the Pope. The defeat of the Pataria and the election of Tedald by the suffragan bishops of Milan had occurred earlier in the year, but Henry was then perhaps contemplating imperial coronation, and even the victory on the Unstrut had not achieved the submission of Saxony. When this was certain, he invested Tedald with the archbishopric and sent the embassy to Italy which was, probably designedly, responsible for the rupture with the Pope. Once more his position in Germany seemed strong enough to justify the recovery of the authority that had been lost in Italy. And the moment seemed to be well-chosen, because he could count on the enthusiastic support of the episcopate in Germany and in North Italy in any venture against Gregory VII. But he had grievously miscalculated the strength of the spiritual power and the greatness of his opponent, and once more he had misunderstood, or foolishly disregarded, the real feelings of the German princes. The absence of the three dukes from the final campaign against the Saxons was ominous, and was certainly not sufficiently accounted for by their plea of the losses they had suffered in the June campaign. As before, it was the completeness of the royal victory, and the arbitrary use that Henry made of it, that caused them to stand aloof. Though their absence was at the time satisfactory to him, he ought to have realised its import and that they too needed to be mastered before he could take in hand the new task of Italy and the Papacy.

The king spent Christmas 1075 at Goslar, and the nobles there present took an oath to accept his son Conrad, born in February 1074, as his successor. Some measure of leniency was shewn in allowing the exiled Saxon bishops to return to their sees pending trial, but of the lay princes Count Otto of Nordheim alone received the king's clemency, and he was even advanced to high office and power in his native land. The king was still at Goslar at the beginning of January 1076 when the papal embassy arrived with the verbal message threatening excommunication if the king refused obedience. This was as unexpected as it was distasteful to the royal dignity. In an uncontrolled passion, which was unusual with him, he summoned the Council of Worms that pronounced Gregory's deposition, and dispatched to Piacenza and then to Rome the messenger to the Lenten synod. Before the papal sentence at the synod reached the king, the murder of Duke Godfrey of Lower Lorraine in February had deprived him of one of his staunchest adherents, and of a strong support of the Empire on its western frontier, where Robert the Frisian, successful in Flanders, whose intrigues probably brought about the murder of Godfrey, was a constant menace. Still confident in his own position, Henry bestowed the duchy on his infant son Conrad, and Godfrey's nephew and heir, Godfrey of Bouillon, had to be content with the Mark of Antwerp.

Then at Easter came the news of the Lenten synod and its decrees, and both the strength of the spiritual power and the weakness of his own position were speedily revealed to the king. The excommunication had an immediate effect in alienating from him his lay subjects. The German bishops, too, who had welcomed the deposition of the Pope, trembled before the papal sentence and again hastily abandoned the cause of the king. Accordingly his summons to diets at Worms and Mayence were practically disregarded, and he was rapidly becoming isolated. His weakness was the Saxon opportunity. The Saxon leaders were able to effect their escape from captivity, or were deliberately released by the nobles to whose custody they had been entrusted. Bishop Burchard took the lead in a new revolt, and, Otto of Nordheim turning traitor once more, the whole of East Saxony was in arms. Henry's one faithful ally, Duke Vratislav of Bohemia, was driven from Meissen by Margrave Ekbert. The victory of 1075 had been completely undone. And, finally, the dukes of Upper Germany saw their opportunity and took it. Acting in unison they had been able to make their intervention effective whether against the king or against the Saxons. Satisfied with the Saxon defeat in June 1075, they had abstained from the further expedition in October, but the king's ability to bring the Saxons to submission without their aid, and his high-handed treatment of them when he had obtained the mastery, must have already determined them to throw their weight into the balance against him. The excommunication and its results gave them the decisive voice in the government of the kingdom. Meeting at Ulm, they decided on a diet at Tribur, where the future of the kingdom was to be debated and the royal authority made subservient to particularist interests. To this diet the Saxon nobles were invited, and the grievances of 1074 were forgotten.

The diet met at Tribur on 16 October 1076. The Saxons came in force, and the papal legates were present, to give spiritual sanction to the triumph of the nobles. The king, to whom this assembly was in the highest degree dangerous, arrived at Oppenheim on the other side of the Rhine with an army. But his chief supporters deserted him to obtain absolution from the papal legates, and he was abandoned to the tender mercies of the diet. The Saxons advocated his deposition and the appointment of a new king. For this revolutionary step the other princes were not yet prepared. The choice of a successor would raise difficulties and jealousies that might dissolve the harmony, and such an action would compromise the high moral pose which they had adopted in their attitude against Henry. The deliberations of the diet were complicated too by the ill-feeling, with difficulty restrained, which still persisted between Saxons and South Germans. But in one respect they were all of one mind: the king must be humiliated, and the government of Germany must be subject to the dictation of the princes. Towards the victory over the king, the papal sentence first, the papal legates later, had largely contributed. The nobles were anxious to retain the valuable papal support, and to represent themselves as fighting for the cause of right against a wicked king. The Papacy, therefore, must be given an important share in the fruits of victory. So, first of all, the king was forced to publish his repentance and his promise of obedience and amendment for the future—to do justice in both the papal and the feudal sense. The diet then proceeded to make two important decisions. Firstly, recognising the validity of the papal sentence, they decreed that Henry would lose his kingdom if he failed to obtain absolution within a year and a day[1] of his excommunication (22 February); secondly, recognising the papal claim to a principal share in the final judgment, they invited the Pope to a council at Augsburg on 2 February 1077, where under his presidency the future of the kingdom was to be decided.

This shews the lengths to which the nobles were prepared to go for their own selfish interests to satisfy papal claims which in different circumstances they were fully prepared to repudiate. It also shews that the Pope held the key to the whole situation, a fact which he and Henry alike were swift to recognise. If it promised the immediate realisation of the Pope's highest ideals, it at the same time revealed to the king the avenue of escape from his dangerous position. The conjunction of his enemies in Germany meant the final ruin of his power; if he could obtain absolution from the Pope in Italy, he not only removed opposition from

---

[1] The regular period of grace, the period too within which a vacant office had to be filled up. This treatment of the royal office by the nobles is significant.

that quarter for a time but also deprived the German nobles of their most effective weapon against him. With this aim in view he made his escape and his memorable journey over the Mont Cenis pass, finally arriving in January 1077 outside the fortress of Canossa. Here by his humiliation and outward penitence he was able to force the Pope to grant him absolution, and the purpose of his journey was achieved. Though the importance of the royal humiliation has been grossly exaggerated, it is equally absurd to proclaim the absolution at Canossa as a striking victory for the king. He had been forced to accept the justice of the papal excommunication, and consequently the right of the Pope to sit in judgment upon him, and by this acceptance the relations of the two powers had been fundamentally altered. The absolution was in a sense a recognition of the king's defeat; on the other hand, it limited the extent of the defeat and prevented a far worse calamity.

Yet, as far as Henry's enemies in Germany were concerned, it was a real victory for the king, and they were staggered at the news. The absolution of Henry they regarded as a betrayal of their cause, and they expressed their indignation as strongly as they dared. They could not, indeed, risk alienating the Pope, whose alliance was so necessary to them; but they were not impressed by his optimistic view that the decision to hold the council in Germany still held good. They did what they could, however, to nullify the effect of the absolution. The story soon became current among them that the absolution had been granted on certain conditions which Henry immediately broke, so that it became void and the king returned to his state of excommunication[1]. The papal legates, though not the Pope, gave encouragement to this view.

Their more immediate need, however, was to complete what had been begun at Tribur, and, with papal co-operation if possible, to prevent the restoration of Henry's authority in Germany and so to counteract the disastrous effects of Canossa. A preliminary meeting at Ulm, in issuing summons to a diet at Forchheim in Franconia, where the last of the German Carolingians (Louis the Child) and the first of his successors (Conrad I) had been elected, shewed that the Saxon proposals had been

---

[1] Bruno, c. 90, SGUS, pp. 66–7, states this very definitely, and it confuses not only his narrative but also his chronology. As the excommunication of 1076, according to his view, prevailed throughout, he makes no mention of that of 1080, and places together in 1076 the documents of both dates. Neither his editor in SGUS, W. Wattenbach, nor K. Heidrich, who in *Neu. Arch.* Vol. xxx investigated the dating of the numerous documents in Bruno, noted that this essential misunderstanding, whether wilful or ignorant, of the facts of Canossa is responsible for his muddled chronology. A complete revision of Bruno's chronology from this point of view is badly needed. I should like to call attention to the possibility that Henry's letter to the Romans (in Bruno, c. 66, and nowhere else) was written in 1080 and not in 1076. I cannot go into the whole question here, but two points may be mentioned: (1) any manifesto (as that in c. 73) dealing with 1080 would have been dated by him to 1076; (2) there is no evidence that Henry appealed to the Romans in 1076, though he did so regularly in 1080 and following years.

accepted. The diet met on 13 March and, in the presence and with the approval of two papal legates, Duke Rudolf of Swabia, with all the customary formalities of procedure, was designated and elected king. This was a reactionary and indeed a revolutionary step, recalling the anarchy of the later Carolingians. The electoral right of the nobles, when it was not a mere formality, had been strictly limited in practice. Ever since the Saxon kings had restored the monarchy, the hereditary principle had been dominant; when there was no son to succeed, the king had been chosen from a collateral branch of the royal family. Now the electors usurped a plenary power—the power to depose the established king and to exercise complete freedom of choice as to his successor. Behind this lay the theory that the relation of king and nobles was one of contract, and that an unlawful exercise of his power justified the breach of their oath of fealty. The bishops at Worms in 1076 had taken this line with regard to the Pope. It was a natural development of feudal ideas, which were not, however, to prevail in the Church as they did in the kingdom. There were other points of novelty in this election. In the first place, the formal right of election, which was the prerogative of all the princes, was here assumed by a small minority. This minority included, indeed, the Archbishop of Mayence, whose right to the *prima vox* was uncontested[1], numerous Saxon nobles, and the three South German dukes; perhaps these latter, in anticipation of fourteenth-century conditions, regarded themselves as adequate to represent their duchies. Secondly, the presence of the papal legates was a recognition of the Pope's claim to a share in the election. And, finally, the electors emphasised the contractual nature of the royal office, and ensured the maintenance of their own control, by imposing conditions on the king of their choice: Rudolf had to renounce the hereditary right of his son and royal control of episcopal elections, while he also made a promise of obedience to the Pope. But the German princes at Forchheim got no advantage from their triumphant particularism; the revolt gained no additional supporter from the fact that its leader styled himself king. On the contrary, their attempt to ride roughshod over tradition and legitimacy put Henry in a strong position; the bishops (except in Saxony), the lesser nobility, the peasantry, and above all the towns, preferred a single ruler, however absolute, to a government dominated by the selfish interests of the princes. All the more, then, had Rudolf and his party to depend on the support of the Church. The Pope certainly recognised the electoral rights of the princes, and accepted the election of Rudolf as a lawful election. He did not, however, recognise their power to depose Henry; this he regarded as a matter for his own decision, and in the meanwhile spoke continually of *two* kings. Yet his legates had been quite decided

---

[1] Cf. Wipo's account of the election of Conrad II (c. 2, SGUS, p. 14), and the statement of Frederick Barbarossa (Otto et Rahewin, *Gesta Friderici imperatoris*, Bk. III, c. 17, SGUS, p. 188).

in their support of Rudolf, and the rebels naturally inferred that the Pope would abide by their decision[1].

Meanwhile Henry had resumed his royal functions in Lombardy, though he had to act with extreme caution. The Lombards resented his refusal to take direct action against the Pope, and Milan, in opposition to its archbishop, had reverted to the papal alliance; nor could he obtain coronation at Pavia with the iron crown of Lombardy. He dared not, moreover, alienate the Pope, while policy made it essential to prevent the journey to Germany on which the Pope had set his heart. Then came the news of the election at Forchheim, and he had to return at once to Germany to counter the revolutionary government of the princes. The sentiment in favour of the lawful ruler, now that he was restored to communion, was immediately made evident. As before, the Rhine towns set the example, beginning with a riot at Mayence where Rudolf was crowned and anointed king by Archbishop Siegfried on 26 March. Rudolf was compelled to abandon Mayence and make his way to Saxony, where alone he could maintain himself as king. In Saxony, with few exceptions, the lay and ecclesiastical nobles were on his side, and to Saxony was his kingdom confined[2]. Elsewhere the balance was predominantly in favour of Henry, especially in the south-east. As Rudolf was still in the Rhine district, Henry returned to Germany by way of Carinthia and Bavaria, in both of which duchies he received an enthusiastic welcome. Carinthia, where Duke Berthold had always been ignored, was wholly on his side; on Bavaria he could also rely, except for the hostility of Margrave Liutpold of Austria and two important ecclesiastics, Archbishop Gebhard of Salzburg and Bishop Altmann of Passau, who however could not maintain themselves in their sees. On Duke Vratislav of Bohemia he could count for loyal assistance, and though King Ladislas I of Hungary, who married a daughter of Rudolf, was hostile, he gave no assistance to Henry's opponents. Burgundy, in spite of Rudolf's possessions there, was apparently solid for Henry, as were the Rhine towns. In Swabia the position was more equal. The bishops and lesser nobles were mainly on Henry's side, but Berthold and Welf had considerable power in their ancestral domains, and the great reforming Abbot, William of Hirschau, organised a strong ecclesiastical opposition which was to be continually dangerous to Henry; his work was to be carried still further by one of his monks, Gebhard, son of Duke Berthold, who as Bishop of Constance and papal legate was more than anyone else responsible for the existence and gradual increase of a strong papal party in South Germany. The

---

[1] The Pope, though not endorsing, did not actually disown his legates' actions; so, as *Vita Heinrici imperatoris* (c. 4, SGUS, pp. 17–18) says, his silence was taken to give consent.

[2] Bruno (c. 121, SGUS, p. 93) speaks of "Saxoniae regnum." So too in the two papal letters quoted in cc. 118 and 120 (*ib.* pp. 90, 92), Gregory addresses the princes "in Teutonico atque in Saxonico regno commanentibus" and "Rodulfo omnibusque secum in regno Saxonum commanentibus."

struggle was thus in the main between Saxony and Thuringia under Rudolf and the rest of Germany under Henry, though in Swabia Berthold and Welf were able to maintain themselves and were supported, in spite of the Pope's neutrality, by an advanced section of Church reformers.

Henry's first move after Rudolf's withdrawal was to raise a force of Bavarian and Bohemian troops and invade Swabia, which suffered terribly from the constant depredations of both sides, neither of which was able to obtain complete mastery. At the end of May he held a diet at Ulm, where the three rebel dukes of South Germany were formally deprived of their duchies. Carinthia was given to Liutold of Eppenstein, head of the most important family in the duchy. Bavaria and Swabia he retained for the time in his own hands. But in 1079 he founded the fortunes of the Hohenstaufen family by appointing to the duchy of Swabia the Swabian Count of Staufen, Frederick, to whom he married his daughter Agnes[1]. From him he obtained loyal support, and Rudolf vainly attempted to create a counter-influence in the duchy by having his son Berthold proclaimed at Ulm as duke, and by marrying his daughter Agnes to Berthold, son of Duke Berthold (who had died at the end of 1078).

During these years Rudolf was bitterly disappointed in his expectation of a direct intervention of the Pope against Henry. The papal legates were as emphatic as he could wish, both at Forchheim in March and at Goslar in November 1077, when the Cardinal-deacon Bernard united with Archbishop Siegfried in excommunicating Henry; but they were not upheld by their master, who persisted in his neutrality. Henry, during the same period, shewed himself in diplomacy to be far astuter than his impetuous rival. He was successful in preventing a conference of nobles on both sides, which Rudolf tried to arrange in 1078 in recollection of the success of this policy in 1073. He contrived, moreover, to prevent a coalition between the forces of Rudolf and his South German allies, though he failed to defeat them separately as he had hoped. On 7 August 1078 he fought an indecisive battle with the troops of Rudolf at Melrichstadt in Franconia, where, though his own losses were the heavier, his enemy was forced to retire; and, on the same day, an army of peasants, hastily recruited from Franconia, was decisively defeated on the Neckar by Dukes Berthold and Welf. But Henry maintained himself at Würzburg, and so prevented the threatened junction of the enemies' forces. Above all he was successful in keeping the Pope neutral, while at the same time disappointing Gregory's hopes of making his judgment decisive between the two kings. He was not, however, on this account any the more compliant with the ecclesiastical decrees. He continued to appoint, as it was essential to him that he should appoint, and invest to bishoprics and abbeys vacant by death or occupied by supporters of his

[1] In these two appointments Henry abandoned the policy of appointing an outsider as duke. He now needed powerful dukes who could be relied on to support him.

opponent. Rudolf imitated his example, though he was careful to leave episcopal elections free, and so, besides the rival kings in the kingdom and dukes in the duchies, there were rival bishops in several sees. Germany was devastated by civil war, in which the peasants, especially in Swabia, suffered the greatest hardships, and the trading opportunities of the towns were severely handicapped. The whole country sighed for peace and order, and it was becoming increasingly evident to the majority that in Henry's victory lay the best hope of this being attained.

So in 1080 he was able to carry the war into the enemy's country and invade Saxony. The battle of Flarchheim in Thuringia (27 January) was indecisive and Henry had to retire again to Bavaria; but his diplomacy was successful in detaching from Rudolf's cause the leaders of the Billung family, Duke Magnus and his uncle Herman, and also Margrave Ekbert of Meissen. And now the time had arrived when the Pope was to make the fateful decision that was to prolong and embitter the struggle of which Germany was already so weary. The moment seems to have been chosen by Henry himself. His envoys to the Lenten synod of 1080 were instructed no longer to appeal, but to threaten the Pope, and Henry had doubtless foreseen the result. He could hardly expect a judgment in his favour, but an adverse decision, while it would be welcomed by few, would be regarded with indignation by the vast majority. He contrived in fact to throw upon the Pope the odium of starting the new struggle. The sentence of Gregory VII not only upset the hopes of peace; it also outraged German sentiment in its claim to depose the king and to set up a successor in his place. The German bishops of Henry's party met at Bamberg (Easter) and renounced obedience to Gregory; a diet attended by king, nobles, and bishops assembled at Mayence (Whitsun) and repeated this renunciation; and finally, in an assembly mainly of North Italian bishops at Brixen[1] on 25 June, Gregory was declared deposed and Archbishop Guibert of Ravenna, nominated by Henry, was elected to succeed him. With his compliant anti-Pope, Henry could now entertain the prospect, impossible in 1076, of leading an expedition into Italy to establish his will by force.

But he could not leave Germany with Rudolf still powerful in Saxony, and he hastened back from Brixen to settle the issue with his rival. In the autumn he collected an army and marched through Thuringia to the Elster; there, in the neighbourhood of Hohen-Mölsen, a battle was fought, in which Henry was defeated. But this was more than compen-

---

[1] The choice of Brixen is curious. One would expect to find the meeting-place of an Italian assembly within the Italian kingdom, and the presence of the Italian chancellor, Bishop Burchard of Lausanne, points in the same direction. But, though 't is always difficult to fix the exact frontier-line, it seems clear that Brixen was on the German side. Perhaps, as Giesebrecht suggests (*Geschichte der deutschen Kaiserzeit,* Vol. III, p. 502), Brixen was chosen because of its isolation and security and the undoubted loyalty of its bishop.

sated by the mortal wound which Rudolf received, from the effects of which he died on the following day. To many this appeared as the judgment of God, not only on Rudolf but on the Pope as well. Though Henry was still unable to win over Saxony by force or negotiations, his position was sufficiently secure in Germany; now at last he could give his whole attention to the decisive contest with the Pope. From the spring of 1081 to the summer of 1084 he was in Italy. He succeeded in defeating his great adversary, he established Guibert as Pope Clement III, and by him was crowned Emperor in St Peter's. At Rome he seemed to have realised his ambition and to have raised himself to his father's height. But he was forced to retire before the arrival of the Normans, he could not overcome the resistance of Countess Matilda, and his Pope did not receive the recognition necessary to make him a useful tool. Imperial authority had been revived in Italy, but not so effectively as he had contemplated.

In Germany, his enemies took advantage of his absence to elect a successor to Rudolf. The obvious candidate was Otto of Nordheim, whose military skill had been conspicuous throughout. But, partly owing to jealousy among the leaders, partly perhaps from the desire to obtain western support, their choice fell on the Lotharingian Count Herman of Salm, brother of Count Conrad of Luxemburg and nephew of Herman, Count-Palatine of the Rhine. At any rate, he failed to win over his powerful relatives, and his kingdom, like that of Rudolf, was confined to Saxony. He had neither the ducal prestige nor the military prowess of his predecessor, nor does he seem to have entered into relations with the Pope; there was nothing to recommend this feeble rival of Henry. Towards the end of 1082 he did indeed advance south into Swabia, and the possibility of his leading an expedition into Italy caused Henry some anxiety. But it came to nothing; the death of Margrave Udo of the North Mark in 1082 and in January 1083 of Otto of Nordheim, whose sons were too young to play any part, deprived him of his chief military support. On the news of Otto's death he hastily returned to Saxony, and henceforward was of no account. So insignificant did he become that in 1088 he retired to his native Lorraine, and shortly afterwards was killed in front of a castle he was besieging.

It was the Church party that formed the chief danger to Henry when he returned to Germany in 1084. Archbishop Siegfried of Mayence had died in February, but his authority in his province had long disappeared; like the two anti-kings he had been forced since 1080 to remain in Saxony. To succeed him Henry appointed Werner (Wezil) as archbishop and arch-chancellor; in the latter office Siegfried had not been superseded—it was clearly a merely titular dignity, and the chancellor did the real work. The organisation of a papal party was actively conducted by the legate Otto, Cardinal-bishop of Ostia and afterwards Pope Urban II. With the assistance of Abbot William of Hirschau he combined monastic reform with opposition to Henry. The election of Gebhard as Bishop of

Constance in December was an important result of their joint efforts; for Gebhard later succeeded Otto as permanent legate, and was probably Henry's most dangerous enemy in Germany for the rest of his reign. In the work of reform, not only did numerous Swabian monasteries adhere to the rule of Hirschau, but the reform attracted laymen of the upper classes who came in numbers to the monastery as *conversi*. From Swabia Otto went on to Saxony. Here his influence was decisive against peace, the desire for which led to a meeting of princes of both sides at Gerstungen in January 1085. The Church party used the excommunication of Henry and his supporters to prevent a reconciliation. In this the legate was prominent, and still more so at a partisan synod held at Quedlinburg just after Easter. The excommunication of the anti-Pope and his adherents was a matter of common agreement, but Otto had the cause of Church reform and reorganisation equally at heart. Decrees were passed asserting the primacy of the Apostolic See and the supremacy of papal jurisdiction; others enforced Roman against local customs and strengthened the central authority by creating uniformity; finally, a few upheld the main principles of Church reform. It was at this point that a cleavage of interests became manifest. The Saxon nobles, who had been most zealous for Church reform when it was a useful weapon against Henry IV, firmly resisted it when it meant the restoration by them of churches and ecclesiastical property in their possession. Otto discovered that the bishops supported their secular allies in this, and that political interests in Saxony over-rode religious considerations.

While discord was thus beginning to make its appearance in Saxony, Henry was establishing his hold more firmly in the rest of Germany. At an imperial diet held at Easter 1085 at Mayence, the deposition of Gregory VII and his supporters and the election of Guibert were confirmed, and the Peace of God was proclaimed. Already in 1081 Bishop Henry of Liège had proclaimed the Peace in his diocese, and in 1083 Archbishop Sigewin of Cologne had done the same in his province. Henry had ratified their action, and now extended it to the whole kingdom. It was a sign, perhaps, of royal weakness that he could not by his own authority enforce the maintenance of peace, but had recourse to an expedient adopted in days of anarchy and royal impotence by the Church in France and Burgundy. It was also an unfortunate moment to choose in which to appeal to the sanction of the Church, when many of his subjects regarded him and his followers as schismatics. But it seemed for a time as if peace would result. Lorraine, which he visited in June, was wholly loyal; Henry confiscated the territory held there by Matilda, and allotted it mainly to Godfrey of Bouillon and Bishop Dietrich of Verdun. There followed a much greater triumph in July, when, taking advantage of the divisions in Saxony to win over the lay nobles, he was able for the first time for many years to enter the duchy in peace, and to progress as far as Magdeburg.

His success, however, was short-lived, and for this his failure to appreciate the Saxon temper was responsible. Many bishops were still hostile, especially the Archbishop of Magdeburg, and Henry proceeded to appoint bishops of his own party to replace them. Nothing was more calculated to cause a revulsion of feeling among the lay nobles than this exercise of royal authority without their concurrence, and the introduction of aliens into episcopal office in the duchy. Accordingly in September Henry was forced to abandon Saxony once more. In the following year (1086) Welf and his Swabian adherents were able to join forces with the Saxons and to besiege the important town of Würzburg. Henry, hastening to its relief with an army mainly composed of peasants and levies from the towns, was severely defeated at the battle of Pleichfeld on 11 August. It was not the usual encounter of knights. The troops of Welf and of the city of Magdeburg dismounted and fought on foot, with the cross as their standard and encouraged by the prayers of the Archbishop of Magdeburg[1]. As a result of the battle, Würzburg was captured and its Bishop, Adalbero, was restored, though only temporarily, to his see. The position of affairs, so favourable to Henry the previous year, seemed to have been entirely reversed. But his enemies were not able to gain any permanent advantage from their victory, or even to retain Würzburg for long. Negotiations were resumed, to break down continually over the impediment of Henry's excommunication and his recognition of the anti-Pope. At last, in the summer of 1088, a renewal of discord in Saxony caused a reaction in Henry's favour, and in a short time, for good and all, the revolt in Saxony was ended.

The most powerful noble in Saxony at this time was Margrave Ekbert of Meissen[2]. Of violent and audacious temper, like his father, he had taken the lead in welcoming the king in Saxony in July 1085 and in expelling him two months later. His Mark had previously been transferred by Henry to Duke Vratislav of Bohemia, who received the title of king in 1085; but Vratislav was unable to enter into possession of it. In 1087 Ekbert came to terms again with Henry, perhaps as the result of a Bohemian invasion. But he immediately broke his word, having conceived the bold scheme of getting himself appointed king in place of the helpless Herman. This was too much for his jealous confederates. The bishops in particular rejected his scheme, and the murder of Bishop Burchard of Halberstadt, who had been in the forefront of every Saxon rising against Henry, was believed to be Ekbert's revenge for his rebuff. The ambition and violence of this noble were more dangerous than the royal authority; the rest of Saxony hastened to make its peace with the

---

[1] This battle is described in some detail by the chronicler Bernold (MGH, *Script.* Vol. v, p. 445) who was himself present.

[2] The Billung family, since their adhesion to Henry in 1080, seem to have taken little part in public affairs. Duke Magnus remained loyal to Henry, and he is mentioned as present at the coronation of Henry's son Conrad as king in 1087.

Emperor[1], and, while safeguarding its own independence, recognised him as king of Germany. The bishops indeed would not recognise Guibert; they compromised by regarding Urban II as the rightful Pope, and at the same time disregarding his excommunication of Henry. Ekbert was isolated, and was condemned at a Saxon diet held at Quedlinburg in 1088; at Ratisbon in 1089 he was proscribed as a traitor, and on Margrave Henry of the East Mark (Lusatia) was conferred the margravate of Meissen. Ekbert remained defiant, and even posed as the champion of the Church against Henry; at the end of 1088 he inflicted a severe defeat on the king in front of his castle of Gleichen. But he was murdered in 1090, and so all opposition in Saxony came to an end. His county of Brunswick passed to his sister Gertrude, who married, as her second husband, Henry the Fat, the son of Otto of Nordheim.

The years 1088–1090 mark the climax of Henry's power in Germany. Except for Margrave Ekbert, against whom he had the assistance of the rest of Saxony, and the few Swabian counts that supported Welf, he was universally recognised as king. The succession had been secured by the coronation of his son Conrad as king in May 1087. The Church party was dispirited and quiescent, and it lost its chief champion in Bavaria with the death of Archbishop Gebhard of Salzburg in 1088. In Lorraine, in 1089, Bishop Herman of Metz was reconciled with the king and restored to his see, and the duchy of Lower Lorraine was conferred on Godfrey of Bouillon. To the see of Cologne, vacant by the death of Archbishop Sigewin, Henry appointed his chancellor Herman; and, during his stay at Cologne for this purpose, he was married (his first wife, Bertha, had died in 1087) to Praxedis (Adelaide), daughter of the Prince of Kiev and widow of Margrave Henry of the North Mark. The marriage was celebrated by Archbishop Hartwig of Magdeburg, with whom, in spite of his prominent share in the king's defeat at Pleichfeld in 1086, Henry was completely reconciled. The archbishop, however, refused to recognise the anti-Pope, and this was the chief weakness in Henry's position. It seems that on more than one occasion he could have come to terms with the Church party and returned to communion, had he consented to abandon Guibert. He was himself unwilling both to betray so faithful a servant and to discard so useful a tool; while many of his chief supporters and advisers among the bishops, feeling that their own fate was implicated in that of Guibert, influenced him in the same direction. He might also have expected the ultimate success of his anti-Pope. There was nothing to lead him to anticipate the fatal results to himself of the election of Urban II as Pope in March 1088. Urban, like his predecessor, had to live under Norman protection, and Guibert remained securely in possession of Rome.

---

[1] But it seems almost certain that he cannot have recovered full possession of the royal domain. Probably the situation in Saxony was a return to the *status quo* of 1069.

As in 1072 and 1075, the position in Germany appeared favourable for the recovery of authority in Italy; and again a situation had arisen vitally affecting imperial interests. In 1089, Countess Matilda of Tuscany, now over forty years of age, devoting herself to furthering the political advantage of the Papacy, had married the younger Welf, a lad of seventeen. The elder Welf, having lost his Saxon allies, had turned his ambitions to the south, and hoped for great things from this marriage. His Italian inheritance adjoined the territories of Countess Matilda, and he doubtless anticipated for himself a position in Italy such as Duke Godfrey, the husband of Matilda's mother Beatrice, had held during the minority of Henry IV. The Emperor came into Italy in April 1090 to counteract the dangerous effects of this alliance, and at first met with considerable success. But the papal party was rapidly gaining strength, and unscrupulous in its methods worked among his family to effect his ruin. The revolt of Conrad in 1093 under Matilda's influence, accompanied by a league of Lombard cities against the Emperor, not only reduced him to great straits but even cut off his retreat to Germany. The next year another domestic blow was struck at the unfortunate Emperor. His wife Praxedis, suspected of infidelity to her husband, escaped to take refuge with Matilda and to spread gross charges against Henry. False though they doubtless were, they were eagerly seized upon by his enemies, and the Pope himself at the Council of Piacenza in 1095 listened to the tale and pardoned the unwilling victim. Praxedis, her work done, disappears from history, she seems to have returned to Russia and to have died as a nun. Her husband, stunned with the shock of this double treachery of wife and son, remained in isolation at Verona. But the conflicting interests of Welf and the Papacy soon broke up the unnatural marriage-alliance. Matilda separated from her second husband as she had done from her first, and the elder Welf, who had no intention of merely subserving papal interests, took his son back with him to Germany in 1095. The next year he made his peace with the Emperor; the road to Germany was opened again, and in the spring of 1097 Henry made his way by the Brenner Pass into Bavaria.

The long absence of Henry in Italy had less effect than might have been expected on his position in Germany. Saxony remained quiet, and the government by non-interference was able to ensure the loyalty of the lay nobles, among whom Henry the Fat, with Brunswick added to Nordheim by his marriage with Gertrude, now held the leading place. In Lorraine the Church party won a success in the adhesion of the Bishops of Metz, Toul, and Verdun to the papal cause. Otherwise the only centre of disturbance was Swabia. The government of Germany during Henry's absence seems to have been entrusted to Duke Frederick of Swabia, in conjunction with Henry, Count-Palatine of the Rhine, who died in 1095. In 1091 the death of Berthold, son of the anti-King Rudolf, brought the house of Rheinfelden to an end. He was succeeded both in his allodial territories and in his pretensions to the duchy of Swabia by his brother-in-law Berthold of Zähringen, son of the former Duke of Carinthia, a far more formidable rival to Duke Frederick. The successes of Henry in Italy in 1091, combined with the death of Abbot William of Hirschau, brought to the king's side many adherents in Swabia. But the disasters of 1093 caused a reaction, and the papal party began to revive under the lead of Bishop Gebhard of Constance, Berthold's brother. An assembly held at Ulm declared the unity of Swabia under the spiritual headship of Gebhard and the temporal headship of Berthold, and a land-peace was proclaimed to last until Easter 1096, which Welf with less success attempted to extend the next year to Bavaria and Franconia. The Church party took the lead in this movement, and papal overlordship was recognised by Berthold and Welf, who did homage to Gebhard as the representative of the Pope. This coalition was entirely ruined by the breach of Welf with Matilda, which led to his reconciliation with Henry and to a complete severance of his alliance with the Papacy.

The comparative tranquillity during Henry's absence was due, not to the strength of the government but in part to its weakness, and above all to the general weariness of strife and the desire for peace. To this cause, too, must be attributed the feeble response that Germany made when in 1095 the summons of Urban II to the First Crusade resounded throughout Europe. Some, and among them even a great ecclesiastic like Archbishop Ruthard of Mayence, were seized with the crusading spirit so far as to join in the massacre of Jews and the plunder of their property. But, except for Godfrey of Bouillon, who had been unable to make his ducal authority effective in Lower Lorraine, no important German noble actually went on crusade at this time. Indeed, it does not seem that the position of Henry was to any material extent affected by the Crusade. But, if the immediate effect was negligible, it was otherwise with the ultimate effect. Important results were to arise from the circumstances in which the crusading movement was launched—the Pope, the spiritual head of Christendom, preaching the Crusade against the infidel, while the Emperor, the temporal head, remained helpless in Italy, cut off from communion with the faithful. Gregory VII in 1074 had planned to lead a crusade himself, and wrote to Henry IV that he would leave the Roman Church during his absence under Henry's care and protection. This plan was typical of its author, though it was a curious reversal of the natural functions of the two heads of Christendom. Had Pope and Emperor been working together in the ideal harmony that Gregory VII conceived, it would certainly have been the Emperor that would have led the crusaders to Palestine in 1095, and under his suzerainty that the kingdom of Jerusalem would have been formed. As it was, the Papacy took the lead; its suzerainty was acknowledged; in the war against the infidel it arrogated to itself the temporal as well as the spiritual sword. And not only was the Emperor affected by the advantages that accrued to his great rival. His semi-divine character was impaired; when he failed to take his natural place as the champion of the Cross, he prejudiced his claim to be the representative of God upon earth.

At any rate, on his return to Germany Henry found but slight opposition to his authority. The reconciliation with Welf was confirmed in a diet at Worms in 1098, and was extended to Berthold as well. Welf was formally restored to his duchy, and the succession was promised to his son. The rival claims to Swabia were settled: Frederick was confirmed in the duchy, Berthold was compensated with the title of Duke (of Zähringen) and the grant of Zurich, to be held as a fief directly from the Emperor. At the price of concessions, which implied that he had renounced the royal ambitions of his earlier years, Henry had made peace with his old enemies, and all lay opposition to him in Germany ceased. At a diet at Mayence the princes elected his second son Henry as king, and promised to acknowledge him as his father's successor; the young Henry took an oath of allegiance to his father, promising not to act with independent authority during his father's lifetime. For the Emperor, though anxious to secure the succession, was careful not to allow his son the position Conrad had abused. The young Henry was anointed king at Aix-la-Chapelle the following year; on the sacred relics he repeated the oath he had taken at Mayence, and the princes took an oath of fealty to him.

Ecclesiastical opposition remained, but was seriously weakened by the defection of Berthold and Welf. It gained one notable, if not very creditable, adherent in the person of Ruthard, who had succeeded Werner as Archbishop of Mayence in 1089. The crusading fervour had manifested itself, especially in the Rhine district, in outbreaks against the Jews, who, when they were not murdered, were maltreated, forcibly baptised, and despoiled of their property. Henry on more than one occasion had shewn special favour to the Jews, who played no small part in the prosperity of the towns. Immediately on his return from Italy, he had given permission to the victims to return to their faith, and he was active in recovering for them the property they had lost. Mayence had been the scene of one of these anti-Jewish outbreaks, and the archbishop was suspected of complicity and of having received his share of the plunder. Henry opened an enquiry into this on the occasion of his son's election, to which the archbishop refused to submit and fled to his Thuringian estates. Apart from this, there is, until 1104, a period of unwonted calm in Germany, and in consequence little to record. During these years the chief interest lies in Lorraine, owing to the ambition of Count Robert II of Flanders and the recrudescence of a communal movement at Cambrai. Defence against the count was its object, and so the commune received recognition from the Emperor and Bishop Walcher; but it found itself compelled to come to terms with the count, who made peace with Henry in 1103. Having enjoyed independence, the commune continued to exist, and entered into a struggle with the bishop, who was handicapped by a rival and pro-papal bishop. For a time it maintained its independence, until in 1107 it was overthrown by Henry V and episcopal authority restored.

Henry, then, might seem to have at last accomplished his object in Germany, and by the universal recognition of his authority to have achieved the mastery. But in reality he had failed, and the peace was his recognition of failure. For it was a peace of acquiescence, acquiescence on both sides, due to weariness. The nobles recognised him as king, and he recognised the rights they claimed. Not as subjects, but almost as equals, the Saxons, Welf, Berthold, had all made terms with him. No concessions, however, could reconcile the Papacy. The death of Urban II in 1099 made no difference; his successor, Paschal II, was even more inflexible. There seemed a prospect of peace when the anti-Pope Guibert died in 1100, and a diet at Mayence proposed an embassy to Rome. The following year Henry proposed to go to Rome himself. In January 1103, at another diet at Mayence, besides promulgating a land-peace for the Empire for four years, Henry announced his intention, provided he could be reconciled with the Pope, of going on pilgrimage to the Holy Land. But to all these proposals the Pope turned a deaf ear. Henry had been excommunicated and deposed, and the sentence was repeated by Paschal in 1102. There was no hope of ending the schism during Henry IV's lifetime.

This state of affairs led to the final catastrophe. To no one did the situation give so much cause for dissatisfaction as to the heir to the throne—the young Henry V. The longer his father lived the weaker he felt would be the authority to which he would succeed. Self-interest determined him, in defiance of his oath, to seize power before matters became worse. He knew that he might expect the reconciliation with the Pope that was denied to his father, and that the Germans would willingly accept the leadership of one who was at the same time lawful king and in communion with the Pope. Probably the disturbances that broke out at Ratisbon while the court was staying there at the beginning of 1104 decided him in his purpose. Many nobles had disliked the promulgation of a land-peace, which interfered with their customary violence; then the murder of a Bavarian count by one of his own *ministeriales*, and the Emperor's neglect to punish the offender, provoked such discontent that Henry IV found it wiser to leave Bavaria and go to Lorraine. Henry V went with him, but he had already the nucleus of a party and began to mature his plans. In Lorraine his father was among friends, but when at the end of the year he marched north to punish a breach of the peace by a Saxon count, the young Henry decided that the moment was ripe for his venture. At Fritzlar on 12 December he escaped by night and went rapidly south to Ratisbon, where he placed himself at the head of the discontented nobles. His father, abandoning his expedition, returned to the Rhine; he was broken-hearted at his son's treachery and made frantic appeals to him to return. Henry V sanctimoniously refused to listen to an excommunicated man, and made overtures to the Pope which were immediately successful.

The revolt was well-timed, and events turned out as Henry V had planned. The papal legate, Bishop Gebhard of Constance, met him in Bavaria and gave him the papal absolution. The Saxon and Thuringian princes, with whom was the exiled Archbishop Ruthard of Mayence, sent him an invitation which he eagerly accepted, and with the papal legate at his side he arrived at Quedlinburg for Easter 1105. A synod was held at Nordhausen on 21 May, at which he adopted an attitude of humility that was immediately successful. The Church party was won over by his action against imperialist bishops, and by his placing in the forefront the excommunication of his father as the cause of his revolt; the lay princes were equally attracted by his promise to act always in accordance with their direction. He could now count on Saxony wholly, and largely on Bavaria; Duke Welf seems on the whole to have remained neutral. He was fortunate, too, in the death this year of his brother-in-law, Duke Frederick of Swabia, whose sons were too young to intervene.

He now took the field against his father, and marched on Mayence with the intention of restoring the archbishop. But the Rhine towns stood firm in their loyalty, and, after taking Würzburg, he was forced to retire to Ratisbon. His father followed hard on his tracks, retook Würzburg, and nearly surprised the son at Ratisbon. Here the Emperor was reinforced by Margrave Liutpold of Austria and Duke Bořivoi of Bohemia. Henry V marched against him, and managed to entice from his father his two chief supporters. The Emperor found himself abandoned on all sides, and had to make a hurried escape to avoid capture. After an adventurous and perilous flight through Bohemia and Saxony, he arrived safely at Mayence at the end of October. Driven from there by his son's approach, he took refuge at Cologne, and then followed the second and most shameful treachery of the young Henry[1]. Promising to assist his reconciliation with the Pope, he persuaded his father to meet him and accompany him to Mayence. Nothing was wanting that hypocrisy could suggest—tears, prostration at his father's feet, solemn and repeated pledges of safe-conduct. By these means he induced him to dismiss his retinue, and, on arriving at Bingen, represented the danger of going to Mayence and enticed him into the castle of Böckelheim, where he kept him a close prisoner. At Christmas a diet was held at Mayence in the presence of papal legates, who dominated the proceedings. The Emperor was brought before the diet, not at Mayence where the townspeople might have rescued him, but at Ingelheim; crushed in spirit by his sufferings in prison and in fear for his life, he surrendered the royal insignia, promising a humble confession of his misdeeds and even resignation of his throne. It was a scene that moved the lay nobles to compassion, but the legates, having gained their ends,

---

[1] K. Hampe, *Deutsche Kaisergeschichte im Zeitalter der Salier und Staufen*, p. 70, calls it "the most devilish deed in all German history."

declared themselves not competent to grant absolution. Henry V was
equally obdurate, and his father was kept in confinement at Ingelheim.
An invitation was sent to the Pope inviting his presence at a synod in
Germany. Henry V for his own purposes was willing to allow the papal
decision so much desired by Gregory VII.

But the year 1106 saw a change of fortune. The Emperor escaped
from captivity and was strongly supported in Lorraine and the Rhine
towns. In the spring Henry V was severely defeated outside Liège by a
coalition of Duke Henry of Lower Lorraine, Count Godfrey of Namur,
and the people of Liège; in the summer he signally failed before Cologne.
In face of this devoted loyalty to his father he was powerless; then suddenly death came to his aid, and the opposition collapsed. The Emperor,
worn out by sorrow and suffering, fell ill at Liège and died on 7 August.
On his death-bed he sent his last message to his son, requesting pardon
for his followers and that he might be buried beside his father at Spires.
His dying appeal was disregarded. Henry V deposed the Duke of Lower
Lorraine, and appointed Godfrey of Brabant in his place; the town of
Cologne was fined 5000 marks. The Pope refused absolution and Christian burial to the excommunicated Emperor. The people of Liège, in
defiance of king and Pope, had given his body a royal funeral in their
cathedral amid universal lamentation; the papal legates ordered its
removal. It was taken to the cathedral at Spires, where again the people
displayed their grief and affection. The bishop ordered it to be removed
once more to an unconsecrated chapel. Five years later, when Henry V
wrung from the Pope the cession of investiture, he also obtained absolution for his father, and on 7 August 1111 the body of Henry IV was at
last solemnly interred beside those of his father and grandfather in the
cathedral he had so richly endowed at Spires.

The story of this long reign of fifty years reads like a tragedy on
the Greek model. Mainly owing to conditions for which he was not
responsible, Henry was forced to struggle, in defence of his rights, against
odds that were too great for him, and finally to fall a victim to the
treachery of his son. The mismanagement of the imperial government
during his minority had given the opportunity for particularism in
Germany and for the Papacy in Italy to obtain a position from which
he could not dislodge them. As far as Germany was concerned, he might
have been successful, and he did at any rate acquire an important ally
for the monarchy in the towns, especially in the Rhine district. How
important it was is seen in 1073–4, when the example set by Worms
turned the tide that was flowing so strongly against him; and, more
notably still, in the resistance he was able to make to his son in the last
year of his life. But the reason that prevented his making full use of this
alliance prevented also his success in Germany. The fatal policy of Otto I
had placed the monarchy in a position from which it could not extricate
itself. Essentially it had to lean on ecclesiastical support, and from this

two results followed. In the first place, as the important towns were under episcopal authority, a direct alliance with them took place only when the bishop was hostile to the king. Secondly, the success of Otto I's policy, in Germany as in Italy, depended now on the Papacy being subservient, or at least obedient, to imperial authority. The Papacy regenerated by Henry III, especially with the opportunities it had had during Henry IV's minority, could not acquiesce in its own dependence or in the subordination of ecclesiastical appointments to lay control. A contest between *sacerdotium* and *imperium* was inevitable, and, as we can see, it could only have one end. Certainly it was the Papacy that caused the failure of Henry IV. He was unfortunate in being faced at the beginning by one of the greatest of all the Popes, and yet he was able to defeat him; but he could not defeat the Papacy. It was the long schism that partly prompted the revolt of Henry V, and it was the desire to end it that won him the support of most of Germany. Papal excommunication was the weapon that brought Henry IV to his tragic end, and avenged the death in exile of Gregory VII. And, apart from this, it was owing to the Papacy that his reign in Germany had been unsuccessful. He made peace with his enemies, but on their conditions; and the task that he had set out so energetically to achieve—the vindication of imperial authority—he had definitely failed to accomplish.

With the passing of the old king, many others of the leading actors disappear from the scene. Especially in Saxony, old houses were becoming extinct, and new families were rising to take their place in German history. The Billungs, the Counts of Nordheim, the Ekberts of Brunswick, had each in turn played the leading part against the king; and now the male line had failed in all these families, and the inheritance had fallen to women. In 1090 by the death of Ekbert II the male line of the Brunswick house became extinct; his sister Gertrude was left as heiress, and she married (as her second husband) Henry the Fat, the elder son of Otto of Nordheim. He was murdered in 1101, his brother Conrad suffered the same fate in 1103, and the elder daughter of Henry and Gertrude, Richenza, became eventually heiress to both these houses[1]. Lothar, Count of Supplinburg, by his marriage with Richenza in 1100, rose from an insignificant position to become the most powerful noble in Saxony. In 1106 died Duke Magnus, the last of the Billungs. His duchy was given by Henry V to Lothar, his family possessions were divided between his two daughters: the eastern portion went to the younger, Eilica, who married Count Otto of Ballenstädt and became the mother of Albert the Bear, the Saxon rival of the Welfs; the western portion to the elder, Wulfhild, who married Henry the Black, son of Duke Welf of Bavaria.

---

[1] Gertrude had been married first to Count Dietrich of Katlenburg; on the death of Henry the Fat she married Henry of Eilenburg, Margrave of Meissen and the East Mark. He died in 1103, and his posthumous son Henry died childless in 1123. Gertrude herself died in 1117.

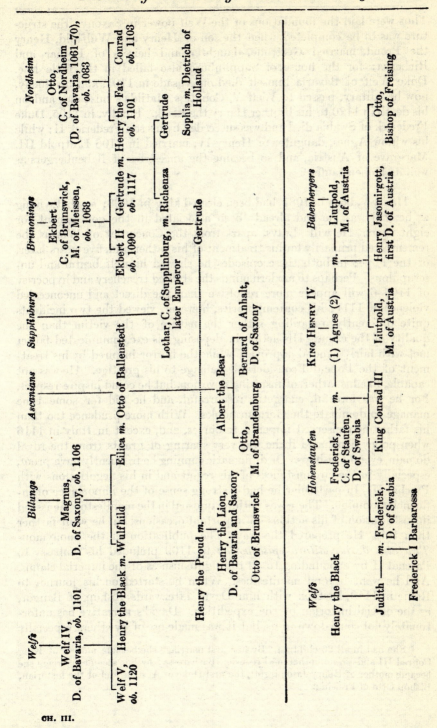

Thus were laid the foundations of the Welf power in Saxony; the structure was to be completed when the son of Henry and Wulfhild, Henry the Proud, married Gertrude, daughter and heiress of Lothar and Richenza; for the house of Supplinburg also failed in the male line. Duke Welf of Bavaria himself died on crusade in 1101, and his duchy, now hereditary, passed to Welf V, Countess Matilda's husband, and on his death in 1120 to his brother Henry the Black. Finally, in 1105, Duke Frederick of Swabia died and was succeeded by his son Frederick II; while his widow Agnes, daughter of Henry IV, married in 1106 Liutpold III, Margrave of Austria, and so became the ancestress of Babenbergers as well as Hohenstaufen[1].

Henry V, born in 1081, had been elected king in 1098; so that, young as he still was, he had already been associated in the government for eight years. He will always, apart from the Concordat of Worms, be remembered primarily for his treatment of his father and, five years later, of the Pope; in both these episodes he shewed himself brutal and unscrupulous. Perhaps to modern minds the studied treachery and hypocrisy of 1105–6 will appear more repulsive than the direct and unconcealed violence of 1111; his contemporaries, however, viewed the two incidents quite differently, regarding rather the nature of the victim than the quality of the crime. His action in deposing his excommunicated father met with fairly general approval; while the horror inspired by his treatment of the Pope did considerable damage to his prestige. He was not capable, like his father, of inspiring devotion, but he could inspire respect. For he was forceful, energetic, resourceful, and he did for some time manage to dominate the German nobles. With more prudence too than his father he conserved imperial resources, and, except in Italy in 1116 when policy demanded it, he was very sparing of grants from the royal domain, even to bishops. Of diplomatic cunning he frequently gave proof, especially in the circumstances of his revolt and in his negotiations with Paschal II. In particular he had a strong sense of the importance of influencing opinion. There was nothing unusual in the manifestoes he issued in justification of his actions on important occasions, but he went farther than this. He prepared the way. The publication of the anonymous *Tractatus de investitura episcoporum* in 1109 preluded his embassy to Paschal II by expounding to all the righteousness of the imperial claims. And he went beyond manifestoes. When he started on his journey to Rome in 1110, he took with him David, afterwards Bishop of Bangor, as the official historian of the expedition. David's narrative has unfortunately not come down to us, but it was made use of by others, especially

---

[1] She had in all 23 children. By her first marriage she became mother of King Conrad III and grandmother of Frederick Barbarossa; by her second marriage she became mother of Henry Jasomirgott, the first Duke of Austria, and of the historian, Bishop Otto of Freising.

by the chronicler Ekkehard. It was assuredly propaganda, not history; but it was an ingenious and novel way of ensuring an authoritative description of events calculated to impress contemporary opinion.

To prevent the further decline of imperial authority, he had allied himself with the two powers responsible for that decline. His real policy was in no whit different from that of his father, so that he was playing a hazardous game; and it is doubtful whether, even from his own purely selfish standpoint, he had taken the wisest course. To obtain the assistance of the Pope, he had recognised the over-riding authority of the *sacerdotium*; he had justified his revolt against his father on the ground of the unfitness of an excommunicated man to be king, and had used the papal power of absolution to condone his perjury. To obtain the co-operation of the nobles, he had to abandon for a time the support of the towns and the reliance on the *ministeriales* which had been so valuable to his father. The nobles were, as usual, anxious to make their fiefs and offices hereditary, to obtain the recognition of independent powers, and to prevent the establishment of an over-riding royal justice. This they expected to ensure by the participation in the government that Henry had promised, and in this he humoured them for the time. Their names appear as witnesses to royal charters; all acts of government, even the nomination of bishops, are done *consilio principum*. For their support was still necessary to him, and he skilfully made use of it to oppose a united Germany to the claims of his other ally, the Pope. He had allowed the legates to sit in judgment on his father, and to wreak their vengeance to the full; he had shewn himself zealous in deposing schismatic bishops at their dictation. All this was to his interest; but, his father dead, he was not long in throwing off the mask. It was essential that the bishops should be loyal subjects, and so he was careful to control elections; and, worst of all to the mind of Paschal II[1], he refused to discontinue the practice of lay investiture. In this, and against all claims of the Pope to interfere in the affairs of Germany, he had the nobles, lay and ecclesiastical, almost to a man enthusiastically on his side.

For the first five years of his reign the issue with the Pope was the leading question. Apart from Count Robert of Flanders, against whom Henry had to lead an expedition in 1107, there was no serious disturbance in Germany. In 1108–9 he was principally occupied on the eastern frontiers, where he successfully asserted himself in Bohemia but failed signally in his attempt to intervene in Hungary and Poland. All this time negotiations with the Pope had been in progress, without any satisfactory result, and at last in 1110 Henry decided to go to Rome to effect a settlement in person and to obtain the imperial crown. At the diet at Ratisbon at which he announced his intention, the nobles unanimously

---

[1] It is perhaps remarkable that Paschal in 1105, when he had the chance, did not take the opportunity to obtain assurances from Henry V on investiture or on any other point.

pledged themselves of their free will to accompany him. The summons to the expedition was universally obeyed, and it was at the head of an imposing army that he entered Italy in August. The absence of incident in Germany in these years, and the ready response to the summons, shew the unity of the country both under the king and against the Pope. The events of 1110–11 established his authority in Italy and over the Pope as well. He wrung from the Pope the concession of investiture and received from him the imperial crown. Countess Matilda shewed herself well-disposed; the Normans in South Italy were overawed by the size of his army. At the end of 1111 his power in both kingdoms was at its height.

But it rested on insecure foundations. He had dominated the Pope by violence, and had extracted from him a concession which provoked the unyielding hostility of the Church party. Already in 1112 Paschal retracted his concession, and in Burgundy in the same year Archbishop Guy of Vienne declared investiture to be a heresy and anathematised the Emperor, undeterred by the efforts of Henry to rouse the nobles and bishops of Burgundy against him; while Archbishop Conrad of Salzburg, who had always opposed Henry's ecclesiastical policy, abandoned his see and took refuge with Countess Matilda. Moreover, Henry's government of Germany was only government by consent; it depended on the good-will of the princes. Some of the bishops were alienated by his treatment of Paschal II; the lay nobles, who had concurred in his ecclesiastical policy, were justly apprehensive of the independence and high-handedness of his actions in 1111.

He was determined to free himself from their tutelage, now that they had served his purpose. So he returned to the policy of his father of relying on *ministeriales* and lesser nobles, whose share in the government, dependent as they were on his favour, would be effective in his interests and not in their own. Above all, he concentrated on the royal domain, and was so sparing in his grants that he gave the appearance of miserliness. He had not followed the common practice of making himself popular by large donations on his accession. He bountifully rewarded faithful service, but that was all. Such grants as he made to ecclesiastical foundations were usually of little importance and for purely religious purposes. The bishops fared especially badly under his regime, but, with the working of the leaven of reform and the increasing authority of the Papacy, they were becoming less reliable as agents of monarchical government. To him, as to his father, the building of castles was a necessary step to protect the royal estates from the continual encroachments of the nobles. They too had adopted the same method of protecting their own domains, and against this usurpation of his prerogative he used his best endeavours, on the whole not unsuccessfully. It was, however, one of the causes of friction between him and his two chief enemies—Duke Lothar of Saxony and Archbishop Adalbert of Mayence. Like his father again, the rich domain in Saxony at first attracted his main attention; it was there that he went immediately after the successful inauguration of his revolt in Bavaria in 1105. But after his defeat in 1115 Saxony had to be abandoned. He then turned to a new quarter, to the south-west, where lay the rich lands of the middle and upper Rhine. We find him engaged in exchanges, revocations of previous grants, even confiscations, which all point to the policy of creating in this new region a centralised and compact domain. Finally, he attempted to revive the alliance with the towns. Especially to Spires in 1111 and to Worms in 1114 he gave important charters[1], which raised the status and independence of the citizens by removing the most vexatious of the seignorial powers over their persons and property. He could not, however, count on their loyalty. Worms revolted more than once, Mayence was won over by privileges from its archbishop, Cologne was sometimes for and sometimes against him. He was unable to win their confidence fully or to inspire the devotion that had been so serviceable to his father.

In all this he was engaged in building up his resources, and in attempting to establish a basis for the royal authority which would make it independent of princely support. But he was by no means content merely to shake off their control. He was determined to enforce the recognition of his sovereign rights, and opposition only enraged him and revealed the arbitrary tendency of his ideas. In January 1112, at Merseburg, he intervened as supreme judge to prohibit the unjust imprisonment of Count Frederick of Stade by Duke Lothar of Saxony and Margrave Rudolf of the North Mark. When they refused obedience to his judgment, they were deprived of their dignities, which were only restored after they had made submission and released Frederick. Two other Saxon counts were punished with close confinement for a breach of the peace. In July, at Mayence, he exercised another sovereign right in sequestrating the fiefs of Count Udalric of Weimar who had died without heirs; he also, it seems, with the consent of a diet, added the allodial territory to the royal domain. Siegfried, Count-Palatine of the Rhine, claimed to succeed as next-of-kin to Udalric; and, in his disappointment, he started a conspiracy among the Saxon and Thuringian nobles, which was joined by Lothar and Margrave Rudolf, and eventually the whole of Saxony was ablaze with revolt. Finally, as Henry was preparing an expedition to Saxony, came the breach with his former chancellor, now the greatest ecclesiastic in the land, Archbishop Adalbert of Mayence[2].

---

[1] F. Keutgen, *Urkunden zur städtischen Verfassungsgeschichte*, Berlin, 1901, pp. 14 sqq.

[2] The province of Mayence covered nearly half the German kingdom. It included 14 (or, if Bamberg is taken into account, 15) suffragan bishoprics and extended as far as southern Saxony and Bohemia, and southwards to Chur at the Italian frontier. The archbishop had precedence over all nobles, lay and ecclesiastical, and as the leading official played the principal part at royal elections. The potentialities of this exalted office had been obscured by the mediocrity of the three previous archbishops

Adalbert, son of Count Sigehard of Saarbrücken, owed his rise to fame almost entirely to the favour of Henry V. By him he had been appointed chancellor in 1106, before the death of Henry IV, and had received lavish preferment and grants from his master. On Archbishop Ruthard's death in 1109, Adalbert was nominated as his successor by the king, who, perhaps because he did not wish to be deprived of Adalbert's assistance on his important expedition to Italy, deferred investiture; the see remained vacant for two years, during which Henry, by virtue of his rights of *regalia*, doubtless enjoyed its revenues. On his return to Germany in 1111, he immediately invested Adalbert, who thereupon entered into possession of the temporalities of the archbishop, though not yet consecrated. At once a change was manifest. As chancellor he had been an ardent imperialist, the right-hand man of the king, who recognised his services and rewarded them with his confidence and with material benefits. He was probably the chosen instrument of Henry's policy of emancipation from the control of the nobles. But as archbishop his interests diverged, his ambition led him to independence, and the cause of the princes became his. He took a strong Church line, and professed an ultra-papalist standpoint, though it was he who had been chiefly concerned in all the leading events of 1111; it was interest and not principle that influenced his change of view. Personal ambition was the mark of his career. His great aim was to establish an independent principality. At first he planned this in the Rhine district, and, as this brought him into contact with the royal domain, he was soon in conflict with the king. Thwarted in this endeavour, he later turned his attention with more success to the eastern possessions of his see, in Hesse, Thuringia, and Saxony[1].

In November 1112 the breach took place which definitely ranged Adalbert on the side of the king's enemies. It was only a year after his investiture, but Adalbert had already had time to realise his new environment and to adopt his new outlook. It is probable that a leading cause of friction was the king's exercise of the rights of *regalia* during the two years' vacancy[2]. The final cause seems to have been a quarrel over two castles in the palatinate, which Adalbert refused to abandon. At any rate the breach was complete, and the king's indignation, which found expression in a violent manifesto[3], was unbounded. He, like

in this period—Siegfried, Werner, and Ruthard. Adalbert seized upon them at once, and founded the greatness of his successors.

[1] Cf. K. H. Schmitt, *Erzbischof Adalbert I von Mainz als Territorialfürst* (*Arbeiten zur deutschen Rechts- und Verfassungsgeschichte*, No. 11), Berlin, 1920.

[2] Meyer von Knonau, *Jahrbücher Heinrichs IV und V*, Vol. vi, p. 263. Doubtless Henry IV had exercised the same rights during the exiles of Siegfried and Ruthard, and it is probable that there had resulted serious encroachments on the temporalities of the see, which Adalbert was attempting to recover.

[3] Published by Giesebrecht, *Geschichte der deutschen Kaiserzeit*, Vol. iii, pp. 1269 sq.

Henry II of England afterwards, raised his faithful chancellor to be the leading archbishop of his kingdom, expecting to gain a powerful supporter, and found in him his most dangerous opponent. Adalbert set off to join his new associates in Saxony; the king was marching thither at the same time, and their ways converged. The quarrel broke out afresh. Adalbert firmly refused to yield what he held; he was taken prisoner and exposed to severe privations. This arbitrary act, in which the judgment of the princes played no part, increased the alarm and suspicion which had already caused revolt to break out in Saxony.

The first revolt against Henry V was ill-organised, and was effectively suppressed in 1113. The royal army under Count Hoier of Mansfeld won a decisive victory at Warmstadt near Quedlinburg. Siegfried died of wounds, and the palatinate of the Rhine was conferred on Henry's faithful supporter, Count Godfrey of Calw. Count Wiprecht of Groitsch was taken prisoner and condemned to death; the sentence was commuted to three years' imprisonment, but his possessions were confiscated and his two sons rendered homeless. Of the other leaders, Count Louis of Thuringia and Bishop Reinhard of Halberstadt made submission and received the royal pardon. Henry was triumphant, and hoped that Adalbert would have learnt from their failure and his own sufferings the folly of resistance; the archbishop was brought before the king at Worms, but he refused to yield and was taken back to his prison. The next year, on 7 January 1114, the Emperor celebrated his victory by his marriage at Mayence with Matilda, the eleven-year-old daughter of Henry I of England. To Mayence came Duke Lothar to make humble submission and to be restored to favour. But the concord was immediately broken by Henry's sudden and arbitrary imprisonment of Count Louis of Thuringia. This further breach of the custom, by which the nobles claimed to be condemned only by the sentence of their peers, roused wide-spread resentment, and in other quarters besides Saxony. To Henry's arbitrary treatment of the archbishop and the count may be ascribed the disasters that immediately followed.

They started in an unexpected quarter. Henry had just commenced a punitive expedition against the Frisians in May, when the town of Cologne suddenly revolted. It was not left alone to face the wrath of the Emperor. Not only the Archbishop, Frederick, but also the leading nobles of Lorraine, the lower Rhine, and Westphalia joined in the insurrection. Henry failed before Cologne, and on 1 October was decisively defeated at Andernach in Westphalia. The news of his defeat gave the necessary encouragement to the disaffected nobles in East Saxony and Thuringia. This time the revolt was better organised, with Duke Lothar at the head, and all the other nobles, lay and ecclesiastical, participating. The two armies met at Welfesholze on 11 February 1115, and again Henry suffered a severe defeat. Utterly discomfited, he was forced to abandon Saxony and retire to Mayence, where he negotiated for peace; but Lothar refused his terms. And meanwhile the Saxons revived their old alliance with the Church party, which was able to take advantage of Henry's defeat to raise its head in Germany once more. First the Cardinal-bishop Cuno pronounced excommunication on Henry at Cologne and in Saxony; then the Cardinal-priest Theodoric, who had been sent as papal legate to Hungary, came by invitation to a diet at Goslar, and repeated the same sentence. In the north and north-west Henry was practically friendless. But he was not reduced to the humiliation of his father in 1073 and 1076. The southern nobles did not join in the revolt; and, though only his nephew Duke Frederick of Swabia was actively on his side, the other leading princes at any rate remained neutral. They did not make use of his weakness to acquire a share in the government.

At this moment the death of Countess Matilda of Tuscany (24 July) made it imperative for Henry to proceed to Italy to make good his claim to her inheritance. It was all the more necessary to procure peace in Germany. A diet for this purpose was summoned to meet at Mayence on 1 November. Henry waited there in vain; his enemies refused to appear, and only a few bishops obeyed the summons. Taking advantage of his weakness, the people of Mayence suddenly assailed him in force and compelled him to release their archbishop, giving securities for his good behaviour; and at Spires in December Adalbert was reconciled with the Emperor, taking an oath of fealty and giving his nephews as hostages. The hardships suffered during his three years' imprisonment had not daunted the spirit of the archbishop. Neither his oath nor the safety of his nephews deterred him from his purpose of active hostility. He went at once to Cologne, where the bishops under Archbishop Frederick, the nobles under Duke Lothar, were awaiting the arrival of the Cardinal-legate Theodoric to complete the plans of the new alliance. The legate died on the journey, and Adalbert soon dominated the proceedings. First of all he was consecrated archbishop by Bishop Otto of Bamberg; for, though he had been invested four years previously, he had not yet received consecration. Then, in conjunction with Archbishop Frederick of Cologne, he held a synod at which the ban of the Church was pronounced against the Emperor. Henry sent Bishop Erlung of Würzburg to negotiate on his behalf, but Erlung himself was won over, and on his return refrained from communion with the Emperor. In revenge Henry deprived him of the semi-ducal position held by the Bishops of Würzburg in Eastern Franconia, and conferred the judicial authority there, with the rank of duke, on his nephew Conrad, brother of Duke Frederick of Swabia[1].

In spite of the dangerous situation in Germany, Henry embarked on his second expedition to Italy in Lent 1116 and was absent for two years. In the acquisition of Matilda's allodial territories, as well as the disposition

[1] This *iudiciaria potestas* was, however, restored to the bishop in 1120. Conrad seems to have retained the ducal title.

of the fiefs she had held from the Empire, he obtained considerable advantages. He was able naturally to increase the royal domain, to acquire a new source of revenue, and also to gain adherents among the towns by generous grants of charters. His further attempt to crush papal resistance and to establish an anti-Pope was, as usual, a failure. His absence made little difference to Germany. The north was hopeless from his point of view, and the southern nobles remained quiet. The government of Germany was entrusted by him to Duke Frederick of Swabia and Godfrey, Count-Palatine of the Rhine. They performed faithfully and with no small success the task entrusted to them. The position rather improved than otherwise; the area of disturbance was at any rate diminished. The centre and mainspring of revolt was Archbishop Adalbert; his settled determination was to injure the royal power by every means at his disposal, to win over or to ruin all Henry's supporters. Without him the desire for peace might have prevailed, but he kept alive the civil war. We read of continual fighting, though always on a small scale, of sieges and counter-sieges, of attempts at negotiation that came to nothing, and of a general disregard for law and order which gave to the robber and the brigand an undreamt-of security.

At last, however, events in Italy affected the German situation and necessitated the Emperor's return. The definite revival of the schism between Empire and Papacy with the excommunication of Henry V by Pope Gelasius II in April 1118, and the activity of the Cardinal-bishop Cuno as papal legate, gave renewed vigour to the Church party in Germany. Adalbert ensured the fidelity of Mayence by an important grant of privileges, and the Bishops of Worms and Spires (the latter his own brother) now joined him. The episcopate as a whole was no longer subservient to the Emperor, whose control of elections had been considerably weakened; while Adalbert, on the other hand, by his appointment this year as papal legate, gained increased authority over it. The anti-imperialists, lay and ecclesiastical, now revived the plan of 1076 of a diet, to be held at Würzburg, to which the Emperor was to be summoned to answer the charges against him. Henry returned from Italy in August, just in time to prevent this, and his appearance in Lorraine speedily restored the balance in his favour. The situation did not permit of his acting with the masterfulness that had given so much offence before, but his diplomatic skill was able to make use of the strong desire for peace. He gave earnest of his own intentions when he opened negotiations with the new Pope, Calixtus II, in 1119; he could hardly be blamed for their failure, and he was little affected by the renewal of excommunication. In Lower Lorraine his position decidedly improved, especially when the town of Cologne declared for him and expelled its archbishop. Frederick made his way to Saxony, but even that duchy was no longer a sure refuge for the Emperor's enemies. For Henry himself was at Goslar in January 1120, able to visit his Saxon domain for the first time since his defeat in 1115;

and a number of Saxon nobles, including Duke Lothar, were with him at court. The bishops, obedient to the papal sentence, held aloof, but the lay nobles were anxious above all for peace, though a peace of their own making. Henry wisely took no steps to revenge himself for the excommunication, and, by withholding support from the anti-Pope, facilitated the re-opening of negotiations. Adalbert alone was stubborn against reconciliation, but his very obstinacy caused the German princes to take action. When in June 1121 he marched with an army from Saxony to the relief of Mayence, which was threatened by the Emperor, they intervened decisively for peace, and a diet was summoned to meet at Würzburg.

The diet met on 29 September, and an armistice was arranged which, besides re-establishing order in Germany, created the necessary conditions precedent to a settlement of the issue between Pope and Emperor. Henry was to recognise the Pope, and meanwhile king, churches, and individuals were to be in undisturbed possession of their rights and lands; bishops who had been canonically elected and consecrated were to be left in peaceful occupation of their sees, and the Bishops of Worms and Spires were to be reinstated, though the town of Worms was to remain in royal hands; prisoners and hostages were to be mutually restored. The princes then bound themselves to use their mediation between Emperor and Pope to bring about a settlement on the question of investiture which would not impair the honour of the kingdom, and on the other hand to act in concert against any attempt of the king to avenge himself on any of his enemies. The Bavarian nobles, who were not present at Würzburg, gave their assent to these conditions on 1 November. The princes had thus taken affairs into their own hands, and by their unanimity had restored peace and order to the kingdom. In this they rendered it a great service, and probably the same result could have been achieved in no other way. But it was a restoration of their control of the government, and was a measure of the weakness of the royal authority. The king had no alternative but to acquiesce; and indeed he welcomed their intervention as a means of extricating himself from the impasse in his relations with the Pope. An embassy was sent at the beginning of 1122 to Rome, where it was well received by Calixtus, and three cardinal-legates with full powers were dispatched to Germany[1]. Archbishop Adalbert alone, in spite of a letter from the Pope expressing his earnest desire for peace, did his best to prevent a reconciliation, and made what use he could of the disputed election at Würzburg which followed on the death of Bishop Erlung. But the papal legates resisted his attempts to promote discord, and by their tactful management of the difficult preliminaries were able to get general consent to the holding of a council. This was summoned by them to meet at Mayence on 8 September. The place of meeting was, however, naturally distasteful to Henry, and, as a concession to him, the Council eventually took place at Worms on 23 September 1122.

[1] Of these legates, two became Popes—Honorius II and Innocent II.

The Concordat of Worms was a treaty for peace between the two great powers, the spiritual and the temporal heads of Western Christendom. As such it gave public recognition to the position the Papacy had acquired in the course of the struggle. It gave recognition too to another fact—the distinction between the spiritual and the temporal functions of the episcopate. Over the bishops in Italy and Burgundy royal control was appreciably diminished; in Germany it was in effect retained. The king abandoned investiture with ring and staff, but he could now claim papal sanction for his control of elections, and the grant of the *regalia* was recognised as implying the performance of duties to the king—*quae ex his iure debet*—in return. On 11 November a diet was held at Bamberg, composed mainly of the princes who were not present at Worms. They unanimously ratified the Concordat, which thereby became a constitution of the kingdom. The relations of the king with the bishops and abbots of Germany were thus put on a legal basis, and the election of Udalric as Abbot of Fulda gave an immediate occasion to put the new practice into effect. Even Adalbert had been constrained to subscribe at Worms, but he immediately wrote to the Pope attempting to prejudice him against the Emperor. He was quite unsuccessful, however. He saw his old associates welcoming the Concordat at Bamberg; and finally the ratification of the Church was given at the Lateran Council in March 1123, to which the Pope, in anticipation of the greatness of the event, had issued a general summons in June of the preceding year, and which ranks as the First Ecumenical Council to be held in the West. The concord between Empire and Papacy was not to be broken again in Adalbert's lifetime.

Peace without mastery was the conclusion of Henry's struggle with the Pope. In Germany he achieved neither peace nor mastery. The course of time had produced a great change in the relation of the nobles, originally royal officials, with the king[1]. The counts had in many cases ceased to hold directly from the king, and as a result of marriages, divisions of the inheritance, and the like, their possessions often bore little relation to their titles. Above all the dukes, whose power and independence the first two Salian kings had successfully combated, had during the long civil wars and the Church schism recovered much of their old authority. In Bavaria the Welfs were creating an almost independent state: a hereditary duchy with the subordinate nobles—margraves and even the count-palatine as well as ordinary counts—in a vassal relationship to the duke. There was no hostility to Henry V who did not interfere, but Bavaria seems to hold itself aloof and to act as a separate unit; at the Diet of Würzburg in 1121 Bavaria was not represented, but gave its assent later. The Hohenstaufen were working to the same end in Swabia, but the influence of the Dukes of Zähringen prevented them from achieving complete mastery, and their participation in the govern-

[1] Cf. Giesebrecht, *op. cit.* Vol. III, pp. 960 sqq.

ment of the kingdom was more important to them than a policy of isolation. But both Duke Frederick and his brother Conrad were actively employed in increasing the Hohenstaufen domains, and in protecting their acquisitions by castles[1]. This was likely soon to conflict with the similar policy of the Emperor in the neighbouring districts, and perhaps it is for this reason that signs of friction between Henry and his nephews began to appear towards the end of his reign. No such policy was possible in Lorraine, where the division into two duchies, the weakness of the dukes, and the strength of the other nobles, lay and ecclesiastical, had destroyed all cohesion; in this region and in Franconia it was more possible for royal authority to recover ground.

But the most important centre of particularism had always been Saxony, and it became increasingly so under Duke Lothar. The son of a petty count, he had acquired the allodial territories, and the consequent prestige, of the two most powerful antagonists of Henry IV—Otto of Nordheim and Ekbert of Brunswick. He held a position greatly superior to that of his predecessors, the Billungs, and by his victory in 1115 became the acknowledged leader of the Saxons. His intention evidently was to unite Saxony under his rule and to exclude the royal authority. The Saxon nobles were by no means prepared to submit to the first part of this programme, but Lothar vigorously encountered opposition and usually with success; his activity extended to expeditions against the Wends, and by these aggressive measures he protected the north-eastern frontiers. His policy of isolation was indicated by his abstention from the Diet of Würzburg and the Concordat of Worms He departed from it to some extent in 1123 when he supported, rather half-heartedly, his step-sister Gertrude of Holland, who was allied with Bishop Godebald of Utrecht against the Emperor. But he was quite determined to resist royal interference within his duchy. On the death in 1123 of Henry, Margrave of Meissen and the East Mark and step-brother to Lothar's wife, the Emperor appointed Herman II of Winzenburg to Meissen and Wiprecht of Groitsch (a former rebel, now tamed to loyalty by imprisonment) to the East Mark. Lothar treated these appointments as being in his own gift, and gave Meissen to Conrad of Wettin and the East Mark to Albert the Bear, son of Count Otto of Ballenstadt and grandson of Duke Magnus. Henry V summoned Duke Vladislav of Bohemia to support his candidates, but Lothar successfully resisted him and made effective his claim to usurp a sovereign right. In 1124 Henry, victorious over Gertrude and Godebald, assembled a diet at Bamberg before which Lothar was summoned to appear. He did not obey the summons, but the expedition decreed against him was deferred owing to Henry's preoccupations in the west. Lothar remained defiant, and no further action was taken against him.

[1] Frederick was famous as a builder of castles; cf. Otto of Freising, *Gesta Friderici imperatoris*, Bk. i, c. 12, SGUS, p. 28.

Unsuccessful in the internal struggle, the king could not restore imperial authority in the eastern states once subject to the Empire. In the peaceful years at the beginning of his reign he had made a determined effort. In Bohemia his suzerainty was recognised, and his decision was effective in favour of Svatopluk who expelled his cousin Duke Bořivoi in 1107, and on Svatopluk's murder in 1109 in favour of Vladislav, Bořivoi's son; from both he obtained the payment of tribute. But, like his father, he had to be content with Bohemian allegiance. His intervention in Hungary (1108) and in Poland (1109) ended in hopeless failure. Immediately afterwards his attention was diverted to his Italian expedition, and he had no opportunity, even if he had the inclination, to intervene again. But, in the north-east, German influence began to spread by another agency. The great missionary work of Bishop Otto of Bamberg in Pomerania started at the end of Henry V's reign; idols and temples were overthrown, and eight churches built. This was a revival of the old method of penetration by missionaries, and though Otto's work was done by the invitation and under the protection of Duke Boleslav III of Poland, who wished to Christianise where he had conquered, it was German influence that permeated the country; the new churches were closely attached to Bamberg, and the first bishop in Pomerania was Otto's friend and helper, Adalbert. This was to be the beginning of a new wave of German penetration among the Slavs.

Henry V, indeed, had no part in this. In the last year of his life he was turning his attention to a novel foreign policy. He had come into close touch, owing to his marriage, with the English king, and he was induced by Henry I to enter into an alliance against King Louis VI of France, from which he hoped perhaps to recoup himself by conquest for his loss of authority in his own kingdom. But the expedition was unpopular in Germany; he could only collect a small force, and he was obliged to retire ignominiously before the large army which assembled to defend France from invasion. In 1125 he is said to have conceived the plan, also suggested by his father-in-law, of raising money by a general tax on the English model; it would have made him independent of the nobles, who strongly resisted the innovation[1]. The only result was to add to his unpopularity, which was increased by a severe famine and pestilence; though this was the natural result of two hard winters, the common people attributed to him the responsibility for their sufferings. It was in these circumstances that he fell ill and died in his forty-fourth year on 23 May 1125. On his death-bed he made his nephew, Duke Frederick of Swabia, his heir and named him as his successor; the royal insignia were placed in the castle of Trifels under the charge of the Empress Matilda. At Spires the last of the Salian house was given royal burial beside his three predecessors, but there were few to mourn the ruler who had been able to win the affection of none. Fear he had

[1] Otto of Freising, *Chronica*, Bk. VII, c. 16, SGUS, p. 332.

inspired, and there were soon stories current that he was not dead, and a pretender even arose in Burgundy claiming to be Henry V; no one wished him back, but there was much popular apprehension of his return.

His personality was such as to inspire fear but not affection. The one was a useful attribute in dealing with the nobles, but without the other he could not gain the support necessary to keep them in check. The middle and lower classes in the towns, and the lower classes in the country-side as well, had felt a regard for Henry IV which was not merely due to privileges obtained from him. Henry V was never able to win this regard despite his privileges, and the revolts of important towns were often a serious handicap to him. So the nobles, whom he had used to defeat his father and to defeat the Pope, had proved too strong for him in the end. Only by their renewed participation in the government was peace restored to Germany and the schism in the Church healed. And so particularism prevailed, and ducal authority rose again even in Swabia and Bavaria, but especially in Saxony, where Lothar had challenged an undoubtedly royal right by his claims to appoint his subordinates. To the end he was defiant, a rebel against royal authority. But the imperial idea was still strong, and so too was the hereditary principle. Had Henry had a son, he would doubtless have succeeded to the throne with fair chances of success. That Henry died childless was a fact of the first importance in the history of Germany, and incidentally in the history of England as well. His bitterest enemy, the Archbishop of Mayence, was still alive, and it was the Archbishop of Mayence who by prescriptive right had the first voice in the election of a king. Skilfully Adalbert used his advantage to get possession of the royal insignia and to defeat the candidature of Henry's heir, Duke Frederick of Swabia. Led by him, the princes triumphantly vindicated the claim they had vainly tried to assert at Forchheim in 1077, and deliberately rejected the next-of-kin. The election of Lothar was a step forward towards the eventual victory of the electoral over the hereditary principle.

CHAPTER IV.

(A)

THE CONQUEST OF SOUTH ITALY AND SICILY BY THE NORMANS.

When the Normans made their appearance at the beginning of the eleventh century, South Italy was divided into a large number of small states. Sicily was occupied by the Saracens, Apulia and Calabria by the Byzantines; Gaeta, Naples, and Amalfi were all three republics; Benevento, Capua, and Salerno were the capitals of three Lombard principalities, which were bounded on the north by the Papal State.

In spite of this subdivision caused by the anarchy which had prevailed throughout the south of the peninsula during the ninth and tenth centuries, Byzantine historians imply that South Italy had not changed in any particular and that the Greek Emperors still maintained their predominance. It is indeed true that the continual warfare and constant rivalries between the principal towns of South Italy often led one of the combatants to have recourse to Byzantium; appeals thus made to the sovereign authority of the Emperor no doubt contributed to the maintenance in Constantinople of the idea that the imperial sovereignty was still recognised by provinces which seem in fact to have been absolutely independent. The Byzantine possessions properly so called now consisted only of Apulia, the region of Otranto, and Calabria, and, although the Greek Empire gained much prestige by the reconquest of Italy undertaken by Basil II, yet—even in the territory under its sway—it only exercised a somewhat feeble authority and its power was by no means firmly established.

In spite of the attempt at Hellenisation made in the tenth century, Byzantium only partially succeeded in its efforts to assimilate the inhabitants of the territory taken from the Lombards. Only Calabria and the district of Otranto really succumbed to Greek influence. There was not the same result in Apulia, where Byzantium encountered a very strong and persistent Lombard influence which could neither be crushed nor undermined. It was thus that the Lombards retained the use of Latin, and obliged the Greek Emperors to allow the maintenance of Latin bishoprics in many towns, to tolerate the practice of Lombard law, and to admit native officials into the local administration. Thus the links which bound South Italy to Constantinople were very weak. Byzantium had shewn itself incapable of defending the country and giving security

The position arising from the strength of the native element and the weakness of the central power favoured the development of autonomy in the cities and led to the establishment of real communes. On the other hand, there were many burdens on the inhabitants, and the country was crushed under the weight of taxes and military levies. Thus the advantages derived by the populations under Byzantine sway from their submission to the Empire did not seem commensurate with the burdens they had to bear, and there arose a general state of discontent, which at the close of the tenth century found expression in the frequent assassination of Byzantine officials and in constant revolts; these were facilitated by the organisation of local bands—the *conterati*. It was easy for Byzantium to overcome the first isolated attempts, but her task became more difficult when there arose leaders capable of attracting malcontents, organising their forces, and directing the struggle with the Greeks in a firm resolution to attain the freedom of their country. The first great revolt was that of Melo.

Melo belonged to the Lombard aristocracy. He was a native of Bari, and exerted considerable influence not only in his birthplace but throughout Apulia. Openly hostile to the Byzantines whose yoke he wished to cast off, Melo first sought to rouse his countrymen in 1009. He was secretly supported by the Lombard Princes of Capua and Salerno. This first attempt failed, and the Lombard leader, forced into exile, probably betook himself to Germany, and besought the Emperor Henry II to intervene in the affairs of South Italy. By 1016 he was back in his own country. In that year he entered into negotiations with a band of Norman pilgrims who had come on pilgrimage to the shrine of St Michael on Monte Gargano, and begged for their help in driving out the Greeks. The Norman knights did not accept the offers made to them, but promised Melo that they would encourage their compatriots to join him.

The Norman knights of Monte Gargano may probably be identified with the pilgrims spoken of by the chronicler Aimé of Monte Cassino. According to him, at a time when Salerno was besieged by the Saracens, a band of Norman knights returning from the Holy Land disembarked there. Scarcely had they landed before they fell on the infidels and put them to flight. Amazed at the courage of these unexpected allies, Guaimar IV, Prince of Salerno, and the inhabitants of the city begged them to remain, but the Normans refused. In view of this refusal Guaimar thereupon decided to send back messengers with the pilgrims to raise a body of Norman auxiliaries in Normandy itself.

If we admit the identity of the pilgrims of Salerno with the pilgrims of Monte Gargano, which is almost inevitable, we are led to believe that the meeting of Melo and the Normans was not accidental, but that it was arranged by Guaimar IV, who had already supported the Lombard leader in his rebellion. In any case the body of auxiliaries raised in Normandy on the return of the Norman pilgrims was recruited on behalf of both Melo and Guaimar.

The Lombard envoys easily succeeded in raising a sufficiently powerful body of auxiliaries in Normandy. At this period, indeed, Normandy was pre-eminently the land of adventurers. The frequent emigrations, often referred to, were due not only to a natural tendency of the race but to the existence of a population too dense for the country, part of which was therefore obliged to expatriate itself. Moreover, as a result of the violent quarrels and constant struggles between the nobles, there was always a certain number of men who were obliged, by crime or misfortune, to leave their country. There was no lack of this element in the first band recruited for the Prince of Salerno. The leader who commanded it, Gilbert le Tonnelier (the Cooper, Buatere, Botericus), had incurred the anger of Duke Richard by an assassination. He was accompanied by four of his brothers, Rainulf, Asclettin, Osmond, and Rodolf.

On their arrival in Italy, the Normans divided into two parties, one of which joined Melo, while the other entered the service of the Prince of Salerno. Melo was awaiting the coming of his Norman auxiliaries before making a fresh attempt to drive out the Byzantines. In 1017, supported by Guaimar IV and by Pandulf (Paldolf) III, ruler of Capua, he attacked Apulia, and soon became master of all the country between the Fortore and Trani. In October 1018, however, the Byzantines destroyed the rebel army at Cannae, and the Catapan Boioannes re-established imperial authority throughout Apulia.

While the vanquished Melo sought the support of Henry II and fled to Germany, where he eventually died, the Normans who had come to Italy entered the service of various nobles. Some remained with Guaimar IV, others were engaged by Prince Pandulf of Benevento, others by Atenolf, Abbot of Monte Cassino, and the rest by the Counts of Ariano. Some of this last party entered the service of the Greeks a little later, and were established at Troia by the Catapan Boioannes.

For some years the Normans played only a secondary part in Italy, content to reap an advantage by turning to their own ends the rivalries which sowed discord between the rulers of the Lombard states. After the death of Henry II (1024), Pandulf III, Prince of Capua, who had been made prisoner by the deceased Emperor, was set free by his successor Conrad. With the help of the Greeks, Pandulf regained his dominions, and soon took advantage of the death of Guaimar IV (1027) and the succession of his son Guaimar V (still in his minority) to extend his dominions at the expense of the neighbouring principalities. Sergius IV, Duke of Naples, realising that his state was threatened by Pandulf, whom Aimé refers to as the "*fortissime lupe*" of the Abruzzi, called to his aid the Normans under Rainulf's command. He took them into his service, and conceded Aversa and its dependencies to their leader (about 1029).

This was not the first occasion on which the Normans had been granted territory since their arrival in Italy, but none of the settlements thus founded had ever developed. It was Rainulf's personality which ensured the success of the county of Aversa. He had hitherto played only a secondary part in Italian affairs, but now shewed himself to be a very shrewd and clever politician. He appears to have been the first Norman capable of rising above his immediate personal interest to further the attainment of some future political object. Devoid of scruples, guided only by interested motives, in no way hampered by feelings of gratitude, he possessed all the requisite qualities for arriving at a high political position. Throughout his career he had a marvellous capacity for always attaching himself to the stronger party. In 1034 Rainulf deserted Sergius IV to enter the service of the Prince of Capua, whom he presently forsook in 1037 to join the young Prince of Salerno, Guaimar V. The last-named soon restored the earlier ascendency of the principality of Salerno, thanks to the assistance of the Normans, and his success was crowned in 1038 on the arrival of the Emperor Conrad, who reunited the principality of Capua with Salerno.

The establishment of the Normans at Aversa was followed by a considerable influx of their compatriots, a tendency always warmly encouraged by Rainulf. The new arrivals were cordially received at his court, and very soon Aversa became the centre where all adventurers coming from Normandy could forgather; it was a kind of market where those in need of soldiers could engage them.

Among the adventurers who came thither between 1034 and 1037 were the sons of a petty Norman noble, Tancred de Hauteville, whose name was to receive enduring renown from the exploits of his descendants. Tancred, who held a fief of ten men-at-arms at Hauteville-la-Guicharde near Coutances, was not rich enough to bestow an inheritance on all his numerous children. By his first wife, Muriella, he had five sons, William, Drogo, Humphrey, Geoffrey, and Sarlo; by his second, Fressenda, he had Robert Guiscard, Mauger, William, Auvrai, Tancred, Humbert, and Roger, to say nothing of daughters. The two eldest sons, William and Drogo, realising the modest future which awaited them if they remained under the paternal roof, resolved to seek their fortunes abroad, and started for Aversa.

Not all the Normans who came to Italy entered Rainulf's service, numerous parties remaining either in the service of Salerno or in that of Byzantium. The greater number flocked to join the army which the Greek Empire, when threatened by the Sicilian Saracens, determined to dispatch under the command of George Maniaces. During this expedition (1038–1040) difficulties, either with reference to pay or to the division of booty, arose between the Greek general and his Norman and Scandinavian auxiliaries, who finally left the army. The leader of the Norman forces, a Milanese adventurer named Ardoin, joined the Catapan Michael Doceanus, while his troops dispersed, most of them returning either to Salerno or to Aversa.

Ardoin, who was almost immediately appointed *topoteretes*, or governor, of the district of Melfi, soon realised that the position of the

Greeks in Apulia was very precarious, and that there was a magnificent opportunity for bold adventurers such as those he had lately commanded. At that time, indeed, discontent was rampant in Apulia because of the levies in men and money necessitated by the war in Sicily. Profiting by the reduction of the Byzantine forces due to the Sicilian expedition, the Lombards had resumed their agitation, assassinations of Byzantine officials were becoming multiplied, and Argyrus, Melo's son, was endeavouring to rouse his compatriots; Ardoin therefore visited Rainulf, who was then regarded as leader of the Normans, and raised a force of three hundred men commanded by a dozen leaders, chief of whom were Pierron, son of Amyas, and the two sons of Tancred de Hauteville, William of the Iron Arm and Drogo, who had both become famous during the Sicilian war. Half of the land to be conquered was to be reserved for Ardoin, the other half to be given to the Normans.

With the help of the Normans, the Lombard rebels won a series of victories, the most important being that of Montemaggiore (4 May 1041). Atenolf, brother of the Prince of Benevento, was then chosen as leader by the insurgents. This choice shews clearly that the Normans were not yet masters, and proves the Lombard character of the insurrection. After the victory of Montepeloso in September 1041, Atenolf was superseded by Argyrus, Melo's son, in spite of Guaimar's efforts to be elected as leader (February 1042).

The rebellion came near to being crushed when Maniaces was appointed governor of South Italy in the spring of 1042, but, when he fell out of favour in September of the same year, the Byzantine general crossed the Adriatic to march on Constantinople. He took with him some of the Norman adventurers, who after his death entered the service of the Greek Empire. They were the nucleus of the Norman force which was formed in Byzantium, a force swelled every year by the arrival of other adventurers from Italy. Soon Normans were chosen to fill some of the highest offices at court, and a few years later one of them, Roussel de Bailleul, even aspired to mount the throne of Constantinople.

It was only after the departure of Maniaces that the Normans assumed control of the insurrection. When Argyrus deserted to the Greeks, the Normans took advantage of his treachery to choose the Prince of Salerno as leader. At the same time they divided among their own chiefs the territory at the conquest of which they aimed, and during the following years, under the command of William of the Iron Arm, they pursued the methodical subjugation of the Byzantine provinces. Henceforth the struggle with the Greeks was incessant. and every year the Norman conquest crept further south.

During this period Guaimar remained the ally of the Normans, but his authority was no longer unquestioned. At the death of Rainulf of Aversa in 1045, he was unsuccessful in imposing his candidate, and was obliged to recognise Rainulf II Trincanocte. About the same time William of the Iron Arm died, and his brother Drogo was recognised as leader of the Apulian Normans (1048).

The position of the Normans was not affected by the visit of the Emperor Henry III in 1047; but Guaimar was not so fortunate, as Capua was taken from him and restored to Pandulf III. The years which followed the coming of Henry III were the most active period of the Norman conquest. We know nothing of the details of events, but we can judge what this conquest meant to the unfortunate inhabitants of southern Italy by the adventures of Robert Guiscard, one of the sons of Tancred de Hauteville, a late arrival in Italy.

A fair giant of Herculean strength, with a ruddy complexion, broad shoulders, and flashing eyes—such is the description given by Anna Comnena of the hero who intimidated her father—Guiscard was coldly received by his brothers, and he had an uphill struggle at first, as he passed from the service of Pandulf to that of Drogo. The latter assigned to him the conquest of one of the poorest parts of the country, Calabria, where only a scanty profit could be made. Established first at Scribla in the valley of Crati, subsequently at San Marco, Guiscard led the life of a robber chief, pillaging, destroying the harvests, burning down houses and olive-groves, laying waste the tracts he could not conquer, holding up merchants to ransom, and robbing travellers. Unable to obtain food or horses save by robbery, Guiscard shrank from no violence, and nothing was sacred to him; he respected neither old age, nor women and children, and on occasion he spared neither church nor monastery. In these circumstances Robert gained the reputation of a bold and resolute leader, and his support was soon sought by Gerard, lord of Buonalbergo, who joined him and brought with him two hundred knights. From that day Robert's fortune was made, and he began to "devour" the earth.

The life led by other Norman chiefs differed in no way from that of Guiscard; we can therefore easily imagine the unhappy lot of the wretched population of South Italy while the Norman conquest was in progress. From their midst there soon arose a clamour of distress and a cry of hate against the oppressors, which reached the Pope, Leo IX. Touched by the complaints of the victims of Norman cruelty, the Pope, who blamed the conquerors above all for making no distinction between the property of God and the property of the laity, determined to intervene. His first visit to South Italy (1049) led to no result. Leo IX then begged for the support of Henry III. On his return from Germany, he received an embassy from the people of Benevento, who, to save their city, handed it over to him (1051). Being therefore more directly interested, and supported moreover by the Emperor, the Pope henceforward intervened much more actively in the affairs of southern Italy.

In these circumstances a wide-spread plot was organised to assassinate all the Normans on the same day. This attempt failed, only Drogo and some sixty of his companions being massacred (1051). Drogo's death had considerable importance, because by the position he had acquired he stood for the type of Norman who had succeeded, who maintained a degree of order in his territory and was no longer a mere brigand chief. After his disappearance there was no one with whom the Pope could negotiate. Henceforward anarchy increased, and for some time the Normans were without a leader.

Leo IX determined to have recourse to arms, and collected around him all the native nobles with the exception of Guaimar V, who refused to fight against his allies. The situation was not changed by the assassination of Guaimar (June 1052), for the Normans, led by Humphrey, established Gisulf, son of the dead prince, at Salerno, although their support cost him very dear. The following year (1053), having recruited troops even as far as Germany, Leo IX marched against the Normans, after having come to terms with Argyrus, who represented the Greek Emperor at Bari. His force was defeated at Civitate on the banks of the Fortore, and he himself was taken prisoner (23 June 1053). The conquerors knelt before their august prisoner, but did not release him until he had agreed to all their demands. We know nothing of the agreement thus signed.

The death of Leo IX (19 April 1054) was followed by a long period of unrest. Richard, Count of Aversa, nephew of Rainulf I and son of Asclettin, extended his possessions at the expense of Gisulf of Salerno, of the Duke of Gaeta, and of the Counts of Aquino. The Normans still advanced southward; they reached Otranto and Lecce; Guiscard took Gallipoli, and laid the territory of Taranto waste. In Calabria he came to terms with Cosenza, Bisignano, and Martirano. He also attacked the principality of Salerno, and his brother William, appointed by Humphrey as Count of the Principato, conquered the territory which had been granted to him at the expense of the State of Salerno. In 1057 Humphrey died, and Guiscard was called to be his successor (August 1057). He at once appropriated the heritage of his nephews, Abelard and Herman; then, resuming his victorious advance southward, he threatened Reggio. In the region of Monteleone near Bivona he established his brother Roger, who had just arrived to seek his fortune in Italy. Robert had soon to return, because the Norman nobles of Apulia refused to recognise him, and it was by force that the new count taught his rebellious vassals that they had now a master who knew how to make his authority respected.

In these early struggles Robert Guiscard was supported by his brother Roger, who likewise assisted him in a new and vain attempt to take Reggio in the winter of 1058. In the course of that year they quarrelled, and Roger made an alliance with William of the Principato. Roger settled at Scalea and in his turn led the life of a brigand chief, but it was his brother's territory which suffered most from his depredations. The year 1058 was remarkable for a great famine in Calabria. This is not surprising if we consider the systematic destruction of harvests, the usual procedure of the Normans in war. The general misery caused a revolt, and the Calabrians attempted to take advantage of the quarrel between the two brothers to avoid military service and to refuse tribute; they even came to open resistance and massacred the Norman garrison of Nicastro. Guiscard realised that if the rebellion spread he ran a great risk of losing Calabria, and determined to treat with Roger. He conceded him the half of Calabria whether in his possession or to be acquired, from Monte Intefoli and Squillace to Reggio. By this it must be understood that the two brothers shared equally in each town. At about the same time Gisulf of Salerno determined to treat with Guiscard. The latter thereupon repudiated his wife Auberea, by whom he had a son Bohemond, in order to marry Gisulf's sister Sykelgaita.

The year 1059 marks an important date in the history of the Normans in Italy—their reconciliation with the Papacy. This reconciliation was due to a somewhat curious evolution in papal policy. The continuation of the struggle with the Normans had been one of the articles of the programme which the party of reform in the Church led by Hildebrand aspired to realise. To attain this much-desired object, the successors of Leo IX—Victor II and Stephen IX, encouraged by the future Gregory VII —had recourse to external aid, the former to the German Emperor, the latter to his own brother, Duke Godfrey of Lorraine, on whom he intended to bestow the imperial crown, when his pontifical career was cut short by death. The party of the Roman aristocracy which was hostile to reform now triumphed and proclaimed Benedict X as Pope, while Hildebrand favoured the election of Nicholas II. The approval of this election by the Empress Agnes soon confirmed the legitimacy of Hildebrand's candidate, and Nicholas II shortly afterwards obtained possession of Rome. This double election deprived the party of reform of all the ground so laboriously gained. Again the Papacy had found itself between the Roman aristocracy and the Empire, and had only triumphed over the former by placing itself in dependence on the latter, and again the legitimacy of the Pope had been established by the recognition of the imperial court. If the work of reform were to be carried out, the Papacy must be rendered independent both of the Emperor and of the Roman aristocracy. The Pope now risked a very grave step: with remarkable political insight he realised the changes which were beginning to appear in the various states of the southern peninsula, and appealed to the only Italian power capable of supporting him—the Normans. To appreciate the audacity of this policy we must remember the reputation of the Normans, which was moreover richly deserved; they were regarded as freebooters and Saracens.

It seems, however, that the idea of this alliance, which was to lead to such grave results, did not occur immediately to Hildebrand. The Pope required soldiers to oppose the partisans of Benedict X, who were in the field, and, probably by the suggestion of Desiderius, Abbot of Monte Cassino, he applied first to Richard of Aversa, now ruler of Capua. The latter had already acquired a certain respectability, and had become sufficiently powerful to act as the head of a state rather than as a robber chief. He complied with the Pope's request. Nicholas II had full cause for self-congratulation in his first dealings with the Normans, who enabled him to restore order. Therefore, when in 1059 he promulgated his decree on papal elections, he sought for an ally in view of the dissatisfaction which the proposed measures were certain to excite at the imperial court, and appealed to the Normans. The interview between the Pope and the two Norman chiefs, Richard of Capua and Robert Guiscard, took place at Melfi in August. The Normans had already tried to obtain from Leo IX the recognition of the states they had established; this was now conceded by Nicholas II. The Pope received an oath of fealty from Robert Guiscard and probably also from Richard of Capua; he conferred on the latter the investiture of the principality of Capua, and on the former that of the duchy of Apulia, Calabria, and Sicily. We have no record of Richard's oath, but Guiscard in his undertook to pay an annual tribute to the Pope, and to be faithful for the future to the Pope and the Church. He promised to be the ally "of the Holy Roman Church, so that she might preserve and acquire the rights of St Peter and his dominions," to help the Pope to retain the see of Rome, and to respect the territory of St Peter. Finally, in the event of an election he bound himself to see that the new Pope was elected and ordained according to the honour due to St Peter, as he should be required by the better part of the cardinals and by the Roman clergy and laity.

By what title did the Pope bestow the investiture of territory which had never belonged to his predecessors? The terms used undoubtedly imply that Nicholas II based his action partly on Charlemagne's Donation, granting the duchy of Benevento to the Roman Church, and partly, as regarded Sicily, on the theory shortly afterwards expressed by Urban II, that all islands appertained to the domain of St Peter in virtue of the (spurious) Donation of Constantine[1].

After his recognition at Melfi as rightful Duke of Apulia, Robert Guiscard had to defend himself during the ensuing years against the other Norman chiefs, who at first refused to admit the supremacy of one of their number. The opposition encountered by the new duke caused him most serious difficulties and favoured the return of the Byzantines. In 1060 Guiscard had taken Taranto, Brindisi, and Reggio from the Greeks, and as soon as the last-named place had fallen, he and his brother Roger were irresistibly attracted to Sicily; but events in Italy detained the duke in Apulia. First, there was a revolt of the Norman

---

[1] Jaffé-Löwenfeld, *Regesta*, No. 5449.

nobles in the north of Apulia, which favoured a resumption of hostilities by the Greeks. Guiscard thereafter lost Brindisi, Oria, Taranto, and Otranto, and the Byzantines laid siege to Melfi. The duke returned from Sicily, and restored his ascendency during the early months of 1061, finally recapturing Brindisi in 1062. Two years later (1064) some Norman nobles—Geoffrey of Conversano, Robert of Montescaglioso, Abelard (Humphrey's son), Amyas of Giovenazzo, and Joscelin—entered into negotiations with a representative of the Greek Emperor at Durazzo. With the help of the Byzantines they rose in the spring of 1064. For four years it was with difficulty that Guiscard held his own. Finally, the duke's victory was assured by the successive defeats of Amyas, Joscelin, and Abelard, and the capture of Montepeloso from Geoffrey of Conversano. Robert now realised that he could only hope to complete the conquest of Sicily when he had no cause to fear a revolt of his vassals in Apulia; consequently, to be sure of their absolute obedience, he must above all deprive them of Greek assistance. The ensuing years were therefore devoted to the task of wresting from the Byzantines their remaining territory. This was more easily done because the Basileus, Romanus Diogenes, was engaged in a bitter struggle with the Turks in Asia. In 1068 Guiscard was victorious at Lecce, Gravina, and Obbiano, and in the summer of the same year he laid siege to Bari. As supplies reached this city by sea, it held out for three years; finally the Norman fleet overcame the Byzantine ships which were bringing reinforcements, and the inhabitants entered into negotiations with Guiscard and surrendered the town (April 1071). The capture of Bari marks the real fall of Byzantine power in Italy; moreover it brought Guiscard another advantage, ensuring him a fortified place of the first rank in the very heart of Apulia, which assisted him greatly in maintaining his authority over his vassals.

Relieved of anxiety regarding Apulia, Guiscard was now again free to deal with Sicily. The capture of the island from the Saracens had been the object of the Normans ever since their arrival at Reggio. Their cupidity was excited by its riches and fertility, and, moreover, the proximity of the Saracens constituted a permanent danger to their possessions. Guiscard, however, was detained during the early years of the conquest by events in Italy, and played a somewhat secondary part in the conquest of Sicily, leaving the principal part to his brother Roger.

The Norman conquest was further facilitated by the quarrels of the Muslim emirs who shared the island; 'Abdallāh ibn Ḥauqal held Mazzara and Trapani, Ibn al-Hawwās was in possession of Girgenti and Castrogiovanni, and Ibn ath-Thimnah was at Syracuse. Ibn ath-Thimnah, having been defeated by the Emir of Girgenti, called for the help of the Normans, who since 1060 had been vainly endeavouring to take Messina. At Mileto the emir came to terms with Roger, who at a renewed attempt succeeded in laying waste the region of Milazzo. The capture of Messina in the summer of 1061 provided the Normans with a base of operations, but the invaders failed to take Castrogiovanni, nor were they more successful at Girgenti, although they succeeded in establishing themselves at Troina. The death of Ibn ath-Thimnah in 1062 deprived the Normans of a valuable ally, and they had to retire on Messina. In the same year Roger was dissatisfied because Guiscard paid him in money instead of in land, and quarrelled with his brother, so that another war began between them. Only the fear of an insurrection in Calabria brought them to terms. Threatened with the prospect of a revolt, Guiscard consented to share his Calabrian territory with Roger, and the treaty then concluded established a kind of condominium of the two brothers over every town and every stronghold. The struggle with the Saracens was resumed at the end of 1062, and continued during the following year. During this first period the Normans only succeeded in establishing themselves at Messina and Troina, the rest of the island remaining in the hands of the Saracens. In 1063 the latter attacked Troina, but were overwhelmingly defeated near Cerami. In 1064 Roger and Guiscard vainly attempted to take Palermo. The following years the conquest advanced slowly towards the capital. At Misilmeri in 1068 the Normans defeated Ayyūb, son of Tamīm, the Zairid Emir of Africa, who had been summoned to help the Sicilian Saracens. Ayyūb had succeeded Ibn al-Hawwās. After his defeat Ayyūb returned to Africa, and the Saracen party became disorganised.

The struggle was interrupted by the siege of Bari, but was resumed immediately after the fall of that city. Guiscard, realising the necessity of having a naval force, had succeeded in equipping a fleet, by the help of which the Normans occupied Catania and then proceeded to blockade Palermo; on 10 January 1072 the city fell into their hands, and, as a result of this success, the Saracens of Mazzara capitulated.

The first stage in this conquest of Sicily closed with the capture of Palermo; for the next twelve years the Normans, having but weak forces at their disposal, could only advance very slowly. As they were masters of Mazzara, Messina, Catania, and Palermo, they encircled the territory of the Emirs of Syracuse and Castrogiovanni in the north, who, however, succeeded in prolonging the struggle for a considerable time.

Sicily was divided by Guiscard as follows: for himself he retained the suzerainty of the island, with Palermo, half Messina, and Val Demone, while he assigned the rest to Roger. It must be noted that the position in Sicily differed greatly from that of South Italy. In Italy the leaders of the original Norman forces were at first equal among themselves, and consequently they for long refused to recognise Guiscard's authority, which had to be forcibly imposed. In Sicily, on the contrary, the conquest was achieved by troops in the pay of Guiscard and his brother Roger; consequently, they possessed all rights over the conquered territory, and their vassals received the investiture of their fiefs from them; and both were careful not to bestow too much land on their followers, whereby they made sure that none of their vassals would be powerful enough to rival them.

After the capture of Palermo, Robert Guiscard remained some months there, consolidating his gains. In the autumn of 1072 he had to return hurriedly to Italy, where his Apulian vassals had again taken advantage of his absence to revolt. At the head of the movement were Amyas, lord of Giovenazzo, Peter of Trani, and Abelard and Herman, Humphrey's two sons; the rebels were upheld by Richard, Prince of Capua, whose power had increased to a remarkable extent since the Treaty of Melfi. He was the protector of Pope Alexander II, who had only been able to maintain himself from 1061 to 1063 by Richard's aid, and the latter had attempted to force recognition of his suzerainty over all the petty nobles whose possessions surrounded his own. He had been energetically supported by Desiderius, Abbot of Monte Cassino, who realised that only a powerful state could restore the peace so incessantly broken by wars between nobles. On the other hand, Alexander II was disturbed by the growth of the Capuan state, which adjoined the papal dominions. He actually came to an open rupture with Richard, who in 1066 revenged himself by laying waste the Papal State up to the very gates of Rome. For a while the Romans hostile to the Pope even thought of electing the Prince of Capua as Emperor. But the latter became reconciled with Alexander II when Godfrey of Lorraine took up arms; we know, however, nothing of the grounds of conciliation. Nevertheless the Pope did not forgive Richard for his aggressive policy, and he tried to excite disorders in the principality of Capua by means of another Norman, William of Montreuil. Thereby Alexander II inaugurated a new policy, to be hereafter pursued by the Papacy, which, not having reaped all the expected advantages from the Norman alliance and being unable to overcome the Normans by arms, applied itself henceforward to reducing them to impotence by inciting one leader against another.

Such, therefore, was the position in the autumn of 1072 when Guiscard returned to Italy. The duke very soon brought his vassals back to obedience, but hardly had he dealt with them when he found himself in difficulties with Gregory VII, the successor of Alexander II. The new Pope, who had inspired the Norman policy adopted by his predecessors, saw with irritation that the Papacy had not derived those benefits from the Norman alliance which had been hoped for, and that as a whole it was Richard and Robert who had reaped advantage from the Treaty of Melfi. Moreover, Gregory VII was particularly annoyed to see the Normans beginning to extend towards the north in the region of the Abruzzi, near Amiterno and Fermo, where several chiefs had established themselves—notably, Robert, Count of Loritello.

After the first interviews which he had with Robert Guiscard at

Benevento (August 1073), Gregory VII, who displayed his usual stubbornness in the negotiations, came to an open breach with the Duke of Apulia. It was probably on the question of the conquest of the Abruzzi that the conference was wrecked. Having broken with Guiscard, Gregory VII turned to the Prince of Capua, who accepted the proposed alliance. Henceforward for some years war was resumed with great energy throughout southern Italy. Guiscard fought in Calabria against his nephew Abelard, in the neighbourhood of Capua with Richard, and meanwhile succeeded in establishing himself at Amalfi (1073).

As a result of these violent conflicts, the anarchy prevailing throughout South Italy reached such a height that the destruction of the Normans became the first condition necessary for the realisation of all the plans which Gregory VII had formed for the succour of the Greek Empire, now threatened by the Muslims. In March 1074 Guiscard and his partisans were excommunicated, and the Duke of Apulia must have feared at the time of the expedition in June of that year that the Pope would succeed in his plans, but the quarrels which arose between the Pope's allies caused the enterprise to fail dismally. Cencius, the leader of the Roman aristocracy and of the party hostile to the Pope, now offered to make Guiscard Emperor if he would help them to expel Gregory VII. The Duke of Apulia was too well aware how little he could count on the Roman nobles, who were incapable of upholding their candidates, and he did not accept their proposition.

After the agreement between the principality of Capua and the Pope, the hostilities between Robert and Richard continued until 1075, when Guiscard was invited by Henry IV to abandon the papal for a royal alliance. He refused. This circumstance decided the two Normans to combine against the common enemy, and their reconciliation was the prelude to a general coalition between the Normans. Desiderius, Abbot of Monte Cassino, who brought all his influence to the cause of peace, tried to arrange a treaty between Gregory VII and Guiscard, but failed, because the Pope, in spite of the critical position in which he was placed by the breach with the king, refused all the concessions which the Duke of Apulia, taking advantage of the papal necessities, impudently demanded.

Without any further consideration for the Pope, Robert and Richard took up arms and together besieged Salerno and Naples. They also combined their forces to make some successful expeditions into papal territory. At the very moment when Gregory VII was triumphing over Henry IV and obliging him to come to Canossa, Gisulf, Prince of Salerno, the only ally remaining to the Pope in South Italy, was deprived of his states by Guiscard (1077), and in December of the same year the bold Duke of Apulia laid siege to Benevento. This attack directed against a papal possession must have exasperated Gregory VII, who was already indignant with Robert, to whom fortune had never been kinder than since the day he was excommunicated. At the Council of Rome in March 1078 the Pope pronounced the excommunication of "those Normans who attack the territory of St Peter, *i.e.* the March of Fermo and the duchy of Spoleto, those who besiege Benevento and dare to lay waste the Campagna, the Marittima, and Sabina." The Pope forbade any bishop or priest to allow the Normans to attend the divine offices.

The excommunication pronounced by Gregory VII brought discord between the Normans. When Jordan, son of Richard of Capua, found that his father was seriously ill (Richard died on 5 April 1078), he feared lest the Pope should raise obstacles to his succession, and went to make his submission at Rome; as soon as his father died, he forced Guiscard to raise the siege of Benevento; shortly afterwards the new Prince of Capua played an important part in the preparation of the rebellion which, towards the end of 1078, again set the duke and his Apulian vassals at odds.

On the occasion of the marriage of one of his daughters, Guiscard for the first time demanded from his vassals the levy due to the lord when his daughters married. No one dared resist openly, but the duke's demand excited great discontent. Probably inspired by Gregory VII, who visited Capua in 1078, Jordan called Geoffrey of Conversano, Robert of Montescaglioso, Henry, Count of Monte Sant' Angelo, and Peter, Count of Taranto, to join him. The insurrection at once spread not only to Apulia but to Calabria and Lucania; Bari, Trani, Bisceglie, Corato, and Andria all revolted, and sent their troops to swell the ranks of the insurgents (1079).

After Calabria had been pacified, Guiscard repaired to Apulia with considerable forces and soon dispersed the rebels; he then at once marched against Jordan. The Abbot of Monte Cassino succeeded in inducing the two princes to make peace. Then returning to Apulia, Guiscard recaptured the rebel towns one by one. Several of the revolting nobles fled to Greece to escape the punishment due to them; amongst these was Abelard, the duke's nephew. After the suppression of the revolt (1080), Guiscard was more powerful than ever, at the very moment that Gregory VII finally excommunicated and deposed Henry and recognised his rival, Rudolf, as King of Germany. As Gregory VII feared that Guiscard might form an alliance with Henry, he determined himself to treat with the Duke of Apulia. The negotiations were conducted by Abbot Desiderius, and ended in the compromise of Ceprano, where on 29 June Guiscard took an oath of fealty to the Pope. He swore to be the Pope's man, with a reservation as to the March of Fermo, Salerno, and Amalfi. Gregory VII recognised the conquests of the Count of Loritello, on condition that for the future the territory of St Peter should be respected. The duke moreover promised that he would help the Pope to defend the Papacy. On the whole, at Ceprano Gregory VII had to yield all along the line; he preserved appearances by reserving the most vexed questions, but in reality on 29 June 1080 it was the Norman who triumphed over the Pope and obliged him to recognise his achievements.

After the meeting at Ceprano, Guiscard's insatiable ambition was far from being satisfied, and, master of South Italy, he now attempted to realise his long-cherished project of mounting the throne of Constantinople. On the one hand the Duke of Apulia wished to punish the Greek Emperor for the support given to the rebel Normans, whose headquarters were now in the Byzantine territory in Illyria, and on the other hand, consciously or unconsciously, the Norman had succumbed to the attraction which Byzantium and the Byzantine world exercised over all the West. Already in Italy Guiscard had come to be looked on as the legitimate successor of the Emperors, whose costume he affected, going so far as to copy their seal. Moreover, how was it possible for Guiscard to imagine that the conquest of Byzantium could offer any difficulties to him, the mighty Duke of Apulia, when quite recently two poor Norman knights, Robert Crispin and Roussel de Bailleul (of whom the former had served under the orders of Richard of Capua and the latter with Robert himself), had almost succeeded in mounting the throne of Constantinople? Guiscard had long felt attracted to Constantinople; and for their part the Emperors could not ignore their powerful neighbour, and sought his alliance. About 1075 the negotiations which had been entered on ended in the betrothal of one of Guiscard's daughters to the son of Michael VII. This projected marriage served as a pretext for a declaration of war by Guiscard, when in 1080 he determined to profit by the disturbances which had broken out in the Greek Empire, and to attempt to seize Constantinople. At the accession of Nicephorus Botaniates, Guiscard's daughter had been relegated to a convent; under the pretext of defending his daughter's rights, the Duke of Apulia became the champion of the dethroned Emperor. As his plans aroused only moderate enthusiasm among his vassals, the Duke of Apulia determined to carry out a fraud, and in the middle of 1080 he presented a Greek named Rector as the real Michael VII escaped from a monastery, where he had been imprisoned by Botaniates. By this means the wily Norman hoped to inflame his vassals and conciliate the Greek population.

Gregory VII fell in with the views of Guiscard, who persuaded him that the proposed expedition would realise the projected crusade which had been near the Pope's heart for some years, and would end the schism and bring about reunion with the Greek Church. In July 1080 the Pope wrote to the bishops of Apulia and Calabria, exhorting them to favour the duke's plans. In 1081, at the end of May, Guiscard took the field and landed at Avlona. His son Bohemond had already taken Avlona, Canina, and Hiericho. Soon Corfù fell into the hands of the Normans, who next laid siege to Durazzo. Although they were defeated at sea by the Venetians, whom Alexius Comnenus had summoned to his aid, the

Normans nevertheless continued the siege of the Illyrian capital. On 18 October they defeated the army which the Emperor had brought to relieve the besieged city, and on 21 February 1082 Durazzo was taken.

In the spring of 1082 Guiscard was obliged to return. Gregory VII had sent him urgent appeals for help, threatened as he was by Henry IV's expedition to Italy. On the other hand, Alexius Comnenus was subsidising the German king, and at the same time, by means of Abelard and Herman, Robert's nephews, had succeeded in exciting an insurrection in Apulia. Leaving Bohemond to continue the war against the Emperor, Guiscard returned to Italy, and spent some time in re-establishing his authority in Apulia (1082 and 1083). In May 1084 he marched on Rome which was occupied by the German Emperor; Henry did not await the coming of the Normans, but his retreat did not prevent Guiscard from entering the city in force; he sacked it and freed Gregory VII, whom the partisans of the anti-Pope, Clement III, were besieging. As soon as the Pope was free, Guiscard placed him in Salerno for safety, and immediately returned to the conquest of Constantinople.

After his father's departure, Bohemond had again defeated the Greeks at Joannina and Arta; he had then occupied Ochrida, Veria, Servia, Vodena, Moglena, Pelagonia, Tzibikon, and Trikala, but in 1083 he was defeated outside Larissa by Alexius Comnenus, and was shortly afterwards obliged to return to Italy, as his troops were clamouring for pay. After this the Byzantines regained the advantage, and the Normans lost all the places they had occupied, including Durazzo.

When Guiscard took the field in the autumn of 1084, he had consequently no foothold on the other side of the Adriatic. While his son Roger occupied Avlona, the duke proceeded to Butrinto, whence in November he arrived at Corfù. Although twice defeated near Cassiope by the Venetian fleet, Guiscard soon took his revenge when he won an overwhelming victory near Corfù, which fell into his hands as a result of this success. The duke sent his army into winter quarters on the banks of the Glycys, while he went to Bundicia; during the winter an epidemic ravaged the Norman army, but hostilities were resumed at the beginning of the summer, and Roger sallied forth to attack Cephalonia. On the way to join his son, Guiscard fell ill; he was obliged to halt at the promontory of Ather, where he died on 17 July 1085 in the presence of his wife Sykelgaita and his son Roger.

With Guiscard closed what may be called the heroic era of the history of the Normans in Italy. Robert's immediate successors, being unable to maintain their authority, abandoned his plans, which were only resumed on the day when the Counts of Sicily became kings and consolidated the work of conquest.

The reign of Guiscard's son, Roger Borsa (1085–1111), was a period of absolute decadence in the duchy of Apulia; the prince was too weak to make his authority respected, and he was bitterly opposed by his brother

Bohemond, of whom he was relieved by the First Crusade, and also by most of his vassals, who shook off the yoke imposed by Guiscard. In 1086, however, it was again the Duke of Apulia who, assisted by the Prince of Capua, restored Rome to the successor of Gregory VII. A few years later, during the pontificate of Urban II (1088–1099), it was no longer Roger who protected the Pope but the Pope who extended his protection to the duchy of Apulia, and exerted himself to re-establish order in the sorely troubled land. The only political success achieved by Duke Roger was the recognition of his suzerainty by Richard, son of Jordan of Capua, who sought his aid to enter into possession of his paternal inheritance (1098). Then for the first time, in theory at least, the authority of the Duke of Apulia extended throughout the Norman possessions.

In the midst of all the difficulties surrounding him, the Duke of Apulia found a supporter in his uncle Roger I, Count of Sicily. During the years which followed the fall of Palermo, Guiscard's brother played only a secondary part in Italian affairs, for he was detained by the conquest of Sicily, a long and troublesome undertaking. Twenty years elapsed after his establishment in Palermo before the Normans succeeded in totally expelling the Saracens. Syracuse was not taken until 1085, Noto and Butera, the two last places retained by the Saracens, not until 1088 and 1091. Although the Saracens were still powerful in 1072, this mere fact is not enough to explain the slow progress of the conquest, and we must attribute the delays of the Normans to other causes. During all this time, and especially at first, Roger was left with only his own troops; generally he had but a few hundred knights under his command, so that it was with greatly reduced forces that he had to carry on the struggle. It was because of this that the Count of Sicily was obliged to avoid great undertakings and confine himself to guerilla warfare, which was the only method which his weak forces permitted.

Gradually, as the conquest proceeded, the count felt that the strength of his infant state was increasing, and the time came during his nephew's reign when he represented the only power in the midst of general anarchy. Called to arbitrate between the parties, Roger of Sicily was quick to realise how to profit by the situation. In return for his services, he successively extorted from the Duke of Apulia the abandonment of the strongholds in Calabria which they had hitherto held in common, as well as the half of the city of Palermo. Roger also obtained a promise of half of Amalfi and, when Richard of Capua sought his aid, he demanded that all rights on Naples should be abandoned to him.

Supported by a powerful military force, a considerable part of which consisted of Saracens, Roger of Sicily thus became one of the leading personages of Europe, and his alliance was sought by Count Raymond IV of Saint Gilles, Philip I of France, Conrad, son of Henry IV, and Koloman, King of Hungary, all of whom aspired to marry his daughters.

The position of protector of the Holy See, which the Duke of Apulia was powerless to retain, was offered to the Count of Sicily by Urban II, who, in 1098, had to concede the privilege of the Apostolic Legateship, whereby for the future papal intervention in Roger's states was to be exercised only through the count himself. When Guiscard's brother died on 22 June 1101, he left his successor a state possessed of cohesion, wherein the authority of the overlord was everywhere recognised. The last survivor of the heroic age of conquest disappeared with him; his successor was rather a politician than a soldier, and, although Roger II succeeded in establishing his supremacy over all the Norman provinces in Italy, it was to a great extent because his father had established his Sicilian state on so solid a foundation.

(B)

THE NORMAN KINGDOM OF SICILY.

In 1103, after the death of young Count Simon, who had succeeded Roger I in 1101, the county of Sicily passed to his brother, Roger II. The new count remained under the guardianship of his mother Adelaide until 1112, and very little is known about his early years. According to some authorities Robert of Burgundy was Adelaide's favourite, but he became so powerful that the countess-regent grew uneasy and caused him to be poisoned; unfortunately all our information on this point lacks precision. Towards the close of her regency, Adelaide was sought in marriage by King Baldwin of Jerusalem, who wished to repair his fortunes by a wealthy marriage. Before leaving for the Holy Land, Roger I's widow stipulated that if her union with the King of Jerusalem were childless, the crown of Jerusalem should revert to the Count of Sicily. This agreement remained a dead letter, for the deserted and betrayed queen died miserably in Sicily, but it is of interest as revealing the dreams of future greatness cherished even at the beginning of his reign by the youthful Roger II.

Boundless ambition was, in fact, the ruling characteristic of the founder of the Norman monarchy; Roger II was bold and adventurous and always intent on extending his dominions, while his thirst for conquest was insatiable. Even at the beginning of his reign he conceived the daring plan of concentrating all the commerce of the Mediterranean in his states by obtaining command of the two most important maritime routes. By his possession of Messina he already controlled one, and he sought to attain the other by the conquest of the Tunisian coast. The first Norman attempts to establish themselves in Africa were unsuccessful (1118–1127), and Roger II was obliged to seek for allies. At the very moment when he had signed agreements with Raymond-Berengar III, Count of Barcelona, and with the city of Savona, the death of his cousin William I, Duke of Apulia, induced him to postpone for a time his plans for an African war, because, before he undertook distant conquests, the Count of Sicily wished to unite in his own hands all the Norman states of South Italy.

Duke William's reign (1111–1127) had been even more disastrous than that of his father Roger Borsa. Incapable even of preserving the inheritance, already sadly diminished, which he had received, he died leaving South Italy almost in the same state as it was before Guiscard's reign. The title of duke was an empty word, for the duchy of Apulia now existed only in name; it had in fact been dismembered and consisted of a number of independent seigniories.

As Duke William had died childless, the most direct heir was Bohemond, son of Bohemond I, then at Antioch. The Count of Sicily was a degree further off in relationship to the deceased duke. As soon as he heard of his cousin's death, Roger II determined to seize the inheritance so as to present an accomplished fact to this possible rival. The rapidity with which he appeared outside Salerno and induced the inhabitants to treat with him disconcerted his opponents. The intervention of Pope Honorius II, who feared above all things that the Count of Sicily might succeed William, came too late, and he had to resign himself to the fact that the union of the duchy of Apulia with the county of Sicily disturbed the balance of power which the Papacy, in its own interests, had endeavoured to maintain between the various Norman states. Although he had sided with the Normans who refused to recognise Roger II, Honorius II was, in 1128, obliged to invest the Count of Sicily with the duchy of Apulia. In the following year the new duke finally crushed the chief rebels and obliged the ducal towns to ask for terms, while the Prince of Capua himself recognised Roger II as his suzerain. In order to secure the submission of the rebels, the duke displayed great leniency and granted important privileges to the towns. In particular, several of these obtained the right of themselves defending their walls and citadels. As soon as his authority was established, Roger revoked a concession which rendered his authority absolutely precarious.

The new duke's conception of his authority differed entirely from that of his two predecessors. In September 1129 he expounded it to his vassals assembled at Melfi. After they had taken the oath of fealty to his sons, Roger and Tancred, he instructed them in the rules of government which he insisted all should observe; he forbade private feuds, imposed on the nobles the obligation of handing over criminals to the ducal courts of justice, and ordered that the property and persons not only of ecclesiastics, but also of pilgrims, travellers, and merchants, should be respected. It was not easy to impose such habits of discipline on, nor to ensure respect for ducal authority from, the Norman feudatories,

CH. IV.

who had hardly submitted to Guiscard's iron rule. It took Roger nearly ten years to make his vassals obey his wishes.

In 1130 for the first time all the principalities founded by the Normans in Italy were united in a single hand. Roger II considered that the title of duke was therefore inadequate, and decided to make his state into a kingdom. To attain this object, he made very skilful use of the schism which followed the double election of Anacletus II and Innocent II in February 1130. He promised to support the former, and received in return "the crown of the kingdom of Sicily, of Calabria, and Apulia, the principality of Capua, the honour of Naples, and the protectorate of the men of Benevento" (27 September 1130). As soon as the Pope's consent was obtained, Roger II held an assembly near Salerno, where he caused his vassals to entreat him to take the title of King. Then on Christmas Day 1130, in the cathedral of Palermo, his coronation closed the first chapter in the history of the descendants of Tancred of Hauteville, whose grandson thus became King of Sicily.

"Whosoever maketh himself king in Sicily speaketh against Caesar." These words, addressed by St Bernard to the Emperor Lothar, were true not only as applied to the Germanic Empire but also to the Greek Empire. Neither of the two Empires had ever regarded as legitimate the Norman occupation of territories over which both claimed rights. Therefore, alike in Germany and in Byzantium, the establishment of the Norman kingdom was regarded as a flagrant insult. United by an equal hatred of the common enemy, the two Empires sought by means of an alliance to crush their adversary. Both Roger II and his successor had to employ almost all their energy, either in fighting the two Emperors singly or in preventing the Germano-Byzantine alliance from producing its full effect.

During the whole course of its existence the kingdom of Sicily had to struggle with a third enemy. Never did the Papacy submit to the establishment of a powerful state in South Italy, even when its recognition was inevitable. As soon as the Papacy was on good terms with the Germanic Emperor, it incited him to destroy the Norman state, and if, on the contrary, its relations with the Empire became less cordial, the Popes gladly fell back on the support of the Norman sovereign. This explains the alternations of policy pursued by the Papacy throughout the twelfth century as regards Roger II and his successors.

The organisation which Roger II insisted on establishing in his states, and the manner in which he demanded respect for his authority from his vassals, excited general discontent, which in 1131 caused a revolt led by Tancred of Conversano and Grimoald of Bari. Although the king met with some successes, the insurrection spread, Rainulf, Count of Alife, and Robert, Prince of Capua, joining the movement at the instigation of Pope Innocent II; and Roger was severely defeated on the banks of the Sabbato (1132). The coming of the Emperor Lothar to

Rome, where he established Innocent II, was certainly connected with the revolt of Roger's vassals. They were seriously disappointed when they realised that the Emperor did not intend to invade South Italy. During the summer of 1133 Roger resumed the struggle, and succeeded in restoring order in Apulia; when he returned to Sicily the rebel party was disorganised. The conflict was continued only by the Duke of Naples, the Prince of Capua, and the Count of Alife, who wished to secure the assistance of the Pisans. The year 1134 witnessed further progress by the king, who succeeded in crushing the rebels, but all the effect of the success attained was destroyed by a false rumour of Roger's death, which caused a general revolt in the winter of 1135. The king had again to fight the rebels, and had not quite subdued them when in 1136 the Emperor Lothar at length invaded his dominions in response to the appeal of Innocent II. At the approach of the Germans the whole country rose in arms against the king. Lothar encountered hardly any resistance; his two most notable successes were the taking of Bari and Salerno. The Emperor, however, did not seek to push his advantage any further, for most of his vassals begged him to return north. He was obliged to consent, but before his departure he invested Count Rainulf of Alife with the duchy of Apulia. It took the King of Sicily three years to destroy the organisation established by the Germanic Emperor. His task was facilitated by Rainulf's death on 30 April 1139, as well as by the failure of Innocent II.

When the schism was ended by the abdication of Victor IV, successor of Anacletus II, Pope Innocent II vindictively pursued all the partisans of the anti-Pope. Amongst these Roger II was not overlooked, as it was by his help that Anacletus had been enabled to maintain himself in Rome. In the spring of 1139 the King of Sicily was excommunicated, and in the early summer the Pope, at the head of all the forces he could muster, set out for the south to restore the condition of affairs established by Lothar. It was an unlucky venture; on 22 July on the banks of the Garigliano, near Galluccio, he was defeated and taken prisoner by Duke Roger, the king's son, who also seized the pontifical treasure. Like Leo IX in bygone days, Innocent II beheld the Norman leader kneeling for his blessing, but to obtain his liberty he had to grant to Roger II the investiture of his states as bestowed by Anacletus II. This royal success led to the collapse of the rebellion; the king shewed himself relentless in repression so as to discourage future revolts; to escape punishment many of his vassals fled to Germany and Byzantium, among them Robert of Capua. The rebel cities forfeited most of their privileges.

Concord between the king and the Pope was not of long duration; and in 1140 a fresh rupture was caused by the conquests of the king's sons in the Abruzzi. To bring Roger to terms, Innocent II utilised the question of episcopal elections, which had not been settled in 1139.

The King of Sicily, in virtue of the Apostolic Legateship, which he claimed to exercise throughout his states, demanded the right of interference in episcopal elections. Innocent II denied him this privilege, and refused canonical investiture to the bishops of the kingdom of Sicily.

There was no change in the position under Celestine II (1143–1144). It was otherwise with Pope Lucius II, who, requiring the support of the Normans to secure Rome, concluded a seven years' truce with Roger II in October 1144. The same consideration influenced the conduct of Eugenius III, who succeeded Lucius. On his return to Italy in 1148, he concluded a four years' truce with Roger II; the Pope confirmed the privilege of the Apostolic Legateship, but seems to have reserved the question of episcopal elections. In return Roger II supplied the Pope with men and money; thanks to this, the Pope succeeded in entering Rome. The King of Sicily had hoped that, in exchange for the services rendered, the Pope would come to a final agreement; on the contrary, Eugenius III, counting on the approaching descent into Italy of King Conrad III to settle the question of the Norman kingdom, refused to renew the investiture of Roger with his states. By 1151 the breach was complete, and it was without the Pope's consent that Roger II had his son William crowned at Palermo on 8 April. Henceforth Eugenius III definitely sought an alliance with the King of the Romans.

As soon as he had destroyed the organisation established in South Italy by Lothar, Roger II, realising clearly that the Germanic Empire would not submit meekly to such a check, and anxious to prevent a repetition of such an intervention, sought to create every possible difficulty for Conrad III, Lothar's successor. It was for this reason that he supplied Welf, brother of Henry the Proud, with subsidies, and thus succeeded in prolonging the revolt of the German nobles against their new king. By this means he contrived to keep the King of the Romans busy in his own dominions, and prevented him from lending a favourable ear to the appeals for intervention in Italy which were addressed to him by all the Norman nobles who had taken refuge at his court.

Above all Roger II feared lest the King of the Romans and the Greek Emperor, united by their common hatred of the kingdom of Sicily, should enter into an alliance against him. John Comnenus had already approached Lothar on this subject, and the negotiations were resumed with Conrad in 1140. To prevent this alliance, Roger sent an embassy to Constantinople to solicit the hand of a Byzantine princess for one of his sons. This embassy coincided with the death of John Comnenus (3 April 1143). The negotiations were continued by Manuel Comnenus, but ended in a breach, and the Basileus about 1144 reverted to the German alliance.

At the very moment when the alliance between the two Empires was about to be concluded, the preaching of the Second Crusade averted the danger. After vainly attempting to turn the Crusade to his own advantage, Roger resolved to profit by the embarrassment caused to Manuel Comnenus by the presence of the crusaders, and to invade the Greek Empire. While the crusaders were still outside Constantinople, the Normans took possession of Corfù, occupied Neapolis, laid the island of Euboea waste, and, on the homeward journey, penetrated into the Gulf of Corinth, pillaging and destroying Thebes (end of 1147 and beginning of 1148). The Byzantines did not recover Corfù until 1149.

On his way home from the Crusade, Conrad met Manuel Comnenus, and the two monarchs agreed to attack the King of Sicily in the course of 1149. In preventing the execution of this plan Roger shewed extraordinary activity. He again supplied Welf with money, and induced him to organise another league against King Conrad; at the same time he started the idea of a league to include all the states of western Europe, intended in the first instance to punish the Greek Emperor, to whom the failure of the Crusade was ascribed, and subsequently to succour the Christian communities of the Levant. Roger succeeded in converting to his views not only King Louis VII of France and his minister Suger, but also St Bernard, who at that time exercised great influence on European opinion. The projected alliance failed to come into being because of the opposition of King Conrad, but fortune again favoured the King of Sicily, for at the very moment when, by agreement with Manuel Comnenus, Conrad was about to invade Italy, he died (February 1152), whereby the Norman kingdom escaped the danger of a coalition between the two Empires.

In spite of the failure of his early expeditions, Roger II never abandoned his intention of attacking the coast of North Africa, and his attempts to get a foothold there constitute one of the most curious features of his reign. Almost all his expeditions were led by the Grand Emir (Admiral), George of Antioch, who with his father had been in the service of Tamīm, the Zairid prince of Mahdīyah. He next entered the service of the King of Sicily, where, by his knowledge of Arabic and his familiarity with the Muslim world and the African coast, he was an invaluable auxiliary to Roger II. Taking advantage of the internal quarrels which continually broke out between the chiefs of the petty Muslim principalities of Africa, Roger first took under his protectorate Ḥasan, prince of Mahdīyah (1134), and then occupied the island of Gerba, at the foot of the gulf of Gabes. In 1143 he took Djidjelli, near Bugia; and in 1145 Bresk, which lies between Cherchell and Tinnīs, was pillaged, as also the island of Kerkinna. In 1146 Tripoli fell into the hands of the Normans. Until then Roger II does not seem to have contemplated establishing himself in Africa; he was content to dispatch his naval forces each summer on a privateering expedition, to loot and burn the towns which they surprised. After the capture of Tripoli, he established his power in Africa on a regular basis. A garrison was placed in each captured town, but the native population was governed by a Wālī and judged by a Cadi, chosen from among the Muslims.

The fall of Tripoli had a great effect in Africa, and was quickly followed by that of Gabes, Mahdīyah, and Sūs (1148). The progress of conquest was not arrested by the death of George of Antioch, and in 1153 the Normans occupied Bona. At this moment the Norman dominion in Africa reached its greatest extent; the authority of Roger II stretched from Tripoli to Tunis, and in the interior from the desert of Bakka to Qairawān. Roger appears to have proportioned his aims to the forces at his disposal, and to have been content to occupy the most important commercial centres without attempting to advance far inland. For some years the King of Sicily was actually master of the communications between the two basins of the Mediterranean. Unfortunately his work did not endure. The results obtained by allowing the natives to enjoy religious, judicial, and administrative liberty were lost when the conquerors wished to interfere in religious questions, and tried to make the people of Tripoli abandon the party of the Almohades. Under the influence of religious prejudice, an insurrection broke out which destroyed in one day the work of the Norman conquest. This mistake, however, was not made by Roger II, who died at Palermo in the height of his glory on 26 February 1154.

When the founder of the Norman monarchy died, the political horizon of the kingdom of Sicily was heavy with ominous thunder-clouds. None of the vital questions affecting the welfare of the new kingdom had received any solution. Even the genius of Roger II had been unable to find any means of settling the problems which had arisen; he had only succeeded in postponing the moment of settlement. Internally the calm which had reigned since the last revolt of the aristocracy and the cities was more apparent than real. The exiled Norman nobles had not given up hopes of regaining possession of their confiscated property and were in communication with their partisans. The inhabitants of the cities, kept in subjection by the royal garrisons which occupied the citadels, still deplored their lost liberties; fear had indeed compelled all heads to bow before the king, but regret for the past was deeply enshrined in all hearts. The aristocracy, systematically excluded from any share in public affairs by Roger II, looked on jealously while the king governed with the help of men derived from the inferior classes of the country, for whom were reserved the highest offices at court. Here also submission was only apparent, and the nobles impatiently awaited an opportunity of claiming both their former independence and a share in the government.

Abroad the Papacy remained hostile to the kingdom of Sicily; in 1153 Eugenius III and the new King of the Romans, Frederick of Swabia, had concluded an agreement entirely to the detriment of the Norman kingdom (Treaty of Constance). As the Greek Empire also remained hostile, there was no change in the situation, and an alliance between the two Empires against the Normans was always a possibility to be feared.

Roger II was succeeded by William I, last survivor of the sons born of his wife Elvira, daughter of Alfonso VI of Castile[1]. William I has for long had a very bad reputation among historians, and by universal consent the epithet of the Bad was attached to his name. Only in recent years has it been discovered that this reputation was scarcely deserved, and a more critical study of documents has revealed the fact that Roger's son has been the victim of the pamphleteer Hugo Falcandus, a passionate opponent of the policy followed by the new king. William was pre-eminently the inheritor of his father's political work; he made no innovations, and only followed the course which Roger had traced out. Brought up to distrust the nobles, he continued to deprive them of power, and surrounded himself with his father's old servants, to whom he gave his confidence. Less energetic than Roger II, he devolved the exercise of power upon his ministers, and was content to live in his palace surrounded by his harem like an oriental sovereign. Only some very urgent necessity for his personal intervention could induce him to emerge, but when once he overcame his natural indolence the king displayed an incredible energy in executing the measures on which he had decided. During all the early part of the reign power was exercised by the Emir of Emirs (Admiral), Maio of Bari, son of a judge of Bari; he also had passed his whole life in the law-courts, and his high place in the king's favour excited the hatred of all the nobles.

In the very year of William I's accession, Frederick Barbarossa determined to descend into Italy. In order to avert the danger of an alliance between the two Emperors, the King of Sicily offered to make peace with Manuel Comnenus; he would even have consented to restore all the booty taken at the sack of Thebes. Manuel refused the offers made to him, but on the other hand the Norman king succeeded in making peace with Venice, whereby in case of war Byzantium was deprived of the support of the Venetian fleet.

The negotiations which had been entered upon between Manuel and Frederick Barbarossa proved abortive, very likely because the latter refused to admit the claims of the Basileus to South Italy. When Manuel learned of the arrival of the King of the Romans in Italy, he feared lest Barbarossa's enterprise undertaken without him was aimed against him. He therefore sent Michael Palaeologus to Italy with orders to approach Frederick anew, and if he failed to take some action on his own account. As the negotiations with Barbarossa were inconclusive, Palaeologus established himself at Ancona, and entered into relations with William I's

---

[1] Roger was married a second time to Sibylla, daughter of Hugh of Burgundy, and a third time to Beatrice, daughter of the Count of Rethel, who gave birth to a posthumous daughter, Constance.

cousin, Robert, Count of Loritello, who had just revolted. Assisted by the exiled Norman nobles who flocked back in large numbers, and also by those who had adhered to the Count of Loritello, the Byzantines invaded William's states and were extraordinarily successful. At first under the command of Palaeologus, and after his death under John Ducas, the Greeks occupied most of the large towns, Bari, Trani, Giovenazzo, and Molfetta, and advanced to Taranto and Brindisi. Meanwhile Palaeologus came to terms with Pope Hadrian IV. The latter had experienced grave disappointment when Barbarossa retired directly after his imperial coronation, for he had always expected that the German Emperor would settle the question of the Norman kingdom Manuel Comnenus made very skilful use of the situation, and wished to play the part of protector of the Papacy which Barbarossa had relinquished. His designs very shortly became apparent, when he demanded that the Pope should restore the unity of the Empire in his person. The first offers of the Basileus were accepted, and it was by means of Greek subsidies that Hadrian IV paid the troops with which he invaded the Norman kingdom. This intervention resulted in the restoration of Robert, Prince of Capua, to his dominions (October 1155).

The progress of the Byzantine and papal troops was greatly facilitated by the serious illness of William I (September–December 1155) and by the revolt of some Sicilian vassals. The royal army assembled by the Chancellor, Asclettin, to resist the German invasion, was disorganised by the revolt of the Italian vassals; and it could not be reinforced, because the rebellion of the Sicilian vassals prevented the withdrawal of troops from the island.

It was only at the end of the winter of 1156 that William repaired to Butera to besiege Geoffrey, Count of Montescaglioso, the leader of the rebels who demanded the dismissal of Maio. As soon as this insurrection was crushed, William I prepared to attack Italy. He tried to negotiate with the Pope, to whom he offered highly advantageous conditions in exchange for his investiture. But Hadrian IV preferred the Byzantine alliance. The successes of the troops led by William I, however, soon caused the Pope to regret his decision. The Byzantines indeed lost their conquests even more quickly than they had achieved them. After their total defeat outside Brindisi (28 May 1156), the Greek troops were unable to retain the towns they had taken. William I was relentless in repression; he ordered a large number of rebels to be hanged, blinded, or thrown into the sea. These executions inspired terror everywhere, and when the Norman army reached Apulia no city dared to offer resistance; none the less the king made an example of Bari, and destroyed it. In the north of the kingdom resistance ceased; the Prince of Capua fled, and the dispersal of his allies left Hadrian IV alone in opposition to the Norman king, who besieged him in Benevento.

Forced to treat, Hadrian IV had to agree to all the demands of the conqueror. The treaty therefore settled all the questions pending between the kingdom of Sicily and the Papacy. Hadrian IV granted to William I the kingdom of Sicily, the duchy of Apulia, the principality of Capua with Naples, Amalfi, Salerno, and the district of the Marsi (since the time of Gregory VII the Papacy had refused to recognise the last-named conquests). The King of Sicily took the oath of homage, and agreed to pay a tribute of 600 *schifati* for Apulia and Calabria, and 500 for the district of the Marsi. The questions relating to ecclesiastical discipline which had been raised in connexion with the privilege of the royal legateship were arranged by a compromise. The treaty made a distinction between Apulia and Calabria on the one hand, and Sicily on the other. In Apulia and Calabria the Pope secured the right of appeal by clerics to Rome, the right of consecration and of visitation except in those cities where the king was residing, and finally the right of summoning councils. In Sicily the Pope might summon ecclesiastics to attend him, but the king reserved the right of preventing their obedience to the Pope's command. The Pope could only receive appeals and send legates at the king's request. The clergy nominated the bishops, but the king had the right of refusing to accept their election. The Papacy obtained the right of consecration and visitation, but not that of nomination, over certain monasteries and churches, the prelates of which had to apply to Rome only for consecration and benediction. Thus the Treaty of Benevento confirmed in favour of the King of Sicily all the privileges granted by Urban II to Count Roger, and Hadrian IV further had to recognise all the Norman conquests. Moreover, the King of Sicily obtained the erection of Palermo into a metropolitan see.

These advantages were certainly considerable, but the Treaty of Benevento was to have far wider consequences. Possibly when he signed the Pope did not realise that he was severing the link which had united the Papacy and the Germanic Empire ever since the Treaty of Constance. Barbarossa was indignant at the attitude of Hadrian IV, and notwithstanding the efforts made by the Pope to remain on good terms both with the Emperor and the King of Sicily, a rupture was inevitable. The Papacy was consequently obliged to seek support and strength from the Norman kingdom.

Barbarossa had been very ill-content at the Greeks' successes in Italy, but the tidings of their reverses removed his uneasiness, and during the years 1156–1157 negotiations between the two Empires were resumed. Again they failed to reach an agreement. Meanwhile William I, having treated with the Genoese so as to deprive the Byzantines of the possible support of the Genoese fleet (1157), arranged a great expedition to ravage the coasts of the Greek Empire. This took place in 1157; the rich ports of Negropont in Euboea and Almira (Halmyrus) in Thessaly were pillaged, and according to some chroniclers the Norman fleet even appeared outside Constantinople. In the same year Manuel resumed hostilities, sending Alexius, son of the Grand Domestic Axuch, to Ancona, where he raised a force and entered into relations with some Normans, among whom was Count Andrew of Rupis Canina (Raviscanina, near Alife). The Byzantines and their allies attacked the Norman kingdom on its northern frontier.

In the spring of 1158 peace was signed between Manuel and William I, thanks to the intervention of Hadrian IV (1158). After the rupture with Barbarossa (1157), the Pope had made friends with the Greek Emperor, and, wishing to form an alliance against the Germanic Empire, succeeded in bringing about peace between Byzantium and Sicily. Henceforth Manuel Comnenus designed to obtain from the Pope the restoration of the unity of the Roman Empire; consequently, with this larger scheme in view, the question of the Norman kingdom lost much of its importance in his eyes. On the other hand, the new claims of the Basileus were disliked at Palermo, where the treaty of 1158 was regarded as a truce which left in abeyance all the questions pending between the two states.

During the ensuing years the papal alliance was to be the pivot of the Norman policy, for it was well known at the Norman court that Barbarossa had not abandoned his designs on South Italy. Henceforward the Pope and the King of Sicily sought to create every possible difficulty for Frederick, so as to keep him far from Rome and South Italy. When the Milanese revolted in 1159 they were encouraged by both Pope and king. As protector of the Papacy William I had great influence at the papal Court, and his party secured a conspicuous success in 1159 while the Pope was at Anagni; here was formed the league between the Pope, Brescia, Piacenza, and Milan to resist the imperial pretensions. During this same visit the partisans of William I set about choosing a successor for Hadrian IV, who died on 1 September 1159. The strongest proof of the importance of the Sicilian party at the papal Court is the number of votes obtained by William's candidate, Cardinal Roland, its leader, who actually received twenty-three votes out of a total of twenty-seven. His election as Pope Alexander III was therefore a personal triumph for the King of Sicily.

The disorder which prevailed in Italy during 1155 and 1156 had its counterpart in the Norman possessions in Africa. On 25 February 1156 there was a massacre of Christians at Sfax; then the insurrection spread to the islands of Gerba and Kerkinna, and finally to Tripoli. In this city the military commandant had attempted to make the imāms preach against the Almohades, whose growing power was causing uneasiness at the court of Palermo. This order gave rise to a wide-spread conspiracy. The conspirators made an unexpected attack on the Normans (1158), who were driven out of Gabes and only succeeded in holding their ground at Mahdīyah until January 1160. With the fall of this town perished the Norman dominion of Africa. At first sight it seems as though William I did little to defend his African possessions. Very probably the abandonment of Africa was dictated by political necessity. At Palermo it was regarded as inadvisable to undertake a struggle with the mighty Almohad Empire at the very moment when war with Barbarossa seemed imminent; and it was preferable to keep intact the forces of the kingdom, which might soon have to struggle for its very existence.

At the beginning of 1160 the position of the kingdom of Sicily, which was at peace with the Greek Empire and allied with the Pope and the Lombard towns, was unquestionably much stronger than at the accession of William I, thanks to the policy pursued by the Grand Emir, Maio of Bari. It was at the very moment when the latter might have hoped to reap the harvest of his skill that he was assassinated.

Since the revolt in 1156, Maio's influence had constantly increased, to the great dissatisfaction of the nobles, who regarded the minister as responsible for the severe measures taken after William's victory, and were profoundly irritated because they were not allowed a share in the government of the State. Maio was equally unpopular with the inhabitants of the large towns, where he was blamed for the royal decisions which had attacked their municipal liberties, and also for the increase of the financial burdens which weighed on the bourgeois. A plot against the all-powerful minister was organised, in which the principal part was assigned to the Italian vassals of the King of Sicily. Richard of Aquila, Count of Fondi, Gilbert, Count of Gravina, and Roger, Count of Acerra, were the leaders of the movement. They came to an understanding with the exiled Norman nobles and with the inhabitants of certain towns. When the revolt broke out, the leaders of the movement declared that they desired only to deliver the king from an imprudent minister who aspired to usurp the throne. In reality the conspirators were equally hostile to William I, whom they wished to replace by his son Roger. On 10 November 1161 one of the conspirators, Matthew Bonnel, assassinated the Grand Emir. For some time William did not dare to take vengeance on the guilty, but was forced to entrust the government to Henry Aristippus, Archdeacon of Catania, who was friendly with Maio's murderers. Emboldened by their impunity, the conspirators succeeded in taking possession of the royal palace of Palermo, where they seized the person of the king (9 March 1161), who only owed his deliverance to the popular riots excited by the bishops then present at court. Even when set at liberty, the king had still to disguise his wrath and to treat with the rebels. But as soon as he felt himself strong enough, William I arrested Matthew Bonnel, whose eyes were put out. Immediately after Easter (16 April) 1161, the king marched against the Sicilian rebels, who were forced to treat with him; they only obtained pardon on condition that they left the kingdom. Sicily being subdued, the king crossed to Italy, where the revolt headed by Robert of Loritello had spread on all sides. Calabria, Apulia, and the Terra di Lavoro were

CH. IV.

forced in turn to recognise the royal authority. Anxious to make examples, the king imposed on all the towns a supplementary tax called *redemptio*; moreover he ordered Salerno to be rased to the ground, and it was only saved by the intervention of Matthew of Ajello, one of the principal officials at court, who was a native of the city. This successful campaign enabled the king to punish the most highly-placed culprits; on his return to Palermo he threw Henry Aristippus into prison, and pursued all the supporters of Matthew Bonnel with the utmost severity.

After the arrest of Henry Aristippus, William entrusted the government to Count Silvester of Marsico, to Richard Palmer, the Bishop-elect of Syracuse, and to the Master Notary, Matthew of Ajello; after Silvester's death the Grand Chamberlain Peter was associated with the other two. Trained in the school of Maio, Matthew of Ajello was the inheritor of his political traditions, and up to the end of William's reign Norman policy pursued the same course.

The great aim of this policy was to prevent Barbarossa from invading South Italy. Frederick indeed had not abandoned his plans of intervention. The alliance with Sicily was one of his chief grounds of complaint against Alexander III, and in 1160 he resumed negotiations to gain the support of Manuel Comnenus. After the fall of Milan he formed a treaty with Pisa and Genoa to conquer the Norman kingdom (March 1162). The expedition, which was constantly postponed, appeared at last about to start in 1164; but the league of Verona prevented Barbarossa from realising his designs.

Meanwhile the King of Sicily remained obstinately faithful to the cause of the Pope and benefited by the progress made by him. From 1159 to 1161 Alexander III, who had not been able to hold his own in Rome, remained almost continually close to the Norman frontier ready to apply for shelter to William in case of need. After his return from France in 1165, the Pope landed at Messina, and it was Norman troops who, on 23 November 1165, established him in the Lateran.

The reinstatement of the Pope in Rome was the last success achieved by William I, who died on 7 May 1166. Even to the last the King of Sicily was faithful to the papal alliance, and on his death-bed he bequeathed to the Pope a considerable sum.

Judged as a whole, William's reign was not devoid of greatness, and it is evident that he has been unfairly treated by historians. Placed in particularly difficult circumstances, he succeeded in averting the dangers which threatened his dominions. He undoubtedly displayed excessive severity in repressing rebellions by his subjects, but it must not be forgotten that these occurred when the enemy was at the very gates of his kingdom. There are consequently many excuses to be found for him, and it must also be remembered that even his bitterest enemy, the chronicler Hugo Falcandus, was forced to regret him when he contemplated the anarchy which followed his reign.

Duke Roger, the king's eldest son, had been killed by a stray arrow on the occasion when the king was liberated by the people; the crown consequently devolved on the second son William. On his death-bed William I entrusted the regency to his wife Margaret, daughter of Garcia VI Ramirez, King of Navarre, and recommended his chosen counsellors as worthy of her confidence.

The accession of the new king aroused great hopes in all his subjects, and his youth caused everyone to regard him with sympathy. It was expected that the queen-regent would be more lenient than her husband, and that she would be forced to make concessions to the nobles and the cities. Margaret wished to call a new man to her assistance in governing, and having summoned her cousin, Stephen of Perche, from France, she bestowed on him the appointments of Chancellor and Archbishop of Palermo. This choice was unpopular with everyone, and the new chancellor encountered formidable opposition. The leading nobles of the kingdom and the councillors of the queen-regent combined against him, and were joined by all those who considered themselves injured by the reforms which the new chancellor attempted to introduce into the administration, or by the favours granted to the Frenchmen who had come in his train. Stephen of Perche succeeded in foiling the first plot; but the conspirators contrived to obtain possession of Messina, and on receipt of these tidings an insurrection broke out at Palermo. Stephen was besieged in the campanile of the cathedral, and was obliged to treat with the rebels. His life was spared on condition that he left the kingdom.

The coalition which achieved Stephen's downfall was the logical consequence of the aristocratic attempts to reduce the royal power. A common hatred of foreigners reconciled all the parties which had hitherto striven with one another in rivalry. For some time the queen-regent was entirely deprived of any exercise of authority, as the rebels established a council consisting of ten members of the royal Curia—Richard Palmer, Bishop of Syracuse; Gentile, Bishop of Girgenti; Romuald, Archbishop of Salerno; John, Bishop of Malta; Roger, Count of Geraci; Richard, Count of Molise; Henry, Count of Montescaglioso; Matthew of Ajello; Richard the Kaid; and Walter Ophamil, Dean of Girgenti (like Palmer, an Englishman), who was the king's tutor and was consecrated Archbishop of Palermo in September 1169. He soon played a very important part, and appears to have deprived the Council of Ten of the powers which they had usurped. Supported by Matthew of Ajello, Walter excluded the representatives of the aristocracy from the council, and very soon reverted to the governmental tradition of Roger II and William I. And when William II reached his majority, the Archbishop of Palermo still retained his confidence.

Under William II Norman policy as regards the Papacy and the Germanic Empire for many years remained identical with that of the previous reign. The King of Sicily was the more inclined to support the papal cause, because in 1166, when Barbarossa invaded Italy, everyone thought that the Emperor intended to attack the Norman kingdom in the following year. But when Frederick was about to advance towards the south, he was summoned to Rome by the victory of Christian of Mayence at Monteporzio. In these critical circumstances Alexander III found support from the Normans, and the Sicilian galleys penetrated the Tiber as far as Rome. Alexander III did not take advantage of the proffered assistance, preferring to remain in the Eternal City, but a little later, when he took refuge at Benevento, he was again protected by Norman troops. The formation of the Lombard League prevented Barbarossa from interfering in South Italy, as before he could deal with the Norman kingdom he had to conquer North Italy, the whole of which was in arms. William II on his side did not stint his subsidies to the League; and in 1173, when Frederick tried to detach him from the papal alliance, the Norman king refused to fall in with the imperial views. At the Peace of Venice the Norman envoys played a leading part in the negotiations which preceded the conclusion of peace, and it was owing to their support that Alexander III succeeded in overcoming the difficulties raised by the Emperor and the Venetians. By the Peace a truce of fifteen years was assured between the Norman kingdom and the Germanic Empire. But henceforward William II modified his attitude towards the Papacy. When Lucius III, who succeeded Alexander III, was in his turn on bad terms with the Emperor (1184), William refused to side with the Pope. Intent on distant conquests of which we shall presently speak, the King of Sicily saw no use in risking a struggle with the Empire. The Treaty of Constance (1183) had put an end to the Lombard League, and William II was faced by the possibility of being the Pope's only champion in a conflict; he preferred to come to terms with Barbarossa, who had recently approached him to obtain the hand of Constance, Roger II's daughter, for his son Henry. As William II was childless, the Emperor hoped that the Norman kingdom might be secured for his son, Constance being the legitimate heir. On 29 October 1184 the betrothal was announced at Augsburg, and on 28 August 1185 Constance was handed over to the imperial envoys at Rieti.

His alliance with Alexander III had enabled William II to play an important part in the great events which occupied European diplomacy during his reign. He was brought into relations with the King of England in connexion with Henry II's quarrel with Thomas Becket, and eventually in 1176 he married Henry's daughter Joan. This marriage brought the two countries closer together, and many Englishmen came to settle in Sicily.

Norman policy towards the Greek Emperor underwent a series of changes during William II's reign. About 1167 Manuel Comnenus definitely demanded from Alexander III the restoration of imperial unity, with himself as sole Emperor of East and West. As he feared that the King of Sicily would oppose this plan, he at once approached the court of Palermo with an offer to marry his daughter Maria, heiress to his dominions, to the young King William II. Nothing further is known as to the relations between the two courts until 1171, when owing to his quarrel with the Venetians Manuel reverted to this proposed marriage, and it was agreed that the Byzantine princess should arrive in Taranto in the spring of 1172. But when William went to meet his bride on the appointed day, she was not there. Probably by that time Manuel had entered on fresh negotiations with a view to arranging the marriage of his daughter to Barbarossa's son.

William II was deeply offended at the insult offered him, and resolved to be avenged. He began by forming an alliance with the Venetians (1175) and the Genoese (1174), thus depriving the Byzantines of possible allies, and as soon as a favourable opportunity occurred he dispatched troops to conquer Constantinople. When after Manuel's death Andronicus Comnenus dethroned Alexius II (1184), the King of Sicily took advantage of the disturbances which broke out in the Greek Empire to declare war. As in bygone days Guiscard had used a pseudo-Michael VII, so William now made use of a spurious Alexius to gain partisans among the Byzantines. From the Norman kingdom an army of, it is said, eighty thousand men was gathered under the command of a certain Baldwin and of Richard, Count of Acerra. The fleet was commanded by Tancred of Lecce. In June 1185 the Normans took Durazzo and advanced on Salonica, which was invested at the beginning of August. After the fall of this town, they marched on Constantinople and proceeded as far as Seres and Mosinopolis. Near the latter town was fought the decisive battle, wherein the Normans, treacherously attacked while negotiations were proceeding, were overwhelmed by the Byzantines. All the conquered cities were quickly recaptured from the invaders, only Durazzo remaining in their hands for a time. William II indeed carried on the war by sending his fleet under the command of the Admiral Margaritus to support Isaac Comnenus who had been proclaimed Emperor; but he came to terms with the Emperor Isaac Angelus before 1189, although we do not know the exact date when the war ended.

In sending his troops to attempt the conquest of Constantinople, William II was reverting to the grandiose policy of expansion formerly pursued by Robert Guiscard and Roger II. His Moorish policy was derived from the same sources. It is, however, specially in these matters that we can trace the personal influence of the king, for we know that his ministers were opposed to these distant expeditions; moreover, when he dispatched his ships to attack the Moorish possessions, William II was not only considering the Sicilian trade, he was not only seeking to assure communications between the Western world and the Holy Places, but he was ambitious to pose as the protector of the Christian communities of the Levant. This explains why in his reign the Norman fleets specially directed their attacks against the Muslims of Egypt. Only the Normans supported the King of Jerusalem in his proposed campaign against Egypt, which was prevented by his death (1174)[1]. In like manner during the ensuing years, even while William was treating with the Almohades, he continued to send his sailors to lay waste the coasts of Egypt and to pillage Tinnīs (1175–1177). These naval expeditions were interrupted by the war with the Greeks, but were resumed when the Christians of the Levant appealed to the West. The King of Sicily was one of the first to assume the cross on the occasion of the Third Crusade. He aspired to lead the expedition, and the engagements he entered into with some of the leaders of the Crusade caused serious embarrassment to his successor. Death prevented William II (18 November 1189) from realising his design, but the Norman fleet had already set sail for the East, and the exploits of its admiral Margaritus off the coast near Laodicea (Lāṭiqīyah) cast a halo of glory round the last days of his reign.

Of all the Norman sovereigns William II is the one of whose character we know least. He seems to have been devoid of the vigorous qualities of his race, for he never took personal command of his army and preferred a life of ease and pleasure in the seclusion of his palace to the life of the camp. But it was precisely this contrast to his predecessors which caused his popularity. People were weary of the despotic authority exercised by Roger and William I; they breathed a sigh of relief at the accession of William II, and the tranquillity of his reign was almost too much appreciated, while deep gratitude was felt towards the sovereign who had bestowed these benefits. Regretted by his subjects, William "the Good" continued to be regarded in Italy as the ideal type of king,

> Rex ille magnificus,
> Pacificus,
> Cuius vita placuit
> Deo et hominibus;

and when Dante gave him a place in Paradise he was only echoing popular sentiment[2].

As William left no children, Constance, daughter of Roger II, was legitimate heiress to the crown of Sicily. Before her departure for Germany, William II had made his vassals swear fealty to her, thus clearly indicating his wishes, which were however disregarded. While one party, led by Walter, Archbishop of Palermo, was anxious that the royal will should be executed, two other parties, which had nothing in common save their hatred of the Germans, wished to elect a king, one supporting

---

[1] Cf. *infra*, Chapter VIII, and *supra*, Vol. IV, Chapter XII, p. 377.

[2] *Paradiso*, xx, 66. The Latin threnody is by Richard of San Germano, MGH, *Script.* XIX, 324 (SGUS, p. 5).

Roger of Andria, the other Tancred, Count of Lecce, illegitimate son of Duke Roger, and thus grandson of Roger II. Tancred was chosen (January 1190?), thanks to Matthew of Ajello, who was rewarded with the appointment of Chancellor. From the very outset he was faced by the most serious difficulties. A Muslim insurrection broke out in Sicily; in Italy the partisans of Roger of Andria revolted and espoused Henry VI's cause out of hatred for Tancred; finally, the arrival of the Third Crusade at Messina was the source of the gravest embarrassment to the new king.

Richard of Acerra, Tancred's brother-in-law, succeeded in restoring order in Italy and in seizing Roger of Andria, while Tancred conceded numerous privileges to the burghers of the towns and thus sought to secure their support against the feudal nobility. At the same time the king was carrying on very troublesome negotiations with the crusaders in Italy. Richard Coeur-de-Lion had complained even before his arrival in Messina that his sister Joan, widow of William II, was detained in captivity and had not received her jointure. Moreover, he demanded an important legacy bequeathed by the deceased king to Henry II of England, to wit, a golden table twelve feet in length and a foot and a half in breadth, a silken tent large enough to contain two hundred knights, twenty-four golden cups, a hundred galleys equipped for two years, and sixty thousand loads of wheat, barley, and wine.

Tancred met these demands by setting Joan at liberty and giving her a million *taris* as jointure, but Richard was annoyed because all his claims had not been satisfied and, on his arrival at Messina, he occupied Bagnara on the Italian coast; subsequently, disagreements having arisen between the English and the people of Messina, he took possession of the city by force and built a wooden tower which he mockingly called "Mâte Grifon" (Slaughter-Greek). In the end Tancred came to terms with the irascible King of England; he indemnified Queen Joan by giving her another twenty thousand ounces of gold. In return for an equal sum Richard I renounced William II's legacy and agreed to arrange a marriage between his nephew Arthur of Brittany and one of the King of Sicily's daughters. Moreover Richard promised to uphold Tancred as long as he remained in the latter's dominions. There is little doubt that the alliance was directed against Henry VI, Constance's husband, but this clause of the treaty was of no assistance to Tancred's interests, for after the departure of the crusaders for the Holy Land (March and April 1191) he remained in isolation to confront the German invasion.

Ever since 1190 Henry VI had determined to claim his wife's inheritance by force. He was delayed by the death of his father, which took place during the Crusade, but was soon in a position to resume his Italian plans. In March 1191 he renewed the treaty of 1162 with Pisa; about the same time he entered into negotiations with Genoa, which were concluded a little later. He appeared outside Rome just after the death of Pope Clement III, and the cardinals hastened to elect a successor before the arrival of the German troops (30 March 1191). The new Pope, Celestine III, was called upon to crown the Emperor the day after his own consecration (15 April). Immediately afterwards Henry VI directed his march towards southern Italy. There flocked round him not only the exiled Normans but also a large number of the nobles who had taken part in the last insurrection. The German expedition advanced with great ease, and it was almost without serious fighting that the Emperor laid siege to Naples, where the Norman troops had concentrated. While Henry was besieging Naples, the people of Salerno made their submission. The Empress Constance then repaired to Salerno and established herself in the royal palace of Terracina, where she remained when, in the course of the summer, an epidemic forced the Emperor to raise the siege of Naples and retire to the north. But he left garrisons in all the towns that had adopted his cause, and retained occupation of the conquered territory.

After the departure of the Germans, the people of Salerno were much ashamed of their disloyalty, and to conciliate Tancred they handed over Constance to him. During the summer of 1191 Tancred crossed to Italy; he succeeded in wresting several towns from the Germans, among them Capua. He could not however drive out Henry's troops; hostilities continued for some years, and the Germans managed to hold their ground in the district of Monte Cassino, while on the other hand the King of Sicily established his authority in the Abruzzi.

In expectation of the German Emperor making a fresh attack, Tancred sought to secure the aid of Byzantium, and arranged a marriage between his son Roger and Irene, daughter of Isaac Angelus. At the same time, in order to obtain the protection of Pope Celestine III, the King of Sicily agreed by the concordat of Gravina (1192) to relinquish the rights which the Treaty of Benevento had granted to the kingdom of Sicily. The mediation of the Pope with the Emperor, however, was unsuccessful, and Celestine III proffered no other assistance to Tancred. He even gave him the unpalatable advice to liberate Constance. Tancred followed this unhappy suggestion, and thus deprived himself of the hostage whom chance had placed in his hands.

Tancred, however, did not live to witness the victory of Henry VI, for he died on 20 February 1194. He has been held up to ridicule by Peter of Eboli, who gloats over his ugly face and dwarfish stature; but he does not deserve the jibes of this poetical adulator of the German conquest, for it cannot be denied that during his short tenancy of the throne he displayed rare qualities as a military commander, which enabled him to offer resistance under almost hopeless conditions.

The king's elder son and crowned colleague Roger having predeceased him, the crown devolved on the second son William III, who was still very young. The regency was in the hands of the queen, Sibylla, sister of

Count Richard of Acerra. The German Emperor had therefore only a woman and an infant to oppose him in the conquest of the Norman kingdom. Henry VI indeed had not relinquished his plans; he had been delayed by events in Germany, but was ready to take the field in 1194. In January of that year he concluded the treaty of Vercelli with the Lombard towns, so as to ensure that neither the Pope nor the King of Sicily should find allies among them. Having quelled in March 1194 the revolt of the house of the Welfs in Germany, Henry VI opened the campaign. He carefully arranged that he should be supported by the fleets of Pisa and Genoa.

The characteristic feature of the expedition was the ease of his conquest. There does not seem to have been any attempt at resistance, as from the outset the cause of William III was regarded as hopeless. As soon as Henry VI appeared outside a town, its gates were thrown open to him. Only the people of Salerno, who feared chastisement for their treachery, dared to resist, whereupon their city was taken by storm. In Sicily Sibylla vainly endeavoured to withstand him; she suffered the mortification of seeing the inhabitants of Palermo open the gates of the capital to the Emperor (20 November 1194). Having fled to Caltabellotta with her son, she accepted the peace proposals made by Henry VI, who offered William the county of Lecce and the principality of Taranto, and on Christmas Day 1194 the Emperor was crowned King of Sicily at Palermo in her presence and that of her son. Four days later, on the pretext of their complicity in a plot, the queen and the principal nobles of the kingdom were arrested. The Emperor has been severely blamed for these arrests, and has been accused of having forged all the documents proving the existence of a plot and of having caused the death of the prisoners. He has been partially exonerated on this score. In 1194 there was no blood-thirsty repression, and there apparently was a plot. On the other hand, there is no doubt that, after the great insurrections against the German domination which broke out in 1196 and 1197, Henry VI did order wholesale executions. He not only punished the instigators of the revolt, but also directed that some of the prisoners of 1194 who had taken no part in it should have their eyes put out. Consequently, even if we adopt the most favourable hypothesis, Henry VI's conduct must appear excessively cruel, as he punished individuals who, having been in German prisons for two years, must necessarily have been innocent of complicity in the later events.

The fate of William III, last of the Norman kings, is unknown; according to some reports Henry VI caused him to be mutilated, according to others Tancred's son became a monk.

The administrative organisation established by the Norman kings in South Italy and Sicily was not less remarkable than their political achievement. Two facts dominate the history of the Norman organisation and explain its methods: the very small numbers of the conquerors and the sparseness also of the indigenous population. Even after the conquerors had been strengthened by a further immigration, still none too large, of their compatriots, they were never sufficiently numerous to outweigh the native races; they were obliged to attract settlers from all parts to populate vacant lands, and to retain their ascendency they were led to concede equal importance to the institutions, customs, and characters of all the races they found represented in the regions they subjugated.

Hence although French remained the court language, the Norman Chancery made use of Greek, Latin, or Arabic, according to the nationality of those to whom they dispatched the royal diplomas. The same principle recurs in private law, and in the preamble of the Assises of Ariano in 1140 the greatest Norman king decreed as follows: "The laws newly promulgated by our authority are binding on everyone...but without prejudice to the habits, customs, and laws of the peoples subject to our authority, each in its own sphere...unless any one of these laws or customs should be manifestly opposed to our decrees." We find an expression of the same spirit in the manner in which Roger II and his successors borrowed from various legal systems those elements of public law which they considered most advantageous to their dynasty and most easily applicable to the conquered country. Thus Norman public law seems to be a mixture partly of Justinianean and Byzantine, partly of feudal law. Recently H. Niese has endeavoured to prove that in Sicilian law there was an element of Norman law, the importance of which he may have exaggerated.

The greatest social change which the Normans introduced into their new domain was, perhaps, feudalism in the true sense of the word. Neither the Lombards of the south nor the Byzantines had known vassalage or fiefs, however much hereditary counts and nobles may have formed a fitting prelude to feudalism proper. But by the reign of Roger II we find a feudal hierarchy of princes, dukes, counts, and barons, holding fiefs by military tenure under homage and fealty, and usually enjoying feudal jurisdiction, at least in civil causes. Below and beside them stand the simple knights with or without fiefs. Roger II, by decreeing that only the son of a knight could himself be knighted, endeavoured to form the whole feudal body into a kind of caste. In its general outlines this system was not different from that of Normandy. The mass of the peasantry were either actual serfs, bound to their plots, many of whom (the *defensati*), not unlike the German *ministeriales*, were specially liable to military service, or men who, though personally free, held their land by servile tenure. The new settlers, called in to people vacant lands, were naturally favoured by their own customs. But there were also large, if diminishing, survivals of non-feudal freeholders, mostly townsmen, who fully owned their property *absque servitio*. Slaves were not very numerous, and no Christians, save Slavs only, could by custom-law be bought and sold as such. The non-noble population as a whole were liable to the *angariae, i.e.* the repair of roads and castles and the like. The peasants had already adopted the habit of living together in small towns for the sake of safety, and, just as happens to-day in Sicily, a man's plot of ground might lie some miles from his dwelling-place. The burdens on the peasant were indeed heavy and his lot was hard, but it was mitigated by the growth of custom, favoured by his value to his lord and by the strictness of the royal administration.

From a religious point of view the Norman kings borrowed their conception of a theocratic monarchy from Byzantium, but their spirit of tolerance mitigated the exaggerated results which might have attended this principle. The "pious" king, the "defender of the Christians," insisted that he was "crowned by God" and is shewn in the mosaics of the churches receiving the diadem from Christ. It was, said Roger II in his Assises, "equal to sacrilege (*par sacrilegio*) to cavil at his judgments, his laws, deeds, and counsels." Further, the privilege of the Apostolic Legateship conferred on the Norman sovereigns an authority over part of the Latin clergy in their dominions such as was possessed by no other monarch of that period. Nevertheless they allowed free exercise of their religion to the Muslims from the start, and to the Greeks after a comparatively short interval from the conquest.

The administrative organisation established in their states was the most characteristic creation of the Norman rulers. At the heart of this skilfully constructed system was the king, who governed with the assistance of the *Curia Regis*, in whose hands were concentrated all powers. Gradually there came into being various departments, a Court of Justice side by side with a Financial Council (Archons of the Secretum) which was itself divided into several sections (*dohana [diwān] a secretis, dohana baronum*), equipped with official registers, according to the business with which it had to deal. In the Curia we find both lay and ecclesiastical vassals, as well as chosen counsellors of the king, the *familiares*, from whom were recruited the members of the Privy Council (ἡ κραταιὰ κόρτη), known as the Lords of the Curia (*Domini Curiae*). Among them the great officials of the kingdom held the chief place. The Emir of Emirs or Admiral (*ammiratus ammiratorum*) had at first perhaps the charge of the Muslim population as well as the command of the fleet, a duty from which the modern title Admiral for a naval commander is derived, but under Roger II the Admiral George of Antioch became practically a prime minister or Grand Vizier. The office was left unfilled after the death of Maio, and the Chancellor, whose office was also often left vacant, was, when nominated, the chief royal minister. Over the finances was set the Grand Chamberlain, who became the chief of the Financial Council when that emerged. Dependent on one or other of the two great bodies—the Court of Justice or the Financial Council—there were ranked the officials of the provinces. These by the time of William II consisted of the Master Justiciaries, Master Chamberlains, and Master Constables (all over groups of provinces), and the older posts of Justiciars (for justice), Chamberlains (for finance), and Constables (for troops), each for a single province. They had under their orders local subordinates, *e.g.* catapans, strategi, viscounts, *baiuli*, cadis, judges, many of whom still retained the old Greek, Lombard, or Saracen titles.

Thanks to this hierarchy of officials, royal authority was in all parts powerfully exercised over its subjects. This is particularly shewn by two facts. None of the cities in the Norman kingdom ever succeeded in constituting itself a free town; even the greatest of them had at its head an official appointed by the king. And, with very rare exceptions, none of the vassals of the Crown, whose obligations towards the king were regulated by feudal law, possessed the right of trying criminal cases; these the king reserved for himself.

The power of the monarchy at home and abroad was increased by its wealth. From many sources a treasure was amassed which was still considerable when Henry VI captured it at Palermo. In addition to the revenue derived from the royal demesnes, the profits of justice, and the usual feudal aids (called in the Norman kingdom the *collecta*), including purveyance, the kings raised a variously-named tribute analogous to the English Danegeld, and drew large sums from tolls and duties, such as the lucrative port-dues levied on the ships which thronged their harbours. The kings themselves engaged in trade. The manufacture of silk, introduced by Roger II, was a royal monopoly, and his royal mantle still preserved shews how exquisite the new art could be.

Even in art we find the combination of various elements resulting in a new and harmonious whole As creators or promoters of a civilisation which was enriched on all sides by the most varied influences, the Norman kings aspired to leave behind them witnesses of their achievements— monuments capable of attesting the power and originality of a conception which sought to recognise every living element in the races they governed and to represent truthfully the particular nature, spirit, and quality of each of these races in the close collaboration of all. Although some of the monuments erected under their supervision have a definitely Eastern character, such as the palaces of La Zisa or La Cuba, most of the buildings which they constructed present a happy combination of Norman, Byzantine, and Saracenic art. As the finest examples of this composite art it is enough to mention the Cappella Palatina at Palermo, the cathedral of Monreale, and the church of Cefalù.

The mosaic of manners and customs due to the juxtaposition of different races was also evident in the life of the great cities of the Norman kingdom. Never indeed was there any fusion between the races existing therein. Greeks, Italians, Normans, Saracens, all continued to dwell in the same towns subject to the same authority, but faithful to their own customs and traditions.

The court at Palermo exhibited the same diversity as was elsewhere visible. There the king appeared in a costume derived alike from Byzantine ceremonial, from Western chivalry, and from the magnificence of the Saracenic East. For his protection there were two bodyguards, one of knights, the other of negroes under the command of a Muslim. In the army there was the same mixture, Norman knights arrayed beside Saracen troops in striking costumes. In the train of the sovereign, Latin, Greek, and Muslim officials were in constant intercourse. At Roger II's court the Arab geographer Idrīsi, the Greek author Nilus Doxapatrius, and the Emir Eugenius who translated Ptolemy's *Optics* into Latin, might be found side by side. Arabic poets composed poems in honour of the royal family. Abū-ad-Dah bewailed the death of Duke Roger; 'Abd-ar-Raḥmān sang the charms of one of the royal palaces. At William I's court Henry Aristippus translated the works of St Gregory Nazianzen by desire of the king, and undertook the translation of the *Phaedo* and the fourth book of Aristotle's *Meteorologica*.

Affected by contact with Eastern civilisation, the Norman sovereigns allowed themselves to adopt the morals of their Moorish courtiers with a facility which was a credit to their eclecticism, but which gradually weakened their energy and dignity; and their example was undoubtedly followed by most of the nobles at court. If the sons of the Norman conquerors all suffered more or less from the pernicious influence of these new customs combined with the effect of an unaccustomed climate, nowhere was this degeneracy so rapid and so intense as in the royal family. Most of the sons of Roger II died young; the number of children diminished with William I, and William II was childless. The extinction of the royal family only preceded the fall of the Norman domination by a few years; it was at once a cause and a sign. Between the various elements which formed the Norman kingdom, elements which differed too widely ever to blend into a coherent and durable whole, the person of the king supplied the only link, a link which necessarily disappeared with his disappearance, for Constance was not regarded as the daughter of Roger II but as the German Empress. With Henry VI there began a new period in the history of South Italy and of Sicily, and it may be said that the conquest in 1194 marked the close of the Norman domination.

CHAPTER V.

THE ITALIAN CITIES TILL *c.* 1200.

No more characteristic phenomenon of the prime of the Middle Age can be found than the self-governing town. It existed, more or less fully developed, in the chief countries of the West, and we shall hardly err in attributing its rise and growth to economic causes of equally general prevalence. It was the resurgence of trade, of manufacture for a wide market, after the anarchic, miserable ninth and tenth centuries, which produced town and townsman, merchant and craft. The conditions of the times imprinted on the medieval town other universal characters. Safety and orderly life were impossible save in association, in group life, and the associated burghers replaced or competed with the feudal or kinship groups which preceded them. Local and personal law was the rule, and the law of merchant and town took its place by the side of other local and class customs. Central authority in greater or less degree was shattered, and the town, like the baron, obtained its fraction of autonomy. Whatever the degree of their independence, the shackled English boroughs, the French towns in all their varieties, the republics of Flanders and the Hanse, and the Italian communes, obey the same impulse and bear a family resemblance.

Yet while the medieval towns are obviously akin, the divergences among them in character and history are deep and wide; and most aberrant from the rest, if the most pronounced and perfect of the type, are the Italian city-states. Like their congeners, indeed, they owed their florescence ultimately to geographical factors. Some, like Venice and Pisa, were ports on the sea; others were halting-places at the fords or junction of rivers, like Cremona; others, like Verona, were at the mouths of passes; others punctuated the immemorial roads, like Siena or Bologna; others, perhaps, were merely safe centres in a fertile land, clots of population, which could produce un-bled by feudal tyranny. The whole land, too, had a temporary geographical advantage: Italy was the half-way house between the East (and Constantinople), with its civilisation, its luxury, and its arts, and the West, hungry for these amenities, the most extravagant of purchasers. But, save the last, these advantages of site were old, and the Italian cities, for the most part, were old too, or at least conscious children of the past like Venice, and in their history their inheritance counts for much. Bruges and Bristol were new growths,

Padua and Milan started as cities on their medieval career. In the wreck of the Roman Empire, at the coming of the Lombards, they had indeed lost, even in Byzantine territory, the greater part of their city institutions of antiquity. They were transformed beyond recognition perhaps, but not beyond identity. The attempts of historians to shew a continuous existence of the main institutions of civic government from Theodosius to Frederick Barbarossa have failed, though in rare cases an office or a title might outlive the welter; but civic instinct, civic co-operation could survive and blend with new elements under new conditions after centuries of revolution. For the understanding of the new growth it is necessary first to look, though too often by a flickering and uncertain light, at the dubious remnants of the ancient order.

It is natural that the clearest traces of late Roman institutions should be found in those Italian cities which fell into Lombard hands either late or never. A general description of their government before the Frankish conquest has already been given in a previous volume[1], and here it will only be necessary to touch on their organisation in Frankish and post-Frankish times. We find that at Ravenna and Naples the *curiales* are no longer a governing magisterial assembly, but a college of notaries; in fact the town office-staff had survived the assembly they had served. Ravenna, however, still possessed a Senate of nobles, though it may be questioned if it ever met as an administrative body. Its chief members, the *dukes*, who belonged to but a few great families, had individually judicial and administrative powers; and its secondary members, the *consuls*, may have had some functions. At Naples *consul* was merely a title enjoyed like other Byzantine ranks by many of the nobility, *i.e.* of the wealthier landowners. At Rome the Senate as an assembly had disappeared, although the title *Senator* belonged to the greatest noble family. There the *consules et duces*, a combined title for which that of *consules Romanorum* was substituted before A.D. 1000, had some of the functions of the Ravennate dukes, while the plain *consuls* seem merely to hold a title, and possibly might not be of noble birth[2]. The city-militia, ranged in twelve local regiments (*numeri, bandi*, or *scholae*), formed the nearest approach to a popular assembly in Ravenna and Rome, while at Naples the *milites* were more like a warrior caste beneath the nobles. In all three towns there are traces of the ancient trade-corporations (*scholae*) still subsisting. Alike in all, however, real authority is derived, in Byzantine fashion, from the ruler, the Duke at Naples, the Pope at Rome, and is wielded by his bureaucracy, of which the dukes at Ravenna and the *consules et duces* at Rome were only subordinate

---

[1] Vol. II, Chap. VIII (A)

[2] But the notaries who were consuls (L. Halphen, *Études sur l'administration de Rome au Moyen Âge*, p. 29, n. 3) may well have been nobles like those of Ravenna in the eleventh century. See G. Buzzi, *Le curie arcivescovile e cittadina di Ravenna*, BISI, 35, p. 54.

members. The distance of Ravenna from Rome, and the desire of its archbishop to rule it in opposition to the Pope's rights, may have allowed a Ravennate Senate to continue; the material power of the great Roman landowners and the local patriotism of the Roman militia may have raised Alberic as their elected prince to exercise the temporal prerogatives of the Popes; but in the tenth century no commune, no republican city, save Venice perhaps, exists in Italy.

The break-down of the institutions of the ancient Empire was of necessity far more complete in the territory conquered by the Lombards, which accounted for the greater part of Italy. The Lombards came as barbaric enemies of Rome; they replaced Roman organisation by simpler institutions of their own. Here and there so-called *curiales* or similar officials might exist as petty tax-gatherers and notaries. Here and there might continue a trade-corporation, like the soap-makers of Piacenza who at some time before 744 were paying annually thirty pounds of soap to the king. The number of survivals may be increased by further research. But in general the elaborate Roman administration disappeared. It could hardly be otherwise. Depopulated and in stagnation, with the self-sufficing great estate or *curtis* as the typical economic unit, with the mass of the population *aldii* or half-free peasants, with the growing class of Roman freemen in the towns for long officially ignored by the Arian Lombards, only the most elementary and hardiest Roman organisations could be expected to survive. Some such, however, there were, and the course of time increased their importance. From the first the towns could not be deprived of their position as economic centres of their surrounding countryside; the *curtis* often had surplus produce to dispose of; Roman crafts were torpid, not dead—the Lombard merchant and the Italian shipwright became known abroad. The conversion of the Lombards to Catholicism, and the inevitable intermixture of race, ended in the official recognition of Roman as well as Lombard law by the time of Liutprand (712–744), and the ranking of freemen in the army on a pure property basis by King Aistulf in 750.

It is in close connexion with their ecclesiastical arrangements, themselves founded on the civil organisation of the falling Empire, that we find the earliest germs of the later North Italian communes. The diocese corresponded usually with the Roman *civitas*, the unit of secular administration. The largest subdivision of the diocese was the *plebs* or *pieve*, presided over by its archpriest and having its centre in the baptismal church (*ecclesia*), in which alone for long the chief rites of religion could be performed. The *plebs* was in its turn subdivided. In the country it was a collection of villages each of which in time had its own oratory (*capella*) and bore, at least later, some such name as *vicinantia*. The bishop's city, however, with its suburb stretching a mile or so beyond the walls, formed a *plebs* by itself, a fact of which the baptisteries of Italian cities still remind us. Its subdivisions, or parishes in modern language, each with its *capella*, formed the *vicinantiae, populi*, or *contratae* of the city. A *vicinantia* in town or country usually possessed, or had the use of, common lands, pasture and wood, as an economic necessity, and the meeting of the *vicini* (parishioners, neighbours) perhaps round the village elm or at the door of the *capella* to arrange such matters can hardly ever have gone out of use. To this day the use of certain Alpine pastures is managed by similar meetings of the hereditary users[1]. Nor in such meetings can the personal status of the *vicini* have formed a bar to participation. Later under the communes the *vicinantiae* were to play a part in the city-administration. In the country the *plebs* had at least its little market for exchange on holy days before its *ecclesia*, and often, it seems, the use of common lands to manage in customary fashion. But in the towns we see an intermediate and purely secular subdivision, the quarters or gates (*portae*), going back to Roman times. The first duty of the quarter was the repair and guarding of the walls, or that share of the work (one-third) which did not fall on the State or the Church. The city *plebs*, too, was not without its assembly and its elementary functions. There were common lands of the city needing some management. There were proclamations to be made, public burdens perhaps to be apportioned, as in the country. As early as Rothari's time (636–652), strayed animals were cried in the *conventus ante ecclesiam*. And perhaps there was the election of a bishop or the alienation of church-lands to be formally approved. In Carolingian times we find sure evidence of the existence and occasional activity of this city-assembly in Lombard Italy. About 790 Charlemagne's son Pepin of Italy forbade the men of Piacenza to receive *aldii* in the city by *their* decree (*praeceptum*); and at Piacenza the general assembly (*contio*) long met in front of the old cathedral of Sant' Antonino, a proof of the assembly's existence before the new cathedral of Santa Giustina was built in 877.

Two features with far-reaching effects characterised the assembly. First, it was composed of dwellers within the walls alone. Even if this character does not go back to late Roman times, the fact that in the suburb outside the walls there would be in depopulated Lombard Italy but scattered hamlets at most would sufficiently account for it. Its importance needs no stressing. The walled city, forming a separate *plebs*, exceptional in population, duties, and power, is the starting-point of the urban Italian commune, cut off from the countryside and, apart from the State-administration, possessing as its ultimate authority a general

---

[1] Cf. A. Serpieri, *Studio sui pascoli alpini della Svizzera*, pp. 185–8; at Cortina certain hereditary groups each dispose of the usufruct of a portion of the alp, and elect their officers in a meeting of the group in front of the church. F. Schneider, *Die Entstehung von Burg und Landgemeinde in Italien*, would apparently restrict the managing use of common lands to the settlements of *Arimanni, i.e.* in this connexion, free warriors specially assigned to the frontier-strips or other garrison-duty. But his evidence is insufficient.

assembly of the city dwellers. Secondly, there is the close connexion of the city with its bishop. Protector of the plain subject in late Roman times, head of his Catholic flock while the Lombards were still Arian, chief citizen and a public official under the Carolingians, surrounded by a throng of vassals in town and country, it was the bishop, whether much or little privileged, who brought the formless assembly and the elementary machinery of quarters and *vicinanze* into working order as a substitute for decaying government. How strong the feeling of city unity was, and how intimately linked with the city's church, is seen as early as 715 when the dispute over the diocesan boundaries of Siena and Arezzo led to armed conflict between the two cities in which the Sienese people appear as a self-acting body.

The effect of the strictly Carolingian period was to intensify the existing current of development. Freemen, whether Frank, Lombard, or Roman, or of some other race or personal law, were privileged according to their rank in society, not by their racial descent, although the offspring of Germanic conquerors were naturally still predominant among them. And a mixed customary law, containing elements both Lombard and Roman, was evidently growing up locally even in the *vicinanze*, and even among a serf-population. The *loci consuetudo* had been already acknowledged by King Rothari, and King Liutprand in 727 admitted its mingled, local, and popular character. The development of such local *usus terrae* in the towns at least must have been assisted, and the training of the notables in law and government must have been increased, by Charlemagne's institution of the *scabini*[1]. These law-experts and life-assessors in judgment, chosen *totius populi consensu*[2] by the *missi*, produced a competent professional class of lawyers among the very men who would naturally take the lead in the affairs of the city and its church.

A far more powerful impulse, however, towards city-autonomy, was given by the disasters of Italy during the age of anarchy following the deposition of Charles the Fat in 887. The civil wars, the weakening of the degenerate kingship, the rapid changes among the provincial wielders of the public power, left the state unable to exercise its rights, to levy its dues, or to protect its miserable subjects. Against the Hungarian or Saracen ravagers the only sure defence lay in the guard of the walled towns or castles by their inhabitants. *Castra* (*castelli*) began to spring up in the countryside through the unprompted co-operation of the neighbouring population, who would there find a place of refuge for themselves and their property. The cities were similarly a place of refuge, but their defence fell on the permanent inhabitants, whose organisation of quarters (*portae*) and *vicinantiae* regained for military purposes its full significance.

---

[1] See *supra*, Vol. II, Chap. XXI, p. 668.
[2] *Capitulare Wormatiense*, A.D. 829, MGH, Capit. II, p. 15.

A song of the city-watch has been transmitted to us from this time, a prelude in Latin of Italian verse.

> "Fortis iuventus, virtus audax bellica,
> vestra per muros audiantur carmina:
> et sit in armis alterna vigilia
> ne fraus hostilis haec invadat moenia."[1]

It was the bishop who appeared at the head of his fellow-citizens (*concives*) in this work of co-operation and defence. Thus in 904 King Berengar permits Hildegar, Bishop of Bergamo, and his *concives* to guard against the heathen raids and the oppression of the great nobles by rebuilding the city walls and towers, and in the same diploma to the bishop and his see were granted those walls and the public jurisdiction within them. Other grants of the kind were to follow. Under the Holy Roman Emperors it was the public policy to hand over the comital powers in cities and a radius round them to their bishops. But how much these grants merely ratified an existing or impending situation is seen in Tuscany, where few bishops obtained them yet all were closely concerned with the dawn of city-autonomy. Looking from above, the Emperor let slip powers of his own or of the great vassals into the hands of his own episcopal nominees who could effectively administer them. Looking from below, the city notables obtained a greater voice in the city government through its formal conferment on their episcopal chief, of whom they were the customary and recognised councillors and generally the vassals.

In spite of the disasters of the times, the effort for self-defence and the restoration of the walls, not to mention the acquisition of local State-administrative powers by rulers on the spot, could not fail to promote the prosperity of the cities. Their population, too, must have increased, if only owing to the inrush of refugees who did not always return to their ruined homes in the countryside; while, after the Ottos had excluded heathen ravage, their progress was comparatively rapid. It is natural that we should trace signs of greater civic self-consciousness and self-dependence in the larger and wealthier centres. In Milan this took an ecclesiastical form. The townsmen fought for five years (948–953) in support of the canonically-elected Adalman against the royal nominee Manasse, who was favoured by the nobles of the countryside. The same people *c.* 980 shew a more pronounced communal spirit when they drove out their archbishop, the tyrannous great noble Landolf II, and only received him again after a battle and a treaty. Considerable must have been the internal cohesion of the city and of its rudimentary organisation to enable its notables to enter even into an informal contract. And their collective character was gaining some sort of recognition too from the royal government. It was to his subjects and inhabitants of Genoa, with no mention of bishop, count, or marquess, that Berengar II in 958 con-

---

[1] MGH, *Poetae Carolini aevi*, III, pp. 703–5.

firmed their local customs and privileges; and when Count Nanno of Verona, acting as imperial *missus*, tried the case of Ratherius, the saintly and fractious Veronese Bishop, he appealed formally for their opinion to the townsmen (*urbani*) gathered *en masse* before him. Their answer, if expressed (so the bishop says) with "porcine clamour," was articulate and resulted in Ratherius' deposition. In both these cases, however, the breach between citizens and bishop remains personal, not constitutional, in its nature, for neither at Verona nor at Milan did the prelate exercise the powers of a count in his city. But a deliberate effort to replace the bishop in some of his governmental rights appears at Cremona, where he was endowed with comital authority over the city and a radius of five miles round it. In 996 the Emperor Otto III granted to the free citizens, "rich and poor," the absolute use of their common rights of pasture and of the river-transit in the *contado* as well as the State rights annexed thereto. The bishop, Ulric, when he heard of the grant, was up in arms, for his were the profitable dues and tolls affected; and soon the unprecedented diploma was quashed.

Thus we can sum up the results of the Ottonian peace on the cities. More populous, more wealthy, more secure, their embryonic institutions were allowing them to act collectively, however heterogeneous their population of nobles, great and small, and plebeians might be. As a rule, doubtless, their bishop was still their protector, the nucleus round which their rudimentary assemblies could cohere. At this very time, in the transaction of the bishopric's secular affairs we find the bishop surrounded by a council which included lay vassals of his and notables, and the steward of his lands, the *vicedominus*, was in many cases becoming lay and hereditary. But if such incidents as that of Cremona were exceptions which chequered a usually good understanding, they nevertheless go to shew the sense of an independent corporate existence among the citizens, that they were not merely the prolongation of the bishop's shadow. Pisa, early mature through her shipping, could wage a city-war with neighbouring Lucca in 1004, and in the same year King Henry II was receiving hostages and collective oaths of fealty from the Lombard towns[1]. Communes and consuls there were none as yet, but notables and assemblies could already act in concert, though all the powers of State-government, strictly speaking, still belonged to imperial or feudal officials. The slowness of the change may have been partly due to the fact that some of these officials or vassals were the leading notables of the town.

In fact, the impulse to association and to the formation of local custom was shewing itself even in the feudal countryside, especially in the little towns (*castelli*) which grew out of the castles of refuge. These were cooperative from the start, in spite of the extreme inequality in the rights

---

[1] Adalbold, *Vita Heinrici*, 41, MGH, *Script.* IV, p. 693: "Civitates etiam, ad quas rex nondum venerat, obsides ultro transmittunt fidemque debitam per sacramenta promittunt"

and status of their denizens, ranging from few lords to many oppressed serfs. The evidence for them, indeed, mostly dates from a later time, but it still allows us to draw some conclusions as to their earlier existence, and as to the economic necessities which compelled some collective action within them. Like the tiny *vicinanze* they possessed common rights to pastures and woods ; there was watch to be kept on the walls, and necessary repairs of their fabric ; and a chief-watchman (*portinarius*) to be appointed by common consent of the feudal lord and his subjects of all degrees. In the rare cases when there was no lord or compossessing family of *signori*, the denizens stepped into his place, as we can see in a unique diploma of Otto II in 983 to the men of Lazise on Lake Garda. These eighteen men, who seem to be merely the chief free men of the *castello*, receive collectively the right to levy tolls and dues, as if they were feudal magnates. They had outrun their city neighbours in this prophetic grant because no feudal lord stood between them and the Emperor.

A variant of these primitive arrangements of the north Italian towns may be seen in the contemporary institutions of Venice, where the continued connexion with the East Roman Empire led both to the earlier foundation of a republican government and to its retention of a quasi-monarchical administration. In Venice ultimate power resided in the tumultuary mass-meeting of the citizens, the *arengo*, which elected the Doge, and approved peace and war and the most important State decisions. The Doge (*Dux*), as befitted the lineal successor of a Byzantine provincial governor, with the aid of his nominees exercised the whole executive, but around him in his solemn court for judgment and consultation gathered the notables, clerical and lay, the *maiores, mediocres, et minores* citizens. These *boni homines*, as they were often called, among whom naturally the landowners (at Venice identical with the chief shippers) predominated, formed a kind of representation of the community, and their presence was practically necessary to an act of State.

In every circumscription in the *Regnum Italicum*, whether *vicinantia, plebs*, or *comitatus*, the *boni homines*, or notables, appear. They were assessors in the courts, witnesses of deeds, arbitrators in voluntary jurisdiction, advisers of the higher authorities, interpreters of local custom. They were not a noble class, but in the city were normally free landholders, preferably of some rank. Among them would be the *iudices* (the legal experts, earlier called *scabini*), the holders of *curtes* (manors) within the walls, and a selection of lesser nobles and freemen who had become well-to-do in trade. It was the *boni homines*, a composite collection of notables long-practised in local affairs, who were to be the animating nucleus of the future commune.

The first movement towards city-autonomy, strictly speaking, seems to have taken place in southern Italy. There, outside the limits of the *Regnum Italicum*, among warring, fragmentary states and laxly-held Byzantine territories, the notables, with the active or passive assent of

CH. V.

the population, could form a more or less comprehensive league of townsmen and extort, or take unheeded, from their sovereign part at least of the functions of government. "*Facta est communitas prima,*" we read in the *Annals of Benevento* under 1015[1]. The pact of Sergius IV, Duke of Naples, with his subjects *c.* 1030 recognises such a *societas*, though perhaps of nobles only, and engages that peace or war shall not be declared, nor customs changed, nor a noble tried, save with the consent of the nobles. Still earlier, during the minority of their Duke Atenolf II, *c.* 1000, the nobles and *boni homines* of Gaeta obtained a share in political power. The participation of the wealthy shippers in the government of Amalfi was at least as large. All these towns, however, were the capitals of hereditary princes; and more real communal forms are to be dimly discerned in the restless cities of Apulia under the weak Byzantine rule. Thus at Bari the *Fraternitas Sanctae Mariae*, headed by the archbishop, appears to have taken a leading part in the faction-fights, defence, and effective government of the town. The city of Troia enjoyed practical autonomy, at the price of a tribute, from its foundation by the catapan Boioannes in 1018. Assembled in the bishop's court, the chief citizens (*seniores* and *boni homines*) chose their judge and turmarch (commander-in-chief) and directed affairs. In these Apulian proto-communes, the scanty evidence gives the impression that they were more strictly oligarchic in character than their congeners in the north. The bishop and the *nobiliores homines* seem to act for their fellow-citizens with no appeal to a city-assembly. It was a difference more in form than in substance, which was due perhaps to Byzantine, anti-popular influences, and in any case was obliterated by the appearance of an assembly when in the twelfth century the Apulian cities take rank as full-fledged, but definitely subject, *universitates* under the Norman dukes.

The fact, however, that the Apulian towns fell under Norman rule before their institutions were fully developed, separates them sharply from the city-states of North Italy, which in fact, if not in theory, were in their maturity independent republics. In the eleventh century the northern towns were only in process of attaining internal solidarity and self-government. There it was only gradually, and so to say blindly, through many tentative variations, that the sworn league (*coniuratio*), which appears perhaps[2] as early as the tenth century among sections of the *bourgeoisie*, coalesces with the city-assembly in a *commune*. We may assume, arguing from later custom, that it was probably the city-assembly, the mass-meeting of inhabitants, which took the collective oath of fealty to Henry II in 1004, and at Ivrea to Marquess Ulric-Manfred II of Turin

---

[1] *Annales Beneventani* (*S. Sophiae*), BISI, 42, p. 131. The *coniuratio secundo* of 1041(2) (*ibid.* p. 135) gives a valuable light on the meaning of *communitas* and the method of forming a commune.

[2] For the term *coniuratio* for the league of the Milanese *c.* 980 against Archbishop Landolf II is only used by the chronicler Arnulf (*c.* 1070).

c. 1016 in terms which hint at the process by which the sworn association long after became identical with the city-state[1]. But the special protection which Henry II granted in 1014 to *omnes maiores homines* dwelling in the *castello* (borough) of Savona, and to *cunctos arimannos* dwelling in the city of Mantua, can only refer to definite classes of the population. Leaving aside, however, such a special kind of landholder as the *arimannus* of the eleventh century, we find the population of the north Italian cities falling into three main divisions, the *capitanei*, the *valvassores minores* or *secundi milites*, and the plebeians[2], *i.e.* roughly speaking, the barons, the knights and squires, and the non-nobles. The two first classes were by no means composed solely of nobles who held manors or fiefs in the city proper. A large number of the countryside nobles resided for a part of the year within the walls. This was an immemorial custom in town-loving Italy, and had been given a stronger hold by the barbarian ravages of the tenth century. In consequence in the early class-warfare we cannot precisely distinguish in their case between town and country, nor can we indeed draw any hard and fast line of demarcation in later times. The plebeians, however, when town-bred, are townsmen only. A further characteristic of these nobles, and indeed of their times, is the rapid multiplication when once devastation and anarchy had been removed by the Ottonian peace. It was favoured by the room made by previous de-population, and by the practice of compossession, or at the least of equal subdivision of inheritances, which was all but universal in Italy. Thus the families of *capitanei* already amounted to a respectable fighting force, especially as they were at the head of numerous *masnadieri* (to use a later term) or unfree retainers, while the lesser vavassors were naturally very numerous. In the end, indeed, both classes in the countryside were impoverished by their own numerousness. The twelfth-century *cattani* (*capitanei*) of Tuscany were often little better than small country squires, and there the term *Lombardi* occasionally comes to mean groups of freed *masnadieri* as well as survivors of the older nobility.

The habit of sworn associations among classes of the population first comes clearly to light in the war (1035–1037) between the *capitanei* of the Milanese province, headed by Archbishop Aribert, and the lesser vavassors, in which the vavassors, partly by the aid of the Emperor Conrad II, finally gained the day[3]. Henceforward the minor nobility had the same security of tenure (*i.e.* practically the full property) of their fiefs as their privileged suzerains. The opposition, however, remained between the two orders, occasioned by difference of wealth and status,

---

[1] "*Communiter* cives sibi iurare fecit." Bloch, *Neu. Arch.* XXII, 17. Cf. the acceptance by the Lodese *c.* 1027 of a new bishop on the nomination of Archbishop Aribert of Milan: "in *commune* deliberant suscipiendum episcopum." Arnulfus Mediol. II, 7.

[2] Cf. *supra*, Vol. III, Chaps. VII, pp. 174–5, X, p. 221, XI, p. 265. The term *valvassor* became appropriated to the *valvassores minores* in common usage.

[3] See *supra*, Vol. III, Chap. XI, pp. 265–7.

and even of profession, as commerce increased and some minor nobles became traders; and to it was added the enmity between both and the third class, the plebeians, or to use the later vernacular name, the *popolani,* whose leaders were naturally the merchants, *negotiatores.* The rise of the plebeians was indeed intimately connected with the increase of population and trade. Italy produced more; her consumption of necessaries, such as salt and cloth, and of luxuries, *e.g.* silk and spices, was greater. From her seaport towns, along the natural arteries of the Lombard rivers, over the chief Alpine passes, the transport of foreign and native wares grew in volume. Her manufactures, such as they were, began to flourish with the enlarged home and foreign demand, trivial indeed if we compare present-day statistics, but highly wealth-bringing then. There was already noticeable a drift of peasants to the cities where such gains and comparative freedom were to be had. We may almost say that these plebeians were recruited for two centuries from the enterprising and adventurous.

The life of the Italian cities, and later of their communes, was almost inextricably intertwined with their church and its head, the bishop. Civic patriotism, religious emotion, and the ordinary transactions of life, the market and the festival, all clustered round the city-saints and their fanes, and it is barely possible to define the relative shares of the religious, the political, or the economic motive. When Aribert was imprisoned by the Emperor Conrad during the war of the vavassors, a mixture of civic, religious, and even national enthusiasm swept over the Milanese. The citizens, with the exception we may assume of the vavassors then withdrawn to the countryside, rushed to arms, were enraptured at their archbishop's escape, and successfully withstood an imperial siege[1]. Whether the league[2] on this occasion strictly included more than *capitanei* may be doubted, but the practical co-operation of the plebeians is none the less clear. It only required the peace between *capitanei* and vavassors for them to form a party of their own. Already Aribert had invented the standard of the future commune, which became the emblem of civic liberty all over North Italy. Round the *carroccio,* the ox-drawn waggon with its pole and flag, the citizens henceforth rallied in battle.

Aribert had not long been reconciled with the Emperor Henry III, when the new development took place at Milan. Whatever grudges existed between *capitanei* and vavassors, they united in insolence to the plebeians. The ancient authority of the Marquess-Count of Milan, an Otbertine, had decayed, the Archbishop was himself the greatest of the *capitanei* by blood, and the oppression of many noble tyrants became intolerable. In 1042 the explosion came when a plebeian was slain by a knight in a private quarrel. The ever-enduring feuds among the nobles were to be a continual advantage to the *popolani,* and now the people

---

[1] See *supra,* Vol. III, Chap. XI, pp. 266–7.

[2] Wipo, *Gesta Chuonradi,* xxxv, "tumultus…populi Mediolanensis quaereutis ab imperatore si vellet favere coniurationi eorum."

found a leader in the *capitaneus* and jurist Lanzo, notary and *iudex Sacri Palatii*. With slaughter and rapine the whole body of nobles was driven out: Aribert himself, no longer a popular idol, decamped; and a new siege was endured for three years with fierce heroism until weariness, the threatened intervention of Henry III, and the statesmanship of Lanzo led to an accommodation in 1044. The nobles returned under terms of mutual oblivion of the past, but "the state of the city and its Church had been changed."[1] Henceforward the plebeians form a separate power, and the curious tripartite constitution of the later Milanese commune had begun. Henry III, perhaps, thought to take a middle course when he appointed a vavassor, Guido, to succeed Aribert as archbishop, but neither the fissure between classes was to be healed, nor the instinct for self-government to be conjured, by the fact that the archbishop was not formidable either by birth or character.

None the less, we still find the archbishop taking the lead in the next corporate act of his city, the war of Milan with Pavia in 1059; it needed the convulsion of the religious struggle lasting over twenty years from 1056 to shatter finally the archiepiscopal authority, as that of the marquess, last effectively exercised shortly after Guido's accession, had long been made obsolete. The strife, however, not only ousted the archbishop from power; it enabled a real commune to be formed by merging class-distinctions in religious factions. If the conservatives, who upheld the autonomy and ancient usages of the see of St Ambrose, included most of the nobles, and the reformers had a majority among the plebeians, especially among the poorest class, from which their derisive name of Patarines, "rag-pickers," was derived, yet the reforming leaders who led the agitation for clerical celibacy and the abolition of simony belonged to noble houses, and had many associates of their own rank[2]. The greatest of them, the *capitaneus* Erlembald, taught autonomy to his fellow-citizens. The lean, red-bearded man, with his flashing eyes, could carry with him any assembly, great or small, and dominated the people by his oratory. A council (or was it an executive committee?) of thirty surrounded him, but in these times of revolution the *arengo* played a part it never did in the settled constitution. When that was really established in Milan we do not know, but in 1097 we find the first mention of the *consuls* of the city[3]; and the existence of consuls implies that of the *commune* of which they were the elected rulers.

Every commune had its peculiar features, due to its local characteristics and local history, and Milan was especially marked by the share the nobles of the countryside took in the commune from the start, and

---

[1] Arnulfus Mediol. II, 18, "adeo execrandum...ut...immutatus sit status urbis et ecclesiae." That nobles and plebeians each formed sworn leagues is implied by "partium fiunt iuramenta quam plurima." [2] See *supra*, Chap. I, p. 40.

[3] "Actum in ciuitate Mediolani in consulatu ciuium" in a Cremonese document (P. Del Giudice, *Di un recente opuscolo ecc.* See Bibliography III). Cf. *Gli Atti del comune di Milano*, Introd. pp. xxviii–xxxi.

by the strict division of orders in the state. An unusual number of nobles from at least three surrounding counties dwelt partially in the greatest city of the plain; the plebeians rose early to wealth; and the rapid succession of class and religious wars crystallised distinctions of rank at an early date into their final forms. Thus the consuls were carefully divided among the classes; in 1130 seven were *capitanei*, seven were vavassors, and six plain citizens. It is another aspect of the same circumstances that Milan had little trouble with her dependent *contadi*, where the feudal lords were her own chief citizens. Her early wars were only with weaker cities such as Lodi and Como, or with rivals like the ancient capital Pavia.

Most northern cities, either by their institutions or by their recorded history, give evidence of class-warfare[1] as one cause of the emergence of the commune, although this was by no means universal. The civil discord, which seems almost invariable, might be due to the dissensions of the nobles among themselves, each faction with their abettors among the plebeians. While at Lucca the people, aided here by the clergy and some nobles, rose against their reforming bishop Anselm and Countess Matilda and established consuls c. 1080, at Pisa we find the popular Archbishop Daimbert, with five colleagues, publishing c. 1090 an award limiting the height of the towers from which the nobles warred on one another. As we might expect in this undeveloped time, the *commune colloquium*, *i.e.* the *arengo*, is the chief constitutional instrument[2], but something like a council is indicated, and c. 1084 Pisa already had consuls. The commune may have been established by the earlier *securitas* or award of Bishop Gerard (1080–1085).

All over North Italy, however, at the commencement of the twelfth century, consuls, the indubitable evidence of the full-fledged commune emerging from the semi-autonomy of the eleventh century, were appearing, here earlier, there later, according to the events of local history or the chances of the preservation of the evidence to our days. Thus in Lombardy, consuls are mentioned at Asti in 1093, at Pavia in 1105, at Brescia in 1127, at Bologna in 1123; the first known consuls of Genoa date from 1099; in Tuscany, Siena has consuls in 1125 and Florence in 1138, while in the documents of Arezzo they first appear in 1098. It has become increasingly plain of late years[3] how they arose. During the

---

[1] At Piacenza in 1090 (? 1091) circumstances were much like those in Milan in 1042: a *miles* fights a *pedes*. See Codagnelli, *Ann. Placentini* (SGUS), p. 1. The *milites* abandoned the city, re-entered it during the absence of the army of the *pedites*, and finally a *concordia et pax* was agreed to.

[2] In 1081 the Emperor Henry IV promises to appoint no fresh Marquess of Tuscany without the assent of twelve Pisans to be elected in the *commune colloquium*.

[3] This view was put forward by R. Davidsohn, *Entstehung des Consulats*, in *Deutsch. Zeitschrift f. Geschichtswissenschaft*, VI, p. 22, 1891, and still earlier by A. Mazzi, *Studi bergomensi*, 1888, whose works did not attract attention for some years.

growth of civic freedom in the eleventh century, the city-notables, the *boni homines*, like the more numerous notables of the several subordinate *viciniae* among whom they were also counted, played an increasingly important part. It was the *boni homines*—mostly greater or lesser nobles, with jurists and a sprinkling of wealthy traders—who advised the bishop in his *curia*, the count or marquess in his *placitum*, and took the lead in the *commune colloquium*, the *parlamento* or *arengo*, of the whole city. As the need for a more definite city-executive grew, a commission of *boni homines* would be appointed, often *ad hoc* for some special business[1], but soon permanently with the name of consuls. For instance twelve *boni homines* represent Siena in business at Rome in 1124, but next year consuls are in office. Occasionally we find the documents allow for the possibility that not consuls but *boni homines* may be in power in some future year[2], there being yet no absolute permanency of the office. In Genoa, till late in the twelfth century, the *compagna* of the citizens, which established *consuls* and a common government, was renewable every few years[3].

This very conservative habit of Genoa emphasises another aspect in the rise of the commune. It was intended to include the whole city; it was established by the *commune colloquium*; but it was in origin a private sworn association for the maintenance of peace and the common advantage of those who swore to it. It started from the *coniurationes* we have marked among classes or persons. When the *arengo* was called upon to swear collectively to such a league, we may say it became a commune[4]. We still find in 1162 at Pisa, in 1143 at Genoa, a kind of boycott and denial of aid and justice contemplated for such notables as refused to join the league[5]. With the establishment of consuls two oaths were taken in the *arengo*, the one by each consul binding him to certain duties for his term of office, the other by a representative in the name of the assembled people, which must have included from the first a promise to

[1] See the instance of Pisa, *supra*, p. 220, n. 2.

[2] *E.g.* at Lucca in 1147, and at Colle and S. Gimignano in 1199; see Davidsohn, *Origine del Consolato*, ASI, Ser. v, Vol. ix (1892), pp. 240–1.

[3] Cafarus, *Annales Ianuenses*, ad annos. Cf. the *Statuta Consulatus* in MHP, ii, *Leges munic.* i, c. 241 sqq., and the *Breve compagne*, MHP, xviii, *Leges Genuen.* c. 5 sqq.: "iuro compagnam usque ad annos quatuor."

[4] More stress is here laid on the importance of the collective oath of the *arengo* as establishing the commune than is usual. Cf. *supra*, p. 216, n. 1.

[5] For Genoa see the *Statuta Consulatus Ianuensis* of 1143, MHP, ii, *Leges munic.* i, c. 243: "Si quis Ianuensis ab aliquo ex nobis specialiter et nominatim vocatus vel a pluribus publice vocatus...fuerit intrare in nostram compangnam, et infra xl dies non introierit, non illi debiti erimus et personam eius et lamentationes eius per hos iii annos non recipiemus...neque aliquod officium de communi illi dabimus...et laudabimus populo ut personam eius...et pecuniam suam per mare non portet." For Pisa see the *Breve consulum* of 1162, Bonaini, *Statuti inediti di Pisa*, i, 9: "Eorum autem reclamationes qui sacramentum consulatui non fecerint inquisiti, nisi a...consulibus remissum fuerit, mea sint voluntate."

obey the consuls[1]. These oaths which gave definite authority to an elected magistracy could scarcely have been exchanged until such a magistracy was established in the consulate, with which therefore we may date the beginning of the commune proper[2].

There has been debate on the origin of the new title. It was known, we saw, in North Italy at Ravenna and Rome as a title of dignity, and in eleventh-century Rome the *consules Romanorum* exercise functions in the city government. These, and the style *consul et dux* borne by the rulers of Naples and Gaeta, may have suggested or kept alive the title, but it was probably a conscious return to Roman tradition, kept up in so many cities by the schools of grammar, which led men to choose with striking unanimity the classic term for a collegiate republican magistracy. The influence of education is, indeed, not to be disregarded in the formation of Italian communes. Proud of their civic traditions and their Roman past, the city-nobles received a more learned education than the illiterate Transalpines. Besides schools of grammar there existed schools of law, where nobles obtained the legal knowledge necessary for the function of *iudices*, or jurists, and notaries, to which many of them were addicted almost by hereditary succession. The Pavese jurist, Archbishop Lanfranc of Canterbury, was no exceptional portent, and the increased study of Justinian's Code towards the close of the eleventh century synchronises with the emergence of the commune. Thus the adoption of the term consuls for the chief magistracy is more than a choice of words; it symbolises the classic learning, the legal training, the heritage from the ancient world, which made the city-state, so to say, natural in Italy.

If religious, economic, and cultural phenomena all played parts in the birth of the commune, the purely political circumstances of the Holy Roman Empire also had most important effects. The Saxon and Salian Emperors inherited a monarchy already debilitated, and were of necessity absentees. Although Otto the Great might shrewdly balance bishop against marquess, yet in the end his successors could never favour any local magnate in the subject *Regnum Italicum* without reserve. An archbishop of Milan might be as dangerous to his distant foreign suzerain as a marquess of Tuscany. A feudal monarch was not unnaturally but half a friend to his great vassals. Like Conrad II he might deliberately weaken them at a critical time, and, unlike more lasting kingdoms, in Italy the monarch was seldom present to take their place in government. Hence throughout the eleventh century it is not only the functions of the king that are exercised at spasmodic intervals and wither, but those

---

[1] The *sacramentum consulatui*, which became later the *sacramentum sequimenti potestatis*. The words at Genoa in 1157 were (MHP, xviii, *Leges Genuen.* c. 5): "quodcumque ipsi electi consules laudaverint aut statuerint secundum quod in eorum brevibus determinatum est...observabo et operabor."

[2] Evidence for the contemporaneous institution of consuls and *compagna* may be seen in the townships subject to Genoa, *e.g.* "faciemus compagnam et consulatum in plebeio Lavanie" (1157). Caro, *Die Verfassung Genuas*, p. 73, n. 123.

of the great vassals too, episcopal or lay. The citizens, favoured like the Savonese by Henry II or the Lucchese and Pisans by Henry IV, were quick to take advantage of the weakness of their rulers, whether it was due to revolts, invasions, religious wars, feuds, or the mere break-up of the great fiefs by the practice of compossession, which subdivided for instance the great Otbertine house into five or six numerous branches. In Tuscany, which retained primogeniture, the power of the marquess, although even there endangered, outlasted in the person of Countess Matilda that of all its unwiser compossessing competitors. And the strength and the practical efficiency of the citizens were mounting steadily as those of the official holders of the public power declined. The functions, legal and executive, of these became formal, and the groups of citizens, themselves largely composed of secondary nobles, could by co-operative action and voluntary jurisdiction leave little room for the count, and in the end usurped the undoubted powers of the State. The same decadence of the official government had aided in the establishment of proto-communes in Byzantine Apulia. It was not unanalogous to the genesis of feudalism itself, and an age of feudal lords, of private wars, and of local custom, saw little strange in cities making wars and internal leagues save their odd capacity of acting in concert and enforcing their common regulations.

The usurpation of public functions and attributes by the communes was also rendered easier by the status of some of their members. The branches of the vicecomital house remained the leading members of the *compagna* of Genoa; the Viscounts (*Visconti*) of Pisa and Milan, and the *Vicedomini* (*Visdomini*) of Florence, were chief clans in their respective communes. Above all the bishops, who even when they had been elbowed out of their comital rights were usually reconciled to the new state of affairs in the first half of the twelfth century, were invaluable allies to their fellow-citizens. They at least held a position of unquestioned legality in the feudal chain; they could, even when not invested with comital powers, yet at least for their episcopal fiefs (*episcopium*) receive homage and conclude recognised feudal contracts. Thus the Archbishop of Pisa and the Bishop of Siena are all-important for the enlargement and formation of their communes' dominion over the *contadi* (counties) surrounding them. The lords of the countryside, new allies or vanquished enemies, surrendered their lands to the bishop and his city or to the bishop alone, and, by contracts which no feudal lawyer could impugn, became subjects to a private power as yet non-existent or incapable of such action in the eyes of feudal jurisprudence.

The enlargement of the rule of the city-commune over the county (*contado*) and diocese of which it was the centre was the most natural of developments, an aggression which was barely distinguishable from defence. From the beginning, the city-notables headed by the bishop, and the city itself, had lands in the *contado*; and these links were rendered more numerous by a process in the countryside too which was in full activity early in the twelfth century. With their multiplication, the nobility did not grow less oppressive to their serfs; in fact, poorer by reason of their numbers, they were the more inclined to heap abuse on abuse (new exaction, uncustomary, *ab usu*)[1] on their serfs. But these, too, were more numerous and restive, more inclined and able to resist, if their lords were not too great dignitaries. Hence, there is a double stream of immigration to the cities: one of lesser nobles, seeking a new way of livelihood, such as the historic Buondelmonti who thus joined the original city-nobility, the Uberti and others, at Florence; the other of peasants, *contadini*, lured by the comparative freedom of the town. For some cities this voluntary adhesion of the countryside nobles continued to be the chief means of gaining control of the *contado*. The greatest lords round Pisa, the Gherardesca and the Upezzinghi, along with a crowd of lesser feudatories, were glad to be enrolled, whether as vassals of the archbishop or without an intermediary, as Pisan citizens.

But there were motives which urged the communes to forcible expansion as well. There was the city food-supply to be assured; there was the security of the citizens, new and old, and their lands outside the walls; there were inherited feuds and claims, ecclesiastical and secular; there were the freedom and safety of roads, the abolition of tolls and blackmail, and the exit and entrance of the commerce, which took an ever larger share in the city's thoughts; there was the independence of the city itself to be preserved from ancient or invented feudal claims. If lesser nobles could be both troublesome neighbours and a tempting prey, it was the surviving greater houses, strong in fiefs and vassals, who were most dangerous. For many years Florence waged war with her neighbours, the Counts Guidi, heirs in some degree of Matilda, and the Alberti of Prato, thus gaining by slow progresses, and the capture of castle after castle, the control of her immediate surroundings. Siena slowly mastered the powerful counts around her in the same twelfth century. One usual condition of peace enforced by the victorious commune was the compulsory citizenship and partial residence within the walls, say for three months a year, of her vanquished enemies. This was only doing by compulsion what so many nobles had done and were doing of their free will, but while it gave the commune a stronger hold on the countryside, it also, as we shall see, intensified the native disorder prevalent among the half-feudal clans of the city.

Thus, as the twelfth century wore on, the great communes were securing control of the greater part of their diocese or *contado*. It was the commune which superintended in the last resort justice and peace, and levied its vassals for war. There did not thence follow any difference in the status of the serf, who remained subject to his immediate lord, or the city which succeeded him. Nevertheless, a very considerable change

---

[1] An *ab-usus* was a regular new exaction, a *supra-usus*, a capricious one.

was taking place over tracts of the countryside in North Italy. The inhabitants of the *castelli* or fortified townships, and even of lesser places, were forming communes of their own, arising out of the necessary co-operation between compossessing lords and *vicini*. As early as 1093 the Counts of Biandrate in Lombardy shared the jurisdiction over their town of Biandrate with twelve consuls of the *habitatores*, appointed seemingly from the ranks of the *rustici*, the peasants. They made a separate grant to vassal nobles, *milites*, but these submitted to the consuls' jurisdiction. All through the twelfth century we find petty communes arising and developing in Tuscany. They might begin from groups of lesser vassals or freeholders or of freed *masnadieri*, organised in a community known as *Lombards*—in this fashion we find the commune of the men of San Gervasio in Val d'Era assenting to the sale of their *castello* and *curtis* by the count whose fief it was to the Bishop of Lucca. They might be similar associations of the *villani* or serfs of a *vicinia* or of a whole *pieve*. The two communities often subsisted together in the same district, but they end in being united as a *communis et populus*. With an infinite variety of constituents and history, they were approaching throughout the twelfth century a common type, the rural commune of landholders of different status, governed by its elected consuls. It was rather local administration, land-rights, and cultivation, than politics proper which formed the subject of these township-communities. What was in process was the decease of feudalism as an economic and administrative system, and its replacement by co-operative arrangements which drew their origin eventually from immemorial methods of using and sharing the land, all quickened to new growth by a new prosperity.

To sum up this aspect of the theme: towards the close of the twelfth century North Italy was subdivided into a considerable number of city-states, the great communes, for the most part, though not all, ancient episcopal sees. They were rapidly growing in wealth and population, how rapidly may be gathered from the new and wider circuits of walls they were constrained to build. Pisa already had her new walls by 1081, Piacenza before 1158; Florence was building her Second Circle in 1172–4, Modena in 1188, and Padua in 1195; and the fact implies the existence of important suburbs outside the old walls for some time previously. These vigorous towns were in perpetual strife with one another and with the surviving great feudal lords, who like the Pelavicini, the Estensi, the Marquesses of Montferrat in Lombardy, the Malaspina in Lunigiana, or the Aldobrandeschi in Tuscany, held out amid the mountains and the marshes. With these exceptions, they were ruling in various ways and degrees their *contado*, the county and diocese surrounding them, ruling from one point of view over a strange medley of feudal vassals, freemen, and serfs of all degrees, from another over an assemblage of petty communities, all illustrations of that method of self-management by association and league, which was necessary for safety,

CH. V.

which was dictated by tradition and material circumstances, and which was provoked by the decadence and abuses of outworn feudalism.

The energies of the communes were far from being wholly absorbed in self-government, in internal production, and in the annexation of their *contadi*. The inter-city wars went on with unceasing fury from year to year, it might be said from century to century. Not till Siena was annexed by Cosimo of Florence in 1557, was their series over. In some degree these conflicts had their rise in sheer antipathy and jealousy. The strongly-marked character of each commune, its intense local patriotism, made its neighbours its enemies. Old disputes over diocesan boundaries, as between Pisa and Lucca, Siena and Arezzo, or over feudal claims of superiority, as between Milan and Lodi, furnished grounds for dispute where sentiment had free play. The moral shortcomings of each Italian town are enshrined in civic proverbs and in Dante. But far more important were the causes of strife which arose from the mutual relations of towns depending on commerce for their prosperity and independence. Geography and trade in combination were the most explosive compound of nature and art. Seaports were rivals in a narrow but profitable market, when piracy and trading went hand in hand. By land there was the outlet to the sea, or a toll-free road by land, as well as rivalry in manufacture, to create discord. Commercial competition for the protection of home-industry or the possession of the carrying-trade was the staple of these city-wars.

Effective though the Crusades were in making the Italian seaports European powers, in increasing their wealth and the scope of their enterprise, and in enlarging the mental horizon of all Europe, they did not begin the career of the maritime republics. The trade of these was of natural growth, and it was rather in the pre-crusading wars with the western Saracens, in the abolition of Muslim piracy, and in the opening of sea-routes to the Ponent (the West) and the Levant (the East), that they secured their pre-eminence. Venice, by taming the Slav pirates of Dalmatia and defeating the Sicilian Muslims at Bari in 1002, was in a way to become queen of the Adriatic. Pisa, sacked by Saracens in 1004 and 1011, could yet defeat them near Reggio in 1005 and, in concert with Genoa, rescue Sardinia from Mujāhid of Denia in 1016. This victory began the long wars of Pisa and Genoa, fought for the trade of the Mediterranean and more especially for the exploitation of Sardinia and Corsica. They were still allies against their common enemy, the Saracens, but their joint capture (1087) of Mahdīyah in Barbary from Tamīm the Zairid, and the famous temporary conquest (1113–15) of the Balearic Isles by the Pisans and Christian allies from the neighbouring coasts (with the exception of Genoa), together with the Norman conquest of Sicily (1061–1091), established Christian supremacy in the Ponent. Thereafter, Pisans and Genoese fought one another with little relaxation in East and West. Amalfi, once first in the Levantine trade, faded under its Norman masters, and its sack in 1135 by the Pisans, in the service of Pope and Emperor, hastened its decline. But the bull (1133) of Innocent II which assigned Sardinia and half Corsica to the Pisan sphere of ecclesiastical influence, and the rest of Corsica to the new Genoese archbishopric, only resulted in a truce. The two cities fought for influence in Sardinia, for trade with Sicily and the Ponent, and in the East there was a three-cornered struggle between them and Venice. The strife of Pope and Emperor, the Crusades, were incidents in and opportunities for this civic rivalry. If Pisa at first took the lead and was predominant in Sardinia at the close of the twelfth century, she was, nevertheless, fatally hampered by her open *contado* and strong Tuscan neighbours. Genoa, once she had subdued her Riviera, was secured by the Apennines from inland rivalry; and during the thirteenth century Pisa slowly lost ground.

The geography of Tuscany was largely responsible for the inland rivalries of the province. Across the encircling Apennines came all-important roads from the north. By the Monte Bardone (now the Pontremoli) Pass came the Via Francigena from Parma (joined by the land-route from Genoa) to Lucca. Then it crossed the River Arno near Fucecchio and struck south to Siena and Rome. From Bologna, the chief junction-city on the Emilian Way, came two roads, one through Pistoia, the other straight across the Apennines to Florence. From Florence again two roads led to Rome, one westerly to Poggibonsi, where it joined the Via Francigena and also a direct route from Pisa, through Volterra, to Siena, and the other, the ancient Via Cassia, easterly, past Arezzo, down the valley of the Chiana, under Montepulciano, to Orvieto and Rome. From Florence, too, flowed the natural artery to the sea, the River Arno, with its port at Pisa. To these trade-route factors should be added finally the lure of fertile stretches of countryside for food, for produce, and for men. Each commune was anxious for trade-outlets under its own control, the power of controlling the outlets of its neighbours, and for a wide subject-territory. Nowhere was the theory of territorial corridors better understood than in medieval Tuscany.

As a result Pisa and Lucca were early mortal enemies. There were disputed tracts of fertile *contado*. Lucca held both the northern outlet of the Via Francigena and its crossing at the Arno. Pisa held its gate, and that of most Tuscany, to the sea. Pisa fought to gain a footing on the Via Francigena before it reached Lucca, to control the mouth of the Lucchese river, the Serchio, and to remove Lucca's grip on the middle Arno at Fucecchio. The Lucchese sought to compel all trade from the north to halt in their city and pay dues there, and to prevent a Pisan wedge intervening between them and Siena. Already in 1003 the two cities, not yet communes, were fighting. Early in the twelfth century, the struggle took a more permanent form, and the Lucchese became the born allies of the Genoese in their war with Pisa.

While her manufactures, chiefly of cloth, were of small account,

Florence was seldom Pisa's enemy. They were not next-door neighbours and Lucca's hold on the Arno was vexatious to both. As late as 1171 they allied against Genoa and Lucca, at the price of free trade and equal opportunity for the Florentines in Pisa. But the terms were burdensome to Pisa, and the Florentine advance southward was causing an opposition of interests. Florence was endowed with a large *contado* and was anxious to extend it, but was also anxious to free her roads to Rome and the west. Thus she was hostile to Arezzo, a backward feudal hill-town, and still more to Siena. Florence wished for the Val Chiana and its road, and for Monte Pulciano, which would give her free exit to Orvieto and Rome. She was also eager to wrest the cross-roads at Poggibonsi from Siena, so as to have a footing on the Via Francigena and the road to Pisa. The wars caused by this enmity, pursued through the twelfth century, led to Florence ousting the Sienese from Poggibonsi in 1208 and repelling them from Monte Pulciano. With these minor communes in the Florentine sphere of influence, with the Florentine acquisition of Empoli on the lower Arno in 1182, with the rapid increase of Florence's manufacture, wealth, and power, the Pisans could no longer favour their new rival's prosperity. The Italian communes, no more than ancient Greek cities, were able to live and let live; their passionate patriotism was wholly local; their institutions, sprung from small local units and dictated by local needs, were by nature incapable of territorial extension; their interests were sharply antagonistic. No city could share its freedom with another; rather, full freedom and independence were only obtainable by the depression or even subjection of rivals. Thus we find Pisa, which had of late immensely profited by its services to the Empire, holding aloof in 1197, together with threatened Pistoia, from the Tuscan League of San Genesio, which was led by Florence and promoted by the Papacy so as to reduce the imperial interference, lately made so real by Henry VI, in the province. Rupture and war with Florence did not come till 1218, but it thenceforward continued with intervals till the fall of Pisa in 1405. In the thirteenth century, the foes of Florence are the Ghibelline Pisa, Siena, Pistoia, and Arezzo, those neighbouring communes in fact whose submission was requisite and whose rivalry was to be dreaded for the free development of her commerce. Lucca was a faithful friend, but to Pisa's enemy.

The circumstances of the central band of Italy, of the Roman Campagna, the Duchy of Spoleto, and the March of Ancona, seem altogether more primitive than those of the great commercial cities of the north. Besides the Tuscan roads to Rome, the chief commercial and military routes were the coast-road (Via Apruntina) past Ancona to the south, and that roughly in the line of the ancient Flaminian Way which crossed the Apennines from Fano and led by two main tracks past a string of cities, like Perugia, to Rome. But these small towns fought rather for land than for commercial supremacy. They were cramped for room in their narrow Umbrian valleys. Yet even in Umbria there appears a tendency for the cities in connexion with the western route to group round its central town, Perugia, in hostility to the cities on the old Roman Way, with their leader, Spoleto.

It was partly disputes over their respective boundaries, partly the desire for free, or rather preferential, outlets for their trade, which made the communes so frequently enemies of their immediate neighbours and allies of the city from which they were divided by those neighbours; and these tendencies were increased by the fact that while a petty commune not unusually accepted cheerfully a great city's overlordship and protection, those of middle size fought desperately for their full autonomy and all autonomy could give. These characteristics are marked when we turn to the geography and politics of Lombardy and the Romagna.

The whole of Lombardy between the Alps and the Apennines was linked together by its natural artery, the River Po and its tributaries, with the assistance of a few subsidiary streams, like the Adige, to the east. Along these waterways the commerce of the land had arisen; they remained the cheapest form of transit. The commercial outlets to the north were by a series of Alpine passes: the Mont Cenis and Mont Genèvre, debouching into the plain at Susa in the territory of the Count of Savoy; the Great St Bernard coming from Savoyard Aosta to Ivrea; the Splugen, the Septimer, and the Stelvio entering Italy at Como; the Brenner, whence routes ran to Verona and Brescia; and the less known Strada d'Alemagna reaching to Vicenza and Padua. To the south the chief outlets were the ports of Venice and Genoa. At Venice was the meeting-place of the trade from the Po and the Brenner and that from the Levant. At Genoa the sea-trade similarly met that from the western Alpine passes, focussed on the way at Asti and Vercelli. But there were also the land-exits to the south. From Piacenza on the Po the Emilian Way went through a series of wealthy cities till it reached Rimini on the Adriatic. Leading from it there were the Via Francigena, branching off at Parma, the roads to Florence, branching off at Bologna, and the Flaminian Way from Rimini to Rome. Favourable positions on all these routes brought wealth and greatness. It was the aim of every city to control as long stretches of them as possible, and if possible to control exits over the mountains and by the sea.

To the west Genoa was fortunate in an early domination of her narrow Riviera and in the formidable barrier of the Apennines in her rear. Her cue was merely to be sure that trade flowed steadily from the inland emporiums which needed her more than she needed them. Asti was mainly preoccupied in securing free transit from the passes; her chief enemies were the feudal marquesses (the Aleramids of Montferrat, Saluzzo, etc.) who survived in backward Piedmont; it became her ambition to dominate the little communes which sprang up in the twelfth century on the routes to the Western Alps, as it had previously been to enlarge

CH. V

her direct *contado*. Milan, in the centre, was a more potent focus of disturbance. An ancient capital, populous and powerful as the centre of a wide champaign, a seat of manufacture at the meeting-place of almost every route, she had every temptation for aggression. First, she is seen gaining outlets; she conquers and reconquers in 1118 and 1127 Como, which blocked the way to the Alps[1], and Lodi (1027, 1107–11), which lay between her and the Po. Almost at the same time[2] began her enmity, soon to become traditional, with the other capital, Pavia, and Cremona, rival centres these of the transit commerce, and keys of the Po, no mere entrances to it. Milan's natural allies were Crema and Tortona, threatened respectively by Cremona and Pavia with the same fate which Lodi and Como had undergone from Milan. By the usual chequer-pattern of these feuds, Brescia and Piacenza were inclined to Milan, Bergamo and Novara to Pavia. The oft-repeated wars were still being waged when Barbarossa entered Italy and by his claims and actions gave rise to the Lombard League.

Along the Emilian Way, for the same reasons, each city was the enemy of its immediate neighbours. Piacenza and Reggio were at odds with Parma, Cremona, and Modena. Through Piacenza and Cremona this southern system was related to the central wars and alliances; through Modena with feuds farther east. For Modena stood in dread of and enmity with Bologna. *Docta Bononia,* the centre of legal studies, was great not only through her university but through her cross-roads. She was eager to increase her *contado,* and eventually to dominate the minor Romagnol cities to the coast, an aim which for a while she achieved in her best days in the thirteenth century. This, however, was not yet. She had not even entered on the wars connected with Venetian ambitions, which gave some consistency to the politics of the Trevisan, or Veronese, March. Venice aimed at controlling all exits to the sea from Ravenna northwards at least, if not from Ancona. Against her, but severed by their own disputes, stood Padua, Treviso, Ferrara, and Ravenna. But Padua and Treviso were likewise on uneasy terms with their northern neighbours and outlets, Verona and Vicenza, as well as at some variance with the branch of the Otbertine marquesses who, being eliminated from Milan, had their chief possessions round the small town of Este, and thence were soon to take their title and surname. Mantua, impregnable amid her marshes, was on her side at war with Verona over the important limits of their respective *contadi.* To sum up, when the Hohenstaufen came, there were systems of alliance and enmity ready-made, to be decorated and in some degree inspired by the contest of Papacy and Empire. It was in spite of these ingrained feuds, and as a testimony to the desire for

---

[1] Most Lombard towns seem to have aided Milan in this long war, a fact which shews how important the three northern passes were to them.

[2] 1110 for Cremona, c. 1129 for Pavia, but cf. *supra,* p. 219 for Milan's earlier rivalry with Pavia.

their city-autonomy and to aversion for an effectual foreign rule, that the Lombard Leagues were made; it was because of them that the Leagues were never complete, and so ready to dissolve.

The communes obtained their jurisdiction in their own cities in some degree by the exercise of functions, like that of arbitration or of garrison, which lay outside the customary sphere of State-authority, but for the most part they occupied or usurped rights which the State-authorities had long neglected or were forced to resign. These *regalia*, or State-rights vested immemorially in the kings, included both coinage, tolls and customs of all kinds, and the functions of police, justice, and war, enfeoffed to the mostly hereditary marquesses and counts. Large numbers of tolls and the like dues had been granted formally to bishops and lay nobles, and the bishops of many Lombard towns[1] had also received the countship over their city and its environs, or even over the whole *contado*. Hardly ever had jurisdiction or even tolls been granted to the citizens themselves[2], and never over the surrounding *contadi*. The citizens governed themselves in the first instance in the collapse of the kingship during the Wars of Investiture, and gained dominion in the *contadi* by a series of private agreements with greater or lesser feudatories very commonly made in the name of the bishop. For the first usurpation they could indeed claim the tacit consent of the kings. Henry V, Lothar III, and Conrad III in his rebel days, had acquiesced in the city-communes, and on the rare occasions when they were asked and no bishop's rights stood in the way had granted vague diplomas, the language of which referred to the "liberties" of the Lombard towns in general[3]. But to the alienation of fiefs in the *contado* to a new suzerain they had never consented; in fact Lothar III in 1136 by a *Constitutio* forbade the alienation of fiefs by under-vassals without the consent of their lord[4]. This, however, was ineffectual, even when not disregarded, for the tenants-in-chief too

[1] Acqui, Alba, Albenga, Asti, Bergamo, Brescia, Cremona, Feltre, Ivrea, Lodi, Mantua, Modena, Novara, Padua, Parma, Piacenza, Ravenna, Reggio, Savona, Tortona, Trent, Treviso (?), and Vercelli, at Barbarossa's accession; and, in Tuscany, Arezzo, Fiesole, Luni, and Volterra.

[2] To Pisa in 1081 the confirmation by Henry IV of the *Consuetudines quae habent de Mari* implies the power to enforce them.

[3] Cremona, 1114, "bonos usus"; Mantua, 1116, "eam consuetudinem bonam et iustam quam quelibet nostri imperii civitas optinet"; Bologna, 1116, "antiquas etiam consuetudines" (doubtful diploma); Novara, 1116: "omnes bonos usus illorum...et consuetudines.... Turres quoque, quas pro munitione nostrae ciuitatis erexerunt"; Turin, 1116: "omnes usus bonos eorum...in eadem libertate in que hactenus permanserunt deinceps permanere...ea uidelicet condicione ut nulli mortalium deinceps nixi (*i.e.* nisi) nobis seruiant salua solita iustitia Taurinensis episcopi"; *ibid.* 1136, with significant variations: "eandem quam cetere ciuitates Italice libertatem habeant...saluo...iure nostro seu comitis illius cui uicem nostram comiserimus."

[4] MGH, *Constit.* i. pp. 175–6: "nemini licere beneficia, que a suis senioribus habet, absque eorum permissu distrahere."

could be compelled by the communes to consent to their own spoliation.

With the local holders of public jurisdiction within the cities there were diverse methods of dealing. The marquess or count, if he still existed, was usually simply excluded, which was all the more easy as his chief interests lay in his estates in the countryside. Thus we find Count Uberto of Bologna intervening formally to obtain an imperial charter for the city with whose government he did not meddle. Lucca had revolted from Countess Matilda *c.* 1080, Mantua in 1091, with the Emperor's approval. The Counts of Siena play an obscure part in the *contado* in the twelfth century. But the Counts of San Bonifazio, who, though like so many other "rural counts" they took their title from their chief castle, were Counts of Verona, became citizens of the commune, and may have retained some feudal dues thereby.

The viscounts, on the other hand, were mainly city-dwellers and took a large share in forming the communes. Their official rights in the city seem to have slowly merged in the communal jurisdiction. In the case of Pisa, where perhaps at first the viscount was a consul by right of office, he is last known to have exercised jurisdiction in 1116, and after a sanguinary struggle the compossessing house was in 1153 summarily deprived of its financial rights and dues derived from the office of gastald or steward of the royal demesne.

The bishop's position in the city bore commonly some analogy to the viscount's. If he held by imperial diploma the comital functions, he would usually enfeoff or merely allow to the consuls a large part of his powers in the city, reserving some profits or functions for himself, reservations it was hard to maintain. Thus at Piacenza in 1162 there was made out a long list of the bishop-count's prerogatives. The bishop shared, at first at least, in the government of Arezzo and Bologna, nominating one or more of the consuls. Indeed the communes of these towns thus obtained something of a legal status. But disputes were very liable to occur, and the bishop would be made to feel he was a subordinate politically, even with regard to his domains in the *contado*. In 1154 the Bishop of Treviso was compelled to cede a great part of his feudal rights on his church's lands. Midway in the twelfth century the communes are ceasing to use their bishop as a legal figurehead for the acquisition of dominion in the *contado*. Towards its close the bishop is generally an undisguised, if sometimes reluctant, subject of the commune for his feudal estates.

At the base of the commune, thus formed and master in its own house, was the general assembly, the *arengo, parlamento, concione*. In early days, summoned *sonantibus campanis*, by its shouts of *fiat, fiat*, it legislated, declared peace or war, ratified treaties, approved the election of consuls. But these proceedings, save under great excitement, were of a formal character. There was no debate. The generality of citizens were bound more to duties than rights. They were to swear obedience to the consuls and thereby to membership of the commune, to attend the assembly, to serve in the host. And from the mid-twelfth century onwards the mob-like *arengo* meets more and more rarely, till once a year is usually sufficient for the taking of the usual oaths between rulers and ruled. Frequent meetings become the sign of revolution, for which the *arengo* provided an apt and legal means.

The true core of the city-state was formed by the magistracy of the consuls. The office was practically the monopoly of those families of notables whose private league had become a State-government. Characteristically, the outgoing consuls had a leading voice in electing their successors. Their office was almost invariably annual[1]. The board varied in numbers not only from city to city, but from year to year in the same city: at Genoa in 1122 there were four, in 1127 six; at Milan in 1130 there were twenty, in 1172 twelve; the more usual numbers ran from four to twelve, and in all cases seem fixed with some regard to the quarters of the city. The functions of the consuls were all-embracing; they led the host, administered the commune, saw to legislation, justice, and order. They inherited the voluntary jurisdiction by arbitration which had always been vested in each body of *vicini* and naturally included all disputes arising out of the *consuetudines* of each town, but they did not delay to usurp the public *placita* of count, bishop, or viscount. Subdivision of duties, however, was soon introduced. At Genoa in 1133 subordinate *Consules de placitis* were appointed, and shortly after 1150 Consuls of Justice (*consules iustitiae*) appear in most towns to preside in the tribunals and execute judgment, at first as specialised members of the consular college, later as a separate institution. Their functions and authority varied indeed, but their general character was the same.

Other officials of various titles appear as administering departments under the consuls. The *iudices*, trained jurists, tried cases under the consuls, and perhaps on occasion by the fact of appointment by some imperial authority provided the formal legal link between the upstart jurisdiction and the old. The notaries were concerned with official documents. For financial officials the most current title was *camerarius* (chamberlain), but at Siena, for instance, the power of the consuls was early limited by the institution of the *Provveditori della Biccherna*, to whom the *camerarius* was subordinated. The *boni homines* (soon styled consuls) of the *portae* commanded their quarters in the army, and acted as the lieutenants of the consuls of the commune in the city. The *vicinanze* (town-parishes) were responsible for the roads, canals, etc. within them. In Bologna they elected their own *ministrales contratarum*, whose title shews the antiquity of their office.

After the consuls, however, the most essential organ of city-government was the Council, most usually called the *Consiglio della Credenza* (Council

---

[1] At Genoa, however, till 1122 the consuls are elected for periods of three, four, and finally two, years.

sworn to secrecy), although on occasion it was classically named the Senate, as at Pisa. It was the natural development of the meetings of notables from which the commune sprang, and we may doubt if the consuls had ever acted without the advice of the Wise Men (*sapientes, savii*). These meetings were very soon crystallised as a formal council, the parent of all later councils of the commune. Its numbers varied from city to city and from time to time; perhaps from 100 to 150 was the average. Its object may have been partly to check and advise the consuls, but still more to express and collect the opinion of the oligarchy of notable families who ruled the State. This led to complicated developments. At Florence the meeting (*pratica*) of *Savii* merely invited by the government never went out of use, and was more important for initiative than all the formal councils. In order to be large enough for legislative purposes, the Credenza by the end of the century had become very generally a numerous body, the Great Council of the Commune; in the same way, in order to be small enough for secret business, a certain number of its members had become the Special or Lesser Council of the Commune. The dates, however, of these changes differed greatly from town to town and range over a century. We see a beginning of the process at Piacenza in 1144, when a city-law is passed, not by the *arengo*, but by the Council in the presence and with the consent of many non-councillors. It was not long, in fact, before the powers of the Council grew, in relation both to the consuls and to the *arengo*. They legislated, shared in elections, and guided the executive, and thus formulated and possibly accentuated the oligarchic character of the commune. In the late-born commune of Rome[1] even, the Senate of some fifty-six members[2] established by the revolution of 1143 did without consuls, though some of them (*senatores consiliarii*) served as an executive committee, until Innocent III contrived to replace the whole body by one or two Senators, resembling the North Italian *podestà*.

The law of each commune presented a peculiar mixture, and was enlarged and developed by different concomitant, yet in the end harmonising, processes. Omitting the foreign Germanic codes, which soon became obsolete in Italy, there were two general Laws, the Roman and the Lombard. Of these, the Roman, by its intrinsic superiority, by force of sentiment, by the studies of the jurists, kept gaining ground, and was more and more considered the normal law. But the Lombard Law was strongly rooted in family custom; in some ways its less civilised *dicta* were more suitable to the early Middle Age; and its influence was more lasting and wide-spread than would be gathered from contemporary statements. Further, while the Roman Law the jurists spread was that of Justinian's Code, the traditional Roman Law in the customs of North Italy went

---

[1] See *infra*, Chap. xi, pp. 369–370.

[2] Under the Roman Senate there was a body of *consiliarii* somewhat like the Great Council of a North Italian commune.

back mostly to the times before Justinian, to the Theodosian Law. Thus, the third original element, the local *consuetudines* or *usus*, besides being based on local needs and peculiarities, were a blend of Lombard and pre-Justinian Roman Law ; they grew, partly governed by local circumstances, partly under the influence of Justinianean jurists. Some of this growth was spontaneous and merely written down in and added to the *usus*. But local legislation was also a factor in development. Special laws were passed for this or that object in the *arengo* or the council throughout the twelfth century, edicts might be issued by the consuls as at Genoa, and all became part of the body of local law. Lastly, there were the *brevia* or oaths of office of the consuls, councillors, and other officials, and the *breve communis*, by which the citizens annually swore to perform their obligations under the commune and to obey the consuls. Current legislation tended to be taken up into these *brevia*, dealing with the powers and duties of office, which became longer and longer, till in the thirteenth century they were frequently fused into one multifarious code, the Statute of the Podestà, to which the chief magistrate of the commune swore on his accession to office. The method of growth was characteristic. A board of *emendatores*, *arbitri*, or the like, was elected at first annually, later at frequent intervals, and this commission revised the *brevia* or Statute *en bloc*. Thus the stable laws of the city were distinguished, at least in theory, from the *Provisions* of temporary application only, emanating from the councils.

The development of the commune was naturally enough from the simple to the complex. City law and constitution, however, by no means regulated all the activities of the citizens. As their wealth and numbers grew, they more and more found their interest in subordinate associations. Each group in short, as it became strong enough to be self-conscious, formed a petty commune. The impulse spread from above till, so to say, the single-celled state of 1130 became the multiple-celled community of 1250. While in Milan and a few other Lombard towns the older subdivision of the nobles into *capitanei* and vavassors was preserved, in most cities we find the inhabitants in the mid-twelfth century more simply divided into *milites* and *pedites*. This classification had a military basis in the communal army. Men whose property was estimated at a certain amount were obliged in war-time to attend the levy with horse and knight's armour ; those below the knight's assessment took the field on foot with a simpler equipment. Roughly speaking, this was a distinction between noble and plebeian, but the dividing line was drawn more according to wealth than birth. It was not only that the non-noble families who early became rich in a city joined the ranks of the *milites* without abandoning their merchandise, but many minor or even greater feudal families added trade to their real property. This was early a marked feature of Asti and Genoa and Pisa. The Visconti and other great families never had disdained to arm galleys and combine a carrying-trade with war and piracy. Their shipping gave them a greater hold on their respective communes than their like possessed elsewhere. But this mainly feudal origin gave a definite stamp to the whole class of *milites*. The persistence of the Germanic kinship, modified in some degree by the Roman *patria potestas*, was seen in the strict maintenance of the agnatic family groups, linked together by compossession and the duty of blood-revenge (*vendetta*). A family could increase with extreme rapidity—in a century the agnates descended from one man could number from 50 to 100 men—and further the agnatic group could be extended by voluntary alliance with one or more others. Thus in the noble's life the *consorzeria*, the family group, was the leading factor. The *consortes* placed their houses side by side; if the family was very great, it would have a covered *loggia* in the midst for festivities and meetings; in any case it would compossess a lofty tower for attack and defence, and thus the Italian medieval town shewed a forest of towers within its walls, the rallying-points of the incessant blood-feuds of the *consorzerie*. Organisation did not, however, cease here. There grew up leagues of *consorzerie*, the Societies of the Towers (*Società delle Torri*), and in the last half of the twelfth century we find all the *milites* of a city grouped under consuls of their own, who in treaties are already recognised as state-functionaries. To sum up, by the year 1200, the *milites* form a sharply separate class, marked off not so much by birth or the source of their wealth as by traditions and habits of life. They, or their principal families, have the chief say in the commune.

The *pedites* or plebeians appear at first as less organised than the higher ranks, or rather the local organisation of *vicinanze* and *portae* was sufficient for them while the volume of trade was still small. Men of the same craft dwelt almost wholly in the same quarter or even *vicinanza*, and, although in the once Byzantine cities of Ravenna and Rome some ancient gilds (*scholae*) seem to have continued, it needed a period of prosperity to incite craftsmen in general to tighten their trade, as opposed to their local, inter-connexion. The first to emerge separately were naturally the merchants (*mercatores* or *negotiatores*), who for the most part were concerned with import and export and the transit trade It was for them the profits were largest and the dangers greatest; they most needed corporate action and influence for their wealth and for mere safety in their voyages and journeys. Accordingly, half-way through the twelfth century, we find consuls of the merchants recognised officials in the communes of Pisa, Piacenza, and Milan, and every decade added evidence of their appearance in other cities. The Merchants and Money-changers (*campsores*, *cambiatores*), however, were like their allies the Jurists (*iudices*, *notarii*) largely drawn from the ranks of the *milites*, the composite nobility of the commune. They form a class through their particular economic interests. More closely connected with the plebeians

were the more specialised manufacturing, craft, and retail gilds, which
sprang up in their footsteps, and gained at the close of the twelfth
century recognition or toleration from the commune. Certain crafts
were then outrunning the others in the race for wealth, and beside the
Merchants there appear according to the various circumstances of each
city such gilds as those of Wool (*Arte della Lana*), the Apothecaries
and Spicers (*Speziali*), the Furriers (*Pelliciai*). The most common term
for them is Art (*Arte*), although *Mestiere* (*ministerium*) and *schola* are
also used. They were organised on the model of the commune, with a
general meeting of masters, a council, and consuls and subordinate
officials. The community of interest in each Art, its strict supervision
of its members, and their close mutual association in daily life, soon
made the Arts as a whole the bodies with greatest inner solidarity in
the communes.

Both the emergence of new classes, with the reassortment of members
of the old, and the exasperation of the inner divisions, partly social,
partly merely old blood-feuds, in the ruling oligarchies, seem to have
caused the gradual complication and development of the city-constitu-
tions. Thus the consuls of the Merchants and of the *Milites* become
powerful officials of the State; they take part in treaties, perform State-
functions; in their wake, *e.g.* at Florence in 1193, we find the chiefs of
a federation of more specialised handicraft Arts, whose trade was local,
sharing in the government. At Florence the inner feuds of the aristocracy
seem to have hastened the movement; in 1177 civil war broke out
between the Uberti and the group of consular families then in power.
At Milan, and generally in Lombardy, distinctly class warfare was the
cause of change. In Milan itself we find the lesser traders, butchers,
bakers, and the like, forming a league, the Credenza di Sant' Ambrogio,
which combined with the Motta, or association of the wealthier traders,
to wrest a share of power from the Credenza dei Consoli in which the
capitanei, strengthened perhaps by the war with Barbarossa, were
dominant. The merchants of Milan seem still to have retained their
association. Elsewhere, the struggle is between *milites*, whether traders
or not, and the *pedites*, whose wealth, if yet acquired, was new. The
expulsion of the *milites* from the city, which had occurred in the pre-
communal age, began to reappear as a feature of class-warfare.

The immediate result of these broils and social changes, however
caused and carried on, was the institution of a new single executive, the
Podestà (*Potestas*). An occasional single ruler, called by the vague title
of *Rector* or *Potestas*, was no novelty. From 1151 to 1155 Guido da Sasso
so ruled Bologna, and during the foundation of the Roman commune
Jordan Pierleoni ruled with the title of Patrician. But after Barbarossa's institution of imperial Podestàs[1], evidences of a tendency to

[1] Cf. *infra*, Chap. XIII. An official in each town to exercise and exact the
regalia recovered by the crown in 1158.

supersede the board of consuls by a single man multiply. At Pisa a *rector* is regarded as possible from 1169; at Milan the first known is of 1186, at Florence of 1193. At first an exceptional magistrate, as at Piacenza in 1188, the Podestà grew to be a permanent institution. The consuls who alternated with him were elected more and more rarely, and about the year 1210 he had become the normal ruler in all communes. By then the office had acquired a definite character. Though native Podestàs appear and are usually dangerous to liberty, the typical Podestà is a foreigner, *i.e.* from another city. He must be a knight, *i.e.* a noble; he brings with him his *familia* or household of knights and jurists; he is held strictly to account by a *syndicate* at the close of his year's or half-year's office, and is carefully segregated from the social and faction life of the city. Nor, partly through the natural elaboration of the State, partly from jealousy of power, was he allowed the full functions of the native consuls. He led the army, summoned the Councils, supervised police and criminal justice; but legislation, finance, and foreign policy were withheld from him, while in his own sphere he was surrounded by a Special Council, which often had direct connexion with the Consulate, and he was guided by the Great Council, which had now become the central organ of the commune. Even so the Podestà had to be a man of great natural gifts for rule and of elaborate training in law and affairs. A special tract, the *Oculus Pastoralis*, was written as a guide to his duties. For a century it was a kind of profession for the ablest city-nobles. They went from commune to commune, administering, warring, judging among an infinite variety of routine, of debate, and of emergencies, and such men as Brancaleone the Bolognese, and Corso Donati the Florentine, give much of its brilliance to Italian history in the thirteenth century.

It has been much debated what party had its way in the institution of the Podestà in the later twelfth century. First of all, undoubtedly the State: for the unity of the executive enabled the commune to survive the feuds and amateurishness and dissensions of the board of consuls; nor was self-government lessened, since the Great Council became the directing body of the commune. Next, we may probably say, the *pedites*, for affairs were no longer transacted by an oligarchic, quasi-hereditary board, but by the single foreign official and a Council in which the *milites* were no more than preponderant. It was in fact a step, like the admission of the wealthier Arts to a share in government, towards a wider basis for the State. But it was not a long step; the nobles were still dominant, and their lesser members benefited, perhaps, most by the supersession of the narrow ring of consular families. The further development, by which the non-nobles (*popolani*), or the people (*popolo*), erected a fresh organisation, the *popolo*, and secured power over the State, belongs to a later volume.

The Peace of Constance and the niggardly diplomas of the Emperor

Henry VI finally admitted the communes into the feudal chain, and it continued for many generations to be their endeavour to express their relations of territory and dominion according to the reigning feudal law. But this should not conceal the fact that the cities by their very nature were anti-feudal; they and their very nobles were trading, manufacturing, not chivalrous, in a word they were *bourgeois*. Their trade, as we have seen, long ante-dated the Crusades, which gave it so powerful a stimulus. From the first the exchange of goods between East and West formed a chief part of it. From Constantinople and the Levant the Italians brought the much desired spices, sugar, silk and cotton, rare fabrics, dye-woods, and wine, objects of art and luxury, and soon corn and fish from the Black Sea. From Africa came gold, ivory, indigo, and lead. In return they exported metal and building-woods, furs, linen, cloth, and wool. To the Transalpines they handed on the Oriental and African products, with a slowly increasing quantity of their own cloth[1], and received cloth, wool, hides, and furs in exchange. The chief manufacture of Italy was to be the finer qualities of dyed cloth. In the later twelfth century the ascetic, half-heretical fraternity of the Umiliati gave a re-markable impulse to the cloth industry in Lombardy, and they and their methods were introduced farther south. In the next century the Art of the Merchants of Calimala in Florence became specialists in dyeing and dressing Transalpine cloth, and in almost every town the Arte della Lana (Gild of Clothmakers) was among the wealthiest.

This trade was vigorously organised. From the seaports *caravans* (merchant fleets, escorted by galleys) sailed twice a year to the Levant. At Constantinople and the Syrian ports existed colonies of Venetians, Pisans, and Genoese, governed in a fashion we should now call extra-territorial by consuls or *baili*, with store-houses (*fondachi*) for wares and ship-tackle. It was the aim of each city to gain exclusive privileges and turn out its rivals, and much of their best energy was spent in these bitterly-fought commercial wars. One rival they overcame; the Byzantines faded from the sea and from their own export-trade. In the West, the merchants trooped by road and river to the great fairs of Champagne, of which six were held in the year. Here, too, men travelled in caravans; but there was no question of extra-territoriality, though trade-concerns might be settled by Law-merchant, the custom of traders. Security and toll-freedom were the things aimed at, if only very partially obtained.

It was the Transalpine trade which gave the Italians their pre-eminence and ill-fame in the thirteenth century as bankers and money-lenders. Merchants whose business stretched from the Levant to England had a natural advantage in the handling of money and the organisation of credit. Partners in a firm would reside for long periods abroad; there was always an agent at least, and money-values could pass from Paris to Siena by note of hand. Almost all the great merchant houses took up

[1] Salt was a staple export of Venice.

banking and with it usury, from which they reaped in the thirteenth century enormous profits. The levying of the papal revenue fell into their hands. They knew and dealt in the coinage of Europe in all its varieties and degradations. It is a testimony to the inflow of the precious metals into Italy that the Gild of Money-changers (*Campsores, Arte del Cambio*), who dealt in banking in their native town, was next in wealth to the Merchants. The Italian, or "Lombard," banker was indeed hated abroad, and often at home, for his usury, both fair and unfair. The risk was great, the monopoly hard to break through, the interest usuriously high. Then, although a logical series of exceptions and relaxations was gradually worked out, the trade of money-lending, the taking of interest, was in principle forbidden by Canon Law. The perplexing limits within which interest could be taken were always being overstepped, and we have the curious spectacle of the merchant-class, the factors of the Papacy, making their living by a mortal sin, as they thought it, and perhaps the more extortionate because a reasonable profit on a loan was in theory forbidden.

The great firms might be either family businesses of many kinsmen, or as time went on more frequently voluntary partnerships. The several partners subscribed the capital, traded, travelled, served in the commune's army, held state-office, met in their gild and religious confraternity, co-operated in their *consorzeria*, and in the *portae* and *vicinanze* of their city. It was a full life, and, when citizen and commercial organisation grew more complicated in the thirteenth century, it is no wonder that short terms of office and each man taking his turn on council and board of officials were the rule. The drain on the citizen's time as well as civic and class jealousy made it necessary. But the citizens also knew well that unfettered power made the tyrant. The one true single official, the Podestà, was fettered and supervised in a healthy state. The commune had begun by association and it lived by corporate action and impersonal decisions. Personal fame in it is a sign of disease and decay. At its best we hear only of the commune, the *milites* and *pedites*, the *consorzeria* and the gild.

These collective units, however, gave ample opportunity for broils, which always hampered and eventually wrecked the communes. Class-warfare and its early effects have already been mentioned; it was to transform the commune. But it was partly caused and its method was perniciously affected by the blood-feuds which existed from generation to generation among the *consorzerie*. The nobles, often of Germanic descent, and always adopting feudal, Germanic traditions, were perhaps somewhat antipathetic to the thrifty Latin plebeians, although this must not be pressed far. But it was their turbulent, tyrannous habits that became ever harder to bear. They rioted in the streets like Capulet and Montague, they fought round their towers, they were fierce and insolent to their inferiors. However given to commerce they might be, the *vendetta* was a sacred duty, and by its nature it could only end, if it did end, with the extinction of a stock. Thus, whether the *milites* fought among themselves for power or vengeance, or the plebeians took up arms to tame them, the city was a victim of civil fighting. Now and again the flimsy wooden houses would be destroyed over parts of the city by accidental or wilful incendiarism. And these methods became normal. There was no rage so furious as that of the Italian bourgeois intent on restoring peace and order.

In fact the intensely strong family and group feeling of the citizens is in strange contrast to their European trade and policy. Next to the Roman Curia, they have the widest, most civilised outlook of the Middle Ages. Strangers from all climes jostle in their streets. They themselves have a cult of efficiency and energy. They are the most original devisers of laws and constitutions, the acutest in jurisprudence and organisation, innovators at last in literature and romance. It is hard to exaggerate their devotion to their group or their commune. But on the other side is their narrowness. For his *consorzeria* the citizen at his best will devote everything; to his gild he will be staunch; to his city, if these allow. well-meaning and fiercely loyal. But these associations are exclusive. City wars down city with relentless rivalry; family, class, and gild struggle mercilessly for dominion within them. It was only the danger to the autonomy of all which produced the Lombard League, and in that perhaps, as in other manifestations, it is the triumphant *genius loci*, the immediate character and communal will of each city, which dominates medieval Italian politics.

CHAPTER VI.

ISLĀM IN SYRIA AND EGYPT, 750–1100.

WITH the accession of the first of the Abbasid Caliphs (A.D. 750) it became clear that the dominions of Islām would consist, henceforth, of a number of separate and independent Islāmic states. Even in the time of the Umayyad Caliphs the unity of the Muslim Empire was maintained with difficulty and was never quite complete. In Arabia, the birthplace and the original home of the new world-power, there was neither the military strength nor the political organisation required for the rule of the conquered lands. The movement of the seat of government to Damascus under the Umayyads is, in one aspect, a practical acknowledgment of this fact. For a time the Arabian families who ruled the subject provinces were a connecting link and a partial bond of unity. But even they adopted and so perpetuated the national governments of Persia and Syria and Egypt, and thus the Muslim Empire was from the first a loosely-knit federation of Muslim states. The superiority of Mesopotamia and Persia over Syria and Arabia was declared by the triumph of the Abbasids. It was symbolised by a further movement of the capital from Damascus to Ambār and finally to Baghdad. But, inevitably, this movement of the capital to the distant east weakened the control of the Abbasid Caliphs over the lands of the far west. An Umayyad prince became ruler of Muslim Spain in A.D. 755, and founded a dynasty which afterwards claimed the Caliphate and assumed the much disputed title of "commander of the faithful" (A.D. 929). In Morocco Idrīs ibn 'Abdallāh, a descendant of 'Alī, established in 788 the first Shī'ite Caliphate. The dynasty of the Idrīsites, so established, maintained their power for about 200 years (788–985). In Tunis Ibrāhīm ibn Aghlab (800–811) was the first of another line of independent emirs with a brilliant history (800–909). This process of disintegration continued in all parts of the Muslim dominion. Every provincial governor was potentially an independent ruler. National traditions and aspirations reinforced the drift to separatism. Egypt and Syria and Arabia and Persia once more fell apart. The Arab conquest created a permanent international brotherhood of learning, literature, and religion; it achieved a spiritual federation and affinity between much-divided races and nationalities; it encouraged and made easy the migration of individuals from one land to another; but it did not permanently obliterate national boundaries and national rivalries.

Parallel to the development of Islām as a world-power went the development of the Caliphate, its highest dignity. On the political side this office was an adaptation to new conditions of the ancient city governments of Mecca and Medina. Yet its holder was, essentially, a successor of the Prophet and so the supreme head of Islām. Local traditions and needs were bound to yield to this pre-eminent fact. When the Caliphs ceased to reside in Arabia, their local functions were soon practically abrogated. Only the restriction that they must be descended from the ancient ruling families of Mecca long remained to mark their political ancestry[1]. The sovereign power inherent in the Caliphate was most fully realised in the case of the Umayyad princes. After them, in the Abbasid period, the authority of the office was circumscribed and diminished by the existence of rival Caliphates and by the disappearance of the political unity of Islām. The Caliphs of Baghdad drifted towards the condition of being a line of Muslim princes with a specially venerable ancestry. From this destiny they were partly saved by a further transformation of their position. They surrendered their political authority, even in their own territories and capitals, first to Persian and then to Turkish sultans, whose mere nominees they became. The Caliphate was now a dignity conferred by certain Muslim princes upon the descendants of an old Arabian family, which had formerly ruled Islām and still had a recognised hereditary right to its position. Some forms of power remained to it, which expressed respect for an ancient tradition and occasionally decided the course of events. The case of the Frankish kings of the seventh century, who ruled by the grace of the mayors of the palace, may be referred to as a parallel. It may not be superfluous to add that in this phase the Caliphate cannot be described as having been reduced to a purely spiritual function. The office is not a kind of Papacy. In name, if not in fact, the Caliphs have always been great Muslim sovereigns. The separation of Egypt and of Syria from the jurisdiction of the Abbasid Caliphs and the subsequent conflicts between them and their Fāṭimite rivals, to be narrated in this chapter, are essentially a sequence of military and political events[2].

The distinctive principles and the historical origin of the Shīʿite party, who supported the exclusive claims of ʿAlī to the Caliphate, have been explained in a previous chapter. Having failed to secure the succession for one of ʿAlī's descendants when the Umayyads were overthrown, they turned their intrigues and plots with increased energy against the Abbasid usurpers. Two branches of this Shīʿite agitation, with apparently a

[1] The restriction was observed until the Ottoman Sultans assumed the title of Caliph (*circa* A.D. 1517). The legitimacy of their Caliphate has been challenged and its authority widely rejected by Muslims on the ground that it did not possess this hereditary qualification.

[2] It should be borne in mind that the successive phases through which the Caliphate has passed make it difficult, perhaps impossible, to sum up its essential character satisfactorily in any brief statement.

common origin, have a notable influence on the history of Egypt and
Syria in the ninth and tenth centuries. One of the Shī'ite sects is known
as the Ismā'īlian, because its adherents believed that the Mahdī, who was
to establish their cause and set the world right, would be a son or
descendant of the seventh Imām, Ismā'īl. About the middle of the ninth
century a certain 'Abdallāh ibn Maimūn, a Persian, gained a position of
great influence among these Ismā'īlians, and directed a wide-spread propaganda from Salamīyah, his headquarters in northern Syria. At least
two of his descendants, Aḥmad ibn 'Abdallāh and Sa'īd ibn Husain,
succeeded him as the heads of the organisation which he established. In
the beginning of the tenth century the supporters of Sa'īd gained
sufficient power in North Africa to enable them to overthrow and depose
the last of the Aghlabite emirs. In 909 they proclaimed a certain
'Ubaidallāh ibn Muḥammad as the Mahdī and the first of the Fāṭimite
Caliphs (909–934)[1]. There is strong reason to believe that this personage
was actually Sa'īd ibn Husain, who had disappeared from Salamīyah
some years previously. But his followers held that he was a descendant
of 'Alī and of the Prophet's daughter Fāṭimah. In 969 the fourth
Fāṭimite Caliph conquered Egypt, and soon afterwards Egypt became the
seat of the dynasty, with Cairo as its capital.

The Qarmaṭians were another offshoot of the propaganda organised
by 'Abdallāh ibn Maimūn. They became a political power in Baḥrain and
amongst the Arabs on the borders of Syria and Mesopotamia, towards
the end of the ninth century. Their special name is derived from the
name (or nickname) of the agent whose preaching converted them to
Shī'ite doctrines. They are alleged to have been to some extent under
the secret control of the Fāṭimite Caliphs, who are thus supposed to have
been the heirs of the authority of 'Abdallāh ibn Maimūn and his successors
in Salamīyah. During the tenth century the Qarmaṭians were persistent
and formidable enemies of the Abbasid Caliphs. Their repeated attacks
on the pilgrim caravans to Mecca and their famous seizure of the Black
Stone, which they kept in Baḥrain for 21 years (930–951), are evidence
of the looseness of their attachment to Islām.

Aḥmad ibn Ṭūlūn (870–884) was the first of the Abbasid governors
of Egypt to make himself practically independent of the Caliphs and to
transmit his emirate to his descendants. He invaded Syria in 878, and
joined it and a large part of Mesopotamia to his dominions. His territory
extended to the borders of the Greek Empire, with which he came into
conflict. His successor, Abu'l-jaish Khumārawaih (884–896), on the

---

[1] His recognition may be dated from the capture of Sijilmāsa in August 909.
His Caliphate is usually made to commence on the day of his triumphal entry into
Raqqādah, which is dated by Jamāl-ad-Dīn al-ḥalabī on Thursday, 21 Rabī' ii A.H.
297 and treated as equivalent to 7 January 910. But the conflict between the day of
the week and the day of the month in this date demands the reading 21 Rabī' i
A.H. 297, *i.e.* 7 December 909 (see Stevenson's *Chronology*).

whole maintained his authority in Syria and was confirmed in his position by the Abbasid Caliph. Three other members of the Ṭūlūnite family were also, at least nominally, rulers of Egypt. In 903 the first great Qarmaṭian invasion of Syria took place. The governor of Damascus and the army of Egypt were unable to save the province. Help was asked from Muktafī, the last of the Caliphs of Baghdad to exercise a measure of independent political power. His troops defeated the Qarmaṭians (903), put an end to the authority of the Ṭūlūnites (904–905), and then repelled a second attack of the Qarmaṭians on Syria (906).

For thirty years Egypt and Syria were again ruled by a series of emirs nominated by the court of Baghdad. Their brief terms of office reflect the unstable condition of the central government. The first *'amīr al-'umarā* to exercise supreme power in Baghdad, the eunuch Mūnis (908–933), also effectively influenced the course of events in the provinces. It was he who saved Egypt from the first attacks of the Fāṭimites. Twice (914–915 and 919–920) an invading army captured Alexandria and occupied part of the country for several months, but was in the end repulsed. During the next fifty years the Fāṭimite Caliphs had little leisure to pursue their scheme of annexing Egypt. They made one slight attempt in 935–936. In 935 the Emir of Damascus, Muḥammad ibn Tughj al-Ikhshīd, obtained the governorship of Egypt. He lost his Syrian possessions for a time to Muḥammad ibn Rā'iq of Aleppo. But after the death of this rival (942) he reoccupied Syria and obtained the governorship of Mecca and Medina on the nomination of the Abbasid Caliph.

About this time the most powerful emirs in Upper Mesopotamia were two rulers of the Arab house of Ḥamdān, Nāṣir-ad-Daulah Ḥasan of Mosul (936–967) and Saif-ad-Daulah 'Alī of Diyārbakr (935–944). This house now began to play an important part in the history of Syria. In 944 Saif-ad-Daulah seized Aleppo and became master of northern Syria. An attempt to occupy Damascus was not permanently successful (spring of 945) and a battle fought with the army of Ikhshīd, near Qinnasrīn, was indecisive. In the autumn of 945 peace was made between Saif-ad-Daulah and Ikhshīd, on the terms that the former should hold northern Syria as far as Ḥimṣ and the latter Damascus and southern Syria. The line thus drawn is the usual line of division in the tenth and eleventh centuries between the territory of Aleppo and the territory ruled by the sovereigns of Egypt. Antioch and a large part of Cilicia were also dependencies of Aleppo when the peace of 945 was made.

When Ikhshīd died (July 946), he was nominally succeeded first by one son and then, after an interval, by another. But the real ruler of Egypt in these two reigns was a native African, Abu 'l-mish Kāfūr (946–968). He defeated a second attempt of Saif-ad-Daulah to seize Damascus (946), and then renewed with him the previously existing agreement, modified somewhat to his own advantage (947). Henceforward Kāfūr's rule was undisturbed by foreign attack. He successfully promoted the internal development of his own dominions, and made no attempt to encroach on the territory of his neighbours.

In northern Syria during the period of Kāfūr's reign Saif-ad-Daulah waged a desperate and continuous warfare with the Greek Empire (944–967). First the Muslims, and then after some years the Greeks, were the chief aggressors. But for nearly twenty years the character of the warfare was substantially the same. Each year some raid or expedition was launched far over the enemy's borders by one or both of the combatants, and yet no decisive success was secured by either side. A notable victory is sometimes ascribed to Saif-ad-Daulah (*e.g.* in the year 953), but more often he seems to have suffered serious defeat (*e.g.* in November 950 and November 960).

During these years Aleppo was the seat of a court which attracted to it poets and men of learning from all the lands of Islām. Saif-ad-Daulah was himself a poet and a man of letters, and also, literally, the hero of a hundred fights. His character and his court are illuminated for us by the poems of one of the most famous of Arabic writers, Aḥmad ibn Ḥusain, al-Mutanabbi.

The first campaign of Nicephorus Phocas in 962 marks the commencement of a change in the scene and character of Greek operations. The most striking feature of the campaign was the sack of Aleppo and the occupation of the city by a Greek army for six or eight days (December 962)[1]. But the most important and significant operations were those which aimed at the conquest of Cilicia. Three years were needed to bring them to a conclusion. In 965 Mamistra and Tarsus were both captured, and the annexation of the province was virtually complete[2].

During 965 and 966 Saif-ad-Daulah was engrossed by the distractions of civil strife and Muslim war. His death, early in 967 (in January or February)[3], was a prelude to further dissensions in Aleppo. Rival princes of the house of Ḥamdān and other emirs waged war with one another. Nicephorus, now Emperor (963–969), seized his opportunity. In the autumn of 968 he made a terrifying raid through the greater part of northern Syria, burning and destroying and taking many prisoners from the towns he passed. He marched up the valley of the Orontes, passed

---

[1] Such partial and temporary occupations are frequently mistaken by modern historians for complete captures or permanent conquests. It should not be said without qualification of an oriental town in this period that it has been captured, unless its citadel is known to have been surrendered or stormed. In 962 the citadel ot Aleppo remained intact and Saif-ad-Daulah and the best of his troops lay outside the city undefeated.

[2] The sources which relate the capture of these towns at an earlier date either give the year wrongly or possibly refer to temporary occupations, such as those referred to in last note.

[3] The authorities vary curiously between Friday, 25 January (Kamāl-ad-Dīn), and Friday, 8 February (Yaḥyā, Al-makīn, Ibn Khalliqān).

Ḥamāh and Ḥimṣ, and then turned through Al-Buqai‘ah to the sea. He returned northwards along the coast by Jabalah and Lāṭiqīyah to Antioch. No territory was gained by this invasion, unless possibly the sea-coast town of Lāṭiqīyah. But the display of the Emperor's power contributed to the success of his representative in the following year. Nicephorus, as he withdrew to Cilicia, left a strong garrison in the castle of Baghrās, at the Syrian gates. It was commanded by Michael Burtzes, who soon learned that the people of Antioch, having declared their independence of Aleppo, had no settled government. He secured an entrance into the city by the help of traitors, and took possession on 28 October 969. Two months later he imposed humiliating terms of peace on Aleppo, which was again occupied by Greek troops, as it had been in 962. The boundaries between the dukedom of Antioch and the emirate of Aleppo were minutely defined and remained practically the same for the next hundred years. Ḥārim was the farthest castle of the Greeks on the east and Athārib the corresponding fortress of Aleppo on the west. On the north the territory of Aleppo extended to the river Sajūr and included Mambij. It was a condition of peace that the emirs of Aleppo should pay an annual tribute to the Greeks[1].

The fourth Fāṭimite Caliph, Abu Tamīm Ma‘add al-Mu‘izz (953–975), added much to the fame and power of the dynasty. His success was due to his own qualities of statesmanship and to the talents of his most trusted general, Jauhar ar-Rūmī, originally a Greek slave (*ob.* 992). When Abu 'l-mish Kāfūr died (April 968), Mu‘izz, having established his supremacy in Tunis and Morocco, had already commenced to prepare for the invasion of Egypt. Kāfūr's death was followed by civil strife in Egypt and by circumstances which caused wide-spread distress. A strong party was ready to welcome the Fāṭimite ruler. No one was much opposed to his taking possession of the country. In the summer of 969 Jauhar's invasion met with only slight opposition. Cairo was occupied on 6 July, and the name of the Fāṭimite Caliph quietly supplanted that of his Abbasid rival in the public prayers of the following Friday (9 July). Jauhar's conciliatory policy and the practical benefits of his government secured general acquiescence in the new regime. Mu‘izz did not transfer his residence to Egypt until the early summer of 973, but Jauhar's conquest marks the beginning of a new period in the history of Egypt and of the Caliphate (969). For two centuries the governors of Egypt contested the claim of the Abbasids to the obedience of all Islām. The prestige of its rulers was equal and even superior to that of the Caliphs of Baghdad. The emirs of Syria and Arabia had an alternative Caliph to whom they might transfer their allegiance at choice. During the next hundred years the rulers of Lower Mesopotamia were either too weak or too much engaged elsewhere to exercise any effective control in Syria. The

---

[1] Kamāl-ad-Dīn gives large extracts from the treaty, including a definition of the boundaries on the north and north-west.

histories of Syria and Egypt thus run, for the most part, in one channel. In the extreme north the emirs of Aleppo maintain a precarious independence. But southern and central Syria, which had been subject to the Ikhshīds and to Abu'l-mish Kāfūr, remained normally subject to Egypt until the coming of the Turks.

The disaffection or rivalry of the Qarmaṭians was the chief obstacle to the occupation of Damascus and southern Syria by the Fāṭimites. It seems probable that the Qarmaṭians of Baḥrain had been up to this point secret supporters and allies of the Fāṭimites. It is therefore possible that their invasions of Syria in 964 and 968 were instigated by the Caliph Muʿizz as a step towards his conquest of Egypt and Syria. But now a party held power in Baḥrain whose policy was to oppose the Fāṭimites and to acknowledge the Abbasid Caliphs. Such a complete reversal of the principles of the sect could not fail to shake the confidence of its adherents, and it may be that the rapid decline of the Qarmaṭians from this date onwards is due to the internal schism so introduced[1]. The new policy had only a brief prospect of success. Syria was invaded by one of Jauhar's lieutenants, Jaʿfar ibn Fallāḥ. He defeated the Ikhshīd governor, Husain ibn ʿUbaidallāh, at Ramlah in the autumn of 969 and entered Damascus in the third week of November. The population of Damascus was not disposed to acknowledge a Shīʿite Caliph, and Jaʿfar's position as governor during two years was precarious and uneasy. On the other hand Acre, Sidon, Beyrout, and Tripolis seem to have transferred their allegiance to the Fāṭimites without resistance. The decisive factor in their case was the command which the Egyptian fleet held of the sea. In 971 the Qarmaṭian leader, Ḥasan al-ʿaṣam (Ḥasan al-aʿsham), in agreement with the Emir of Aleppo and the Caliph of Baghdad, invaded Syria. Jaʿfar was defeated and Damascus occupied (autumn 971), and the Qarmaṭians became masters of the interior of southern Syria. During the three years of their occupation they twice invaded Egypt without success (October 971 and May 974). After their second repulse Damascus was reoccupied by Fāṭimite troops for a few months (June 974). But the inhabitants were still opposed to the Fāṭimites, and chose a Turkish emir, Al-aftakīn, to be their governor (spring 975). Al-aftakīn, after an unsuccessful attack on the Syrian coast-towns in 976, was besieged in Damascus for six months by Jauhar (July–December). A Qarmaṭian army came to his rescue, and the allies reoccupied southern Palestine with the exception of Ascalon, which Jauhar held against them for fifteen months. The loss of this city in the spring of 978 was counterbalanced by an Egyptian victory near Ramlah (15 August 978). Al-aftakīn's career was ended by his capture after the battle, but the Egyptians judged it expedient to buy off the Qarmaṭians by promising payment to them of an annual sum of money. Damascus also maintained its independence.

---

[1] So De Goeje.

A Syrian emir named Qassām was chosen governor by the citizens, and remained in power until July 983. During most of his emirate a large part of southern Syria was ruled independently by the Arab chief, Mufarrij ibn Daghfal ibn Jarrāḥ. In 982[1] this chief was driven out of the country, and thus, finally, Palestine was reduced to obedience. In the following year Qassām himself surrendered to an Egyptian army. The Caliph, Abu manṣūr Nizār al-'Azīz (975–996), then secured control of Damascus by appointing as its governor Bakjūr, recently Emir of Ḥimṣ, who was a *persona grata* to the inhabitants (December 983). He ruled five years and was then deposed for disloyalty (October 988). But the series of governors who succeeded him, until the Turkish occupation, were nearly all nominees of the Fāṭimite Caliphs.

By the Fāṭimite conquest of Egypt and the Greek occupation of Aleppo in the same year (969), the way was opened for the clash of two distant powers in Syria. The Syrian coast-towns as far as Tripolis quickly became a portion of the Fāṭimite dominions. In the early part of the year 971 an army sent by Ja'far ibn Fallāḥ unsuccessfully besieged Antioch for some months. The attempt was not followed up because of the resistance that the Fāṭimites met with in Palestine. It was also the condition of Palestine during the Fāṭimite conquest and the Qarmaṭian occupation that induced the Emperor John (969–976) to invade Syria in 975. Aleppo was already a humble tributary, and probably the Emperor expected to reduce a large part of the country to the same condition. The fullest description of his campaign is contained in a letter that he wrote to an Armenian prince[2]. The expedition lasted from April to October. The farthest point reached by the main army was the plain of Esdraelon (Marj ibn 'Amir). From Antioch the Greeks marched past Ḥamāh and Ḥimṣ, then through the Biqā' and the valley of the Jordan as far as Baisān. From Baisān they turned westward to Acre, and from there along the coast back again to Antioch. No hostile army attempted to stop their progress. Most of the Syrian emirs professed submission in order to save themselves from attack. Al-aftakīn of Damascus and others purchased immunity by paying considerable sums of money. Baalbek was besieged and captured, and Beyrout was successfully stormed. Tripolis was besieged for forty days without success. The real gains of the expedition were made on the coast just to the south of Antioch and in the hills facing Jabalah and Lāṭiqīyah. From now onwards Jabalah was an advanced post of the Greek Empire, facing Tripolis and the territory of the Fāṭimites. In the hills Ṣahyūn and Barzūyah became Greek strongholds. Beyond these limits nothing was gained. The southern emirs, who promised to pay an annual tribute, and even signed treaties to

---

[1] Possibly in the beginning of 983; at all events before the Egyptian attack on Qassām.

[2] Matthew of Edessa (trans. by E. Dulaurier, 1858), pp. 16 sqq.

this effect, were beyond the reach of the Emperor's troops in ordinary times and never fulfilled their promises[1].

In Aleppo after the death of Saif-ad-Daulah (967) the authority of government was usurped by Turkish slaves, of whom Farghūyah (Qarghūyah) was the chief. In the following year Saif-ad-Daulah's son, Saʿd-ad-Daulah Abu 'l-maʿālī, was expelled from the city (968). When Farghūyah submitted to the Greeks (970), as previously described, Saʿd-ad-Daulah was allowed to retain Ḥimṣ. In 975 Farghūyah was thrown into prison by an associate, the emir Bakjūr, part of whose later history has already been narrated. This encouraged Saʿd-ad-Daulah to attempt the recovery of his father's capital (976). Bakjūr was compelled to come to terms, and received Ḥimṣ in compensation for the surrender of Aleppo (977).

The chief feature of the remainder of Saʿd-ad-Daulah's emirate is the oscillation of Aleppo between dependence upon the Greeks and alliance with the Egyptians. Saʿd-ad-Daulah wished to be quit of the burden of tribute due to the Emperor, and was willing to make concessions to the Caliph in return for his help. But ʿAzīz hoped to reduce northern Syria to the same state of obedience as Palestine, and for this and other reasons Saʿd-ad-Daulah was compelled at times to ask protection from the Greeks. His first revolt, in 981, quickly collapsed owing to lack of support from Egypt. In 983 Bakjūr of Ḥimṣ, having quarrelled with Saʿd-ad-Daulah, attacked Aleppo with the support of Fāṭimite troops (September). The siege was raised by a relief force from Antioch under Bardas Phocas. Bakjūr fled to Damascus, and Ḥimṣ was sacked by Greek soldiers (October). Even in these circumstances there was friction between Saʿd-ad-Daulah and his protectors. The dispute was settled by the payment in one year of two years' tribute[2]. During 985 and 986 Saʿd-ad-Daulah was again in revolt. The principal events were the capture of Killiz by the Greeks (985) and their siege of Fāmīyah (986). Fāṭimite troops captured and held for a short time the castle of Bulunyās. Most likely it was the determination of ʿAzīz to make peace with the Greeks that led to Saʿd-ad-Daulah's submission to the Emperor on the same terms as before. The amount of the annual tribute was 20,000 dinars (400,000 dirhems).

The career of Bakjūr, which is characteristic of the period, may here be followed to its close. After ruling Damascus for five years in dependence on ʿAzīz (983–988), he was deposed by his order. He fled to Raqqah, on

---

[1] Gustave Schlumberger, who gives a brilliant account of all these events, over-estimates the results of the campaign of 975, and misapprehends the position held by the Greeks in Syria at this date and later.

[2] There was fighting between the allies after the retreat of Bakjūr. The cause is not mentioned by the sources. Possibly Bardas Phocas demanded payment for his help either in money or in some other way. Kamāl-ad-Dīn is wrong in stating that the Greeks were defeated and driven away from Aleppo by Saʿd-ad-Daulah. His narrative under this year is confused, and includes events that happened in 986.

the Euphrates, and from there once more plotted against Sa'd-ad-Daulah. In April 991 he was defeated, captured, and executed by his former master and rival. In this battle Greek troops from Antioch again assisted the Emir of Aleppo.

In 987 or 988 (A.H. 377) the first of a series of treaties between the Greek Emperors and the Egyptian Caliphs was made. The scanty details which are preserved suggest that it followed the lines of the better-known treaties of later date. If so, the outstanding feature is that the Emperor exercises his influence on behalf of the Christian subjects of the Caliph, and that the Caliph similarly acts as protector of the Muslims of the Empire. It is significant that under this arrangement the Fāṭimite Caliph is recognised to the exclusion of his Abbasid rival. Under the treaty there was an exchange of prisoners and the duration of peace was fixed at seven years[1].

Sa'd-ad-Daulah was succeeded nominally by his son Abu'l-fadā'il Sa'īd-ad-Daulah (December 991). But the effective ruler throughout his reign was the *wazīr* Abu Muḥammad Lūlū al-kabīr (Lūlū the elder). It was presumably hostility to him that drove a number of the mamlūks of Aleppo about this time to seek refuge in Egypt. Their support encouraged 'Azīz to attempt again the conquest of Aleppo. This led to a renewal of war with the Greek Empire also. The governor of Damascus, Man-jūtakīn (Banjūtakīn), commanded the Egyptian army. He invaded the territory of Aleppo and conducted operations there for thirteen months (992–993). A Greek force from Antioch under Michael Burtzes was repulsed (June 992). But Manjūtakīn's operations were not energetic, and in the spring of 993 he returned to Damascus owing to lack of provisions. Next spring (994) 'Azīz sent reinforcements and supplies to Syria, and with these at his service Manjūtakīn attacked Aleppo early in June. A relief force from Antioch was severely defeated on the banks of the Orontes (14 September 994). Scarcity of food, caused by the closeness of the blockade, now reduced the defenders of Aleppo to desperate straits. In their extremity they were saved by the sudden and unexpected arrival of the Emperor Basil (976–1025). He rode through Asia Minor in sixteen days at the head of 3000 horsemen. The alarm caused by his arrival was so great, the numbers of his army probably so exaggerated, that Man-jūtakīn burned his tents and equipment and made off in panic, without risking a battle (end of April 995). Basil followed southwards as far as

---

[1] The Muslim historians Abu 'l-maḥāsin and Al-'ainī (Rosen, p. 202), who are our authorities, particularly mention that prayers were to be said in the mosque at Constantinople in the name of 'Azīz, and that the Emperor agreed to release his Muslim prisoners. Al-'ainī, however, also says that the Emperor sent materials to Jerusalem for the repair of the church of the Resurrection, and this, doubtless, was in accordance with the terms of the treaty. See *infra*, pp. 256–7. The dates of the later treaties between the Empire and the Caliphate are A.D. 1000, 1027, and 1037.

Al-Buqai'ah, and then turning down to the coast marched northwards by the Mediterranean to Antioch. Prisoners were taken from Rafanīyah and Ḥimṣ, but as dependencies of Aleppo they were presumably not seriously injured. Tripolis was besieged without success for more than forty days. Ṭaraṭūs was occupied, and garrisoned by Armenian auxiliaries.

'Azīz now began to prepare extensively for war with the Emperor. He made terms with Lūlū, who formally acknowledged his Caliphate (995). But the only fruit of these preparations was an expedition to recover Ṭaraṭūs. 'Azīz died on 13 October 996, and revolts in southern Syria against the authority of Ḥasan ibn 'Ammār, who ruled in the name of the new Caliph, made foreign wars impossible. For three years the governor of Antioch carried on an active border warfare and somewhat strengthened his position in the direction of Tripolis. In 998 he besieged Famīyah which was held by a Fāṭimite garrison. The Egyptians sent a relief force and the besiegers were severely defeated (19 July 998). This defeat brought the Emperor Basil once more to Syria (October 999).

Basil's second Syrian campaign lasted almost exactly three months. Two months were spent in raiding the province of Ḥimṣ as far as Baalbek. Shaizar was occupied and garrisoned. Several castles were burned and ruined (Abu-qubais, Maṣyāth, 'Arqah, and the town of Rafanīyah). It is not likely that Ḥimṣ itself was much injured. A large amount of plunder and many captives were secured. From 5 December to 6 January Tripolis was invested, without success. The Emperor spent the rest of the winter in Cilicia. Affairs in Armenia now claimed his attention, but even apart from this Basil probably desired to make peace with the Caliph of Egypt. It may be that the ten years' truce concluded about this time was ratified before the Emperor left Cilicia in the summer of 1000[1].

In the second half of the tenth century Egypt enjoyed a period of much prosperity and internal peace. This was principally the merit of the Caliphs Ma'add al-Mu'izz (953–975) and Nizār al-'Azīz (975–996). They were just and tolerant rulers and fortunate in the generals and officers of state who served them. Art, learning, and manufactures were fostered and flourished. Numerous public buildings and other works of public utility date from this period. The burdens of taxation were somewhat lightened and more equally distributed. Much of the kaleidoscopic life of the *Thousand and One Nights* was actually realised in the Cairo of those days.

The instability of fortune and the caprice of rulers never found more striking illustrations than in the reign of the sixth Caliph, Abu 'Alī al-

---

[1] The Egyptian plenipotentiary in the negotiations was chosen by Barjuwān, who was assassinated on 4 April 1000. Basil seems to have opened negotiations during his Syrian campaign, so that the treaty may have been concluded by the spring of 1000. The conditions of peace are not specified by Yaḥyà, from whom the particulars of this paragraph are taken.

Manṣūr al-Ḥākim (996–1021). His minority was a time of chaos, when the chiefs of the Berber and Turkish guards fought and schemed for supremacy. The native historians relate strange and incredible stories of his personal government, out of which it is nearly impossible to make a coherent picture. He is represented as arbitrary and cruel beyond measure and as the persecutor of every class in turn. He kept his position only by unscrupulous assassination and by playing off against one another the Arab, Turkish, Berber, and Negro factions which mingled in his court. On the other hand, measures are attributed to him which have been interpreted as the conceptions of a would-be reformer and unpractical idealist. In part of his reign he seems to be a rigid Muslim, persecuting Jews and Christians against all tradition and in spite of the fact that his mother was a Christian and his uncle at one time Patriarch of Jerusalem. At another period his conduct suggests that he was influenced by the esoteric doctrine of the Ismāʿīlian sect to which his ancestors belonged. Towards the end of his life he seems to have countenanced sectaries who proclaimed him to be an incarnation of deity. The mystery of his death was a fitting close to a mysterious life. He left his palace one dark night (13 February 1021) never to return; the presumption is that he was assassinated. But some declared that he would yet return in triumph as the divine vice-gerent, and the Druses of Lebanon are said to maintain this belief to the present day.

The revolts in southern Syria at the beginning of Ḥākim's reign reflect the strife of parties in Egypt and did not threaten the authority of the Caliphate itself. This distinction helps to make intelligible the maze of revolts and depositions and revolutions in which the governorship of Damascus was now involved. In twenty-four years and a half there were at least twenty changes in the occupancy of the post. Two governors between them held office for nine years, so that the average term of the remainder was less than ten months each. More than one was deposed within two months of his appointment. Generally the only cause of change was the arbitrary disposition of the Caliph or an alteration in the balance of power amongst the emirs of his court. Sometimes the new governor had to establish his authority by force of arms.

On one occasion in these years there was a revolt of a more serious character. Early in 1011 the Arab chief Mufarrij ibn Daghfal ibn Jarrāḥ, having defeated the Caliph's representative, became ruler of inland Palestine for the second time. He failed to occupy any of the coast-towns but held possession of the interior for two years and five months, until his death (1013). A peculiar feature of this revolt was the acknowledgment by Ibn Daghfal of the *sharīf* of Mecca, Ḥasan ibn Jaʿfar, as "commander of the faithful." This personage was a descendant of the Prophet and so possessed one outstanding qualification for the Caliphate. But his only supporter was Ibn Daghfal, and his phantom authority lasted less than two years. Ibn Daghfal's sons were defeated by Ḥākim's troops immediately after their father's death, and the control of Palestine passed again to the governor of Damascus.

An event of special interest to Christendom occurred in Jerusalem during Ḥākim's Caliphate, namely, the profanation and ruin of the church of the Holy Sepulchre (commencing 27 September 1009). It is unlikely that the fabric of the church was seriously injured. Ḥākim ordered its relics to be taken away and its monuments, including the Holy Sepulchre, to be destroyed. The portable furnishings of the church and its treasures were carried into safety before the Caliph's agents arrived. But the Holy Sepulchre and other venerated shrines were destroyed as completely as possible. The interior must have been left in a very mutilated condition. Mufarrij ibn Daghfal began the work of restoration when he was ruler of southern Palestine (*i.e.* between 1011 and 1013)[1].

Saʿīd-ad-Daulah of Aleppo having died early in January 1002, Lūlū banished the surviving members of the Ḥamdān family to Egypt and assumed the emirate. He acknowledged the Fāṭimite Caliph, Ḥākim, and also continued to pay tribute to the Greek Emperor. His rule is praised as having been wise and just. After his death (August 1009)

---

[1] The intention of the Caliph and the extent of the destruction of the church are to be ascertained chiefly from the narratives of Abu Yaʿlà (pp. 66–68) and Yaḥyà (p. 195 sq.). The former conveys the impression that a primary object of the Caliph was to plunder the treasures of the church. His version of the Caliph's order particularly specifies the destruction of the monuments (*athar*, which, however, is an ambiguous word and might signify relics). When the historian says "its structures were ruined and uprooted stone by stone," he refers, presumably, to such buildings as the shrine of the Holy Sepulchre. Yaḥyà's account would harmonise completely with this view but for his summary statement "it was thrown down completely to the foundations, except what could not be ruined and was too difficult to uproot." If the subject of the first verb is the church, then obviously the expression "to the foundations" cannot seriously be pressed, and the amount of damage to the walls and fabric remains obscure. But the subject in the original is quite vague, and the reference may be principally to the monuments and the interior structures. The brief statements of other writers, Eastern and Western, are no proof of such a complete destruction of the church as modern writers have assumed. The exact date is supplied by Yaḥyà (Tuesday, five days from the end of Ṣafar, A.H. 400). This agrees so far with the statement of Ademar (Lequien, III, 478) that the Holy Sepulchre was destroyed on 29 September (A.D. 1010). Yaḥyà (p. 201, lines 9 sqq.) relates that Ibn Daghfal began the work of restoration; he observes particularly that "he restored the places in it" (*i.e.* the shrines?). Possibly Ḥākim also authorised its repair, under the influence of his Christian mother and uncle (cf Glaber). In A.H. 411 (A.D. 1020) the church is described by Yaḥyà (p. 230) as still in a ruined condition. The relevant extracts from the Latin historians are given by Lequien, *Oriens Christianus*, III, 475 sqq. Other references will be found in Ibn al-athīr, IX, 147, Maqrīzī, II, 287 (Kitāb al-khiṭaṭ, Bulak edit., 1853–1854), Abu 'l-mahāsin, II, 64 (from Adh-dhahabī), and II, 101, Cedrenus (*Corp. Script. Byzant.*), Vol. II, p. 456. Forty-five years before this, in A.D. 966, this church had been seriously injured by the local Muslim and Jewish population (Yaḥyà, p. 125 sq.). The dome of the Holy Sepulchre and the roof of the adjoining main church were then both destroyed, and the necessary repairs had been completed only a short time before the events of 1009.

Manṣūr his son, although unpopular, held the emirate for some years against the Ḥamdān family and the attacks of the Banī Kilāb under Ṣāliḥ ibn Mirdās. Finally he was expelled from Aleppo by an insurrection (6 January 1016), headed by the governor of the castle, Mubārak-ad-Daulah Fataḥ, and, having escaped to Antioch, became a pensioner of the Greeks. These events increased the authority of the Egyptians in northern Syria. About a year later, Mubārak-ad-Daulah was made governor of Tyre, Sidon, and Beyrout by Ḥākim, and 'Azīz-ad-Daulah Fātik, an Armenian, was installed as governor of Aleppo (3 February 1017). As so often happened in such cases, the new governor began to act as an independent emir, and his assassination (13 June 1022) was probably instigated by Sitt-al-mulk, Ḥākim's sister, now regent. During the next two years and a half an Egyptian garrison held the citadel of Aleppo, and a series of Egyptian governors controlled the city.

The seventh Fāṭimite Caliph was Abu 'l-ḥasan 'Alī aẓ-Ẓāhir. He was a boy when he succeeded his father and he never exercised much influence in the government of his dominions (1021–1036). For the first three years of his reign Ḥākim's sister, Sitt-al-mulk, was regent. Soon after her death the Arab tribes on the borders of Syria made a league against the Caliph, hoping to conquer and rule the country (1024). The leaders of the revolt were Ṣāliḥ ibn Mirdās, chief of the Banī Kilāb, who lived in the neighbourhood of Aleppo, Sinān ibn 'Ulyān, chief of the Banī Kalb, near Damascus, and Ḥassān, a son of Mufarrij ibn Daghfal, whose home was in southern Palestine. The confederates were at first successful both in Palestine and northern Syria. Aleppo was captured by Ṣāliḥ ibn Mirdās (January 1025)[1], and Ḥimṣ, Baalbek, and Sidon soon acknowledged his authority. Thus a new dynasty, that of the Mirdāsites, was established in Aleppo (1025–1080). In Palestine the Caliph's representative, Anūshtakīn ad-dizbirī, was more than once defeated and was driven out of Syria. The least successful of the allies was Sinān ibn 'Ulyān. After his death in July 1028, his successor deserted the alliance and submitted to the Caliph. In the following year a decisive battle was fought at Uqḥuwānah, south of Lake Tiberias, between Ṣāliḥ and Ḥassān on the one side, and the Egyptians and their allies on the other (14 May 1029). Ṣāliḥ was killed and Ḥassān's power was completely broken. From now onwards Anūshtakīn was governor of Damascus and the most powerful emir in Syria (1029–1041).

[1] The citadel did not surrender until five months later (June 1025). Cf. note *supra*, p. 246. As illustrating the textual criticism that must always be applied to the dates of Arabic historians, it may be pointed out that 13 Dhu 'l-qa'dah 415 in Kamāl-ad-Dīn's text (date of the capture of Aleppo) should be 23 Dhu 'l-qa'dah 415, and that 1 Jumādà ii 416 (date of the surrender of the citadel) should be 1 Jumādà i 416. These are typical errors. The correct dates are given by Yaḥyà (pp. 246, 248), along with the week-days, which provide the necessary test of accuracy. See Stevenson, *Crusaders in the East*, appendix on Chronology.

During the period of this rebellion, in 1027 (A.H. 418), an interesting treaty of peace was made between the Fāṭimite Caliph and the Emperor Constantine VIII. It was provided that the Caliph's name should be mentioned in the public prayers of the mosques throughout the Empire, to the exclusion of his Abbasid rival. This arrangement was continued until the year 1056, when it was reversed at the instance of the Turkish Sultan Ṭughril Beg. A further recognition of the representative character of the Fāṭimite Caliph, and another concession to Islām, was contained in the provision that the Caliph might restore the mosque in Constantinople and appoint a muezzin to officiate there. The counterpart of these provisions gave the Emperor the right to restore the church of the Holy Sepulchre in Jerusalem. It is not to be assumed that the church had lain in ruins since its profanation by Ḥākim's orders in 1009, nor, perhaps, that much was actually done at this time in the way of restoration[1]. Another concession made by the Caliph was that those Christians who had become Muslims by compulsion in the time of Ḥākim might again profess Christianity without penalty. It may be assumed that the treaty of peace, as usual, was valid for a limited period only; but the term is not specified by the only source that mentions the treaty.

Naṣr Shibl-ad-Daulah, son of Ṣāliḥ ibn Mirdās, was permitted to succeed his father as ruler of Aleppo on the condition that he acknowledged the Fāṭimite Caliph in the customary manner, on his coinage and in the public prayers of Friday. His emirate did not include Ḥimṣ or Ḥamāh, but extended north-eastward to the Euphrates. The Greeks, who had recently been losing ground in Syria, now seized what seemed to them an opportunity of improving their position. The territory of Aleppo was twice invaded (1029 and 1030), both times unsuccessfully. The Emperor Romanus shared in the second invasion, a very ill-judged attempt. The Greek army suffered so much in the neighbourhood of ʿAzāz from the hot season, lack of water, and fever that it was compelled to retreat in a few days and lost heavily as it retired (August 1030). The Emir of Aleppo, reckoning his triumph an occasion of conciliation and not of defiance, at once opened negotiations for peace. A treaty was signed on terms that were distinctly unfavourable to the Muslim city. Aleppo again became tributary to the Empire, and a Greek deputy was allowed to reside in the city and watch over the due performance of the conditions of peace (April 1031).

---

[1] Maqrīzī (Khiṭaṭ, p. 355, lines 9 sqq.) is here the chief authority. He does not name the Emperor, but does mention Ẓāhir. William of Tyre also refers to a restoration of the church by permission of "Daher" (=Ẓāhir), and Cedrenus, II, 501, implies that the restoration was permitted by a son of the Caliph who destroyed the church. The brief statement of Cedrenus is obviously very confused and inaccurate (cf. *infra*, p. 257, n. 3). If Maqrīzī were the only authority it might be conjectured that his date A.H. 418 was an error for A.H. 428 (*i.e.* A.D. 1037). See p. 257.

At this date the territory of the Greeks in Syria extended eastward from Antioch to Ḥārim and southwards along the coast as far as Maraqīyah. The hillmen of the Jabal Anṣarīyah, who adjoined this territory, were partially held in check by strong castles such as Bikisrāyil, but still maintained their independence. After the defeat of Romanus, one of the chiefs of the hill tribes, Naṣr ibn Mushraf, captured Bikisrāyil and a general rising took place. Maraqīyah was besieged by Ibn Mushraf and the Emir of Tripolis. Nicetas, the new governor of Antioch, took prompt action against a very dangerous situation. He raised the siege of Maraqīyah (December 1030), and during the next two years systematically besieged and reduced the castles of the hillmen (1031–1032). Balāṭunus, Bikisrāyil, and Ṣāfīthā were among the fortresses now garrisoned and held by the Greeks.

These events brought about a resumption of hostilities between the Empire and the Egyptian Caliph. Anūshtakīn of Damascus and the Emir of Tyre had given a timorous support to the mountaineers in their struggle with Nicetas. Rafanīyah was therefore attacked and captured by Greek troops. A Byzantine fleet threatened Alexandria and the mouths of the Nile. Both parties desired a stable peace, but the task of settling the matters in dispute proved to be long and difficult. The chief obstacle to a settlement was the demand of the Emperor that Aleppo should be treated as a Greek dependency[1]. The negotiations were continued, or resumed, after the death of Romanus (April 1034), and peace was signed, perhaps in the autumn of 1037[2]. Each party pledged itself not to assist the enemies of the other, and their respective spheres of influence in northern Syria were defined. The Greek deputy whom Romanus had stationed in Aleppo had been driven out soon after that Emperor's death, so that Aleppo probably secured its independence. The right of the Emperor to renovate the church of the Holy Sepulchre was acknowledged, and possibly the privilege of appointing the Bishop of Jerusalem. In return Michael IV set free 5000 Muslim prisoners. The duration of the peace was fixed at thirty years. The Emperor sent builders and money to Jerusalem, but the repairs to the church were not completed until the reign of his successor Constantine IX[3].

[1] Full details of the negotiations are given by Yaḥyā (p. 270 sq.). His account throws light on the terms of the treaty of 1037, and has been used above to supplement the meagre details of that treaty preserved by others. Unfortunately Yaḥyā's narrative, at least as printed, breaks off before the year 1037 is reached.

[2] This date is derived from Yaḥyā, who seems to fix it as being three and a half (Muslim) years after the death of Romanus. Barhebraeus gives A.H. 427, but his narrative, on the whole, is not strongly against A.H. 428, which would agree with Yaḥyā. On the other hand, Cedrenus (vol. II, p. 515) gives A.M. 6544 (= A.D. 1035–1036) and Abu 'l-fidā (III, 96) and Ibn al-athīr (IX, 313) both A.H. 429.

[3] The authorities are those of the last note. The renovation of the church must have been considerable and not merely a repair of the damage done by Ḥākim. Cedrenus (II, 501) wrongly makes Romanus commence the work and Michael com-

The eighth Fāṭimite Caliph, Abu tamīm Maʿadd al-Mustanṣir, was only seven years old when his father died (June 1036), so that his reign began with a succession of regencies. The Caliph's mother, an African woman, exercised a considerable amount of influence. The contemporary Persian traveller Nāṣir-i-Khusrau records very favourable impressions of the prosperity and tranquillity of the country while the Caliph was a minor.

Early in this reign peaceful relations between Aleppo and Egypt were broken off. Naṣr ibn Ṣāliḥ was defeated and slain in battle with Anūshtakīn (May 1038), and Aleppo was captured and garrisoned by Egyptian troops for a few years (1038–1042). The disgrace of Anūshtakīn, followed immediately by his death (January–February 1042)[1], weakened the Fāṭimite dominion all over Syria. Aleppo was recovered by Naṣr's brother, Muʿizz-ad-Daulah Thumāl (March 1042). He resumed payment of tribute to the Greeks and so secured himself in that direction. The terms of the rulers of Egypt were not so easily satisfied. Envoys came and went between the parties. Attacks were launched against Thumāl by the Emirs of Ḥimṣ and Damascus, acting in the name of the Caliph (1048–1050). At length, in 1050, an agreement satisfactory to both sides was arrived at.

Two isolated events, which are a part of the history of the Fāṭimite Caliphs, deserve mention here. In 1049[2] Muʿizz ibn Bādīs, the Zairite Emir of Tunis, ceased to pay tribute to Mustanṣir and transferred his allegiance to the Abbasid Caliph. His family had ruled in Qairawān, in practical independence, since 973, when the Fāṭimite Caliph of the day made Cairo his residence and capital. But the formal separation, signalised by the acknowledgment of the Caliph of Baghdad, took place only now. On the other hand, for the greater part of the year 1059 the Caliphate of Mustanṣir was acknowledged in Baghdad itself. Such acknowledgments were now symbols of the triumph of political parties and alliances. The Turkish Sultan Ṭughril Beg identified his cause with that of the Abbasid Caliphs, with the result that his enemies in

plete it. William of Tyre, also, says that Romanus received permission to restore the church. Possibly the explanation of these statements is that during the negotiations of 1031–1034 the article regarding the restoration of the church was agreed to (so Yaḥyà), although the treaty of which it was part was not signed until the reign of Michael. William of Tyre seems to imply that not much progress was made with the repairs until the reign of Constantine. He gives 1048 as the date when the work was completed; similarly Abu 'l-fidā (A.H. 440). There was a severe earthquake in Jerusalem in January 1034 (Yaḥyà, p. 272; cf. Cedrenus, II, p. 511), which may possibly have caused some of the injury that was afterwards repaired.

[1] 1042 according to Kamāl-ad-Dīn and Ibn al-athīr, 1041 according to Abu Yaʿlà.

[2] So Ibn ʿAdhārī (A.H. 440), who further states that Ibn Bādīs struck new coinage in Shaʿbān 441 (end of 1049 or beginning of 1050). Ibn al-athīr is inconsistent with himself, giving both A.H. 435 and A.H. 440. Abu 'l-maḥāsin gives both A.H. 435 and A.H. 443, preferring the latter.

Mesopotamia were disposed to favour recognition of the Fāṭimite Caliphs in those districts and cities where they triumphed. In 1059 Baghdad was occupied by a Turkish emir, Arslān al-Basāsīrī, who, being an enemy of the sultan, acted in the manner just described. The occasion was hailed in Egypt as an extraordinary triumph, and in fact probably marked the highest point of superiority to the Abbasids ever reached by the Fāṭimite Caliphs.

When Mustanṣir came of age he shewed such feebleness and incapacity that he was treated by all parties as a cypher in the government. The ministry of Ḥasan al-yāzūrī (1050–1058) was still, on the whole, prosperous and considerate of the general welfare. But after his death there recommenced a bitter struggle for power between the leaders of the Turkish and those of the negro troops. The country was devastated and impoverished by civil war, and finally lay at the mercy of the unscrupulous and cruel Turkish leader Nāṣir-ad-Daulah ibn Ḥamdān (1062–1073). Prolonged drought and famine increased the miseries of the unhappy people. The influence of Egypt upon foreign affairs fell to its lowest ebb. It was in no way able to share in the defence of Syria against the Seljūq Turks.

The rule of Muʿizz-ad-Daulah Thumāl in Aleppo was mild and generous, and therefore popular. His greatest troubles were caused by the unruly Arabs of the district, the Banī Kilāb, and latterly by the Seljūq Turks, already planted at Raḥabah on the Euphrates. In January 1058, feeling no longer equal to the tasks of his position, he abdicated and left an Egyptian governor and garrison once more in power. These were soon expelled by the citizens assisted by the Banī Kilāb (September 1060), and shortly afterwards Muʿizz-ad-Daulah was persuaded to return to his former post (April 1061). During his second brief emirate the Greeks provoked hostilities by repairing some border castles, and Arṭāḥ was taken from them. Peace with them was renewed during the civil war that followed Muʿizz-ad-Daulah's death (November 1062). Arṭāḥ appears to have returned to its former owners.

Thumāl's brother, Asad-ad-Daulah ʿAṭīyah ibn Ṣāliḥ, was his successor. His title to succeed was challenged by a nephew, Maḥmūd ibn Naṣr, and the brief period of his emirate was one of civil war (1062–1065). It was at this date, just before the Norman conquest of England, that the Seljūq Turks entered Syria.

From the ninth century onwards, Turkish governors and Turkish generals and Turkish mercenaries play an important part in the history of Syria and especially of Egypt. The Ṭūlūnites were a Turkish family and were served by Turkish officers and soldiers. So also were the Ikhshīds. In Mesopotamia, from which these viceroys came, Turkish slaves held the highest place, subject only to the nominal authority of the Caliphs. In Egypt the Fāṭimite dynasty retained and added to the Turkish household troops of their predecessors. Turkish, Berber, and Negro factions struggled for supremacy, and the Fāṭimite governors of

Syrian towns in the tenth and eleventh centuries were often Turkish Mamlūks.

Before the middle of the eleventh century, a new wave of Turkish migration, under the great Sultan Ṭughril Beg (1037–1063), swept into Lower Mesopotamia from the north and threatened Armenia and Upper Mesopotamia. It was the precursor of the conquest of Syria by the Seljūq Turks. The manner of their conquest is representative of many other periods in Syrian history. Bands of horsemen, a few hundred strong—seldom as many as a thousand—rode under adventurous leaders who sought their fortune and lived by their swords. They took service with any ruler for money or for lands, and gained their chief advantage where local feuds were being waged. Some novelty in their arms or in their way of fighting might give them an advantage in battle. In any case they were always on the war-path, and so could finally wear down the resistance of cities which depended upon the cultivation of the land or upon peaceful industry. The inland towns of Syria—Aleppo, Ḥimṣ, Baalbek, Damascus, Jerusalem—yielded first and most completely to the Turks. Once established, the way of the conquerors was smoothed by their being Muslims. Their introduction of the nominal authority of the Caliphs of Baghdad was almost a matter of indifference to their subjects. The rule of Turkish emirs was already familiar in Syria. The invaders were backed by the prestige of the Seljūq sultans, but only to a slight extent occasionally by their armies.

A conquest of the character just described implies, of course, that Syria was in its normal state of political disintegration. It was, in fact, even less united than it had been for some time past. Aleppo was an independent territory and was rent by civil war. The Arabs hung loosely on the borders. The hillmen of the Jabal Anṣarīyah took no interest in the fate of the neighbouring plains. Antioch and its dependencies were under the rule of foreigners. Damascus and the coast towns from Tripolis southwards had cut themselves adrift from Egypt, which was in the throes of revolution. They were governed by independent emirs, antagonistic to one another. Only the south-west of Palestine was still closely attached to Egypt. After the great defeat of the Greeks at Manzikert (1071), Antioch was almost left to its own resources. Even the Armenians, who had long given soldiers to the Greeks on the eastern borders of the Empire and in Syria, now preferred to make terms with the Turks.

Hārūn ibn Khān was the first of the Seljūq Turks to gain a footing in Syria. About the end of 1064 he and his thousand followers turned the scale in favour of 'Aṭīyah ibn Ṣāliḥ against his rival Maḥmūd. When, however, 'Aṭīyah and the citizens of Aleppo rose against their deliverer and massacred his followers, he made off with the survivors to Maḥmūd and helped him to victory at the battle of Dābiq (16 June 1065). After the surrender of Aleppo to Maḥmūd (13 August 1065), Hārūn was given the little township of Ma'arrat-an-Nu'mān in fief, and settled there with a mixed following of Turks, Kurds, and Dailemites.

In the summer of 1067 another Turkish leader, 'Afshīn by name, raided the territory of Antioch and carried off great booty. His prisoners were so many that "a girl was sold for two dinars[1] and a boy for a set of horseshoes." In the following year 'Afshīn besieged Antioch and was bought off by the payment of a large sum of money (1068). At the same time there was war between Aleppo and Antioch, and Artāḥ was captured by Hārūn ibn Khān after a five months' siege (1068). In the following year a Greek army, under the Emperor himself (Romanus Diogenes), recovered Artāḥ and captured Mambij. Before the close of the year the Armenian governor of Antioch (Kachatur) made peace with Maḥmūd on terms that were favourable to the latter.

In 1070 a Turkish leader, known as Zandīq, entered Syria at the head of large forces and ravaged the territories of Aleppo, Ḥamāh, Ḥimṣ, and Rafanīyah. This was the first devastation of Muslim Syria by the Turks. It decided Maḥmūd to seek the protection of the Sultan Alp Arslān (1063–1072), and at the same time, in consequence, to transfer his allegiance from the Fāṭimite to the Abbasid Caliph. Prayers were said in the mosques of Aleppo for the new Caliph and for the sultan on Friday 30 July 1070[2].

Alp Arslān now demanded that Maḥmūd should engage in war with Antioch and with the Fāṭimite emirs. Maḥmūd having at first refused, the sultan invaded Syria (spring of 1071). Two months were spent in negotiations, and during another month Aleppo was blockaded. Then Maḥmūd submitted and became the sultan's vassal. The historian of these events comments especially upon the discipline of Alp Arslān's army. The persons and the property of the country people were respected. Even the forage that the soldiers used was often paid for. Aleppo was neither ruined nor pillaged. Fasdiq, where Alp Arslān pitched his tent during the expedition, was henceforth known as the Sultan's Hill (Tell-as-sulṭān).

Maḥmūd does not seem to have shewn much zeal in the fulfilment of his pledge to the sultan during the remainder of his emirate (*ob.* 10 January 1074). His sons Naṣr (1074–1076) and Sābiq (1076–1080) were the last of the Mirdāsites to rule Aleppo. Fresh bands of Turks were pouring into Syria. Rafanīyah was occupied by Jawālī ibn Abaq (1075), who raided the territory of Aleppo until he was severely defeated by Aḥmad Shāh, another Turkish leader, in the service of Naṣr ibn Maḥmūd and afterwards of his brother Sābiq. The assassination of Naṣr and the accession of Sābiq illustrate the influence now exercised by the Turks over the internal affairs of Aleppo. Sābiq was opposed by two of his brothers and by the Banī Kilāb, but defeated his enemies with the help of Aḥmad

---

[1] Fifteen dinars may have been a normal price.

[2] The same change was made in Mecca in this same year. But the acknowledgment of the Fāṭimites was resumed there again in 1074 or 1075.

Shāh and other Turks (July 1076). Naṣr and Sābiq both waged war inter-mittently with the Greeks. In 1075 Mambij was recovered by the former.

The principal Seljūq emirs of the north of Syria were 'Afshīn, Zandīq, and Muḥammad ibn Dimlaj. In the summer of 1077 they were ordered by Alp Arslān's successor, Malik Shāh (1072–1092), to unite under the command of his brother Tāj-ad-Daulah Tutush. In the spring of 1078 Tutush attacked Aleppo at the head of a large force, which included the Banī Kilāb and the soldiers of Sharaf-ad-Daulah Muslim of Mosul (1061–1085). The siege lasted four months and its failure was attributed to the action of Sharaf-ad-Daulah, an old ally of the Turks, who was now turning against them. Next year (1079) Tutush resumed his operations in Syria, with some success. Mambij, Buzā'ah, and other places sur-rendered or were captured. Then an invitation from the Turkish Emir of Damascus, At-sīz ibn Abaq, drew his attention southwards.

The first mention of the presence of Seljūq Turks in Palestine be-longs to the year 1070[1]. The authority of Nāṣir-ad-Daulah, governor of Egypt, did not extend at that time beyond the south of Palestine. Acre and Sidon were governed by an Armenian, Badr-al-jamālī, who had played a prominent part in Syrian affairs since 1063. Damascus, Tyre, and Tripolis were in the hands of other independent emirs. The Arab tribes on the southern and eastern borders were their own masters. After the assassination of Nāṣir-ad-Daulah (10 May 1073), Mustanṣir appealed to Badr-al-jamālī to end the régime of the Turkish slaves in Egypt. At the head of his Syrian troops he occupied Cairo (February 1074), and in a few years restored unwonted peace and order to the country. He was the all-powerful ruler of Egypt for twenty years (1074–1094).

Several Turkish leaders shared in the conquest of southern Syria, but they all, in a measure, seem to have obeyed At-sīz ibn Abaq[2]. His first acquisition was 'Ammān, an Arab stronghold in the Balqā (1071?)[3]. From there he became master of the south of Palestine, including Jeru-salem and Ramlah. Jerusalem capitulated on terms, and suffered nothing from its change of rulers. For several years At-sīz, having marked Da-mascus as his prey, ravaged its territory, especially at harvest time, and levied contributions from the coast-towns as the price of their immunity. In 1075 he captured Rafanīyah and gave it over into the charge of his brother Jawālī. In the summer of 1076 Damascus at last sur-rendered to him. After this he ventured to invade Egypt and was severely defeated in the neighbourhood of Cairo (January 1077)[4]. His

---

[1] A.H. 462 (Ibn al-athīr, x, 40; Kamāl-ad-Dīn, p. 77).

[2] His name first appears in the year 1071 (A.H. 463). Qarlū is the only leader mentioned by name in the previous year (A.H. 462).

[3] Quatremère, p. 413 f.

[4] The date is from Sibṭ ibn al-Jauzī. The general sequence of events suggests a year later. Cf. *infra*, p. 263, n. 1.

bold challenge prompted Badr-al-jamālī to seek the recovery of Palestine and Damascus. At-sīz, fearing the issue of the conflict he had provoked, invited Tāj-ad-Daulah Tutush to his aid. The result might have been expected. Tutush took possession of Damascus and put At-sīz to death (September 1079)[1]. Badr-al-jamālī withdrew his forces from Palestine. The emirs of the coast-towns, for the most part, paid tribute to Tutush rather than submit to their ancient rival, the governor of Egypt.

Finding himself secure in Damascus, Tutush at once sent most of his army back into northern Syria. 'Afshīn, his general, laid waste the country from Baalbek to Aleppo and ravaged the territory of Antioch. In consequence of this attack Sābiq and the citizens of Aleppo surrendered the town to Sharaf-ad-Daulah Muslim of Mosul (June 1080). Sābiq retired to Raḥabah, and Muslim and Tutush stood opposed as well-matched antagonists.

As matters turned out, there was little actual fighting between the rivals. For two or three years Muslim strengthened his position in northern Syria and Upper Mesopotamia, held communications with Badr-al-jamālī, and sought to divert the tribute of Antioch from the sultan to himself. During part of this time Tutush was absent from Syria, engaged in war with his brother Malik Shāh. After his return he captured Ṭaraṭūs and some neighbouring castles from the Greeks (1083). Muslim's one attempt on Damascus (1083) was broken off because Badr-al-jamālī failed to co-operate as he had promised, and a revolt in Ḥarrān called for attention. Next year was occupied by war in Mesopotamia with Malik Shāh. Towards the end of that year Sulaimān ibn Qutulmish, a Turkish emir who ruled a large part of Asia Minor, intervened in Syrian affairs. Antioch was surrendered to him by traitors (December 1084)[2], and Muslim fell fighting against him in the following year (21 June 1085). These events altered the whole situation. Badr-al-jamālī again retired from Syria, which he had invaded. Sulaimān and Tutush became rivals for the possession of Aleppo. The former was defeated and slain in June 1086. Soon afterwards Malik Shāh intervened to settle the division of the Syrian conquests. Tutush was left in possession of Damascus and southern Syria.

[1] The date is fixed by a consideration of Tutush's movements in northern Syria. Abu Ya'là gives Rabī' i, 471 (instead of Rabī' i, 472).

[2] Except that there was delay in the surrender of the castle, Antioch was yielded by its inhabitants almost without resistance, and with little loss of life. Philaretus (Philard or Firdaus), the governor, was an Armenian by birth, with possessions in Euphratesia which belonged to him before he was called to administer Antioch and its territory. He maintained friendly relations with the Turks and was unpopular with many of his Christian subjects. Sulaimān was hurriedly invited to seize Antioch on an occasion when Philaretus was absent from the city. Muslim disliked the change of government, particularly because Sulaimān would not continue to pay the annual tribute that had been received from Philaretus. Antioch had paid tribute to Muslim for 2 or 3 years, and previous to that to Malik Shāh. The sources consulted by the present writer do not shew when the payment of this tribute began. Both the last two governors of Antioch appear to have been Armenians.

Qasīm-ad-Daulah Āq-sonqor, father of the famous atābeg 'Imād-ad-Dīn Zangī, received Aleppo. Antioch was given to Yaghī Bassān[1]. Khalaf ibn Mulā'ib of Ḥimṣ and 'Alī ibn 'Ammār of Tripolis remained attached to the Egyptian alliance which Muslim had formed. In 1089 (A.H. 482) Acre, Tyre, Sidon, and Jubail (Byblus) submitted to Badr-al-jamālī for the sake of protection against the Turks. In the following year Khalaf was overpowered by a combination of the Turkish emirs. Thus all northern Syria, as far as Tripolis, was now securely in the hands of the Seljūq Turks.

The assassination of Niẓām-al-mulk (October 1092), Malik Shāh's great vizier, followed soon by the sultan's own death (November 1092), opened a period of civil war and political decay in the history of the Seljūq dominions. The rival claims of the sultan's children served as a welcome shelter to the ambitions of the powerful emirs who supported them. Tutush of Damascus was a candidate for the sultanate. He defeated, captured, and put to death Āq-sonqor of Aleppo (summer of 1094). Then he marched into Mesopotamia, where he met his own fate (February 1095). After this Aleppo was ruled by Fakhr-al-mulūk Riḍwān, son of Tutush, and Damascus nominally by another son, Shams-al-mulūk Duqāq, under the guardianship of the emir Ṭughtigīn. Antioch remained in possession of Yaghī Bassān. In the summer of 1097 Ḥimṣ again became independent, under Janāḥ-ad-Daulah Ḥusain. The coast-towns from Tripolis southwards were still dependencies of Egypt. The scene was now set for the entrance of the crusaders into Syria (autumn of 1097).

In December 1094 the long reign of the Caliph Mustanṣir (1036–1094), one of the longest reigns in Muslim history, came to an end. He was succeeded by his son, Abu 'l-qāsim Aḥmad al-Musta'lī (1094–1101), the ninth Fāṭimite Caliph. Earlier in the same year Shāh-an-shāh al-Afḍal, son of Badr-al-jamālī, succeeded his father as *'amīr al-juyūsh*, and so as the actual ruler of Egypt (1094–1121). In the summer of 1098 he seized Jerusalem from its Turkish governor and regained the whole of the south of Palestine from the Turks. Thus two groups of foreigners governed Syria just before the advent of the First Crusade—Turkish emirs whose power lay mostly in the north and the east, and Egyptian garrisons who occupied the central and southern coast-towns and a part of Palestine. Neither of these groups could depend upon the loyalty of the Syrian people, and neither of them was disposed to unite with the other in joint opposition to the invaders from the west.

[1] This name appears in Arabic MSS. as Yaghī Siyān and Baghī Siyān. Van Berchem (*Zeitschrift für Assyriologie*), gives reasons for preferring the form Yaghī Bassān

religious opportunity. The direct line of approach to the history of the crusading movement is a survey of the Muslim attack on Western Europe which was a sequel to the great Arabian uprising of the seventh century.

After the Muslim conquest of North Africa, Spain (eighth century), and Sicily (ninth century), all the southern coast of France and the western coast of Italy, with the islands of Sardinia and Corsica, lay at the mercy of hostile fleets and of the forces which they landed from time to time. The territories and suburbs of Genoa, of Pisa, and of Rome itself were raided and plundered. The Italian cities of the north had as yet no fleets, and the Muslims held command of the sea. In the south of Italy and in southern France Muslim colonies established themselves and were the terror of their Christian neighbours. During the tenth century the Byzantine Emperors made vain attempts to shield their possessions in South Italy, and were actually compelled to pay tribute to the emirs of Sicily. The defeat of the Emperor Otto II near Rossano in 982 marked the failure of the imperial power of the West in its traditional part of political defender of the faith. On the other hand the Muslims had already occupied lands more extensive than their numbers as yet permitted them to hold securely. They were weakened by political divisions and by frequent dynastic changes in North Africa, which was the chief seat of their power. The Muslim settlers in the south of France were expelled by the year 975 and those in South Italy, excluding Sicily, never gained more than a temporary and precarious foothold. In North Italy, Genoa and Pisa began to build ships to protect their coasts, and to further a commercial policy in which Venice, on the Adriatic shore, already led the way. In the early part of the eleventh century there was civil war amongst the Muslims in Africa, Spain, and Sicily, and the balance of power began significantly to alter. The occupation of Sardinia by the Muslims from Spain, and their descent from there on Luni in the gulf of Spezia, drove Genoa and Pisa into an alliance which was crowned with success. Sardinia was recovered, and a first clear step was taken in asserting the Italian mastery of the Tyrrhenian sea (1015–1017). Italian fleets now ravaged the coast of Africa and imposed treaties in furtherance of their growing commercial interests. Mahdīyah, the capital of the Muslims in Tunis and the chief harbour of their fleets, was menaced as Genoa and Pisa had been a hundred years before. In South Italy the Byzantine generals were still unsuccessful against Muslim raids, but their place was being taken by an ever-increasing number of Norman knights (from A.D. 1017 onwards). The victories of the Normans over the Greeks in this period were supplemented by successful war against the Muslims. When Sicily was finally plunged into a state of complete anarchy, the Normans began to make conquests there also (1060). The capture of Palermo (1072) was a significant token of their progress. Italian fleets co-operated in these Norman enterprises. When Genoa and Pisa in 1087 made a joint expedition, for the second time, against Mahdīyah, captured the town, burned the ships in its harbour, and imposed terms of peace on its ruler, the command of the Western Mediterranean passed finally to the Italian republics. The event is a landmark in the history of the medieval struggle between Islām and Christendom. Even the final conquest of Sicily by the Normans, which followed it very closely (1091), is not so important. In Spain the same work of reconquest made steady progress after the middle of the century. Here too Norman valour and Norman swords played an efficient part. Expeditions from South France, and probably also ships from Italy (1092–1093), joined in the war. Normans, Italians, and southern French, were thus already practically leagued in warfare against the common foe. The First Crusade joined to these allies other peoples, more widely separated, and bore the contest from the Western to the Eastern Mediterranean. But the contest remained the same, and the chief combatants on the Christian side were still Normans, Italians, and Frenchmen.

The recovery of Italy and Sicily and a large part of Spain from Muslim rule gave an impulse to the victors which could not fail to carry them to further enterprises. The defeated enemy had territory in Africa and the nearer East which invited attack. Pisa and Genoa were engaged in an oversea traffic which beckoned them eastwards. Sicily, in Christian hands, offered them ports of call and harbours of refuge on their way. Amalfi already traded actively with Syria, Egypt, and North Africa; Venice more particularly with the possessions of the Greek Empire. Italian commerce had everything to gain from Christian settlements in the East. An enterprise for the conquest of Syria and of Egypt was assured of the welcome and support of the Italian republics. The adventurous Normans too, as they spread from land to land with never-failing audacity and success, had found the Muslim East, had seen its treasures, and had heard its call. Their conquest of Muslim Sicily gave them a stepping-stone to Egypt and to Syria. From Italy they were already overleaping the narrow sea which separated them from the Greek Empire. War with the Muslim East may well have lain within their destiny independently of Pope Urban's summons, to which they so willingly responded.

The relation of the Popes to the age-long Muslim war is easily understood and simply stated. As the primates of the Church their most sacred interests were always imperilled by Muslim victory. Inevitably their authority and influence were cast into the balance against the spoilers of the Church's patrimony. No partial triumph could extinguish their hostility, least of all while the holy places of the faith remained an infidel possession. Direct political interest also for a time stimulated their activity. But at the period of their greatest political power they were influenced chiefly by the hope of realising their far-reaching vision of a universal Church. In the ninth century and in the early part of the tenth century, Rome was within the territory threatened by the Muslim invaders of Italy, and local circumstances drove the Popes to concert measures against them. Gregory IV (827–844), Leo IV (847–855), John VIII (872–882), and John X (914–928), all took an active part in the Muslim war. Their successors in the eleventh century were not, in all probability, the actual instigators of the Norman and Italian enterprises of the period, as some of the chroniclers assert, but at least they gave them every countenance and support. Benedict VIII (1012–1024), an Italian count and successful soldier before his consecration, approved and assisted the expeditions against the Muslim conquerors of Sardinia in 1015–1016. Gregory VII (1073–1085), by his advocacy of the cause of the Greek Empire, prepared the way for more distant enterprises. Victor III blessed the standard of the expedition against Mahdīyah (1087) and declared remission of sin to all who took part in it. From the middle of the century, under the guidance of the great Hildebrand, both before[1] and after he became Pope Gregory VII, the Papacy asserted and in a measure secured its claim to be the ecclesiastical "emperor" of Christendom. Granted that all secular power was subject to the control of the Church for ecclesiastical ends, the Pope became the predestined head of any great united enterprise against the Muslims. The part played by Pope Urban in rousing Europe to the First Crusade was suggested from the outside, and actually became a means of realising the papal claims. Still, the suggestion that he should take action was made because he actually represented the unity of Christendom and alone could issue an appeal which would be listened to with general respect. The Pope was an international power much more truly than the Emperor. He controlled an organisation through which he could exert influence upon every country from within. He best could maintain the "truce of God," which secured peace at home while the crusaders were absent on their enterprise. It is not clear that the Pope's initiative was essential to the starting of the First Crusade, but his intervention at some point was inevitable and his authority was one of the great forces which maintained the movement.

The date at which Europe became ready for a united attack on the Muslim East cannot be put earlier than the last quarter of the eleventh century. The enemy were then at last driven out of the home lands, excepting Spain, and the Western Mediterranean was again a Christian sea. As long as the struggle in the West was proceeding, schemes for the conquest of Palestine were impracticable. These facts must be kept in mind in any consideration of the alleged bull of Sergius IV (1009–1012), in which he announces the recent destruction of the Holy Sepulchre in Jerusalem (September 1009) and declares his wish to overthrow the

[1] For a different view on this point see *supra*, Chapter II, pp. 52–53.

Muslims and restore the Sepulchre. His intention is to equip a thousand ships for the purpose of his expedition, and he says that word has already come from the Italian coast towns to the effect that preparations there have been begun. Assuming the genuineness of the document, which is seriously disputed, it may be noted that the preparations reported may not really have been carried very far, nor indeed even commenced, and that the circumstances which suggested the expedition were very transitory. The reported destruction of the Holy Sepulchre was indeed an event likely to awaken the resentment of Christendom, and it may possibly have originated the earliest formulation of the crusading idea that has been preserved. But nothing came of Pope Sergius' intention; the Italian cities were not yet able to fit out the armada he proposed, and the Sepulchre, only partially injured, was soon restored without Western intervention[1]. Neither the alleged destruction of the Sepulchre nor the Pope's daring thought, if it actually was his, had any direct influence on the origin of the First Crusade. At most they may have increased the animosity of war in the West and stirred the Christians there to renewed exertions.

The feature of the First Crusade that most struck the imagination and stirred the fervour of its supporters was its declared purpose of delivering Jerusalem from the hands of the infidels. Extreme veneration for Jerusalem and its sacred sites was fostered by the whole system of Latin Christianity, and especially by its encouragement of pilgrimages. Frequent pilgrimages to local and national shrines were crowned by the necessarily less frequent pilgrimage to Palestine. In the eleventh century pilgrimages *en masse*, in which hundreds journeyed together to Jerusalem, led by some bishop or noble, were not unknown. One such notable pilgrimage was from Normandy in 1064; another was headed by Count Robert I of Flanders (1088–1089). Individual pilgrimages also grew more frequent as the century advanced and the way became easier. The Cluniac revival gave fresh life to this part also of the Church's ancient practice. Devotion to the cradle of Christianity was nurtured and stimulated even amongst those who never adventured on the distant journey. The indignities which Christians suffered in Jerusalem at the hands of the Muslims thus became familiar in Western Europe. It is not likely that the occupation of Jerusalem by the Turks (1071) stirred feeling in any special manner. But the capture of Antioch from the Greeks (1085) may have done so. Some part of its former population seems to have reached Europe, and to have roused animosity against the Turks by a recital of its misfortunes. In this and other ways the victories of the Turks over the Greek Empire influenced popular feeling and at the same time the policy of those at the helm of state. It was the situation of the Greek Empire and the advance of the Turks in Asia Minor which finally called Europe to arms on behalf of Jerusalem

---

[1] See *supra*, Chapter vi, p. 254.

and the Eastern Churches. A sense of obligation to the Holy City and to Christians in the East, long expressed in other ways, now took the form of the First Crusade.

The long history of warfare between the Muslims and the Byzantine Empire has been told in another volume of this work. In the crisis which followed the fatal battle of Manzikert (26 August 1071), the Emperor Michael VII conceived the idea of calling to his assistance his Christian brethren of the West. His appeal was directed to Pope Gregory VII, as the supreme representative of Western Christianity and more truly its common head than the greatest of its secular potentates. The Emperor's petition fell on willing ears, for Gregory saw in it an opportunity of restoring the East to the Roman obedience, and at the same time of practically realising his great principle that the kings of Christendom are the liege servants of the Church. For several months the Pope was full of the project of a mighty expedition to the East, in which he thought of personally taking part, and for which his letters claim that he received substantial promises of support (1074). But pre-occupations in Italy made it impossible for him to carry out his intention. The Greek Emperor was left to wage an unequal war with the Turkish invaders of his dominions. They overran Asia Minor and came within striking distance of Constantinople itself. The Emperor Alexius (1081–1118) saved a part of his Asiatic territory by acknowledging defeat and making what terms of peace he could. His position was weakened by the frequent wars he had to wage with the vassals of the Empire in Europe. When at length these wars were ended (1094) and the recovery of lost Byzantine territory in Asia became again feasible, it is not surprising that Alexius bethought himself of the powerful help which had once been so nearly granted to his predecessor. In 1090 he had been assisted against the Turks by Count Robert of Flanders. Such another expedition, but on a considerably larger scale, was no doubt what he desired and hoped for. His appeal was directed to Pope Urban II, Gregory's successor in spirit as well as in office (1088–1099). Once more the Byzantine proposal was favourably received, and on this occasion nothing intervened to prevent the Pope from executing his resolve. At his summons Western Europe eagerly prepared to make war with the Muslim East.

The First Crusade by proceeding through Constantinople and Asia Minor accomplished for Alexius even more than he can originally have expected to obtain from his Western allies. Not the least achievement of the crusading movement, considered in its ultimate results, was that it postponed the Turkish capture of Constantinople for 300 years. But the crusaders never regarded themselves as the mere auxiliaries of the Greek Empire, nor was their chief purpose to aid the Emperor against his Muslim enemies. Pope Urban's official utterance declared the general purpose of the Crusade to be the deliverance of the Christians of the

East. The danger of the Greek Empire is therefore one motive to action, explicitly stated, but much more stress is laid on the situation in Palestine. There and not in Asia Minor lay the supreme object of the enterprise for the peoples of the West. Their conception of the Crusade may be said to differ from that of the Emperor only in the emphasis which they laid on one part of a complex whole. Alexius' appeal, in general terms indeed, was also doubtless on behalf of the Christians of the East, and possibly his ambassadors spoke of the deliverance of Jerusalem as something to be aimed at ultimately by the allied forces. But the mere change of emphasis exercised a transforming influence. Very quickly it appeared that all the Latin interests, religious, commercial, and political, lay in these remoter achievements in which the Emperor had no direct concern. Thus the Crusade had one aspect for the Latins and another for the Greeks. The two parties were engaged in appearance in a common enterprise. Each quickly found the other disloyal to the common cause, because their conception of that cause was not the same. All the history of the relations between the Greeks and the Latins, in the First Crusade and afterwards, must be read in the light of this fundamental discrepancy.

Assuming now that a proposed expedition on behalf of the Greek Empire and the Eastern Churches could thus become one for the deliverance of Jerusalem and the Holy Land, we can better estimate the significance of Pope Gregory VII's scheme in 1074. It has been argued that his intention was quite different from that of the crusaders of 1096, and that if his project had been realised there would have been an expedition to the assistance of the Greeks but no crusade. In reality the comparison in these words does not lie between two quite disconnected schemes, and it seems more than probable that, if events had progressed further in Gregory's time, they would have taken the course they did afterwards in Urban's. It is significant that one of Gregory's letters shews that Palestine was thought of as the goal of his enterprise[1]. It is true that this goal is not yet the chief object which he has in view. But neither was it so at first in the time of Urban. It was only after consideration, and when it had been decided to inaugurate a great international enterprise (*i.e.* between the dates of the Councils of Piacenza and Clermont), that Pope Urban and his councillors began to define the issue in a specially Latin sense. It is not extravagant to suppose that Gregory would also finally have done the same. Still, it remains to the credit of Urban and his advisers that they saw there was a distinctive Latin view which it was for them to enunciate, and that this was done in the Pope's great speech at Clermont.

It must be added that the part played by Alexius in the inception of the Crusade has been variously estimated, and that recent writers of

[1] "Iam ultra quinquaginta milia...contra inimicos Dei volunt insurgere et usque ad sepulcrum Domini, ipso ducente, pervenire." *Gregorii VII Reg.* II, 31.

authority have denied it altogether. These writers are entirely justified when they insist that the number of the crusaders was a cause of surprise and of serious trouble and anxiety to the Emperor, and that he did not propose a crusade in the sense of the actual movement, if that be defined as "a religious war, properly so called, induced by the assurance of spiritual privilege and undertaken for the recovery of the holy places."[1] Admitting this, however, it may still be asserted that letters of the Emperor to the Pope formulated the first draft, as it were, of a scheme for which the West had long been ripening, and which came into being in the shape of the First Crusade. Ekkehard and Bernold of St Blaise supply the necessary proof so far. If so, the Turkish advance and the need of the Greek Empire must be included amongst the determining causes of the crusading movement. The expedition of Robert of Flanders, recorded by Anna Comnena and already referred to, then also becomes a precursor of the First Crusade. The alleged letter of the Emperor to Robert, asking for help, may or may not be genuine in its present form. The supposition to which recent critics incline, that it is a modified edition of the original letter, seems best to account for its conflicting features. But that some such letter was written by the Emperor to Robert is both credible and probable.

Pope Urban's first public appeal on behalf of the Christians in the East was made at the Council of Piacenza in March 1095. The humiliation of the Eastern Church and the danger of Constantinople were described to the Pope and the Council by ambassadors from the Greek Emperor. Urban espoused their cause so warmly that some pledged themselves at once to go to the rescue of the imperial city. There is no allusion to the Holy Land in the one report (that of Bernold) which we have of these events. The decision to rouse Christendom to a united attack on Islām must have been arrived at in the summer months which followed the Council of Piacenza. The direction of such an enterprise, its prospects of success, and the motives to which it might appeal for support, must all have been considered. In this interval, we may suppose, Jerusalem became the hoped-for prize of the Muslim war and the chief incentive to it. There are indications that even certain details had been arranged before the Council of Clermont, *e.g.* the time of starting, the declaration of a three years' truce for the security of the crusaders' homes and property, and their solemn pledge, marked by the assumption of a cross on the cloak or tunic. It can hardly be doubted that the Pope had assurance of influential support before he delivered his speech at Clermont. The circumstances of the adhesion of Raymond of Toulouse imply that he was previously aware of the Pope's intention and had been invited to join the movement. Thus prepared for, Pope Urban's eloquent speech on 27 November 1095 met with an enthusiastic reception and definitely committed the Church to a movement in full accord

---

[1] This is substantially Riant's view.

with its genius and history. On the following day, in a council of the bishops, Ademar of Puy was chosen to be the papal representative during the Crusade. Other matters connected with its organisation were doubtless at the same time provided for. During the next six months a host of preachers, both official and voluntary, carried the Pope's appeal into every part of France and even beyond its borders. Urban's personal share in this missionary work cannot be too highly estimated. His association with the Cluniac movement, his French nationality, his eloquence and energy and organising power, were all of conspicuous influence in determining the result. For nine months he travelled from place to place with the special purpose of stirring enthusiasm for the Crusade. He traversed Western France as far as Le Mans. At Tours he held a synod from 16 to 23 March 1096. From there he turned southward to Bordeaux and then eastward through Toulouse, Montpellier, and Nîmes. He did not return to Italy until the month of September 1096. The first proclamation of the Crusade at Clermont, the ensuing journey of the Pope through France, and the enthusiasm with which he was received, account in large measure for the extent to which the Crusades became and continued to be a French national movement.

Neither King Philip of France nor the Emperor Henry IV was on such terms with the papal court as to make it possible for them to join the First Crusade. None of the great nobles who therefore became its chiefs had any good claim to authority over the others. Ademar of Puy was the principal ecclesiastic in the army but not its military commander. As a Provençal bishop he was in fact a vassal of Raymond of Toulouse. The composite character of the Crusade, its association of men of different nationalities, naturally suspicious of and hostile to one another and without any supreme leader, thus provided sure causes of disunion and discord. Even the common purpose of the national chiefs, their intention to conquer and occupy Syria or Palestine, was a further cause of separation. Those at least who intended to settle in the East were prospective rivals in the apportionment of the conquered territory. Thus when the crusaders assembled at Constantinople they did not become one united army, but remained a loose confederation of forces, whose individual characters and rivalries did much to determine the subsequent failures of the First Crusade, and indeed of the whole crusading movement.

A brief notice of each of the more important leaders will therefore suitably clear the way to an understanding of the events of the Crusade. Hugh, Count of Vermandois, brother of the French king, was in some degree his royal brother's representative. But neither his army nor his war-chest were commensurate with his apparent rank, and he did not play a distinguished part during the Crusade. He intended to settle in Palestine, although he did not carry out his intention. The oldest and the wealthiest of the crusading leaders was Raymond of Saint Gilles, Count of Toulouse since 1093. His army was from the first probably the most considerable and his wealth enabled him to maintain its strength. He had fought with the Muslims in Spain, and his third wife was Elvira of Castile. During the Crusade he claimed a foremost place, and doubtless expected to become a prince in the Latin East. With him went Ademar of Puy. Robert of Normandy, son of the Conqueror, was fitted for leadership neither by character nor by military capacity, but was of importance because of the number of Norman nobles who followed him. Godfrey of Bouillon, Duke of Lower Lorraine, had similar resources to those of Robert, but in character and capacity he stood much higher. His dukedom was a barren title, and he sold his small estates to provide himself with means for the Crusade. He is described as being equally fit to be the light of a monastery or the leader of an army. During the Crusade he distinguished himself as a brave soldier, although in no sense, of course, its supreme commander. His brothers Baldwin and Eustace gave added strength to his position. The latter had already been an ally of Robert of Normandy against William Rufus. Robert II of Flanders (1093–1111) was pre-eminent for his soldierly qualities and had greater monetary resources than either Robert or Godfrey; but as a leader of the Crusade he stood in the second rank. By far the most able of the crusading chiefs and the best fitted to establish a Latin princedom in Syria was Bohemond of Taranto. The Norman knights from Southern Italy who accompanied him, including his bold nephew Tancred, were sufficient in numbers to make his force important apart even from his own capacity. There is strong reason to suspect that he was resolved from the first, by one means or another, to make himself lord of Antioch. He had Muslim troops in his army, and Tancred, if not Bohemond also, could speak Arabic. Having experience already in Muslim warfare, he displayed during the Crusade a resourcefulness and a military capacity in which he had no equal.

Three chief ways to Constantinople were open to the crusaders. One starting from the Rhine passed by Nuremberg and Ratisbon, down the valley of the Danube, and through Hungary. It was already a pilgrim road familiar to many. Another passed through Dalmatia, and was accessible from the north of Italy and the south of France. The third was the ancient Appian Way through the centre of Italy, and involved a short sea passage from Bari or some other Italian coast town. Each of these was used by some of the numerous bands and armies which marched to Constantinople from the spring of 1096 to the spring of 1097. None of the leaders whose names have been enumerated started before 15 August 1096. This was the date fixed for the departure of Ademar of Puy, and had been announced to others as an indication of the time when they should be ready. But the spring of 1096 may have been named by some of the earlier preachers, and by that date a popular movement, for which little preparation was required, was already afoot. The first crusaders whose start can be dated were Frenchmen from districts visited by Peter the Hermit. They left home in March, and seem to have included only eight who could be ranked as knights. Five of these were of one family, Walter Sansavoir (the Penniless) of Poissy on the Seine, with his uncle and three brothers. They are said by Orderic Vitalis to have been a part of Peter's own expedition as far as Cologne and to have separated from him there. In Christian Hungary they were well received by King Koloman and passed through his territories without any special incident. At Belgrade, which lay just on the Bulgarian frontier, the account that they gave of themselves was disbelieved and they were refused provisions. This led to a general plundering of the district by the crusaders and to severe retaliation by the Bulgarians. Walter hurriedly fled as far as Niš, where the Greek governor of the province was stationed and where he was recompensed for his losses and given a safe-conduct for the remainder of the journey. It is calculated that he arrived in Constantinople soon after the middle of July.

Peter the Hermit was one of the most successful of the preachers who stirred enthusiasm after the Council of Clermont. He preached at first in Berry in central France, and afterwards, perhaps, chiefly in the districts to the north and north-east of his starting-point. He, like Walter, made his way to Constantinople through Germany and Hungary. He is known to have passed Trèves on 10 April 1096, but before he finally turned eastwards he preached the Crusade for a week at Cologne (12–19 April). In South Germany he and his French followers were joined by considerable numbers of Germans gathered from those districts which favoured the Pope in his quarrel with the Emperor. Walter of Teck and Hugh of Tübingen, Count-Palatine of Swabia, are two of some twenty knights who were their leaders. Whatever authority Peter may have enjoyed among the French peasantry whom he had stirred by his preaching, it cannot be supposed that he was in any way recognised as a leader by this German contingent. Possibly the Germans followed at some distance, even some days' march, behind Peter's Frenchmen. Albert of Aix's history, our only source, refers chiefly to the latter. Hungary was traversed peacefully and uneventfully as far as Semlin (Malevilla), just on the Bulgarian border. Here the French crusaders stormed and plundered the town, on the alleged ground of injuries recently done to stragglers in Walter's army. In Bulgaria, which they now entered, they were beyond the reach of Hungarian retaliation, and having given hostages to Nikita, its governor, they were permitted to purchase provisions in Niš. Here again, however, trouble arose, owing, it is said, to the burning of some mills and houses by a party of Germans. Peter's baggage train, including his money-box, was completely plundered by the Bulgarians, numbers of women and children were taken captive, and Peter himself and his followers were driven in headlong flight into the woods. In

Sofia the fugitives found a harbour of refuge, and were overjoyed to receive a message from the Emperor to the effect that they had already suffered sufficiently for their wantonness and that they might be assured of his protection during their further journey. They reached Constantinople and encamped alongside of Walter's followers on 1 August 1096.

The trans-shipment, five days later, to the coast of Asia Minor of all the crusaders who had now reached Constantinople, was no doubt at the instance of the Emperor Alexius. He may already, in this short time, have had experience of conflicts arising between the Greeks and the Latins. At least he foresaw that they were sure to arise. There is no ground for the suspicion that the Emperor shewed unfriendliness by his action and deliberately sent the crusaders to meet their doom on the other side. Provisions were regularly supplied to their camp at Cibotus, and if the pilgrims had remained quietly there until reinforcements arrived, as they were advised to do, they would have been undisturbed by the Muslims. About the middle of September, however, first a party of Frenchmen ravaged the neighbourhood of Nicaea, and then an expedition of Germans followed and captured a castle close at hand (Xerigordon). Dā'ūd Qilij-Arslān, Sultan of Rūm, after a week's siege recaptured the castle (7 October), and then, having made the necessary preparations, led an army against the Latins at Cibotus. The crusaders marched out against him as he approached and were utterly defeated (21 October). More than half the Latin knights were slain. Hugh of Tübingen, Walter of Teck, Walter Sansavoir and two of his brothers, were amongst the number. Most of those who escaped took refuge in the citadel at Cibotus, from which they were rescued by Greek ships. The more important of the survivors afterwards joined the forces of Godfrey of Bouillon. Many sold their weapons and gave up the crusade altogether.

Following Peter's expedition came several bands which did not reach their destination at all. One passed through Saxony and Bohemia, headed by a priest named Volkmar. It may be identified with those crusaders who persecuted the Jewish colony at Prague (30 May). Further on, at Nyitra (Neutra) in Hungary, most probably owing to their own excesses, they were attacked by the Hungarians and completely dispersed. The survivors probably returned home. The identification of Volkmar with Fulcher of Orleans, afterwards referred to as one of Peter's companions, is too precarious to be relied on.

Another German expedition from the Rhine had been stirred by Peter's preaching and by that of a priest, Gottschalk by name, who marched with it. Inspired no doubt by what had already taken place, as we shall see, in the cities on the Rhine, they commenced a persecution of the Jews at Ratisbon (23 May). They were well treated by the Hungarians in Wieselburg (Meseburg), but behaved so badly there that they were attacked some distance farther on by the orders of the Hungarian king and utterly cut to pieces. Very few of them escaped.

From the valley of the Rhine also, somewhat later, came an expedition whose chief leader was Emico, Count of Leiningen, between Worms and Spires. He made himself notorious by commencing a persecution of the Jews in the Rhine cities. Previous to the crusades the Jews had been living on quite friendly terms with their Christian neighbours, and although the new movement had stirred religious animosity against them they had not hitherto been molested. Count Emico was most likely chiefly influenced by the hopes of the plunder which he secured in the Jewish quarters of Spires (3 May), Worms (18–20 May), and Mayence (27 May). He initiated a persecution which extended to other cities. That in Trèves (1 June) is attributed by the Jewish contemporary account to the agency of visitors from the towns just mentioned. The synagogues and Jewish houses in Cologne were plundered by crusaders chiefly from Lorraine, on their way up the Rhine to join Emico (early in June). The Jews of Cologne took refuge in the country villages round about and it was in them that the worst massacres took place (end of June). The crusaders whose evil work this was may have come from France or from Flanders and Lorraine, and they must ultimately have joined Emico on the borders of Hungary. Emico's army included finally a considerable number of Frenchmen, in addition to his own German followers. Amongst these were Clarebold of Vendeuil, Drogo of Nesle, and perhaps William of Melun, known as Charpentier, "the carpenter," because of his fighting prowess. This expedition found its progress barred at the Hungarian frontier by King Koloman, who was posted with an army in the strongly fortified city of Wieselburg (middle of June). The king's hostile attitude is fully explained by his recent experiences, not to mention the reputation of Emico's followers which had probably been reported to him. The crusaders besieged Wieselburg for six weeks with an increasing prospect of success, until one day, as they pressed their attack, a sudden sally of the besieged threw them into a panic. They were quickly routed and completely dispersed (beginning of August). Emico escaped and returned home. Others joined the army of Godfrey, which was now advancing. Some of the French knights made their way into Italy and there joined the forces of Hugh of Vermandois.

The incredible estimates of the numbers of those who joined in the First Crusade still given in modern histories of deserved repute make it necessary to discuss this subject specially and somewhat fully. At this point it will be sufficient to indicate the nature of the evidence in the case of the disastrous expeditions of which an account has just been given. The statements of our sources to the effect that Walter had 15,000 followers and Peter 40,000, or that the crusaders when encamped at Cibotus numbered 25,000, are to be regarded as possessing no evidential value at all. Such numbers in medieval sources when they can be brought to a definite test are invariably proved to be unreliable. Albert of Aix is our chief authority for the events in question, and his use of numbers may be illustrated from one chapter[1] in his history. There we read that Peter's host of 40,000 was dispersed by the Bulgarians, that only a party of 500 remained with Peter and the other leaders, that these by making signals and blowing horns reassembled 3000 more by evening, and that after three days 30,000 men, shewing a loss of 10,000, resumed their march together. Such an account only tells us that the crusaders were routed and scattered and gradually reassembled, and that they lost a large part (one quarter) of their total number. Even in this form the narrative may not be reliable history. But in any case the numbers are not records based on observation or tradition, nor even of the nature of statistical estimates. They are a mere fashion of speech intended to express proportions and relations, and may be called illustrative or pictorial numbers. In another chapter[2] there is a good illustration of the merely pictorial use of a number. Instead of relating how a band of hot-headed youths made an unjustified attack on Niš and were immediately joined in their attack by another similar band, the writer states that the attack was made by 1000 men ("mille insensatorum hominum iuventus"), and that these were immediately followed by another thousand like them ("mille eiusdem levitatis"). Here 1000 is used where another writer would consider 500 or 300 appropriate. Almost everything depends on the numerical scale in use, almost nothing on the actual figures. These may be quite unknown to the writer, and then of course cannot influence his choice of a number. Those who recognise that such numbers are unreliable often say that they are "exaggerated." This criticism does not go far enough if it implies or is understood to imply that the numbers bear some proportion to reality and may be taken as a starting-point for an estimate of the actual numbers. Pictorial numbers in most writers are essentially fictitious, and are only at best of occasional use to the historian by setting an upper limit to the figures which he is in search of.

Any estimate given of the numbers, say of Walter's followers or of Peter's, must start from another kind of evidence. Some of the experiences of the crusaders indicate their relatively small numbers. Walter's followers were put to flight by a force of which the greater part seems to have consisted of the garrison of Belgrade; Peter's host was easily dispersed by the troops assembled in Niš. Both expeditions seem to have obtained sufficient supplies of food without difficulty from the markets of the towns they passed through. Even allowing in the one case for the presence of undisciplined peasant pilgrims, with some proportion of women and children, and in the other for provisions carried with them, these facts are significant. If the first narrative summarised above be historical at all, it cannot describe what happened to 40,000 people, nor even to 10,000. Only by making it refer to Peter's own French

[1] Book i, Chap. 13.   [2] Book i, Chap. 12.

followers and by numbering these in hundreds instead of in thousands do the difficulties disappear. If the number of knights be taken, as it usually may, to be an indication of the number of efficient soldiers in the two expeditions, we reach a total of a very few thousands as our maximum. The defeat of the crusaders at Cibotus by an army such as that of Qilij-Arslān is also an evidence of numerical weakness. In conclusion, however, we can only guess at the numbers who marched through Hungary with Peter and Walter. If the guess be made of 4000 to 5000 for Walter and 6000 to 7000 for Peter, these figures are maxima which may still be much too high. They are large in proportion to the numbers of the disciplined armies which followed, under Godfrey and the other leaders, of which a better estimate can be given[1].

By the end of October Alexius was fully informed of the magnitude of the crusading movement and had decided what policy to follow. His first aim was to minimise the disturbance and loss of property which the march of the crusaders through his European territories necessarily involved. This he sought to do by giving a friendly reception on the borders to each fresh arrival, and by provision of supplies to the various armies on the march. At the same time he posted troops along every line of approach to Constantinople with instructions to deal severely with plunderers and to repel force by force. Alexius had also reason to fear that the leaders of the Crusade might not respect his claims to the countries they were about to reconquer from the Muslims. Bohemond, at least, who had been a recent invader of his territory, was certainly not to be trusted. If the Latins chose to act in combination they were formidable enemies and perhaps irresistible. But they came professedly as friends. The circumstances thus pointed to a definite agreement with them as a solution of this part of the Emperor's difficulties. It may be supposed that he was indifferent regarding the future government of Palestine. But Asia Minor and Northern Syria were, in virtue of tradition and long association, essential parts of the Empire and could not be alienated voluntarily. On the other hand, guidance through an unknown country, abundance of provisions up to a certain point, subsidies of money, the use of Constantinople as a starting-point for the march through Asia Minor, possibly the assistance of Greek troops and ships and a free hand in Palestine, were all substantial advantages which could be offered in exchange for a recognition of imperial claims. Taking advantage of Western feudal customs, Alexius decided to demand from each crusading chief an oath of allegiance and a promise that the ancient possessions of the Empire which might be reconquered should be restored to him. Of course the oath of allegiance could only apply to the crusaders as holders of land in the East, which they were to occupy as the Emperor's vassals. So understood, it was a reasonable settlement of the future relations between the Latin settlers and the Greek Empire, assuming,

[1] See *infra*, pp. 297-8.

that is, that they really came to deliver the Christians of the East and therefore the recently enslaved lands of the Empire. Of course if the crusaders fought merely for their own gain and recognised no obligation to the Emperor, they might well regard Alexius' proposal as unwarrantably to his own advantage. But this was not the footing on which they presented themselves. They were permitted to enter Greek territory only as allies, already bound implicitly to render assistance to the Greeks against their Turkish enemies. The Emperor's proposal when it was put before them was received with dislike by some; but most seem to have recognised that it was a proper way of making definite the understanding created by their presence and of regulating their future relationship. If the Emperor continued the support he had already commenced to give, they were prepared to regard their conquests as ultimately a part of the Greek Empire. It was indispensable that many of the Latin knights should settle in the East, and it was agreed that they should do so as vassals of the Empire and not as independent Latin rulers. The special promise to restore the lost lands of the Empire to Alexius was no doubt intended to be realised in large measure by the establishment of Latin fiefs, and thus was not an irreconcilable alternative to the Latin occupation of Syria.

Obviously the foregoing interpretation and estimate of Alexius' policy depend to a considerable extent on the view taken of the origin and purpose of the Crusade. It has been argued by some modern writers that the Emperor should have welcomed the establishment of the Latins in Syria on any terms, that he tried to impose impossible conditions upon them, and that he roused their enmity by his jealous and suspicious conduct. Such criticism assumes that the Crusade was not organised even in part on behalf of the Empire, and ignores the almost complete certainty of friction and discord arising in any case. It also, in particular, undervalues the importance of Antioch for the Empire, and underestimates the danger arising from the establishment there of an independent Norman state.

Hugh of Vermandois was the first crusader of the highest rank to reach Constantinople. He came through Italy, and crossed from Bari to Durazzo probably before the end of October 1096. Many of the French knights who might have accompanied him marched through Germany and Hungary. Others were lost in a storm during the crossing from Italy, and those who remained were few in number. Hugh received, nevertheless, a cordial reception from the Emperor and gifts in due proportion to his rank. In return he took the oath of allegiance which Alexius desired. Some sources suggest that he was practically compelled to take the oath. But such compulsion, however small Hugh's following, was neither politic nor possible.

The next arrival was Godfrey of Bouillon. He left home about the middle of August and reached Tuln, near Vienna, soon after Emico's defeat. There he spent three weeks negotiating with the Hungarian king regarding his further progress. Koloman agreed to allow him to proceed if he gave sufficient hostages for the good behaviour of his troops. Godfrey's brother Baldwin and his family having been accepted as hostages, the crusaders marched through Hungary under strict discipline and closely watched by the king in person. Provisions were abundantly supplied, and at the frontier Baldwin and his family were released. At Belgrade Godfrey received assurances from Alexius that the crusaders would find abundant markets open to them on their route if they refrained from ravaging his country. The Emperor kept his word and all went well as far as Silivri (Selymbria), two days' march from Constantinople. There the Latins encamped for a week, and the country was laid waste by Godfrey's orders. The explanation of the Latin historian Albert is that Hugh of Vermandois was a prisoner and that the Emperor had given no satisfaction to an embassy which Godfrey sent to him from Philippopolis. He further states that Godfrey's action secured Hugh's release. Evidently, as Godfrey approached Constantinople he became suspicious of the Emperor's good faith, and possibly he made some demand which Alexius refused. When he encamped outside the gates of the Greek capital and was met by Hugh and representatives of the Emperor (23 December), his suspicions remained and he refused the Emperor's invitation to an interview. Anna's narrative suggests that the cause was his unwillingness to take the oath of allegiance required of him. Albert indicates rather a general suspicion of the Emperor's good faith. Reading between the lines, in the light of the final issue, we may conjecture that Godfrey at this stage asked for hostages as a guarantee of his safety, and that the Emperor considered this demand an insult to his dignity[1]. Rather than have the surrounding country plundered by the Latins, Alexius continued his permission to them to purchase provisions, and four days after Christmas he invited them to leave their tents and take shelter in a suburb of the city. As the weather was inclement, this proposal of the Emperor was accepted. An interchange of messages went on until the middle of January 1097, Greek soldiers all the time keeping strict watch to see that the Latins did not issue out to plunder. The conflict which ensued was inevitable in the circumstances and is not to be attributed to a deliberate act of policy on either side. The sources disagree, of course, as to which party was the aggressor. The Latins burned the suburb in which they were quartered and took up their position under the walls of the city. From there they plundered the country round for a week. But both sides had reason to desire peace, and quickly came to terms. The view we take of the cause of this dispute decides the question of which side now yielded most to the other. The Emperor sent his son John as a hostage, and at the interview which

---

[1] It is not impossible that Godfrey feared to trust himself in the Emperor's power because the ravaging of the country round Silivri had no sufficient justification (being due perhaps to false information regarding Hugh's position).

followed Godfrey took the required oath of allegiance (latter part of January 1097). Hugh of Vermandois assisted in bringing matters to this conclusion, and the royal hostage was released immediately after the interview. Some weeks later the Latins were transported to a camp on the opposite coast, no doubt in order to make room for other crusaders, who were now at hand (end of the third week in February). In their new quarters they were still supplied with provisions by the Emperor, and the poor among them were substantially helped by his bounty[1].

Bohemond was the next to arrive in Constantinople with a few knights (beginning of April). He seems to have crossed from Italy at the end of October 1096. But his forces followed slowly in separate bands for which he waited, and the united army was just at Castoria by Christmas. They crossed the river Vardar, not much farther on, on 18 February. Here there was a skirmish with Greek troops, who attacked them presumably because of their previous depredations. From this point they were under the guidance of a high official sent from Constantinople, and by his care obtained abundance of supplies. Rusa was reached on 1 April, and there Bohemond left his army for Constantinople. Tancred remained in command, and finally crossed into Asia Minor without entering Constantinople. Bohemond was an hereditary enemy of the Greek Empire, and now as at all times ready to take up arms against Alexius if he saw any advantage in doing so. He intended to secure a princedom in the East, and most probably had already fixed his choice on Antioch. Before taking the oath of allegiance he endeavoured to obtain a promise from the Emperor to support his scheme. Alexius' answer no doubt was that such requests were premature, and that everything would depend on the issue of the Crusade. It is unlikely, in spite of the definite statement of the *Gesta Francorum*, that Bohemond was now promised territory in the neighbourhood of Antioch. At most the Emperor may have indicated that he would afterwards consider favourably such claims as the Norman chief might be able to present.

Robert of Flanders accomplished the first part of his journey through France and Italy in the company of Robert of Normandy. He crossed from Apulia in December 1096, and did not advance farther towards

---

[1] The attitude of the modern historian to Anna Comnena's narrative of these events is decisively important for the view to be taken of them. Her account is interpreted by some to mean that Alexius finally compelled Godfrey, by force of arms, to take the oath of allegiance. This is no doubt the impression she conveys, but in view of Albert's narrative the Greek account may be regarded as patriotically overdrawn at this point. The view that the essential matter in dispute between Godfrey and Alexius was the oath of allegiance is a possible one, but Godfrey's yielding (without defeat) on such a point is more difficult to understand than Alexius' yielding on the point of the hostages. The very improbable date that Anna gives quite incidentally at one point ("Thursday in holy week" = 2 April 1097) has not been satisfactorily accounted for by those who reject it (cf. Kugler). May there not be a confusion with Christmas week, in which, according to Albert, *there was a cessation of hostilities* out of respect to the season? Christmas Day in 1096 *was a Thursday*.

Constantinople until the spring. He arrived later than Bohemond, and readily took the oath of allegiance.

Raymond of Toulouse, having left home, perhaps, about the end of October 1096[1], came by the north of Italy and the eastern shore of the Adriatic Sea. Passing through Dalmatia in the winter, his army suffered from the inclemency of the season, from scarcity of food, and from the attacks of the inhabitants of the country, so that large numbers of the crusaders lost their lives. At Durazzo messengers from the Emperor brought assurances of friendship and promised supplies. Beyond this point, however, there was frequent fighting between the crusaders and the Greek mercenaries who watched their progress. The Provençals considered themselves the aggrieved parties, and retaliated by destroying the suburbs of Rusa and plundering the town. At Rodosto, four days' journey from Constantinople, Raymond received a request from the Latin leaders already in Constantinople to hurry on, because they were preparing to start and were making arrangements with the Emperor to which it was desirable that he should be a party. When he reached Constantinople (perhaps in the third week of April), he decisively refused to take the now customary oath of allegiance. If the Emperor put himself at the head of the expedition and came with them, he would become his follower, he said, not otherwise. News of a shameful defeat of his army, in a conflict in which they were afterwards judged to have been in the wrong, only increased his determination not to yield. Finally, under pressure, he only consented to take an oath that he would do nothing against the life and honour of the Emperor. In consequence of his attitude he received, as the Provençal historian notes, little of the Emperor's bounty.

Last of all came Robert of Normandy, with his powerful brother-in-law, Stephen of Blois, and with Godfrey's brother Eustace, Count of Boulogne. Their army included the first expedition of " Englishmen and Britons " to join in the Crusade. Robert left home in September and had spent the winter in the south of Italy. He embarked at Brindisi on 5 April 1097, and reached Constantinople about the middle of May. After spending a fortnight in the Greek capital he proceeded to the siege of Nicaea, which had already begun.

The Emperor Alexius had good reason to be satisfied with the initial result of his negotiations with the Latins. Formally, at least, he had secured from the leaders of the Crusade the acknowledgment he desired. Even Raymond of Toulouse seems finally to have admitted the Emperor's claims in Asia Minor and Syria[2]. An agreement so important and so

---

[1] The date rests on a doubtful calculation. Vic and Vaissete, *Histoire générale de Languedoc* (1733), Vol. ii, p. 628.

[2] It is not easy to say when Raymond became the friend and partisan of the Emperor, which he shewed himself to be in Antioch. Albert, xi, 20, implies that it was previous to the march of the crusaders through Asia Minor. The Emperor may

intricate must have been put in writing and signed by the contracting parties[1]. If it did not specify all the lands which the Emperor claimed, it probably named at least the territories and towns in which he desired to place Greek governors, and some also of those which might be held by the Latins in fief. The plunder of all the captured cities may have been assigned to the Latins, and the Emperor certainly promised military assistance to his allies. The obligations of the Latin feudatories must have been defined, and, it may be, also the conditions on which they would obtain recognition as lords of the conquered territory. Of course the adherence of the crusaders to this agreement depended entirely on the Emperor's fulfilment of his promise to render them further assistance. If he failed in this obligation, the Latins were inevitably released from their pledges to him. But meantime the leaders were won partly by the personal charm and lavish gifts of the Emperor, partly, it may be added, by the reasonable character of his proposals, so that they judged their treaty with him to be of value to their enterprise. It is true that there was at the same time, especially among the rank and file, a strong undercurrent of suspicion and hatred of the Greeks. Godfrey's troops and Raymond's had already been engaged in serious fighting with them.

have gained Raymond's concession by a definite pledge, in the formal treaty which regulated the relationship of the parties, to bring an army to the assistance of the Latins. Even Raymond's oath in Constantinople may have guaranteed the Emperor's territorial claims, although it was not an oath of allegiance. To the view that Raymond suddenly changed his attitude in Antioch out of hostility to Bohemond, it may be objected that there is no suggestion in the sources of any inconsistency in his attitude, nor of any difference between the obligations of the individual Latin leaders towards the Emperor. The hostility of the Provençal historian, Raymond of Agiles, expressed in his description of the occurrences at Nicaea and elsewhere, is not a certain indication of the attitude of Raymond of Toulouse at the time. This historian, and the Provençals generally, never shared Raymond's partisanship for the Emperor. Raymond's remaining in the camp at Nicaea in June 1097, when the other chiefs went to visit the Emperor after the capture of the city (Hagenmeyer, *Epist. et Chart.* p. 140), must be regarded as merely incidental, on the view here taken of his final reconciliation with the Emperor.

[1] This is also F. Chalandon's view. There is a small amount of documentary evidence in its favour, viz. *Alexias*, XIII, 12, where the reference to a treaty with Bohemond may be understood of a general treaty made with the Latin chiefs, and Hagenmeyer, *Epist. et Chart.* No. 12, from which it may be inferred that the date of the agreement was the middle of May. The terms of the treaty, as these are suggested above, are inferred from narratives of what took place after the captures of Nicaea and Antioch and from the terms of the later treaty with Bohemond in 1108 (*Alexias*, XIII, 12). The alleged grant to Bohemond of territory in the neighbourhood of Antioch at this time (*Gesta Francorum*) may be interpreted to mean that this territory, although not assigned to any individual, was actually designated in the treaty as a prospective Latin fief. The exclusion of the city of Antioch suggests that it was to be placed in the hands of a Greek governor. Albert, V, 2, states that the Latin leaders had sworn specifically to hand over Antioch and Nicaea (if captured by them) to the Emperor (cum omnibus castellis et urbibus ad regnum eius pertinentibus). Raymond, ch. IV, shews that certain rights were conceded to the Latins in these Greek towns (in Nicaea a monastery and a hospital).

The Normans were really bitter and contemptuous enemies of the Greeks, although Bohemond judged it to be expedient to acquiesce in a general treaty, and required Tancred, much against his will, to take the common oath of allegiance. At the same time the marked hostility of the Western sources to the Emperor in their narratives of these events reflects largely the anger and disappointment of a later period. The Greeks and Latins had important interests in common, and it is likely that the policy inaugurated by the Emperor would have held them together until at least the foundations were laid in Syria of one Greco-Latin state. It was Alexius' own failure to implement his promise that finally turned the Latins into declared and irreconcilable enemies.

Before the Latins left Constantinople, their route through Asia Minor and their plan of operations had been decided on. In the first place the Muslim capital of Nicaea, about six days' march overland from Scutari, was to be taken. The Emperor provided siege engines and food supplies but only a small detachment of troops. Nicaea was very strongly fortified and was protected on the west side by the waters of a lake. The disposition of the crusading army illustrates the separation caused by national divisions. Bohemond's forces encamped on the north, Godfrey and the Germans on the east of the city (6 May 1097). When Raymond's troops arrived they occupied the south side (16 May). On the day of Raymond's arrival a small force of Muslims attempted to throw themselves into the city and were beaten off. Robert of Normandy and his men joined the besiegers on 1 June; their position also was on the south side. The siege operations, begun on 14 May, were pressed strenuously with little result for nearly five weeks. At length the ruin by Raymond's engineers of a large tower on the south side brightened the prospects of the besiegers. This and the launching on the lake of Greek vessels, brought from the sea, decided the defenders to surrender. They opened negotiations with the Greek commander, and capitulated to him on condition that their lives should be spared (19 June 1097). Most likely they were allowed to remain undisturbed in their homes if they chose to transfer their allegiance to the Emperor. In order to prevent wanton plundering and destruction, the Latins were allowed to enter the city as visitors only and in small parties. As previously arranged, the spoil of the town, or its equivalent, was distributed among the crusaders, and their leaders received in addition handsome gifts from Alexius. No doubt the sparing of the lives of infidels became a cause of reproach to the Emperor in the Latin camp, and perhaps the precautions taken to protect the city from plundering were resented. But the Latins do not seem, on this occasion, to have been unfairly treated[1], and some of them settled in Nicaea as the Emperor's subjects.

[1] Raymond's account brings no specific charge against Alexius, although it shews that he was disliked and hated by the Provençals.

After the capture of Nicaea the proximate goal of the crusaders' march was Antioch on the Orontes. It may be assumed that Alexius urged the siege and capture of a city which had been for a century an outpost of the Empire, and the occupation of which would be an important initial step in the conquest of Syria. Besides, the "deliverance" of Antioch had been from the first one of the specific objects of the Crusade. The way through Asia Minor was familiar to the Greeks and in any case easily found and followed. It leads through Dorylaeum and Iconium and then over the passes of the Taurus into Cilicia. But in order to rescue Armenia Minor from the Muslim yoke and to secure for themselves friendly support in a district near Antioch, the main body of the crusaders kept eastwards to the anti-Taurus mountains, and then came southward to Antioch by way of Geuksun (Coxon) and Mar'ash. Cilicia, in which there was also a friendly Armenian population, was secured by Tancred and by Godfrey's brother Baldwin. The Latins sent letters to the Armenians of Euphratesia, most probably from Nicaea, and Baldwin was joined there by an Armenian exile who accompanied and advised him during the march through Asia Minor. This alliance with the Armenians was afterwards of great value during the siege of Antioch, and by it the crusaders were enabled to make their first settlements in the East.

When the Latins left Nicaea—those who moved first started on 27 June—some cherished the hope that they might reach Jerusalem in five weeks, if Antioch did not prove a serious obstacle in their way. It was three months before they approached Antioch and nearly two years before any of them reached Jerusalem. Qilij-Arslān, having assembled his army too late to save Nicaea, attacked the Latins near Dorylaeum on 1 July. The crusaders were in two divisions, two miles apart, on separate roads. The first encounter was between the whole Turkish army, which consisted exclusively of horsemen armed with bows, and the smaller part of the Latin host, which included the Normans only, under Bohemond, Tancred, and Robert of Normandy. An attack of the Norman knights was repulsed by the Turks, whose advance, in turn, was checked by the spears and bows of the Latin infantry, upon whom the knights fell back[1]. The encircling Muslims now employed their usual elusive and harassing tactics and the Normans fought a desperate battle, until they were relieved by the arrival, in successive bands, of Godfrey and the other leaders. The Turks having retreated on to a hill-side, the crusaders formed themselves into line of battle and broke and scattered their opponents by one irresistible charge. In the shock of direct encounter the light Turkish horsemen had no chance of success. The fight before

---

[1] The fullest account of the first stage of the battle is given by the *Gesta Tancredi*. This source alone explicitly mentions the decisive action of the infantry (densissima pedestrium hastarum silva nunc fugam impedit, nunc extinguit). The part played by the Latin infantry in these battles with the Muslims is frequently ignored by the sources (cf. *infra*, p. 290, note 1).

Godfrey's arrival may have lasted two or three hours and the second stage of the battle, including the pursuit, three hours more. The enemy were pursued for several miles, and great booty was obtained from the captured Muslim camp[1].

During the march beyond Dorylaeum the Latins found the country laid waste for a considerable distance, and suffered greatly from want of food and water as well as from the excessive heat. They lost a large number of their horses and baggage animals. Most probably the crusaders now marched in one main force, where all the baggage was placed, and in several smaller forces under independent leaders such as Tancred and Baldwin. From Iconium eastwards the conditions seem to have improved, and of course in Armenia Minor the friendship of the Christian population made the way easy. The Muslims were nowhere in sufficient force to venture another attack after their defeat at Dorylaeum. In Armenia Minor the Turkish garrisons, which had not long been in possession, were expelled and Armenian supremacy was restored. Several Western knights settled in the conquered strongholds, but the only leader of importance to remain in the district was Baldwin, Godfrey's brother, afterwards his successor in Jerusalem. Baldwin was the founder of the first of the crusading states in the East. After passing, as we shall see, through Cilicia he reached the main army at Mar'ash. But while it went on to Antioch he remained to establish a Latin princedom in Euphratesia. His first capital was Tell-bāshir (October 1097). Afterwards, when he became ruler of Edessa (spring of 1098), he made that city his capital. His forces in themselves were not at first large, but the friendship of the Armenian princes secured his position. After the fall of Antioch, Godfrey came to his assistance, and from that time he was quite able to maintain himself. Undoubtedly, if the Latins had continued to co-operate with the Armenians, this northern state would have been a much more effective bulwark of their power than it ultimately proved to be.

No doubt Baldwin's settlement in Edessa was made with the consent and approval of the Latin leaders. It was in some measure due to him, since he had recently resigned to Tancred his claim on Cilicia. As the crusaders arrived in the districts where the first permanent conquests were attempted, it became perfectly clear that each leader fought not merely for the common cause but also for a share in the territory that was being

---

[1] Oman's representation that Godfrey and the others were six or seven miles distant from the Normans and that Bohemond fought alone for five hours (*Art of War*, 1st ed. p. 275 [2nd ed. I, p. 277]), seems to lack foundation. The distance between the divisions was two miles according to Raymond, who is confirmed by Albert's statement (II, 35) that the intention was that the divisions should march one mile apart. The *Gesta Francorum* makes the battle last from the third hour to the ninth, and Fulcher says that the enemy were routed at the sixth hour. This seems to indicate that the six miles pursuit (Albert, II, 42) lasted about three hours. Fulcher is vague regarding the time of the commencement of the battle, for which he names both the second hour and the first.

conquered. In the smaller undertakings each national army made its own conquests and of course claimed to retain what it thus won. The events in Cilicia are narrated at full length by the sources, and may be taken as the best available illustration of what has just been said. The occupation of this province was probably part of a general scheme suggested by Armenians who accompanied the crusaders from Nicaea, and it may have been included in the plans of the leaders from the time they left that city. But since Baldwin and Tancred were rivals in their operations in that province from the first, it is not hazardous to conclude that one at least was deputed to protect national interests against the action of the other[1]. Tancred left the main army at Heraclea and made directly for Tarsus, which he hoped to gain with the help of Armenian friends. He had encamped beside the town and was negotiating its surrender, with every prospect of success, when Baldwin came on the scene with much larger forces[2]. It is uncertain whether Baldwin had left the main army at Heraclea, or had separated from it much earlier than Tancred and had reached Tarsus by a different road. The result of his arrival was that the Turkish garrison deserted the town and the inhabitants prepared to surrender formally to Tancred. Baldwin, in virtue of his superior strength, required them, however, to surrender to him, and Tancred retired in anger without fighting. At Adana he found the Turks already driven out and an Armenian governor installed[3], from whom he received a welcome. Mamistra, the next town on the way, was occupied without difficulty, for the garrison fled almost as soon as Tancred approached the city. Meantime Baldwin was joined at Tarsus by a fleet of Flemings and Frisians, which had been cruising for some years in the Mediterranean and was commanded by a certain Winemar of Boulogne. Having left a garrison in Tarsus, Baldwin marched on to Mamistra, where he encamped outside the walls. Either party may have been the aggressor in the fighting which followed. But Baldwin had now designs further east, so that peace was quickly re-established and Tancred was left in possession. Before the Norman leader left Cilicia, he had established a claim to possession which Bohemond and he, as princes of Antioch, afterwards strenuously maintained against the armies of the Empire. Meantime most of the population favoured the Latins, and the small Turkish garrisons were cowed by the numbers

---

[1] If both left the army at Heraclea they may have been declared rivals from the first, or Tancred may possibly have tried to outstrip Baldwin and thus have provoked the final conflict. On the other hand, if Baldwin left the main army considerably earlier on the march from Nicaea, then Tancred must have entered Cilicia with the purpose of securing the province for the Normans with the knowledge that he would probably have to compete with Baldwin for its possession. Both Baldwin and Tancred were advised by Armenian friends.

[2] The *Gesta Tancredi* estimates Tancred's force at 100 knights (*loricas*) and 200 bowmen (ch. XXXIII), Baldwin's at 500 horsemen and 2000 foot soldiers (ch. XXXVII).

[3] Ralph of Caen. Albert makes the governor Welf, a Burgundian, who had also separated himself from the main army.

of their opponents. Only a fortnight or three weeks were required to subdue the principal towns of the province. Three or four weeks more were spent in the neighbourhood of Antioch, subduing castles there. Iskanderūn (Alexandretta) was one of Tancred's acquisitions and probably became his headquarters. It is significant that Raymond of Toulouse and Robert of Flanders also sent on a part of their forces to make conquests in Northern Syria before the main body of the army arrived. Each leader was thus fighting for his own hand and anxious not to be outdone by his rivals. The result was that before the siege of Antioch began the Latins had gained a secure footing in Syria and Euphratesia. These preliminary conquests, and especially the establishment of friendly relations with the native Christian population, were the essential conditions of further success.

It was perfectly evident soon after the main army reached Antioch (21 October 1097) that the crusaders were not able to press the siege of such a strongly fortified city. Lack of siege engines and the moderate number of efficient fighting men in the army may have been contributory causes. No attempt was made to undermine the walls or to take the town by storm. For four or five months the city could not even be said to be strictly invested. The Latins were encamped together, with the exception of one small party under Tancred, just on the side where they had reached the town. The besieged still had almost complete liberty of exit, especially by the river gate on the north side. The fighting was only a series of skirmishes on the plains to the north of the Orontes, and on the roads eastward to Hārim and westward to St Simeon. Although the Turkish garrison was not more than 5000 strong, and the auxiliary troops cannot have been numerous[1], the Latin army was evidently not the overwhelming force dreamed of by poets and imaginative historians. Still the chief cause of the weakness of the Latin army was its deficiency in supplies. In December 1097 and in the earlier months of 1098 the number of horses, so vital to the strength of the army, was reduced to a dangerously low figure[2]. The privations of the crusaders themselves would have been intolerable but for the assistance of their Armenian and other native Christian allies. As many as could be spared from active service were dispersed through the conquered towns and castles of Cilicia along the coast and the neighbouring country. It was not until fleets from England and other countries arrived in the spring that the strain of the situation was

[1] Stephen of Blois, *Epist.* (Hagenmeyer, *Epist. et Chart.* p. 150): "milites Turci plusquam v milia...exceptis...Arabibus, Turcopolitanis...aliisque gentibus diversis." Raymond (MPL, p. 598): "duo millia optimi milites et quatuor vel quinque millia militum gregariorum atque decem millia peditum et eo amplius." This latter may be regarded as a genuine attempt at an estimate, but the 10,000 foot can only represent the whole male population of the city and that at its maximum.

[2] According to the *Gesta*, not more than 1000 war horses (cf. Albert, III, 60); according to Anselm, *Epist.* (Hag. 157) only 700. The Provençals at this same time are said to have had no more than 100 horses (Raymond d'Agiles, MPL, p. 602 c). Compare also *infra*, p. 290, note.

relieved. On the other hand, during the winter the Muslim garrison does not appear to have suffered much from lack of provisions. A large part of the non-combatant population, especially Armenian and Syrian Christians, were dismissed at the beginning of the siege. In early spring the Muslims were still able to pasture their horses in relays outside the city. It was only from March or April that the besieged began to suffer serious privation. Their numbers were then reduced not only by death but by desertion. Finally, it was the treachery of a discontented soldier which secured an entrance for the enemy (3 June 1098).

The chief events of the siege were the battles which the crusaders fought with the relief armies of other Syrian emirs. Yaghī Bassān, the Turkish governor of Antioch, had no reason to expect cordial assistance from his neighbours. They did not desert him altogether, but the ease with which they were repulsed is as much an indication of their lukewarmness as of the superiority of the Latin arms. In November, raiders who probably came from Ḥārim, a strong castle on the way to Aleppo, were ambushed and severely defeated by Bohemond, Robert of Normandy, and Robert of Flanders. These same leaders were sent out in December to bring in supplies, and at Al-Bārah they encountered and repulsed troops from Damascus and Ḥims̱ which were on their way to relieve Antioch (31 December 1097). In the beginning of February 1098 the Latins learned that a Muslim army, consisting chiefly of troops from Aleppo, was close at hand. It was decided that they should be met a few miles away at a narrow point on the road by the full force of the Latin cavalry, 700 strong[1]. The foot-soldiers and unmounted men were left to guard the camp. The Muslims were attacked where they could not employ their customary enveloping tactics, and their crowded rear increased the confusion rather than the strength of the ranks in front. The first charge of the crusaders was checked, but the onset of the reserve under Bohemond was irresistible. The Latin victory (9 February 1098) was specially welcome because it secured fresh supplies of provisions and of horses, and was followed immediately by the surrender of the strong castle of Ḥārim.

[1] This number is given by Raymond d'Agiles, Anselm, Albert, and Cafaro. Possibly Raymond's knights remained with him in the camp. On the other hand a small number of foot-soldiers may have accompanied the horsemen (Anselm). As a contribution to the vexed question of the numbers of the crusaders and their opponents, it may be noted that Raymond in describing the other engagements of this paragraph estimates the Latin knights at 150 and 400 (*v.l.* 300) respectively. In December the Latins, including infantry, are said to have numbered 2000 (*Gesta*) or 5000 men (*Hist. Pereg., Rec. Hist. Cr.* III, 187). Presumably footsoldiers were employed in November also, although they are not mentioned by the sources. The almost exclusive reliance upon the knights in February was quite exceptional. The Latins probably outnumbered their opponents in November and December, although not in February. 3000 is a reasonable estimate of the strength of the Muslim army in February (Cafaro). The Muslim slain, whose heads were cut off as trophies, are reckoned at 100 (*Gesta*) or 200 (Anselm, Albert). It is very unlikely that as many as 400 Muslims were slain in the fight in November (Anselm).

As already observed, the investment of Antioch by the crusaders was not complete until March or even April. The city lay at this time wholly on the south bank of the Orontes, with its northern wall[1] running roughly parallel to the river. The Latin camp was on the same side of the Orontes, round the north-east corner of the wall. In this position the crusaders blockaded three of the city gates, which opened here on the northern and eastern sides. They built a bridge of boats across the river to be a means of communication with the plain on the other side, in front of the city, and later a fort on the hill slopes beside them to protect their exposed flank on the south. Tancred remained separate from the main army in occupation of a monastery on the west side of the city, no doubt in order to maintain communication with the sea and the port of St Simeon, ten miles away. The gate in the centre of the north wall, where it approached the river most closely, was the principal gate of the city and opened on-to a bridge over the Orontes. By this the Muslim garrison issued out to intercept the provision trains, which began to come more frequently in spring from St Simeon to the Latin camp. In front of the bridge was a low mound with a mosque and a burying-ground upon it. In order to frustrate the sallies of the garrison, the crusaders at length determined to seize and fortify this post. On 1 March[2] Bohemond and Raymond rode with a strong escort to St Simeon in order to obtain workers and tools for the fortification of the mound, and with the intention of escorting a provision train on its way to the camp. A party of the garrison set an ambush for them as they marched back (5 March). The knights seem to have saved themselves at the expense of their companions, many of whom lost their lives. Meantime Godfrey and the other leaders in the camp had become aware of what was happening, and prepared to intercept the victorious Muslims. Bohemond and his horsemen joined the main army in time to share in this counter-attack. The garrison attempted to rein-force their comrades, but this only increased the magnitude of their disaster. Next day the work of fortifying the rising ground in front of the river gate was begun. The gravestones on the hill supplied welcome material to the builders. The graves themselves were desecrated, to the distress and indignation of the Muslim spectators[3]. After the fort was

---

[1] More exactly, the wall which faced N.W. Similarly, what is called the western wall faced rather S.W.

[2] This date is arrived at by reckoning four days back from the day of the return, which was 5 March according to *Epist. Lucc.* (in Hagenmeyer, *Epist. et Chart.* p. 166). The interval of four days is given by Raymond d'Agiles. Hagenmeyer in his *Chronologie* makes the day of departure 5 March and the day of return 6 March.

[3] The narratives of Raymond and the *Gesta* here demand special scrutiny because they indicate how, in this case, the number of the Muslim slain was computed at 1500. The basis of the calculation seems to have been the number of bodies ex-humed from the burying ground (Raymond). But in spite of the definite assertion of the *Gesta* it is extremely improbable that those slain on 5 March had already been buried in the cemetery, and certainly the bodies exhumed included more than these.

CH. VII.

completed it was occupied by Raymond's troops. Early in April Tancred's position was strengthened, and the only other important gate, that on the western side, was now completely blocked. The garrison was quite unable to dislodge the crusaders from their new position, and provisions could no longer be brought into the beleaguered city.

In May 1098 word reached the crusading chiefs that a great army under the command of Karbōghā of Mosul, with the approval of the Caliph of Baghdad, was on its way to the relief of Antioch. The Latin position was now extremely perilous. Fortunately Bohemond was already in communication with an officer who commanded one of the western towers, and through him the Latins gained an easy entrance into the city on the night of 3 June. Although the citadel at the southern extremity of the town did not surrender, the crusaders were now protected by the walls of Antioch itself against the army of Karbōghā. On 5 June the Muslim host encamped at the "Iron Bridge," eight miles away, and that same day, or the day before, a party of their horsemen was seen from the walls of Antioch and skirmished with the Latins. From 8 June to 28 June the crusaders were besieged in Antioch. Some of the nobles lost heart at once and deserted their comrades. The ships in the harbour of St Simeon began to set sail, crowded with fugitives. Had Karbōghā's army arrived four days sooner, it is not improbable that the crusading movement would have been extinguished at the gates of Antioch. As it was, the Latins endured three weeks of continuous fighting and terrible privation.

In these circumstances the crusaders took an unprecedented step. Neither on the march to Antioch nor during the siege had their operations been controlled by one supreme commander. The current modern belief that Godfrey of Bouillon was the leader of the whole Crusade has no foundation in fact. But now it was decided that one chief should take command and the choice of the leaders fell on Bohemond[1]. Enthusiasm

Reading between the lines it may be concluded: (a) that the Latins found on the hill some of the recently slain Turks, probably unburied (should Raymond's *in vallo* be *in valle*?); (b) that some graves were opened during the digging of the ditch of the fort, and that this led to the deliberate desecration of other graves; (c) that the cemetery had been used as a burying-ground by the besieged throughout the siege; (d) that 1500 may have been an estimate of the total losses of the Muslims up to this time; (e) that if this number was based at all on the number of the bodies exhumed it included a very liberal allowance for those known to have been slain and not buried in the cemetery.

[1] The choice of the battle-ground and the plan of battle on 9 February were probably due to Bohemond, and he may, therefore, have exercised the chief command during that engagement also. But there was probably no formal appointment then such as there was now. Stephen of Blois in the winter of 1097 is known to have been appointed *provisorem et gubernatorem* by the leaders in council. But he was never distinguished as a military leader; so that his office can hardly have been that of commander-in-chief. More probably he acted as an executive officer, and saw that certain decisions of the leaders were carried out.

had already been stirred by supernatural visions and by the finding of the Holy Lance (14 June), and thus encouraged the leaders had decided to put all to the hazard of a single battle. Bohemond's part was to direct the preparations, to marshal the army, and to exercise the chief command during the fight. His supreme authority was to remain intact for a fortnight beyond the day of battle. It is probably not accidental that the chosen day (28 June) was a Monday, the second octave of the finding of the Holy Lance.

The hazardous operation of crossing the bridge into the plain north of the Orontes, where the Muslims lay, was accomplished without dangerous interference from the enemy. Karbōghā's army included the troops of the brothers Duqāq of Damascus and Riḍwān of Aleppo, who were deadly rivals, and Arab forces upon whom small reliance could be placed. When it was known that the Latins intended to march out from the city, there was hot debate regarding how they should be met. Those who wished that they should be attacked as they issued from the bridge were overruled, and some in consequence rode away almost before the fight began. The Latins took up their position in the plain, with their front to the east, in three divisions, stretching from the river to the hills. Bohemond with strong forces posted himself in the rear, facing westward. It is not clear that the Muslims had a well-arranged plan of battle. Evidently the Syrian, Mesopotamian, and Anatolian troops operated separately, and their chief attack was from the west and north-west, although their main strength faced the Latins on the east. The crusaders, therefore, were able to transfer reinforcements from the east front to the west, and to rout the enemy in the rear before they began their decisive movement forward[1]. Karbōghā, who was posted on the right flank of the Muslim army, remained strangely inactive. When he saw that the attack from the west had failed, he drew back to his camp, set fire to his tents, and made off in hasty flight. The number of the Muslim slain does not seem to have been large. Yet the Latin victory was the turning-point in the history of the First Crusade and decisive of its ultimate success. The defenders of the citadel of Antioch now made overtures of surrender, and the Latins took possession in the beginning of the following week. It was determined in council that the march on Jerusalem should not be resumed until 1 November.

The final disposal of Antioch after its capture was complicated by jealousies and rivalries and doubtful questions of interpretation. Certainly

---

[1] The distribution of the Latin forces is plainly given by Raymond, and the battle is most fully described by Albert. A large force under Qilij-Arslān threatened the Latin rear from the N.W. and was opposed by troops taken from the Latin left. A strong attack on Bohemond was made later by the horsemen of Aleppo and Damascus, who seem to have crossed from the south side of the river. To repel them it was necessary to bring large reinforcements from the Latin centre and right wing. Oman's *Art of War* does not distinguish the two forces operating against the rear of the crusaders.

it had been assigned by treaty to Alexius, but only on condition that he brought in person a sufficient army to help the crusaders. What period might he claim for the fulfilment of this promise? In 1097 and 1098 the naval and military forces of the Empire were chiefly engaged in subduing Muslim towns in the west of Asia Minor[1]. But in June 1098 Alexius had already marched with a considerable army half way to Antioch, following the road traversed in the previous year by the crusaders themselves. Unfortunately for all concerned, he listened at Philomelium to the alarmist stories of Stephen of Blois and the other fugitives from Antioch who met him there. They probably told him that the crusading host had been irretrievably defeated, and that a Turkish army was already marching against him. He turned back to protect his recent conquests in Asia Minor. Naturally this action was judged by most to be a surrender of the Latin cause. At the best Alexius was now in a position hard to retrieve. There are two accounts of the message which the crusaders sent him in July. Albert of Aix says that the envoys were instructed to tell the Emperor that he had been untrue to his promise, and thus had nullified his treaty. This may have been the opinion of most of the Latin leaders, but, as their attitude in November shewed, they were not yet prepared completely to break off relations with the Emperor. The *Gesta Francorum* says that the envoys were told to invite Alexius to fulfil his promise and come to receive possession of Antioch. It may be that something of this kind was said, with qualifications, setting a limit to the delay which would be considered reasonable, and referring to the Emperor's recent retreat. Presumably the envoys were empowered to adhere in substance to the original treaty, provided the Emperor agreed to carry out his engagements effectively and quickly. It is not known what reply Alexius sent to this communication. It may be that he felt the difficulty of his position so keenly that he sent no immediate reply. In the spring of 1099 he promised to join the crusaders with an army on St John's day (24 June), if they would wait for him until then. Perhaps he was encouraged by the support of Raymond of Toulouse. But his proposal came too late. The Crusade was nearing a successful conclusion without the Emperor's assistance. All the leaders except Raymond now held that the treaty had lapsed, and that the Emperor had not fulfilled his obligation.

Bohemond, Prince of Antioch as he now became, profited most by the Emperor's mistake. Before the capture of the city he had manoeuvred dexterously to establish his claim to it. Under pressure of Karbōghā's approach, the leaders had reluctantly assented to his proposal that the lordship of Antioch should fall to anyone who secured its capture or betrayal. Before Bohemond made this proposal he had arranged for the betrayal of the town. Of course the rights of the Emperor were duly reserved, but after the defeat of Karbōghā's army Bohemond was practi-

[1] *E.g.* Smyrna, Sardis, and the towns in the district of the Meander valley.

cally ruler of Antioch[1]. In November he urged that the Emperor's claim had already lapsed. The other leaders would not yet make the declaration he desired, but Raymond was the only one to maintain that Alexius' right was beyond dispute. Provençal troops held strong posts in Antioch until January 1099. Their ejection in that month marked Bohemond's final triumph.

The six months that followed Karbōghā's defeat were spent by the crusaders partly in recuperating their strength, partly in extending their conquests. Baldwin of Edessa gained especially by the help which he received at this time from Godfrey and other crusaders. Bohemond strengthened his position in Cilicia. Raymond, and no doubt other leaders also, sought to occupy the Muslim castles on the way to Aleppo and in the valley of the Orontes. Plague raged in Antioch and St Simeon for several months, so that few remained there of choice; its most distinguished victim was Ademar, Bishop of Puy. The quarrel between Bohemond and Raymond regarding the lordship of Antioch further delayed the march of the Crusade. At last Raymond in despair yielded to the clamour of his Provençals and started for Jerusalem, accompanied by Tancred and Robert of Normandy (13 January 1099). They marched slowly as far as 'Arqah near Tripolis, to which they laid siege (14 February), and where they were joined by Godfrey and Robert of Flanders a month later. Here, on 8 April, the unfortunate finder of the Holy Lance, Peter Bartholomew, submitted himself to an ordeal by fire. When he died, after twelve days, the nature and cause of his injuries were a matter of dispute between the believers and the unbelievers. The siege of 'Arqah was abandoned in the middle of May (13 May), and the remainder of the march to Jerusalem by the coast route was accomplished without any special incident. Ramlah, between Jaffa and Jerusalem, was occupied on 3 June, and on the morning of 7 June the crusading army at length encamped outside the walls of the Holy City.

The arrival of the crusaders at their destination obviously put fresh heart into the rank and file and fresh energy into the action of their leaders. Jerusalem was strongly fortified and well supplied with mangonels, and its garrison of 1000 men fought bravely. Perhaps, indeed, the civilian population was ill-disposed to their Egyptian governor or was intimidated by the numbers and the reputation of the Latins, and so did not second the efforts of the garrison. At all events the siege was quickly brought to a successful issue. The first attempt to storm the city failed because the besiegers were not equipped with the necessary ladders and siege-engines (13 June). Two siege-towers, a huge battering-ram, and a quantity of mangonels were constructed before the next attack was made. Some Genoese ships which reached Jaffa on 17 June brought

---

[1] In July 1098 he granted by charter to the Genoese a church, a warehouse, and a number of dwelling-houses. In return they promised to defend the city against all comers, excepting Raymond of Toulouse, in whose case they were to stand neutral.

a welcome supply of provisions and also workers skilled in the construction of siege material. The scarcity of water was the chief inconvenience from which the Latins suffered. A solemn procession round the town, when the preparations were nearly complete (8 July), raised general enthusiasm. The second assault was begun late on 13 July, was continued next day, and was finally successful on 15 July. Godfrey's men were the first to storm the walls, with the help of a siege-tower at the north-east corner. Raymond on the south was less successful, but the great "tower of David," in which the Egyptian commandant was stationed, surrendered to him. The celebration in the church of the Holy Sepulchre, where men wept together for joy and grief, and the merciless slaughter of the inhabitants, well express, in combination, the spirit of the Crusade. Raymond, however, at the cost of some opprobrium, escorted safely on the way to Ascalon those who had surrendered to him.

A prince to rule Jerusalem and the south of Palestine had now to be chosen. On 22 July the crusading chiefs met for this purpose. Some of the clergy thought that a high dignitary of the Church should be the only ruler in Jerusalem, and Raymond favoured their view. Raymond himself was the first to be offered the princedom, but declined it because of his ecclesiastical sympathies. Finally, Godfrey of Bouillon, rather unwillingly, accepted the distinguished and difficult post, and thus became Defender of the Holy Sepulchre (*Advocatus Sancti Sepulcri*). He was always addressed as *dux* or *princeps*, never as king. But his successors were crowned as kings, and so he may be called the first ruler of the Latin kingdom of Jerusalem.

The defeat of an Egyptian army near Ascalon on 12 August may be reckoned as the last achievement of the First Crusade. Palestine was then governed in part by Turkish emirs and in part by representatives of the Egyptian Caliph[1]. Jerusalem and Ascalon were subject to the same Egyptian governor. The Muslim army, which the Latins now defeated, was probably levied to protect the Holy City when the final movement of the crusaders from 'Arqah became known in Egypt. The Egyptians seem to have put forward their full strength, and so may possibly have mustered an army of 20,000 men. Godfrey's troops may be reckoned at half that number[2]. By taking the initiative he probably forced the Egyptians to an engagement before they were quite ready. The extension of the Latin line from the shore to the hills, in three divisions, neutralised the numerical superiority of their opponents. The left wing, which Godfrey commanded, was echeloned behind the other divisions as a reserve. An attempt of the Muslims to envelope the

---

[1] See *supra*, Chap. vi, p. 264.

[2] Raymond's estimate is not more than 1200 knights and 9000 foot-soldiers. An official letter of the crusaders (Hagenmeyer's *Epistulae*, p. 172) gives not more than 5000 knights and 15,000 foot-soldiers against 500,000 Muslims! Fulcher makes the numbers 20,000 Latins against 300,000 Muslims.

Latins from the side of the hills was frustrated. The decisive movement was the charge of the knights of the Latin centre, which completely broke the opposing line. The battle was over in less than an hour. The victors gained great spoil of provisions and animals, especially sheep and camels. But the prestige of the victory was of much greater value. It was several years before any considerable movement was again attempted by the Egyptians against the newly-established state.

The statements of the best contemporary sources regarding the number of men bearing arms who joined the First Crusade[1] are quite irreconcilable. These discrepancies and the estimates of Muslim armies that the same sources give[2], which are impossible, make it clear, as already explained, that all these general estimates are merely pictorial in character. Even the lowest of them, if that be 60,000, cannot be admitted to be approximately correct merely because it is the lowest. 60,000 is a stereotyped expression used by writers of the period for a very large number.

On the other hand, scattered through the sources there is a considerable amount of what may be accepted as approximately accurate information about the numbers of the crusaders engaged in particular fights or slain on particular occasions, and about the numbers of the knights and men who served individual leaders. From such details a reliable estimate of the military efficiency and numerical strength of the Crusade may be obtained, and the partial figures when taken in combination indicate a range within which the grand total probably lies. Raymond d'Agiles supplies more material of this kind than any other writer, and his general consistency is itself evidence of considerable value. He uses pictorial numbers occasionally, especially in reports of rhetorical speeches and in estimates of Muslim armies. But most of his figures harmonise with their context and present an appearance of tolerable exactness. His general narrative also is particularly clear and convincing and full of detail[3]. His account of the three battles fought during the siege of Antioch may be referred to in illustration of the moderate numerical estimates which are characteristic of him[4]. It must be remembered that he speaks only of the knights who fought in these battles, and also that the number of these able to take the field at the time was greatly reduced by the dearth of horses. Besides, as already explained, the total strength of the crusaders was never gathered at any one time in the camp at Antioch. Still, it is noteworthy that the knights in these engagements are numbered by hundreds and not by thousands. The scale thus provided is amply confirmed by what we are

[1] 600,000 (Fulcher and Albert); 300,000 (Ekkehard); 100,000 (Raymond d'Agiles).
[2] At Dorylaeum: 150,000 (Raymond); 260,000 (*Epist. Anselmi*); 360,000 (*Gesta* and Fulcher); in Karbōghā's army: 100,000 (Cafaro); 200,000 (Albert).
[3] For a general estimate and criticism see Clemens Klein.
[4] See *supra*, p. 290, note.

bound to suppose were the numbers of the Muslims. An expedition from Aleppo or Damascus might number 500 horsemen or 1000 or 1500, very rarely more. These figures set a clear upper limit to the numbers of the Latins on the supposition that the Muslims were superior to them in number.

Such being the character of Raymond's history, great importance must attach to his making what may be regarded as a serious attempt to estimate the number of the crusading army during the siege of Jerusalem. Excluding non-combatants, his total is 12,000 of whom 1200–1300 were knights[1]. Now this implies that the more important leaders had an average of something like 2000–3000 men including 200–300 knights. This agrees with all the estimates of the forces of these leaders in which any confidence can be placed. Reference may be made to one of these. Albert of Aix's narrative, in spite of its defects, contains a great deal of exact information, especially about Godfrey of Bouillon. Now Albert says that Godfrey commanded 2000 men during the battle against Karbōghā. In this battle there were five or six leaders whose forces, on an average, would be equal to Godfrey's. Thus the army of the crusaders at Antioch would be similar in size to Raymond's estimate of that which besieged Jerusalem. In both cases the estimate is rather too high than too low. The numbers in Karbōghā's army supply a vague standard of comparison. If it numbered 12,000 it was a large army for the circumstances of the time. It is unlikely that the Latins were as numerous. Perhaps at this time the crusaders actually under arms in Syria, Cilicia, and Edessa numbered 12,000–15,000 men.

In estimating the sum total of those who joined the Crusade, we have to add such as lost their lives or deserted the cause during the siege of Antioch and the march through Asia Minor. Non-combatant priests and women and various ineffectives have also to be allowed for. But this latter class cannot have been so great as to prejudice the military effectiveness of the Crusade. Perhaps it is not too great a venture to suggest that 25,000 or 30,000, all told, marched through Asia Minor to Antioch; and it seems to the writer that this estimate is more likely to be above reality than below it. Of course many left their homes who never reached Constantinople, and those who accompanied Walter and Peter suffered heavy loss in Asia Minor before the arrival of the organised expeditions. Something has been said of their numbers already. But to attempt an estimate of all the men and women and even children (?) who left their homes in Western Europe for the Crusade would be merely to pile conjecture upon conjecture. Yet perhaps this may safely be said: that the number, if stated at all, should be in tens of thousands and not in hundreds of thousands.

---

[1] De nostris ad arma valentes, in quantum nos existimamus, numerum duodecim millium non transcendebant sed habebamus multos debiles atque pauperes. Et erant in exercitu nostro mille ducenti vel trecenti milites, ut ego arbitror, non amplius.

As Peter the Hermit still plays an important part in the popular accounts of the origin of the First Crusade, some additional observations regarding him may be permitted in conclusion. His actual rôle as an early and successful preacher of the Crusade has already been indicated. His legendary history originated, we must suppose, amongst those who were stirred by his preaching, and who knew him as the originator of their crusade. Along with other legends it was elaborated in the popular songs of the period, the *chansons de geste*. From there it made a partial entrance into the narrative of Albert of Aix, and in a more developed form entered the history of William of Tyre. Through William of Tyre it has so fixed itself in modern literature that no historian of mere fact seems able to root it out.

According to legend Peter stirred the Pope and all Western Europe to the First Crusade. The four writers who were present at the Council of Clermont report Pope Urban's words in terms which are quite inconsistent with this representation. Besides, the chief authorities for the history of the Crusade make it clear that Peter began his preaching after the council and in consequence of it. His journey as far as Constantinople has already been related. In the later stages of the Crusade he appears as a personage of some influence among the poorer classes, but not as one whom the leaders particularly respected. His volunteering, with a comrade, to take a message to Karbōghā in July 1098, has no clear significance. Perhaps it was simply a reaction from his failure in the beginning of the year, when for a time he was a deserter. In March 1099 the duty of distributing alms to the Provençal poor was entrusted to him. In August 1099 he was one of those who organised processions and services of intercession for the victory of the Latins before their battle with the Egyptians. Between Nicaea and Jerusalem he plays a recorded part five times in all. This minor figure is not even an appropriate symbol or representation of the mighty forces, religious, political, and economic, that created the First Crusade.

CHAPTER VIII.

THE KINGDOM OF JERUSALEM, 1099–1291.

WHEN, a week after the fall of Jerusalem, the crusaders met to choose a king for the new kingdom, one after another of the greater princes refused the proffer of a barren and laborious honour. Godfrey of Bouillon, upon whom the choice at last fell, had been foremost in the capture of the Holy City; but otherwise there was little in his early career in the West or as a leader of the Crusade to mark him out. His selection was indeed rather in the nature of a compromise, as that of one who was equally acceptable to French and Germans. Nevertheless, in the piety with which he refused the royal title and desired to be styled only Baron of the Holy Sepulchre, and in the high purpose which he shewed in his brief reign, there was much to justify the glamour which has gathered about his name. From the next generation onwards he was linked with Arthur and Charlemagne as one of the three Christian heroes who made up the number of the nine noblest. Romance has converted History to find in Godfrey the typical hero of the Crusade.

Had Godfrey presumed to style himself King of Jerusalem his title would have been no more than an empty show, for as yet the crusaders held little but the Holy City and the places which they had captured on their way thither. Still, his victory over the Egyptian invaders at Ascalon in the first months of his reign secured for the moment the southern frontier of the intended kingdom. This was followed by at least the show of submission from Acre and other cities of the coast, and immediately before his death, on 18 July 1100, Godfrey had secured the Christians in the possession of Jaffa, a necessary port for the Italian traders, upon whom the fighting Franks in Syria were always in great measure to depend. Thus early do we find the religious enthusiasm of the crusader interwoven with commercial enterprise. Godfrey's endeavours had, however, been hampered by the ambitions of other crusading nobles, and in particular of Raymond of Saint Gilles. Commercial rivalry and princely jealousies were to be the bane of the Frankish settlers in Palestine, and already they began to cast their shadow on the infant kingdom.

Later historians and lawyers found in Godfrey the creator alike of the material kingdom and of its theoretical institutions. But the actual conquest of the land was the work of his first three successors, and it was only by a slow process that the institutions of the kingdom grew to something like the theoretical perfection with which the jurists of the next age invested them. At its widest extent the kingdom of Jerusalem properly so called reached from Al-'Arīsh on the south to the Nahr-Ibrāhīm just beyond Beyrout on the north. For the most part its eastern boundary was formed by the valley of Jordan; but in the extreme north the small district of Banias lay beyond the river Liṭanī, and on the south an extensive territory on the east of the Dead Sea reached for a brief time to Elim on the Gulf of 'Aqabah. The whole region of Frankish rule was, however, much greater. Immediately to the north the county of Tripolis formed a narrow strip along the coast as far as the Wādī Mahik, near the modern Bulunyās. Beyond it the principality of Antioch reached to the confines of Cilicia, and at one time even included the city of Tarsus; on the east at its greatest extension its territory came within a few miles of Aleppo; it was the earliest and on the whole the most permanent conquest of the Franks, who held the city of Antioch for 170 years. Finally, in the extreme north-east was the county of Edessa, the capital of which was the modern Urfah; the eastern limits of the county were never well defined, and here a small body of Frankish lords held rule for less than half a century over a mixed population of Armenians and Syrians.

Edessa had been conquered by Godfrey's brother Baldwin in 1097. When Baldwin was called to the throne of Jerusalem, he gave his county to his kinsman and namesake Baldwin du Bourg. Baldwin II in his turn succeeded to the kingdom in 1118, and gave Edessa to Joscelin of Courtenay, after whom his son Joscelin II maintained a precarious rule till 1144. But if the hold of the Franks on Edessa was precarious it was none the less important, for the county formed a strong outpost against the Muslims of Mesopotamia, and its loss meant a serious weakening of the defensive strength of the Frankish dominion.

Antioch was secured as a principality by Bohemond at the time of its capture in 1097. In July 1100 Bohemond was taken prisoner by the Turks near Mar'ash. After over two years' captivity he was released early in 1103, only to suffer a disastrous defeat at Ḥarrān in the following year. He then crossed the sea to seek aid in the West, and never returned to his principality. Bohemond's nephew Tancred governed Antioch during his uncle's captivity, and again for eight years from 1104 to 1112. He was one of the foremost of the early crusaders, and the virtual creator of his principality by constant warfare against the Greeks on the north and the Muslims on the south. Tancred's successor was his nephew Roger Fitz-Richard, a less vigorous ruler, who was slain in battle with Īl-Ghāzī near Athārib in 1119. The government of Antioch was then assumed by Baldwin II of Jerusalem during the minority of the son of Bohemond. When Bohemond II came from Italy in 1126, he married Baldwin's second daughter Alice, but reigned only four years; after his death Antioch was again in the king's hands till a husband was found in 1136 for Bohemond's daughter Constance in the person of Raymond of Poitou.

Tripolis had been marked out as a county for Raymond of Saint Gilles; but when he died in 1103 only a beginning of conquest had been made. The city of Tripolis was not captured till 1109, when the county was secured to Raymond's son Bertram. Three years later Bertram was succeeded by his son Pons, whose reign lasted five and twenty years.

Some brief account of the three great fiefs has seemed needful before we could discuss the relation of their rulers to their nominal overlord at Jerusalem. In theory the Prince of Antioch, the Counts of Edessa and Tripolis, all owed fealty to the king at Jerusalem as their suzerain. The king on his part had to give them his aid and protection in case of need. Thus Baldwin I went to the aid of Baldwin of Edessa against the Turks in 1110, and Baldwin II was called in by Roger of Antioch when hard pressed by Īl-Ghāzī in 1119. Also it was the king who had to intervene in the disputes of his feudatories, as for instance between Bertram of Tripolis and Tancred in 1109, and again between Tancred and the Count of Edessa next year. The reality of the royal authority was shewn even more clearly when Baldwin II intervened in the affairs of Antioch after the death of Roger, and Fulk after the death of Bohemond II. But though Baldwin and Fulk both assumed for a time the government of the principality as part of their kingly duty, neither desired to find an opportunity for an extension of their personal power, and they were glad when the choice of a new prince relieved them of an onerous charge. Geographical conditions did not favour the concentration of power under a central authority. The long and narrow territory of the Franks was affected by a diversity of interests between the component parts, and this was shewn not only in the disputes of the great feudatories between themselves but also in their attitude to their suzerain. If it served their own advantage the Frankish princes were ready to seek Musulman aid against their Christian rivals, and even against the king himself. However incontestable the king's rights might be in theory, in practice his authority was under normal conditions limited. The Prince of Antioch and the Counts of Edessa and Tripolis were virtually sovereigns in their own states.

In the kingdom of Jerusalem properly so called there were four greater baronies, the county of Jaffa and Ascalon (which in later times was an appanage of the royal house), the lordship of Karak and Montreal, the principality of Galilee, and the lordship of Sidon. In addition there were a dozen lesser lords, some of whom, like the lords of Toron, were important enough to play a great part in the history of the kingdom. The royal domain, besides Jerusalem and its immediate neighbourhood, included the two great seaports of Tyre and Acre.

The kingdom of Jerusalem, established in a conquered land at the time when the feudalism of Western Europe was at its greatest strength, put into practice in their purest form the theoretical principles of the age. Though the monarchy, elective in its origin, soon became hereditary, the barons never entirely lost their right to a share in the choice of a new king. The king, though by virtue of his office chief in war and in peace, remained always under the restrictions which a fully organised feudal nobility had imposed on him from the start. As Balian of Sidon told Richard Filangieri, who was bailiff of the kingdom for Frederick II: "This land was not conquered by any lord but by an army of crusaders and pilgrims, who chose one to be lord of the kingdom, and afterwards by agreement made wise statutes and assises to be held and used in the kingdom for the safeguard of the lord and other men." In the Assises of Jerusalem we have indeed the most perfect picture of the ideal feudal state, and they are themselves the most complete monument of feudal law. They do not, however, so much describe the kingdom of Jerusalem as it ever actually existed, as the theoretical ideal of the jurisconsults of Cyprus by whom they were first drawn up in the thirteenth century. John of Ibelin, one of the first of these lawyers, relates that Godfrey, in the early days of the kingdom, by the advice of the patriarchs, princes, and barons, appointed prudent men to make enquiry of the crusaders as to the usages which prevailed in the various countries of the West. Upon their report Godfrey adopted what seemed convenient to form the assises and usages whereby he and his men and his people, and all others going, coming, and dwelling in his kingdom, were to be governed and guarded. The Code thus drawn up was then deposited under seal in the church of the Holy Sepulchre, whence it received the name of *Lettres du Sépulcre.* The consultation of the Letters was hedged about by elaborate precautions, and the Code (if it ever existed) could not have been really operative. In any case it perished at the capture of Jerusalem in 1187, and the tradition of its existence may well have been invented to give authority to the later Assises. It is certain, however, that during the twelfth century there had grown up a body of usages and customs, the collection and writing down of which in the next age formed the basis of the existing Assises.

There is evidence in the Assises themselves that they were, in part at all events, an adaptation of Western usages to the needs of a conquered land where an ever-present enemy made war almost the normal state. All who owed military service must come when summoned, ready with horse and arms to serve for a full year in any part of the kingdom. Such a provision differed essentially from the feudal customs of the West, but must have been necessary in the East from the earliest times. From the Assises we learn that the king, whose legal title was *Rex Latinorum in Hierusalem,* had under him great officers, Seneschal, Marshal, Chamberlain, Chancellor, and others. For the administration of justice there was the High Court at Jerusalem, which was originally intended to have jurisdiction over the great lords, but gradually became in effect the king's Council of State dealing with all political affairs; its powers were extended over the lesser lords of the kingdom proper by Amaury I. The seignorial courts in other places were governed by the customs of the High Court at Jerusalem. In Jerusalem and all towns where the Frankish settlers were sufficiently numerous there were Courts of the Burgesses, presided over by the viscounts, who were sometimes hereditary officers and, like the sheriffs of Norman England, combined financial and judicial functions. The Assise of the Burgesses appears to date from the reign of Amaury I. Other courts were those of the *Fonde* for commercial matters, of the *Chaine* for maritime affairs in the ports, and the courts of the *Reis* for the native Syrians. The whole organisation was perhaps more elaborate and complete than anything of the kind that then existed in the West.

The Assises of Jerusalem do not survive in the actual shape given to them by John of Ibelin and his contemporary Philip of Novara in the middle of the thirteenth century; for, since they served for the kingdom of Cyprus, they were from time to time revised during the next three hundred years. Yet in the *Assises de la Haute Cour* we can trace the most ancient and pure expression of French feudalism, and in the *Assises de la Cour des Bourgeois* we have a faithful picture of life in the Latin kingdom. The principality of Antioch and county of Tripolis had each their own Assises. The short-lived county of Edessa had also, no doubt, its own body of customary law, though it is not unnatural that no trace of it has survived.

The kingdom of Jerusalem was fortunate in its early rulers, who were all men with the qualities needed in a youthful state which had to fight for its very existence. Baldwin I (1100–1118) was named by his brother Godfrey as his successor and was confirmed as king by the choice of the barons, in spite of some opposition from Daimbert the Patriarch, who asserted the superior claims of the ecclesiastical authority. Baldwin had little of the religious character with which tradition has invested his brother, though William of Tyre described him as looking in his chlamys more like a bishop than a layman. He was a typical knight-errant, eager for adventure, valiant but rash. Nevertheless, though hampered always by lack of money and men, and not always successful in war, he did much to consolidate his kingdom. On the coast, aided by the Genoese and Venetians, he reduced the important ports of Arsūf, Caesarea, Acre, Sidon, and Beyrout; on the east he carried his arms beyond Jordan, where in 1116 he built the strong fortress of Montreal. Beyond the limits of the kingdom proper he helped Bertram to win Tripolis in 1109, and gave his aid to Baldwin of Edessa and Tancred of Antioch in their warfare with the Muslim.

Baldwin II (1118–1131) was his predecessor's nephew, and came to the throne after nearly twenty years' experience of Eastern warfare. His first years were occupied with the defence of Antioch and Edessa, and in

1123 he had the misfortune to be taken prisoner by the Turks. When after a year's captivity at Kharput he purchased his release, he renewed his warfare and in 1125 inflicted a severe defeat on the Emir of Mosul. But the greatest conquest of his reign was the capture of Tyre in 1124, which was accomplished by Eustace Grener, then guardian of the kingdom, with the aid of a Venetian fleet. Baldwin II had married one daughter to the youthful Bohemond of Antioch; for his elder daughter Melisend he found, with the consent of the lords of his kingdom, a husband in Fulk V of Anjou. Fulk had been Count of Anjou since 1109; thus he was a tried ruler; he was also no stranger to the Holy Land, where he had spent a year as a pilgrim in 1120. An Angevin of the Angevins, in character not unlike his grandson Henry II of England, he was well fitted for his new task. Fulk came to Palestine in 1129 and, two years afterwards, on the death of his father-in-law, succeeded to the throne. A reign of thirteen years (1131–1144) was troubled by calls for the king's intervention in the affairs of Tripolis, Antioch, and Edessa, by constant warfare with the Turks, by threatened encroachments of the Greek Emperor, and even by the turbulence of the barons of his own kingdom. Nevertheless it was on the whole a time of progress, and the year of his death may be said to mark the greatest extension of Frankish power in Syria.

Had the first crusaders and their immediate successors been dependent solely on their own efforts, it would be strange that they should have accomplished as much as they did. But we have seen how under Baldwin I and Baldwin II the work of conquest had been aided by Genoese and Venetian fleets. The establishment of the Franks in Palestine had opened a new field to the commercial enterprise of the Italian merchants, whose support was not less helpful to the prosperity of the new realm than the conflicting interests which they introduced were to prove baneful at a later time. Nor was it only the trader who was attracted Eastwards. The spirit of adventure or the zeal for religion brought a steady stream of reinforcements. "God," wrote Fulcher of Chartres, "has poured the West into the East; we have forgotten our native soil and become Easterners." Those who stayed settled down to become a source of strength; others who had come but as soldier-pilgrims were sometimes a source of embarrassment, eager to provoke the conflict which was the reason of their coming, reluctant to accept the advice and authority of the lords of the land. Nevertheless it was due to the zeal of these religious adventurers that the great Military Orders, which were to become the mainstay of the Christians in the East, were established.

There had been a Hospital of St John at Jerusalem for the aid of sick and poor pilgrims since the early years of the eleventh century. Gerard, who was its Master at the time of the First Crusade, was called the devoted servant of the poor; but it was not until after his death that the Order became a military body. The idea of a body of knights sworn to the service of the Cross was first conceived by Hugh de Payen, who in

the reign of Baldwin I joined with eight other knights in the task of
protecting pilgrims on the road to Jerusalem. They were already under
the triple vows of chastity, obedience, and poverty, like regular canons,
but it was only when Baldwin II in the first year of his reign gave them
a dwelling near the Temple of Solomon that they came to be known as
the Knights of the Temple. A little later under Raymond du Puy a
similar organisation was adopted for the Hospital of St John. The two
Orders thus established grew rapidly in wealth and power, and acquired
great possessions in Palestine and the West. Already in the reign of
Fulk they had begun to be an important element in the military strength
of the kingdom, and a generation later the Hospitallers furnished
Amaury I with five hundred knights for his Egyptian campaign, and
William of Tyre says that in his time the Templars numbered three
hundred knights. Wealth and power brought abuses in their train. Even
in the twelfth century the pretensions of the two Orders began to be
troublesome, and the Templars in particular won an evil name for avarice
and arrogance. At a later date the rivalry of the two great Orders became
a serious danger. But in their prime they were an efficient military organisation, whilst the wealth, which enabled them to maintain a steady
flow of reinforcements from the West, gave them always an advantage
over the native lords of the land. The minor Orders, like the Teutonic
Knights, the Knights of St Thomas of Acre, and the Knights of the
Holy Ghost, did not grow up till much later.

The success of the early crusaders was, however, due more to the
division of their enemies than to their own valour. It was during the
confusion and civil war that followed on the death of the great Seljūq
Sultan Malik Shāh in 1092, that the First Crusade was launched. No
moment could have been more auspicious, and a generation was to pass
before the Muslim power was again to be gathered in a single hand.
Nevertheless the Frankish conquest was far from complete. Even within
the limits of the actual kingdom and its subordinate principalities it was
little more than the armed occupation of a land where the old inhabitants
still formed the bulk of the population, at all events in the rural districts.
Nor was the occupation, such as it was, ever carried far enough to make
the conquest secure; Damascus, Emesa (Ḥimṣ), Ḥamāh, and Aleppo
were still under the rule of Muslim princes, and there was but a small
part of the Christian territory that was beyond the reach of a sudden
raid. So long, however, as these cities remained under separate rulers,
the Franks also might carry their own raids far and wide, and the balance
of success rested with them. The man who was to find a remedy by
restoring unity amongst the Musulmans was ʿImād-ad-Dīn Zangī, who
became Atābeg of Mosul in 1127.

Zangī's first aim was to establish his rule in Muslim Syria, and within
three years he made himself master of Ḥamāh and Aleppo. He was
more intent upon the consolidation of Musulman power than on active

conquest from the Franks, and though in 1135–6 he made a successful campaign against Antioch, the conquest of Edessa, which he achieved near the close of his career, does not appear to have been an essential aim of his policy. Joscelin of Edessa had been a restless fighter, whose name was a terror in all Musulman lands. So long as he lived, Edessa was a strong outpost of the Christians in the most dangerous quarter. His death in 1131 coincided with the rise of Zangī. His son Joscelin II, though a valiant soldier when he chose, preferred a life of ease to the hardship of frontier warfare. So he left Edessa to the care of unwarlike Armenians and ill-paid mercenaries, and withdrew to the luxurious comfort of his Syrian lordship at Tell-Bāshir. For a time Zangī was busy with the attempted conquest of Damascus, which Mu'īn-ad-Dīn Anar, its ruler, defeated by making common cause with the Franks. When, however, Zangī turned his attention northwards, Edessa fell an easy prey (25 December 1144). To the Muslims it was "the conquest of conquests," and the first step to the destruction of the Franks. Zangī did not long survive his victory; for within two years he was murdered by some of his own Mamlūks. The work which he had begun was continued by his son Nūr-ad-Dīn, who in 1150 captured Tell-Bāshir and in 1154 by the conquest of Damascus brought all the Musulman cities of Syria under a single ruler.

In Western Europe the fall of Edessa was recognised as a disaster which threatened the very existence of the Frankish conquest. St Bernard of Clairvaux came forward as the apostle of the Second Crusade, and at his bidding Conrad of Germany and Louis VI of France both took the Cross. Conrad and Louis started independently on their long journey by land in the spring of 1147. Both met with utter disaster in Asia Minor, and it was by sea that the remnant of their hosts reached Syria a year later. Louis went first to Antioch, where Raymond would fain have diverted him to a war against Nūr-ad-Dīn in the north, which was indeed the most dangerous quarter. Conrad had already reached Acre, and when the whole host was at length assembled it was resolved to make the capture of Damascus the object of the war. A siege was begun with good prospect of success. But between the Syrian Franks and their Western allies there were bitter jealousies of which the Saracen emir was quick to take advantage. By specious argument and perhaps by bribes he worked on the Easterners so effectually that the enterprise was abandoned. Conrad presently went home in disgust, and though Louis stayed a little longer he could effect nothing.

To Western Europe the fiasco of the Second Crusade was a keen humiliation. St Bernard found in it "an abyss so deep that I must call him blessed who is not scandalised thereby." To the Syrian Franks the Crusade had brought no advantage; it had done little to check the growth of Muslim power, but had rather tended to throw Damascus into the arms of Nūr-ad-Dīn. Amongst the Christians themselves it had sown the seed of dissension which was to bear bitter fruit.

However, for some years to come Nūr-ad-Dīn was busy with the establishment of his authority in Muslim lands. Meantime the Franks, under the vigorous rule of Baldwin III (1144–1163) and Amaury I (1163–1174), were able to maintain at least the semblance of power. Baldwin III was a boy of thirteen at the time of his father's death, and ruled conjointly with his mother till 1152. The first year of his sole reign was marked by the capture of Ascalon, which for fifty years had been an open sore in the side of the Franks towards Egypt. Four years later he attempted to recover Caesarea on the Orontes, which had been lately taken by Nūr-ad-Dīn. This enterprise, in which Baldwin was assisted by his brother-in-law Theodoric (Thierry) of Flanders, was likely to have proved successful. But Theodoric and Reginald of Chatillon, whom Constance of Antioch had taken for her second husband, both laid claim to the unconquered town; their rivalry led to such hot dissension amongst the crusaders that they abandoned the siege altogether. Baldwin III was more than a mere soldier; he had a high repute for his familiarity with the customary law of his realm, and more than a little of that literary culture which seems to have been a common characteristic of the Frankish nobility. He had sought to strengthen his position by a marriage with the sister of Manuel Comnenus, the Emperor of Constantinople, but at his death in 1163 he left no children and was succeeded by his brother Amaury I.

In Syria Nūr-ad-Dīn at Damascus and Amaury at Jerusalem now stood face to face as leaders of the rival races. It was becoming clear that the victory would rest with the one who could make himself master of Egypt. The Fāṭimite Caliphs at Cairo had sunk to be the puppets of their viziers. In January 1163 the vizier Shāwar was expelled by a rival called Dirghām, and fled for aid to Nūr-ad-Dīn. Dirghām unwisely refused to pay the tribute which for some years past had been rendered by Egypt to the King of Jerusalem. Thereupon Amaury made war and defeated Dirghām in battle; but, when the vizier flooded Egypt by breaking the dams of the Nile, he was forced to retire on some sort of composition. Nūr-ad-Dīn perceived his opportunity, and in 1164 sent Shāwar back to Egypt with an army under Shīrkūh, the uncle of Saladin. Too late Dirghām sought a reconciliation with Amaury. Shāwar, however, soon found his tutelage irksome, and in his turn called in the Frankish king. Amaury invaded Egypt in 1167, and was so far successful that a treaty was made under which the Saracens withdrew their army. Next year Amaury was persuaded against his own judgment to break the peace and again invade Egypt. As the king had foreseen, this act threw Shāwar once more into the arms of Nūr-ad-Dīn, and the return of Shīrkūh forced the Franks to retire from before Cairo. Shīrkūh soon found an excuse to put Shāwar to death, and became vizier in his place. After only three months he died and was succeeded by Saladin. A renewed attempt by Amaury, with the aid of the Emperor Manuel, to capture Damietta in the autumn of 1169 ended in disaster. Thus was the conquest of Egypt for Nūr-ad-Dīn accomplished by the man who was destined to complete his work in Syria.

Nūr-ad-Dīn and Amaury both died in the summer of 1174. The sons of both—Baldwin IV at Jerusalem, and Ṣāliḥ at Damascus—were mere boys. It was not long before Saladin displaced his master's heir, and with Syria and Egypt in the hands of the same ruler the Franks were between the nether and the upper millstone. In Saladin the Muslims had obtained a great leader, whose single purpose was the recovery of Jerusalem. But amongst the Christians there was no one with enough authority to repress the mutual jealousies which spoiled all their endeavours. It was only after some dispute that Raymond III of Tripolis (1152–1187) was chosen to be guardian of the kingdom, and as long as he held the position he was hampered by the disputes of rival factions. The troubles of the reign were increased by the fact that Baldwin was a leper, whose disease before his death had crippled him altogether. Baldwin had two sisters: Sibylla, who was married in 1176 to William of Montferrat but lost her first husband within a year; and Isabella, who in 1183 became the wife of Henfrid IV of Toron. The prospect of the king's early death made the marriages of Sibylla and Isabella the sport of political intrigue, in which the chief opposing parties were the lords of the land and the soldiers of fortune from the West. These disputes were to be the undoing of the kingdom.

Baldwin IV in early manhood was able to take an active part in the war. A disastrous defeat in 1179 made the Franks welcome a two years' truce. When it expired, they had a further brief respite whilst Saladin was busy beyond the Euphrates. Meantime another husband had been found for Sibylla in the person of Guy de Lusignan. Guy was a foreigner, and when in 1183 Baldwin made him his lieutenant the native lords refused to obey one whom they despised as a man "unknown and of little skill in war." The jealousies were so bitter that an attempt was made to obtain another solution by crowning Sibylla's little son by her first husband as Baldwin V. The native party then obtained the reappointment of Raymond as regent, whilst Guy withdrew in dudgeon to his county of Ascalon. Guy was supported by the aliens or Western adventurers like Reginald of Chatillon (now lord of Karak), and by the Knights of the Temple and the Hospital. With them the one idea of policy was war, but the native lords, who had more at stake and had acquired the habits and ideas of the East, were not unwilling to make terms with their Muslim neighbours. When Baldwin IV died in 1185, Raymond as regent at once concluded a four years' truce with Saladin. But the death of the child-king Baldwin V next year gave his opponents their opportunity.

Gerard de Rideford, a French knight who had recently become Master of the Temple, had a personal feud with Raymond of Tripolis. He now conspired successfully to secure the crown for Sibylla and her husband.

The opposite party made an attempt to put forward Henfrid of Toron as a rival candidate. But Henfrid was unwilling, and the majority of the Frankish lords then accepted Guy as king. Raymond, however, withdrew to Tripolis, whilst others held aloof, and it was with difficulty that the outbreak of civil war was prevented. Raymond is alleged to have intrigued with Saladin. It is more certain that Reginald of Chatillon provoked war by a flagrant breach of the truce. On 1 May 1187 a Saracen force crossed the Jordan, and taking the Christians by surprise inflicted a disastrous defeat on the Templars and Hospitallers at Nazareth. For a moment all feuds were hushed and Raymond gave Guy his whole support. Under the influence of Gerard de Rideford, Guy nevertheless rejected the cautious advice of Count Raymond, and on 4 July was compelled to give battle at Ḥiṭṭīn on unfavourable terms. That day saw the virtual destruction of the kingdom of Jerusalem. Guy, with many other of the leaders, was taken prisoner. Raymond escaped from the battle only to die of despair a few days later. Of the chief lords there was none alive and free save Balian of Ibelin. One after another the towns and fortresses of the kingdom fell into the hands of the Saracens. Jerusalem was taken by Saladin on 2 October 1187, and within a few months Tyre was the only place of importance in the kingdom that remained in the hands of the Christians.

The fall of Jerusalem stirred every heart in Western Europe, and provoked the Third Crusade. All the great princes in turn took the Cross, but the Emperor, Frederick Barbarossa, was the first to take the field in May 1189. Marching overland, the German host met with the usual difficulties and delays that attended that route. Frederick himself was accidentally drowned in Cilicia, and it was not till late in 1190 that the remainder of his army reached Syria.

Guy de Lusignan had obtained his freedom in July 1188, and during the next few months gathered a little army at Antioch, with which in the spring of 1189 he marched south to Tyre. But Conrad of Montferrat (brother of Sibylla's first husband), who held the city, would not admit him. Guy was, however, gradually reinforced by the arrival of knights and soldiers from the West, and in August felt himself strong enough to undertake the siege of Acre. The crusading army continued to grow in numbers, and secured some successes, but could not establish a complete investment. Presently they were themselves invested by a Saracen army, and though food grew scarce within the town the condition of the Christians in their camp was little better. This double siege had lasted eighteen months before Philip of France arrived, and it was not till 8 June 1191 that Richard of England (who had tarried to conquer Cyprus) appeared. Acre was then on the point of falling, and on 12 July the Christians recovered the city, which had of late years almost supplanted Jerusalem as the royal residence, and was the most important port of Palestine.

Quicker progress might have been made before Acre had it not been for the continued feuds of the crusading leaders. Sibylla had died, leaving no children, at the end of 1190. Thereupon the native party induced Isabella to consent to a divorce from Henfrid of Toron and to a marriage with Conrad of Montferrat. Guy on his part was naturally unwilling to resign the crown. He appealed to Richard of England, whilst Conrad obtained the support of Philip Augustus. Eventually, after the fall of Acre a compromise was effected, by which Guy retained the title for life, whilst the succession was secured to Conrad. It was a misfortune for the Christians that their two chief leaders should have taken opposite sides in this quarrel. It helped to revive the national rivalry of the French and English, at a time when the personal dissensions of Philip and Richard were already threatening to wreck the Crusade. "The two kings and peoples," wrote an English chronicler, "did less together than they would have done apart, and each set but light store by the other."

Richard was at his best as a crusader with his whole heart in the war. Philip remained the unscrupulous intriguer intent on his own gain. Soon after the fall of Acre the French king found an excuse to go home, though he left part of his followers behind under Hugh, Duke of Burgundy. Richard had now at all events the advantage that there was no one to dispute his place as the foremost leader of the Crusade. In August he marched south, inflicted a severe defeat on Saladin at Arsūf on 7 September, secured Jaffa, and at the end of the year advanced to within twelve miles of Jerusalem. But he was forced to fall back to the coast, where he busied himself with the restoration of Ascalon. The old feuds had broken out with new violence. Most of the French left the army and went back to Acre, where they found open discord between the supporters of Guy and Conrad. The Pisans were in arms for Guy, and the Genoese for Conrad. The French joined forces with the latter, and the English king was compelled to intervene. Richard consented reluctantly to acknowledge Conrad, whilst he consoled Guy with the gift of Cyprus. A month later, in April 1192, Conrad was murdered, and his party then chose Henry of Champagne as king and husband of the widowed Isabella. Henry of Champagne had the fortune to be Richard's own nephew, and this choice restored at least the appearance of unity. In the summer the crusaders again advanced to Bait Nūbah, twelve miles from Jerusalem. A bold dash might have recovered the Holy City, but cautious counsels prevailed. Other successes, however, followed, and Saladin began to incline to peace. Richard also was now anxious to return home, and, after a brilliant victory over the Saracens before Jaffa on 5 August, consented to a three years' truce.

Under the truce the Christians secured a narrow strip of coast from Ascalon to Acre with the right of access to the Holy City. Such a result was entirely out of proportion to the greatness of the effort put forward, or to the halo of glory with which romance has invested the Third Crusade. If we would seek the causes of this failure we should find them in the personal enmities of the great princes, the national rivalries of their

followers, and the mutual jealousies of the native lords. That the Third
Crusade was not in fact and in history such a fiasco as the Second was
due mainly to the personal greatness of the two chief actors : to Richard
as the whole-hearted champion of the Cross, and to Saladin as the
pre-eminently wise and just restorer of Muslim power. " Were each,"
said Hubert Walter, " endowed with the virtues of the other, the whole
world could not furnish such a pair of princes." The great Saladin died
within a few months, in February 1193, and Richard returned to a troubled
kingdom and an early grave in the West.

The loss of Jerusalem and the failure of the Third Crusade marked
the end of the kingdom as an organised state. Here then we may stop
to consider briefly the social life of the Franks in Syria. Outwardly, at
all events, the Frankish nobles lived much the same life as their contemporaries in the West, with like pursuits and like ideals. The great
lords dwelt on their fiefs in their castles, the finest of which, like
Karak, Ṣāhyūn, Krak des Chevaliers, and Markab (the two last belonged
to the Hospitallers), were amongst the most splendid monuments of
medieval military architecture. But in later days many of them had
also their palaces in such towns as Antioch, Tripolis, and Acre. In the
second generation most of the Franks had adopted the luxuries, manners,
and even the dress of the East. The dwellers in the land established in
the intervals of peace friendly relations with their Musulman neighbours, and this association led not only to a change in habits but to
a wider culture. This difference of mental attitude contributed almost
as much as difference of interest to keep the native lords apart from the
Western soldiers and adventurers who had no personal ties in the East.
But the aristocracy of knights and nobles did not stand alone; there was
a large class of burgesses, many of them the offspring of marriages with
Syrian women and known as *Pullani*; they, even more than their rulers,
had adopted luxurious habits and, with the growth of commercial interests,
had lost their zeal for the war. Amongst the knights there was a class of
mere adventurers like Reginald of Chatillon, whose predatory instincts
made them a bane to the older settlers. But a worse class were the men
of lower rank who had gone on the Crusade to escape the consequences
of their crimes and in the East reverted to their evil ways. During the
whole period of the kingdom these wastrels were a constant source of
danger. Far otherwise were the foreign merchants, "a folk very necessary
to the Holy Land." It has been remarked before how closely commerce
and military enterprise were interwoven in Frankish Syria. The foreign
trade was almost entirely in the hands of the Italians, and above all of
the Genoese, Pisans, and Venetians. All of them had rendered good service
in the early days of the kingdom, and all of them had been rewarded with
privileges and their special quarters in the towns; hence they acquired a
political influence which was to bear evil fruit. From the first there was
much commercial rivalry between them, and from the Third Crusade

onwards, when the power of the nobles had become less and the importance of the merchants greater, their dissensions were a potent factor in the final downfall of the kingdom. In these ill-assorted strata of separate classes there was little material for a unified nation, and it must not be forgotten that the great mass of the agricultural population still consisted of the ancient inhabitants. The fatal lack of unity was not the least of the causes which prevented the permanence of the Frank colonies.

Of the ecclesiastical hierarchy nothing has yet been said. Under the two Patriarchs of Jerusalem and Antioch there were eight archbishops and sixteen bishops, with numerous abbeys and priories of the Latin rite. If there was more culture amongst the laymen in the East than amongst their kinsmen in the West, much of the work of actual administration rested in the East as in the West on ecclesiastics. The Patriarch Daimbert, at the time of the election of Baldwin I, put forward pretensions of the loftiest character, which, if they could have been established in their entirety, would have made the kingdom a theocratic state. Except for a brief period under Baldwin II when Stephen of Chartres laid claim to Jaffa and Jerusalem, his successors were content to work in harmony with the king. Nevertheless the Latin Church with its privileged position and immunities, supported by the vast wealth which it possessed not only in Syria but in every country of the West, formed a power which was dangerous to the unity of the kingdom. Jacques de Vitry, who was Bishop of Acre in the thirteenth century, roundly charges the clergy of his time with greed and avarice. But, whatever the faults of some, there were great names amongst the churchmen of the East. William of Tyre, archbishop, chancellor, and historian, was pre-eminent; whilst, amongst lesser names, an English writer must not omit his countryman, Ralph, Bishop of Bethlehem, who was chancellor under Baldwin III and Amaury.

After the Third Crusade the kingdom of Jerusalem was little more than a shadow. For the most part it consisted of a narrow strip along the coast, and such strength as it retained rested upon the possession of the important ports from Jaffa to Beyrout, and above all of Acre. Further north the Christians still held a more substantial territory, though Bohemond III of Antioch, the son of Raymond and Constance, was hard pressed by the Christian princes of Armenia. The county of Tripolis gained strength from the presence within its borders of some of the greatest fortresses of the Military Orders. Raymond III, at his death in 1187, left the county to his godson Raymond, son of Bohemond III. But after the death of Bohemond III in 1201 Raymond resigned Tripolis to his brother Bohemond IV, and henceforward the Princes of Antioch were also Counts of Tripolis.

In the kingdom proper the native lords would have been content to enjoy the small remnant of their former possessions, and it was against their will, when German crusaders came to Acre in 1197, that the war was renewed. In that same year Henry of Champagne died and his widow married for her fourth husband Amaury de Lusignan, who had succeeded his brother Guy as King of Cyprus. The Lusignans ruled prosperously in Cyprus for over three centuries, and from this time the fortunes of the kingdom of Jerusalem were linked closely with the island. The reign of Amaury II witnessed some recovery of territory on the mainland, and more might have been accomplished had not the Fourth Crusade been diverted to the conquest of Constantinople, an ill-advised enterprise which did great injury to the Christian cause in the East. Amaury II died in 1205, and his infant son Amaury III a year later. Then the kingdom of Jerusalem passed to Mary, Isabella's daughter by Conrad of Montferrat. For Mary a husband was found in John de Brienne, a French knight, who came to Acre in 1210. John, though a man of modest rank, was a skilful soldier, whose incessant raids on Saracen territory did something to stay the waning fortunes of his kingdom. It was in answer to John's appeal that Innocent III in 1216 proclaimed a new crusade. In the autumn of 1217 a great host assembled at Acre. By the advice of King John it was determined to make an expedition to Egypt by sea, and accordingly in May 1218 the crusaders laid siege to Damietta. There they were joined by further reinforcements from the West, including the four English Earls of Chester, Arundel, Salisbury, and Winchester; Robert de Courçon, an English cardinal, also came as one of the Pope's representatives, though he died within a few weeks of his arrival. The siege lasted over a year, and it was only on 5 November 1219 that the crusaders fought their way into the city. This success brought the Saracens almost to despair. They offered to surrender most of Palestine, if only Damietta were restored to them. But the crusaders refused, in the vain hope that the Emperor Frederick II would come to aid them in the conquest of all Egypt. After long delay, in the summer of 1221 an advance was made towards Cairo. Soon the crusaders found themselves in a perilous position, from which they were glad to purchase their release at the price of the surrender of Damietta. Well might Philip of France say that the men were daft who for the sake of a town had refused the proffer of a kingdom.

John de Brienne had not been responsible for the folly which threw away the fruits of the victory he had planned. In 1222 he went to Europe, where in 1225 he found a husband for his daughter Yolande in the Emperor Frederick II. Frederick soon quarrelled with his father-in-law, and dispossessed him of his kingdom, which he claimed for himself in right of his wife. He was already in the throes of his conflict with the Pope, but in 1228 he paid a visit to the Holy Land, where by negotiations with the Sultan Kāmil he obtained a partial surrender of Jerusalem, together with Bethlehem and Nazareth. His enemies the Templars found a new grudge against him, in that their great church at Jerusalem was left to the Muslims, and Pope Gregory denounced the treaty as a concession to Belial. Frederick's brief Crusade added only to his own troubles, and it brought little good to his Eastern subjects. The Saracens soon broke the treaty, and reoccupied Jerusalem. Frederick then sent Richard Filangieri to Palestine as his bailiff; Richard fell out with the native lords under John of Ibelin, who called in the King of Cyprus to their aid. After some years of strife, in 1236, when Yolande was dead, Queen Alice[1] of Cyprus, who was a daughter of Henry of Champagne, persuaded the native party to take her then husband, Ralph of Soissons, as bailiff.

When the Emperor had received the crown of Jerusalem it must have appeared that the kingdom was assured of a powerful protector. But in the issue Frederick's rule only embittered the old enmities, whilst his quarrel with the Papacy introduced a new cause of discord. The results might have been even more disastrous had it not been for the unsettled condition of the Musulman state. Saladin's brother 'Ādil (Saphadin) was succeeded in 1218 by his son Kāmil, whose reign of twenty years was troubled by pressure from the Turks in the north and the Tartars advancing from the east. At Kāmil's death in 1238 his sons fell to civil war, so that the moment was not unfavourable for the new Crusade which was launched next year. In this crusade none of the great princes took part. The chief leader was Theobald, King of Navarre. The French nobles, who were his principal followers, persisted in making a series of desultory raids, which ended in most of them being taken prisoners. Earl Richard of Cornwall, who came to Acre in the following year, was able through his great wealth to procure their release; but the quarrels of the Military Orders prevented any prospect of successful war, and the English earl soon went home. The Templars and Hospitallers continued to dispute as to the relative advantages of alliance with Damascus or Egypt. In the end the former prevailed, and in 1244, by a treaty with Ismā'īl of Damascus, the Franks secured the whole land west of Jordan. There was a brief period of rejoicing in Christendom that all the holy places had at last been recovered. Then Ayyūb, the Sultan of Egypt, called to his aid the predatory horde of the Khwārazmian Turks, who fell upon Jerusalem and massacred its inhabitants (23 August 1244). The Muslims of Ḥamāh and Damascus united with the Franks to meet this common danger, but their joint army was utterly defeated by the Khwārazmians and Egyptians under the Mamlūk emir, Baibars Bunduqdārī, at Gaza on 17 October 1244. This was the greatest disaster that had befallen the Franks since Ḥiṭṭīn, and swept away nearly all that had been so painfully recovered in the last fifty years.

The destruction of Jerusalem and the disaster of Gaza led directly to the first crusade of Louis IX. Frederick, who should have been the natural protector of his distant kingdom, was too deeply involved in his own troubles, and Louis was the only one of the great princes of the West who had both the will and the power to help. Though he took the Cross early in 1245, it was not till the end of 1248 that he reached Cyprus, where he spent six months. The ill-omened precedent of thirty

[1] Alice had married Hugh de Lusignan, King of Cyprus 1205–18.

years before was followed for the plan of campaign with remarkably similar results. Damietta fell on this occasion, almost without a blow. Then there followed a long delay in waiting for reinforcements, amongst whom there came a small body of English under William Longespée, Earl of Salisbury. When at the end of November 1249 the crusaders began their advance on Cairo, they soon found themselves entangled in the difficulties of the Egyptian Delta. A rash attack on Manṣūrah on 8 February 1250 ended disastrously. The crusaders could not advance, and when, a few weeks later, sickness and lack of food compelled them to retreat, they found the way blocked by their enemies. In the end Louis and his army were obliged to surrender, and then to purchase their freedom at the price of Damietta and a huge ransom in money. Louis with the remnant of the crusaders reached Acre about the end of May. He spent nearly four years in the Holy Land, and, though not able to attempt any great enterprise, did something to strengthen the Franks by repairing the fortifications of the seaports, and especially of Jaffa, Caesarea, and Sidon.

Frederick II had died in 1250. During his twenty-five years' reign the royal power had been virtually in abeyance, or exercised by bailiffs whose authority was disputed by those whom they were supposed to rule. The conflict of interests, political, military, and commercial, amongst the Franks in Syria had thus, through the lack of control, free scope to develope. The native lords, strengthened by their association with the prosperous island kingdom of Cyprus, grew more impatient of an outside authority. The jealousies of the Military Orders, enormously increased in wealth and power and opposed to one another in policy, became more acute. The Italian merchants, on whose commerce the prosperity of the seaport towns, and therefore of the kingdom, depended, gained greater importance and added political disputes to their commercial rivalry. The dislike of the native lords for the rule of the Emperor's bailiff had led to bitter strife in 1236, and the rivalry of the two Military Orders went much deeper than the conflict of policies which had crippled the crusades of Theobald of Navarre and Richard of Cornwall. In 1249 there was actually open warfare for a month between the Pisans and Genoese at Acre. The greatest service which Louis IX rendered during his four years' sojourn in Palestine was that the weight of his authority did something to check dispute. But on his departure the old feuds soon broke out once more. The trouble began with a quarrel between the Venetians and Genoese in 1256, in which all other parties were soon involved. Four years of civil war exhausted the Latin communities at a time when all should have been united to build up the falling state.

The title of Frederick to the kingdom of Jerusalem passed ultimately to his grandson Conradin, at whose death in 1268 the line of Yolande came to an end. Up to that time the royal authority had been exercised nominally by bailiffs. On Conradin's death the succession was disputed between Hugh III of Cyprus and Mary of Antioch. Both claimed to represent Isabella, daughter of Amaury I, the former through Alice, daughter of Henry of Champagne, and the latter through Melisend, daughter of Amaury de Lusignan. The Hospitallers and the Genoese, who had supported Conradin, favoured Hugh, who was actually crowned King of Jerusalem at Tyre in 1269 and maintained some shew of authority till 1276, when he was forced by the opposition of the Templars to leave Acre. The jealousies of the Italian merchants of Genoa, Pisa, and Venice, and the rivalry of the two great Military Orders, thus again prevented any unity among the Franks at the time when it was most needed.

In 1259 the Tartars had appeared in Syria and threatened Muslim and Christian alike. They were defeated next year by Quṭuz, the Sultan of Egypt, who on his return home was murdered by his Mamlūks. This double event really sealed the fate of the Franks in Palestine. Baibars Bunduqdārī, the victor of Gaza, who now became Sultan, was to prove the most relentless foe that the Christians had had to encounter since the death of Saladin. As soon as he had established his authority in Syria, he set himself to destroy the remnant of Frankish rule. In 1265 Caesarea and Arsūf were taken, and other captures of less importance followed, till in 1268 first Jaffa and then Antioch fell into his hands.

The fall of Antioch was the occasion for the last great Crusade under Louis IX of France and Edward of England. Louis turned aside to attack Tunis, where he died, whilst Edward, thus left to himself, only reached Acre in the spring of 1271. He came in the nick of time to save the city from a threatened attack, but, though during an eighteen months' stay he achieved a series of minor successes, his Crusade brought only a transient relief. Before he left Palestine Edward procured for the Christians a ten years' truce, which on its expiration was again renewed by the then Sultan, Qalā'ūn, for a like period. The Franks made but an ill use of this breathing space, and their domestic feuds continued with all the former persistence.

Qalā'ūn was at first disposed to peace, but in 1285, provoked by an attack which the Hospitallers made on a caravan, besieged and captured their great fortress at Markab. In 1289, on a pretext that the treaty had expired, Qalā'ūn appeared before Tripolis. After a month's siege that great city, which was so rich and populous that four thousand weavers are said to have found employment in its factories, was taken and sacked with all the horrors of war. Those who escaped aboard ship took refuge at Acre, as many from other towns and places had done before. Thus, in the expressive words of an English chronicler: "There were gathered in Acre not as of old holy and devout men, but wantons and wastrels out of every country in Christendom who flowed into that sacred city as it were into a sink of pollution."

Though some minor places like Sidon still remained to the Franks,

Acre stood out as their chief stronghold, and it was clear that Acre must soon share the fortune of Tripolis, unless some great deliverance came to it from the West. There was, however, little practical enthusiasm for a new crusade. Pope Nicholas IV and most of the greater princes were more intent on schemes of aggrandisement nearer home, and though Edward of England had never lost his interest in the East he was too deeply engaged in his own affairs to take the Cross once more. The Pope, it is true, sent a force of 1600 mercenaries, for whom the republic of Venice provided shipping. But these mercenaries did more harm than good, and the most effectual assistance was perhaps that which Edward sent by his trusty knight, Sir Otto de Grandison, who, however, brought more money than men.

In the tragedy of Acre all the main causes that had led to the downfall of the kingdom were brought, as it were, to a focus. In Acre during its last days, the legate of the Pope and the bailiffs of the Kings of England, France, and Cyprus, all exercised their authority in independence; whilst the lords of the land, the Military Orders, and the traders of the Italian towns had all their strong towers and quarters fortified, not against the common foe so much as in hostility to their Christian rivals. Thus within the walls of one city there were seventeen separate and distinct communities; "whence," wrote Villani, "there sprang no small confusion."

Nevertheless the manifest peril of Acre after the fall of Tripolis restored for the moment some unity of purpose, and all joined in accepting the leadership of Henry of Cyprus, who was also titular King of Jerusalem. Henry made it his first care to conclude a two years' truce. But the old feuds soon broke out again, and when the papal mercenaries arrived they fell through lack of discipline to plundering the Saracen villages. Provoked by this breach of the truce, Qalā'ūn's son Khalīl, who had but lately succeeded as Sultan, took the field early in 1291. Had there been any unity of command in Acre it is just possible that the city might have been saved. But from the first the defence was hampered by the bitterness of the ancient jealousies. The rival parties each fought bravely enough in their own quarter, but would give no help to one another. So when, after a six weeks' siege, the Saracens began their assault, many, like the King of Cyprus, sailed away in despair. For four terrible days those who remained fought stubbornly, though even in such a crisis the Knights of the Hospital and the Temple could not lay aside their mutual enmity. Acre was finally stormed and taken on 18 May, though the Templars with Otto de Grandison held out for ten days longer in their castle by the waterside. Some of the Christians made good their escape by sea, but many were drowned in the attempt, and a far greater number perished by the sword or were carried into captivity[1].

[1] See, for a full narrative, *Transactions of the Royal Historical Society*, 3rd Series, III, 134–150.

The fall of Acre was the death-knell of the Latin kingdom of Jerusalem. One after another, the remaining strongholds of the Franks were abandoned or surrendered, amongst the last to go being Sidon and Beyrout about the middle of July. Pope Nicholas IV, whose schemes for the conquest of Sicily had made him half-hearted whilst there was yet time, was stirred by such a disaster to make a vain effort to revive the crusading spirit. But the old enthusiasm lingered only in the visionary ideals of men like Philip de Mézières, and it was a mockery of fate that for centuries to come the phantom title of King of Jerusalem was claimed by princes whose predecessors had failed to defend its reality.

CHAPTER IX.

THE EFFECTS OF THE CRUSADES UPON WESTERN EUROPE.

THAT eastward adventure of united Christendom which we call the Crusades, the common endeavour of all Europe to recapture the home of its religion and to subdue the rival faith of Mahomet, has naturally exercised a strong fascination over the minds of later ages. With the rediscovery of the Middle Ages in the nineteenth century, with the realisation that, after all, what the rationalism of the eighteenth century had been inclined to regard as a period of static misery was in fact a time of steady and fruitful growth, the crusading movement began to be studied with renewed interest, and the marked development of European civilisation during the two centuries from A.D. 1100 to 1300 was, on the principle of "post hoc, ergo propter hoc," assigned to its influence. So Michelet and Heeren attribute to it all those changes in Western Europe which make its condition in 1300 so marked a contrast to that of two hundred years before. The rise of the French monarchy, the growth of towns all over Europe, the great increase in international trade, the development of the Universities, the decline of feudalism, the opening up of Asia, the thirteenth-century Renaissance in literature, philosophy, and art—all this was regarded as due to the stir and movement introduced by the Crusades into a sleeping Europe. If such a view is too facile and enthusiastic, it is perhaps no less difficult to accept the more cynical estimate of the Crusades which would regard them as marauding expeditions disguised by a profession of piety, momentarily successful, but incapable, by their very nature, of leaving a permanent mark upon the West.

The Crusades were initiated by the Papacy, and from the moment of Urban II's appeal to the Council of Clermont down to the fall of Acre—and indeed for long after—they remained one of the first preoccupations of every Pope. Describing the policy of the Curia of so late a date as the middle of the fourteenth century, Viollet remarks that "Rome ne cessait guère, dans l'intérêt général de la chrétienté, d'entretenir de grands mais stériles projets de Croisade; c'est pour elle un impérissable honneur." And what was true of the French Papacy of Avignon was far more true of the Popes of the twelfth and thirteenth centuries at the height of their power. It were strange if this continuous direction for two hundred years of the armed forces of Europe in the campaign against the infidel should have left no mark upon the Papacy itself.

When Nicholas II, in 1059, issued the decree regulating the election of future Popes, the great effort of the Church to emancipate itself from the secularisation involved in its acceptance of a feudal constitution began. The long struggle with the Empire, which opens between Hildebrand and Henry IV, and which continued relentlessly throughout the period of the Crusades, was an attempt—successful in the main—to organise the Church as a "societas perfecta," to use a phrase of later controversy, independent of the secular power within its own sphere, and only dependent upon that power in so far as it needed the sword of material force to carry out the sentences of spiritual judgment. In all other respects the Divine Society was to be as superior to the secular as its very nature demanded. The attempt to attain this ideal, with all its tremendous implications, involved the Popes not only in continual warfare with successive Emperors but also in decisive conflict with the Kings of England and France, and, in an increasing degree, it involved the secularisation of the Papacy itself. To be successful its occupants must be statesmen first and men of God second; to carry on war they must raise men and money, and resort to shifts of all kinds to do so; to seize every advantage, to shape policy to fit every change of circumstance, they must be prepared to use diplomatic dissimulation and, if necessary, to lie with hardihood. That this process of degradation, from the lofty heights of spiritual control to the lowest levels of political expediency, set in, is not difficult of proof; it suffices to compare Gregory VII with Innocent IV, or the enthusiastic response with which the call to the First Crusade was met, with the indifference and even hostility which greeted such appeals in the later thirteenth century. The wheel had gone full circle, and the attempt to free the members of the Church from secular control ended in a more subtle secularisation of its very heart—the Papacy itself.

In that process the Crusades played an important part. They were one of the main sources of papal strength throughout the twelfth century, for they provided the Popes with the moral support of Europe, and placed the Papacy in a position of acknowledged leadership which was of the greatest value in the struggle with the secular powers. The literal mind of the Middle Ages found it more easy to understand the task of succouring the earthly Jerusalem by force of arms than that of gaining the heavenly Jerusalem by the practice of the Christian virtues, and in this case the natural man could at once find an outlet for his martial energies and also, by virtue of the indulgence attached to the Crusade, make certain of attaining the heavenly reward. Every motive of self-sacrifice or self-interest, every desire for glory or for gain, was appealed to by the call to the Crusade. The noble could hope to carve out a principality in the East; the merchant to make gain by transporting the crusading armies and supplying their necessities; the peasant to escape from the crushing burdens of his servile status. But foremost in the minds of all, at least in the early days, was the unselfish desire to regain for Christ the city made sacred by His life and death, and, inspired by this common aim, men of every class and country of Europe flocked to take the Cross at the instigation of the one authority acknowledged by them all—Christ's earthly Vicar. Here for the first time Christian Europe gave expression to a common mind and will, and it is of the highest significance that this mind and will had been formed and educated by the Church and was now placed at the service of the Church's head.

There can be little doubt that this moral enthusiasm of Europe proved in the twelfth century an almost incalculable assistance to the Papacy in its struggle with the Empire. To this force of a united Christendom behind them the successors of that Gregory VII who died in exile owed much of the great advance which they were able to make in the century after his death. For the Crusades were a living parable of the doctrine of the superiority of the spiritual sword. They were organised by the Popes and directed by their legates, and, what was more, all those who took the Cross became by that act the subjects of the Papacy in a new and special sense. Their goods during their absence, themselves before they departed and until they returned with their vows fulfilled, were removed from secular and placed under ecclesiastical jurisdiction. The Kings of France or England, of Hungary or Naples, the very Emperors themselves were, as crusaders, at the orders of the Pope, and the value of the moral compulsion of public opinion upon which the Popes could rely in forcing reluctant monarchs to take the Cross is clearly evidenced by the example of Henry II in his extreme old age, or of Philip Augustus, or of Frederick II. It is difficult indeed, except by this explanation, to account for the amazing difference between the position of the Papacy at the accession of Urban II, staggering under the defeat of Gregory VII and the schism which followed, faced too with a Church as yet but half-hearted in support of the reforming policy, and the position of almost undisputed supremacy occupied by Innocent III. After making all allowances for the ability of Alexander III and the persistence with which the "Hildebrandine" policy was pursued, after taking into account all the circumstances which were favourable to Innocent III's own assertion of his claims—the folly of John, the death of Henry VI, and the youth of Frederick II—there remains the fact that in an age when emotional religion was becoming steadily more powerful, the Pope, as leader of the conflict with the infidel, was enabled to command to an unprecedented degree the devotion of the faithful.

Yet, in the thirteenth century, much of this prestige and much of this popular devotion were lost. It was not merely that the Holy Land little by little fell into the hands of the Saracen and that the respect given to success was withdrawn when failure followed. The Papacy might have retained undiminished reverence had it failed, as St Louis failed, with clean hands and for no lack of high courage. But the very success which had attended the crusading appeal proved too strong a temptation to the Popes, and the appeal to take the Cross not only ceased to attract but definitely alienated the faithful when it was used as a weapon in the struggle against the Hohenstaufen. The list of so-called crusades in the thirteenth century, not directed against the Saracen, makes sad reading. No good Christian, indeed, was likely to be shocked by an appeal to take the Cross against the infidels of Provence, though a full Holy Land indulgence for forty days' service might seem almost too easily won when "the greater part of the faithful returned home after the forty days were over"; but since the expedition of Prince Louis against the English king was announced as a crusade, since the papal feud with the Hohenstaufen, so obviously maintained to safeguard the Papal States from danger, was provided with religious sanctions, it is not improbable that Matthew Paris represents a genuine popular reaction, and not merely his own opinion, when he writes of the "crusade" of 1255: "When the faithful heard this, they marvelled that he should promise them reward for shedding the blood of Christian men that was in former time promised for the shedding of infidel blood."

But, apart from the direct effect upon public opinion of this misuse of the Crusade for party ends, there emerged from the crusading movement two financial weapons of lasting importance to the papal armoury—the indulgence and the tithe.

It would, indeed, be untrue to assert that indulgences originated in the Crusades, but there can be no doubt that the indulgence as a financial expedient is a direct outcome of them. More than this, the practice had been instituted by Gregory VII of granting absolution from their sins to those who, in particular localities, fought on the Pope's side in a holy cause[1]. Urban II applied this to the whole of Christendom by his assurance that "those who die there in true penitence will without doubt receive indulgence of their sins and the fruits of the reward hereafter." The plenary indulgence to crusaders marks an epoch in the development of the system.

It is not, however, till the end of the twelfth century and the beginning of the thirteenth that the indulgence began to be used as a source of revenue. In 1184 those who cannot themselves take the Cross are bidden to give alms to support the Crusade and, in return for these contributions and for a threefold repetition of the Paternoster, are promised a partial indulgence. In 1195 Celestine III writes to Hubert of Canterbury as his English legate that "those who send of their goods in aid of the Holy Land shall receive pardon of their sins from their bishop on the terms that he shall prescribe." In 1215 the Fourth Lateran Council goes a step farther and promises a plenary indulgence to those who shall contribute to the crusading funds in proportion to their means. With that step the downward path was begun, and in the thirteenth century

---

[1] *Gregorii VII Reg.* II, 54, VII, 12 *a ad fin.*, VIII, 6.

the process of degeneration went steadily on. The demand for exemptions from actual service—at first the pretext for a monetary transaction—ceased to be more than a form, and the oratory of the mendicants stirred the ignorant to buy what they at least thought to be a certificate of admittance to Paradise. The Pardoner became a characteristic figure of medieval life, and the abuse of indulgences, after rousing the protests of Wyclif and of Hus, increased steadily till it provoked the avenging wrath of Luther.

If the Crusading Indulgence formed a lucrative and welcome addition to the papal revenues, the Clerical Tithe, another crusading device, proved even more profitable. Before the Crusades papal taxation in the strict sense did not exist. Romescot was a gift and not a tribute, and the Popes had not yet developed the system of annates and first-fruits which later provided them with a large part of their revenues. In 1146, however, the necessities of the Second Crusade led Louis VII of France to impose a tax upon all clerics under his jurisdiction of a tithe of their moveables, and this innovation was taken over by Richard I and Philip Augustus in the "Saladin Tithe" of 1188. The secular princes had here taken the initiative, and the tithe may be regarded as of first-rate importance in the general history of taxation as almost the first recorded step in the substitution of national taxes based on property values for the ruder and less profitable feudal taxation. But, important as the tithe may be in the history of secular, it is still more important in the history of ecclesiastical taxation. The Popes could not afford to allow ecclesiastical property to become the basis of national revenues. A tithe for a crusade might soon become a tax for foreign aggression, and when Louis VII in 1163 repeated his fruitful experiment, the Council of Tours of that year forbade bishops to pay tithe under penalty of deposition. The position was further defined by the Third Lateran Council of 1179, which allowed tithes to be levied by princes, subject to the consent of the clergy; but Innocent III thought this concession too great, and desired to monopolise the new invention as far as clerical property was concerned. The Fourth Lateran Council of 1215 decreed, therefore, that bishops should never pay tithe without first applying to Rome for the Pope's consent, whilst Innocent at the same time definitely adopted the system of tithe as a source of papal revenue by imposing a half-tithe on all the clergy of Christendom for the Crusade. From that year onwards the new weapon was constantly in use, and the list of tithes imposed during the thirteenth century is too long to reproduce. But that the Crusades provided first a reason and later an ever-ready excuse for the enormous extension in the thirteenth century of papal control over all ecclesiastical revenues is certain, and but for the Crusades the position adopted by Boniface VIII might never have been reached. "The Apostolic See has the absolute power of administering (the ecclesiastical property). It can dispose of it without the consent of anyone. It can exact, as it sees fit, the hundredth, the tenth, or any other part of this property." The absolutist theory of Hildebrand may have contained this doctrine implicitly; it was the needs of the Crusades which made possible its practical application.

One further result of the crusading movement on the life of the Western Church was more obviously consonant with its Founder's teaching than those already mentioned. Before the date at which our period closes—the fall of Acre—the most truly religious minds of the West had begun to turn from the propagation of the Kingdom of Heaven by force to the project of converting the heathen by persuasion, from militant Crusades to peaceful Missions. St Francis of Assisi, after two unsuccessful attempts, reached Egypt in 1219 and preached before the Sultan; and his followers, as well as those of St Dominic, continued during the first half of the thirteenth century their attempts to convert the Muslim world. St Louis, for whom the Crusade in every form was the passion of his life, gave a new turn to missionary effort when in 1252 he sent the Franciscan William of Rubruquis to the Great Khan in Central Asia, in the hope that the new Mongolian Empire, once converted to Christianity, might descend upon the rear of the Turks and render the recovery of Palestine easy of accomplishment. At his instance, too, Innocent IV formed in 1253 the first "Missionary Society" since the conversion of the West—the "Peregrinantes propter Christum"—who were, for the most part, Franciscans and Dominicans. But the foremost figure in the development of the policy of the peaceful "Crusade" of persuasion was Raymond Lull, who devoted his life to the organisation of missionary work, and found a martyr's death in attempting to execute his projects. A Spaniard himself, the conversion of the Arab invader was his first concern, and in 1276 he persuaded the King of Majorca to found the College of the Holy Trinity of Miramar. Here Lull, who had learnt Arabic himself, trained the brothers for their work as true followers of Christ and His apostles, whose only weapons for conquest of the heathen had been "love, prayers, and the outpouring of tears." After ten years of this work of preparation, he began a career of incessant activity amongst the Tartars and Armenians of the East and the Muslims of North Africa, only interrupted by his efforts, constantly renewed, to persuade Popes and kings to engage their energies in missionary enterprise. To his efforts the decision of the Council of Vienne in 1311 to establish six schools of oriental languages in Europe must be attributed, and only his death by martyrdom, in 1314, put an end to his strenuous attempts to persuade Western Europe that the way to recover the Holy Places was to convert the heathen into whose hands they had fallen.

The missionary effort thus begun as a reaction from the methods of the Crusades, as well as a result of the interest in the East created by them, continued throughout the Middle Ages. In particular it was successful in Asia. Here Buddhism was an enemy less energetic and less directly hostile to Christianity than the faith of the Prophet. Political conditions, too, were favourable during the thirteenth and fourteenth centuries, and bishoprics were set up not only in Armenia, Persia, and the Kipchak in Western Asia, but right across China to the Pacific coast. The twenty-six years' journey of Orderic of Pordenone between the years 1304 and 1330 shews that at that time there was Christian missionary work in active progress in Persia, India, China, and Tibet; and for a time, in the fourteenth century, it must have seemed possible that the dreams of Raymond Lull were about to be fulfilled, and that the West, having converted the Mongol Empire to the faith of Christ, would be able to recover the Holy Land by a concerted movement of West and East upon the centre of Christian devotion. But Asia was not yet to be converted. The slackening of the activities of the Western Church produced by the Babylonish Captivity and the Great Schism was felt in the failure to give adequate support to the eastern missions; in the latter half of the fourteenth century the constituent portions of the Mongol Empire were rapidly converted to Islām, and with the rise of Tīmūr and his dreams of a reconstitution of the Caliphate the opportunity of converting Asia had definitely passed.

But if ultimate failure descended upon the missionary side of crusading activity, as it had fallen earlier upon the Christian states set up and maintained by force of arms in Syria, the effort was not all lost. Both from the Crusades proper and from the missionary activity which resulted from and succeeded them the peoples of Europe learned much of the world which they had not known before. One of the first-fruits of the Crusades is to be seen in the numberless itineraries written by those who had taken part in them for the benefit of future crusaders or pilgrims. Such writings appeared, indeed, before the Crusades began, but their number very greatly increased afterwards and, as Dr Barker says, "there were medieval Baedekers in abundance for the use of the annual flow of tourists who were carried every Easter by the vessels of the Italian towns or of the Orders to visit the Holy Land." Naturally these "Itineraria" are mainly concerned with Europe and Syria; the different routes to and from the Holy Sepulchre are their obvious subject, and in the latter half of the thirteenth century so intelligent a man as de Joinville could exhibit the grossest ignorance about the countries beyond the crusading area, could speak of the Nile as rising in the earthly paradise from which "ginger, rhubarb, wood of aloes, and cinnamon" floated down the stream to enrich the happy fishermen who cast their nets in its upper waters. Of the route from India to Egypt, indeed of the existence of India, he plainly had no conception. Such a combination of knowledge and ignorance is characteristic of the Middle Ages, and it would be easy to exaggerate the number of those who shared the new knowledge of the world which was brought back to the West by crusaders. For example, the traders of the Italian cities undoubtedly increased their knowledge of Mediterranean geography enormously during the crusading period, and examples of accurate and detailed charts for the use of their navigators can be found dating from the late thirteenth century at least. But that such knowledge was very far from being universally shared is shewn plainly enough by a monastic map like the famous Mappa Mundi of Hereford, to which the date 1280 is assigned, and in which even Europe appears as an almost incomprehensible maze. Further knowledge of the East was provided by the story in which William de Rubruquis narrated the adventures of his mission for the benefit of his royal patron St Louis. But it was not until the fourteenth century, when the book of Marco Polo began to be widely read, and when the Christian missions had spread throughout the vast Mongol Empire, that the conception of the vastness of Asia began to take hold upon the consciousness of the West. Moreover it is at least doubtful whether this new knowledge can be regarded as directly a fruit of the Crusades. The Polos were traders not crusaders, and it was Marco Polo's story far more than any other which captured the imagination and attention of Europe. Even so it was Mediterranean Europe, and in particular the seafarers of the Italian towns, who were interested. Europe north of the Alps had other things to think of in the fourteenth and fifteenth centuries when England and France were at grips in the Hundred Years' War. Even the Church lost its interest in the East after the overthrow of the missions in the late fourteenth century, and was more absorbed in the struggles of the Schism and in the settlement of its internal difficulties in the Councils than in the affairs of Asia. The knowledge of the East accumulated by its missionaries lay unused in the papal archives, and it was left to the discoverers and merchant adventurers of Portugal and Spain in the fifteenth and sixteenth centuries to prove the value of Marco Polo's stories, and to renew the direct contact of the West with the riches of India and China.

The effects of the Crusades on the economic and social life of Western Europe are, in the nature of the case, almost impossible to disentangle from the general process of growth of which these effects are but a part. To attribute to the Crusades the rise of the cities of Italy in particular, or of Western Europe as a whole, is to ignore the fact that the towns of the West had been steadily recovering for centuries before the Crusades began, and, even if that movement had never taken place, there is good reason to suppose that they would still have won their emancipation from feudalism, have created their organs of local self-government, and developed their trade with its system of internal organisation. Gibbon writes: "The estates of the barons were dissipated and their race was often extinguished in these costly and perilous expeditions. Their poverty extorted from their pride those charters of freedom which unlocked the fetters of the slave, secured the farm of the peasant and the shop of the artificer, and gradually restored a substance and a soul to the most numerous and useful part of the community. The conflagration which destroyed the tall and barren trees of the forest gave air and scope to the vegetation of the smaller and nutritive plants of the soil." The rhetorical method of writing history is a pleasant one, but we are no longer permitted the untroubled serenity of the classical historian.

It is, indeed, impossible to set down any general effects which the Crusades had upon feudal society as a whole. Many of the "tall and barren trees of the forest" were destroyed in the East, and much of the martial energies of the nobles of the West found an outlet in crusading less destructive of civil peace than they could have found at home. By so much the task of kingship, especially in France, was lightened, the growth of the central power at the expense of feudalism made easier. The Counts of Toulouse, of whom four in less than fifty years died in the East, provide an example of the failure of a house to consolidate its fiefs because of a too passionate love of crusading. So also the lands of the house of Bouillon passed into the female line for a similar reason, to be absorbed by marriage into other fiefs. Yet the total extinction of a noble house was not a common event, and the most striking example of the union of a great fief with the royal demesne in twelfth-century France—a union which, in the event, was only temporary—was solely due to the failure of male heirs to the house of Aquitaine and had nothing to do with the Crusades. The charters of liberties obtained by the French and English towns cannot, for the most part, be attributed to the Crusades, though exception should be made for Richard Coeur-de-Lion's great auction of liberties before his departure to the Holy Land. Yet, at the most, such charters were only ante-dated by the necessities of their grantors. They could not exist had not towns been quietly growing during the eleventh and twelfth centuries, had not groups of merchants, or of tenants acquiring a mercantile character, formed themselves to purchase exemption from feudal dues. The Crusades in some cases certainly provided opportunities for the towns; they did not create the civic demand for "liberties."

So too, in the general question of the relation of the Crusades to the development of European commerce, it is impossible to make the progress of the twelfth and thirteenth centuries depend upon them. The case is best illustrated with reference to the Italian cities, in particular to Venice, Genoa, and Pisa. It has been very clearly shewn, as for example by Heyd, that before the Crusades began the products of the East, silk, sugar, and spices especially, were reaching Europe not only by land from what is now Russia but even more by way of Italy. Here, before the First Crusade, Amalfi and Venice were the two chief agents in supplying Western Europe with the Eastern luxuries which her developing civilisation led her to desire. Amalfi fell out of the race with the Norman Conquest of South Italy and the attempt of the Norman rulers to regulate commerce too rigidly in the interests of politics. Venice therefore was left, at the period when the Crusades began, as the chief agent of the Levantine trade in Italy, and her position was rendered the more advantageous by the large concessions in Constantinople and the Eastern Empire granted in 1082 by Alexius Comnenus when Amalfi had fallen under the power of Robert Guiscard. But this position was not to remain unchallenged. The crusaders, as they poured into Italy for the journey to Palestine, sought transport and maritime assistance not only from Venice but from Genoa and Pisa as well, while these two cities were not slow to perceive in the needs of the crusading hosts a source of profit to themselves, and in the conquests that might be made in Syria a means to obtain secure access to the trade between East and West. In the first three Crusades, and in the intervening years between them, Venice, Genoa, and Pisa all took an active part, not merely in trans-shipping crusaders but in the actual work of conquest. The Genoese were largely responsible for the capture of Arsūf, Caesarea, and Acre, the Pisans for that of Laodicea, the Venetians for that of Sidon and Tyre. Moreover, the diversion of the crusading effort to capture these towns, strategically sound as it was for defensive purposes, was dictated mainly by trading interests. All three cities received wide privileges both in the seaports and inland towns of all the crusading states of Syria, and they all benefited equally in one respect—that they had for almost a hundred years secure markets for their Eastern trade. Further, the crusaders who had settled in Palestine depended upon the West for vital necessities, for armour, for horses and ships, for wine and woollen goods, and, above all, for reinforcements to maintain their position. Pilgrims flocked to see in security the newly-recovered Holy City, and a very large proportion of all the carrying-trade for this flow of people to and from Palestine was in the hands of the Italian cities. More shipping was required and was built; every year Venice sent two fleets to Syria; Genoa and Pisa did the same. The rivalry of the Eastern Empire, the necessity for dependence upon Constantinople as a market, was almost removed, and there can be no question but that the Crusades brought to all three cities in the twelfth century a steady increase of prosperity and wealth. Statistics, unhappily, do not exist by which this increase can be measured, but one event stands out as evidence of the height of power and success to which the events of the twelfth century had brought Venice.

The Fourth Crusade could not have been planned by the Venetians of 1100 with any hope of success. Yet in 1204 they were able to provide the naval equipment for a force consisting of "4500 horses, 9000 squires, ...4500 knights, and 20,000 sergeants on foot," to pay the expenses of the whole, and to overturn the Empire which it had been the primary object of the First, as it was professedly the object of the Fourth, Crusade to protect. In the division of the spoils which followed the capture of Constantinople Venice received her reward. One-third of the great city itself fell beneath her sovereignty, and all the ports and islands of the Eastern Empire were secured for her commerce to the exclusion of her rivals. It is true that Venice was unable to retain her monopoly intact, for the Genoese and Pisans intrigued with the representatives of the deposed Emperors at Nicaea and received concessions in the ports which remained under their control; but this did not prevent the Venetians from reaping a rich harvest from their new dominions during the thirteenth century. Venice took then a position of superiority over the other Italian cities which she never lost, even when the Latin Empire had fallen and the kingdom of Jerusalem had perished with the fall of Acre. And, as the prosperity of Venice depended on the development in north-western Europe of markets for the products of the East which she supplied, the Crusades must be regarded as an important cause of the development of the chain of commercial republics along the Rhine Valley into Flanders, as also of the increased prosperity of Marseilles and the towns of southern France. Undoubtedly the more constant intercourse with the East aroused a new demand for the luxuries which it alone could supply, and the silks, sugar, and spices which flowed through Damascus and Egypt became the indispensable necessities of the nobles and their ladies, to say nothing of the rich bourgeois, of France, Germany, and England. On the other hand it is impossible to claim that the Crusades introduced these Eastern products to the West; nor must it be forgotten that the development of creative manufacture in the towns of Western Europe had begun before the Crusades started, and that, without the wealth produced in steadily increasing quantities by the gildsmen of the West, Europe would have had no means of purchasing the Eastern wares to satisfy the craving which the experience of crusades and pilgrims taught.

If an indeterminate answer must be given to the question "What effects had the Crusades on the economic life of Western Europe?" it is equally difficult to define their relation either to the growth of a sense of nationality in the Western nations or to the great development of Western thought which took place during the twelfth and thirteenth centuries. The term "nationality" is not easy to define, but, by the end of the period with which this volume deals, " Frenchmen " had a feeling of their difference from "Englishmen," "Germans," or "Italians," more acute than at the beginning of the Crusades. That, like other international movements, the Crusades accentuated the sense of national unity and even of a natural hostility between nations is, à *priori*, likely enough and, so early as 1146, evidence of this can be found in the account of the Second Crusade written by Odo of Deuil, who certainly nourished a hearty dislike for both Greeks and Germans as such. His dislike for the Greeks may have been stimulated by their heretical opinions, though it is rather their excessive flattery and their guile that appear to have aroused him; at any rate no such explanation will account for his hard sayings about the Germans. "Nostris etiam erant importabiles Alemanni," he says, and goes on to give instances of the trouble created by King Conrad's host for the French who followed after, and of the direct affronts offered to the French by German soldiers, finishing his complaint by saying, "Thus the Germans, going before us, disturbed everything; so that the Greeks fled from our peaceful army."[1] Further evidence tending in the same direction may be seen in the national name and character of the Teutonic Order, founded in 1190, which are in striking contrast to those of the older international Orders of the Hospitallers or Templars. Yet it is not often that this note of national separateness and rivalry is sounded in the chronicles of the Crusades, and the development of "nationality" can only be in part attributed to the rivalries which arose in the mixed hosts of Christendom travelling towards or engaged in the Holy War.

The coincidence of the thirteenth-century "Renaissance" with the period of the Crusades is striking, and it would be rash to deny any share in the outburst of intellectual energy which marks the thirteenth century to the new ideas and broadened outlook of those who, having gone on crusade, had seen the world of men and things in a way to which the society of the tenth and eleventh centuries was unaccustomed. But it must be admitted that a man may travel much and yet see little, may preserve intact the narrowness of vision with which he set out. St Louis, as Joinville shews him to us, or Joinville himself, was not intellectually changed by his crusading. And when we examine the great motive force of the thirteenth century "Revival of Learning" it is Aristotle from whom the impulse proceeded, and Aristotle first brought back to the West by way of Spain and the Moorish versions of his works. It is true that, so early as 1128, James of Venice translated into Latin some of the works of Aristotle, but the greater impulse to the absorption of Greek philosophy by the Western Church came from the study and translation of the Arabic versions of the Aristotelian writings and the commentaries upon those writings made by the scholars of Musulman Spain, in particular by Avicenna and Averroës. In the thirteenth century, however, the conquest of the Eastern Empire by the crusaders of 1204, and the discontent felt by Western scholars with the versions of Aristotle which had come to them at second hand, led to the direct translation of Aristotle's works from the Greek, as well as to Latin versions of other Greek writings. Thus Robert Grosseteste translated the *Analytica Posteriora* and is said to have written a commentary upon the *Nicomachean Ethics*, while later in the century St Thomas Aquinas, refusing to rely upon the faulty Arabic versions, was able to find in William of Moerbeke, Archbishop of Corinth from 1275 to 1286, a Greek scholar capable of translating the whole of Aristotle's writings from the original Greek into tortured Latin. In this task William of Moerbeke may have received some assistance from another

---

[1] MPL. CLXXXV, *S. Bernardi Clarae-Vallensis opera*, IV, col. 1217.

member of the Dominican order, Henry of Brabant, and, in view of the enormous influence exerted by the theological writings of St Thomas, it is at least interesting to be able to point to these translations as the source upon which he relied in the task of incorporating the thought of Aristotle in his great *Summa Theologiae*. Yet in general the course of the great movement of medieval thought which began soon after the year 1000 gives little evidence of having been affected by the Crusades. To them indeed we owe the work of the greatest medieval historian, William of Tyre, and, on the purely literary side with which we cannot here deal, their influence was profound in the development of vernacular romances. But the growth of an articulated system of philosophy, theology, and politics began before the Crusades, and went on steadily throughout their course with no more assistance from that movement than was given by such improvements in the Aristotelian texts as we have already mentioned.

It remains to consider the military results of the Crusades upon the West. Their influence on the improvement of the art of war and military architecture must be left to be described in special chapters in a future volume. With regard, however, to the ever-wavering frontier of East and West, it is clear that the foundation of the Latin States of Syria during the First Crusade and the course of the twelfth century checked for the moment the Muslim advance upon Constantinople which had threatened its very existence. But against the assistance rendered to the Eastern Empire in the First Crusade must be set its overthrow in the Fourth—a blow from which, despite its revival at the end of the thirteenth century, it never wholly recovered. Whether therefore it is fair to attribute to the Crusades the delay of nearly three hundred years in the Turkish advance into the Balkan lands is a problem perhaps incapable of decision, though the diversion of Muslim effort to the Holy Land probably outweighs by much the disintegrating effect of the Fourth Crusade and the foundation and fall of the Latin Empire. And on this view the Crusades must be given credit for providing Western Europe with time to consolidate itself into centralised national States, far better able than those of the eleventh century to defend themselves against the renewed Muslim advance when it came in the sixteenth century. Nor, in that renewed struggle between East and West, must the gallant defence of Rhodes and Cyprus, and later of Malta, by the crusading Knights of St John, be forgotten.

It was however another and younger order of crusading Knights which left the deepest mark upon the history of Europe. Founded in 1190, during the Third Crusade, by certain citizens of Bremen and Lübeck as a hospital, and raised in 1198 to the rank of an order of Knights, the Teutonic Order under its great Master, Hermann von Salza, transferred its energies from the Holy Land to the forcible conversion of infidels nearer home. Already in East Prussia the Knights of the Sword of

Livonia were engaged in the difficult task of converting the mixed heathen population of Letts, Slavs, and Wends to Christianity, and the Teutonic Knights, after absorbing this order in 1237, carried on the same work with great energy and striking success for the next eighty years. They founded Thorn, Königsberg, Marienberg—to which in 1309 they transferred their headquarters—and finally, in 1311, they captured Dantzig. They allied themselves with the Hanseatic League, and sought by every means to develop trade in the dominions won by their swords. To their activities in the thirteenth and early fourteenth centuries is due the Germanisation of East Prussia, as to their weakness in the fifteenth century, to their defeat at Tannenberg and the recovery of Dantzig and the mouth of the Vistula by the Polish kingdom, is due the problem of giving Poland access to the sea which has cost so much anxiety since the Treaty of Versailles. The junction of the lands of the Teutonic Order with those of the Hohenzollern house at the Reformation brought Prussia into the affairs of Western Europe.

Yet, despite the tangible conquests of the Teutonic Order in north-eastern Germany and, what should not be forgotten, the assistance given by such Orders as those of Calatrava, Santiago, and Alcántara to the Christian monarchs who reconquered Spain from the Moors, it is perhaps in the realm of ideas that we must seek for the most permanent influence of the crusading movement. Just as it was itself the product of a Christendom that at the outset of the struggle felt itself morally united, so it has in turn been the exemplar in later times of many movements undertaken on a smaller scale indeed, and using the weapons of reason rather than of war. Never since the fall of Acre has " Christendom " acted as a united whole; for never since has it enjoyed unity. Yet the memory of the failure in which the Crusades ended has only served to heighten the value of the ideal which created them and won, especially in the First Crusade, all their success. Our modern use of the word "Crusade" is in fact a testimony of our belief in the effectiveness of action possible where large groups of men share a common ideal, and the grounds of that belief are to be found in the events narrated in this volume.

CHAPTER X.

GERMANY, 1125–1152.

The Saxon wars, the imperial struggle with the Papacy, had brought to the front a new nobility. The Hohenstaufen, the Wittelsbachs, the Wettins emerge to replace the families which, in consequence of the wars, had become extinct. In like case Lothar, the son of a petty count, one Gebhard of Supplinburg, rose to the first rank among German princes. By his marriage he acquired a pre-eminent position in Saxony; for his wife Richenza was the heiress of Henry of Nordheim and Ekbert of Meissen. In 1106, on the death of Magnus, Duke of Saxony, the last of the Billungs, he succeeded to the duchy and to the power which that family had sedulously built up since the time of Otto the Great. During the reign of the Emperor Henry V, Lothar as Duke of Saxony had been conspicuous for his activity in extending his influence in the Wendish districts and for his constant opposition to the Salian house. In 1125 he was raised to the throne.

His election marks a change in the German kingship. Though always elective in theory, owing to the strength of the Saxon and Salian rulers it had been rendered in practice hereditary. At the diet of Forchheim in 1077 the German princes passed a resolution, accepted by the Pope, in favour of spontaneous election[1]. Effect was given to this resolution in 1125. Henry V died childless, his nephew, Frederick of Swabia, was passed over, and Lothar without a shadow of hereditary claim—his pedigree is lost beyond one generation—won the throne by right of election. During the twelfth century the elective principle becomes firmly established. Lothar is succeeded by his rival Conrad, and Conrad's son is passed over in favour of his nephew. The attempt of the Hohenstaufen Emperors to restore the principle of hereditary succession meets with very limited success. The Electoral College of princes is gradually forming itself and establishing its control.

It is fortunate that of an election so important in the history of the German kingship a detailed and contemporary account has come down to us[2]. Immediately after the completion of the obsequies of the late Emperor, writs of summons were issued to the princes to attend an electoral council at Mayence on the feast of St Bartholomew (24 August).

[1] Bruno, *De Bello Saxonico*, SGUS, ed. Wattenbach, p. 67.

[2] The author of the *Narratio de Electione Lotharii* (MGH, *Script.* XII, 509–512) is unknown, but he is presumed to have been one of the clergy present at the election from the diocese of Salzburg, and a member of the extreme Church party.

The gathering was a large one[1]; it included, besides the German princes and their vassals, two papal legates and Suger, Abbot of St Denis, the famous minister of the French King Louis VI.

The natural choice would have been Frederick of Swabia. He was nearly related to the Salian house, he was executor of the late king, heir to his private estates, guardian of his widow Matilda, the daughter of Henry I of England, to whose care were entrusted the imperial *insignia*; he was well qualified by age—being then thirty-five years old—and by his personal character and attainments. The head of the house of Hohenstaufen, he was possessed of considerable private wealth; in addition to his own duchy of Swabia, he could command the interest of Eastern Franconia, over which his younger brother Conrad exercised ducal powers. But he was out of sympathy with the Church party; and the Church party was strong under the able leadership of Archbishop Adalbert of Mayence. Already before the meeting at Mayence Archbishop Frederick of Cologne had dispatched an embassy to Charles, Count of Flanders, inviting him to stand for election; the count however declined the offer. Archbishop Adalbert was more successful. His candidate Lothar commended himself to the Church dignitaries on the ground of his enmity to the Salian house, to the lay princes because he was advanced in years[2], destitute of a male heir, and therefore unable to found a dynasty to deprive them of their power of election.

At Mayence the business of selection was delegated to a committee of forty[3], ten representatives from each tribe, Bavaria, Swabia, Franconia, and Saxony. Three names were submitted: Frederick, Leopold, Margrave of Austria, and Lothar. From this moment the skilful diplomacy of Archbishop Adalbert comes into play. He had already, by means not too reputable, if we are to believe Bishop Otto, succeeded in persuading the Empress to surrender the *insignia*; now, by addressing awkward questions to the candidates, he managed to place Frederick in a dilemma.

---

[1] It is often stated, on the authority of Ordericus Vitalis, xii, 43, that 60,000 persons were present at the election. So *e.g.* Giesebrecht, *Kaiserzeit*, iv, 7; Zeller, *Histoire d'Allemagne*, iv, 9. This figure was however commonly used to denote a large indefinite number, and very frequently by Ordericus, who *e.g.* estimates the attendance at the famous meeting at Salisbury in 1086 at 60,000 (vii, 11), and reckons also the number of knight's fees in England at 60,000 (iv, 7). The usage may be traced to the Babylonian numerical system; see Johannes Schmidt, *Die Urheimat der Indogermanen und das europäisch. Zahlsystem*, p. 46 sq. in *Abhandlungen der Akad. d. Wiss. zu Berlin*, 1890.

[2] Probably fifty years of age; he was born according to the *Ann. Disibodi* a few days before the battle of the Unstrut, 9 June 1075, at which his father was killed. Cf. *Neu. Arch.* xliii (1922), p. 641.

[3] Wichert, *Die Wahl Lothars*, FDG, xii, 96 sq., and xvi, 374 sqq. and Schirrmacher, *Entstehung des Kurfürstentums*, p. 8, hold that the committee was composed of only ten members in all, that in consideration of the limited number of princes qualified to vote at the preliminary election the number forty was too large. The committee of forty is however generally accepted. See *e.g.* Bernhardi, p. 31 sq

Lothar and Leopold had first with unnecessary humility declined to come forward, and later agreed to abide by the decision of the electors. Frederick, on the other hand, "ready to be chosen but not to choose a king," refused to give a direct answer to the question whether he would submit to the result of election; he must, he said, consult his followers; and he left the council. By this action he lost the confidence of the assembled princes; he appeared to deny the doctrine of free election and to set his reliance on hereditary right. The question was settled by the turbulent mob of Saxons, who broke up the deliberations of the council by their shoutings and acclamation of Lothar as king. He was raised on the shoulders of the enthusiastic crowd amidst a tumult only calmed by the intervention of the papal legate. The Bavarians refused to comply with this irregular ending of the proceedings in the absence of their duke. But their duke's son was already the affianced husband of Lothar's only child; there was no danger from that quarter. The Duke, Henry the Black, hurried to the scene, and Lothar III was duly elected on 30 August. A fortnight later, 13 September, he was solemnly crowned at Aix-la-Chapelle.

The opening years of the reign were marked by widespread unrest. In Bohemia, in Lorraine, even in his own dukedom of Saxony, the authority of the new king was disputed or openly disregarded. In Swabia and Franconia the party of the Hohenstaufen was in the ascendant. Duke Frederick had eventually done belated homage to Lothar, but almost immediately quarrelled with him over the issue of the Salian inheritance. After his coronation the king proceeded to Ratisbon, where he held a diet in November. To the assembled princes he put the question whether estates that had been confiscated from outlaws or had been acquired by exchange with imperial lands should be regarded as imperial or private property. The problem was raised on general grounds, but its real application was obvious. The Salian Emperors had largely increased their territorial position by both these means, and the lands so acquired were included in the Hohenstaufen inheritance. The diet decided against Frederick; he refused to give up the fiefs in question, was found guilty of high treason at the Christmas court at Strasbourg, and at Goslar in January 1126 was placed under the ban of the Empire.

Lothar's position, by no means strong, was sensibly weakened by the conspicuous failure of his first military enterprise. It arose over the question of the succession to the Bohemian dukedom, in which, with singular lack of judgment, he supported the weaker claims of Otto of Olmütz against those of the popular candidate, Soběslav, a brother of the late King Vladislav I (*ob.* April 1125). Otto appealed, not in vain, for Lothar's assistance at the diet of Ratisbon. In midwinter the king crossed the Erzgebirge into Bohemia with a small band of Saxons. Wearied by long marches through the snow-covered mountains and exhausted by lack of provisions, they emerged into the valley of Kulm to find a large force of Bohemians under Soběslav awaiting their coming (February 1126). The advanced troops were all but annihilated by the overwhelming numbers of the enemy; and Lothar had no choice but to make terms. The death of his protégé on the battle-field facilitated matters, and Lothar found in his conqueror a submissive and loyal ally. Soběslav recognised Lothar's election, did homage for his dukedom, and in after time proved his loyalty by signal services in the field.

The king could not press forward the punitive expedition against Frederick of Hohenstaufen which had been arranged for Whitsuntide 1126 until his own position in Germany was more secure. The uselessness of doing so had been proved by an abortive campaign in Swabia in the autumn of 1126. The prospect brightened a little with the death in December of Henry the Black, Duke of Bavaria, who shortly before had withdrawn from the world to spend his closing years in the monastery of Weingarten. His son and successor Henry, called the Proud, was young and energetic, the heir to enormous wealth, the chosen husband of Gertrude, Lothar's only child. His inheritance comprised, in addition to the duchy of Bavaria, the greater part of the private property of his family in Bavaria and extensive possessions round Lüneburg in Saxony which passed to him through his mother Wulfhild, daughter of Magnus Billung. The rest of the inheritance in Bavaria and Swabia fell to Henry's younger brother Welf VI[1]. The projected marriage, which was in after years to upset the balance of ducal power in Germany by the union of Saxony and Bavaria in the hands of one man more powerful almost than the king himself, was carried out on the borders of Swabia and Bavaria near Augsburg on 29 May 1127. The immediate result was that Lothar could now in co-operation with Henry of Bavaria prosecute the war against the Hohenstaufen with vigour and with fair prospects of success. His position was further improved by his alliance in the same year with Conrad of Zähringen. In March William, Count of Burgundy (Franche Comté), was murdered. His inheritance fell naturally to his cousin Rainald, who immediately occupied the lands without waiting to be formally invested by the king. Lothar took advantage of this remissness and granted the rectorship of Burgundy to Conrad of Zähringen who was also connected with the late count, thereby not only gaining a new ally for himself but also detaching a strong supporter from the party of the Hohenstaufen.

Yet the tide of events still went against the king. Nuremberg successfully resisted his attack. For ten weeks the armies of Lothar, supported by the levies of Henry and Soběslav from Bavaria and Bohemia, invested the town. The Bohemian allies ravaged the country, burnt the

[1] There were also claims upon lands in Italy through Azzo, Marquess of Este, who married Cunegunda, sister of the childless Welf III. Henry the Proud and Welf VI were their great-grandsons. But these claims were not made good till 1154.

churches, and so incensed the population that they had to be sent home. At last Conrad of Hohenstaufen, lately returned from the Holy Land, advanced with fresh troops for its relief. Without risking a battle, Lothar withdrew first to Bamberg, then to Würzburg, whither he was pursued by Conrad, who however contented himself with celebrating a tournament at the very gates of the town as a mark of his disdain and returned, as he had come, to Nuremberg.

The efforts of the Hohenstaufen had met with such success that they now purposed to wrest the crown itself from Lothar. Frederick waived his claim of seniority in favour of his brother Conrad, who was duly elected king by his supporters on 18 December 1127. Spires declared for him and drove out its bishop; but this was the last triumph of his party. The election of Conrad was the turning-point in the conflict. By it not only the German kingship but also the German Church was assailed; the whole weight of the ecclesiastical power was thrown into the scale on the side of the legitimate king. Realising that the odds against him in Germany were too heavy, Conrad, early in the year 1128, crossed the Septimer to try his fortunes in Italy.

The Rhenish town of Spires now became the centre of the Hohenstaufen resistance. After a siege of nearly three months the burghers asked for terms, agreed to give hostages, and made promises for their future loyalty (November 1128). Lothar was now free to attend to business in other parts of his kingdom. Lorraine was hostile to him; a rising of the citizens of Aix-la-Chapelle during his stay in the town in January 1127 was only pacified by liberal concessions; Godfrey the Bearded, Duke of Lower Lorraine, supported the pretensions of the Hohenstaufen. The duke was drawn into a dispute over the inheritance of Charles the Good, Count of Flanders, who in March 1127 had been murdered in the church of St Donatian at Bruges, on the side of William Clito the son of Duke Robert of Normandy. While he was thus engaged, Lothar seized his duchy and handed it over to Walram, Count of Limburg, the son of Henry, Godfrey's predecessor in the dukedom. Godfrey soon succeeded in recovering the greater part of his possessions, and the only result of Lothar's intervention was the further dismemberment of the old Lotharingian duchy.

In the meanwhile Henry of Bavaria remained in the south to cope with Frederick of Swabia. The latter was keeping Lent at the monastery of Zwifalten on the banks of the Danube when Henry happened to be visiting his family estates in the same neighbourhood. The opportunity of finding Frederick unaware of his presence and with but a few companions was too much for his sense of honour. Coming one night to the monastery with a body of armed followers, he set fire to the dwelling-rooms of the monks in which he rightly imagined Frederick to be. The latter escaped from the flames with the help of the monks and took refuge in the church tower. Henry surrounded the church, broke in the doors, even disturbed the brethren at their prayers with threats of death, but all to no effect.

Frederick, safe in his tower, defied his sacrilegious assailant, who not only had to retire in disgust but had to pay for his scandalous behaviour by forfeiting the advocacy of the monastery. The Hohenstaufen still had a strong position in Franconia and Swabia; there was yet hope in the Rhine country in spite of the submission of Spires. The insincerity of the promises made to Lothar on the occasion of its surrender was revealed when Frederick proceeded there with the view to making it again the centre of resistance. The townsmen readily threw over the king for the duke. The fortifications were strengthened, the garrison increased; Frederick himself after completing his arrangements departed for Swabia, leaving the conduct of affairs in the city to his wife Agnes of Saarbruck. In June 1129 Lothar appeared before the walls. Month after month the siege dragged on without either side shewing signs of giving in. At last the king in despair sent an urgent appeal for help to his son-in-law, who was engaged in besieging a rebellious subject, Frederick of Bogen, in his castle of Falkenstein. Henry, leaving the siege in charge of his sister Sophia, responded immediately to the royal summons with a body of six hundred Bavarian knights. The joint strength of Bavaria and Saxony turned the scale. From midsummer till past Christmas the townsmen, under the gallant leadership of Agnes, held out in spite of every hardship and privation. Eventually deprived of all hope of relief, for a force brought to their aid by Frederick was driven off, they submitted and on the feast of Epiphany 1130 opened their gates to the king.

With the capture of Spires the opposition in the Upper Rhineland was crushed. Before long Nuremberg, the chief strong-point of resistance, fell before Lothar's attack; and with it went all hopes of success for the party of the Hohenstaufen in Germany. In Italy too Conrad's initial success was not long maintained. Notwithstanding his excommunication by Honorius II he was welcomed at Milan, crowned by its archbishop at Monza and again in the cathedral of St Ambrose with the Iron Crown of Lombardy. But this was the limit of his achievement. An attempt to acquire the possessions of the late Countess Matilda ended in failure the towns of Lombardy which had at first received him declared against him; his supporters one by one abandoned his cause and left him almost alone. In despair he gave up trying to establish himself in Italy and re-crossed the Alps (1130), only to find that in Germany also the family cause was as good as lost.

Yet years dragged on before the brothers admitted defeat. Their opponents were too busily occupied with other matters to press the issue to a conclusion. The petty quarrels and rivalries of ambitious princes kept Saxony in ceaseless turmoil. Albert of Ballenstädt and Henry of Groitsch, Conrad of Wettin and Herman of Winzenburg, each strove to increase his own power at the other's expense. The murder in one of these feuds of a trusted follower of the king, one Burchard of Loccum, by Herman of Winzenburg, Landgrave of Thuringia, called for Lothar's intervention in the affairs of his old duchy. Herman was found guilty of high treason in December 1130, and sentenced to the confiscation of his fiefs. Before another year was out Albert the Bear for some similar offence was deprived of the East Mark. The rebellious town of Halle suffered the severest of punishments. It fell before Lothar's assault, its inhabitants were put to death, mutilated, or in some cases allowed their safety on payment of heavy fines. By such stringent methods as these Lothar restored the peace of Saxony.

The fate of Augsburg affords another example of the stern measures employed by the king to suppress local risings, but in this instance he had less justification for his action. On the journey to Italy in August 1132, a dispute arose in the market between the townsfolk and the soldiers and quickly spread through the whole city. The king, suspecting treason, ordered the troops to punish the burghers. From noon till night the town was in a tumult; men, women, and children were massacred in the streets and houses; churches and monasteries were broken into, plundered, and burnt. As on previous occasions the Bohemian troops in the royal army were conspicuous for their barbarity and excess. In a state of complete desolation Augsburg was left as a warning to other towns not to risk the king's displeasure.

During Lothar's absence in Italy (September 1132–August 1133) Henry of Bavaria remained in Germany to deal with the Hohenstaufen. But rebellions in his own duchy kept him too busily occupied to effect a decision. The appointment of Henry of Wolfratshausen in August 1132 to the see of Ratisbon against the wishes of the king and himself led to serious trouble. The bishop, aided by his advocate, the duke's old enemy Frederick of Bogen, made stubborn resistance. For some months fighting continued, the armies plundering and burning after the manner of medieval warfare round Ratisbon and Wolfratshausen, a castle near the site of the present town of Munich. At last the two armies, the bishop's strengthened by the adhesion of Leopold of Austria, faced each other on the banks of the Isar to bring matters to a final issue. At the critical moment Otto of Wittelsbach, the count palatine, intervened as mediator and reconciled the contending parties.

It was not till August 1134 that the Emperor and his son-in-law were free to deal decisively with the Hohenstaufen. The Swabian town of Ulm had now become the centre of resistance. After a short siege Henry captured the town, which was thereupon almost totally destroyed by the devastations practised by the Bavarian soldiers. Lothar had in the meanwhile overrun Swabia without opposition. The brothers were in desperate straits: their castles were captured; their supporters deserted. Frederick was the first to realise the futility of further resistance; he approached the Empress Richenza and begged her to intercede on his behalf. At Fulda towards the end of October the reconciliation was effected. The terms of his submission, settled at the crowded diet of

Bamberg (March 1135), were favourable in the extreme: he was freed from excommunication, and received back his dukedom and his possessions; for his own part he had only to promise to accompany the Emperor on the Italian campaign which had been planned for the next year—a condition imposed no doubt at the request of St Bernard who was present at the court in the papal interest. Conrad held back for some months longer, but finally made his peace with the Emperor at Mühlhausen in September under the same lenient conditions as those imposed upon his brother.

Lothar owed his crown to the support given him by the leaders of the Church hierarchy. Did he reward their confidence by granting on that occasion definite concessions? The question is crucial and controversial. That some settlement was reached seems clear, but its precise nature cannot be determined. We have no reliable information. A famous passage[1] formulates a position, but it is more likely the position at which the leaders of the party aimed than the one actually attained[2]. More profitable results may be found from the evidence of Lothar's actual relations with the Church during his reign. After his election we are told he neither received nor exacted homage from the spirituality, contenting himself merely with the oath of fealty; and even this he remitted in the case of Conrad, Archbishop of Salzburg, in deference to the latter's scruples in the matter. The most important change was with regard to the royal presence at elections. Here again Lothar bent to the wishes of the Church party and refrained from exercising the right granted him by the Concordat of Worms[3]. Two elections took place within a month of his accession—Eichstätt and Magdeburg—and in neither case was he present. Indeed there is scarcely an instance during the first five years of his reign of his disturbing episcopal elections by his presence[4]. The ecclesiastical princes had no cause to complain of the conduct of the man they had set upon the throne. Lothar even if he wished it could not afford to quarrel with the Church; but to support the orthodox Church party was natural to him. As Duke of Saxony he had been bred up to

---

[1] *Narratio de Electione Lotharii*, MGH, *Script.* XII, c. 6.

[2] See Hauck, *Kirchengeschichte Deutschlands*, IV, p. 118, n. 2. The passage in the *Narratio* mentions three points: 1. Free election without the presence of the king; 2. Investiture with the *regalia* by the sceptre after consecration; 3. The right of the king to exact the oath of allegiance. As the citation of the wording of a document this breaks down on the second point; for the old practice of investiture with the *regalia* before consecration continued to prevail.

[3] Or were the concessions granted in the Concordat by Calixtus II only intended for Henry V personally, and not for his successors? There is no mention of the latter in the document, and Otto of Freising (*Chron.* VII, 16) expressly tells us that at Rome it was interpreted in this way "hoc sibi soli et non successoribus datum dicunt Romani." See D. Schäfer, *Zur Beurteilung des Wormser Konkordates*, in *Abhandlungen der Akad. d. Wiss. zu Berlin*, 1905.

[4] See Hauck, *op. cit.* p. 128, n. 1; also for the whole question Bernheim, *Lothar III und das Wormser Concordat*, Strasbourg, 1874.

the traditional policy of opposition to the anti-hierarchical Salians; and this policy he maintained as king.

When Honorius II died in February 1130 and the two factions in Rome each chose its own candidate to fill the papal throne, Lothar was faced with the necessity of making a momentous decision. Though not as yet crowned Emperor, the long attachment of the imperial title to the King of Germany gave Lothar the unquestioned position of temporal ruler of Christendom. The rival Popes Anacletus II and Innocent II, the one master of Rome, the other a refugee in France, each appealed anxiously to him for recognition. Each had his supporters in Germany. Anacletus found an advocate of his pretentions in Adalbero, Archbishop of Bremen, who happened to be in Rome at the critical moment; Innocent saw his claims upheld by the most advanced Churchmen, represented by Conrad of Salzburg, Norbert, and Otto of Bamberg. But Lothar hesitated. Perhaps he feared a split in the ranks of the Church party on whose support he relied so much. It was not till Louis VI of France at Étampes, under the influence of Bernard, had declared for Innocent that Lothar, urged also by Innocent's legate Walter of Ravenna, consented to take action. He summoned a meeting at Würzburg in October to discuss the question. Only sixteen bishops presented themselves, but the sixteen were unanimous for Innocent. Lothar accepted the decision without hesitation, and immediately sent Conrad of Salzburg and Ekbert of Münster to carry Germany's recognition to the Pope in France.

At Innocent's suggestion a personal interview between Pope and king was arranged; Liège near the French frontier was chosen as a convenient meeting place for both parties. Thither on 22 March 1131 came Innocent accompanied by thirteen cardinals, a large number of French bishops, and the indispensable Bernard. Lothar received him with due humility; he performed the office of groom for the pontiff when he dismounted, signifying by his act that he claimed to be but the servant of the Bishop of Rome; he made promises to enter Italy to destroy the invaders of the Holy See. But these cordial relations were almost upset at the very meeting which had given them birth. Lothar, it seems, raised the vexed question of episcopal elections; he evidently wished to recede from the concessions he had made at the time of his accession, to revive the royal influence over elections, in short to claim those privileges which the Concordat had granted to the Crown. A quarrel was prevented by the eloquence of Bernard. It is impossible to say whether any understanding was reached. But a change of attitude is perceptible in Lothar's dealings with the Church during the year following: he appears to have tried to exert some control over elections to bishoprics[1]; but the Church party

---

[1] Notably in the cases of Adalbero of Münsterol to the archbishopric of Trèves at Easter 1131, and of Henry of Wolfratshausen to the see of Ratisbon 19 August 1132. See Hauck, *op. cit.* IV, p. 151 sq.

resented his action so strongly that rather than quarrel he tacitly relinquished his pretensions.

The relations with the Pope continued to be friendly. In August 1132 Lothar carried out his promised campaign in Italy to end the schism, and on 4 June 1133 at the Lateran received as his reward the imperial crown. Again Lothar took occasion to raise the crucial subject of episcopal elections, and, in spite of loud protests from the Gregorian party in Germany, obtained concessions contained in a document dated 8 June 1133 which amounted to a confirmation to himself of the rights allowed to the Emperor in the Worms Concordat[1]. We should expect to find a complete reversal of policy in consequence. Nothing of the sort is perceptible. Lothar too well realised the value of the Church support; he used his power with a refinement of tact; he was often present at elections but his presence was scarcely felt. The settlement at the Lateran, which came so near to disturbing the peaceful relations between Church and State, in practice made little or no change in Lothar's attitude of conciliatory friendship towards the Church. The reign of Lothar from the point of view of Church politics marks the consummation of the victory of the hierarchy.

Throughout his reign we see Lothar, with an energy surprising in a man of his age, busily occupied in a succession of wars both at home and abroad: now he is campaigning against the Hohenstaufen, now settling contested claims to an inheritance, now fulfilling the supreme function of his imperial office by taking up arms against the enemies of the Church. But more enduring results matured from the work which alike as duke and king had always been nearest to his heart—the expansion of Germany eastwards, the revival of German influence, the re-establishment of the Christian religion and civilisation in the Wendish regions. In this sense an annalist is justified in describing Lothar as "the imitator and heir of the first Otto."[2] Since the tenth century nothing had been done, and even the districts then brought under German influence had since lapsed once more into paganism and barbarism. Lothar was ready to promote with his support and encouragement every enterprise which led in this direction. So Otto of Bamberg was able to make his second journey to Pomerania in 1127, and to see his work established on a firm basis. So also the Premonstratensians were able to pursue their missionary labours in Brandenburg with the co-operation of Albert of Ballenstädt, who in 1134 was enfeoffed with the North Mark as a reward for his services

---

[1] Nos igitur, maiestatem imperii nolentes minuere sed augere, imperatoriae dignitati(s plenitu)dinem tibi concedimus et debitas et canonicas consuetudines presentis scripti pagina confirmamus. Interdicimus autem, ne quisquam eorum, quos in Teut(onico) regno ad pontificatus honorem vel abbatiae regimen evocari contigerit, regalia usurpare vel invadere audeat, nisi eadem prius a tua (potes)tate deposcat, quod ex his, quae iure debet tibi, tuae magnificentiae faciat. MGH, *Const.* I, 168 sq and printed in Bernheim, *Quellen zur Geschichte des Investiturstreites*, II, p. 70.

[2] *Ann. Palidenses* sub anno 1125. MGH, *Script.* XVI, 77

in the Italian campaign, and on the death of Pribislav of Brandenburg without heirs received that district in addition. The priest Vicelin made progress in Holstein and the district about Lübeck.

It was the king's activities in Nordalbingia which involved him in the tangled affairs of Denmark. In 1131 the land was plunged into civil war by the murder of Canute, the son of the late King Eric, at the hands of Magnus, the son of the reigning King Niel. Canute was ruling in Schleswig, and had also been enfeoffed with the county of Wagria and the land of the Obotrites by Lothar. His firm hand kept the turbulent Wendish population under control; the country prospered; Christianity and civilisation began to revive. But the success of his rule and the uncertainty of the succession to the Danish throne brought upon him the jealousy of his cousin Magnus. His assassination was the result. Lothar could not allow the murderer of his vassal to go unpunished. In the summer of 1131 he advanced as far as the Eider, but being confronted there not only by the troops of Niel and Magnus but also by rebels "as innumerable as the sands of the sea," he wisely contented himself with a fine of four thousand marks and the homage of Magnus. Canute's Nordalbingian possessions were divided between two Wendish princes, Pribislav and Niclot, the former receiving Wagria and Polabia, the latter the land of the Obotrites. Lothar led his army across the Elbe and received homage from these princes. But with two Wendish chieftains, who owed only a nominal recognition to the German king, ruling the country, the development of civilisation which had been making rapid progress under Canute and his predecessor, Henry son of Gottschalk, received a set-back; every hindrance was placed in the way of Vicelin the German missionary, who brought his complaints and remedial proposal to the king. His suggestion was the erection of a strong fortress in a commanding position on a hill, Segeberg, near the banks of the Trave. To the disgust of Pribislav and Niclot, who saw in the plan the German yoke falling on them, the fortress was built and garrisoned with Saxons; with military protection behind him Vicelin was now able to proceed unhindered on his missionary enterprise.

The pacification of Denmark was likewise unsatisfactory. Niel and Magnus pursued Canute's brother Eric with relentless hostility. Driven from Schleswig he took refuge in Zealand, where even his brother Harold turned against him. The German settlers at Roeskilde on the island were murdered, mutilated, or expelled. It was clearly time for Lothar to intervene once more in the affairs of the north. But no campaign took place. Magnus presented himself at the Easter court at Halberstadt, indemnified himself for his misdeeds with large sums of money, and became the vassal of the German king. Nevertheless, while Niel and Magnus lived and reigned there could be no peace in Denmark. Their deaths, the one assassinated by the burghers of Schleswig, the other slain in battle, cleared the field. Eric, left in undisturbed possession, sent ambassadors to the court at Magdeburg at Whitsuntide 1135 and received the Emperor's recognition of his title.

At the same diet a quarrel, in which all the eastern neighbours of Germany—Hungary, Poland, and Bohemia—were involved, was also brought within sight of determination. It arose on the death of Stephen II of Hungary. His crown was disputed between his blind cousin Béla and his half-brother Boris; the former was supported by Soběslav of Bohemia, the latter by Boleslav of Poland. All the three countries engaged sent embassies to Lothar at Magdeburg. But the Emperor required Boleslav's personal attendance. He appeared at Merseburg in August, paid twelve years' arrears of tribute, and took the oath of allegiance; he was in some measure compensated by the acquisition of Pomerania and Rügen as fiefs of the German crown. An armistice was arranged between Bohemia and Poland pending a definite peace. Boris gave up the struggle, and Béla remained in secure possession of the Hungarian throne. To the Merseburg diet came also ambassadors from the Eastern Emperor John Comnenus and from the Doge of Venice offering help against their common enemy, Roger of Sicily. "So highly was the Emperor Lothar esteemed by kings and kingdoms," writes the chronicler, "that he was visited with gifts and embassies from Hungarians, Ruthenians, Danes, French, and many other nations. The Empire enjoyed peace and plenty, religion in the monasteries flourished, justice reigned, iniquity was repressed."[1]

The year 1135 was indeed a year of reckonings. It witnessed the results of a decade of masterful rule. Since the days of Henry III German prestige had not risen so high. It is marked by the ending of quarrels, by reconciliations, by peace. At the diet of Bamberg in March, which brought to a close the long-contested fight with the Hohenstaufen, a peace to last for ten years was proclaimed throughout Germany. This state of peace and prosperity the Emperor was only destined to enjoy for one year more on German soil. Towards the end of the summer of 1136 he crossed the Alps to take the field against Roger of Sicily. On his return in the following autumn he fell sick at Trent, and barely had sufficient strength to reach his own country. He died in a peasant's hut in the Tyrolese village of Breitenwang on 4 December 1137.

Lothar, by an arrangement with the Pope in 1133 had secured under certain conditions the allodial estates of the Countess Matilda for his son-in-law Henry the Proud[2]; he had also before his death granted him the duchy of Saxony and entrusted to him the imperial *insignia*, thereby designating him as his successor to the throne. With two dukedoms, with extensive possessions of his own in Germany and in Italy, with rich lands in Saxony by right of his wife, there was no man in Germany who could compete with Henry in power and wealth. Yet the Church faction which had raised Lothar to the throne disapproved of his

[1] *Ann. Saxo*, MGH, *Script.* vi, 770. [2] MHG, *Const.* i, 169.

appointed heir. On the Italian campaign he had neither shewn deference to their wishes nor a bearing likely to command their confidence. Still less was he acceptable to the lay princes; they feared his overwhelming power; they were above all anxious to avoid the foundation of a dynasty and to prove their right of election by passing over the man designated by the dead Emperor. Neither the spiritual nor the secular princes wanted the Welf candidate.

The see of Mayence was vacant; the Archbishop of Cologne, but just elected, had as yet not received the *pallium*; it was only natural in these circumstances that the direction of affairs should fall to the third great ecclesiastical prince, Archbishop Adalbero of Trèves, between whom and Henry a long-standing enmity subsisted. He summoned a meeting at Coblenz—a singularly unrepresentative gathering, for neither Saxons nor Bavarians were present—and at his proposal Conrad of Hohenstaufen, Lothar's rival, was chosen on 7 March 1138. Ten days later he was crowned at Aix-la-Chapelle by the papal legate. "A mere mockery of right and custom,"[1] yet however irregular the procedure may have been the result was popular. The princes of Germany flocked to the court at Bamberg on 22 May to do homage to the new king; Leopold of Austria, Conrad of Zähringen, Soběslav of Bohemia, even the widowed Empress Richenza, put in an appearance.

Duke Henry was absent from the court at Bamberg; a diet was fixed to assemble at Ratisbon, and there Henry appeared ready to deliver up the royal *insignia* in his keeping in return for confirmation in the possession of his two dukedoms[2]. But here lay the difficulty; apparently already at the diet of Bamberg Conrad had promised Saxony to Albert the Bear. The king disliked the notion of two dukedoms united in the hands of one man. He succeeded, nevertheless, by diplomacy, by vague promises no doubt, in extracting the *insignia* from Henry, and fixed a meeting at Augsburg for a final settlement. But here again no agreement was reached. Conrad, fearing Henry's threatening attitude, left for Würzburg, where the duke was put under the ban (July 1138). Saxony was bestowed upon Albert; Bavaria, which was confiscated a little later at Goslar, after a short retention in the king's hands, was disposed of to Leopold of Austria.

Before the year 1138 was far advanced Saxony and Bavaria were ablaze with civil war; the old feud of Welf and Hohenstaufen, which had disturbed the peace during the greater part of the previous reign,

---

[1] Giesebrecht, *Kaiserzeit*, IV, 171.

[2] The accounts of these events differ considerably in their details. The comparatively late *Annales Palidenses*, MGH, *Script.* XVI, anno 1138, mention that Conrad besieged Henry at Nuremberg and forced him to give up the *insignia*; whereas Otto of Freising, *Chron.* VII, cap. 23, expressly states that the *insignia* were given up at the diet held at Ratisbon. Cf. Giesebrecht, *op. cit.* IV, 175 sq. and 459, and Bernhardi, *Konrad III*, 49 sq.

broke out once more with renewed bitterness. The Empress Richenza
by her vigorous energy in the cause of her son-in-law won the support of
many of the Saxon princes, who looked upon Albert the Bear as an
upstart. But Albert was too quick for them; he attacked before their
preparations were completed, defeated them decisively, and occupied the
Welfic possessions of Lüneburg and Bardowiek. The king, however,
deceived himself into thinking the opposition in Saxony crushed; the
sudden appearance of the banished duke in his northern dukedom altered
the situation. Town after town fell into his hands, even the lands of
the usurping margrave were no longer secure, and by the spring of
1139 Albert with his chief supporters, Bernard of Plötzke and Herman
of Winzenburg, was driven to seek shelter with the Archbishop of
Mayence at Rusteburg in the Eichsfeld.

The royal army which assembled at Hersfeld in July for the recovery
of Saxony was imposing enough; the Archbishops of Mayence and Trèves,
the Bishops of Worms and Spires, the Duke of Bohemia, the new Dukes
of Saxony and Bavaria, Louis of Thuringia, Herman of Winzenburg, all
appeared with their levies. But a strong army was required, for Henry
had behind him the weight of Saxony, and the history of the past had
shewn that Saxony, when its heart was in the struggle, was all but invin-
cible. The two armies confronted each other at Kreuzburg in Thuringia;
the leaders of the royal army hesitated, a council of war voted for arbitration, finally a day was fixed to settle the issue at Worms at Candlemas.
The conference was however a mere farce, and nothing was done; the two
parties, laying aside the business for which they had come together, gave
themselves over to amusement and feasting, the latter much embellished
by the thirty tuns of wine which, we are told, the Archbishop of Trèves
carried with him on the campaign and lavished upon the negotiators.
He, it is scarcely necessary to add, was the only man to benefit by the
affair; he was rewarded with the abbey of St Maximin at Trèves, the
richest in his diocese, a possession however not entirely advantageous, for
it brought the new possessor into a feud with the monks and their
advocatus which after a long and devastating struggle was only closed,
like many similar feuds, by the Second Crusade. In other respects the
existing state of things continued; Henry remained master of Saxony,
Albert, deserted even by the few Saxon princes who had previously
joined him, had to console himself with the empty and portionless title
of duke.

In Bavaria Henry's supplanter received a warmer welcome. Leopold,
with the help of his brother Bishop Otto of Freising, the historian, had
in a remarkably short time gained a firm hold over his new subjects.
Henry, now secure in Saxony, prepared to recover Bavaria. His army
was mustered in readiness at Quedlinburg when at the moment of starting
he fell sick and died. His youth, the suddenness, the unaccountableness
of his death, most of all the advantage it gave to his antagonists, gave

rise to the suspicion, whether with justice it is impossible to say, of poison. His premature end was certainly a terrific blow to the Welf cause. Henry's heir and namesake was but a boy of ten years old; the fortunes of his house depended on the resources of two women, the little Henry's guardians, Richenza and her daughter the duke's widow Gertrude. Nevertheless the death of Henry the Proud did not have the expected result upon Conrad's fortunes. Both in Saxony and Bavaria the war continued with undiminished vigour. The attempt of Albert the Bear to recover Saxony was a complete failure; he suddenly appeared at Bremen on All Saints' Day, and put forward his claim at an assembly of princes and people, but met with the most hostile reception. Surrounded by enemies, he barely escaped with his life. The Saxon princes under the leadership of Frederick, the count-palatine, and Conrad, Archbishop of Magdeburg, firm in their loyalty to the boy-duke, were even strong enough to take the offensive, and to make plundering raids into Albert's country, capturing many of his castles. In vain Conrad tried to put an end to the quarrel, but the Saxon chiefs refused to obey the imperial summons to diets held at Worms in February and at Frankfort in April 1140. The king's attitude moreover was not conciliatory; he demanded unconditional surrender and refused a safe conduct to the Saxons for the negotiations. So the war was pursued with energy; and Albert, driven from his March, fled to the king for help.

But Conrad's attention was directed to a rebellion in the south which threatened to be even more dangerous. There Welf, Henry's uncle, had taken up the family cause, perhaps with the idea of acquiring for himself the Bavarian dukedom[1]: no friction however appears to have existed between the two branches of the house at this time, though doubtless Welf hoped to obtain a share of the family inheritance in the event of success. In the summer of 1140 he attacked Leopold, who was besieging a castle on the river Mangfall, and inflicted upon him a defeat which seemed likely to undermine his authority in the duchy. Conrad, at the duke's urgent appeal, hastened into Swabia, accompanied by his brother Frederick, against the Welfic fortress of Weinsberg. In vain he battered at its strong walls; the stout resistance of the loyal inhabitants parried every attempt, till he was obliged to turn from the town to face Welf himself who was hurrying to its relief. The battle that ensued unexpectedly redeemed his fortunes: the defeat was crushing; Welf only with difficulty effected his escape; Weinsberg despairing of relief opened its gates on 21 December. Two legends make the siege of Weinsberg famous in history and romance. In the heat of the fierce fight on the banks of the Neckar the rival leaders, it is said, urged on their followers with the battle cries of "Hi Welf!" "Hi Weibling!"—the first time, if there

---

[1] *Hist. Welf. Weingarten*, MGH, *Script.* xxi, 467, "ipse enim Gwelfo praefatum ducatum iure hereditatis ad se spectare proclamans." Cf. Otto of Freising, *Chron.* vii, 26.

be truth in it[1], that these names, so famous in after years, were used to designate the opposing factions in German politics. Jacob Grimm has included among his *Märchen* the story of the capitulation of the Weinsbergers. The tale, though seemingly unhistorical, has a basis in an early authority. The women alone were spared with what they could carry away with them. The sturdy Swabians, it is said, came down from the town bearing their condemned husbands upon their shoulders[2].

The effects of Conrad's victory were far reaching. It not only crushed, for the moment at least, the rebellion in the south, but it also changed the aspect of affairs in the north. It is significant that many Saxon princes presented themselves at the Whitsun feast at Würzburg in 1141, though no solution to the questions at issue was then reached. The Welfic cause suffered another severe blow by the death on 10 June of the Empress Richenza, by whose energy and enterprise the struggle had been maintained and the diverse elements of the opposition to the Hohenstaufen had been kept together. Her daughter Gertrude, who had shared with her the guardianship of the young Henry, was a woman of a different stamp; incited by no inveterate hatred, like Richenza, to the Hohenstaufen, actuated rather by personal animosities than by the interests of her family, she was in no way qualified to act as the leader of a great party. The number of her supporters dwindled; the war was pursued but half-heartedly. However with Richenza's death the greatest obstacle to a compromise was removed. The moment was favourable. In the south after a period of intermittent warfare Duke Leopold had died in October. Conrad granted the margravate of Austria to Leopold's brother Henry Jasomirgott, but kept the duchy in his own hands, pending a decisive settlement. Marculf, a skilful diplomat who had recently been raised to the primacy of Mayence, was entrusted with the negotiations. Preliminaries were drawn up, and a diet was summoned at Frankfort in May 1142 to give effect to them. Henry received Saxony, Henry Jaso-

---

[1] It is condemned as unhistorical by Jaffé, *Konrad III*, p. 35, n. 22. It is first mentioned in 1425 by Andreas presbyter Ratisponensis, Schilter, *Script. rer. Germ.* 1702, p. 25, "clamor vero exhortationis ad resistendum et fortiter pugnandum, in exercitu Welfonis fuit talis: *Hye Welff.* Unde Fridericus ad confusionem Welfonis praecepit clamari in exercitu suo, *Hye Giebelingen.*"

[2] The truth of the story rests on the question whether the passage in the *Chronica Regia Coloniensis* "descendebant viros humeris portantes" existed in the contemporary annals of Paderborn, which is the original source of the Cologne chronicle for these years. The Pöhlde annals which drew their information from the same source say nothing of the Weinsberg women. Scheffer-Boichorst, who reconstructed the text of the *Annales Patherbrunenses*, accepts the story. Bernheim, *Historisches Taschenbuch*, 1884, p. 13 sq. is sceptical. The point has been much under discussion of recent years, but the two articles by R. Holtzmann, *Die Weiber von Weinsberg. Zugleich ein Beitrag zur Kritik der Paderborner Annalen* (Stuttgart, 1911), and *Die Trauen Weiber von Weinsberg*, HVJS, XVIII, 1918, have gone far to prove the presence of the passage in the contemporary annals, and so the authenticity of the story.

mirgott Bavaria, while Albert the Bear, who had, since the end of the previous year, renounced the title of duke, was re-established in the North Mark. A general pardon was granted to all who had taken part in the rebellion, and finally a seal was set upon the general pacification by a marriage, which immediately followed at Frankfort amid great festivities, between Gertrude and the new Duke of Bavaria.

The settlement appeared more complete than in fact it was. Otto of Freising gives the truer interpretation of the results when he concludes his account of these events with the remark: "it was the seed of the greatest discord in our land." It failed to satisfy any of those concerned; Welf refused to accept the alienation of Bavaria from his family, and soon reopened the struggle against the new duke. Frederick of Swabia was dissatisfied; he grudged the favour shewn to Henry Jasomirgott and threw in his lot with the Welfs. Although soon reconciled, he was never again a trusted friend to Conrad; later he even appeared together with Welf in alliance with Conrad's dangerous enemy Roger of Sicily. Further, it remained to be seen whether the young Duke of Saxony, when old enough to manage his own affairs, would be content with the portion of his father's possessions allotted to him. Finally, the peaceful designs of Conrad received a fatal blow by the death of Gertrude. She died in childbed, when journeying to Bavaria to join her husband on 18 April 1143.

The struggle of the two great families of Welf and Hohenstaufen was not the only source of trouble which disturbed the peace of Germany. Since the king's accession Lorraine was the scene of a civil and an ecclesiastical dispute. The deaths of Walram in 1138 and of Godfrey a few months later gave rise to a conflict between their successors, Henry and Godfrey the younger; the former, who had held the ducal title during his father's lifetime, was naturally dissatisfied with the king's action in granting the duchy of Lower Lorraine to the latter[1]. War was the result, and Henry of Limburg was compelled to renounce his claim to the title. Godfrey, however, only enjoyed his dukedom for a short while; he died in 1142 and was succeeded by his one-year-old son.

The ecclesiastical difficulties were less easily ended. The gift of the abbey of St Maximin to the Archbishop of Trèves, already mentioned, was bitterly resented by the monks themselves, who found a keen champion of their rights in their *advocatus*, Henry, Count of Namur and Luxemburg. The election of an abbot without the knowledge of the archbishop brought the matter to Rome. Innocent II took up the cause of the monks, and in May 1140 issued a bull in which he declared the monastery to be subject only to Rome and the Empire; at the same time he wrote to Adalbero bidding him remove the sentence of excommunication which he had imposed upon the newly appointed abbot. The truculent archbishop

---

[1] The reason may be found for this in the marriage connexion between Conrad and the young Godfrey; the latter had married the king's sister Ermingarde

treated the Pope's missives with open defiance, refused even to obey a summons to Rome, and was in consequence suspended from his office. Luckily for him, however, his cause was taken up by St Bernard, whose influence with Innocent was predominant. The suspension was removed, and a bull, dated 20 December 1140, was issued cancelling the previous one and granting the posssession of the abbey of St Maximin to the archbishop and his successors in perpetuity. It was a solution, but not one which was acceptable to the monks or their advocate. For seven years the rich lands round the Moselle were laid waste by incessant war, until at the great diet held at Spires in December 1146 for the proclamation of the Crusade the two antagonists, at the instance of St Bernard, agreed to lay aside their quarrels and allow peace to be restored to their impoverished country.

Conrad's difficulties may in large measure be attributed to his family connexions. His mother Agnes had married, after the death of Frederick of Swabia, Leopold III of Austria; by the two marriages she was the mother of twenty-three children. The elevation of his family seems to have been a guiding motive with the king; we have already noticed how the grant of the duchy of Lower Lorraine to his brother-in-law Godfrey led to a feud in that country. The situation in Bavaria was complicated by the establishment of the Austrian Babenbergers, half-brothers of the king, as Bavarian dukes. The marriages of two half-sisters, the one to a claimant of the dukedom of Poland, the other to a claimant of the dukedom of Bohemia, involved Conrad in wars with these countries.

The death of a ruler in the half-civilised lands which bordered the German kingdom to the east was almost inevitably followed by a war of succession. Boleslav of Poland died in October 1139, leaving a disposition whereby the country was to be partitioned among his four sons, the eldest of whom, Vladislav, was to have a certain pre-eminence with the title of grand-duke. This prince at once attempted to use his exalted position to develop his own power at the expense of his brothers, an enterprise in which he confidently relied on the support of Conrad, his brother-in-law. Early in the year 1146 he appeared at the German court and was enfeoffed with the whole of Poland. A strenuous and not unsuccessful resistance was made by his brothers, Boleslav and Mesco; Posen withstood his attack, the Archbishop of Gnesen excommunicated him, his own town of Cracow was taken and destroyed; finally, he himself was driven into exile. Conrad made a campaign into Poland on behalf of his vassal, but, unable to make any headway, entered into negotiations and withdrew to Germany with Vladislav, who continued to live in exile while his victorious brothers established their authority securely in Poland. The only result which emanated from Conrad's intervention was the diminution of German influence in that region.

The king's dealings with Bohemia had a more successful end. When Soběslav appeared at the diet of Bamberg in 1138, Conrad guaranteed the succession of the dukedom to his son Vladislav. On Soběslav's death in 1140 Conrad, despite his former promise, disposed of the dukedom to a nephew of the late duke also named Vladislav who had married his half-sister Gertrude. Dissatisfaction at his rule led to a rebellion in the interests of the other Vladislav instigated by Otto of Olmütz, the son of that Otto who fell in Lothar's army at Kulm. Vladislav the son defeated Vladislav the nephew of Soběslav at Wysoka to the west of Kuttenberg on 25 April 1142. The latter fled to Germany to seek help from Conrad; the king took up his cause and accompanied him back to Bohemia. The rebellion collapsed without a fight; on 7 June the royal army entered Prague and restored Vladislav II securely in his duchy.

Boris, the unsuccessful aspirant to the Hungarian throne whose pretensions Lothar had set aside, again came forward, backed by the support of Duke Vladislav II of Bohemia and the influential Babenbergers. By a lavish distribution of money he had built up a strong position for himself; he was regarded with favour by Conrad, with whom he had an interview at Aix-la-Chapelle early in the year 1146. A band of his followers, among them a number of *ministeriales* of Henry Jasomirgott returning to Hungary, made a sudden night attack upon the frontier fortress of Pressburg. The garrison was killed, captured, or dispersed. Géza, the Hungarian King, collected an army, moved on Pressburg, and recaptured it. He imputed, not without good grounds, the blame for this outrage to Conrad and the Duke of Bavaria, and only awaited an opportunity to take vengeance upon them. The moment came in September 1146. With an army reckoned at the incredible figure of seventy thousand men the King of Hungary crossed the frontier, fell upon the duke's army near the banks of the Leitha, and after a fierce battle threw the German soldiers into confusion; the victory was complete; the Duke of Bavaria himself only with difficulty reached the shelter of Vienna.

The Babenbergers, who had thus been largely responsible for Conrad's implication in the affairs of Poland, Bohemia, and Hungary, had in their own duchy of Bavaria disturbed the peace by a bitter feud, the origin of which is unknown, with the Bishop of Ratisbon. The city of Ratisbon was besieged by Duke Henry; the country was burnt and plundered. The duke and his supporters, among them his brother-in-law the Duke of Bohemia, Frederick of Bogen, the cathedral *advocatus*, and Otto of Wittelsbach, the count-palatine, were placed under the ban of the Church by the bishop and his metropolitan Conrad of Salzburg. Conrad at last intervened, held a diet at Ratisbon, and reconciled the contending parties.

To add to the misery of war and devastation from which the country suffered, a famine of unheard-of severity broke out and spread through the whole of Germany. Every chronicler fills his narrative of the year

1146 with lamentations over the afflictions and misfortunes which heavily oppressed their unhappy land. Prices rose to unprecedented heights; in one place thirty-four shillings had to be paid for a measure of wheat; many sustained life merely on a diet of roots and herbs; many succumbed to a death from starvation.

But the troubles which beset Germany lost significance in the minds of men when the news of great disasters in the East reached Europe. Edessa fell in 1144; Jerusalem itself was threatened. Pope Eugenius III entrusted to Bernard of Clairvaux the preaching of a Crusade. In France the project was taken up with enthusiasm, and Louis VII himself took the cross at Easter 1146. The crusading spirit spread across the Rhine, but there St Bernard's emissary, Ralph, a monk of Clairvaux, damaged the cause by raising the cry against the Jews instead of against the Turkish infidel. Persecution of the unhappy Israelites was the first sign of crusading ardour among the German people. St Bernard himself had to hasten into the country to counteract the misplaced zeal of his fellow-worker; but he had another end in view in this visit—it was to win Conrad for the enterprise. Early in November he reached Mayence, and proceeded almost at once to Frankfort, to meet the king. But Conrad hesitated; the condition of his kingdom hardly, he thought, justified his absence. At home and abroad he was faced with determined enemies; the Welfic party, still unsubdued, were in the pay of Roger of Sicily, who hoped that by subsidising Conrad's opponents at home he might prevent him from coming to Italy. However at the Christmas festival he was won over by the eloquence of the great preacher in the cathedral of Spires[1]. The danger of leaving Germany at such a critical time was much lessened by the fact that many of the chief princes of the Empire, among them Welf and Henry, Duke of Bavaria, had either already taken the cross or now prepared to follow their king's example. A great diet was held at Frankfort in the following spring (19 March 1147) to make the necessary arrangements for the expedition and for the government of Germany in the king's absence. Conrad's son Henry, a boy of ten years old, was elected king and crowned a week later at Aix-la-Chapelle; he was entrusted to the care of the Archbishop of Mayence, while the direction of the affairs of the kingdom was placed in the capable hands of Abbot Wibald of Stablo. To lighten the burdens of government a general peace was proclaimed throughout Germany. The large concourse of crusaders came together at Ratisbon in May 1147. Conrad himself by boat, the army along the bank, set out down the Danube, pursuing the overland route to Constantinople and Pales-

---

[1] According to H. Cosack, *Konrads III Entschluss zum Kreuzzug*, MIOGF, xxxv (1914), the decision was due not to the preaching of Bernard but to the news that Conrad's enemy Welf VI had taken the cross on Christmas Eve. On the other hand, it is by no means certain that Conrad was in possession of this information when he took the decisive step.

tine. Some few days later another vast army—the French crusaders—
assembled at Metz and followed in the footsteps of the German host
on its way eastward.

In Saxony also the crusading spirit penetrated; but the princes obtained leave from the Pope to direct their energies not against the Turk
but against the heathen Slav[1]. On the death of Lothar development in
these regions had received a sharp set-back. The civil war which followed
Conrad's accession was the signal for a Wendish rebellion. The strong
fortress of Segeberg was taken, the German settlements destroyed; the
town of Lübeck was burnt, the surrounding country devastated. The
danger spread to Holstein, where the quick action of Henry of Badwide
alone saved the situation: he took the field in mid-winter (1138–9) and
drove the Wends back across the Trave. But further progress was impossible while Saxony was in the throes of civil war. Only when peace
was restored in 1142 was the work of German expansion again undertaken.
The revival was due to the energy and enterprise of the Count of Holstein,
Adolf of Schauenburg[2]. In 1143, once more in possession of his county,
he threw himself into the work of Germanising the Slavonic country with
renewed vigour. Immigrants poured in from the over-populated districts
of Westphalia, Frisia, and Holland, and received lands under the most
favourable conditions of tenure. Lübeck was rebuilt and, owing to its
excellent harbour, soon became the station through which all the trade
between Scandinavia and Southern Europe passed; Adolf formed an
alliance with Niclot, prince of the neighbouring Wendish tribe, the Obotrites, to secure the protection of his town. Over and above its commercial
advantages it became one of the centres for the work of conversion of
the heathen, to which the priest Vicelin for many years past had devoted
his life, and for which on 29 June 1147 the Saxon princes assembled at
Magdeburg in fulfilment of their crusading vows. The news of the
intended campaign roused the Wends to rebellion. Niclot, notwithstanding his alliance with Adolf, sailed up the Trave against Lübeck.
The citizens, engaged in celebrating the feast of SS. John and Paul
(26 June) and too drunken to offer effective resistance, were brutally
massacred; the Slavs followed up their success, overran the whole province
of Wagria to the very walls of Segeberg, its chief stronghold, burning
and plundering as they went, killing those who resisted, and carrying the
women and children into slavery. Their course was not however entirely
unchecked; the colonists of Eutin and Süssel effectively withstood the
invaders who, hearing that Count Adolf was about to take the field

---

[1] The Saxon princes received all the privileges usually granted to crusaders;
but they wore, as a mark of distinction, the cross surrounded by a circle. Otto of
Freising, *Gesta Friderici*, I, 40.

[2] He had been the victim of the personal animosity of Gertrude, who had con-
firmed the grant of Holstein made by Albert the Bear to Henry of Badwide.
Helmold, *Chron. Slav.* I, 56. After Gertrude's death the country was restored to
Adolf, while Henry of Badwide was compensated with lands elsewhere.

against them, wisely retired with their booty to the fortress of Dobin on the Lake of Schwerin.

In the meanwhile the preparations for launching the Crusade were nearing completion. All the foremost men in Saxony, among them the young Duke Henry and his rival Albert the Bear, and from the south Conrad of Zähringen, gathered with their levies on the feast of SS. Peter and Paul at Magdeburg. But there were yet more to come in; without waiting for the loiterers, one part of the army, numbering some 40,000 men, under the leadership of Duke Henry, Conrad of Zähringen, and Archbishop Adalbero of Bremen, set off against the rebellious Niclot in the fastness of Dobin. The Saxon host was reinforced by an army from Denmark, which had suffered severely from the inroads of the Slavs; and, though the country had been lacerated by civil war since the death of Eric III in 1146, the two claimants to the throne, Svein and Canute, had put aside their internal controversies in order to crush their common enemy. But the Crusade was doomed to failure. Private interests interposed, and the aim that they set out to accomplish was neglected; disputes arose over territory not yet won, while the Saxon and Danish chiefs failed hopelessly to maintain any unity of action. On 31 July the Danes met with a serious defeat, and it was said the Germans received bribes to leave their Danish allies to their fate. When at last they succeeded in bringing Dobin to submission they granted very easy terms to the garrison; it was in the interest of the princes to keep a tributary population, and therefore they abstained from anything in the nature of annihilation; hence to accept Christianity, to free the Danish prisoners, to cease from making devastating attacks across the border, were the only conditions imposed on the conquered Slavs. Even these moreover were not strictly enforced. They received Christianity only to renounce it as soon as they secured their liberty; of the Danish prisoners, only the old and infirm gained their freedom, while the more vigorous were retained as slaves.

Hardly more successful were the achievements of the second army. Sixty thousand men under the command of Albert the Bear and a number of North German bishops, supplemented by large contingents from Poland and Bohemia, crossed the Elbe and advanced northward through the Havel country, while the Wends retreated into the inaccessible swamps and forests of the interior. The crusaders besieged the town of Demmin, and pushing on into Pomerania would have attacked Stettin had it not been for the Pomeranian Bishop Adalbert, the pupil of Otto of Bamberg, who realised that it would mean the undoing of the life-work of his master. They turned back from the Oder and early in September recrossed the Elbe, having accomplished nothing. The whole enterprise had entirely failed in its avowed purpose. The princes had made the crusading badge the pretext for a war of personal profit; the work of Adolf and Vicelin was retarded rather than promoted by these campaigns. The German colonists had to bear the brunt of the widespread devastation and its resultant, severe famine. It was with the greatest difficulty that they were persuaded not to abandon their new homes, where they found it, in the circumstances, far from easy to maintain a livelihood.

The years following the Wendish Crusade witness the rapid development of the power of Henry the Lion. The main obstacle in his path of progress was Hartwig, first provost, then, in 1148, Archbishop of Bremen, a man of worldly ideas, greedy of material wealth, ambitious for hierarchical power, whose aim was to restore the old supremacy of his see in northern Germany. As early as 1144, when Henry was but fourteen years old, the two had come to blows over a disputed inheritance, consequent upon the childless death of Count Rudolf of Stade. Conrad intervened and ultimately decided against the young duke, who had in the course of the quarrel given offence by capturing and imprisoning not only his rival Hartwig but the Archbishop Adalbero of Bremen himself. The result was a lifelong enmity between Henry and Hartwig and strained relations between Henry and the king. Hartwig, on his accession to the see in August 1148, first attempted to recover the suffragan bishoprics of Scandinavia which had been lost by the creation of the metropolitan diocese of Lund in 1104; but as the Pope refused to consider his request he turned his attention to the east, to the three bishoprics of Slavonia: Oldenburg, Mecklenburg, and Ratzburg. Oldenburg was given to Vicelin as a reward for his thirty years of missionary work, and Mecklenburg to a fellow-worker named Emmehard; good as the appointments were, they were made without reference either to Duke Henry or to Count Adolf; the former, who claimed the right of investiture, refused to give the lay support necessary for the progress of Vicelin's work, the latter cut off the tithes on which the church depended for its maintenance. Proselytism among the Wends remained at a deadlock until Vicelin, realising that only submission to the duke could enable him to continue his labours, despite the wishes of his metropolitan, received investiture from Henry's hands at Lüneburg (1151).

In the summer of 1149 Conrad, after the disastrous failure of his Crusade, was again in Germany. His intention was now to make his long wished-for campaign to Italy with the twofold purpose of receiving the imperial crown and of subduing his enemy, Roger of Sicily. For the latter project he had, while staying at Constantinople on his return from Palestine, definitely clinched the alliance with the Eastern Emperor, Manuel, which had for some time past been the subject of negotiations and which had been strengthened by Manuel's marriage with Conrad's sister-in-law Bertha of Sulzbach in 1146. At the meeting of the two Emperors a joint expedition against Roger was arranged. This move was parried by a counterstroke from Roger; he had an interview with Welf, who returned from the East by way of Sicily, and agreed to pay him the yearly sum of a thousand marks for keeping the German king busy in his own kingdom. Conrad's schemes for a visit to Italy were again frustrated;

he found on his return to Germany that the work on his hands would keep him engaged north of the Alps for some time to come.

At the great diet of Frankfort, when the plans for the Crusade had been arranged, Henry the Lion had raised his claim upon the dukedom of Bavaria; he had denied the finality of the settlement reached and accepted by his guardians in his name at Frankfort five years earlier. Without giving a decisive answer Conrad postponed the question till his return; it now required an answer, and it became daily more certain that if the answer should be unfavourable to Henry there would again be recourse to arms. For war Conrad was but poorly equipped. Whereas Henry's position during the last two years had been steadily growing stronger, Conrad's had grown perceptibly weaker. He had, for instance, by his injudicious interference in the affairs of the Burgundian kingdom estranged the powerful Swabian family of Zähringen; Conrad with his son Berthold definitely declared for the Welfs, and sealed the alliance by a marriage between his daughter Clementia and the Duke of Saxony. On the other hand, in Saxony itself the king could rely on some support. Henry's strong rule had made him enemies, his increasing power in the country beyond the Elbe was not entirely popular with the Saxon princes, and, most important of all, his rival Albert the Bear had recently strengthened his hand by the acquisition of the district which about this time came to be known under the name of its principal town, Brandenburg[1]. Immediately on Conrad's return, Henry renewed his claim upon the duchy of Bavaria, and, as the king took no steps to deal with the matter, quietly assumed the title of Duke of Bavaria and Saxony[2].

Tedious negotiations, frequent diets, underhand diplomacy, characterise the development of the dispute during the remainder of Conrad's lifetime. The impetuous and premature campaign of Welf in Swabia in February 1150, his siege of the Hohenstaufen castle of Flochberg, and his utter defeat at the hands of the young King Henry, made little difference to the situation. An equally ineffective and brief campaign by Duke Henry himself in Bavaria, the details of which are unknown, resulted only in a truce and more negotiations. Conrad's feverish anxiety to make his journey to Rome (he was urged on by embassies from Venice and Constantinople, and 8 September 1152 had been fixed for the setting-out of the expedition) is the only justification for the means he now employed during time of truce to crush his rival. With the object of undermining Henry's authority in Saxony itself, he sent his chaplain, Herbert, to sow dissension among the Saxon princes, and he himself soon followed to Goslar

---

[1] It was bequeathed by the Slavonic prince Plotislav, who died childless in 1150. Cf. Henricus de Antwerpe, *Tractatus de Captione urbis Brandenburg*, MGH, *Script.* xxv, 482, "Et cum non haberet heredem, Marchionem Albertum sui principatus instituit successorem."

[2] "Dux Bavariae et Saxoniae" appears in a document of 13 September 1149 Bernhardi, *op. cit.* 839, n. 3.

with the intention of besieging the duke's capital, Brunswick. The
strictest secrecy was observed with regard to his plans and movements,
while a close watch was kept upon Henry, who was then in Swabia, to
prevent him returning to his duchy where his personal influence would be
the undoing of the king's plans. Henry, however, eluded his watchers,
escaped in disguise from Swabia (December 1151), and after five days
hard riding appeared unexpectedly at Brunswick. Conrad's schemes completely collapsed; and having no heart to continue the struggle he
withdrew hastily to Goslar and soon abandoned Saxony altogether. This
unlucky and degrading enterprise was the last event in a far from brilliant
career; Conrad fell ill at Bamberg, and died on 15 February 1152.

Failure was the keynote of the reign of the first king of the house of
Hohenstaufen. Failure dogged his steps in every enterprise. In spite of
long fighting and interminable diplomacy, the Welfs remained unsubdued:
a brilliantly equipped expedition to Syria had ended in a dismal
catastrophe; the king's intervention in the quarrels of his neighbours
achieved nothing; for the first time since the revival of the Empire by
Otto the Great the German king had not been crowned at Rome. The
early promise of Conrad as the young, energetic, popular anti-king to
Lothar remained sadly unfulfilled when he came to rule as a lawful
sovereign. Yet it is difficult to see the cause of this almost uninterrupted
misadventure. The bulk of his subjects, jealous of the over-great power
of the Welfs, were ready to give him their support and accept him as
their champion. Nor had his difficulties their origin in the fatal quarrel
with the Church which had been the undoing of the Salian Emperors.
On the contrary he was in harmony with Rome, he interfered not at all
in ecclesiastical elections, his zeal for the protection of the Church and
its property against lay aggression was worthy of all praise; he was a
devoted son of the Church. "Never," says Giesebrecht, "had the concord
between Church and State been greater." His character and attainments
would justify the highest hopes for the success of his rule. The poet-
chronicler Godfrey of Viterbo compares him to the ancient personifications
of the virtues: "a Seneca in council, a Paris in appearance, a Hector in
battle."[1] Abbot Wibald of Stablo, a man of shrewd judgment and great
sincerity and candour, cannot speak too highly of his Emperor's character;
piety, clemency, moderation, generosity, intellectual ability, sense of
humour are all the subject of his praise[2]; bravery and tireless energy
were his to a remarkable degree. Such in the eyes of contemporaries was
the man who beyond a doubt lowered the prestige of Germany. The
difficulties with which he was confronted were certainly great; to the
political troubles were added those arising from bad harvests and consequent famine and discontent. In spite of his many fine qualities he

---

[1] MGH, *Script.* xxii, p. 263, 51.
[2] See *e.g. Epistolae* 364 and 375 in Jaffé, *Monumenta Corbeiensia.*

seems to have lacked foresight and statesmanship; his policy was often undecided or injudicious. Disappointment at his initial lack of success brought out the weaker sides of his character, and the chaotic state of things which prevailed during his last years was the result. It is curious to notice that but one contemporary writer connects the disorders of the kingdom in any way with its ruler. The royal chronicle of Cologne, after eulogising the king's merits, remarks: "under him the country began to be ruined by misfortune." Indeed it required all the powers of statesmanship with which his nephew Frederick Barbarossa was so richly endowed to extricate Germany from the disruptive condition in which Conrad left it.

CHAPTER XI.

ITALY, 1125–1152.

THE treaty which was concluded at Worms in 1122 between Pope Calixtus II and the Emperor Henry V marks the close of a great period of history. With that treaty the long contest which took its name from the question of Investitures ended, when its chief interest was becoming exhausted and new times were bringing new tendencies. Neither power could boast a complete victory. The strength of an idea, the unity of Christendom, which animated both Empire and Papacy, formed a bulwark to each institution against every attempt of the other towards full supremacy. Yet, during the strife, the Papacy had vastly improved its political position, more especially in relation to the Empire. Raised to a great moral height by the internal reform which had been effected, chiefly by the impulse given by the genius of Gregory VII, the Papacy had conquered in the world a very different position from that which it had held in the time of the Ottos and the early Henries. The universality of its spiritual jurisdiction was now recognised, and, if causes of new discords could arise with regard to the frontiers between that jurisdiction and other powers, at least the Papacy's independence of those powers was securely established. On its side, the Empire had contested with energy the papal claims and the tendency of the Church to withdraw itself, even in temporal things, from the dominion of every royal right, and to create almost a State within the State. Owing to this opposition, the Church had been obliged to accept limits and restraints for its aggressive and domineering inclinations. Still, the long resistance of the Papacy, and its preaching of the First Crusade, which it proclaimed to the world while the Empire, its foe, could take no part therein, diminished the ideal conception of the universal power of the Emperor. He was in so far placed in a position of inferiority towards the Pope, who was establishing himself securely as lord of souls and spiritual director of the world.

Meanwhile, in Italy throughout the eleventh century there were developing the hidden seeds of a great transformation. The ancient Latin civilisation, torpid for centuries but never dead, was slowly awaking. The new elements in the population, which one after another had penetrated into Italy, had at last completed their laborious fusion with the ancient elements, which, as they absorbed them, joined with them in unfolding the beginning of a new life. In North Italy the distance of the imperial authority had favoured the almost unnoted development of another factor in Italian life, the Commune, which speedily grew vigorous, especially in Lombardy, and diminished or annihilated the strength of feudal institutions, and was soon to stand proud and threatening even in face of the Emperor. Intellectual culture, which had never entirely failed among Italian laymen even when it had sunk to its lowest point among the clergy, took on a new development; at the same time as agriculture, manufactures and commerce began to flourish in Lombardy and Central Italy, and, reaching the sea-routes, came to Venice, to Pisa, and to Genoa, whose maritime power spread daily more and more. The exuberant growth, the wealth, the vigour of the communes nourished in them a need of independence, which, on one side, undermined the foundations of the power of the feudal nobility, and, on the other, rendered those sturdy plebeians impatient of the rights and authority which were claimed over them by the Empire. Southern Italy and Sicily contained districts which were prosperous owing to the richness of the soil and the long tradition of maritime commerce; and there the Norman princes were gathering together in one dominion the various elements which co-existed in regions occupied for centuries by rulers so diverse in tendencies of civilisation, in religion, and in race. It was a combination not yet close and united, but already strong through the energy, the wealth, and the fine political ability of the Norman dynasty, ever on the watch to draw new advantages from the various relations, sometimes friendly, sometimes hostile, in which it stood with the Empires of East and West, and the near and jealous authority of the Roman pontiffs. The Norman princes aroused both the good wishes and the fears of the Church; the Papacy saw in their growing power the possibility of a support for itself, but still more the development of a neighbour which was too strong and ever determined to use its strength without scruple.

The new period of the relations of Italy and the Papacy with the Empire began soon after the conclusion of the Concordat of Worms, on the death of the Emperor Henry V in 1125 and the extinction of the Franconian house. In Germany there was discord over the election of a new king. At the Diet of Mayence, on 30 August 1125, Lothar of Supplinburg, Duke of Saxony, was elected King of the Romans, but not without opposition. A powerful party favoured another candidate, Frederick of Hohenstaufen, Duke of Swabia. He was considered both the natural successor of Henry V to whom he was nearly related, and the heir of the political traditions of the Salian house. The ecclesiastical party in Germany, on the other hand, favoured Lothar, and it was possible for Pope Honorius II, in supporting the Saxon, to shew clearly all the weight and importance of his aid. Lothar was elected, but Frederick of Swabia did not submit to the election, and civil war burst out in Germany, putting the Crown in a danger which the beginning of an unfortunate war with Bohemia rendered the more serious. In such grave circumstances, Lothar naturally appreciated all the value of the Church's help, and he found the Pope eager to give it, whether in order to profit thereby in gaining a better position in his relations with the Empire, or because of the fear with which the anti-papal tendencies of the Hohenstaufen inspired him.

In fact, the Pope, on his side, had need of Lothar, and understood all the opportunities offered by an alliance with him. While the principle of papal authority had been so exalted in the face of the royal authority and in the conscience of distant peoples, the Pope did not find close at hand that deference and submission which would allow his activity to develop. In South Italy, the Norman policy upset all the papal schemes and claims. William, Duke of Apulia, died childless at Salerno in 1127, and Roger II, Count of Sicily, who claimed to be his natural heir, hastened to Apulia to take possession of his lands. The Pope, invoking his feudal suzerainty over William's territories, proceeded to Benevento, and hurled sentence of excommunication against Roger, who, far from being terrified, countered him by laying waste the Beneventan countryside. The Pope stirred up Robert, Prince of Capua, and many barons against his foe, but was soon, against his will, obliged to yield, and in August 1128 had to submit to invest Roger with the duchy of Apulia and Calabria. Thus a strong monarchy was founded, while for the moment there remained no other advantage to the Papacy than a theoretic right of suzerainty over it.

Meanwhile, in Latium the more powerful barons exercised a lordship against which the forces of Honorius were spent in continual war. Rome itself, although always divided by the factions of the more powerful families, seems to have allowed him to enjoy some kind of peace; but it was a truce rather than a peace, as his successors were very soon to learn. The ferment of political life, which was raising up the other Italian communes, was working too in Rome, and rendered the citizens ever more impatient of the pontifical rule, to which they had never felt themselves wholly subject. Never quite autonomous, never quite subjects either of Pope or Emperor, the medieval Romans were for centuries in a truly singular position. At this time events were pending which were to determine Rome's tendencies towards communal autonomy, and cause the vain dream of lost greatness to hover over the Capitol.

To these diverse circumstances, which caused Honorius to desire the coming of Lothar, there was added another which gave him motive and opportunity to repeat the invitation to hasten to Rome for the imperial crown. In Germany, the party favourable to the house of Swabia not only was still in revolt but in December 1127 at Spires had raised up another king against Lothar in the person of Conrad of Hohenstaufen, brother to Frederick of Swabia, who agreed to the election. Conrad, leaving his brother in Germany to defend his cause in arms, descended into Italy, where Anselm Pusterla, Archbishop of Milan, placed the Iron Crown on his head; and the new king immediately advanced his claims to the inheritance of Countess Matilda. These claims alone, without any other reasons, would have sufficed to make Honorius his enemy; and the Pope did not hesitate to excommunicate him along with the archbishop who had crowned him. In spite of the excommunication, however, Conrad maintained himself in Italy, and found his chief support in the Milanese, who were to be later such bold and tenacious adversaries of his house.

On 13 February 1130 Honorius II died at Rome, and his death was the beginning of a most dangerous schism in the Church. On the same day Cardinal Gregory, titular of Sant' Angelo, and Cardinal Peter, titular of St Calixtus, were elected almost at the same moment, and took respectively the names of Innocent II and Anacletus II. Both were members of powerful Roman houses: Innocent belonged to the Papareschi, Anacletus to the Pierleoni[1]. Their elevation threw Rome into discord. Both elections had been hasty, both perhaps hardly canonical; but there were plausible reasons for maintaining the validity of either, and the case was doubtful. Without delay both the claimants vigorously maintained their pretensions before the world, and both turned to Lothar with the object of attracting his support; but Lothar, doubtful and occupied with German affairs, at first avoided declaring for either. It was indubitably most important to obtain the recognition of the Emperor-designate, but other powerful influences affected Christendom and served to decide its future. From the beginning, while Christendom was still uncertain between the two rivals, Innocent appeared more confident in himself and in his right, and this confidence was not without its value. Thanks to the great power of the Pierleoni, who held the upper hand in Rome, Anacletus, master of the Vatican and supported by the greatest Roman nobles, soon forced Innocent to take to flight; he went by sea to Pisa, and thence by way of Genoa betook himself to France. He found his chief stay in St Bernard, who after a brief hesitation espoused his cause. This extraordinary man, whose fascination drew his contemporaries irresistibly whithersoever his inspired zeal called them, soon saw with what troubles a schism at that time would be charged, and threw himself into a combat for the unity of the Church. His influence had the greatest weight. The Kings of France and England decided for Innocent, and one after the other in January 1131 met him with every demonstration of reverence and honour. Their example was soon followed by the King of the Romans. On 22 March 1131, Innocent and Lothar met at Liège, where the Pope held a synod, in which he hurled the anathema against Anacletus and against Conrad and Frederick of Hohenstaufen. A few days later, on 29 March, Innocent repaired to the cathedral with great

---

[1] The Pierleoni were descended from a converted Jew, Benedict, who lived *c.* 1020, a relative of whom Pope Gregory VI (John Gratian) seems to have been. Cf. R. L. Poole, *Benedict IX and Gregory VI, Proc. Brit. Acad.* Vol. VIII.

pomp, while the king acted as his squire and held the bridle of his horse; then the Pope solemnly placed the royal crown on the heads of Lothar and of his wife Richenza. At the meeting at Liège it was settled that Lothar should proceed to Rome to receive the imperial crown, and to recover for Innocent the city from the anti-Pope. Taking the opportunity, Lothar attempted to re-open the question of Investitures, and to recover the advantages which the Empire had lost; but he met with a firm resistance, and St Bernard, along with the German prelates who were in favour of the rights of the Church, supported the Pope. Lothar understood that it would be unwise to insist, and was obliged to yield and abandon the attempt.

The schism could now be considered as overcome in the main; but Anacletus had still sufficient strength to resist the recognised Pope. The cities of north and central Italy, intent on their special interests, had not been much excited over the schism, but sided in general with Innocent, with the exception of Milan, which favoured Anacletus more owing to its political opposition to Lothar than for any other reason. Yet Anacletus was master of Rome, and, strongly established there, had turned to the south for aid and become closely allied to Roger of Sicily. The shrewd Norman was not slow to see the profit which he could gain from this alliance. He met Anacletus at Avellino on 27 September 1130, and, in return for an annual tribute in recognition of the papal suzerainty, obtained the title of "King of Sicily and of the Duchies of Apulia and Calabria." Thus the foundation of a southern monarchy, to which Honorius II had formerly agreed with reluctance, was now consecrated by the concessions of an anti-Pope, which in the sequel were to be confirmed and permanently recognised by the legitimate pontifical authority.

Although the state of the German kingdom was anything but quiet, it was indispensable that Lothar should turn his thoughts to Italy, and, after making his authority prevail there, come back to Germany with the prestige and strength which the imperial crown would gain him. In the summer of 1132 he started; but the harassing circumstances of the time did not allow him to collect a strong army. Accompanied by Queen Richenza, he passed the Alps and descended into Italy. From the first, owing to the scanty forces at his disposal and the hostility of powerful communes like Verona and Milan, he could make little show of authority. He attempted in vain to subdue Crema, and, after having lost a month in the useless siege, had to cross Lombardy warily, avoiding the places which shewed themselves hostile and approaching those cities which favoured him more by reason of their enmity to Milan than because of their reverence for the Empire. In November, he met Innocent, who had preceded him to Lombardy, and on the plain of Roncaglia held a diet, in which he consulted on the general condition of the Church and the Empire with the Pope and such Lombards as had answered his summons. Together with the Pope he marched from Piacenza towards

Rome, slowly journeying amid populations which greeted him with coldness or hostility. His position could have become very dangerous, if Roger II had been in a condition to face him and annihilate his forces at one blow, and so assure Rome to Anacletus and to himself the unquestioned recognition of his kingdom of Sicily. But in the summer of 1132 a revolt of the barons of the Regno[1], followed by a severe defeat, put Roger's crown in peril; he was obliged to withdraw to Sicily to prepare a reaction, whilst Benevento, rebelling against Anacletus, opened its gates to the legates of Innocent II. Even with this advantage, however, the Pope and Lothar were in the midst of great difficulties, and the advance towards Rome proceeded most slowly. Quitting Lothar, the Pope went to Pisa, where, aided at Genoa by St Bernard, he succeeded with much ado in composing a peace between the Pisans and Genoese, which assured him the assistance of the two rival sea-powers. He joined the king again at Viterbo, and went thence with him to Rome. Some attempts of Anacletus to justify his claim before Lothar gave rise to negotiations which had no success.

Lothar remained some weeks at Rome, while these negotiations continued; perhaps he and Innocent craftily hoped to gain by them possession of the church of St Peter, and to perform there according to ancient custom the ceremony of coronation. But St Peter's, like the greater part of the city, remained in the hands of Anacletus and his partisans. On 4 June 1133 Lothar and Richenza assumed the imperial crown in the Lateran, after Lothar had taken the customary oath to the Pope and guaranteed the privileges of the city. The aid given to Innocent in Rome had amounted to very little, and a longer stay in Italy was impossible for Lothar, who was obliged at once to think of his return. Before separating, however, Pope and Emperor confirmed in substance the Concordat of Worms, and came to an agreement over their respective claims to the inheritance of Countess Matilda. The Pope conceded the use of it to Lothar and his son-in-law Henry, Duke of Bavaria, for their lifetime; they were to hold it of the Church, to which it should return at their deaths. Thus Matilda's lands were held by the Emperor as a fief from the Pope. Morally the Papacy rose ever higher in comparison with the Empire. The coronation and its significance were commemorated in a painting placed in the Lateran, which represented Lothar at the feet of the Pope at the moment of receiving the crown; and beneath it were to be read these two lines, which were later to give rise to bitter complaints, for they contained a bold assertion of the complete supremacy of the Papacy:

> Rex stetit ante fores, iurans prius Urbis honores;
> Post homo fit Papae, sumit quo dante coronam.

[1] We adopt on occasion the convenient Italian use of "the Regno (Kingdom)" as a general name for "the kingdom of Sicily, and of the duchies of Apulia and Calabria," to avoid unnecessary confusion with the island of Sicily.

The return of Lothar to Germany left Innocent II in an extremely perilous situation in Rome, confined as he was within a small district of the city, and almost besieged by the powerful Anacletus and his more numerous partisans. King Roger, with fresh troops collected in Sicily, had returned, victorious and menacing, to Apulia. Thereon Innocent was forced once more to flee from Rome and take refuge at Pisa. But his situation was far from being desperate. Their jealousy of Roger's sea-power silenced for a moment the rivalry of Genoa and Pisa, and united the two republics in favour of Innocent, who therefore met with an honourable reception at Pisa, and there held a synod. Although an exile from his see, he was now universally recognised as head of Christendom, and the little opposition that was left continually decreased. Even the Milanese yielded to the fiery fascination of St Bernard, who had visited them; they came over to Innocent's side, and abandoned their Archbishop, Anselm Pusterla. The schism, now confined to Rome and South Italy, could not have long duration.

The auguries were more propitious for Lothar in Germany, and, now that his prestige was increased by the imperial crown, the current of opinion flowed in his favour. Neither Conrad of Hohenstaufen in Italy nor his brother Frederick in Germany had succeeded in gaining the upper hand, in spite of the faction-discords which disturbed Germany and weakened the royal power. An energetic campaign soon compelled Frederick of Swabia, and then Conrad, to submit. The Emperor shewed generosity to them. He left them in possession of their lands and honours on condition that they accompanied him in his second descent into Italy; thither the Pope had recalled him, and he himself felt the need of returning in order to establish his authority in Lombardy and to destroy the power of Roger.

With German affairs thus settled, the Emperor, in a diet held at Spires at the beginning of 1136, announced his approaching expedition to Italy, and devoted himself to the preparations. In August he left Germany, and, by the Brenner Pass, descended into the Valley of Trent with a great following of soldiers and barons, chief among them Conrad of Hohenstaufen, who was now high in his favour. Faced by such great forces, the Lombard cities did not offer any noteworthy resistance, and Lothar could traverse Upper Italy, meeting no ill reception, and making the fear of his authority and the advantages of his protection felt both by hostile and friendly districts.

But, far more than Upper Italy, the Emperor, incited by Venice and by the Byzantine Court, which were jealous of Roger's growing power by sea, aimed at the South, where he was ambitious of reviving the power of the Empire after the fashion of Otto the Great and Henry III. Dividing his army into two corps, he entrusted one to his son-in-law Henry, Duke of Bavaria, who with three thousand men-at-arms was to restore throughout Tuscany the imperial authority, and then together with the Pope to pass through the States of the Church. Meanwhile, the Emperor with the main body was to reach Apulia by the eastern route through the March of Ancona, and there to meet the other corps. The two armies both made their strength severely felt on the districts they traversed, wasting them and compelling them to submit. Duke Henry met the Pope and marched with him southwards without touching at Rome, so as not to delay the enterprise against Roger. The Emperor and the Pope in their victorious career joined forces at Bari at the end of May 1137, and the submission of Bari decided that of a great part of Apulia and Calabria. Meanwhile, the ships of Pisa and Amalfi attacked the coastal cities and especially Salerno, but a dispute which arose between the Pisans and the Pope and Emperor prevented the capture of the fortress of Salerno, which remained in the hands of Roger's garrison. Roger, feeling that he could not repel this impetuous invasion, had retired to Sicily to await events and the opportune moment. The Pope and the Emperor, thus become masters of South Italy, thought of entrusting the duchy of Apulia to Rainulf, Count of Alife, whose strength and fidelity, they were sure, would hold the duchy against Roger. But at the moment of investing him there broke out a grave dissension between Lothar and Innocent, which marked once again how delicate and difficult the relations between Pope and Emperor always were, even when they most sought to act in accord. Each of them claimed the suzerainty over the reconquered lands and the right of investing Rainulf. It was a bitter dispute which lasted almost a month, and was finally removed by a kind of simultaneous double investiture. Pope and Emperor, each holding at the same time the symbolic banner of investiture, gave it together to Rainulf. And this was not the only cause of dissension which arose at this time, when the interests of the moment were able to lull, but not to extinguish, the profound antagonisms which lay hid in the relations between the Empire and the Church.

In September 1137 Innocent and Lothar started on their return. Re-entering Roman territory, they proceeded to the monastery of Farfa in Sabina, and Lothar continued his way to Germany. Like many other imperial expeditions in Italy, that of Lothar did not leave behind it durable results, but it had served to recall to men's minds the authority of the Empire, and had secured to the Pope the means of re-entering Rome and putting an end to the schism. It seemed that Lothar, on his return to Germany, would be able to extend his power and guide with confidence the fortunes of the Empire. But those fortunes were about to be entrusted to other hands. Scarcely had he surmounted the Alps, when the old Emperor died on his march through the Tyrol on 4 December 1137, and the Empire again lacked a ruler. The fear of a fresh civil war, and the suspicions which the power of Lothar's son-in-law, Henry of Bavaria, aroused, smoothed the way for Conrad of Hohenstaufen, who was elected King of the Romans on 7 March 1138 and on 13 March was crowned at Aix-la-Chapelle. With him began that powerful dynasty which was to exercise so unique an influence on the history of Italy.

The abasement of Roger's power had so lamed the strength of the Pierleoni that the Frangipani, getting the upper hand once more, could lead back Innocent II and give him again authority in Rome; while the eloquence of St Bernard aided the Pontiff to blot out the last traces of the schism and was detaching from the anti-Pope Anacletus the adherents who were left him. Meantime, scarcely had Lothar gone, before Roger left Sicily and disembarked his forces at Salerno, bent on recovering his lost lands. The new Duke of Apulia attacked and routed him; but Roger did not therefore give up his enterprise. St Bernard, meanwhile, visited him, and sought to induce him to abandon the anti-Pope; and Roger, seeing the profit to be gained, proposed a conference of three cardinals of Innocent and three of Anacletus to discuss the proposals on each side. The conference took place, and St Bernard succeeded in detaching from Anacletus his most authoritative and best reputed partisan, Cardinal Peter Pisano. With this desertion the schism could be said to be at an end; but the crafty Roger did not yet abandon Anacletus, and, when the anti-Pope died (25 January 1138), caused the few remaining schismatic cardinals to elect a new anti-Pope, who took the name of Victor IV; but he held out only a little time, and was soon obliged to renounce his pretensions. Roger continued the contest, though avoiding a pitched battle, and throughout 1138 South Italy was desolated by the war. Next year, fortune became favourable to the King of Sicily. The death of Duke Rainulf removed the most formidable of his competitors, and he could more energetically undertake the recovery of the Regno. Innocent II, after he had held a council (the Second Lateran), in which he annulled all the appointments made by Anacletus and with his own hands stripped the schismatic bishops of the ensigns of their dignity, marched in arms against Roger, who surrounded him, took him prisoner, and, shewing him great respect, treated with him for peace. The Pope was compelled to recognise Roger's royal dignity and to confirm as valid all the concessions he had obtained from Anacletus. Thus ended the war between the Pope and the Norman prince; Innocent, like Leo IX, returned humiliated to Rome; there new mutations awaited him.

That tendency which had already raised to such strength the cities of Lombardy and Central Italy, and had caused municipal life and liberties to grow so exuberantly in them, began to make itself felt in Rome also, although the city was under different conditions, which were not favourable to the development of a potent communal life. Situated in the midst of a region rendered unhealthy by long neglect and not made prosperous by agriculture or trade, torn by the factions of a rude and powerful nobility, in theory the seat of the Empire which still claimed its rights over it, and lastly the seat of the Popes who considered it as their patrimony and subject to their rule, Rome could with difficulty produce a commune which would be capable of rising to the dignity and strength of an independent State. But the spirit which animated other cities had also entered into Rome, and made it feel more vividly the desire of asserting itself, especially when causes of dissension arose between the citizens and the Pope. In the last years of Innocent this spirit of independence flamed out more hotly, and caused the beginning of a new and not inglorious period in the life of the commune.

Little by little, amid the factions which split up the great baronial families, and under the insecure rule of the Popes, there had gradually formed in Rome a kind of lesser nobility, which had similar interests to the people's, and thereby, in alliance with the people, gathered strength. From it the people acquired a consciousness of itself and of its civil rights. The re-awakening of the ideas of antiquity, which began to spread widely in Italy at this time, could not be without influence in Rome, where the memory of ancient greatness had been a vain but continual regret through the centuries. The union of the people with the growing minor nobility had furthered the organising of their forces, of which even the Popes had sometimes made use.

The Romans had favoured Innocent II's enterprise against Roger, and when the Pope was compelled to make peace they, in discontent, wished the Pope to tear up the treaty to which he had been forced to subscribe when he was a prisoner at the mercy of his conqueror. Innocent did not agree, and the Romans were irritated; but a graver cause of dissension became manifest soon afterwards in a question which touched them more nearly. Among all the surrounding districts, Rome was specially hostile to Tivoli. In 1141, to subdue this city, the Pope sent the Romans to besiege it; they were driven back and withdrew from the siege, meditating revenge. When they returned to the attack, Tivoli surrendered to the Pope, who concluded peace without consulting Rome, and Rome, aflame with wrath, demanded of the Pope that he should dismantle and completely destroy the rival town. The Pope would not yield, and there followed a revolution which changed the state of the city.

The insurgent Romans, in 1143, proclaimed on the Capitol the constitution of the republic, "renewed" the Senate[1], excluding therefrom the Prefect, the ancient warden of order, and almost all the greater nobility, although they may have had Jordan Pierleoni, a brother of Anacletus, as their leader. While they declared that they recognised the imperial authority which was far away and not too burdensome, they asserted especially their independence of the Pope, whom they wished to be despoiled of his temporalities, saying that he ought to live on offerings

---

[1] It is disputed whether the term "Senators," when it occurs before 1143, denotes really a consultative assembly or is merely a collective term for the greater nobles. See L. Halphen, *Études sur l'administration de Rome au moyen âge* (751–1252), who decides for the second alternative. The passage in the text has been slightly revised in view of M. Halphen's work.

and tithes. In these straits Innocent died (24 September 1143); he was succeeded in the space of a few months first by Celestine II and then by Lucius II, who wrote to King Conrad, stating his grievances against the Romans, and asking for his protection. The Romans meanwhile (1144) raised Jordan Pierleoni to the, perhaps dictatorial, office of Patrician, a reminiscence of the days of the Crescentii. Lucius even attempted to take the Capitol by force and overturn the Senate; but he was repulsed, and one report says that he was wounded with a stone during the attack. Shortly afterwards he died, worn-out and discouraged, on 15 February 1145.

Terrified amid the armed Romans, the cardinals immediately agreed on the election of the Pisan Bernard, Abbot of Sant' Anastasio *ad Aquas Salvias*, a disciple of St Bernard; he was very apprehensive at his election, and to the cardinals who chose him he wrote in wonder and fear lest he should be unequal to the heavy burden in such difficult times. He took the name of Eugenius III, and shewed as time went on much greater capacity in the government of the Church than St Bernard had suspected. Hardly was he elected when he was obliged to quit the city, which rioted for the recognition of the Senate and the Republic. He was consecrated in the monastery of Farfa, and then betook himself to Viterbo, while Rome consolidated its new state and rendered for the moment his return impossible.

The constitution of the republic did not, however, imply in the mind of the Romans the cessation of the idea of an imperial and papal Rome, which to the thought of medieval Christendom was, so to say, the pivot of the social unity of mankind. In fact, the Romans desired to shake off the yoke of the Pope's temporal sovereignty, and to live as a free commune; they associated with the idea of independence the vast and confused memories of the greatness of the Empire in which they placed their pride, without being aware that the Empire was now German, and that the glorious name of Rome served to cover the German pretensions to rule in Italy. These feelings of the Romans found characteristic expression in a letter which they addressed later to King Conrad, inviting him to come to Rome to receive the imperial crown, and there to take up his residence.

"All that we do," they wrote, "we do for your honour and in fealty to you." And they assured him that they had restored the Senate in order to exalt the Empire to the rank it held in the times of Constantine and Justinian, and that they had destroyed the houses and towers of the barons of the city who were preparing to resist the Empire in alliance with the Pope and the King of Sicily. None the less the Romans soon began to experience the difficulty of realising their intentions. The Pope found aid in the jealous distrust inspired by the new-born republic, which desired to extend its supremacy outside Rome and to dominate its neighbours. The imperilled cities round, and the high Roman nobility threatened in its possessions in the Campagna, whence it drew its strength, all joined the papal side. The city was obliged to yield to their united forces, receive the Pope anew within its walls, restore the authority of the Prefect, and recognise the sovereignty of the Church. Thus at the close of 1145 the Pope could re-enter Rome and there celebrate Christmas with solemn pomp; yet he, too, had not the strength to maintain himself. In spite of the concessions it had made, the new republic remained firmly seated on the Capitol, and the authority of the Senate continued to hold its own in face of the Pope. New dissensions soon broke out, and Eugenius, unable to make his will prevail, was constrained after a few months to abandon the city a second time, and repair again to Viterbo, whence he betook himself to Pisa.

This second exile shewed clearly that Eugenius could not hope that his throne in Rome would be stable without Conrad's help; and so he would have wished the king to hasten to Italy for the imperial coronation. But the king was preoccupied with German affairs, and, without refusing point-blank, avoided giving a definite reply; he continued to defer it, unmoved even by the fiery appeal of St Bernard, who exhorted him to go to defend the Church against the Roman people, a people accursed and riotous, incapable of rightly measuring their own strength, who in their folly and rage had attempted a great sacrilege. In spite of the exhortations of Bernard, who warned him not to listen to opposite counsels, Conrad, who had his own plans with regard to Italian affairs, continued to temporise. He aimed at linking his expedition to Italy with an entente with Constantinople, and perhaps too he was not wholly grieved at seeing the Pope entangled in difficulties, and reduced to such conditions as rendered the royal position towards him now far more favourable than had been that of Lothar towards Honorius and Innocent.

Meanwhile, the breach between the Romans and the Pope became ever wider and deeper. A remarkable man had appeared among them to fire them with his own passionate ardour for citizen liberty and the reform of the Church. This was Arnold of Brescia, who for some time both in Italy and beyond the Alps had in perfervid discourses championed new ideas, full of peril according to many, on the state of the Church and its reform. The renascence of philosophical ideas and of classical culture, which developed so swiftly and widely in Europe at the dawn of the twelfth century, stirred in men's minds, and incited them to debate problems and intellectual novelties which disquieted them and alarmed the guardians of the recognised religious and social doctrines. After early studies in Italy Arnold had gone to Paris and become a disciple of Abelard; he had been his devoted follower, and had shared his disasters with a tenacious faith and a firmness of character greater than his master's. But an apostolic fervour which summoned him to action was stronger in him than Abelard's spirit of subtle enquiry. Perhaps, living among the people as he did, he loved and welcomed their favour; but he felt to the core a holy zeal for liberty and the purification of the Church, and persecutions and obstacles only inflamed it the more. Pious, pure, and austere, his greatest adversaries bore unanimous witness to the sanctity of his life, while they combated his doctrines and his actions. "Would that he were of sound doctrine," exclaimed St Bernard, "as he is austere in life! A man who neither eats nor drinks, he only, like the Devil, hungers and thirsts for the blood of souls." It does not appear that his eloquence was turned against dogmas. Only one contemporary, Otto of Freising, relates an uncertain rumour, that he did not think rightly concerning the sacrament of the altar and infant baptism; and the story of his last hours could perhaps raise a doubt on his doctrine with regard to confession. Rather than at doctrine he aimed at discipline. He vehemently attacked the clergy, denied to clerics and monks the right to possess property, and to bishops the right to the *regalia*; he bitterly denounced the way of life of the ecclesiastics. In the Lateran Council of 1139 Innocent II had blamed him, and condemned him to silence. Forced to leave Brescia, he had returned to France, and had been an unshakeable defender of his master Abelard in opposition to St Bernard, who became his enemy.

When Abelard yielded before his mighty adversary, Arnold continued the struggle at Sainte-Geneviève among poor students, and probably mingled with his teaching violent invectives against the corruption of the clergy. He could not resist for long in France, but betook himself to Zurich, where he found new followers and new persecutions, and thence joined the train of Cardinal Guido, legate in Germany, who protected him. He returned with the cardinal to Italy, and at Viterbo saw Eugenius III, who absolved him and prescribed as his penance a pilgrimage to the graves of the Apostles and to the churches of Rome.

The place was not adapted for the hoped-for repentance of Arnold; the Pope had sent fire to a volcano. At that time Rome was both the most fertile soil in which he could sow the seed of his doctrines, and itself a stimulus and inspiration for the thoughts which dominated his life. The heights of the Capitoline hill, sacred to history, and the ruins of the Forum, the ancient churches and the graves of the martyrs in the catacombs, must have spoken a mysterious language to the soul of Arnold of Brescia, and have called him to his mission with energy renewed. The republican movement and the Patarine traditions diffused among the people in Lombardy found their consecration in Rome from the history told by her ruins, and from the churches and sacred memories of Rome the spirit and the humility of primitive Christianity seemed to ask of God a reform to free the Papacy from worldly interests and mundane pomp. The fervid, vehement words of the Brescian apostle fascinated the Romans, ever ready listeners to eloquence which evoked the memories of their past greatness. The republic was strengthened by him, and he had a large share in the counsels and regulation of the city. To the

Senate already constituted there was added, in name at least, an equestrian order[1] probably composed of the lesser nobility and richer citizens; and thus there was created at Rome, in imitation of the Lombard republics, a nucleus of picked militia; the Capitol was fortified; and the constitution of Rome became in substance similar to that of the other Italian communes.

Rome's example was followed in the surrounding territory: other communes began to be organised in the Patrimony of the Church, and rendered the position of the Pope with regard to Rome ever more difficult. But for the moment the Papacy was obliged to direct its solicitude elsewhere. The Muslim power, which had been checked in its career by the First Crusade, again appeared threatening and awoke anxiety in Europe, and with the anxiety almost a fever of desire for a new crusade. The discords between the Christian rulers in the East, the close neighbours of the Musulmans, had borne their natural fruit, and opened to the Saracens the way to the re-conquest of the lands torn from them by the First Crusade. Zangī, a resolute and bold Muslim warrior, led the attack, to which the Christians could not oppose an efficacious barrier. When Edessa fell into Zangī's hands at the end of 1144, a bulwark was lost without which all the Christian Levant was placed in grave peril. It seemed evident that, if Antioch, too, was taken, Jerusalem itself would not be safe, and perhaps all the work of the First Crusade would totter and crumble to nothing. The weak and discordant Christian princes turned anxiously to the West for aid; they sounded the alarm and called Europe to the defence of Christendom. France more especially felt the force of this appeal, and shewed herself inclined to respond to it with the same *élan* as to that for the First Crusade. Eugenius received at Viterbo messages from the Levant, and understood that now was the moment for him to imitate Urban II's example, and summon Christendom to the counter-attack. He was the more willing to do so because he hoped that the movement he was about to initiate might serve also to bring the Eastern Churches closer to Rome. He turned first to France, where the king, Louis VII, and his people were easily gained over, although his chief and wisest minister, Abbot Suger, was against the enterprise. The Crusade was decided on, and the king took the Cross. The Pope, involved in his struggle with the Romans, could not go at once to France, and entrusted to St Bernard the preaching of the Crusade. Convinced that he spoke by divine inspiration, the Saint infused in others his own conviction, and the enthusiasm he evoked surpassed all expectation; it seemed a miracle. "Cities and castles are emptied," he wrote to Eugenius III, "and there is not left one man

---

[1] Does this classic name (Otto Frising., *Gesta Friderici I imp.* I, 28, ed. Waitz-Simson, SGUS, p. 44) cover a reform of the ancient *scholae* of the militia, or the institution of the body of Councillors, *Consiliarii*, who at Rome represented the Great Council of other Italian communes?

to seven women, and everywhere there are widows of still living husbands."

It was needful that the ardour of Germany should correspond to that of France, and Bernard hoped to revive it by his eloquence and to induce King Conrad to take the Cross and join with the King of France in the great enterprise. In a first interview at Frankfort at the end of November 1146, he was unable, although honoured on all hands, to win Conrad to take the crusading vow. At the close of December he met the king again at Spires and returned to the charge. At first Conrad resisted: the internal troubles of Germany, his delicate relations with Constantinople and Roger of Sicily, made him hesitate to embark on an adventure so far from his realm. But he was carried away by the general excitement; and at a solemn service in the cathedral, in answer to an unpremeditated exhortation of St Bernard, he took the Cross. The German nobles vied with one another in following their sovereign's example, among them his nephew, the young Frederick of Swabia, who thus took the first step in a career destined to enrol his name amid the greatest and most glorious of Germany.

Although Eugenius was himself on the point of crossing the Alps to increase the impetus of the Crusade and watch over the great expedition, he did not share the joy of St Bernard when he knew that Conrad had yielded to the Saint's inspiration and was preparing to leave Europe. Although the peril of the Holy Places moved the Pontiff, not even that made him forget the circumstances of the Papacy in Rome and Italy, and the necessity of the speedy and sure help which at that moment he hoped for from Germany. Conrad's absence could not be short, and the needs of the Pope were pressing. Further, Eugenius could easily foresee that this absence would weaken still more the imperial authority in North and Central Italy. Here the cities continued in perpetual war with one another; but they did not seem to be enfeebled thereby, and the spirit of civic liberties did not only nourish in them the sentiment of independence towards the imperial claims. Among the people and the lower clergy there were growing sentiments of independence towards ecclesiastical authority, which disturbed the Pope and had caused him several times to call the attention of the bishops, especially in Lombardy, to these, and to exhort them to deal sternly with the dangerous novelties which crept into their dioceses. And from the Crusade there might arise between the crusading monarchs, the Eastern Emperor, and Roger of Sicily relations not devoid of disquiet to the Pope. King Roger, most sagacious, ambitious, and ready to snatch every opportunity to assure and enlarge his power, sought to draw profit from the Crusade. To the request of the King of France he replied with large proffers of ships and victuals, offering to join the Crusade in person or to send one of his sons; but like proffers were also made by the Emperor Manuel Comnenus, and were accepted, much to Roger's annoyance, who desired to draw the

King of France to himself and separate him from Conrad in the Eastern enterprise. He knew that Conrad was in secret treaty with the Emperor Manuel for an alliance against himself, and he wished to isolate him. His envoys left France predicting the harm that the fraud of the Greeks would occasion to the crusaders, and they were not false prophets.

Eugenius III, who had set out for France, sent messengers to Conrad with letters in which he could not refrain from complaining that the king had decided to take the Cross without consulting him. Conrad justified himself by alleging the irresistible impulse to which he had suddenly yielded. "The Holy Ghost," he wrote to the Pope, "Who breatheth where He listeth, Who cometh on a sudden, did not allow me to delay that I might take your counsel or that of any other, but in a moment touched my heart to follow Him." Understanding that the Pope needed reassuring, he announced to him that he had made arrangements for the time of his absence, and had had his son Henry crowned king, who would govern in his stead; he invited the Pope to proceed to Germany from France for an interview with him, and to treat personally of the affairs of the realm and the Crusade.

Eugenius did not accept the invitation, but he could not undo what had been done, and it only remained for him to push on events in the best manner possible. He met Louis VII in France, and had leisure to confer with him before he started for the expedition, on which Conrad III had already preceded him. But the history of this disastrous Crusade does not belong to this chapter; and we must confine ourselves to recording the consequences it had for Italy and the relations of the Empire and the Papacy.

The chief reaction on Italy from the Crusade was felt in its relations with the Byzantine Empire and with the African coasts of the Mediterranean. King Roger of Sicily did not fail to seize the occasion of drawing advantage from a movement which was bound to occupy the forces and the solicitude of the Emperor Manuel Comnenus. The continuous increase of Roger's power had been from its commencement a cause of suspicion and disquietude to the Byzantine monarchs, who saw in it a menace to their possessions and influence in the Adriatic, and also looked on the steady expansion of the Sicilian domination on the African coasts and Roger's pretensions to the principality of Antioch as perilous to themselves. The policy of the Comneni necessarily tended to oppose the ambitions of the Norman prince, and to try if it were possible to wreck them and substitute for his realm a restored Byzantine dominion, or at least a marked influence, in South Italy. Roger, aware of this policy, and of the negotiations for an alliance against him which had several times taken place between Manuel and Conrad III, thought that it was time to act. Preparing a powerful fleet, he undertook an energetic expedition by sea, seized on and fortified Corfù, and placed there a Norman garrison to secure its permanent possession. Setting sail again, he became master of Cape Malea and the island of Cerigo, both of which he also fortified; then, penetrating the Gulf of Corinth, his troops sacked Corinth, and marching by land reached Thebes, which underwent the same fate. From Thebes, which then was flourishing through the silk manufacture, he took not only plunder but some artificers, who were brought to Sicily and afterwards aided there in the development of the silk industry. Having thus displayed its standards in the Grecian seas, Roger's fleet, loaded with booty, returned to Sicily about the beginning of 1148.

The Emperor Manuel Comnenus was grievously and profoundly moved by these events, and he actively bestirred himself in devising a remedy. After his overtures for an alliance with Louis VII, who was still in Asia, had failed, he turned with better results to the Venetians, who also took umbrage at the growing extension of the Norman power in the Adriatic and willingly became his allies. The result of this alliance was a long and chequered sea-campaign, in which Manuel succeeded in recovering Corfù (summer of 1149). Encouraged by this success, Manuel thought of closing on Roger and realising his plans in South Italy. After the disastrous ending of the Crusade, the Byzantine Emperor turned with many blandishments to Conrad III, whose presence in the East no longer inspired him with any fear, and renewed and completed the negotiations for an alliance which had been often begun and interrupted. It was a formidable league, and Roger, who saw the danger, employed all his sagacity to hinder its effects and to turn it from himself. Profiting by the inner dissensions of Germany, he attempted, even by giving subsidies, to raise against Conrad a league of German barons, which should force the King of the Romans, immediately on his return to Europe, to hasten to Germany and turn away from any enterprise against Sicily. At the same time Roger sought a *rapprochement* with the papal party at Rome by means of its chief, the powerful baron Cencio Frangipane. Thus he might separate from Conrad the Pope, who was displeased with the Byzantine alliance, and induce him to favour the German barons, who were opposed to their sovereign.

The history of the relations of the Popes with their Norman neighbours consists of an alternation of hostility and *rapprochements* occasioned by the perpetual alternation of the mutual distrust and political necessities of the two parties. Eugenius III, after the departure of the crusaders for the Holy Land, had sojourned in France and Germany, occupied with the ecclesiastical affairs of the two countries, and awaiting the opportune moment for re-entering Italy. He held several councils, and in them, especially at Rheims where the opinions of Bishop Gilbert de la Porrée were laboriously discussed, there was manifested all the anxiety of the Church to secure the orthodoxy of theological doctrines from the subtle perils which were created by the extension of philosophic thought, by a pronounced tendency towards investigation, and by a bold and restless desire for speculation. Meanwhile, there arrived gloomy news from the East. The disastrous result of the Crusade, proclaimed with such assurance of victory, as if God Himself had directly inspired its initiation, turned against Eugenius and St Bernard the minds of the peoples who most felt the weight of the calamity. Eugenius saw that a sojourn in France and Germany, both embittered by their disillusion, was no longer suitable for him, and took the road for return. In July 1148 he held a council at Cremona, in which he confirmed the decrees of the Council of Rheims. It is probable that in it he also treated of the conditions of the Church of Rome, where Arnold of Brescia was exercising his influence. Certain it is that a few days later at Brescia the Pope, in a warning addressed to the Roman clergy, complained that some Roman ecclesiastics, following the errors of the schismatic Arnold, were refusing obedience to the cardinals and their other superiors; and he ordered that all contact with Arnold should be avoided. Thus from the moment he put foot again in Italy, Eugenius aimed at Rome, and frankly renewed the struggle.

Quitting Lombardy in October 1148, the Pope halted some time at his native city of Pisa, which he drew to his support for his imminent action against Rome, and then went to resume his residence at Viterbo. The league concluded between Manuel Comnenus and Conrad troubled him, and, on the other hand, he was oppressed by the necessity of prompt aid to return to his see. Roger of Sicily, wholly intent on his secret manoeuvres against Conrad, found at this moment a readier hearing from the Pope. Eugenius, supported by the Frangipani and the other Roman barons, who were impatient of the rule of the democracy in the Capitol, had at great expense collected troops to attempt the re-conquest of Rome. To gain the Pope for his schemes, Roger offered him a contingent in aid; but in spite of this *rapprochement*, it is not easy to say how far the Pope shewed himself disposed to support the King of Sicily and the German barons who were conspiring against Conrad. Undoubtedly Eugenius, while outwardly reconciled to his powerful neighbour, was obliged to be reserved and wary. Nor did he abandon his reserve when the King of France, on his return by way of Roger's dominions from the Crusade, met him at Tusculum, and disclosed to him the project of a new crusade, including the formation of a league destined to strike at the heart of the Byzantine Empire, which Louis VII held to be the principal cause of his own disasters. The diplomacy of the Roman Curia saw at once that such a league would increase Roger's power too much, and let the proposal drop. Nevertheless, ever intent on regaining full possession of Rome, Eugenius with the help of the soldiers of the Sicilian king succeeded in seating himself by force in the Lateran; but the Roman Senate did not therefore submit, and maintained its power in the face of the Pope: it upheld the rights it had acquired and its protection of Arnold of Brescia, who remained in the city.

Meanwhile, scarcely had Conrad III left the East, when he moved with the greatest speed towards Germany with a view to restoring order to the realm, vexed by dissensions and revolt. Shortly after his arrival he was attacked by an illness which lasted six months; but his presence induced an improvement, and a defeat which his son, the young King Henry, inflicted on the rebel barons (1 February 1150) secured the fortunes of the kingship and raised its diminished prestige. There then began a very active interchange of diplomatic moves, which tended both to form and to break up alliances, to insinuate and to dissipate distrust and suspicion. Conrad, fixed in the idea of destroying Roger's power, endeavoured to confirm the agreement made with Manuel Comnenus for common action in South Italy, and asked at Constantinople for the hand of a Greek princess for his son King Henry. The Pope, while attempting to erase the unfavourable impression occasioned by his momentary *rapprochement* with Roger, sought for means to estrange Conrad from the Byzantines; but on this point the king gave vague and evasive replies. The Romans, by repeated letters and embassies to Conrad, strove to emphasise the Pope's relations with the King of Sicily and the German rebels, and to increase to their own profit his distrust of the Roman Curia. Meanwhile, Roger, supported by Louis VII, who thought of retrieving his defeats in Asia, importuned Conrad to induce him to change his policy and turn against Constantinople.

Thus Conrad became still more an uncertain element in the various currents of European politics; and amid such alternation of contrary proposals he did not let himself be moved. The ardour that was manifested in France for a new crusade left him cold. The exhortations sent him by some eminent French ecclesiastics, such as St Bernard and Peter of Cluny, only aroused his suspicions of Rome, so that the Pope had to hasten to declare that those personages had acted of their own motion, and that he was quite a stranger to their overtures. Conrad and his counsellors saw clearly that the King of France was a tool of Roger for thwarting his plans in Italy and for making war on Constantinople; and the Pope himself, although he could not oppose it openly, had no faith in the possibility of a fresh expedition to the East.

Constrained after a few months' residence to quit Rome anew and retire near to Roger's borders, the Pope met the Sicilian king at Ceprano, and there they discussed many ecclesiastical questions in regard to the Regno, which were in great part adjusted. But on an essential point, the full recognition of Roger's sovereignty, they did not reach an understanding; and they parted with outward friendship but now definitely alienated from one another. The Pope could only turn, without further vacillation, to a complete understanding with Conrad, who also recognised the importance of such an accord for the preparation of his expedition to Italy, and for the securing of results from it. The king sent the Pope an embassy, which was to settle the basis of the agreement. Doubtless it was then determined that the king should receive the imperial crown at Rome, and, in return, force the Romans into subjection to the Pope. It was bound to be more difficult to arrive at an understanding concerning Conrad's alliance with Manuel Comnenus, which had been the principal reason that the Pope had leant towards the King of Sicily; but the dispatch of the Cardinals Jordan of Santa Susanna and Octavian of Santa Cecilia as legates to Germany shewed that the Pope was resolved to smooth over every difficulty in order to bring the matter to a satisfactory conclusion. Both these cardinals were notable personages of the Curia, and one of them, Octavian, was later destined, as the anti-Pope Victor IV, to play an important part in the relations of Papacy and Empire. Nobly born, fond of pomp and show, free with his money and liberal in granting favours, he aimed perhaps already at the Papacy, and sought to win the good-will of the Germans, just as he had sought, though without much success, to win that of Rome. On this occasion he became acquainted with Frederick, the young Duke of Swabia, and thus established relations with the future Emperor who was to become his mainstay. The two legates stayed long in Germany, arranging many pending ecclesiastical questions, and treating with Conrad concerning his Italian expedition. This was solemnly announced at the diet of Würzburg in September 1151; but time was necessary if it was to be undertaken energetically and with durable results. On the one hand, a large force was needful to control the autonomous tendencies of the free communes and to destroy Roger's power; and on the other, it was necessary to be sure that Germany was in such order as to permit a long absence of the king and his most powerful adherents without harm. A year was allotted for the preparations, and it was decided that Conrad with his army should start on 11 September 1152 to cross the Alps. There was still a serious task for the king to perform in Germany before his departure, for Henry the Lion, Duke of Saxony, was in full revolt, and it was necessary to subdue him and leave him incapable of doing harm. While attending to this, Conrad yet took the utmost pains to prepare for his descent into Italy, which now occupied the chief place in his thoughts. A little previously he had suffered a grievous blow in the death of his son, the youthful King Henry; for him he had been negotiating that marriage with a Byzantine princess which was to draw tighter still the bonds of the alliance with the Eastern Court. Since the son who was left him was a mere child, Conrad, although he was getting into years, thought of resuming the negotiations on his own behalf, and for that end sent an embassy to Constantinople.

At the same time he sent ambassadors into Italy, his chancellor Arnold, Archbishop-elect of Cologne, Wibald, Abbot of Stablo, and the notary Henry, all three trusty counsellors experienced in State affairs. They were sent to the Pope, but were commissioned to conduct negotiations on their road which would assure the unhampered progress of the expedition. They bore a royal letter to Pisa, with which they were especially to negotiate for the preparation of a fleet to be employed against the King of Sicily. Taking the opportunity of this embassy, Conrad at last accorded a reply to the letters which the Romans had repeatedly addressed to him. It was a reply of mingled condescension and arrogance, in which he skilfully announced his speedy arrival with large forces in Italy, and recommended to them his ambassadors, from whom the Romans would learn with certainty his will and intentions. In reality, his envoys, and especially Wibald, were charged to mediate concerning conditions of peace between the Pope and the Romans. In the very valuable collection of Wibald's letters is found a kind of draft of these conditions, from which we can infer the existence of the negotiations which must have taken place under the circumstances. But the Pope, relying on the hope of Conrad's coming, did not profit by Wibald's intervention, and did not follow his counsels of moderation, missing thereby the opportunity of reconciling himself with the Romans. Perhaps he was convinced that a peaceful solution of the controversy would not be lasting, and trusted only to the argument of victorious force. Now that he was entirely alienated from the King of Sicily, he was determined to smooth Conrad's road and thus facilitate in every way his early arrival in Rome; the ambassadors took their leave elated with concessions and promises.

But they were not to bring back to their master the messages of the Pope. While still on their journey, they received the news that Conrad had died on 15 February 1152 at Bamberg, whither he had gone to hold a diet. All the preparations for the Italian expedition were thus unexpectedly interrupted. The relations between Germany and Italy, the condition of Germany itself, not yet issued from a long period of confusion and discord, and the consolidation of the Empire, might relapse into a state of danger and incertitude if a firm and vigorous hand did not succeed in taking the reins and steadfastly guiding the realm. Conrad III on his death-bed understood the needs of the moment, and indicated as his successor his nephew Frederick of Swabia, to whom he entrusted the royal insignia and the wardship of his child son. The magnates of the realm followed Conrad's counsel, and on 4 March 1152 Frederick of Hohenstaufen was elected at Frankfort. With him the star of the Empire was to shine with renewed lustre.

CHAPTER XII.

FREDERICK BARBAROSSA AND GERMANY.

THE campaigns of Frederick Barbarossa in Italy form the most celebrated feature of his reign; they reveal his great qualities as a soldier and as a statesman in times both of victory and of defeat; they form a part, and a very important part, of the great contest between Empire and Papacy. The peculiar interest attached to this side of Frederick's activities has often led historians to under-estimate the value of his work in his native kingdom. Yet it is in Germany that the enduring marks of his boundless energies are to be sought. He succeeded to the throne of a kingdom in a state of complete disintegration; a great family feud divided the land into factions in open hostility; internal discord and wide-spread unrest prevailed everywhere; the country was exhausted by civil war and by the plundering and burning which accompanied it, the people by famine and want which was its natural consequence. The royal authority in the hands of Conrad was too weak to check the lawlessness of the nobility, hopelessly incapable of dealing with the crucial question of the position of the Welfs. Within four years of his coronation Frederick, by his masterful rule, had transformed Germany. Feuds were healed, enemies reconciled; *Landfrieden* were proclaimed in all the duchies, and offenders were dealt with by stern punishments. Order was restored and the rule of law was established.

Conrad's elder son Henry had died two years before, and the dying king realised that where he had so signally failed his younger son Frederick, a boy of but six years old, was unlikely to succeed. He therefore designated as his successor his nephew Frederick of Swabia and entrusted to him the royal insignia. He was a man of remarkable promise, of suitable age, and with a distinguished career behind him; and what was of still greater importance he was connected by equal ties of kinship to the two rival houses of Hohenstaufen and Welf. His father was the late King Conrad's elder brother Frederick; his mother, Judith, was the sister of Henry the Proud. He had already on more than one occasion acted as mediator between the two parties; his sympathies were equally divided; indeed no man was more favourably circumstanced for healing the quarrel which had for so long disturbed the peace of Germany. Seldom during the Middle Ages has a king been chosen to rule Germany with greater unanimity on the part of his subjects[1]. The formalities of

[1] Henry, Archbishop of Mayence, appears to have raised objections to Frederick's election (see the passage in the royal chronicle of Cologne, SGUS, ed. Waitz, p. 89); but evidently he was unable to press them far. Cf. Simonsfeld, *Jahrbücher*, pp. 19 sq.

election were carried through with scarcely a hint of opposition, and with a promptness and ease truly amazing considering the state of the country at the moment of Conrad's death. On 15 February 1152 the king was dead; on 4 March Frederick was chosen king by the princes at Frankfort; on the next day he set out for his coronation, travelling by boat down the Main and the Rhine as far as Sinzig and so by road to Aix-la-Chapelle. There on 9 March he was crowned by Arnold, Archbishop of Cologne. Immediately after the event, emissaries—Eberhard, Bishop of Bamberg, Hillin, Archbishop-elect of Trèves, and Adam, Abbot of Ebrach—were dispatched to Rome with letters to Pope Eugenius III in which the king announced his election, promised his obedience, and declared his readiness to protect the Holy See.

The man thus chosen to rule Germany was in the prime of life, some thirty years old, vigorous in mind and body, a fine figure of a man of rather more than middle height, and of perfect proportions; his personal appearance was remarkably attractive, with his fine features, his reddish curly hair, and his expression so genial that, we are told by Acerbus Morena who knew him well, he gave one the idea that he always wanted to laugh; even when moved to anger he would conceal his indignation beneath a smile. Brave, fearless, a superb fighter, he regarded war as the best of games; he gloried in the hardly-contested battle; he was the very embodiment of medieval chivalry. Though no scholar, he was not without intellectual tastes; he could understand, if he could not speak, Latin, and in his native tongue he was even fluent; he was interested in history, in the deeds of his ancestors. With the qualities necessary for ruling a great empire he was singularly well endowed: shrewd judgment, rapid power of decision, untiring energy, the highest sense of justice. Frederick was no respecter of persons; though normally his temper was of the gentlest, he was inexorable towards wrong-doers, and even on the festive day of his coronation he is said to have refused forgiveness to a malefactor; "I outlawed you not out of malice," he declared, "but in accordance with the dictates of justice; therefore there is no ground for pardon." A friend of distinguished Roman lawyers he was himself a lawgiver of no slight ability, and his public acts bulk large in the volumes of Constitutions of medieval Emperors[1]. Not only among writers of his own country or of his own way of thinking is Frederick regarded as nearly reaching to human perfection according to the ideals of the time. German and foreigner, friend and foe, have but one opinion on the character of the great Emperor; they must go back in their histories to Charles the Great to find a worthy parallel.

At the time of the coronation, so Abbot Wibald reports to the Pope,

---

[1] Some idea of the amount of his legislative work may be gained from the fact that his Constitutions and Public Acts occupy no less than 273 quarto pages of the *Monumenta Germaniae Historica*, whereas those of his predecessors from Henry the Fowler to Conrad III occupy together only 190.

there was talk among the bishops of an immediate expedition to Italy. The more prudent counsel of the lay princes, however, prevailed; and the new king turned his first attention to the more pressing and no less difficult problems of his German kingdom. The promulgation of a general land-peace was the preliminary step in this direction. This ordinance is a striking advance on the meagre, temporary, local enactments of former kings; it was universal in its application to all parts of Germany, it was intended to be permanent, it was comprehensive in character. Breaches of the peace were punishable by the strictest penalties: murder and theft (when the value of the stolen goods exceeded five shillings) were punished with death; smaller offences, such as assault and petty larceny, by fines, mutilation, or flogging. There were reforms too in criminal procedure and in the settlement of disputes over possession of land. The price of corn was to be fixed annually after the harvest by the count of the district and a committee of seven; selling above the fixed price was henceforth to be treated as a breach of the peace. This regulation was intended to remedy the abuse of forcing up the price by holding back the grain in times of shortage. In 1158 at the Diet of Roncaglia a peace constitution was issued not only for Germany but for the whole Empire; all persons between the ages of eighteen and seventy were bound to swear to maintain the peace, and their oath was to be renewed every five years.

The most significant feature in this legislation was its treatment of private war. The *Landfrieden* had grown up in the early years of the twelfth century with the object of checking unjustifiable feuds. The principle emerges that private war, so characteristic of medieval social life, was only permissible under certain prescribed conditions; otherwise it was a crime, a violation of the *Landfrieden*, a breach of the peace. In the *Constitutio pacis* of 1158 it was forbidden altogether. Presumably, however, the machinery of justice and modes of redress were still too rudimentary to admit of so sweeping a reform; and in the last of Frederick's peace enactments, the Constitution against Incendiaries promulgated at the Nuremberg Diet in 1186, the feud was once more conditionally permitted. Perhaps these constitutions do not bear the stamp of originality; they were based no doubt on previous enactments of a like nature; so for example the Nuremberg Constitution may have its origin in those issued against incendiaries by Innocent II, Eugenius III, and Alexander III. But it was not so much in their novelty as in the fact that they gave uniformity in the penal law and procedure throughout the Empire that their true value lies. Nevertheless, in spite of this comprehensive general legislation, the old provincial land-peace was not entirely superseded. Frederick himself confirmed many local peaces: in the first year of his reign he confirmed a Swabian land-peace at Ulm; and after the settlement of the Bavarian question at Ratisbon in 1156 one was sworn for that duchy. The peace promulgated at Weissenburg in 1179 for Rhenish Franconia, which in character is not unlike the

Treuga Dei, has a special interest attaching to it: it professes to be the renewal of a peace which has existed from time immemorial, for so long indeed that it has come to rank as an ordinance of Charles the Great. The legislative achievement of Frederick bears a favourable comparison with that of his great English contemporary, Henry II. The uncompromising measures employed in its execution are thus summarised by the chronicler: "much blood was shed by King Frederick for securing peace, very many persons were hanged, many churches, towns, and castles were destroyed by fire." But if we deplore the crude violence of the method, we can only praise the result, for, we are told, he so successfully crushed the disturbers of the peace that in a very short time the firmest peace was restored by the fear of his coming.

During the royal progress the work of reconciliation went on apace. Acting on the dying wish of King Conrad, he enfeoffed his young cousin, Frederick of Rothenburg, with the duchy of Swabia, and created his uncle Welf VI Marquess of Tuscany and Duke of Spoleto. A feud between the bishop and the townsmen of Utrecht, which Conrad's efforts had failed to determine, was immediately ended at his first diet at Merseburg; he arbitrated between the rival candidates for the Danish throne, and extended the authority of the house of Zähringen over Burgundy and Provence; at Constance in March 1153 he concluded a close alliance with Pope Eugenius III; and before the first year of his reign had drawn to a close he had approached the most difficult problem of all—the position of the Welfs.

Hitherto Frederick had shewn favour but not undue partiality to his cousin Henry; and in a dispute in which the latter became involved with Albert the Bear over the inheritances of two Saxon nobles, Hermann of Winzenburg and Bernard of Plötske, he had decided the matter in the most equitable manner by assigning one inheritance to each of the disputants. But with wide and ambitious schemes in view he could not afford to delay a settlement of the vital question of the Bavarian duchy. The success of his plans moreover depended in no small measure on the full co-operation of the powerful head of the house of Welf, to whose influence, perhaps, he partly owed his crown[1]. The first years were occupied with tentative negotiations rendered difficult by the uncompromising attitude of Henry Jasomirgott, who, by the late king's arrangement, was in possession of the Bavarian duchy. Diet followed diet in rapid succession, resulting only in delay and postponement. Henry Jasomirgott, summoned to Würzburg in October 1152, failed to appear; he was

---

[1] So Haller, *Der Sturz Heinrichs des Löwen*, p. 297, on the authority of the late (written *c.* 1230) *Chronicon S. Michaelis Luneburgensis*, MGH, *Script.* XXIII, 396, 'qui (Henricus) eum ad imperialem promoverat celsitudinem.' But cf. Simonsfeld, *Jahrbücher*, p. 26. It is, however, possible that Henry had come to an understanding with Frederick before his election that he would satisfy Henry's claim to Bavaria. See Giesebrecht, v, p. 9.

summoned twice in the following year before the Court, at Worms (Whitsuntide) and at Spires (December), but in each case he evaded a decision by finding a flaw in the summons. At last on 3 June 1154 the princes, wearied by the seemingly interminable proceedings, met at Goslar and resolved to bring the matter to a conclusion. The elder Henry was again absent; his continued defiance of the royal authority was sufficient pretext for depriving him of his position. Henry the younger, who had already assumed the title of Duke of Bavaria and Saxony, was now therefore duly awarded the vacant duchy. After his return with the Emperor from the Italian expedition (1154–5), in which he had conspicuously distinguished himself, he was formally invested with the dukedom of Bavaria at Ratisbon (October 1155). But the settlement lacked finality. Henry Jasomirgott obstinately refused to yield to the conciliatory advances of Frederick. It was not until a year later that an arrangement satisfactory to both parties was concluded at Ratisbon on 17 September 1156. It was a diet of the first importance, for it established the power of Henry the Lion and it created the duchy of Austria.

The ex-duke did not enter the town; he set up a magnificent encampment some two miles from its walls, and there the solemn scene, which witnessed the end of the long drawn-out struggle, took place. The details had already been prepared and the terms engrossed in a document[1] read aloud to the assembled princes by Vladislav II of Bohemia. Henry the elder surrendered the seven flags, the insignia of the Bavarian dukedom; these in turn were handed over to Henry the younger, who forthwith returned two to the Emperor, relinquishing by this act all claim to the Austrian March. With this insignia the Emperor enfeoffed Henry Jasomirgott with the now created duchy of Austria. With it the new duke received an enviable list of privileges, such indeed as no other prince of the Empire might enjoy. The duchy was granted in fee to Henry and his wife Theodora jointly, and to their children whether male or female; if they should die without issue, they had the right of bequeathing the duchy by will[2]; no one was permitted to exercise jurisdiction within the duchy except with the consent of the duke; furthermore the duke was only liable for attendance at diets held in Bavaria and for military service in Austria or in its neighbourhood[2].

Frederick's policy towards the great princes of Germany was at first therefore to strengthen their position with the hope that they would reward his confidence with their loyalty and co-operation. The duchy of Bavaria was not the only accretion to the power of the house of Welf. There were claims also to Italian territories. A Welfic heiress four

---

[1] MGH, *Const.* I, 220, the *privilegium minus* which is the genuine document. The *privilegium maius, ibid.* I, 683, is a forgery of Rudolf IV of Austria made in the winter 1358–9, see Huber, SKAW, xxxiv, pp. 17 sq.

[2] According to W. Erben, *Das Privilegium Friedrichs I für den Herzogtum Oesterreich* (1902), these clauses were later interpolations.

generations back, Cunegunda, sister of the childless Welf III, had married Azzo, Marquess of Este, and through her the line descended. While the imperial army was encamped near Verona, Henry the Lion had a meeting with his Italian cousin and acquired the family inheritance in return for a payment of 200 marks. At the same time his uncle Welf VI, with Frederick behind him, was able to make good his claim to the wide possessions of the Countess Matilda.

Heinricus Leo dux Bawariae et Saxoniae: such was the name now borne by the great Welf. He ruled an *imperium in imperio*, but he did not abuse his privileged position; his rule for the twenty years which followed the settlement of Ratisbon was beneficial to Germany, if it was detrimental to the interests of individual princes. Henry threw himself with all his energy into the work of German expansion, the promotion of commercial enterprise, the development of municipal life.

The northern frontier had been disturbed for ten years past by a civil war in Denmark. Eric III died in 1146, and Svein the son of Eric II and Canute the son of Magnus disputed for the throne. The rivals had laid their pretensions before Frederick at his first diet at Merseburg (18 May 1152), but the decision had satisfied the successful hardly more than the defeated candidate; for Svein in return for the recognition of his claims had had to acknowledge himself the vassal of the German king, and to compensate his opponent with the island of Zealand. Their feud unappeased, the rival claimants continued their war of devastation, now one, now the other, gaining a temporary advantage. In 1154 Svein, alienated from his subjects on account of his cruelty, and at the end of his resources, fled to Saxony, where he lived for upwards of two years with his father-in-law, Count Conrad of Wettin. In 1156, when the latter withdrew to a monastery which he had founded at Lauterberg, Svein again went in search of help to recover his lost throne. He found the Saxon princes ready for the enterprise; the services of Henry, just returned triumphant from the Diet of Ratisbon, were easily secured in consideration of a subsidy. The campaign was opened with success; Schleswig and Ripen fell into Svein's hands; but a national resistance and the treachery of the Slavs serving in the German host checked its progress. They withdrew therefore with hostages from the captured towns. Henry, however, did not relinquish his efforts on behalf of his allies; with the help of the Slavonic prince Niclot and by judicious bribery he once more gained a foothold on Danish territory. Thus matters stood when the Danish Church under the guidance of the Bishop of Ripen exercised its influence to end the terrible disorders by means of compromise. There were now three aspirants to the throne, for Waldemar, the son of Canute, the late Duke of Schleswig[1], had recently advanced his claim. Among these three the country was equally partitioned. Three days later, 7 May 1157, Svein's character was revealed in its true colours. Suddenly, at

---

[1] See *supra*, p. 344.

a feast held in honour of the reconciliation, he fell upon his opponents: Canute was killed, Waldemar, though wounded, managed to escape under cover of darkness. Svein's conduct effectively disposed of his chances of the throne. His disgusted supporters deserted in numbers to Waldemar, who was able to win a decisive victory at Viborg. Svein was killed in the battle, and Waldemar, the sole survivor of the three rivals, became the undisputed sovereign of Denmark.

In the exhausted state of the country the new king was powerless to withstand the constant attacks of the Slavonic pirates upon the Danish coasts. He put himself therefore under the protection of the man most capable of defending his kingdom, Duke Henry. In this way Henry established that influence in Danish politics which was to continue for more than twenty years. The influence certainly was not always congenial to Waldemar, who on one occasion even took arms against his protector. He had in 1168 with the help of Henry's vassals captured the island of Rügen; Henry demanded in accordance with an alleged covenant a half-share in the conquest. The king's refusal caused a war which lasted till 1171. Then at a conference on the Eider the old alliance was restored; Waldemar yielded to the duke's demands, and the relations were drawn still closer by the marriage of their children, Canute and Gertrude, the widow of Frederick of Rothenburg.

In the intervals between his Italian campaigns Frederick paid hurried visits to Germany to set in order what had gone amiss during his absence. While he was in the kingdom the peace was well kept, but when he was safely beyond the Alps the old feuds broke out once more; private war for the righting of wrongs, for the settlement of disputes, was too much engrained in the feudal nobility to be crushed out in a moment by peace ordinances or by the rule of a strong but absent Emperor. The diocese of Mayence affords a good example of this. Archbishop Arnold soon after his election quarrelled with the nobles of the surrounding country, at the head of whom was Herman of Stahleck, Count-Palatine of the Rhine; on his return from his first Italian expedition Frederick suppressed the rebellion with strong measures at the Christmas court (1155) at Worms. There was an old custom among the Franks by which men found guilty of offences of this kind were obliged to undergo the ignominy of carrying certain objects varying according to their rank: for the noble it was a dog, for the *ministerialis* a saddle, for the rustic the wheel of a plough. It was this penalty that Frederick imposed on the Count-Palatine; he and ten other counts, his accomplices, carried dogs for a full German mile. When, we are told, this dreadful punishment was made known, "all were seized with such terror that they preferred to live at peace than to devote themselves to the turbulence of war." Soon after, the Count-Palatine died, and Frederick strengthened his own resources by conferring the Palatinate on his half-brother Conrad, who, since the death of the old "one-eyed" Duke Frederick II of Swabia, had come into the Hohenstaufen patrimony in Rhenish Franconia. The difficulties of the Archbishop of Mayence were not, however, at an end; in 1158, when somewhat reluctantly he had obeyed the imperial summons to take part in the second Italian campaign, Arnold imposed a war tax on the *ministeriales* and citizens of Mayence. Again there was rebellion and terrible disorders throughout the city. The climax was reached when the archbishop returned triumphant after the fall of Milan. He laid the city under an interdict, but the trouble continued; he prepared for war, but was himself attacked; he sought sanctuary at the monastery of St James, but the monastery was put to the flames and he was butchered at the gates by the infuriated mob (1160)[1]. Not only the perpetrators but the whole town suffered punishment for the infamous act when the Emperor returned from Italy in 1163; many were fined, the city was deprived of its privileges, and its walls were destroyed. Two elections to the see were quashed before a man was found who met with the Emperor's approval; and even he, Conrad of Wittelsbach, had afterwards to be removed for the offence of espousing the cause of Pope Alexander III. The diocese of Mayence had a stormy history until in 1165 it fell into the capable hands of Archbishop Christian.

During the third Italian expedition the peace of Germany was disturbed by a feud between Duke Welf and Hugh of Tübingen, the latter supported by Frederick of Rothenburg, Duke of Swabia; the Emperor settled the affair when he was back in Germany in the autumn of 1164, but he was no sooner off again to Italy than it broke out afresh with renewed vigour and on a wider field, for now the house of Zähringen was enlisted on the side of Welf and the King of Bohemia lent aid to Hugh. It was not until 1166 that the Emperor, by severe punishments, forced Hugh to submit. These are but instances; there were many other similar quarrels: Rainald of Dassel against the Count-Palatine of the Rhine, Henry the Lion against the rival princes of Saxony. They were the inevitable consequence in these times of the absence of a king from his kingdom. A king was accounted to have done well if he succeeded in maintaining the peace when he was at home and was strong enough to restore order when he returned after an absence.

The border countries of Bohemia, Poland, and Hungary had been the source of much trouble to Frederick's predecessors; their rulers found, however, that disobedience to Frederick was a more serious matter. In Poland, Boleslav, having driven out his refractory elder brother Vladislav (Wladisław), had acquired the government himself (1146); he now refused to pay homage and the accustomed tribute of 500 marks. In the summer of 1157 Frederick set out across the Elbe to punish him for his defiance; in a letter to Wibald of Stablo he describes the difficulties of the journey through the dense forests, the surprise and dismay of the Poles when

---

[1] Cf. *Vita Arnoldi Archiepiscopi*, ed. Jaffé, *Bibl. rer. Germ.* iii; and for the value of this source, P Amandus G'sell, OSB, in *Neu. Arch.* xliii, 1920–1.

they saw the German army reach the Oder and the soldiers in their eagerness leaping into the great river and swimming across; he describes the flight and the pursuit to Posen and the humble submission of the duke. Boleslav had to pay a heavy price for his rashness: he not only had to do homage, but also to pay large fines, 2000 marks of gold to the Emperor, 1000 to the princes, 20 to the Empress, and 200 marks of silver to the court. He had further to allow his brother to return from exile and to bring the complaint he had against him before the imperial court at Magdeburg the following Christmas; finally he engaged himself to accompany Frederick on the forthcoming Italian expedition. The Emperor then returned, taking with him hostages as an assurance of the duke's good faith. Géza II of Hungary, who had been for some time past on bad terms with the Empire, voluntarily presented himself at a diet at Würzburg and promised to join the Italian expedition. In return for the cession of Bautzen and the elevation of his duchy into a kingdom, Vladislav II (I) of Bohemia made a similar promise of assistance. He alone of the three princes who had promised to take part in the second Italian campaign fulfilled his engagement.

During the rest of his reign Frederick had need to pay little attention to the affairs of his eastern neighbours. In 1172 he was called upon to settle an internal feud in Poland and a disputed succession in Hungary: but in each case he managed to avoid recourse to armed interference. In Bohemia the cordial relations established in 1158 continued till the appointment in 1168 of Vladislav's son, Adalbert, to the archbishopric of Salzburg. Adalbert, being a supporter of Alexander III, was soon deposed, and an estrangement sprang up between the two courts. Without consulting the Emperor or the Bohemian nobles, Vladislav abdicated in favour of his son Frederick; the Emperor cancelled the arrangement and appointed Soběslav II, the son of that Soběslav who preceded Vladislav II in the Bohemian duchy, as the successor to the dukedom. But he was so unpopular among his subjects, and made himself so troublesome to his neighbours, that not long after he was removed from his position. Vladislav's son Frederick was now raised to the dukedom with the Emperor's approval and was duly enfeoffed. Peace was thus satisfactorily restored.

The German kings had never succeeded in making their authority felt in their Burgundian kingdom. Lothar had improved the position by bestowing on the powerful Swabian house of Zähringen the title and duties of *rector Burgundiae* (1127), and Duke Conrad had striven hard to secure the interests of Germany; but Conrad was dead (1152), and his son Berthold IV had not yet been able to establish his influence in Burgundy. Trouble arose in the county of Burgundy. Count Rainald died leaving only a daughter Beatrix; his brother Count William of Mâcon not only seized the custody of the inheritance but thrust the heiress into prison and tried to get her possessions permanently into his own hands. It was to the interest of Frederick no less than of Berthold that strong measures should be taken. At the Diet of Merseburg in 1152 the authority of Berthold as Rector was confirmed and extended; he was to be practically autonomous in Burgundy and Provence in the absence of the Emperor; for his part he agreed to assist Frederick in the projected Italian campaign with a Burgundian contingent of 500 heavy-armed knights and 50 archers. The difficulties with regard to the Count of Mâcon were to be settled by the judgment of the princes when Frederick should himself visit Burgundy in the following year. In accordance with this plan, in February 1153 Frederick held his court at Besançon; many Burgundian nobles assembled to do him homage, and among them William of Mâcon; but whether any action was taken against the latter on this occasion, or who retained possession of the countship of Burgundy, is a matter of uncertainty. It appears at any rate that the bargain made at Merseburg was not carried out. It was not till the troublesome Count William was dead that Frederick inaugurated any real change in his Burgundian relations, and the motive was a new one. Some years previously, at Constance in 1153, the Emperor, under circumstances none too creditable it would seem, divorced his first wife Adelaide of Vohburg. He turned to Burgundy in 1156 with the object of making the rich and attractive Beatrix his wife. The pair were married in gala fashion at Whitsuntide in the town of Würzburg. The lands which thus came under his sway by right of his wife became the nucleus of a real imperial power over Burgundy; an independent authority such as the Zähringen had possessed no longer suited the Emperor's schemes, and the compact of 1152 remained unfulfilled; by way of compensation Berthold received the advocateship of the three sees of Lausanne, Geneva, and Sion.

The eventful Diet of Besançon in October 1157, with its brilliant gathering of representatives from all parts of Italy, from France, England, and Spain, was no doubt held with a view of impressing upon the inhabitants of the newly-acquired county a sense of the imperial power. The papal legates brought with them letters from Pope Hadrian complaining of an outrage which had been perpetrated against Eskil, the Archbishop of Lund, in imperial territory. The aged prelate, while journeying homewards after visiting the Pope, was attacked by bandits; his property was seized, he himself, after some rough handling, was carried off into captivity. Hadrian's letter complains of the fact that, although he had informed the Emperor of these distressing events, the perpetrators remained unpunished. The Pope continues by reminding Frederick of his previous kindness towards him in those famous words which hastened on the rupture of the friendly relations which till now had existed between Pope and Emperor. He speaks of "conferring the imperial crown" and of his willingness to bestow upon him "even greater *beneficia* if it were possible," and concludes by imputing the blame for Frederick's lapses to evil counsellors—a dark reference no doubt to the Chancellor, Rainald of Dassel, Archbishop of Cologne. Now the words *conferre* and *beneficium* have technical meanings: they are the terms used in feudal phraseology to connote the grant of a fief by a lord to his vassal. It will never be known what Hadrian himself meant to imply. If he intended his words to be interpreted in the sense that he had bestowed the Empire upon Frederick as a papal fief, there was an end to all amicable relations between the ecclesiastical and secular lords of Christendom. And such indeed was the interpretation put upon it by one of his envoys, in all likelihood Cardinal Roland: "From whom then does he hold it if not from the Pope?" Feeling ran high among the outraged German princes, and Otto of Wittelsbach would have run the audacious prelate through the body had not Frederick himself interposed to prevent the shedding of blood. The Emperor was, however, deeply incensed; the legates were sent packing to Italy with all haste. He realised that a rupture with the Papacy was imminent, and took steps to secure the loyalty of the German Church by stating his case in a letter. He relates the episode of the Besançon diet; he tells how he has searched the baggage of the cardinals and has found many other letters of a similar tenour and even blank mandates, sealed by the papal Chancery, for the legates to fill in arbitrarily to supply a sanction for their nefarious work of despoiling the churches of Germany[1]. Frederick concludes by refuting the papal claims of overlordship and by stating his own theory of the Empire: it is the doctrine of the two swords, the Empire is an independent and divinely instituted lordship held direct "from God alone by the election of the princes." Frederick's attitude was upheld by the German bishops; their reply to Hadrian's letter soliciting their support, though moderate in tone, was an emphatic assertion of their belief in the Emperor's right. Hadrian did not feel sufficiently prepared for the contest which he had brought upon himself, more especially as he could not count on the support of the clergy beyond the Alps; more tactful legates were dispatched, who, after suffering capture and robbery at the hands of Alpine brigands, ultimately succeeded in reaching the Emperor's court at Augsburg. Frederick, like Hadrian, had no wish to precipitate a struggle. He was willing enough to listen to the conciliatory letter read out by Bishop Otto of Freising: *beneficium*, the letter stated, in Rome, as in the Scriptures, had not the technical feudal sense; it implied simply a *bonum factum*, a good deed; the crowning of the Emperor was admittedly "a good deed." When we say "we have conferred" the crown, we merely mean "we have imposed" the crown upon the royal head. By such quibbles the Emperor's anger was appeased, and the legates returned to their master loaded with gifts and messages of friendship.

Ever since the time of Gregory VII extreme papalists had been arguing

---

[1] Cf. H. Schrörs, *Untersuchungen zum Streite Kaiser Friedrichs I mit Papst Hadrian IV* (1157–1158), Bonn. Univ. Progr. 1915. The Curia, following on the successful advance made in its position in the time of Conrad III, proposed to undertake a wide visitation of the churches in the Empire by its legates. This fact helps to explain the blank mandates with which the legates were armed. Frederick's measures were directed against further encroachments of papal influence.

the theory of the feudal subjection of the Empire to the Papacy. Pope Innocent II had caused the coronation of Lothar III to be commemorated in a picture hung in the palace of the Lateran. The Emperor was portrayed kneeling and receiving the crown from the enthroned Pontiff; below was inscribed this significant couplet:

Rex venit ante fores, iurans prius Urbis honores,
Post homo fit Papae, sumit quo dante coronam.

A picture and inscription so derogatory to the imperial dignity was, we need scarcely remark, destroyed at Barbarossa's instance; but it revealed a tendency, and with this in our minds it is difficult to avoid the inference that the Curia, in dispatching the famous letter, had intended to set a subtle trap into which it was hoped the Emperor would fall and, by accepting the letter, would tacitly acknowledge the papal overlordship claimed in those both vague and technical phrases. Frederick's legal mind and his astute Chancellor Rainald were not to be so easily caught, and the Curia had to recede along the path of verbal sophistry.

The royal influence in ecclesiastical matters had sensibly diminished during the reigns of Lothar and Conrad III. St Bernard had jealously guarded the Church's interests, and even the rights left to the king by the Worms Concordat were by no means always enforced. Gerhoh of Reichersperg, the powerful champion of Church pretensions, was able to write in Conrad's time: "Thanks to God, episcopal elections now take place without the presence of the king."[1] But Bernard died in 1153, and a man was on the throne of Germany who would brook no interference with his rights or what he deemed to be his rights, would suffer no encroachments upon the position the law allowed him. Frederick was determined that his influence should be felt in the elections of bishops and abbots. Within two months of his accession he interfered, and interfered with success, in the election to the vacant see of Magdeburg. The votes of the Chapter were divided between the provost, Gerhard, and the dean, Azzo. Frederick himself appeared in the midst of the wrangling electors and recommended Wichmann, Bishop of Zeitz, who was duly chosen and immediately invested with the *regalia* of his see. It was a bold stroke, justified, it is true, so far as interference in a disputed election went, by the Concordat; but his action was open to attack on other grounds: it was contrary to Canon Law to translate a bishop without a licence from the Pope. Wichmann's election, though upheld by the German bishops at Ratisbon, was denied at Rome. Eugenius III remained firm till his death in the summer of 1153; but his more compliant successor Anastasius IV yielded, and granted the pallium to the archbishop of Frederick's choice. But the king would not often disturb the electoral gathering with his presence; he would rather work through trustworthy representatives, or he would send letters indicative of his will. So on the death of Rainald he wrote to the electors

[1] Gerhoh, MGH, *Libelli de Lite*, iii, 280.

of Cologne recommending his Chancellor Philip of Heinsberg as his successor, "him only and no other we wish to be elected without delay"; Arnold was appointed to the archbishopric of Trèves in succession to Hillin "at the suggestion or advice of the Emperor." The Concordat had also conceded to the king the right of deciding disputed elections—a right which Conrad had allowed to slip from his grasp. As we have seen, Frederick had exercised his authority in this respect in the case of the disputed election to the see of Magdeburg soon after his own accession, and had established a practice known as *Devolutionsrecht* to meet such cases, whereby the nomination devolved upon the Emperor; both candidates were set aside and a third, his own nominee, was chosen.

This policy, boldly and successfully carried out, completely changed the character of the German episcopate. The bishops of Frederick's choice are men of practical experience, of administrative ability, men trained in the imperial Chancery; Philip, the Chancellor, is appointed to the metropolitan see of Cologne for his skill in statecraft. Frederick's bishops are politicians first, and only in the second place good churchmen. But they are nevertheless distinguished men—Rainald of Dassel and Christian of Mayence are notable examples; they are men capable of governing the extensive dioceses of Germany.

Moreover he made the weight of his influence felt in other spheres of the Church's work; he claimed certain powers of jurisdiction over the clergy. In the peace ordinance of 1152 it is laid down that a clerk committed for breach of the peace shall be punished in the local lay court, that of the count of the district, and in case of disobedience he shall be deprived of his office and benefice. At Ulm in the same year it was decreed that a man accused of damaging the property of the Church shall only be punished if he is found guilty in the lay court. He clung tenaciously to the rights of *regalia* and *spolia*. A doctrine had been growing up that property once bestowed upon the Church belonged to the Church for ever without the re-grant to a new bishop[1]; this theory made the investiture of the *regalia* by the Emperor a matter of mere formality. Frederick determined that it should be a real thing, and heavily fined a bishop, Hartwig of Ratisbon, for disposing of the fiefs of his church before he had been duly invested with them. Further, he claimed that what he had granted he could likewise take away from those who did not fulfil their duties of vassalship. So in 1154 he deprived Hartwig of Bremen and Ulrich of Halberstadt of the *regalia* for refusing to perform their military service on the Italian campaign. He appropriated the revenues of vacant churches and the moveable property of deceased bishops, and in the exercise of this last right, the *ius spolii*, caused much bitterness among the bishops; nevertheless, though strongly attacked by Urban III, the vexatious practice continued.

These measures and these claims are characteristic of Frederick's whole attitude towards the relations of Church and State; the exercise of a certain

[1] Gerhoh, *loc. cit.*

control over the affairs of the Church was part of his duty as Emperor. His ecclesiastical policy was essentially conservative: he wished only to recover and to retain that authority over the Church which had been wielded by his predecessors; he looked back to the tradition of the great Emperors of the past, of Henry III, of Otto I, perhaps even of Charles the Great whom he caused to be canonised in 1166. We are struck by the boldness of such a policy, but more surprising still is the ready compliance with which it was received by the German episcopate, and the comparatively mild treatment meted out by the Curia. The legates at Constance in March 1153 had no doubt their own axe to grind, but it is indeed extraordinary to find them a month or two later sanctioning the deposition of Henry of Mayence on the sole ground that he had opposed the election of Frederick Barbarossa; moreover the royal nominee, the king's own Chancellor Arnold, was raised to the thus vacated archbishopric without the slightest demur. Several others on purely political grounds were removed from their sees, Henry of Minden, Burchard of Eichstätt, Bernard of Hildesheim. Frederick began his reign with a definite and reactionary Church policy, and he carried it through with remarkably little opposition. The Gregorian party could count but few sympathisers among the German bishops; those who, like Eberhard of Salzburg or Eberhard of Bamberg, approved of the hierarchical views of the Curia, were unfitted to organise and lead a great political party; they were not militant, they were not politicians, perhaps they were too loyal. At any rate Frederick in these early years was able to establish his control firmly over the German Church, firmly enough to be able to count on its support when at a later time he was to create a schism in Europe. The schism, it is true, roused Eberhard of Salzburg to declare himself openly on the side of Alexander III, and his example was followed by the Bishops of Brixen and Gurk; but his influence did not penetrate beyond the boundaries of his province. The rest of Germany stood firmly by Frederick and his Pope Victor IV till the latter's death in April 1164. Then it was that the German clergy adopted a different attitude; the bishops, who had readily accepted Victor, found a difficulty in accepting Paschal III. Not only was his election outrageously uncanonical, but an obvious opportunity of ending the schism had been allowed to slip by owing to the headstrong action of Rainald of Dassel. Opposition to Frederick's policy was no longer confined to the province of Salzburg. The Archbishops of Mayence, of Trèves, and of Magdeburg changed sides; the Archbishop of Cologne, the promoter of Paschal, stood alone among the metropolitans of Germany to champion the imperial cause. It required much compulsion and not a few depositions to bring the German clergy to heel. The oath of Würzburg, May 1165, never to recognise Alexander or one of his party as Pope, was extorted from an unwilling clergy and a not over-zealous laity under threat of the severest punishments. But it was Frederick's strong personality and his immense energy which carried the day in Germany. Resistance continued only in the province of Salzburg, and with this Frederick dealt with a high hand. The fiefs of the Church were confiscated and given to laymen; the Archbishop himself, Conrad, Eberhard's successor, was declared an enemy to the Empire and was obliged to flee his diocese to the shelter of the monastery of Admont where he died shortly after (1168). His place was taken by Adalbert, a son of King Vladislav of Bohemia and a nephew of the Emperor; when he too declared for Alexander, in spite of his personal relationship to Frederick, he lost his see; but he was a young man and lived to be reappointed to his archbishopric ten years later, when the struggle had long passed by, and to hold it till the end of the century.

Thus Frederick's position in Germany was gradually retrieved; vacant sees were filled with staunch imperialists, and Frederick could once more enter Italy with the solid support of the German episcopate at his back. But if the German bishops stood loyally by Frederick, he stood loyally by them. He might have made a satisfactory, if not a glorious, peace in 1169 by the sacrifice of his bishops. Alexander refused to admit the validity of their ordination, while Frederick made it an essential preliminary to peace. The negotiations of 1175 broke down on the same point. After Legnano, Wichmann of Magdeburg, Conrad of Worms, and, a little later, Christian of Mayence, proceeded to Anagni to discuss terms. Both Frederick and Alexander were anxious for peace; the Pope's authority and prestige had suffered more from the schism than had the Emperor's; peace was even more essential to the conqueror than to the conquered[1]. The crucial question of the German bishops was again raised, and this time not in vain; the bishops were confirmed in their sees. The authority which Frederick had acquired over the German Church survived the peace of Venice unchanged. Frederick continued to control elections, to insist that no vacancy should be filled without his consent, to exact homage and the oath of fealty from the bishop-elect before consecration; he continued to claim and to exercise the right of nomination in cases of disputed elections. In one instance of this kind Frederick was near being beaten; in 1183 the electors to the archbishopric of Trèves were divided; the Emperor supported one candidate, the other appealed to Rome, and after a struggle won his case. But even on this occasion Frederick eventually had his way, and the papal candidate had to give place to one who met with the Emperor's approval. So Frederick's ecclesiastical policy from the beginning to the end of his reign was successful. Nevertheless, it is open to much criticism: it was too conservative, too reactionary; it took no account of changed conditions; it could be maintained by a strong personality such as Frederick possessed, but it could not last. The forces to which Frederick's predecessors had submitted, and against which Frederick himself had striven, would revive ere long and ultimately triumph.

That Frederick weathered the many storms to which the papal schism gave rise was due in large measure to his own personality and force of

[1] Hauck, iv, 302.

character; but a share, and a large share in the success of the Emperor's policy must be set to the credit of his Chancellor, Rainald of Dassel. The well-built, thick-set figure of Rainald is ever at the Emperor's hand. He was a man of learning and of great statesmanlike qualities; in character headstrong, but generous, cheerful, and affable. Trained, like his great opponent Alexander III, in the schools of Paris, and with practical experience gained as provost of the cathedral churches of Hildesheim and Münster, he was raised in 1156 to the office of Imperial Chancellor. Henceforth he devoted all his energy and all the ability with which he was so plentifully endowed to the service of the Empire. He is diplomat, administrator, organiser of the imperial policy; he is a good soldier too, fearless and unhesitating in battle. His obstinacy of purpose carried his master through the difficult crises which the schism engendered, carried him farther perhaps than he would himself have liked to go. Had it not been for the influence of Rainald the schism might well have died with Victor IV in 1164; it is perhaps idle to speculate whether, had Rainald not succumbed to the pestilence in 1167, Legnano might not have been an imperial victory, the peace of Venice an imperial triumph[1].

It is Rainald who is entrusted with the delicate negotiations which brought about the numerous changes in the imperial foreign relations during the schism. Frederick was guided in his policy by the attitude adopted by the European powers towards the schism. Conrad III's last efforts had been directed towards a close understanding with the Byzantine Emperor, and on his death-bed he had urged his successor to continue this policy. The interests of both Empires were alike threatened by the Norman kingdom. Frederick, though less eager than Conrad, was not averse to the alliance, and in 1153 he even sent ambassadors to Constantinople with proposals for a marriage with a Byzantine princess. On the other hand neither Pope nor Emperor wished to see a revival of Greek influence in South Italy; and this was soon manifestly revealed as Manuel's intention. By the compact of Constance (1153), therefore, both Pope and Emperor bound themselves to concede to Manuel no Italian territory and to expel him if he should attempt a landing. This was virtually the end of the friendly relations between the Eastern and Western Empires. It was followed by the renewal of the Papal-Norman alliance, the victory of the Normans over the Greeks, and, as a result, a truce between these two powers. The Pope and the Eastern Emperor, who at the outset of the reign were allied with Frederick against the Normans, were now allied with the Normans against Frederick. With the schism came the need for allies. The Emperor therefore turned his attention to the West of Europe, to the Kings of France and England. Louis VII and Henry II were keen rivals; neither was anxious for a German alliance or to recognise an imperial Pope, but still less did either wish to see the other reap the advan-

[1] See the laudatory verses of the Archipoeta, ed. Manitius *Münchner Texte*, vi, 1913.

tage which such an alliance would yield. So their attitude remained undecided; the attempt of Henry of Troyes, Count of Champagne, to bring Frederick and Louis together on the Saône (1162) broke down. The quarrel of Henry II and Thomas of Canterbury made the prospect of an English alliance more hopeful; in 1165 Rainald of Dassel visited England and succeeded in bringing about the desired result; the English ambassadors at the Würzburg diet went so far as to promise recognition to Paschal. But the alliance served little useful purpose and was soon at an end. More important and more permanent results emanated from the second attempt on the part of the Count of Champagne to bring about an alliance between the Hohenstaufen and the Capetians; a meeting of the two monarchs actually took place on 14 February 1171 between Toul and Vaucouleurs. The friendly relations established on this occasion matured later (1187) into a close alliance. Louis VII was now dead, but his son and successor Philip Augustus met Frederick in a conference near Mouzon on the Meuse and there the alliance was sealed. It was a natural one; both kings had over-powerful vassals to cope with, and these vassals, Henry II of England and Henry the Lion of Saxony, were united by a marriage tie, the importance of which was disclosed after the fall of the Saxon Duke. It was to endure, in spite of rash attempts of King Henry to interfere in French affairs on behalf of Philip's enemies in 1185–6, till the joint forces of Welf and Angevin were finally shattered on the field of Bouvines in 1214.

While Frederick was engaged in fighting for his imperial rights in the Lombard plains, Henry the Lion was building up a strong, well-ordered state in the north-east of Germany. The conquest of the Wendish lands beyond the Elbe, which had never hitherto been successfully achieved, was now systematically undertaken. For the first time in history this country became permanently subjected to German rule. Instead of the haphazard plundering raids, useless burnings, and wholesale massacres which characterised the border warfare of the past, Henry employed the most up-to-date methods of military science; he had learnt at the sieges of Milan and Crema how a siege should be conducted, and the strongholds of the Slavs could not stand against the new forms of siege-engines and battering-rams which he applied to their walls; organised campaigns rapidly put an end to such resistance as they were able to make in the open. They had no choice but to submit or to retire into the swamp and forest land of the interior. There were of course outbreaks of rebellion. In Henry's absence in the south the Slavs would strike a blow for their lost independence, would take to their ships and ravage the coasts of Denmark; but the years 1160–1162 saw the last serious attempt to throw off the German yoke. In the summer of 1160 Henry crossed the Elbe, while his ally Waldemar advanced with Danish troops from the coast; the Slav strongholds, Ilow, Mecklenburg, Schwerin, and Dobin were abandoned and destroyed; the Slavs themselves retired inland as the German army advanced. At Mecklenburg the sons of Niclot, the chief of the Obotrites, attempted to resist, but they were easily defeated, and Niclot himself fell in a skirmish with a foraging party. So ended the campaign of that year. But the sons of the fallen chief, Pribislav and Vratislav, were yet to give trouble. Of their father's possessions the fortress of Werla alone had been restored to them; the rest Henry had bestowed upon his followers, the most conspicuous of whom, Guncelin of Hagen, became Count of Schwerin, and it was against him that the attack of 1161 was in the main directed. Count Adolf with his Holsteiners penetrated into the swampy waste whither Pribislav had withdrawn, while Henry and Guncelin attacked Vratislav in his fortress of Werla. After an obstinate resistance the place fell into Henry's hands, and with it Vratislav whom Henry retained a captive at Brunswick. His brother held his own for another year. In February 1162 he attacked Mecklenburg, captured and burnt the town, massacred the garrison, enslaved the women and children. The prompt action of Guncelin of Hagen alone prevented further calamities; marching straight for Ilow, the place next threatened, he frustrated the attempts of the Slav prince and compelled him to retreat. Vratislav was hanged for complicity in the plans of his elder brother. Then Henry himself, supported by many of the neighbouring princes, Waldemar, Albert the Bear, and Adolf of Schauenburg, took the field. The previous tactics were again adopted: the Danish king attacked by sailing up the river Peene, Henry by marching across country against the fortress of Demmin. An advance guard was sent forward under Adolf, Guncelin, and Christian of Oldenburg. The necessary precautions were, however, neglected, and a catastrophe followed. On the morning of 6 July, the camp was surprised and, in spite of a brave defence, in which Count Adolf lost his life, the Slavs were temporarily successful. But while the victors were scattered through the camp in search of booty, the German troops rallied under their leaders, made a counter-attack, and little by little regaining the lost ground, finally turned the disorganised ranks of the enemy to flight. Henry arrived in the evening to find the day which had begun so disastrously ended in a brilliant success. Having joined forces with Waldemar, the duke followed up the victory and drove the Slavs, who had fired the fortress of Demmin and retired inland, to surrender. Thus ended the last serious campaign which Henry had to make on his eastern frontier. But its success was overcast by a great blow, the death of Count Adolf of Schauenburg. He it was who had been responsible for much of the development in the Wendish country. Holstein under his organisation had prospered as it had never done before; however, the young colonies no longer needed his firm hand and his watchful care; they were now, thanks to him, strong enough to continue their growth unaided.

Christianity too made rapid progress. The Church in Slavonia had passed through many vicissitudes. The see of Oldenburg, founded by Otto I in 968, was divided by Adalbert, Archbishop of Bremen, into three parts, Oldenburg, Mecklenburg, and Ratzeburg (1052–1054); but, shortly after, the three bishoprics became vacant and remained so for 84 years until they were re-established by Hartwig of Bremen in 1149. Their existence nevertheless continued to be precarious, and it was only when at the Diet of Goslar in 1154 Henry, in spite of the protests of Archbishop Hartwig, was granted the right of investiture to the three bishoprics and to any others which should be founded in the Wendish country hereafter, that substantial headway could be made[1]. This imperial concession moreover later received papal confirmation. That the administration of Church and State should be controlled by one hand was almost essential to the success of a country in the earliest stages of its civilisation, and henceforth the missionary work in Slavonia made steady progress. Henry was content not merely with sanctioning appointments made by the Chapter, but himself took the initiative; Gerold, for example, Vicelin's successor at Oldenburg, was the duke's chaplain and formerly *scholasticus* and a canon at Brunswick. The task of this new bishop was not an easy one; he arrived at Oldenburg to find, instead of the flourishing town of Vicelin's day, a deserted ruin; a half-destroyed chapel alone stood to mark the once busy missionary centre. There can moreover have been little real enthusiasm among the Slavs for the new religion. Life was difficult; taxation was onerous; the new civilisation brought with it new burdens. Henry was a hard task-master; obedience to him was all they understood. "There may be a God in Heaven," Niclot answered to Henry's exhortations, "he is your God. You be our God, and we are satisfied. You worship Him, we will worship you." Nevertheless, in spite of all, progress was made; the churches were rebuilt, and received generous endowment from Henry's treasury.

Moreover there was peace in the land. Helmold, the simple parish priest of Bosau, who chronicled the events that were passing in the country around him, speaks with unbounded enthusiasm of the great duke and of the beneficial results of his energy and enterprise. "He says peace, and they obey; he commands war, and they say: 'we are ready.'" So he writes at the conclusion of his *Chronicle of the Slavs*. And again, "All the region of the Slavs from the Eider, which is the boundary of the kingdom of the Danes, extending between the Baltic Sea and the Elbe through long tracts of country to Schwerin, once bristling with snares and almost a desert, is now, thanks to God, become one united Saxon colony, and cities and towns are built there, churches and the number of Christ's servants are multiplied." These words contain no exaggeration. Westphalian, Frisian, and Flemish colonists had now firmly established them-

---

[1] This is not an isolated example of the grant of such a privilege: similar grants were made to Count Thierry of Flanders in respect of the bishopric of Cambray and to Duke Berthold of Zähringen in respect of the bishopric of Lausanne; the former privilege was afterwards revoked in deference to the protest of the bishop concerned. See Hauck, *Kirchengeschichte Deutschlands*, IV, 210.

selves in the newly-acquired territory; the country was administered and kept at peace from strongholds such as Schwerin, Malchow, and Ilow, fortressed and garrisoned by German troops. Even in distant Pomerania a significant advance was made when in 1163 it became subject to Henry; German influence began to penetrate deep, and the Cistercians and the Premonstratensians successfully pushed forward the work of conversion.

Of the numerous activities of Henry the Lion perhaps his patronage of commercial and municipal development had the most lasting results. In this direction, it must be admitted, his policy was often carried out at the expense of others. The new city of Lübeck, founded by Count Adolf of Schauenburg in 1143, was already shewing signs of its future commercial greatness and was rapidly absorbing the trade of the Baltic; the duke's town of Bardowiek suffered in consequence. Henry demanded a half-share in the profits of the market of the city; the demand not unnaturally was refused, and the market of Lübeck was closed by the duke's order (1152). A fire destroying the greater part of the city completed its ruin. At the request of the citizens a new town was built for them in the neighbourhood, called after its founder Löwenstadt. But the narrowness of its harbour, which could admit only the smallest ships, hampered its trade, and the town failed. Nevertheless it served its purpose, for Count Adolf was forced to yield to the duke's will. The abandoned city was rebuilt under the auspices of Henry, the burghers returned, and trade once more flourished in the port of Lübeck[1]. Under Henry's patronage the town developed with extraordinary rapidity; in 1160, by the removal thither of the seat of the Bishop of Oldenburg, Lübeck acquired an ecclesiastical, in addition to its commercial, importance. In Bavaria also Henry stimulated trade, and it was to a trade dispute between the duke and Bishop Otto of Freising that Bavaria owes the early prosperity of its modern capital. The rich supplies of salt from the Reichenhall mines were carried along the road from Salzburg to Augsburg and crossed the Isar at Vehringen, a little town belonging to Bishop Otto, who drew a handsome revenue from the tolls. By the building of a bridge at Munich, then an insignificant village, and by the destruction of the old one, Henry not only diverted the trade

---

[1] Henry's charter to Lübeck contained the grant of mint, toll, and market. Rietschel in a paper on the town policy of Henry the Lion read before the International Historical Congress at Berlin, 1908, tried to prove that Henry was the first to develop the constitution of the *Rath*. His evidence is the charter of 1188 to Lübeck in which Frederick concedes *omnia iura que primus loci fundator Heinricus quondam dux Saxonie eis concessit et privilegio suo firmavit*. The charter, however, though partly based on a genuine original, is a forgery of the years 1222–5. The *Rath* does not emerge until the last fifteen years of the twelfth century, and then it makes its first appearance in the Rhine district—between 1185–1198 at Basle, Strasbourg, Worms, Spires, and Utrecht. The first evidence for it at Lübeck is in 1201. Cf. Hermann Bloch, *Der Freibrief Friedrichs I für Lübeck und der Ursprung der Rathverfassung in Deutschland. (Zeitschrift des Vereins für Lübeckische Geschichte und Altertumskunde*, Vol. XVI, Lübeck, 1914.)

through his territory and the revenues to his treasury, but raised the little place to a city of the first importance. The bishop's remonstrances went unheeded by the Emperor, who sanctioned Henry's arrangements at the court at Magdeburg in 1158.

But Henry's rule threatened the independence of the nobility; for he did not confine his almost sovereign power to the frontier and to the newly-won Wendish lands, but exercised it in Saxony itself. The traditional policy of the Billung dukes had been to interfere very little in the affairs of the duchy except on the border and in their own personal possessions. Henry, regardless of tradition, interfered everywhere, strained the use of his jurisdiction to the utmost limits, and attempted even to transform the countships into administrative offices under his immediate control. He sought further to increase his power and possessions by claiming the inheritance of counts who left no direct male heir. As early as 1144 he had thus laid claim to the inheritance of the murdered Count Rudolf of Stade, territory of the first importance to him, for it commanded both banks of the mouth of the Elbe, but by so doing he involved himself in a life-long feud with the count's brother, Hartwig, afterwards Archbishop of Bremen; he laid claim to the lands of Christian of Oldenburg despite the claims of the count's son who was a minor (1167); to those of the Count of Asseburg despite the claims of the count's daughter (1170). Had it not been for the imperial support, Henry could not have stood against the opposition he was creating; but for the first twenty-five years of the reign Emperor and duke were the best of friends. The success of their respective activities depended largely on this mutual understanding; Frederick, relieved of the burden, which had borne heavily on his predecessors, of protecting the eastern frontier of his kingdom, of maintaining the peace of Germany, could devote himself whole-heartedly to his Italian policy; Henry with the free hand allowed him by the Emperor could increase and consolidate his unrivalled position north of the Alps.

Nevertheless the Saxon princes were not prepared to stand idle when their independence was at stake. Conspiracies were common, and when the Emperor left for Italy in the autumn of 1166 the struggle began in earnest. Many princes and bishops were united against him: Wichmann of Magdeburg and Herman of Hildesheim; Louis, the Landgrave of Thuringia, and Henry's old associate in the Slav campaigns, Christian of Oldenburg; and there was of course Henry's keenest rival in East Saxony, the Ascanian, Albert the Bear, and his four sons, each of whom was to rise to a powerful position after the death of their father four years later. Fighting at first centred round Haldensleben, Goslar, and Bremen; with these attacks Henry was well able to cope, but the prospect looked more serious when the Archbishops of Magdeburg and Cologne joined in an offensive and defensive alliance directed at his overthrow. The sudden death of Rainald in Italy in 1167 and of Hartwig in the following year relieved the situation, and the return of Frederick settled the matter in Henry's favour. For the moment there was peace; Albert the Bear, the leader of the opposition among the East Saxon princes, died in 1170, so that Henry could safely leave the charge of his affairs to his English wife Matilda, daughter of Henry II, whom he had married in 1168 at Brunswick, and could set off on a pilgrimage to Jerusalem (1172).

On Henry's return to Germany there are no obvious signs of a change of attitude in his relations with the Emperor. They meet frequently, and apparently on cordial terms of friendship. There were nevertheless grounds for friction. Old Welf VI, since the loss of his son by the pestilence in Italy (1167), thinking that in his advanced age he could make better use of money than of land, resolved to sell his inheritance. He offered it first to Henry who, though accepting the proposal readily enough, was tardy in the matter of payment; Welf therefore approached his other nephew, Frederick, who concluded the bargain forthwith. Henry was thus deprived of a rich portion of the estates of his family, lands on both sides of the Alps, on which he had surely counted. This was a grievance but not the only one that rankled in the heart of Henry. Frederick had attempted, it was said, to get into his hands the disposal of Henry's inheritance in the event of the latter's death in the Holy Land. Nor was the bitterness all on one side ; the Emperor too had cause to complain of his cousin. Henry had been drawn into relations with foreign powers who were not in sympathy with Frederick's Italian policy—with the Eastern Emperor Manuel who was aiding the Lombards, with Henry II of England, his father-in-law, who had recognised Alexander III.

So the breach widens. The collapse of the great Welf power was at hand. A campaign to Italy was arranged for the autumn of the year 1174, and in this campaign Henry took no part. Frederick, whose Lombard adversaries had grown in strength, had become more united, more stubbornly resolved to resist to the last, could ill afford to dispense with the troops which Henry could bring into the field. It is unlikely that he willingly left the duke in Germany even for so important a task as the maintenance of peace; nor in the circumstances was Henry, surrounded as he was by personal enemies, very likely to succeed in this. The two met for the last time on terms of friendship at Ratisbon in May 1174. Their next meeting, if indeed it is historical, is the famous interview at Chiavenna. This is altogether a very mysterious episode. The chroniclers who refer to it are so confused in their knowledge that many scholars are led to the conclusion that the whole thing is a myth, a legend spread by ballad singers after Henry's death in 1195; and their contention is so far supported in that we possess no account of it written near the time it was supposed to have taken place. With the exception of Gilbert of Mons, who probably wrote in 1196, and the Marbach Annals, which are attributed to the year 1184, all our authorities belong to the first quarter of the thirteenth century. Yet it is difficult to understand how such a widely, though inaccurately, known story could have arisen entirely without foundation. It was after his army had suffered severe losses at the siege of Alessandria that Frederick in the spring of 1176 sought a personal interview with his cousin. They met at Chiavenna, and the Emperor begged for the other's assistance; he even humbled himself before his proud subject, for, it seems, he realised that he must make amends for something, presumably his conduct while Henry was in Palestine. Henry, on the other hand, felt himself in a position to dictate terms, and he demanded the restoration of Goslar, which he had ceded to the Emperor as the price of peace in 1168, as a fief; the terms were too heavy, and the two parted in enmity. So runs the story and, in spite of the difficulties, we may accept the substance of it. Moreover it has an important bearing on what followed. Though the refusal of help and the subsequent trial cannot be regarded as cause and effect, it is impossible to deny the influence of the one on the other. The breach between the former friends was now almost, if not quite, irreparable; the Emperor would no longer arbitrate in the duke's quarrels as a friend, not even as an impartial judge, but as a man determined on the duke's ruin; and it was a quarrel between the duke and the Saxon princes which gave rise to the famous trial.

The quarrel centred round the bishopric of Halberstadt. Its Bishop, Ulrich, as long ago as 1160 had been deprived of his see for the attitude he had adopted in the papal schism; for he had recognised Alexander III. His place had been filled by one Gero, a close friend of the duke. By the terms of the agreement reached at Anagni and confirmed at Venice, Ulrich was restored to his old see, and he immediately set about undoing all the acts of the usurper; he claimed back the fiefs of his church which had been granted to Henry; he dismissed from their benefices the clergy appointed by Gero under the duke's patronage. Henry was engaged in a campaign in Pomerania, and was besieging the fortress of Demmin, when the news of these events reached him. Having hurriedly concluded a truce with the Slavs, he hastened back to Saxony. The last move of the bishop was still more threatening; on a hill in the near neighbourhood of Halberstadt he built a fortress, obviously as a basis of operations against the duke. Twice was the stronghold destroyed and twice rebuilt. A command from the Emperor in Italy, bidding the princes to refrain from repairing the obnoxious fortress, for the moment restored peace. But Henry's position was becoming daily more hazardous; a portion of his army had suffered a severe defeat and the loss of more than four hundred prisoners at the hands of Bernard of Anhalt; then early in the year 1178 an offensive and defensive alliance was concluded against him at Cassel between Ulrich and the formidable Philip of Cologne. The duke's castles and lands in Westphalia were attacked and plundered, and it was only with difficulty that Archbishop Wichmann of Magdeburg succeeded in preventing further hostilities till the Emperor's return. He returned towards the end of October, and both parties laid their complaints before him at a diet held at Spires on 11 November 1178.

We are now launched into a sea of uncertainty and doubt. Innumerable questions arise: What was the Emperor's attitude? What were the grounds of complaint against the duke? What course did the proceedings follow? According to what law was he judged? Where and when was the case heard? All and each of these questions are capable of more than one answer. The only incontrovertible authority is the document drawn up at the Diet of Gelnhausen on 13 April 1180, which, while having as its main object the partition of the Saxon duchy, gives an official account of the course of the trial. This too is not free from criticism. The original manuscript is in parts wholly illegible; we have to rely on a transcript made in 1306; it is open to a variety of interpretations according to the way in which it is punctuated. But still it tells us much that we wish to know; it makes it clear that there were two distinct legal processes, one according to customary law, *landrecht*, one according to feudal law, *lehnrecht*. In the former there is a single summons[1], the Swabian princes —Henry's tribal peers—are the judges[2], the sentence is the ban; in the latter there are three citations, the princes without differentiation of tribe are the judges, the punishment is the loss of fiefs. The document tells us further that it was the complaints of the princes which initiated the proceedings; for Henry "had sorely oppressed the liberty of the Church and of the princes of the Empire by seizing their possessions and by threatening their rights."

He was summoned to Worms on 13 January 1179 to answer to the charges but failed to appear, and a new hearing was arranged for 24 June at Magdeburg. Here, as Henry was again absent, the ban was pronounced against him according to customary law. Now new charges are brought into court: Henry in spite of warnings has continued his aggressions against the princes; a Saxon noble, Dietrich of Landsberg, declared that at Henry's instigation the Lusatians had made an incursion into his territory, and was prepared to prove his assertion by battle—a challenge which Henry refused; Henry had shewn contempt of the imperial commands. It is now "evident high treason," and the suit according to

[1] The rule in customary law was that three summonses should be issued to the defendant with terms of fourteen days intervening. But could these three intervals be made consecutive in one long term of six weeks? Suits by customary law were commonly of a local character and were heard in local courts. The short terms were therefore quite practicable. When however the suit was cognisable in the imperial court, which was always moving about, frequent short summonses were difficult. One peremptory citation after a six weeks' interval would be an obvious and natural evasion of this inconvenience. Güterbock, *Der Prozess Heinrichs des Löwen* (1909), pp. 131 sq., cites eight instances of this practice: Otto of Nordheim, Lothar of Supplinburg, Frederick of Swabia, Conrad of Salzburg, Otto of Wittelsbach, Frederick of Isenburg, Ottokar of Bohemia, and Guy of Flanders. Haller, *Der Sturz Heinrichs des Löwen* (1911), contests this view and believes there were three citations in both suits, pp. 367 sq.

[2] The tribe was determined by the situation of the family castle (in the case of the Welfs, Altdorf in Swabia), *i.e.* by descent.

feudal law goes forward. A second hearing was fixed for 17 August at Kaina, and a third for 13 January 1180 at Würzburg, where—on the ground of contumacy, the repeated neglect of the imperial summons—the sentence, the loss of his fiefs, fell. We are told[1] that Henry made an attempt to secure a reconciliation, perhaps the removal of the ban, after the Diet of Magdeburg. A meeting between Henry and the Emperor apparently took place at Haldensleben, where the price of peace was set at 5000 marks; Henry refused to pay so large a sum, and the negotiations broke down. The law therefore took its course. At the Diet of Geln-hausen, 13 April 1180, the duchy of Saxony was partitioned. Westphalia, severed from the duchy, was granted with ducal powers to the Archbishop Philip of Cologne; the remainder, the portion east of the Weser, with the title of Duke of Saxony, was conferred upon the Ascanian prince, Bernard of Anhalt, the younger son of Albert the Bear. But Henry in the course of his career had accumulated a number of Church fiefs in his hands; these now reverted to the bishops, leaving to the new duke but a comparatively small portion of Henry's extensive territorial possessions in east and middle Saxony. In the Bavarian capital, Ratisbon, a diet was held on 24 June 1180. Its object was twofold: first, as a year and a day had elapsed since the publication of the ban at Magdeburg, Henry's complete outlawry, the *oberacht*, was pronounced, and a campaign to give effect to the sentence was arranged to open on 25 July. Secondly, Henry's Bavarian duchy and fiefs were declared forfeit. Three months later (16 September), at Altenburg, Bavaria was subjected to a treatment similar to that of Saxony. The March of Styria was completely detached and raised to the position of an independent duchy under Ottokar, its former margrave; the dukedom thus diminished in extent was conferred upon Otto of Wittelsbach.

No single event in the Middle Ages so profoundly altered the map of Germany as the fall of Henry the Lion. In place of the four or five large compact duchies, the conspicuous feature of the Germany of the Saxon and Salian Emperors, we have now some few duchies, relatively small, and innumerable independent principalities, little and great, scattered broad-cast over the country. The duke moreover no longer stands in a place apart, unrivalled in his wealth, power, and magnificence; there are others as powerful as or more powerful than he: the Margrave of Brandenburg, the Landgrave of Thuringia, the Count-Palatine of the Rhine. The day of the tribal duchy has passed away.

Henry was condemned but not subdued; all this time, while the long and dreary trial was going forward, warfare between the ducal and the anti-ducal party had continued unceasingly, and fortune had on the whole favoured Henry. Halberstadt had been captured and burnt by the duke's men, and its Bishop Ulrich made prisoner; the Archbishops of Magdeburg and Cologne had laid siege to the duke's **town of Haldens-**

[1] Arnold of Lübeck, II, 10.

leben, but in spite of every effort they were forced after some months to abandon the attempt to take it. A truce gave both parties a much-needed rest during the early months of the next year, 1180; but in April fighting began again, and still Henry was successful. Though he failed to capture Goslar, to which he laid siege, he gained an important victory over an army led by Louis of Thuringia and Bernard of Anhalt at Weissensee on the Unstrut, pursued the enemy as far as Mühlhausen, and returned triumphantly, with more than four hundred prisoners, among them the Landgrave Louis himself, to Brunswick. At the duke's bidding, the obedient Wends swept ravaging through the Lausitz. On 30 July Bishop Ulrich of Halberstadt, the source of much of Henry's trouble, died, and two days later came the news of a considerable victory in Westphalia. There a number of discontented vassals rose against their feudal lord; a strong army under Henry's old associates in the Slav campaigns, the younger Adolf of Schauenburg, Bernard of Ratzeburg, and Guncelin of Schwerin, joined battle with them at Halrefeld, and after hard fighting utterly routed them.

But this was the last of Henry's triumphs. The Emperor himself had taken the field in July; after capturing Lichtenburg, an important stronghold of the duke, he held a diet at Werla whence he issued a decree commanding Henry's vassals to join his standard. A large number of desertions was the result. Henry moreover had failed in his attempts to secure foreign aid; he had approached Denmark and England. But his old ally Waldemar was now strong enough to rest on his own resources; his dependence on Henry was irksome, and he was only too glad to stand by and watch the discomfiture of his former master. Henry II of England, though full of good intentions towards his son-in-law, was not prepared single-handed to entangle himself in so large an enterprise as war with the Emperor would entail. One after another Henry's supporters fell away and surrendered their castles; one after another his strongholds opened their gates to the Emperor. The burghers of Lübeck put up a gallant fight, for they owed much of their prosperity to the duke's paternal care. But Waldemar of Denmark had now openly declared himself on Frederick's side; between the Danish fleet and the German troops the town was so closely invested that further resistance was useless; the citizens, not however before they had obtained the express permission of their patron, surrendered their city. The fall of Lübeck crippled Henry's resources. He attempted to negotiate, he attempted to make a last stand at Stade; but the time had passed for negotiations, and the town of Stade fell into the hands of Philip of Cologne; it remained only for him to submit. He appeared at a diet held at Erfurt, bowed himself before the Emperor, who characteristically raised him from the ground and kissed him amid tears. He was granted the two cities of his patrimony, Brunswick and Lüneburg, but it was considered, and, as events proved, with justice, unsafe to allow him to remain in Germany. He was therefore banished under oath not to return without Frederick's leave. The terms were hard, and foreign powers viewed with alarm the total collapse of the great Welf power. Henry II of England, Pope Alexander III, Philip Augustus, and Philip, Count of Flanders, used their endeavours to persuade the Emperor to a more lenient course; and their efforts were not without success: the term of banishment was limited to three years and a portion of his revenues was allotted to the exiled duke. So in the summer of 1182 Henry with his family left Brunswick to spend the years of banishment at the court of his father-in-law in Normandy and England.

For the general peace of the country it was no doubt better that Henry should be out of Germany, but it is none the less true that his overthrow and banishment caused a serious set-back to his work on the eastern frontier. Duke Bernard had neither the ability nor the resources necessary to carry it on effectively; he had little influence among the East Saxon nobility, who quarrelled among themselves and threw the country into anarchy. "In those days there was no king in Israel," laments Arnold of Lübeck, "and each man ruled in the manner of a tyrant." Denmark took the opportunity to re-assert its independence; Canute VI, who had succeeded his father Waldemar in May 1182, soon gained ascendency in Holstein and Mecklenburg; he defeated Bogislav of Pomerania and made him his vassal; finally he refused his homage to Frederick.

But these disasters were confined to the north-east corner of Germany; elsewhere the Emperor's power and prestige were greater than they had ever been. Here the chronicler tells a different tale; "all the tumult of war has been stilled," and the brilliant festival of Mayence at Whitsuntide 1184 bears testimony to the success of the Emperor's rule. In the broad meadows on the banks of the Rhine a vast city of wooden palaces and bright-coloured tents was erected to house the multitude of princes and foreign envoys that came thither to witness the knighting of the two elder sons of Frederick, King Henry and Duke Frederick of Swabia. For three days the large company were entertained as the Emperor's guests with festivities and tournaments. To Henry, thus ceremoniously knighted, was entrusted the regency during the Emperor's absence (1184–5). Born in 1165, he was crowned at Aix-la-Chapelle when but four years old; now at the age of nineteen he was called to a position of the highest responsibility and difficulty; and if his youthful efforts at administration were not entirely successful, it was because unaided he had to deal with problems which might well have baffled more experienced rulers. There was no Rainald of Cologne, no Christian of Mayence, no statesman-bishop on whom he could rely for assistance. Philip of Cologne, the most powerful man at the moment, was already adopting a hostile attitude towards the crown, which was soon to be aggravated into open hostility when the young king early in 1185 imposed a fine upon him for breaking the peace in a feud with the burghers of Duisburg.

A dispute over the archbishopric at Trèves made matters worse.

Two candidates claimed to have been elected to the see in May 1183—
Rudolf of Wied, provost of the Cathedral, and the Archdeacon Folmar.
Frederick summoned the electors to a diet at Constance, on the advice of
the princes ordered a fresh election, and subsequently invested the successful candidate Rudolf with the *regalia*. Folmar, who had originally
received a majority of the votes, vigorously protested against the whole
proceeding, against Frederick's interference, and most of all against the
election of his rival. He appealed to the Pope, and even used armed force
to keep Rudolf from entering upon his duties; in Germany his cause was
championed by Philip of Cologne, Rudolf's by King Henry who impetuously took up arms against the supporters of Folmar. Pope Lucius III
hesitated to give a decision on the appeal; but his successor, Frederick's
old enemy Archbishop Humbert of Milan, as Pope Urban III, immediately confirmed the appointment of the anti-imperialist candidate
and consecrated Folmar. Henry, by way of retaliation, was sent on a
plundering expedition into the papal patrimony. The Trèves election
dispute in this way brought the Emperor once more into hostility with
the Curia. Moreover other issues were involved: the still undecided
claim to the inheritance of the Countess Matilda, and the coronation of
his son. To this last demand both Lucius and Urban were deaf. It
was not possible, they said, that two Emperors should rule the Empire
at one and the same time. Frederick therefore took the matter into his
own hands; at the feast which celebrated at Milan the nuptials of
Henry and Constance of Sicily he had his son crowned King of Italy at
the hands of Ulrich, the Patriarch of Aquileia, and associated him
with himself in the government of the Empire.

Philip, Archbishop of Cologne, formerly the zealous champion of the
imperial cause against Alexander III, had now, as we have seen, set himself at the head of the opposition to Frederick and his son in Germany.
Having, on the fall of Henry the Lion, acquired the duchy of Westphalia,
he had become a territorial prince with interests of his own to follow,
interests which clashed with those of the Empire. He had behind him,
moreover, a considerable party; many of the bishops, especially those of
his metropolitan diocese, sympathised with the attitude he had adopted
in the papal-imperial controversy, and more especially was this the case
when Urban III retaliated against the Emperor by an attack on the
latter's rights to the *regalia* and *spolia*, vexatious rights which they would
gladly see abolished. Many of the lay nobles, on the other hand, saw in
his policy the advancement of particularist as opposed to national or imperial interests; so we find enrolled among Philip's partisans Louis, the
Landgrave of Thuringia, and Adolf, Count of Holstein. For foreign
allies he could reckon of course on the Curia, perhaps on Denmark and
England. To the latter court he had paid a visit apparently with the
object of arranging a marriage between Prince Richard and a daughter
of the Emperor; it is not impossible that he used the occasion to come

to an understanding with the banished Henry the Lion at the same time; however, when the duke returned from exile about Michaelmas 1185, he seems to have lived peaceably at Brunswick without taking any active steps to support the great coalition which was gathering against the Emperor.

The situation was serious; but Frederick was equal to the occasion. He hurried back from Italy in the summer of 1186. Having tried without success to settle matters at a personal interview with Philip, he summoned a diet to Gelnhausen in December, himself addressed the bishops in a long speech in which he expatiated on his grievances, especially regarding the Trèves election, and finally won them over to his way of thinking. Conrad of Mayence, on behalf of the German clergy, made known to the Pope the result of this assembly. Urban retorted with threats of every kind, but he died suddenly while journeying from Verona to Venice in the following autumn, 20 October 1187, stubborn but unsuccessful. Philip, but now the head of a dangerous coalition, was gradually being isolated from his previous allies till he stood almost alone. He was already deprived of the support of the Pope and of the German bishops; the value of his allies on the lower Rhine, the Count of Flanders and the Duke of Brabant, was counteracted when at Toul Frederick won the services of Count Baldwin of Hainault by the recognition of his claims to the inheritance of Namur; finally the Emperor entered into a close alliance with Philip Augustus against Henry II of England which disposed of any hopes Philip of Cologne may have entertained of help from that quarter. His refusal to present himself to answer to the charges brought against him at the imperial court at Worms in August and at Strasbourg in December 1187 alienated his German supporters; further resistance would have been useless. Cardinal Henry of Albano, the zealous preacher of the Third Crusade, exerted his influence in the interests of peace, and finally Philip appeared before the Emperor at Mayence (March 1188), cleared himself on oath of the charges raised against him, and was restored to the good graces of Frederick.

With the death of Urban III all hindrances in the path of Frederick's Church policy were withdrawn. Urban's successors were compliant to the imperial will. Their energies were devoted to arousing Christendom to action for the recovery of Jerusalem, which on 3 October 1187 had fallen into the hands of Saladin. Gregory VIII in a busy pontificate of less than two months restored peace and friendly relations with the Emperor; Clement III deposed Folmar from the archbishopric of Trèves, and Henry in his turn restored the papal lands which he had occupied in the course of the struggle with Urban.

For Frederick, as for many great men in history, the East had a singular fascination. After the battle of Legnano he is said to have exclaimed: "Happier Alexander, who saw not Italy, happier I, had I been drawn to Asia." It was appropriately on the fourth Sunday in Lent,

named from the introit *Laetare Hierusalem*, that Frederick pledged himself
to recover the Holy City by taking the cross from the Cardinal-bishop of
Albano (Mayence, 27 March). His example was followed by his second
son Frederick, Duke of Swabia, by Leopold of Austria, and by large
numbers of other princes both lay and ecclesiastical. Frederick had
accompanied his uncle the Emperor Conrad III on the Second Crusade,
and had experienced the mismanagement of that ill-starred expedition.
He therefore took every precaution; he admitted into his army only
those who could maintain themselves at their own cost for a two years'
campaign. He wrote to the King of Hungary, to the Emperor of Constantinople, to the Sultan of Iconium, demanding an unmolested passage
through their respective dominions. He wrote even to Saladin requiring
the restitution of the lands he had seized, and warning him in the event
of his refusal to prepare for war within a twelvemonth of the first
of November following. Saladin in a respectful but boastful letter
accepted the Emperor's challenge, and the latter hurried forward his preparations for the expedition.

His son Henry, already crowned king and Emperor-elect, was to take
charge of affairs in the West during his absence; but Frederick was
anxious to remove as many difficulties as he could from the path of the
young and inexperienced ruler. Henry the Lion, who since his return
from banishment had remained tolerably peaceable at Brunswick, was
now shewing signs of restiveness; he was still, though in advanced years,
active and ambitious, too ambitious to rest quietly content with the
humble position which remained to him; there was not a little discord,
we are told, between him and his supplanter, Duke Bernard. At a diet
at Goslar in August 1188 he was given the choice between three alternative proposals: either he must content himself with a partial restitution
of his lands, or he must accompany the Emperor on the Crusade at the
latter's expense on the understanding that on his return he should be
completely restored to his own, or finally he must leave Germany with his
eldest son for a further period of three years. At first sight it seems
strange that Henry should choose the third alternative; but it was the only
one of the three which left him with a free hand. If he had accepted the
first offer he must renounce for ever the remainder of his former possessions, if the second he saw little likelihood of Frederick's having either
the power or the inclination to make him the promised full restitution of
lands which had already been granted away to others. So at Easter 1189
he once more withdrew to the court of his father-in-law, there to scheme
and plot with his English kinsfolk for the recovery of his lost possessions by force of arms.

There was another important matter which the Emperor wished to
see settled. His friendly relations with the French court drew him inevitably into the political turmoil of the western border-countries—Flanders,
Champagne, Brabant, Namur, Hainault. The centre of interest is Baldwin,

Count of Hainault, of whose doings we have a full account from his Chancellor, Gilbert of Mons. He was heir to his childless brother-in-law, Philip of Flanders; he was heir also to his blind, elderly, and also childless uncle Henry II, Count of Namur and Luxembourg. Such rich expectations brought upon him the jealousy and hostility of his neighbours. However he could look for support in the highest places; his sister had married Philip Augustus, and Philip was on terms of friendship with the Emperor. It was to the imperial court therefore that he looked for, and from which he gained, a guarantee of his rights of succession to the countship of Namur. Thus matters stood when to the surprise of everyone, and not the least of himself, the aged Count of Namur became the father of a daughter, Ermesinde, who before she was a year old was betrothed to the Count of Champagne with the inheritance of Namur as her promised dowry. Baldwin once more sought the help of Frederick, but the final decision was postponed till the return of King Henry from Italy. Then at Seligenstadt in May 1188 the Emperor not only confirmed him in the succession, but raised the county into a margravate, thereby exalting Baldwin to the rank of a prince of the Empire. Frederick's policy was to create a strong outpost on the north-west frontier of his dominions. Baldwin did not live to occupy this powerful position; but it passed to his second son Philip, while his elder son united the counties of Hainault and Flanders and was destined to become the first Latin Emperor of Constantinople.

At the head of an army of some twenty thousand knights Frederick left Ratisbon early in May 1189. The journey eastward was likely to prove difficult, for Isaac Angelus, who was on anything but friendly terms with Frederick since the conclusion of the German-Sicilian alliance, had opened negotiations with Saladin. All kinds of obstructions were thrown in the path of the imperial army. The crusaders had scarcely left Hungarian soil before they encountered hostility from the Bulgarians, instigated by the perfidious Emperor of Constantinople; the ambassadors, the Bishop of Münster and others, sent forward to the Greek capital as an earnest of Frederick's good faith, were thrust into prison. Nevertheless fear of the German arms was stronger than hatred; the inhabitants of Philippopolis and Hadrianople fled at their approach and left the cities deserted; Isaac Angelus, dreading an attack on Constantinople, had to submit. He agreed to provision Frederick's army, to transport it to Asia Minor, and to provide hostages for his good conduct. Isaac had given way none too soon; for Frederick, disgusted with his behaviour, had written to his son in Germany with instructions to collect a fleet from the maritime towns of Italy and to get the Pope's sanction to a crusade against the Greeks. Timely submission alone prevented Barbarossa from anticipating the work of the Fourth Crusade.

Without entering the Greek capital the German army moved southward from Hadrianople and crossed from Gallipoli into Asia Minor. Here too unexpected difficulties were encountered: the promises of the Sultan of Iconium on which Frederick had reckoned were as valueless as those of the Emperor of Constantinople; the line of march of the crusading army was continually harassed by Turkish bands; supplies were cut off and famine was added to the other difficulties which beset their path. Iconium had to be captured before Sultan Qilij Arslān would fulfil his compact, grant them a safe passage through his dominions, and provide them with the necessary supplies.   With Armenian guides they proceeded on their way across the Taurus till they reached the banks of the Cilician river Salef. There the great Kaiser met his end. How precisely, we cannot tell; there are many versions of the story. Frederick, perhaps, chafing at the slow progress of his army over the narrow bridge, rode impetuously into the stream and was borne under by the swift waters, or, wearied by the tedious march across the mountains, he may have wished to refresh himself in the cool stream and found the current too strong for his aged limbs. Certain it is that his body was drawn lifeless from the river.

The memory of Frederick Barbarossa was not extinguished when his bones were laid to rest in the church of St Peter at Antioch. He has lived on in the minds of his fellow-countrymen as the truest expression of German patriotism. It is but a little more than a century ago that his name was first linked with the well-known Kyffhäuser Saga; the hero of that famous legend is his gifted, brilliant, yet far less patriotic grandson. Rückert and Grimm[1], with a keener perception of the fitness of things, make not Frederick II but Frederick Barbarossa sleep in the solitary cave on the mountain side with his great red beard growing round the table at which he sits; twice his beard has encircled the table; when it has done so a third time he will awaken and fight a mighty battle, and the Day of Judgment will dawn.

---

[1] Rückert, *Patriotische Gedichte*, 1813; J. and W. Grimm, *Deutsche Sagen*, 1816, p. 29. Cf. also Grimm, *Deutsche Mythologie*, 1854, pp. 906 sq.

CHAPTER XIII.

FREDERICK BARBAROSSA AND THE LOMBARD LEAGUE.

WHEN the votes of the Electors called the young Duke of Swabia, Frederick of Hohenstaufen, to the throne, men's minds turned to him in anxiety yet in the fulness of hope. Germany had need of settled government in order to reunite her inherent forces and to raise the fallen dignity of the Empire to the high level once attained by Charles and Otto the Great. The character of the young monarch who now undertook to direct the destinies of the Empire was not unequal to the task, and the manly ambition which glowed within him found in the example of those great predecessors a spur and inspiration fraught with promise. His person seemed a symbol of domestic peace to the Germans who had raised him to his throne. His father had transmitted to him the Ghibelline blood of the Hohenstaufen with all the other imperial traditions of the Franconian house. On his mother's side he was related to the Welfs, and thus seemed to form a reuniting link of friendship between the two great parties so long at variance. He was a voice calling upon the scattered forces of Germany to combine and work in harmony for common interests.

Gifted with a good memory and a keen intelligence, Frederick spoke his native language eloquently but was not at home in the Latin tongue, although he read Latin authors with pleasure and took a delight in those narratives of Roman history which brought before his mind, yearning for greatness and fame, memories of that bygone Roman Empire on the restoration of which his heart was set. Like all men of a higher cast of character, he opened his ears to the spirit of his age and yielded to the influences of the revived classical learning. His mind was full of the revived conceptions of the Roman imperial law, of which the Italian jurists saw in him the embodiment. They did not, however, understand that the Empire transplanted into German soil was not the Empire of old, and that in Frederick of Hohenstaufen they had before them the most authentic representation of the good and evil of Germanic power against which, as by an inevitable antithesis, the free Lombard communes were to rise. Frederick was the successor of Charles the Great rather than of Augustus, and his counterpart was the new Italy which had taken the place of the ancient Rome.

The crown was hardly on his brow when he sent to Italy ambassadors, who presented themselves to the Pope and were well received. Eugenius III, in May 1152, had at once written to Frederick from

Segni congratulating him on his election and announcing the dispatch of a legate who would acquaint him with his intentions. The Pope, in expressing his confidence that the king would maintain the promises made by Conrad III to himself and the Roman Church, hinted at an early visit to Rome. With a bearing on this subject which lay so near his heart, Eugenius wrote on 20 September 1152 to Wibald, Abbot of Corvey (Stablo), informing him of the machinations set on foot in Rome by the popular faction at the instigation of the heretic, Arnold of Brescia, unknown to the nobles and leading personages of the city. About two thousand of the common citizens had met secretly to arrange for the election of one hundred senators for life and two consuls, and to vest the supreme authority over them and over Rome in one man holding the rank of Emperor. The Pope enjoined Wibald to inform Frederick of this secretly in order that he might take steps to meet the occasion. Frederick stood in need of no incitement from the Pope to turn his thoughts to Italy, and in the very first days of his reign he had discussed the matter in council with the princes. His ecclesiastical advisers would have liked him to have given effect without further negotiations to the engagements made between Conrad III and the Holy See, and then to have proceeded to Rome to receive the crown and re-establish the impaired authority of the Pope. But the lay princes were opposed to this immediate absence from Germany, either because the position of the kingdom was still too unstable or because they thought it expedient to wait for a fresh invitation from the Pope. Frederick, although anxious to receive the crown and feeling that it was important to do so quickly, saw the necessity of first dealing with the affairs of Germany. In the case of the election of Wichmann[1] to the archbishopric of Magdeburg the interpretation of the Concordat of Worms was involved, and this introduced a serious cause of disagreement with the Pope.

In spite of this incident, friendly relations were maintained between the Pope and the king. It was a matter of pressing importance for both that the coronation at Rome should not be long deferred. While settling the affairs of Germany, Frederick kept his attention steadily fixed on Italy, and in giving his decision in favour of the Saxon Henry the Lion, whom he liked and wished to reconcile to the Empire, in the dispute between that prince and the Duke of Bavaria, he aimed at securing powerful co-operation in his expedition into Italy. Invitations to enter upon this expedition were many and fervent. The rebel barons of Apulia pictured to him the easiness of an enterprise against the King of Sicily; many Italian cities asked his aid against other and more powerful cities, especially against the powerful and haughty Milanese whom they had not sufficient strength to oppose. Anastasius IV, who had succeeded Eugenius III in July 1153, confirmed the proposals of his predecessor, and went so far as to grant the pallium to Wichmann for

---

[1] See *supra*, Chapter XII, pp. 392–3.

the see of Magdeburg, while urging Frederick to come to Rome. The moment had come, and the young restorer of the Empire set out in October 1154 from the Tyrol for Italy. In November he encamped near Piacenza, on the plains of Roncaglia, in order to hold, according to custom, his first Italian diet. A few days afterwards, on 3 December 1154, Anastasius died at Rome, and with his successor a new era opened, in which the story of the House of Swabia up to its end was inextricably bound up with that of the Papacy.

The new Pontiff was known as Hadrian IV. He was born in England, at Langley near St Albans, in poor circumstances, and his name was Nicholas Breakspear. He had left his native country in youth and wandered through various districts of France in search of instruction. After a stay of some duration at Arles, his studies being now complete, he was received into the monastery of Saint-Ruf in Provence, where his good looks, well-weighed speeches, and prompt obedience made him a favourite. There he was able to turn to account his intellectual gifts, and made such advance in his studies and in the esteem of his fellow-religious that he was raised to the rank of abbot. In this office, however, he did not obtain the same sympathies as before, either because the monks found the rule of a foreigner irksome, or that he had heaped up resentments against himself by his unflinching severity. Thus disputes arose between him and his monks which brought him to Rome to Eugenius III. In this way the Pontiff learned to estimate his true worth and, removing him from the abbacy, appointed him Cardinal-bishop of Albano and then placed him at the head of the Norwegian missions. By carrying the Gospel into these distant regions and there organising the Church, he secured such a reputation at Rome and among the cardinals that they, on the day after the death of Anastasius (4 December 1154), soon after his return from his mission, elected him to the Papacy.

A strong man, called upon to face difficult times, he entered on his sacred office with a very lofty conception of the supreme mission for which this office had been instituted on earth by God. The zeal and piety which inspired him were combined with a capacity for public affairs bordering on astuteness, while the suavity of his manner was accompanied by a strength and tenacity of character which looked straight forward, without swerving, to the end in view. He had scarcely become Pope when an occasion arose for displaying his firmness. The Romans, in the last days of the pontificate of Eugenius, had consented to a sort of truce which had enabled the Pope to re-enter Rome and establish himself in the Vatican within the precincts of the Leonine city. But it was a truce which both parties viewed with suspicion. Arnold of Brescia with his followers was still in Rome, and his presence encouraged the popular faction to contend for communal liberty against pontifical supremacy. This new Pope, a foreigner, confident of his authority and hostile to the teaching of Arnold, could not be acceptable to the Romans, whose discontent reached at last the pitch of violence.

One day when Cardinal Guido of Santa Pudenziana was returning from the Vatican, he was attacked and seriously wounded by Arnold's followers. Hadrian in return for this grave outrage unhesitatingly launched an interdict against the city, declaring that it should not be removed until Arnold and his party were banished from Rome.

Never before had this heavy sentence fallen upon the city, and the unforeseen event spread terror in men's minds. Easter was close at hand, Holy Week had begun, and the churches were prayerless and shut against the faithful. Hadrian remained unmoved amidst the amazement of the panic-stricken people. Urged by the clergy and the populace, the senators sought the Pope's presence and swore to banish Arnold and his followers. While wandering in the Campagna he was taken prisoner by members of the papal party, but being rescued by some friendly barons who revered him as an apostle he found refuge in one of their strongholds. His rebellious adversary having thus been got rid of, Hadrian was able at last to issue forth from the Leonine city and proceed with great pomp to the Lateran, where he presided at the Easter solemnities.

While things were thus happening in Rome, fresh causes of anxiety had arisen in the south, where the quarrel between the Curia and the King of Sicily, William I, was once more active. The new king, who had but recently succeeded Roger, began his reign under difficult circumstances. Harassed by rebellion within and by hostility on the part of the Eastern and Western Emperors without his dominions, he thought of reverting to the subtle traditional Norman policy by trying to renew friendly relations with the Pope and thus separating him from Frederick. On the election of Hadrian he had sent ambassadors to discuss terms of peace but without success. Later, towards March 1155, the Pope, alarmed perhaps by the arrival from Sicily of William at Salerno, sent to him, in return, Henry, Cardinal of SS. Nereus and Achilleus, with letters apostolic. In these letters, however, William was addressed ambiguously as Lord instead of King of Sicily. He therefore sent back the cardinal to Rome without even receiving him, a treatment which was greatly resented by the Curia and the Pope. All probability of agreement being thus upset, the king, notwithstanding his domestic troubles and the movements among the hostile barons who were hoping great things from Frederick's approach and were inclining towards him, sent out an expedition against the papal territory under his Chancellor, who set siege to Benevento, laying waste many districts, and burning among other places Ceprano, Bauco, and Frosinone. On his return he pulled down the walls of Aquino and Pontecorvo, and expelled almost all the monks from Monte Cassino on the suspicion that they were partisans of the papal cause. Hadrian could do nothing in his own defence except put William under excommunication and place all his hope on Frederick.

The Pope had pursued steadily the negotiations relative to the visit of the future Emperor to Rome. The agreements arrived at under Eugenius III were confirmed, and the two potentates entered into a close alliance, the terms of which included the submission of the Roman Republic to the Pope, hostility towards the King of Sicily, and an embargo on the acquisition of any Italian territory by the Emperor of the East. Frederick, however, had scarcely set foot in Italy before he perceived that he was walking on a volcano. The lofty notions of domination of the Roman-Germanic Emperor were met by a burning sentiment of liberty, which was the breath of life to those prosperous cities wherein had originated a new phase of civic existence and commerce. It was clear that Frederick could never hope to have supremacy in Italy and to hold aloft the imperial authority, if he did not first subdue the strength of those self-reliant republics which in spite of their intestine feuds shewed little willingness to submit. At Roncaglia the representatives of the republics had appeared and had shewn a certain degree of respect for the imperial authority, but it was not difficult to see what fire was smouldering under the ashes. Pavia, Lodi, and some other towns favoured Frederick out of hatred for Milan, to which they were subordinate, but Milan was the soul of Lombardy and could not endure the imperial yoke. During the diet Frederick had adjudicated and settled terms of peace in the disputes between the different cities, especially between Pavia and Milan, but the latter gave clear signs of disinclination to bend to his will. It was necessary for Frederick to use force and bring his heavy hand to bear. He very soon found an opportunity of shewing his hostility to Milan. His temper had been aroused by the conduct of the Milanese in guiding his army through their territory along bad and inconvenient roads. He entered Rosate, a strong *castello* of the Milanese, and, driving out the inhabitants, gave it over to fire and pillage. In the same way the *castelli* of Trecate and Galliate were entirely destroyed. The cause of the Empire in Italy was bound up with that of feudalism, which was waning every day before the growth and emancipation of the communes. The city of Asti and the *castello* of Chieri had rejected the authority of the Marquess of Montferrat, and Frederick, on an appeal from the marquess, put them to fire and sword. But these acts of destruction were not sufficient to prove his power and determination. The opportunity had not come for carrying his power against Milan. That city was too powerful and too well stocked with provisions and means of defence. A siege would have exposed the army of Frederick to too serious a test and would have delayed too long his coronation. It was better to attack some other places faithful to Milan and, by thus weakening the strength of her allies, to spread through Lombardy the terror of his arms and unbending purpose.

Pavia, always a relentless enemy, pointed out to him Tortona which, when asked to separate from Milan, firmly refused. Frederick, supposing that her subjection, like that of other strongholds, would be easy, laid siege, supported by the forces of Pavia and of the Marquess of Montferrat, but met with a stubborn resistance which gave earnest of obstinate struggles to come. The fury of the assaults, the gallows on which Frederick had the prisoners hanged in order to strike terror into the besieged, the pangs of hunger, availed nothing during two months to shake their determination. It was only at the beginning of April that they were compelled to surrender through thirst. The inhabitants' lives were spared but they were scattered abroad, and Tortona was razed to the ground and utterly destroyed. All Lombardy rang with the news of this event.

Frederick had spent so much time on this siege and had used up so much of his strength upon it that he had to renounce all thoughts of the entire subjugation of Lombardy. In the meantime he had taken steps to secure the friendly assistance of the great maritime cities, Venice, Genoa, and Pisa, in view of an expedition against the King of Sicily and, after keeping Easter with great magnificence at Pavia, he moved towards Rome. His route lay through Tuscany, where he intended to meet the Pope, who was then at Sutri. His journey was so rapid that the Curia felt some suspicions. Recollections of the violence used scarcely half a century before by Henry V to Paschal II in St Peter's, in order to wring from him concessions in the matter of the investitures, may perhaps have occurred to Hadrian and the cardinals at this moment. After consultation with the latter, with Peter, prefect of the city, and Otto Frangipane, the Pope sent two cardinals to Frederick with special instructions to settle the conditions of their interview. The cardinals found Frederick at San Quirico near Siena and were received with marks of honour. They explained the object of their mission, and among other requests asked that Arnold of Brescia should be handed over to the Pope, who felt anxiety at his being a fugitive at large. The request was a small one and was at once granted. Frederick caused one of the barons friendly to Arnold to be made prisoner and compelled him to surrender the unfortunate refugee. The hour of martyrdom had now come for the apostle of Brescia. He was condemned to death by the prefect of Rome and fell a victim to his consuming zeal for the purity of the Church. His death perhaps occurred at Civita Castellana, but the exact day and place are unknown. He encountered the stake without fear; he made no recantation; he murmured a silent prayer to God; and committed himself to the rope and the flames with such calmness and serenity that even his executioners gave way to tears. His ashes were cast into the Tiber lest the Romans should preserve them as relics for veneration and as incentives to revenge, but his words long re-echoed in the ears of the people. By the martyrdom of Arnold an ill-omened seal was set to the compact between

Pope and Emperor which was only to bear fruit in bloodshed and was soon to be dissolved. Frederick had not hesitated to comply with the first request of the papal ambassadors, but with regard to their other demands he replied that he had already sent to the Pope Archbishop Arnold of Cologne and Anselm, Archbishop-elect of Ravenna, to discuss these points, and therefore could give no answer until they returned. The dispatch of these ambassadors, when made known to the Pope, increased his suspicions. He feared some underhand dealing and, giving up his original intention of proceeding to Orvieto, withdrew to Civita Castellana, a strong and well-fortified place. There he received the imperial envoys, whom he informed, in his turn, that he could give no reply until the cardinals whom he had sent to Frederick should have returned. Thus both embassies turned back, leaving things where they were. Meeting however on the way, they resolved to return together to the king, who had reached Viterbo. There the negotiations were concluded, the king swearing to respect the life and liberty of the Pope and to observe the stipulations as agreed before. Among those present at the conferences was Cardinal Octavian of St Cecilia who, it would appear, was not in agreement with the other cardinal-legates of the Pope. Probably already at that time he represented in the Curia the leaning towards closer ties with Germany and greater compliance with the policy of the Emperor. It is certain that he was already on friendly terms with Frederick and an object of suspicion to the dominant and stricter party who, as we shall see later on, were not without reasons for suspicion. The conditions and place of meeting having been settled, the Pope and the king moved forward. Frederick with his court and army encamped at Campo Grasso in the territory of Sutri, and the Pope, now assured of his personal safety, left Civita Castellana and came down to Nepi, where on the following day he was met by a large company of German barons who accompanied him in solemn procession along with his bishops and cardinals to the tent of the king.

But here a new surprise awaited him, reviving all his doubts and suspicions. Frederick, on the Pope's arrival, did not advance to offer his services as squire to hold Hadrian's bridle and stirrup. The cardinals were thrown into great excitement. The Pope himself, disturbed and uncertain what to do, dismounted unwillingly and seated himself on the throne prepared for him. The king then knelt before him and kissed his feet and drew near to receive the kiss of peace. But the Pope firmly refused. "Thou hast denied me," he said, "the service which, out of reverence for the Apostles Peter and Paul, thy predecessors have always paid to mine up to the present time, and until thou hast satisfied me I will not give thee the kiss of peace." The king replied that he was not bound to this act of service. Through the whole of that day and of the next the dispute on this point of ceremonial went on. So obstinate was the contention that some of the cardinals, either from exasperation or fear, left the camp and returned to Civita Castellana. The question was more serious than it seemed to be, for Frederick by his refusal wished to shut out even the semblance of homage to the Pope, and by so doing implicitly denied that he was in any way indebted to the Pontiff for the imperial crown. But the unshakeable firmness of the Pope carried the day. The existence of ninth-century precedents for the papal claim was a notorious fact, and among the followers of the king the older men could remember having seen the Emperor Lothar pay this very service to Innocent II. Frederick besides had too many reasons for hastening on the coronation to put obstacles in his own way over a matter of form. The camp was moved a little farther away to the neighbourhood of a lake in the district of Nepi, and here, according to arrangement, the king and Pope met, coming from different directions; Frederick, in the presence of the army, fulfilled the functions of squire, holding the Pope's bridle for about a stone's throw and the stirrup as he dismounted. Agreement having thus been secured, Hadrian and the king advanced towards Rome together, journeying and halting in company and keeping up friendly conversations, in the course of which the Pope reiterated his grievances against the Romans and the King of Sicily, calling upon Frederick to give him his promised help in restoring the papal authority in Rome, and in providing him with security against his powerful and aggressive neighbour in the south. As they drew near to Rome, they were met by the ambassadors sent by the senate and people of Rome to greet Frederick. The Pope's presence and his evident alliance with the king had not yet quelled the high spirit of the Romans. They still felt conscious of a strength real enough to contest the possession of Rome, and, with the glamour of ancient Roman greatness before them, they used the language of lords and dispensers of the Roman Empire, demanding a tribute and sworn guarantees for the safety and liberties of the city. Frederick, in agreement with and at the advice of the Pope and the cardinals, haughtily repulsed their audacious requests. The ambassadors withdrew to the Capitol in wrath, there to convey the news of the rejection. Wounded in their pride and determined not to surrender the liberty won after so many years of conflict with the Popes, the Romans made ready to avenge this outrage. The Pope, who understood the Roman temper, advised the king to act quickly and cautiously. The Leonine city was still the Pope's. It was necessary to keep it in their hands, and therefore a strong band of men was at once sent to occupy it by night. In order to reassure Frederick, the Pope proposed that Cardinal Octavian, his faithful adherent, should act as their leader. Without waiting for the Sunday, on the following day (Saturday, 18 June 1155), preceded by Hadrian, who went to await him on the steps of St Peter's, Frederick came down from Monte Mario at the head of his army and, in great pomp, surrounded by his princes and barons, entered the church and went with the Pope to worship at the tomb of the Apostles.

Here, according to the accustomed rites, he received at the Pope's hands the imperial crown amid such loud acclamations from the Germans that the roof of the church seemed to send back peals of thunder.

While Frederick re-entered his camp without the walls of the city, the unexpected news of the coronation reached the Capitol, where the Romans had assembled to discuss the best means of preventing the ceremony. Finding themselves thus over-reached, their indignation knew no bounds, and they seized their arms and rushed to the Leonine city in fury. Some German soldiers who had remained behind, and some followers of the Pope and of the cardinals, were killed by the populace. The tumult was great, and Hadrian and the cardinals were in personal danger. The report of the commotion reached the camp at the point nearest to the city, where Henry the Lion, Duke of Saxony, was encamped. He rose in haste and entered by a breach in the walls, which had been left open since the days of Henry IV, to meet the Romans, followed quickly by the Emperor with all his forces. There followed a terrible struggle which lasted persistently throughout the day, accompanied by great slaughter. At last towards nightfall the disciplined soldiery of a regular army got the better of the stubborn fury of the populace. The Romans were driven back over the Tiber, with great loss in killed and wounded and leaving behind them some hundreds of prisoners.

Frederick was boastful of his victory, but, if by rapidity of movement he had been able to carry out his coronation undisturbed, the bloodshed which followed it did not give him possession of Rome and could not secure it for Hadrian. It was out of the question to make his way into the city by force, nor was it expedient, even if possible, to remain where he was. The infuriated Romans refused all intercourse with him and would not supply him with the means of victualling his army. The only course open was to strike his camp and, taking with him the Pope and the cardinals, to retire towards the Sabina and make for a crossing over the Tiber near Soracte, at some distance from Rome. After a brief rest at the monastery of Farfa, he led his army to an encampment in the valley of the Tiber on the banks of the Aniene near Ponte Lucano. Here the Pope and the Emperor celebrated the festival of SS. Peter and Paul (29 June 1155), and it is said that on this occasion the Pope absolved the soldiery from the guilt of the bloodshed in Rome, declaring that he was not guilty of murder who slew another in fighting for his own sovereign.

From Ponte Lucano they went on to the territory of Albano and Tusculum. Since it was impossible to make an immediate attack on Rome and obtain mastery over the city, the Pope urged Frederick to seize the favourable opportunity and move against the King of Sicily, now that his barons, emboldened by the Emperor's presence in Italy, had risen in open rebellion. Frederick was inclined to listen to him and his ecclesiastical advisers were in favour of the design, but fever was already making inroads on his army, and the lay barons strongly opposed it and insisted on his return to Germany. The Emperor abandoned the expedition, and took leave of the Pope with promises of a speedy return with stronger forces to subjugate Rome and Sicily. They parted with all the forms of friendship, but the Pope felt his disappointment and isolation bitterly. On his way Frederick set fire to Spoleto, which had offered him resistance, and at Ancona he met with the Byzantine ambassadors of the Emperor Manuel Comnenus, who offered him money and help towards the Sicilian expedition, an aid which he was obliged to refuse on account of his homeward journey. He continued his march in speed to Verona, where he met with an unfriendly reception. At the defile of the Adige he encountered obstinate resistance which he overcame with courage and skill, leaving traces behind him of his stern severity as a warning to those who were inclined to oppose him. In this way he reached Germany with no other gain than the imperial crown, but he had learned to know the Italians and had taught the Italians to know him. He knew henceforward what kind of obstacles he had to expect and what amount of strength would be required to overcome them. The crown of Empire was his, but it behoved him to make it the symbol of real power and of intrinsic greatness, and to guard it not only from the claims of the Papacy as of old but from the rising popular forces of the free communes which seemed to have sprung as by enchantment from the soil. A conflict there was bound to be, and it was imperative that he should be prepared.

The departure of the Emperor rendered the condition of the cities favourable to the Empire more serious, for Milan and the communes in alliance with her became increasingly aggressive throughout the cruel and incessant warfare waged between the cities of Lombardy. Frederick had scarcely turned his back when Tortona, notwithstanding the opposition of Pavia, sprang again into life with the help of Milan in money and men, and her newly reconstructed walls once more raised a bulwark of defence for the citizens who had already shewn such a heroic capacity of resistance. The hegemony of Milan established itself more firmly than ever, and thanks to her well-chosen alliances with other cities this predominance bore with increasing weight on the other communes. The cities thus held within her grasp looked to the Germanic Emperor as their only means of salvation.

The Emperor, in the meantime, strengthened by the prestige of the imperial crown and the renown of his military exploits in Italy, had turned energetically to the restoration in Germany of the imperial authority and the organisation of the State[1]. Having divorced his first wife, he had married Beatrix, the heiress of the County of Burgundy, thereby extending his influence towards Provence and bringing the frontiers of his effective rule nearer to Italy, never absent from his thoughts. After having received, along with the Empress, the homage

[1] For events in Germany see *supra*, Chapter xii.

of Burgundy at Besançon, he returned to Germany in January 1158. Scarcely two years had passed since his coronation in Rome; the whole of Germany regarded with pride and wonder the sovereign who had led her back to the position of the central power in Europe.

But this conception of universal influence had its roots in Italy, and it was in that country that the foundations of the Empire must be laid if they were to rest on a stable basis. In northern Italy it was necessary to have a firm foothold in order to confront the Papacy, from which the Empire could not sever itself but towards which it was yet indispensable to assert full independence. It was equally necessary if the imperial influence was to be efficacious in the political affairs of southern Italy and in the relations between Germany and the Empire of the East. Frederick never lost sight of the imperial idea amid all the pre-occupations of his German kingdom. He knew henceforward what difficulties he would have to struggle against before reaching his goal, and made his preparations by keeping a watchful eye on his adversaries and combining the forces necessary for their overthrow. Difficulties had in fact increased since his return from Italy.

Milan and the communes friendly to her had renewed their strength and were haughtier and more aggressive than ever, while the papal policy was moving in a direction the reverse of favourable to the Empire. Hadrian IV, bitterly disappointed in the hopes which he had placed in Frederick, found himself in a very critical situation. Rome was closed against him and the King of Sicily threatened his borders, while he had no aid or defence except among the rebel Sicilian barons. The harassing uncertainty of his position was aggravated by divided opinions among his councillors. The rising divisions among the cardinals had now become sharply accentuated, and two parties had been formed in favour of opposite courses of action. One side held fast to the continuance of the alliance with the Emperor, the other, distrustful of Frederick and mindful of the ancient enmity between Papacy and Empire, stood for a renewal of the Hildebrandine policy of close relations with the Norman princes. Each of these two parties had a powerful leader. At the head of the first party was Octavian, Cardinal of Santa Cecilia, who had powerful family connexions in Rome, and on account of his intimate personal relations with Frederick had been chosen to conduct his advanced guard into the Leonine city at the time of the coronation. The other party was led by Roland, Cardinal of St Mark and Chancellor of the Church, a learned expert in the canon law, a firm, sagacious man, a sharer in the councils and policy of Hadrian, convinced like him of the Church's supremacy and resolved to maintain it. Amidst such conflicting views the Pope, in November 1155, yielding to the incitements of the rebel barons of Apulia, betook himself to Benevento and there became the chief pivot of the revolt against King William. The latter, seeing that the Pope was joining hands on the one side with the insurgents and on the other with the Eastern Emperor then preparing an expedition against him, was in such difficulties that he reopened negotiations, offering very favourable conditions of peace. The Pope was inclined to accept them, but the anti-Sicilian party prevailed, and the majority of the cardinals would not consent to listen to the advantageous terms proposed. The hour of regret came quickly. William made an energetic movement against the rebels and the Byzantines, and after defeating them turned back against the Pope and threatened Benevento. The Curia had no way of escape and was forced to yield. Hadrian sent Roland and two other cardinals to sue for the peace which he had just rejected, and obtained it under much less favourable conditions than those before offered.

With this peace began a political estrangement between the Pope and the Emperor. The new situation irritated Frederick, and was regarded with dislike also by the German clergy. The treaty between the Pope and King William seemed a treacherous infraction of the terms agreed upon at Constance in 1153[1], and there certainly seemed to be grounds for believing that the Pope had fallen short of that understanding. On the other hand Hadrian had as an excuse the Emperor's abandonment of him and the calamitous situation in which he found himself at Benevento without hope of assistance. In every way the relations between the Pope and the Emperor had become clouded by suspicion and bitterness, when an incident occurred which led to the first open rupture. Eskil, Archbishop of Lund, on returning to his see from Italy, was made prisoner in Germany and detained until he paid a ransom. In spite of the Pope's entreaties Frederick had done nothing towards liberating him. Hadrian was deeply offended, and in October 1157, when the Emperor took formal possession of the Burgundian kingdom at Besançon, he sent two legates, the Chancellor Roland and Bernard, Cardinal of San Clemente, to obtain Eskil's freedom and to treat of the political relations as modified by recent events. Frederick received the legates courteously, but their greeting struck him as a strange one. "The Pope and cardinals salute you, he as father, they as brethren." Received in solemn audience the next day, they presented the Pope's letter. Its tone was severe and haughty. Hadrian rebuked Frederick for having allowed the Archbishop of Lund to be despoiled and imprisoned with impunity in German territory, and for having consciously connived at this act of sacrilege. The Pope added that such dissimulation and negligence he could not understand, since he was quite unconscious of having given any cause of offence. The Emperor would do well to remember that the Church had received him joyfully and had *conferred* upon him the imperial crown. That step the Pope had never regretted, and would rejoice to be able to bestow upon him even greater *benefits*. He feared lest some one were sowing tares of

[1] See *supra*, Chapter IV (B), p. 190.

discord between them, and ended by recommending to him the two cardinals who had full powers to treat with him.

On the Chancellor Rainald reading this letter aloud, the princes present rose in a storm of indignation. They were especially incensed at the allusion to the imperial dignity as *conferred* by the Pontiff and at the word *benefits* (*beneficia*) which the German chancellor had evidently translated by *fiefs*, the sense it bore in feudal law. They recalled the rash assertions of Rome that the Empire and the Italian kingdom were gifts of the Pontiffs, and remembered the picture in the Lateran representing Lothar at the feet of the Pope with the humiliating inscription which declared him to be the Pope's liegeman (*homo papae*), and how Hadrian renouncing such vain pretensions had promised to have the picture destroyed. The legates were not intimidated by this tumult; indeed it seems that one of them exclaimed: "And from whom does the Emperor hold the Empire if not from the Pope?" The composure of the legates fanned anger into fury, and the Count-Palatine of Bavaria, Otto of Wittelsbach, advanced with drawn sword against one of the cardinals. Frederick's authority, however, assuaged the tumult and saved the cardinals from danger. On the following morning they were both dismissed with stringent orders to return directly, without diverging to right or left into episcopal or abbatial territory. Frederick at once wrote to the German clergy to inform them of the incident before Rome had time to speak. In a circular sent out through the whole kingdom, he explained the tenor of the papal manoeuvre and the indignation of the princes. He added that the legates had been immediately dismissed because blank letters were found in their possession with the papal seal to enable them to strip the altars and carry off the treasures of the German churches. The Empire was his by the choice of the princes, and he held it direct from God. To affirm that the imperial crown came to him as a *beneficium* from the Pope was a lie against an institution of God and a denial of the teaching of St Peter. He exhorted the clergy to rally to him against such pretensions, since he would without hesitation encounter death rather than submit to such contumely. At Rome the legates on relating their bad reception at Besançon were judged in accordance with the different opinions prevailing in the parties to which the cardinals belonged. The Pope on his part wrote to the German bishops in terms of grave complaint, calling upon them to intervene and obtain from the Emperor that Rainald of Dassel and Otto of Wittelsbach, who were the worst offenders against the persons of the cardinals, should make satisfaction to the Church. But the Pope's words were not well received by the bishops. They replied respectfully but coldly, shewing plainly that they took the part of the Emperor. It was evident that the answer had been written in agreement with the Emperor, whose claims were put forth more firmly than ever along with counter-allusions to the papal aggressiveness. The divine institution of the Empire was insisted on, and the treaty with the King of Sicily condemned. The bishops finally advised the Pope to issue new letters to soothe the angry feelings of the Emperor. The Welf Duke Henry the Lion made a similar recommendation.

Hadrian perceived that this was not the time for a stubborn obstinacy. Prudence was all the more necessary as the descent of Frederick with a formidable army behind him was becoming more imminent day by day. Already the Chancellor Rainald and Otto of Wittelsbach had preceded him into Italy to prepare for the expedition and to secure the fidelity and aid of the Italian cities. In June 1158 two other cardinals appeared before Frederick in Augsburg. In much more obsequious fashion they handed in the letters in which the Pope explained in satisfactory terms the expressions in the previous letters which had aroused such wrath. Frederick received the communication with apparent good-will and treated the cardinals with every courtesy; but in his heart his distrust still rankled, although he did not wish to give the Pope a pretext for joining his enemies while he was on the point of entering Italy.

The Emperor's two envoys, Rainald of Dassel and Otto of Wittelsbach, had worked hard to smooth the way for the expedition. Having taken possession of Rivoli and secured the defile of the Adige, they received oaths of fealty from many Italian cities. Beginning at Verona they went down the Po to Ferrara, then visited Modena and Bologna, going on from thence to Ravenna and Ancona, which latter place they secured for Frederick, ousting the Byzantine emissaries who were there trying to obtain a footing. Turning back they wrested Piacenza from the league made with Milan. Thus so far as was possible all was made ready for the expedition, and the road to Italy lay open to the Emperor. In July 1158, accompanied by the King of Bohemia and the flower of the German nobility, Frederick crossed the Alps at the head of the greatest army seen in Italy for centuries, and turned towards Lombardy with the determination to subdue it and stamp out all forces of resistance to the Empire. The cities which sided with him rallied to him, but those which were hostile he found ready to oppose him in combination, with Milan as their centre of union. His faithful Lodi had been destroyed, and not only was Tortona rebuilt but many other fortresses were rendered capable of checking the advance of an enemy. Hostilities began at Brescia, which was quickly forced to submit by the Bohemians who formed the advanced guard. The rebuilding of Lodi was soon set on foot, and Frederick, after proclaiming the ban of the Empire against Milan, passed the Adda by a bold manoeuvre, took possession of the fortress of Trezzo, and laid siege to Milan. He was aided by all the cities unfriendly to their powerful rival, especially by Pavia and Como. In spite of the great force arrayed against her, Milan made a stiff resistance and gave occasion for remarkable displays of prowess on both sides. After a siege of a month, the Milanese were compelled to surrender, famine having made its ravages quickly felt in so populous a city. Frederick offered terms which were relatively lenient. Como and Lodi were to be rebuilt without hindrance, many hostages handed over, a large indemnity was to be paid, and, worst of all, there was to be a great curtailment of their liberties. The Milanese submitted perforce, but in their hearts they were resolved to shake off their yoke at the first possible opportunity.

On receiving the homage of the Milanese, Frederick dismissed a large number of his German barons, and after a short expedition into Veronese territory he proceeded to Roncaglia, where he had convoked many Italian barons, representatives of the cities, and numerous bishops of upper and central Italy to a diet. The presence of the bishops and their assent was a matter of considerable importance, because in times gone by they had been the foremost representatives and ministers of the Empire in Italy. There, before a people who had just witnessed his great power, the triumphant monarch proposed to arrange the relations between the Empire and the cities of the Italian kingdom. Never perhaps had the imperial rights been so proudly proclaimed, and at that moment the authority of the Empire appeared absolute in Italy and as if it were to last for ever. The jurists, led by the celebrated doctors of the Bolognese school, carried away by the memories of ancient Rome and the reviving study of the Justinianean code, proclaimed in the monarch's name his absolute supremacy, appealing as to a dogma to the famous axiom " quod principi placuit legis habet vigorem."

To the principles extracted from Roman legislation were added others which derived from German notions of law and in reality formed the basis and the bulk of the constitutions of Roncaglia. All the *regalia* were the Emperor's, his all feudal rights, the mints, the customs, the mills, and all other rights, even that of appointing the city consuls, the podestà, and other civic magistrates. And he who had thus been declared lord over the whole world, and whose will was law, dictated in the diet other rules all tending to restrict the rights of the communes, and settled differences between various cities, not without a sense of justice, yet often diminishing the power of the allies of Milan, from which city he also took away the dominion over Monza and the counties of Seprio and Martesana. Frederick had reached the summit of his ambition. The Lombard cities now had their wings clipped, and could venture no more on any dangerous flights. Frederick's only possible opponent was the Pope, whose sole support was the King of Sicily, occupied at home with rebellion and abroad with the ambitious schemes of Byzantium. The glory of his power would soon rival that of Charlemagne and Otto.

But Frederick did not realise that he was pursuing the phantom of an irrevocable past. Soon in Lombardy the rights claimed at Roncaglia began to appear excessive even to the cities which supported the

Emperor. Their imperial tendencies had sprung principally from hatred of their neighbouring enemies, and, when they perceived that their interests and municipal liberties were infringed, their zeal began to cool and symptoms of discontent to appear. Genoa was the first to shew resistance to the interference of the Emperor in her domestic affairs and the government of the city. Safe on the side of the sea, the Genoese sought to gain time by negotiations, while at the same time at great expenditure of labour and money, men and women combining in the work, they strengthened the defences on the land side and made themselves safe against a sudden attack. Pavia and Cremona as partisans of Frederick accepted obediently the podestà appointed by him to each, and Piacenza, although secretly attached to Milan, had not the courage to resist. On the other hand the little city of Crema, in alliance with Milan, stoutly refused to dismantle her walls and fill up her trenches as Frederick demanded. The latter had been offered a large sum of money from the Cremonese to insist upon this demand. The Milanese, not one whit less stubborn, did not feel beaten after their siege. Their irritation was still great at the loss of Monza and the territories wrested from them by the decrees of Roncaglia, when Frederick sent them two legates, the Chancellor Rainald of Dassel and the Count-Palatine of Bavaria, Otto of Wittelsbach. The authority of these two personages did not intimidate the Milanese, who, knowing that they had come to establish officials of imperial appointment, rose against them with such fury that they had to make good their escape in secret. Frederick felt the insult bitterly, and realised the necessity of striking Milan a deadly blow if he were to be supreme in Lombardy. Meanwhile the Milanese declared open war, attacked and took possession of Trezzo, making prisoners of its German garrison, and tried several times, but in vain, to destroy the new city of Lodi which was being built under the auspices of the Emperor. Brescia also shook off the imperial authority and joined Milan, while Piacenza, which had yielded perforce, left Frederick under no delusion as to her aversion. The Emperor, then at Bologna, again proclaimed the ban of the Empire against Milan, and wrote to Germany demanding reinforcements, which were promptly granted, and which arrived led by Henry the Lion. With him came the Empress and Duke Welf VI, uncle of the Emperor, who had just been invested with the lands of the Countess Matilda, to which the Pope laid claim. Advancing into Lombardy, and aided chiefly by Pavia and Cremona, Frederick began to ravage the country, in order to weaken Milan and cut off the supply of provisions necessary for her defence. Afterwards, in July 1159, he laid siege to Crema with a great force. The heroic resistance of this small city for seven months against the great besieging army of Frederick has been handed down as an object of admiration to later ages. The siege, conducted with obstinacy and savage fury, was endured by the besieged with a firmness of mind which nothing could bend, not even the sight of their own kindred who had been taken prisoner being bound to the machines with which the enemy advanced to make their attacks upon the walls. Undaunted, the Cremaschi repelled their onsets, without compassion for their own flesh and blood, and with no other thought than to defend their native city to the last. It was only in January 1160, after a six months' struggle, when all their forces were exhausted and further resistance was impossible, that these valorous citizens surrendered. Their only conditions were that their own lives should be spared, and the lives of those Milanese and Brescians who had joined with them in the defence. Crema was destroyed, and her rival Cremona was able to exult with unseemly joy over her ruins.

Meanwhile the disputes between the Pope and the Emperor had broken out again more hotly than ever. An impassable abyss lay between them, for the irreconcilable principle of two supremacies rendered their two representatives irreconcilable also, and provided endless subjects of disagreement. Frederick, already disposed to take offence, had become hardened in his resentment because the Pope refused to confirm the nomination of Guido, son of the Count of Biandrate, to the archbishopric of Ravenna. Much greater was his indignation when a letter arrived from Hadrian carried by a messenger of mean appearance who disappeared immediately after consigning it. The letter was marked by a renewal of the bitter tone which for some time past had dropped out of their correspondence, and was full of complaints against the recent exactions made by the imperial officers on ecclesiastical possessions. Frederick, more incensed than before, ordered his Chancellor in answering it to place his name before the Pope's and to address him in the second person singular *tu* instead of by the customary plural *vos*. In this way he thought to remind the Pope of the old imperial supremacy. But the Pope stiffened himself all the more, in spite of the great but unavailing efforts of Eberhard, Bishop of Bamberg, to soothe the two antagonists. The bishop writing of Frederick to a cardinal said: " You know what he is. He loves those who love him and turns away from others, not having yet thoroughly learned to love also his enemies."

The exhortations of Eberhard bore no fruit. The Pope, it is true, sent four cardinals to the Emperor to discuss the points of disagreement between them, but with conditions which seemed too hard. All magistracies and *regalia* of Rome, the Pope affirmed, belonged to St Peter, and therefore the Emperor had no right to send his envoys direct to the Romans; the estates of the Pope were not to be subject to *fodrum* except at an imperial coronation; Italian bishops owed the Emperor no homage but only an oath of fealty, and were not obliged to entertain imperial envoys in their palaces. Restitution was to be made to the Pope of the possessions of the Roman Church—Tivoli, Ferrara, Massa, Ficarolo, the lands of the Countess Matilda, the territory from Acquapendente to Rome, the duchy of Spoleto, and the islands of Sardinia and Corsica. Frederick was certainly not the man to submit to such exaggerated claims. He repelled them, not without expressions of irony, by saying that he would not require homage from the Italian bishops if they would give up those of their temporalities which were *regalia*; further, imperial envoys would have no right to be entertained in the bishops' palaces if these happened not to be built on lands held from the Emperor; but normally they were so built, and were imperial palaces. Then the Pope's affirmation that imperial envoys could not be sent direct to the Romans, since the magistracies at Rome and the *regalia* were papal, would imply that he, Roman Emperor by right divine, was a mere phantom sovereign, bearing an empty name.

Such was the situation when some ambassadors from the city of Rome came to Frederick with offers of recognition of the imperial rights in return for his recognition and protection of the Roman Senate. Frederick grasped the opportunity, received the Roman envoys with marks of honour, and dismissed them not without hope. He then proposed to the legates that a committee of arbitration should be formed consisting of six cardinals on the Pope's side and six bishops on his own, and informed them that he would send ambassadors to Rome to treat with the Pope and the Roman citizens, thus inserting a threat amid the formalities of friendship. Ambassadors were sent, but Hadrian absolutely refused arbitration, admitting no tribunal above his own, and the Romans themselves shewed a suspicious temper, fearing that the Emperor, in restoring the banished prefect of the city, wished to introduce a magistrate of his own, and while retaining the semblance to destroy the reality of an independent senate. Here, as on other occasions, Frederick ran counter to the sentiment of municipal freedom widespread throughout Italy. Hadrian again, recognising the power of this sentiment, turned his eyes towards Lombardy in the hope of securing the assistance of the communes. A first attempt at a league between the citizens of Milan, Brescia, and Piacenza agreed at Anagni with Hadrian to come to no terms with the Emperor without the consent of the Pontiff and that of his successors, and the people of Crema, still besieged within their walls, sent their oath to the same effect. The Pope made like promises to the leagued cities, and announced to them that he would within forty days place Frederick under excommunication. But before he could put into effect such a serious resolution, an attack of angina suddenly brought about his death at Anagni on 1 September 1159.

The election of his successor was bound to be a stormy one. The two divergent policies among the cardinals were inevitably brought into collision at a moment when the whole future direction of the Church depended upon the preponderance of one or other of the two parties. The majority of the cardinals favoured the election of Cardinal Roland, a supporter of Hadrian's policy and of the alliance with Sicily, while a small minority gave a stubborn support to Cardinal Octavian, head of the party bent on agreement with the Emperor. After Hadrian had been laid to rest in the Vatican, the cardinals assembled in the church of St Peter, and on 7 September 1159 the majority succeeded, after a sharp struggle, in electing Roland, but the opposing party would not admit their defeat, and proclaimed Octavian as Pontiff. In the tumult of this double election, while the two Popes-designate were struggling for the possession of the papal mantle[1], the doors of St Peter's were opened to the armed partisans of Octavian who was proclaimed by the name of Victor IV.

Roland and his cardinals, fearing personal violence, retired into the fortress annexed to the church and remained shut in there for several days, unable to move owing to the armed strength of the opposite faction. Afterwards Roland, who had managed to be conveyed to Trastevere, made a successful attempt at escape from his opponents. But, although on regaining his freedom he was triumphantly acclaimed by his own party, he did not feel himself sufficiently strong to remain in Rome, and had to betake himself elsewhere. At Ninfa he was consecrated Pope as Alexander III, and after a short stay at Terracina he went to Anagni. Neither could Octavian hold out long at Rome. His consecration took place at the monastery of Farfa, whence he went to Segni. Thus the two rivals, in near touch with Rome and only a few miles distant from each other, began to hurl anathemas the one against the other. A great schism rent the Church afresh, and rendered her path more difficult at a moment when dangers and pitfalls threatened on every side. The contending parties lost no time in presenting their cases to the tribunal of Christendom, and sent legates and letters to sovereigns and bishops relating the story of the election each in his own way. In a situation so uncertain, the attitude of Frederick might have great weight, not only in Italy and Germany where he exercised direct influence, but also throughout the rest of Europe where his name was a force and his ideal position as the temporal leader of Christendom was recognised. He perceived his advantage. As soon as the news of Hadrian's death reached him, while the siege of Crema was yet in progress, he wrote without delay to Eberhard of Salzburg a letter which clearly shewed his intentions. In it he said that the successor of Hadrian must be one who would reform the condition of the Church in the direction of a pacific union, and treat the Empire and the loyal subjects of the Empire with greater consideration. He had heard with great regret that the election was already the cause of factions; he therefore warned him not to give his adhesion precipitately to the Pope-elect, whoever he might be, without first consulting him (the Emperor), and enjoined him to communicate the same advice to his suffragans. He also

---

[1] Octavian tried to seize it from Roland; failing in this, he snatched a duplicate from his chaplain, but, in his haste to be the first to be invested, he put it on the wrong way round.

informed him that he was negotiating for a firm understanding between himself and the Kings of France and England, and had instructed his ambassadors to come to an agreement with them as to the most suitable candidate for the Papacy, so that no election should be accepted without the common consent of the three sovereigns. He added in conclusion that letters were being sent on this matter to Germany, Burgundy, and Aquitaine, in order that all his subjects might know that he would not on any consideration suffer so great a dignity to be filled by anyone who was not unanimously chosen by the faithful for the upholding of the honour of the Empire and the peace and unity of the Church.

It was not likely that Roland and his partisans would find favour with a prince thus disposed. Even if his grief at the schism were sincere, it was only natural that Frederick should have wished for the triumph of Octavian, of whom he felt secure. Either acting on secret instructions from the Emperor or more probably on their own initiative, the two imperial ambassadors who happened to be in Rome at the time shewed themselves favourable to the election of the imperial cardinal, while the latter and his followers, in the letters sent by them to the bishops and princes of the Empire, dwelt strongly on the alliance of Roland with the King of Sicily and his antipathy to the Empire. The letters of Alexander III, more elevated in tone and shewing greater confidence in his claims, displayed in turn a suspicion of the imperial attitude, and the Alexandrine cardinals in writing to Frederick did not conceal this, but openly accused Otto of Wittelsbach of opposing their Pope and themselves and of having violently entered the Campagna with Octavian, trying to make the territory subject to him. Reminding the Emperor that it was a duty incumbent on his office to defend the Church against heretics and schismatics, they concluded by saying: "Our wish is to honour you as the special defender and patron of the Roman Church, and as far as in us lies we desire the increase of your glory. Therefore we supplicate you to love and honour the Holy Roman Church your mother; to watch over her peace as becomes your imperial excellence and not to favour in any way the great iniquity of the invading schismatic." Their firm language and austere admonitions shewed that the traditions of Hadrian IV were still in force, and that his successor, even in the anxious moments which ushered in his pontificate, was not one to bend in face of difficulties.

The memory of those of his predecessors who, like Otto the Great, had brought the imperial authority to bear in all its fulness on the Papacy, could not fail to recur to Frederick's mind and dispose him to try to become an arbitrator in the contest, thus resuming the ancient claims of the Empire from which the Church by slow degrees had become emancipated. He therefore decided to convene an assembly of prelates, while inviting the two contending parties to be present and submit their reasons to its judgment. Two bishops were charged to convey the letters in which Frederick ordered the two claimants to appear. Alexander was well aware that a refusal might be taken to mean that he was uncertain of his cause, but a refusal was inevitable. Not only had Alexander and his followers reason to fear the bias of a council convened in the Emperor's name and placed under the aegis of his power, but to acknowledge such an assembly and participate in it would be dealing a fatal blow at the great principle at stake, the superiority of the Church to every earthly authority. In agreement with his cardinals, Alexander rejected the proposal, and expressed his sorrowful surprise that the Emperor should have overstepped in this manner the limits of his dignity, and presumed, he the champion of the Church, to dictate terms to the Pontiff as though he were his sovereign. The imperial legates withdrew, ill-content with such an answer, and betook themselves to Octavian who, on the other hand, accepted the invitation without hesitation and set forth for Pavia.

Frederick at last had brought Crema to surrender, and had given orders for the demolition of the heroic city and the dispersal of the citizens. In February 1160 he opened the Synod of Pavia with an oration in which, notwithstanding the vagueness of the phraseology, his thoughts concerning the relations of the Empire and the Church were transparent enough. "Although," he said, "in my office and dignity of Emperor I can convoke councils, especially in moments of peril for the Church, as did Constantine, Theodosius, Justinian, and in later times the Emperors Charlemagne and Otto, yet we leave it to your prudence and power to decide in this matter. God made you priests and gave you power to judge us also. And since it is not for us to judge you in things appertaining to God, we exhort you so to act in this matter as though we awaited from you the judgment of God." Thus speaking he retired, leaving the Council to their deliberations. At this Council were assembled many abbots and lesser ecclesiastics, but only fifty of the rank of bishop and archbishop, the majority of whom were Germans or northern Italians. From other countries hardly any had come, and some foreign sovereigns had sent in adhesions couched in vague terms which were received and registered as if they had a positive value. Octavian had no difficulty in establishing the validity of his cause, all the more so since Alexander was not present, owing to his refusal to recognise the synod, and thus did nothing to vindicate his case. Alexander besides had to reckon with the accusation of his hostility to the Empire and alliance with the Sicilians and the Lombards. Octavian was acknowledged to be Pope and honoured as such by the Emperor. On the following day he launched a fresh excommunication against Roland and severe admonitions to the King of Sicily and the Lombards.

The schism had now become incurable. Alexander did not stagger under the blow. He issued an excommunication against Frederick and renewed the ban already laid on Octavian and his party. Thus asserting his authority, he released Frederick's subjects from their obedience, encouraged the Lombards to revolt, and fomented the internal discords of Germany. Meanwhile he maintained his cause throughout the rest of Europe, writing to the bishops at large, and exhorting them to support him among their flocks and before their sovereigns. The support of the episcopate was in fact of great use to him in the various courts of Europe, and especially in those of France and England, two centres of influence of the highest importance. Frederick made vain efforts to gain the kings of these countries; they maintained a prudent reserve, which after some hesitation settled down into an attitude decidedly favourable to Alexander.

The part taken by the Emperor in this struggle for the Papacy did not turn him from his fixed resolve to subdue Lombardy to obedience, and root out all possibility of resistance by bringing Milan to his feet. The calamities and destruction of Crema did not avail to break the spirit of the unyielding Lombard towns opposed to the Emperor, and they rose again in arms, reinvigorated by their alliance with the Pope. In order to assert his sway it was necessary for Frederick to strike a mortal blow at Milan and thus cut out the heart of the Lombard resistance. But it was not an easy undertaking, and all Barbarossa's power might have been shattered but for the assistance of the cities which stood by him faithfully. Their municipal hatred of the great sister city waxed ever stronger as the struggle went on, and caused a wretched denial in the face of the foreigner of those bonds of unselfishness and of blood which ought to have drawn them closely together. With such auxiliaries Frederick began operations against Milan, and for a whole year there was constant warfare in the surrounding territory, with alternating success and a cruel destruction of the great Lombard plain. In the spring of 1161 Germany and Hungary sent the reinforcements necessary for the campaign, and the Emperor was able to shut in the city more closely. A long siege followed, lasting yet another year. The defenders held out as long as was possible with unshaken tenacity, but in the end the forces of resistance failed. The flower of the garrison had fallen at their posts, disease and hunger were rapidly cutting off the remnant, munitions of defence had given out, all resources were exhausted. There was nothing to be done but to make terms, and all attempts were vain to secure some favourable agreement previous to surrender. In March 1162 the vanquished city had to stoop low and submit at the conqueror's discretion. The sight of the misery and fall of so great and noble a city aroused pity even in her enemies, who could not refrain from appealing to the clemency of Frederick. The stern ruler would not bend, but turned a heart of stone to their prayers. For him harshness in this case was justice. The imperial majesty must be vindicated by a signal example of rigour which should extirpate all hope of future conflict. Milan, given over to pillage and fire, seemed buried for ever beneath the mass of her own ruins.

To those Milanese who survived the siege were assigned four localities where they might settle, not very far from the ruined city. It was a grievous dispersion, yet a contemporary chronicler accused Frederick at a later date of a want of foresight in having allowed the Milanese to remain so near to the ashes of their fallen city. But how could it have been possible to imagine a speedy resurrection after such a fall, and that Milan might rise again, when Frederick's power had reached such a height and was inspiring everywhere both reverence and terror? All opposition gave way before him. Piacenza and Brescia had to accept his stern conditions. Their walls were demolished; the imperial officials were received; tribute and hostages were rendered to the Emperor; the imperial Pope was recognised, while the Bishop of Piacenza, whose loyalty to Alexander was untainted, passed into exile. Other cities underwent the same ordeal. The imperial claims asserted at Roncaglia held the field. The dissensions of the Lombard cities had borne the bitter fruit of misery and servitude, but a fruit destined in its bitterness to be one of remedy and healing.

The victories in Lombardy now strengthened Frederick's projects with regard to Sicily and the East, where the help of maritime forces was indispensable. He therefore first offered inducements to Pisa and then to Genoa to form an alliance with him. Both consented, although each was distrustful of the other, and Genoa in particular gave adhesion from motives of expediency rather than from any friendly intention. The position in northern Italy being thus secured and a powerful naval connexion being established on the sea, Frederick might well feel assured that within his grasp lay the dominion of all Italy, and that he was on the verge of entering upon the lordship of a genuine and incontestable empire. But Alexander III, despite the grave anxieties of his position, was keeping a watchful eye on this policy with the intention of arresting its achievement. While the war in Lombardy lasted, the Pope, unable to keep a footing in Rome, had remained in the Campagna. In spite of Frederick, all Europe outside the Empire and the Latin East now acknowledged him, but his material resources were such that he was bound to quit Italy and throw himself upon the traditional hospitality of the French kingdom. He embarked at Capo Circello on a galley of the King of Sicily, and after a halt at Genoa entered France through Provence, where he was received everywhere with signs of deep devotion. Well aware of Frederick's commanding influence, he turned to Eberhard of Salzburg, the prelate most loyal to him in Germany, who had brought all his authority to bear on Frederick in order that he might relinquish the schism and make peace with the Church. But the Pope could only put slender trust in these pacific proposals, and within a short month, in May 1162, the struggle still continuing, he renewed his excommunications against Octavian and the Emperor in a solemn act of promulgation at Montpellier. In the meantime, Alexander was keeping up his relations with France and England with a view to gaining their decisive adherence to his cause. Nor did he neglect any means of attracting German sympathy and that of Italy, and by raising difficulties in the path of Octavian of dealing a blow at the policy of Frederick. Octavian, in his turn, in two synods held at Lodi and Cremona, had confirmed the decisions of the Council of Pavia, but it was not difficult to see that Alexander's adherents were gaining in number and that Octavian's party was lukewarm and more of a make-believe than a reality. Alexander could only be overcome by shattering his foundations and depriving him of the asylum which was at once his refuge and his strength.

While he appeared to be preparing for an expedition in the South, Frederick turned back and, leaving his representatives in Lombardy charged to keep that province in subjection, he crossed the Alps. Taking advantage of the disputes between England and the French King Louis VII, he turned to the latter in the hope of making him an ally and separating him from the Pope. Louis hesitated; at the instigation of certain councillors who were strongly in favour of an alliance with the Emperor, he began to treat with Frederick and finally with Octavian, while at the same time he made no break in his relations with Alexander, who watched with anxious attention this turn in French policy. It was settled that the two sovereigns should meet on 29 August 1162 at St-Jean-de-Losne on the frontiers of France and the County of Burgundy, now subject to Frederick. Henry of Champagne, brother-in-law of King Louis, was the soul of these negotiations, and it suited his interests to separate Louis from Henry II of England. The two sovereigns were to bring with them the two pretenders to the Papacy and to arrive together at a final recognition of the true Pope, but if one of the two rivals refused to appear then the other was to be recognised on the spot. Later the king asserted that Henry had gone beyond his instructions in accepting this condition; but meanwhile Alexander, perceiving the serious danger of such an interview, made every effort to prevent its taking place. He was in time to have a conversation with Louis, and if he did not succeed in dissuading him from the meeting he at least was able to convince him that he, the Vicar of Christ, could not bow to the decision of the proposed tribunal. Louis, shaken by the Pope's arguments, made his way to the banks of the Saône in an uncertain mood and anxious to find a means of extricating himself from the complications in which Henry of Champagne had involved him. He was also apprehensive of the show of force with which the Emperor came to meet him, and Frederick himself had his own suspicions. The latter arrived with his own Pope, Victor IV, at the place of meeting, but, not finding the king there, withdrew. Soon afterwards Louis arrived, and hearing of the Emperor's withdrawal took his departure without waiting to see if he would return. Thus the interview between the two sovereigns never took place.

Perhaps there was no real wish on either side for the meeting. But

Henry of Champagne in his vexation threatened to transfer his allegiance to the Emperor, and so constrained Louis to promise to return in three weeks in readiness to accept, along with Frederick, the decisions of a congress. This was a mortal blow for Alexander, but he did not lose courage. He brought every kind of influence to bear on Louis, and shewed great political shrewdness in turning to the King of England who was suspicious of an alliance between France and the Emperor, even succeeding in bringing about an understanding between him and the King of France. Thus when Frederick felt most sure of his position he found himself threatened by an unexpected danger, and made up his mind to withdraw from the conference. The Emperor's defection caused no regret to Louis. He returned to Dijon freed from the obligations into which he had entered almost against his will. Before leaving Burgundy, Frederick had held a diet in which Victor IV, while affirming his rights, had excommunicated Alexander III. The latter, in the meanwhile, had enjoyed a triumph at Coucy-sur-Loire. There the Kings of England and of France paid him reverence together and declared him to be the valid and legitimate Pope. In the presence of this triumphant success the anti-Pope's importance was diminished. The struggle between the Papacy and the Empire reverted to great principles and issues, and although the two chief litigants were then at a distance, both appealed to the name of Rome, and the name of Rome once more localised in Italy the arena of combat.

In Italy signs were not wanting that Frederick, notwithstanding the destruction of Milan and the dismantling of the cities in alliance with her, was far from having stamped out all resistance. The heart of the people was unconquerable, and beat in expectation of the hour when they could rise again for the struggle. The affairs of Germany held the Emperor there under weighty responsibilities, while his representatives in Lombardy were imposing cruel exactions on the subject populations. These called in vain for justice. Day by day their yoke became more galling, and if the terrible fate of Milan warned them to endure the burden, still the germs of revolt were ripening below the surface. The Chancellor Rainald of Dassel was indefatigable in checking disaffection and in preparing the naval expedition against Sicily, in the absence of the Emperor, but his adversaries were not idle. Alexander III, the Kings of Sicily and France, the Emperor of Constantinople, Venice, and the Lombard cities, had come to an agreement among themselves. The forces of resistance were quickened into life. When in October 1163 Frederick with a small army re-entered Lombardy, he was met on all sides by complaints of the rapacity of his agents and by appeals to mitigate the hardships of the oppressed populations. But Frederick gave little heed to such appeals, and the sufferers felt that succour must be sought amongst themselves. Venice gave them encouragement. While the Emperor was engaged in appointing one of his creatures as king in Sardinia without estranging Genoa and Pisa, who were disputing with each other the possession of this island, Verona, Padua, and Vicenza rose in joint rebellion to offer a common resistance and to maintain the rights which ancient custom had handed down. Frederick was suddenly faced by the fact that the league might embrace a wider compass and, being without sufficient force to quell the insurgent communes, he made efforts to pacify them. In this attempt he failed. He therefore sought aid from Pavia, Mantua, and Ferrara, whom he loaded with privileges, trying to move them to hostile action against the League. But the allies appeared in such strong force that he had temporarily to renounce the hazard of battle.

In the meanwhile the anti-Pope Victor had died, in April 1164, at Lucca. The position of Alexander III being thenceforth secure, Frederick might not have been altogether indisposed to renew attempts at reconciliation, but the Archbishop of Cologne, Rainald of Dassel, the implacable enemy of Alexander, stood in his way and obtained the immediate election of another anti-Pope. This was Guido of Crema, who took the name of Paschal III. From the moment of his election the Emperor took him under his protection, and, on his return to Germany, tried to make the German and Italian bishops acknowledge him, but this scheme met with open opposition in the episcopate of both countries. Among the Germans, the Archbishop-elect of Mayence, Conrad of Wittelsbach, rather than yield went into exile in France, near Alexander. The Archbishops of Trèves, Magdeburg, and Salzburg, and the Bishop of Brixen held out, refusing to accept an election so patently uncanonical; while many others of less courage submitted in appearance only to the imperial will.

This opposition, which augmented Frederick's difficulties in Germany, also encouraged the Lombards to shake off their yoke. Alexander III, now that hope of reconciliation with Barbarossa had proved fallacious, was doing all in his power to spur on the resistance of Lombardy, relying on the determination and love of liberty among the communes. Thus by stirring up the cities to rebellion and by devising means for drawing together more closely the adverse powers of Europe, the able policy of Alexander aimed at isolating Frederick and placing him in a position of marked inferiority in his struggle with the Church. The Emperor, wishing to break through the ring of hostile influences which encompassed him, turned to Henry II of England. This monarch was bound to the King of France by very fragile ties, and had deep causes of dissension with the Pope, owing to the struggle which had arisen with Thomas Becket. This dispute was undoubtedly the source of serious difficulties for Alexander III, difficulties which only came to an end on Becket's tragic death. The Emperor and the King of England took advantage of this event to draw closer together, yet without essentially modifying the Pope's position towards Frederick. Alexander was now recognised as the uncontested head of Christendom. He felt strong enough to reoccupy his see and carry on the struggle, which threatened to be renewed with greater tenacity than ever. Through the aid of his vicar, the Cardinal of SS. John and Paul, the Pope had secured guarantees for his safe residence in Rome, and in October 1165 he left France where his reception had been so generous. He travelled to Messina by sea. From Palermo the King of Sicily sent him gifts and ordered an escort of galleys to convey him honourably to Rome, where the Pope made a solemn entry on 23 November. He at once took up his residence in the Lateran. From Germany, whither he had returned and which he was striving to pacify, the Emperor could not fail to perceive that the triumphs of his rival in Rome were a source of dangers which it would be necessary to dispel. He felt that the loyalty of the Lombard cities was no longer to be reckoned upon, and therefore began to recruit an army powerful enough to be confident of success and capable of crushing any resistance from one end of Italy to the other. In order to conjure back more and more the majesty of the Empire, he had Charlemagne canonised by the anti-Pope Paschal III on the Christmas festival of 1165. But times had changed and altered situations had arisen for the Papacy, the Empire, and the peoples now awakened to a new life. Frederick Barbarossa in his lofty aspirations had no conception that he was summoning from the tomb of his great predecessor in Aix-la-Chapelle the phantom of a past for which there was no longer a place amid the living.

The absence of Frederick made it more easy for the Lombards to come to agreements preliminary to common action. The signs of resistance arose quickly on all sides. In the cities tumults frequently broke out and in Bologna the imperial podestà was killed during an uprising of the populace. William I of Sicily had died and was succeeded in 1166 by the child William II, whose mother the Regent maintained friendly relations with the Pope and an antagonistic policy towards the Emperor. She was encouraged by Manuel Comnenus, who aimed at gaining a foothold in Italy and showered attentions on the youthful king, while he was trying to flatter the Pope by holding out to him the mirage of reunion of the two Churches, asking in return the Roman crown of Empire. Alexander placed no reliance on this project, but shewed himself ready to negotiate in order to add to the dangers of Frederick's position. Venice entered into alliance with Sicily and Constantinople, forming thus a joint domination over the Adriatic, while Pisa and Genoa, although in league with Frederick, were mutually so quarrelsome and jealous of each other that the warmth of their devotion could not be safely depended upon. Only one way lay open to Frederick, and that was the reconquest of Italy by force.

He collected a considerable army, and in October 1166 set out accompanied by the Empress. By the middle of November he was in Lombardy and held a diet at Lodi, but he quickly saw that hostility was greater than ever, and that he aroused an atmosphere of hatred to the highest intensity. The cities which had at first favoured him had turned lukewarm or unfriendly, and the two on which he most relied to give effect to the expedition against Sicily, Pisa and Genoa, came to Lodi only to dispute rival claims, thus emphasising a discord which was of evil omen. Instead of moving directly upon Rome in order to dispatch the business of Alexander and scatter the forces of William of Sicily and the Byzantines, Frederick was obliged to tarry some time in Lombardy, making destructive raids on the territory of Brescia and Bergamo. Thence he advanced on Bologna and compelled that city to give hostages before betaking himself to Ancona by the Romagna. He sent a portion of his army towards Rome under the command of Rainald, Archbishop of Cologne, and another warrior-archbishop, Christian of Buch, whom he had substituted in the see of Mayence for Conrad of Wittelsbach, a partisan of Pope Alexander. The immediate descent on the south made it necessary that he should have a base on the Adriatic and that the approach to Abruzzo by the Marches should be free. He therefore determined to invest Ancona in person.

He met with a stubborn resistance. Lombardy in the meantime, determined to throw off his yoke, was emboldened by the League of Verona, and one city after another entered into a joint compact to prepare for an act of liberation. The confederates resolved, as a symbol of their union, to restore Milan from her ruins, construct her moats, and set up her walls anew as a bulwark. On 27 April 1167, the allied forces appeared before the fallen city bent on the work of reconstruction and of warding off any possible attacks, especially from Pavia, always the faithful ally of the Empire. Milan rose again as if by enchantment and the spirit of independence seemed to live again within her. The cities in their rekindled life built fortifications, and all through Lombardy ran the thrill of coming war.

Alexander III saw in this harmony his greatest hope of safety and hailed it with fervour. His position was a very serious one. He had succeeded in gaining to a certain extent the favour of the Romans, thanks to their hatred of the neighbouring cities, who seemed to be biassed towards the Empire, especially Tusculum. But the two German archbishops at the head of their forces were masters of the Campagna, and had reduced that district into obedience to the anti-Pope Paschal, who had made Viterbo his headquarters. The Roman militia were sufficiently numerous to place in danger Rainald of Dassel, who was occupying Tusculum with a slender force, but the Archbishop of Mayence advanced to the succour of Rainald. The Romans, in spite of the Pope's dissuasions, advanced against this combined array trusting in their own numbers, but, being hemmed in on both sides, suffered a terrible defeat on 29 May 1167 and were pursued to the very gates of Rome, leaving in their flight many dead and many prisoners behind them. The discouragement in Rome was great. Alexander rallied together as many soldiers as he could, and prepared to offer resistance to the imperial troops now before the city.

Frederick, having made peace with Ancona, made a rapid march on Rome, and on 24 July 1167 appeared with his army on Monte Mario. The day after he made an unsuccessful attempt to storm the walls. Subsequent assaults were more fortunate, and opened to him the defences of St Peter's. The neighbouring church of Santa Maria in Turri was set fire to by the assailants, who amid blood and slaughter forced their way to the sacred basilica itself, compelling the papal soldiers to surrender. The anti-Pope being in possession of the church renewed the Emperor's coronation with great solemnity and placed the crown on the imperial consort's head.

Frederick, however, was not yet master of the left bank of the Tiber. The Pope had taken refuge in a stronghold of the Frangipani near to the Coliseum, and was in constant deliberation with his cardinals and other adherents. The King of Sicily had sent him by the Tiber two galleys and a sum of money. The money was distributed amongst his defenders, while the galleys were sent away with two cardinals. The Pope himself remained in Rome. Grave as the situation appeared to be, Alexander did not despair, and thought perhaps that some means of understanding with Frederick was not impossible. Conrad of Wittelsbach, the dispossessed Archbishop of Mayence, who held to the Pope, went to visit the Emperor. The latter enjoined upon him the task of proposing to the Alexandrine cardinals and bishops that both Pope and anti-Pope should resign in order to make way for a fresh election. At the same time he acquainted the Romans with this proposal, promising them that, if it were carried out, he would return the prisoners and the booty captured on 29 May. The bishops with one voice rejected the imperial offer, but the Romans urged the Pope and cardinals with pressing insistence to yield and to set them free from their privations. Alexander's position in Rome was no longer endurable, and he suddenly and stealthily disappeared. Three days afterwards he was seen near Monte Circello, then at Terracina and Gaeta, and thence he went to Benevento, where he was joined by the cardinals whose loyalty had remained unshaken in the hour of danger.

The appearance of eight Pisan galleys on the Tiber and the expected approach of a great fleet of ships ready to attack Rome and Sicily brought the Romans to make terms with the Emperor and to submit to him the nomination of the Senate. Frederick could now look upon himself as supreme master of Italy. Rome was his, and the army behind him with the Pisan fleet guaranteed to him a victory over the Sicilian king, whose strength was shaken by internal discords, and whose defeat would render certain the suppression of the revolt of Lombardy. The Empire of Charlemagne was on the point of revival in all its pristine majesty. But the decrees of history were otherwise written. The scorching August sun was oppressing the German forces in the Campagna when a slight rain came to refresh them, but on the following day sudden destruction fell upon their encampments. A deadly fever spread through the ranks and those attacked by the sudden malady died in crowds. The panic was great, heightened by religious terror, for this mysterious and violent destruction appeared to be an act of divine vengeance for the profanation of St Peter's. The imperial army, decimated, terrified, and demoralised, was routed by an unseen enemy, and Frederick was compelled to break up his camp. He led the remnants of his army across the Tuscan Apennines, his path of retreat strewn with dead and dying. The flower of his army, the pick of his captains, had fallen. In this conjuncture Frederick's magnanimous strength of will shewed itself in full force. He was suddenly bereft of the most valuable and staunchest supporters of his throne; his best councillors, his most valiant warriors were wrested from his side. His nephew Frederick of Swabia, the Archbishop of Cologne, Rainald of Dassel, the Bishops of Liège, Spires, Ratisbon, Verden, and Duke Welf VII of Tuscany, were all struck down, and hundreds of other nobles and churchmen. He dragged behind him as best he could the surviving few, and being unable to follow the open roads from Tuscany, since the Lombards in arms held the passes, he took to the hill paths of Lunigiana and by a difficult circuit came down on loyal Pavia. Here he gathered together his available forces, and, aided by some cities still faithful, by the Count of Biandrate and the Marquess of Montferrat, he attempted some attacks on the Milanese territory, but the Lombards pressed him so closely that it was only with great effort that he could extricate himself in safety and get beyond the frontier of Italy. Under the protection of Humbert, Count of Maurienne, he reached Susa with a small following, but the city displayed such a menacing demeanour that he was forced to escape under cover of the darkness of night. The powerful monarch who had descended on Italy certain of victory returned to his own country alone, disarmed, a fugitive; but his mind was undaunted and his ambition was bent more than ever on the re-affirmation of his rights and the restoration of lustre to the waning star of Empire.

The Lombards, who had felt so heavily the weight of Barbarossa's arms, knew that the struggle was not yet at an end and that there must be a fierce renewal of the contest if their liberties were to be re-won and maintained. They set to work. The League added to its numbers, and in a short time the greater part of the cities of Venetia, Lombardy, and Piedmont were confederated and ready to act on the defensive against the Emperor and those barons and cities, such as Pavia, which still stood by him. As a greater safeguard the League decided to build a strong city at the confluence of the Tanaro and the Bormida, in such a position as to command every point of entrance into the plains of Lombardy. The city rose rapidly, not rich indeed in fine buildings but fortified to its utmost capacity, and was soon able to reckon a population of 15,000 citizens to man and defend it. As a symbol of alliance with the Papacy the name given to the city was Alessandria, and the Pope, on his part, aided by the Lombard clergy, did all he could to encourage the League and to tighten the bonds between himself and his other allies. The Emperor's influence in Italy was steadily losing ground. Genoa, without actually joining the League, regarded it with favour, and, when Pisa entered into friendly relations with Sicily, did the same. The court of Sicily, at the same time, seeing what a safeguard the League might become, gave assistance in money, and so did Manuel Comnenus, ever mindful of his own interests and of his ambitious hopes regarding Italy.

While the struggle was thus in preparation, the shuttle of papal diplomacy was moving incessantly and working to keep France and England aloof from Frederick. Alexander III had been recognised by Denmark, and little by little this recognition had spread over the greater part of northern and eastern Europe. Towards the Byzantine Emperor, who adhered to his design of uniting the Eastern and Western Empires, the Pope shewed great courtesy but maintained an attitude of non-committal friendliness. His strength had its foundation in the King of Sicily and the Lombards. The latter pre-eminently were his first bulwark against the attacks of Frederick. As had always been the case, his weakest point was Rome, where permanent habitation was difficult, so much so that he had for several years to be contented with Benevento or some town of the Campagna as a settled residence. The anti-Pope was always face to face with him, although devoid of an authority in Christendom adequate to challenge that of Alexander. On the death of Paschal III in September 1168, a successor had been found in Abbot John of Struma, called Calixtus III, whom Frederick hastened to acknowledge. Although the schism had spent its force, an anti-Pope could always be used as a handy instrument against Alexander by an able and determined adversary.

On his return to Germany in 1168, the Emperor bent all his energies to the restoration of order in the kingdom distracted by civil dissensions and to the establishment of peace between his most powerful vassals, the Saxon Henry the Lion and the Margrave Albert the Bear, two implacable enemies. While endeavouring to bring them into friendly accord, Frederick was inclined to favour Henry, to whom he was attached by old ties of friendship, and to whom he looked for support. But the power of these barons made him feel the need of making provision for the security of his own house, and in April 1169 he caused his son Henry to be elected King of the Romans and had him crowned at Aix-la-Chapelle by the new Archbishop, Philip, of Cologne, the successor of Rainald of Dassel. From the old Duke Welf VI, who now had no heirs, he bought the right of succession to his estates in Swabia and Tuscany, but this acquisition, which certainly made a notable accession to his power in Germany and Italy, alienated from him the sympathy of Henry the Lion, who had himself aspired to the whole Welf inheritance.

The internal affairs of Germany did not exclusively occupy the mind of Frederick, and he was also giving his thoughts to the state of Italy and his relations with the Church. If the anti-Pope Calixtus III was an embarrassment and a difficulty to Pope Alexander, his force and authority were not to be compared with those which the Cardinal Octavian had wielded in the early days of the schism. Prudence also kept Frederick from putting difficulties in the way of the barons who were summoned to Bamberg to elect his son as King of the Romans. It seemed to him wise, at this juncture, to make an attempt at conciliation which, without admitting any compromise in regard to the existing dispute, might be a means of shewing to Germany his good intentions regarding the close of the schism, and also of arousing suspicion against the Pope among the Lombards and in Sicily. Eberhard, Bishop of Bamberg, was chosen as the messenger of conciliation. His wisdom and moderation were acknowledged by all parties. He was under strict obligations to disclose his proposals to the Pope only. The latter was not without his misgivings. He foresaw that the negotiations might be regarded with suspicion by his Lombard allies, and arranged that certain faithful citizens should be deputed by the cities of the League to come immediately to Veroli and assist at the conference with the imperial envoy. Eberhard, however, insisted on a confidential explanation with the Pope of his mission. The Emperor made some concessions, but did not make an explicit avowal of his readiness to accept the validity of Alexander's election. At the bottom of his heart he probably clung to the often-expressed idea of a simultaneous renunciation on the part of the two pretenders, followed by the election of a third party to the Papacy. The negotiations fell to the ground completely. The Pope in the presence of the Lombard delegates rejected the imperial proposals, and all hope of conciliation vanished.

War was once more the arbiter. The alliance of the Lombards with the Pope and with Sicily could only be broken up by force. The League was dominant in upper Italy, and Pavia had at last to bow to its authority. A fresh expedition into Italy had become a vital necessity for the Emperor, though he was still hampered by the complicated affairs of Germany. He had to dispatch a first army corps under Christian of Buch, Archbishop of Mayence, whose political and military task was to consist in preparing the ground by consolidating friendships and inspiring with fear the pride of the rebellious cities. Christian's principal object was to bring Genoa into closer relationship with the Emperor, and to gain as much as possible the goodwill of Tuscany. His next endeavour was to secure for the imperial army a base on the Adriatic, and to carry out afresh the investment of Ancona. The city held out stoutly for six months until the succour of her allies compelled the army to raise the siege.

Frederick, as soon as his hands were free in Germany, concentrated his army for the Italian expedition and again crossed the Alps at its head. He had a strong force at his disposition—a certain number of barons and bishops followed him—but it was much inferior to that which he had on the previous occasion. The most conspicuous gap was that caused by the absence of Henry the Lion, the comrade of his choice. Internal conditions in Germany and the disastrous end of the last expedition into Italy had chilled the enthusiasm of the Germans and their inclination to carry war beyond the Alps. He opened his campaign at the end of September 1174 by the destruction of Susa, an act of reprisal for the ignominy of having had to escape from it when he left Italy. He then came down through Piedmont and moved on the borders of Lombardy. Asti surrendered at once, and the Marquess of Montferrat, with the cities of Alba, Acqui, Pavia, and Como, finding themselves strengthened by his favour, deserted the League and turned to him. Frederick, emboldened by these adhesions, presented himself before Alessandria. This town, with its name taken from his enemy, appeared to him as the symbol and bulwark of rebellion which must disappear from the face of the earth.

But the determination of the Emperor to crush the Lombards was not greater than their determination to oppose him, and to defend their liberty to the last gasp. This stubborn opposition hardened into obstinacy Frederick's resolve to obtain the mastery. The city was beleaguered on every side, but held out firmly. The winter, always severe around Alessandria, was in this year of exceptional rigour, and increased beyond measure the difficulties of the siege and the sufferings of the besiegers. The confederates meanwhile were combining their forces in order to fall upon the Emperor and destroy the army which was wearing itself out in the attacks on the city. Barbarossa, intent on dividing and thwarting the enemy, sent Christian of Buch into the Romagna and the Bolognese territory, thus succeeding in diverting and holding in check no inconsiderable portion of the allied armies. He redoubled his efforts to carry Alessandria by storm, but all his attempts were ineffectual, being repulsed with heavy losses. After six months of unsuccessful siege, in April 1175, knowing that the allies were close at hand, he tried to penetrate the city by means of mines and take it by surprise, but the soldiers employed in the mines were discovered and killed, and in a spirited sortie the defenders raided the Emperor's camp and destroyed by fire his best siege machinery. With his quick resolution Frederick then raised the siege without delay, and advanced rapidly against the army of the League. The two armies met in the territory of Pavia, and pitched their camps between Casteggio and Voghera at three miles distance from one another. Just as a battle appeared imminent, negotiations for peace were suddenly begun between the Emperor and the League, although it is not clearly known from which side the initiative came. Perhaps the Lombards were not entirely confident of their strength, and certainly Frederick must have found the moment opportune for a truce, in order to reinvigorate his troops, exhausted by the unfortunate enterprise against Alessandria. For a moment peace appeared to have been concluded, but all at once the negotiations were broken off. Other negotiations were opened through three cardinals, in order to see if it were yet possible to come to some agreement with the Church, but this attempt also came to nothing, and hostilities began anew. For the remainder of the year 1175 the war dragged on without any important engagements. The Lombards seemed to keep a watchful attitude, looking for the opportune moment, and Frederick stood on the defensive waiting for reinforcements from Germany before striking a decisive blow. Germany shewed no great willingness to reply to his appeals, and when at last in the spring of 1176 the reinforcements did arrive they were not accompanied by Henry the Lion. The Emperor had gone in person to Chiavenna in order to confer with him, and to impress upon him the supreme importance of his co-operation in the interests of the Empire. All was in vain. Henry's proud spirit was deaf to the voice of an old friendship, and refused to recall the acts of kindness of his imperial relative spread over many years. Frederick gained nothing from this interview save a chilling refusal, and the painful impression that, where he had looked for friendship, he had only found the foreshadowing of rebellion.

Frederick had advanced to meet his fresh supports with the determination of opening a vigorous campaign with a battle in the open field. Having collected a contingent from Como, he moved on Pavia in order to form a conjunction with the remainder of his army before delivering an attack on the Lombards. The latter, who had his movements under observation, came forward rapidly and cut off his approach. The hour on which the issue of the long contest depended had now struck. On 29 May 1176 the two armies engaged near Legnano in a battle which was keenly contested on both sides. At first the Germans seemed to have the upper hand. Their heavy cavalry broke through the front ranks of the Lombards and threw them into confusion. But round the *Carroccio* the German onset was checked, and was of no avail to shatter the desperate resistance of the handful of heroes who defended this central point. It became the centre of the battle now resumed with fierce determination. Frederick encouraged his troops in vain by plunging into the thick of the fight with his wonted courage. In the struggle he was unhorsed, and amid the confusion and the groups of combatants vanished from sight. The defeat of the Germans was complete and great their slaughter. The exultant Milanese wrote to their brethren of Bologna: "Glorious has been our triumph over our enemies. Their slain are innumerable as well as those drowned and taken prisoners. We have in our hands the shield, banner, cross, and lance of the Emperor, and have found in his coffers much gold and silver, while the booty taken from the enemy is of great value, but we do not consider these things ours, but the common property of the Pope and the Italians. In the fight Duke Berthold was taken, as also a nephew of the Empress and a brother of the Archbishop of Cologne; the other captives are innumerable and are all in custody in Milan."

Frederick had no small difficulty in reaching Pavia in safety with the remnants of his army which had made good their escape from the hands of the victors. He had fought and lost. It would have been folly to suppose that Germany would have followed him in any scheme of reconquest. One of his highest qualities as a statesman was his ready and intuitive perception of changed situations. He accepted facts and determined to consider some other policy which would reconcile the order of things created by the Lombard victory of Legnano with the dignity and majesty of the Empire. The desire for peace which had gradually arisen in his own mind and that of his counsellors now ripened, and inclined him to open negotiations which would lead finally to an honourable and lasting conclusion. Four times he had entered Italy with an armed force, and still the Italians met him undaunted face to face. The Pope, now enjoying an uncontested authority, by his excommunication was stripping the imperial crown of its halo of sanctity. He had failed to carry his arms against the King of Sicily, and Constantinople might still become a menace. It was time to make approaches to peace while the Empire was yet strong and formidable.

His first considerations were not in the direction of Lombardy. The primary object of reconciliation was the Church. By restoring friendly relations with his foremost adversary, he would be in a position at once to allay the scruples of Germans disturbed by the papal schism and to smooth the way for understandings with Lombardy and Sicily. In October 1176 Frederick sent to Anagni the Archbishops Wichmann of Magdeburg and Christian of Mayence, Conrad Bishop-elect of Worms, and the protonotary Wortwin, with full powers to conclude peace. The Pope received them honourably and expressed his fervent desire for peace, but declared that it must be extended to his allies the King of Sicily, the Lombards, and the Byzantine Emperor. To this the ambassadors agreed, but asked that the negotiations might be carried on in secret, since there were in both parties persons who were more disposed to enmity than to concord. They thus gained the advantage of holding the first deliberations privately and solely with the Pope.

The long and detailed discussion lasted more than two weeks, involving the relations between the Empire and the Church, and a variety of questions affecting important personages connected with the schism. The terms of agreement were at last fixed. The Emperor recognised Alexander as Pope, restored to the Church her possessions and the right to appoint the prefect of Rome, and promised to all ecclesiastics the restitution of all that had been taken from them during the schism. The Empress and King Henry also recognised the Pope, and undertook the same obligations as the Emperor. The latter and King Henry bound themselves to enter into a fifteen years' peace with the King of Sicily, and also to make peace with the Emperor of Constantinople and the other allies of the Pope. Christian of Mayence and Philip of Cologne were to be confirmed in their sees, notwithstanding the schismatic origin of their elections, while Conrad of Wittelsbach, the legitimate Archbishop of Mayence, was to be provided for with the first vacant archbishopric in Germany. The anti-Pope Calixtus was to be appointed to an abbacy, and for other ecclesiastics provision was made in various ways. The Pope recognised Beatrix as Empress and her son Henry as King of the Romans, and promised to crown them either in person or by deputy. He undertook to convene a council speedily, in order to promulgate the peace with penalty of excommunication against its violators, and to have it confirmed on oath by many nobles of Rome and the Campagna, while the Emperor and King Henry promised to keep the peace for fifteen years with the King of Sicily, and a truce of six years with the Lombards.

Such were the principal provisions of the Treaty of Anagni. In order to obtain a definite conclusion, the participation of the Sicilians and Lombards was necessary; it was therefore resolved that the Pope with his cardinals and the Emperor should meet in Lombard territory. Bologna was agreed upon as the place of meeting, and on 9 March 1177 Alexander and his cardinals betook themselves to the Adriatic coast, where they embarked at Vasto on Sicilian galleys waiting to escort them to Venice, along with Roger, Count of Andria, Grand Constable of the kingdom, and Romuald, Archbishop of Salerno, the historian of these events. They landed at Venice, where Alexander was received with great honours. The Emperor, who was then in the Romagna, sent messages to the Pope asking him to alter the place of meeting. In order to treat better with the Lombards it was important for Frederick to isolate them and separate them from the Pope. Bologna, loyal to the League, was suspect to the Emperor. The Pope answered that he could not give a decided assent until he had come to an agreement with the Lombards, and made his way to Ferrara, in order to discuss the matter with the representatives of the League.

On 17 April 1177, in the church of St George, the Pope addressed a solemn discourse to the Lombards, who had met him at Ferrara, magnifying the victory of the Papacy over the Empire, and declaring that it was not a work of man but a miracle of God that an aged and unarmed priest should have been able to resist the fury of the Germans, and without striking a blow subdue the power of the Emperor. But, he added, though the Emperor had offered peace to him and the King of Sicily, he had declined to conclude it without them, and on this account had engaged on a long and perilous journey.

The Lombards, to whom the Treaty of Anagni, concluded without their participation, had given offence and cause of suspicion, answered respectfully, but not without a touch of bitter irony. They thanked him for having come. The persecutions of the Emperor were known to them, not by hearsay only, but from hard experience. They had been the first to sustain in their own persons the fury of the imperial attack in order to avert the destruction of Italy and the Church, and for the honour of both they had exposed property and life to extreme danger. It was only just and reasonable that he should not have consented to terms of peace without their adhesion, seeing that they had often refused to listen to proposals which had not been referred to him. The fatigues and dangers of his journey were very different from those to which they had exposed themselves on behalf of the Church, offering up their substance, themselves, and the lives of their children. "Let your Holiness know," they added, "and let it be known to the imperial power that we, so long as the honour of Italy is safeguarded, are willing to accept peace and favour from the Emperor provided our liberties remain intact. The tribute due to him of old from Italy shall be rendered and his ancient rights acknowledged, but the liberty inherited from our sires and forefathers can only be surrendered with life itself, and to us a glorious death would be preferable to an existence dragged out in wretched servitude."

When the imperial delegates arrived and the various mediators had been chosen, the question as to where the discussion should take place broke out afresh. The Imperialists refused to hear of Bologna, while Venice was displeasing to the Lombards. In the end Venice was accepted, on the condition that the Emperor should not enter the city without the consent of the Pope. The disputes over the conditions of peace at Venice were long and often bitter. The imperialist claims were obstinately resisted by the Lombards. The latter were determined not to admit the privileges conceded to the Empire at Roncaglia, but to restrict them solely to the rights enjoyed by Lothar and Conrad III. Definite peace with the Lombards ceased to be thought of, and in its place was proposed a preliminary truce for six years. In order to expedite matters, Frederick was allowed to come to Chioggia, but, taking advantage of a rising of the popular party in Venice, he tried to force the doge to allow him to enter the city. The Lombards in anger left Venice and retired to Treviso. The Pope was in a great strait and peace seemed once more to be in danger. The Sicilian legates saved the situation. Seeing that the doge was wavering, they made ready their galleys with great ostentation and then, reproaching the doge with breach of faith, they threatened to leave Venice and trust to their king to take his revenge. This was tantamount to saying that the many Venetians in the kingdom of Sicily would be made prisoners and their goods confiscated. The popular party had to give way before the attitude of the rest of the community, and the doge was able to keep the Emperor at bay during the period of the negotiations, which now were resumed and went on more rapidly. On 23 July 1177 peace was concluded with the Pope, a truce of fifteen years with Sicily and of six with the Lombards. At the request of the Pope, the Venetian galleys went to Chioggia to bring Frederick to San Niccolò del Lido, where a commission of cardinals absolved him from excommunication, while the imperialist prelates abjured the schism. On 24 July the doge, along with the Patriarch of Aquileia, went to the Lido and meeting the Emperor escorted him to Venice with great pomp. There in front of St Mark's, amidst a reverent and deeply-moved assemblage, the two champions met after a struggle of eighteen years for the ideal supremacy which each deemed granted him by God. The moment was full of solemnity. The Emperor, overcome by sentiments of reverence for the aged man who received him, threw off his imperial mantle and prostrated himself before him. The Pope, in tears, raised and embraced him, and leading him into the church gave him his benediction. The next day the Pope said mass in St Mark's, and on his quitting the church the Emperor held his stirrup and made ready to conduct the palfrey. The Pope, however, gave him his blessing, at the same time dispensing him from accompanying him to his barge.

On 1 August the peace between the Church and the Empire, and the truce with Sicily and the Lombards, were solemnly ratified. The Pope in a council held in St Mark's pronounced anathemas against any who should dare to disturb the peace now concluded. The Emperor in the meantime displayed particular friendliness to the ambassadors of the King of Sicily, and in the conversations with them laid special emphasis on the common interests which bound together the two sovereigns and on the possibility of a future alliance. Probably Frederick's active mind was already turning over the new direction which might be given to his relations with southern Italy and was preparing the way for a new development of his aims.

After settling some minor points which were still pending, the Emperor and the Pope parted company towards the end of September. Frederick remained in Italy until the end of 1177, and Alexander returned first to Anagni and thence to Rome, where he met with an enthusiastic reception. This cordiality, however, was of short duration. The old motives of discord were still active, and the opposition between the temporal claims of the Pope and those put forward by the party of municipal liberty were quickly renewed. The Treaty of Anagni had again given to the Pope the right of investing the prefect of Rome, but the prefect in office refused to pay homage and withdrew to Viterbo, continuing his support of the anti-Pope. The Archbishop of Mayence, who represented the Emperor in Italy, tried ineffectually to recall him to obedience. But Alexander instead, by more diplomatic means, won him over, and thus compelled the anti-Pope to surrender and turn to him as a suppliant. The Pope received him and provided for him generously.

Another anti-Pope lasted for a few months, but having been taken prisoner was shut up in the abbey of Cava.

The long travail of the Church was at an end, and it seemed a first necessity that in the face of the world the pacification of consciences should be ratified, the evils of the long schism healed, and the recurrence of fresh divisions in the Church of Christ checked once and for all. In March 1179 Alexander III summoned the Third Lateran Council, which was attended by a great concourse of bishops and prelates from all quarters. Many ordinances were proclaimed for regulating the lives of the clergy; the rights and privileges of the Church, independent of lay authority, were affirmed; abuses and customs contrary to the sanction of civilisation and the feeling of Christianity were prohibited. All the ordinances of the anti-Popes were annulled, and in order to prevent the renewal of schismatical elections to the Papacy it was decreed that, in the case of a contested election, the candidate who obtained two-thirds of the votes should be declared elected. With this council the long and laborious work of the pontificate of Alexander III may be said to have come to an end. For two years longer he ruled the Church, not without difficulties arising from his various relationships with the Lombards, the Emperor, and the Romans, who were always jealous of papal authority and inclined to revolt. On 30 August 1181 he died at Civita Castellana. His pontificate was without doubt one of the most remarkable in the history of the Church. For twenty-two years he had guided her in times of singular difficulty with great prudence and firmness through a schism of the most serious nature. His enemies were numerous, and he was in open conflict with the Empire presided over by one who was among the greatest wearers of the imperial crown. The champion of the Emperor and the champion of the Papacy each represented in this strife contrasting ideals which hardly admitted of reconciliation, and the strife was waged on both sides with vigour because both the champions were animated by a profound faith in the ideals for which they fought.

Lucius III, who succeeded Alexander, found a question of debate with the Empire still undecided. This was the question of the inheritance of the Countess Matilda, which the Treaty of Venice had settled only provisionally and in terms lacking in precision. Nor was this his only difficulty. The Romans held up their heads more proudly than ever, bent on asserting their independence as opposed to the temporal pretensions of the Popes. Lucius was soon forced to leave Rome and shift from place to place in the Campagna until, his situation in the neighbourhood becoming daily more precarious, he had to make up his mind to retire still farther, and in July 1184 he transferred himself to Verona. The principal reason for fixing on this place of residence was his desire to regain the friendship of the Lombards who, since the peace of Venice, had kept much aloof from the Church. He also wished to discuss with Frederick the questions which still remained over for settlement. The Emperor, after the peace of Venice, had set himself strenuously to restore order in Germany, and had quelled by force of arms the open rebellion of Henry the Lion who, in November 1181, was compelled to sue for peace at Erfurt and then to seek refuge in England as an exile for several years. Frederick, in the meanwhile, was not neglecting Italy. His long conflict with that country had brought him gradually to recognise both the powers of resistance that the republics possessed, and the advantages that might accrue to him from their friendship. He turned over in his mind a new scheme of policy. The negotiations for a definite peace with Lombardy were facilitated by the discontent of the Lombards with the Pope, while they saw that Frederick and the King of Sicily were at peace and that, by the death of Manuel Comnenus, they could no longer count on help from Constantinople. On these grounds their minds were now occupied in securing in a friendly way the liberties so dearly fought for and not in meditating fresh hostilities. The peace was first negotiated at Piacenza and then concluded at Constance in June 1183. It was an honourable arrangement. The high sovereignty of the Empire was admitted without question and its ancient rights were recognised, but in such a way as not to interfere with the freedom of the republics or with their development. They were invested by the Emperor or by their bishop, according to their status, with the *regalia*. The cities were allowed to elect their own consuls or podestàs, who were to administer justice according to their laws. They could also raise taxes without the Emperor's special consent, although an appeal to him was conceded. All the ancient customs were recognised. The allies were to fortify their towns and castles, and their League was to continue unimpaired with power of renewal. All offences were forgiven; the prisoners were exchanged; bans, confiscations, and all other penalties were annulled; the city of Alessandria was admitted to the imperial favour, under the condition, not of long duration, of taking the name of Cesarea. Thus the imperial claims put forth at Roncaglia were curtailed at Constance, and the proud but sagacious prince became reconciled to the noble people who had defended their liberty with such valour and such tenacity.

With Germany restored to order and Italy pacified, Frederick might well look backward over the thirty years of a glorious reign and feel pride in the achievements of his career. In order to celebrate the termination of so many vicissitudes, he commanded a great festival to be held at Mayence on Whitsunday in the year 1184, a festival which long survived in the lays of the Minnesingers and the legends of Germany.

During these festivities, in a tournament in which the Emperor himself took part, the young King Henry VI won his spurs. He was a young actor making his first entry on the stage of history. Frederick's chivalrous designs were henceforward to be turned in a new direction. While maturing in his mind the plan of a new and sacred enterprise, he was preparing his son to rule the State and testing his capacities in various ways so that the lofty Empire to be committed to his charge might be upheld in undiminished greatness. With this aim he proposed and concluded the contract of marriage between Henry and Constance, the heiress of Sicily, thus hoping to achieve his design of linking southern Italy with the Empire. In September 1184 he re-entered Italy as a friend, with a great suite of nobles but no army, and was received with a cordial welcome from the Lombards. He wished to come to a closer understanding with them, and to obtain from the Pope the imperial crown for his son Henry. Pope and Emperor met at Verona, both in a conciliatory mood, but it soon appeared how difficult would be the process of coming to agreement. The Emperor insisted that the Pope should confirm the orders conferred by the schismatic bishops, and the Pope, after some hesitation, declared that before this step could be taken it would be necessary to have conciliar authority, and proposed to summon a synod at Lyons. This procrastinating reply did not please Frederick and made more difficult than before the solution of the questions relating to the inheritance of the Countess Matilda, which Frederick in the meantime held and had no intention of giving up. Another source of discord was the archbishopric of Trèves, where in 1183 a double election had occurred, the Pope favouring one candidate and the Emperor the other. But the most delicate point of all was the Emperor's persistent demand of the imperial crown for his son Henry. The Pope objected, adducing as his reason that, notwithstanding precedents, the contemporaneous existence of two Emperors was incompatible with the very nature of the Empire itself. The Pope's refusal was perhaps not altogether without support from the German nobility, who may have seen in such a coronation a tendency to make the Empire hereditary. It is probable that the suspicions and fears raised in the Curia by the approaching marriage of Henry and Constance had a strong influence over the Pope. In spite of the strained situation, the personal relations between Lucius and Frederick remained cordial, and in their conversations at Verona they had opportunity for enquiring together into the imminent necessity of carrying succour to the Christians of the East, exposed to serious danger by the enterprises of Saladin. But on 24 November 1185 Lucius III died at Verona, and was succeeded by the Archbishop of Milan, who took the name of Urban III. He was an unbending and vigorous man, with little friendship for the Emperor and ill-disposed to concessions. With him was reopened the quarrel between Church and Empire, and the imperial policy was turned more decisively to the path on which it had first entered. Thus, as at the end of the struggle of the investitures, so now, after a long contest, neither party could claim the full victory or acknowledge entire defeat.

CHAPTER XIV.

THE EMPEROR HENRY VI.

THE Emperor Henry VI presents both in character and appearance a striking contrast to his father; instead of the fine figure, the attractive mien, the charm of manner which distinguish the personality of Frederick Barbarossa, we are confronted with a man, spare and gaunt, of an unprepossessing appearance, which thinly disguised the harsh, cruel, unrelenting qualities of his character. Instead of the fearless and skilful soldier, the very personification of all that was knightly in an age of knights, we see a man whose honour even among friends could not be trusted, whose cruelty would stop short at nothing when it suited his purpose; a man who cared not for the field of battle, and whose only active pursuit was falconry and the chase. Certainly it was not Henry's personal attributes that made him a great Emperor, nor was it in field-sports or deeds of arms that Henry excelled; it was as a man of learning, as one "more learned than men of learning,"[1] as a man of great business capacity, that Henry impressed his contemporaries. One writer will dwell on his eloquence and on his prudence, another will praise his intellectual attainments, his knowledge of letters and of canon and secular law. "I rejoice," writes Godfrey of Viterbo in his dedication of the *Speculum regum* to Henry, "that I have a philosopher king."[2]

But if the characters of the two Emperors have so little in common, there is a striking similarity in their political outlook. Henry inherited from his father not only the problems that required solution, but the methods and the ideas with which to solve them. The Peace of Venice, though the end of one phase of the struggle, was also the beginning of another. Frederick's last years, which coincide with Henry's first, are occupied with the solution of the old problem on new lines; the three powers whose combined strength had defeated him, the Papacy, the Lombards, and the Normans, must be separated and separately dealt with. The first step in this direction was achieved when Alexander III, who had long been excluded from his capital, and who hoped with the Emperor's aid to become once more master in Rome, was induced to sign the Peace of Venice from which the Lombards and the Normans were excluded. These had to content themselves with truces, the former for six, the latter for fifteen years. As in the famous dramatic episode at Canossa a hundred

---

[1] "Literatis ipse literatior." Gervase of Tilbury.

[2] MGH, *Script.* XXII, 21. Cf. also *Memoria seculorum*, MGH, *Script.* XXII, 103, "Tu vero, Henrice regum omnium felicissime, sicut a pueritia curasti phylosoficis inherere doctrinis."

years before, the Emperor cloaked a diplomatic triumph under the guise of abject humility. Considered by results it is not too much to say, with a recent writer[1], that the Pope entered Venice as judge and left it as protégé of the German Emperor. That Frederick remained with the upper hand seems proved from the fact that, in spite of the agreement at Anagni, he refused to evacuate the *terra Mathildis* which he claimed as of right to be imperial territory. Moreover Alexander gained little by his compliance; he was, it is true, reinstated at Rome by Christian of Mayence and German soldiery, but only to be hounded once more from the city to die, two years later, in exile at Civita Castellana. Alexander's successor, Ubald, Cardinal-bishop of Ostia, who took the name of Lucius III, was a man of advanced years and well-disposed towards the Emperor; he would, he declared, deny him nothing; nor could he well do otherwise, for he too after a short struggle was forced to abandon Rome, a fugitive from the hostile Romans. Pope and Emperor were now working for the same object—a durable peace; but there were still questions to be settled, above all the question of the lands of Matilda. In the course of the negotiations which occupied the years 1182-3 the Emperor through his representatives suggested two solutions: first, that the disputed territory should be definitely assigned to him, while he in return should compensate the Pope with a tenth, the cardinals with a ninth, of the revenues; or secondly, that a commission appointed from both parties should revise the boundaries and, by means of mutual exchanges, arrive at a settlement agreeable to both of them. However, neither plan commended itself to Lucius, who proposed a personal conference at Verona, where he had taken up his residence in July 1184 and whither the Emperor came in the following October.

Here the issue was complicated by new difficulties: the demand of Frederick for the reinstating of the Bishops of Metz, Strasbourg, and Basle, who had been deposed in accordance with the second decree of the Third Lateran Council (1179) which pronounced the ordinations by schismatic Popes to be invalid; the demand for the imperial coronation of the young King Henry; the question of the disputed election at Trèves. Lucius was prepared to fall in with Frederick's wishes as far as he could, but he was old, weak, and procrastinating; he would gladly restore the deposed bishops, but a decision of a General Council could only, he thought, be reversed by a similar body. He may not have been entirely averse to crowning the young king, and according to one authority it was the cardinals and not the Pope who stood in the way; but he soon seems to have come round to the view that there could not be two Emperors reigning simultaneously, and that Henry could only acquire the title if Frederick was himself ready to abdicate in his favour. As regards the Trèves election dispute there is little doubt that Lucius had every intention of satisfying the Emperor, was willing, that is to say, to consecrate

---

[1] Haller, *Heinrich VI und die römische Kirche*, MIOGF, xxxv, p. 388.

the imperial candidate; but the matter was not a very simple one. In June 1183 one party of the electors had chosen Folmar, the archdeacon, the other party the provost Rudolf. The dispute was referred to the Emperor, who decided for the latter and forthwith invested him with the *regalia* of his see; the disappointed Folmar thereupon appealed to the Pope. Lucius procrastinated *more curiae*, as the Trèves historian comments. At last the cardinals decided that as the appeal had been made the case must, at least as a matter of form, be heard, and Rudolf was summoned to Verona; this all meant further delay, and no decision was reached when Frederick in November 1184 left the conference. But what is of importance is that Frederick left Verona under the strong impression that all was going well, that a decision favourable to him would ultimately be pronounced; and so no doubt it would, had not Henry taken precipitate action in Germany—he treated Folmar and his supporters as traitors and seized their property—and had not, soon after the news of this ill-judged act reached the papal Court, the well-intentioned Lucius died.

It has been generally stated that the mild old man sitting at Verona was struck as it were by a thunderbolt by the news from Augsburg of the betrothal on 29 October 1184 of Henry with the aunt and heiress of the reigning King of Sicily, and in consequence all hope of a peaceful settlement between Pope and Emperor was at an end[1]. At one blow the Curia would be deprived of its strongest ally, the Empire of its most formidable enemy; in the next phase of the papal-imperial contest the southern kingdom would be on the side of the Emperor, the Pope would be between two fires. But it must be remembered that Lucius meant that there should not be another phase of the hitherto incessant struggle. Professor Haller has gone far to prove that this betrothal was not, as usually supposed, a devastating blow to the Pope—for the simple reason that the Pope himself had planned it[2]. Nor was the event so certainly to lead to the union of the Empire and Sicily. When the scheme was set on foot, Constance was not heir-apparent but merely presumptive, and the presumption rested on the fact that William II and Joanna, whose respective ages in 1183 were 30 and 18, would die childless: the birth of an heir was still within the bounds of possibility, even of probability; Constance herself at the age of 40 gave birth to the future Emperor

---

[1] This hypothesis suggested by Adolf Cohn in 1862 (FDG, I, p. 441) was accepted as a fact by all writers for half a century, until Haller re-examined the whole evidence in 1914 (MIOGF, xxxv, pp. 414 sqq.).

[2] This view rests principally on the testimony of Peter of Eboli (the physician and court-poet of Henry VI), *Liber ad honorem Augusti*, lines 21-24,

> Traditur Augusto coniunx Constantia magno;
> Lucius in nuptu pronuba causa fuit;
> Lucius hos iungit quos Celestinus inungit;
> Lucidus hic unit, Celicus ille sacrat.

Frederick II in the ninth year of her married life. Barbarossa was in-fluenced, no doubt, by the results the alliance might yield, but he must also have been aware that the incorporation of Sicily in the Empire was as yet but a possible eventuality. Lucius was perhaps less far-sighted; he saw that the independent kingdom in the south was an obstacle in the way of a durable peace with the Empire, that the surest way to attain his object was to unite the two enemies in a family alliance, and he laid his plans accordingly[1]. While he was conferring with the Emperor over the boundaries of papal territory at Verona, the seal was set to his marriage-project at Augsburg. A year later, 25 November 1185, Lucius died, believing till the end that his cherished scheme for a lasting peace between the spiritual and temporal rulers of Christendom would yet come to pass.

At Rieti on 28 August 1185 Constance was handed over to the German envoys, who conducted her to Milan. This town, the arch-enemy of Frederick in the days of the Lombard League, had been won over to the imperial friendship by the grant of a comprehensive charter of privileges in February 1185, and here, at the request of the Milanese themselves, Constance and Henry were married on 27 January of the year following, in the presence of a large concourse of German and Italian princes. The marriage festival marks the triumph of Frederick's diplomacy. The enemies who had threatened his position in Italy for twenty critical years of his reign were now bound to him by close ties of friendship. The ceremonies were concluded by three coronations: Frederick himself received the Burgundian, Constance the German, Henry the Italian crown. If Henry had been denied by the Pope the insignia, he had now at least the substance, of imperial power. Since the age of four he had been King of Germany; he was now King of Italy also. For all practical purposes he was co-Emperor. He was given in fact the title of *Caesar*. When Frederick in the following August returned to Germany, Henry remained behind in charge of the administration of the Italian kingdom.

In spite of his strong position in Italy, the task was not altogether an easy one. Urban III, who had succeeded Lucius on the papal throne, did not succeed to his policy; he was an old enemy of the Hohenstaufen; he was a Milanese, and his family had suffered in the destruction of Milan at Frederick's hands in 1162. He hated the Sicilian marriage, hated too, no doubt, the cordial relations of his native city with the Emperor. On personal grounds, if not on political, he was determined to resist the rapidly developing imperial domination in Italy. Henry's ambassador, Conrad of Mayence, with untiring patience tried to reach a settlement by mutual concessions: Urban should cede the lands of Matilda, while Henry in return should subdue Rome and restore the Pope to his

---

[1] The marriage commended itself to William II, who required the support of Frederick in his designs against the Eastern Emperor.

capital. But Urban was not of a conciliatory turn of mind; he raised new issues, the renunciation of the *ius spolii* among others; he demanded the unconditional surrender of the occupied territories; and on 17 May he took the decisive step—he confirmed the appointment of Folmar, and a fortnight later consecrated him Archbishop of Trèves. It was a declaration of war, and he risked the inevitable break, relying on the difficulties with which the Emperor was faced. There were weak links in the imperial armour: there were popular risings in the Tuscan towns, especially in Siena, the rebuilding of Crema led to the revolt of its rival Cremona; in Germany the rebellion of Philip of Cologne threatened to become general[1]. These rebellions the Pope fostered by every means in his power; he forbade the towns and bishops under threat of excommunication to assist in the suppression of Cremona. But he had underrated the strength of his opponent. Henry in alliance with the Tuscan nobility speedily put down the rising of the Sienese, and deprived them of many of their privileges; while his father, after a siege of a few weeks, forced Cremona to submission. By way of retaliation for the part the Pope had played in the revolts, Frederick commanded his son to overrun the Campagna. Henry carried out his task with a thoroughness which characterised all his actions; he devastated the country to the frontier of Apulia, received the oath of allegiance from the towns and nobles of the Campagna and Romagna, and by the end of the year 1186 almost the whole of northern and central Italy were under imperial control.

Urban's efforts to promote discontent in Germany met with little better success. Though the new issues he had raised, the question of the *ius spolii*, of the lay advocacies, of the taking of ecclesiastical tithes by laymen, all long-standing grievances of the clergy, were framed with the object of winning the German Church to his side, the bishops, with but few exceptions, stood firmly by Frederick (Gelnhausen, December 1186). Urban, isolated and deserted at Verona, perhaps in a moment of weakness, perhaps under pressure from the imperialist section of the cardinals, changed his front, abandoned Folmar, and agreed to a new election. This was in the summer of 1187. But before his death in the following October he had once more reverted to his former attitude of bitter hostility. He left the imperialist Verona for the papalist Ferrara, where he died, cogitating, it is said, the excommunication of both the Emperor and the king.

That the cardinals sympathised little with Urban's policy seems clear from their choice of a successor. The aged Albert of Morra, who now as Pope took the name of Gregory VIII, had been the chief confidant of the Emperor among the cardinals; Gervase of Canterbury would even have us believe that he kept the Emperor informed of the secret counsels of the Curia, and in his official capacity of papal Chancellor he would have the best opportunities of furnishing him with accurate reports. But

---

[1] See *supra*, Chapter xii, pp. 408 sq.

from political as well as from personal motives Gregory was anxious to re-store the harmony between Empire and Papacy. The Christians in Syria had been defeated at Ḥiṭṭīn on 4 July 1187, and the ill-tidings are said to have hastened the death of Urban; on 3 October Jerusalem was in the hands of Saladin. Gregory devoted the last energies of his life to the organisation of the Third Crusade, for the success of which the co-opera-tion of Frederick was essential. In his two months' pontificate he worked hard to undo the mischief done by his predecessor; the question of the disputed lands falls into the background, papal support is withdrawn from the anti-imperialist Archbishop of Trèves, and the scribes of the papal Chancery are bidden to address King Henry as Roman Emperor-elect. Frederick on his side was not behindhand in meeting the Pope's advances; he sent instructions to Leo de Monumento, the Roman Senator, and to other princes to conduct the Pope to his capital, and it was on the way thither that Gregory died at Pisa on 17 December.

Clement III, equally well-disposed towards the Emperor, continued the work of conciliation which his predecessor had begun. He regained Rome, not by the help of German arms but by a somewhat disgraceful bargain with the Romans; he agreed to sacrifice the loyal Tusculum, totally to demolish it in the event of its falling into his hands, and, if it should not, to excommunicate its inhabitants and to employ the troops of the Papal States to accomplish its ruin. The terms, which, to their honour, Alexander and Lucius had refused as the price of recovering their capital, were ultimately carried into effect by Clement's successor in co-operation with Henry VI. The negotiations between Pope and Emperor dragged on for another year; but the fruits of that year's work, engrossed in a document dated at Strasbourg on 3 April 1189, mark the final triumph of the imperial policy. The Emperor agreed to evacuate the Papal States with a reservation of imperial rights; Folmar, who had failed to answer the Pope's summons to Rome, was set aside, and John the imperial Chancellor became Archbishop of Trèves with the Pope's sanction; finally, Clement promised the imperial crown to King Henry when he should come to Rome to obtain it.

Henry was not, however, destined to be crowned Emperor while his father yet lived; after the latter's departure for the Holy Land at Easter 1189, the king took over entire charge of the affairs of the Empire, and the work kept his hands fully occupied. Frederick, before he left, had done all in his power to smooth the path; unity between Empire and Papacy had been completely restored, the troublesome affair of the Trèves election had been happily solved, Philip of Heinsberg, Archbishop of Cologne, had made his submission, and remained a loyal supporter of the crown during the rest of his life; the difficulties in the lower Rhenish districts had been peaceably settled[1]; the leader of the Welfs, Henry the Lion, had withdrawn once more into banishment at the English court.

---

[1] See *supra*, p. 410.

Nevertheless, in spite of Frederick's wise precautions, Henry's task was not altogether an easy one. Saxony and the neighbouring districts to the east had been in a perpetual state of unrest since the fall of Henry the Lion in 1180. Bernard of Anhalt, the new Duke of Saxony, was at once unpopular and inefficient, lacking in decision and judgment, and his authority was disregarded by princes and people alike. The man most capable of maintaining order, Count Adolf of Holstein, had gone off with Frederick on Crusade, leaving the care of his lands in charge of his nephew, Adolf of Dassel. The opportunity was too tempting for the banished Welf; encouraged by the Kings of England and Denmark, actuated also by the death in the summer of his wife Matilda whom he had left to manage his affairs at Brunswick, Henry the Lion broke his oath and returned to Germany (October 1189). At first his enterprise met with astonishing success; he was welcomed by Hartwig, Archbishop of Bremen, who enfeoffed him with the county of Stade; he was joined by many of his old vassals, Bernard of Ratzeburg, Helmold of Schwerin, Bernard of Wölpe; many of the Holsteiners even transferred their allegiance to him. Town after town fell into his hands, and the helpless Adolf of Dassel fled with his family to Lübeck. On his way thither in pursuit, Henry met with resistance at Bardowiek, which he stormed, captured, and destroyed. When he reached Lübeck in November he found the inhabitants willing to open their gates on the condition that Adolf should be allowed to withdraw in safety; this was granted and Henry entered the town. The successful campaign of the autumn of 1189 was concluded by an attack on the strong fortress of Lauenburg which Duke Bernard of Saxony had built on the banks of the Elbe; after a month's siege the fortress fell. Holstein was his, save only the town of Segeberg which stood loyally by its absent count. It was while besieging this place that the tide of fortune turned; the garrison put up a brave resistance, and Henry's besieging troops were finally defeated by a force under Duke Bernard (May 1190). Moreover the young king himself had taken steps to check the progress of the rebellion. At a diet at Merseburg (October 1189) he had proclaimed a campaign; but except the devastation of the country round Brunswick and the burning of Hanover nothing was accomplished, and the hardness of the winter made it necessary to postpone further operations till the next spring.

In the meantime events had occurred which made the king anxious for peace: William II of Sicily died on 18 November, and Henry, by right of his wife, was heir to the Sicilian crown. Through the mediation of the Archbishops of Mayence and Cologne peace was concluded at Fulda in July: Henry the Lion agreed to rase the walls of Brunswick and to destroy the fortress of Lauenburg; he was permitted to retain half the city of Lübeck on the understanding that Adolf should have undisturbed possession of the remainder. As surety for the fulfilment of his obligations, the ex-duke handed over his two sons Henry and Lothar as hostages. Peace was restored, but Henry the Lion felt no compunction in disregarding the terms; he delivered over his sons, one of whom—Henry—was destined to accompany the Emperor on his first Italian expedition, to escape, and to play a part in the mighty conspiracy of 1192; but the walls of Brunswick continued to stand, the fortress of Lauenburg remained undestroyed, nor had Henry the least intention of surrendering half of Lübeck, as he had promised, or indeed any other of the Holstein lands he had occupied, to the absent Count Adolf.

It was the situation in Sicily which hurried King Henry into concluding a makeshift treaty with the Welfs. It was at once clear that the inheritance of his wife was not to be won without a struggle. There was a curiously strong national sentiment among the heterogeneous population which composed the kingdom of Sicily; correspondingly, there was a deep hatred, especially manifest in the island, to the idea of German domination, which the succession of Constance would inevitably bring with it; the children, we are told, were terrified by the raucous tones of German speech. Constance herself was not disliked; she was a member of the family of Hauteville, the founders of Sicilian greatness; but it was her German husband against whom their patriotic feelings revolted. Constance had been recognised conditionally by her nephew William II as his heir, and the chief barons had taken to her the oath of allegiance[1]; the oath seems to have been repeated by some of the barons, and among them Tancred of Lecce, at Troia immediately after William's death. But the national party under the able leadership of the Chancellor Matthew of Ajello had soon brought nationalist candidates into the field. Two names were proposed: Count Roger of Andria and Count Tancred of Lecce. Tancred, both because he was of royal blood—he was a natural son of Duke Roger of Apulia, the son of King Roger—and because he was the choice of the clever and influential Matthew, was selected. The consent of Rome was secured[2], and at Palermo in January 1190 the Archbishop Walter placed the crown of Sicily on the head of Tancred.

"Behold an ape is crowned," wrote Peter of Eboli, and indeed, if the illuminator of Peter's manuscript portrays him with any faithfulness, the simile is not inept. The small, misshapen, and horribly ugly appearance of Tancred disguised, however, a fine and brave character. His military

---

[1] This probably happened in 1174 after the death, a couple of years before, of William's brother, Prince Henry of Capua. See Haller, *op. cit.* p. 429, and the evidence of the *Gesta Henrici II et Ricardi I* (Rolls Series, ed. Stubbs), ii, pp. 101 sq. That homage was done to Constance at Troia in 1186, as is usually stated (*e.g.* Toeche, *Heinrich VI*, p. 127; Chalandon, *Hist. de la Domination Normande en Italie et en Sicile*, ii, p. 387), is unlikely. Cf. Haller, *op. cit.* pp. 425 sqq.

[2] The motives of Clement in thus turning round against the Emperor, whose interests he had hitherto been so anxious to promote, are difficult to perceive. It may have been, as one contemporary suggests, that out of the confusion which was bound to follow he hoped to be able to appropriate Apulia, and to add it to the States of the Church. See Haller, *op. cit.* pp. 550 sq.

prowess had won for him in the past high commands both on land and sea; his practical efficiency had been rewarded by the grant of administrative posts of great responsibility. He was in fact Grand Constable and Master Justiciar of Apulia and of the Terra di Lavoro. He was a man, too, of some intellectual capacity, familiar with the Greek tongue, versed in a knowledge of astronomy and of the peculiar Arabic-Byzantine culture which characterised the Norman kingdom of Sicily and South Italy.

Tancred's election had not been carried through without the shedding of blood; and much more was to be spilt in his attempts to maintain himself on the throne thus won. In Sicily the Saracens, seizing the favourable opportunity to pay off old scores—in particular a massacre of their people perpetrated by the Christians of Palermo—revolted. The suppression of the Muslims occupied Tancred's attention during the greater part of the year 1190. In the Norman provinces of South Italy, in Apulia, Salerno, and Capua, Tancred's election was regarded with disfavour. The supporters of Constance and the supporters of the rejected candidate, Count Roger of Andria, made common cause, and under the leadership of Count Roger himself the malcontents took up arms. Then, in May 1190, Henry of Kalden, Marshal of the Empire, crossed the Norman frontier near Rieti with the first detachment of German troops.

In conjunction with Count Roger of Andria, the German commander pushed along the coast of the Adriatic for the invasion of Apulia. At first he encountered but little resistance; when, however, he struck westward across the Apennines to join forces with the rebels of Capua and Aversa, he received a check. And the German army had to retire before the attack of Count Richard of Acerra, the brother-in-law of Tancred; the Count of Andria fell into a trap, was captured, and shortly afterwards put to death. The optimistic report, *omnia facilia captu*, of Henry's Chancellor Diether, who was sent in the summer to reconnoitre the position, was hardly warranted by the facts.

In September Philip Augustus and Richard Coeur-de-Lion arrived at Messina on their way to Palestine. Their presence, especially that of the English king, was an additional embarrassment to Tancred; there were constant broils between the unpopular English troops and the people of Messina and the surrounding districts; Richard himself made extravagant demands on Tancred both on his own behalf and on that of his sister Joanna, the widow of William II, whom Tancred had imprudently thrust into prison. At last, however, in November the two kings came to an agreement, and a treaty was concluded according to the terms of which Richard promised, so long as he remained in the Norman dominions, to lend aid to the Sicilian king in his struggle with Henry VI.

With the opening of the new year Henry had entered in earnest upon the long-delayed[1] Italian campaign; he spent a month in strengthening

---

[1] The army was assembled at Augsburg in the autumn, and everything was in readiness to start when news arrived of the death before Acre of the Landgrave

his position in Lombardy; he secured on 1 March the assistance of the Pisan fleet for the conquest of Apulia by the confirmation and augmentation of the charter of privileges granted by Frederick Barbarossa in 1162; he then resumed his journey Romeward. He was, it appears, already in communication with Clement, who seems to have been prepared to fulfil his earlier promise to grant Henry the imperial crown, stipulating only for the confirmation of the rights and possessions of the Romans. Then in the spring, towards the end of March, Clement died; and for the better part of a month Henry was forced to linger in the neighbourhood of the city, while a successor was appointed and new conditions for Henry's coronation were arranged[1]. Clement, whether from inability or from disinclination it is impossible to say, had not carried out the compact, by which he had gained admission into his capital in 1188, with regard to Tusculum. Nor yet had Henry complied with the condition of the Peace of Strasbourg (1189) which related to its evacuation, for there was now a German garrison in the fortress. The vigorous old cardinal Hyacinth—he was well past eighty years old—who was now Pope Celestine III, belonged to the family of Bobo, a branch line of the Orsini; the interests of the Roman Senate were the interests of his own house. Perhaps, too, he still had dim memories of how in his youth he had espoused the cause of Arnold of Brescia and brought upon himself thereby the rancour of St Bernard[2]. It was no doubt the Senate that urged him to make Henry's coronation conditional upon the surrender of Tusculum. Henry complied, for not otherwise could he acquire the imperial title which he regarded as indispensable; but by his compliance he suffered something in prestige. So at least thought the chroniclers of the next generation. "He had," they said, "brought not a little dishonour upon the Empire." But were it not for the high reputation Celestine enjoyed for honourable conduct—"to see or hear him was to learn the meaning of honour," wrote a contemporary—one would impute rather to him the responsibility for the black deed; for he it was who delivered the hapless town, as the price of his own security in his capital, to the mercy of the Romans. But the Romans shewed no mercy; not a stone was left standing, scarcely a man left alive or unmutilated.

Louis of Thuringia without direct heirs. Henry hurried northward to attempt to get the vacant fief into his own hands. However, in deference to the strong protests of the princes, who thought that the hereditary character of fiefs was endangered, he was forced to grant it to Herman, brother of the late landgrave. This affair delayed the Italian campaign for two months.

[1] The statement of Arnold of Lübeck, v, 4, which has been followed by the majority of recent historians, that Celestine III postponed his own consecration in order to avoid crowning Henry is probably mere gossip. Celestine was elected probably on 30 March; it is quite understandable that he should postpone his coronation for a fortnight in order that the ceremony might take place on Easter Day, which fell in that year on 14 April. See Haller, *op. cit.* pp. 556 sq.

[2] John of Salisbury, *Historia Pontif.* cap. 31.

The significance of this event lies in the fact that the Pope was now once more reconciled with the Romans. Safe in Rome he could steer his course independently of the Emperor; he could and did defy the Emperor, and spent the closing years of a long life in championing the cause of the Church against his encroachments. He failed, but his failure was due not to his own lack of effort but to his opponent's strength. His work was not wholly unrequited, for by his policy he prepared the way for the triumph of his successor Innocent III.

On 15 April Henry was crowned; a fortnight later, in spite of the Pope's remonstrances, he, with the Empress Constance and the German army, crossed the Norman frontier at Ceprano. The bulk of the feudal aristocracy of southern Italy stood, it appears, on the side of the Emperor; Tancred therefore looked chiefly to the towns for support, and won their interest by lavish grants of privileges. He organised his defences round two strong points: first round a group of towns in the heel of the peninsula, Brindisi, Taranto, Lecce, and secondly round Naples. Henry delivered his attack against the latter point, which was defended by Tancred's brother-in-law, Richard, Count of Acerra. The campaign opened propitiously: Arce after a short siege, Monte Cassino, San Germano, Capua, Aversa, and many other towns, opened their gates; and an ever-increasing number of the Norman feudatories deserted Tancred to swell the ranks of the imperial army; the walls of Naples were reached with scarcely any serious resistance. But the fortifications of Naples were strong and withstood Henry's repeated attacks; only by cutting off supplies from the sea could the place be captured. But the Pisan fleet deputed for this task was defeated by Tancred's admiral Margaritus, and the Genoese, whose aid was bought by the grant of a charter on 30 May, arrived too late. The siege dragged on; the summer came, and with it disease and death. Many perished, not a few deserted; to crown all, the Emperor himself was attacked by the prevailing sickness; and the Welf hostage, the younger Henry, escaped from the camp at Naples to spread wild rumours in Germany of the Emperor's death and of the crushing disasters which had befallen his army. In the face of these overwhelming troubles he could do nothing else than raise the siege and make his way back to Germany (August). But before he quitted the Norman dominions he received yet another blow; the people of Salerno had revolted and had captured the Empress Constance who had taken up her residence there during the siege of Naples. By the end of the year 1191 most of the German garrisons left in the captured towns, in spite of the efforts of Diepold of Vohburg, had been expelled by Tancred's generals. In the course of the following year the Pope took a more decided line with regard to Sicilian affairs; he excommunicated the monks of Monte Cassino and placed the abbey under interdict for favouring the cause of Henry; he attempted mediation and failed; and finally he took the decisive step—he invested Tancred with the kingdom of Sicily. But

although Tancred now had official recognition of his status, the concordat
sealed at Gravina in June 1192 robbed him of many of the valued
privileges which his predecessors had wrung from former Popes. Celestine
continued to intrigue in the hope of getting Henry to renounce his
claims; with this end in view, he induced Tancred to liberate the
Empress Constance, intending himself to use her as a pawn in the
negotiations; but Constance eluded him on her road to Germany.

In the meanwhile, the Emperor had hastened homeward, stopping
only at Pavia and Milan to settle disputes which had arisen during his
absence among certain of the Lombard cities. Before Christmas 1191 he
was once more in Germany. It was but a gloomy prospect that awaited
him here: the north-east of Germany was in a state of the wildest confusion; nobles formed themselves into bands to rob and plunder their
neighbours; families were divided amongst themselves; Albert of Wettin,
for example, had to return from Italy to defend his March of Meissen
against the attacks of his brother Dietrich. In Saxony the war continued
unabated. Adolf of Holstein, hearing at Tyre that his lands had been
invaded by the Welfs, had hurried home; before Christmas 1190 he was
in Germany, but barred from entry into his own territory by Henry the
Lion, who was in possession of the strong places around the mouth of
the Elbe. However, with the help of the brothers Bernard, Duke of
Saxony, and Otto, Margrave of Brandenburg, he succeeded at last in
forcing his way through, and at once set to work to recover Holstein.
Lübeck, the first object of his attack, resisted all attempts made against
it, and even when the sea-approach was blocked by a boom thrown across
the mouth of the Trave, it continued to hold out until relief came.
But the tide of events now turned in Adolf's favour; he won a decisive
victory at Boizenburg on the Elbe; he captured the town of Stade; and
Lübeck itself at last capitulated. With the fall of Lübeck, Adolf was
once more master of his country. Nevertheless, the position of the
Welfs was far from hopeless; the political situation in the Empire gave
them ample ground for encouragement. The Pope, anxious above all
things to frustrate the Emperor's Sicilian policy, was secretly abetting
the disturbances in Germany; in August 1191 he granted to Henry the
Lion a privilege protecting him and his sons against ecclesiastical
punishments. Moreover the Welfs were able to rely on the support of
powerful secular princes, of Tancred and of Tancred's ally, Richard of
England, with whom they were connected by ties of blood, and of Canute
of Denmark. Henry VI's high-handed methods had alienated not a few
of his earlier supporters; the Landgrave of Thuringia and even the Duke
of Saxony appear to have sympathised with the opposition which was
rapidly forming against the Emperor. Unhappily also, the wisest and the
most loyal of the royal supporters in that region of discontent, Wichmann,
Archbishop of Magdeburg, who had, by his moderation and skilful
management of affairs, many a time saved the Emperor and his father

from critical situations, died in the summer of 1192. The death of old Duke Welf VI in December 1191 was more cheerful news for the Emperor in these months of gloom; for his rich property in Swabia and his numerous fiefs were a substantial accession of strength to the house of Hohenstaufen which he had made his heir.

As so often in the twelfth century, a disputed election to a bishopric played a prominent part in the great rebellion which now broke out against the Emperor. With regard to ecclesiastical appointments Henry adopted the policy established and maintained with such success by his father. He took care that candidates to his liking were chosen; occasionally he would himself be present at the electoral gathering; in 1190 he even went so far as to procure the see of Würzburg for his brother Philip, a boy of some fourteen years of age. His influence was often resisted, sometimes with success: Bruno of Berg in 1191 was elected to the see of Cologne against the imperialist candidate Lothar of Hochstadt. In cases of dispute he himself exercised the right of nomination on his father's principle of the *devolutionsrecht*, and it was on this principle that he acted, with the express consent of the German bishops, in the case of Liège. The electors were divided; the majority gave their votes for Albert, brother of Henry, Duke of Brabant, the minority for Albert, uncle of Baldwin, Count of Hainault. Both appealed to the Emperor, and both were set aside in favour of a third, Lothar of Hochstadt (Worms, 13 January 1192). Albert of Brabant refused to submit to the decision; he appealed to the Pope, went himself to Rome, and there obtained confirmation of his election. The appeal to Rome was in itself an attack on the imperial position in regard to Church matters; still more so was the Pope's method of executing his judgment. He ordered the Archbishop of Cologne to consecrate Albert, but, in the event of his expected refusal, he directed that the ceremony should be performed by the Archbishop of Rheims; and by this prelate Albert was duly consecrated at Rheims in September 1192.

War between the two parties was the result; Albert, it seems, was regarded by the Emperor as guilty of high treason; the property of certain of his supporters at Liège, we are told, was confiscated; he himself, though vigorously backed by Celestine, who pronounced excommunication against those who denied his claims, and by the majority of the nobles in the district of the lower Rhine, was driven from his diocese, while his brother, Henry of Brabant, was forced to take the oath of fealty to his rival Lothar of Hochstadt. Prospects were brightening for Henry, when the untoward event occurred: Albert was murdered at Rheims by a party of German knights on 24 November 1192. The Emperor, it was said, had a hand in the deed; the charge, though in all probability groundless, was given countenance by the fact that Henry only inflicted slight punishments on the perpetrators, and it had the serious effect of uniting together the various elements of opposition.

Frederick in his last years had been at pains to promote rivalry and so to keep apart the two centres of danger to the Hohenstaufen power—Saxony and the lower Rhine—the combination of which it had been the aim of Philip of Cologne to achieve. This unlucky incident of the murder of Albert brought about the result which Philip had struggled for in vain: it united the Welfs with the princes of the Netherlands—a union which was responsible for such influence as in after years the Emperor Otto IV was able to exert. Then in December Richard of England, returning from the Crusade, fell into the hands of Duke Leopold of Austria, who agreed to surrender his prisoner to the Emperor (Würzburg, 14 February 1193). The imprisonment of a crusader was regarded almost as an act of impiety, and the resentment against Henry was increased.

These events were the signal for a general and widespread insurrection, in which many of the leading nobles from all parts of Germany were ready to play a part: the Archbishop of Mayence, the Landgrave of Thuringia, the Margrave of Meissen, the Dukes of Bohemia and Zähringen, were to be found on the side of the malcontents; deposition and a fresh election were freely discussed. The rebels could moreover rely on the sympathetic encouragement, if not the active support, of Pope Celestine, from whom Henry was now definitely estranged. For he had answered the Pope's enfeoffment of Tancred by aggressive measures: he had prevented the German clergy from going to Rome; he had captured and imprisoned the papal legate, Octavian, Cardinal-bishop of Ostia; for two years negotiations with the papal Court entirely ceased. Celestine threatened the Emperor with excommunication, but he could do no more, for he was weak in Italy and Henry was strong; the infirmity of old age no doubt prevented him from promoting the rebellion in Germany by more energetic methods. He probably realised too that the political situation required careful handling. Henry's position in the winter and spring of 1193 was certainly extremely critical. But Richard's capture had supplied him with a trump card, and with skilful play the game might yet be his. It was indeed the masterful manner in which Henry, armed with his valuable prisoner, dealt with the situation that saved him his kingdom.

What the Emperor's enemies feared, what the Pope, the Welfs, the princes of the lower Rhine, the regents in England, dreaded above all, was that Richard should be handed over to Philip Augustus, an event which seemed only too probable considering the friendly understanding which already existed between him and the Emperor. Philip himself made overtures to Henry with this object; he and the treacherous Prince John offered large sums of money for Richard's person or, failing that, for the prolongation of his captivity[1]. It was necessary for Richard's allies to prevent this

[1] Such was their anxiety to gain this end that in January 1194—a month before Richard's final release—they were prepared themselves to pay the full amount of the ransom, 150,000 marks, for the surrender of Richard to them or for his retention by the Emperor for the space of another year. Hoveden, iii, 229.

at whatever cost. Henry could therefore impose almost any terms he chose to dictate, holding the threat of the surrender of Richard to the French king over the heads of his opponents. The negotiations were opened on behalf of Richard by Savaric, Bishop of Bath, a kinsman and trusted friend of the Emperor. But the issues were complicated; many interests were involved; and it was not till 29 June at Worms that the terms of release were finally settled; and even then many months had to elapse before Richard gained his liberty on 3 February 1194 at Mayence. In addition to the payment of an enormous ransom—100,000 marks of silver—Richard had to yield up his kingdom and to receive it back as a fief of the Empire; he had further to undertake the submission of the Welfs and to throw over his former ally, Tancred. His honour, however, forbade him to comply with the condition of assisting personally in the conquest of Sicily, and he procured his release from it by the payment of an additional 50,000 marks.

The conditions were certainly hard, but a great advantage had been gained: the alliance between the Hohenstaufen and the Capetian was, temporarily at least, broken. The suddenness of the event is striking; a meeting of the two sovereigns was arranged to be held between Toul and Vaucouleurs on 25 June. That meeting did not take place; instead on that very day the imperial court assembled at Worms, and after a discussion lasting four days agreed to the terms of Richard's liberation. The proposed meeting near Vaucouleurs was certainly meant as a threat, and it had its effect inasmuch as Richard and his friends hastened to bring about the much desired reconciliation between the Emperor and the kinsmen of the murdered Bishop of Liège, and it also made them listen more readily to the exacting terms which were pronounced at the meeting at Worms. But welcome and important as these results were to Henry, they do not adequately account for the complete reversal of his policy towards the King of France; other considerations must have influenced his mind. It was in this same summer of 1193 that Philip Augustus sought a second wife, and he sought her in Denmark. The political motive clearly was to detach Canute VI from alliance with the Welfs and with England, but the alliance of France and Denmark could not but be regarded as threatening to the security of Germany as well. Henry's sudden abandonment of the Capetian alliance was no doubt also and mainly due to his policy of universal empire. Richard with his extensive dominions in France was now his vassal; through him he intended to bring the French King himself to subjection. Innocent III writing to Philip Augustus some years after Henry's death asserted that Henry had declared that he would force Philip to shew fealty to him[1], and he was

---

[1] Affirmans quod te de cetero ad fidelitatem sibi compelleret exhibendam. *Reg. Innocent. III de negotio Romani Imperii*, No. 64 (MPL, ccxvi, col. 1071). Cf. Hoveden, iii, 301. Notum enim erat regi Angliae, quod praedictus imperator super omnia desiderabat, ut regnum Franciae Romanorum imperio subiaceret.

not using mere idle words. The Emperor's whole attitude to Richard points in the same direction; he was continually urging him to fresh activities against the King of France[1]. This too was the object of the enfeoffment of Richard with the kingdom of Arles. German control over Burgundy, never very great, had sensibly decreased since the time of Frederick Barbarossa; the policy of strengthening it by setting up a strong vassal-power there had been attempted with some success by the Emperor Lothar in his grant to the Dukes of Zähringen; Henry had the same end in view when he proposed to transfer the Burgundian crown to Richard, who as Duke of Aquitaine had already a strong position in the south-east of France. But the scheme never matured; it died as soon as it was conceived[2].

When the King of England was finally liberated in February 1194 the Welfs were still unreconciled with the Emperor. It was a slow and difficult business, but the marriage in 1193 between Henry, the eldest son of Henry the Lion, and the Emperor's cousin Agnes, the daughter of Conrad, the Count-Palatine of the Rhine, made it easier, and at last it was accomplished in March 1194 at Tilleda near the Kyffhäuser; the eldest son of the old duke agreed to prove his loyalty by accompanying the Emperor on his campaign to South Italy, the other two sons, Otto and William, were retained as hostages. Henry the Lion himself in the absence of his sons was sufficiently powerless to be left with his liberty; he was indeed old and worn out and well content to spend his closing days quietly at Brunswick. There he busied himself in intellectual and artistic pursuits; the magnificent church of St Blaise, which he had begun on his return from Palestine in 1172, he now had leisure to complete; under his direction his chaplain prepared a kind of encyclopaedia of knowledge to which Henry gave the title *Lucidarius*, a book which is not without interest as an early example of a prose work in the middle high German dialect; he also, we are told by the annalist of Stederburg, ordered "the ancient chronicles to be collected, transcribed, and recited in his presence, and engaged in this occupation he would often pass the whole night without sleep."[3] Poets and Minnesingers thronged his court, where they looked upon the old duke as their enlightened patron and made him the hero of their ballads and legends. Thus peaceably he ended his long and stormy career; he died on 6 August 1195 and was buried beside his second wife, the English Matilda, in his church of St Blaise at Brunswick.

In the meanwhile, in Sicily and South Italy Tancred had been

---

[1] In 1195 he used his authority as overlord to prevent Richard from making peace with Philip. Hoveden, III, 302.

[2] It is perhaps noteworthy in this connexion that Hoveden (IV, 30) speaks of Savaric, Bishop of Bath, as the Emperor's Chancellor of Burgundy in the year 1196.

[3] MGH, *Script.* XVI, p. 230. The editor, Pertz, suggests that perhaps the Annalista Saxo is referred to.

strengthening his position in every possible way. He had entered into alliance with the Eastern Emperor, Isaac Angelus, and had married his elder son Roger to the Emperor's daughter Irene. His armies had constantly harassed the imperial troops left by Henry to guard the frontier fortresses. But the German position had sensibly improved since the disastrous winter of 1191–2, and much ground had been recovered by the active imperial commanders, Diepold of Vohburg, Conrad of Lützelinhard, and Berthold of Künsberg. Tancred indeed found himself obliged to visit the mainland in person to restore his fortunes. His campaign was a rapid series of successes. Berthold, the ablest of the German commanders, died at Monte Rodone. Conrad was less capable and less popular, and there were desertions from the German ranks; one after another of the fortified places surrendered to Tancred. His triumphant progress was only checked by sickness. He was compelled to return to Palermo, where he died on 20 February 1194.

Freed from enemies at home, Henry could once more turn his attention to the conquest of the Sicilian kingdom. The project was supported by the princes of Germany; it was financed by English gold. No obstacle now lay in the path of success. In the campaign of 1191 Henry had been dogged by misfortune at every step, in the campaign of 1194 he was favoured by fortune in an astonishing degree. His enemies, through his diplomacy, were now isolated; they had been deprived of their former allies, the King of England and the Welfs; they could not expect the Lombards to put any check or hindrance in the way of Henry's advance, for Henry had secured their loyalty by the treaty of Vercelli in the previous January. And now with Tancred's death they were left leaderless; the elder son, Roger, had died a few weeks before his father, and the younger, William, was still a mere boy when he was called upon to represent the interests of the national party in Sicily. Nor was this all: the young William III was left without experienced advisers, for Matthew of Ajello, the Chancellor, to whose skilful statesmanship was due in large measure the transient success of Tancred, had himself died in the summer of the previous year. His son Richard, who succeeded to his office, was not possessed of his father's ability; certainly neither he nor the Queen-mother were capable of handling the almost desperate situation in which they found themselves on Tancred's death.

Henry's task was therefore an easy one. At the end of May he crossed the Splügen pass; by Whitsuntide he was at Milan. On his way southward he secured the very essential co-operation of the fleets of Genoa and Pisa. The delicate business of getting the two rival maritime powers to work in concert was achieved by the Steward of the Empire, Markward of Anweiler, who was entrusted with the command of the joint fleets. Naples, whose obstinate resistance had caused the failure of Henry's first attempt to conquer the kingdom, surrendered at once; Salerno tried in vain to hold out, but it was taken by storm, sacked, and in part destroyed, in revenge for its perfidious action of delivering the Empress Constance over to the enemy. The fate of Salerno effectively crushed any inclination to resist which the towns of Apulia and Calabria may have entertained. It was a triumphant progress rather than a campaign; by the end of October the Emperor had crossed the Straits to Messina, was master of South Italy, and prepared for the conquest of the island. The only serious engagement that took place was a long and bloody battle between the Pisan and Genoese fleets. But before Henry had landed, the subjugation of Sicily was already well advanced; Markward, with the fleet of Genoa, had received the submission of Catania and Syracuse; when the feeble opposition raised by the Queen Sibylla had been suppressed the road to Palermo was open. Henry had but to enter the capital. He was met on his approach by a delegation of citizens offering their submission; the Queen and her family fled to Caltabellotta; the Admiral Margaritus surrendered the castle; and on 20 November Henry entered the town. On Christmas Day he was crowned King of Sicily in the cathedral of Palermo.

The whole campaign had been carried through with the greatest moderation. With the exception of the destruction of Salerno, for which there was ample justification, no scenes of violence, no acts of wanton cruelty, no plundering or devastation, defile the history of the conquest of the kingdom of Sicily. This fact must be borne in mind in judging the Emperor's conduct towards the family of Tancred. They were at his mercy in the castle of Caltabellotta; he could have attacked the place, and it would have fallen instantly. Instead, he opened negotiations and offered generous terms: the young William was to receive his father's county of Lecce together with the principality of Taranto. The terms were accepted and Sibylla, her son, three daughters, her daughter-in-law Irene, and a number of Sicilian barons, returned to Palermo to be present at Henry's coronation. We next hear, a few days later, of the whole party being seized and sent into exile in Germany on the pretext of conspiracy. It is possible, and not out of keeping with Henry's character, to conceive that the charge was trumped up as a means of clearing the field of persons who were likely to be the source of danger and rebellion in the future. On the other hand it would have been contrary to the policy which Henry had hitherto pursued on the Sicilian campaign; his object had been, not to terrorise, but to conciliate the Norman population. It seems more reasonable to believe, as indeed Innocent III himself believed, that a conspiracy actually had been formed against the Emperor, and that the latter was acting only with justifiable prudence when he banished the remnant of the royal house of Sicily and their adherents to Germany.

In the spring of 1195 a great diet was held at Bari to complete the arrangements for the administration of the newly-won country. The government was entrusted to the Empress Constance who, Norman by blood and sentiment, was well qualified to continue the tradition of the Norman kingdom. The German commanders who by their services during the campaign had earned the Emperor's gratitude were either now or shortly before rewarded with fiefs and administrative offices: thus Diepold of Vohburg became justiciar of the Terra di Lavoro, Conrad of Lützelinhard became Count of Molise. The latter had previously held the March of Ancona and the Romagna, which now with the additional title of Duke of Ravenna was bestowed upon the man to whose enterprise was largely due the success of the campaign—Markward of Anweiler; besides these tokens of Henry's favour he was granted his freedom—he had been hitherto an unfree *ministerialis*—and raised to the position of prince of the Empire. Conrad of Urslingen, who since 1183 had held the duchy of Spoleto, was made vicegerent (*vicarius*) of the kingdom of Sicily, and finally Philip of Hohenstaufen, who after the death of his brother Frederick (*ob.* 1191) had abandoned his ecclesiastical career, was granted the duchy of Tuscany. The whole of southern and central Italy therefore was dominated by a group of German officials, and Rome was isolated.

At the same time that a large concourse of nobles was assembling at Palermo to witness the coronation of Henry VI as King of Sicily, a numerous gathering of distinguished persons was collecting round a tent erected in the midst of the public square of the little town of Jesi in the March of Ancona. The object of this gathering, which is said to have included no less than fifteen cardinals and bishops, was to witness the birth of the last Hohenstaufen Emperor (26 December 1194). The number of credible witnesses seems a surprising but, as after events shewed, a not unwise precaution; Constance was not young, and she had been married and childless for nine years; it was only natural that enemies of the house of Hohenstaufen should call in question the legitimacy of the all-important child. Even such careful precautions did not prevent a relatively honest man like Innocent III or a sinister figure like John of Brienne from uttering their disbelief in Frederick's legitimacy, or monastic chroniclers from weaving elaborate tales to explain Frederick's origin from other than royal parents.

Henry's rule now stretched from the North Sea to the coast of Africa, for the Almohades of North Africa sent embassies and paid him tribute. England was his vassal kingdom and he had, as we have seen, the intention of reducing France to a similar state of dependence. He had designs also of extending his power beyond the Pyrenees; the overlordship of the kingdom of Aragon he had proposed to include in the grant of the Arelate to Richard of England; when this plan failed he tried another. The Genoese had been cheated of their promised rewards in the Sicilian kingdom; they had already been established by Henry on the Burgundian coast—at Monaco and elsewhere; they were now by way of compensation given authority to conquer the kingdom of Aragon[1]. The maritime republic however did not avail itself of Henry's offer.

[1] Otobonus, MGH, *Script.* xviii, 112.

The acquisition of Sicily opened up new possibilities for the extension of the Empire. Henry adopted the traditional policy and aspirations of the Norman kings towards Africa and the Byzantine Empire—namely, the establishment of a hegemony in the Mediterranean. Already he had under his influence two outposts in the eastern Mediterranean, the kingdoms of Little Armenia and Cyprus, whose rulers, Leo and Amaury of Lusignan, had received their crowns from him (1194, 1195), thus recognising their dependence no longer on the Eastern but on the Western Empire. In pursuance of his ambitious design of extending his influence over the Byzantine Empire, he sought to profit by the ever-recurrent revolutions at Constantinople. Isaac Angelus, who ten years before had deposed and tortured to death the last of the house of Comnenus, the Emperor Andronicus, was now in his turn attacked, mutilated, and deposed by his own brother, the Emperor Alexius III. In his attempt to ward off the approaching danger, Isaac had turned to Henry VI for help. Henry's demands were of the most extravagant nature; he regarded himself, writes the Byzantine historian Nicetas, "as though he were lord of lords, emperor of emperors." But Isaac was in no position to haggle over terms. His daughter Irene, the widow of Tancred's son Roger, had been found by Henry in the palace at Palermo and given in marriage to Philip of Hohenstaufen. This pair the hapless Emperor was prepared to recognise, if we may believe the evidence of Otto of St Blaise, as heirs to the Byzantine throne; the Eastern and Western Empires would then be united in the family of Hohenstaufen. However the success of the revolution which gave the crown to Alexius III prevented Henry from reaping the fruits of this project. Nevertheless, by a skilful use of the threat of war he was able to exact from the usurper large sums of money which helped to finance his Eastern policy. Moreover he had devised other means to obtain the same end. Already before the fate of deposition had overtaken the hapless Isaac, on Good Friday, 31 March 1195, in the presence of but three chaplains, the Emperor had received the cross from the hands of the Bishop of Sutri; on Easter Day the Crusade was publicly proclaimed at the diet of Bari. The Crusade was to serve a double purpose: besides promoting his Eastern policy, it was to be instrumental in bringing about a reconciliation with the Pope which Henry regarded as essential to the successful accomplishment of his schemes.

Since the conquest of Sicily the papal and imperial courts had become more than ever estranged. Henry might occupy the Papal States, but he had no foothold in Rome; there the Pope was secure and unassailable, and in no immediate need of the Emperor's help. To Henry on the other hand the Pope's co-operation was all important; he was strong in Italy, but his position was to some extent unauthorised; his title to the lands of Matilda had never been admitted, and his right to the occupied territory in central Italy was more than questionable.

Sicily added a new complication: it was a hereditary monarchy, which hitherto had owed allegiance to the Holy See. Was Henry also to recognise this papal overlordship? Not only its relation to the Papacy but also its relation to the Empire presented difficulties; Sicily was hereditary, Germany and the Empire were elective. Henry wished Sicily to be an integral part of the Empire. This problem, with many others which exercised the mind of Henry, would be solved in that most chimerical of all his ideas, the plan to alter the imperial constitution with the object of making the Empire itself hereditary in the house of Hohenstaufen.

For all these reasons friendship with the Pope was an urgent necessity. Negotiations had been tried, but had failed to bring about the desired result; the offer to go on crusade was one which Celestine could hardly refuse to accept. As an earnest of his good faith, Henry had already issued orders for the recruiting of 1500 knights and as many squires for the enterprise. Never was a crusade pushed forward so impetuously by an Emperor or more tardily by a Pope. But little though he might desire it, Celestine could not resist the friendly overtures of a man who was prepared to render the highest service to Christendom, and at last, on 4 August, four months after Henry himself had taken the cross, Celestine wrote the formal letter to the German bishops bidding them to preach the crusade.

Towards the end of June 1195 Henry returned to Germany. Here he busied himself in actively promoting the crusade; recruits were enlisted, the date of departure was fixed for Christmas 1196; the enormous wealth of the Sicilian treasury which he had brought to Germany[1] provided him with ample resources wherewith to finance the expedition. But the crusade was not the only nor yet the chief project which occupied the attention of the Emperor during his year's stay in Germany. He was anxious above all that the great position he had won should be retained for ever in his family. His first step was to try to secure the election of his two-year-old son as king, but when this failed, apparently owing to the opposition of Adolf of Altena, Archbishop of Cologne, he brought forward a "new and unheard-of decree" at the diet of Würzburg in April 1196. The exact nature of this extraordinary proposal, the circumstances attending it, and the means employed by Henry to carry it through, have all been matter of keen controversy[2].

---

[1] From the treasury at Palermo he brought also the magnificent coronation robes of Arab workmanship used by the Norman kings since the time of Roger II. These were deposited in the castle of Trifels, and were used at imperial coronations for many centuries.

[2] See K. Hampe, *Zum Erbkaiserplan Heinrichs VI.* MIOGF, xxvii, 1906; M. Krammer, *Der Reichsgedanke des staufischen Kaiserhauses* (*Untersuchungen zur deutschen Staats- und Rechtsgeschichte*, ed. Gierke, No. 95), Breslau, 1908; and especially J. Haller, *Heinrich VI und die römische Kirche.* MIOGF, xxxv, 1914.

The sources of our information are meagre, ambiguous, and often conflicting; the two principal narrative accounts[1] were written by men
belonging to opposing political parties, the one attached to the Emperor's
court, the other to the court of the Emperor's opponent, Herman,
Landgrave of Thuringia; the one is short and tolerably reliable, the
other is full, but confused and inaccurate. The "new and unheard-of
decree" was no less than a fundamental alteration of the constitution
with the object of making the kingship hereditary. After preliminary
negotiations among the princes who composed the intimate court-circle,
Henry laid the proposal before a full diet at Würzburg, and persuaded—
or, the Reinhardsbrunn Chronicle would have us believe, bullied—the
majority of princes, 52 in number, to give a reluctant consent in writing
under seal. In return they were to receive certain concessions, slender,
they seem, when weighed beside what they were asked to renounce—the
most highly valued privilege of electing the king and Emperor designate:
the secular princes were to have the unrestricted right of inheritance in
their fiefs not only in the male but in the female and collateral lines,
the ecclesiastical princes were to have the free testamentary disposal of
their movable property. The true value of these concessions is difficult to
estimate. Strong Emperors no doubt could and did deny inheritance to
other than a direct male heir; only the year before Henry had withheld
the March from the brother of the Margrave of Meissen who died without
a direct heir, absorbed it as a vacant fief, and contrary to custom did not
re-grant it after the lapse of a year and a day; moreover his action gave
rise to no protest[2]. On the other hand some princes, the Duke of Austria
or the Margrave of Namur, for example, already had these rights of
succession by special privilege, and no doubt many others hoped to acquire
them without making so large a sacrifice in return. The Emperor's exercise of the *ius spolii*, which he was prepared to renounce as a compensation to the ecclesiastical princes, had long been contested and regarded
as an abuse—it had been one of the grounds of dispute in Frederick
Barbarossa's quarrel with Urban III; the removal of an abuse was scarce
adequate compensation for the surrender of an important and undoubted
privilege. The minority, composed chiefly of princes of Saxony and of
the Rhine country, though inconsiderable in number, could not be ignored;
again it was headed by the Archbishop of Cologne who claimed the right,
sanctioned by long custom, of crowning the king-elect at Aix-la-Chapelle.
This ceremony, hitherto all-important, would lose much, if not all, its

It is the conclusions of this last writer which have been in the main followed in the
text. See also the bibliography of this chapter.

[1] *Annales Marbacenses*, ed. Bloch, SGUS; *Cronica Reinhardsbrunnensis*, MGH,
Script. xxx.

[2] Cf. however the case at the death of the Landgrave of Thuringia, when Henry
had to yield to the demands of the princes and to grant the vacant fief to the brother
of the late landgrave (1191). See *supra*, p. 462, note 1.

significance, would become in fact a mere form, if the person crowned was inevitably the eldest son of the late monarch.

Without making any attempt to overcome the opposition in Germany, Henry began once more to negotiate with the Pope. The correspondence between the two courts was now of a more cordial nature, and Henry expresses his wish to assist the Pope in the suppression of heresy and even announces his intention of coming to Italy himself. His intention was no sooner announced than acted upon, and by the end of June 1196 the Emperor was on his way to Rome. Far from abandoning his scheme for a hereditary monarchy, he hoped now to reach it by a different path—by means of the Pope. Peace with Celestine, which, he repeatedly insists, is the principal object of the journey, was more essential than ever. The Emperor was accompanied by only a scanty following, which was the cause of derision among the Italians; but it was part of his policy. His object was not to excite alarm, not to use force, merely to seek peace. His eagerness is remarkable; the sacrifices he was prepared to make are, at first sight, astonishing. Indeed it required much zeal, much steadfastness of purpose, to persevere in the face of the cold reception his overtures received at Rome. For Celestine's letters, judging by Henry's replies, had assumed once more an antagonistic tone; he raked up a number of old complaints mainly respecting Henry's government in Sicily and his brother Philip's encroachments on papal territory. He had no doubt heard of Henry's new plan and disapproved of it. Nevertheless the Emperor did not lose heart; he pushed forward up to the very gates of Rome, and stayed in the neighbourhood of the city for more than three weeks (20 October–17 November).

The object of the negotiations which passed between the two courts during these weeks was the baptism and the anointing of the young prince Frederick as king[1]. The natural person to perform this function was the Archbishop of Cologne who was himself the leader of the opposition to the design of a hereditary monarchy; this antagonism led Henry to try the expedient of getting the Pope to do it instead, thereby dispensing not only with the German election but with the German coronation as well. This plan would also serve another purpose. The union of Sicily with the Empire was an important consideration; indeed, according to one authority, Henry had promised it to the princes in return for their surrender of their right of election. Two coronations would militate against a close union of the two kingdoms. The Archbishop of Palermo, to whom the right of crowning the King of Sicily by tradition belonged, would not lightly yield his claim to a German bishop,

---

[1] Interim missis legatis suis, imperator cepit cum apostolico de concordia agere volens, quod filium suum baptizaret—nondum enim baptizatus erat—et quod in regem ungeret. *Ann. Marbac.* sub anno 1196. Bloch, Hampe, and others interpret *regem* as *imperatorem*. But the annalist, as Haller, p. 630 points out, is singularly accurate in his use of titles, and is not at all likely to have written "rex" when he meant "imperator." Cf. also Krammer, *Der Reichsgedanke*, pp. 13 sqq.

whereas to the Bishop of Rome he could scarcely refuse it. Henry's plan of a coronation of Frederick as King of the Romans by the Pope was, in short, a simple method of evading a number of difficulties.

The Pope's co-operation was therefore all-important to Henry's schemes. But what had Henry to offer in order to induce Celestine to make such large sacrifices of power as these changes necessarily involved? The Emperor's personal participation in the crusade was obviously not a sufficient inducement[1]. Moreover Henry himself asserts that he has offered to the Roman Church more substantial concessions than any of his predecessors had done; what these substantial concessions were we are not so certainly informed. Giraldus Cambrensis, who visited Rome on three separate occasions between the years 1199–1202 and who may therefore be presumed to have good information on such matters, speaks enthusiastically of Henry's good intentions towards the Church; he tells us further how Henry proposed a plan for the secularisation of the states of the Church which were in foreign hands (those actually in the possession of the Church were to remain so). In place of this theoretically powerful but practically valueless domain, Henry was ready to grant to the Pope and to the cardinals very material financial benefits from the revenues of the churches throughout his Empire. In view of the policy which the Church had pursued for the last hundred years, this suggestion seems preposterous. On the other hand the territory over which the Papacy could exercise any real control was exceedingly small, and was indeed to be retained under Henry's scheme; from the rest little or no revenues were forthcoming, with the result that the Curia was reduced to considerable financial straits. The Emperor's proposal, though obliging it to abandon its ambitious claim to be an independent world-power by becoming a pensioner—and the prospect of independence for the moment was overshadowed—would at least establish its finances on a sound footing.

The second offer is more startling; and it is the one on which, if Professor Haller interprets the matter aright, Celestine gave Henry to understand his plan must stand or fall. This was no less than to concede to the Pope what Innocent II and Hadrian IV had vainly tried to exact from Lothar and Frederick Barbarossa, the feudal lordship over the whole Empire. The evidence for this strange and daring proposal comes from a no less credible witness than Pope Innocent III himself, who, after expounding his theory of the translation of the Empire in the opening sentences of the *deliberatio* on the respective claims of the rival German kings, Philip and Otto, proceeds to declare that Henry had recognised this feudal superiority of the Pope over the Empire and had "sought to be invested of the Empire by the Pope through the symbol of a golden orb."[2]

[1] Though this is stated as the inducement in the Marbach Annals.

[2] This interpretation of the words of the *deliberatio* is, however, not free from difficulties and has been severely criticised by M. Tangl, *Die Deliberatio Innocenz III*, SPAW, LIII, 1919. Cf. also Haller's reply in HVJS, xx, 1920.

To such lengths was Henry, it seems, prepared to go for the attainment of his end; on the other hand it must be borne in mind that, considered in connexion with Henry's whole policy, the consequences of such a concession need not perhaps have been very serious. If the imperial office were hereditary and included an effectual rule of all Italy, it might be of less consequence that it was held in vassalage of a Pope surrounded by the imperial power; it might seem but a form, a ceremony, lowering somewhat the prestige of the Empire but its power not at all. In fact it would clear away many problems—the position of Sicily for example —the solution of which meant additional strength rather than weakness to the Empire; it meant further a corresponding weakening of the papal position, an abandonment of the independent policy which the Curia had hitherto pursued. And seeing it in this light, the experienced and far-sighted statesman Celestine resisted it. Not at once, it is true; for he allowed the negotiations to drag on for some time till the favourable moment came. He may have heard that trouble was brewing in Sicily, that a formidable conspiracy against German domination was in process of formation; almost certainly he was kept informed of the march of events in Germany, and was even fomenting resistance there to Henry's plans. In the middle of October 1196 at the diet of Erfurt, the proposal for setting the German kingship on an hereditary basis was again before the princes, and this time it met with the determined opposition of a powerful group under the leadership of the Landgrave of Thuringia. It is not unlikely that Celestine was acting largely on the strength of this opposition when he signified to Henry on 17 November that he must postpone a decision till Epiphany. This virtually ended the negotiations.

The Emperor, realising his defeat, left the neighbourhood of Rome for the south. He also sent instructions to Germany that the letters of the princes promising their support to his scheme should be returned to them and that his son should be elected king in the customary manner; this the princes readily conceded, and Frederick was unanimously chosen king at Frankfurt (December 1196).

But that Henry did not despair of peace with the Curia is evident from the fact that as early as February 1197, smothering his not unnatural resentment, he addressed a letter to the Pope written in terms of due humility and moderation. But Celestine turned a deaf ear; the letter, it seems, remained unanswered. Nevertheless the Emperor was not at the end of his resources. Age was on his side: Celestine was very old, and he was in the prime of life. He was not without influence with the cardinals which he might exert to gain a more pliant successor to Celestine. There was also the crusade, which might serve his purpose well; it was his hope that, having recovered Jerusalem, he could approach the Pope once more and win, as reward for the services he had rendered to Christendom, the much-desired peace. In such circumstances the Pope could hardly deny him his request. Moreover everything promised well for the success of the enterprise: the usurper Alexius III was ready to pay an annual tribute to the Emperor of the West in return for recognition; Irene, the daughter of the deposed Isaac, was now in 1197 the wife of the Emperor's brother Philip of Swabia. There was no fear of interference from Constantinople. Even in Syria itself the outlook was favourable. Since the death of Saladin in 1193, civil war had raged among the sons of the great Sultan and their uncle Saphadin ('Adil).

So Henry pressed forward his preparations with still greater energy. Then in the midst of his work he was interrupted by the news of the imminent outbreak of a widespread rebellion, affecting not only Sicily and South Italy but even Rome and Lombardy. It was the result of a growing feeling of resentment against Henry's harsh rule. The previous Christmas at Capua he had done to death in the foulest manner Richard of Acerra, one of the most prominent leaders of the national party. Such acts were not likely to win the confidence or affection of his Norman-Italian subjects. In February a plot was formed to put Henry to death and to raise up a new king in his stead. The Empress Constance herself and Pope Celestine cannot be acquitted of the charge of being privy to the conspiracy. Warned in time by an informer, Henry fled to Messina where he was among friends, Markward of Anweiler and Henry of Kalden, and with their help he suppressed the rising with savage and revolting cruelty: those who were not visited by instant death were reserved for more terrible ends, for crucifixion or torture. Even the Sicilian barons who since 1194 had been confined in German prisons were not spared, but were blinded by Henry's orders.

The conspiracy suppressed, the Emperor once more turned his attention to the crusade. Early in September the main body of the German crusaders under the Chancellor Conrad, Archbishop of Mayence, embarked for the East; Henry himself was to follow shortly, when he fell ill while hunting on a cold night in the swampy woodlands of Linari. Never physically strong and always subject to attacks of fever in the unhealthy climate of his southern kingdom, he rallied only sufficiently to be removed to the neighbouring Messina; he hoped to reach the Sicilian capital but on 28 September death from dysentery supervened. His body was carried to Palermo and buried in the cathedral.

Henry VI was perhaps in character the least attractive of the great Holy Roman Emperors of the Middle Ages; cruel, relentless, and entirely lacking in human sympathy, he had many faults which it is difficult to excuse. Yet there is something in the magnitude of his outlook and in his astonishing success which commands admiration. His career exhibits what a ruler with immense energy and remarkable diplomatic ability could achieve in a short space of years. Under him the idea of a universal Empire, of world-domination, came nearest to realisation during the

CHAPTER XV.

THE DEVELOPMENT OF THE DUCHY OF NORMANDY AND THE NORMAN CONQUEST OF ENGLAND.

KING EDWARD, son of Aethelred and grandson of Edgar, died on 5 January 1066, being the eve of the Epiphany. On 6 January he was hurriedly buried before the high altar of his new minster-church at Westminster, which had been consecrated just nine days earlier. On the very same day Harold, son of Godwin, Earl of the West Saxons, alleging that the old king on his death-bed had committed to his keeping not only his widow but his kingdom, had himself formally elected to the kingship by a small and probably partisan assembly of magnates. And thereupon he was straightway hallowed King of the English people by Ealdred, the Archbishop of York, within the very precincts and almost at the very spot where some six hours before Edward's body had been laid to rest.

The unprecedented haste and indecent callousness of these proceedings speak for themselves. Whether Edward with his last breath had really attempted, as his biographer and the Peterborough chronicle report, to designate Harold as his successor can never be certainly known; but at any rate, if precedent and the customs of Wessex counted for anything, the crown of England was not his to bequeath; nor had Edward ever brought himself to make any such recommendation when fully possessed of his faculties. What alone is clear is that Harold had no intention of allowing any real debate on the succession to take place among the magnates as a whole. For it is impossible to believe that the great men of the Midlands and of the North, or even of East Anglia or Devon, were then gathered in London. Evidently, as soon as ever it had become apparent that Edward's recovery was unlikely, Harold had made up his mind to set aside Edgar the Aetheling, the sole surviving representative of the old royal stock, who was, it seems, about sixteen years old, on the plea of his youthfulness, and had determined to snatch the crown for himself on the double ground that, being over forty and a statesman of many years' experience, he was far better fitted than the Aetheling to be king, and that he was the only man in England who could be relied on to keep order and defend the realm from its foes. When therefore the moment came for action, all his plans were fully matured; and so it came about that in the course of a single morning, without any public murmurs of protest, the right kin of Egbert and Alfred, which could trace its ancestry back to Cerdic and which for the last two hundred years had played the leading part in England on the whole with credit and success, was displaced in favour of the semi-Danish house of Godwin, which had only emerged from obscurity some half a century before, and then only as the favoured instrument of the alien conqueror Knut. That the *coup d'état* of 6 January was a gamble on Harold's part cannot be doubted; for most men, he was aware, would regard him as a usurper, while it was plain that he could not really count on the support of either the house of Leofric or of the thegns north of the Humber, even if the young Earls Edwin and Morkere were for the moment acquiescent. Looking at the question, however, from the other side, it must be owned that England at the moment wanted a full-grown king and a man of experience, who would be feared and respected; and Harold was undoubtedly the foremost personage in the kingdom, and so wealthy that his mere accession almost doubled the revenues of the Crown and at the same time eliminated its most formidable competitor in all the southern shires. Harold too cannot but have had before his mind the similar change of dynasty which had been brought about in France only eighty years before when the Carolingian line was finally set aside by Hugh Capet. If the Duke of the Franks had been justified in 987, the Earl of the West Saxons in 1066 may well have persuaded himself that he had an equally good case; for his material resources were greater than those of the Capetian, and the need of England for an active leader was patent to all. Lastly, in justification of his decision it can always be urged that it was plain to Harold, from his personal knowledge of Normandy and his misadventures there, that Duke William really was set on claiming the English crown on the ground of his kinship to Edward, by consent if possible, but by force if need be, and would leave no stone unturned in the attempt to achieve his purpose. Year by year men had seen the Norman Duke grow more powerful, and both Harold and his partisans may quite honestly have argued that the sooner an experienced and capable man was placed in Edward's seat, the more likely it would be that William's plans would be brought to naught; whereas his chances of succeeding in his designs would be deplorably increased, if the kingly office were not quickly filled and Englishmen instead drifted into disputing how best to fill it.

If this interpretation of Harold's behaviour may be adopted as the most plausible one and the best suited to account for his inordinate haste, it follows that we must also hold that Harold and his advisers not only considered a struggle with the Norman Duke to be inevitable, but also considered that the danger which threatened England from that quarter was of the greatest urgency. Harold of course knew that he might also have other foes to reckon with, such as his exiled brother Tostig and his cousin Svein Estrithson, King of Denmark (1047–1075), who as nephew of Knut had dormant claims on England which would revive when he learnt of Harold's accession. But Tostig was not really formidable, and might probably be placated, if compensated for his lost possessions;

while Svein was of a cautious disposition, and unlikely to move at all quickly. Harold need not, therefore, have acted with any precipitancy merely to meet such contingencies, nor even to forestall internal opposition within England. It can only have been William that he deemed an immediate menace. But why should he think William so formidable? Normandy as compared with England was only a small state. From Eu, its frontier town in the north-east, to Rouen and thence by Lisieux and Falaise to the river Couesnon in the south-west, where the duchy marched with Brittany, was a journey of less than 190 miles, about the same distance as would be covered by a horseman riding from Yarmouth through Ipswich and London to Salisbury, while the breadth of the duchy from north to south was nowhere more than 70 miles. A considerable portion of the province too was covered by forest; nor was the fertility of its fields and meadows, so far as we know, any greater than the fertility of the fields and meadows of Wessex. Even if Normandy possessed a more enterprising and more vigorous upper class than England, the whole Norman territory was only equal in area to five-sixths of Wessex, and all round its borders were other feudal lordships which had constantly harassed its rulers in the past, and which bore no goodwill to its present duke. Bearing all these points in mind, it would seem at first sight as if William must be attempting an impossible task if he set out to conquer England, and as if Harold might safely have ignored his threats. But nevertheless, as the course of events was to shew, Harold's instinct of fear was right. Though William's dominions were small in extent, William himself, ever since 1047, when he had taken the conduct of affairs into his own hands, had been giving the world proof after proof that he possessed not merely energy and ambition but a gift for leadership and a power of compelling others to do his will which almost amounted to genius. During the last nineteen years he had succeeded in all his undertakings, whether as a leader in war or as a ruler and diplomatist, so that in all northern France there was no feudal prince who had a greater prestige, or one who had achieved a more unquestioned mastery of his own subjects. Normandy too was far better organised internally than were other parts of France, and was governed under a system which really did impose restraints, both on feudal turbulence and on ecclesiastical pretensions. If then we wish fully to understand the risks run by Harold in challenging William, it will be well to make a short digression before describing the struggle between them and to study the steps by which the Norman duchy had acquired its peculiar characteristics and its ruler his remarkable prestige.

To understand the Normandy of 1066 it is not necessary to go back to the foundation of the duchy in 911 by the Treaty of Saint-Clair-sur-Epte, or to attempt to dispel the fog that surrounds the careers of the first three dukes. These princes, Rollo (911–931), his son William Longsword (931–942), and his grandson Richard I surnamed the Fearless (942–996), were all undoubtedly men of mark; but nevertheless for this period there are really very few reliable details available. Dudo, dean of Saint-Quentin, who wrote about 1020, indeed professes to tell their story, but his work is fundamentally untrustworthy and for the most part based on legend and hearsay. Some important points, however, can be established about the development of the duchy during the tenth century. The first is that by the end of the reign of Richard I the descendants of the original Norse settlers had become not only Christians but in all essentials Frenchmen. They had adopted the French language, French legal ideas, and French social customs, and had practically become merged with the Frankish or Gallic population among whom they lived. The second is that, as in other French districts so in Normandy, most of the important land-owners by this date held their estates on a feudal tenure, rendering the duke military service and doing him homage. Allodial ownership, however, was not altogether obsolete. The third is that the land-owning class had abandoned the old Scandinavian method of fighting on foot, and had adopted fighting on horseback. They no longer relied, like the English and the Danes, on the battle-axe and the shield-wall, but were renowned for their skill and efficiency as knights or heavy cavalry.

With the accession of Richard II, in 996, we reach a somewhat less obscure period. As the title "the Good" indicates, Richard II was much influenced by the ideals of ecclesiastical reform which had spread from Cluny in the tenth century, and was a much more active patron of monks than his ancestors had been. Mainard, a monk of Ghent, had indeed obtained permission in the tenth century from Richard the Fearless to revive the ruined abbey of Saint-Wandrille on the Seine. Thence about 966 he had moved on into the Avranchin and re-established monks in the abbey of Mont-Saint-Michel. The third duke, however, had shewn his zeal for religion rather by re-organising the seven bishoprics of his duchy than by founding monasteries; and when he founded Fécamp about 990, he organised it merely as a house for canons. Richard the Good, on the other hand, like his contemporary King Robert of France (996–1031) with whom he was ever on the best of terms, undoubtedly believed that monks were superior to canons. He therefore about 1001, acting under the advice of the well-known Lombard, William of Volpiano, the Cluniac monk who had risen in 990 to be Abbot of Saint-Bénigne at Dijon, re-organised Fécamp and substituted monks for the canons. His wife Judith also founded a monastery at Bernai. Richard's zeal on behalf of monasteries further induced him to issue a number of charters in their favour, granting them liberal endowments and privileges of many kinds. Several interesting examples of these charters have come down to us, especially those in favour of Fécamp, and it is chiefly from their contents that it is possible to piece together a few facts as to the nature of the ducal system of government in the first quarter of the eleventh century.

To begin with, if we analyse the witnesses to Richard's charters, we find that the Norman Duke was served by certain household officers. The complete household of a feudal prince does not, it is true, come before us, but we find mention of a constable, a chamberlain, a chancellor, and a *hostiarius*. More prominent, however, among the witnesses than the household officers are the duke's local officials, styled *vicecomites*. As many as thirteen *vicomtes*—it seems rather confusing to English ears to call them *viscounts*—attested the charter for Bernai, issued in 1025. It is permissible, however, to assume that all the *vicomtes* were not present at the duke's court when that charter was granted, and from later evidence it can be shewn that there were more than twenty *vicomtés* in Normandy, each under its *vicomte*. It is impossible to say when the *vicomtés* were originally established or how far they were based on older Frankish subdivisions, such as the *pagi* and *centenae*. In the tenth and eleventh centuries *vicomtés* were the common units for administrative purposes in all parts of France, and in some provinces not a few of these jurisdictions had developed into important feudal principalities. In Normandy, on the contrary, it is clear from their number that the *vicomtés* were of no great size, nor should they be regarded as the equivalent of the shires in England. The majority of them were probably larger than Middlesex, but few can have been as large as Huntingdonshire. They compare best in fact with the rapes of Sussex in area. As to the position of the *vicomtes* politically, it is clear that they had not succeeded in making their offices hereditary except in one or two instances. They were still at Richard's death public officers, appointed by the duke and removable at his will, who acted as his agents for all purposes of civil government. The duties laid upon them were not only fiscal, but judicial and military, the chief being to manage the duke's estates situated within the *vicomté*, to collect the duke's rents arising from them, whether in money or in kind, to lead the local levies in time of war, to maintain order in time of peace, and to administer justice in the name of the duke and collect the fines imposed on delinquents. Besides the *vicomtés* there also existed in Normandy under Richard II four or five districts distinguished as *comtés* (*comitatus*). These were the *comtés* of Mortain, of the Hiesmois, of Évreux, of Brionne, and of Eu. They were clearly appanages in the hands of the duke's kinsmen; for under Richard II the first was held by his second son, and the rest by his brothers or nephews. In area these *comtés* were not more extensive than the *vicomtés*, nor were their revenues greater. The difference between the two jurisdictions lay in the fact that in the *comtés* the duke retained no important estates in his own possession and left the local administration to the counts, whereas in the *vicomtés* he always owned several estates of importance, and as often as not one or more castles as well for their protection. A *vicomté* indeed might easily be changed into a *comté*, as was the *vicomté* of Arques shortly after Richard's death simply as the result of a grant transferring the ducal interests there to William of Arques, who was the duke's illegitimate son; and then become a *vicomté* again upon the death or forfeiture of the grantee. In no instance, however, be it noted had a *comté* ever been set up in Normandy in favour of a baron who was unrelated to the ducal house.

Besides telling us something about the officials of Richard's day, his monastic charters also throw a faint light on the machinery of government. For example, they shew fairly clearly that there was already in existence an organised ducal treasury. They not only refer to the *fiscus dominicus*, but make a distinction between the regular revenues of the *fiscus* and the occasional or extraordinary revenues of the *camera*. For example, in 1025 the monks of Fécamp were granted the tithe of the duke's *camera*, and a hundred pounds from the same source was at another time given to the monks of Saint-Bénigne at Dijon. Special dues levied from market towns and on the profits of the duke's mint are also mentioned. For example, we hear of the tolls from the *burgus* of Caen, and also of the tolls of Falaise, Argentan, Exmes, Arques, and Dieppe. Rights of jurisdiction, on the other hand, and immunities are not so clearly referred to. In the charters granted to the monks of Saint-Ouen, Jumièges, Fécamp, and Bernai, there are clauses it is true which somewhat obscurely guarantee to each abbey the possession of its endowments "free from disturbance by any secular or judicial powers," but what this implied is doubtful. These slight hints of course do not enable us to form any clear picture of the administrative system under Richard II, but they go some way to form a basis from which discussion may start. The fact too that these charters of Richard II do not deal in vague generalities, but are characterised by preciseness and a good deal of detail, adds considerably to their value. On the other hand, being solely concerned with monastic privileges they leave us entirely in the dark as to the relations of the duke with the bishops and secular clergy of the province, and with the mass of the feudal vassals, both matters which are of capital importance for the understanding of Norman conditions. To obtain any light on such questions, we must go outside the monastic charters; but, as there are no written laws whether secular or ecclesiastical to turn to as in England, we have only the very scrappy and obscure information to rely on which can be gleaned from the narratives of the few chroniclers who collected the traditions as to Richard's reign some two or three generations later. As regards the bishops, one point, at any rate, emerges clearly, namely, their practical subordination to the duke. Unlike many bishops in other parts of France or in Germany, not one of the seven bishops of Normandy was uncontrolled master and lord of his episcopal city, still less of any county or jurisdiction attached to it. Each bishop had a *vicomte* by his side as a rival power reminding him of the duke's authority. In Rouen itself there was a *vicomte* of the city, and the archbishop apparently had no special *burgus* of his own exempt from the *vicomte's* interference. Again, in the matter of appointing bishops the duke paid the scantiest attention to the wishes of the cathedral clergy; for the most part he regarded bishoprics as scarcely differing from lay fiefs, and when vacancies occurred bestowed them, wherever it was possible, on his kinsmen. Richard the Fearless, for example, shortly before his death appointed his younger son Robert to the archbishopric of Rouen. Robert was already Count of Évreux, and he held both offices for nearly fifty years. At his death in 1037 his *comté* descended to his son Richard, while the archbishopric was bestowed on Malger, a bastard son of Richard the Good. Once appointed, the bishops in theory had considerable powers over the chapters of their cathedral churches and over the parochial clergy, and, as regards some moral offences, over the laity as well; for we meet with references to the *Episcopales Consuetudines* and to the jurisdiction exercised by archdeacons, and see the monks constantly endeavouring to withdraw their lands and tenants from the bishop's jurisdiction. In the duke's view, however, the bishops enjoyed their authority rather by his leave and license than as an indefeasible right arising under the universal law of the Church; and if there was any doubt or dispute as to the extent of a bishop's powers, it was brought before the duke and settled by his authority.

The position of the laity, whether the military classes or the peasantry, cannot be very summarily dealt with. As to the former, three obscure problems confront the inquirer. They may be stated as follows: firstly, on what conditions of tenure did the substantial landowners hold their estates? secondly, how large were the ordinary baronies, that is to say, the baronies held by men who could claim no kinship with the duke? and thirdly, had any precise amount of military service been already fixed for each barony? As to tenure, we find that an estate in some cases would be referred to as an *alodus*, in some cases as a *beneficium*, in others as a *feudum*. The contrast, however, between these tenures is evidently vanishing, and the one is no more precarious in its nature than the other. The "alod" in particular no longer, as in earlier days, implied absolute ownership. It was held of a lord, and the allodial owner, if he wished to dispose of it, had to obtain the lord's consent. The lord, on the other hand, was free to dispose of his rights over the allodial owner to a third person. We find Richard II, for instance, giving the monks of Saint-Wandrille an "alod" which he describes as held of himself by tenants named Osbern and Ansfred. Again, though Richard II alludes in one of his charters for Fécamp first to certain *hereditates quas paterno iure (fideles mei) possidebant*, and afterwards to certain *beneficia quae nostri iuris erant*, thereby seeming to imply that there was some contrast between them, it is evident that in general the fiefs whether of the barons or their knights were held on hereditary tenure, and were neither estates for life nor estates at will. It seems clear too that there was no attempt as yet, on the part of the duke, to insist that fiefs were indivisible. In the absence of any special agreement, when a succession occurred, all the sons had rights in the inheritance and, in default of sons, daughters might inherit even the largest fiefs. It is not so clear what happened if the heirs were

under age. In one case Richard II seems to dispose of the hand of a
vassal's daughter; but our sources are too scanty to inform us whether
the so-called feudal incidents of later times, the right of the lord to
reliefs, wardships, and marriage, had as yet been systematically introduced.

Evidence as to the size of the baronies is also scarce; but by good
fortune we have a fairly detailed description of the barony of a certain
Géré, which seems typical of the medium-sized Norman fief. This is preserved in the remarkable account given of the origins of the monastery
of Saint-Évroul by Ordericus Vitalis, a monk of that house, who wrote
only a century after Richard II's death, and who piously put on record
all the traditions which he could collect about the ancestors of the men
who had founded the monastery in 1050. Géré, who was of Breton
descent, began his career as a vassal of the lords of Bellême, holding lands
on the southern frontier of Normandy and in Maine, with a castle at
Saint-Céneri on the river Sarthe near Alençon. While still a young man,
he came under the notice of Richard II, who granted him in addition the
barony of a Norman named Heugo, situated in the southern part of the
diocese of Lisieux in the district of Ouche. The demesne lands of this
barony, as described by Ordericus, consisted of about half-a-dozen detached
manors spread out over thirty miles of wooded and hilly country, the
chief being Montreuil and Échauffour, the one lying north and the other
south of the site of Saint-Évroul. Even in his own district Géré had many
formidable neighbours, of whom the chief were the Count of Brionne and
the lord of Montgomeri; but none the less he is put before us as a man
of some importance, whose daughters all married well, whose sons after
his death were able to stand up against the Count of Brionne, and who
himself was rich enough to build and endow six parish churches for the
use of his tenantry. Compared with the estates of many a king's thegn in
England, Géré's barony was clearly insignificant; but this only emphasises
the fact that Normandy was quite a small principality, in which there
was no room for really large fiefs, and in which the great majority of the
duke's vassals were men of quite moderate estate, more or less on an
equality with each other. To shew that Géré's barony really may be
regarded as a fair specimen of the medium Norman fief, we have to rely
on much later evidence, namely, the returns to the inquest ordered in
1172 to ascertain what services were then due to the Duke of Normandy
from his various barons. In these returns[1] we are informed that the
barony of Montreuil and Échauffour still belonged to the house of Saint-
Céneri, that the number of knights holding of it was twenty, and that its
lord owed the duke the service of five knights. If, however, we analyse
the whole of the returns collected in 1172, we find that the total number
of knights enfeoffed on the Norman baronies, after allowing for some
missing returns, was about 1800 knights; that the total service due to
the duke from all the baronies put together was about 800 knights, and

[1] *Red Book of the Exchequer*, p. 645.

that, though there were some two dozen larger baronies which owed the duke the service of ten to twenty knights each, the great mass of the baronies were no larger than Géré's and owed the duke either a service of five knights, like the barony of Montreuil and Échauffour, or even a smaller service. In the period of 150 years between 1025 and 1172, we must, of course, allow for the break-up and reconstitution of some of the Norman baronies; but, as there is no good reason to suppose that the majority of them were materially altered in either extent or character during that time, this later evidence, besides testifying to the size of the baronies, gives us a much-needed means of estimating roughly what number of fully-armed mounted knights could take the field when summoned for service by Richard II. And this is a matter of some importance, if we are to have any just idea of Norman conditions; for historians have often spoken, when describing Normandy, as if the Norman dukes could rely on several thousands of knights, whereas in all probability in the middle of the eleventh century the number of fully-equipped knights existing in the duchy can hardly have exceeded twelve hundred. It is a further question how many of this total were really bound to render the duke service on expeditions outside the limits of the duchy. As already stated, in 1172 the duke only claimed to be entitled to the service of some 800 knights, though by that date his barons had sub-enfeoffed more than double that number of knights on their lands. It seems hardly probable that any of the earlier dukes could claim the service of a larger body; for if so, then, as the duchy grew more populous and more organised, the liability to find knights for offensive purposes must have been reduced. But this we can hardly believe; and it is altogether more reasonable to assume that the obligation to provide 800 knights or thereabouts for the duke's service was an arrangement made in quite early days and applied in the middle of the eleventh century as well as in the middle of the twelfth. On the other hand, we can hardly assume that the precise number of knights, twenty, fifteen, ten, five, and so on, due in 1172 from individual baronies, had been fixed for each by the end of Richard's reign. Such fixed quotas might indeed have been agreed upon at any date; but in the case of the lay baronies their continuance unaltered over a long period of years seems hardly feasible, so long as inheritances were regarded as divisible among sons. The maintenance of fixed quotas of service seems in fact bound up with the adoption of primogeniture as the rule of succession to land, and with the development of the doctrines that fiefs were indivisible and that younger sons, to share in the succession at all, must become under-tenants of the eldest son. Exactly when these customs were introduced, it is impossible to say. There are indications, however, that fixed quotas of service had been imposed on some of the ecclesiastical baronies by the middle of the eleventh century.

Lastly, a few words may be hazarded about the peasantry and other classes below the grade of knights. As in the rest of the feudal world, the general body of the peasantry in Normandy were tied to the soil and in return for their holdings were bound to labour on the demesnes of their lords and render them in addition many special dues and services. There were, however, it would seem, on Norman estates very few actual slaves who could be treated merely as chattels; and this has been held to differentiate Normandy from other French districts, as it certainly distinguishes it from southern England. In Norman legal documents the ordinary term for a peasant tied to the soil is either *villanus, conditionarius*, or *colonus*, but a considerable class, described as *hospites*, is also frequently referred to. It may be presumed from their name that this latter class, in theory at any rate, had originally not been tied to the soil in the same way as the *villani*, but the evidence about them is too scanty to say to what extent it was still possible for them to move from one lordship to another. The real difference in Richard's day may have been that, unlike the *villani*, they were not bound to regular week-work, but only rendered the lord occasional services, like the sokemen or *radmanni* in England. Finally, above the *hospites* came the *vavassores* or smaller freeholders. These men seem to have been bound to military service, like the knights; but most of them served in war-time on foot, not being individually wealthy enough to provide themselves with a knight's full equipment. Groups of vavassors, however, might in some instances be jointly liable to provide a fully-armed knight to serve in the field for them. Lastly, there was a small class engaged in industry and commerce, for the Normans had inherited the trading spirit from their Norse ancestors. These men dwelt chiefly in the seven episcopal cities and in the duke's *burgus* of Caen. Outside these eight towns there were as yet, so far as we can tell, no urban centres of any importance; such places as Lillebonne, Fécamp, Arques, Eu, Argentan, Falaise, Mortain, and other sites of castles, indeed had their markets, but these places still remained essentially rural in character and their inhabitants are not referred to as "burgenses."

Duke Richard II died in 1026, leaving two legitimate sons by his Breton wife Judith. The elder son, Richard III, only survived his father a year, dying, it is hinted, by poison. The younger son, Robert I, who must have been born about 1010 and who had been made titular Count of the Hiesmois, the district with Falaise for its centre, then succeeded and ruled as duke from 1027 to 1035. At first he was influenced by evil counsellors, and indulged in planning foolish schemes, such as a raid on England in the interest of his cousin, the exiled Aetheling Edward; but this was frustrated by a storm. Tradition also has it that he might have married the widowed Estrith, Knut's semi-Swedish, semi-Danish half-sister, who must have been some ten years his senior, but he neglected Knut's overtures. He began, however, as he grew older, to shew his family's normal ability, and he quite came to the front in French politics in 1031, when he helped Henry I, the new King of France, to secure his throne in despite of the Queen-mother and the Count of Blois, who wished to set him aside. In return for this service, King Henry is said to have ceded to Robert the mesne feudal suzerainty over the barons of the French Vexin, the district between the Epte and the Oise, which ecclesiastically was part of the diocese of Rouen; but in the end this grant remained inoperative, being always ignored by the Counts of Mantes, who were determined to remain direct vassals of the French crown. Duke Robert, like his father, was as a rule well disposed to the reforming party in the Church, and is represented as placing much reliance on the counsels of Richard, the famous Abbot of St Vannes near Verdun, while Odilo, the fourth Abbot of Cluny, is found witnessing one of his charters. Robert too, in spite of his short career, was a builder of monasteries, being the founder of the abbey of St Vigor at Cerisy and also of the first Norman nunnery, which he placed at Montivilliers near the mouth of the Seine. Cerisy and Mont-Saint-Michel, it should be noted, were as yet the only monasteries founded in the western half of Normandy; but whereas the famous Mount, lying on the very confines of Brittany, hardly extended its influence beyond the Avranchin, Cerisy, lying twelve miles west of Bayeux, was well placed for influencing both the Bessin and the Cotentin. Charters still in existence further shew that Robert's liberality was not confined to his own foundations. Though they unfortunately add little to our knowledge of Norman institutions, they attest Robert's interest in Fécamp, Mont-Saint-Michel, Saint-Ouen, Jumièges, and Saint-Wandrille, as well as in the cathedrals of Rouen and Avranches. More important still, they reveal the fact that a desire to found monasteries was now beginning to arise among the greater Norman barons, and that the movement was encouraged by ducal approval. This is a most noticeable development and led to three non-ducal monasteries being founded, La Trinité-du-Mont at Rouen in 1030 by the *vicomte* of Arques, Préaux near Pontaudemer by Humphrey de Vetulis of Beaumont in 1034, and a third on the fief of Gilbert, Count of Brionne, by his knight Herluin. This last was shortly afterwards moved to Bec near Brionne, and in a very few years became one of the leading centres of piety and learning in northern France. An equally important event, but of a different kind, which also befell in Robert's reign, was the founding of the first Norman principality in South Italy. Ever since 1016, bands of Normans had been taking a part in the conflicts between the Lombards and the Greeks and Saracens. The Greek armies, we are told, disappeared before them "as meat before devouring lions." Consequently they were much prized as allies by the Princes of Salerno and other Italian barons. About 1030, however, they set up a petty state of their own at Aversa just north of Naples, a small beginning, but one destined to have important consequences, like the founding of Bec. In these adventures Duke Robert took no part personally, but in 1034 he determined to follow the example of Fulk Nerra of Anjou and see the world by making a pilgrimage to

Jerusalem. Pilgrimages to the Holy Land had at this date become quite common undertakings for Frenchmen; but in Robert's case it entailed a difficulty, for being still unmarried he had no direct heir who would automatically take his place if he did not return. He had, however, when only Count of the Hiesmois, formed an irregular union with a low-born maiden named Arlette, the daughter of Fulbert a tanner of Falaise, and had by her a son named William. For this bastard son, who was now about seven years of age, and for Arlette, Robert had a great affection, and he was determined that the boy should be his successor, especially as his legitimate heir, his sister's son, was a Burgundian and even younger than William, while his own half-brothers, Malger and William, were both illegitimate. He therefore summoned a council and proposed to his barons that they should undertake to accept his bastard son, should misfortune befall him on his travels. This, it appears, they consented to do, though doubtless the proposal was distasteful to some of them. Whereupon four guardians of the duchy were chosen to conduct the government for the little William, should his father fail to return. The guardians selected were Gilbert, Count of Brionne, Osbern the duke's seneschal, Thorold of Neufmarché, probably the duke's constable, and Alan, Count of Rennes, the duke's cousin. Approval for these arrangements was also obtained from the King of France as overlord of Normandy. As Duke Robert was only about 25 years old and in perfect health, it perhaps did not seem probable that the question of the succession would become of immediate importance. Robert's journey, however, turned out to be an ill-fated one. He reached Jerusalem safely, but fell ill at Nicaea in Asia Minor, on his way home, and died there on 2 July 1035.

As soon as Robert's death was reported in Normandy, feudal turbulence broke out in most parts of the duchy. The young William was, it is true, proclaimed duke without demur, for the barons never anticipated that in a few years the bastard would become their unchallenged master, still less that their children would one day acclaim Arlette's child as the Conqueror of England. What they looked forward to was the possibility of exploiting a long minority in their own interests. William's guardians, it would appear, tried to do their duty to their ward; but how critical the times were can be seen from the fact that at least three of them came to violent ends, Osbern the seneschal being actually assassinated in William's bed-chamber by a member of the house of Montgomery. It is by no means clear who took charge of William's education after the deaths of his guardians. Some writers think that he became a ward of the King of France; but it is equally probable that he was protected by the Archbishop of Rouen, who naturally desired to have control of the boy duke's ecclesiastical powers and who was at the same time his most prominent kinsman. At the date of William's accession to the dukedom the archbishopric was still held by his great-uncle Robert, who was also Count of Évreux. But Robert died in 1037 and was succeeded in the archbishopric by William's uncle Malger. Now it was under Malger's auspices in 1042 that the "Truce of God" for limiting private war to three days in the week under pain of severe ecclesiastical penalties was first proclaimed in Normandy, a circumstance which at any rate shews that he busied himself with the suppression of feudal turbulence. And if he was active in that direction, the further inference that he took upon himself the protection and education of his nephew seems fairly justifiable. The promotion of Malger's younger brother William to be Count of Arques at this time also points the same way; and so does the appointment of Ralf de Wacy to lead the duke's men against Thurstan Goz, the *vicomte* of the Hiesmois, who had treacherously seized Falaise; for Ralf was a younger son of Archbishop Robert and Malger's first cousin. Ralf de Wacy himself had rather an evil reputation; but a certain amount of calm nevertheless seems to have followed on his appointment, and it is interesting to note that three more baronial monasteries arose about this time, the first being founded at Conches by Roger de Toeni, standard-bearer of Normandy, the second at Lire by William the son of the murdered seneschal Osbern, and the third at Saint-Pierre-sur-Dives by Lescelina, Countess of Eu. It was also during this period that Robert, Abbot of Jumièges, was summoned to England by King Edward to become Bishop of London, and that Robert Guiscard left his village home at Hauteville near Coutances to seek his fortune in Apulia and become the founder of the principality which in due time grew into the kingdom of Sicily. It is not, however, till 1047, when Duke William had reached the age of twenty, that we really get any precise news about him personally. By that time it is clear that the more turbulent barons, especially those whose fiefs lay in the Bessin and the Cotentin, were beginning to be afraid of him, with the result that an organised movement was set on foot for getting rid of him on the ground of his bastard birth, and substituting in his place his Burgundian cousin Guy, who already had a footing in the duchy as lord of Brionne and Vernon. The leaders of this movement were Ralf of Briquessart and Nigel of Saint-Sauveur, who were respectively *vicomtes* of the Bessin and the Cotentin. They began operations by trying to capture William by treachery at Valognes. William, however, was warned in the nick of time; and making his escape rode right across Normandy to Poissy near Paris to ask for help from the King of France. King Henry was not unwilling to repay the service which he had himself received in like circumstances from William's father sixteen years before, and so William was enabled before long to take the field against the rebels at the head of a mixed force of Normans and Frenchmen with King Henry at his side. The rival forces met at Val-des-Dunes, a few miles east of Caen, and the day ended in a complete victory for the Bastard, who soon followed it up by taking Brionne and driving Guy of Burgundy out of Normandy.

The victory of Val-des-Dunes marks William's accession to power, and a year later he still further enhanced his fame by leading a large band of Norman knights into Anjou to assist King Henry in an attack on Geoffrey Martel. On this expedition he shewed such daring in the field and such skill as a military leader that Geoffrey Martel himself declared that there could nowhere be found so good a knight as the Duke of Normandy.

Having made such a successful début, William was not the man to let the grass grow under his feet, but quickly set to work to make it clear to all who were in any way inclined to thwart him that he "recked nought of them and that if they would live or would keep their lands or would be maintained in their rights they must will all that he willed." If not, whether kinsman or vassal, bishop or monk, rich or poor, he would sweep them from his path, sparing no man. The first to feel the weight of his wrath were his kinsmen, William Count of Mortain, William Busac of Eu, and William Count of Arques. In turn they all challenged the duke's authority, and for their temerity were deprived of their estates and driven into exile, the first to Apulia, the second to Boulogne, and the third to the court of the French King. Shortly afterwards William also fell foul of Archbishop Malger. The quarrel arose primarily because William resented the attitude which the leaders of the Church had taken up in the matter of his marriage. As early as 1048, William made overtures to the Count of Flanders, Baldwin V, for the hand of his daughter Matilda. The Count approved of the match, but on some obscure grounds the clergy objected to it, and bringing the matter before Pope Leo IX at the Council of Rheims in 1049, obtained a decree forbidding William and Matilda to marry. As soon, however, as William heard in 1053 that Pope Leo had been beaten and taken prisoner at Civitate, he set the Church's ban at defiance, and boldly married Matilda in the minster at Eu. Malger, who was smarting over the outlawry of his brother the Count of Arques, thereupon excommunicated William, with the result that two years later he was himself deposed by a council summoned by William, on the charge that he was too worldly a prelate, while his see was bestowed on Maurilius, a monk of Fécamp. It was in the middle of this period of family strife in 1051 that William visited England and came back believing, as he afterwards declared, that he had received some sort of promise from his kinsman King Edward that he would be nominated by him as his successor. At the moment, of course, this promise could make no practical difference to William's position. It was otherwise, however, with his marriage to Matilda; for the alliance with Flanders upset the balance of power in northern France and led Henry I to abandon the traditional friendship of the Capetian house towards the lords of Rouen and to take up the cause of William's dispossessed kinsmen. This new policy led to two invasions of Normandy by French forces, but on both occasions Henry's arms met with crushing defeats, in 1054 at Mortemer, not far from Aumâle, and in 1058 at Varaville, near the mouth of the Dives.

These victories greatly increased William's confidence in himself, and turned his thoughts towards enlarging his dominions at the expense of his southern neighbours. Already in 1049 he had made a beginning by seizing the hill-town of Domfront and the surrounding district of the Passais in the north-west corner of the county of Maine and annexing them to Normandy; but in 1051 Geoffrey Martel had made further expansion in this direction difficult by driving Herbert, the young Count of Maine, out of his patrimony, and annexing his territories to Anjou. After the victory of Mortemer William advanced beyond Domfront another twelve miles into Maine and built a castle at Ambrières in defiance of Geoffrey. This was a serious menace to Geoffrey of Mayenne, the leading baron of western Maine, who appealed to Geoffrey Martel for assistance; but their united efforts to demolish the fortress only led to the capture of Geoffrey of Mayenne, who, a little later, was forced to do homage to William for his lands in order to regain his freedom. In eastern Maine, however, where lay the see and castle of Le Mans and the chief demesnes of the count, Geoffrey Martel's position remained unaffected, and the most William could do was to prepare for the future by betrothing his infant son Robert to Count Herbert's infant sister Margaret, with the understanding that Herbert's right to Maine, if he died childless, should pass to the heir of Normandy as Margaret's destined husband. In 1060 both Henry of France and Geoffrey of Anjou died, and the way became open for Count Herbert to recover his patrimony. But in 1062 Herbert also died, whereupon William at once advanced down the valley of the Sarthe and occupied Le Mans in Margaret's name, in opposition to the wishes of the inhabitants, who rose in favour of Herbert's aunt Biota, the wife of Walter, Count of Mantes. A year later the little Margaret died before any marriage had taken place between her and Robert. The only excuse for holding Le Mans therefore vanished; but William none the less determined to retain his prize and shortly afterwards himself assumed the title of Count of Maine. In normal times this step would have provoked strong opposition both from the King of France and the Count of Anjou; but Philip I, the new King of France, was at the time a minor, and in the guardianship of William's father-in-law, the Count of Flanders, while the Angevin inheritance was in dispute between Geoffrey Martel's two nephews. William accordingly in 1064 had a free hand. His overlordship nevertheless was not really acceptable to either the clergy or the barons of Maine, who, if they must submit to a stranger, much preferred an Angevin master. In the long run, therefore, the acquisition of the overlordship over Maine, partly by force and partly by chicanery, brought William little real strength, though it undoubtedly increased his reputation for luck and cunning. Meantime on his eastern border William had also profited by the victory of Mortemer to compel the Count of Ponthieu to do him homage; and thus it came about that Harold was handed over to William and became his unwilling guest when he was wrecked in the count's territory.

By 1065, then, William was a far more commanding French feudatory than he had been in 1047. Within his duchy also he had taken steps which greatly consolidated his authority. For example, he had fixed the quotas of military service for his barons and rigidly enforced the rule that no castle should be built without his leave; he had made his half-brothers, Robert and Odo, the sons of Arlette by a marriage with Herluin of Conteville, respectively Count of Mortain and Bishop of Bayeux, and had bestowed on each of them very extensive fiefs. He had also, in 1059, obtained a dispensation for his marriage from Pope Nicholas II on the condition that he and his wife should each build and endow a monastery. This reconciliation with the Church had been negotiated in Rome by the Italian Prior of Bec, Lanfranc of Pavia, who, in spite of his original opposition to William's marriage, had become his closest friend and adviser. And this was very important, for Lanfranc was not only the finest teacher of his day and renowned for his successful disputations with the heretic Berengar, but was also a most subtle lawyer and a statesman of genius. Born about 1008, he was some twenty years older than William; but, once they had made friends, the difference of age and training was no bar to the completest sympathy arising between them, and so a relationship arose which was of the utmost value to William, as it put at his service one of the keenest and most practical intellects in Europe. At the same time, it must not be thought that either William's reconciliation with the Papacy or his friendship for Lanfranc had made him in any way abandon the claims of his ancestors to be supreme over the Norman clergy. On the contrary, in 1065 there was hardly any continental Church so much under the control of the secular power as that of Normandy. Not only did the duke nominate all the Norman bishops and invest them with their privileges, but he was regularly present at the meetings of Church councils and no ecclesiastical decrees were issued without his sanction. His influence over the clergy, however, seems to have been almost wholly a good one. For just as he himself in his private life was an earnest and religious man and an exemplary husband, so in his public capacity, as protector of the Church, he took the greatest pains to foster discipline and piety among the parish priests, and saw to it that the prelates whom he selected were men of learning and character who would do their best to promote reforms and rebuke evil-doers. He also took an active part in broadening the range of monastic influence. In obedience to the Pope's decree, he set himself about building two monasteries at Caen, one for men and the other for women, and he did his best further to improve discipline and learning in the older ducal abbeys. His example too was an incentive to several of his greater vassals, with the result that some six or seven baronial minsters were founded between 1050 and 1065. The chief of these were

St Évroul and Cormeilles in the diocese of Lisieux, St Martin at Séez, and Troarn near Val-des-Dunes in the Bessin, the last two, it should be noted, both being founded by Roger of Montgomery. Normandy could therefore boast in 1065 of twenty-one monasteries for men, eight of which were in the patronage of the duke and thirteen in the patronage of the leading barons. There was, however, still no monastic foundation in the diocese of Coutances.

The foregoing sketch of the development of Normandy and of William's career down to 1066 has been given in order to shew clearly the nature of the risks deliberately accepted by Harold when he seized the English crown. However confident he might be that he could deal with the Earls of Mercia and Northumbria—and he at once tried to conciliate them by marrying their sister Ealdgyth—Harold knew that his most dangerous rival was William and that it would be very difficult to come to terms with him. Nor did William long leave any one in doubt as to his intentions. As soon as he heard of Harold's coronation, he sent messengers to England, reminding him of his oath and demanding his allegiance. At the same time he proclaimed to all the world that Harold was a usurper, and sent envoys to Pope Alexander II denouncing Harold as a perjurer and asking for a blessing on his proposed invasion of England. To this appeal the Pope gave a favourable ear; for the English Church in the eyes of the Curia was much in need of reform, and might well be brought by such an expedition more under papal authority. Alexander, therefore, by the advice of Archdeacon Hildebrand, sent William a consecrated banner as a token of his approbation, and thus gave the duke's piratical adventure almost the character of a holy war. Pending the result of their negotiations, William summoned a council of his barons to meet at Lillebonne, and asked them to support his enterprise. It was only with difficulty that they were persuaded to help him. Feudal law gave the duke no right to call for their services out of France, and to most of them it seemed doubtful whether a sufficiently strong force could be got together for so great an undertaking, or, even if got together, whether it would be possible to build and man sufficient transports to carry it across the Channel. The first objection was met by asking for volunteers from outside Normandy and promising them a share in the plunder of England. And as for the second objection, William would not listen to it for a moment, but ordered transports to be built in all parts of the duchy and stores of arms and provisions to be made ready by harvest time. In these deliberations the most active advocate of the duke's project was his seneschal William Fitz Osbern, who perhaps knew something of southern England at first hand, as his brother Osbern Fitz Osbern already held an ecclesiastical post in Sussex, being Dean of Bosham, together with an estate in Cornwall[1]. The appeal for volunteers soon brought adventurous spirits from all

---

[1] *Domesday* I, 17 a. Boseham; 121 b. Stratone.

quarters to William's standard. The largest number are said to have
come from Brittany, led by Brian and Alan of Penthièvre; but the
number of Flemings was almost as great. There were also strong contingents from Artois and Picardy, while Eustace of Boulogne, who had
a long-standing feud with the house of Godwin, offered his services in
person. On the other hand very little help came from Maine or Anjou,
and only a handful of knights from more distant parts, such as Champagne, Poitou, or Apulia. One would fain know the total number of
William's host, but as usual the figures given by the chroniclers are
merely rhetorical. Several considerations, however, strictly limit the possible numbers. In the first place, we can be sure that the Norman contingents outnumbered the auxiliaries from other parts. But, as we have
already seen, it is very unlikely that Normandy at this time could put more
than 1200 knights into the field. Again, the Bayeux poet Wace, who
describes the expedition in great detail in *Roman de Rou,* a metrical
chronicle written about 1172, states that his father had told him that
the number of transports of all kinds was not quite seven hundred; and,
as the Bayeux tapestry testifies, the largest of these were only open barges,
with one square sail, not capable of holding more than a dozen horses,
while the majority were still smaller and less capacious[1]. It seems then
that the most plausible number we can assume for William's army is
somewhere round about 5000 men. Somewhere about 2000 of these were
probably fully-equipped knights with trained horses, of whom about 1200
hailed from Normandy and about 800 from other districts, while the
remaining 3000 men would be made up by contingents of footmen and
archers and the crews who manned the ships. In that age, however, even
5000 men were an almost fabulously large force to collect and keep
embodied for any length of time, nor were there any precedents for
attempting to transport a large body of cavalry across the sea. No viking
leaders had ever done that. Their fleets had only carried warriors, and
their first operation after landing had always been to seize horses from
the invaded territory. William's knights, on the contrary, must have
their own trained horses; and so William had to provide for bringing
over at least 2500 horses in addition to his men, and this too in small
open boats which were unable to beat to windward; nor could he reckon
on any docking accommodation, either for embarking or disembarking
them. The mere crossing of the Channel, then, would be a remarkable
and very novel feat; and if the weather turned stormy or the tide were
missed, a very hazardous one. Nothing indeed brings out the duke's
prestige so plainly as the fact that he was able to persuade his followers
to take so tremendous a risk. By harvest time, as arranged, his preparations were fairly complete, and the contingents from western Normandy

[1] The reasonableness of Wace's figure is strikingly illustrated by William of
Malmesbury's statement that in 1142 the Earl of Gloucester used 52 ships to transport some 360 knights from Cherbourg to Wareham.

and Brittany lay ready with their transports at the mouth of the Dives[1]. There they remained windbound for four weeks, and it was only in the middle of September that they were able to move eastwards to Saint-Valery in the estuary of the Somme and join the contingents from eastern Normandy and Picardy. At Saint-Valery the invaders were about 60 miles as the crow flies from the Sussex coast, instead of about 105 miles as they would have been had they started from the Dives; but still there was no sign of a fair wind for England, and whispers began to spread that William's luck had deserted him.

Meantime, events were taking place in England which greatly improved William's chances. All through the summer Harold had kept both men and ships in readiness on the south coast for William's coming. But when September came the men insisted on going to their homes to see after the harvest. Scarcely, however, had they disbanded, when Harold received the unwelcome tidings that his exiled brother Tostig in alliance with Harold Hardrada, the great warrior-King of Norway, had entered the Humber with a large fleet and was threatening York. Harold at once got together his house-carls and such other men as he could lay hands on, and started to cover the 200 miles between London and York by forced marches to succour the Yorkshiremen. Before he reached Tadcaster, news arrived that the Earls Edwin and Morkere had been defeated at Fulford outside York, that the city had submitted, and that the invaders had moved off eastwards to plunder Harold's own manor of Catton by Stamford Bridge on the Derwent[2]. Harold accordingly marched past York and fell on the invaders by surprise. A long and desperate fight ensued, in which both Harold Hardrada and Tostig were killed, while only a remnant of their men survived to regain their ships and betake themselves home. This splendid victory was gained on Monday, 25 September, and at any other time would have made Harold's position secure. Almost at the same time William at Saint-Valery, in total ignorance of what Harold was doing, was organising processions of relics to intercede for more favourable weather. In most years equinoctial gales might have been expected, but suddenly fate smiled upon him. The weather became fine, the wind veered round to the right quarter, and on Thursday, 28 September, he was able to embark all his men and horses. By nightfall all was ready, but he still had to wait for the tide. The actual start was not made till near midnight, William leading the way with a lantern at his mast-head in the Mora, a fast-sailing craft which had been specially fitted out for him by his wife. The probable intention was to land near Winchelsea in the great manor of Brede (Rameslie), which for over 40 years had been in the possession of the monks of

[1] William of Poitiers states that the whole armament was first assembled at the Dives. It would, however, have been senseless to bring the eastern contingents so far west, only to lengthen the crossing.

[2] *Domesday* i, 305a. Cattune.

Fécamp by the gift of Knut and Emma[1]. The wind and tide, however, carried the flotilla farther to the west, and in the morning William found himself off the small haven of Pevensey, with no obstacle to bar his entrance. Pevensey itself at this time was a small borough of 52 burgesses[2]; but they could only look on helplessly while William's transports were one by one beached and unloaded. Once safe ashore, no time was lost in moving eastwards to the larger borough of Hastings, where orders were immediately given for the building of a castle.

On the news of William's landing being brought to York, Harold at once rode south to London to collect fresh forces, leaving Edwin and Morkere to follow. Many of his best house-carls had fallen at Stamford Bridge, but a very powerful force of thegns could soon have been mustered from the shires south of the Welland and Avon if only Harold would have played a waiting game. He was, however, in no mood to remain on the defensive. He had just won a magnificent victory, and it seemed to him a cowardly plan merely to stand by and let the invaders overrun his native Sussex without hindrance. He therefore, after a few days' halt, set out again, having with him only such levies as had hastily come in from the districts nearest London. Passing through the Weald, he led his forces towards Crowhurst and Whatlington, two villages lying northwest of Hastings[3], which had formed part of his personal estates before he became Earl of Wessex, and on 13 October, the eve of St Calixtus, he encamped on an open ridge of down which lay midway between his two properties some six miles from the sea. Early next day William, eager to attack, marshalled his army near the high ground of Telham, two miles away, and then advanced in three divisions having the Breton contingents, say 1000 men, on the left, the Flemings and Frenchmen, say 1000 men, on the right, and the Normans, say 2400 men, in the centre. A slight valley intervened between the two armies, and across it William could see Harold's forces posted in close formation several ranks deep along the crest of the ridge, having a front of perhaps 500 yards. The English in accordance with their national custom were all on foot, the house-carls and thegns being armed with two-handed axes and kite-shaped shields. Some of Harold's men, however, were just peasants, armed only with javelins and stone-tipped clubs. The whole body probably outnumbered the invaders, but Harold knew that he was at a great disadvantage in having very few archers, and no mounted troops to match William's 2000 horsemen. He consequently gave his men orders to stand strictly on the defensive, and on no account to leave their position, which was one of advantage, as the enemy would have to attack up a fairly

[1] *Domesday* I, 17 a. Rameslie. Cf. also Haskins, EHR, Vol. xxxii (1918), p. 342.

[2] *Domesday* I, 20 b. Pevensel.

[3] *Domesday* I, 18 b. Crohest, Watlingetone.

steep slope, whether in front or on the flanks[1]. William's men, undeterred by that, came on steadily, the front ranks in each division being made up of archers and cross-bowmen, followed by lines of heavily-armed footmen (*loricati*), while the knights brought up the rear. For some hours all attempts to storm the hill were in vain, and at one moment William had great difficulty in preventing the Bretons from retreating in a panic. At last, however, by the stratagem of a feigned flight on the right, a number of the English were induced to rush down the hill in pursuit, whereupon the Norman knights wheeled their horses round, and easily cut them to pieces. This gave the opening which William was looking for. Renewing the attack, slowly but surely the Norman knights pressed back the depleted English shield-wall, until at last Harold was mortally wounded by an arrow in his eye. For a space some leading thegns still held out round the king's dragon standard; but one by one they too were hewn down, so that by nightfall the English army was reduced to a mere leaderless rabble which scattered and fled into the woods. The disaster to Harold's cause was complete. The deaths of his brothers, Earls Gyrth and Leofwin, together with the slaughter of so many leading men, made it impossible for the supporters of the house of Godwin in eastern Wessex to make another stand. Duke William, on the other hand, was too cautious to press on quickly; and it was not till five days after his victory that he set out from Hastings to get possession of Canterbury, moving by Romney and Dover. Meantime, in London, the leaders of the English Church, headed by Stigand, acting in co-operation with the chief landowners of the Midlands and the Eastern counties under the guidance of Aesgar the Staller, the leading magnate in Essex, declared for setting Edgar the Aetheling on the throne. In this decision Edwin and Morkere outwardly acquiesced; but secretly the two earls were intriguing to prevent the crowning of the young prince—he was hardly yet seventeen, it would seem—and they soon retired to their estates without summoning their men to fight for him. Once more it was clearly shewn that the English race had as yet developed no true national feeling. Perhaps what the earls hoped for was a partition of the kingdom between themselves and William, the duke contenting himself with Wessex. While still at Canterbury, the news was brought to William that Queen Edith and the men of Winchester were prepared to recognise him. This made it safer for him to advance on London; but before actually attacking the city, he thought it more politic to secure as strong a foothold as possible south of the Thames. He therefore marched past Southwark and Kingston and up the Thames valley, harrying a wide belt of country, until he came to the borough of Wallingford, at that time the chief place in Berkshire. Crossing the Thames at this point, he doubled back eastwards to Berkhampstead in Hertfordshire, so as to threaten London

---

[1] Freeman's view, that the English line was protected by a palisade, has been strenuously contested by Mr Round, and seems quite untenable.

from the north-west and cut it off from possible succour from the Midlands. As Edwin and Morkere still remained inactive, the magnates in London decided that armed resistance was hopeless. They accordingly went to meet William, and made their submission, the king-elect, Edgar the Aetheling, being one of the party. The Norman forces thereupon advanced unopposed to London; and on Christmas Day 1066 William, like Harold only a year before, was hallowed King of the English in Edward's new church at Westminster by Ealdred the Archbishop of York, Stigand of Canterbury's services being refused, on the ground that he had received his pallium from an anti-Pope.

When once William had been crowned with the traditional rites, his attitude towards those who had submitted to him necessarily changed from that of an invader bent on promoting terror and havoc to that of a lawful sovereign anxious to stand well in the eyes of his new subjects and eager to give them as good peace as he had already given to Normandy. Nevertheless, William was faced with a dilemma; for he could not safely allow his new dominions to remain without a Norman garrison, or risk offending the soldiery to whom he owed his triumph by disappointing them of their promised rewards. To feel secure he had to allot extensive estates to his chief followers, which they, in their turn, could deal out to their retainers, and also build castles up and down the land for their protection. As he surveyed his position, however, after the coronation, William might well think that he had gained sufficient territory to reward his men lavishly. The area acknowledging his authority was already much larger than Normandy, and it included a considerable proportion of the most fertile and best populated parts of the country. It comprised, moreover, the estates of nearly all those who had actually fought against him, including a large proportion of the estates of the house of Godwin; and all these he could legitimately regard as confiscated for treason and available for distribution. The areas, too, which had not as yet actively opposed him, such as West Wessex, North Mercia, and Northumbria, might well submit voluntarily if given more time. He therefore decided to adopt a waiting policy, and to direct his immediate efforts to organising the south-eastern half of the country, giving out at the same time that the English laws and customs would be maintained, and that even those who had helped to set up Edgar the Aetheling might make their peace by paying suitable fines and providing hostages. In Essex and East Anglia there was really little doubt that leniency would be the best policy, as William knew that several of the leading landowners, such as the Bishop of London, the Abbot of Bury St Edmunds, Ralf the Staller, and Robert son of Wimarc, were definitely on his side, being men of French extraction who had been installed and promoted by King Edward. The policy of waiting, however, quickly bore fruit in the Midlands as well, and before long many of the leading Mercians, headed by Edwin and Morkere, betook themselves to William's court at Barking and did him homage. The two earls, in fact, as they had not fought against William, were well received and confirmed in all their possessions on the condition that they remained in his company. Meanwhile castle-building and the assignment of confiscated lands to Normans were pressed on steadily, and by March William felt himself sufficiently secure to risk a visit to Normandy, for the double purpose of making a triumphal progress through the duchy and of impressing his continental neighbours. To grace his triumph he took with him Edgar the Aetheling, Archbishop Stigand, Earl Edwin, Earl Morkere, Earl Waltheof, and many other leading Englishmen, and also a great quantity of gold and silver and plate and jewels, seized from the conquered districts, for distribution as a thank-offering among the churches of Normandy. In England he left the direction of affairs in the hands of his half-brother, Odo, Bishop of Bayeux, and of his seneschal William Fitz Osbern, the former having his head-quarters in Kent and Essex, and the latter apparently in Hampshire and the Isle of Wight, together with the custody of more distant strongholds in Gloucestershire and Herefordshire. For eight months these two governed as joint-regents; and if they did not foster, at any rate they did little to repress, the rapacity and licence of the rank and file of the intending settlers. No serious risings of the English, however, occurred, the only disturbance of note being an unsuccessful attempt made by Eustace of Boulogne, helped by the men of Kent, to oust Odo of Bayeux from Dover, a stronghold which the count claimed ought to have been entrusted to him and not to the bishop.

In December 1067 William returned from Normandy, and soon realised that the remoter shires were not going to submit to his authority without compulsion. To begin with, Harold's mother, Gytha, was still holding out in western Wessex; and though the men of Somerset had apparently by this time deserted her cause, it required a march by William in person to Exeter, and an eighteen days' siege of the borough, before the men of Devon and Cornwall would come to terms with him. Then, soon after Whitsuntide 1068, came the news that Edwin and Morkere, disgusted at the slights put upon them, had broken into revolt, that Edgar the Aetheling with his sisters had set out for the north, and that Gospatric, who had been recognised by William as Earl of Bernicia, was inclined to set Edgar up as king. William, thus challenged, at once marched his forces into Yorkshire. The rapidity of his movements and the prompt building of castles at Warwick, Nottingham, and York, quickly cowed Edwin and Morkere into renewing their allegiance; but Edgar and Gospatric took refuge at the court of Malcolm Canmore, the King of Scots (1054–1092), who received them honourably. William himself did not go beyond York, but turned south again, and spent the autumn in erecting castles at Lincoln, Huntingdon, and Cambridge. Being determined, however, to get a footing in the north, he offered the earldom of Bernicia to one of his Flemish followers, Robert of Commines, and sent him early in 1069 with a force of 500 horsemen to Durham. This move ended in disaster, for the Northumbrians at once rose and massacred Commines and his men; whereupon Edgar, helped by Earl Waltheof, reappeared in Yorkshire and laid siege to William's forces in York. Once more William hastened to York and gave orders for a second castle to be built there. But even so the Yorkshiremen were only temporarily quelled, and soon took heart again on hearing that Svein Estrithson of Denmark was at last fitting out an army to enforce his claim to the English crown as Knut's heir. The Danish expedition set out in August 1068, and after ineffective attacks on Kent and East Anglia, joined forces with Edgar the Aetheling in the Humber. The fall of York followed towards the end of September, Waltheof taking a prominent part in the attack. For a moment the situation looked serious; for a revolt was also in progress in Shropshire and Staffordshire led by a thegn named Eadric the Wild, while only a month or two earlier some of Harold's illegitimate sons, sailing from Dublin, had effected a landing near Barnstaple in Devon. There was, however, no real co-operation between William's enemies, and the crisis soon passed away. Leaving the Bishop of Coutances and Brian of Penthièvre to deal with the danger in the south, William himself marched upon Stafford, scattering the rebels before him, and then into Yorkshire, at the same time sending detachments into Lindsey under the Counts of Mortain and Eu. South of the Humber these leaders were successful in capturing several parties of Danes, but William himself was held up at the river Aire by floods for over three weeks. His mere proximity, however, demoralised the Danes; and when at last he renewed his advance, he found that the main body had evacuated York and retreated to their ships. The way was thus cleared for William to punish the Yorkshiremen. Thrice they had defied him, and he was determined that it should never occur again. He therefore gave orders that the country from the Humber to the Tyne should be systematically devastated. For several weeks the cruel work went on, the villages one after the other being burnt, while the inhabitants and cattle were either killed or driven away. As a result, the whole of the diocese of York, stretching from the North Sea to the Irish Channel, became so depopulated that even twenty years later the greater part of it still remained an uncultivated waste. Nothing in William's career has so blackened his reputation as this barbarous action; but it led quickly to Gospatric and Waltheof's submission, and at any rate freed the Normans from all further danger. In 1070 Cheshire and Shropshire were both overcome without any serious fighting, and by March William was back at Salisbury and able to disband his forces. After that, only one more rising of the English is reported. This was led by Hereward, a petty Lincolnshire landowner, and was no more than a forlorn hope, provoked by the arrival of the Danish fleet in the fenlands surrounding Ely. The Danes indeed effected little beyond the sack of Peterborough, but Hereward held out in the

Isle of Ely for over a year. The fall of his stronghold marks the completion of the Conquest. By the close of 1071, William was in full possession of every English shire; Earl Edwin was dead, Earl Morkere a prisoner, and Edgar the Aetheling was once more a fugitive in Scotland.

Having followed in outline the five years' struggle by which William gradually obtained full mastery over his kingdom, it is time to turn to the measures which he took for its reorganisation and government. At the outset, as we have seen, it was by no means his intention to make many sweeping changes. He claimed to be Edward's lawful heir, and from the first he gave out that it was his will that "all men should have and hold Edward's law." Such surviving writs and charters as date from the years 1067 and 1068 shew that at first he acted partly through Englishmen, while to some extent he even seems to have employed the English local levies in his military operations. The prolonged resistance, however, which he encountered in so many districts, inevitably led the Conqueror to change this policy, and gave him an excuse for treating all the greater English laymen as suspected, if not active, rebels and for confiscating their estates. He thus by degrees seized nearly all the best land, with the exception of the broad estates owned by the Church and the monasteries, and was able to reward his leading fighting-men not merely handsomely, but with fiefs often ten or even twenty times as valuable as the lands they possessed across the Channel. And even so he by no means exhausted the land at his disposal, but was able to retain for himself far more and far better distributed crown-lands than had been enjoyed by any English king before him. He was able further to set aside a sufficient amount of land to provide wages or maintenance for some hundreds of minor officials and domestic retainers, such as chaplains, clerks, physicians, chamberlains, cooks, barbers, bailiffs, foresters, falconers, huntsmen, and so forth, whom he employed about his person or on his wide-spread estates, or whose past services had entitled them to either pensions or charity.

The process by which the conquered land was parcelled out into fiefs for William's fighting-men can unfortunately only be surmised; for no documents have survived, if any ever existed, recording his grants or the terms on which they were made. The outcome of the process on the other hand is very completely set before us, as the resulting fiefs, or "baronies" to use the technical French term which now came into use, are all described in minute detail in the "book of Winchester," the unique land-register, soon nicknamed "Domesdei," which the Conqueror ordered to be drawn up in 1086. This wonderful survey, which we know as Domesday Book, covers the whole kingdom with the exception of the four northern counties and a few towns, London and Winchester being unfortunately among the omissions. Internal evidence shews that the survey was made by sending several bands of commissioners on circuit through the shires, who convened the shire-moots and got the information they required from local juries, containing both Normans and Englishmen, drawn from each hundred. The resulting returns, which are set out in Domesday Book county by county and fief by fief, are clearly answers to a definite schedule of questions which were put to the juries, and which were designed to elicit how many distinct properties, or "manors" as the Normans termed them, there were in each hundred, by whom they had formerly been held in King Edward's day, and to whom they had been allotted, how far they were sufficiently stocked with peasantry and plough-oxen, and what was estimated to be their annual value to their possessors, both before the Conquest and at the date when the survey was made.

Particulars were also called for, which enable us to ascertain the categories into which the peasantry were divided, the distribution of wood, meadow, and pasture, and the amount of taxation to which each manor was liable in the event of the king levying a Danegeld. Unfortunately the clerks who compiled the record in its final shape at Winchester, and re-arranged the returns by fiefs instead of as originally by hundreds and villages, were not directed to summarise the information collected about each fief; and so the survey contains no totals either of area or value for the different fiefs by which they can be conveniently compared and contrasted one with another. With patience, however, such totals can be approximately worked out, and sufficiently accurate statistics compiled to shew relatively how much of England William reserved for himself and his personal dependants, how much he left in the hands of the prelates and monastic houses, and how much he assigned to the various lay baronies which he created to reward the soldiery by whose help he had effected the Conquest. In making such calculations, however, it is not so much the acreage or extent of any given fief which it is important to find out as its total annual value. Any wide-spread estate, of course, gave importance to its possessor from a political point of view; but in the eleventh century, just as to-day, acreage was only of subsidiary importance, and the effective power of most of the landed magnates at bottom depended, not on the area but on the fertility and populousness of their manors and on the revenue which could be obtained from them either in money or in kind. It is in fact as often as not misleading to count up the number of the manors on different fiefs, as some commentators on Domesday Book have done, and contrast, for example, the seven hundred and ninety-three manors allotted to the Count of Mortain with the four hundred and thirty-nine manors allotted to the Bishop of Bayeux, or both with, say, the hundred and sixty-two manors allotted to William Peverel. For "manors" or holdings were of every conceivable extent and variety, just as estates are to-day, and might vary from petty farms worth only a few shillings a year, in the currency of those times, to lordly complexes of land stretching over dozens of villages and worth not infrequently as much as £100 a year or more. Even neighbouring manors of similar acreage might vary enormously in value in proportion as they were well or badly stocked with husbandmen and cattle; while in some parts of England whole districts remained throughout William's reign so badly devastated that to own them was far more of a liability than an advantage, in view of the large expenditure required for reinstatement.

To take a leading example, Hugh, the *Vicomte* of Avranches, was allotted almost the whole of Cheshire with the title of Earl, a wide territory which in later centuries gave considerable importance to his successors; but in Hugh's day (1071–1101) the revenue which could be derived from all the manors in Cheshire put together was estimated to be little more than £200 a year. In Middlesex on the other hand the single manor of Isleworth was estimated to be worth £72 a year in 1086 and the manors of Fulham and Harrow £40 and £56 a year respectively; nor were manors such as these by any means the most valuable which then existed in fertile and populous parts of England. It seems clear then that the *Vicomte* of Avranches did not derive his undoubted importance and power in England so much from his Cheshire estates, in spite of their extent, as from other far better stocked manors which William allotted to him in Lincolnshire (£272), Suffolk (£115), Oxfordshire (£70), and elsewhere, which were together worth over £700 a year, and without which he and his retainers could hardly have supported the expense of defending the marches of Cheshire against the tribesmen of North Wales.

Let us take then the estimated annual value put upon the various manors and estates by the Domesday juries in 1086 as the most illuminating basis of calculation open to us. If this is done, it will be found, after a reasonable allowance has been made for ambiguous entries and entries where the value has been inadvertently omitted by the scribes who wrote out the final revision, that the total revenue in the money of the period of the rural properties dealt with in the survey, but exclusive of the revenue arising from the towns, may be thought of in round figures as about £73,000 a year.

To this total the ten shires of Wessex south of the Thames contributed about £32,000, the three East Anglian shires about £12,950, the eight West Mercian shires about £11,000, the seven shires of the Southern Danelaw lying between the Thames and the Welland about £9400, the northern Danelaw between the Welland and the Humber about £6450, and finally the devastated lands of Yorkshire and Lancashire about £1200. If it were possible to ascertain the corresponding values at the date when the estates first came into the hands of their new owners, the figures would in each case be much smaller; but though there are some returns in Domesday which give the values "when the lands were received," these are far too fragmentary to furnish the data necessary for calculating such general totals. To make up totals from averages is all that could be done for the earlier date, which would be unsatisfactory;

and, after all, the values for 1086 are perhaps more to our purpose, as they indicate better the potentialities of income to which the new landowners could look forward in 1070, however much for the moment the country-side had been impoverished by the fighting in the previous four years.

Reckoning then that the income from land which the Conqueror had at his disposal, exclusive of the rents and other profits of the boroughs, was potentially about £73,000 a year, Domesday Book, when further analysed, shews that the distribution of this sum resulting from the king's grants for the five main purposes for which he had to provide was roughly as follows: (*a*) £17,650 a year for the support of the Crown and royal house, including in that category himself, his queen, his two half-brothers, and King Edward's widow; (*b*) £1800 a year for the remuneration of his minor officials and personal servants, later known as the King's Serjeants; (*c*) £19,200 a year for the support of the Church and monastic bodies; (*d*) £4000 a year for the maintenance of some dozen pre-Conquest land-owners and their men, such as Ralf the Staller, Robert son of Wimarc, Alured of Marlborough, Colswegen of Lincoln, and Thurkil of Arden, who for one reason or another had retained his favour; and (*e*) £30,350 a year for the provision of some 170 baronies, some great and some small, for the leading captains, Norman, French, Breton, and Flemish, and their retainers, who had risked their lives and fortunes in the great adventure of conquering England.

The figures just given, though of course they only claim to be approximately accurate, are of great interest, revealing as they do that William retained nearly a quarter of the income of the kingdom from land for the use of the royal house, and that he assigned little more than two-fifths of the total for rewarding the chiefs of the great families who had fought for him, and their military and other followers. Even if the two fiefs, worth together about £5050 a year, which William assigned to his half-brothers, the Bishop of Bayeux and the Count of Mortain, be reckoned to the share of the baronage rather than to the share of the Crown, the income allotted for baronial fiefs must still be thought of as considerably less than half the total income of the estates in the kingdom. With these two fiefs deducted, the share of the Crown may be thought of as about £12,600 a year; but as some £1600 a year of this was assigned to Queen Edith and her retainers for her life, William and Matilda's potential income from their manors before 1076 was roughly £11,000 a year. Even this smaller figure is about twice the amount of the Crown's revenue in King Edward's day as estimated by the Domesday juries. The estates, too, retained by the Conqueror for the Crown were more evenly distributed over the kingdom than Edward's estates had been, so that the power of the Crown in many districts was much increased. In the last years of his reign Edward had possessed no manors in Middlesex, Hertfordshire, Essex, Lincolnshire, Rutland, Cheshire, or Cornwall, and comparatively few in Norfolk, Suffolk, and Yorkshire. As arranged by William, the

Crown had a substantial share everywhere except in Sussex and in the three counties along the Welsh border, in which districts he parted with all the old Crown manors and erected marcher fiefs of a special kind, apparently for military reasons. The ultimate increase in the revenue of the Crown from land was not, however, solely due to a retention of a larger number of manors for the royal use, but arose partly from raising the rents at which the manors were let to farm to the sheriffs and other reeves, who took charge of them as speculative ventures and recouped themselves in their turn by raising the dues and increasing the services exacted from the cultivating peasantry. To what extent these augmented rents were justifiable or oppressive we cannot tell; but Domesday often records a thirty, and sometimes a fifty, per cent. rise above the estimated values of King Edward's day, and in not a few instances the remark is added that the cultivators could not bear these increased burdens.

Turning from the Crown to the Church, let us next analyse the revenue of about £19,200 a year set aside for the support of the various classes of the clergy. This substantial sum is made up of four items as follows: (*a*) £8000 a year assigned for the maintenance of the secular clergy, that is to say of the fifteen bishoprics and of the houses of secular canons, some thirty in number, but exclusive of the endowments of the parochial clergy; (*b*) £9200 a year appropriated to some forty monasteries for men; (*c*) £1200 a year appropriated to some ten nunneries; and (*d*) £800 a year appropriated, by the gift of either Edward or William, to Norman and other foreign monasteries.

In one sense of course very little of this revenue can be said to have been assigned to the Church by William, for the greater proportion of the manors which produced it had long been devoted to religious purposes. The Conqueror, however, as a matter of policy acted on the principle that not even the oldest grants to the Church were valid until he had re-confirmed them. As a result, the Church suffered not a few losses; but she was at the same time recouped by many new grants of great value, and on the whole gained considerably. In particular, the poorly-endowed sees of the Danelaw acquired a great increase of temporalities. In some cases, however, such new acquisitions seem to have been purchased. The see of Canterbury, as might be expected, enjoyed the wealthiest fief, with a revenue of about £1750 a year, the see of Winchester coming second with a revenue of over £1000 a year. In general, however, the greater monasteries controlled more valuable fiefs than the lesser bishops. The seven richest houses, that is to say, Glastonbury (£840), Ely (£790), St Edmund's Bury (£655), the old Minster at Winchester (£640), Christchurch at Canterbury (£635), St Augustine's (£635), and Westminster (£600), were assigned between them a revenue of nearly £4800 a year, whereas the ten poorer bishoprics had less than £3000 a year between them. The see of Selsey for example had even in 1086 only a revenue of £138 a year, and the see of Chester even less. It is true the secular clergy had other sources

of revenue besides their manorial incomes; but none the less it remains one
of the most outstanding features of the society of the day that the monks
and nuns, who can hardly have numbered all told a thousand individuals,
should have had control of so large a share of the rental of England.

Having provided for himself, his half-brothers, his personal servants,
and the Church, William still had an income of over £34,000 a year from
land at his disposal. Some £4000 of this, as already noted, was either
restored to or bestowed on favoured Englishmen and their retainers; but
these doles were on too small a scale to affect the general character of the
Conquest settlement, and so they need not detain us. It is, however, interesting to observe that Archbishop Stigand occupied an important place
in this category; for he appears in Domesday as having held till his death
a personal barony worth some £800 a year in addition to his immense
Church preferments, and so as a landowner he ranked with the wealthiest
of the barons. Let us pass on then and consider the general body of the
military fiefs, the "baronies" or "honours" as the Normans termed them,
which were created to reward the invading armies, and which form one of
the corner-stones of the English social system for some three centuries. It
is here that the Domesday evidence is particularly welcome, the evidence
of the historical writers being for the most part vague, and limited to too
few fiefs to give a true picture. Domesday on the other hand enables us
to analyse and compare all the fiefs, and shews that there were at least one
hundred and seventy baronies, without counting as such the petty fiefs
held directly of the Crown with incomes of less than £10 a year, which
were also numerous but only of subsidiary importance.

As with the "manors," the first thing to note about the "baronies"
is that they were of many different types and varied not only in size and
value, but in compactness and to some extent in the conditions of tenure
under which they held. What a contrast one barony might be to another
can best be seen from the fact that the list of baronies comprises fiefs of
all grades, starting from quite modest estates producing incomes of only
£15 a year or less and gradually advancing in stateliness up to two
princely fiefs with revenues of about £1750 a year each. Another characteristic is that there were no well-marked groups in the list corresponding to definite grades of rank; nor is there any indication that the
Conqueror distributed his rewards in accordance with any pre-arranged
scheme. A clear idea of the nature of his distribution, however, can only
be gained by attempting some classification; and so it will be well to
divide the baronies arbitrarily into the five following groups: Class A,
containing baronies valued at over £750 a year each; Class B, containing baronies having revenues between £650 and £400 a year; Class C,
containing baronies having revenues between £400 and £200 a year;
Class D, containing baronies with revenues between £200 and £100 a
year; and Class E, containing baronies valued at less than £100 a year.

Working on these lines, Domesday enables us to say that in Class A there were eight baronies, having an aggregate of about £9000 a year; in Class B ten baronies, with revenues aggregating about £5000 a year; in Class C twenty-four, with revenues aggregating about £7000 a year; in Class D thirty-six; and in Class E between ninety and one hundred. The two wealthiest baronies were those assigned to William Fitz Osbern and Roger of Montgomery; and next in order came the fiefs allotted respectively to William of Warenne, Hugh of Avranches, Eustace of Boulogne, Richard of Clare, Geoffrey Bishop of Coutances, and Geoffrey de Mandeville. In Class B the richest fief was that assigned to Robert Malet, and several other famous names figure in it, such as Ferrers, Bigod, Giffard, Braiose, Crispin, and Taillebois; but it is not till Class C is reached that we come to the equally famous names of Peverel, Lacy, Montfort, Toeni, Mortimer, and Vere, and only at the very bottom of Class C that we find Beaumont and Beauchamp. It remains to be said that if we insert the English survivors into these classes, Ralf the Staller and Stigand take rank in Class A, Earl Waltheof in Class B, and Robert son of Wimarc in Class C. Similarly as regards the bishoprics. The sees of Canterbury and Winchester, both be it noted held by Stigand, are the only sees which rank in wealth with the first class of baronies. The sees of London (£615), Dorchester (£600), Salisbury (£600), Worcester (£480), and Thetford (£420) rank with the second class; the sees of Exeter (£360), Wells (£325), York (£370), Hereford (£280), Rochester (£220), and Durham (£205) with the third, Chichester (£138) with the fourth, and Chester (£85) with the fifth. York and Durham, however, are not fully accounted for in Domesday, and so possibly these sees should be reckoned as baronies of the second class.

The spoils of victory being thus parcelled out, we must next inquire under what conditions of tenure the baronies were held. On this point the Domesday survey is unfortunately silent, no questions as to tenure being put to the hundred juries, and so we have to fall back on inferences drawn from the conditions of tenure found in force in England a generation or two later, supplemented by the few vague hints which can be gleaned here and there from monastic chronicles. There can, however, be hardly any doubt that William from the outset insisted that the baronies should be held on the same conditions of tenure as the baronies in Normandy, nor can the barons themselves have desired to hold by any tenure other than the one they were accustomed to and understood. This means that the English methods of land-tenure were not adopted, and that the barons obtained their fiefs on the four conditions of (*a*) doing homage to the king and swearing fealty, (*b*) providing definite quotas of fully-equipped knights, if summoned, to serve in the king's army for 40 days in the year at their own cost, (*c*) attending the king's court when summoned to give advice and assist the king in deciding causes, and (*d*) aiding the king with money on the happening of certain events.

CH. XV.

If these obligations were not sufficiently performed, it was recognised that the baronies were liable to be forfeited. As to the rules of succession, it was recognised that no baron had any power to dispose of his barony or any part of it by will. If a baron died leaving no heirs, the barony escheated, that is, fell back to the Crown. If there were male heirs it descended to them, subject to the payment of a relief to the Crown; but already there was a tendency for the king to claim that fiefs were indivisible and to insist on enforcing a rule of primogeniture. If there were only female heirs, the fief was partitioned amongst them provided the king did not interfere. If the heirs were minors, the king had the right of guardianship, and in the case of female heirs the right of bestowing them in marriage. A further question, about which there has been a good deal of discussion, is how were the quotas of knights to be provided fixed for each barony. There has been a tendency to suppose that the number of knights demanded must have borne some fixed relation either to the size or to the value of the barony. All the evidence, however, tends to prove that in this matter there was much caprice and no uniformity, and it seems probable that the king was able to fix the amount of military service arbitrarily when the baronies were created, and perhaps solely in accordance with his personal estimation of the merits of the various barons. As a result the quotas which he imposed, the *servitium debitum* as it was called, were for most baronies a round number of knights—5, 10, 15, 20, 40, 60, and so on, the feudal armies being organised on a basis of constabularies of ten knights. Quotas of forty or more knights were imposed on most of the baronies having revenues of over £200 a year; quotas of between twenty and forty knights on most of the baronies having revenues of between £200 and £100 a year. It appears, however, that several of the poorer baronies had to find comparatively large quotas, and on the whole the burden of knights' service was lightest for the richer baronies. It is certainly curious that William was satisfied with such small quotas, for the system is only designed to produce a force of some 4200 knights. He made up his mounted force, however, to 5000 knights by imposing tenure by knights' service on all the bishoprics and on a number of the richer abbeys, and he evidently regarded these selected ecclesiastical fiefs in many respects as baronies. One more matter requires elucidation. It is commonly supposed that there was a castle at the head of each barony, but at any rate in William's day this was not the case. It is true that William himself ordered many castles to be built, but these were on his own estates; it is also true that many castles were erected by William Fitz Osbern, Roger of Montgomery, and Hugh of Avranches, the three barons with special powers put in charge of the Welsh marches; but elsewhere William insisted that no castles should be built without his licence. A small number of barons only were accorded this special mark of favour, and those who obtained it were not always the barons with the largest fiefs. Most of the barons, it would seem, far from having castles of their own, were saddled on the contrary with the obligation of finding garrisons for the royal castles, a service that came to be known as "castle-guard."

Having set out the baronies and defined their military liabilities and conditions of tenure, William to all appearances left each baron full discretion to deal with his barony as he liked. The various manors composing it were handed over as going concerns with the peasantry living upon them, and each baron selected for himself which manors he would keep as demesnes for himself and which he would sub-enfeof. The king did not even insist that enough knights should be enfeoffed to perform the *servitium debitum* of the barony. If the barons preferred it, they had full liberty to farm out their lands to non-military tenants, who held not by knights' service but by the tenure known as "socage," that is to say, by the payment of rents in kind or in money, together with some light agricultural services. It thus came about that, though the baronies in their entirety were held by knights' service, only a portion of the lands which they comprised were actually held by military tenants. It must not be supposed, either, that when subtenancies were created the barons only gave them to their kinsmen or retainers from overseas. The returns in Domesday shew clearly that on all baronies many men were granted subtenancies who were of English descent, and some of these undoubtedly held their lands by knights' service subject to the same conditions as their Norman neighbours. As to the peasant classes, it was not to the interest of either the barons or their subvassals to expropriate them to any extent. The invaders were few and could not provide a peasantry from their own ranks. Their interest lay in having as numerous a population as possible on their estates, in order that they might obtain increased dues and increased labour services from them, and in time bring more land into cultivation. At the same time the new landlords could see no use in preserving the numerous distinctions which had differentiated the "geneat" from the "gebur" or the "soc-manni" from the "liberi homines." They found it much more convenient to regard the peasantry as all equally bound to the soil and all liable to similar dues. In particular they were hostile to the system of commendation under which some of the cultivating classes had been free to select and change their lords. As a result commendation was entirely swept away, and the men in every manor, whatsoever their social status, became bound to their lords by an hereditary tie. This meant a considerable social revolution, especially in the eastern half of England. To a great extent the freer classes were merged into the less free, absorbed into manors, and compelled to do unfree services. Every lord of a manor was allowed under the new system to maintain a court for his tenantry and could compel them to bring their civil disputes before it, provided tenants of other lords were not involved. The net outcome no doubt was increased exploitation of the peasantry, but at the same time the advent of the new landowners also meant greater activity in farming. When once the turmoil of the Conquest and reallotment of the land was over, the new lords set to work with a will at reinstatement, and they not only, in a few years, restocked the greater proportion of the wasted manors, but are soon found encouraging the assartation of woodlands, the drainage of the fens, the building of mills and churches, and the planting of new urban centres. There were of course black sheep among them, stupid and avaricious men, of whom little good is reported; but such men were hardly typical and, at any rate as long as William lived, they had to keep in the background and curb their passions.

The allotment of the land was perhaps the most complicated and critical task that William had to undertake. At any rate it was the most revolutionary of his measures; for it established in England the cardinal feudal doctrines that all land is held of the king, that all occupiers of land except the king must be tenants either of the king himself or of some lord who holds of the king, that the tie between the lord and his tenants is hereditary, and that the extent of each man's holding and the nature of his tenure determine in the main his civil and political rights. William in fact, whether consciously or not, brought about a reconstruction of society on a new legal basis, and so in a sense turned England into a feudal state. But though this is so, William also took very good care that he himself should not become a feudal king after the pattern of the king in France or the Emperor in Germany. In Normandy he had established his ascendency over the baronage and had shewn how feudalism could be combined with personal government. In England he worked out exactly the same result on a larger scale. Rich and magnificent as were some of the new baronies, he never allowed any of their holders to become petty kings in their own fiefs, to make private war on their neighbours, or to acquire a jurisdiction over their tenants which would entirely exclude his own. To this end he maintained intact the courts of the shire and hundreds, and to some extent the Anglo-Saxon system of police. To this end he created only six or seven earldoms, with strictly curtailed spheres and privileges, and in the rest of England retained all the fiscal rights that had attached to the office in his own hands. To this end he insisted on the rule that all tenants by knights' service owed that service to the king alone and not to the barons from whom they held their knights' fees. To this end he maintained side by side with the new feudal cavalry-force the right to call out the old national infantry levy. Taxation was not feudalised. The obligation on all freeholders to pay "gelds" was maintained as well as the obligation to serve in the "fyrd"; and for both purposes William quickly realised that he must put on record the details of the ancient hidage scheme from which alone each man's liability could be ascertained. Lastly, he never allowed his advisory council to take a definitely feudal shape. As supreme feudal lord he constantly held courts for his immediate tenants; but, the kingdom being large and the tenants widely dispersed, he soon established the practice of summoning only a portion of the tenants to any particular court. As a result the court of barons, the "Curia Regis," as it was called, easily became a very elastic body, very like the old "Witenagemot" in composition, in which the king could take the advice of whom he would, but still need never hamper himself by summoning too many of those who were likely to oppose his wishes. So completely indeed was this principle established, that mere gatherings of the king's household officers, the steward, the butler, the chamberlain, or the constable, reinforced by one or two prelates and perhaps one or two barons of moderate estate, came to be regarded before William died as a sufficient meeting of the "Curia Regis" for all but the most important sorts of business, and the way became cleared for future kings to utilise their feudal court as the chief organ of government, out of which in due time the various departments of state for special purposes were each in turn developed. There were, however, no developments of this nature in William's day. Confident in his own powers and determined to be master in everything, his numerous "writs" shew that he settled nearly every detail himself, and made little use of any subordinates other than the staff of royal chaplains who prepared the writs under the supervision of his chancellor, and the local sheriffs to whom the writs were addressed, who presided in the shire-courts, had charge of the collection of the revenue, and farmed the royal manors. So confident indeed was he, that he frequently employed barons of the third grade as sheriffs; but it is clear that he dismissed them at will, and we never find them in league against him or attempting independent action. Looked at broadly, the outcome of the Conqueror's policy was the establishment of a monarchy of such an absolute type that it could ignore all provincial differences of law and custom; and so William's measures tended to bring about a real unity in the kingdom such as had never been known under the Saxon kings.

One set of deliberate reforms has still to be mentioned. Before the Conquest the English Church organisation was very defective. Synods for promulgating ecclesiastical laws had ceased to be held, nor were there any special ecclesiastical tribunals or any definite system of archdeaconries. The special jurisdiction of the bishops was exercised in the shire and hundred moots, with the result that the enforcement of moral discipline was at the mercy of doomsmen who were ignorant of Canon Law and very possibly themselves offenders. Even the powers of the primate over his suffragans were far from clear; and the two archbishops, instead of working together, were in dispute as to their spheres of jurisdiction. In addition to these defects, there was little zeal shewn anywhere for either discipline or learning. The monasteries had not adopted the Cluniac reforms. Simony, pluralities, and worldliness were everywhere rampant. The authority of the Papacy was only formally admitted, while the primate himself had been uncanonically elected. To continental observers such a state of affairs was intolerable; nor could William as a zealous Churchman, whose expedition had been blessed by the Pope, afford to ignore it. As soon therefore as he felt himself secure, he took the matter up, assisted by three papal legates who arrived in England early in 1070. The first matters taken in hand were the deposition of Stigand and three other bishops, the appointment of Lanfranc, the great Italian scholar and theologian of Bec and Caen and William's trusted friend, to be Archbishop of Canterbury, and the appointment of Thomas, a canon of Bayeux, to the see of York, which had fallen vacant by the death of Archbishop Ealdred. Under these new shepherds the English Church was soon put in better order. One after another, as vacancies occurred, the bishoprics and abbeys were put in charge of carefully selected foreigners. The holding of synods was revived. Monastic discipline was tightened up. Study and learning were encouraged. The canons of cathedrals were made to observe celibacy. Sees, such as Dorchester and Selsey, which had been situated in villages, were removed to populous towns, while everywhere there arose a movement, headed by Lanfranc at Canterbury, for building more magnificent churches. Most far-reaching of all were two reforms introduced in 1072. These were the definite subordination of York to Canterbury, and the creation, as in Normandy, of a distinct set of ecclesiastical courts, the so-called "Courts Christian," in which in future the bishops were to be free to deal with ecclesiastical causes and to receive the fines arising from all matters *contra christianitatem*, unhampered by lay interference. The latter change was perhaps not altogether wise; for it set up rival jurisdictions side by side which sooner or later were bound to come into collision, and also gave an opening for the Papacy, as the source of the Canon Law, to claim the legal sovereignty of the Church in England. These dangers, however, were remote, and William could afford to ignore them, being quite accustomed to such courts in Normandy and confident that he would not fall out with Lanfranc. Nor did he fear the Papacy, not even in the person of Hildebrand, who just at this moment was elected to succeed Alexander II. On the contrary, when in 1080 Gregory VII demanded that he should do fealty as the Pope's vassal, William refused point-blank; nor did he ever admit that anyone but himself had any right to control the English Church. Throughout his reign he not only appointed bishops and abbots at will but also invested them with their spiritualities, and in his determination to be master went so far as to insist that no Pope should be recognised without his leave, that no papal letters should have any force in his dominions until he had approved them, and that none of his officers or barons should be subjected to excommunication without his consent. So uncompromising an attitude naturally led to strained relations between himself and Gregory; but in view of the Conqueror's proved zeal for clerical efficiency, the great Pope never thought it politic to begin an open quarrel.

The events of the last fifteen years of William's career, when once he had brought unity and order into his new dominions, are not of the same interest as the story of the Conquest or even of his early days. Both in England and Normandy men feared to provoke him, and his most serious preoccupations were not at home but with the outside world, especially with the county of Maine, where his claim to exercise over-lordship on behalf of his son Robert entailed the constant hostility not only of the local baronage but also of Fulk le Rechin, the Count of Anjou. Much of his time was accordingly spent in Normandy, English affairs being entrusted as a rule to Lanfranc. His foreign difficulties began in 1069, when Azzo, an Italian marquess who had married a daughter of Count Hugh III, was acclaimed Count of Maine in opposition to the youth-ful Robert. Azzo was really put forward by Geoffrey of Mayenne, William's old antagonist; and he soon went back to Italy, leaving his wife Ger-sindis and a son to carry on the struggle under Geoffrey's protection. For three years William had no time to deal with the revolt, yet Gersindis made little headway, having compromised herself by becoming Geoffrey's mistress, while Geoffrey's own arrogance drove the townsmen of Le Mans, in 1072, to set up a government of their own and to summon Fulk le Rechin to their aid. This popular rising in Le Mans in opposition to the exactions of the neighbouring baronage has an interest as one of the earliest attempts in North France to form a *commune* based on an oath of mutual assistance, but it was really a very ephemeral affair leading to nothing but the occupation of Le Mans by Fulk[1]. In 1072 William himself was occupied partly in Northumberland, where he set up Waltheof as Earl, in place of the half-Scotch Gospatric who had bought the earldom in 1069, and partly in leading his forces into Scot-land against Malcolm Canmore, who had recently married as his second wife Edgar the Aetheling's sister Margaret, and who was harbouring Edgar and other English refugees. Malcolm, realising that his men were no match for Norman knights, retired before them, but came to terms when William reached Abernethy near Perth, and agreed to expel Edgar. At the same time Malcolm did some kind of homage, sufficient at any rate to enable men in after days to boast that William had reasserted the old claim of the English crown to suzerainty over Scotland. This suc-cess left William at last free to attend to Maine, and in 1073 he set out for Le Mans, taking it is said some English levies with him. On this occasion the Norman force advanced from Alençon down the Sarthe valley, and though it met with some resistance at Fresnay and Beaumont from the local *vicomte*, Hubert of Sainte-Suzanne, easily reached Le Mans, only to find that Fulk le Rechin had retired. Once more William had triumphed; but the successes of 1072 and 1073 were not really con-clusive. Neither Malcolm nor the men of Maine nor the Count of Anjou

---

[1] Le Mans was, even in 1100, economically little more than a market town. Cf. EHR, Vol. xxvi (1911), p. 566.

were cowed, and all three continued to seize every opportunity of annoying him. In 1076, for example, Fulk attacked the lord of La Flèche on the Loir, an Angevin upholder of the Norman cause in Maine, and also dispatched assistance to the Breton lords who were defying William at Dol. In 1079 Malcolm overran Northumberland as far as the Tyne, an act which led to the foundation of Newcastle as a defence against further Scotch raids. In 1081 Fulk, assisted by Hoel, Duke of Brittany, burnt the castle of La Flèche before the Normans could gather their forces, and even when William did come in person to the rescue of his adherents, he found it politic to avoid a battle and agreed to an arrangement known as the Peace of Blanchelande, under which Robert, now perhaps 26 years of age, was recognised by Fulk le Rechin as Count of Maine, but only on the condition of accepting Fulk as his overlord and doing him homage. Even this peace was not well kept; for in 1083 Hubert of Sainte-Suzanne and others of Maine once more took up arms against the Norman domination over their fiefs, and for three years defied all attempts made by William to subdue them. The fact is, in spite of much rhetorical talk about William's conquest of Maine, the greater part of the county was never thoroughly in his grasp, and as years went by the influence of Anjou kept increasing.

During all this time we hear of no challenge to William's autocratic rule either in England or in Normandy, except in 1075, when a handful of barons plotted a rising, but with such little general support that William did not even return to England to deal with it. The chief conspirators were two rash young men who had recently succeeded to their fathers' baronies, Roger, Earl of Hereford, the son of the trusted William Fitz Osbern who had been killed in Flanders in 1070, and Ralf of Guader in Brittany, the son of Ralf the Staller, who had been recognised by William as Earl of East Anglia. These two earls were aggrieved, partly because William had forbidden Ralf to marry Roger's sister and partly because the sheriffs claimed jurisdiction over their estates. They accordingly took up arms and for a moment enticed Waltheof, Earl of Northumberland, to dally with their schemes. Waltheof, however, soon repented and disclosed their intentions to Lanfranc, who had no difficulty in rallying the mass of the barons to the king's side and easily dispersed the forces of the rebels both in Worcestershire and in Norfolk. Ralf was wise enough to flee the country, but Roger was captured and sentenced to perpetual imprisonment. It was harder to deal with Waltheof, who had not called out his men and who was married to Judith, the Conqueror's niece; but after five months' hesitation William ordered him to be executed, possibly to please the loyal barons, who were indignant that so much favour had been wasted on an Englishman.

The only serious domestic trouble of William's later years came from his eldest son Robert, who, though not wanting in courage, early shewed himself a spendthrift and quite destitute of statesmanlike qualities. To some extent the friction between them was William's fault; for, like many other men with strong wills, the Conqueror could not bring himself to depute any part of his authority to his son, not even in Maine where Robert was ostensibly count. Not unnaturally Robert as he grew up resented being kept in tutelage more and more, until at last he quarrelled openly with his father and betook himself, after some aimless wanderings, to Paris. Philip, the King of France, always ready to harass William, took pains to welcome the fugitive, and in 1079 established him at Gerberoi near Beauvais, where he could attack Normandy. A personal encounter followed between the father and son, in which Robert actually wounded William. This scandalous episode, however, led to a reconciliation, and Robert returned for a time to his father's court. But the two could never work together; and after Queen Matilda's death, which occurred in 1083, Robert again went abroad and never returned in his father's life-time. Of minor troubles in these years, two perhaps should be mentioned. The first is the murder in 1080 of Walcher, the Bishop of Durham, who had been put in charge of Northumberland after the execution of Waltheof. This murder was the work of an English mob, and shews that William's peace was never properly established north of the Tees. The second is the outbreak of a quarrel between William and his brother Odo, leading to the arrest and imprisonment of the bishop in 1082. This dramatic step fairly astounded Norman society; for Odo was Earl of Kent and the holder of the wealthiest fief in England, and only two years before had been in full favour and entrusted with the punishment of the Northumbrians. Some have supposed that William feared Odo's ambition; but Odo's hostility to Lanfranc and mere greed on the king's part may really have been the moving causes. Anyhow he kept the bishop a prisoner at Rouen for the rest of his reign and sequestrated his large English revenues. That William in old age became avaricious is attested not only by the Peterborough chronicler, who had lived at his court, but also by his public measures, such as the levy of a triple Danegeld in 1083 without, it would seem, any real need, and the compilation of the Domesday Book in 1086. This failing comes out too in his refusal to give Robert a position and income suitable to his expectations. As the chronicler says grimly, "the king loved much and overmuch scheming to get gold and silver and recked not how sinfully it was gotten." But of course that is only one side of the picture, and it was just because he paid such close attention to his finances, and thought it no shame to set down "every ox and cow and pig" in his great survey, that he was able to found a unique type of feudal monarchy in England, in which the king's wealth was adequate to his needs so that he could "live on his own" and pay his way, and not be merely *primus inter pares* in his dealings with his vassals. From this point of view the making of Domesday was William's greatest exploit, not merely because of the novelty of the undertaking, but because the inquiry proceeded on the theory that all

CHAPTER XVI.

ENGLAND, 1087–1154.

A. REIGN OF WILLIAM RUFUS (1087–1100).

WILLIAM RUFUS set out for England even before the Conqueror expired, and made direct for Winchester to secure the royal treasury. That
done he repaired next to Lanfranc, and on 26 September was crowned king
at Westminster without overt opposition, just seventeen days after his
father's death. In spite of the general calm, men foresaw that the separation of England from Normandy must bring trouble, as it placed all
the barons who had estates on both sides of the Channel in a dilemma,
and meant that sooner or later they would be forced to choose between
their allegiance to the duke and their allegiance to the king. For Robert,
on returning from exile, naturally denounced William as a usurper, and
found himself supported not only by those who honestly thought that
the Conqueror's arrangement was a blunder, but also by a body of turbulent spirits both in England and Normandy who, knowing the characters of the two brothers, thought that the elder would prove the easier
master and less likely than Rufus to stand in the way of their ambitions.
The leader of this section was the Earl of Kent, Bishop Odo of Bayeux,
who emerged from his five years' imprisonment thirsting for vengeance
on Lanfranc, whom he regarded as the instigator of his disgrace, and
determined to upset the Conqueror's dispositions and make himself again
the chief man in England. He accordingly betook himself to his Kentish
estates, and after some months spent in secret plotting put himself openly
at the head of a league for deposing William in favour of Robert. It is
usually alleged that Odo took the field supported by more than half the
baronage, but the accounts that tell the story by no means bear out such
a conclusion. Sporadic risings did indeed take place in districts as far
apart as Norfolk, Somerset, and Herefordshire, led by Roger Bigod,
Geoffrey Bishop of Coutances, and Roger de Lacy respectively; but
these movements were isolated and easily suppressed, and the only real
danger arose in Kent and Sussex, where Odo had the support of his
brother Robert of Mortain, aided by Gilbert of Clare and Eustace of
Boulogne, and could base his movements on four strongholds, Dover,
Rochester, Pevensey, and Tonbridge. Rufus, on the other hand, was supported not only by the men of the royal demesnes and by all the prelates
of the Church, except William of St Carilef, Bishop of Durham, but, so
far as can be seen, by the greater part of the baronage in the Midlands

and in Eastern England, headed by such magnates as the Earl of Chester, Count Alan of Richmond, William of Warenne, Walter Giffard, Geoffrey de Mandeville, Robert Malet, and Roger of Beaumont. From the very outset, in fact, it was clear that Odo had grievously miscalculated his influence. Even the native English were all on the royal side, so that Rufus was able to add largely to his forces by summoning foot-soldiers to his aid as well as the feudal levies, especially from London and the estates of the archbishopric of Canterbury. As a result the struggle, though sharp, was of brief duration. By the end of June the rebel fortresses had all fallen, and Lanfranc could congratulate himself that for a second time he had driven Odo out of England. Duke Robert, meanwhile, impecunious as ever, had hardly moved a finger to further his own cause beyond encouraging Robert of Bellême, the eldest son of Roger of Montgomery, and Robert of Mowbray, the nephew of Bishop Geoffrey of Coutances, who was now Earl of Northumberland, his former associates in his quarrels with his father, to join in the rising. It was to young men such as these, the duke's special friends, that William was most severe after his victory, making them share Odo's banishment; but all the other leaders were treated with great leniency, except the Bishop of Durham, who, having been one of Rufus' confidential advisers, was put on his trial for "deserting his lord in time of need." This trial is somewhat famous. The bishop pleaded that he could only be tried by an ecclesiastical court; William, on the other hand, backed by Lanfranc, insisted that he was charged not as a bishop but as a baron enfeoffed with extensive territories, and so must answer in the *Curia Regis*. The case dragged on for some months and in the end the bishop was allowed to appeal to the Pope on the point of jurisdiction, but had to surrender Durham Castle.

Odo's rebellion, if hardly more formidable than the rebellion of the earls in 1075, at any rate served to shew that Rufus had all the determination of his father and could not be trifled with. His subjects, however, were soon to learn that though he had his father's strong will and plenty of energy he had neither his respect for religion nor any regard for justice. While Lanfranc lived, he did not shew his true colours; but the aged archbishop passed away in 1089, and immediately there was a great change for the worse. Being now free to please himself and to indulge his rapacity, Rufus took for his favourite adviser Ranulf Flambard, the rector of Godalming, one of the royal chaplains, a self-made man who had held minor posts under the Conqueror, and who won Rufus' attention by his skill in devising ways of raising money. This unscrupulous man, being made treasurer, soon became notorious for his ingenious and oppressive exactions, and earned the hatred of every class; but his extortionate methods only delighted William, who by degrees placed him in supreme control of all financial and judicial business. His first opportunity came when he advised the king to postpone filling the vacant see of Canterbury, and to take the revenues for his own uses;

and soon this became the regular practice with all benefices in the royal gift, unless some cleric could be found willing to purchase the preferment. We are also told that he vexed all men with "unjust gelds," that he levied excessive and novel feudal dues, both from the baronage and the clergy; that he "drove the moots all over England" to inflict excessive fines, that he increased the severity of the game laws, and that he even tried to re-assess the Danegeld, though this probably only means that he ignored the reductions of assessment that had been granted by King Edward and the Conqueror. Hated as all these measures were, William's prestige was so great after his victory over Odo that he only once again was faced with armed opposition. This occurred in 1095 under the leadership of Robert of Mowbray, who had been permitted to return to Northumberland, backed by Roger de Lacy and William of Eu. This outbreak, however, only led to their ruin, William of Eu being sentenced to mutilation, Mowbray to life-long imprisonment, and Lacy to forfeiture.

William Rufus' real preoccupations were not with feudal or popular unrest but with schemes for the enlargement of his dominions and especially for the recovery of Normandy. He wished to be a conqueror like his father, and he knew that if he succeeded he could snap his fingers at discontent. His first move against his brother in 1090 was designed to take advantage of the discontent of the barons of eastern Normandy with Robert's feeble rule. Here he easily established himself; for the great men of the locality were the Counts of Eu and Aumâle, William of Warenne, Walter Giffard, and Ralf of Mortimer, all of whom, having still larger interests in England, were afraid of his displeasure and willing to further his designs. Their men and their fortresses were consequently at his disposal, and even in Rouen a party was formed in his favour led by Conan, one of the richest citizens. In central Normandy, on the other hand, Duke Robert's position was less precarious, for he could count on the loyalty of Caen and Falaise, while the chief landowners, such as the Bishop of Bayeux, the Count of Évreux, William of Breteuil, and Robert of Bellême, who had been put in possession of his mother's Norman fiefs, had either little or no stake in England or had fallen out with Rufus. Here then opposition might be serious, and a struggle seemed probable. But William, in 1091, was quick to see that the position in western Normandy offered him a better alternative. There the leading man, since 1088, had been his younger brother Henry, the third surviving son of the Conqueror, who had purchased all Robert's estates and ducal rights in the Cotentin and the Avranchin with the money that had been bequeathed to him by his father, and now called himself Count of the Cotentin. But Robert, shifty as ever, had quickly regretted this deal with his brother and wished to recover the ducal property. William, knowing this, instead of attacking Robert in central Normandy went to meet him at Caen and offered to assist him in attacking Henry and in recovering Maine, on the condition that the duke should cede to him Cherbourg and Mont-Saint-Michel as soon as Henry had been expelled from them, and also his ducal rights in Fécamp and parts of eastern Normandy. The terms offered were very one-sided, but Robert thought it safest to accept them; and shortly afterwards the two elder brothers advanced against Henry and having ousted him from all his purchases divided the spoils between them. With this result William might well feel satisfied. In eighteen months he had acquired a firm grasp on the duchy both in the east and the west, and what is more he had achieved his success by a treaty with Robert without any serious fighting.

Meanwhile news came through that Malcolm Canmore had again overrun Northumberland. Rufus accordingly left Normandy and hurried north to retaliate. On reaching the Forth, he found Malcolm repentant and willing to buy him off by doing homage and becoming his man on the same terms as the Conqueror had exacted in 1072. In 1092, however, Rufus broke the peace in his turn and overran the districts in Cumberland and Westmorland, which had been regarded as parcel of the Scottish kingdom ever since King Edmund had ceded them to Malcolm I in 945. Not unnaturally Malcolm protested, and came in person to Gloucester to treat with Rufus. But the English king refused to meet him and required him as a vassal to submit his case to the *Curia Regis*. At the same time he ordered English settlers to be planted in the valley of the Eden and founded a castle at Carlisle. Malcolm went home indignant and a year later again invaded England, but was slain in an ambush near Alnwick. Here, too, William must be credited with a distinct success. Henceforth the boundary of England was fixed for good at the Solway, and within a few years Cumberland and Westmorland came to be reckoned as English shires. Queen Margaret, who had done much to introduce English ways into her husband's kingdom, died of grief on hearing the news of his death, whereupon a struggle arose between the Celtic and the English factions in Scotland as to the succession. The Celtic party set Malcolm's brother Donaldbane on the throne in preference to any of Margaret's sons, hoping thereby to put an end to the spread of English influences; but four years later Rufus took up the cause of the English party and sent Edgar the Aetheling into Scotland with a force of Norman knights, who drove out Donaldbane and made Margaret's son Edgar king. This prince made the Lowlands his favourite abode, and being largely dependent on Norman support never sought to deny that Rufus was his feudal superior.

William's advance in the North had its counterpart also in Wales; but there the lead was taken by various barons independently and not by the Crown. The Conqueror's general policy had been to leave all responsibility for dealing with the Welsh in the hands of the three specially privileged earls who had been granted the marcher lordships of Chester, Shrewsbury, and Hereford. At the Conqueror's death, as Domesday shews, his lieutenants had already pressed into northern and mid Wales beyond the line of Offa's dyke at several points, especially in Gwynedd where Robert of Rhuddlan had established his outposts on the Conway, and in Powys where Roger of Montgomery had reached the sources of the Severn near Plynlimon. In South Wales on the other hand there had been little advance since the death of William Fitz Osbern in 1071. The frontier still ran roughly along a line from Radnor through Ewyas to Caerleon; and though the Conqueror himself in 1081 had ridden west as far as St David's, he had been content to leave Deheubarth and Glamorgan in the hands of a Welsh prince called Rhys ap Tewdwr, exacting from him only an annual tribute of £40. It was in 1088 that new advances began. In that year Robert of Rhuddlan, soon after returning from the siege of Rochester, fell a victim to a Welsh attack. But almost immediately afterwards the Earl of Chester got possession of the districts round Snowdon. Thence he advanced into Anglesey, and in 1092 we find a Breton named Hervé appointed to be Bishop of Bangor. It was also in 1088 that the Normans under Bernard of Neufmarché, the son-in-law of the lord of Richard's Castle, first advanced against Brecknock, while a year or two later they overran Glamorgan led by Robert Fitz Hamon of Évrecy near Caen, a Kentish landowner who had come to the front in the struggle against Bishop Odo, and who had been rewarded for his services to the Crown by a grant of nearly all the lands which had once belonged to Queen Matilda. In 1093 came another wave of conquest. In that year Rhys ap Tewdwr was killed near Brecknock. In the confusion which followed Roger of Montgomery dashed into Deheubarth, and having established himself at Cardigan pushed on thence into Dyfed, where his son Arnulf soon built a castle for himself at Pembroke. About the same time William of Braiose, a Sussex baron, acquired a lordship at Builth on the upper Wye, and William Fitz Baldwin, coming from Devon, erected a fort on the Towy near Carmarthen. Such persistent encroachments led in 1094 to a furious counter-attack by the Welsh, which brought about the withdrawal of the Normans from Anglesey and the destruction of a great many of the new castles. Next year the Welsh even took Montgomery Castle and repulsed a royal army which Rufus himself led into Gwynedd. In 1096 they besieged Pembroke, but the castle held out bravely under Gerald of Windsor, and thenceforth the marcher barons in South Wales nearly always held the upper hand. In Gwynedd on the other hand the Normans failed to recover the ground lost in 1094, in spite of serious efforts made by Rufus in 1097 and by the Earls of Chester and Shrewsbury in 1098. North Wales never was reduced but remained an independent principality under a Welsh prince named Gruffydd ap Cynan.

At home the chief event during these years of external expansion was William's quarrel with the Church. Irreligious and venal, the king saw no reason at first for putting any curb on Flambard's systematic spoliation of Church revenues. But in 1093 he fell ill, and fancying himself face to face with death was seized with remorse. In this mood he gave way to the general desire that the see of Canterbury should not remain vacant any longer, and offered the archbishopric to Anselm of Aosta, a saintly Italian scholar, who had been Lanfranc's favourite pupil and who for the last fifteen years had been Abbot of Bec. Anselm himself in no way desired the appointment; but as it was clearly the desire of the English magnates both lay and clerical, as well as of the king, he eventually consented, stipulating however that the lands of the archbishopric must all be restored to the see and that he himself should be free to recognise Urban II as Pope rather than his rival Clement III, the imperial candidate. But William, as soon as he was well again, forgot his repentance, and not only retained a good deal of the property of the archbishopric but made heavy demands on Anselm for aids and refused to allow him to initiate any Church reforms or hold any synods. Anselm refused to pay the aids in full, and in 1095 exasperated the king by asking leave to go to Rome to obtain his pallium from Urban. William did not wish to be committed to either claimant for the Papacy, and like his father he claimed that no Pope should be recognised in England without his permission. The matter was referred to a council of magnates held at Rockingham. The lay barons took Anselm's side and Rufus had to give way. William next tried to negotiate with Urban for Anselm's deposition; but he was outwitted by the Pope's legate, who obtained the king's recognition of Urban and then refused to move against Anselm. Two years later, in 1097, William again attacked the archbishop, charging him with breach of his obligations as a tenant-in-chief. Realising that he could do no good in England, Anselm again preferred his request to be allowed to visit Urban. At first William refused to acquiesce, but finally he changed his mind; and, as soon as Anselm had sailed, once more took possession of the revenues of the archbishopric. Anselm remained abroad for the rest of William's reign, universally regarded as a martyr, though at Rome he got little active support. By his firmness, however, he had set up a new standard of independence for the English clergy, and had made the opening move in the struggle between Church and State in England.

To return to secular affairs, William's desire to acquire Normandy had only been whetted by the gains made in 1091. He therefore took no pains to observe his treaty with Robert, and three years later resumed hostilities. His forces invaded central Normandy, hoping to acquire Caen, but they had little success; for King Philip of France came to Robert's aid, with sufficient men to enable him to drive William's captains out of Argentan and the neighbouring district of Le Houlme. They then together crossed the Seine to attack William in eastern Normandy, but the king saved himself by bribing Philip to desert his ally. In 1095, William, being too much occupied in England with Mowbray's rebellion and the quarrel with Anselm to come to Normandy, opened negotiations with his brother Henry, who had two years before found an asylum at Domfront, and persuaded him to take up the struggle for him. This move, however, proved to be unnecessary; for in 1096 the adventure-loving Robert, carried away by Pope Urban's call for volunteers to deliver the Holy Sepulchre, took the Cross regardless of his ducal interests, and to obtain funds offered to mortgage his ducal rights in Normandy to his brother for 10,000 marks. William quickly found the money, and in September Robert set out for the East, taking Odo of Bayeux and Edgar the Aetheling with him.

Being at last in temporary possession of Normandy, but fully convinced that Robert would never be in a position to repay the loan and redeem his patrimony, William applied himself with a will not only to the task of restoring the ducal authority, but also to the recovery of Maine. That county, owing to Robert's weakness, had fallen completely into the hands of Hélie, lord of La Flèche; but in 1098 William captured Hélie and soon afterwards, in spite of the opposition of Fulk le Rechin of Anjou, took possession of Le Mans. He had, however, to conquer the town a second time in 1099. He also undertook operations for the recovery of the French Vexin. In 1100, growing still more ambitious, he began negotiations with the Duke of Aquitaine, who wished to go on crusade, for taking over the ducal rights in Poitou on the same kind of terms as had been arranged in the case of Normandy. But this fanciful scheme was destined to remain a dream. On 2 August, while hunting in the New Forest, William fell, shot by an arrow from an unknown hand. He was buried next day in Winchester Cathedral, some of the churches in the city refusing to toll their bells. A brother-in-law of Gilbert of Clare, Walter Tirel, lord of Langham near Colchester and of Poix in Picardy, was thought to be responsible. But no inquiry was ever made. Men were just content to know that their oppressor was dead. And yet William, despite all his vices and violence, had done a great work. As a man he had been detestable; but as a king he had known how to make himself obeyed, and though he pressed his feudal claims too far, he had maintained unflinchingly his father's two great principles, that peace and order must be respected and that the king's will must be supreme.

B. Reign of Henry I (1100–1135).

The sudden removal of William Rufus at the age of forty, leaving no children behind him, gave his brother Henry an easy opening for making himself King of England. Not only was he on the spot, having been one of the hunting party in the New Forest, but he was well acquainted with the state of opinion in England, having lived, since 1095, on friendly terms with Rufus and his various ministers. He was, moreover, confident in himself. He knew well that all men had a contempt for his eldest brother; and he could urge, like Rufus before him, that if the

magnates set Robert's claims aside a second time they would only be
carrying out the Conqueror's wishes. Duke Robert, on the other hand,
was still far away in Sicily, and though he had somewhat redeemed his
character by his prowess in Palestine, had no supporters in England except a turbulent section of the baronage who hated peace and order
and saw in the duke's weakness a golden opportunity to attack their
neighbours. Henry knew that this section was not formidable, if boldly
confronted. He therefore made straight for Winchester as soon as he
heard that Rufus was dead, and seized the royal treasury. Here the
Treasurer opposed him, but William Giffard, the Chancellor, took his
side, and also the Count of Meulan and the Earl of Warwick, that is to
say, the two brothers Robert and Henry of Beaumont, the only barons
of importance who seem to have been present. These greeted him as king,
whereupon he started with them for Westminster, and two days later
had himself crowned by the Bishop of London without any opposition.

To strengthen his position he next issued a manifesto intended for
publication in all the shire-courts, in which he promised redress of
grievances, and as a sign that he was in earnest ordered the arrest of
Ranulf Flambard, who only a year earlier had been made Bishop of
Durham by Rufus as a reward for his zealous services. This manifesto,
usually known as Henry's "Charter of Liberties," contains many specific
promises to the Church and the baronage, as for example that benefices
should not be kept vacant or sold for the benefit of the Crown, or that
baronial demesnes should be exempt from Danegeld; but its main gist
is simply that Henry would restore his father's system of government
and abolish the evil innovations introduced by his brother in the matter
of reliefs, wardships, marriages, and murder fines. This programme he
knew would be popular, and the list of witnesses to the document shews
that in advancing it he had the support of the bishops and of such leading
barons as Walter Giffard, now Earl of Buckingham, Robert Malet of
Eye, Robert de Montfort, and Robert Fitz Hamon. Nor was Henry himself altogether insincere in his professions. Though only thirty-two, he
had been well schooled in adversity and had grown up the very antithesis
of his two brothers. Cool-headed, clear-sighted, and patient, a methodical
man of business, and for a prince well educated, he hated all waste, violence, and disorder, and he honestly wished to revert to the methods
which had made his father's reign the wonder of Western Europe. Foremost among these was the maintenance of harmony between Church and
State, to promote which Henry not only began to make appointments to
the sees and abbacies kept vacant by Rufus, but also sent messengers to
Anselm requesting him to return to England. The archbishop was at
Cluny and at once obeyed the summons; but no sooner did he meet
Henry than his actions quickly shewed that peace between himself and
the king was hardly to be expected, and that he was in no mood to play
the part of Lanfranc.

Meantime Henry decided that the time had come for him to marry, and gave out that the lady of his choice was Edith, the sister of the King of Scots. This alliance was doubly advantageous, as it would secure him the friendship of Scotland and also please the native English, Edith being descended through her mother Margaret from the royal house of Wessex. Some Normans of course scoffed at the idea of an English-speaking queen, and also tried to make out that Edith had been professed a nun; but Anselm brushed this latter objection aside, and himself officiated at the wedding ceremony. To please the Normans, Edith's name was changed to Matilda; but the king's example must have done something to encourage intermarriage between the Normans and the English and so helped to bring about the eventual fusion of the two races.

While Henry was thus making himself popular in England, Normandy was slipping back into disorder. Robert reached home in September, bringing with him a Sicilian bride, but men soon learnt that the duke was as easy-going as ever. Partly from laziness, partly from lack of funds, he took no steps to prevent the re-establishment of Hélie de la Flèche as Count of Maine; and so that county fell once more under the influence of Fulk le Rechin of Anjou, who two years earlier had affianced his son to Hélie's only daughter. Nor did Robert shew much desire to intervene in England until he was persuaded by Ranulf Flambard, who had escaped from his English prison, that there was a party in England who wished to make him king. In this belief he sailed for England in the summer of 1101, helped by William of Warenne whom Rufus had made Earl of Surrey, and by Count Eustace of Boulogne who, though he had just become Henry's brother-in-law, had fallen out with him about his English fief. Robert soon found that the mass of the English baronage had no intention of helping him openly, and that his only course was to make the best terms he could with his brother. Accordingly, by a treaty made at Alton, he surrendered his claim to England in return for a promised pension of £2000 a year. Henry on his side gave up all claim to be Count of the Cotentin under his earlier bargain with Robert in 1088, restored Eustace of Boulogne to his estates in England, and promised his assistance against Hélie de la Flèche. This arrangement probably suited Robert, who was desperately in need of money; but it is typical of Henry's duplicity, as he had no real intention of paying the pension and meant himself to make a bid for Normandy as soon as the duke's misgovernment should afford him a colourable excuse. Meantime the task immediately before him was that of humbling the restless elements in the English baronage and of finding pretexts for ridding himself of those who had secretly favoured Robert, though they had not dared to support him openly. The chief example of this class was Robert of Bellême. That vicious, cruel, turbulent man had succeeded in 1098 to the wide estates in Shropshire, Sussex, and elsewhere which formed the earldom of Shrewsbury, and was also the greatest of the feudatories in Normandy, being the possessor of the extensive lordships of Alençon and Montgomeri, and in addition Count of Ponthieu in right of his wife, *Vicomte* of Argentan and Falaise, and lord of a score of castellanies in the borderlands of Perche and Maine. With Bellême near at hand, Henry knew that he never could feel really safe; and so in 1102 he deliberately picked a quarrel with him and summoned him to stand his trial before the *Curia Regis* on some forty-five separate charges. As Henry no doubt expected, the Earl of Shrewsbury preferred to fight rather than to plead, and was supported in his revolt by his two brothers Roger of Poitou and Arnulf of Montgomery, lords respectively of Lancaster and Pembroke, and also by the Welsh of Powys. This combination, though formidable, was quite unable to withstand Henry, who within a month captured the earl's castles at Arundel and Bridgnorth and forced the earl himself to surrender at Shrewsbury. This was the end of feudal risings in England in Henry's lifetime. Bellême and his brothers were allowed to leave the country, but their fiefs were all confiscated, and for the next thirty-three years no baron ever ventured to take the field against the Crown. Several, indeed, fell out with the king, as for example his cousin the Count of Mortain, who was outlawed on trivial pretexts in 1104; but even he, wealthy and proud as he was, with his four castles of Pevensey, Berkhampstead, Montacute, and Trematon, never attempted any armed resistance to Henry in England.

With nothing to fear in his kingdom, Henry was free to turn his attention to the acquisition of his father's duchy. Like Rufus he utilised the disorder prevailing in Normandy as a pretext for intervention, posing not so much as a rival to Robert as the champion of the English barons who had estates on both sides of the Channel. In particular he claimed that his friends must be protected from the outrageous violence of Robert of Bellême, who was venting his wrath upon them to avenge himself for his English losses. The duke, however, was quite powerless to do anything of the kind, and so in 1104 Henry himself crossed the Channel attended by a formidable array of Anglo-Norman barons and sought out his brother to remonstrate with him personally. At his wits' end to know how to satisfy Henry, Robert offered to cede to him the overlordship over the Count of Évreux, and thus for the moment put off an open quarrel. But only for the moment. In 1105 the situation became more strained than ever, as Robert of Bellême joined his forces with those of the Count of Mortain, and the pair then deliberately ravaged the Cotentin where Henry had many trusted friends. Worse still, Duke Robert connived at the arrest of Robert Fitz Hamon, the lord of Évrecy and Glamorgan, and imprisoned him at Bayeux. This act determined Henry to make war in earnest. He accordingly invited Hélie de la Flèche to attack Robert from Maine, and himself crossing to Barfleur burnt Bayeux and occupied Caen. All men could now guess that he meant to dispossess his brother, but it was not till 28 September 1106 that the decisive encounter took place not far from Tinchebrai, a castle belonging to the Count of Mortain and situated some twelve miles north of Domfront. In this battle, fought exactly forty years to a day after the Conqueror's landing at Pevensey, Henry utterly routed the duke and took him prisoner, whereupon the duke himself gave orders to Falaise and Rouen to surrender and formally absolved his vassals from their allegiance. Such a complete collapse can hardly have been expected even by Henry's adherents; but no one seems to have doubted that it was irretrievable, so that even Robert of Bellême abandoned his hostility and for a time acknowledged Henry as his lawful overlord. As for Duke Robert, he never regained his freedom, though he survived for another twenty-eight years; but his claims passed to his infant son William, usually called "the Clito," who, being left at liberty, became, when he grew up, a centre for renewed intrigues and disaffection.

Throughout the years spent in driving Bellême from England and in acquiring his father's duchy, Henry was continuously engaged at home in a stubborn controversy with Anselm over the question of clerical immunities. While in Rome, in 1099, Anselm had taken part in the council held at the Lateran by Pope Urban in which bishops and abbots had been forbidden either to receive investiture from laymen or to do homage to them. As a result he came back from his exile holding more extreme views on the relations of Church and State than he had previously held, and began at once to put them into practice by refusing to do homage to Henry for his temporalities, though he had not scrupled to do homage to Rufus; and a little later he went further and refused to consecrate the new bishops and abbots whom Henry had appointed, on the double ground that they had not been freely elected by their chapters and had received investiture with the symbols of their office from the king. To these challenges Henry had replied that, while he could not abandon the ancient customs of the realm, he was willing to refer the matter to Rome and see if the new Pope, Paschal II (1099–1118), would modify his predecessor's decrees. Meantime, he allowed Anselm to hold a synod and issue canons with regard to the celibacy of the clergy and other disciplinary matters of such a sweeping nature that they created consternation in all ranks of society. Nothing, however, came of the application to Paschal, and so in 1103 it was agreed, at the king's suggestion, that Anselm himself should go on a mission to Rome to see if he could not arrange some way round the difficulty. Again Paschal proved obdurate, with the result that Anselm remained abroad, while Henry appropriated the revenues of Canterbury to his own uses. For two years after that matters remained in suspense; but in 1105 Paschal began to threaten Henry with excommunication, a move which so alarmed Henry's sister, the Countess of Blois, that she persuaded him to meet Anselm at L'Aigle, near Évreux, and reopen negotiations. Once more envoys from the king went to Rome, and this time they found Paschal ready for a compromise, but it was not till April 1106 that he notified Anselm of his new intentions, and not till the very eve of the Tinchebrai campaign that Henry met Anselm at Bec and, adopting a scheme worked out by Lanfranc's famous pupil, the great canonist Ivo of Chartres, effected a common-sense settlement satisfactory to both parties. The terms of the compromise were briefly as follows: bishops and abbots were for the future to be canonically elected by cathedral or monastic chapters and were no longer to receive the ring and staff on investiture from lay hands; but the elections were to take place in the king's presence, and those elected were to do homage to the king for their temporalities like the lay barons. This arrangement, which was finally ratified by an assembly of magnates in 1107, might seem to embody distinct concessions by both sides; but in practice Henry retained nearly all that he really wanted, the prelates being relieved of none of their feudal obligations, whereas the king was left with a sufficient power of influencing the electors to secure that his nominees would usually be elected. Anselm, on the other hand, by forcing the king to negotiate with the Pope had established a striking precedent for appeals to Rome, and so made it easier for future Popes to interfere in England, and for future bishops to resist the royal supremacy. Despite all his tenacity Anselm had not gained his immediate point; but he had demonstrated to the world that the English Church could not and would not be the obedient servant of the State.

The settlement with the Church, followed two years later by the death of Anselm, brings to an end the first phase of Henry's reign, during which he was winning his spurs as a ruler. The rest of his reign, which was to last for over a quarter of a century, has a totally different character in England, being notable not so much for exploits in the field or for brilliant strokes of policy, as for the measures which the king took to improve the system of government and set up a routine of law in the place of an ill-regulated despotism. Not that Henry can be credited with any lofty motives in pursuing these ends. He pursued them, both in England and Normandy, chiefly because he hated waste and loved money, and had the wit to perceive that the surest way to fill his coffers was by methodical pressure applied by well-trained agents in accordance with definite rules, and not by handing over his subjects to rapacious farmers and tax-gatherers, each acting as a law to himself. Henry was probably quite as unscrupulous and quite as avaricious as Rufus; but he had the temper of a shrewd, calculating, self-controlled man, and put his faith from the outset in the wise selection of subordinates, in recourse to litigation rather than to force, in the suppression of robbery and disorder, in the development of trade and industry, and in the maintenance of a business-like administration of justice and finance.

To attain these ends Henry had perforce to work either through the superior officers of his household or else through the agency of the *Curia Regis*, that elastic advisory council being the only central organ of government as yet in existence. When, however, he became duke as well as king, the affairs of Normandy and the intrigues of Louis VI, the new King of France (1108–1137), frequently prevented him for months or even for years together from being present at the sessions of the *Curia* or giving any attention to the supervision and control of the household officers; and so he was obliged to make use of a deputy or confidential chief minister to preside over the administration in his absence, and to issue writs in his name and deal with urgent matters. The man whom Henry chose for these important duties, and who, as long as Henry lived, occupied the position of regent, whenever the king was absent, with the title of *iusticiarius totius Angliae*, that is to say, "president of the Curia," or "justice-in-chief," was Roger his sometime chaplain, a native of Caen, whom he had promoted to be chancellor on his accession, and who two years later was made Bishop of Salisbury (1102–1139). On his appointment to the bishopric, Roger, in obedience to precedent, ceased to be chancellor, but became treasurer, a significant change of office, as it placed him in the shoes of Flambard and gave him control of the revenue; but exactly when he became permanent deputy for the king is not recorded. It seems probable, however, that for some time Roger combined the offices of regent and treasurer with such success that Henry came to regard a permanent deputy as indispensable on both sides of the Channel, and appointed John, Bishop of Lisieux (1107–1141), to hold a similar position in Normandy.

Very little detailed information is forthcoming as to Bishop Roger's activities year by year during his long tenure of the post of chief minister, but such glimpses as we do get, coupled with the veneration in which we know his name was held by the officials of the next generation, shew that he must have been a very able man, and that he may be credited with several innovations of permanent value. The one among them which perhaps struck the imagination of his successors most was the development, within the *Curia Regis*, of a board or group of barons specially charged with the duties of auditing the sheriffs' accounts and trying causes which concerned the collection of the various items of the king's revenue. This board sat for auditing purposes twice a year, at Lady Day and Michaelmas, and was known as the *Scaccarium* or "Exchequer." It acquired its curious name from the chequered table-cloth which was spread before the board to facilitate the reckoning of the sheriffs' accounts by means of counters, the system employed being an adaptation of the *abacus* method of working sums which had recently come into vogue in Germany and France at the schools of Liège and Laon. The permanent members of the board, known as "barons of the Exchequer," were Roger himself, who was the presiding officer, the treasurer, the chancellor, the constable, the marshal, and two chamberlains, assisted by the keeper of the king's seal and sundry clerks, one of whom had to keep a written record of all the sums of money accounted for, the wording of the enrolments being dictated by the Treasurer. This annual record, known as the *rotulus de thesauro*, and in later days as the *magnus rotulus pipae*, or "Pipe Roll," may be taken to be one of Roger's most practical and important innovations, for it not only gave Henry a handy means of checking his officials, but served as the model for nearly all English account-keeping for several centuries. Unfortunately only one roll compiled under Roger's supervision survives, namely the Pipe Roll for the financial year ended Michaelmas 1130, but from it can be seen all the items of the revenue and how very carefully they were collected, and what a great amount of detail had to be furnished each year to the barons of the Exchequer by the sheriffs and other local officials before they could obtain their discharge.

Besides developing the Exchequer, Bishop Roger surrounded himself by degrees with a group of assistant justiciars, in whom we may see the rudiments of the future bench of judges, though at this date they were not in any sense professional lawyers. Some of them, like Roger himself, owed their elevation entirely to their own abilities. Of this class were Ralph Basset and his son Richard, the latter of whom is sometimes called *capitalis iusticiarius*. Some of them on the other hand were undertenants, like Geoffrey de Clinton, who became a chamberlain in the king's household, and some were barons of medium rank like Walter Espec of Malton or William de Albini of Belvoir. At first these justiciars confined themselves to hearing causes in which the king's interest was concerned, but as time went on their reputation as skilled and experienced judges attracted other litigation to the king's court, and great men found it worth their while to pay the king considerable sums to be allowed to bring their grievances before them. By degrees, too, the practice grew up of sending the justiciars on circuit round the shires to try the so-called "pleas of the Crown"; and here too they gradually extended their jurisdiction by the simple device of maintaining that all matters which endangered the king's peace were matters that concerned the king and so came into the category of pleas that should come before a royal official. By this means a beginning was made towards bringing the local courts into touch with the *Curia Regis*, and towards disseminating through the land a common standard of law based on the practices of the king's court. But it must not be thought that there was any intention as yet that the justiciars should supersede the local courts. On the contrary, the king's court was far too irregular in its sessions and the king's justice far too expensive to be of much service to ordinary suitors. For their suits and the repression of every-day crime, the shire and hundred courts remained the regular tribunals, and the only surviving ordinance of Henry's reign is in fact one which strictly enjoins all men to attend the local courts at the same times and in the same localities as in the days of King Edward. So far as the local courts were in danger, it was not from the interference of the king's justiciars, but from the rivalry of the baronial and manor courts; and here too Henry protected the ancient communal tribunals, laying it down that suits between the tenants of different lords must be tried in the shire courts and not in the court of either lord. We can also see that throughout Henry's reign quite serious attempts were being made to state the old English law, which was enforced in these courts, in an intelligible and rational way. Both the Conqueror and Henry had confirmed the *laga Eadwardi*, but the Norman sheriffs had great difficulty in ascertaining what that law was. To help them, divers men set themselves to work not only to translate the old English dooms but also to systematise them, and as a result produced a number of very curious legal tracts which purport to harmonise the old English customary rules and set them forth in practicable form. The two most important examples are the tract called *Quadripartitus* and the so-called *Leges Henrici*. These were compiled apparently between the years 1113 and 1118 by anonymous French writers; and, though their authors had set themselves tasks which were quite beyond their powers, they nevertheless tell us many things of great value and shew especially that the Norman sheriffs were still gallantly attempting to maintain the old English ideas as to *sake* and *soke*.

If the foregoing fiscal and judicial measures may probably be ascribed to Bishop Roger, there were many other developments during the reign in which we can trace the hand of the king. It is impossible to specify them all, but a selection may be mentioned to indicate their width of range. Such are the creation of the new dioceses of Ely and Carlisle in 1109 and 1133; the appointment of the first Norman bishop to St David's in 1115; the acceptance of *Scutage* from the Church fiefs, that is to say, of money contributions in lieu of the render of military service; the restoration of capital punishment; the settlement of a colony of Flemings in Pembrokeshire; the reform of the coinage, first in 1108 and then a second time in 1125; the institution, recorded in the famous *Constitutio Domus Regis*, of a new scale of stipends and allowances for the officials of the king's household; and finally the supersession in 1129 of the sheriffs of eleven counties and the appointment of two special commissioners in their place to act as temporary *custodes* or joint sheriffs, so that the king might be made acquainted with all the details that went to make up the farms of the counties and be in a position to insist on his dues being paid to the uttermost farthing.

Varied as were these developments, there yet remain two matters which cannot be altogether passed over, if we wish to outline Henry's chief activities. The first is the king's dealings with the baronage, the second his dealings with the merchants and craftsmen. As to the former, the view usually held seems to be that Henry always looked upon the mass of the barons as his enemies, and that, so far as he did make grants of land, he deliberately endowed a class of ministerial nobles "to act as a counterpoise to the older Conquest nobility." This view, however, fails to take account of a number of facts which point to other conclusions. It has of course some truth if applied to the first five years of Henry's reign. In those years Henry without doubt had reason to suspect quite a number of the barons. But this early period is very distinct in character from the remaining thirty years of the reign, and after 1105 it is really a misconception to picture either England or western Normandy as scenes of baronial insubordination. In eastern Normandy, in the Vexin, and round Évreux, Henry had trouble enough, culminating in open rebellions in the years 1112, 1118, and 1123; but in these districts he had to contend not only with a "perpetual pretender" in the person of his disinherited nephew William Clito, but also with persistent intrigues fomented by Louis VI. These factors kept the valleys of the Seine and Eure in a state of constant unrest. But the disaffection in these districts was not really formidable; for the men who proved disloyal were not the men with great fiefs on both sides of the Channel like the Giffards or Mortimers or the house of Warenne, but were either French counts whose territorial possessions were only partly in Normandy, such as Amaury de Montfort, the claimant to the county of Évreux, or Waleran Count of Meulan, or else the owners of border fiefs such as Hugh of Gournay or Richer of L'Aigle, whose position as marcher lords made them specially liable to be seduced from their allegiance. How far these two classes were made use of by Louis VI in his endeavours to arrest the expansion of Henry's power can be read at length in the contemporary French and Norman chronicles; but their double dealing had little effect in the long run, and their treacheries are mainly of interest because the repeated failure of their schemes made it plain to Henry that he need not fear his vassals or abstain for fear of ulterior consequences from the normal feudal practice of creating fiefs to reward his favourites. His feudal policy, at any rate in England, lends itself best to this interpretation. For hardly had he seized on the widespread fiefs held by the Malets and the Baignards, the Count of Mortain, and the houses of Grantmesnil and Montgomery, than he set to work to establish fresh baronies in their place which were just as extensive and just as formidable. Leading examples of such creations are the baronies given to the brothers Nigel and William de Albini; to Alan Fitz Flaald of Dol, the ancestor of the famous house of Stuart; to Humphry de Bohun and to Richard de Redvers; the honour of Wallingford conferred on Brian Fitz Count; the honour of Huntingdon made over to David of Scotland; and the still more important honour of Gloucester created for the king's eldest illegitimate son, Robert of Caen. This latter fief, which had for its nucleus the English and Welsh lands of Robert Fitz Hamon, was erected into an earldom in 1122. It fairly dominated the southwestern counties and was as wide-spread and valuable as any barony created by the Conqueror. It was not, however, unique among Henry's grants, but was matched in splendour by a rival barony which he built up in the east and north as an appanage for his favourite nephew Stephen of Blois, by throwing together the three great honours of Eye, Boulogne, and Lancaster, in addition to creating him Count of Mortain in Normandy and securing for him the hand of the heiress of the county of Boulogne in France. It may perhaps be argued that family affection blinded Henry to the dangers involved in making Robert and Stephen so powerful; but no such plea can be advanced to account for his policy as a whole which included many grants to the Giffards and the Beaumonts and to the great houses of Clare and Bigod. Evidently his practice was founded on the conviction that the traitor barons had learned their lesson and that the Crown had grown powerful enough to be indifferent to would-be rivals. Other signs that point the same way are the restoration of Ranulf Flambard to the see of Durham and a marked relaxation of the Conqueror's rule about the building of castles.

To appreciate Henry's dealings with the craftsmen and trading classes it is necessary to obtain some notion of the number and size of the urban communities—"ports" as the English termed them—which existed in England in his day. When the Domesday survey was compiled in 1086, there were just about one hundred localities—styled for the most part "boroughs"—in which portmen (*burgenses*) or chapmen (*mercatores*) were to be found. Such particulars as can be gleaned from the survey about their organisation and customs are unfortunately difficult to interpret, owing to the scantiness of many of the returns and their entire lack of uniformity. But they are sufficient to shew that the word *burgus* stood indifferently for several types of trading centre, including on the one hand walled "ports" of ancient fame, such as London, Oxford, and Stafford, and on the other tiny urban hamlets recently planted by Norman barons near their newly-built castles, as at Wigmore and Rhuddlan. The cardinal fact to be grasped is that the average *burgus* at the beginning of the twelfth century was quite an insignificant community and often largely agricultural in character. In more than fifty instances the number of portmen (*burgenses*) is returned in the Domesday survey as less than a hundred, and in some thirty of these instances as less than fifty. On the other hand there are only some twenty boroughs where the record reports the existence of more than 500 portmen; and even boroughs of the rank of Gloucester and Chester were probably not much more populous than the small market-towns of to-day having populations of 3000 to 4000 souls. From the territorial point of view the lands and houses (*masurae*) comprised within the urban areas were in most boroughs held by a number of different lords, a feature which has been described by the term "tenurial heterogeneity"; but as the Conqueror had arranged the distribution of the spoils, the king had the lion's share, being possessed usually of not only the haws (*hagan*) and messuages (*mansiones*) which had formerly belonged to King Edward but also of those which had belonged to the earls. We may in fact think of some seventy of the *burgi* as king's boroughs, in so far as the king had the largest share of the house-rents (*gafol*), and the king's officers the control of their government. And from these urban properties the Crown was receiving in 1086 a revenue whose yearly value was round about £2400. The sums at which the profits of London and Winchester were let to farm are nowhere recorded; but York, Lincoln, and Norwich, the three boroughs next in importance, were farmed for £100 a year each, Thetford and Bristol for about £80 each, Oxford, Wallingford, Gloucester, and Hereford for £60 each, Canterbury, Wilton, and Stamford for £50 each, Ipswich for £40, Colchester, Huntingdon, Nottingham, and several others for £30, Yarmouth for £27, Hertford for £20, Buckingham for £16, and so on. There were also considerable sums derived from the mints, and various casual profits. The collection of this urban revenue was entrusted to the sheriffs and portreeves, who further were charged with the holding of the borough courts (*portmanmoots*) and with the maintenance of law and order. Of the "ports" in which the king had no interests the most important in 1086 were Sandwich, Hythe, Lewes, Chichester, Bury St Edmunds, Dunwich, Shrewsbury, and Chester.

During the next fifty years a few new boroughs were founded by the barons on their fiefs, and one by Henry himself at Dunstable; but the Pipe Roll of 1130 shews that the relative importance of the boroughs as a whole did not change much, except that Wallingford and Thetford somewhat decayed. The king, however, handed over his interests in Leicester and Warwick to the Beaumonts but, on the other hand, he recovered control of Shrewsbury and Chichester. The real interest of the Crown always lay in developing the boroughs as sources of revenue. That most of them did develop in population and trade under Rufus and Henry there can be little doubt; otherwise it would have been impossible for them to support the very heavy taxes which were imposed upon them. But it is not easy to point to any very definite measures undertaken by Henry for the benefit of the towns as a whole, other than his strict maintenance of peace and order. There is ample evidence, on the other hand, as to his schemes of taxation, his chief measure being the abolition of the practice of taking Danegeld from the more important boroughs and the imposition in its place of much heavier levies known as "aids." In 1130 these aids varied in amount from £3 in the case of Winchcombe up to £120 in the case of London. Here and there, however, Henry did do a little to encourage the beginnings of municipal self-government. He allowed the men of York and Wilton for example, and perhaps of Salisbury and Lincoln, to form merchant gilds, or voluntary societies, for the regulation of trade; he sold the right of farming the revenues of their borough to the men of Lincoln, thereby exempting them from the control of the sheriff in financial matters; and he issued charters confirming the men of Bury St Edmunds, Leicester, and Beverley in the privileges which they had obtained from their immediate overlords. These measures would seem to have been tentative, and can hardly be construed as evidence of a definite policy pursued systematically throughout the reign. But just at its close Henry did in the case of London grant its burghers some extraordinary political privileges, which at any rate shewed that he did not regard them as a danger to his authority. London was in the peculiar position of being the largest borough in the kingdom but situated in the smallest shire, and in one moreover where the king had no rural demesne manors. The sheriff of Middlesex, on the other hand, except for his duties with regard to London, had very little to do. It seemed therefore obvious, if the Londoners were to farm the revenues of their borough like the men of Lincoln, as they wished to do, that there was little to be gained by maintaining a separate shire organisation. Henry, accordingly, leased to the Londoners the shrievalty of Middlesex *en bloc* and made them farmers of both Middlesex and London at an inclusive rent of £300 a year. At the same time he permitted them to appoint their own sheriff and their own justices, who were to keep and try the pleas of the Crown to the exclusion of every other justice. The Londoners thus acquired a very privileged and a very exceptional position, but one that they were not destined to maintain.

The sketch just attempted of Henry's domestic measures in England will have indicated how important they were in view of the future development of English institutions. To Henry himself, however, this side of his activities probably did not seem as important as his relations with his French neighbours; for out of the twenty-nine years which elapsed between 1106 and his death, he spent no less than seventeen years in Normandy. His contest with Louis VI dragged on intermittently till the death of William Clito in 1128; but already in 1119 by a victory at Brémule, in the Vexin, Henry had virtually got the upper hand, and after that he only encountered minor troubles in the regions round Évreux and Breteuil. Even before his triumph at Brémule he had come to terms with Fulk V of Anjou, and arranged a match between his eldest son, who was just sixteen, and Fulk's daughter. By this means he hoped eventually that the Norman house might recover the possession of Maine, as it was agreed between their parents that that county should be settled on the young pair. But in 1120 this cherished design was wrecked by a sudden catastrophe, which left the whole future of Henry's dominions in complete uncertainty. This was the tragic death of the young William, who was drowned with his brother Richard and a number of other nobles while crossing the Channel. As the loss of the two princes left Henry without a legitimate male heir and as his wife Matilda had died in 1118, Henry's thoughts naturally turned to a second marriage, and early in 1121 he contracted an alliance with Adelaide, the daughter of the Duke of Lower Lorraine. But this marriage proved childless, and for four

CH. XVI.

years the question of how to provide for the succession still vexed the king, as he was loth to see it pass to his nephews of the house of Blois. He still had one legitimate child, his daughter Matilda, but she had been married in 1114 to Henry V of Germany, which seemed an insuperable bar to any plan of making her his heiress. To Henry's relief this bar was removed by the death of the Emperor in 1125; whereupon Henry summoned Matilda back to England, and in 1127 he held a great council at which he required all the prelates and chief barons of England, headed by David of Scotland, Stephen of Blois, and Robert of Gloucester, to swear to accept her as their future sovereign. This arrangement many of them very much disliked, as it was unprecedented that England or Normandy should be ruled by a woman; nor was it yet disclosed what plans Henry had for providing her with a second husband. On this point Henry himself had unpopular but far-sighted views. He still desired to recover Maine, and so he approached the Count of Anjou again and proposed that the Empress should be married to Fulk's son and heir, Geoffrey, nicknamed in later days Plantagenet. This of course was acceptable to Fulk, for it meant that on Henry's death Geoffrey would not only unite Normandy to Anjou and Maine but would also become King of England and so be one of the most powerful princes in Western Europe. This prospect quite gratified Henry's dynastic ambition, but it was viewed with extreme dislike both in England and Normandy, as most men of Norman blood regarded it as a disgrace that they should have to accept the rule of their hereditary foe. Henry, however, would not listen to any protests, and in June 1128 he brought his daughter to Le Mans, where she was married to Geoffrey in the presence of a brilliant assembly. Even then his anxieties for the future were not at an end. Geoffrey was not yet fifteen; and Matilda, who was twenty-five, and of a haughty disposition, soon quarrelled with her boy-husband. Many of the barons also declared that, as they had not given their consent to the match, they were no longer bound by the oaths as to the succession. Henry met this objection by demanding, in 1131, a renewal of their oaths; but it was not till 1133 that he had the satisfaction of hearing that the Empress had borne a son, whom she duly christened Henry and whose advent seemed to place the question of the succession at length beyond dispute. Henry was now at the close of his sixty-fifth year. As he was still apparently quite vigorous, he hoped to see his young grandson reach an age when he might be accepted as king under his mother's guardianship, and so obviate any opposition arising to a female succession. But this was not to be. In August 1133 the king crossed once more to Normandy anxious to see his little heir, but soon found himself involved in troubles with Geoffrey, who was now the reigning Count of Anjou, having succeeded his father in 1129, when Fulk had withdrawn to Palestine to become King of Jerusalem. We are told that Geoffrey wanted castles in Normandy; and as Henry would not accede to his wishes, he provoked William Talvas of Bellême to revive his hereditary grievances and stir up trouble in the country round Séez. Henry replied by outlawing Talvas, and in 1135 laid siege to his castle at Alençon. The fortress did not hold out long against him, but the expedition was Henry's last effort. A few weeks later he was taken suddenly ill while hunting in the Vexin, and died on 1 December at Lyons-la-Forêt, having reigned a little over thirty-five years.

C. REIGN OF STEPHEN (1135–1154).

As soon as Henry's death was known, it rapidly became apparent that his cherished schemes for his daughter's succession were not likely to be carried out. Had his little grandson been older, a considerable party would no doubt have favoured his accession and been willing to risk the dangers of a long minority; but, as things were, hardly anyone wanted the crown to pass to the Empress, not only because there were no precedents for the accession of a woman, but because she was personally disliked for her arrogance and because men of Norman blood hated the idea of having to submit to her Angevin husband. Even the Earl of Gloucester made no move, so far as we know, in favour of his half-sister; and such magnates as were gathered at Rouen began openly to discuss whether the succession should not be offered to Theobald, Count of Blois, as being the Conqueror's eldest male descendant and the person best able to withstand the claims of the Count of Anjou. This discussion, however, led to no decision; and meanwhile Theobald's brother Stephen, who was at Boulogne when Henry died, without consulting his fellow-magnates, made up his mind to bid for the crown himself, and embarked for England with the intention of playing the same part as his uncle Henry had done thirty-five years before. There can be no denying that, if the oaths of allegiance taken to Matilda in 1127 and 1131 were to be disregarded, Stephen's territorial position as Count of Mortain and lord of the wealthy honours of Boulogne, Eye, and Lancaster made him a much more suitable candidate for the throne than Theobald. For Theobald, though prominent in France, was practically a stranger in England; whereas Stephen had lived among the English for some thirty years and had married a lady who, like the Empress, could claim descent from the old Saxon kings. Stephen, too, was known as a brave and affable prince, who was quite a favourite with the Londoners; and he had also gained credit with the Church by establishing a band of monks from Savigny at Furness on his Lancashire fief, thereby introducing a new monastic order into England. It is not surprising then that, when he presented himself in London and no other candidate's name was put forward, the citizens, alarmed at the prospect of an interregnum, at once declared in his favour and encouraged him to hurry on to Winchester to win over the officials of the Exchequer and secure the royal treasury. At Winchester

he was welcomed by the citizens, as he had been in London, and also by
his younger brother Henry of Blois, the powerful bishop of the diocese,
who was not only prepared to disregard his oath to the Empress, but also
eagerly lent his aid in persuading others and especially William of Corbeil,
the Archbishop of Canterbury, to do likewise. The archbishop was
full of scruples, but was at last persuaded to accept Stephen in return for a promise that he would restore to the Church its liberties;
and so also were the Bishop of Salisbury and the chamberlain, William
de Pont de l'Arche, the heads of the administration, who placed the
royal treasure and the castle of Winchester at his disposal. Thus
strengthened Stephen returned to London and was duly crowned at
Westminster within three weeks of receiving the news of his uncle's death.
The attendance of barons at the coronation was small, but no one
challenged its propriety; and as soon as the news of it reached Rouen,
the barons who were in Normandy, such as the Earls of Leicester and
Surrey and the Count of Meulan together with all the Norman bishops
acquiesced in the decision. Count Theobald too, bearing his brother's
success with equanimity, took up his cause and negotiated a truce on his
behalf with Count Geoffrey of Anjou. The Empress, however, was not at
all content, and at once appealed to Pope Innocent II against Stephen's
usurpation; nor did the Earl of Gloucester give in his adhesion. For
the time, however, Stephen had clearly triumphed, and a little later he
was also successful at the Curia, his emissaries backed by the influence of
the King of France getting the better of those sent by the Empress and
obtaining a letter from Innocent in which he recognised Stephen as King
of England and Duke of Normandy. As the oaths of fealty which had
been sworn to Matilda were Stephen's greatest stumbling-block, this
recognition by the power which could absolve men from their oaths was
a great feather in Stephen's cap, and for the time made him feel
fairly secure as regarded the future. And so no doubt he would have
been, had he possessed the cunning of his predecessor, or even sufficient
foresight and tenacity to strike at his probable enemies before their
preparations were matured. Such ideas were, however, entirely foreign to
Stephen's nature; and hence, instead of making good his initial success,
and devising means to remove all supporters of the Empress' cause, as
King Henry in his day had removed Robert of Bellême, which would have
impressed his subjects, he merely rested content with the position he had
so recklessly snatched, or at best tried to win over those whom he suspected of being disloyal by concessions. Even this timid policy, though
expensive, might have succeeded, had Stephen only had men of his own
calibre to fight against. In the Empress, however, he had opposed to him
a most tenacious woman, who had at her side in the persons of her
husband Geoffrey and her half-brother Robert two very sagacious
captains, who knew how to wait and scheme and take advantage of
Stephen's difficulties. The result was that before two years were gone by

Stephen's influence began to wane, and on both sides of the Channel men began to whisper that he was a mild and soft ruler, and to realise that he was quite incapable of maintaining the good peace which had persisted so long under his predecessor.

The first persons to oppose Stephen openly were the *vicomte* of the Hiesmois who admitted the Empress to Argentan and Exmes, William Talvas of Ponthieu and Bellême who regained Alençon, and David of Scotland who made a raid into Cumberland and Northumberland nominally in the interest of his niece but really to secure those districts for his son Henry. Leaving Normandy to be dealt with later, Stephen promptly hurried to Durham, and in February 1136 came to an agreement with David by the simple process of granting half his demands. The terms agreed were that David should acknowledge Stephen as king, and that Stephen in return should grant Cumberland to Henry as a fief, and also put him in possession of the honour of Huntingdon, which had long been held by the King of Scots in right of his wife. Stephen seems to have considered this settlement a good bargain, and in a way it was something of a family arrangement, Henry being Stephen's nephew; but as Stephen was soon to discover it had two drawbacks. It did not really satisfy David, and it offended the powerful Earl of Chester who, having himself claims on Cumberland, was converted into a life-long adversary. Returning to London, Stephen celebrated his first Easter as king by holding a magnificent court, at which his wife Matilda was crowned. This court was attended by no fewer than nineteen bishops, English and Norman, and by at least forty barons drawn from all parts of the kingdom. The paucity of magnates at his own coronation was thus fully made good; and a little later even the Earl of Gloucester crossed the Channel and outwardly came to terms with him. The only overt opposition to his rule during the rest of this year came from Hugh Bigod in Norfolk, and from a petty rising in Devon headed by Baldwin de Redvers and Robert of Bampton. These troubles however were easily met, and in 1137 Stephen found himself free to cross to Normandy, where he remained for nine months.

Though the Empress was still in possession of Argentan and some other castles, Stephen, had he played his cards well, ought to have had no difficulty in dispossessing her; for he had the support of Louis VI of France, who in May invested him with the duchy, while Geoffrey of Anjou had bitterly incensed the inhabitants of central Normandy in the previous year by a futile raid on Lisieux in which his men had been guilty of many outrages. Unfortunately, Stephen brought with him a band of Flemings led by his personal friend William of Ypres, and in resisting a renewed invasion by Count Geoffrey he gave great offence to the Norman leaders by entrusting the chief command to this Flemish knight. This act was a far-reaching blunder, as it not only alienated such important men as William of Warenne and Hugh of Gournay, but led to fresh quarrels with Robert of Gloucester, who accused the Fleming of suspecting his loyalty and of attacking him treacherously. Gloucester was thus thrown once again on to the side of his half-sister, which meant that Stephen was unable to dislodge the Empress and consequently his position in Normandy, especially in the Bessin where Gloucester's Norman fiefs lay, was left even more insecure when he re-embarked for England than when he had landed. When he departed he left the government of Normandy in the hands of William of Roumare, lord of the honour of Bolingbroke in England, a half-brother of the Earl of Chester, who is spoken of as justiciar. Under him the ducal administration was maintained in eastern Normandy for some time longer, but Stephen himself never returned to his duchy.

The year 1138 must be reckoned the turning-point in Stephen's fortunes. Left to his own devices in Normandy, Robert of Gloucester soon formed a definite alliance with Count Geoffrey, and in May sent a formal defiance to Stephen, declaring him a usurper and renouncing his allegiance. This action almost immediately brought about in England the defection of a number of west-country barons who were Gloucester's neighbours or kinsmen, such as William Fitz Alan of Oswestry, Ralph Paganel of Dudley, and several Somerset and Dorset landowners, headed by William de Mohun, lord of Dunster. Nor were these the only malcontents whom Stephen found himself called upon to meet. For quite early in the year Miles de Beauchamp, a Bedfordshire knight, provoked by a decision to confer the Beauchamp barony on a cadet of the house of Beaumont, had fortified Bedford castle against him, while in the north King David once more invaded Northumberland. As before, David's main object was to secure Northumberland as an earldom for his son; but this time he was much more bent on his scheme than in 1136, having gauged Stephen's character. Foiled in his first attack in the spring, he renewed his inroads in the summer, and having been joined by Eustace Fitz John of Alnwick pressed forward through Durham into Yorkshire. By this time Stephen had too many troubles to meet in the south to come north himself; but the general alarm, coupled with the exhortations of Thurstan, the venerable Archbishop of York, led nearly all the important northern barons, with the exception of the Earl of Chester, to take the field and join their forces to the levies of the archbishop in order to bar David's farther progress. The battle which ensued in August near Northallerton, known as the battle of the Standard because the English had in their midst a waggon bearing the consecrated banners of the archbishop's three minster churches —St Peter of York, St John of Beverley, and St Wilfrid of Ripon—ended in a rout for the over-audacious Scots. But there was no pursuit. David merely retreated to Carlisle, and in the following spring his niece, Queen Matilda, negotiated a permanent peace with him, acting on her husband's behalf, under which Henry, the heir to Scotland, who was already Earl of Huntingdon, was created Earl of Northumberland as well and was invested with the Crown lands in that county with the exception of the castles of Bamburgh and Newcastle. Meanwhile Stephen had done his best to cope with the risings in the south and west; but though he had reduced Shrewsbury and several castles in Somerset, he had hesitated to attack Bristol, which was the chief stronghold of the Empress' party. His efforts were consequently ineffective; nor were his lieutenants in Normandy any more successful in coping with the Earl of Gloucester, who went so far as to invite Count Geoffrey to Caen and Bayeux. In fact by December 1138 men could see that Stephen's initial luck was deserting him, and that it was certain that the Empress would not abandon her claims without a severe struggle.

In the spring of 1139 Stephen's position was still comparatively advantageous. He had settled with the Scots. The wealthiest districts of England and Normandy favoured his cause, and so did the Church, whose liberty he had publicly confirmed by a charter granted in accordance with his coronation promises. As for the control of the Church, he had quite recently secured the archbishopric of Canterbury for Theobald, Abbot of Bec, his own nominee, and he had obtained the still higher post of legate for his brother Henry. He had control of the exchequer and the judicial system. His revenues were still ample, and the Empress and Gloucester had not ventured to cross the Channel. But in June Stephen by his own act, perhaps to please the Beaumonts, forfeited the Church's support by requiring the Bishops of Salisbury and Lincoln to surrender their castles. Roger of Salisbury, the old justiciar, and his nephew Alexander had no doubt grown exceedingly arrogant, and in time of peace it might have been politic to curtail their pretensions. But it was unwise to attack them just when the real struggle for the throne was beginning, and stupid to submit them to indignities and throw them into prison when they refused to comply with the royal demands. It was in vain that Stephen urged the familiar plea that they were arrested as barons and not as bishops. Immediately all the English prelates were up in arms, led by the Bishop of Winchester who, acting under his commission as legate, called together a synod at which he denounced his brother's actions. Stephen, however, would give no redress, and three months later, on the death of Bishop Roger, seized all his plate and treasures.

It was in the midst of these dissensions that the Empress and the Earl of Gloucester decided to come to England. They landed in the autumn at Arundel, bringing 140 knights with them. This was the signal for civil war to break out in earnest. At once Miles of Brecknock, who was also constable of Gloucester, and Brian Fitz Count, the lord of the honour of Wallingford, threw off the mask and joined the Earl of Gloucester at Bristol, two adhesions which gave the Empress control of the upper Thames region; and soon the whole south-west from Wiltshire to Cornwall was practically lost to Stephen, together with Herefordshire. But elsewhere very few barons joined Matilda's standard openly, the most notable man to do so being Nigel, Bishop of Ely, who had shared in the indignities meted out to his uncle Bishop Roger and who was eager for revenge. The main object of the Empress was to expand her influence eastwards and get possession of London and Winchester, the acknowledged seats of government; for it was idle to proclaim herself queen until she could see her way to secure coronation at Westminster. Events were to shew, however, that her military forces were too weak for this purpose, unless she could win over one or more of the greater magnates in the eastern counties and so undermine Stephen's hold on that side of England. But this she never really accomplished, in spite of some momentary successes; and so the struggle, after dragging on for some eight years, was, in 1148, dropped without achieving anything beyond a pitiful devastation of the countryside and the total disorganisation of Henry I's elaborate system of government. In 1140 the chief fighting was in Wiltshire and was characterised by many excesses and cruelties on the part of the Empress' men. But the raids and sieges had no marked effect on Stephen's defences and did not even deter Louis VII, who had become King of France in 1137, from betrothing his sister Constance to Stephen's eldest son. It would seem, however, that Stephen's confidence was shaken, for the year is marked by the creation of three new earldoms in favour of Hugh Bigod, William of Roumare, and Geoffrey de Mandeville. These three barons became respectively Earls of Norfolk, Lincoln, and Essex; and as they all later on played Stephen false, it certainly looks as if these new dignities were conferred in the hope of binding men to his side whose allegiance was known to be wavering. If so, Stephen's action may be criticised as unwise and weak and as shewing his want of foresight. At the same time it should be noted that the recipients of his favour were all magnates of the first rank and quite able to support these dignities out of their own resources; nor was the policy of creating additional earls a novelty in 1140. Both Rufus and Henry I had adopted it sparingly; and Stephen himself in 1138, before he was in any danger, had made William of Aumâle and Robert de Ferrers Earls of York and Derby respectively, to reward them for their services in repelling the Scots, and had further set up a marcher earldom of Pembroke for Gilbert of Clare in the hope of providing a leader to repel the Welsh princes who, in 1136, had slain Clare's elder brother Richard Fitz Gilbert and overrun the cantrefs of Cardigan and Dyfed and the vale of Towy.

The first of the magnates advanced by Stephen to comital rank to desert his cause was the Earl of Lincoln, who was dissatisfied because his Norman estates were in danger and because the custody of the royal castle at Lincoln, which he claimed as heir of the house of Tailbois, had not been entrusted to him by the king as well as the earldom of the county. To shew his displeasure the earl, with the help of his half-brother Ranulf, Earl of Chester, who had equally large interests in Lincolnshire and his own grievances to avenge, seized Lincoln Castle at Christmastide 1140; and, when Stephen hurried thither with a royal force to drive them out, sent messages to the Earl of Gloucester asking him to come and assist them. Naturally Earl Robert seized so favourable an opportunity to obtain a footing in the eastern counties; and on 2 February 1141 a battle was fought outside the gates of Lincoln, in which Stephen, though he had the assistance of six earls, was beaten and himself captured. So unexpected a stroke of fortune, after a period of almost stalemate lasting some sixteen months, seemed at first a decisive triumph for the Empress. Not that the victory gave her the control of Lincolnshire. The brother earls were merely fighting for their own hands and had no more desire to see her in real authority than the easy-going Stephen. Nor were the citizens of Lincoln and the minor landowners of the shire won over. But still the possession of Stephen's person seemed everything; and Earl Robert, to whom he had surrendered, at once carried him off to Gloucester and a few days later lodged him in Bristol Castle for safe keeping.

The Empress herself, on hearing her good fortune, was intoxicated with joy, and at once started for Winchester with the object of securing the royal treasure and the king's crown, which were kept in the castle. It was at this juncture that Stephen's folly in offending the churchmen made itself felt. Instead of opposing the Empress, Henry of Winchester, the legate, came to meet her at Wherwell and agreed to recognise her as "Lady of England" (*Domina Angliae*), on the condition that he should have his way in all ecclesiastical matters. This conditional adhesion of Stephen's brother was followed by the surrender of Winchester Castle, and on 3 March the Empress was able to have herself proclaimed Queen of England in Winchester market-place. But she had yet to be elected and to secure London, before she could be crowned with the traditional rites in Westminster Abbey. A month later, in the absence of the Empress, the legate called another synod together at Winchester and in the name of the Church declared her elected, but it was only towards the end of June that she was able to enter London. Meantime she had been acting as *de facto* sovereign, appointing a bishop of London, and creating new earldoms of Cornwall, Devon, and Somerset for her half-brother Reginald and her well-tried supporters, Baldwin de Redvers and William de Mohun. Oxford, too, had been surrendered to her and the Earl of Essex brought over to her side by the grant of a number of valuable Crown estates, and by his appointment as hereditary sheriff and justiciar of his county. The Empress, however, was not destined to be actually crowned. During her brief tenure of power she had excited general disgust by her intolerable arrogance; and she reached London with only a small following to find herself almost immediately threatened by the advance of Stephen's queen on Southwark with a considerable force. This marks the turn of the tide. Immediately the Londoners rose and forced the Empress, who had tried to tax them, to an ignominious flight, whereupon Henry of Winchester went back to his brother's side. To avenge this the Empress besieged him at Winchester, but Queen Matilda, with the Londoners and many barons, came to the rescue and not only routed the Empress' forces but took the Earl of Gloucester prisoner. The Empress' cause was at once ruined. On 1 November Stephen was released in exchange for Gloucester, and at Christmas he was re-crowned at Canterbury by Archbishop Theobald.

The restoration of Stephen to power in eastern and central England in no way put an end to the civil war. All through the spring and summer of 1142 the Empress remained in possession of her advanced post at Oxford, eager to march again to London, and it was not till the Earl of Gloucester had departed to Normandy to seek help from the Count of Anjou that Stephen renewed his attacks. Meantime, both leaders had been bargaining for support. Stephen, for example, late in 1141 created two more earls, making the head of the great house of Clare Earl of Hertford, and giving the earldom of Sussex to William of Albini, who, as husband of Henry I's widow, had possession of the honour of Arundel in addition to his extensive Norfolk fief. These grants seem to have been made in reply to the Empress, who somewhat earlier had created Miles of Gloucester and Brecon, her staunchest supporter, Earl of Hereford. Stephen also journeyed north to York and came to terms with the Earls of Chester and Lincoln. The stiffest bargaining, however, was over the allegiance of the crafty Geoffrey de Mandeville, Earl of Essex, who was hereditary Constable of the Tower of London. He had at once deserted the Empress when the Londoners expelled her, and at Christmas 1141 had obtained an extraordinary charter from Stephen which made him hereditary Sheriff and Justiciar of Middlesex and Hertfordshire as well as of Essex, and bestowed upon him and his son lands worth no less than £500 a year. But even this enormous endowment at the expense of the Crown did not keep the earl faithful for many months. In June the Empress again won him over by yet more lavish promises and by conferring an English earldom on Aubrey de Vere, Count of Guisnes and Chamberlain of England, his wife's brother, who took Oxfordshire for his county though his lands lay near Colchester. Such preposterous bids and counterbids apparently shew that both sides considered Mandeville's support the key to victory, carrying as it did the control of the Tower of London; but the extravagance of these concessions should not be regarded as typical of the methods of either leader. If they had been, neither Stephen nor the Empress would have retained any resources. Only one other person, in fact, is known to have received exceptionally large grants of land. This was the Fleming, William of Ypres; but he received no offices and well repaid Stephen's generosity by his devoted services.

The pause for negotiations was followed in the autumn of 1142 by a determined attack on Oxford. The town was easily occupied, but the Empress held out in the castle for three months, and eventually escaped

on a snowy night by climbing down a rope hung from the battlements, and
got away to Wallingford. By this time the Earl of Gloucester had returned
from Normandy bringing the Empress' little son Henry with him and
a force of 360 knights. But this reinforcement was inadequate to restore
his sister's fortunes and only enabled him in 1143 and 1144 to maintain
his hold on Dorset and Wiltshire. Meantime Stephen took heart, and
late in 1143 forced the Earl of Essex to surrender his castles. This
move gave Stephen undisputed control of London and Essex, but Mandeville himself set up his standard in the fenlands, and having seized
Ramsey and the Isle of Ely, held out there, plundering the surrounding
country like a brigand until his death from a wound nine months later.
A terrible account of his cruelties, especially of his pitiless attacks on
villages and churches and of his extortions and use of torture, can be read
in the Peterborough Chronicle; for there can be little doubt that the
much-quoted picture of Stephen's reign, with which the Chronicle ends,
though it professes to be a picture of all England, was really inspired by
memories of the outrages which the monks had seen enacted in their
own neighbourhood in 1144. With the removal of Mandeville and the
return of Vere to his allegiance the Empress' chances of success finally
faded away. For three years more the Earl of Gloucester kept up a desultory struggle; but he too died in 1147, and early the next year Matilda,
convinced that all hope of gaining her inheritance was gone, left England
for good, her little son Henry having departed some time previously.

Freed of his rival's presence, Stephen had a second chance of making
himself master of England. The Angevin party was at a very low ebb,
and had he made a determined effort to secure Wallingford, Gloucester,
and Bristol, he might have reduced it to submission. He was, however,
much too easy-going to seize the opportunity, and allowed five years
(1147–1152) to pass away, during which no active operations are recorded,
except a half-hearted attempt to take Worcester from the men of the
Count of Meulan, who had declared definitely for the Empress to escape
losing his Beaumont patrimony in Normandy. Even when the young
Henry reappeared in England in 1149 to rally his depressed friends,
Stephen made no attempt at all to interfere with his movements, but
allowed the youth to journey unmolested all the way to Carlisle to visit
his great-uncle King David. When he heard that the Earl of Chester,
who desired to secure Lancaster, had also gone to Carlisle, he was indeed
obliged to take some notice; but his action took the unwise form of
bribing the earl to remain loyal by extravagant grants of land in Nottinghamshire and Leicestershire and by allowing him once more to take
possession of Lincoln Castle. This undignified move achieved its purpose
for the moment; and Henry, who was only sixteen, retired to Normandy
having effected nothing. That Henry's visit was so peaceful shews that
both sides were tired of fighting; and evidently Stephen, provided he was
left in peace, was quite content to let south-western England alone. It

did not seem to matter to him that his writs did not run there. In the bulk of England on the other hand, where the popular sentiment was on his side, he still maintained his predecessor's forms of government, appointing sheriffs and justices and holding the royal and communal courts; but such scraps of evidence as we have shew that his revenues were carelessly collected, and that the standard of order which he maintained was a very low one, each petty baron being allowed to build himself a stronghold and pursue his private feuds with his neighbours without much hindrance. The simple explanation is that Stephen was fast ageing. In 1147 he must have been nearly sixty, and it was only in ecclesiastical matters, where fighting was not needful, that he seems still to have desired to get his way. But even this display of will was unfortunate, as it led him into a serious quarrel with Pope Eugenius III over filling the archbishopric of York and into a rash attempt to prevent the Archbishop of Canterbury from attending a council held by the Pope at Rheims in 1148. In both matters Stephen could plead that he was following in the footsteps of Henry I; but the ecclesiastical world regarded his actions as breaches of his promise that the Church should be free. The result was that both the Papacy and Archbishop Theobald became his declared enemies; and when in 1151 Stephen desired to have his son Eustace crowned and formally recognised as his successor, they both refused to permit any prelate to perform the ceremony, even though Stephen gave way in the matter of the archbishopric of York. In spite of this rebuff, as he had survived so many difficulties, and as the Count of Anjou and his wife continued to leave him in peace, Stephen at this time probably considered his son's succession reasonably certain. But the reality was different. The real danger lay not in England but in Normandy, where the Count of Anjou had been steadily gaining power year by year ever since Stephen had turned his back on the duchy in 1138. As a prudent man, Count Geoffrey had never shewn any desire to help his wife in England; but in the duchy he had made the most of every opportunity for establishing her claims, and by patience had not only conquered the land but by his good government had almost brought the inhabitants to forget their anti-Angevin bias and become supporters of his family interests. He had first begun to make progress in 1141 when he got possession of Falaise and Lisieux. In 1142 he acquired the Avranchin and the Cotentin. By the end of 1143 the majority of the Norman prelates and fief-holders joined him, led by the Count of Meulan; and in 1144 even the capital and the Archbishop of Rouen submitted, whereupon Geoffrey publicly assumed the title of duke. A little later Louis VII formally invested him with the duchy, and by 1145 only the castle of Arques still held out for Stephen. Having conquered the duchy, Geoffrey at once set to work to restore it to order, but he was wise enough to make it clear that he held his prize for his son Henry and not for himself. Wherever he could, he continued the institutions and policy of Henry I, and made no attempt to introduce Angevin customs. He suppressed the justiciarship and made Rouen much more the capital than it had been before, but he retained all the traditions of the Anglo-Norman chancery, and when he wanted new officials drew his recruits from Normandy and not from Anjou. He had his son instructed by the most famous Norman scholar of the time, William of Conches, and in issuing charters, though he ignored the Empress, frequently joined the young Henry's name with his own, and declared that he was acting with his advice and consent. Finally, as soon as his son, in 1150, reached the age of seventeen, he invested him with the duchy and himself withdrew to Anjou. The very next year Count Geoffrey in the prime of his manhood died suddenly of a fever, and the young Henry unexpectedly found himself Count of Anjou and Maine as well as Duke of Normandy, and secure at any rate on the continent in the position which his grandfather Henry I had so ardently desired should be in store for him. The sudden elevation of the young Henry to a position of power and prestige was a threat to Stephen which he could not well have anticipated; and the menace became even greater in May 1152, when the young duke was married to Eleanor of Aquitaine, the divorced wife of Louis VII, and in her right became Count of Poitou and overlord of all the fiefs in south-western France from Limoges to the Pyrenees. At a stroke Henry had become feudal head of territories as large as Stephen's, and it was only to be expected that, as soon as he possibly could, he would make a serious attempt to regain his mother's English inheritance.

The imminence of the danger woke up Stephen. As soon as he heard of Henry's doings, he renewed his demand that Eustace should be crowned and also ordered an attack on Wallingford, the unsubdued stronghold whence Brian Fitz Count had defiantly upheld the cause of the Empress in the Thames valley for nearly fourteen years. The resumption of active measures, however, came too late. Rather than obey Stephen, Archbishop Theobald fled across the Channel, and before the resistance of Wallingford could be overcome Henry himself arrived in England with a small force of knights and foot-soldiers. He landed in January 1153 and at once received an offer of support from the Earl of Chester. A few weeks later he captured Malmesbury and relieved Wallingford. But the desire for peace was so general that a truce was agreed upon for negotiations. This enabled Henry to visit Bristol, whence he set out on a march through central England, visiting in turn Warwick, Leicester, Stamford, and Nottingham. The reception he met with was a mixed one, but clearly the midlands were wavering. Meantime Stephen was detained in East Anglia, having to face the Earl of Norfolk who had seized Ipswich in Henry's interest. So matters stood six months after Henry's landing, when suddenly England was startled by the news that Stephen's heir Eustace had died at Bury St Edmunds. Only a year before Stephen had lost his devoted wife, and this second family catastrophe seems to have deprived him of all desire to prolong the dynastic struggle, even though he had another son in whose interest he might have gone on fighting. He accordingly permitted his brother the Bishop of Winchester to join with Archbishop Theobald in mediating a peace, by which it was arranged that he should remain King of England for his life but that Henry should be recognised as his successor and should in future be consulted in all the business of the realm. This settlement, which was ratified in November by Henry and his partisans doing homage to Stephen at Winchester before an assembly of magnates, was welcome to all parties; to Stephen because he was old and broken, to Stephen's heir William because he was unambitious and was guaranteed the earldom of Surrey in right of his wife and also the succession to all his father's private fiefs, to the barons because it freed them from the fear of the rule of the Empress and secured them the restoration of their Norman estates, to the leaders of the Church and the Papacy because it meant the humiliation of a prince who had tried to thwart them, and to the mass of the people because it promised the return of order after fifteen years of license and the destruction of the mushroom castles which had been dominating the country-side. To the young Henry the slight concessions made to Stephen were unimportant. He was still under twenty-one and could well afford to wait for an undisputed succession. Besides he had plenty of problems to occupy his attention in his continental duchies and could not afford to remain indefinitely in England. As it turned out, Henry had not to stand aside for long. Having set the work of restoration on foot he withdrew about Easter 1154 to Normandy, but six months later Stephen died and in December Henry returned to London for his coronation at Westminster, determined to re-establish his grandfather's system of government in every particular.

The years which witnessed the struggle for the throne between Stephen and Matilda form a dismal and barren period when compared with the thirty years of peace and progress enjoyed under the elder Henry. It is doubtful, however, whether historians have not been inclined to paint them in too sombre colours, indulging in generalisations which seem to assume that all parts of England were plunged into anarchy for fifteen years. So far as fighting is concerned, this clearly was not the case. At times and in certain districts, chiefly in the valley of the upper Thames and in the fens round Ely and Ramsey, there was no doubt serious havoc; but in the greater part of England the fighting was never very serious or prolonged. What the people had to complain of was the failure to put down ordinary crime and robbery and the ineffectiveness of the courts of justice. They could see the feudal lords constantly arrogating new powers to themselves, and attempting new exactions. But it is impossible to suppose that the feudal lords as a whole were guilty of the crimes and outrages which undoubtedly were committed by some of the Empress' captains in Wiltshire and by Geoffrey de Mandeville. The pictures painted in the Peterborough Chronicle and by monastic writers generally are certainly overdrawn. If some feudal lords were turbulent and cruel, it cannot be overlooked that a considerable number of the magnates from Stephen downwards were remarkable at this period for their works of piety. It was in Stephen's reign that the only English monastic order was founded by Gilbert of Sempringham, that the canons of Prémontré first came to England, and that the Orders of Savigny and Cîteaux spread over the country. In all more than fifty religious houses were founded and endowed by the baronage at this time. Castle building and priory building in fact go very much together. Another point to be remembered is that for the most part the boroughs were free from exactions throughout the reign. A few were the scenes of fighting, but none had to pay the heavy aids which Henry had imposed. It was the same with the Danegeld. So far as is known Stephen never attempted to levy it. The charge against him is, not that he was avaricious but that he failed to get in his revenues. All accounts agree that he was genial and generous. He had no ambition to play a part on the continent or to be an autocrat; and so he let the powers of the Crown be curtailed, and lived on his own revenues. His reign in fact was disastrous for the autocratic ideal of government set up by the Conqueror and elaborated by Henry; it also witnessed a growth in the pretensions of the clergy, and the practice of appealing to the Pope. But to those who do not place order above everything and who realise how oppressive Henry's government was becoming in spite of its legality, it must always remain a moot question whether Stephen's reign was such a total set-back for the mass of the people as the ecclesiastical writers of the day would have us believe. At any rate, in the sphere of the arts, of learning, and of manners there were movements which are hard to reconcile with an age given over to anarchy. In architecture, for instance, the activity, which under Henry's orderly rule had perhaps culminated in Flambard's buildings at Durham, by no means ceased. On the contrary, it was under Stephen that the great naves were erected at Norwich and Bury St Edmunds by Bishop Eborard and Abbot Anselm, that the minster arose at Romsey and the noble hospital of St Cross at Winchester, that the pointed arch was introduced at Fountains and Buildwas, that stone vaulting began to be used for large spans in place of the flat painted wooden ceilings, and that sculptured doorways became numerous. In literature and learning it was the period when Geoffrey of Monmouth published his epoch-making romances and was rewarded by Stephen with the bishopric of St Asaph; when Adelard, the pioneer student of Arabic science and philosophy, wrote his treatise on the astrolabe at Bath and dedicated it to the young Henry Plantagenet; when Robert of Cricklade abridged Pliny's *Natural History*, and when John of Salisbury acquired his love of the classics. It was the period when the ideas of chivalry began to take hold of the baronage, and when tournaments first became popular. Finally, it was a period when no attempt was made to debase the coinage, and when the two races, French and English, began to be blended into one nation.

CH. XVI.

that thereafter all the business of the kingdom was done through him. In any case, the work of demolishing the unlicensed castles of the anarchy was begun before Stephen's death, although the slowness with which the work was accomplished almost caused a rupture between Henry and Stephen. As king, Henry carried on the work, and used in the administration men who had served Stephen before him. Archbishop Theobald of Canterbury, Robert, Earl of Leicester, Richard de Luci, had all played their parts in Stephen's reign. They now became Henry's chief advisers, together with Reginald, Earl of Cornwall, his uncle, and Thomas Becket, one of Theobald's clerks, whom Henry made Chancellor on the archbishop's advice. Nigel, Bishop of Ely, Henry I's treasurer, was called in to re-organise the Exchequer.

The assertion of royal authority was made without difficulty. Ranulf, Earl of Chester, who had nearly created for himself an independent principality in central England, died in December 1153, leaving a child as his heir. No one seems to have considered the possibility of making Stephen's surviving son, William, king. The Church was on Henry's side, and the baronage, tired of a weak king, accepted the situation. After keeping his Christmas court at Bermondsey, Henry visited the northern and eastern parts of his kingdom. On 23 January he was at Lincoln with the Archbishop of Canterbury and the Master of the Templars in England[1]. In February he was at York, and William of Aumâle, Earl of Yorkshire, surrendered the castle of Scarborough. Thence Henry went to Nottingham, and William Peverel of Nottingham, the greatest baron of Nottingham and Derby, suspected of poisoning the Earl of Chester, took shelter under the cowl. The only serious opposition to the surrender of castles was in the west. Roger, Earl of Hereford, fortified Hereford and Gloucester; Hugh Mortimer fortified Wigmore, Cleobury Mortimer, and Bridgnorth. The Earl submitted on the persuasion of the Bishop of Hereford, Gilbert Foliot, but the subjugation of Hugh Mortimer's castles occupied most of the summer of 1155.

At a great council held at Wallingford in April Henry tried to secure the succession to the throne. He caused all the magnates to swear fealty to himself and his heirs, William, who was not yet two, and, failing William, Henry, born in the preceding February. At the Winchester council in September he put forward his plan of conquering Ireland, to make a principality for his younger brother William. It seems to be this proposal, together with the Toulouse war of 1159, that has made historians talk of Henry as of one who set order in his kingdom that he might engage in wars of conquest. It is the prerogative of youth to dream, but history suggests that Henry's dreams were short. There was sound political reason for the Irish proposal of 1155: William's support was necessary, for Henry's second brother, Geoffrey, was making trouble by insisting on his claims to Anjou and Touraine. To suppress him,

---

[1] Cott. Vespasian E. xviii f. 73d.

and to assure himself of the loyalty of Aquitaine and Normandy, Henry left England in January 1156. The capture of Geoffrey's castles of Mirabeau and Chinon ended his revolt. He was satisfied with compensation in money and permission to accept the invitation of the men of the eastern part of Brittany and make himself Count of Nantes. In his attitude towards Brittany, both now and later in his reign, Henry was but maintaining the policy of his ancestors who claimed overlordship of that province. In his relations with continental powers the same feeling can be traced, a desire to lose nothing that had come to him by inheritance or marriage; no right must be given up, no claim allowed to lapse. But Henry was only an aggressor in so far as he forced others to recognise claims which they would rather see forgotten. The war of Toulouse which occupied the July, August, and September of 1159 was undertaken to recover Toulouse, to which Henry inherited a title through his wife. When the King of France interfered, Henry gave up the war; to continue it against his overlord would have been going beyond his right.

The question of Henry's relations with Wales and Scotland had to be faced early in the reign. Both countries had gained by the anarchy in England. David of Scotland had been succeeded in 1153 by his grandson Malcolm IV, who visited Henry in England, and agreed to surrender Northumberland and Cumberland, with the castles of Bamburgh, Newcastle, and Carlisle. Either at Peak Castle or at Chester he did homage to Henry for his English lands, the honour of Huntingdon. A Welsh expedition was not only essential from the standpoint of general policy; it was a means of securing the gratitude of marcher lords who had lost land in the time of Stephen. The object of Henry's attack was the northern kingdom of Gwynedd, where Owen Gwynedd had built up a principality which Ranulf, Earl of Chester, himself had feared. The succession of a child of six to the earldom exposed it to Owen's attacks. Henry's Welsh expedition of 1158, though not a brilliant military success, achieved for the moment its end; Owen was forced to give hostages, and his activities were checked for a time. Rhys ap Gruffydd, the ruler of Deheubarth, the southern kingdom, after some hesitation, acknowledged the overlordship of Henry. The Clares and Cliffords were restored to the lands that Rhys had conquered in the previous reign. Neither Rhys, however, nor Owen was prepared to acquiesce in any reduction of power, and in 1162 Rhys took Llandovery Castle from Walter Clifford. In the next year Henry led an expedition into Wales, passing through Carmarthen and taking Rhys prisoner at Pencader. Rhys was allowed to do homage and return to his principality, but he immediately re-opened war, ravaging Cardigan until little more than the castle and the town remained to the Normans. Henry's absorption in the Becket quarrel after 1163 encouraged Rhys and Owen to make a combined attack on the marcher barons. The lesser princes of Wales were attracted into the alliance by the prestige of the two leaders. The failure of Henry's great expedition of 1165 to suppress the coalition secured for the Welsh another hundred years of freedom. Henry made no other great effort, and from that time his attention was confined to strengthening the border castles. His concern was not to restrain the Welsh princes or keep their lands for the marcher lords, but merely to retain the overlordship of the two kingdoms of Deheubarth and Gwynedd. In the troubles of the rebellion of 1173-4 the Welsh princes were faithful to Henry.

The minister to whom Henry from the first gave his fullest confidence was Thomas Becket, his Chancellor. The office of chancellor involved the custody of the king's seal and constant attendance on his person: Becket is almost always a witness, often the sole witness, to the charters and writs of the early years of the reign. His power, however, depended not on his office, but on his intimacy with the king. It was at Henry's gift that he received the custody of vacant benefices, not by virtue of his office as chancellor. Becket acquired wealth and became a leader of fashion. Too busy to return to his archidiaconal duties, he earned but mild reproaches from his archbishop and requests that he would forward certain business with the king. Through him the king might be approached not only by schemers like Arnulf, Bishop of Lisieux, but by such men as John of Salisbury. The circumstances of Becket's death have secured the preservation of masses of material, not only relating to his life as archbishop, but also to his time as chancellor. His work can also be traced in the official language of the Pipe Roll clerks. He was concerned in the restoration of order, in the administration of justice, in diplomatic business at the French court. His writ could authorise the payment of money out of the treasury, a right that later in the reign belonged only to the Justiciar. It was with reason, though in flattery, that Peter, Abbot of La Celle at Troyes, wrote: "Who does not know you to be second to the king in four kingdoms?"

Archbishop Theobald died in April 1161, and a year passed before Henry decided that Becket should succeed him. The stories of Henry's announcement of his decision to Thomas and Thomas' unwillingness to become primate were probably invented to fit the history of the struggle. The *nolo episcopari* of Thomas was probably no less common form than that of most contemporary bishops; there is nothing in his career to suggest an unwillingness to accept great office. He was a man of high ambitions. Of undoubted ability, he was, however, not fitted to be Lanfranc to Henry's William. He had neither the training nor the sanity of that great archbishop and administrator, nor among the churchmen of Henry's day would it have been easy to find a second Lanfranc. Henry's hesitation may mean that he was not sure of Becket. There is no evidence that he was obnoxious to the ecclesiastical party as a whole; Gilbert Foliot, Bishop of Hereford and afterwards of London, was never his friend, but Theobald seems to have desired him for a successor. Once Becket was consecrated, he tried to be the perfect archbishop. He resigned the chancellorship, though he did not give up the archdeaconry of Canterbury until the king forced him to do so. He played the ascetic as perfectly as he had played the courtier. There was no insincerity in this changed way of life.

He shewed from the first a determination to let go no right which the Church could claim. His attitude was natural, for it must have seemed a noble thing to be head of the Church in England. He set about winning back for his own Church of Canterbury the lands and rights which it had lost. No claim was too shadowy for him. He demanded from the king the custody of the castles of Rochester, Saltwood, and Hythe, from the Earl of Hertford, Roger de Clare, his homage for Tonbridge Castle. Forgetting his own past, he deprived clerks in the king's service of the benefices in the see of Canterbury that they held as their reward. As archbishop he claimed rights of patronage over all benefices on land held by tenants of the see; he excommunicated William of Eynsford, a tenant-in-chief for other lands, for resisting the application of this claim. He came into conflict with the king over a matter of general administration. In July 1163 at the council of Woodstock, Henry proposed that the sheriff's aid should be paid into the royal treasury. Becket's opposition was so vigorous that Henry dropped the plan. Flagrant cases of the inadequacy of ecclesiastical punishment for crime, and of abuse in ecclesiastical courts, came to complete the estrangement. On 1 October 1163 at the council at Westminster the question of criminous clerks was discussed at length. The king and his advisers demanded that accused clerks should answer the accusation in the lay court, that they should be handed over to the ecclesiastical court for trial and judgment, and that if the accused were found guilty he should be degraded and given up to the secular power for punishment. Warrant for this procedure could be found in Canon Law. Becket, with the support of the bishops, answered, not that Henry's interpretation of Canon Law was unjustifiable, but that "God will not judge a man twice for the same offence." Realising that Becket would continue to evade the question of law, Henry fell back on custom, and asked whether the bishops were prepared to observe the ancient customs of the kingdom. After discussing the matter among themselves, they said that they were prepared to observe them, "saving their order." Hilary, Bishop of Chichester, alone promised to observe them without this reservation. Henry broke up the council in exasperated fury.

The king used every means in his power to overcome the clerical opposition. He removed his heir from Becket's charge, and he took from Becket the custody of the castles and honours of Eye and Berkhampstead. He did his utmost to make a party against Becket among the bishops, and the Archbishop of York and the Bishop of London promised to observe the customs. In the last three months of 1163, Arnulf, Bishop of Lisieux, and Richard of Ilchester, afterwards Bishop of Winchester, are said to have crossed the sea six times to gain the Pope's assent to the customs. The Pope himself, exiled from Rome and travelling in northern France, was unwilling to offend Henry. He obviously wished Becket to moderate his opposition, although he did not immediately accede to Henry's requests that Roger, Archbishop of York, should be appointed legate in succession to Theobald, and that the bishops should be ordered to obey the customs. Before the end of the year Becket gave way to the expostulations of the bishops and the fears of the Pope and cardinals; he promised his consent to the customs.

A council was therefore summoned to meet at Clarendon in January 1164 at which Becket might give his formal assent. He is said to have come repenting his promise and prepared to withdraw it. The king in the meantime must have caused the customs to be carefully drawn up and engrossed. The writing of the Constitutions cannot have been left, as some authorities would have us believe, until the council was in actual progress; they were produced on the first day of the council. Becket was only induced to agree to them by the persuasions of bishops, two knights of the Temple, and the two senior earls, Cornwall and Leicester. After giving his unqualified assent to the Constitutions and allowing the bishops to do the same, Becket refused to take the irrevocable step of sealing the document. The Constitutions had been engrossed *modo cirografi*, that is, they had been written out three times on one piece of parchment. Before the parchment was severed into three, the two archbishops and the king should each have affixed his seal to each copy of the Constitutions. Since Becket refused his seal, the document apparently unsealed, was cut into three parts. One part was given to the Archbishop of York, one was thrust into Becket's hand, and the third was laid up in the royal treasury.

There is no evidence that the general body of English clergy felt that the Constitutions of Clarendon were any other than Henry claimed, that is, an accurate representation of the customs of his grandfather's time. The relations between Church and State had never exactly been defined before. Such hesitation as the bishops may have felt in agreeing to the Constitutions was probably due to a natural dislike of definition and fear of precedent. The Church won little by Becket's death because it wished to win little. It was not an aggressive body, and many of the judges in its courts had been trained, some were still actually engaged, in the king's service. To say that the king's policy at this time meant an inevitable quarrel between Church and State is to go beyond the evidence. What might have been expected was an assertion of the right of the king's court to define the limits of ecclesiastical jurisdiction, and, thereafter, competition between the Church courts and the lay courts for jurisdiction over individual cases. Henry did not begin the quarrel by attempting a general revision of ecclesiastical justice. His ultimatum, in the Constitutions, was as much directed against and caused by Becket's

general attitude of arrogant and aggressive rectitude as by the abuses of
ecclesiastical courts. A few years later, at the time of the Inquest of
Sheriffs, the barons submitted to a far more drastic supervision of feudal
justice than Henry ever proposed in the case of the courts of the Church.
Thomas was an exception among the churchmen of his day. He would
have found a congenial atmosphere in the Curia of Boniface VIII.

The fate of the Constitutions indicates the attitude of the English
Church to Henry's claims. Only in regard to criminous clerks and appeals
to the Pope was Henry forced to give way. Both sides laid particular
emphasis on the clause dealing with criminous clerks. Opinion among
canonists as to the validity of Henry's claims was divided. Passages in
Canon Law could be interpreted to mean that clerks found guilty and
degraded in the ecclesiastical court should be handed over to the lay
court for punishment. It does not seem to have been the opinion of
canonists that this procedure was contrary to the dictum so constantly on
Becket's lips. The archbishop was no canonist, and there were those who
said that he was not even scholar enough to make a speech in Latin.
He concentrated on the question of punishment. His murder secured
for clerks immunity from lay punishment for their first crime. But it
should be remembered that, when Henry submitted on this point, and
indeed throughout the next century, the word clerk had not the wide
interpretation that it received in later times. In the twelfth and thirteenth centuries a clerk had to prove his ordination, at least to the
sub-diaconate, before he was handed over to the official of the Church
to be tried in Court Christian. Moreover Henry succeeded in forcing
accused clerks to appear in the lay court to prove their clergy, although
Canon Law gives no justification for the practice. So much he gained.
His unfortunate surrender of the right to punish the guilty clerk left an
opening for private revenge. In 1202, in a trial for murder at Lincoln,
it was stated that the murdered man had been degraded from the
diaconate for killing a relative of the defendant.

The king retained without serious question much of what the Constitutions gave him. Advowsons remained lay property; the king kept
control over the churches of his fee; elections to bishoprics were conducted as before in the king's chapel. For the rest, the relations between
Church and State were left to be worked out in the practice of the courts.
By the Constitutions the king had agreed that jurisdiction over land
held in free alms belonged to the Church courts; but he had secured to
his own court the right of adjudging, in accordance with the verdict of a
jury, whether the land at issue were lay fee or free alms. Had the
Church courts been able to keep all the jurisdiction this clause would
have given them, much business would have been lost to the king's court;
for during the last half of the twelfth and throughout the thirteenth
century innumerable grants of lands were being made to religious houses
in free alms. By John's day it was highly exceptional for this procedure

by the assize *utrum*, as it was called from the words of the writ which began it, to be a prelude to a suit in the ecclesiastical court. The assize rolls shew the religious houses using the layman's forms of action in the lay courts. The assize *utrum* was already almost entirely confined to rectors of parish churches, who without it would have found difficulty in proving their right to the lands of their church appropriated by laymen. If the jury's verdict in such a suit declared the land to be free alms the parson recovered his land without further process of law. In this respect at least the king had won far more than the customs of Henry I would have given him. But the king's courts found it difficult to maintain what Henry had asserted at Clarendon, jurisdiction over debts where the bargain had included the formal pledging of faith. No one doubted that it belonged to the Church courts to deal with questions of broken faith. Henry declared in effect that the *affidatio*, or pledging of faith, was not essential to the legal validity of a bargain, and that suits touching the bargain must be heard in his court. The lay court won in the end, but it had to contend not only with ecclesiastical courts more eager for jurisdiction than those of the twelfth century, but also against the religious feeling of the English people.

Becket never intended to observe the Constitutions. He abstained from the service of the altar as a penance for his weakness in ever promising to observe them; and he even made an ineffectual attempt to leave the country. The Pope took neither side, not daring to offend Henry nor wishing to desert Becket. The next move came from the king. An officer of the court, John the Marshal, father of the famous William Marshall, Earl of Pembroke, complained to the king that the archbishop's court had failed in justice in a plea which he had brought for the recovery of land held of the see of Canterbury, and Becket was summoned to answer for the failure of his court. Instead of sending an essoin, a formal excuse for non-attendance, he sent four knights with letters from himself and the sheriff of Kent to answer on his behalf. The case was adjourned, and Becket was summoned to appear at a great council at Northampton in October, to answer both for his previous contempt of the king's court and for the failure of his own court to do right to John the Marshal. Becket came to Northampton. He sought the king on 7 October, and his case was heard the next day. On the original question, the case of John the Marshal, the archbishop was successful, but the barons, both lay and ecclesiastical, adjudged him guilty of contempt of the king's court, and he therefore fell into the king's mercy. Although protesting that no court had the right to try him, Becket was persuaded to offer to make fine with the king for his amercement. The king, on the other hand, seems to have come to Northampton with the intention of forcing Becket's hand by attacking him in every possible way. He demanded an account of the sums which Becket had received as *custos* of the honours of Eye and Berkhampstead, of five hundred marks which he had received from the king for the Toulouse campaign, of another five hundred marks for which the king had been his pledge to a certain Jew, and finally of the issues of the vacant sees which had passed through Becket's hands while he was chancellor. Becket was forbidden to leave Northampton until he had given the king security for the whole amount. The third day of the council, Saturday 10 October, was passed by Becket in discussing with the bishops and abbots the course that he should take. However ungracious the king's demands, they did not alienate either the bishops or the laity; some bishops even urged Becket to resign the archbishopric and put himself in the king's mercy. On the following Tuesday, Becket made up his mind to defiance. He forbade the bishops to associate themselves in any judgment on him with regard to his conduct as chancellor, he appealed to the Pope, and he ordered the bishops to excommunicate all who dared to give effect to the judgment of any lay court upon him, thus directly contravening the Constitutions of Clarendon. His action placed the bishops in a difficult position. They must either endure the king's anger for breaking the eleventh clause of the Constitutions of Clarendon or the censures of the Church for disobedience to their archbishop. They evaded the dilemma by abstaining from judgment upon the archbishop, but appealing to the Pope for his deposition on the ground of his perjury in withdrawing the assent which he had originally given to the Constitutions. The king's court never delivered its judgment upon Becket. The barons, headed by Robert, Earl of Leicester, *qui dux erat verbi*, went to pronounce it, but Becket did not stay to hear it. He left the castle; next day he left Northampton; by 2 November he had crossed the Channel as a fugitive.

The quarrel begun unnecessarily by Becket was pursued unmercifully by the king. He exiled all the archbishop's kinsfolk, of whom there seem to have been many. They had become rich with drippings from Becket's abundance, and their departure impressed contemporaries so much that private documents may occasionally be found dated "in the year in which the king caused the kinsfolk of the archbishop to cross over."[1] Becket's exile lasted for six years. To a man of his temper it must have been hard to bear, and its influence upon his character was lamentable—he became fanatic. The Pope was still unwilling to commit himself. Henry tried to intimidate him by negotiations with the Emperor, but it was obvious that opinion in England, although almost wholly on Henry's side in his struggle with the archbishop, was not favourable to dealings with the anti-Pope. Alexander forbade Becket to take any irrevocable step until Easter 1166. By the time the truce expired, the Pope was back at Rome, and ready to support the archbishop. Becket was authorised to excommunicate all who had occupied the lands of Canterbury since his flight, and was given a legatine commission over all England except the see of York. At Vézelay on Whitsunday Becket excommunicated John of

[1] Cott. Nero C. III f. 200.

Oxford, afterwards Bishop of Norwich, and Richard of Ilchester, afterwards Bishop of Winchester, for communicating with the supporters of the anti-Pope. They had been Henry's ambassadors to the Emperor in 1165. Richard de Luci, the Justiciar, and Joscelin de Balliol were excommunicated as the authors and fabricators of the Constitutions, and Ranulf de Broc, Hugh de St Clare, and Thomas fitz Bernard for having occupied Canterbury lands.

The sentences brought Becket little good. The armies of Frederick Barbarossa were coming south, and the Pope himself dared not attack Henry openly. He received Henry's embassy sent to prosecute a renewed appeal on behalf of the English bishops against Becket. One of the ambassadors was John of Oxford, whom the Pope allowed to clear himself by oath of the imputations which had been the ground of his excommunication. Legates were appointed to bring about peace, but both antagonists had gone beyond reason. At Clairvaux in April 1169 Becket excommunicated Bishops Gilbert Foliot of London and Joscelin of Salisbury. Foliot had opposed Becket from the first, and had brought to his opposition a bitter wit and a gift of sarcasm which Becket could not match.

As time went on, new matters of dispute made hopeless the original quarrel over the Constitutions of Clarendon. Becket demanded all the revenues of the see of Canterbury which had accrued during his exile. In the meantime, the king had been providing for the apportionment of his possessions among his sons, and wished his heir, his eldest surviving son, Henry, to be crowned King of England. In Becket's absence, the ceremony was performed on 14 June 1170 by Roger, Archbishop of York. It is easy to understand Becket's anger at this infringement of an undoubted prerogative of his see. The bitterness had never gone out of the struggle for primacy between successive Archbishops of York and Canterbury, and Roger had never made a profession of canonical obedience to Thomas. Becket had a further, though unacknowledged, reason for resentment. Roger de Pont l'Évêque had been a senior clerk in Archbishop Theobald's household when Thomas of London had entered it from a merchant's office[1]. It is hard to understand Becket's willingness to agree to a reconciliation with Henry at Fréteval on 22 July 1170 which left every matter at issue unsettled.

The king's attitude was plain. The Pope had commissioned the Archbishop of Rouen and the Bishop of Nevers to make peace. Becket was not to insist on the arrears of the revenues of his see, and the question of the Constitutions was not to be raised until peace had been secured; in that event, the king was to be persuaded to moderate them. If Henry refused to be reconciled to the archbishop within forty days of the receipt of the Pope's letters, his continental lands were to be laid under an interdict.

---

[1] Thomas of London is the last, and Roger de Ponte episcopi the first, in a group of Archbishop Theobald's clerks who attest an archiepiscopal writ in favour of Southwark Priory. Cott. Nero C. III f. 188.

The reconciliation of Fréteval was a mere form. Nothing was said of the Constitutions, for Henry meant to maintain them, and Becket knew it. The question of the arrears was not raised, for Becket meant to have them, and Henry knew it. The king promised amends for the injury done to the archbishop by the coronation, but refused to give him the kiss of peace. Becket demanded it, though he meant war. At Becket's request, the Pope had given him letters suspending the prelates who had taken part in the coronation. These letters he sent to England before he himself landed on 1 December. On Christmas Day in Canterbury cathedral, he violently denounced his enemies, especially those who had entered upon the possessions of his see. The end of his story, which came four days later, is well-known, but Becket's secret thoughts and hopes, which undoubtedly precipitated the tragedy of 29 December, remain mysterious. There is much in his conduct at the end to suggest that he desired the martyr's crown. In Becket's heart there had always burned a fierce desire to excel. He had enjoyed the highest secular power he could hope to win; the highest ecclesiastical position in England had been his. Neither Church nor State had suffered from his exile, and even the Pope had not unreservedly supported him. He hoped to be a second and a greater Alphege; by his death he won what to him was sweeter than life.

The news of the murder reached Henry at Argentan on 1 January 1171. He is said to have spent three days in solitude. The Pope had previously instructed the Archbishops of Sens and Rouen to lay an interdict on Henry's continental lands if the archbishop were arrested. On 25 January the Archbishop of Sens published the interdict, but the Archbishop of Rouen and the Norman clergy refused to recognise the sentence. They appealed against it, and the archbishop with three bishops and three clerks set out to prosecute the appeal at the papal court. In considerable anxiety as to Alexander's attitude, Henry sent an embassy, and the excommunicated bishops sent messengers. Alexander waited until April; then he confirmed the interdict and the excommunication of the bishops. Against the king personally he took no other action than to forbid him to enter a church; legates were to be sent later to announce the terms on which absolution would be granted. After a few days the Pope was persuaded to send permission for a conditional absolution on behalf of the Bishops of London and Salisbury because of their age and infirmity. In the meantime Henry had spent the months of March and April in Brittany. England must have been simmering with excitement, for the miracles of Thomas began almost as soon as he was dead. The first miracle occurred in Sussex on the third day after the martyrdom, and the second miracle at Gloucester two days later. By Easter time "miracles came in crowds."[1] But at first it was the humble who believed. Brother Elias of Reading dared not tell his abbot of his visit to the shrine of Thomas to win a cure for his leprosy; he had asked leave to visit the

[1] Abbott, *St Thomas of Canterbury*, I, p. 249.

health-resort at Bath. Though the better-informed may have been sceptical of the miracles, the unforgiven king must have been glad to leave England for Ireland, to pass the time there until the legates should come to absolve him.

Recent events in Ireland combined with the murder to suggest that the invasion proposed in 1155 should at last be carried out. Ireland in the twelfth century resembled Britain in the days of Gildas. The position of high-king was a dignity to be fought for continually, but it gave to the winner only a nominal supremacy, a cattle tribute, and jurisdictional rights so vague as to be indefinable. In theory, each of the five divisions of Ireland—Ulster, Munster, Leinster, Connaught, and Meath—had its king. In fact, the boundaries of the provinces shifted with the varying power of the kings, whose very existence depended on success in war and the reputation which it brought. The chief preoccupation of each king was to keep his family in power against other families, and himself as against other members of his own family; no thought of establishing order in their kingdoms troubled them. Indeed, if it had, their period of power would have been short. The Scandinavian settlements along the coast, Dublin, Limerick, Waterford, Wexford, were centres where the Irish tribesmen disposed of their furs and hides, and obtained the produce of civilisation. A poor country, ridden by war, Ireland was never previously conquered because it was not worth conquest.

The immediate occasion of Norman intervention in Ireland was an appeal for help from the exiled King of Leinster, Dermot Mac Murrough. Henry gave him presents, received his homage, and issued letters patent allowing any of his subjects to assist Dermot to recover his kingdom. Dermot found help among the Norman colonists in Wales. Richard Fitz Gilbert, whose father had been created Earl of Pembroke by Stephen, was anxious to win a position in another land. The marcher lords of South Wales were steadily losing ground before the encroachments of Rhys ap Gruffydd. Richard, generally known by his father's nickname of Strongbow, bargained for Dermot's daughter in marriage, with the reversion of Leinster, and made his expedition conditional upon Henry's consent. By the end of 1169, Dermot had recovered Leinster with the help of small bands of Norman adventurers from Wales. In spite of Henry's withdrawal of his permission for the expedition, Strongbow himself landed in Ireland in August 1170, married Eva, Dermot's daughter, and succeeded him, not without opposition, on his death in May 1171. Henry, unwilling that a subject should make a kingdom in Ireland, prevented reinforcements from reaching Strongbow, and recalled him. On the news of Henry's intended expedition to Ireland, Strongbow crossed to Wales, and met the king on his way to Milford Haven. Henry allowed him to do homage for Leinster on condition that he surrendered the seaports. The king stayed in Ireland for six months, from October 1171 to April 1172, in which he took homage from many Irish chiefs, summoned a council of the Irish Church at Cashel, and authorised a programme of ecclesiastical reform. The chief seaports were garrisoned. Hugh de Lacy, in command at Dublin, was appointed Justiciar of Ireland, and was allowed to create for himself a feudal principality in Meath. The lordship of Ireland had been easily won. The Irish had no castles, their armies were only undisciplined rabbles, and the Church was on the side of the invaders. But Henry left Ireland to be subdued by the adventurers. Not trusting them, he tried to balance the native chiefs against them, and the country was therefore never conquered. When, in 1185, a great expedition was entrusted to John, Henry's youngest son, it proved an utter failure[1].

Henry left Ireland in April 1172 to meet the legates and hear the Pope's judgment. At Avranches on 21 May he received absolution. The terms of reconciliation were light. The king submitted to a public penance. He swore that he did not command nor wish the archbishop's death, that when he heard of it he grieved exceedingly, that he would give satisfaction because he could not produce the murderers, and because he feared that words of his had given occasion for the crime. He also swore that he would not withdraw from Pope Alexander and his successors, and that he would allow appeals in ecclesiastical causes, provided that, where there was any suspicion of disloyalty, security should be given that the appeal was not to the hurt of the king or kingdom. He vowed to undertake a crusade, and to give to the Templars as much money as was in their judgment necessary to maintain two hundred knights in the defence of the Cross for one year. He pardoned all those who had been exiled for St Thomas' sake, and swore that the possessions of the Church of Canterbury should be as they were one year before the murder. He swore also to destroy all the customs adverse to the Church introduced in his time, a vague promise which king and Pope could each interpret as he chose. The king, most unhappily, gave way in the matter of the criminous clerks. In regard to the other principles laid down in the Constitutions of Clarendon, there was to be a trial of strength between the king and the Pope, or rather between the king's justices and ministers and the ecclesiastical courts, a struggle none the less real because it was conducted without advertisement. Something has already been said of the struggle and its issue.

The oath to go on crusade was lightly taken. Henry evaded the obligation by promising to build three monasteries, a promise which he fulfilled at the least possible expense. Before the final ratification in September of the agreement at Avranches, Henry had known that trouble was brewing in England. His sons, encouraged by their mother, were meditating rebellion. The young king bore the style King of the

---

[1] For a short, but convincing, summary of the arguments with regard to the Bull *Laudabiliter* (authorising Henry II to conquer Ireland), see Orpen, *The Normans in Ireland*, Vol. I, Chapter IX.

English, Duke of the Normans, and Count of the men of Anjou[1]. He had done homage to the French king for Anjou and Brittany. Geoffrey, the second son, had done homage to his brother for Brittany, and had himself received the homage of the men of the province. For Aquitaine, which lay outside the young king's titles, Richard had done homage to the King of France. No independent power had been given to any of the king's sons. The young king's wife had not been crowned with her husband, a grievance to Louis VII, and after the agreement at Avranches the young king was crowned again, and his wife with him. He had his own seal and his own court, but ministers of his father composed his court and doubtless directed him in the use of his seal. That Henry should commit the rule of any part of his dominions to the reckless youth of his sons was inconceivable.

The occasion of their rebellion was Henry's attempt to provide for his youngest son John, born in 1166 or 1167. Early in 1173, a marriage was arranged between John and Alais, heiress of Humbert III, Count of Maurienne. In return for the provision that the greater part of Humbert's possessions should descend to John and his wife, Henry proposed to settle on them the three castles of Chinon, Loudun, and Mirabeau, formerly granted as an appanage to his second son Geoffrey. The young king refused his consent, and fled to the French court in March 1173. His brothers Richard and Geoffrey followed him, and Eleanor, their mother, set off to raise Poitou for Richard. She was taken and kept in confinement. Richard Barre, to whom Henry had entrusted the young king's seal, brought it back to the king, and the other ministers whom Henry had placed with his son returned to Henry, bringing with them the young king's baggage. Henry, always generous to his sons, sent back the ministers with rich gifts, but the young king dismissed those of them who would not swear fealty to him against his father. Walter the chaplain, Ailward the chamberlain, and William Blund the usher, returned to the old king; of the labours of the two last in the king's service the Pipe Rolls give ample evidence.

Barons of every province of the continental Angevin dominions joined the rebellion. The Counts of Flanders and Boulogne and William, King of Scots, gave their support. To secure it, the young king made lavish grants. His charters were sealed with a new seal which the King of France had had made for him. All Kent, with the castles of Rochester and Dover, was to go to the Count of Flanders; Carlisle and Westmorland were promised to the King of Scots; the earldom of Huntingdon and the county of Cambridge, to which the King of Scots had inherited a claim, were promised to his brother David. In England, the rebels were joined by Hugh, Earl of Chester, Robert "Blanchesmaines," Earl of

---

[1] The young king's style is so recorded in a writ, the original of which has survived, issued on behalf of the priory of St Frideswide, Oxford. *Bod. Lib. Oxford, Charters,* 59.

Leicester (son of Henry's justiciar), William de Ferrers, Earl of Derby, Hugh Bigod, Earl of Norfolk, and Roger de Mowbray, a great baron in Yorkshire and north Lincolnshire. They brought to the cause of the young king a great stretch of England and many castles. Leicester was a centre for the rebels, with Leicester Castle supported by Groby Castle five miles to the north-west and Mountsorrel seven miles to the north. The Ferrers castles of Duffield in Derbyshire and Tutbury in Stafford-shire, the Bigod castles of Bungay and Framlingham in Suffolk, and the Mowbray castles of Thirsk and Kirkby Malzeard in Yorkshire, were all held for the young king.

On Henry's side were the mass of the clergy. The legates sent to give Henry absolution remained to attempt a reconciliation between him and his sons. At their suggestion, Henry proceeded to fill all vacant bishoprics and abbeys. It was not Henry's fault that the see of Canter-bury had not been filled before, for the perennial quarrel between the prior and monks of Canterbury and the provincial bishops delayed every election. The six bishops now appointed were all chosen for their politics rather than for their religious zeal. Richard of Ilchester, elected Bishop of Winchester, was a skilled financier. Geoffrey Ridel, elected Bishop of Ely, had suc-ceeded Becket as Archdeacon of Canterbury and had borne the king's seal. Both of them were bitter opponents of Becket, and had been excom-municated in the course of the struggle. The king's illegitimate son, Geoffrey, was elected Bishop of Lincoln. In June, the monks of Canter-bury were conciliated by the election of Richard, prior of St Martin's at Dover, to the archbishopric. The young king's attempt to prevent the consecration of the prelates probably did much to confirm the eccle-siastical order in its support of his father; the only English bishop who finally joined the rebels was Hugh Puiset of Durham.

Among the barons, there were on the king's side his uncle Reginald, Earl of Cornwall, his half-brother Hamelin, Earl Warenne, his cousin William, Earl of Gloucester, William de Mandeville, Earl of Essex, Simon de Sentliz, Earl of Northampton, and William de Albini, Earl of Arundel. Although the most powerful of the earls were in revolt, the baronage as a whole was on the king's side. The rebel castles were more than balanced by the royal castles and those of loyal barons. The fee of the Earl of Derby was roughly balanced by the honour of Peverel, then in the king's hand, with its castles of Nottingham, Bolsover, and the Peak. John de Lacy, constable of Chester, was on the king's side, and his loyalty made Roger de Mowbray's defection of less moment. In East Anglia, the Warennes balanced the Bigods, and in the west, the loyal marchers and the king's Welsh auxiliaries balanced the Earl of Chester. In the north, the Umfravilles, Vauxes, Vescis, Bruces, Balliols, and Stutevilles, balanced the King of Scots. The mass of men, the lesser baronage, the sheriffs, and above all the new ministerial class, were solidly on Henry's side. Richard de Luci the justiciar, himself an Essex baron holding the castle and honour of Ongar, raised forces and garrisoned castles. The Kymes of Lincolnshire, richer than most baronial families, were active in the king's support. If Henry's sons expected a glad response in England to the call of anarchy, they were disillusioned.

The rebellion began with an attack upon Henry's position in northern France. The Earl of Chester, hereditary Viscount of Avranches and Bayeux, ravaged Brittany, in association with Breton nobles. The young king, with the Counts of Flanders and Boulogne, advanced from the east, while the King of France laid siege to Verneuil. Louis VII, though he could intrigue, could not carry through a war. He and his allies had no concerted plan; the brains were all on Henry's side. His castles were ready to stand siege, and he himself with a competent force could go where he was needed. Brittany was cleared of rebels by the end of July 1173, and the Earl of Chester was taken prisoner with many other nobles. The King of France did no more than sack Verneuil and then retreat before Henry. The rebel forces operating in the east took Aumâle, but after Matthew, Count of Boulogne, had been mortally wounded did no more. At a meeting between Trie and Gisors in September, Henry made generous offers to his sons, though denying them independent rule; his terms were refused, and after the meeting the rebels and their allies seem to have concluded that an attack on England must be made.

In England, the centres of war were the midlands, the north, and the east. There also no definite plan can be traced. No other warfare was possible at this period than a series of sieges and counter-sieges, raids and counter-raids, for neither side could call itself victorious while the other side still held unreduced castles. The justiciar took the offensive by laying siege to Leicester, and if he could have taken it, the fall of Groby and Mountsorrel would soon have followed. The town of Leicester was almost entirely destroyed by an accidental fire. The townsfolk came to terms, but the castle still held out. The justiciar arranged a truce that he might be free to meet a Scotch inroad, and together with Humphrey de Bohun, the king's constable, he chased the Scots into Scotland; but he was then obliged to make a truce with them until 13 January 1174, in order to turn south to meet an invasion by the Earl of Leicester with a body of mercenaries. The earl was one of Henry's bitterest opponents at this time. He may possibly have felt slighted because he had not succeeded his father as justiciar, though his conduct during the rebellion gives no indication that he had any of the ability necessary for such an office. He landed at Walton near Felixstowe about 18 October 1173. Walton was a royal castle, and the earl failed to take it. He joined the Earl of Norfolk at Framlingham, and together they attacked and took the great castle of Haughley, held for the king by Ranulf de Broc. At Bury St Edmunds, on his way to Leicester, the earl heard of the approach of the royal army under the constable, supported by the Earls of Cornwall, Gloucester, and Arundel. He retreated before they came up, and tried to escape to

Leicester by passing to the north. They met him at Fornham St Gene-
vieve three miles north-west of Bury. "In the twinkling of an eye" the
battle was over, and the earl and his wife were prisoners. Winter was
now coming on, and a truce was made with the Earl of Norfolk, to last
until 19 May 1174, on condition that his Flemish mercenaries were sent
back over sea. The Bishop of Durham arranged for a prolongation of
the truce with the Scots until the end of March, and the Northumbrian
barons paid the King of Scots two hundred pounds for the respite.

The winter was passed in preparation for the final struggle. The
Bishop of Durham, abandoning his pretence of loyalty, fortified his episcopal castle of Northallerton, while Roger de Mowbray strengthened his
castles of Thirsk and Kirkby Malzeard, and put into a defensible state a
derelict castle at Kinnard Ferry in the Isle of Axholme, of which he was
lord. The site of the castle can still be seen at Owston Ferry by the
lower Trent. A typical Norman motte and bailey, it had probably been
an adulterine castle of Stephen's time, from which the broad and fertile
flats of Axholme could be protected. The castles of Bamburgh, Wark,
and Carlisle, the border fortresses of Liddel and Harbottle, Prudhoe
Castle on the Tyne, Appleby and Brough-under-Stainmoor, were all held
for the king. The rebel plan for 1174, as for the previous year, seems to
have involved a threefold attack on Henry's supporters. The King of
France intended that the young king and the Count of Flanders should
land in East Anglia to join the Earl of Norfolk. In the midlands, the
Earl of Derby, David, the Scottish Earl of Huntingdon, and Anketill
Mallory, the constable of Leicester, tried to reduce the neighbouring
towns. In the north, the King of Scots attacked the northern castles.
He was supported by the Bishop of Durham, who was arranging for his
nephew Hugh de Puiset, Count of Bar, to bring troops to northern
England. The King of Scots began operations in April, but failed to
take Bamburgh and fell back on Berwick. In May he advanced again,
failed to take Wark, and passed on to lay siege to Carlisle. While main-
taining a close siege, the king himself led out detachments against other
castles. One such raid secured Liddel and Harbottle, another Appleby
and Brough-under-Stainmoor. Meanwhile, in East Anglia, a body of
Flemings sent in advance by the Count of Flanders joined the Earl of
Norfolk; with their help he took Norwich in June. In the midlands,
Nottingham was sacked by a raiding party from Leicester under David,
Earl of Huntingdon, and Anketill Mallory raided north Oxfordshire and
Northamptonshire, defeating the townsmen of Northampton who came
out to attack him.

On 5 May Geoffrey, the Bishop-elect of Lincoln, took the castle of
Kinnard Ferry. Roger de Mowbray, on his way to seek help at Leicester,
was taken prisoner by "the rustics of the Clay," the thickly-populated
district west of Trent which now forms the North and South Clay divisions of Bassetlaw wapentake. Much of this district was ancient demesne

of the Crown, and the king's humble tenants had nothing to gain from baronial anarchy. With the support of the Archbishop of York, Geoffrey took the castle of Kirkby Malzeard, and fortified Topcliffe, which he gave in charge to William de Stuteville to control Roger's remaining castle of Thirsk. Contemporaneously with these events the Justiciar laid siege to Huntingdon. Failing to take the castle, he built a counter-work against it, and placed Earl Simon of Northampton, who claimed the earldom of Huntingdon, in charge of operations. Messages were sent to the king to ask him to cross over. While Henry was landing at Southampton on 8 July, the King of Scots, having brought William de Vaux to promise to surrender Carlisle if it were not relieved by Michael-mas, was planning an attack on Prudhoe. Henry's first care after landing was to perform an elaborate penance at Becket's tomb. In the mean-time, the loyal barons of the north, under the sheriffs of York and Lancaster, were quelling the rebellion. The King of Scots began the siege of Prudhoe on Tuesday, 9 July, but on Thursday he abandoned it, hearing that the northern barons were gathering at Newcastle. The invading army ravaged far and wide, while the King of Scots rode to-wards Alnwick. A mist lay over the valley of the Alne. The English forces approached Alnwick as the mist lifted, and found the King of Scots with a few followers. The king charged, but capture was inevitable: Ranulf de Glanville took custody of him, and sent a messenger to Henry, who heard the news on 17 July. On 21 July Henry in person received the surrender of Huntingdon. From Huntingdon he went to Sileham, a village midway between the two Bigod castles of Framlingham and Bungay. The Earl of Norfolk surrendered; and Henry then turned west-wards to Northampton, where the King of Scots was brought to him, and the rebels made their submission. It only remained for Henry to return to Normandy and shew himself ready to take the offensive, and the King of France abandoned the siege of Rouen, which he had begun after Henry's departure. The threatened invasion of England never took place.

The rebellion was suppressed, but not without two summers of warfare which must have reminded old men of the days of Stephen. After the first few months there can have been little doubt which side would win. The king's sons relied on their powerful allies and assumed a feudal hatred of order which might exist in France but was not felt in England. They forgot that alliance with the King of Scots would secure the sup-port of the northern barons to their father, and that though some barons might resent order the masses of men loved it. Henry's position in England was never threatened again. The King of Scots was not only compelled to do homage for his kingdom as English barons did homage for their baronies; he was forced to allow Henry to garrison the castles of Berwick, Jedburgh, Roxburgh, Stirling, and Edinburgh. Peace was made with France, and lasted until Louis' death, when it was Henry's support which secured Philip Augustus in his position. To the young king,

Henry gave a competent revenue, but no share in the government of his dominions.

The subsequent rebellions by which Henry was troubled were no more than attempts on the part of his sons to anticipate his death; they belong rather to French than to English history. In securing Philip Augustus on the French throne, Henry had done the one thing that ensured the ultimate disintegration of his own dominions, for Philip lost no opportunity of encouraging Henry's sons in their rebellious attitude. In 1175 Henry entrusted the government of Aquitaine to Richard. The rebellion of 1181 began as a quarrel between Richard and the young king. In that year, Henry issued the Assize of Arms in England, which provided for the arming of men according to their degree, and forbade the export of arms. There was no fear of rebellion in England; Henry could rely on the respect which men felt for his government, and arm them to defend it against invasion. The war in France dragged on until the young king's death in 1183. In the next year, it was renewed by Richard, unwilling to surrender Aquitaine to John. Henry gave way, and the Irish expedition was fitted out for John in 1185. Its failure was the less serious in that Geoffrey, Duke of Brittany, died in 1186, leaving Henry with two sons only for whom to make provision. The long-expected fall of Jerusalem in the next year postponed the imminent war between Henry and Philip. Public opinion demanded a crusade, and the Kings of France and England could do no other than follow it; Henry, Richard, and Philip took the cross. Henry, who had evaded a crusade for so many years, cannot have meant to undertake one when old age was creeping upon him; in fact, both kings were willing to assist the cause with money, but neither wished to leave his kingdom. Of pretexts for war between Philip and Henry there were many; Philip claimed the wardship of Geoffrey's heir, and demanded the marriage of Richard and his sister Alais, so long promised. The war began in the south-west, with aggressions by Richard on Toulouse and counter-attacks by Philip, but it soon changed its character. When Henry crossed to Normandy in 1188, Richard and Philip became allies fighting for the recognition of Richard's right to succeed his father in all his dominions. Ill and prematurely aged, Henry was no match for the military skill of Richard and Philip. He was forced to surrender, and having agreed to Philip's terms, overcome with his illness and shame for his failure, he succumbed to the shock of learning that John, too, had deserted him.

II.

The essential feature of English history in the twelfth century is the development of a reasoned system of law for the whole land. The change from the archaic law of the conquered English, modified by new Norman elements, to the law described in the treatise known by Ranulf de

Glanville's name, was the work of Henry II and his ministers. Henry's reign witnessed a change that was almost a revolution. His early years carry on the tradition of the previous reigns. He was then a very young man, and the first necessity was to secure England and to consolidate his continental dominions; the interest of that time lies in political events. The Becket quarrel came to hinder, though for a time only, what must have been an extensive programme of reform. The charters and writs of these earlier years are very similar in form and wording to those of the reign of Henry I; they suggest the influence of the individual circumstance. Those of the latter part of the reign suggest the routine of a government bureau. In the latter years there were few political events in England to be recorded; the interest of that time lies in the detail of administration. No precise date can be taken as marking the change between the earlier and later parts of Henry's reign, but it seems to fall between the deaths of Henry's first two justiciars, Robert "Bossu," Earl of Leicester, and Richard de Luci, that is, between 1168 and 1179. Between these years fall Becket's murder and the rebellion of 1174, each of which helps to mark the close of an epoch.

Little can be learned about the personnel of the administration from the chronicle accounts of Henry's earliest years. The re-organisation of the Exchequer is unnoticed. From the second year of the reign, the Pipe Roll of each year, or, as it was more properly called, the Great Roll of the Exchequer, records the financial administration of the year. The early rolls are small. They shew that the king and his ministers had to contend with the financial difficulties presented by land wasted in the anarchy, or granted away to buy support for the king. Nigel, Bishop of Ely, nephew of Roger, Bishop of Salisbury, remained treasurer until he bought the office for his son Richard, who was to become the author of the treatise known as the *Dialogus de Scaccario*[1], and who continued as treasurer into the reign of Richard I. To these men is due the honour of elaborating the system of the Exchequer. Richard is not known to have taken an active part in any other administrative work; unlike most Exchequer officials, he did not act regularly as a judge. He writes of the Exchequer as a man writes whose life-work lies in the subject of which he treats. When he wrote the *Dialogus*, the business of the Exchequer was transacted at two great annual sessions at Easter and Michaelmas, over which the Justiciar presided. Already in Henry's fifth

---

[1] The dates of both the beginning and end of Richard's official career are uncertain. The date generally accepted for the purchase of the office on his behalf by Nigel is 1158, but at the Easter session of the Exchequer in 1162 a quittance from Danegeld was attested by Nigel, Bishop of Ely, Robert, Earl of Leicester, and the other barons (Lincoln Cathedral, *Registrum Antiquissimum*, f. 36). It is generally stated that Richard held the office until his death, but at some date after 1194 he granted certain houses in Westminster to his beloved kinsman William, the king's treasurer (Cott. Faust. A. III f. 248). The word *consanguineus* is important as proving kinship between William of Ely and Richard Fitz Nigel.

year, John, the king's Marshal, when granting land, states that his charter was sealed at the Exchequer in the Easter term and before Robert, Earl of Leicester, and Richard de Luci.

This great department of State was inherited from Henry I and Roger, Bishop of Salisbury. Each officer of high rank had his definite seat there. The Justiciar sat at the head of the exchequer board, a rectangular table, five feet by ten, covered with a chequered cloth; on his left sat the Chancellor, and on his right, when Richard wrote, the Bishop of Winchester, Richard of Ilchester, sat by the king's command. These three filled the head of the table. On the Chancellor's left, though not at the table, sat the Constable, the Chamberlains, and the Marshal. Along the side of the table to the right of the Bishop of Winchester sat the Treasurer and the clerks. At the foot of the table, opposite the Bishop of Winchester, sat another skilled financier, master Thomas Brown, and next to him, opposite the Justiciar, sat the sheriff or other person who was rendering account. Along the remaining side sat the tally-cutter, the calculator, and the clerk who was at the head of the writing office. At the same side of the table sat other "discreet men sent by the king," a phrase which must have had a wide application. Most men who were employed on the king's business did at times sit at the Exchequer. It was far more than a financial office; it was the heart of the government. Becket's biographer, William Fitz Stephen, says of the Exchequer that there the pleas of the king were wont to be heard; and the surviving final concords of Henry's reign illustrate the judicial business that was done there. Many if not most of the judges employed by Henry in his latter years were Exchequer officials, "barons of the Exchequer," men who normally sat there; such persons must be understood by the phrase "discreet men sent by the king." They were barons of the Exchequer, although they did not hold any definite office there or have any definite seat. The duties of such men were doubtless undefined; they took their share in whatever work there was to do, judicial, financial, or administrative. Exemption from fiscal burdens *per libertatem sedendi ad scaccarium* was enjoyed by men who are not known to have held any of the definite offices of state.

The Justiciar presided over the Exchequer, because by origin it was a session of the king's court and the Justiciar was the man who represented the king in his absence. By the end of Henry's reign, the dignity and work of the office of Justiciar were well defined. He was second to the king in the kingdom, and governed the country when the king was abroad in accordance with the directions sent him by the king. At such times he disposed of every sort of business that arose, whether it concerned the Church, the State, or the king's private affairs. He presided at the election of bishops; he saw to the fortification of castles; he sat as a judge; he provided for the sending of necessaries to the king for his hunting, or for other purposes. His duties were less onerous when the king was in England, but even then there was much routine work to be done. The Pipe Rolls shew that throughout the late twelfth century the Justiciar actually sat at the Exchequer for the ordinary business of the session. By the middle of Henry's reign it was established that he alone among officials could issue writs in his own name to authorise the payment of the king's moneys out of the king's treasury. To the end of John's reign, the Justiciar normally presided over the king's court of justice at Westminster. From the sixth year of Richard I, the Feet of Fines, which begin at that date, shew the Justiciar sitting there, day after day, the chief among the judges. Difficult cases were referred to him by the justices itinerant in the shires. The evidence which has survived from the reign of Henry II suggests that the same practice was already usual in Henry's later years. From time to time, the Justiciar himself led parties of justices itinerant. His title, *Capitalis Iusticiarius Regis*, expresses the truth; he was the chief justice in actual fact. But he was also at the same time a politician, a soldier, and a financier. The king's service in the twelfth century did not admit of specialisation.

It is in the conception of the position and duties of the Justiciar that the difference between the earlier and later parts of Henry's reign is most clearly shewn. It is doubtful if the idea of a permanent head of the administration was fully developed in 1154. Under Henry I, Bishop Roger of Salisbury had held a position comparable to that of the later Justiciar. But in that reign, although Roger used the definite title *Procurator*, applied by some chroniclers to the Justiciars of Henry II, it was possible for Henry I's queen to do work which later in the century would have fallen to the Justiciar. Moreover, although Roger presided at the Exchequer, Ralf and Richard Basset, father and son, seem to have acted in turn as the head of the judicial body. There is no record of the appointment by Henry II of his first two Justiciars, Robert, Earl of Leicester, and Richard de Luci, nor is it easy to find evidence of their labours in the early years of the reign. The fact that they were presiding together over the Easter Exchequer of Henry's fifth year shews that the control of finance was already an essential part of their duties. Both of them had served Stephen, and Richard had served him consistently to the end; both were past their youth in 1154. It was natural that Henry should have been unwilling to allow them in the early years of the reign the wide powers which belonged to the later Justiciars. They were mainly occupied with routine work; the king's confidence was given to Thomas of London, his Chancellor.

Viceregal power did not automatically belong to the Justiciar. That Queen Eleanor should act in Henry's place in Aquitaine was natural, for the land was her inheritance, but, like the queens of William I and Henry I before her, she seems to have acted in a similar capacity in England. The Pipe Rolls of Henry's earliest years contain numerous entries of money paid out or pardoned on her writ. In one instance, the writ of "the queen and the Justiciar" is said to be the authority. A writ of the king from over-sea was her authority for issuing a writ at Oxford forbidding that the abbey of St Benet of Holme should be impleaded in the king's absence[1]. The queen's writ was attested by Richard de Luci. Later in the reign, the young king had his brief period of delegated power. Although its limitations caused him to rebel, he certainly exercised some of the powers of a Justiciar[2]. The king wrote to him to announce the end of the Becket quarrel, and to command him to cause the archbishop to be put into possession of his lands. In writs of which copies have survived, the young king commands Peter of Studley to observe the agreement which he has made with Godwine of Warwick[3], and commands Roger Foliot to warrant to the monks of Biddlesden the land which he has given them[4]. When a collection of the young king's writs has been made, it will certainly shew him to have been entrusted with considerable administrative responsibility in England in the time immediately preceding his rebellion.

In the early years of the reign, the Justiciar was not, as at a later time, the only officer whose writ could authorise the payment of money from the Treasury. The establishment of this Exchequer rule seems to coincide with Becket's resignation of secular power. Becket himself took an important part in the business of financial administration. The Pipe Roll of 1162, the last year of his chancellorship, records no less than nine writs by which Becket either authorises the payment of money from the Treasury or pardons debts. The Earl of Leicester issued only one such writ in this year, while Richard de Luci issued none, though three separate payments are said to have been made "through" him—*per Ricardum de Luci*. Although in each year previous to 1162 payments were made either "through" Richard de Luci or by his command—*precepto Ricardi de Luci*—it is not until 1163 that the Roll records a financial writ issued in the joint names of the two justiciars. In the years before 1162 it was not Richard de Luci but the queen or the Earl of Leicester who issued the recorded writs on which the Treasury officials took action. The rolls of those years record many payments made "through" or "by command of" other persons—the Chancellor, or, on rare occasions, Nigel, Bishop of Ely. Payments on the Earl of Leicester's writ are recorded on each successive roll from 1159 to 1163. The king's presence in England between January 1163 and March 1166 meant that the Pipe Rolls offer little evidence of the financial authority of his justiciars, but the roll for 1167 shews the earl and Richard in full control of the administration; it records fourteen writs issued by Richard and twenty-one issued by the earl. The king

---

[1] Cott. MSS. Galba E. ii f. 33d.

[2] He presided over a session of the Exchequer at Winchester. EHR, vi (1891), p. 364.

[3] P.R.O. Exchequer K. R. Misc. Bks. 22 f. xxxix.

[4] Harl. MSS. 3688 f. 20.

was sending his writs to them, and they were acting on the commands contained therein. The impression created by the Pipe Rolls is that in the early years of the reign the control of finance was not yet concentrated in the hands of the justiciars.

With few exceptions, the chroniclers say little of the Justiciar's work in the early years of the reign. Gervase of Canterbury speaks of the Earls of Leicester and Cornwall as wise, famous, and most powerful in the kingdom, but he nowhere gives to the Earl of Leicester the title of justiciar. Of Richard de Luci, Gervase states, under the year 1166, that he had the rule in England—*prefecturam agebat in Anglia.* Roger of Howden records an assertion by Becket that the barons of the Exchequer and Richard de Luci, "Justiciar of England," had given him quittance of his accounts before he was elected archbishop. Ralph de Diceto applies the phrase *justiciarius regis* to both the Earl of Leicester and Richard de Luci. The judicial work of the justiciars had little interest for the ordinary chronicler, unless his own house was concerned in a plea. The most familiar illustrations of their activity come from the History of Abingdon and the Chronicle of Battle. Between 1160 and 1164, the Earl of Leicester presided over a plea in the shire-court of Berkshire touching the right of the Abbot of Abingdon to hold a market there. The earl first heard the plea by virtue of the king's writ from over-sea. When Henry returned in January 1163, the case came up again before his justices at Oxford. Opinions varied, and the earl, who was present as *justiciarius et judex*, did not presume to give judgment, but went to consult the king. Between 1139 and 1171, Richard de Luci's brother Walter was Abbot of Battle. The Chronicle of that house describes at length an important plea which he prosecuted against the Bishop of Chichester in 1157. The Earl of Leicester was present among the barons, but his office is not mentioned, nor does he appear to have taken a prominent part in the discussion; Richard de Luci acted on his brother's behalf. The Chancellor seems to have led the debate, and the suit ended in a compromise to the abbot's advantage, arranged by the king. In a suit against Gilbert de Balliol, the abbot, though his brother was Justiciar, had some trouble in obtaining a hearing in the king's court. At last it was heard at Clarendon before the king. Richard de Luci, *vir magnificus et prudens*, "at that time chief justice of the king," was present, but only appears in the account of the plea as the advocate of his brother's cause. When the king sat in person, the Justiciar was present in court as a baron, not as a judge. Isolated administrative documents which illustrate the Justiciar's activity suggest that his position was more important than would be gathered from the accounts of famous pleas before the king. Between 1156 and 1165, the Earl of Leicester presided over the knights of Nottinghamshire when they defined the boundary between the land of the Archbishop of York and the king's forest of Sherwood[1]. By virtue

---

[1] Thoroton, *History of Nottinghamshire*, ed. 1790, Vol. II, p. 160.

of the king's writ from over-sea, he commanded "the king's barons of Hastings to allow the Abbot of St Benet of Holme peaceable possession of his lands in Yarmouth."[1] The king laid on him the duty of constraining the Earl of Norfolk to do the castle-guard at Norwich which he held of St Edmund[2]. *Magnus fuit hic.*

Until within a year of his death in 1179, Richard de Luci continued to perform the duties of Justiciar. No discreditable tales are told of him. The worst that can be said is that he supported his brother, the Abbot of Battle, in his efforts to give effect to the claims of his house, and it is very doubtful if he went beyond the law in his support. He was honest enough to oppose the king when Henry began to prosecute men for forest offences which he had himself allowed at the time of the rebellion of 1174. Richard must have been an able administrator and a skilled judge; many of the reforms of Henry's reign in legal and administrative matters were initiated while he was Justiciar. His successor was a man no less able but more unscrupulous, Ranulf de Glanville, who was appointed Justiciar in 1180. Of an East Anglian family of no special importance, Ranulf early entered the king's service, and already in 1164 was sheriff of Yorkshire. His conduct as sheriff cannot have been beyond reproach, for he was deprived of his office between 1170 and 1175, doubtless as a result of the Inquest of Sheriffs in 1170, but he was reinstated after the rebellion of 1174. The part which he took in the capture of the King of Scots may well have been the cause of his reinstatement. The Pipe Roll of 1177 contains a curious entry that Ranulf has accounted for more than fifteen hundred pounds derived partly from the county and partly from the lands of Everard de Ros which he had held in custody. The king pardoned the whole amount, but the entry suggests that there may have been good reason for Ranulf's removal from his sheriffdom. Further light is cast on the Justiciar's character by a story told by the chronicler known as Benedict of Peterborough and corroborated by entries on the Pipe Roll of 1184. There seems little doubt that Ranulf strained the law in the hope of securing the execution of Gilbert de Plumpton, in order that his widow, an heiress, might become the wife of Reiner of Waxham, Ranulf's steward. Whatever his faults, Ranulf suited Henry, whose service demanded ability and fidelity rather than too strict an honour, and during the last ten years of Henry's reign Ranulf was the dominating figure in English administration. That he wrote the legal treatise which bears his name is most probable; it must have been written while he was Justiciar. It has been suggested that it was written by his nephew Hubert Walter, himself afterwards Justiciar and Archbishop of Canterbury. Hubert had been brought up by Ranulf de Glanville and his wife, and that he should write an account of the practice of the king's court at his patron's request is not in itself unlikely. Yet even if the words in which Roger of Howden, the chronicler and judge, introduces the earliest text of the treatise do not prove that

---

[1] Cott. Galba E. ii f. 33d.   [2] Brit. Mus. Add. MSS. 14847 f. 37.

Glanville himself wrote it, they certainly imply that it was written at his inspiration and, in all probability, under his guidance[1].

Between the earlier and later parts of Henry's reign there occurred a remarkable change in the personnel of the administration. Richard de Luci was one of the last men in constant touch with the king who had shared in the early labours of re-organisation. There was, in particular, a definite break in the development of the office of Chancellor. Throughout the twelfth century, the importance of any individual *curialis* depended rather upon his relations with the king than upon the office which he held. The peculiar importance of the chancellorship in the early years of the reign was due to Becket's intimacy with Henry. Between the time of Becket's resignation and the spring of 1173, the king's seal was apparently kept by Geoffrey Ridel, Becket's successor as Archdeacon of Canterbury. Although Geoffrey seems to have done the Chancellor's work, it is not certain that he was ever appointed to the office. In 1173, Henry appointed Ralf de Warneville Chancellor. This appointment coincides nearly, though not precisely, with a remarkable change in the royal style. Until at least May 1172, charters composed in the royal chancery uniformly style the king *Rex Anglorum et dux Normannorum et Aquitannorum et comes Andegavorum.* In charters known to issue from the chancery after May 1173 these titles are preceded by the formula *dei gratia.* It is difficult to find evidence of Ralf's presence in England, where he seems normally to have been represented by Walter of Coutances, then Archdeacon of Oxford, afterwards Bishop of Lincoln, Archbishop of Rouen, and for a short time Justiciar of England. The last Chancellor of the reign was Geoffrey, the king's illegitimate son, who in 1181 resigned the see of Lincoln before consecration in order to take the office.

The office of Treasurer remained with the kin of Roger of Salisbury not only throughout Henry's reign but into the reign of Henry III[2]. The Treasurer's work was more specialised than that of any other official, and he was essentially a financial officer. Until the appointment of Eustace de Fauconberg early in the reign of Henry III, the treasurers were not much concerned with general administration; Richard Fitz Nigel rarely appears among the persons who attest the writs and charters of Henry II. The names which are most prominent in the attestation clauses of Henry's charters belong to a small number of men who, in the strict sense of the word, may be styled *curiales.* Few of them held high baronial rank, and most of them possessed definite office in the king's household. In the first years of the reign, Thomas Becket, the Chancellor, was generally with the

---

[1] "...cuius sapientia conditae sunt leges subscriptae quas Anglicanas vocamus." Howden, II, 215. Maitland's doubt as to Glanville's authorship of the treatise rests on an unusual translation of the verb *condo.* The normal translation of *condo* in this context would be to write down or compile. A comparison of the treatise with the surviving judicial records of the early thirteenth century shews that it is the work of a practised judge.

[2] Cf. *supra* p. 573, note.

king. Manasser Biset the steward, Warin Fitz Gerald the chamberlain, Richard de Humez the constable, were his constant companions. Until his disgrace, Henry of Essex, as constable, was constantly attendant on the king. Unlike his fellows of the household, he was of baronial rank. His forfeited honour was given by the king to Henry Fitz Gerald, brother of Warin, and like him a chamberlain. In the later years of the reign, the personnel of the court was more varied; judges, and other men who served the king without definite office, appear beside the regular household officials. Much research remains to be done upon the *curiales* of Henry II. That he reposed great confidence in them is certain. He rewarded them with land, but not lavishly, though some of them have left their names to English villages: Manasser Biset is immortalised in the name of Preston Bisset in Buckinghamshire. Before the end of the reign there are definite traces of the organisation which was to develop into the wardrobe of the thirteenth century. The names of many chamber-clerks appear on twelfth-century Pipe Rolls. They were already employed in administrative work as well as in purely household functions. It is only from the examination of unprinted documents that more can be learned of their origin and status.

If the men in the king's immediate service are as a body obscure, his sheriffs are all known by name, and their territorial position can often be ascertained precisely. The office still gives a field for research, but it is certain that during the reigns of Henry II and his sons the sheriff took the first and all-important steps towards his present position of forgotten dignity. The Norman kings had suffered from the over-mighty sheriff, and had tried to check his power. Henry I had often put his own *curiales* into sheriffdoms and united several counties in the hands of one or two trusted ministers. But the lists of sheriffs in Henry II's early years still shew baronial names. In Devonshire, the earl was sheriff until 1157. Northumberland was held by William de Vesci from 1157 to 1170, and by Roger de Stuteville from 1170 to 1185. William de Beauchamp was sheriff of Worcestershire from 1155 to 1169, of Gloucestershire from 1157 to 1163, and of Herefordshire from 1160 to 1169. Wiltshire was held by Patrick, Earl of Salisbury, from 1155 to 1160. Throughout the reign, Shropshire was held by local magnates. A baron was not inevitably the king's opponent, and a baronial sheriff may have been as good an officer as any *curialis*. Moreover, many sheriffs of baronial rank held their offices because they had become *curiales*, and were competing for the prizes which the king's service offered. Ranulf de Glanville was the chief among many such men. Many of Henry's sheriffs were undistinguished knights in the counties they held. Adam de Catmere, sheriff of Berkshire from 1160 to 1170, and of Oxfordshire from 1164 to 1170, held half a knight's fee at Catmore in Berkshire of William, Earl of Derby. The south Lincolnshire knight, Alfred of Pointon, sheriff of Lincolnshire in 1166 and 1167, and again from 1170 to 1174, held three knight's fees of Maurice de Craon, and was his steward. Even at the beginning of the reign, some shires were held by *curiales*. The important county of Hampshire was held by a succession of them. Turstin, sheriff until 1160, had been the clerk of a chamberlain in the reign of Henry I[1]. His son succeeded him, and was followed from 1170 to 1179 by Hugh de Gundeville. From 1174 to 1177 Hugh was also sheriff of Northamptonshire, from 1177 to 1179 he was sheriff of Devon, and his name frequently occurs in lists of Henry's judges. From 1155 to 1160 Northamptonshire was held by another minister who often served as judge, Simon son of Peter of Brixworth in that county. By the end of the reign it was the rule rather than the exception that the sheriffs should be *ministeriales*. The change was probably the result of Henry's policy rather than the policy itself. Henry was controlling the excesses of sheriffs, and at the same time increasing their work, so that barons may have become less anxious to hold the office. The large sums offered, though not always paid, for shrievalties at the beginning of Richard's reign may suggest that the buyers hoped for laxer administrative control under a new king—a hope that was not realised.

The judicial reforms introduced by Henry II materially increased the labours of the sheriff. In addition to the financial and military responsibilities which had lain upon him in the Norman time, he was now required to give effect to an elaborate system of centralised justice. The earliest rolls of the itinerant justices reveal the unceasing labours of the sheriff in the time of Henry's sons. He was responsible for the most minute details of judicial administration; he must receive and produce the writs which began the innumerable pleas resulting from Henry's legal reforms; he was responsible for summoning every person necessary for the conduct of a plea; he had to give effect to the justices' decisions, and keep a record of his action; he must answer for the most meagre chattels of criminals that had fallen in to the king. Any failure in the performance of these duties meant that he would be called to account before the justices. It is not remarkable that *curiales* appear in increasing numbers among the sheriffs of Henry's later years. Unless the sheriffs were brought into close relations with the king, his plan of a judicial organisation extending over the whole land and centring upon his court was bound to be fruitless.

In 1170 Henry sent bodies of commissioners or justices round the country to inquire touching the behaviour of the sheriffs, their bailiffs, and all who were doing the king's business in the shires. Generally known as the "Inquest of Sheriffs," the inquiry had a much wider scope. It entered into the financial relationship between lords and their men, with which the king had normally no concern. It covered only the four years of Henry's recent absence abroad. Two fragments of the original returns have survived, relating respectively to East Anglia and

---

[1] Round, *The Rise of the Pophams*, in *The Ancestor*, VII, 59.

the borough of Worcester. The East Anglian fragment relates almost exclusively to the payments made to the Earl of Arundel and other barons by the men on their own land and on land held in custody. Payments were made to the earl to help him in his work on the Marches of Wales, in his expedition to France, in his difficulties with the Jews, in his contribution to the aid for marrying the king's daughter, and in his journey to Saxony with her. The Worcester fragment, on the other hand, deals almost entirely with payments to the sheriff. It shews that the sheriff, William de Beauchamp, took from the borough forty-two pounds in the first two years in question, and fifty pounds in the last two years. The farm of the borough was fixed at twenty-four pounds when, at a later time, the burgesses were allowed to pay it direct into the Exchequer. The burgesses also made payments to him for the conveyance of treasure and prisoners, and on the occasion of his daughter's marriage. William de Beauchamp was one of the sheriffs removed before the inquiry was made, and many others were removed afterwards. Only in Cumberland, Devon, Kent, Rutland, Staffordshire, Surrey, and Wiltshire, was the custody of the shire in the same hand for any appreciable period before and after 1170. Of these counties, Rutland was held by the king's constable, Richard de Humez, and Surrey and Kent were in the custody of Gervase of Cornhill, a member of a family which owed its wealth to London trade and had entered the king's service. It is evident from the fact of the enquiry that the king did not intend the government of the shires through sheriffs and other officers to rest on exploitation. No other enquiry was made in this reign with the principal object of discovering the abuses in local government, but, when the king's justices went round the country, people had the opportunity, if they dared to use it, of expressing their grievances. On the Lincoln Assize Roll of 1202 occurs an entry to the effect that certain sums of money have been taken from merchants to the use of the sheriff, his bailiff, and his bailiff's clerk, for the right of leading corn from county to county through England.

It must have been possible for the sheriff to make considerable profits in a legitimate way. The amounts of his profits from the local courts of justice must have depended on the justice he gave, and a period of peace and careful management meant that the value of the royal land farmed by the sheriff increased considerably. That Henry II had no intention of allowing the sheriff to obtain the whole of this increment is shewn by the fact that he had to account for variable amounts, known later as *incrementa*, apart from and in addition to his farm. Even so, the sheriff must have made money on his farm. The *incrementa* were unpopular alike with the sheriffs and the people, and the first issue of Magna Carta declared that counties should be at their old farms, without any increment, a clause that, for obvious financial reasons, it was impossible to retain. When lands escheated to the king, they were generally farmed by the sheriff or by some magnate or *curialis* who was recompensed for his trouble by the amount he raised beyond the sum for which he farmed the escheat. But sometimes escheated lands were held *in custodia*, that is, the holder strictly accounted for them to the king. Like that of his father, the reign of Richard I was a time of administrative reform. The large amount of land that came in to the king in 1194, mainly as a result of his brother's rebellion, necessitated fresh arrangements. Two escheators were appointed, William de Sanctae Mariae Ecclesia, and Hugh Bardolf, who held the escheats in custody, and rendered detailed accounts for them. William held the escheated lands in the southern and Hugh in the northern part of England. It was doubtless experiments like this, compelled by the pressure of increasing business, which suggested the practice, developed in the next century, of sometimes letting shires themselves to their sheriffs *in custodia* instead of *ad firmam*.

In addition to profits of uncertain amount and diverse origin, the sheriff was entitled to a customary payment from the men of the shire, known as the sheriff's aid. This payment enters into general history as one of the causes of dispute between Henry II and Becket in 1163. The king is said to have wished to annex the money given to the sheriffs to his own revenues. It is probable that he intended the sheriffs to account at the Exchequer for the sheriff's aid as for the money which they collected on the king's behalf. The significance of his proposals can only be conjectured, for they were abandoned in face of the archbishop's protest. That Henry wished to take possession of the sheriff's aid without compensation to the sheriffs for its loss is highly improbable; he depended too much on his sheriffs to alienate them by an arbitrary measure of confiscation. He may well have been feeling his way towards an increased centralisation of local government, and wished, as a step towards this end, to appropriate the ancient sheriff's aid and compensate the sheriffs by a payment direct from the treasury. It is also probable that his proposals were suggested by the close resemblance between the sheriff's aid and the Danegeld. The sheriff's aid was a geld, a tax laid upon land according to the assessment which determined the incidence of the Danegeld; it descended from the fiscal system of King Edward's day. Various passages in private charters shew that it was paid four times a year. A Lincolnshire charter of the reign of Henry II refers to it as the "four aids of the sheriff," a Leicestershire charter as the "four gelds of the shire."[1] It was natural that Henry should wish the sheriff's aid to follow the other ancient gelds into his treasury. Had it done so, its amount and incidence would be less obscure at the present day. In the reign of Edward I, the sheriff's aid in the counties of Cambridge and Huntingdon seems to have brought in approximately thirty pounds a year. It was not an adequate recompense for the sheriff's manifold labours, but the income which it brought him was not negligible.

[1] Stenton, *Danelaw Charters*, p. 127. Haverholme Cartulary, *Lincs. Notes and Queries*, Vol. XVII, p. 48.

Even under the Norman kings, the sheriffs had not been the sole dispensers of royal justice in the shires. Apart from the sporadic appearance of royal officials sent round the country to do justice, there is evidence that already in the reign of William II local officers known as justiciars were in existence. The local justiciarship can be traced through the reigns of Henry I and Stephen, but it is not generally realised that the office still existed in the reign of Henry II. In writs of Henry II, few of which have yet been printed, there are definite references to the justiciars of Lincoln[1], Norfolk[2], Warwick[3], Sussex[4], York, and Nottingham[5]. It is probably to these officers that William of Newburgh refers when he states, under the year 1154, that Henry "appointed in all the districts of his kingdom ministers of right and law, to coerce the boldness of the wicked, and do justice to those seeking it, according to the merits of the cases." The relation of the local justiciar to the sheriff and the shire-court is uncertain, but it is certain that he took precedence of the sheriff in the shire.

The little that is known of these local justiciars suggests that Henry did not long continue the practice of appointing them. In matters of justice, he seems in his earliest years to have adopted his grandfather's expedients, both employing local justices and sending out officers of his court to do justice over a great stretch of the country. The year 1166 may be regarded as a turning-point. The Assize of Clarendon, issued in that year, opens a new phase in the history of criminal jurisdiction in England. The king then commanded that twelve lawful men of every hundred and four lawful men of every village should declare on oath if any in their hundred or village had been accused or suspected of being a robber, murderer, or brigand, or a harbourer of such, since Henry became king. The presentments of these jurors were to be taken before the sheriffs and again before the justices. Those who were apprehended by reason of such presentment were to have judgment before the king's justices only, they were to go to the ordeal by water, and the chattels of the guilty were to go to the king. Men of ill repute proved innocent by the water were nevertheless to abjure the realm. Gaols were to be built in counties where there were none, for the custody of prisoners awaiting the coming of the justices. In the case of those apprehended in any other way than through presentment, the procedure was to remain "as it was and ought to be," a provision which allowed the sheriff to deal with crimes other than those specified, and with many minor offences, such as petty assaults. This measure was a long stride towards centralisation. Ten years later, the Assize of Northampton, reinforcing that of

---

[1] B.M. Harl. MSS. 742 f. 265. Cott. Vesp. E. xvii f. 19 b.
[2] B.M. Cott. Galba E. ii f. 31 d and 33 d. Cott. Claud. D. xiii f. 41.
[3] P.R.O. Exchequer K. R. Misc. Bks. 22 f. cxxv.
[4] B.M. Cott. Faustina A. iii f. 74 b.
[5] B.M. Cott. Vesp. E. xix f. 7.

Clarendon, gave to the justices cognisance of other grave crimes which had lain outside the scope of the earlier assize. For the first time in English history, criminal justice was to be administered all over the land in accordance with the same rules.

The years between 1166 and 1180 were years of experiment in the centralisation of justice. The Assize of Clarendon was enforced by Earl Geoffrey de Mandeville and Richard de Luci. The *justiciarii* or *barones errantes* who conducted the Inquest of Sheriffs were large companies of barons and clergy. But the judges who from 1168 onwards were doing justice and assessing tallages in the shires were household and Exchequer officials of the king. The Assize of Northampton of 1176 was put into operation by six groups of three justices, whose work was made heavy by the disturbance of the rebellion. When the king returned from Normandy in 1178, he recalled the eighteen judges, and appointed five, who were not to depart from his court but were to remain there to hear complaints, so that if any matters needed special consideration they could be determined by the king with the advice of his counsellors. This provision originated no new court; it was an arrangement by which the king, exercising his ancient prerogative of justice, might inspect the work of his judges. He spent his time in England going from place to place, and the five judges doubtless travelled with him. Richard de Luci retired from the justiciarship in the next year, and Henry did not immediately appoint a new Chief Justiciar. He divided the country into four districts for the purpose of judicial administration. Ranulf de Glanville and five other judges were placed in charge of the north; the three southern districts were each put in charge of a bishop, who was also a *curialis*. In 1180 Glanville became Chief Justiciar. From that time, justices visited the shires in almost every year. They inspected the local administration, inquired into the king's rights, and assessed taxes; justice was only a part of their work. These justices were intimately connected with the Exchequer. It was thence they set out, and they returned there to hand in their rolls; so the fact that the Exchequer was at Westminster meant that Westminster became the centre of the judicial system. There, judges sat almost continuously, for the Exchequer officials were the judges. The justices *de banco* are the justices of the bench at Westminster. They did not form a different court from that of the justices on eyre; there was but one court, and that the king's. The distinction between the judges who sat at Westminster and those who went round the country was narrow. The justices on eyre were governed by the terms of a commission; those who sat at Westminster sat there primarily to deal with pleas brought up by people who wished for the best available opinion on their suits, and with pleas transferred from the justices itinerant in the country.

The procedure described in Glanville's treatise is that of the end of Henry's reign, when the king's judges appeared constantly in the shires, and when his court was within the reach of every free man deprived unjustly of his land. Of the means by which Henry brought about this result all too little is known. The king could not force men to seek his court for civil litigation; he could only attract them to it by giving better justice than the courts of honours and manors, shires and hundreds. No one doubted that it belonged to the king, if he chose, to see that justice was done to those who sought it; appeal to the king was always possible. The work of Henry II in centralising justice in the king's court must not be overrated. The writs of Henry I suggest that the rule of law, familiar to readers of Glanville, that no one need answer for his free tenement in his lord's court without the king's writ or that of his justiciar, may have been already established before 1135. Glanville speaks of it as according to the customs of the kingdom, not as though it were a recent enactment. The writ of right may well have been known by that name before Henry became king; Conan, Earl of Richmond, refers to it by name in a charter which must be earlier than 1158[1]. The procedure by which a plea was removed from the feudal court to the shire-court on the plaintiff proving in his lord's court before the sheriff that his lord had failed to do justice was probably the same as that described by Glanville, even in the first half of the century. The king could always send his justices into the shire-courts to hear the suits in process there. But the first condition to be fulfilled before the king could take justice into his hand was the frequent appearance of royal justices in the shires; only then would it be worth men's while to appeal to the king.

With the advice of his barons, the king could always make general statements of law. He could also send men round the country to inquire into his rights by means of the sworn inquest. It is probable that Henry's first step towards the centralisation of justice was to combine these prerogatives. At or about the time of the Assize of Clarendon, he must have declared that no man might be disseised unjustly and without judgment of his free tenement, and commanded his justices to inquire touching such disseisins within the period covered by the Assize. Ten years later, in the Assize of Northampton, he made a general statement that a man's heir should have such seisin as his ancestor had on the day when he was alive and dead, and he commanded that, where the lord of the fee had prevented this, the justices should inquire touching the dead man's seisin and restore it to his heir. The justices were again commanded to inquire into disseisins committed within the limit of time covered by the Assize. These two enactments lie behind the procedure begun by the writs of Novel Disseisin and Mort d'Ancestor, but they did not immediately create those writs and that procedure. It appears as though Henry at first made his benefits for a time compulsory that he might make people realise their advantages before he put up definite

[1] Harl. Chart. 48 G 41.

writs and a definite procedure for sale. That the result of these enactments was the taking of possession under the royal protection is true, but it is certain that Henry and his justices did not set out deliberately to protect possession. Their aim was to quell the disorder of self-help, and to provide a speedy remedy for the man unjustly dispossessed of his tenement or prevented from entering into his inheritance. Writs of previous kings shew that here, too, he was working on foundations already laid[1]. Henry II's genius lay in subtly devising a single means to fit the many slightly varying circumstances.

It was not the partiality of feudal lords but the inadequacy of feudal procedure that ultimately brought all free men into the king's court. Feudal justice was slow. It was felt that a man must be present in person to conduct his suit. Hence, there was developed a complicated law of essoins, of excuses for non-attendance; an unwilling suitor could prolong his plea almost indefinitely by making full use of his essoins. When the justices of John's reign investigated complaints that a feudal court had failed to do justice, the evidence often shewed, not that injustice had been done, but that the plaintiff had brought his troubles on himself by refusing to answer in his lord's court or by expecting his essoins to avail him too long. Moreover, the ownership of land was decided in the feudal courts by the issue of the duel between two champions who were supposed to be ready to fight because they were witnesses of the truth. It was difficult for the king to interfere in such pleas, where the lord of the court was giving the best justice that feudal law permitted. Hence it was that he allowed to the defendants in such suits the *regale beneficium* of the Grand Assize. Dr Round has shewn that the Grand Assize, the Assize of Windsor as it is sometimes called, was probably issued in 1179. The tenant alone could avail himself of this royal benefit. If he put himself on the Grand Assize, the case was removed from the feudal court into the king's court, and judgment was given in accordance with the verdict of twelve knights of the shire chosen by four knights summoned by the sheriff for the purpose. The question of the truth of the case, whether this man or that has the greater right, was put to the jury. That the king's barons were conscious of the shortcomings of feudal procedure is evident from the fact that the Grand Assize was issued by the king with the advice of his barons, *consilio procerum*.

Although the king was always regarded as the fountain of justice, his duty was rather to see that justice was done than to do it himself. It is

---

[1] *E.g.* P.R.O. Ancient Deeds, B. 11342. "S. Rex Angl' Waltero filio Gisleberti et preposito suo de Mealdona salutem. Si canonici Sancti Martini Lond' poterint monstrare quod Oswardus de Meldona iniuste et sine iudicio illos dissaisierit de terra sua de Meldon' de burgagio tunc precipio quod faciatis illos resaisiri sicut saisiti fuerunt die qua rex Henricus fuit vivus et mortuus...Et nisi feceritis Ricardus de Luci et vicecomes de Essexa faciant fieri ne audiam inde clamorem pro penuria recti." I owe this reference to Mr Lionel Landon.

evident from Glanville's words that some suits were felt to be rightly brought in the first instance into the royal court, and that the king could if he wished order that others should come to it too. The disputes of tenants-in-chief for land held in chief of the king came naturally into the king's court. The writ that brought suits directly to the royal court was the writ *Precipe*, so called from its first word. It was addressed to the sheriff, and told him to command the defendant to restore to the plaintiff the land or other property of which he had deforced him or to be before the king or his justices on such a day. Although Glanville says that the king may if he wishes issue this writ, it is clear that he felt that suits touching the ownership of land held by sub-tenants ought not to be begun in the king's court where the lord's court was ready to do justice to the plaintiff. The aim of king and barons alike in the legal reforms of the reign was to secure quicker justice and thus maintain better order in the land. It was not the mere bringing of suits to the king's court that secured speedy justice, it was the employment of further expedients to secure quicker action, expedients which the king alone could sell. The plea which settled a man's right to the ownership of land was of necessity long in whatever court it was heard.

As in the feudal courts, so in the king's court, cases concerning the ownership of land were decided in accordance with the issue of the duel, unless the defendant put himself on the Grand Assize. The law of essoins ruled in every court alike. Although Glanville says in praise of the Grand Assize that it did not admit of so many essoins, and therefore allowed an earlier decision, it was sufficiently tedious in fact; to carry through a suit for the ownership of land might take many years. The case of Richard of Anesty is always quoted to prove the delay in law-suits in the Angevin period. But Richard's sorrows, though great, have been given undue prominence. His case fell early in Henry's reign; he began it before the Toulouse expedition, and it involved the papal as well as the royal court. In every way it was exceptional. The time taken by the ordinary suit in the king's court at the end of Henry's reign can best be judged by the records of proceedings in the reigns of his sons. But the gaps in the series of extant rolls make difficult the tracing of suits. There are few parallels to the statement in a roll of 1194 that Simon Grim has followed the same suit "for seven years in divers courts."[1]

In addition to the fact that many years might elapse before the question of the ownership of land was settled by the judgment of a court, the plaintiff in a plea of right was in an unfavourable position. The defendant had the choice of procedure, the duel or the Grand Assize. The defendant also had the land. Men, sure of the fact that they had been unjustly evicted from their land, or prevented from entering into their inheritance, could afford to forgo the security which a judgment in their favour in a writ of right would give. They could well be content

---

[1] *Rotuli Curiae Regis*, i, p. 68.

with a speedy judgment by which they could be put in immediate possession, in seisin, of their land. Hence it was that, when Henry passed from making compulsory inquiries into unjust and extra-judicial disseisins to allowing the purchase of writs which ordered the summons of a jury to answer definite questions with regard to the seisin of land, he found people ready to take advantage of his devices. The jury summoned by the writ of Novel Disseisin answered the definite question: Has the plaintiff been disseised unjustly and without judgment within the period covered by the assize? The writ of Mort d'Ancestor ordered the summons of a jury to answer the questions: Was the ancestor of the plaintiff seised of the land at issue on the day he died? Did he die within the period covered by the assize? Is the plaintiff his next heir? A third recognition, known as Darrein Presentment, was devised probably about the year 1179. Advowsons were a fertile source of litigation, and a new parson could not be appointed to a church the advowson of which was in dispute. The Lateran Council of 1179 required the diocesan bishop to fill the vacancy if the patron delayed too long in making his presentation. The writ of Darrein Presentment ordered the summons of a jury to inquire who presented the last parson to a vacant church in time of peace, and it was adjudged that he or his heir should present again. The three recognitions begun by these writs became in a few years extremely popular. They were speedy, for few essoins were allowed. Few indeed were necessary, for a favourable judgment under one of these assizes gave the winner no right of ownership in the disputed land or advowson; the loser could still bring the writ of right in his lord's court. Barons used the new procedure, which was meant as much for them as for the humble freeman. It is customary to speak of these devices as though they were directly aimed against the barons and their courts. But to say that Henry deliberately set out to protect possession or seisin in order to deprive the baronial courts of their jurisdiction is completely to misunderstand the conditions of the time. The curtailment of suits was as much to the advantage of barons as to that of other men. It was also to the general good that men should not be tempted to self-help by the law's delays. Moreover, such was the love of litigation at this time that it is doubtful if the new recognitions made very much difference to the volume of business in the feudal courts.

The *Leges Henrici Primi* shew that in the reign of Henry I a court of justice was regarded as a place where men might either be brought together in love or separated in judgment. It was as much the duty of the judge to end litigation by arranging an agreement as by delivering a judgment. The famous pleas of the early years of Henry II were often ended by a compromise. In the course of the reign, the idea of embodying the agreement so arranged in the form of a chirograph, an indenture, was elaborated by the development of a definite formula for the record of the convention. Written twice, head to head, on one piece of parchment, the text recorded the place and date of the agreement and the judges before whom it was made. It then proceeded to recite the terms of the agreement. The authenticity of the text was guaranteed by the device of severing the parchment through the word CYROGRAPHUM written between the two copies. Originally devised with the object of curtailing and preventing litigation, the final concord came to be regarded as the ideal way of making an agreement touching ownership; for the king's court would enforce its observance. It soon became worth men's while to bring a fictitious action as the formal preliminary to a pre-arranged agreement, in order to enjoy the security given by a final concord made before the king's justices. The final concord had before it a longer history than either Henry or Glanville can have foreseen.

The year 1166, in addition to being a turning-point in legal history, has been claimed as marking a revolution in financial organisation. In that year the policy which ultimately assimilated towns to the royal demesne, and made them with it subject to aids or tallages assessed by royal justices, was definitely entered upon. Also in that year Henry required his tenants-in-chief to send him a sealed return, informing him how they had arranged the details of their knight-service. He did not ask the amount of the knight-service that they owed, the *servicium debitum*. He asked how many knights had been enfeoffed before the death of Henry I, and how many since, and how many, if any, remained to be provided for by the tenant-in-chief himself. He asked, in fact, how many knights were of the old enfeoffment, how many of the new, and how many "in demesne"; the names of the knights enfeoffed had also to be returned. The object of this enquiry has generally been regarded as financial. Dr Round has pointed out that after 1166 tenants-in-chief paid on their *servicium debitum* only in those cases where they had enfeoffed fewer knights than the amount of the knight-service that they owed the king. Where for any reason the tenant-in-chief had enfeoffed more knights than his actual service required, he paid after 1166 on the number of knights that he had actually enfeoffed and not on his *servicium debitum*. Dr Round has therefore argued that the object of the returns was to secure "a new feudal assessment." That Henry did in fact compel some of his tenants-in-chief to pay on more knights than their old *servicium debitum* is certain, but there remained many cases in which no difference in the assessment or in the amount paid was made[1]. It is also highly probable that Henry's object in making the enquiry was in part at least political, and that the Archbishop of York is accurate in his statement that the king has asked the questions because he wishes to know the names of the knights, in order that those who have not done allegiance, and whose names are not written on the king's roll, may do allegiance before a certain date.

It is on his achievement in setting English lawyers upon the paths

---

[1] More research into this matter is needed.

that they have trodden for seven hundred years, and are indeed treading yet, that the fame of Henry II rests. He was the greatest and the richest king in western Europe. One of his daughters married the King of Sicily, another the Duke of Saxony, Henry the Lion. The latter marriage made much history. But the triumph of his reign lay, not in his riches or alliances, but in the fact that his contemporaries recognised in him the greatest lawyer of his day. Kings came to him for judgment. If in his enforcement of the forest laws Henry shewed himself not only ungenerous but unjust, it was a matter of gratulation and wonder that the poor could come to his court and win justice against the rich. The men about his court were not mere judges and administrators, they included men of letters. Henry was fortunate in his servants, but the court of those days was what the king made it. Henry's greatness has always been recognised, and much that was done by previous kings has been in the past assigned to him. Of late years, justice has been done to the work of his predecessors. It has been realised that Henry worked on foundations already laid. But the foundations were slight—a few formulas, the beginnings of an idea.

CHAPTER XVIII.

FRANCE: LOUIS VI AND LOUIS VII
(1108–1180).

The history of France throughout the reigns of Louis VI (1108–1137) and Louis VII (1137–1180) is completely dominated by two apparently contradictory factors. We see on the one hand the persistent extension of the Anglo-Norman domain, which, from the day that it passed into the hands of the Counts of Anjou, gradually increased until it included more than half of France; while on the other hand it is obvious that the king's power was daily becoming more firmly established, daily gaining as much in strength as it lost in extent through the growing predominance of Normandy and Anjou. Philip I's two immediate successors concentrated nearly all their energies, though not with equal zeal, upon a twofold task: to oppose the English monarch's invasion of the kingdom, and to recover authority over all the territory that was normally subject to the Crown.

The most urgent matter was to secure obedience from the barons of the royal domain, whose turbulence and insubordination threatened to make the sovereign's authority of no effect, even in the Isle de France. This was the task to which Louis VI especially applied himself. Even in his father's lifetime, as we have seen[1], he had attacked the problem with energy.

No work could have better suited this vigorous soldier-king, in whom courage was carried to the point of temerity. In person he was tall and strong, with a tendency to corpulence that earned him the nickname of *le Gros*, and, to his great sorrow, began to unfit him for the rough profession of arms when he was no more than forty years of age. A large eater, and a lover of freedom and gaiety, he was at the same time honest and upright, cheery and easy of approach; and his contemporaries charge him with but one serious failing, that of cupidity. All are agreed in praising the rare energy and valour of which the record of his actions is sufficient evidence.

Of the first years of his reign, indeed, hardly one passed that did not see him actively employed in fighting and chastising his turbulent vassals. The massive castles by means of which they dominated the highways had

[1] *Supra*, Vol. III, Chap. v.

become mere dens of brigands, and the terror that they inspired is described in vivid terms by the chroniclers of the day. A traveller from Paris to Orleans, for instance, was threatened at every step by some fresh danger. Whether he were minded to follow the highroad, or to avoid it in the hope of escaping " the ravening wolves," the lord of some castle would be lying in wait to fall upon him and rob him. The owners of the fortresses of Montlhéry, Châteaufort, La Ferté-Alais, and Le Puiset were masters of this part of the country, and had reduced it to such a "chaos of confusion," says one of the chroniclers, "that it was unsafe to venture upon the road without either obtaining their consent or securing a considerable escort." If a man were bound for Melun he found his way barred by the fortress of Corbeil; if for Mantes, Dreux, or Chartres, he was forced to reckon at least with the castles of Chevreuse, Épernon, Rochefort, Gometz, Montfort-l'Amauri, Montchauvet, Houdan, and Maule.

Everywhere the barons, safeguarded by their fortresses, perpetrated the same excesses: these usually consisted, not only in robbing merchants and pilgrims, but also in fleecing the peasants, in seizing their wine, corn, and cattle, and in pillaging the property of the neighbouring churches and abbeys, invading the abbeys themselves, and making imperious demands for food and shelter for all their suite. It was these last misdoings that drew down upon them, not unnaturally, the worst imprecations of the writers of their day, who were nearly all clerics. There were certain barons who went even further than the rest, and took pleasure in posing as veritable *dilettanti*, so to speak, in the arts of brigandage and cruelty. The most famous example of this type was the son of Enguerrand of Coucy, that Thomas of Marle of whom a contemporary chronicler, Guibert, Abbot of the neighbouring monastery of Nogent, has given us an imperishable portrait.

After a youth spent in debauchery, and in robbing unfortunate pilgrims bound for the Holy Land, Thomas had come to take a positive delight in murder. His cruelty, says the worthy Guibert of Nogent, "so far exceeded previous experience that men who were notoriously cruel killed cattle, apparently, with more regret than he shewed in slaying men." He slaughtered without cause for the sheer pleasure of it; and he exhibited great ingenuity in devising horrible deaths for his victims. Sometimes, it was said, he would hang a man by his thumbs or some other part of the body, and shower blows upon him till he died. Guibert of Nogent declares that he was present one day when Thomas of Marle had the eyes of ten of his victims torn out, with the result that they immediately expired. On another occasion he asked a peasant who had angered him why he did not walk faster, and on the man answering that he was unable to do so—"Wait a moment," cried Thomas; "I'll make you bestir yourself!" and leaping from his horse he drew his sword and cut off both the peasant's feet at a single blow. The poor wretch died; and Guibert, who tells the story, adds: "No one can imagine the number of those who perished in his dungeons, from starvation, from torture, from filth."

Fortunately, not all the petty barons by whom the king was confronted were fashioned after this pattern; but the evil was deeply rooted everywhere, and it was necessary for Louis VI to complete without delay the purge which he had begun even in his father's lifetime. The two *seigneurs* who gave him the most trouble were this very Thomas of Marle whom we have just described, and Hugh, lord of Le Puiset. The latter, though not so perverted as Thomas, was the terror of the country round Chartres, which he ravaged, pillaged, and devastated with fire, without intermission and without mercy. In March 1111, when Louis VI was holding his court at Melun, the charges brought against this brigand were particularly vehement and urgent. To the complaints of Theobald, Count of Chartres, were added those of the Archbishop of Sens, the Bishops of Chartres and Orleans, the abbots of such monasteries as were especially open to attack, and many canons and priests, all of whom besought the king to rid them of this "rapacious wolf," to "tear from the monster's jaws" their property, the fertile fields of Beauce that he "was devouring." On being summoned to the king's presence to answer for his depredations, Hugh, not unnaturally, evaded the summons. He was promptly declared to have forfeited his fief by this refusal to appear, and Louis VI, after calling upon the rebel to surrender, gathered an army and, supported by the Count of Chartres, laid siege to the castle of Le Puiset. It was only after a fierce struggle that he succeeded in reducing it. Hugh was taken prisoner, and the castle was burnt and razed to the ground.

But Hugh was one of those men whom misfortunes only exasperate. No sooner had the king, in 1112, been rash enough to release him than, with renewed ferocity, he returned to his evil courses, "as a dog that has been chained up too long," says Suger, "will bite and tear everything that comes his way." The king was engaged in a war with Henry of England and Theobald of Chartres; and Hugh, taking advantage of his embarrassment, raised a band of marauders and proceeded to ravage the country. Pillage, robbery under arms, imprisonments, were resumed with fresh energy; and one day, when the king arrived in haste to put a bridle on the robber's daring, he found that the castle of Le Puiset had arisen from its ruins. Hugh, who on this occasion had the help of the Count of Chartres, held his own against his sovereign, who was repeatedly repelled, and only overcame the terrible baron after the Count of Chartres had withdrawn from the struggle. Hugh was despoiled of all he possessed and his castle was again destroyed, the walls razed, the moats filled up, the soil levelled. This was trouble thrown away, however; for hardly was the king's back turned before the demolished fortress rose again as though by magic. Hugh, who was pledged to return to the place no more, promptly entrenched himself within its walls, and continued, as before, to terrorise his neighbours. This time the victory remained with Louis VI, who besieged Le Puiset in 1118 and finally stripped the baron of his possessions. Before surrendering, however, Hugh had at least the pleasure of killing, with his own hand and lance, the king's seneschal and faithful friend, Anseau of Garlande. He was destined soon afterwards to lose his own life in an expiatory pilgrimage to the Holy Land.

These episodes in Louis VI's conflict with one of the most unruly barons in his domain are an indication of the difficulties he had to overcome. Against Thomas of Marle he was obliged to organise a regular holy war. In the town of Laon, at this time, the fury of the populace had broken loose and the most dreadful excesses were being committed. Bishop Gaudri and his followers, who had tricked the townsfolk and had suppressed their commune with the king's consent, had been murdered in a riot, the prelate's body covered with wounds and mutilated, the houses of the nobles and clergy sacked, and the churches and episcopal palace set on fire. This was in April 1112. The townspeople, fearing the consequences of the king's anger, appealed to Thomas of Marle, who eagerly granted them his protection and enrolled them in his band of robbers. He removed from his path by murder Gautier, the Archdeacon of Laon, and took possession of two properties belonging to the abbey of Saint-Jean-de-Laon, Crécy-sur-Serre and Nouvion-l'Abbesse. Here he took shelter behind massive walls and strong towers, whence he only emerged to fall upon his prey. The dignitaries of the Church were roused; and in December 1114, at a council held at Beauvais under the presidency of Cono, Cardinal-bishop of Palestrina and legate of the Holy See, Thomas was excommunicated, placed under the ban of Christendom, and pronounced unworthy henceforward to bear a sword. The king was implored to lose no time in suppressing the insane audacity of this protector of Bishop Gaudri's murderers, this rifler of churches and pilgrims. Thomas was pursued by the reiterated anathemas of prelates in council and synod, and of every parish priest; he soon found himself held at bay by the popular levies, whom the summons of the clergy had gathered in large numbers to fight in the pious cause under the king's banner. The fortresses of Crécy and Nouvion fell in turn into Louis VI's hands, and were utterly demolished (1115). Thomas was surrounded in his castle of Marle, and was forced to beg for absolution from the Church and for mercy from the king.

Louis, who at the time had a good deal of other business on his hands, was imprudent enough to pardon him, and was hardly out of sight before the robber's acts of violence began again. For fifteen long years he was able to indulge in these practices to his heart's content, while no one, not even the king, dared to oppose him. In the meantime, on the death of his father Enguerrand in 1116, Thomas had become lord of Coucy and Boves, and seemed able to defy all attacks; until, in 1130, Louis VI was driven by the constant complaints of the clergy and the urgent entreaty of Ralph, Count of Vermandois, to organise an expedition against him. It was only by a stroke of good fortune that the king was enabled to end the matter quickly. Thomas, being taken by surprise before Coucy and mortally wounded, fell into Louis' hands, and died at last, to the great relief of the whole district. To the very end he obstinately refused, in spite of his sufferings and the threats and entreaties of others, to order the merchants whom he had robbed and imprisoned to be set at liberty.

With opponents such as this, as may easily be imagined, Louis VI found that the task to which he had resolved to devote himself, of bringing peace into the royal domain, was an arduous undertaking, and one that required persistent effort on his part. Even in 1108, immediately on his accession to the throne, he was involved in war with Hugh of Crécy, who, not content with ravaging the country, had crowned his offences by capturing Eudes, Count of Corbeil, and imprisoning him in the dungeons of La Ferté-Alais. To set him free it was necessary to besiege that fortress, which only surrendered to the king after a long struggle, full of vicissitudes.

A few months later, in the spring of 1109, Louis VI was again in the field. This time he was besieging Mantes, which he recovered after a strenuous fight from his half-brother Philip, the son of Bertrada of Montfort. This count, like the barons of less distinguished descent, spent his time in the sordid plundering of the churches and peasants of the neighbourhood. Moreover, he formed dangerous conspiracies against the Crown.

Hardly was this danger averted before an equally serious one arose: the lords of Montfort-l'Amauri were threatening to cut off all the king's communications with the country south of Paris. Amauri of Montfort, who was already in possession of the castles of Montfort, Montchauvet, Houdan, and Epernon, had married his daughter to Louis VI's recent opponent, Hugh of Crécy, and was willing to help his son-in-law in the conquest of the castle of Montlhéry and its dependencies, notably the castle of Arpajon. All these fortresses, combined with Hugh's other castles of Crécy-en-Brie, Châteaufort, and Gometz, and those of Amauri's brother Guy of Rochefort at Rochefort-en-Iveline, Chevreuse, and Bréthencourt, would, if linked to one another, have interposed a continuous barrier between the king and a considerable portion of his domain. Louis VI, however, hastened to forestall his enemies, and, before Hugh of Crécy could interfere, seized Arpajon and handed over Montlhéry to Milo of Bray, Viscount of Troyes, who claimed it on the ground of hereditary right. This occurred at the end of the year 1109. In the meantime Hugh of Crécy was forced to fly precipitately. This turbulent vassal, who was nearly as redoubtable as Hugh of Le Puiset or Thomas of Marle, and like them had earned a sinister reputation for robbery and murder (this "tool of the devil," as a contemporary chronicler calls him), was destined to be a source of trouble to the king for many years after this. In 1112 he was one of the most ardent supporters of Hugh of Le Puiset and Theobald, Count of Blois, in their rebellion, and he was the life and soul of the league that was formed at that time against the king by a handful of petty barons: Lancelin of Bulles, lord of Dammartin, Païen of Montjay, Ralph of Beaugency, Guy of Rochefort, and Milo of Bray-sur-Seine, the very man whom Louis VI had weakly allowed to take possession of Montlhéry. In 1118 Hugh of Crécy put the finishing touch to his misdeeds by treacherously seizing this Milo (who was his cousin-german), keeping him in chains in a dungeon at Châteaufort, and finally strangling him and throwing his remains to the winds. This was more than could be borne. Hugh was excommunicated and left without a friend, his castle at Gometz was seized by the king, and he himself threatened with the severest penalties. Seeing that his only safety lay in penitence, he implored the king's pardon, which he only secured at the price of losing all his estates and assuming the monastic habit. In this garb he was left for the rest of his days to meditate on the difference between massacring a few common peasants and murdering a baron.

It was thus, by means of a ceaseless struggle, of which the episodes recorded are merely a few examples, that Louis VI gradually achieved the establishment of the royal authority within the limits of his domain.

But Louis and his counsellors were becoming more and more alive to the fact that it was the king's duty to see that peace and justice were respected throughout the length and breadth of his kingdom; and that by appearing everywhere, even in the most distant fiefs, as the protector of the oppressed and the defender of law and right he would revive the monarchical tradition, and would become really king of all France. A letter addressed to him in 1114 by Ivo, Bishop of Chartres, reminded him that "it behoved the King's Majesty to prevent the violation of the covenant of peace, for which he had pledged himself, under Divine inspiration, to enforce respect in his kingdom"; and Suger repeatedly insisted that the sovereign was bound by his office to "curb the audacity of the tyrants" who robbed and oppressed the people, destroyed churches, and disquieted the whole country.

Louis VI did all he could to fulfil this obligation. Vassals, who for long years had never thought of their sovereign except to take arms against him, he unhesitatingly summoned to appear before his tribunal; nor, if any of them refused to obey, did the king fail to raise an army and set out upon a costly and fatiguing expedition, with a view to teaching the rebel a proper respect for law and order, and obedience to the royal will. One day he was on the point of starting upon one of these petty campaigns when he was reminded, not only that there were many difficulties in his way, but that he might even find it impossible to reduce a castle that had the reputation of being impregnable. With great spirit Louis answered indignantly: "We decided, in a council held at Laon, to make this expedition, and there is nothing in the world that could make us change the decision to which we then came. What a disgrace it would be for the majesty of the Crown if we were to hold back for fear of a bandit!" This answer shews us the whole man.

A few examples of Louis' intervention will reveal, not only the high ideal that he had of his office, but also the increasing confidence with which the oppressed, in every part of France, turned to him as to their recognised protector. At the very beginning of his reign, in 1108 or 1109, a seigneur named Aymon Vaire-Vache unblushingly seized the lordship of Bourbon, although its rightful inheritor was his nephew Archambaud, at that time a minor. The king was informed of the matter and was implored to maintain the boy's rights. As Aymon refused to appear before the royal tribunal to explain his conduct, Louis VI promptly crossed Berry with his troops, besieged the rebel in his castle of Germigny-sur-l'Aubois, forced him to surrender at discretion, and took him back to Paris, where he was condemned to restore all the property that he had unlawfully seized. This rapid success was bewildering. "Kings have long arms!" exclaimed Suger on this occasion, turning to account a line of Ovid.

Perhaps even more characteristic was his behaviour in 1122, when Aimeri, Bishop of Clermont, on being driven out of his episcopal town by William VI, the Count of Auvergne, appealed to the king. Louis, without a moment's hesitation, set off to punish the delinquent, after in vain summoning him, both by word of mouth and by sealed letters, to appear before the royal Court. Mustering at Bourges a large army which included some of his most important vassals, such as the Counts of Anjou, Brittany, and Nevers, the king marched rapidly into Auvergne, seized as he passed the fortress of Pont-du-Château on the Allier, and fell upon Clermont, which Count William and his men abandoned in disorder. They had to submit to the triumphant return of the king's protégé, the bishop.

Four years later the Count of Auvergne thought the moment had come to take his revenge. But Louis VI was able to shew that his will must be obeyed. He entered upon a new campaign with undiminished energy, though the summer heat was overpowering and his stoutness increasing so much that, young as he was, the active life of a soldier became more difficult for him every day. He advanced swiftly to Montferrand, which he burnt, seized Clermont for the second time, and, leaving the country settled and at peace, haled the rebel before the royal Court at Orleans to render account for his latest misdeeds.

In the following year there occurred a still more serious episode. On 2 March 1127, the Count of Flanders, Charles the Good, was assassinated in the church of St Donatian at Bruges while actually engaged in his devotions. The story of this grievous scandal spread like wildfire through the kingdom, and even to England; the news was known in London in less than forty-eight hours. Louis VI instantly set out for Arras, and arrived there less than a week after the murder. Here he remained, holding himself in readiness for any emergency. The crime demanded an exemplary punishment, and the Flemings had turned to the king for help as promptly as he had hurried to their aid. The question was complicated, however, by difficulties in the matter of the succession. The Count of Flanders had left no direct heir, and while the country was in a state of hopeless confusion and the Flemings were occupied in dealing with the murderers, a variety of claimants sprang up on all sides and fell upon the quarry. William of Ypres, who was a natural son of the murdered man's uncle and was popularly accused of complicity with the murderers, succeeded in the course of a few days in taking forcible possession of some of the strongest fortresses in Flanders. Other claimants were Thierry of Alsace, son of Gertrude, Countess of Holland, who based his pretensions on the fact that Robert the Frisian, Count of Flanders (*ob.* 1093), was his maternal grandfather; Arnold of Denmark, nephew of Charles the Good, who seized Saint-Omer; Baldwin IV, Count of Hainault, who, though his only claim was through his great-grandfather Baldwin VI of Flanders (*ob.* 1070), proceeded to occupy Oudenarde; and several others, notably Godfrey the Bearded, Duke of Brabant, who, profiting by the prevailing confusion, suddenly discovered claims of his own, and hastened to vindicate them by force of arms.

The king determined to assert himself. While occupied in concentrating his troops at Arras he sent an urgent summons to the Flemings, bidding them elect a new count in his presence without delay. Louis had a candidate of his own, William Clito the son of Robert Curthose, who had been disinherited by his uncle Henry I of England, and has been justly called "a perpetual pretender to the duchy of Normandy." His right was certainly no better than that of Baldwin of Hainault, seeing that his only connexion with the House of Flanders was through his maternal great-grandfather, Baldwin of Lille, Count of Flanders (*ob.* 1067), father-in-law to William the Conqueror. But he was the king's candidate, and on 23 March 1127 the Flemish delegates hastened to elect him as their suzerain in the presence of Louis VI at Arras. The election was at once confirmed by Ghent, Bruges, Lille, and Saint-Omer; and the king, accompanied by the new count, whom he was fully determined to keep in a state of strict pupillage, advanced rapidly into the heart of Flanders, announcing in a circular letter his intention of making an example of the murderers and restoring order to the country. By 2 April he was at Ghent; on 5 April he reached Bruges, where the murderers were blockaded in the tower of St Donatian and forced to surrender; a few days later, on 26 April, he took Ypres, captured William of Ypres, confiscated his property, and dispatched him to a dungeon at Lille; on the following day he reduced Aire, Cassel, and all the towns in which William of Ypres had obtained recognition; and finally, on 6 May, he was able to set out on his return journey to France by way of Arras. But first, he saw the murderers executed—hurled, under his eyes, from the top of the tower in which they had taken refuge. He had, it seemed, imposed the suzerain of his choice upon the whole of Flanders.

That a king of France should be in a position to act with so much daring and resolution shews plainly how much ground the Crown had recovered. His success, it is true, was short-lived; but this was the fault of the young count, whose blundering stupidity compromised the whole situation as soon as his royal protector left him to himself. In a country where the bourgeois were predominant, where commercial and industrial interests prevailed, and where social development was far more advanced than in that of its neighbours, William Clito imagined that he could ignore the people and rely on the nobles alone. The barons and knights thought that the moment had come for them to take their revenge, and a period of feudal reaction followed. Almost immediately riots broke out in the towns; the evicted claimants plucked up courage; Ghent and Bruges opened their gates to Thierry of Alsace; Saint-Omer recalled Arnold of Denmark, who was secretly supported by the King of England. Disorder once more reigned supreme.

Louis VI tried to intervene, thinking he could take a high tone with the rebels. "I desire you," he wrote to the people of Bruges on 10 April 1128, "to send eight notables to me at Arras on Palm Sunday (15 April); I will summon as many from each of the towns of Flanders, in order to inquire, in their presence and in that of all my barons, into the reasons of your disagreement and of your conflict with your Count William, and I shall make it my business forthwith to establish peace between you and him. If there be any man among you who dares not come to me, I will give him a safe-conduct, both for coming and for going." But this time his authoritative tone made no impression on the men of Bruges, whose answer was a haughty and violent indictment of the King of France. They accused him of selling their country for a thousand marks, denied him all right of interference in the election of their suzerain, and condemned in very energetic language the treacherous treatment they had received from William Clito. They, moreover, had settled the question for themselves. They announced without further ado that in place of William Clito, who had played them false and had been expelled by them, they would recognise no suzerain in future but Thierry of Alsace, "who had a stronger hereditary right to be their count, was a wise and loyal man, and had been raised to power in accordance with the custom of the country. To him who so admirably adhered to the manners and customs of his predecessors they had pledged their faith and homage." This was a direct declaration of war.

Louis VI, who was at the moment engrossed in other difficulties, doubtless understood that the game was lost. The rapid successes of

Thierry of Alsace, who made his entry into Lille on 11 April 1128, left no room for hope. He contented himself with convening a great assembly at Arras, in which Thierry was excommunicated, and with making a demonstration before the walls of Lille. Then, having satisfied his conscience, he abandoned William Clito to his unhappy fate (May 1128). William's death at the siege of Alost (27 July 1128) hastened the end. The whole country submitted to Thierry, and Louis VI was obliged to ratify the accomplished fact by giving investiture to the conqueror. This time the king had overrated his powers; the hour had not yet come for great conquests and the subjection of the great fiefs. It was the head of the Anglo-Norman monarchy who was to be the chief instrument in proving this fact to Louis.

Ever since the middle of the eleventh century the kings of France had been making ceaseless efforts to arrest the dangerous and ever-increasing expansion of the Norman dominion. Philip I, as we have seen[1], was as eager as his father Henry to seize every possible chance of embarrassing this formidable vassal and supporting his enemies. But the King of France had a redoubtable foe to deal with. The Conqueror's third son, Henry Beauclerc, was not the man to be intimidated by the Capetian. Having deprived his brother Robert Curthose of his duchy of Normandy and sent him into captivity, declaring, not without reason, that he was incapable of maintaining order and peace in his dominion (1106), Henry I hastened to take possession of the castle of Gisors. This fortress on the right bank of the Epte formed, it is true, an integral part of the Norman Vexin, but such was the strategic importance of its position commanding the road from Rouen to Paris, that when Henry I did homage for Normandy to the King of France they made a special agreement on the subject. Both were pledged never to occupy the place in person, but either to leave it in the hands of a neutral castellan, at that time Païen of Neauphle, or else to demolish it.

Louis VI lost no time in protesting. He called upon his vassal to observe the conventions of the treaty, and summoned him to account for his conduct in the presence of his suzerain, whom he was to meet on the frontier of their respective dominions, at the bridge of Neauphle on the Epte. Both kings came there in force. Henry refused to submit to the demands of the King of France, whereupon the latter naively, if courageously, offered, if need were, to prove his right by meeting the King of England in single combat. To the bearers of this strange message Henry replied: "When the King of France attacks me I shall know how to defend myself!" This incident happened about March 1109.

This meant war—a war that was destined to drag on for twenty years, interrupted from time to time by a truce or a sham peace which enabled each of the two foes to keep his eye upon the other while awaiting a

---

[1] *Supra,* Vol. III, Chap. v.

propitious moment to renew the attack. The tactics of the King of France, in his efforts to arrest the growth of the power of Normandy, were simple. They consisted in allying himself with the Count of Anjou, and favouring the Angevin intrigues in Maine, with a view to keeping the Norman from that province, and finally himself attacking him at his most vulnerable point, the Vexin, in order to free the royal domain from the perpetual menace that threatened it if Gisors remained in the hands of the English king. As for Henry, his policy was to secure freedom of action by seizing every possible chance of creating difficulties for the King of France in his own dominions; and, while seeking to be on good terms with the Count of Anjou, to lend his support to Theobald, Count of Blois and Chartres, who was to wage perpetual war against Louis, harassing his army in the rear as his Norman foes slowly advanced.

In 1109, at the beginning of hostilities, the alliance between Henry of England and Theobald of Blois was not yet concluded, and at one time it almost seemed as though Louis VI were about to triumph. He crossed the Epte, repulsed Henry's troops, and pursued his victorious way through part of the Norman Vexin. But in 1111 everything was changed. Theobald, who in 1109 had figured in Louis VI's army, suddenly changed sides, and by the spring of the following year had succeeded in bringing together a formidable coalition against the King of France. This coalition was composed, as we have already seen[1], of Henry of England and a host of petty barons: Lancelin of Bulles, lord of Dammartin, Païen of Montjay, Ralph of Beaugency, Milo of Bray-sur-Seine, Hugh of Crécy, Guy of Rochefort, and Hugh of Le Puiset himself, not to speak of Hugh, Count of Troyes. This time Louis was forced to yield. He succeeded, it is true, in overcoming the coalition of French barons and in repulsing Theobald; but he found it impossible to defeat the English monarch. Not only was there now no question of obliging him to abandon Gisors, but a treaty was signed before the walls of that fortress at the end of March 1113, by which Louis agreed, perforce, to recognise Henry I as suzerain of Brittany as well as of Maine, which in 1110 had come by marriage into the hands of the Count of Anjou.

Three years were hardly gone before war broke out again (April 1116), a war of constant skirmishes on the confines of the Norman and the French Vexin, in which each king captured in turn the strongholds of his rival. Louis VI, encouraged by several successes, of which the most brilliant was the surprise and capture of Les Andelys, early in 1119, by means of treachery within the walls, thought the hour had come for a decisive engagement. He suddenly offered battle to Henry I in the plain of Brémule, not far from Noyon-sur-Andelle. The result was disaster. The troops of the King of France were seized with panic when confronted by the large and well-disciplined army that the English king had at his disposal, and took to flight, carrying Louis with them in their stampede.

[1] See *supra*, p. 597.

He fled precipitately to Les Andelys, where he succeeded in finding a refuge, but only after wandering alone in the forest of Musegros; his war-horse and banner he left in the hands of the enemy (20 August 1119). In his rage and humiliation he vainly tried, a month later, to avenge himself by attacking the district of Évreux; but, though he captured and burnt Ivry, he failed before Breteuil, which was the object of the expedition. In the meantime his son-in-law William of Chaumont was being equally unsuccessful at the siege of Tillières, where he fell into the hands of the enemy. Louis was again forced to beat a retreat, and such was his fury that he was on the point of burning Chartres, to vent his wrath at the expense of Count Theobald.

And now his failing health, and his weariness of this long struggle that had brought him only mortification, prompted Louis to negotiate for peace. He appealed to the supreme arbitrator, Pope Calixtus II, on the occasion of a council held by the latter at Rheims on 20 and 21 October 1119. The Norman monk, Ordericus Vitalis, has given us in his chronicle, if not the exact words, at least the substance of the speech delivered on this occasion by the "strongly-built, pale, corpulent, eloquent" king, whom he seems himself to have seen and heard. The speech was a veritable indictment, a denunciation of Henry I's conduct from first to last. Nothing was overlooked, from the iniquitous imprisonment of Robert Curthose to the arrest of Robert, lord of Bellême, who had been sent on a mission to Henry by the King of France in 1112. "The King of England, who was long my ally, has been guilty of constant acts of aggression and violence at my expense, and at that of my subjects; he took forcible possession of Normandy, which forms part of my kingdom; he has treated Robert, Duke of Normandy, shamefully, in defiance of law and justice. Ignoring the fact that Robert was my vassal and his own brother and lord, he subjected him to all manner of vexations, and finally imprisoned him. Even now he has him fast in his dungeons. And here before you stands the son of this unhappy duke, William (Clito), who has come hither with me, having been driven into exile and disinherited by the King of England! By the mouths of bishops and counts and many others, I have called upon him to restore to me the duke whom he holds imprisoned; but I have obtained no satisfaction. Robert of Bellême, my ambassador, whom I sent to signify my will to him, was arrested by his orders in his palace. He loaded him with chains, and has kept him to this day in a cruel prison." Finally, Henry was also accused of inciting to rebellion that Count of Blois, Theobald, whose shameful excesses had disturbed the whole kingdom. The Pope promised to intervene. But this *ex parte* statement of Louis VI, who had omitted to say that he himself, in 1107, had connived at the spoliation of Robert Curthose, was met by Henry I with another that was no less biassed, and was moreover supported by various gifts on the occasion of an interview that he had with Calixtus II at Gisors in the following November. Henry agreed, however, to enter into negotiations with the King of France, and in 1120 peace was concluded on these terms: the two adversaries were to restore their respective conquests, and Louis VI was to receive homage for the duchy of Normandy from William Aetheling, only legitimate son of Henry I and heir apparent to the throne of England. In the matter of Gisors Louis was obliged to yield. This was a decided set-back.

On both sides underhand hostilities continued. On 25 November 1120, Louis VI's hopes were revived by the unexpected death of William Aetheling in the White Ship; and in 1123 a coalition of Norman and French *seigneurs* was formed with the object of expelling the King of England from the duchy of Normandy and replacing him by William Clito. Henry I stoutly held his own against this coalition, while at his instigation his son-in-law, the Emperor Henry V, made ready to fall upon Rheims in order to hamper Louis VI's actions (August 1124). The latter, however, succeeded in diverting the storm. With the most remarkable eagerness and unanimity the entire country rose at the king's appeal, and rallied round him to repel the national danger. Thereupon Henry V, daunted by finding a whole nation in arms, beat a hasty retreat. But Louis could not recover the upper hand in Normandy. Henry I triumphed over all his enemies, and contributed by his manoeuvres and aggressions towards the frustration of the French policy in Flanders. He even went so far as to ally himself with the Count of Anjou by marrying (1127 or 1128) his widowed daughter Matilda, the sole survivor of his legitimate children, to Geoffrey the Fair, heir to the fiefs of Anjou and Maine. This marriage was a terrible menace to hang over the head of the French king, and it was not long before Louis VII felt its fatal effects.

And yet, as the time drew near for Louis VI to die, it seemed that the French monarchy was in a good position. Henry I of England had died on 1 December 1135, and Stephen of Blois, who obtained the English crown, was fully occupied at home with difficulties that quite prevented him from meditating any kind of intervention on the Continent. Count Theobald, who, since the death of his uncle Hugh I of Champagne in 1125, had been lord over all the territory of the ancient House of Blois —namely Champagne, Blois, and Chartres—had at last laid down his arms and rallied to the Capetian cause. And finally, an unexpected windfall had just placed the whole duchy of Aquitaine in the hands of the future king. Duke William X, who had died on 9 April 1137, during a pilgrimage to the shrine of St James of Compostella, had upon his death-bed confided to Louis VI the care of marrying his daughter and heiress Eleanor; and Louis had promptly taken steps to get his son accepted as her husband. The future Louis VII was occupied in taking possession of Aquitaine when the death of his father on 1 August 1137 placed him on the throne of France.

During the first few years of his reign the new king, who thus became his own master at the age of sixteen or seventeen, displayed more activity than discretion. It is possible that the suggestions of his young queen, Eleanor, on whom he lavished, says one of the chroniclers, "an extravagant love," may sometimes have misdirected his energies; and the counsels of the discreet but somewhat ingenuous Suger were inadequate to counteract this influence. Without disturbing himself in the least, or putting the smallest obstacle in the way, Louis allowed the Count of Anjou to increase his territory so rapidly that his power was every day a greater menace, and in the meantime threw himself heart and soul into rash undertakings which, being ill-organised and ill-executed, brought him nothing but mortification.

Not content with the acquisition of Aquitaine, which he had already found sufficiently hard to control, he bethought him soon afterwards, in 1141. of insisting upon the rights to the county of Toulouse that his predecessors in the duchy had several times claimed. Accordingly he organised an expedition against Count Alphonse-Jourdain. Towards the end of June a considerable army marched rapidly upon Toulouse under the king's leadership; but after a few weeks he was obliged to retrace his steps without having gained any advantage.

It was not long before the young king was concerned with more serious affairs. For more than two years he squandered the strength of the monarchy in a twofold and sterile struggle against the Papacy on the one hand and Count Theobald of Champagne on the other. On the death of the Archbishop of Bourges in 1141 two candidates were put forward to succeed him: Cadurc, the king's Chancellor, and Peter of La Châtre, a near relative of the Chancellor of the Roman Church. The one was the king's candidate, the other the Pope's. The second was elected, in spite of the fact that Louis forbade the clergy to choose him. Louis in a fury swore upon the sacred relics that, as long as he lived, Peter should not enter Bourges. The sovereign pontiff, Innocent II, calmly retorted by consecrating Peter with his own hands at Rome, and, since Bourges still remained closed to him, by laying an interdict on every town, village, or castle that should shelter the king. "The King of France is a child," the Pope is declared to have said, "and must be educated, and prevented from acquiring bad habits." In the meantime Count Theobald had added fuel to the fire by taking part openly against his sovereign and receiving Peter of La Châtre in his domain. This was enough to exasperate Louis VII, who already had a subject of complaint against this vassal, in that he had twice refused his feudal contingent—in 1138, on the occasion of an expedition against the rebels of Poitou, and more recently when Louis had marched against Toulouse.

A fresh incident occurred to aggravate the dissension and hasten the rupture. Ralph, Count of Vermandois and Seneschal of France, having repudiated his first wife, Theobald's niece, in order to marry

Queen Eleanor's sister Alice (also called Petronilla) of Aquitaine, three bishops of the royal domain consented to dissolve the first marriage on grounds of consanguinity, and to bless the second. It was not long before protests were raised; and, at a council held under the presidency of a papal legate at Lagny-sur-Marne, the three accommodating prelates were excommunicated, their decision reversed, the second marriage annulled, and the territory of the Count of Vermandois laid under an interdict. In itself the incident was commonplace, and the history of the times records a score of similar episodes. But the young king, stimulated by Queen Eleanor, took the matter as a personal insult. Here again he was confronted with Count Theobald. The council that had annulled the marriage of Ralph and Petronilla was held at Lagny-sur-Marne, on the territory of the Count of Champagne, who openly took the part of his niece, Ralph's repudiated wife. This was enough to make the irascible King of France hold Theobald responsible for the whole affair. With an outburst of fury that took his enemy by surprise, Louis VII descended on Champagne, attacked Vitry-sur-Marne, captured it, and left it in flames. Hundreds of the inhabitants—thirteen hundred, it is said—perished in the burning church. Theobald, whose turbulent habits and baneful energy had gradually given place of late years to a spirit of devotion and a zeal for good works, assumed a pathetic attitude that earned him the ridicule even of his own subjects. "Why," they asked, "has not Count Theobald spent his time and his money in more useful ways? He has what he deserves: for knights he has monks; for bowmen, lay brethren. He sees now how little such as these can avail to serve him!" The clergy of Champagne, who had suffered cruelly from the royal invasion, were at a loss to determine what to do.

But Louis VII, no doubt, was equally embarrassed. His victory brought him no practical advantage; it merely increased the unpopularity of his cause. He was only too thankful, in the summer of 1143, to accept terms that pledged him to evacuate Champagne on condition that Theobald—through the good offices of Bernard, Abbot of Clairvaux—should secure the removal of the ban that had been laid upon the Count of Vermandois and the queen's sister.

It was not long before Louis perceived that the venerable Abbot of Clairvaux, who had conducted all the negotiations, had taken unworthy advantage of his inexperience. Hardly had he restored his conquests to Theobald before Ralph and Petronilla, who refused to be separated, were excommunicated for the second time. The young king's wrath was boundless, and he swore to be revenged upon Count Theobald. Bernard of Clairvaux only incensed him the more by affecting airs of innocence. What, asked the abbot, had he and Theobald done to deserve the king's reproaches? Was it their fault if Ralph had behaved in such a way as to merit excommunication? Had not Count Theobald done his utmost, had he not even done violence to his conscience, to secure Ralph's absolution on the first occasion in the face of a thousand difficulties? And what could he do against this fresh excommunication?

The war was resumed. Louis VII again occupied a portion of Champagne, and refused to allow the appointment of bishops to vacant sees. Theobald's attempt at retaliation was to form a feudal league; he allied himself with the Counts of Flanders and Soissons. Every day the conflict became more bitter, without any advantage accruing to either party. Suger and St Bernard were in favour of peace, and perhaps also the immediate circle of the new Pope, Celestine II, who had just (26 September 1143) succeeded Innocent II, but it was not without difficulty that they prevailed over the obstinacy of the young king. After stubbornly seeking for months to wreak his vengeance upon Theobald, he was forced to yield at all points: to evacuate Champagne entirely and unconditionally, to abandon Ralph of Vermandois to his fate, and to recognise Peter of La Châtre as Archbishop of Bourges. This was indeed a triumph for the Papacy.

It was fully time for Louis to pull himself together and turn his attention towards the west. For, while he was thus exhausting his strength in fruitless efforts, the Count of Anjou and Maine, Geoffrey the Fair, was taking advantage of every opportunity to extend his dominions. While his wife Matilda in England was carrying on a ceaseless struggle with its king, Stephen of Blois, in defence of the rights that she had inherited from her father Henry I, Geoffrey descended upon Normandy and conquered it by slow degrees. In the course of the successive campaigns in which he engaged almost yearly between 1136 and 1144 he won nearly the entire province. There remained at last only Rouen; and on 23 April 1144 that town also yielded. Louis had no choice but to accept the accomplished fact, and to recognise his powerful vassal as the possessor of the conquered duchy. He had the acuteness, however, to prevail upon Geoffrey, in exchange for this concession, to evacuate Gisors, the strategical importance of which we have already seen. This was, at all events, some compensation.

It may be thought that by this time the king would have learnt wisdom and, profiting by the experience of these early years, would take up the reins of government with a firm hand. But hardly was his desperate struggle with the Church at an end, before he became possessed by a spirit of mystic piety which prompted him to desert his kingdom and go forth to fight the infidels in a distant land.

The news of the capture of Edessa by the Atābeg Zangī of Mosul on 25 December 1144 had recently filled the whole of western Christendom with consternation. On Christmas Day 1145, when Louis was with his court at Bourges for the ceremony of wearing his crown—a solemnity that was customary at the great festivals—he suddenly informed the barons of his intention to take the Cross, and exhorted them to follow his example. This suggestion they received with so little enthusiasm that it was found necessary to postpone the final decision to another court to be held at Vézelay the following Easter. The pious Suger himself advised the king against this enterprise; and St Bernard, on being entreated to use his influence for the furtherance of the Crusade, dared not take upon himself so serious a responsibility, and therefore referred the question to the Pope. We have seen in an earlier chapter[1] how the latter decided to espouse the cause, and how St Bernard, in accordance with the Pontiff's urgent desire, preached the Crusade with enthusiasm and became its life and soul. He it was whose eloquence, at the assembly at Vézelay on 31 March 1146, succeeded in rousing a fresh outburst of zeal for the holy war; it was he who kindled the ardour of the Germans and overcame the resistance of King Conrad III, and who was responsible for the organisation of the expedition, for all the preparations and arrangements. When Louis VII's army set out on 11 June 1147, success appeared certain. We know how these hopes were frustrated: by the discord that so soon broke out between French and Germans, and weakened their attack upon the common enemy; by the disasters that overtook both armies, the Germans at Dorylaeum and the French near Laodicea; and finally by the deplorable repulse of the crusaders before Damascus in July 1148, after which the greater number of them gave up the struggle.

Louis VII, however, was quite content to linger in the Holy Land, visiting the sacred places and forgetting his own kingdom while he devoted himself overseas to pious works. The Abbot of St Denis, Suger, who had carried on his shoulders nearly the whole weight of the regency since the day of the king's departure, urged him to return. Hitherto the abbot had succeeded admirably in keeping order in the kingdom; but the king's brother Robert of Dreux had lately returned, and the malcontents had begun to gather round him. There was even some talk among them of deposing Louis and making Robert their king. Happily Suger contrived to frustrate these intrigues, and, when at last, at the beginning of November 1149, Louis made up his mind to return to his kingdom after an absence of nearly two years and a half, he found the country at peace.

Louis VII at last realised where the true interests of the monarchy lay. During the early years of his reign he had allowed the whole of Normandy to be appropriated by the Count of Anjou, Geoffrey the Fair; and the energetic campaigns conducted by Geoffrey's wife Matilda and their son Henry Plantagenet—afterwards Henry II—plainly shewed whither the dangerous ambitions of the House of Anjou were likely to lead. The security of the Crown imperatively demanded that the king should employ every possible means, if indeed it were not already too late, to undermine this formidable power, which was infinitely more menacing

---

[1] See *supra*, Chap. xi, pp. 373–75.

than the Anglo-Norman power had ever been in the days of Henry I of France.

It was an incident of minor importance, the siege of Montreuil-Bellay by Geoffrey the Fair, that supplied the pretext for a rupture. Gerald, the lord of this little Angevin fortress, had placed himself at the head of a strong coalition formed against his suzerain, Count Geoffrey, who had retaliated by laying siege to the rebel's stronghold. But Gerald was the king's protégé and his seneschal in Poitou; Louis therefore made his cause his own, and called upon Geoffrey the Fair to raise the siege (1150). Suger, who was in this, it must be owned, more remarkable for uprightness than for political insight, succeeded for a time in warding off the storm; but on 13 January 1151 he died, and since Gerald still held out stubbornly against Geoffrey the Fair, and Geoffrey continuously refused, not unnaturally, to comply with the royal command, hostilities broke out.

Louis had already decided upon a line of conduct. His policy consisting in putting forward Eustace of Boulogne, the son of King Stephen of England, as a rival to the Count of Anjou and his son Henry Plantagenet, to whom Geoffrey had transferred the duchy of Normandy at the beginning of 1150. Acting in concert, Louis and Eustace made a sudden descent upon Caux in May or June, 1151, and repulsed Henry at Arques; then, in July, they advanced as far as Séez, which they burnt. In the following month, when Louis was preparing to invade the duchy of Normandy anew at the head of a still stronger army, a sudden attack of fever obliged him to suspend operations. Geoffrey the Fair and his son were only too glad to seize this opportunity of coming to terms; and towards the end of August a treaty was signed in Paris by which they surrendered to the king, not now Gisors alone, but the whole of the Norman Vexin.

Unfortunately Louis then made an irreparable blunder. His love for his wife Eleanor, which had been so ardent during the first years of their marriage, had gradually cooled; while the queen, for her part, having grown more and more indifferent to Louis, had been led into frailties, or at least into follies, that were by no means pleasing to her husband. This state of things had at last resulted in an open rupture between them, and Louis, to whom personal feelings were of more importance than reasons of State, prevailed upon a council held at Beaugency on 21 March 1152 to dissolve the marriage on grounds of consanguinity. Barely two months later (May 1152) Eleanor married Henry Plantagenet, who, on the sudden death of his father Geoffrey the Fair on 7 September 1151, had succeeded to the county of Anjou. Since, naturally, the daughter of Duke William X took her dowry with her to her second husband, this marriage not only meant a loss to the monarchy of the whole duchy of Aquitaine, but also a new and formidable acquisition of territory for its rival.

Too late, Louis recognised the mistake that he had made. He hastened to take up arms once more, and, as Henry was preparing to cross the Channel and fight King Stephen for the English crown, he again invaded Normandy. With his army marched, not only Eustace of Boulogne but also Count Robert of Perche, Henry the Liberal, Count of Champagne, and even the Count of Anjou's own brother Geoffrey, who was to oppose Henry Plantagenet on many more occasions than this. Had the attack been conducted with vigour it might have proved disastrous for the young Count of Anjou. It was, however, conducted timidly and half-heartedly: Louis contented himself with besieging a few places on the frontier, of which Neufmarché was the only one he captured. He retreated hastily to the shelter of his own castle-walls as soon as Henry shewed signs of retaliating. Moreover, when Henry, whose affairs demanded his presence in England, proposed a truce at the end of August 1152, Louis—with almost incredible weakness—instantly agreed to the suggestion.

For eight months he remained inactive. At a time when an energetic attack on Normandy might perhaps have been fatal to Henry's success in England, and might even have undermined his position on the Continent, Louis abstained from action. At last he decided to cross the Norman frontier, to besiege Vernon and make a demonstration before Verneuil. He even succeeded, after two sieges, in entering Vernon (August or September 1153); but he was content to do no more, while Henry calmly pursued his advantages in England. By the time the latter returned to Normandy in April 1154, his recognition by Stephen of Blois as the heir to the English throne had been brought about by the death of Eustace of Boulogne; and Louis VII in alarm hastened to sign a treaty of peace (August 1154). This peace really amounted to a capitulation on his part. By it he engaged, in return for an indemnity of 2000 silver marks, to restore the two fortresses that were all he had succeeded in capturing, Vernon and Neufmarché, and to relinquish the title of Duke of Aquitaine, which he had hitherto continued to use. On 25 October following Stephen of Blois died, and a few weeks later (19 December 1154) Henry was crowned at Westminster without any attempt on the part of Louis to hamper the movements of his formidable enemy.

At an age when most men are in the full exercise of their powers Louis VII, whose blundering impetuosity had once been so much to be deplored, seemed suddenly to have become irresolute and almost sluggish. Those who were much with him at this time lay stress on his simplicity, his gentleness, his placability, and his piety. A certain monk of Vézelay frankly declares that the king always inclined to compromise, that he loved quiet and detested conflict. Another writer recalls having seen him in the midst of a procession, modestly mingling with the crowd of clergy. Upright and loyal himself, he had confidence in the honesty of others. He was in the habit of walking alone amid his subjects, and it is even told of him that one day he lay down in a forest and slept profoundly with only two knights to guard him. When someone expressed surprise, the king answered: "I can sleep alone in perfect safety, because no man wishes me ill." He carried this confiding spirit into all his dealings, without any regard for the subtleties of the statesman. A contemporary chronicler, Gervase of Canterbury, tells us that he was "a very Christian king, but somewhat simple-minded." " A very pious man" is the description of another writer, "a friend to the clergy, a devout servant of God, one who was deceived by many and himself deceived none."

To the end of his reign his policy towards Henry II consisted in perpetual retreat. Any attempt at resistance on the part of the King of France invariably ended in a treaty that gave fresh advantages to his opponent.

Hardly had Henry II established his authority in England before he undertook the task of extending his dominions in every direction on the Continent. In the north it was the Norman Vexin that he desired to recapture from the King of France; in the west it was Brittany that he aspired to make his own; in the south it was the county of Toulouse that he demanded as a dependency of Aquitaine. This gigantic programme he promptly set to work to carry out.

In 1156, amid the domestic dissensions that had harassed Brittany from time immemorial, the county of Nantes had submitted to Geoffrey of Anjou, Henry Plantagenet's brother. When Geoffrey died on 26 July 1158, Henry claimed the succession to the county, and, as he was quite prepared to support his claim by force of arms, his authority was recognised at Nantes. Not only did Louis VII abstain from opposing him, but he even went so far, it seems, as to smooth his enemy's path by authorising him to enter Brittany with the title of Seneschal of France, which must doubtless have given an air of legality to the King of England's act of usurpation.

The two kings at this time were firm friends. They met near Gisors on 31 August 1158, when Louis VII unhesitatingly agreed to betroth his third daughter, Margaret, an infant six months old, to the King of England's eldest son, Henry, whose age was then three years, and pledged himself to give the bride for marriage-portion the whole of the Norman Vexin. This dowry, till the children were of marriageable age, was to be left in charge of the Templars. The "good and gentle" king had no suspicions; he welcomed his rival to Paris as though he were his best friend, and allowed him to take away the little princess. So delighted was he with his new friendship that he even made a pilgrimage across Normandy to Mont-Saint-Michel, accepting the attentions and marks of affection that Henry lavished upon him during the journey without for a moment doubting their sincerity. He was entirely absorbed in pious thoughts. The pilgrimage to Mont-Saint-Michel failing to satisfy his devotion, he planned a great crusade against the Moors of Spain. He made sure that his dear friend Henry would accompany him.

The latter, however, was of a more practical nature, and, having gathered a considerable army and formed a sound coalition, was preparing to enforce his rights over Toulouse at the expense of Count Raymond V. Recalled thus roughly to the world of reality, Louis VII at last awoke and attempted to negotiate. Henry humoured him, and conferences were held at Tours (March 1159) and Heudicourt (6–8 June 1159). But the King of England had already resolved upon his course of action. At the end of June his army set out towards Languedoc, occupied a portion of that province, and proceeded rapidly in the direction of Toulouse. The town would doubtless have fallen if Louis VII, who had followed his rival with a few troops, had not decided, after fresh delays and renewed attempts at negotiation, to intrench himself within the walls (September 1159). Henry dared not take so serious a step as to besiege his suzerain the King of France; and as Louis, who was delighted at the success of a manoeuvre that called for no effort, resolutely remained in Toulouse, the King of England contented himself for the moment with establishing his troops firmly in Cahors. He then hastened back to Normandy.

It was not long before Louis learnt the reasons for this rapid retreat. Henry had gained the adherence of Theobald of Blois, Seneschal of France, and had proceeded without delay to attack the Beauvaisis in person. Louis had barely time to hasten thither; and when he found that the Count of Évreux had also deserted him, and had handed over to the King of England the castles of Montfort-l'Amauri, Rochefort, and Épernon, he was only too glad to obtain a truce (December 1159). This truce was followed, in May 1160, by a treaty of peace. The King of France, while confirming the former agreement with regard to the Norman Vexin, confined himself to stipulating, on behalf of the Count of Toulouse, for a year's truce. Henry II, whatever befell, was to keep the fortresses he had captured in Languedoc until the expiration of the truce.

The treaty was hardly signed before the English king, without a word of warning, celebrated the marriage of his son Henry to Margaret, the little princess whom Louis had so confidingly entrusted to his care (2 November 1160). The young husband was only five-and-a-half years old, and the bride was certainly not yet three! But the King of England was impatient to lay his hand upon the dowry, the Norman Vexin, which he succeeded in obtaining from the Templars in whose charge it had been placed. Once more the simple-minded Louis perceived that he had been outwitted; once more he hankered after revenge. He arranged with Theobald, Count of Blois, that Chaumont-sur-Loire should be made the centre for an attack on Touraine; but in December 1160 the King of England took possession of the place. In the following spring, after allowing his adversary ample time to fortify himself in Gisors and to garrison all the frontier fortresses, Louis made a show of preparing to recover the Vexin at the point of the sword; but after a few skirmishes he consented to a new truce. In September 1162—yielding as usual to the force of circumstances—he agreed to sign a treaty of peace which was an open confession of weakness.

It was at this juncture that the case of Thomas Becket came into prominence. We have seen in an earlier chapter[1] how the Archbishop of Canterbury, at the end of the year 1164, fled from England, where his position was imperilled, and took refuge in France. Louis VII, who was delighted to revenge himself upon his enemy without having recourse to arms, and was also, no doubt, honestly distressed by the misfortunes of the prelate, had declared openly for him at the very beginning. He gave his protection to the exile in spite of the protests of the English king, who declared that the treaty of 1162 contained a clause to the effect that neither of the monarchs should receive in his dominions any rebellious subject of the other. When Henry, in one of his letters of protest, referred to Becket as the "ex-Archbishop of Canterbury," the King of France exclaimed: "What! Ex-Archbishop? Why, the King of England has no more right than I to depose even the humblest of his clergy!" Yet for two years the matter dragged on, while every day the discussion grew less amicable, and a fresh rupture more inevitable. War broke out in June 1167; but again nothing was effected on either side save a few skirmishes on the frontier. When each had burnt a village or two and a few castles, the two kings were ready to come to terms. Henry could employ his time more profitably than in continuing so fruitless a struggle, and Louis was even less disposed than usual to take advantage of his enemy's many difficulties and to conduct the war with spirit. In August they agreed to lay down their arms until Easter 1168. On the renewal of hostilities Louis acted with his habitual irresolution and weakness, chiefly confining himself to supporting the rebellions in Aquitaine and Brittany against Henry. The month of August saw fresh negotiations, which led to new truces and new ruptures. Finally, on 6 January 1169, the two kings again met at Montmirail, near the frontier of Maine, to arrange a peace, and at the same time to come to some conclusion on the question of Thomas Becket, which was still unsettled. Louis VII, true to his character, was content to receive purely nominal satisfaction, such as the homage of the younger Henry for Normandy, Brittany, Maine, and Anjou, and that of the English king's second son, Richard, for the county of Poitou. As for the questions that had caused the war, they were not considered. The Vexin, which Henry had so unceremoniously annexed, remained in his possession; his rights over Brittany, which he had conquered, received formal recognition; even Thomas Becket was almost sacrificed as well. It was not till many months had passed, and many conferences had been held, that an apparent reconciliation was effected between him and Henry.

Shortly after the tragic end of the Archbishop of Canterbury on 29 December 1170, the opportunity came at last to Louis VII for a

---

[1] See *supra*, Chap. XVII.

striking act of vengeance. Henry II, who pursued his policy of invasion untiringly, had succeeded in securing the homage of the Count of Toulouse (January 1173), and his power on the Continent seemed to be more firmly established than ever, when suddenly his sons broke out into rebellion. We have already seen[1] how his son Henry, whose disaffection against his father had been carefully nourished by the King of France, had (8 March 1173) suddenly fled to the French court, where his two brothers Richard and Geoffrey soon joined him, at the instigation of Queen Eleanor. At last Louis seemed determined to take a firm line; strong in the support of a powerful faction, which included the Counts of Flanders, Champagne, Boulogne, Blois, Sancerre, Dreux, and others, he at last shewed a warlike spirit. When the envoys of King Henry—Rotrou, Archbishop of Rouen, and Arnulf, Bishop of Lisieux—came to negotiate with Louis, he turned upon them with bitter complaints of his adversary's encroachments. "Why," he asked, "has the King of England, in spite of his solemn pledge, kept Margaret's dowry, Gisors and the Vexin? Why does he seek to incite against their rightful sovereign the people of France, from the mountains of Auvergne to the Rhone? Why did he receive the liege homage of the Count of Toulouse? Tell your master that I swear I will never make peace with him without the express consent of his wife and sons!" Not only was Henry the Younger received at the court of France with every sign of favour, but Louis VII affected to regard him as the true King of England. He had a royal seal made for him, and took a solemn pledge to help him in the winning of the crown. Henry the Younger received the homage of a great number of barons, who had followed him in his rebellion.

There can be no doubt that a prompt and energetic attack would have placed Henry II in a peculiarly dangerous position. But Louis was no more capable than on previous occasions of acting swiftly and striking with a firm hand. While Henry the Younger, in concert with the Counts of Flanders and Boulogne, invaded the country round Bray, to the north of the Seine, the King of France lingered over the siege of Verneuil; and when, on 9 August, Henry II's army drew near, he immediately decamped and began to parley with the enemy. In the following year he made a final effort against Rouen; but again, on the approach of the King of England, he beat a shameful retreat, burnt his engines of war himself (14 August 1174), entered into negotiations, and finally deserted the cause of the rebels, whom he forced to implore pardon of the King of England at Montlouis (30 September 1174).

Thus Louis VII, with his customary indolence, let slip this unexpected opportunity of driving the English monarch into important concessions. He allowed Henry II to reduce at his leisure his English and continental subjects, who had risen at the call of his rebellious sons, and to enlarge

---

[1] See *supra*, Chap. XVII.

his dominions still further at the expense of the French monarchy by the acquisition of the county of La Marche (1177). There was even a time, shortly before his death, when Louis seemed to cherish the illusion that he had transformed Henry II into a faithful friend of the Capetian monarchy.

Yet, feeble as this " good" king appeared in his struggle with the enterprising and active English sovereign, so strong was the force of circumstances that, in spite of everything, he left the French monarchy more firmly established than he found it—left it with its prestige definitely restored, and its position in Europe such that it was thenceforward a power to be reckoned with.

And first, within the limits of his own kingdom we find that Louis VII pursued, not unsuccessfully, the work of pacification and concentration that his father had begun with so much energy. In the preamble to one of his charters we read that " it is the office of the Crown to crush those who evade justice, and to support the obedient and submissive and secure to them their rights." Louis VII indeed was as ready as Louis VI to face hardships, and at times to embark upon long expeditions at the call of the oppressed, in order to make the royal tribunal respected throughout the country and thereby secure recognition of the king's supremacy. In 1153, for instance, when Hervé of Donzy complained that his father Geoffrey of Donzy was trying to deprive him unjustly of the fief of Gien, Louis proceeded thither without delay, captured the town, and forced the unnatural father to respect the laws of feudal heredity. A few years later the king responded to an appeal from Dreu of Mouchy, whom Névelon of Pierrefonds had driven out of Mouchy. Louis mustered some troops and obliged the offender by force of arms to shew a proper regard for justice. On two occasions, in 1163 and 1169, the canons of Clermont and of Brioude appealed to the king as their natural protector to save them from the violence of the Counts of Auvergne and their agents; and Louis unhesitatingly plunged into the mountains of central France to inflict exemplary punishment upon the delinquents, whom he even kept for some time imprisoned. In 1166 the Count of Chalon, too, who had dared to lay his hand on the property of the great monastery of Cluny, felt the weight of the king's displeasure. The count, though repeatedly summoned to answer for his misdeeds, refused to appear; whereupon Louis marched into his territory, took forcible possession of it, and confiscated it. In 1173 it was the turn of the Viscount of Polignac, whom the royal troops pursued, captured, and imprisoned, for molesting the canons of Le Puy.

As time went on the royal court of justice became able to take a more commanding tone, and to insist that the great vassals of the Crown should obey its summons. The Count of Nevers, the persecutor of the monks of Vézelay, for instance, was forced in 1166 after many evasions to appear before the king's tribunal in Paris and to abjure his turbulent ways. Louis VII's words to the injured monks at the beginning of this long affair were significant: " I have sent my messengers to summon the count. As to what he will answer or what he will do I know nothing as yet; but you may rest assured that if he held as much land as the King of England in our kingdom I should not allow his violence to go unpunished." It is also noticeable that as a rule this determined language took effect, and that the nobles brought an ever-increasing number of cases to be tried before the king's tribunal. Thus in 1153 the Bishop of Langres and the Duke of Burgundy travelled as far as Moret to lay their differences before Louis.

From all quarters of France, even the most distant, appeals were addressed to the king. In 1163 the inhabitants of Toulouse, whom he had recently defended against Henry II, wrote to express their devotion and to beg for further support: " Very dear lord, do not take it amiss that we write to you so often. After God, we appeal to you as to our good master, our protector, our liberator. Upon your power, next to the divine power, we fix all our hopes." A certain lord of Uzès wrote to him to complain of the illegal dues levied by the Count of Melgueil, and to beg for the king's intervention. Again, in 1173 Ermengarde, Viscountess of Narbonne, entreated him in the most urgent terms to hasten to the rescue of Languedoc, which was threatened by Henry Plantagenet. " We are profoundly distressed, my fellow-countrymen and I," she wrote, " to see this country of ours—owing to your absence, not to say your fault—in danger of being subjected to the authority of a foreigner who has not the smallest right to rule over us. Do not be angry, dear lord, at the boldness of my words; it is because I am a vassal, especially devoted to your crown, that it grieves me to see the lightest slur cast on your dignity. It is not merely the loss of Toulouse that we are threatened with, but that of our whole country from the Garonne to the Rhone, which our enemies are confident of conquering. I feel that they are even now making all the speed they can, so that, when they have subjected the members, they may the more easily overcome the head. I entreat you of your valour to intervene, and appear among us with a strong army. The audacity of your foes must be punished, and the hopes of your friends fulfilled."

Beyond the frontiers of the kingdom, too, the prestige of the King of France was steadily growing. From the kingdom of Arles came numerous promises of fealty, if in return the king would grant his intervention. Raynald of Bâgé, lord of La Bresse, cried urgently for his help: " Come into this country, where your presence is as necessary to the churches as it is to me. Do not fear the expense; I will repay you all that you spend; I will do homage to you for all my castles, which are subject to no suzerain; in a word, all that I possess shall be at your disposal." In Dauphiné, when Louis VII's nephew Alberic of

Toulouse married the heiress of Viennois, it was considered a matter for rejoicing that the French influence had gained ground in that direction.

Thus it is not surprising to find Louis VII in 1162 playing his accustomed part of arbitrator in the great papal schism between Alexander III and Victor IV, the candidate of the Emperor Frederick Barbarossa. To tell the truth the king's rôle was not always very brilliant, nor did it reflect much credit on his perspicacity. In August and September 1162 Frederick, with the connivance of the Count of Champagne, entangled him in a web of mystification which at one time nearly had disastrous consequences. It will be well to relate the circumstances, as we may gain from them some idea of the weaving and unravelling of intrigues that went on round this "good" king, Louis VII.

When Hadrian IV died in 1159 two Popes had been elected at the same time : Cardinal Roland under the name of Alexander III, and Cardinal Octavian under that of Victor IV. Alexander III, who was elected by a majority of the cardinals, represented the party that was opposed to the absolute power of the Emperor, the party of Italian independence. Between him and Frederick Barbarossa there was no possibility of agreement, whereas naturally an alliance existed between the Emperor and Victor IV. Alexander III, who had obtained recognition both from Louis VII and from the King of England immediately after his election, took refuge in France. But, whether because he had not held the balance sufficiently equal between Louis and his rival, or because the King of France was reckoning on the advantage over Henry II that an understanding with the Emperor might secure for him, the end of the year 1161 saw the opening of negotiations between Frederick and Louis. The question of the schism was naturally placed first on the programme.

Now, at the court of France there existed a Germanophil party headed by Louis VII's own brother-in-law Henry the Liberal, Count of Champagne. He it was whom the king chose to be the principal negotiator; and moreover Louis made the further blunder of giving a prominent part in the affair to the Bishop of Orleans, Manasse, who from the first had shewn decided hostility towards Alexander III. So successfully did these two, Henry of Champagne and Manasse, conduct the affair in the direction of their wishes, that Louis found himself involuntarily and almost unconsciously led into far closer relations with Frederick than he had desired. The bishop, writing in his sovereign's name to convey final instructions to the Count of Champagne, abused Louis' confidence so far as to insert, on his own initiative, a phrase that gave the count full authority to make pledges for the King of France. Count Henry lost no time in coming to terms. It was agreed that the two monarchs should meet on a bridge that crossed the Saône at Saint-Jean-de-Losne on 29 August 1162; that each of them should bring his Pope with him; and that, then and there, a mixed commission of arbitrators should be chosen from the clergy and laymen of the two parties to adjudicate between the two Pontiffs. Both sovereigns were pledged to abide by this judgment; and in the case of Louis refusing to acquiesce in these arrangements, or to accept the decision of the arbitrators, Count Henry took a solemn oath to abjure his fealty to the King of France and to give his allegiance to the Emperor.

In the meantime Louis, who was still ignorant of the engagements entered into by the Count of Champagne, had made every effort to persuade Alexander III to be present at the projected meeting. At an interview between them at Souvigny in August 1162, the king had in vain urged the Pope to yield in this matter, expressing surprise, with more or less sincerity, "that since the Pontiff was conscious of the justice of his claim he should miss this opportunity of upholding it by a public statement of his case." Alexander was immovable. He agreed to send four cardinals as delegates, but would do no more; he refused to accompany the King of France. The latter, chagrined, reached Dijon on 28 August, and found there the Count of Champagne, who revealed to him all the clauses of the treaty and placed him—should Alexander persist in his refusal—in this dilemma: he must either recognise Victor IV as Pope, or he must lose the province of Champagne to the Emperor. "What!" exclaimed the king, "you presumed to take it upon yourself to make such an engagement for me without my knowledge, without consulting me!" Henry quoted the letter that he had received from Manasse, giving him full powers. The King of France perceived that he had been tricked. It was too late for him to retire; but what could be hoped from negotiations that were founded on misunderstandings such as these?

On 29 August the Emperor Frederick came at dawn of day from Dôle, accompanied by his Pope, to the bridge of Saint-Jean-de-Losne. Finding no one there he went away, leaving only a few members of his suite upon the spot. A little later Louis VII arrived in his turn from Dijon, and begged Frederick's representatives to consent to a delay, since it was only on the previous day that he had heard the terms of the convention. At the same time he promised to secure the presence of Pope Alexander. On the following morning the Count of Champagne, who played a dubious part throughout the affair, came to Louis to remind him that, should he reject the terms of the treaty, he—Count Henry—was pledged by them to transfer his allegiance to the Emperor. "However," added this sanctimonious individual, "I have prevailed on the Emperor to grant a delay of three weeks, on condition of your promising to be present, with Alexander, at another meeting at the end of that time, and to accept on that occasion the arbitrators' judgment between him and his rival. You must bind yourself by securities, in case you fail to abide by their award, to give yourself up as a prisoner into the Emperor's hands at Besançon." Louis again naively accepted the terms, and gave as his hostages the Duke of Burgundy and the Counts of Flanders and Nevers.

He hoped to persuade Alexander to accompany him; and indeed a good deal of anxiety was felt at this time by the adherents of the Pontiff. But a fresh comedy was about to be enacted. Frederick's army, being short of provisions, had gradually broken up and disappeared; and at this moment the King of England, who feared nothing so much as an alliance between Louis VII and the Emperor, responded to an appeal from Alexander III by arriving on the scene in full force. Frederick had but one desire—to withdraw, but to put a good face upon it. On the morning of the appointed day, 22 September, Louis again repaired to Saint-Jean-de-Losne, where he found no one but Rainald of Dassel, the Chancellor of the Empire, who feigned ignorance. Never, he declared, could it have entered his sovereign's head to submit the decision on the pontifical election to a commission drawn from France as well as from the Empire, seeing that none but the Emperor and the bishops of his dominions were qualified to give judgment in such a case. Louis then turned to the Count of Champagne, who was standing beside him, and begged him to repeat the clauses of the convention. "Well, you see!" exclaimed the king when this had been done, "the Emperor, who should be here, has not appeared, and his representatives have just changed the terms of the treaty in your very presence! You are witness to it."—"That is true," answered the count.—"I am freed, then, from all my engagements, am I not?"—"Certainly you are free," replied Henry. Then the king turned to the barons and prelates of his suite. "You have all heard and seen," he said, "that I have done everything in my power. Am I still bound by the convention?"—"No," answered they all, "you have redeemed your word." Then, wheeling his horse, Louis galloped away upon the road to Dijon, turning a deaf ear to the Emperor's representatives, who tried to detain him.

Such was the end of the tragi-comic adventure into which Louis had so imprudently allowed himself to be drawn. It put an end for ever to any inclination on his part to come to an understanding with the supporters of Victor IV, and it was on the morrow of the meeting at Saint-Jean-de-Losne that he appeared before the world as the protector of the true Pope. Alexander III was lodged in the royal town of Sens; his protector Louis VII carried on a regular and constant correspondence with him; and his close alliance with the Capetian monarchy during the crisis that followed his election contributed not a little to increase the prestige of that monarchy, and to give it the position in Europe that was established so firmly in the days of Philip Augustus.

Not only did Louis VI and Louis VII succeed in extending their supremacy, but they contrived to place the government of their constantly increasing kingdom upon a firm basis. They strengthened their authority by perfecting the machinery of the administration, and by replacing the useless and dangerous feudal element at the court by men whom they could trust, men of humble origin, who were well under control and of tried wisdom.

At the accession of Louis VI all the administrative authority of the monarchy was in the hands of the high officials of the Crown. The men who held the great offices were all, or nearly all, chosen from among the barons, and had but one idea—to obtain a monopoly of important posts for their own families, and thus to secure, at the expense of the sovereign, a position of supreme authority in the kingdom.

At the time with which we are concerned, an ambitious family, to whom no act of effrontery seemed amiss, the family of Garlande, had marked down as their own the chief offices at the court. Of these the post of seneschal was undoubtedly the most important. For the holder of this office was not only in command of the royal troops, but also exercised authority over a large part of the king's officials, was the chief administrator of the royal demesne, and, finally, played a considerable part in the dispensing of justice. It has been said, with perfect truth, that his position at this time was that of a "deputy king." This was the office to which the Garlandes first laid siege. In Philip I's reign two of them, Païen of Garlande and after him his brother Anseau, had already succeeded in securing it temporarily (1101, 1104) in despite of the lords of Rochefort-en-Iveline, who were themselves trying to acquire it for their own family. By 1107 the post of seneschal was again held by Anseau of Garlande, who succeeded in keeping it until the day of his glorious death in the king's service at the siege of Le Puiset (1118).

But before that day came two of his brothers, Gilbert and Stephen, had cast covetous eyes on other great offices. In 1106 Stephen, who was a clerk in holy orders, obtained the position of chancellor; in 1112 Gilbert secured for himself the post of chief butler; and on the death of Anseau it was yet another of the Garlande brothers, William, who succeeded to the seneschalship. It seemed that the ambition of this family now knew no bounds. When the seneschal, William, died in 1120, his brother Stephen, although in orders and already chancellor, acquired the seneschalship for himself rather than allow it to be lost to the family.

Rarely has a man been known to abuse his position with such unconcern. It seemed indeed as though the State held nothing that did not exist solely for the enrichment and promotion of this scandalous priest, who deemed it quite natural that the functions of the king's Grand Chaplain and of the supreme head of the army should be united in his person. In his clerical capacity he laid his hands on all the ecclesiastical benefices of which the king could easily dispose. We find him figuring simultaneously as Canon of Étampes, Archdeacon of Paris, Dean of the Abbey of St Geneviève at Paris, Dean of St Samson and of St Avitus at Orleans;

and one chronicler—rather a slanderous one, it is true—Guibert of Nogent, declares that when in 1112 Stephen wished to add to all these benefices the deanery of the cathedral church of Orleans, a bishopric was hastily bestowed upon the existing dean in order that this desire might be complied with. On two occasions about this time he even intrigued to add to his acquisitions the bishopric of Beauvais or that of Paris; but this was too much, and the king was obliged to submit when Pope Paschal II formally prohibited the appointment.

This did not prevent Stephen of Garlande from attaining to a degree of power that excited jealousy on every hand. The clergy raised a chorus of protest against their unworthy brother, whom Ivo, the austere Bishop of Chartres, described—probably with a certain amount of exaggeration—as "an illiterate gambler and libertine," and St Bernard denounced as a living scandal in the Church. "Who, without surprise and horror," he cried indignantly, "can see this man serving both God and Mammon— at one moment clad in armour at the head of armed troops, and at the next robed in alb and stole, chanting the gospel in a church?"

It was, however, not so much the unedifying character of his life as his abuse of power that at last made him unendurable. "The kingdom of France," says a contemporary chronicler, "was entirely at his mercy," and "he seemed not so much to serve the king as to govern him." The day came at length when Louis VI awoke to the danger. Urged by his wife, Adelaide of Maurienne, whom Stephen very foolishly had treated with disrespect, the king resolved to shake off the yoke with a determined hand. Stephen, who shewed an increasing tendency to regard the seneschalship as his own property, was suddenly deprived of office and driven from the court, together with his brother Gilbert. His fall (1127) was as dramatic as his rise. He did not yield without a struggle; and for three years (1128–1130) stoutly fought his master. "Remember your past power," wrote one of Stephen's friends to him at this time, "remember your riches, and what is still more important, the skill with which you handled the affairs of this world. Of the great officers of state (*palatini*) you were the first; the whole kingdom of France was at the disposal of your caprice. Like Solomon you desired to undertake great enterprises, to raise towers, to build superb palaces, to plant vineyards, to gather round you an immense household of male and female serfs. You demanded gold and silver in heaps; in a word, you had your fill of every delight that is possible to humanity. But pause a moment, and consider the instability of earthly things. This king, whose affection seemed to you the strongest support you could have, at whose side you constantly lived in virtue of your office and the friendship he bore you, this king now pursues you with his enmity; you are now forced to defray the expenses of the war with the money you amassed in time of peace, and to keep a watch over your personal safety night and day, lest the threats of your enemies should be fulfilled." At last, however, Stephen was obliged to yield and humble himself and give up the seneschalship; and indeed he could think himself fortunate in that he recovered not his influence—for that was gone for ever—but at least his title of chancellor.

The lesson was a costly one for the Crown, but it was not forgotten. There were thenceforward no more omnipotent officials before whom the king himself was obliged to bow. Louis VI left the office of seneschal vacant for four years, and when at last he filled it gave the appointment to Count Ralph of Vermandois, a kinsman of his own, on whose fidelity he could rely; and when Ralph died Louis VII left the office vacant for two years before giving it to the Count of Blois. These men, it is true, were important personages, and capable of commanding an army with brilliant success; but it has been pointed out that, since the new seneschals lived on their own lands at a distance from the court, they were as a rule no longer dangerous. They could no longer domineer at court, and their functions tended to become merely honorary.

Louis VI and Louis VII followed the same tactics with regard to the other great officers of state: sometimes leaving their posts vacant, as in the case of the chancellorship, to which, in Louis VII's time, no one was appointed for seven years (1172–1179); sometimes contriving to reduce their powers to privileges of a purely honorary kind. There was an increasing tendency to put all the work into the hands of docile subordinates, who could be easily dismissed. And sometimes auxiliaries, who had no official connexion with the government, would be called upon to lend their aid, men chosen from the clerical rather than the baronial world or *bourgeois* who understood the conduct of business affairs.

Of these confidential advisers of the Crown in the twelfth century some are known to us—as for instance Brother Thierry Galeran, of the Order of the Temple, who from 1132 was for thirty years or so one of the most active agents of the King of France; and Bouchard le Veautre, and Cadurc, and above all the famous Abbot of St Denis, Suger. Of this last, who was a true statesman, we have already had occasion to speak. For his able government as regent during Louis VII's absence on the Second Crusade he well deserved the title that his contemporaries gave him, the Father of his Country.

This is not the place to give a biography of this eminent monk, who, though of obscure and humble origin, succeeded by sheer strength of intellect, combined with remarkable tenacity and an orderly, well-balanced mind such as was rarely met with in his day, in winning his way everywhere without ever resorting to intrigue. Little by little we see his influence replacing that of Stephen of Garlande with Louis VI, who called him "his intimate and his faithful counsellor." From the year 1130 onwards he was always at the king's side, and always ready with a wealth of wise and moderate advice. We find him again with Louis VII, constantly striving—sometimes to excess, as we have seen—to avoid contention and maintain peace at any price. As regent, during the

Second Crusade, he shewed especial ability in the administration of the royal revenue, and was most skilful in his avoidance of all kinds of friction. "There is nothing more dangerous," he said, "than to change the personnel of government without due thought. Those who are discharged carry off with them as much as they can, and those who take their place are so fearful of receiving the same treatment as their predecessors that they proceed, without loss of time, to steal a fortune." His policy, in a word, was above all a policy of tact. It had a firm basis of strength, but its aim was to avoid all direct opposition and to evade obstacles rather than contend with them. He was a man of affairs, whose ambition was to govern the State with the same honesty and scrupulousness that he shewed in the government of his abbey. And in this respect he is one of the most characteristic representatives of that new class of officials to whom Louis VII, more and more as time passed, sought to confide the care of the administration.

CHAPTER XIX.

THE COMMUNAL MOVEMENT, ESPECIALLY IN FRANCE.

Never was the need for united action more urgent than in the Middle Ages. The individual counted for very little. A great feudal noble might stand alone, might build up his own independent power, maintain his own privileges and rule his own vassals; but in the humbler walks of life one man alone could do little in the struggle for existence. The Church encouraged the spirit of association for prayer and service; no trade could be undertaken on a large scale, save by a commercial gild or society; rights, privileges, and property were in the hands of groups of men, who held together for the maintenance of common interests. The communal movement was one very important aspect of this spirit of association. It was a movement not confined to any one country, which spread almost simultaneously throughout Germany, Italy, England, Flanders, and France—an international movement, which may to some extent have been independent of national boundaries, but which each country worked out on its own lines, according to its own circumstances and national characteristics. Similar causes led to the formation of the German stadt, the Italian city, the English borough, and the French commune, and certain essential points of resemblance can be found in all of them, but the actual form which the communal association took, its nature, its strength, and its duration, varied not only from country to country but from district to district—even from town to town.

In no country can this communal movement be better studied than in France. Perhaps it was there that the spirit of association was most widespread, and even in Italy the success of the movement was scarcely more rapid or more marked. On the other hand, it was there also that the results achieved were least permanent, and that the original aim and ambitious character of the communal movement were most completely lost. The southern towns of France were little less strong at one time than the Lombard communes, but their independence was of much shorter duration.

The chief period of communal history falls between the dates 1100 and 1400. A few towns acquired self-government as early as the eleventh century, and a few preserved their independence beyond the fourteenth; but in France this was the exception. It was in the twelfth century, however, that the effort to develop by means of union and association was most successful, and that the urban communes acquired their highest powers. The century which followed marked for most of them the beginning of decline, the gradual loss of independence, the substitution of privileges for rights, the dropping of one ambition after another. In the fourteenth century the true commune almost entirely disappeared. The townsmen had not sufficiently stood together. The union had been local not national. Each separate unit was far too weak to hold its own against the ever-growing power of the monarchy. Financial difficulties gave the impulse which led to the downfall of many struggling associations; the upper classes were not content to share power with the poorer members of their body, and internal dissensions weakened the commune against external foes; royal support insidiously paved the way for royal predominance, and the result was the end of one of the most interesting attempts at achieving success and progress by means of local union and communal life.

It is impossible to give any definition of a French commune which would be universally true. The communal movement may be taken to mean the general spirit of association which affected the country, particularly in the eleventh and twelfth centuries, and which gave rise to many different communal types. It is the purpose of this chapter to consider as far as possible the causes of this movement, the principal aim which inspired burgesses in the towns and peasants in the country to form themselves into groups for mutual protection and self-government. First, however, a brief review is necessary of the varying types of association which resulted from the communal spirit. Only here and there was the highest stage of development reached and real independence obtained; but the varying degrees of success all help to illustrate the communal struggle.

A medieval commune, in the fullest meaning of the word, might be regarded as a collective person: a body which could hold property, exercise rights, possess vassals, and do justice. In the feudal world it took rank by the side of the great lords of the land; like them it could both perform and exact homage and hold courts for its tenants, and with them it could treat on practically equal terms. It was in fact a "seigneurie collective." Sometimes a commune could even declare war and peace and make treaties and alliances without the license and control of any overlord. The signs of its authority were the possession of a belfry, from which could be rung out the signal for its general assemblies, and a public hall, in which business could be transacted, meetings held, and justice done; the proof of its corporate existence was the common seal, which could be affixed to all its documents and public acts. All communes had their own officials, elected or nominated, to carry on communal business; and the two powers most eagerly coveted and most generally secured, though in varying degree, were the administration of justice and the control of finance. Both town and country, as has been already said, could and did acquire some form or other of communal organisation, but the urban communes were as a rule in the vanguard. They were the first to form themselves into corporate bodies, and the best able to assert communal authority.

The true urban communes were most numerous in the north and south of the country; in the centre some towns were privileged but less independent. In the north these communes were known as *Communes jurées*, in the south, where independence was still more marked, as *Consulates*. The term *Commune jurée* meant that all the members bound themselves together by a mutual oath of association, which was the essential feature, the most important bond of unity, and a method of safeguarding their mutual rights. In these towns the burgesses were often known as *jurés de commun*; and, as the charter of Beauvais says, all men "infra murum civitatis et in suburbiis commorantes communiam jurabant." Besides this mutual oath which formed the collective body, a commune might be in the position of a feudal vassal and then an oath had also to be taken to the overlord. At St Quentin a charter of the eleventh century speaks of the oath taken by members of the commune, who "jurerent firmement par sermens a warder et a tenir, sauve la feuté de Dieu et de Saint Quentin, sauve le droiture de Comte et de Comtesse—ens jurerent ensement chescun quemune ayde a son jure et quemun conseil et quemune detenanche et quemune deffence."

Of these communes of Flanders and northern France some occupied very independent positions while others exercised comparatively limited powers; but each one was largely a self-governing body, formed by an oath of association and able to act as a legal person. A few examples only can be given. St Quentin was one of the earliest of all towns to gain municipal organisation. In the eleventh century a charter of Count Hébert (*ob.* 1080) recognised and extended the privileges of the town, granting to it a democratic constitution and almost complete independence under a mayor and *échevins*. To this commune all classes took an oath, not only burgesses but also clergy and knights; a very unusual circumstance in the north.

Rouen illustrates another type of commune, for it was a town possessing the minimum of independence compatible with communal existence. Rouen had worked its way very gradually into importance, through the growth of its commerce and consequent increase of wealth, and in the twelfth century acquired a charter from Geoffrey Plantagenet (1145), which spoke in general terms of "the commune" and conferred judicial powers upon it. At the close of the reign of Henry II of England, Rouen was governed by a mayor and *échevins*, assisted by a fortnightly meeting of *cent pairs*, to consider all questions of public interest; but the mayor was chosen by Henry as Duke of Normandy from a list of names presented by the hundred peers, and it was the duke, not the commune, who exercised rights of high justice and was able to demand military service. Even the oath which formed the *commune jurée* was almost as much the oath of a feudal vassal to the duke as the genuine bond of communal unity. But, despite these limitations, few towns have exercised greater influence on the spread of communal organisation, and traces of the *établissements de Rouen* can be found throughout all those parts of France which fell at one time or another under the rule of the Angevin dynasty.

In Amiens, even more than in Rouen, a good example can be found of communal union resulting from commercial development. No charter of creation exists for Amiens, but in the twelfth century various documents confirm the municipal organisation which the town had already worked out for itself. Here the mayor and *échevins* exercised seignorial powers of administration and justice, although the king kept in his own hands the highest rights of jurisdiction.

In the south of France the *consulates* occupied a still more advanced position than that of the *communes jurées* of the north; in most cases they had obtained a more complete emancipation from the feudal yoke and the establishment of almost independent authority under their own consuls. Nowhere was the communal movement more widespread. Throughout Roussillon, Provence, Languedoc, parts of Gascony and Guienne, and as far north as Limousin and La Marche, not only towns of importance but even tiny villages aimed at acquiring some form of consular government. The powers which all towns coveted, here as in the north, were judicial and financial, to which were often added rights of local legislation and of military control. Besides their almost complete autonomy, another feature which seems to distinguish the southern communes from those of the north was the greater share taken by the nobles in their formation. Whereas in the north it is rare to find the upper classes even admitted as members of the commune, in the south nobles almost always occupied some of the municipal offices, and the consular body was frequently composed half of knights and half of burgesses. As a rule also, an assembly of inhabitants plays a larger part in the southern communes and appears more frequently than in the northern towns.

Here as elsewhere great variety prevailed as regards powers and independence. Marseilles, for a short time, was practically a republic. Probably municipal officers existed there from very early times; consuls were certainly in existence at the beginning of the twelfth century. No distinction was made here between nobles and burgesses; both held office indifferently. Laws were the same for all, officials were elected by all, and a great part was played in town government by the *grand conseil* of elected representatives and the *cent chefs de métiers*, artisans chosen by their colleagues; on special occasions a general assembly of all citizens was summoned to consider the most important questions. To their suzerain, the Count of Provence, the townsmen appear to have owed little but military service, and the statutes of the city were drawn up by the Marseillais themselves without any seignorial assistance.

Another important town, Montpellier, which dates its communal government from the twelfth century, was recognised as a republic in 1204 by the King of Aragon, whom the burgesses had wanted to choose as their lord. It had its own elected officials and had erected careful safeguards against seignorial encroachments; but it was never absolutely independent. The lord's bailiff attested the acts of the consuls and authority was, at least nominally, shared between lord and commune.

In Toulouse we have an example of a commercial commune with great external influence and practical sovereignty throughout the neighbouring country, but with a less advanced political constitution, since the count always exercised considerable municipal powers.

To complete this brief summary of the principal types of southern towns, the *cité* of Carcassonne may be taken as representing the specially military commune, and Lézat the almost wholly rural town. In the latter, the consulate was evidently organised for the benefit of cultivators and proprietors, both within and without the town walls, and the authority shared between the abbot and the consuls of the town was largely concerned with rural matters.

It was not always possible for the efforts of the burgesses to succeed in establishing so complete a measure of self-government as in the communes described above; and in France a third type of town is found under the title *ville de bourgeoisie* or *commune surveillée*, which possessed certain communal characteristics without real political power. It formed, in fact, a privileged community rather than a free commune. Such communities were scattered throughout all parts of France, but in the centre they formed the prevailing type and were on the whole both prosperous and durable; Paris herself, though with certain special characteristics of her own, belonged to this category. Towns on the king's demesne almost always took this form in response to the communal tendency. The townsmen combined to obtain privileges, but royal officials retained full judicial powers, or at most shared them with the town magistrates. The same might happen in the case of seignorial towns, where the lords were induced to make certain concessions but still retained political powers. In some cases a town might have a municipal body wholly nominated from without. This was the case at Troyes, where the count chose thirteen *jurés*, who themselves selected one of their number as mayor. In other cases only the head official might be nominated and his assessors elected by the town—a method adopted at Orleans, where the king's bailiff or *prévôt* was ultimately supreme. Some royal towns were rather more independent than others. At Senlis, Philip Augustus handed over to the town magistrates all his rights of justice, except in cases of murder, rape, and homicide (1212); but later the town itself begged to renounce powers which it could not afford to maintain, and the royal *prévôt* was again reinstated in his original position of supremacy (1320). At Blois, the *boni viri* had no political or judicial functions and divided the administration with royal officials. At Beauvais the *universitas* shared authority with the bishop as well as the king. At Lorris, as Thierry says, the greatest amount of civil liberty existed without any political rights, jurisdiction, or even administrative power.

Many more examples could be given to shew how authority was shared and to illustrate the nature of the privileges sought for by these royal and seignorial towns. But the chief point to notice is the very arbitrary character of the division between these *villes de bourgeoisie* and the actual communes. No really hard and fast line can be drawn between them. A privileged but dependent town is easily distinguished from a republic such as Arles or Marseilles; but it is not so easy to mark off a *ville de bourgeoisie* from a commune of the less advanced description. Royal officials had almost as much authority at Rouen as at Senlis. Even some of the southern consulates were not wholly free from seignorial interference. In Toulouse, the count had a court of justice, and at one time even exercised the right of choosing consuls. Many communes passed through this stage of semi-independence (Bayonne in 1173 was a *ville de prévôté*) on their way to freedom; only a few towns successfully emerged with full powers; almost all sank back to this condition after a brief period of glorious victory. Thus Bordeaux had its mayor nominated by the English king from 1261 onwards; Marseilles, at about the same date, was receiving a representative of the Count of Provence and a judge appointed by him. This was almost always the first step in communal decline; a *commune jurée* could very quickly turn into a *commune surveillée*. Despite their lack of independence, the *villes de bourgeoisie* illustrate an important development of the communal movement, and arise out of that same spirit of association which under more favourable circumstances led to the organisation of true communes.

The same may be said of the *bastides* of the south, and the *villes-neuves* of the north—small rural towns actually created by kings or by seigneurs and endowed from the first with common privileges and common rights, under the safeguard of a charter granted by the king himself, or by the immediate lord with the sanction of the sovereign. These small privileged towns began to spring up as early as the twelfth century under the name of *sauvetés*, created by churches and monasteries, either alone or in conjunction with a lay lord, as new centres of population. In the thirteenth century a great number were added, known as *villes-neuves* when they were more particularly of an economic type, *bastides* when their military character predominated. A lord, anxious to increase the number of his vassals, to attract population, and to win support, was ready to offer inducements to newcomers by promising protection, enfranchisement from serfdom, and the right of electing their own officials. The *bastides* of the south were always strongly fortified and endowed with privileges of a similar character. In many cases they were little more than walled villages; but they had distinct communal existence and a measure of self-government, though always under the protection of their suzerain and dependent upon his will. They became very numerous and very popular. The kings, both of France and of England, constructed them frequently in order to win support and strengthen their rival authority. The fixing of payments and the limitation of dues and labour services which the inhabitants obtained, readily attracted population and increased their well-being and industry.

Besides these small rural towns, the result of direct seignorial creation, there were also rural communities of a somewhat different type. The peasants from the country, either following town example or impelled by their own needs, sought to help on their own prosperity by means of association. Sometimes the inhabitants of a country village would band together for the maintenance of their rights and would win a charter from the overlord granting privileges to the whole body. Such were the communities of Rouvres and Talant in Burgundy, Esne in Cambrésis, and many others. More frequently, however, several villages would combine to secure communal rights, and the village federations of the north gained for themselves positions of considerable strength and importance. One of the best known of these confederations was the commune of Laonnais, a union of seventeen hamlets formed round Anizi-le-Château, which bought a charter of privileges from Louis VII in 1177, and tried to hold its own by force of arms against its ecclesiastical overlord. Round Soissons also village federations were formed which endeavoured so far as possible to imitate the organisation of the commune itself; and in Burgundy eighteen villages, with St Seine-l'Abbaye as the centre, purchased important communal privileges in the fourteenth century. In the mountains natural federations were formed by the character of the country, and the valley communities of the Pyrenees and the Vosges were often almost independent bodies, free from all but very nominal subjection to their feudal overlord.

Many theories have been brought forward to explain this communal movement and to account for its widespread and apparently spontaneous character. Naturally, it is impossible to trace any single line of development for a movement which itself ran in so many different channels. Causes are almost as numerous as communes, each of which was moulded by the circumstances of its history and by the character of its seigneur. On the other hand, no theory can be completely disregarded. They all illustrate different aspects of the movement. Nevertheless, in spite of this complexity and variety it may be possible to find some universal and essential element out of which all the immediate causes grew, some underlying impulse present in every variety of development; and thus to explain why, not only all France, but all Western Europe was tending to develop in a similar direction at the same time, to shew how the same spirit of association could affect places of such very different character, spreading as it did through royal boroughs, seignorial estates, active commercial centres, rural districts, and obscure hamlets.

The earlier writers on communal history advocated the theory of Roman influence and the continuity of the old municipal organisation. They urged the importance of the old Roman cities, the respect of the barbarians for the civic institutions, and the very early existence of communal union long before the grant of charters, which as a rule confirmed rather than created rights of self-government. St Quentin, Metz, Rouen, Bourges, Rheims, and in the south of France almost all the important towns without exception, were cited by these historians as Roman municipalities, whose liberties either survived or were sufficiently remembered to be considered an influential factor in the growth of later communal rule. This theory has, however, been rejected by the majority of later writers, who have shewn how completely Roman municipal institutions had decayed at the time of the fall of the Empire, how the inroads of Saracens and Northmen in the ninth century completed the work of destruction in the towns, and how the communes of feudal times had to be constructed anew, on their own lines and to meet their own individual difficulties. The complete absence of documentary evidence to connect the Roman towns with the later communes, the weakness of analogy as an argument, and the certainty in most cases of municipal ruin and reconstruction, have led to the almost complete abandonment of the Roman theory. For the northern towns it can now find no serious supporters. In the south there is much to be said against it. Certain important Roman centres can be proved to have lost all their old rights and to have built up a wholly new communal government in later days. Bordeaux, though it preserved some degree of municipal organisation under Visigoths and Franks, entirely lost its early civilisation with the attacks of the Northmen; and when after three centuries its history can once more be continued, all traces of municipal institutions have disappeared. A similar fate seems to have befallen Bayonne; while Lyons, Toulouse, Perpignan, and many other old Roman towns, can be shewn to have built up their communal powers as a new thing and on feudal lines. Even though it is often true that communal government and elected officials were in existence long before their formal recognition by charter, and apparently independent of any seignorial grant, it is unnecessary to connect these self-won liberties with the long-past Roman organisation. At the same time, there is no doubt that in the south Rome had more permanent influence than in the north; not so much by direct survival, as by traces of Roman law and perhaps some vague remembrance of earlier independence. It has indeed been pointed out that in south-eastern France the Northmen's invasions had less influence than elsewhere, that feudal oppression was slight, and that the Crusades found the communal movement already far advanced. But at least it can be maintained that no direct survival of Roman institutions need be considered, and that the medieval commune can be studied quite apart from the Roman town.

Another theory, almost as extreme in the opposite direction, was that which suggested a direct Germanic origin for the commune, and connected the urban community with the rural mark. Its supporters pointed to the development of the rural communes through the possession of common property and the acquisition of common rights. This was specially urged for German towns, but French and Italian development was also ascribed to similar causes. However, the Mark Theory has been abandoned for lack of evidence, and it is impossible to maintain that the communal movement originated in rural communities rather than in urban centres. A material town—the houses and the population—may have grown from a thickly populated village, but the village community in fact constantly copied the town community in its organisation, and petitioned for urban privileges when it sought for a charter of incorporation. Scarcely any rural communes obtained formal recognition before the thirteenth century, although natural communities existed in a primitive form long before. But while realising the insufficiency of this second suggestion as to communal origin, the truth underlying it can be recognised in the undoubtedly important part played by common property as a bond of connexion, and in the fact that a great deal of early advance was along the lines of economic and agricultural development.

The *Échevinage* Theory, as it may be called, is almost a corollary to this Germanic theory, since it suggests a connexion between the town *échevins* and the Carolingian *scabini*, judicial officers of the Frankish hundred or *centena*, the subdivision of the county, who were generally chosen by the count with the consent and sanction of the people. Scholars, writing of northern Gaul, have pointed out the existence of a body of judicial *échevins* in the towns, previous to the formally recognised communal government, and have suggested that this may have been a stepping-stone between the old organisation of the hundred and the later and more independent jurisdiction of the commune. At Verdun the *échevinat du palais* seems to have been a sort of dependent municipality in the eleventh century, whereas the town only became an imperial commune in 1195. Bruges had local magistrates, called *échevins*, in 1036. Dinant had a body of *échevins*, nominated by the Bishops of Liège before the *jurés* elected by the community; the Archbishop of Rheims abolished the *échevinage* of the town in 1167, but it was restored with elected officials in 1182. In St Quentin and a few other towns a curious double government existed for a time. The early *échevinage*, instead of merging as usual into the communal government, continued, and the tribunal of the *échevins* represented the justice of the sovereign, distinct from the justice of the town in the hands of the mayor and *jurés*, who had a considerable police jurisdiction and the power to punish offences against their own body.

In 1320 the king, after a dispute ending in the suspension of the commune, allowed the *échevinage* to continue: "qui noster est, et totaliter a communia separatus." But despite evidence of the existence of these early *échevins*, it is impossible to prove any certain connexion between them and the Frankish *scabini*, and between the town and the *centena*. An attempt has been made to prove that early towns were actually small hundreds; and in England we know that the old *burhgemot* coincided very closely in power with the hundred moot, and that for the collection of geld a borough originally was roughly valued at half a hundred; but that only proves influence, not direct connexion. Pirenne entirely repudiates the idea, and urges that the *centena* hardly ever coincided with the town, and that an urban court was a new creation, necessary when the burgesses came to claim trial within their own walls. In any case, however, whatever may be the exact origin of the early *échevinage*, it is at least interesting as a preliminary step to fuller communal rights. It is one of many proofs that liberties nearly always existed before charters, and that the towns were painfully working out their own independence step by step.

We are on firmer ground in a later group of theories concerning communal growth; theories which all contain part of the truth and supplement one another by accounting for different aspects of the development.

In connexion with the *royal* theory, it has been suggested that the kings themselves formed the communes, that they were particularly the work of Louis the Fat, and that his successors continued his policy and allied themselves with the towns against their over-mighty feudal vassals. It is easy to refute a claim that the kings were true friends to communal independence. The monarchy was a determined enemy to local unions, which would inevitably place obstacles in the path of centralisation, and organisations pledged by their very character to oppose arbitrary power. It was the growing power of the Crown which eventually caused the destruction of the communal movement, and it was the pretended support of the king which turned many an independent commune into a royal *prévôté*. On the other hand, it is quite true that the kings for many reasons found it to their interest to grant charters and to confirm customs. They might be in immediate need of money or support, and the sale of concessions was their easiest way of obtaining both. The privileges granted to *villes de bourgeoisie*, the formation of *villes-neuves*, even the recognition of the more limited communes, such as those which the English kings favoured in all their dominions, were repeatedly the work of the monarchs. But their friendliness or the reverse depended entirely on the circumstances of the moment, and their influence was always fatal in the end. They did not favour real municipal independence, and that commune was doomed which sought for royal protection or once admitted royal officials to interfere in its administration.

There are plenty of examples to shew the real policy of the kings, their desire to undermine independent power, their grant of charters only when something could be gained thereby, their universal interpretation of protection as interference. In his French dominions John of England granted fresh privileges to Rouen (a town, it will be remembered, with the minimum of political rights), and extended its organisation to other towns, in the vain hope of increasing his popularity and averting disaster. Edward I, the most active of the English kings in Gascon government, who made a vigorous attempt at successful and popular administration, created numerous *bastides*, and granted favours to Bordeaux, but he took the appointment of the mayor into his own hands and exacted a communal oath of allegiance every year. The customs of Lorris, a privileged town but not a commune, were granted originally by Louis VI, and confirmed by his successors, who extended them to neighbouring villages to curb the power of feudal lords and to remedy the severe depopulation of the country. Beauvais was also favoured by Louis VI, because it took his side in a quarrel with the cathedral chapter; Louis VII confirmed a communal charter in 1144, when he was in great need of money for the Crusade; but the king retained much authority, and attempts at independence ended in severe repression and the strengthening of the royal power by Louis IX. Figeac, which petitioned for the king's support against its feudal superior, was declared a royal town in 1302 and became more subject than before. Lyons in similar difficulties called in St Louis to arbitrate in its quarrels. He took the inhabitants under his protection, and established three royal officials. Again and again the same thing occured. The king was just as much an enemy to the communal spirit as he was to feudal independence. Although he did not actually suppress many communes, as he did that of Laon, nevertheless he opposed the communal movement all the more surely and brought about its downfall.

The attitude of the Church was not unlike that of royalty. An *ecclesiastical* theory claims the Church as one of the greatest supporters of the communal movement; but history proves that a spiritual seigneur could be quite as hostile to town development as a lay lord, for municipal organisation inevitably meant some loss of Church authority in the town. Direct help was only given to a commune when some obvious advantage was to be gained—money in pecuniary necessity, support against some powerful rival, or the like. At Rheims, Archbishop Samson (1140–61) favoured the commune because he needed the support of the inhabitants against his chapter; but his successor attacked the judicial rights of the burgesses, with the result that he was driven out by the town, and constant struggle followed. At Beauvais, in 1099, the bishop granted certain privileges and recognised the commune, at a time when he was involved in difficulties with the king, the chapter, and the châtelain of the town, and therefore eager for the friendship of the burgesses, who had driven out his predecessor not so many years earlier. In various southern towns the bishop allied himself with the commune against the lay lords, but claimed in return a certain position in the town government. He is called in several places the "first citizen of the republic." Thus, the commune of Arles in 1080 was established by Archbishop Aicard, who was trying to increase his temporal authority at the expense of the count; but evidently the ecclesiastical lord was not always popular with the citizens, for in 1248 the general assembly of the town proclaimed that no townsman should speak to the archbishop, set foot in his palace, or do any service for him. The instances of Church opposition are far more frequent than these cases of self-interested support. The clergy, as a rule, distinctly opposed the communal revolution, which was in many instances in direct opposition to ecclesiastical authority. At Cambrai, in the eleventh century, the bishop betrayed the commune which the burgesses had just established. At Corbie, a series of heated disputes between abbot and town were settled in 1282 by a compromise, which meant the real supremacy of the ecclesiastical lord. The opposition of Bishop Albert to the commune of Verdun led to civil war (1208), and the town secretly obtained a charter from the Emperor in 1220, a step which was not likely to lead to internal peace. In Laon, the bishop, who plotted against the commune and obtained its abolition from the king, lost his life in the struggle which ensued (1112). It is unnecessary to multiply examples. Clearly the Church was not a friend to communal development when it meant a diminution of ecclesiastical control.

However, even though the direct action of ecclesiastical lords was not as a rule favourable, there were indirect ways in which Church influence helped on the communal movement. Those historians who maintain the survival of Roman influence explain the growth of democratic powers and ambitions by the share allowed to the people in the election of bishops in early times. In 533 a Church council at Orleans declared that bishops should be elected by clergy and people; at Paris in 559 it was proclaimed that no bishop had valid authority unless the people had shared in his election. This canonical regulation was particularly enforced in the Reform Movement of the eleventh century by papal and synodal decrees. But at the time when the communes were beginning to grow, the ordinary burgess did not play an important part in episcopal elections. In any case, this power could only give to the people a very vague idea of combination; it can have done little actively to develop the communal spirit.

Another theory of Church influence, but one which is practically un-supported by modern authorites, is to link the medieval commune with the Peace of God. The arguments for it rest more on verbal resemblances than on actual facts. Towards the close of the tenth century the Church, endeavouring to diminish anarchy and deeds of violence, proclaimed the Peace of God, which was supplemented *c.* 1050 by the Truce of God. By the latter, from sunset on Wednesday until Monday morning, all hostilities were to cease, all private wars were to be suspended. To maintain this peace, many dioceses formed what were known as *conféderations de la paix*, with mayors at their heads and members known as *jurés*. These communities, it has been urged, would combine to acquire communal charters, until the *jurés de la paix* became the *jurats* of the town, the *maison de la paix* the town hall, and the *paix* itself the commune. It is true that town communities were occasionally given the name of *paix*; the charter of Laon in 1128 is called *institutio pacis*. Little but the name, however, connected the urban organisations with the earlier institutions for the maintenance of peace. The word *paix*, when referring to a commune, frequently signified a treaty which ended some communal strife; and whereas the latter lay associations were generally composed of burgesses united to oppose feudal oppressions, the original institutions were more particularly for the nobles, who had to take the oath for the preservation of the peace, and they secured no actual privileges for the lower classes and townsmen as such. The special "peace" which a town is often said to have was simply a body of local bye-laws and regulations which the inhabitants were bound to respect. No movement, however, which encouraged the idea of combination was wholly without influence, and the burgesses may have learnt a lesson of association and a desire to unite to limit feudal oppressions from the Peace of God, even though the commune they formed was something completely distinct from it.

The ecclesiastical *sauvetés*, privileged districts under Church jurisdiction, did help the growth of the earliest *villes-neuves*, as has already been said; and many towns sprang up in the neighbourhood of monasteries (*e.g.* La Réole in that of Regula), for the obvious reason that a market was at hand for their produce; but this does not necessitate the growth of a commune. In many large towns the *sauvetés* continued as isolated districts within the walls, subject to ecclesiastical jurisdiction instead of being under the rule of the communal officials. In Bordeaux both archbishop and chapter retained certain portions of the city under their direct control apart from the authority of mayor and jurats.

The Crusades have also been named by many writers as an indirect way in which the Church influenced the communal movement, since this great ecclesiastical war did so much to awaken commercial enterprise and to encourage the sale of town privileges by needy kings and crusaders. This is doubtless true; but many towns had acquired self-government before the Crusades could have had much effect on social conditions, and charters were the result rather than the cause of communal rights. Every influence, however, which tended to economic advance and social progress must be reckoned among the many causes of communal development, and the Crusades undoubtedly helped in this direction. Parish organisation also may have given another indirect impulse towards the spirit of association and thus lends support to the ecclesiastical theory. The Church, in so far as it encouraged progress, union, and the education of the people, helped to create a condition favourable to the development of the commune, even though ecclesiastical lords themselves were in frequent opposition to the growth of municipal independence.

One theory which has been advanced by some of the chief authorities on medieval towns is that which connects the growth of the commune with the merchant gild. But it has been proved that, in the case of the English boroughs, gild and commune were not necessarily identical; and for the French towns also it may be said that the gild was only one of many ways in which towns developed, and that, as a general rule, its organisation was distinct from that of the commune. But there is no doubt that the extension of trade was one of the principal reasons for the progress made by the towns, and that in their associations for trading purposes the burgesses learnt to unite for judicial and administrative business also, and to acquire self-government in addition to commercial privileges.

The most important towns, in all countries, sprang up on the great trading routes, and gilds both lay and ecclesiastical were generally formed for the organisation of this trade. It was in the north especially that these mercantile associations were very prominent, and they played a great part in the town life of Flanders and Belgium. It has been considered that it was round these societies of merchants that population clustered and organised itself, first for trade, then for town government. Valenciennes, in 1070, had a gild or *charité*, with a house for common councils. The *charité* at Arras was in part religious, in part commercial, in part connected with the municipality. It has been claimed for St Omer that here at least the gild was actually transformed into the commune. In several towns of France the gilds likewise played an important part in town growth. At Amiens the gild was "the cradle of the commune"; the *Confrèrie de St Esprit* at Marseilles took over the administration and claimed rights of jurisdiction and finance. But it can be asserted with confidence that gild and commune were not generally identical, and that a society of merchants was no necessary and universal preliminary to municipal self-government. At Montreuil-sur-Mer a quarrel between the town and the gild-merchant, ending in the victory of the mayor and *échevins*, proves conclusively that here at least they were two separate bodies. There were many towns which advanced to communal rank without ever having possessed a trading association; others had numerous craft gilds but not one organised group of merchants to encourage the idea of complete incorporation; a rural commune might have little but agricultural interests. The merchant gild in France, as Maitland says of that in England, was one of many elements which went to the building up of a free borough, but not the essential and universal element.

There still remains one other problem in the history of town development to be considered. Were the communes the result of a fierce struggle against feudalism? Is the term "revolution" the best word with which to describe this communal movement? Or were they the result of peaceful and gradual advance, winning their privileges by purchase, by mutual agreements with their lords, or even by voluntary concessions on the part of their feudal superiors? Here again generalisation is impossible. The position which some towns gained at the cost of war and bloodshed, others obtained in the natural course of events. In some cases a town charter took the form of a treaty between hostile factions; in others a written title was scarcely necessary to confirm privileges which had grown up so gradually and naturally that they hardly excited notice, far less opposition. There are examples in plenty of both lines of development. The struggle against feudal oppression may have stirred up the burgesses in some instances, but was not a universal cause of the communal movement. The struggles at Laon, in the early twelfth century, are a typical example of the turbulent acts which sometimes marred the development of communal powers. The town was in a state bordering on anarchy; the bishop at that time was a man of brutal and violent temper; feudal oppressions, heavy dues, and servile disabilities were still prevalent. A charter, purchased by the townsmen from the king during the temporary absence of their ecclesiastical lord, was annulled on his return, in spite of promises to the contrary, and a revolt was the result. The bishop himself was murdered by the rioters and excesses of every kind were committed. The *Charte de Paix*, which eventually ended this struggle, was far from establishing permanent peace; and for a little over a century the commune of Laon had a stormy and precarious existence, and its charter was finally annulled. Rheims, which tried to imitate Laon in its privileges, succeeded in imitating, to some extent, its violence also. It engaged in a fierce struggle with the archbishop over communal rights, and in 1167 drove him from the town. John of Salisbury writes at that date: "A sedition having again broken out at Rheims has plunged the whole country into such disorder that no one can go in or out of the town." Louviers, which was striving to form a commune as late as the fourteenth century and insisted on holding general assemblies, was the scene of such disorder that the affair was laid before the Parlement of Paris and decision given against the town. "Les diz commun et habitans confessent que ilz n'ont corps, ne commune, ne puissance d'eulx assembler sans license du dit arcevesque ou de ses officiers...lequel congié l'en leur doit donner quant besoing est."

In the south, Montpellier passed through various periods of violence. In 1141 the townsmen rose against their seigneur William VI, although no record is preserved of any specially oppressive actions on his part, and finally drove out the ruling family altogether. The revolution ended in the commune choosing the King of Aragon as their lord and forcing him to promise obedience to their customs. Lyons "gained its rights by a century of struggle." In 1193 the inhabitants revolted on account of heavy taxation. In 1208 the citizens, after a struggle against archbishop and chapter, had to promise not to make any "conjuration de commune ou de consulat." In 1228, 1245, and 1269 the burgesses were again in arms, and refused to come to terms unless they received official sanction for their commune, which they gained by charter in 1320. At Béziers a riot was caused in 1167 because a burgess ventured to insult a noble, and in the struggle which followed the viscount himself was murdered by the townsmen. Cahors, Nîmes, Manosque, all had struggles, but in each case they arose after the formation of the commune, not as part of its development. Thus, though some towns won their freedom by force and others were involved in struggles for the maintenance of their rights, this was due to special circumstances. The communal movement was not in necessary opposition to feudalism as such. On the contrary, it was very distinctly in harmony with feudal tendencies and a true commune was in the position of a feudal seigneur. In some cases, no doubt, the members of the old nobility objected to the rise into their ranks of this upstart community; but in others they held out to their new comrade the right hand of fellowship.

Frequent examples of peaceful communal progress are found in Champagne, Burgundy, Flanders, the Angevin dominions, and throughout much of southern France. Naturally the least advanced type of commune excited the least opposition; *villes de bourgeoisie* had very little difficulty in securing privileges; rural communes often developed with little or no struggle. A community which would be content with moderate liberty could hold its own and possibly gain all but nominal independence, when a commune which aimed at complete emancipation and self-government might lose all in the effort to gain too much. As time went on, the lords found it to their interest to favour the towns, and began to create *villes-neuves* and *bastides* on their own account. Sometimes the burgesses were useful allies in struggles between rival seigneurs and had to be conciliated; at other times they could quietly build up their power undisturbed while their overlords were occupied in their own private quarrels. Moreover, the grant of a charter meant a considerable sum of money in the pocket of the grantor, and in France, as in England, many towns bought their privileges little by little, until they were able to take the rank of free boroughs. In Champagne, very little revolutionary sentiment existed. The counts were kind, the population was peaceful and well-to-do, and the example of Flanders encouraged the communal tendency. Meaux received a charter from Count Henry the Liberal (1179), who took, however, an annual tribute of £140 from the town. The charter prescribed that all the inhabitants were to swear to help and support one another, to take an oath of allegiance to their lord, and to attend the general meeting on pain of a money fine. Theobald IV did the same for Troyes and Provins. He was at war with his baronial vassals, and as a chronicler of the time expressed it, "trusted more to his towns than to his knights." In these cases, though considerable powers were given to the town officials, it was the count who chose them, and he retained the right of hearing appeals from their judgments. In Burgundy very similar conditions prevailed; the dukes granted communal charters readily in return for money. There were a good many rural communities and communes in this part of the country, and all seem to have risen peacefully to varying degrees of independence.

In southern France, though various cases of individual violence and civil war have been already noticed, the general tendency was towards the formation of consulates without a struggle. The nobles were often members of the town and favoured the independent government, in which they took part. Feudal tyranny was less extensive here than in the north. There were many private wars, but more frequently between lord and lord than between lord and town; the citizens combined for common defence in times of such constant turbulence and to consider difficulties arising from their two great enemies in the Middle Ages—plague and famine. Consular government was so usual that its existence was scarcely questioned. Local life and local union were very strong in a country where each district, sometimes each town, had its own *fors* or customs which the inhabitants combined to carry out and defend. Many rural towns were created to improve the condition of the country and to attract population. In Roussillon, places such as Perpignan obtained communal government without a struggle, for they added considerably to military defences which were greatly needed; and lords as well as burgesses were glad to encourage the growth of these fortified strongholds. On the whole the communal movement in the south was favoured by the feudal lords, who realised the value of having the towns as their friends and allies. The consulates fell eventually before the growth of royal power and administrative centralisation, not in consequence of seignorial opposition.

The more this communal movement is studied, the clearer it becomes that it was simply a natural stage in economic development. Economic progress is the only one universal cause which can be found underlying all the variety of immediate reasons, all the complex forms of individual development. Society in feudal times was, as it were, in the stage of childhood. Defence from above in return for service from below; the one class to fight and the other to labour; protection rather than competition—such were the ideals of feudalism, which based all these relations and services on land-holding. But even in its most ideal form the feudal system was not progressive; in its least ideal form it was capable of great abuse; protection was apt to turn into oppression, service into servitude. The communal movement was not an attempt to oppose the whole system of feudalism, but it was an effort to guard against its abuses and to advance materially and politically, not only in spite of it, but actually on feudal lines; a town aimed at becoming a landlord. The chief needs in the Middle Ages were defence and progress, and association was one of the most natural means of striving for them. An individual was too weak to strike out for himself or to change existing circumstances, and thus the idea of union and combination arose. As population increased, as wealth was more diffused, and as society advanced, this craving for progress, this tendency towards association, became stronger and stronger. Throughout the whole of Western Europe people lived under very similar conditions; they had common troubles, common needs, common methods of cultivation, and common rights. Feudalism itself had a communal element; every seigneurie was a group of vassals, every manor an agricultural community. The whole tendency of the time pointed to common action as a solution of difficulties and as the best line of advance. Every institution, therefore, which was based on common action, every step which involved common effort, was indirectly an incentive to this spirit of association; every event which encouraged social and economic progress was indirectly a cause of the communal movement. It was not a revolution but a natural development, a sign that society was struggling upward to freedom and civilisation.

Granting that communal growth is an economic question, it follows that certain points must especially be considered in accounting for the development of the medieval communes. First, what were the chief evils which needed reform, if advance were to be made? Secondly, why was the idea of combination, to achieve this reform and assist this advance, so widely diffused? Thirdly, what were the main causes of economic progress, and what direction did it most commonly take? Fourthly, what were the chief aims that burgesses and peasants set before themselves as likely to assist them in this progress? And finally, what circumstances, if any, aided them in their efforts and led to the various forms of communal organisation which have been already briefly described?

The first great necessity for any forward movement in the Middle Ages was to shake off the disabilities of serfdom. In the country, the greater part of the cultivating class was made up of serfs or *hommes questaux*, as they were called in the south; and as the towns, in their early stages, were little more than populous villages, a great many of their inhabitants also were serfs. It was possible for members of the upper class among them to combine in order to improve their condition, to fix their services, and even to get them commuted for money payments, without necessarily rising out of the rank of villeinage; but in urban centres it was more usual for inhabitants to unite to shake off the servile status altogether and for all burgesses to become free men. Examples of serfdom in early towns are numerous, and enfranchisement was one of the first privileges to be gained in any communal charter.

In Champagne and Burgundy, where towns were almost wholly rural in character, serfdom was very prevalent in the twelfth and thirteenth centuries, and local customs went to support the rights of the lords; "coustumes en Champagne que homs de pôté (villeins) ne peut avoir franchise, ne ne doit, ne ne se peut appeler francs, se il n'a de son seigneur lettres ou privilèges." But it was not only in strictly rural districts that serfdom was an obstacle to progress and therefore had to be opposed by the communes. The inhabitants of Laon were not free from *main-morte* and *formariage* till 1178[1]. At Béziers, as late as the twelfth century, the viscount was giving away burgesses as though they were actually his chattels. At Soissons, the desire of the servile population to gain freedom was one of the chief incentives to union, and the same is found in many other places. Town charters aimed, whenever possible, at securing freedom for the inhabitants. Blois was enfranchising serfs in 1196, though they did not disappear in the town until the following century. At Limoges, in customs probably dating from the thirteenth century, freedom from serfdom after residence for a year and a day was decreed—a very usual condition. In Bordeaux, only a month in the town was required to gain liberty. At Oloron, all inhabitants were declared to be "hommes francs sans tâche d'aucune servitude." So much did residence in a chartered town or *bastide* come to imply freedom, that occasionally lords, when founding a *ville-neuve*, would especially stipulate that their own serfs should not be admitted.

In many places not only serfs but free burgesses also suffered from oppressions on the part of their feudal lords, and were encouraged to common action on account of common misery. At Amiens, at the close of the eleventh century, clergy and people united to complain of seignorial abuses, and obtained from the count a promise of fairer justice and lighter payments. At Vézelay, it was pecuniary exactions to which the inhabitants chiefly objected, and in 1137 they claimed to have a voice in taxation, in order that the burden of it might be more fairly distributed: "tam burgensium quam rusticorum, secundum facultatem suam, unus scilicet plus et alius minus talliaretur." At St Quentin, military service and castle-guard had presumably been excessive, since it was conceded in Count Hébert's charter (1045–80) that there should be no castle erected within three leagues of the town and no military service beyond a day's travel. The limitation of military duties was a very usual condition in the south, where feudal quarrels were constant. Only nine days at a time was a fairly common term; but it was also possible to stipulate that a burgess should not be forced to fight so far away that he could not come home to sleep. Actual oppression on the part of the seigneur was an accidental circumstance; but the desire of the towns to break down servile disabilities, to win greater freedom even from a friendly yoke, to manage their own affairs and to settle their own quarrels, was a natural result of progress and became all the more active wherever society was the more advanced.

[1] Special servile characteristics. *Main-morte* implied that serfs could never inherit property. The lord was always the heir, and children of a dead villein had no rights of succession except by his will. *Formariage* was a due paid by serfs marrying outside the estate, which they were not allowed to do without license of their lord.

That this desire to accelerate progress and to defend privileges should take the form of communal association was, as we have seen, almost inevitable. Men acting together could do what each singly could not. Further, communities were often bound together by the possession of common property, common rights, and common customs. When the community desired political as well as civil rights, the organised commune might be evolved. Possibly the rural communes may be considered to have advanced more directly on these lines. The urban communes had other inducements to combine, and were less actuated by the possession of such things as common pasture and common woods; but these influences cannot be wholly disregarded. At Lézat, a rural town, free use of wood and water was demanded for the whole body of inhabitants in their communal charter. In the cartulary of Arbois, certain things are declared to be town property, with which the lord cannot interfere: "costes pendentes, aqua, et li chamois...libere sunt et communes," and the community united to use their own ovens as well as their own woods. The inhabitants of Marseilles were in common possession of certain pasture rights.

The fact that so many southern towns and villages had their own local customs has already been mentioned as a possible bond of connexion for the inhabitants. The *fors, e.g.* of Bordeaux, of Bazas, of Dax, of Bayonne, of Morlas, were all slightly different, and were eagerly defended by the places which possessed them. They represented very early rights and customs, though often not reduced to writing till a comparatively later date. When new privileged towns and *bastides* were constructed, their charters of liberties resembled to some extent the old customary rights of the more ancient centres of population.

Thus the need for combination and the tendency towards it were early in existence, and it was the natural progress of society, both material and moral, which awoke the desire for union into real activity and converted a vague connexion into a living organisation.

The progress of the towns was determined first and foremost by their geographical position. The actual origin of the town itself was due to accumulation of population in a place which was suitable for military defence or for commercial activity; where either fortification and protection was especially needed, or a good market could be established for the produce of the neighbourhood. The more suitable the situation, the more rapidly would the town advance, and the more urgent would become the need for communal action. Bordeaux clearly owed its progress to its superb position. In the heart of the vine country and on a fine navigable river, it early became renowned as a commercial centre of the greatest importance. Soissons, on the high road from Flanders and at the junction of various other routes, soon developed into an important market town, with active trade in all directions. Cambrai had an important position on the frontier of Lorraine; Perpignan was needed for the military defence of Roussillon; Oloron has been called the king of the Pyrenees. In such towns, all of which became communes, their success was doubtless due in great measure to their situation.

Progress could take various directions. Some places long remained almost entirely agricultural, and their markets were only used for the sale of rural produce. Toulon is supposed to have made a very humble beginning in this way, and its commune to have originated out of the assembly which met to discuss pasture rights and rural matters. Others owed their advance to their military importance. Talant was favoured on this account by the Duke of Burgundy (1216), and so were many of the southern *bastides*. But it was through their trade and commerce that most of the leading towns progressed; wealth was a great help in the struggle for independence, and the intercourse with other places which commercial dealings involved brought not only direct ideas from abroad but also a great increase of vigour and civilisation. The commune of Narbonne, though later events robbed it of its greatness, was early rich and powerful, owing to its trade with Spain, Italy, Sicily, and the Levant; Rouen owed its prosperity and doubtless its privileges to the fact that it was a wealthy trading centre; the Flemish towns certainly gained their importance and independence through their commercial development. But whatever line progress and prosperity took, they were the determining causes of the communal movement. The more advance was made in material well-being, the more galling did any social disabilities become, and the more indignation was felt at seignorial interference or tutelage.

The result, therefore, of town progress was to awaken ambitions in the hearts of the burgesses. They desired to secure their property, to gain the full benefit of their wealth for their descendants and their town, to throw off seignorial control, and to work for themselves. The first step was to obtain increased privileges and civil powers, to shake off any idea of servitude and to gain trading rights. The next was to unite for political independence and to win self-government. They desired above all to be free from the abuses of feudal justice, to have courts for their own members, where townsmen could be tried by town judges and according to town procedure. They needed also to secure financial authority and the management of their own taxation, doubtless to avoid excessive pecuniary burdens and the disappearance of town money into the coffers of the seigneurs.

There were various circumstances which aided the towns in their struggle for independence. Both kings and lords were in constant need of money and support. Growth of luxury and expenses for war increased this need, and it was in the towns that the greatest accumulation of wealth was to be found, an important weapon in the hands of the burgesses. The frequent feudal rivalries could be turned by the towns to their own advantage. They might offer support to the highest bidder, or take the opportunity of quiet advance while their lords were too busy to attend to them. Avignon gained its privileges at the end of the war between the

Counts of Provence and Toulouse, who shared the town between them (1085–94). While they were fighting, the citizens were banding themselves together in trade fraternities, and learning the value of union and independence; eventually a municipal revolt ended in the expulsion of both combatants. The fact that so often towns were under mixed jurisdictions helped their cause. When, as in Amiens in the eleventh century, justice was shared between the count, the bishop, and the chapter, it was probably easier to shake off this divided control than the supreme authority of one strong man. Even the long struggle between England and France, together with much misery, brought some benefit to the communes, for the rival kings needed urban support, and both strove to gain it by concessions.

Each town that formed itself into a commune actively helped on the movement, for much was the result of example. Perhaps communal growth was similar in Germany, Italy, England, and France, less because of international connexion than because the root cause, economic progress, was the same in each case; but the action of no country could be wholly without effect on the others. The example of Flanders was influential in northern France, where Calais, Boulogne, and St Dizier all framed their organisations on Flemish lines; and the consulates of the south may have owed something to the great republics of Italy. On the whole, however, outside influence seems to have been slight, and development was largely independent; there was very little intercommunal and still less international solidarity.

The twelfth century was a great period of communal growth, simply because it was a period of active economic development. Material prosperity, moreover, had outstripped social progress; and it was the existence of considerable wealth and an improved standard of living, side by side with dependence and seignorial depression, which, in some cases at least, gave the impulse to the movement. The twelfth century, again, was a fortunate period for the communes, because political conditions helped on this economic progress. The dispersion and division of authority had weakened control, just when the desire for liberty was at its height. The relations between the king and the great lords, between the lay and the ecclesiastical seigneurs, were favourable to the towns. The crusading movement and the consequent need for money amongst the ruling classes coincided with the growing wealth of the boroughs and the growing importance of the burgess class. It was a vital moment, and the communes took advantage of it. The result was a universal spread of communal associations; as Viollet says, "un phénomène social indépendant quant à son essence des races, des langues et des frontières."

In England, although the boroughs did not rise to the independence of the continental communes, there was a steady stream of town charters from the reign of Henry I onwards. The towns purchased their privileges one by one, starting with freedom from serfdom and judicial rights, until little by little self-government was obtained.

CH. XIX.

In Germany communal development was very similar to that in France. The towns were either re-settlements of the old Roman sites, more or less rural in origin, where the bond of common property united the new inhabitants; or newer towns intended as centres of trade from the first. They gradually advanced through the growth of a market and market-place, through trade associations, through the special privileges and judicial rights of the burgesses, until the possession of their own officials and their own *Rat* marked the establishment of communal government. Some of the more important towns, shaking off all intermediate control, retained almost complete independence as Imperial cities. The special characteristics of German towns were chiefly due to the weakness of the central authority. They did not have to reckon with the king from the first, as did the English boroughs; nor did they have to succumb to it in the end, as did the communes of France. The leading towns, therefore, had far more power; affiliation was so strong that the whole country was "a network of inter-dependent municipal courts"; and inter-urban leagues were more possible.

In Italy, the lack of any central authority was even more obvious than in Germany, and the towns were able to profit by the constant struggles between Pope and Emperor. This seems to give the movement a more political character; but, as elsewhere, it was wealth and commercial importance which enabled them to take advantage of the political situation. The Lombard communes began to gain self-government as early as the eleventh century. They resembled the towns of southern France in the character of their government and in the important part played by the upper classes in municipal development. But, while the French communes declined with the decline of feudalism and were gradually subjugated by the monarch, the Italian towns, as the Empire decayed, fell more and more into the hands of great tyrant-dynasties, and maintained political independence at the expense of internal liberty.

In France the movement was particularly marked by its independent character. Though there were local exceptions, the leading communes, especially in the older towns, were the work of the people themselves, formed to protect their own interests, and recognised by charter eventually when the lords were unable to withstand and put down the development which had already taken place. As a rule, the inhabitants began by forming themselves into communal groups, and then little by little these communities acquired self-government. Documents shew this early grouping of town population for common actions. In 962 the men of Arles as a body figure in a treaty; in 1055 vineyards were given "in communitate Arelatensi"; but consular government was not recognised till 1131. In Bayonne, the *prudhommes* were early responsible for the maintenance of old customs, and in 1190 a charter was confirmed by "toute la communauté." The town was already a *commune jurée* when a charter finally recognised its rights in 1215. At Beauvais, where the commune was not formally confirmed till 1122, a trial was held between the chapter and the "universalité des bourgeois" in 1099. Sometimes these communities exercised some form of municipal government, though they had not yet become actual communes. At Dax moderate governmental powers were granted to the *capdel* and *prudhommes* before any sign had appeared of the mayor, *jurés*, and commune of later documents. Probably the *Cinquantine* of Lyons was a communal council leading up to the consulate, though the exact connexion between them is uncertain.

A proof that not only these preliminary communities, but also the communes into which they developed, were the result of a popular movement and the actual work of the townsmen, is to be found in the fact that charters to old towns almost always confirmed rather than granted communal powers. New towns might be privileged from the first and have a certain share in their own government bestowed upon them; but towns older than the communal movement won this for themselves. Occasionally a charter confirms a previous grant, but more frequently still a previous acquisition. In Bordeaux we have a very good example of the independent development of communal government, culminating in a charter which confirmed the popular advance. Although the town had long been an important one, it was not really a commune before the thirteenth century; there was no abrupt change from the government by count and bishop to free municipal organisation. In 1200 a charter was issued "juratis et burgensibus," but no allusion was made to a mayor; in 1205 the remission of a maltolte was granted "dilectis et fidelibus probis hominibus nostris manentibus apud Burdigalensem civitatem." In 1206 for the first time a mention of the mayor appears in the Patent Rolls, when the king actually asks his "maire, jurats, et fidèles de Bordeaux" if they will accept the seneschal he has appointed. There is absolutely no sign that the king grants the mayor and commune, he simply accepts them[1]. At Montreuil-sur-Mer every step in the communal advance was fought for by the townsmen. They proclaimed their own commune in 1137, but not till 1188 was its existence formally recognised by Philip Augustus, who pardoned them for the violence with which they had established it. The charter granted to Rouen in 1145 confirmed the old rights of the burgesses and sanctioned the commune which they had formed. Instances are too numerous to be quoted exhaustively.

Similarly, when once a commune was established, its powers and functions were little by little developed by the town. Communal governments generally exercised some legislative power and constantly published statutes increasing their own authority, or, if this were impossible, further privileges were bought. This, however, is rather a feature of town history than an actual part of the communal movement. All evidence of this

---

[1] A great deal of information concerning Bordeaux has been gathered from some valuable lectures given by Monsieur Bémont in Paris, since published as *Les institutions municipales de Bordeaux au moyen âge*, RH, 1916.

nature, however, helps to strengthen the theory that communal growth was in its origin independent and popular; that its causes are to be found in the progress of the townsmen themselves; that it was only by degrees that the lords realised the possible value of favouring such a development and themselves created new and privileged towns. Probably they also realised that it was wise to gain control of so important a movement and to lead it into channels which would not threaten their own authority too much. Seignorial towns were never dangerous communes; they were rather privileged communities, a source of strength not of weakness to their founders.

Since the communal movement was a natural and economic development, its extent and its results depended upon economic conditions. The powers of a commune, whether urban or rural, varied according to the stage of advance which the town or village had reached when it was struggling for its incorporation and self-government. The more backward a place, the more easily, as a rule, its ambitions would be satisfied; the richer and more prosperous the town, the higher was the ideal at which the burgesses aimed. Something might depend also upon outside circumstances, such as the character of the feudal overlord or the attitude of the king; but it was still more the condition of the town itself which determined the nature and duration of its communal government.

Two other circumstances also tended to influence communal growth: the frequent existence of double towns, and what has been called the affiliation of the communes.

A large number of the older towns, especially in the south, had two parts: the *cité* or fortified portion generally representing the ancient settlement, and quite distinct from it the later *bourg* or mercantile town, side by side with the older *castrum* or else built round it. Thus the military and commercial centres were divided, although occasionally the *bourg* also had its own walls for defence, as at Bordeaux and Carcassonne. The importance of this formation for town development was that the episcopal and more authoritative element tended to concentrate in the *cité* or *civitas*; while in the newer town, where the more democratic buildings were collected, such as the hospital, the market-place, and the town hall, society was often rather more independent and was able to lead the way in the formation of municipal government. This was not, however, invariably the case. In Carcassonne the old *cité* developed municipal organisation almost before the *ville basse* was founded; and at Nîmes the two parts of the town acquired consular government much at the same time, and used to hold joint meetings for subjects of general interest.

The subject of affiliation is a very difficult one and much has been written upon it. The fact that one town influenced another has never been disputed, and certainly imitation must have played a considerable part in the communal movement. Some places formed regular types, from which other towns or villages drew their inspiration and whose privileges they eagerly copied. This imitation, however, was rarely complete; and the influence of one town might be counteracted by the influence of another, or weakened by local circumstances. In France affiliation was certainly less strong than in Germany, where the *Oberhof*, a mother-town to which appeal might be made, could give a final decision on matters concerning one of its imitators. In France, though there are occasional instances of appeal, the idea of a real *chef-de-sens* is never completely worked out. The *jurats* of Soissons were supposed to settle any difficulty of interpretation in the charter of Meaux; Florent had to refer to the rights and customs of Beaumont; while Abbeville had three towns to which it should appeal —Amiens, St Quentin, and Corbie; but, as a rule, appeal to a mother-town was not stipulated for at all. Luchaire has divided French communal development into seven types, originating from seven influential towns, but later writers have considered this division far too simple. Probably the variety of types was far greater and the spread of communal charters was complicated in all sorts of ways. In the north, St Quentin set an example to the neighbouring villages and was in part copied by Abbeville; but its influence over towns such as Laon and Noyon, and the other places which imitated them, has been formerly much exaggerated. The charter of Soissons spread through the surrounding country, was copied more or less by Meaux, Sens, Compiègne, and Dijon, and by means of the latter came to influence the rural communes of Champagne. But this influence was neither direct nor unmixed with others. Soissons itself owed much to the example of Beauvais; so also did Compiègne and Senlis; Sens and Meaux imitated Senlis as well as Soissons. Even some of the village federations of the Soissonais appealed to Meaux in cases of difficulty. Rouen, which was very influential in Normandy and throughout the English dominions generally, taught many of its lessons through intermediaries, especially La Rochelle and Niort. The less advanced charters had generally the greatest direct influence, since the lords did not oppose their propagation. Eighty-three villages are said to have imitated the customs of Lorris; five hundred places in Champagne, in Lorraine, and throughout France, were organised on the lines of the law of Beaumont. But, despite a certain amount of imitation, communal advance was anything but stereotyped, and local characteristics in France were strongly marked.

In some ways the regional grouping of communes is more instructive and more interesting than their division according to types of the leading towns. Geography undoubtedly influenced town development, and the resemblance which many communal charters have to one another may have been due just as often to resemblance of conditions as to direct imitation. Thus, Flanders and northern France might be grouped together as a very independent and commercial region, with St Omer and Amiens as characteristic towns. Lorraine, with old aristocratic families on one hand and servile cultivators on the other, was a district whose advance was chiefly in the direction of enfranchisement and resistance to feudal abuses. Burgundy was in rather a similar condition, though here the friendly relations between lords and people led to very peaceable advance and very early liberties, but, at the same time, to a great survival of seignorial authority. In the cartulary of Arbois a pleasant instance of feudal kindness is given in a charter by which the countess frees a group of serfs from castle-guard. She points out that, after their hard day's work and then the climb up the steep hill to her castle, they are fit for nothing but sleep, and "nature le requiert qu'ils dorment." Champagne was another very rural district, and political powers were in consequence little developed, but Beauvais spread some influence here through trade connexion. The centre of France, having made less economic progress than either the north or the south, was generally contented with *villes de bourgeoisie*, such as Limoges. In Guienne, English influence, trade development, and the existence of local *fors* or customs, all affected urban growth. It was widespread and vigorous, but the royal policy and power prevented complete independence. Bordeaux may be taken as the typical town of this region; and eventually the large number of *bastides* shew how the lords grasped the value of concession and the need for encouraging a loyal population. Provence, even if theories of Roman influence are put on one side, was the home of very early communal independence, in Arles, Avignon, and elsewhere. Here the old general assemblies played an important part in the building up of union and self-government. In Languedoc, towns were either commercial or military. Feudalism was not severe, popular rights were a very natural growth, and committees with consular government were very numerous and very powerful, until royal authority was asserted over them. Albi, Carcassonne, and Toulouse are good examples of towns of this region, which progressed on account of their trade and their military importance. Roussillon was in a district where agricultural progress and the need for military defence were the chief reasons for communal development.

Thus the communal movement was influenced by example, by geographical conditions, and by the circumstances of each town individually; but the whole idea of association was in the air and spread itself almost unconsciously.

The rural communes, so marked a feature of country life in parts of France, require some separate consideration, although in the main their causes and characteristics closely resemble those of the urban communes. Economic advance, and the desire to improve their material and social condition, induced peasants to combine and to struggle for privileges, much as burgesses and townsmen had done. As a rule, political ideas played rather a smaller part in a rural association than in the more enterprising town, but it was the same communal spirit which was inspiring countryman and townsman alike. Differences of degree were due to circumstances, and to the height to which local progress had attained before the formation of the community or commune. As was only natural, the country was generally behind the town. It was the thirteenth century which saw the establishment of most village communities, although in many cases this corporate development was an outcome of older rights and rural freedom in the past.

Rural communes seem to fall into two divisions, although, as often in making distinctions, the line between the two is indefinite and not always easy to trace. There were the self-made communities, villages or federations of villages, which combined largely as a result of town example, to gain material advance, freedom from the worst abuses of serfdom, and a varying degree of self-government. And there were the natural communities, such as the valley communes of the Vosges and Pyrenees, which geographical conditions, old survivals, and the special character of the country, had rendered very independent from the first, where serfdom had never existed in its most extreme form, and where the lords' rights had never been much more than nominal. In some cases, the attempt to get their old rights officially recognised ended in a loss of freedom for these natural communes; but in others the original independence was maintained in a greater or less degree down to modern days.

In both these divisions, however, the idea of combining, for the maintenance of common rights and the increase of material well-being, was always the determining factor in their communal existence. In the northern villages, however, it was the value of example which appears most immediately prominent; in the mountain communes, the union through rights of common property.

It was naturally the rural towns which formed the best example for the villages, and the customs of Lorris and Beaumont were always the first to spread in country districts. The *villes-neuves* and *bastides*, again, themselves little but rural communes, must have done much to lead the still unenfranchised villages to crave for similar privileges. That small rural cultivators like themselves should be granted freedom, defence, and common rights, while they remained under the old conditions, would be naturally galling to any ambitious villagers. It is never so easy to throw off old obligations as to make a wholly fresh start without them; nevertheless, there were various rural settlements which pressed on by their own exertions, and acquired privileges similar to those bestowed from the first on the *bastides*. Some of the villages, especially in the south, fortified themselves; or, if they could not manage to build complete walls and gateways, they made the church a stronghold and centre of their defences in times of danger, and they acquired for themselves rights similar to those of their favoured neighbours. Sometimes it was the *banlieue* of an urban commune, actively influenced by events in the town itself, which spread a desire for equal rights throughout the neighbouring country. Thus, in Ponthieu alone, where the examples of Abbeville and Amiens were before all eyes, thirty-six village communes existed in the fourteenth century.

Although the country profited by town example, the motives which actuated them were not wholly the same, or at least they did not exist in the same proportions. Direct growth from the old free village, the desire to ameliorate servile conditions, and the influence of parish life and church duties, were all more prominent in the country than in the town; while commercial causes, seignorial rivalry, and the desire for political independence, were less general, though not wholly absent. Several isolated villages did organise themselves contrary to the will of their lord, but the result was often fatal, for it was difficult for the peasants to hold their own against opposition. Thus Masnière, a hamlet dependent on the Abbey of Corbie, was put down by the abbot when it had given itself communal government; and the same thing happened at Chablis near Tours. It was to avoid this difficulty that villages came to form federations for mutual support, and when they were near some important urban centre they looked to help from that quarter also. This was not always effective, for the Laonnais group had only a very short and stormy career. It was generally the least ambitious developments which were the most durable, and where advance was very gradual less opposition was excited. Thus a community which united peaceably to maintain old rights, which had assemblies chiefly for agricultural matters, and which elected only a few officials of its own to share in justice and taxation without repudiating the supreme seignorial authority, might very likely get its advance recognised, its privileges confirmed, and its organisation accepted by the lord. He could still exercise influence over the community and at the same time reap the benefit of contented vassals and willing cultivators.

The important part played by common possessions in bringing about union has been already mentioned, but in rural districts this is particularly striking, whether it was actual corporate property the communities acquired or merely common use. In Alsace several villages were often united by the possession of the *almend*, common pasture land for a group of hamlets; just as in the Pyrenees the *ports* or mountain pastures were almost always shared. In some parts pasture was not free, in which case the inhabitants of one or more villages would often combine to pay jointly for pasturing their beasts and gathering wood in the forests; this happened in many rural communities of the Yonne. In Normandy there are many examples of rights in wood and waste shared by the villagers, while any stranger had to pay for the use of it, even for the rights of driving flocks through the land at all. At Brucourt a document shews that here, at least, the pasture was real corporate property: "les communes du dit lieu de Brucourt furent données à la commune de la dite paroisse." At Boismont-sur-Mer, a tiny village in Ponthieu, the habitants had rights of common along the shore, because the land was too poor to be of any use as private property, and they were called *bourgeois* in consequence of being banded together for mutual protection and guarantee of their possession. Similarly, at Filieffes, in the same neighbourhood, two marshes were common to the inhabitants of the village, and a mayor and *échevins* appointed to supervise rural affairs.

Common property led very often to the passing of common bye-laws, and to the appointment of common officials to direct, supervise, and see that these regulations were kept. Constantly the men of a village would appear as joint suitors in a case, or to receive concessions. In 1214 there was a contention "super quaedam communia ab hominibus de Coldres cum hominibus de Nonancourt inita, et super quibusdam consuetudinibus." Elsewhere it was "homines Henrici de Tillao," "homines de Deserto," and others, who owed money "pro recognitione de servicio." In the fourteenth century such instances were particularly numerous in Normandy, and the courts held suits concerning "le commun du hameau du Becquet," "les habitants des cinq paroisses de la forêt de Conches," and so on. In the cartulary of Carcassonne there are many proofs of village claims. The men of Villegly assert that from time immemorial they have had common pasture rights, the common privilege of a sheaf at harvest time, and common liberty to settle amongst themselves what crops they would grow without any seignorial interference (fourteenth century).

The lords, on their side, were also able to enforce common duties. "L'université des habitants" at Villegly owed a pound of wax and were bound to castle-guard in turns. At Gardie, a sum was paid annually "pro omnibus hominibus de universitate predicta." The Church also frequently demanded common dues and services; and sometimes parish officials—syndics and others—were chosen from the whole community to manage the common work of the parish.

The existence of these common rights and duties, the need for agreement as to the cultivation and other local business, led to the holding of popular assemblies in villages and rural groups, which gave an impulse to the idea of self-government. In the county of Dunois, there are frequent examples of general meetings to discuss money payments or military contributions demanded by the lord, or village matters of all sorts, such as the building of enclosures or any public work. At Lutz, in 1387, twenty-seven inhabitants, "faisant la greigneur et plus saine partie des manans et habitans," met to choose representatives to appear before the Parlement on the subject of forced *taille*. In 1440 several villages met to discuss the sending of a body of horsemen which had been commanded by the king. Sometimes the rural communities were so small that about twelve people were all they could muster as their representatives.

Some of the most interesting examples of these village meetings are to be found in the *cours colongères* of Alsace and Lorraine, very independent assemblies, often exercising judicial and administrative powers, evidently survivals of old rights, which they claimed to have existed "from time immemorial." In the Vosges there were a number of these rural groups or *colonges*: associations of hamlets and scattered farms, holding from a lord, but with their own rural regulations, their own tribunals, for low justice as a rule but occasionally for more important cases, and their popular assemblies, without the consent of which the lord was not supposed to interfere in any communal business. Common rights, in particular, were under the supervision of these assemblies, and the lord was often on a par with the villagers, so far as regarded the use of woods and pasture. To be a member of one of these *colonges*, residence for a year was generally required, and the new *colon* was formally received as a member in a general assembly. All had to attend, under pain of a fine, and only four excuses were recognised for absence: war, illness, old age, or deafness. The lord, or his representative, generally presided over this *cour colongère*, but the suitors had final decisions in their hands, and justice was administered by elected *échevins*. Occasionally, greater independence than this was acquired. At Donnelay, near Metz, for example, the inhabitants elected the mayor or president and did justice and levied taxes without seignorial control. No charters to these *colonges* exist before the thirteenth century, some are later still; but they always contain a statement to the effect that they are recognising old rights. These documents shew that the community itself might possess serfs, that it had rural officials, shepherds, foresters, and so forth, and it could buy, sell, or otherwise dispose of its common land according to its will. There are many curious old customs and conditions in these charters, which give a most interesting picture of rural life in these mountain hamlets, but which unfortunately do not throw any special light on the actual communal movement. Here, as time went on, the old free character of the villages was more and more lost. It was territorial sovereignty in this case which was swamping the communes, since in the Empire, of which they were part, central power was not taking the place of the feudal lords, as was the monarchy in France. A letter to the Count of Harbourg in 1529 says: "Votre coulonge a beaucoup de franchises, mais aujourd'hui, hélas, on ne s'en soucie guère." Little by little, this interesting survival of old free rights, which had developed into actual communal organisation, disappeared, and ordinary feudal seigneuries were left in possession of the field.

In the valley communities of the Pyrenees conditions were very similar. Here it was clearly geographical causes which first led to communal organisations. Villages, tiny hamlets, and scattered homesteads, which would have had little importance as isolated units, naturally combined while enclosed in one mountain valley, secure from much outside interference or even intercourse, and already united for the use of pasture land on the slopes of the hills. There was little reason here for much seignorial supervision or interference; little for any lord to gain out of these simple pastoral communities. From early days they had managed their own affairs; during the winter months they were cut off almost entirely from outside relations; and in the summer they were chiefly concerned in arranging for the feeding and management of the flocks and herds which were their chief source of livelihood.

In Roussillon there were seven rural seigneuries, associations of villages, not exactly republics, but with considerable independence, making their own treaties, building their own fortifications, and holding general meetings to regulate local business of all sorts. The little community of Andorra still exists to illustrate something of the condition of these mountain settlements. A group of six parishes, Andorra manages its own affairs and simply pays an annual tribute to its feudal superiors: two-thirds to the government of France, one-third to the Bishop of Urgel in Spain. Though generally called a republic, it is in reality a very independent seigneurie held in *pariage* by two lords.

In the western Pyrenees there were some large and important valleys, which were able to develop considerable powers, free from all but nominal subjection to their overlords. The Vallée d'Ossau still retains its own distinctive dress, though this is fast disappearing, and it keeps its own local archives in the principal village. In the Middle Ages it was directly under the Viscount of Béarn, but otherwise independent. The Vallée d'Aspe was practically a republic. Its narrow defiles and the high mountains blocking it in were natural defences which secured its separate existence, and it had self-government in the hands of its own *jurats*. A document of 1692 speaks of its freedom in ancient times: "elle se conduisoit par des lois et des coûtumes qu'on n'a jamais empruntés, non pas même depuis qu'elle s'est donnée volontairement au seigneur de Béarn." The valley of Cauterets had its own legislative assemblies, composed of women as well as of men, and the fines and profits of justice were shared between the community itself and its ecclesiastical seigneur, the abbot. The Vallée d'Azun had its popular parliament and its local customs for all the inhabitants, which the seigneur confirmed on request of "tot lo pople d'Assun."

These rural communes were known as *beziaus*, the inhabitants as *beziis*, the local word for *voisins*; and it was quite usual for the *bezias* or *voisines* to share equally with the men in government and administration—in any case, when they were householders. The almost sovereign power of these communities is especially shewn in their treaties with other valleys; the *lies* and *passeries* were generally agreements as to pasture-rights, which followed actual warfare between the villages. One of the most famous of these treaties was between the French valley of Barétous and the Spanish community of Ronçal, which was signed in 1373, and arranged for a yearly tribute of three cows to be paid by the Frenchmen. This has given rise to a curious ceremony which was kept up in full until late in the nineteenth century. On the summit of the pass between the valleys, representatives from each side used to meet and, with their hands interlaced on crossed lances, proclaim *Pazavant* (paix dorénavant). After this, the cows, bedecked with ribbons, were led across the frontier, and the day ended in dancing and feasting.

Enough has been said to shew that the Pyrenean valleys were primitive communities which had inherited customs from very early days and which had never been under severe seignorial control. The communal movement in their case was truly a natural growth; but they were so far affected by the general tendency of the twelfth and thirteenth centuries, as to get their rights recognised and their *fors* written down and confirmed. Their special characteristics were elected officials, common rights and common property, and a very popular and independent form of local government.

To sum up shortly the results arrived at in this chapter, two principal conclusions seem to emerge—the difficulty of generalisation and the natural and economic character of the movement.

First, as to the difficulty of generalising. It is almost impossible to argue from events in a few towns the probable course of events in another. Communal growth can best be studied through individual instances, but it is unsafe to draw general conclusions from them as to the line of advance throughout the whole country. Local differences have resulted in a very great variety of local developments and causes, which helped the growth of communes in one part of the country and were often absent in another. The seignorial support, apparently beneficial in one instance, in another may have meant the complete loss of communal independence.

Secondly, as to the natural character of the movement. The communal movement was clearly a stage in economic development; instead of being a break with old conditions and a revolution against feudal ideas, it was consistent with the period of feudalism in which it arose. It was an attempt of communities to rise by force of union in the feudal hierarchy and them- selves to rank side by side with feudal seigneurs; sometimes as their vassals, but whenever possible, as suzerains themselves and tenants-in-chief of the Crown, privileged and independent of all but nominal allegiance.

As a general rule, it may be said that the older towns were the most progressive in their actions, that they developed their own communes and acquired the highest degree of independence for a short time. New towns were often favoured by the lords and became privileged, but under control. Royal towns, though often in earlier possession of charters and privileges, were always less completely free. Rural communities were very frequently peaceful in their development and could trace back their rights to very early days, but the assertion of these rights generally followed the formation of town organisations in point of time, and occasionally the rural commune was a direct imitation of an urban union.

In France this movement was widespread and important but short-lived; for it came at a time when the growth of centralisation was little by little absorbing feudal rights and local independence. The higher the position at which the communes arrived, the more they came into conflict with the development of royal supremacy, and the more completely they were destroyed. But, even though short-lived, the communal movement in France, both urban and rural, had important results which outlasted its own existence. Serfdom was distinctly diminished in severity and extent; local patriotism was excited and continued, even though it might be turned into other channels; commerce and trade were invigorated and the energy of the burgesses could extend in that direction when self-government disappeared; above all, it was the medieval commune which formed the cradle of that important element of French society, the *Tiers Etat.*

CHAPTER XX.

THE MONASTIC ORDERS.

THE Rule of St Benedict was the fountain of monastic discipline in the West, the source, not of a single religious order, but of religious order in the most comprehensive sense of the phrase. Composed in the beginning for a single community of cenobites, it took into account no system which involved the grouping of monasteries in an organised federation or subordinated a number of houses to one common head. The successors of St Benedict at Monte Cassino could make no claim to any but an honorary primacy among Benedictine abbots. The Benedictine monastery was a self-ruling corporation; its abbot, the father of the convent, was supreme in it and in the dependent priories which formed integral, though locally detached, portions of the organism. The Rule supplied the main principle of its life; but in details it was governed by its own customary code, the result of local conditions and individual convenience. Such bodies of customs would necessarily have strong family and local likenesses; but they would shew no trace of a rigid uniformity. Relations between neighbouring communities might be fraternal, but each was a separate household, recognising a common paternity, not in any supreme monastery, but in St Benedict, the founder of the monastic order.

This autonomy of the Benedictine community, with its healthy encouragement to free development on natural lines, was nevertheless not without its drawbacks. The history of such great houses as Monte Cassino and Farfa shews, on the one hand, that a body of monks unprotected by any central authority or mutual bond of union was peculiarly liable to dispersion under the pressure of external attack. During the Lombard invasions in the sixth century, and the Saracen inroads in the ninth, both monasteries were left desolate for long periods. On the other hand, the community ran the continual risk of internal decay. The rule of a weak or careless abbot, under no effective supervision, was inevitably a source of danger; while the growth of temporal possessions, given by benefactors with the best intentions, brought with it temptations to the relaxation of religious observance and to the admission of secular customs out of keeping with the Rule. Both causes, in the disturbed condition of European society, combined against the steady maintenance of the founder's principles. A convent scattered by invaders, and forced to lead a vagrant life in search of casual hospitality, was unlikely, when it was restored to its old home, to enter upon its duties with its pristine zeal and to prefer austerity to comfort.

The restoration of discipline in monasteries was a necessary accompaniment of the establishment of law and order in the Carolingian Empire. Charlemagne, with his sense of the value of learning to civilisation, saw in well-ordered religious houses centres of culture and study which would be an ornament to his realm and exercise a salutary influence upon their surroundings. During his reign, an organised movement towards reform began in the Aquitanian kingdom, with the encouragement of its ruler Louis, his youngest son. The chief agent in this movement was Benedict, Abbot of Aniane. Like many of his followers in the work of monastic administration, he found himself dissatisfied with the normal routine of the religious house in which he had made his profession. As a monk at Saint-Seine, regarding the Rule of St Benedict as a system merely for beginners, he endeavoured to follow the severe practices of Eastern monachism. About 780 he founded upon his inherited estates the monastery of Aniane. At first, the customs which he prescribed to his monks were too drastic; and experience probably taught him the wisdom of the Rule which, in his ardour, he had underrated. After a period of disappointment, Aniane began to flourish. Monks went out from it to spread its teaching in other parts of Gaul; old foundations received new life, and new houses were founded under its influence. Twenty monks were sent from Aniane to colonise Alcuin's monastery of Corméry; William, Duke of Aquitaine, placed others in the monastery of Saint-Guilhem-du-Désert. Benedict gained the favour of Charlemagne as a defender of orthodoxy against the adoptionist heresy of Felix, Bishop of Urgel; and Louis the Pious committed to him full authority to reform the monasteries of Aquitania. When Louis succeeded to his father's dominions in 814, this authority was extended over the whole of Gaul. Benedict was induced to follow Louis northwards, and eventually to take up his abode in the Kornelimünster, an abbey founded by him with the Emperor's help on the Inde, near Aix-la-Chapelle. Here he died in February 822.

In his endeavours for reform, Benedict had to contend with three main abuses. The custom of granting monasteries as fiefs to lay proprietors endangered the whole system. Benedict prevailed upon Louis to appoint only regulars as abbots, and to modify the requisition of services from religious houses. Closely connected with this first abuse was the prevalent abandonment of regular observances. In some prominent houses, such as Saint-Denis at Paris and Saint-Bénigne at Dijon, the inmates had abandoned the title of monks for that of clerks and canons. Saint-Bénigne was brought back to discipline in Benedict's lifetime by its Abbot, Herlogaud. At Saint-Denis his efforts had little success; the monks who were introduced to leaven the house were expelled by the canons; and it was not until some years after his death that the reform was effected by Hilduin and Hincmar. But the crying evil which Benedict recognised as the root of irregularity was diversity of observance. If he was urgent in enforcing the Rule of St Benedict as the foundation of an orderly system, his panacea for disorder was uniformity of custom.

His reform was the first of a series of attempts to mould the monastic life upon a fixed pattern of observance. At the Council of Aix-la-Chapelle in 817 the Rule was interpreted and supplemented by a series of ordinances, the effect of which was to bind monasteries to one scale of simple living. All luxury was forbidden; monks must look after the offices of the house themselves and do their own work. While they were given a somewhat more liberal allowance of raiment than was contemplated by the Rule, they were restricted in the care of their persons. The visits of strangers to the cloister were prohibited, and even visiting monks were to be entertained in a separate dormitory. The abbot's spiritual authority was strongly upheld, but his private liberty was curtailed; he must live as one of the monks over whom he bore rule. The only children who might be taught in a monastery were those who were offered to it by their parents, and these, when they came to years of discretion, should be given a free choice between remaining with the monks or going out into the world. Where a monastery had dependent priories, each must be served by six monks at least, or entrusted to canons. The literary fruit of Benedict's studies in monastic polity is seen in the *Codex Regularum*, a collation of existing monastic rules, and in the *Concordia Regularum*, in which their precepts were applied in the form of a commentary to the governing Rule itself.

It will be noticed that the Council of Aix-la-Chapelle recognised the existence of canons, or persons leading the canonical as distinct from the monastic life, among the constituent parts of ecclesiastical machinery. St Chrodegang, Bishop of Metz (742–766), had composed a rule for the clerks of his cathedral church, by which they were given a quasi-monastic constitution embodying the principles of the common life and community of goods. His rule was the starting-point of reform in similar bodies of clergy, to whose members the title of canons was generally applied. Its origin is sometimes attributed to the canon or rule under which they lived; but it was more probably derived from the canon, the official list or *matricula* of a community. Although this system was in itself an attempt to apply to corporations of secular clerks a constitution upon modified Benedictine lines, its growth presented an alternative mode of life to the inmates of monasteries. The claims of the monks of Saint-Denis and Dijon to be styled canons or regular clerks was a rejection of the mixed constitution of a monastery, in which only a certain proportion of the monks were in holy orders. It also excused the possession of private property by individuals, as the canon had his special allowance from the common fund or, where he was bound by no rule, lived upon the income derived from an individual estate. At Aix-la-Chapelle regulations were also drawn up for canons by a committee of bishops and clerks; and the code attributed to Amalarius, Dean of Metz, on the lines of the Rule of St Chrodegang, was intended for the use, not merely of cathedral and collegiate chapters, but of clerks in general. It was not until a much later date that the so-called Rule of St Augustine was formulated for the use of bodies of clerks vowed to a common life of the monastic type.

For Carolingian monasticism in its full vigour we must look to the abbeys of Gaul and Germany, to Saint-Maur, St Gall, or Fulda. In Italy such monasteries as Monte Cassino and Nonantula flourished under the Carolingian Emperors as centres of civilised and scholarly activity. But the general tendency of the Italian monasteries was towards secularisation. Farfa, between the Sabine hills and the Tiber, was especially favoured by Lothar, the son of Louis the Pious. Its abbot was a prince ruling over a large territory and commanding the allegiance of powerful vassals; he owned no superior but the Emperor, and was able to resist successfully the encroachments which successive Popes, grudging him the privilege of exemption from their authority, made upon his lands. The great monastery, with its circle of embattled walls, its four churches, its imperial palace and splendid monastic buildings adorned with spacious colonnades, was more like a fortified town than a place of retirement from the world. It withstood the attacks of the Saracens for seven years before its eventual fall. Such a foundation was an easy prey to the irregularities against which Benedict of Aniane had striven. Even within the main area of his reform, the dissolution of the Empire of Charlemagne, rent by intestine quarrels and harassed by the invasions of the Northmen, caused the temporary extinction of monastic life after its brief revival. The advance of the northern pirates along the Loire and Seine was marked by the abandonment and pillage of Marmoûtier, the shrine of St Martin of Tours, Fleury, to which the body of St Benedict had been translated after the Lombard destruction of Monte Cassino, and Saint-Denis. The monasteries of the southern coast, such as Saint-Victor at Marseilles and Lérins, formerly a notable link between eastern and western monachism, were sacked by more than one invader during the eighth and ninth centuries. When, after the fury was past, monks returned to these sites, it was with disheartenment and little hope of safety.

A period came, however, when the religious life, under the protection of powerful territorial magnates, had a chance of recovery. In 910 William the Pious, Duke of Aquitaine, founded a monastery at Cluny in the diocese of Mâcon, and set over it Berno, a noble Burgundian, who, as Abbot of Gigny, a house founded by himself upon territory of his own, had already given proof of reforming energy. The monastery of Baume, which had been placed under his direction and furnished with customs closely modelled upon the precepts of Benedict of Aniane, also contributed its example to the new abbey. Cluny, entrusted with the administration of other monasteries, was, before Berno's death in 927, the head of a small congregation, the nucleus of the Cluniac order. Berno, in the last year of his life, resigned his office, and divided his monasteries between his relative Guy and Odo, a monk who had found at Baume the discipline abandoned by his earlier companions, the monks of Marmoûtier. While, under the unworthy Guy, Gigny and Baume became centres of reaction, Cluny and the two other houses given to Odo persevered in the work of reform. Without Odo, indeed, the Cluniac movement might have come to nothing. During the fourteen years between 927 and 941, he earned the title of the reformer of Benedictine observance, not only in France, but in the West generally.

In France, Odo's most remarkable success was the reform of Fleury, to which he was called in 930. At first the monks resisted his entry with violence; but his personal fearlessness overcame opposition, and, with the help of Hugh the Great, the father of Hugh Capet, he purged the convent of abuses and converted it into an active missionary centre, second only to Cluny in influence. In 936, on the invitation of Alberic, the temporal sovereign of Rome, Odo paid his first of several visits to Italy. He was given authority over the monasteries in Roman territory: St Paul's without the walls of Rome was successfully reformed, and other houses followed suit. A beginning was made at Monte Cassino; but Farfa, divided by a schism between two rival abbots who had murdered their predecessor, resisted the introduction of Cluniac monks by Odo and got rid by poison of the abbot whom Alberic installed by armed force. Yet, if Odo's personal success in Italy was limited, he at any rate sowed the seed of a much needed revival. Neither Alberic nor his step-father and rival, King Hugh of Italy, can be credited with an ardent zeal for religion; but both, in the favour which they shewed to the Abbot of Cluny, paid testimony to the importance of religious activity in the restoration of general order.

The work of Odo was continued with unabated energy by his successors. Mayeul (Maiolus), Abbot of Cluny from 954 to 994, was able, with the favour of Otto the Great and his son, to advance the Italian reform in Ravenna, Pavia, and Rome. Through the influence of the Empress Adelaide, the first offshoot of Cluny in the Burgundian kingdom was founded at Payerne (Peterlingen) east of the Jura. Among the French monasteries reformed by Mayeul were Marmoûtier, Saint-Maur-des-Fossés, and Saint-Bénigne at Dijon. He died on his way to Saint-Denis, where his successor Odilo (994–1048) achieved some success. It was under the rule of Odilo that the position of Cluny as the supreme head of a monastic congregation was achieved.

Odo had succeeded to the headship of only half the monasteries which Berno had ruled; and his influence as Abbot of Cluny depended entirely upon his personal gifts and piety, not upon the established reputation of a community which was as yet young and had acquired no great

possessions. Most of the houses which submitted to his guidance were
Benedictine monasteries with a history far older than that of Cluny. In
subjecting themselves to him for a time, they did not surrender their
independence. When he died, the number of houses immediately dependent on Cluny was very small. They were slightly increased under his
next successor Aymard (942–954); but Mayeul, at his accession, had only
five dependent monasteries under his charge. Under Mayeul, again, the
work of reform did not include the principle of submission to Cluny.
Several of the Benedictine foundations whose life was quickened by Odo
and Mayeul initiated reforms of their own which were independent of
Cluniac effort. Thus Fleury and Marmoûtier had each its own congregation of reformed monasteries, which modelled their customs upon those of
the reforming house, but were not members of a distinct order. The Lombard William of Volpiano, to whom Mayeul committed the government
of Saint-Bénigne in 990, migrated from Dijon to Normandy and introduced practices learned from Cluny into the Norman monasteries, either
in person or through his disciples. Yet, though these were closely allied
in ties of friendship, they owned no superior house to which obedience
was due, but preserved the Benedictine principle of local autonomy.

Again, parallel movements may be traced with which Cluny was only
indirectly connected. Thus the reform of monasteries in the Netherlands,
under Gerard of Brogne, and that which proceeded from Gorze in the
diocese of Metz, were purely spontaneous in origin. The monks of
Gorze adopted certain customs which bore a strong resemblance to
those of Cluny; and it is possible that the reform of the Abbey of
Saint-Evre at Toul, achieved by monks of Fleury in 934, brought
them into contact with Cluniac observances. Equally indigenous in its
beginnings was the reform and restoration of the English monasteries,
in which the prime mover was Dunstan, ably seconded by Aethelwold
and Oswald. If Dunstan, during his exile from the court of Eadwig,
learned much from continental monachism in the abbey of Saint-Pierre
or Blandinium at Ghent, his policy had been matured in his own brain
during years of quiet meditation at Glastonbury. The aid of Abbo of
Fleury was subsequently invoked to kindle popular enthusiasm, when
Aethelwold repeopled the ruined monasteries in the east of England, and
when Oswald, in the Severn valley and at Ramsey, founded new houses
in which the Benedictine Rule was strictly observed. Such movements
felt the influence of the Cluniac revival, but were distinct from it. Once
more, the German reform undertaken a century later by William, who,
formerly a monk of St Emmeram at Ratisbon, was elected Abbot of the
distracted monastery of Hirschau in the diocese of Spires in 1069, owed
much to Cluny, then at the height of its power. William modelled his
reform directly upon Cluniac principles; Ulrich's edition of the customs
of Cluny, compiled at his request, was dedicated to him; some of his
monks were sent to Cluny to learn regular observance, and the customs

of Hirschau were compiled from their report. The German congregation, however, owed no allegiance to the monastery to which it was thus indebted. Similarly, the reform of Farfa, achieved by the Abbot Hugh whose purchase of his office in 997 was the unpromising beginning of a praiseworthy career, followed the Cluniac methods which the monastery had rejected at an earlier date. The customs of Farfa, compiled shortly after Hugh's death in 1039, belong, like the *Ordo Cluniacensis* of Bernard and Ulrich's *Antiquiores Consuetudines*, to the main group of authorities for Cluniac practice, and include a most valuable description of the arrangements of a model Cluniac monastery. But Farfa remained outside the Cluniac order.

Odilo's rule at Cluny was distinguished by the intensive application of Cluniac customs to a congregation of dependent houses. Roving commissions to administer the affairs of foreign monasteries became less frequent; we hear more, on the other hand, of gifts of monasteries to Cluny, which were affiliated directly to her as their parent and mistress. The biographer of Odilo enumerates some of the principal churches which he ruled and enriched with possessions, buildings, and ornaments— Payerne and Romainmôtier in the diocese of Lausanne, Saint-Victor at Geneva, Charlieu and Ambierle near Lyons, Ris, Sauxillanges, Souvigny, la Ferté-Hauterive, and Saint-Saturnin in Auvergne, the priory founded by Mayeul at Pavia, and la Voulte-sur-Rhône, founded by Odilo himself in the last years of his life. He adorned the cloister of Cluny with marble columns, shipped from distant places down the Durance and the Rhône, so that he was wont to boast that he had found Cluny of wood and left it of marble.

It may be said with equal truth that he left Cluny, hitherto merely a spiritual power among Benedictine houses, the head of an order, as distinct from a mere congregation of monasteries, within the Benedictine system. Each house of the order owed absolute obedience to the sovereign abbot. Odo had acquired for Cluny the privilege of exemption from any authority but that of the Pope. Her priories, members of the mother-house and incapable of independent action apart from her, were similarly exempt from control by diocesan bishops or secular princes; in whatever country they were founded, they were subjects of Cluny, amenable only to the decrees of the annual chapter at which the priors of the order were gathered together under the presidency of the abbot. The title of abbot, accorded to the head of an old house like Vézelay, which had been drawn within the Cluniac system, did not imply independence of the central government. Certain houses had an honorary pre-eminence, la-Charité-sur-Loire, Saint-Martin-des-Champs at Paris, Souvigny and Sauxillanges, and Lewes, the first Cluniac foundation in England, established in 1077. For visitatorial purposes, the order was divided into ten provinces, for each of which two visitors and other officers were appointed at the general chapter. The provincial organisation, however, did not imply local autonomy; the visitors were responsible to the central autocracy.

This constitutional machinery was perfected during the long rule of Odilo's successor Hugh (1049–1109). His abbacy, glorious as it was in the continual addition of monasteries to the order and in the foundation of the splendid abbey church of Cluny for the 300 or 400 monks for whom the old buildings were insufficient, was in some respects the turning-point of the history of the Cluniac movement. It covered the period of the struggle between the Emperor Henry IV and the Papacy which his father had taken action to reform. In this conflict Cluny was naturally in sympathy with the Pope. Its exemption from local authority made a strong Papacy essential to its undisturbed existence. Its early success had been largely due to its geographical position in a district little affected by the strife of the last days of the Carolingian Empire. But, with the spread of the order over Europe, and with the growth of the spirit of nationality, the safeguard of its central authority was, more than in earlier times, the protection of the supreme spiritual power. On the other hand, while the Papacy was menaced by the power which had restored it, Cluny was surrounded by enemies of the reforms demanded by Gregory VII. It is hardly surprising that its abbot preferred a cautious neutrality to a whole-hearted espousal of the cause of Gregory, and to the consequent risk of provoking the active enmity of Henry IV and the prelates whose jealousy of Cluniac privileges was ready to take advantage of Cluniac weakness. Tradition, founded upon the supposed association of Hildebrand with Cluny, has represented the order as a chief instrument of the policy which, as Pope, he sought to carry out. We may assume with justice that he looked for support to the great influence of the abbot. He found friendship and consolation; the fulness with which he poured out the anxieties of his heart in his letters to Hugh admits of no other interpretation of their spirit. But with these confidences was mingled a tone of impatient reproach which shews that Hugh's regard for him did not go to the length of overt action. The voice of the abbot was not heard in the Pope's synods; Cluny was unprepared to throw its weight into the scales upon his side. As Gregory complained, there were occasions when the abbot's holiness shunned trouble, and when he was slothful in answering the demands of serious business.

The days of Cluniac reform, in fact, were numbered with the settled organisation of the Cluniac order. In a monastery which had increased in power and riches, the mistress of some two hundred priories, piety might still be found and the *opus Dei* still flourish; but its missionary energy had been exchanged for concentration upon internal polity. The patriarchs of Cluny had insisted upon a strict observance of the Rule, upon silence in church and cloister, upon the banishment of meat from the convent table, upon eradication of the *nequissimum vitium* of private property. While this was so, the success of Cluny as an agent of reform was obviously due in no small degree to its moderation and avoidance of extreme forms of asceticism. It presented an ideal which it was possible for the ordinary monk to follow. In spite of its remissness in the cause of Gregory VII, it still sent out great men to champion the papal claims. Urban II, the inheritor of the Hildebrandine policy, had been Prior of Cluny; Paschal II who followed him in the papal chair was also a Cluniac monk. It was to Cluny that Gelasius II, Paschal's successor, came to die, and the next Pope, Calixtus II, was chosen in the abbey. Its fame suffered a temporary eclipse under the rule of Pons, who succeeded Hugh in 1109 and was obliged to resign in 1122; but the wisdom and devout learning of Peter the Venerable, who compiled a revised code of statutes, kept its reputation alive long after. Even so severe a critic as Peter Damian could refer to Cluny in the days of Hugh as "a paradise watered by the streams of the four Gospels, a garden of delights, a spiritual field where earth and heaven meet, a ground of conflict, in which, as in a wrestling-school of the spirit, the frailty of the flesh contends against the powers of the air." St Bernard's quarrel with Cluny arose in the evil days of Pons, when his cousin Robert was enticed from Clairvaux by specious arguments, and his condemnation of the pride and magnificence of Cluny and its preference of the letter to the spirit of the Rule was doubtless affected by this circumstance. Yet this splendour and monastic luxury was not the growth of a few years of misrule; for one point which Bernard attacked, the architectural beauty of the churches and cloisters, with their profusion of ornament and sculpture, we have abundant evidence from the time of Odilo onwards. It was through the imperceptible effect of wealth and power upon a never excessively rigorous system that the state of things arose in which, as Bernard said, the welfare of the order and its observance of religious discipline were held to consist in the magnificence of its feasts, its furniture, and its buildings.

In these respects Cluny set the example to Benedictinism in general. The great revival of monastic life in England which followed the Norman Conquest was a revival of decent order rather than of stringent observance. Lanfranc, in issuing his ordinances to the monks of his metropolitan church, had in view a well-ordered community, pursuing the life of church and cloister with exemplary decorum and following the Rule without extravagant professions of asceticism. The land-owning monasteries of Domesday, the churches whose monks formed cathedral chapters, the splendid buildings which were in progress before the end of the eleventh century, were certainly not homes of an excessively severe discipline. Local instances of disorder, no doubt, occurred; and the strife between William Rufus and Anselm had dangerous effects upon the religious life, exposing monasteries to the intrusion of unworthy nominees of the Crown. It is to be noticed, however, that such movements as that which led in 1132 to the secession of the monks of Fountains from St Mary's at York were due, not to any definite scandals but to the failure of abbots and convents to live up to the stricter precepts of the Rule.

Even in the days of the greatest activity of Cluny, sporadic efforts at a high standard of asceticism are noticeable outside the main movement. In Italy the traditions of the austerities practised by the hermits and anchorites of the East were never dormant. Fonte Avellana in the diocese of Faenza, founded shortly before the year 1000, was a monastery of bare-footed anchorites. Some forty years later, under the guidance of Peter Damian, its strict practices were introduced into other houses, and daughter-monasteries were founded. The mortifications of the community provoked such criticism that the ardent abbot himself felt bound to restrain them. The enthusiasm of Peter Damian, which contributed so much to the revival of the papal authority in Italy, was fostered by the example of Romuald, the founder of the Camaldolese order. The life of Romuald is an extraordinary romance of spiritual fervour. He settled in one hermitage after another, imbuing disciples with his own enthusiasm, establishing communities of hermit-monks, but constantly disappointed by their failure to reach his own almost unattainable standard. The Emperor Otto III found in him a visionary after his own heart, and placed him in charge of the abbey of Sant' Apollinare in Classe near his native city of Ravenna; but here his attempt to impose his severe discipline upon the convent forced him to resign. He was, in fact, wholly unadapted for the cenobitic life; and such success as he achieved was found in solitude and desert places. After abandoning, owing to a sudden illness, a missionary expedition to Hungary, he settled at Camaldoli, near Arezzo, about 1012. Here, on a desolate mountain, he and a few brethren lived in separate cells, attending common offices in their oratory, but passing the rest of their time in silent prayer and meditation, and working on the barren soil for their living. Romuald himself left Camaldoli after a time, migrating to Sitria, near Sassoferrato, where he attracted so many followers that Sitria, says his biographer, became another Nitria, full of hermits, some living in their cells as in tombs. He died in 1027 at Valdicastro, near Camerino, where he had founded a hermitage at an earlier date.

Camaldoli survived the departure of its founder, and became the head of an order of hermit-monks, which received papal approval in 1072. The original severity of the order was modified in the direction of humanity by successive priors of Camaldoli, its permanent generals. An important step was taken in 1102 by the foundation of the monastery of Fontebuono, at the foot of the mountain of Camaldoli, a cenobite establishment which ministered to the wants of the hermits and gave them a place of retirement in case of sickness. Henceforward the double element, hermit and cenobite, existed in the order; and one of the congregations into which it was eventually divided, that of San Michele at Murano, was exclusively cenobite.

Other hermit orders and congregations came into being during the same period. La Cava, near Salerno, was famous as the retreat of St Adalferio, who, falling ill at the monastery of Chiusa in Piedmont, devoted his life to God and made his profession to Odilo at Cluny. His monastery at la Cava, however, was on the hermit model; after his death in 1050, the mountain, covered with establishments of hermits, became a second Mount Athos. Large bodies of monks were sent out to form new colonies, one of which, Monreale in Sicily, became within a few years of its foundation the seat of an archbishop and a monastic chapter. The offshoots of Cava thus reverted to the normal Benedictine model. Vallombrosa, on the other hand, founded in 1038 or 1039 by St John Gualbert on the model of Camaldoli, became the source of another distinctively hermit order. The enthusiasm of the founder was equal to that of Romuald; but his temper was more gentle, and his power of administration probably greater. In the mingling of the cenobite with the recluse element which was characteristic of Vallombrosan houses, an advance is noticeable upon the distinction between them which was preserved by the Camaldolese. At Vallombrosa also we find the first specific mention of the *conversus* who afterwards became a marked feature of Cistercian organisation, the permanent lay brother whose part in the monastic scheme was the exercise of his craft as distinct from the occupation of the monk.

The Camaldolese and Vallombrosan orders had little success outside Italy. In France, the hermit movement developed upon individual lines, and one order, French in origin, spread its branches throughout Europe. The first distinctively French order, that of Grandmont, was inspired from Italian sources. Its founder, St Stephen, as a boy accompanied his father on a pilgrimage from their home in Auvergne to the shrine of St Nicholas at Bari in Apulia. Taken ill on the return journey, he remained in Italy under the care of the Archbishop of Benevento. The holy conversation of some Calabrian hermits impelled him to imitate their life; and, upon his patron's death, he returned, armed with the papal blessing, to his native country. Here he took up his abode on the hill of Muret, near Limoges, where, in 1076, he renounced the world for a life of solitary abstinence and poverty. The usual band of disciples gathered round him, to whom he prescribed a life entirely separate from worldly distractions, avoiding the acquisition of property, and depending upon the voluntary alms of the faithful. After his death, the desert in which he had settled was claimed by a convent at Limoges; and the new prior migrated, to avoid disputes, to a neighbouring solitude at Grandmont. The rule founded upon the counsels of St Stephen, and approved by Hadrian IV in 1156, was that of a cenobite community with common buildings. Each house of the order was divided into *clerici* and *conversi*, the first busied entirely with divine worship and contemplation, the second with the temporal care of the cell, the name applied collectively to the habitation of each convent. The dependent cells, few in number when the rule was composed, were entirely subordinate to the prior of Grandmont, to whose election each sent two proctors. Thus, in general character, Grandmont closely resembled Vallombrosa; while, in its congregational organisation, the method of Cluny was followed. At no time was the order large, and, during its early years, it passed almost unnoticed. But it spread beyond France: small Grandimontine houses were to be found in remote places in England, at Grosmont on the Yorkshire moors and at Craswall on the slopes of the Black mountains in the Welsh march. Its rule underwent various modifications at the hands of the Popes of the thirteenth century; and in 1317 John XXII raised the prior to the dignity of an abbot.

The founder of the Carthusian order was Bruno, a native of Cologne, who, at the time of his conversion to the hermit life, was canon of Rheims and master of the cathedral school there. In 1084, after spending some time in a hermitage near the abbey of Molesme, he and six companions, four clerks and two *conversi*, besought Hugh, Bishop of Grenoble, to grant them a place of settlement in his barren and mountainous diocese. Hugh amply satisfied their ambition for solitude. The desert of Chartreuse, entered by a cleft in the rocks at the top of a steep ascent, inhabited only by wild beasts and generally covered with snow, was, in the bishop's words, more like a prison or purgatory than a human dwelling-place. Bruno and his companions built their church and little cells near the summit of the site, round a spring which gave them their daily drink. The founder himself, called away to Rome by Pope Urban II, sought the congenial society of the hermits of southern Italy, and died in a monastery which he founded at la Torre in the diocese of Squillace. His departure seems to have been followed by the temporary desertion of Chartreuse, which he commended in his absence to the Abbot of la Chaise-Dieu in Auvergne; but it was restored to one of the original inmates, Landoin of Lucca, before Bruno's death in 1101.

The recognition of the Grande-Chartreuse as the head of an order was not fully achieved before 1176; but daughter-houses had come into existence by 1128, when Guigues du Châtel, prior from 1110 to 1137, drew up the *Consuetudines Carthusienses*, at the request of three priors of dependent convents. The essential points in the constitution of the Grande-Chartreuse, as in that of Grandmont, were isolation from worldly affairs and complete poverty. Beyond the bounds of the desert, which surrounded the monastery and afforded some scanty pasturage for a limited number of sheep and cattle, the acquisition of property was forbidden. Any temptation to further possession was checked by the limitation of the conventual body to a prior and twelve monks, sixteen *conversi*, and a few hired servants, shepherds, and herdsmen. As at Camaldoli, the monastery consisted of two distinct parts, the hermitage proper with its separate cells, and the lower house, tenanted by *conversi* and administered by a proctor chosen from among the hermits. Dressed in habits of coarse white cloth, with hair-shirts next their skins, the brethren abstained wholly from meat, fasting three days a week on bread, salt, and water, and on other days eating only vegetables, with the occasional addition of cheese or some milk-food, and drinking watered wine. Not even the sick were permitted the use of meat; gifts of fish were allowed, but not its purchase. The lesser hours were said privately by the monks in their cells; only certain hours were said in church, and in the early days of the monastery mass seems to have been celebrated only on Sundays and feast-days, when the monks left the cells to eat together in the refectory. The life of solitary prayer, varied only by work on the plots of ground adjoining the cells, was the ideal long maintained by the Carthusian community. Guests were merely tolerated. The monastery was founded in the desert to afford refreshment to men's souls, not to their bodies; its site furnished no conveniences for visitors and horses; as for alms to the poor, it was better to send surplus food to neighbouring towns than to attract a crowd of beggars.

The spirit of the Carthusian customs and statutes is a rigorous determination to maintain the strictest self-denial. Those who framed them kept in view all the dangers which beset a nascent order. The novice was warned of the hardness of the life; if its demands were too onerous for him, he was not encouraged to persevere. The poor and compulsorily small monasteries were unattractive homes for men who wished to retire from the world with a certain degree of comfort. From the beginning, Carthusian monks recognised that their life was fit only for the few. They refused to affiliate large houses to their order. When Stephen of Obasine consulted Guigues with a view to uniting his house to some strict order, he was told that the Carthusians had no room for it, and was advised to join the Cistercians, who kept the royal road and whose statutes led to all perfection. The hermit Carthusians admired but had no desire to emulate the rapid growth of cenobite reform under the Cistercians. Their humility and rejection of ambition met with its reward in the later Middle Ages, when, amid the decay of the cenobite orders, they still preserved their pristine zeal.

Another order of a somewhat novel type was developed from experience gained in hermitages. Robert of Arbrissel, a Breton, was, like Bruno, a learned theologian, who left his lectures at Angers to become an anchorite in the forest of Craon, where he was joined by a crowd of imitators. The place was too strait for them all, and they parted to form distinct bands in neighbouring forests. Their leaders seem to have learned by experience that the solitary life in separate cells could not be of the same profit to all. Robert himself founded a monastery for those who preferred a cenobite life. One of his principal followers, Vital, a canon of Mortain, founded the cenobite congregation of Savigny, afterwards merged in the order of Cîteaux; another, Bernard of Abbeville, was the founder of the congregation of Thiron. Robert, however, called upon by Urban II to join in preaching the Crusade, conceived the idea of founding a house

of prayer for those who, smitten with penitence but unable to take part
in the holy war, might compensate for their disability by devoting themselves to God. From the first this house, established at Fontevrault about
1100, was intended to include women as well as men. Nunneries had
played a very small part in the recent history of monasticism. The great
abbeys ruled at an earlier date by women, such as Whitby and Chelles,
had disappeared; others, like Remiremont in the Vosges, seem to have
lost their regular character early, and developed as houses of secular
canonesses. In 1028 Fulk the Black of Anjou had founded a nunnery at
Ronceray, to which he attached four clerks or canons as chaplains: an
arrangement which we find repeated in the canonries annexed to the
important nunneries in the south of England, which owed their origin to
the royal house of Wessex and, whatever decline they may have suffered
during the period before the conquest, recovered their vigour under the
Norman kings. With the approach of the twelfth century, nunneries
began to assume a larger part in religious organisation. The existence of
communities of women, however, raised special problems. Nunneries,
without adequate protection, were exposed to the risk of secular violence;
they needed the ministrations of priests in spiritual things, of manservants
in temporal. Thus there grew up, in more than one order, those double
monasteries in which a cloister of clerks and lay brothers existed side by
side with a cloister of nuns.

The symbolic idea of the double community at Fontevrault, whose
patrons were St Mary and St John, was the care which the beloved
disciple bestowed upon the mother of our Lord. The abbess was supreme
over the monastery. The women, of whom there were 300 in the largest
cloister alone, were consecrated to prayer; the men were charged with
the temporal needs of the house. Cloisters, dedicated to St Lazarus and
St Mary Magdalene respectively, were set apart for the diseased and the
penitent. The Rule of St Benedict was stringently enforced; the use of
meat was forbidden, and the community was ordered to receive no gifts
of parish churches or tithes. In 1106 the new order was approved by
Paschal II, and in 1113 it received the privilege of exemption. Daughter
houses soon grew up in Anjou, Touraine, Berri, and Poitou; and the
success of the order was so great that in 1145 there were said to be more
than 5000 nuns at Fontevrault itself. Nuns were brought from it into
England by Henry II to reform the abbey of Amesbury; others were
settled at Nuneaton and at Westwood in Worcestershire; and the church
of Fontevrault became the chosen resting-place of the Angevin royal
family.

Hitherto, none of the organised congregations which had arisen since
the days of Cluny had produced a far-reaching effect outside certain
localities. Their reforms, moreover, had for the most part pointed away
from the cenobite ideal. The qualified approval which St Benedict had

given to the hermit life was supplanted by a theory which regarded the cenobite system as a concession to human frailty rather than as the normal school of God's service. It was only natural that the devout reformer, face to face with the splendour of Cluny or Saint-Denis, should contrast it unfavourably with the naked simplicity of Camaldoli or the Grande-Chartreuse, and question the spirituality of the system which it represented. But the greatest of the twelfth century reforms was instituted upon strictly cenobite lines; and only in one outstanding detail did it depart from the spirit of the Rule of St Benedict. Even in this, its adoption of the congregational principle, it differed widely from the Cluniac system of centralised government under a single head.

The institution of the order of Cîteaux marks the third great epoch in the history of medieval monachism. The reforms of Benedict of Aniane had been short-lived; the purity of Cluny had become alloyed by customs out of keeping with the intention of its founders. In 1098, Robert, Abbot of the Benedictine house of Molesme in the diocese of Langres, with six of his monks, dissatisfied with the imperfect observance of the Rule in their monastery, migrated, with licence from the papal legate Hugh, Archbishop of Lyons, to Cîteaux, a desolate place covered with thick woods and thorn-bushes in the diocese of Chalon. Here, on Palm Sunday, 21 March 1098, the birthday of St Benedict, the Cistercian order took its beginning. The new monastery was approved by the local diocesan, and the expenses of its wooden buildings were defrayed by Eudes, Duke of Burgundy, who proved a good friend to the struggling community. Robert himself was recalled to Molesme within a year of the foundation; and it was his successor, Alberic, who obtained papal approval of the literal observance of the Rule of St Benedict to which he and his monks devoted themselves. But the monastery was as yet insignificant; during the first years of its existence, its promise can hardly have seemed to contemporary observers as great as that of Fontevrault or Savigny. Its legislator arrived in 1109, in the person of the third abbot, the Englishman Stephen Harding. It was not, however, until 1113 that the event took place which was, within a few years, to raise Cîteaux to a position of unrivalled influence in the Church at large. In that year St Bernard, with thirty companions, including his brothers, made his profession to Abbot Stephen; and in the same year Cîteaux, enlarged in numbers, sent out its first colony to la Ferté-sur-Grosne.

By the time of the promulgation of the *Carta Caritatis*, which was confirmed by Calixtus II at Saulieu on 23 December 1119, the wide expansion of the Cistercian order was a certainty. The foundation of la Ferté was followed by that of Pontigny in 1114. Clairvaux, with Bernard as its abbot, and Morimond, both in the diocese of Langres, were colonised on 25 June 1115. To the abbots of these four houses special pre-eminence was given in the councils of the order; from them and from Cîteaux proceeded those generations of abbeys which in quick succession rose all over Europe. At the date of the confirmation of the Charter of Charity, the order possessed twelve monasteries, of which seven were daughters of Cîteaux, two of Pontigny, and two of Clairvaux. As yet, it had not extended far beyond the bounds of Burgundy and Champagne; but its circle of influence was beginning to widen, and one house, Cadouin in the distant diocese of Sarlat, which owed its foundation to Robert of Arbrissel, had been affiliated to Pontigny.

The Charter of Charity was drawn up to ensure mutual peace and love between the houses of the order. As a constitutional document, its essential point is the position of Cîteaux as the head of the family. The autocracy of Cluny was not copied. Reverence and obedience were due to Cîteaux as a parent; but a certain degree of autonomy was necessary for each house. The order was not composed of an abbot and a crowd of completely dependent priors. Each monastery was ruled by its own abbot, whose responsibility to his superior was purely spiritual. The Abbot of Cîteaux had the cure of souls of the order; but he might levy no temporal exactions upon his spiritual children. In the primitive interpretation of the Rule, in divine service, and in customs, uniformity on the pattern of Cîteaux was to be kept; a monk of one house would find nothing strange or unfamiliar in another. In all houses of the order, the abbots gave place to the Abbot of Cîteaux, if he happened to visit them.

On the other hand, the visitatorial power of the Abbot of Cîteaux was limited. If he practically took charge of a daughter-monastery during his visitation, he might alter nothing without the consent of its abbot and the convent, and the advice of the abbot was necessary to his correction of faults. He might not receive guests in the guest-house, unless the abbot was away. Further, the visitation of each monastery, once a year, belonged to the abbot of the house which was its immediate parent. Thus, among the twelve abbeys existing at the end of 1119, Pontigny and Clairvaux were subject to visitation from Cîteaux, but the Abbot of Pontigny was the visitor of Bouras and Cadouin, and the Abbot of Clairvaux of Trois-Fontaines and Fontenay; and, within a short time, the abbots of these daughters of Pontigny and Clairvaux were exercising the same right over daughters of their own. The order spread in this way by a closely connected system of affiliated houses, each descending in a regular line of pedigree from Cîteaux, the mother of all. At Cîteaux the yearly chapter-general of the order was held, with the abbot as president; at such assemblies and elsewhere where they met, the precedence of abbots was determined by priority of foundation. Measures, however, were taken for holding the power of the Abbot of Cîteaux in check. He himself was subject to visitation by the four prime abbots of the order; if he was unsatisfactory, they were charged with special powers of correction, short of deposition or excommunication, which were reserved to the decision of the chapter-general. Similarly, the settlement of controversies between abbeys belonged to the Abbot of Cîteaux, but not without the choice of such assessors as he might think fit. The removal of other abbots was delegated to the abbot of the parent house with others to help him; while a similar committee presided over the elections of abbots and guided the decision of the convents concerned. To sum up, each house of the order had its place in an hierarchy at the apex of which was Cîteaux; each was under some degree of supervision exercised by the abbot from whose monastery it took birth. The primacy of the whole order was secured for Cîteaux, which had the immeasurable advantage of being the regular seat of the chapters-general; but the monarchy of the Abbot of Cîteaux was limited by necessary safeguards, and his autocracy was impossible without complete subversion of the constitution.

To Stephen Harding, who thus gave the order its constitution, are ascribed also the earliest of its institutes. In enforcing uniformity of custom, he aimed at the removal of all superfluous splendour of furniture and ritual. Gold and silver ornaments were forbidden; only the vessels of the altar were to be of silver or silver gilt. Crosses were to be of painted wood, candlesticks of iron, censers of copper or iron. The vestments were of the most simple kind and material; copes, dalmatics, and tunicles were banished, and the altar coverings were of plain linen without embroidery. The series of Cistercian statutes of which the text has been preserved to us represents a growth of many years and successive codifications from the time of Raynard, who succeeded Stephen in 1134. The body of Cistercian statutes, approved and added to by successive chapters-general, formed no Rule; one essential precept of the order was the uniform interpretation of and loyalty to the Rule of St Benedict. The systematic arrangement of the statutes under inclusive headings was begun in 1203, and the *Institutiones*, revised in 1240 and again in 1256, give a more detailed and comprehensive view of Cistercian customs than the earliest series. Even at the later date, the puritanism of the order and its avoidance of all ostentation were strongly maintained. The choice of remote sites for abbeys, the abstinence from superfluous and curious ornament, were still insisted on. Stained-glass windows and stone bell-towers were forbidden as non-essentials; wooden bell-towers must not be of immoderate height. It is possible to trace some modifications in the later statutes; the prohibition of gold and silver crosses was confined to crosses of large size, and the limitation of the use of meat to the infirmary buildings was not accompanied by its specific limitation to infirm persons. In the dignified simplicity of the services, for which elaborate regulations existed in the early *Liber Usuum*, there was no important change. In theory, at any rate, the Cistercian of the thirteenth century still adhered to the example bequeathed to him by Stephen Harding and Bernard.

The regulations for the foundation of new abbeys implicitly prevented the growth of subordinate priories. When a new house was founded to the honour of St Mary, to whom, in memory of the beginnings of the order in St Mary's at Molesme, all its monasteries were dedicated, the head of the thirteen monks sent out to colonise it was the abbot. Each monastery had its granges, divided from one another by specified minimum distances; but every care was taken that the grange should not become the permanent abode of a small body of religious. No monk save the cellarer, the temporal officer of the abbey, might have charge of it. If monks went, as in harvest-time, to work at the granges, they might pass the night there only in cases of absolute necessity. No churchyards were to be made or burials take place at granges. Such places, in fact, were intended for the support, not for the residence of the community; and their care was entrusted to the *conversi* or lay-brothers.

The *conversus* or *laicus barbatus* was by no means a peculiarly Cistercian institution; but it was in this order that his position was most clearly defined. In a self-supporting community, far from populous places, it was necessary to have workmen on the spot. Although the Rule prescribed manual labour to its followers, the prime duty of a monk was prayer and his proper place was the cloister, not the field or workshop. Thus, when Alberic undertook the rule of Cîteaux, he and his monks decided to receive *conversi*, whom they would treat as themselves in life and death, save that they were not to be admitted as monks. The hire of workmen, however, was also contemplated; and hired artificers and labourers are mentioned in the early statutes. We have no means of estimating how many *conversi* Cîteaux supported at first, or how many were sent out to la Ferté in 1113. It is certainly probable that this consecration of labour received some stimulus from non-Cistercian sources. The community of Thiron, established in the diocese of Chartres about 1114, consisted largely of men who were encouraged by Bernard of Abbeville to exercise in their monastery the trades to which they had been trained; and the enlistment of these *tirones* in the service of God appears to have given Thiron its name. But there can be no doubt that, with the rapid development of Cistercianism after the foundation of Clairvaux and Morimond in 1115, *conversi* entered the order in large numbers. They were admitted purely as labourers; they took the vows, but were prohibited from learning to read or write. They were lodged in the cellarer's building on the west side of the cloister, which frequently, as at Fountains, Ourscamp, and Vauclair, testifies to the very ample accommodation which their numbers required. Their simple offices, consisting of repetitions of prescribed prayers, were said in the nave of the church, before they went out, early in the morning, to the workshops and granges. At the granges, they had intervals at the canonical hours for devotions, led by their appointed overseers. Their chapter-meeting was held every Sunday by the abbot or his deputy. From the early *Usus Conversorum*, which prescribes their manner of life, it is clear that they were intended mainly for field-work, and that batches of them resided temporarily on the granges; while the directions for their habit had field-work mainly in view. There can be little doubt, however, that they made themselves useful in the various offices and workshops which, as at Clairvaux, filled the outer court of the monastery; and, if Cistercian architecture, the natural consequence and appropriate expression of the devotion of the order to ideals which excluded all flattery of the senses, cannot be proved to owe anything to the brain of the *conversus*, it was certainly aided by his hands.

One principle, laid down in the preamble to the Charter of Charity, was the necessity of episcopal consent to the establishment of a Cistercian house in any diocese. In this, no doubt, the collisions between the exempt Cluniacs and the ordinary authority were remembered. The order, however, was exempted in process of time from diocesan authority; and the later statutes uphold its freedom from episcopal visitation. Relations between bishops and Cistercian monasteries were generally friendly: the Cistercian abbot received benediction from the local diocesan or his suffragan, and bishops on their primary visitation tours claimed the right of a night's hospitality as guests in the houses where they could not sit as judges. The secluded sites of Cistercian abbeys brought them seldom, in the ordinary course of things, into conflict with parochial authorities. Their own churches were entirely reserved for the purposes of their communities; the parish altars, found in many Benedictine and Augustinian churches, had no place in their naves. The examples of St Benedict gave no precedent for the possession of appropriated parish churches or tithes, and the founders of the order rejected such gifts. Although their successors abandoned this principle, the appropriation of churches and tithes was less eagerly sought by the Cistercian order than by others; and, at the suppression, Fountains, the best endowed of English Cistercian houses, derived a mere fraction of its income from this source.

The call of the Cistercian order to men to save their souls by retirement from the world to a life of voluntary abstinence and prayer in uninhabited valleys had an extraordinary power. Cîteaux, by virtue of its compact organisation, and with the aid of the missionary zeal and ubiquitous energy of St Bernard, outstripped all other congregations in the rapidity of its growth. In 1120 it set foot in Italy, at Tiglieto in Liguria, founded from la Ferté; while Morimond made its first step eastwards to Bellevaux in Franche-Comté. In 1123 and 1127 Morimond established two important colonising centres in Germany, Camp in the diocese of Cologne and Ebrach in Franconia; from Camp the movement spread into the central and north-western districts of Germany, while the first daughter of Ebrach was Reun in Styria. Meanwhile, in 1128, through l'Aumône in the diocese of Chartres, a daughter of Cîteaux, the Cistercians reached England at Waverley in Hampshire; and the same house in 1131 sent another colony to Tintern, quickly followed in 1132 by Rievaulx, of the family of Clairvaux. In the previous year Clairvaux had established houses in Franche-Comté and the dioceses of Geneva and Mayence. In 1132 she founded Moreruela in the kingdom of Leon, the earliest monastery of the order in Spain. Rievaulx in 1136 became the mother of the first Scottish house at Melrose. Clairvaux reached Flanders at les Dunes and Portugal at Alofoës in 1138, and founded Whitland in South Wales in 1140. In 1142 Irish Cistercianism began at Mellifont, which, through the friendship of Malachy O'Morgair for Bernard, joined the family of Clairvaux; and in 1143 the same family was increased by two Swedish houses, at Alvastra and Nydala. In 1144 Denmark was entered by Cîteaux at Herrevad; and in 1146 and 1147 two English monasteries of the line of Clairvaux, Fountains and its daughter Kirkstead, colonised Lysa and Hovedö in Norway. Hungary, Poland, and Bohemia received their earliest colonists from monasteries of the line of Morimond in 1142 and 1143; and in 1150 Clairvaux founded a house at Cabuabbas in Sardinia.

Many other monasteries were founded during this period; and, apart from the great activity of Clairvaux and Morimond, the younger houses, especially in England, were very prolific. Waverley and Rievaulx produced large families; and Fountains, which, after its secession from St Mary's at York in 1132, joined the order in 1135, owned no less than eight daughters at the beginning of 1151. In Ireland also Mellifont owned five daughter-houses within eight years of its foundation. Progress in the German and Austrian provinces, through Morimond and its offshoots, was remarkable. Throughout the Spanish peninsula the line of Clairvaux spread, monopolising Portugal, Gallicia, and Leon; while the Gascon foundations of Morimond colonised Navarre and Castile, and shared Aragon and Catalonia with the children of Clairvaux, who eventually reached Valencia and Majorca, as the Christian arms advanced against the Moors. In Italy progress was slower; but all the chief houses established their lines in various parts of the country, and that of Clairvaux grew with fair rapidity. St Bernard himself was present at the foundation of Chiaravalle in Lombardy in 1136, and the first abbot of the monastery of SS. Vincenzo ed Anastasio at Rome, Bernard of Pisa, was raised to the Papacy in 1145 as Eugenius III. From 1145 to 1153 the Church was virtually ruled from Clairvaux; and with the deaths of St Bernard and Eugenius in 1153, the great age of Cistercian activity ended.

At the end of 1151 the order numbered 330 monasteries; and the general chapter of 1152 passed a decree that no more were to be founded. Nevertheless, at St Bernard's death on 20 August 1153, the number had risen to 343. Three more were founded within the next month; and the increase, though at a less phenomenal rate, was so steady that, by the end of the thirteenth century, this total of 346 was more than doubled. With the exception of Cîteaux itself, these houses had come into being in little more than forty years. It should be remembered, however, that the process of colonisation was aided by the accession of houses like Fountains, which had begun life by initiating reform on their own lines. The monastery of Savigny, soon after the time of its foundation about 1112, had become the head of a reformed congregation, much on the lines of Cîteaux. In 1147 Savigny, with twenty-seven daughter-houses in

France and the British Isles, was united bodily to the Cistercian order and affiliated to Clairvaux. In the same year the small congregation of Obasine in the Limousin was united to Cîteaux; and later, in 1162, the monastery of Dalon in the same district, with six daughters, joined the line of Pontigny. The wisdom of Cistercian polity was shewn in these cases by the fact that the abbots of the chief monasteries of these affiliated congregations remained the visitors of their daughter-houses, and some indulgence was allowed to existing practices not in harmony with Cistercian customs. Although, in the bull of Eugenius III which united the Savigniac houses to the order of Cîteaux, they are identified with those of the obedience of Thiron, Thiron and its daughters, among which were Kelso and Arbroath in Scotland, remained apart, and eventually were referred to habitually as Benedictine, differing only from Benedictine monks in their grey habit. Similarly, the congregation of Val-des-Choux in Burgundy, founded in 1193, had much in common with the Cistercians and wore a white habit; but their customs were largely derived by their founder, a *conversus* of the Charterhouse of Louvigny, from Carthusian sources, and their priories were subordinated to the parent house on the Cluniac model. Of some thirty priories, three were in Scotland; and the beautiful remains of Pluscarden in the diocese of Moray shew considerable influence, both in plan and architecture, from Cistercian houses.

The immediate influence of Cîteaux affected the movement which took place during the first half of the twelfth century among regular canons. The attempt to enforce a rule of life upon clerks, of which we have seen the beginning, was hampered by the secular preferences both of themselves and of the monks who sought to emulate their comparative freedom from restraint. In 1059 Nicholas II, at the instigation of Peter Damian, held a council at which the duty of the common life and the renunciation of private property were made obligatory upon corporations of canons; and in 1063 these principles were reasserted by Alexander II, who introduced canons of the reformed congregation of San Frediano at Lucca into his metropolitan church of St John Lateran. We have signs of the influence of these reforms in England, in indications of provisions for the common life at Beverley and Southwell in the time of the Confessor, and in the establishment of the Lotharingian system of communal chapters at Exeter and Wells. Mentions of the Rule of St Augustine begin to appear soon after the council of 1063. This Rule, founded upon the famous letter of St Augustine to a congregation of religious women, was supposed to embody the principles upon which he had constituted the common life of his clerks at Hippo. The English churches which have been mentioned never received it; and the normal cathedral and collegiate chapters of canons, both here and abroad, consisted of secular clerks, holding separate prebends of varying value, possessing their own houses, and, if they chose to reside in person, receiving additional allowances from the common fund. But the Augustinian reform had its result, early in the twelfth century, in the frequent substitution of regular for secular canons in churches where the canonical life had fallen into decay, and in the foundation of communities of clerks on what was really a monastic basis, although the Rule which they followed was lighter and admitted of a more liberal interpretation than that of St Benedict. The Rule was enforced upon all canons regular by Innocent II in 1139; but, before this date, houses had come into existence in large numbers in England and France. In France Ivo, Bishop of Chartres, who had received a monastic training at Bec under Lanfranc, promoted the formation of such bodies. In England canons regular of St Augustine seem to have appeared first in 1106 at St Botolph's, Colchester; the order spread within the next few years, and in 1133 the priory church of Carlisle was converted into the cathedral church of a new diocese.

Augustinian, like Benedictine, houses were autonomous communities following their own local customs. As among Benedictines, so here, certain centres of activity, such as the famous house of Saint-Victor at Paris, Saint-Ruf at Avignon, and the Holy Cross at Coimbra, which adopted the customs of Saint-Ruf, formed local congregations with common observances, and occasionally, as in the congregations of Saint-Victor and Arrouaise, with distinctive habits. Some communities from the first appear to have sought a quasi-monastic seclusion; but one powerful reason for the establishment of communities of clerks had been the formation of centres from which neighbouring parish churches could be served. There is abundant evidence in Domesday Book of the presence in England of small "minsters" of secular clerks on these lines. Some of these disappeared, some were continued as secular colleges, and some in process of time adopted the Augustinian Rule; the continuance of the system in Augustinian houses is indicated by the number of parish churches which, in many instances, formed a prominent factor in their early endowments. In later times, ecclesiastical legislation leaned to the natural view that the dispersion of canons in appropriated churches was incompatible with the maintenance of divine service in their monasteries. From the beginning of the thirteenth to the middle of the fourteenth century the practice, although it survived in certain privileged cases, or where custom was too strong to be checked by legislation, was largely discontinued and was discouraged by diocesan authorities. It revived in England during the dearth of priests caused by the great pestilence of 1349, and was very general during the fifteenth century; but by that time the distinction between canons and monks was almost obliterated, and it is probable that the institution of a canon to the vicarage of a church meant little more than that the endowment of the vicarage was ear-marked for his maintenance in his monastery, and that the cure of souls was served for a small wage by a stipendiary chaplain. The privilege, however, of serving parish churches, though generally withdrawn from Augustinians by Canon

Law, was constantly maintained by the order of Prémontré, which laid the strictest interpretation upon the Rule.

The founder of the Premonstratensian order, Norbert, a native of Xanten, underwent the experience, so usual at that epoch, of sudden conversion from a worldly life to evangelical penitence. As a secular canon at Xanten, and afterwards as an inmate of regular houses, his austerities and exhortations made him unpopular. Surrendering his benefices and despoiling himself of worldly goods, he journeyed to Saint-Gilles in Languedoc, and there obtained from Gelasius II a general licence to preach repentance. Travelling northward again with a few disciples, he found a friend in Bartholomew, Bishop of Laon, who offered him the church of Saint-Martin in his episcopal city. The canons of Saint-Martin, however, refused to conform to his strict way of life; and Bartholomew, unwilling to lose his services, gave him his choice of a site in the diocese on which he might found a new church. The place was found in 1120 at Prémontré, over which the Cistercian owners relinquished their claims. Here he and his followers determined to adopt the Rule of St Augustine, with a severity of observance strongly coloured by customs derived from Cîteaux. The constitution of the new order was on the model of the Charter of Charity, with its system of a limited monarchy, affiliated houses, and chapters-general at the parent monastery. In the white habit, in simplicity of dress, ritual, and architecture, in abstinence from flesh-meat and in long fasts, it followed the Cistercian example. Norbert and Bernard of Clairvaux, though not without differences of opinion, were closely united in friendship; and, if Bernard rejected Norbert's views on the reign of Anti-Christ as a present fact, they found common ground in their opposition to the more obvious danger represented by Abailard.

Some twenty years after the order of Prémontré had come into being, Laurence of Liège likened the two orders to the cherubim, spreading out their wings in the midst of the tabernacle on either side of the mercy-seat, and to the two witnesses of the Apocalypse, sent by God at the end of the world, and clothed in the sackcloth of penitence. The repression of the heresy of Tanchelin at Antwerp by Norbert brought the order into the Low Countries; and his promotion to the archbishopric of Magdeburg in 1126 ensured its success in Germany. In 1127, when Honorius II confirmed the order in its possessions, it had nine abbeys, Prémontré, Saint-Martin at Laon, Saint-Michael at Antwerp, two in the diocese of Münster, and one in each of the dioceses of Soissons, Liège, Mayence, and Metz. By 1144, ten years after Norbert's death, the nine had grown to seventy. Some nine years later, the order was to be found in almost every country in Europe and had reached Palestine. The eventual number of its houses is somewhat variously stated, and some estimates appear to be extravagant. The first English monastery, Newhouse in Lincolnshire, was colonised from Licques in the Boulonais in 1143; and eventually the order could count some thirty houses in England and Wales. The establishment of dependent priories, a natural consequence of the connexion of the canons with parish churches, marks a point of divergence from Cistercian custom. There were also several cathedral churches with Premonstratensian chapters, of which we have one British example at Whithorn in Galloway.

In another respect also this order, in its early days, presented a contrast to Cîteaux. The Fontevraldine experiment of monasteries combining monks with nuns was never contemplated by the Cistercians. Women, indeed, soon embraced the Cistercian interpretation of the Rule of St Benedict; and Stephen Harding founded the first Cistercian nunnery in 1120, at Tart in the diocese of Langres. Such nunneries took their place in the line of affiliation; but abbesses were not admitted to chapters-general, and, in time, the nunneries of certain countries held their own general chapters. In England no affiliation between Cistercian nunneries can be traced: these small and poor houses, like Benedictine nunneries, sprang up independently; their connexion with the order was simply their adoption of Cistercian customs; and, like Benedictine nunneries again, their visitors were the diocesan bishops. Where the original link to the main order was closer, the alliance tended to become little more than nominal; and the difficulty of supervision is illustrated by the fact that it was possible in 1210 for the Infanta Constance to usurp the functions of an abbot in the nunnery of las Huelgas at Burgos, founded by her father Alfonso VIII, blessing and instructing novices and hearing confessions. It was perhaps to meet the problems of the effective supervision of nunneries and the proper provision for them of priestly ministrations that the order of Prémontré, at its beginning, admitted women to its houses. It may be noticed, however, that the statute of the general chapter of 1138, which forbade the admission of women, appears to deal primarily with lay-sisters or *conversae,* and refers to separate nunneries of "singing sisters." Be this as it may, the custom of receiving women did not last long. Of the very few Premonstratensian nunneries in England, Irford in Lincolnshire appears to have been always regarded as a dependent cell of the abbey of Newhouse; and similarly the obscure nunnery at Guyzance in Northumberland was under the charge of the canons of Alnwick. The nuns of Swine in Yorkshire, regarded as a Cistercian house, were served by Premonstratensian canons during a considerable period.

The double system was also attempted by Augustinian canons. It is found for a short time in one small Yorkshire house, Marton in the forest of Galtres; but here the nuns, who followed Cistercian customs, were transferred to Moxby, not far away. Again, it played a part in the early constitution of the congregation of Arrouaise, which had some houses in England, and preserved a separate, though somewhat nominal, existence until the later part of the fifteenth century. In this instance, as in that of Prémontré, the system was not long-lived. Its success, however, was achieved in England, though upon a small scale, by the order of Sempringham, which was founded for nuns in 1131 by Gilbert, rector of Sempringham in Lincolnshire. He endeavoured without success in 1147 to induce the chapter-general of Cîteaux to receive his nuns into its order. St Bernard and Eugenius III, however, interested themselves in his venture; and it was with the aid of St Bernard that the Gilbertine statutes were compiled. Canons, following the Rule of St Augustine, and *conversi*, dwelling in a separate cloister, formed after this date an integral portion of each convent. Before Gilbert's death in 1188, thirteen houses had been founded, all in the dioceses of Lincoln and York. Subsequently, the number grew to twenty-six; but, although the double constitution of most of the earlier houses continued until the suppression, all but two of those established after 1188 were for canons only. The prior of the canons in each house, where they were limited to a maximum of thirteen, was the head of the monastery, in direct contrast to the Fontevraldine arrangement. The order was exempt from episcopal visitation and held its chapter-general yearly at Sempringham; but the office of master or general was not attached to the headship of one particular monastery, and might fall by election on any prior or canon who was placed on the list of suitable candidates. Outside England, the order possessed no house, with the exception of one short-lived establishment in Scotland; and its English houses were few outside Lincolnshire and Yorkshire. Cistercian nunneries to which *conversi* were attached were numerous in the same districts; and there are indications that for some of these, like Swine, already mentioned, a constitution resembling that of Sempringham may have been intended. In some, a monk or canon was frequently put in charge of affairs, with the title of master or warden.

At the Council of Troyes in 1128, St Bernard provided the initial suggestions for the Rule adopted by the Knights Templars, a community established at Jerusalem ten years earlier for the defence of pilgrims. The older military order, the Knights of the Hospital of St John of Jerusalem, had some years earlier adopted a Rule modelled on that of St Augustine, which in 1114 had been introduced into the chapter of the church of the Holy Sepulchre. Military orders, while adopting the three substantial vows, were not strictly monastic; the business of the knights was warfare against infidels and heathen, and the preceptories or commanderies in which they were dispersed in Europe and the East were either castles or small manor-houses with little likeness to monasteries. In 1147 the castle of Calatrava in Castile, captured from the Moors, was given to the Templars. They were unable to hold it, and for some years it was defended by Cistercians, chiefly *conversi*, from the Abbey of Fitero in Navarre. This was the origin of the Knights of Calatrava, whose order was approved by Alexander III in 1164, and in 1187 was submitted to the visitation of the Abbot of Morimond. From Calatrava arose the

Knights of Alcántara, formed by the reconstitution on Cistercian lines of an order founded earlier at Pereyro in the diocese of Ciudad Rodrigo. The Portuguese order, known from 1181 as the Knights of Avis, was under the visitation of the Cistercian Abbot of Tarouca; in 1213 it was subordinated to Calatrava, but re-established its independence after the victory of Aljubarrota in 1385. Two other Portuguese orders, those of the Wing of St Michael and of Christ, the latter founded in 1317, were under the jurisdiction of the Abbot of Alcobaça; while the Valencian Knights of Montesa in 1316 received their constitution from Calatrava and were submitted to Cistercian abbots. On the other hand, the Knights of Santiago, founded in 1171, adopted the Rule of St Augustine, which was also the model for the northern order of the Teutonic Knights and the order, which they absorbed, of the Knights of the Sword in Livonia. Various congregations of hospitallers, which afforded lodging to pilgrims on European roads, and in some cases had originally a semi-military character, such as the canons of Saint-Antoine in the diocese of Vienne and of Altopascio near Lucca, and the canons and knights of the united hospitals of the Holy Spirit at Montpellier and Santo Spirito in Sassia at Rome, followed the Augustinian Rule.

It may be noted here that the same Rule, applicable to many diverse communities, was employed by St Dominic in the constitution of the order of Friars Preachers, and was followed by the order of Hermits known popularly as Austin friars. Some orders also, which are occasionally reckoned among friars, were in practice hardly to be differentiated from Austin canons. Such was the Trinitarian order for the redemption of captives, founded at the close of the twelfth century by St John of Matha and St Felix of Valois; the minister and brethren of their chief English house, St Robert's at Knaresborough, were regarded as Austin canons, and were allowed to hold and serve parish churches. Likewise, the Bonshommes of Ashridge and Edington, of whose ultimate origin nothing is known, were not friars, as is sometimes said, but Austin canons; their name appears again in the fifteenth century in Portugal, with customs and a blue habit derived from the secular canons of San Giorgio in Alga at Venice, and was applied later to the Minims in France. Originally they were apparently a congregation which, observing the Rule of St Augustine, maintained a certain individuality in habit and customs.

From the days of Benedict of Aniane to the epoch of the Cistercian movement, the ideal at which monastic reformers aimed was uniformity of practice by means of the congregational system. In France and Italy, at frequent intervals, the customs of individual monasteries had been extended to others, until groups of houses, sometimes attaining to large numbers, had been formed. To speak of such groups as orders is hardly accurate; medieval references to the orders of Thiron or Arrouaise may be found, but the term can only be loosely applied to congregations whose polity was incomplete and the members of which had no very binding connexion with the house whose customs they followed. On the other hand, the congregations of Cluny and Cîteaux, with their definite organisation, became orders in the true sense of the word; Prémontré, Sempringham, the orders of hermits and anchorites who adopted the cenobite life in a modified form, were more than ordinary congregations. The history of the Cistercian order shews clearly how a body with a complete political system was capable of absorbing congregations whose constitution was less sharply defined. Nevertheless, these orders, governed by their own statutes, had no actual rule of their own. Their object was the strict observance of the Rule of St Benedict or of St Augustine; and outside them were the numerous monasteries which followed both these Rules, without ties which bound them to any congregation. The abbey of Saint-Denis might receive the customs of Cluny for a time; its great abbot, Suger, might undertake its reform as the result of the objurgations of St Bernard; but it remained a Benedictine house, without entering the Cluniac or Cistercian systems. Great English abbeys like Peterborough and Ramsey might enter into an alliance of mutual fraternity; the customs of Westminster might be nearly identical with those of St Augustine's at Canterbury; but such monasteries were autonomous bodies. It was also among these houses that the most influential and well-endowed monasteries were to be found in the later Middle Ages. If the wealth of Cluny was great, few of its dependencies could boast more than a modest income. Cistercian abbeys, to judge from the revenues of English houses at the suppression, were seldom well-to-do; and even Fountains or Furness could not compare in income with the great Benedictine houses. The riches of Augustinian canons, many of whose monasteries were small and poor, were certainly not excessive; and their ecclesiastical and political importance was small in proportion to their numbers. But such communities as Cirencester and Bridlington greatly exceeded any Premonstratensian house in wealth. While the papal grant of the use of the mitre to abbots and priors was a privilege which might be conferred irrespective of orders, it was to the heads of prominent autonomous houses that it usually fell. Again, though in the early days of the English parliament Cistercian and Premonstratensian abbots were summoned side by side with Benedictines and Augustinians, the eventual body of spiritual peers, in addition to the bishops, consisted, with some four exceptions, of the chief Benedictine abbots.

Speaking generally, Benedictine and Augustinian houses were subject to episcopal control. The local bishop confirmed elections of abbots and priors, and held periodical visitations. A few important monasteries were subject immediately to the Pope and had quasi-episcopal jurisdiction within their own liberties; in England, St Augustine's at Canterbury, St Alban's, St Edmund's at Bury, Westminster, and Evesham, of the Benedictines, and of the Augustinians, Waltham and St Botolph's at

Colchester, enjoyed exemption. The exercise of control, whether by papal legates or bishops, over monasteries in which the abbot or prior was supreme, was always a difficult problem. The head of the house was a constant factor in its administration; the visitor was an occasional intruder, not always welcome, and sometimes resented by communities which, like St Mary's at York and Glastonbury, attempted more than once to assert that they were exempt. His injunctions had statutory force; but bishops often found that, between visitations, their most careful provisions for the good order of a monastery had been treated as a dead letter.

The famous injunctions addressed by Innocent III to the Abbot and convent of Subiaco, and preserved in the body of the Canon Law, give a comprehensive view of the breaches of monastic order which visitors discovered early in the thirteenth century; and their time-honoured language was employed again and again, during the next three centuries, to clothe similar ordinances where they were necessary. To remedy such irregularities, Innocent III, at the Lateran Council of 1215, resorted to an application of the congregational system. Reform which could not be successfully effected by the *ordinarius loci* might be achieved by a closer association of monasteries. Triennial chapters for Benedictines and Augustinians respectively were established in every kingdom or separate province, at which, on the model of Cistercian chapters-general, statutes were to be drawn up and reforms undertaken, under the presidency of abbots elected by the assembly. Visitors were to be appointed by the chapters, not to supersede the ordinary visitor, but to ensure the supervision of monasteries by a central authority of their own.

At the same time, while the help of Cistercian abbots was recommended in the formation of provincial chapters, no attempt at a subversion of the autonomy of monasteries was contemplated. A federal bond was established in each province, for the sake of greater uniformity; but there was no permanent president or general of the federation, no affiliation to any particular house whose abbot was endowed with primacy. No effort was made to check local customs. The provincial chapter added a new feature to the recognised order of things; the best prospect of its success was the hope that its meetings might do something to raise and maintain at a high level the standard of life prescribed by both Rules. It is possible to criticise the constitutions of Cluny and Cîteaux as foreign to the principle of self-government implied in the Rule of St Benedict. The decree of the Lateran Council, on the other hand, contained no revolutionary element.

Of the internal state of Benedictine and Augustinian houses in England during the thirteenth century we have abundant information in the episcopal registers of its second half; while the *Regestrum Visitationum* of Eudes Rigaud, in the middle of the century, gives a detailed picture of the life of Norman monasteries. The evidential value of episcopal

injunctions has often been disputed, on the ground of the formal language
in which they are cast, and in the absence of reports of the visitations
after which they were issued. More material is available now than formerly
for the critical study of their texts; and it is impossible to avoid the
conclusion that their language refers to faults which had actually been
discovered in the monasteries to which they were addressed. Precautionary
injunctions to a monastery against abuses from which it was entirely free
exist only in imaginations which picture medieval institutions as superior
to the ordinary rules of common sense. There is abundant proof that
these injunctions were composed, as Rigaud wrote of the typical series
directed to the monks of Saint-Ouen at Rouen in December 1249,
secundum ea que inventa fuerunt per visitacionem nostram ibidem.

The decrees of the Lateran Council were followed within little more
than a quarter of a century by the statutes of Gregory IX for the reform
of the Benedictine order. These, involving detailed regulations on points
of discipline and prescribing fixed penalties for their breach, were certainly
not very sedulously regarded. Rigaud, in his visitations, frequently found
that monasteries were without copies of them; and in 1253 the Abbot
and convent of Jumièges, complaining to Innocent IV that they found
the difficulties in maintaining the order of their house much increased by
the rigid wording of the Gregorian statutes, were dispensed from observing
their contents, so far as they were not of the substance of the Rule.
Such a permission might lend itself to a very liberal interpretation. Any
attempt, indeed, to curb laxness of discipline in monasteries by hard-and-
fast legislation was impossible. The natural tendency of establishments
of old foundation was to that type of life which the monks of Fountains
in 1132 had found inadequate for their spiritual needs at York. It was
only here and there that visitors discovered monasteries which were in a
really scandalous condition. Selby, in the second half of the thirteenth
century, under the rule of unsatisfactory abbots, was anything but a
pattern of a respectable and God-fearing life to the neighbouring parts
of Yorkshire. Some of the nunneries of the diocese of Rouen had succumbed to the temptations to which undefended communities of women
were peculiarly liable. Other instances could be cited; but the typical
faults of monasteries were failures to comply with the standard demanded
by the Rule. Heads of houses, moved by family considerations or other
inducements, admitted unsuitable persons to the novitiate and profession.
Accounts were negligently rendered; the common seal of the house was
not securely kept; slackness in the services of the church was observable;
silence was not kept in cloister and the common buildings; fasting and
the prohibition of meat were constantly disregarded. The conduct of the
scattered cells or priories attached to the greater abbeys was a difficult
problem. These, for the most part, were small establishments without
conventual buildings, committed to the charge of a prior and one or two
monks, whose main duty was that of looking after the local estates of

their house and collecting their fruits. Such, with few exceptions, were the numerous priories in England possessed by French monasteries. Sometimes, in direct contravention of the Rule, a single religious without a companion was in charge of a priory; and, even where the requisite pair of monks was in residence, fasts were not kept and flesh-meat was in general use.

Monastic rules, however, are counsels of perfection; and St Benedict had foreseen that his disciples would have to reckon with the constant recalcitrance of human nature. It was inevitable that some monasteries should sink into decay and abandon discipline altogether, and that small breaches of the Rule should become habitual in others. Of the crowds of men and women who flocked into monasteries during the periods of Cluniac and Cistercian reform, many were doubtless prompted by a merely temporary emotion to escape from the world to refuges in the quiet of which they hoped to save their souls, while to others the comparative ease of a life of prayer may have outweighed its prospective hardships. It was certain, at any rate, that no monastery could hope to be without some unfit persons, whom it would tax the energy of the abbot to control. Where the abbot himself was ineffective or engrossed with temporal affairs, the sin of *acedia* was sure to make headway. Grumbling and internal discord were a sure evidence of decline; if, as Rigaud found, the custom of making open complaints in chapter had fallen into disuse, private animosities flourished instead; and where, as at Bardney, in the last years of the thirteenth century, a convent was openly at war with a tactless and overbearing abbot, and the strife became matter of common talk, or where, as at Fountains in the same period, the house was so deeply in debt that the Crown found it necessary to appoint an official receiver, the reputation of a monastery was seriously injured.

The growth of the mendicant orders in the thirteenth century diverted popular enthusiasm from the monastic orders proper. While the Cistercians continued, year after year, to found new monasteries, their rate of progress was much slower than it had been at first; and the other orders were much less active. They had become part of the established condition of things; and the benefactions which had placed them in possession of lands and churches were less numerous than formerly, and were being diverted into other channels. The popularity of the friars was not likely to leave the conduct of the older orders without criticism: it is significant that the two visitors of monasteries at this time from whom we have the most ample records, Archbishops Rigaud and Pecham, were both Franciscans whose zeal in commenting upon monastic abuses can hardly, with the best intentions, have been free from the prejudices of their early training.

By this time, great and far-reaching reforms like those of Cluny and Cîteaux were no longer to be contemplated. The unsettled state of society which had contributed to their success was at an end; with the growth of national institutions and sentiment, the development of another world-wide order, breaking down the barriers of race under the protection of a universal Church, was as impossible as a new crusade. The old quarrel between the keys and the sword was to enter upon a new phase as a merely political contest, the points at issue in which were to be debated by jurists and publicists, and were not to be decided by the missionaries of religion. Henceforward, new orders were of a purely local character, and their outposts beyond the country in which they took birth were few. Reform, moreover, acquired a tendency to lay stress on certain definite points, such as strict enclosure and the change of heads of houses at regularly recurring intervals, which indicate a movement in a different direction from that of the older reforms.

From time to time, new movements, somewhat on the lines of Camaldoli and Vallombrosa, achieved some success in Italy. In the early part of the twelfth century the hermit John of Matera founded the order of Pulsano in Apulia; and his friend and companion, William of Vercelli, the founder of Monte Vergine, became the first general of an order which, with the encouragement of King Roger, was well received in Sicily. The monasteries founded in Calabria and the Basilicata from Flora, the retreat of the famous hermit Gioacchino (Joachim) before 1192, were affected by the influence of the Cistercian monasteries in which he had lived, and interpreted the Rule of St Benedict with such austerity that Gregory IX forbade migrations from them to Cistercian houses, as infringing the prohibition to monks to pass from one order to another of less strict observance. The Rule of St Benedict was also adopted in 1231 at Monte Fano by Silvestro Gozzolini, the founder of the Silvestrines or Blue Benedictines. Rather more than twenty years later, another order of Benedictinised hermits gathered together under Peter of Morrone. After his election to the Papacy in 1294, his monks took the name of Celestines. During his short and inglorious tenure of his office as Pope, he introduced Celestines into Monte Cassino, from which they were quickly removed by Boniface VIII. The order, however, survived its founder and established houses in France and Germany. All these orders were Neapolitan in origin; but in 1313 another was born further north, at Acona in the diocese of Arezzo, to which Bernardo Tolomei and two Sienese noblemen retired. This was the beginning of the strict order of Monte Oliveto, the name given to Acona from the olive-groves which recalled the memory of our Lord's agony in Gethsemane. It had a considerable vogue in Italy, and was permitted to receive members from other orders, the Carthusian excepted.

A comprehensive attempt at monastic reform was made by the Cistercian Benedict XII, formerly Abbot of Fontfroide in the diocese of Narbonne. His constitutions for the Cistercian order, *Fulgens sicut stella*, issued in July 1335, are chiefly remarkable for their regulations against the indiscriminate use of flesh-meat, which had been introduced into certain monasteries, on the plea of custom, upon certain days in the week. It was now banished from the refectory, but permitted, with no very stringent restrictions, in the common hall of the infirmary and at the abbot's table in his lodging; while all flesh-meat was to be cooked in the special kitchen attached to the infirmary. Benedict also attempted to check the construction of private rooms or cells, which led to irregularities. A separate lodging for the abbot had become, in all orders, a permissible transgression of the Rule, due to the necessities of his office; and separate chambers in the infirmary were a convenience that could not easily be disallowed. The division of the dormitory into cubicles was absolutely prohibited; but the prohibition, if observed for a time, was soon disregarded. Clauses against private allowances to monks and the distribution of dividends between the abbot and convent were directed against the growth of *proprietas*; and safeguards were enforced for the financial administration of monasteries.

The constitutions for Black monks (Benedictines and Cluniacs), issued in 1336, and for Austin canons, in 1339, re-enacted the order for triennial chapters, establishing thirty-nine Benedictine and twenty-two Augustinian provinces. These constitutions formed the chief basis on which later visitors of monasteries framed their enquiries. With regard to such customs as the use of flesh-meat their provisions were cautious and lenient; but cells in the dormitory, except for the old and infirm, were as strictly forbidden as in Cistercian houses. The maintenance of the common life and the expulsion of customs tending to the acquisition of private property were insisted upon. Secular persons were, as far as possible, to be banished from the company of the brethren; and monks and canons were not permitted to go outside their monasteries without reasonable cause or without a companion. The integrity of monastic property might not be broken without the deliberation and consent of the whole or a majority of the community; the danger of indiscriminate or improperly conducted sales and leases of land was, as contemporary and later documents shew, one that could not be too sedulously anticipated. While, especially in the case of canons, residence outside monasteries on benefices or in priories was recognised as part of the order of things, it was essential that the numbers of each community should be kept up to their full strength. For monasteries which might decay in observance or in financial resources, regulations were made for bringing in new blood in the first case, and for union with other houses in the second.

Most important are the long and full chapters providing for the support of student monks and canons at universities. Each house of twenty members was to send one; each of above twenty, one or more, according to its resources. Already the Benedictine house at Oxford, Gloucester Hall, had been founded for English monks; and, after the publication of these constitutions, the house for Durham monks came into existence. At Cambridge, no special Benedictine college was founded till the next century; but monks from various East Anglian houses went there earlier, and Benedictines from Norwich, for example, were to be found at Edmund Gonville's Hall of the Annunciation. If these provisions were adhered to, the ordinary monastery of any size would usually contain a few monks who had made a study of theology or Canon Law under qualified teachers; and in later years we frequently find abbots and priors with university degrees, such as William Welles, Abbot of St Mary's, York, who was one of the English envoys to the Council of Basle. Welles and two other abbots of St Mary's with similar qualifications were promoted to bishoprics; St Albans, Gloucester, and other houses also furnished bishops from among their abbots. On the other hand, fifteenth-century visitors in England found this statute often neglected; and in 1438 there occurs the case of a young monk of Spalding who, sent to the university, found his means of support withheld, and was obliged to maintain himself by pawning the books which he had borrowed for his studies from the convent library. Similarly, the constitution which ordained that a teacher should be provided in the monastery for novices and others who wished to learn was often imperfectly observed. If there were learned men in monasteries in the later Middle Ages, it is impossible to avoid the conclusion that monasteries as a whole were not homes of learning. The remarkable activity of monastic chroniclers ceases, with a few exceptions, as the fourteenth century advances; and, if libraries were still enriched with manuscripts and churches with splendid office-books like the Westminster and Sherborne missals, there is no indication that the gifts of writing and illuminating were general. The detailed reports of visitations of monasteries by Bishop Alnwick of Lincoln (1436–1449) leave the impression that learning in religious houses was somewhat deficient. In only three houses was a monk or canon invited to deliver the visitation sermon; and it is significant that when some monks at Bardney wished to draw up a charter, for which they had fraudulently procured the common seal, none of them knew how to do it, and the blank parchment had to be sent to a notary in Lincoln. Neither the Benedictine constitutions nor visitation documents contain information which warrants the supposition, often stated as a fact, that monasteries undertook the education of the children of the neighbourhood. Both are explicit upon the undesirability of admitting secular persons into a monastery; episcopal visitors sedulously strove to limit the admission of children as boarders in nunneries, which was a source of pecuniary profit to the house, as such children generally came from well-to-do families, and afforded more distraction to the nuns than benefit to their young lodgers. So far as the maintenance and education of poor children in the almonries of monasteries was concerned, the custom was gradually falling into disuse in the fifteenth century. Alnwick found, in more than one instance, that their numbers were smaller than those which monasteries could afford to support; and the few maintained at Leicester simply acted as errand-boys for the canons.

Visitation reports and injunctions also disclose that the Benedictine constitutions were constantly transgressed by convents in need of ready money. The bad habit of granting corrodies or allowances in money and victuals to secular persons was forced upon monasteries by patrons who wished to provide for clerks or old servants at a minimum of expense to themselves. But corrodies could also be sold to applicants, and thus a convent was often burdened with a number of lodgers and pensioners who had paid a lump sum for their privileges and became the actual profiters by the speculation. Property suffered by sales and disadvantageous leases; timber was cut down and sold before it was ready for felling. In these circumstances, monastic finance became a difficult problem; the *status domus* often shewed a deficit, and efforts to cut down expenses, where habits of life had become fixed, were unavailing. The evidence shews that the management of finance constantly fell into the hands of a few, who did much as they chose; a masterful abbot or prior could obtain possession of the purse of the convent, or a weak one could leave it to the control of obedientiaries who squandered money and rendered few or no accounts. Petitions for the appropriation of churches contain statements of poverty brought about by the decay of property, rises in prices, heavy taxation, and the exercise of the duty of hospitality to all and sundry, a duty which was profitable where a monastery was a centre of pilgrimage, but irksome where it merely was a resort of casual travellers. But there is no doubt that poverty was the result of careless finance, and, as was natural, brought general negligence and other evils in its train. Even in well-managed and prosperous monasteries, the state of things offered a strange contrast to the requirements of the Rule. The appropriation of a considerable part of the common fund to the abbot, who kept a large household of knights, squires, and grooms, and had his own staff of obedientiaries chosen from the monks, his frequent journeys to London and his manor-houses, were incentives to his monks to live luxuriously, to acquire private property, and to stray outside their house at pleasure. Too much stress may be laid upon the faults of individuals; for a visitor's business was to lay stress on such faults, and he did not waste time in praising cloistered virtue. It was rarely in England that a great monastery was found in such a lamentable state of disorder as existed at Ramsey in 1437, though serious irregularities in smaller houses were not uncommon. It may certainly, however, be said that the patriarchs of western monachism, if they could have visited such eminent houses as Westminster, Durham, or Glastonbury in the fourteenth or fifteenth centuries, would hardly have concluded that they were fulfilling their vocation.

In England, however, from which these general considerations are drawn, conditions were comparatively favourable. If the Benedictine constitutions were not carefully observed, triennial chapters of monks and canons were held, and there was no general call for monastic reform. The pestilences of the fourteenth century worked havoc in many houses and depreciated the value of their property; at this date it seems certain that the great mortality among Cistercian *conversi* eliminated this element from the order, and necessitated the leasing of granges to farmers or their cultivation by hired labour. On the other hand, during the Hundred Years' War, the wisdom of Cistercian polity was exemplified; while Cluniac priories, in common with the small alien cells, were seized by the Crown as members of a foreign order, Cistercian abbeys, with their less exacting bond to Cîteaux, were left untouched. The orthodox Lancastrian kings favoured monasteries, and, even in suppressing alien priories and granting them to non-monastic foundations, they were careful to distinguish between conventual priories, which were preserved, and those which were merely manors belonging to foreign houses. The Wars of the Roses, if they did not encourage monastic discipline, at any rate spared monasteries. Even in face of the serious charges laid to the account of the monks of St Albans by Archbishop Morton, it cannot be said that, in the period immediately preceding the suppression, decline was more evident than it had been at a much earlier date. Abbots were still regulars; the custom, so disastrous in other countries, of granting abbeys *in commendam*, never prevailed in England to any noticeable extent. At the same time, the foundation of monasteries, rare in the fourteenth century, ceased altogether in the fifteenth. Of the few monasteries founded after the beginning of the reign of Edward III, the most important were the seven Charterhouses added to the two previously existing. William de la Pole hesitated over the form of his proposed foundation at Hull, which his son Michael gave to the Carthusians. It was in the prayers of this strictest of orders, living apart from the world in silence and poverty, that the courtiers of the last Plantagenet kings saw the best assurance of salvation. The last monasteries of any importance to be founded in England were Henry V's Charterhouse of Shene and the double house of nuns and canons of the Brigitine order at Syon.

In France, the disasters of the Hundred Years' War, with the prevalence of anarchy, not only destroyed monastic discipline, but left monasteries incapable of recovery. Similarly, in Italy and Germany, disturbed by party factions and intestine warfare, and shaken by the strife of Pope and Emperor and by the great schism in the Church, monastic life was at a low ebb, the Benedictine constitutions were a dead letter, and monasteries ruled by commendatory abbots were virtually secularised. Enthusiasts, however, were not wanting in Italy who sought to establish congregations on lines of strict observance of the Benedictine Rule. Carthusians and Olivetans still set an example of discipline; and Cistercians seem for a time to have remained superior to the general apathy. The small order of Corpus Christi, founded at Gualdo in Umbria in 1318, established the abbey of Santa Maria dei Campi near Foligno in 1373, to which its priories were subordinated. Approved by Gregory XI and by Boniface IX it was affiliated to the Cistercians in 1393. Twenty years later it was freed from this nominal dependence, and, preserving Cistercian customs, remained independent until, late in the sixteenth century, it was merged in the order of Monte Oliveto.

The ruin and revival of the older monasteries is well illustrated by the history of the abbey of Santa Giustina at Padua, which in 1407 contained only three religious. Gregory XII gave it *in commendam* to the Cardinal of Bologna, who attempted to restore it with the aid of Olivetans. The old monks, however, were brought back by the influence of the Venetian republic; and in 1408 Lodovico Barbo, Prior of the canons of San Giorgio in Alga, was appointed Abbot, became a Benedictine, and reinforced the house with two of his canons and two Camaldolese from Murano. From this germ began the reformed congregation of Santa Giustina, which, coming into life in 1421, held its first chapter-general in 1424, and gradually included the older Benedictine monasteries of Italy within its limits. This congregation, which, after the union of Monte Cassino with it in 1504, adopted the title Cassinese, marks the beginning of modern monasticism. Its fundamental principle was essentially different from that of the provincial federations ordered by the Benedictine constitutions. Its chapters were not mere assemblies of a consultative body charged with the preservation of unity between bodies which, for all practical purposes, were self-ruling; they were meetings of a central executive which controlled the congregation as though it were a single monastery. So far, it resembled the Cluniac system; but that system, with a permanent autocrat at its head, was open to abuse, especially in an age when the custom of granting the dignity of abbot *in commendam* to some wealthy ecclesiastic who was not even a monk had done so much to disorganise regular observance. The congregation changed its president, abbots, and other officers at every chapter. Thus not only the individuality of monasteries was suppressed, but their right of free election was taken away; the supremacy of the abbot over the Benedictine house was practically abandoned, and the abbots became merely the obedientiaries of the general chapter.

While the congregational system involved this important change in the Benedictine system of government, it supplied an adequate method for dealing with the critical condition of monastic life in an age which called for wholesale reform. Its rise was contemporary with the conciliar movement; and it was the Pope elected by the Council of Constance who, at the request of Albert of Austria, sent commissaries to reform the monasteries in his dominions. From this source came the reform of Melk in the diocese of Passau, which, beginning in 1418, spread to other Austrian houses. Neither Melk, however, nor Castel in the diocese of Eichstädt, which set the example of reform in Bavaria, organised congregations on the strict model; and their position with regard to the monasteries which imitated them resembled that of the so-called heads of congregations at an earlier date. The reform of Bursfeld in the duchy of Brunswick led in 1464 to the establishment of the first regular congregation in Germany.

One of the most remarkable reforms of this later period sprang from the house of canons regular at Windesheim near Zwolle in Friesland. Its founder, Florens Radewin, was a disciple of Gerhard Groot of Deventer; he after 1374 had gathered round him a body of clerks who, without formal monastic organisation, were called the Brethren of the Common Life and are famous in the annals of Christian mysticism. After Gerhard's death in 1384 his work was carried on by Radewin; and the foundation of Windesheim shortly afterwards fulfilled his ultimate aims. In 1395 a congregation was formed consisting of Windesheim and three other houses; and statutes were promulgated in 1402. In this union the autonomy of the constituent members was respected; the prior-superior of Windesheim was merely a moderator, nor was the expedient of annual or triennial elections of priors adopted. The congregation, however, held tenaciously to uniformity of habit and customs, and was slow to admit monasteries which did not readily conform to its rules. It was only by a compromise on the question of habit that the monastery of Neuss, with some allied houses, was united to Windesheim in 1430. Its influence, however, worked wonders in the Low Countries and in Germany; and one of its sons, Johann Busch, was among the most prominent reformers of claustral discipline in his age. Of the difficulties with which he had to contend and the stern determination with which he met them he has left us a full record. In house after house of canons and nuns, in which the substantial vows were neglected or wholly abandoned, he met with fear, suspicion, or active hostility. His efforts, however, attended with not a little danger, had at least a temporary success, and were undertaken with the concurrence of diocesan authorities who recognised the importance of the restoration of order in the cloister. The congregation of Windesheim maintained the high spiritual ideals of its founder; in some of its houses a Carthusian severity of life was pursued. Groenendael in Brabant, of which the famous mystic Jan Ruysbroek had been prior in the fourteenth century, joined its stricter observance in 1448; and the reputed author of the *Imitatio Christi* was a canon of its monastery at Kempen.

The house of Jesus of Bethlehem at Syon, already mentioned, belonged to an order, established in Sweden in the middle of the fourteenth century, which was in part an Augustinian reform. The order of the Saviour, founded by the Swedish princess St Bridget, was the last attempt at a community of both sexes in one monastery. Side by side with a cloister of sixty nuns there was another, in which thirteen priest-canons, four deacons, and eight *conversi* lived. Thus, as in previous attempts of a similar kind, the spiritual and temporal needs of the nuns were supplied by a male convent; the abbess, as at Fontevrault, being the head of the whole community. The order was approved by Urban V; and, although its monasteries were not numerous, the magnificent endowment of Syon, which at the suppression was among the most prosperous of English houses, gives it a special importance.

No congregational movement was initiated by the Benedictines and canons regular of England before the suppression; and the events of the Reformation period put an end to the congregation of Bursfeld in Germany. In Spain, the gradual growth of a Benedictine congregation proceeded from the priory of San Benito el Real at Valladolid, founded by John I of Castile towards the close of the fourteenth century, which attracted other monasteries into union with it. The congregation, with its system of perpetual enclosure and frequent change of priors, was recognised by Innocent VIII, and the Prior of Valladolid was made an abbot by Alexander VI. If the Papacy throughout the fifteenth century was more remarkable for political than for religious zeal, successive Popes at any rate countenanced the restoration of order in monasteries. Eugenius IV, in his early years one of the founders of the reformed house of secular canons at San Giorgio in Alga, displayed an activity in furthering reform which contrasted favourably with the divided efforts of the Council of Basle to assert its authority against the Pope's. The zeal of Ambrogio of Camaldoli, the faithful henchman of Eugenius, restored discipline in his own order and was used to stir up the flagging energy of others. In 1444 Eugenius, acting upon information from France and Spain, urged the Cistercian chapter-general to take measures to combat slackness. The Cistercians had revised their constitutions in 1350; but growing disunion was felt in their ranks, and in 1426 the forward spirits of the order in Spain had formed a separate congregation under the headship of the Abbot of Poblet, which was eventually recognised by one chapter-general and disowned by the next. The arrest of decline was impossible; when, in 1475, Sixtus IV revived the constitution of Benedict XII against the promiscuous use of flesh-meat, the power of dispensation permitted to abbots led to the complete loss of that uniformity of practice which was a substantive principle of the order. In 1485 came the decision of the chapter-general to allow flesh-meat on three days a week in a separate refectory as the general practice. This concession, however, was no avenue to reform; and in 1487 Innocent VIII issued fresh constitutions for the improvement of monasteries. Early in 1494 a number of French abbots met at the college of the order in Paris and drew up articles of reform which shew that its shortcomings were those habitual in monasteries of other bodies. Monks roamed outside their houses in secular habits; within the monastery they lived too comfortably; the gates were not closed at the proper hours; there was unchecked communication with secular persons, and women were allowed to enter the cloister. It is significant of the strength of the opposition that these articles were quashed on petition by the Parlement of Dijon, on the ground that they had not been drawn up at Cîteaux, within its jurisdiction. The order was saved from extinction only by the perseverance of the Spanish congregation in face of rebuffs, and by the activity of a group of new monasteries in the Low Countries and western Germany. In 1497 a congregation was formed in Tuscany and Lombardy; and, in the century following the Council of Trent, the congregational system was extended to the whole order.

To the same period belongs the extension of the system to France; for, although sporadic reforms had taken place there about the end of the fifteenth century, like that of Chézal-Benoît in the diocese of Bourges, recognised in 1516 as the head of a small congregation, the sufferings of France during the long wars with England, and the civil strife of Burgundians and Armagnacs, had vitally injured her religious life. The growth, however, of later congregations is beyond the scope of this chapter. The Reformation, bringing complete extinction to the monasteries of countries and provinces which rejected the papal authority, put an end to the medieval monastic system. Monasticism, in the later centuries of the Middle Ages, had lost touch with the main currents of progress; once the vital force at the back of ecclesiastical reform, it had now become merely a department of ecclesiastical affairs which exercised little influence. It had long lost the position in which it could control the Papacy and command the reverence of the secular power. Such incidents as the suppression of the Templars, the seizure of the alien priories in England, the summary dissolution of small and inactive houses by papal bulls, were evidences of monastic weakness and precedents for wholesale acts of confiscation and destruction. While Henry VIII took advantage of his breach with Rome to put an end to the English monasteries, the monasteries and military orders of Spain were equally at the mercy of the most Catholic king, if it had been to his advantage to pursue the same line of policy. The monastery, however, is an institution which in every age meets a certain class of human needs. Though deprived of its old prominence, it survived the troubles of the Reformation. Under the fostering care of national congregations, it entered upon a new phase of existence; and, if it was still subject to the inevitable alternation of lapse and revival, such bodies as the congregation of Saint-Maur were still to exhibit a pious fervour comparable to that of Cluny and Cîteaux in their best days, and a learning which more than equalled the best traditions of Monte Cassino and Saint-Victor. If the ordinary medieval monastery has been somewhat overrated as a centre of learning and education, the later achievements of Benedictinism in this direction have renewed the lustre of the age when religious houses, in the midst of a chaotic society, were chief among the formative influences of European civilisation.

CHAPTER XXI.

ROMAN AND CANON LAW IN THE MIDDLE AGES.

I.

THE age of the Crusades was also the age of the revival of legal studies in Italy. These studies were devoted chiefly to two legal systems closely related to each other not only in their historical origin and evolution but also in their form and content. Neither the Civil Law nor the Canon Law had originated in the medieval centuries immediately preceding the Italian legal renascence. Both of these systems were outgrowths of the age of antiquity; both of them were integral parts of the civilisation which the Middle Ages inherited from the ancient world. The Civil Law—the medieval Roman Law—was a system created by the ancient Romans and transmitted by them to the peoples of the East and the West; while the Canon Law, an adaptation and expansion of the Roman Law to meet the purposes of the Christian Church, was in its origins and earlier development not less a creation of the Roman legal genius than the Civil Law itself.

At the time, however, when by slow processes of movement and change ancient society was gradually transforming itself into medieval society, these two bodies of law were in different stages of evolution. The Roman Law had already passed the period of its maturity in the time of the classical jurists and was in process of adaptation to meet the altered social conditions of the world. Canon Law, on the other hand, was still in the earlier stages of its growth. This difference between the state of Roman Law and the state of Canon Law at the beginning of the medieval epoch—a difference marked by the character of the sources and the literature of the two systems and by the scope and manner of the application of these legal materials to human affairs—determined in many ways the main lines of their separate but related histories in the Middle Age. In the case of the Roman Law the work of the medieval centuries was to adapt, modify, and apply a system which the Romans of antiquity had already perfected; while in the case of the Canon Law, on the other hand, the work of the Middle Age was to develop, expand, and apply a system which the ancient Roman world had only begun to evolve for the needs of the youthful Church.

The main purpose of the present chapter is to sketch in outline the history of these two systems of law throughout the medieval age. Two preliminary matters must engage our attention, however, at the very outset of the enquiry. It will be necessary, in the first place, to observe the processes of the inner growth and the world-wide spread of the Roman Law in the age of antiquity, for this earlier development lies at the very basis of the history of the Roman system in the Middle Ages; and, at the same time, we must gain some notion of the nature of the Roman legal materials that were to influence the growth of law in medieval times. A second subject of study, not less important than the first, is the history of the origins of Canon Law in the age of antiquity, and of its general development and its sources in the periods of the Middle Age. Not until we understand these two preliminary matters can we proceed to the study of our main subject, the history of the Roman and Canon Laws in the Later Roman Empire of the East, in the Germanic kingdoms of the West during the early medieval centuries, and in the several national areas—Italy, Spain, France, Germany, and England—of the later Middle Age. What were the processes whereby the Roman and Canon Laws spread throughout the world—in the East as well as in the West—during the medieval epoch? What was the result of the contact of these laws with other legal systems? Where and how were the two Romanic systems studied; and what was the influence of such studies? These are some of the historical problems with which we shall be concerned.

We shall not, therefore, restrict our attention to the age of the Crusades and the revival of juristic studies. To do so would result in the loss of perspective and conceal from our gaze all but a small part of the complete picture. The complete picture, however, must be at best but a rough sketch, an impressionist design. The sources and the literature of the history of Roman and Canon Law in ancient and medieval times fill thousands of volumes. Only a few of these can be drawn upon for the purposes of this chapter[1]. Only a few of the rich and varied colours of medieval legal life can be spread upon our canvas. All but the barest outlines must be left undrawn.

Let us begin with the two preliminary subjects which are to furnish us with the background of our picture.

II.

The history of the evolution of the Roman Law and of its world-wide extension can be traced in unbroken continuity throughout twenty-five centuries. In one sense the ancient history of this greatest of all the legal systems of antiquity reaches its end when the decay of the classical jurisprudence set in, as a part of the general decline of the Roman world, about the middle of the third century after Christ. In another sense, however, the ancient period of Roman legal history does not finally terminate until the completion and promulgation of Justinian's

---

[1] The bibliography to this chapter contains certain of the more important sources and writings.

codification in the first part of the sixth century. The transition from ancient to medieval times was in fact a slow process of centuries; and in no respect is this more noticeable than in the history of the law. Legal decay, adaptation, and transformation were at work in the regions of the West long before the time of Justinian; and from his time onwards these processes also became a marked feature of the legal history of the East. In legal history the chronological boundaries of great eras cannot be marked out with nicety and precision. Transition sometimes takes decades or even centuries.

Let us for the moment fasten our attention upon the authenticated evolution of Roman Law during the ten centuries before the death of Justinian; for the first three hundred years of the city we are without adequate historical evidence. Within this long period of a thousand years[1] the customs of a small city-community were transformed into an elaborate system of justice and extended by conquest to the ancient world. During the epoch from the establishment of the Republic until the subjugation of central and southern Italy, the composite of *fas, ius,* and *boni mores* which characterised the ancient custom of the regal period became the *ius civile,* the *ius proprium civium Romanorum,* and was codified in the *Lex XII Tabularum* (B.C. 451). The latter half of the Republican age was marked by the growth of the *ius gentium* and the *ius honorarium.* Various influences affected both the form and the substance of the law; and among them were provincial conquests, the growth of commerce and the influx of foreigners, the institution of the peregrin praetorship, the simplification of procedure, and the introduction of new remedies under the Aebutian law. The spread of literature and philosophy, as well as the decline of religion and morals, also influenced the law. The growth of the law—which in this period was composed of *ius civile, ius gentium,* and *ius honorarium*—owed little to legislation; but the law's debt to custom, to the edicts of magistrates, and to professional jurisprudence, was very great. The centuries of the Empire before the time of Diocletian were the age of the *ius naturale* and the maturity of Roman jurisprudence; while the age of codification stretched from Diocletian to Justinian—an age when the Emperors were supreme as the sole legislators and when Christianity, as the religion of the State, exerted a powerful influence on legal growth. Within these chief periods of Roman legal history, so briefly sketched, the law was not only altered in its form and substance, but it was gradually diffused throughout all the provinces of the Empire. The inner growth of the law as a system of justice and its world-wide extension went hand in hand as aspects of one and the same historical process. Certain features of this process demand our attention.

Both Roman policy and Roman Law recognised the personality of

---

[1] Details will be found in the two volumes of Karlowa's *Römische Rechtsgeschichte.* A shorter account of Roman legal history is given by Puchta in the first volume of his *Institutionen.*

law as a fundamental principle[1]. By conquest Rome brought within her
dominion many non-Roman peoples in all parts of the ancient world,
peoples who at the time they became subject to Rome were already living
under their own national customs and laws. On the principle of the personality of law the Roman *ius civile* applied only to Roman citizens; while
the *peregrini*, even under Roman rule, continued to live according to
their native systems of law. Thus, there existed under Roman political
sway many diverse legal systems, of which the Roman *ius civile* was only
one; and the Roman Law did not, therefore, dominate the entire territory
of the Roman State from the beginning. Indeed, it was only gradually,
by a long process of development, that the Roman system displaced native
legal institutions in the provinces; and even in the end it did not everywhere supersede them. In many parts of the Empire native systems
persisted and survived Roman rule; they contributed their share to the
development of law in the Middle Ages.

The existence within the Roman domain of many diverse bodies of
law—the *ius civile* of the Romans and the laws of the *peregrini*—raised
the problem as to which of these several national laws should be applied
to the relations of Romans with peregrins and of peregrins of one nationality with those of another. The Romans solved this problem, not by
the development of a system similar to modern international private law,
or the conflict of laws, but by the evolution of a third body of law
different from either one of the national laws of the two parties. This
third body of law was known as the *ius gentium*. Gaius states that the
ius gentium was the law common to all peoples; and the words of Gaius
find their place in due time in the Digest[2]. But this theory of the nature
of the *ius gentium* does not correspond with the facts, for in truth the
ius gentium was a branch or part of the Roman Law itself: it was that
part of the Roman system which had been evolved, both by the edicts of
the Roman magistrates possessing jurisdiction over peregrins and by the
work of the Roman jurists, to regulate the inter-relations of persons of
different nationality. The principles of the *ius gentium* were drawn in
part from the Roman *ius civile*; in part they were new principles, distinct
from Roman *ius civile*, derived in large measure from the national laws
of the peregrins, but shaped, both in form and spirit, in accordance with
Roman ideas of justice. The *ius gentium* embodied the newer legal ideas,
and at many points it was in conflict with the principles of the ancient
ius civile. Applied in the first instance to the cases where there was a
collision of two national laws, the *ius gentium* was later invoked in cases
involving two members of the same nation and thus in cases between two
Roman citizens; and in fact the *ius gentium* was used extensively in the
settlement of disputes between Roman citizens. The evolution of the *ius
gentium* as a new and integral part of the Roman system was thus a

---

[1] See Kipp, *Geschichte der Quellen des römischen Rechts*, 3rd edn, §§ 2, 3.
[2] Gai. i, 1 = D. i, 1, 9.

powerful factor in the spread of Roman Law and in the process of the unification of law throughout the Roman dominion.

Another factor of no less importance was the gradual extension of Roman citizenship to the *peregrini*; for each extension of citizenship meant the extension of the application of the Roman *ius civile*. This development reached its climax in the beginning of the third century, when Caracalla, in his famous Edict (212), abolished the distinction between citizens and *peregrini* by granting full citizenship (*civitas*) to all in the Roman world[1]. In theory at least, the main result of the Edict was that all (*omnes*, πάντες) in the Empire were now amenable both to the *ius civile* and the *ius gentium*. In fact, however, the general application of the *ius civile* throughout the Empire was never fully carried out in practice. Even after the Edict the distinction between citizens and *peregrini* was not completely obliterated; for there still continued to be inhabitants of the Empire who were not citizens[2]. There is evidence, furthermore, that in various parts of the Empire the old national laws of the peregrins survived not only Caracalla's Edict but also the Justinianean legislation. For the persistence of those laws in certain of the eastern provinces of the Empire the Syrian-Roman Law Book[3] is ample authority.

The history of the evolution and spread of Roman Law in the ancient world is in divers ways enlightening to the student of the medieval history of that system. Not only does it give him clear ideas as to the nature of the system, its component parts, its rules and principles, its sources and its juristic literature; but it also shews him that, extensive as was the spread of the Roman Law, it never completely obliterated all the other legal systems of antiquity. Although an account of the concrete rules and principles of Roman Law, as they are to be found in Roman legal sources, more particularly in the Theodosian Code and in Justinian's lawbooks, does not fall within the compass of our present survey[4], we must nevertheless take pains to observe two main results of the evolution and

---

[1] D. I, 5, 17: *Ulpianus libro vicensimo secundo ad edictum.* In orbe Romano qui sunt ex constitutione imperatoris Antonini cives Romani effecti sunt. Scholars are in general agreement that Ulpian's statement of the effect of Caracalla's Edict (the text of which has not been preserved) is too wide. Kipp, *op. cit.* § 3, remarks: *Es ist unzweifelhaft, dass damit zuviel gesagt ist.* On the effect of the Edict, see Girard, *Manuel élémentaire de Droit Romain*, 3rd edn, p. 114; Buckland, *Roman Law from Augustus to Justinian*, 1921, pp. 99–101, where references to the ancient and modern literature of the subject will be found. For a fuller discussion of the subject, see Mitteis, *Reichsrecht und Volksrecht in den östlichen Provinzen des römischen Kaiserreichs*, Chap. VI.

[2] Buckland, *op. cit.* p. 99: "[It] is clear that even under Justinian, barbarian inhabitants of the confines of the empire, some originating there, some immigrant, and some settled by compulsion, were not treated as *cives*."

[3] For a brief account of this remarkable law-book and of recent researches concerning it, see Kipp, *op. cit.* § 23.

[4] See *supra*, Vol. II, Chapter III.

spread of the Roman system during the periods of ancient history, for these results materially affect the medieval development.

Let it be noted, in the first place, that the world-wide diffusion of the Roman Law in antiquity partly prepared the way for its further extension in the Middle Age. The Roman Law penetrated far and wide, in the East and in the West, and gave the ancient world a legal unity such as it had never before enjoyed; and yet this legal unity was of the kind which left in force, even though altered, many local laws and customs of non-Roman origin. Medieval times began, therefore, with the Roman Law in possession of only parts, though extensive parts, of the world-wide legal field. In the East the Greek Law had never been wholly absorbed or obliterated by Roman Law in ancient times; it lived on in many regions under Roman rule[1]. In the period of the Byzantine Empire it continued to come into contact with the Roman Law, more particularly the Justinianean law, and it helped to fashion the Graeco-Roman Law of the East. Likewise in the West the Middle Ages began with Roman Law in only partial occupation of the field. The Western provinces of the ancient Empire had been Romanised in varying degrees of intensity; the Romanisation of Italy differed widely from that of Britain. The differences between the legal histories of Western regions in medieval and modern times are due in no small measure to the differences in the extent of Romanisation in antiquity. The historian of European Law must constantly take account of the fact that the planting of Roman culture, including culture in law, had been intensive in some regions, partial or slight in others. In no extensive region of the West was Roman Law the sole law at the beginning of the Middle Age. Throughout vast areas Germanic racial customs held dominance. Nor were Germanic customs the only rivals of the Roman Law as the world passed into the medieval epoch. In various regions Celtic customs had survived the changes effected by the spread of Roman power and, later, by the migrations of the Germanic tribes. Indigenous customs other than Celtic also lived on during the periods of Roman and Germanic movement and pressure. Here and there Greek Law, planted in southern Europe during the days of Hellenic colonisation, still persisted.

The second main result of the ancient development of Roman Law, in so far as that development affects medieval law, was the accumulation of a mass of legal sources. The history of Roman Law in the Middle Age is, to a large extent, the history of the world-wide diffusion of the manuscripts of these legal texts and their employment by legislators, judges, practitioners, and jurists in the work of adapting Roman Law to medieval social conditions. The facts of this vast process are so complex, so intimately interwoven in the network of medieval events, movements, and tendencies, so bound up with diverse social, political, and economic conditions in the many parts of the world, that they are bewildering even

[1] The establishment of this fact is one of the valuable results of Mitteis' researches.

to one who is trained to single out the main and determining lines of historical development. In truth, to write the medieval history of Roman Law in all its fulness would mean the writing of the history of medieval civilisation—the life of Europe ever moving, ever changing, in the course of the centuries. Not forgetting this wider aspect of Roman legal history in the Middle Age, let us observe that, so far as the diffusion of the texts of the Roman Law is concerned, there are two features of the complex historical process which illumine our path and guide us to understanding.

The first point which we have to note and remember is that the medieval world is not one vast community under a single system of law and government; it is a world made up of many communities, differing one from another in race, in language, in social and legal institutions. Within the Byzantine Empire there is an appreciable degree of political and legal unity; and, at times, there is also political and legal unity of a sort in the West. But the dominant note in the political and legal history of the Middle Age is particularism, diversity, disunion. The system of the personality of law in the early Middle Age means particularism and diversity; and, with the growth of feudalism and the idea that law is territorial, as distinct from personal, regional diversities take the place of racial diversities in law. As a result, there is at first no tendency to uniformity in respect of Roman Law throughout medieval Europe as a whole. A limited legal uniformity is at length introduced by the Frankish Capitularies; but, on the whole, uniformity in law is more marked in modern than in medieval times, and even in modern times it is but a partial uniformity based in large measure on common origins. Since the time of the ancient Roman Empire, Europe has never been one State with one law. Even in the period of the medieval Empire and the medieval Church it was composed of many States, each with its own separate legal system[1].

There is, secondly, the point to be remembered that during the Middle Ages each political unit adopts and adapts in ways of its own the texts of the Roman Law that come to its hands. There is no power from above which imposes certain texts over the whole of Europe[2]. Some of the texts which are adopted and adapted by the separate units are pre-Justinianean, while some of them are parts of Justinian's codification itself. In the early Middle Age in the West the pre-Justinianean texts have at first a preference: it is only gradually that the Justinianean materials acquire a dominance over the earlier ones. Nor is it surprising to find that of all the texts of the Roman Law the institutional treatises and systematic

---

[1] The legal map of medieval Europe is not unlike the legal map of the United States of America to-day; for the States of the Federal Union—nearly fifty in number —all possess their own separate legal systems. Save in Louisiana, where the Civil Law prevails, uniformity in law throughout the Union is based in large measure on the reception of the Common Law of England by the separate States.

[2] The effect of the Frankish Capitularies should, however, be noted. See pp. 727–8, *infra.*

codifications have the greatest influence upon the spread of Roman legal rules and ideas in the Middle Age; for these materials are easier to grasp and to embody in legislation and the practice of courts than are the texts of a more limited and special character. Furthermore, they are more comprehensive and they thus meet more completely the social needs of the time.

Of the pre-Justinianean texts there were three which exerted a far-reaching influence in spreading Roman Law: the two private compilations or codes, known as the *Codex Gregorianus* (about A.D. 300) and the *Codex Hermogenianus* (probably before A.D. 323), and, notably, the great Code of the Emperor, the *Codex Theodosianus* (A.D. 438). Although the Gregorian and Hermogenian Codes were private works, they were nevertheless regarded as authoritative down to the time of Justinian, and they were not superseded by the far more important Code of Theodosius; for while the *Codex Theodosianus* did not embody materials before Constantine, the Gregorian Code reached back to the time of Hadrian[1]. In the East the *Codex Theodosianus* was superseded by the codification of Justinian; but in the West it long influenced legal growth in the Germanic kingdoms, large parts of it being embodied in Alaric's Breviary and other legal sources. In the East, Justinian's codification—gradually moulded, especially in the *Basilics*, to meet Eastern needs—was of paramount importance from Justinian's time down to the fall of the Byzantine Empire and even later. In the West, the pre-Justinianean sources, particularly the Theodosian Code, long continued to play a greater rôle than the texts of Justinian. With the progress of time, however, the Institutes, Digest, Code, and Novels of Justinian spread everywhere throughout the regions of the West. The revival of juristic studies in Italy was by far the most important of all the factors making for this far-reaching influence of the Justinianean law. Not only were the law-books of Justinian the subject of study and instruction in the law schools; they were incorporated in the law itself by the practice of the courts and by the acts of the legislators. Ultimately they became the very essence of the medieval Roman Law of Western countries—the *Corpus iuris civilis*.

Other aspects of the medieval history of Roman Law will be considered in later parts of this chapter. For the moment let us turn our attention to the second preliminary subject of our study—the history of the origins of Canon Law in antiquity and of its general development and sources in the periods of the Middle Age.

III.

While the Canon Law is the law of the Christian Church, a law created and enforced by organs of the Church, it embodies nevertheless rules derived from the Old Testament and thus from times long before the birth of Christ[2]; and, in general, the Canon Law no less than the Civil

[1] Buckland, *op. cit.* pp. 38–40.
[2] Canones et Decreta sacrosancti oecumenici Concilii Tridentini (Sessio Quarta:

Law is a bequest from antiquity. Not only do the earlier stages in the growth of the Canon Law fall within the period from the birth of Christ to the end of the age of antiquity, but the Canon Law itself is in large measure an off-shoot from the main stem of Roman legal growth, deriving from the older system many of its rules and principles. In its origins and in much of its later development the Canon Law is as much the product of Roman civilisation as the Civil Law itself.

From the point of view of medieval history there are, however, many points of difference between the Civil Law and the Canon Law. Not only is the Civil Law primarily the secular law of the State, while the Canon Law is primarily the law of the Christian Church; the difference between the stages of growth reached by the two laws at the close of ancient times also affects materially their medieval courses of evolution. As we have seen, the Middle Age adopts and adapts a system of Civil Law which antiquity had perfected, while it takes over and slowly brings to perfection a system of Canon Law which antiquity had only begun to develop: the Canon Law is the younger system. This difference leaves its mark on the history of the sources of the two systems during the medieval epoch. It accounts for the fact that the historian of Canon Law, as distinct from the historian of Civil Law, must spend much of his time in tracing the evolution of a growing and expanding system and in describing and explaining the successive additions to the sources of that system before, during, and after the formation of the *Corpus iuris canonici.*

The fortunes of the Church followed the fortunes of the Empire, within the frontiers of which it had its origin and earlier growth. The division of the Empire into its western and eastern halves resulted in a corresponding division of the Church. This process of ecclesiastical division was practically complete by the end of the sixth century; but only in 1054 was the schism of Eastern and Western Churches finally consummated[1]. The eastern and the western halves of the Church thus went their separate ways as the Greek Catholic Church and the Roman Catholic Church; and this splitting of the one Catholic Church into two necessarily resulted in the division of the Canon Law into two bodies of rules and principles, the Eastern or Greek Canon Law and the Western or Latin Canon Law. These two bodies of Canon Law possess common elements; they are closely related to each other in various ways; but yet they are distinct one from the other in many other ways and their histories must be separately traced. The early Greek Canon Law consists only of Eastern conciliar canons; it admits no purely Latin elements; and it cannot, therefore, lay claim to universality.

decretum de canonicis scripturis):...*omnes libros tam veteris quam novi testamenti, cum utriusque unus Deus sit auctor...pari pietatis affectu ac reverentia suscipit et veneratur.* According to Gratian only the moral rules of the Old Testament form *ius divinum.* See *Decretum,* prima pars, distinctio VI, c. III; Friedberg, *Kirchenrecht,* 4th edn, § 31. Compare Galante, *Elementi di Diritto Ecclesiastico,* pp. 15–17.

[1] See *supra,* Vol. IV, Chapter IX.

Early Latin Canon Law is itself composed largely of Greek materials; but to this Greek nucleus Latin elements, chiefly the canons of local and ecumenical Councils and the papal decretals, are continually added[1]. The medieval history of both of these canonical systems falls within the compass of our study; but it is the Western Law which must chiefly engage our attention.

In respect of the history of Western Law let us note three main points. In the first place, the history of the Canon Law passes through the same stages of development as does the Church itself. Two of the principal stages we may designate the conciliar and the papal. Corresponding to the constitutional history of the Church the canons of the earlier centuries are chiefly the work of the Councils, whereas in the later centuries the canons are for the most part the product of the legislative power gradually acquired by the Popes and they are embodied in the decretals. In the second place, the term Canon Law has a wider and a narrower meaning; and it acquires its narrower significance only after the law itself has developed into a system and been made the object of study. Whereas in its broader signification Canon Law is the sum or aggregate of the rules which have been recognised or evolved by the organs of the Church for the governance of the ecclesiastical body, in its narrower meaning it is the law contained in a definite and closed group of law-books known as the *Corpus iuris canonici*[2]. Thirdly, let us note that jurists sometimes use the term *ius ecclesiasticum* as equivalent in meaning to *ius canonicum*. This usage leads at times to confusion; for the term ecclesiastical law is also employed to designate a branch of the law of the State as distinct from the law enforced by the Church itself. The κανόνες, *regulae*, were very early distinguished from the secular laws, the νόμοι, *leges*; and hence the Canon Law is sometimes referred to as the *canones, sacri canones*.

Turning to the history of the sources of Canon Law, more especially the sources of the law enforced by the Roman Church, let us observe, in the first place, that they consist of three main kinds: the Holy Scripture, traditions and customs, and the legislation of Councils and Popes. In dealing with these sources, modern canonists draw a chronological and theoretical line of distinction between the ancient and the new law. The *ius antiquum* is the law developed and enforced prior to the time of Gratian; while the *ius novum* is the law embodied in Gratian's *Decretum* and the other parts of the *Corpus iuris canonici*[3]. To distinguish it from the *ius antiquum* and the *ius novum*, the law established by the Council of Trent and subsequent papal consti-

---

[1] See *supra*, Vol. I, pp. 181–2.

[2] Hinschius, *Geschichte und Quellen des kanonischen Rechts* (in Holtzendorff, *Encyklopädie der Rechtswissenschaft*, 5th edn. 1890, pp. 187–8).

[3] This distinction is drawn by Boudinhon. Tardif, *Histoire des Sources du Droit Canonique*, p. 5, says, however, that "le *droit ancien* est le droit antérieur au concile de Trent; le *droit nouveau* dérive de ce concile."

tutions is known to canonists as the recent law, the *ius novissimum*. Canonists also draw a distinction between the *ius scriptum*, the written laws which emanate from Councils and Popes and which are embodied in the collections of sources, and the *ius non scriptum*, or unwritten law, a body of traditional and customary rules based in large measure on natural equity. A further distinction should also be remembered. The common law, the *ius commune*, is the general law intended to regulate the whole ecclesiastical body; while special or local law is the law which, by derogation from or addition to the common law, is concerned with certain categories of persons or certain regions. The function of legislating for the whole Church belongs only to the episcopate, assembled in general or ecumenical Council, and to the Pope as its chief: local councils or individual bishops or prelates have authority to make only special or local laws. Most of the canons which constitute the *ius antiquum*, including such of those canons as are embodied in Gratian's *Decretum*, emanate nevertheless from local councils or individual bishops, not from the supreme authorities of the Church. These canons have gradually come to form parts of the *ius commune* by reason of the fact that canonical collections which include these local canons as their principal element have been adopted generally in all parts of Christendom as of binding authority.

Both the *ius antiquum* and the *ius novum* fall within the compass of our present survey, and of each one of these divisions of the law a few words must needs be said. Let us glance therefore, first of all, at the history of the sources of the *ius antiquum*, the law before the time of Gratian and the formation of the *Corpus iuris canonici*.

In the first centuries of the Christian era, before the close of the period of persecutions, the life of the Christian communities was governed by the Scriptures and by ecclesiastical tradition, the unwritten κανών or *regula*. The various Churches early came to have their own traditions and usages, and these they obeyed as their unwritten customary law; apart from the Scriptures the early Church law was not embodied in any written code. Not until the time of Constantine and the other early Christian Emperors was it possible for the ecclesiastical legislative power to act freely and to create a body of written law. The new position of the Church in its relation to the State formed the constitutional basis of a new movement which led to the establishment of a written law of the Church somewhat after the pattern of the Roman Civil Law. The organs which expressed the mind of the federated Christian communities in the matter of law, no less than in that of creed, were the early ecclesiastical Councils of the fourth century; and the codes formed during the decade 305–315 by the Councils of Elvira, Ancyra, Neocaesarea, and Arles are the earliest of the conciliar materials preserved in the later body of the Canon Law. These codes possessed, however, no binding authority outside the localities in which they were issued. The opportunity to issue a code for the whole Christian Church finally presented itself at the

Ecumenical Council of Nicaea (325): and the issue of such a code of law was a part of Constantine's policy of bringing about the unity of the Church and its close alliance with the Empire. The Nicene canons, in which were incorporated some of the canons of the Eastern Council of Ancyra and of the Western Council of Arles, constitute the earliest code of Canon Law for the whole Church. In the course of time many other codes possessing no connexion with the Nicene Council were placed by collectors of canons in the Nicene code and were thus given its authority. Particularly in the West the Nicene code acquired a position of high authority in the realm of discipline. Innocent of Rome in the cause of St Chrysostom writes that "other canon than the Nicene canons the Roman Church receives not."[1]

The compilation of collections of canons began in the East. The elaboration of these collections, with certain additions drawn from the West, such as canons in the Latin collection of Dionysius Exiguus, resulted ultimately in the formation of the official collection of the Greek Church as it was recognised and sanctioned by the Council *in Trullo* (692). As defined by the Council, the Greek collection consists of several classes of documents: firstly, the eighty-five Apostolic Canons; secondly, the canons of the Councils of Nicaea, Ancyra, Neocaesarea, Gangra, Antioch, Laodicea, Constantinople (381), Ephesus, Chalcedon, Sardica, Constantinople (394), Carthage (the one of 419, according to Dionysius); thirdly, the canonical letters of several great bishops, such as Dionysius of Alexandria, Peter of Alexandria (the Martyr), Athanasius, Basil, Gregory of Nyssa, Amphilochus of Iconium, and Gennadius of Constantinople. To this official collection were added at a later time the twenty-two canons of the Second Council of Nicaea (787). As thus completed, the official canonical collection of the Greek Church had several medieval commentators, such as Photius (883), Zonaras (1120), and Balsamon (1170); but it has remained unchanged down to the present day. As pointed out by Boudinhon, the later growth of the Eastern Canon Law—that is, after the Council of Nicaea (787)—was due to the work of the Byzantine Emperors before the fall of the Empire in 1453.

In its fifth-century state the Greek collection was translated and introduced into the West. The one hundred and two canons elaborated by the Council *in Trullo* (692) did not become part of Western Law until a much later time, and then upon the initiative of Pope John VIII (872–881). Meanwhile local collections of canons were made in the West from the fifth century onwards. Within the sphere of the see of Constantinople a tendency towards the unification of ecclesiastical law manifested itself as early as the fifth century; but in the West collections were purely local until in the eighth and ninth centuries, as the result of passing on the several collections from one region to another, there were the beginnings of a process of unification.

[1] See further, *supra*, Vol. I, pp. 13, 176–182.

The most ancient, and in some respects the most homogeneous and noteworthy, of all these Western local collections is that of the Church of Africa. By the time of the Vandal invasion the African collection had already acquired special importance as an official code; but our knowledge of it is now derived chiefly from incomplete and confused accounts in the collection of Dionysius Exiguus and the Spanish collection known as the *Hispana.* About the middle of the ninth century Fulgentius Ferrandus, a Carthaginian deacon, made a methodical arrangement of the African collection in the order of subjects; and this is now known as the *Breviatio canonum.*

The Roman Church in its early history governed itself largely by its own traditions and customs and by papal letters called decretals. Of non-Roman sources of canonical law it officially recognised, before the sixth century, only the canons of Nicaea and Sardica. At the beginning of the sixth century, however, the Roman Church adopted the double collection —composed of Latin translations of Greek canons and thirty-nine decretals of the Popes from Siricius (384–398) to Anastasius II (496–498) —made by the Scythian monk Dionysius Exiguus; and this collection, its second part receiving successive additions as further decretals appeared, remained the only official body of Canon Law for the Roman Church until the reforms of the eleventh century. Pope Hadrian I in 774 gave this double collection of Dionysius to the future Emperor Charlemagne as the canonical book of the Roman Church; and hence it is known as the *Dionysio-Hadriana.* This collection, officially received by the Frankish Church at the Council of Aix-la-Chapelle in 802, and thereafter recognised and quoted as the *liber canonum,* became the code of Canon Law of almost the whole of the Western Church. In the hands of Pope Hadrian I, and of Charlemagne and the Franks, the work of Dionysius was thus a powerful factor in the growth of a unified Western Canon Law.

Gaul was exceptional in not possessing a code of local Canon Law. The Church had not been centralised, as in many other regions of Europe, round some principal see; and the political territorial divisions had not been stable. In the fifth and sixth centuries only the Church of Arles constituted a canonical centre of any real influence over its surrounding region. The main collection of canonical sources—known from its seventeenth-century editor as the " Quesnel Collection "—contained valuable materials, chiefly Eastern and African canons and papal letters, but no canons of the local Gallic councils. When it was introduced into Gaul, the *Dionysio-Hadriana* did not, therefore, displace any local and generally-accepted collection. Unifying tendencies in the development of Canon Law thus came from without and not within the Gallic Church. In this process the alliance between the Carolingian power and the Papacy, and the acceptance of the *Dionysio-Hadriana,* or *liber canonum,* marked an important stage.

The Spanish Church differed fundamentally from the Gallic; for it had been effectively centralised round the see of Toledo. As a result the Spanish Church possessed an important collection of Spanish Canon Law, the *Hispana*[1], dating from the early part of the eighth century, which, although not strictly speaking an official collection, was everywhere received. The *Hispana* includes in its first part the canons of Greek, African, Gallic, and Spanish Councils, the canons of Spanish Councils forming the local section of the collection; while the decretals of the Popes are in the second part, as in the case of the collection of Dionysius. The *Hispana* emerged into a position of great importance in the period beginning in the middle of the ninth century, for it then served as the basis of the False Decretals.

Although the Churches of the British Isles remained longer than most other Churches outside the centralising movement and the tendency to a unification of Western Canon Law, they contributed nevertheless to the growth of the law as finally embodied in the *Corpus iuris canonici*. This contribution consists fundamentally of two things: firstly, the collections of penitentials, including those of Theodore of Canterbury (*ob.* 690), the Venerable Bede (*ob.* 735), and Egbert of York (732–767); and, secondly, the Irish collection, dating apparently from the eighth century, which introduced the practice among canonists of quoting passages from the Scriptures and the writings of the Fathers. Apart from these two groups of materials, the sources of British local Canon Law were not known to Gratian's predecessors nor to Gratian himself; and they did not, therefore, influence the form and content of the *Decretum*.

About the middle of the ninth century there appeared the famous collection known as the "False Decretals." Round this collection there has arisen a vast controversial literature which it is impossible, within the limits of the present chapter, to summarise or appraise[2]. Certain it is that the collection is based on the genuine Spanish collection known as the *Hispana* or *Isidoriana*. The author, whether he was the mysterious Benedictus Levita, to whom the False Capitularies, a collection closely akin to the False Decretals, have been attributed, or whether he was some other person, assumed the name of Isidore, Bishop of Seville, who had been credited with the greater part of the *Hispana* or *Isidoriana* collection: and hence the False Decretals are sometimes known as the Pseudo-Isidore. Whoever the author may have been, it is now agreed on all sides that the collection had its origin within the Frankish Empire[3].

[1] The collection is also known as the *Isidoriana*, because it has been attributed (but without reason) to Isidore of Seville.

[2] But see the works cited by Hinschius in his *Geschichte und Quellen des kanonischen Rechts* (Holtzendorff's *Encyklopädie der Rechtswissenschaft*, 5th edn. 1890, p. 193). A list of older works will be found in Phillips and Crouzet, *Du Droit Ecclésiastique dans ses Sources*, Paris, 1852, pp. 42, 43.

[3] It was at first thought that the False Decretals originated in the province of Mayence. It is now held by Brissaud and other scholars that the False Decretals must have been written in France, probably at Rheims. See *Continental Legal History Series* (ed. by J. H. Wigmore and others), Vol. 1, (1912), p. 710. Several recent

The collection contains as many canons of councils as papal decretals; and the decretals in it are not all forgeries. It is best described as an amplification of the genuine *Hispana* by the interpolation of spurious decretals. Of the three parts of the collection, the first is completely spurious. It contains, after introductory matter, seventy spurious letters attributed to Popes before the Council of Nicaea (325), all of these letters being the forgery of the false Isidore except two spurious letters of Clement which were already in circulation. The second part of the collection contains the canons of Councils. Most of these are genuine, the few forgeries, including the famous Donation of Constantine, being already known. The third part is a continuation of the series of decretals—which in the first part of the collection had ended with the date of the Nicene Council—down to St Gregory the Great (*ob.* 604); but it contains also one letter of Gregory II (715–731). The authentic decretals of the Popes begin only with Siricius (385), and these the Pseudo-Isidore includes in his collection; but he adds also spurious decretals both for the time before and the time after 385. Most of the forged decretals are not composed entirely of freshly fabricated material. The author draws upon the *Liber Pontificalis* and ecclesiastical writings for some of his matter. Thus, the genuine Councils and decretals, and even this genuine matter falsely put into the mouths of the Popes, served to cloak the skilfully fabricated stuff of the forger and to give it credence.

Blended thus of genuine and spurious matter, the collection rapidly circulated throughout the West and long passed as a valuable source of Canon Law. All the later collections drew materials, genuine and false indiscriminately, from the Pseudo-Isidore[1]. Not until the fifteenth century were suspicions aroused as to the true character of the collection: Cardinal Nicholas of Cusa (*ob.* 1464) and Juan Torquemada (*ob.* 1468) expressed in no uncertain terms their doubts as to its authenticity. In the sixteenth century Erasmus, as well as Dumoulin (*ob.* 1568) and Le Conte (*ob.* 1577), the two editors of Gratian's *Decretum*, decisively refused to accept the Pseudo-Isidore. Gradually the history of the forgery has been pieced together by scholars; and the false character of parts of the collection is now universally admitted.

---

authors have, however, suggested the province of Tours as the home of the collection. See the article on the "Decretals, False" by Boudinhon in the *Encyclopaedia Britannica*, 11th edn, Vol. vii, and the authorities there cited; and Tardif, *Histoire des Sources du Droit Canonique*, Paris, 1887, pp. 140–158.

[1] While the Pseudo-Isidore quickly spread its influence from France to Italy and other European countries, including England, it found a very slow reception at Rome itself. It has been pointed out by M. Fournier and other scholars that, while the collection exerted a slight literary influence on papal letters of the ninth and tenth centuries, the use of the forged material of the False Decretals did not become prominent at Rome until about the middle of the eleventh century. This ultimate reception at Rome was due in large measure to the circulation of the canonical collections in which the False Decretals held a place, no doubt at that time being cast upon the authenticity of the forged documents.

The object of the forger appears to have been the reform, or better application, of the Canon Law. He desired to prevent bishops from being unjustly accused or deprived of their sees, and to protect the property and persons of the clergy against the encroachments of bishops and nobles. He desired also to increase the strength and cohesion of the Churches; and he made the Papacy the very centre of his ecclesiastical edifice. These objects the wide acceptance of the False Decretals no doubt furthered. Certainly they served as a powerful factor in the movement, within the Frankish territories, towards the centralisation of power in the see of Rome.

Opinions differ as to the extent of the modification and corruption of Canon Law itself occasioned by the influence of the False Decretals. However this may be, there is no doubt that by furthering the tendency towards its unification the False Decretals mark an important stage in the history of the law. In yet another respect the Pseudo-Isidore is noteworthy; for it is the last of the long series of chronologically arranged collections of the texts of Canon Law. From this time onwards the canonists arranged the conciliar and papal canons in systematic order according to subject-matter and not according to time; and thus they gradually prepared the way for the systematic codification of the *ius commune* in the *Decretum* of Gratian and the other integral parts of the *Corpus iuris canonici*. Furthermore, from the time of the False Decretals onwards the canonists not only arranged and systematised the materials, gradually bringing local canons into the general mass of the common law; they also added to the bare texts their own conclusions and discussions, thus clothing the texts with canonist learning and theory.

During the three centuries between the appearance of the False Decretals and the time of Gratian about forty canonical collections were made. Among the most important of them are the *Decretorum libri XX* of Burchard, Bishop of Worms, written between the years 1012 and 1023, and the three works—the *Panormia*, the *Decretum*, and the *Tripartite Collection*—attributed to Ivo of Chartres, who studied under Lanfranc at Bec and was the last of the great canonists of the period of the *ius antiquum*. Although many of these collections dating from the middle of the ninth to the middle of the twelfth century were of practical and theoretical value, no one of them rose into eminence as the standard or classical collection which embodied in the most orderly and concordant form the whole mass of the materials of Canon Law that had grown up in the centuries of Christendom. Gratian, garnering the rich harvest which he found in the canonical works of his predecessors, finally provided this standard collection at the very centre of the revival of juristic studies. With Gratian and his monumental *Decretum* the period of the *ius novum* had its beginnings, the period which was to see the completion of the *Corpus iuris canonici*.

The gradual formation of the *Corpus iuris canonici* covers a period of over three hundred years. As finally completed it consists of five separate parts.

(1) Gratian's *Decretum* forms the first and in many ways the most important part: it constitutes in truth the basic part of the entire *Corpus iuris canonici*. It is known that Gratian was a Camaldulensian monk of the convent of St Felix at Bologna, where he taught Canon Law; although only a few details of his life have come down to us. His great work—dated between 1141 and 1150, or, as it is now thought, between 1139 and 1141[1]—bears in the older manuscripts the title *Concordia discordantium canonum*, but is better known as the *Decretum*. The *Decretum* is based on earlier collections, including the works of Ivo of Chartres, but is much more than a compilation or collection. So skilfully has Gratian ordered and treated his materials that his work is essentially a treatise on the Canon Law in which the authorities themselves are included. There are three parts or divisions of the work. The first part deals with the sources of the law and with ecclesiastical persons; the second with ecclesiastical jurisdiction, procedure, property, and marriage; the third with consecration, sacrament, and liturgy. The portions of these parts that are Gratian's own personal contribution are known as the *Dicta Gratiani*, while the notes by Paucapalea, a twelfth-century disciple of Gratian, as well as those of a few other scholars, are called *Paleae*. Very soon after its appearance Gratian's *Decretum* was treated as if it were official; while in the law schools it was used as the foundation of teaching in Canon Law. Like the texts of the Justinianean codification in the hands of the Glossators, the *Decretum Gratiani* was soon provided with glosses. Before 1215 glosses were written by Johannes Teutonicus, and about the year 1236 by Bartholomew of Brescia. It is difficult to overestimate the vast influence which Gratian's work exerted for centuries upon the study and spread of Canon Law throughout the Christian world. No other single book of Canon Law can vie with it in importance and influence.

(2) To complete Gratian's *Decretum*, five compilations—known as the *Quinque Compilationes Antiquae*—were made before the time of Gregory IX. The first of these, compiled by Bernard of Pavia about 1190, was divided into five books, as follows: (1) ecclesiastical hierarchy; (2) procedure; (3) functions and duties of the clergy; (4) marriage; (5) penal law. This order of subjects adopted by Bernard became the accepted order in future compilations of Canon Law. Later scholars have summed it up in the well-known verse: "Judex, Judicium, Clerus, Connubia, Crimen." The last of the remaining four compilations of this group—the *Quinque Compilationes Antiquae*—was an official collection of the decretals of Honorius III, 1216 to 1226.

By the Bull *Rex pacificus* (1234) Gregory IX sent to the Universities

---

[1] On the date of the *Decretum*, see Schulte, *Geschichte der Quellen und Literatur des canonischen Rechts von Gratian bis auf die Gegenwart*, Vol. I, p. 48.

of Bologna and Paris a compilation of the decretals of Popes since the completion of the *Decretum* of Gratian. This official compilation, known as the Decretals of Gregory IX, or "*Extra*" (that is, "Decretales extra Decretum vagantes"), and abbreviated as "X" (meaning "extra"), was in reality a continuation of Gratian's *Decretum*, which now became in law what it had always been in fact—an official Code of Canon Law. The author of the *Extra* was Gregory IX's confessor, Raymond de Peñafort, a Spaniard, who, following the arrangement of Justinian's Code, divided the compilation into books, titles, and canons. Bernard of Parma, who died in 1263, added glosses.

The *Quinque Compilationes Antiquae* were superseded by Gregory's collection and by it deprived of all their authority.

(3) Boniface VIII collected in 1298 the decretals subsequent to the *Extra*; and he published the new compilation in the manner adopted previously by Gregory IX in the case of the *Extra*—by sending it to the Universities of Bologna and Paris. Boniface VIII's collection constituted the *Sextus* or *Liber Sextus Decretalium*, the five earlier books being those embodied in the *Extra*. In 1348 the *Sextus* was glossed by Jean André.

(4) In 1313 Clement V published another collection of decretals, including his own, which is known as the "*Clementinae*." John XXII, Clement's successor, recast the collection and sent it to the Universities in 1317.

(5) The "*Extravagantes*", or the decretals omitted from the above-mentioned compilation ("*extra-vagantes*"), are of two groups: (*a*) the *Extravagantes* of John XXII (twenty constitutions), (*b*) the "*Extravagantes Communes*," including the decretals issued by various Popes, since the publication of the *Sextus*, from Boniface VIII to Sextus IV (1484). The collection of *Extravagantes* differs from the earlier ones just mentioned in not being an official compilation. But it found its place in editions of the *Corpus iuris canonici*; and, inasmuch as all its documents were authentic, it was treated as if it were official.

As completed and closed by the *Extravagantes*, the *Corpus iuris canonici* is thus composed of: (1) the *Decretum Gratiani*; (2) the Decretals of Gregory IX (*Liber Extra*); (3) Boniface VIII's *Liber Sextus Decretalium*; (4) the *Clementinae*; (5) the *Extravagantes*.

The term *Corpus iuris canonici*, used as the antithesis of the term *Corpus iuris civilis* when applied to the whole of the Roman Law, is to be met as early as the twelfth century. In the sixteenth century the term acquired, however, a technical sense, being used to denote the entirety of the five sets of texts already described. From 1563 to 1580 the *correctores romani*, a commission of cardinals and scholars, worked at Rome in order to form a better text than that of the manuscripts and publications then in use. The results of the labours of the commission appeared in 1582, under the pontificate and by the orders of Gregory XIII, as the official edition. Thus formed and completed under the direction of the

Church, the *Corpus iuris canonici* constitutes the *ius novum* as distinct from the *ius antiquum*; and it is still the foundation of the Canon Law. The complete body of Canon Law to-day includes also the *ius novissimum*, the law that has been evolved since the Council of Trent (1545); but the *ius novissimum* forms no part of the *Corpus iuris canonici* in its technical sense.

The gradual evolution of the law embodied in the *Corpus iuris canonici*, a development extending through more than fifteen centuries of the Christian era, is one of the outstanding features of ancient and medieval history. It is an evolution comparable in many ways to the slow growth of the law contained in Justinian's great codification and later in the *Corpus iuris civilis*. With certain aspects of the medieval history of the Canon Law we shall be concerned in later portions of this chapter. We shall see how the Canon Law, as the law of the Church, spread throughout the medieval world, how it influenced secular law and juridical and political theory, how in short it became an integral and vital part of medieval civilisation.

IV.

The history of Roman and Canon Law in the Middle Age falls naturally into two main geographical divisions: the dividing line is formed by the boundary between the East and the West. Although these two parts of our history are closely related to each other—there are legal influences and counter-influences that play back and forth between the two vast provinces of Christendom—we must nevertheless study each part singly ere we can see these relations in their true perspective and gain a complete picture of the vast process of legal evolution in medieval Europe as a whole. First of all, then, let us briefly survey the history of the Roman and Canon Laws in their eastern home within the Later Roman Empire.

Two events of the reign of Constantine the Great mark the definite beginnings of the division of European legal history into its eastern and its western parts. Each one of these events produced far-reaching and lasting results within the domain of law; each one of them shaped and transformed laws and customs in all parts of the world: each one of them was a factor of the highest importance in the history of Roman and Canon Law both in the East and in the West. The first of these two events was Constantine's adoption of Christianity. Henceforth a new order of ideas was given full play in all parts of the ancient world; and these ideas moulded many of the processes of legal growth not only in the period from Constantine to Justinian but throughout the medieval era. The history of Roman and Canon Law among the Hellenised peoples of the East and among the Germanic societies of the West displays in many striking ways the after-influence of the recognition of Christianity in the days of Constantine; and yet these after-influences in the East differ markedly from those in the West. A second event of almost equal significance in the history of law was the making of Byzantium a second capital of the Roman Empire. The centre of gravity in the Empire had been slowly shifting to the East for a considerable time before Constantine; the establishment of Constantinople accelerated this process and gave to the Eastern half of the world-wide imperial domain a definite preponderance. With the loss of the Western provinces, caused by the expansion of the Germanic peoples, the ancient Roman Empire persisted only in the East. Until it finally succumbed to the power of the Ottoman Turks in 1453, this Later Roman Empire—this "Greek" or "Byzantine" Empire —was the true Roman Empire, its Emperors being the legitimate successors of Augustus in an unbroken line of continuity; and down at least to the beginning of its decline in the middle of the eleventh century, except in the lifetime of Charlemagne, it was the first political power in Europe. This transference of the Roman Empire from the West to the East led to legal as well as political results of the highest moment; some of them are to be seen by a comparison of the history of Roman and Canon Laws in their Eastern and in their Western environments.

As the heir of antiquity the Later Roman Empire became the true guardian of the legal traditions of the ancient Empire. In the first half of the sixth century these traditions were, in certain respects, maintained. Justinian, the great codifier of the accumulated mass of Roman legal materials derived from the past, was an Eastern Emperor; his codification was made and promulgated in the East. What, it should now be asked, was the fate of the law of Justinian in its Eastern home? Were the ancient Roman legal traditions still further preserved? Did the law continue to develop in the spirit of the classical jurists? Was the East to inherit the legal genius of the West? The answers to these questions are of far more than ordinary historical interest.

Three main characteristics of the Later Roman Empire determined the future course of legal history and gave to medieval Roman and Canon Laws in this part of the world certain of their marked characteristics. Whereas, throughout the greater part of its history, the ancient Empire had been predominantly Western, Pagan, and Roman, the Later Roman Empire down to its fall in 1453 was fundamentally Eastern, Christian, and Greek. Here we may find the main key to the legal history of the East. The general geographical situation of the Later Roman Empire, particularly its proximity to the Slavs and Eastern peoples, and the social, economic, and religious conditions of its several parts, were determining factors in the evolution of the Roman and Canon Law within the imperial frontiers. But this is only expressing in different terms the same cardinal fact: the Empire was Eastern, Christian, and Greek, and its law evolved along the lines of imperial development.

The history of the Justinianean law in the East may be sketched by a brief consideration of the legal sources in the successive periods of imperial history.

Justinian declared that his codification was to be the sole statement of the law; nothing outside it was to be regarded. In case of need, resort could be had only to the Emperor himself, inasmuch as he was the sole source of the law. The Emperor authorised literal translations into Greek, indexes, and παράτιτλα or summaries of parallel passages or titles; the writing of commentaries and general summaries, as an interference with the Emperor's prerogative of interpretation, was sternly forbidden. But despite these prohibitions—prohibitions designed to restrict the law to the imperial law-books—notes, abridgments, excerpts, general summaries, and commentaries appeared even in Justinian's own lifetime and for half a century thereafter. These writings appear to have been intended chiefly for use in the law schools; most of them were prepared by professors (*antecessores*). Soon, however, they were in the hands of practitioners and judges; and they thus came into general use.

One of the best known of these writings is the Greek *Paraphrase of the Institutes*, which has survived in various manuscripts. It is usually attributed to Theophilus, one of Justinian's commissioners and a professor in the law school of Constantinople; but Ferrini, its latest editor, holds that the authorship of Theophilus rests on inadequate evidence. He contends that the work is a reproduction of Gaius in Greek, that it was originally drawn up at Beyrout, that it was remodelled at a later time on the plan, and with some of the matter, of Justinian's Institutes. The *Paraphrase of the Institutes* formed the subject-matter of commentaries by Dorotheus and Stephanus; while commentaries on Justinian's Digest, Code, and Novels, written by various Eastern jurists, also appeared.

This period of the jurists' study of Justinian's codification soon came to an end. The codification itself had been rendered into Greek and had formed the basis of scholarly, literary treatment; but, once that had been accomplished, juristic studies rapidly decayed. During the profound social disturbances of the seventh century the law-books of Justinian seem to have been hardly understood. The practice of the courts was largely influenced by Greek Christian ideas and ecclesiastical canons; and, with the decline of Roman traditions, these influences shaped legal growth and gave character to the period of legislative activity in the eighth century. Within the domain of legislation the outstanding feature of the century was the appearance of the 'Εκλογή of Leo the Isaurian (740), an abstract of the whole codification of Justinian as amended and rearranged in accordance with Greek and Christian ideas of the time. The legislation of Leo represents indeed a wide departure from the Justinianean rules and principles in nearly every branch of the law, a departure so coloured by ecclesiastical notions of justice that the 'Εκλογή itself has been called a Christian law-book. Thus, for example, while Justinian treated marriage as a contract, dissoluble at the will of the parties, Leo III introduced the Church's doctrine that marriage was an indissoluble bond. The period of the Isaurian (Syrian) and Phrygian (Amorian) Emperors (717–867) was a time in which the law was developed through practice away from the Justinianean model and little or no thought was given to scientific legal studies.

At the beginning of the period of the Macedonian dynasty (867–1057) a great change took place. Basil I (867–886) and his son Leo the Philosopher (886–912), at the end of the ninth and beginning of the tenth centuries, pursued the policy of a return to Justinian's law and a revival of legal studies. Basil repealed the Ἐκλογή of Leo the Isaurian as a departure from Justinian's law which it professed to summarise; and he set himself to the task of producing an authoritative Greek version of the whole of the Justinianean codification, but with the omission of obsolete matter and the introduction of the most desirable parts of the legislation enacted since the death of Justinian. The legal materials were subjected to a treatment somewhat similar to that accorded by Justinian and his commissioners in their day to the writings of the classical jurists and the other accumulated sources. The first result of the new legislative policy was Basil's issue in 879 of a kind of institutional work entitled ὁ πρόχειρος νόμος ("the law as it is"), composed of extracts from Justinian's Institutes, Digest, and Code. This handbook was revised and republished by Leo under the title Ἐπαναγωγὴ τοῦ νόμου. The main work of the Emperors, however, was the famous *Basilics* (Τὰ βασιλικά), a collection of all the laws of the Empire, prepared by legal commissioners. They were begun in the time of Basil and completed under Leo.

The *Basilics* are composed of sixty books, subdivided into titles, in accordance with the general plan of Justinian's *Codex*. Within this framework the law on any particular subject, whether derived from Justinian's Institutes, Digest, Code, or Novels, is arranged consecutively. The so-called παραγραφαὶ τῶν παλαιῶν is an addition to the *Basilics*, consisting of an official commentary collected from the writings of the sixth-century jurists, published by Leo's son, Constantinus Porphyrogenitus. This work, now referred to as the *scholia* to the *Basilics*, has proved of great value to modern civilians in their work of reconstructing the Roman legal texts. Annotations by jurists of the tenth, eleventh, and twelfth centuries, also referred to as *scholia*, are of less value. In many points of civil as distinct from criminal law the *Basilics* discard the rules of the *Ecloga* in favour of those to be found in the Justinianean codification. An example of this tendency of the *Basilics* is to be found in their revival of Justinian's law of divorce, with the result that in the East there thus arose in respect of this matter a contradiction between the Civil and the Canon Law. Although the *Basilics* retained their statutory authority down to the fall of the Byzantine Empire in 1453, they had long before that time been neglected in practice.

The *Basilics* were in fact the one really great codification of Graeco-Roman Law in the Later Roman Empire after the time of Justinian; the successors of Basil the Macedonian and Leo the Philosopher did not legislate on a grand scale. Somewhat more than a century after Leo there was, however, a marked revival of juristic studies under Constantine IX (1042–1054), who founded a new law-school. Many jurists continued down to the fall of the Empire to write commentaries, epitomes, and compendia; but of these jurists only John Xiphilin, Theodore Balsamon, and Constantinus Harmenopulus, of the eleventh, twelfth, and fourteenth centuries respectively, need be mentioned here. The decadence of juristic studies is represented in a striking way by the Ἐξάβιβλος of Harmeno-pulus, a work which appeared about 1345, and which Bruns has characterised as "a miserable epitome of the epitomes of epitomes."

The inner history ot the Byzantine or Graeco-Roman Law—the history, that is, of its rules and principles, as distinct from the history of its sources and general development—is of more than usual interest to the student of the medieval history of Roman Law in central and western Europe. It shews him how the Justinianean law, as embodied in the Institutes, Digest, Code, and Novels, further developed under Eastern conditions; and it thus gives him an opportunity to compare contem-porary development in the Germanic West. By means of comparison he is enabled to see clearly the similarities and the differences between the two evolutionary processes, and to study the underlying social, economic, religious, and political causes which produce divergence and convergence in legal growths. Of special interest is a comparison of legal medievalism in East and in West; for the Byzantine regions, no less than the Romano-Germanic regions of the West, passed through corresponding stages of medieval growth in the domain of law. The medieval legal development of the East, from the sixth to the ninth century, is interrupted by a restoration of the Justinianean law which corresponds in some ways to the revival of the study and influence of that law in Italy and Western Europe from the time of the Glossators to the Reception. Only by bringing into our studies both the Eastern and the Western modes and processes of legal growth, decay, and revival, together with their background of racial, social, and political conditions, ever changing and ever acquiring new colours drawn from the life of civilisation itself, can we hope fully to grasp the nature and significance of the vaster movements in medieval legal history.

In certain parts of Eastern Europe, Graeco-Roman Law survived the fall of the Byzantine Empire and the vicissitudes of the following centuries. The civil code of Moldavia, published in 1816–17, is a codification of Byzantine Law. The civil law of modern Greece is also largely indebted to it. The *Basilics* were sanctioned as law in 1822, but were displaced in 1835 in favour of the epitome of Harmenopulus; although in framing her civil code Greece followed the Napoleonic code as her model, she professes nevertheless to base the law in theory upon the edicts of the Emperors as embodied in this "miserable epitome of the epitomes of epitomes" written by Harmenopulus. In his *Geschichte des griechisch-römischen Rechts* Zachariä von Lingenthal expresses a most favourable opinion of the Moldavian code of Byzantine law; and he regrets that Greece did not adopt it as the basis of her own codification.

In an earlier part of this chapter reference has already been made to the growth of Greek Canon Law during the Middle Ages. Here it is only necessary to observe that the relation between Graeco-Roman Civil Law and Greek Canon Law was very close. Under ecclesiastical influence many of the texts of the Civil Law—the Ἐκλογή, for example—were permeated with the principles of canonical jurisprudence. The evolution of the ecclesiastical law itself was due in large measure to the work of the Emperors. The two bodies of law developed side by side as two aspects of the same historical process. The so-called Nomocanons illustrate this. In these great compilations the imperial civil laws and the ecclesiastical canons on each subject were placed side by side and contrasted. Jurists abridged these compilations and also recast them in systematic treatises (*syntagmata*). The Νομοκανών of John of Antioch, a learned priest made Patriarch of Constantinople by Justinian in 564, was revised and enlarged by Photius and published under Basil in 883. Many of the jurists were as good canonists as civilians. Among the most distinguished canonists were John Zonaras and Theodore Balsamon, both of the twelfth century.

V.

Let us turn our attention from the East to the West. In this part of the medieval world the background of the history of Roman and Canon Law is formed by three vast processes: the decay and fall of the Western Roman Empire; the expansion of the Germanic peoples and the establishment of their several kingdoms; the growth of the Church and of its law. With the history of the Canon Law itself in the Germanic era—the history of its sources and constituent elements—we are not now immediately concerned; but it should be noted that, as the Church developed, its law also developed and that the ecclesiastical courts of Western Christendom everywhere enforced it. Our present object of study is the part played by the Roman and the Canon Law in the life of the Germanic kingdoms during the period of the decay and fall of the Western Roman Empire. What was the influence of those laws on the legislation of the barbarians?

The establishment of the Germanic kingdoms within the Western provinces of the Empire brought Roman Law and Germanic Law face to face. The problem as to which of these two bodies of law should govern was solved by the Germanic rulers on the principle which had already been followed by Rome in meeting a similar problem raised by the spread of Roman power and Roman Law to regions inhabited by non-Roman peoples. On the principle of the personality of law[1] the Germanic rulers allowed the Roman population to live under Roman Law and the Germanic population to live under their own native laws and customs. There were exceptions to this principle, as we shall see; but, in general, it long governed Germanic legislative policy and judicial practice.

Owing to the personality of law the written laws of the Germanic kingdoms were of two main kinds: the so-called *leges romanae*, intended for the Roman population; and the so-called *leges barbarorum*, designed for the Germanic population. Apart from these there were the Capitularies of the Frankish imperial rulers. Our study must now be directed to a brief consideration of these three sorts of Germanic legislation.

In 506 Alaric II, King of the West Goths, gave his Roman subjects their own code of laws, the *Lex Romana Visigothorum*, known also as the *Breviarium Alaricianum*; and this proved to be the most important of all the *leges romanae* of the Germanic realms. Alaric's purpose was to epitomise the leading rules of practice and thus to remove the prevailing confusion and uncertainty due to the many texts of Roman Law then in use. The commission of jurists appointed by the king for the execution of this purpose proceeded upon a plan similar to that adopted by the lawyers of Justinian's commission at a later time. Unlike the compilers of the Justinianean legislation, however, Alaric's commissioners neither altered nor mutilated the passages of the texts which they chose; they simply deleted those portions of the texts which were no longer appropriate to the social conditions then existing. In selecting texts they drew upon both the *ius* and the *lex* of the Roman system. From the *ius* they adopted the *liber Gai*, a condensed re-statement or compendium of the Institutes of Gaius which had been designed for employment in court practice and much used in Roman schools of the fourth and fifth centuries; and they also selected portions of the *Sententiae* of Paulus as well as a passage from the *Responsa* of Papinian. From the *lex* the commissioners took over by far the greater part of the *Codex Theodosianus*, as well as the Novels of Theodosius, Valentinian III, Marcian, Majorian, and Severus, and some constitutions from the private compilations known as the *Codex Gregorianus* and the *Codex Hermogenianus*. The compilers also incorporated in Alaric's Breviary an official but worthless *interpretatio* of all its parts except the *liber Gai*; the latter text, having been originally adapted to practical use, needed no further commentary. The *interpretatio* was not composed, as sometimes thought, by the Gothic compilers of the Breviary; it was drawn from writings of Roman Law teachers of the later period of the Empire in which the earlier texts had been adapted to the conditions then prevailing. When the commissioners

---

[1] But compare Bruns—Pernice—Lenel, *Geschichte und Quellen des römischen Rechts*, § 73 (Holtzendorff, *Encyklopädie der Rechtswissenschaft*, 6th edn, by Kohler, Vol. i).

had completed their task, the Breviary was approved by the popular assembly at Aire in Gascony in the year 506; and it was then promulgated by the king as the sole code for his Roman subjects. Henceforth all other Roman laws were to be ignored.

Alaric's Breviary represents in a striking manner the decay of Roman Law in the West[1]. At best it is a crude and incomplete compilation if we compare it with the codification prepared in the East by Justinian's commission a short time afterwards. But we must not forget that it was the work of a barbarian king and as such a rather remarkable achievement; and it certainly possessed the merit of being adapted to the social needs of the debased Roman population of Alaric's kingdom. Besides, it helped to preserve some of the texts of Roman Law in a part of the old Roman world largely submerged by Germanic barbarians; and it also exerted an influence on the later development of Roman Law in the West which entitles it to a conspicuous place in European legal history. In many parts of Western Europe the Breviary maintained a high authority throughout the Middle Age.

Attention should also be drawn to the *lex romana* of the Burgundians. Gundobad, King of the Burgundians (474–516), promulgated two lawbooks for his subjects. The so-called *Lex Gundobada* was a collection of royal ordinances, issued about the year 495, applicable to the Burgundians and intended also to govern the legal relations between the Burgundians and the Romans. But by issuing the *Lex Gundobada* the king did not deprive his Roman subjects of the privilege of living under the Roman Law; in fact he promised and gave them a Roman code of their own. This code, the so-called *Lex Romana Burgundionum*, embraces criminal, private, and procedural law. It was intended as an instruction to judges and not as a complete codification of the Roman Law; Roman Law not included in the *Lex Romana Burgundionum* continued to have validity. The sources upon which the code is based are the three *Codices*[2], the *Sententiae* of Paul, a writing by Gaius (apparently the Institutes), and school interpretations. After the Frankish conquest the *Breviarium Alaricianum* was used to enlarge or supplement the *Lex Romana Burgundionum*. Owing to the fact that Alaric's Breviary and the *Lex Romana Burgundionum* were often placed together in manuscripts, a stupid mistake arose as early as the ninth century. A short passage from Papinian's *Responsa* formed the conclusion of the Breviary. Hence it was thought that the *Lex Romana Burgundionum*, which immediately followed the Breviary in the manuscripts, was merely a continuation of the passage from Papinian. The *Lex Romana Burgundionum* itself thus came to be known as the "Papian," an abbreviation for Papinian: a designation which, despite the fact that it had and has no meaning, still persists in legal literature.

[1] Cf. Vinogradoff, *Roman Law in Mediaeval Europe*, pp. 6–12.
[2] *Gregorianus, Hermogenianus,* and *Theodosianus.*

The *Edictum Theoderici* holds a special place among the Germanic *leges* which we are studying. In establishing his Ostrogothic kingdom in Italy (493) Theodoric had no intention of obliterating the Roman Law. He differed indeed from other Germanic rulers in making the preservation of the unity of the Roman Empire a cardinal feature of his policy; and many of his constitutional and legal arrangements were based on this conception. The Goths lived in accordance with their own laws, the Romans by Roman Law; while disputes between Goths and Romans were settled in accordance with Roman Law. The *Edictum Theoderici*, promulgated probably between the years 511 and 515, arose out of these conditions. It was based on Roman legal materials, chiefly the three *Codices*, the writings of Paul, and interpretations; but it contained also new rules. It was designed as a means of preventing or settling disputes between Goths and Romans, and was applied to both peoples alike.

The Lombards differed from the Ostrogoths in their determination to preserve intact their own Germanic institutions. When they became masters of northern Italy (568), they treated the Romans as a conquered people and completely set aside Roman administrative arrangements. To the Romans as well as to the Lombards Germanic constitutional law was applied; Germanic law also governed the relations of Romans with Lombards. To the relations of Roman with Roman, as well as to matters of Roman family relationship and inheritance, the Roman Law seems, however, to have been applied. The Lombard Law itself was preserved in its Germanic purity, free from Roman legal influence, down to the middle of the seventh century (*Edictum Rotharis*). Not until the extension and strengthening of the Empire was Roman influence noticeable: as, for instance, in documents. After Charlemagne, in alliance with the Pope, had succeeded in subjugating the Lombards, the Frankish principle of the personality of law—the principle that each people should live under its own laws—was applied; and the Roman Law thus came into full force for Romans in Lombardy.

Although no special code or law-book was promulgated for the Romans within the Frankish realm in northern France, they lived, nevertheless, under Roman Law. From the sixth to the tenth century the Visigothic Breviary of Alaric was used in practice within this region as the general source of the Roman Law; but it was never given real statutory authority. In the north the Roman population seems indeed to have been of far smaller proportions than that of southern France. As a result, the Germanic customary law was of predominant importance in the north, while in the more Romanised south it played a lesser rôle, Roman Law being more generally applied. This early difference lies at the foundation of the later distinction between northern and southern France as the *pays du droit coutumier* and the *pays du droit écrit*[1].

[1] See pp. 749–50, *infra*.

It is to be observed, finally, that the Church as a juristic person or institution—although not the clergy as individuals—was judged by Roman Law in accordance with the principle *ecclesia vivit lege Romana.* This principle was embodied in the earliest Germanic folk-laws; and the reason for its firm establishment among the Germanic peoples is that the Catholic Church had been derived from the Roman Empire and hence had been maintained as a Roman institution. In the legal writings and decisions, as well as in the collections of ecclesiastical law, the validity of Roman Law seems to have been at all times assumed; the principle *ecclesia vivit lege Romana* seems indeed never to have been contested. In the earlier medieval period the chief source of the Roman Law as applied to the Church was Alaric's Breviary; while from the ninth century onwards Justinian's *Institutiones, Codex,* and *Novellae* were also in use. Not until the eleventh century were the *Pandectae* of Justinian similarly applied to the Church.

Especially illuminating as one of the main sources of Roman Law in the early Middle Age is the *Lex Romana canonice compta,* a collection of Justinianean materials for ecclesiastical use dating from the ninth century and originating, to all seeming, in Italy[1]. The chief materials upon which the compiler has drawn are Justinian's *Institutiones* and *Codex* and the collection of Novels known as *Iuliani epitome Novellarum*[2]. These materials the compiler has arranged, in general, according to their subject-matter; but it is difficult, as Maassen points out, to find in the collection a systematic plan consistently carried out. Materials of heterogeneous content are sometimes thrown in at places where one would least expect to find them. The *Lex Romana canonice compta* not only served a practical purpose in providing ecclesiastics with rules of Roman Law that might be useful to them, but it also helped to preserve the texts of the Justinianean law for the employment of future generations[3]. Furthermore, it was one of the many Roman legal materials of the Middle Age which influenced the growth of the Canon Law. Towards the end of the ninth century it was drawn upon by the compiler of the collection of canons that was dedicated to Archbishop Anselm of Milan.

The *leges romanae* of the Germanic kingdoms hold a special place of their own in the history of Roman Law in the Middle Ages. They represent the decay and barbarisation of the law in the West; but at the same time they represent the salvage of a part of the ancient legal culture

---

[1] See the account given by Maassen, *Geschichte der Quellen und der Literatur des canonischen Rechts,* Vol. i, pp. 888–896.

[2] See Krüger, *Geschichte der Quellen und Litteratur des römischen Rechts,* pp. 355, 384.

[3] On other collections of Roman Law for ecclesiastical use, notably the *Mosaïcarum et Romanorum legum Collatio* and the *Excerpta* of Bobbio, see Tardif, *Histoire des Sources du Droit Canonique,* pp. 266–269.

of the Romans in the midst of the vast disturbance and transformation
of European society in the early medieval centuries. The *leges romanae*
were themselves teachers of Roman legal ideas to the Germanic peoples;
they helped to prepare the way for the fusion of Roman and Germanic laws in the legal systems of later times throughout many parts of
Europe.

More significant still, from the point of view of Roman and Canonical
legal influence on Germanic law, are the so-called *leges barbarorum*.
During the period from the fall of the Western Roman Empire to
the beginning of the ninth century the various Germanic peoples who
settled within the former provinces of the Empire put their ancient tribal
customs, or at least a part of them, into writing *juxta exemplum Romanorum*. It seems to have been feared that unless the customs were reduced
to writing they would suffer in their competition with the more highly
developed system of Roman Law. Thus, in addition to the *leges romanae*,
the codes for the Romans in the various Germanic states, there arose
many Germanic popular codes, the so-called *leges barbarorum*. Many of
these codes of Germanic law bear marks of Roman and ecclesiastical legal
influence, not alone in their form but also in their substance. Although
originally the enactments of popular assemblies, they shew an increasing
influence of Rome in that the king acquires more and more power in
legislation; his share in the making of the codes tends ever to increase.
Some of the terms applied to the codes, such as *edictum* and *decretum*,
are merely copied from the phraseology of Roman Law; but certain of
the codes, particularly those in which the people took but a slight share
as compared with that of the king, shew distinct Roman influence in
their subject-matter. Apart from the laws of the Anglo-Saxons, which
are in the native language of the folk, all of the *leges barbarorum* are in
Latin—not the classical, but the low Latin from which in due time the
Romance languages developed; and this use of Latin is a testimony to
the influence of Rome upon Germanic law. Many of the codes shew a
mixture not only of Germanic and Roman elements, but also a mingling
of two or more Germanic systems due to migrations and various counter-
influences.

It is usual to classify the codes in four groups; but this and all other
classifications, particularly those based on resemblances and differences,
must be treated with some caution. On the four-fold classification, the
Gothic group includes the Visigothic and the Burgundian codes; the
Frankish group embraces the Salic, Ripuarian, Chamavian, and Thuringian codes; the Saxon codes include the Saxon, the Anglo-Saxon, and
the Frisian; in the Swabian group are the Alemannic code and its off-
shoot the Bavarian code. The Lombard code is sometimes classed with
those of the Saxon group; but in many ways it occupies a distinct place
of its own.

The codes of the Burgundians and the Visigoths are of special interest from the point of view of Roman influence. Both the Burgundians and the Visigoths had formed kingdoms under the Roman Empire before its fall; and both peoples were deeply Latinised and under the strong influence of the Roman Law. The result is to be seen in their codes, which are attempts to formulate complete systems covering both public and private law, after the Roman fashion, in contrast with the usual Germanic compilation of a limited number of the most important rules. In substance, also, the codes of the Burgundians and the Visigoths shew marked features of Roman origin. The deep imprint of Roman Law on these codes in large measure explains the distinct characteristics of later legal growth in the southern provinces of Gaul—lower France and upper Italy; for, in contrast with the Germanic character of legal growth in the northern part of Gaul, the law in the southern parts was, in a very marked degree, of Roman derivation.

It has already been observed that the Burgundian code of King Gundobad (474–516), known as the *Lex Gundobada*, was applicable to Burgundians and Romans alike in their inter-relations, the Roman Law being left in force for the Romans as their personal law. Roman influence upon Gundobad and his successors is to be seen in various ways, not least in the fact that, like the Roman Emperors, they issued decrees supplementary to the *Lex Gundobada* which were known in Roman fashion as *novellae*. Even after the fall of the Burgundian kingdom (534), the code still possessed validity under Frankish rule as the personal law of the Burgundians.

The Visigothic code, more important than that of the Burgundians, passed through two distinct stages of evolution. As the so-called *Antiqua*, the code contained laws of King Euric (466–483), the first of the Germanic rulers to give written laws to his people, with revisions and enlargements by Leovigild (569–586) and Recared (586–601). The *Antiqua* influenced the Salic, Burgundian, Lombard, and Bavarian codes; and it continued to be the fundamental law of the Visigothic kingdom until changed social conditions necessitated a radical legal reform, resulting in the second Visigothic code, the one known as the *Leges Visigothorum*. Two main factors produced this code: the ever-increasing power of the Church and the slow but well-nigh complete fusion of the Germanic and Roman populations into one people. Owing especially to the latter fact, the existence of two distinct legal systems—the *Antiqua* for the Visigoths and the *Lex Romana Visigothorum* (*Breviarium Alaricianum*) for the Romans—became an anachronism. Inasmuch as it was not possible to give either one of the codes legal validity for the whole population, in the reigns of Chindaswinth (641–652) and Recceswinth (649–672) the two codes were fused into one, to meet the new social needs. Recceswinth abolished Alaric's Breviary of Roman Law; but he preserved parts of the *Antiqua* in the new *Leges Visigothorum*. Promulgated in 654 and made binding on Visigoths and Romans alike, the new code became law throughout the Visigothic kingdom of Spain and southern France. Both in arrangement and in substance the code of *Leges Visigothorum* was strongly influenced by the Roman system, including the Justinianean codification; and this was likewise one of the main features of the later Visigothic compilation which was attributed to King Erwig (680–687) and known as the *Lex Visigothorum Ervigiana*. This latter code of the Visigoths, superior to most if not all of the other Germanic codes and taken as a model in other Germanic kingdoms, followed closely, in many ways, the Roman Law and the canons of the Church.

Many of the other *leges barbarorum* of the Gothic, Frankish, Saxon, Swabian, and Lombardic groups, even the laws of the Anglo-Saxons, displayed the influence of the laws of Rome and the Church in varying degrees of intensity; and this influence tended to increase with the progress of time. The full story of the permeation of the Germanic *leges* with Roman and canonical legal elements is fascinating and of fundamental importance, but it is at the same time long and complex; it cannot be recounted in this chapter.

Let us, however, take note of the fact that the rise of the Frankish Empire as the resurrected Roman Empire in the West meant a vast increase in the influence of the doctrines and rules of Roman and Canon Law throughout Europe. The many peoples united under the single sway of the Franks continued in general to live under their own laws on the Frankish principle of the personality of laws. Charlemagne, indeed, decreed in 802 at Aix-la-Chapelle that all the Germanic customs should be put in writing; and the survival of personal laws was a salient feature of Frankish policy. But over these systems of tribal personal law stood the Empire itself, claiming the prerogative of law-making. The imperial power was in large measure based both on the Roman principle that the Emperor was the source of law and also on the ecclesiastical doctrine that imperial authority was divinely bestowed. Founded thus upon Roman and Christian ideas, the Emperor's authority opened the way for a new and vigorous imprint of Roman and canonical principles upon the law of Europe. Imperial legislation reached to the farthest corners of the Empire, and assisted in moulding the laws of many peoples into forms that fitted them to be the basis of the systems of national territorial law which ultimately developed in the several parts of Europe. The main instruments of the imperial law-making power were the Capitularies; and these were general laws which had application to all subjects of the Empire and which possessed territorial as distinct from personal validity, cutting across and modifying the many systems of personal laws in force throughout the imperial domain. To this there was one important exception. Although on the imperial theory the Frankish Emperor succeeded to the authority of the ancient Roman Emperor, no Capitularies of the Frankish Emperor supplemented the Roman Law as a system of personal law; the reason of the legislators themselves being that no one could imagine the Roman Law capable of improvement. In many directions, however, the Capitularies as general territorial law for the Empire embodied principles of Roman and Canon Law; and these principles the imperial judges applied in their decisions. Judicial power is ever a potent factor in the spread of a legal system. It was potent in the time of the Frankish Empire. It was potent at a later age in the process of the Reception of Roman and Canon Law in Germany. In our own day it has been, and still is, a potent factor in the introduction of English Law into Roman-Dutch and other legal systems within the British Imperial Commonwealth. Not supplanting the pre-existing systems of personal laws, the *leges romanae* and the *leges barbarorum*, but standing beside them, and in a sense over them, the Capitularies as applied by the judges nevertheless aided the development of these laws and produced a certain unity of legal evolution throughout Europe, the effects of which were not fully manifest till later times. Like the Constitutions of the Roman Emperors, the Capitularies of the Frankish Emperors were a civilising and unifying force in which Roman and Canon Law played a rôle of high significance.

The history we have here so briefly sketched is the history of the foundations of the several legal systems of modern Western Europe. These foundations were Germanic customs and Romanic ideas and principles of civil and canonical law. In the period of the Germanic kingdoms these two main legal elements—the Germanic and the Romanic—were partly combined, partly fused. But everywhere, in all the many parts of Europe, the fusions differed one from another in form and scope; everywhere legal growth meant particularism and diversity. Unity there was of a sort, the unity based on the commingling and combination of Germanic and Romanic elements. But within this general scheme of unity there were almost countless detailed combinations, variations, types; and throughout Europe almost innumerable new growths, arising out of economic and social life, added themselves to the luxuriant garden of Germano-Roman stocks.

Another historical factor tended also to produce variety in legal growths. The gradual spread of feudal institutions turned personal laws into territorial laws; the principle of the personality of law gave place to the principle of the territoriality of law. Feudalism meant that law was no longer to be carried about by the members of tribes wherever they might wander; that law was now in a sense affixed to the soil, that it governed the affairs of all the men in a region, a territory. The fact that in the feudal age Europe was composed of a vast number of territorial lordships, large and small, involved the existence of an equal number of feudal systems of law and custom. Feudalism, no less than tribalism, thus led to particularism, multiplicity, and diversity in the domain of law. But in the territorial systems of law that arose as a result of feudalism much of the substance of the supplanted personal systems, including both Germanic and Romanic elements, was incorporated[1].

Still another important feature of the early Middle Age should be noticed. On the map of this age the national lines of modern Europe were nowhere to be seen; but social and political conditions of the time were slowly preparing the way for them. In the course of the eleventh, twelfth, and thirteenth centuries modern geographical and political boundaries were gradually forming themselves; Europe was slowly passing from the age of Germanic kingdoms to the age of the national states of later medieval and of modern times. In our history of Roman and Canon Law we must now take cognizance of these new frontiers in Western Europe; we must deal separately with Italy, Spain, France, Germany (with Switzerland and the Netherlands), and England. In the history of each one of these countries we must, however, go back to the early Middle Age to study the laying of the foundations of the law. Nor shall we find that in any one of these regions of Europe there was much of legal unity. Within each country particularism in legal growth—the particularism of feudal regions, of political divisions and sub-divisions of territories, of towns, of different legislatures and courts —was one of the main features of the time. Only slowly, and in some cases only in modern times, was unity in law attained in the different countries. England, with her centralised and unified system of medieval common law, was the first to attain it.

VI.

Maitland has taught us that "Italy was to be for a while the focus of the whole world's legal history." It is to Italy, then, that we must first direct our thoughts.

From the fall of the Western Empire to the end of the Middle Age— throughout the periods of domination by Ostrogoth, Greek, Lombard, Saracen, Norman, and Frank—the Roman Law never ceased to be in force in the Italian peninsula. Although this continuity in the history of Roman Law in Italy was at one time disputed, it has long since been established by the researches of Muratori, Donati D'Asti, Guido Grandi, and, finally, by von Savigny's great work on the history of Roman Law in the Middle Ages. Despite the decay of Roman political power, Roman civilisation preserved a stronger hold upon Italy, the very centre of Roman history, than upon the other provinces. Roman Law was a vital part of that civilisation, and it persisted tenaciously in the face of all the

---

[1] An interesting illustration is furnished by the history of Catalonian feudalism. The *Usatges*, which Raymond Berengar I put forth in 1064–69, are the earliest known feudal code. They were modified by later monarchs and supplemented by the introduction of Roman jurisprudence. See Merriman, *Rise of the Spanish Empire*, Vol. I, p. 476. On law under the feudal system, see *General Survey of Events, Sources, Persons and Movements* (Continental Legal History Series, edited by J. H. Wigmore and others, Vol. I), pp. 71–83.

foreign invasions. Already entrenched in the life of the peninsula before the fall of the Empire, the Theodosian Code long retained a certain primacy among the sources of the Roman Law in Italy. The Church itself had an interest in maintaining the Code of Theodosius, the ecclesiastical constitution and privileges having been founded under Roman governments prior to the time of Justinian. Likewise the books in use at the bar and in the schools were based on this Code. Nevertheless, the codification of Justinian was put into force in Italy by the enactments of the Emperor himself; and, although it did not supplant at once the earlier Code, making indeed but slow progress in this direction, it ultimately acquired a leading place in the legal life of parts of the peninsula. In the regions that were governed from Byzantium the Graeco-Roman or Byzantine Law—particularly in the form of its elaboration by the legislative reforms of the Eastern Emperors, such as Leo the Isaurian (*ob.* 740), Basil the Macedonian (*ob.* 886), and Leo the Philosopher (*ob.* 912)—was also extensively applied in practice.

Under Lombard rule Roman Law persisted and even influenced the Germanic Lombard Law itself. The legal history of the Lombard kingdom possesses indeed many features of special interest to the student of medieval Roman Law; and certain of these features are brought into clear light only through an understanding of the main characteristics of Lombard civilisation and Lombard law. The Ostrogoths had been mere military adventurers in Italy; and under the Byzantine Empire's reconquest they disappeared both as a national and as a legal influence. Wholly different is the story of the Lombards. When, in the sixth century, they entered Italy, they were in point of civilisation far behind the Roman population. But they were so strong in body and mind and so aggressive in temperament that they soon conquered a large part of Italy and held it tenaciously. Hostile both to the Empire and to the Church, they were determined to control all Italy and to hold fast to their own ancient civilisation and customs.

Our interest for the moment centres in these ancient Lombard customs. Their history in Italy is like that of other bodies of Germanic law in one fundamental particular: contact with the Romans brought about their reduction to writing and their modification in form and substance. Seventy-five years after the entry of the Lombards into Italy, Rothari gave their customary law its written form in his famous Edict of 643. Later kings made supplements to the Edict: Grimoald in 668, Liutprand between 713 and 735, Ratchis in 746, and Aistulf from 750 to 754. What, now, were the Roman influences that played upon this code of Lombard Law? Not only was the idea of a written code derived from the Romans; the designation of the code as an "edict" was a result of Roman conceptions still prevalent in Italy. The very language of the code was that of the conquered people; and it is possible that Romans, more particularly Roman ecclesiastics, took some part in the framing of the Edict and its supplements. The text of the Edict, especially that of the supplements, bears abundant evidences of the incorporation of Roman and Canon Law. In his preamble Rothari transcribes expressions used in the Gothic and Roman codes. The Edict or its supplements contain, in identical or nearly identical words, texts of the imperial decrees, the Bible, the canons, and the Fathers of the Church. Roman and Canonical legal influence tends to increase as the Lombard code is amended and enlarged by the supplements to Rothari's work. This tendency is strikingly illustrated by the supplements of Liutprand (713–735). The influence of Roman Law may be seen in Liutprand's imitation of its ideas and terms and in many points of substantive law; thus, Liutprand introduces reforms, based on Roman Law, in respect of wills, women's rights of succession, the guardianship of minors, prescription, and mortgages. Even more significant is the influence of Canon Law on Liutprand's legislation. During his reign the influence of the Church grew steadily; and he was the Church's main agent in the moulding of Lombard Law in conformity with the Church's law. Many provisions of Canon Law were thus purposely incorporated in the code of the Lombards; for example, canonical doctrines as to impediments to marriage, the privileges of ecclesiastics, the recognition of the pontifical primacy, and penalties upon the pagan practices still surviving. Ratchis and Aistulf followed in Liutprand's footsteps.

Strong ecclesiastical influence on the legislation of Germanic rulers is characteristic of legal growth throughout many parts of the West in this period; but it is especially striking in the case of Lombardic legislation. The permeation of the code of Rothari and his successors by the rules and principles of Canon Law shews us clearly how the Church, as the framer and interpreter of divine law, inspires the modification of secular law to suit the precepts of divine law. Comparisons between legal growth in the West and legal growth in the East, in the successive periods of medieval history, are ever enlightening. Let us not forget, then, that, at the very time when the Church is moulding the Lombardic Law along Latin-Christian lines in the reigns of Liutprand and Ratchis, the same Church influence is effecting a profound change in the law of the East. In the West, Liutprand supplements in 713–735, and Ratchis supplements in 746, the Edict of Rothari; while in the East, Leo the Isaurian's famous Ἐκλογή, an abstract of the Justinianean codification so coloured by Greek ecclesiastical ideas and principles that it may be described as a Christian law-book, appears in 740. Not only in this period does Canon Law exert a moulding influence on secular law throughout the world. Throughout the whole of the Middle Age that influence is continually shaping the form and content of Graeco-Roman Law in the East and Germanic-Roman Law in the West. In some periods the ecclesiastical influence on secular law is stronger than in others; but at all times there is a steady tendency in that direction.

Let us now turn to another aspect of the history of Roman and Canon Law in the Italian Middle Age. Great schools of law arose in Italy in which these two closely related legal systems were studied and taught by scholars. In one sense an account of the rise and the work of these schools belongs to Italian history. But when we contemplate the far-reaching influence of these seats of learning and instruction in Roman and in Canon Law, particularly when we observe Bologna's world-wide effect on constitutional and legal development and on political and juridical thought, we can see at once that we are dealing with one of the most vital aspects of the general history of civilisation. In law, as in art, letters, and other features of culture, Italian history is at the same time world history.

Throughout the darkest period of the Middle Age—from the fifth to the tenth century—legal studies in the West were never entirely interrupted. Although there seem to have been no organised law schools and no juristic studies of the highest order, there was nevertheless, as a part of the general culture of the times, a partial salvage of Roman legal materials and some scholarly attention to their form and content. Monks and ecclesiastics made transcripts and abstracts from the juristic fragments which had survived from antiquity; and these formed the basis of study in the schools of arts. In the curriculum above the rudiments law found its place under dialectic at the end of the *trivium* of grammar, rhetoric, and dialectic. For a long time legal instruction in Italy was for the most part in the keeping of the practitioners of the law; judges and notaries taught their successors and thus preserved from generation to generation the traditions of the profession. The Frankish period marks, however, the beginning of a far-reaching movement. Law gradually came to be regarded more and more as a science. Books were written dealing with the practice, the theory, and the history of the law. The methods of legal education were steadily improved. There arose in Italy great schools or universities of law. The legal renaissance spread from Italy to all parts of Europe.

The Italian law schools of the early Middle Age were of two kinds. There were schools of Lombard Law at Milan, Mantua, Verona, and Pavia; while, apart from schools kept by bishops and monks, the chief schools of Roman Law were at Ravenna and Bologna. The emphasis placed either on Lombard or on Roman Law in each one of these several schools corresponded to the legal conditions prevailing in the localities where the schools were situate. Legal conditions were constantly changing, however, as a result of the struggle between Lombardic and Roman Law in the practice of the courts; and this struggle in legal life was reflected in the work of the schools.

The chief of the schools of Lombard Law was at Pavia, the capital of the Lombard kingdom; and by the close of the tenth century the Pavese school had risen into fame. There had been at Pavia a grammar school, in which law was of course included in the curriculum from an early time; but, chiefly owing to the fact that the Palace Court, the supreme tribunal, was located at Pavia, legal studies were in general in the charge of the judges and practitioners. Out of this system of apprenticeship university instruction in law slowly developed; and, although the precise date of the founding of the Pavese school is no better known than that of the other early Italian schools of law, we learn much of its history from an "Exposition of Lombard Laws" written towards the close of the eleventh century, at a time when the Pavese school of Lombard Law was declining and when the Roman Law was already being cited as the *lex generalis*. From this book it is clear that the Pavese jurists belonged to two distinct schools of thought. The *antiqui* or *veteres* devoted their time and thought to the national Lombardic Law and its interpretation; and these jurists flourished down to the beginning of the eleventh century. The *moderni*, on the other hand, were the jurists learned in the Roman Law and interested in it as the source of rules and principles for the development and improvement of the national Lombardic Law; and in the second half of the eleventh century this modernist school of thought was in the ascendency. The most prominent of the Pavese lawyers belonged to one or other of these two groups. Thus, Valcausus and Bonifilius were among the *antiqui*, while Gulielmus and Lanfranc belonged to the *moderni*. Lanfranc, the son of a judge, early rose to a place of eminence among the Pavese jurists; and, later in life, not only did he found a school at the abbey of Bec, where students flocked to his lectures, but he became adviser to William the Conqueror and Archbishop of Canterbury. The best of the *moderni* were expert Roman lawyers, deriving their knowledge not from mere practice-books, but from the Roman legal sources themselves. In its later period, before its decline towards the end of the eleventh century, Pavia could be reckoned, therefore, among the schools of Roman as well as of Lombard Law.

At Rome itself the teaching of Roman Law, which in the time of the classical jurists had been a voluntary and private undertaking, appears to have continued down at least to the end of the eleventh century. Theodosius seems, however, to have given the Roman schools an official organisation. Certainly before the fall of the Western Empire the teachers at Rome were in receipt of official salaries; and this arrangement was continued by the Ostrogothic kings and by Justinian. By his decree *Omnem* (533) Justinian assigned official schools to Rome and Constantinople, and by his Pragmatic Sanction (554) he decreed that the salaries of law teachers should continue, so that the youth might not fail of good instruction. When the Empire's authority yielded to the Church's authority at Rome, studies in Roman Law suffered a change. Ecclesiastical authorities maintained a thorough acquaintance with Justinian's law-books and an interest in Roman legal science, but by giving to Roman legal studies a purely ecclesiastical tone they deprived the Roman Law of its former Roman spirit and independence of thought. By the end of the eleventh century Rome itself was in a state of decadence, owing to its sack by the Normans in 1084; and Odofred, the Bolognese jurist, tells us that, in consequence, Roman legal studies were transferred from Rome to Ravenna. The origin of the Ravennese school may well go back to the period of the Exarchate, a time when Ravenna was the only seat of Roman authority in Italy; but certain it is that at the close of the eleventh century it was a well-organised and flourishing centre of Roman legal study. Odofred asserts that Ravenna's success as a school was due to the taking of the manuscripts of Justinian's law-books from Rome, and that at a later time Bologna's success was equally caused by carrying them there from Ravenna[1].

Various other causes contributed, however, to the rise of Bologna as the most illustrious of all the Italian law schools of the Middle Ages— the very centre of juristic learning and of its diffusion throughout the civilised world. Bologna's central geographical position and its judicial and commercial importance, the political favour shown to the law school, and the genius of its teachers, were among the leading factors in establishing the fame of the school. But of special importance were the qualities which early distinguished its teaching. The school assimilated and united all of the legal elements derived from the past, and took a broad and independent attitude towards the various divergent tendencies in juridical thought. It adopted and combined the features of legal science already evolved in the schools of Constantinople, Pavia, and Ravenna; and it enjoyed the favouring influences of Pisa and the adjacent Tuscan regions, such as their Renaissance spirit. Byzantine juristic studies formed a background. The method of glosses and of parallel passages already applied by Pavese jurists to the texts of Lombard Law was none other than the method chosen by the early Bolognese glossators. Pisa was long in possession of the most complete and most famous of all the manuscript texts of Justinian's Digest, the manuscript now in the Laurentian Library at Florence; and distinguished Tuscan jurists, such as Pepo and Gratian, the founder of the new school of Canon Law, taught at Bologna. Finally, owing to the political conditions of the time, Bologna possessed the exceptional advantage of being the one city in Italy where Roman legal study could best establish itself afresh, with every prospect of great success, under its traditional imperial patron.

The revival of Roman legal studies at Bologna resulted in a return to the treatment of law as a science which had characterised the work of the classical jurists eight centuries before. The popular Roman Law which

---

[1] On the Pisan (later the Florentine) MS. of the *Digest* and the other MSS. of the Justinianean law at the disposal of the Bolognese jurists, see Krüger, *Geschichte der Quellen und Litteratur des römischen Rechts*, § 52; Bruns—Pernice—Lenel, *Geschichte und Quellen des römischen Rechts*, § 77 (Holtzendorff, *Encyklopädie der Rechtswissenschaft*, 6th edn, by Kohler, Vol. 1).

had been evolved in practice, in response to the social needs of the inter-vening feudal epoch, was disregarded by the jurists, their sole aim being to know the texts of the Justinianean codification and to expound them scientifically. Not only was law separated from dialectic and other branches of study and given its own separate place in education, but it was also deprived of its character as a mere handmaid to the practitioners. These methods and purposes of legal study spread outwards from Bologna. In the course of the thirteenth and fourteenth centuries old law schools were given fresh life and new schools were established. From Bologna there were migrations of teachers to other places where schools were set up; and some of these, such as the schools at Padua, Siena, and Pisa, became permanent and influential seats of legal learning. Rulers also restored or founded schools on the Bologna pattern, this being the origin of the State schools, such as those at Naples and Rome. In many schools Canon Law was added to Roman Law as one of the important branches of study. As the universities grew they sought the support of the Emperor or the Pope; and nearly all of them obtained the privileges and pro-tection afforded by papal bull or imperial charter.

The Bolognese jurists possessed manuscripts of all parts of Justinian's codification—Digest, Institutes, Code, and Novels; and the peculiar state or form of the manuscripts largely controlled the course of their study. Thus, there were several texts or readings of the Digest known as *literae*. The text of manuscripts which were earlier than the Pisan manuscript, or which differed from it, was known as *litera vetus* (*litera communis*, *litera antiqua*); the Pisan manuscript was designated as the *litera Pisana*; while a composite text, formed by a collation of all the other texts for school use at Bologna, was called the *litera vulgata*. Likewise there was a peculiar three-fold division of the contents of the Digest. That part of the Digest which extended from the beginning to Book XXIV, title 2, was known as *Digestum Vetus*; the part onwards to the end of Book XXXVIII was designated as the *Infortiatum*; while the remainder, from Book XXXIX to Book L, was called the *Digestum Novum*. This very remarkable classification of the parts of the Digest, which long persisted in European scholarship, has been explained, on the basis of the traditional views of the glossators, as the result of the transfer of the Justinianean manuscripts from Ravenna to Bologna. Irnerius, when he began to work on the manuscripts at Bologna, did not have the full text of the Digest; and, when he afterwards became familiar with the missing portion in the middle of the manuscripts, he named it the *Infortiatum* (the "fortification" or "fortifying addition"). What-ever may be the value of this traditional view, reported by Odofred, one of the Bolognese glossators, and now generally accepted by scholars, it clearly points to the fact, as Calisse, in his *Storia del diritto italiano*, has pointed out, that this triple division of the Digest's contents must have been made at Ravenna before the time of Irnerius. It was but natural that a long manuscript, such as that of the Digest, should have been physically divided into parts for the scholar's or student's convenience; but, as remarked by Calisse, " why the division should have fallen at those particular books is the unexplainable feature; unless we regard it as a reminiscence of Justinian's own instructions (persisting into the Middle Ages), for the study of his law-books."[1]

The Glossators treated the several parts of Justinian's codification as an entirety and as forming, together with certain other legal sources, the *Corpus iuris civilis*. They distributed the matters of the *Corpus iuris civilis* into five volumes (*volumina*). The three parts of the *Digesta*, formed in the manner already explained, they placed in the first three volumes; while in the fourth volume they put the first nine books of the *Codex*. The fifth volume embraced all the rest of the subject-matter of the *Corpus iuris civilis*, namely, the *Institutiones*, one hundred and thirty-four of the *Novellae* in Latin (known as the *Authenticum*), and the remaining three books of the *Codex* (*tres libri*). In addition to all these Justinianean materials the Glossators also inserted in the fifth book of the *Corpus iuris civilis*—immediately after the *Authenticum*—the text of the Lombard feudal law (*libri feudorum*) and several laws of the Emperors Frederick I, Frederick II, and Conrad. Inasmuch as the fifth volume, with its miscellaneous contents, could not be referred to by its general character, as in the case of the first four volumes, it was known by the Glossators as *Volumen* simply, or, by reason of the fact that it was much smaller than the other volumes, as *Volumen Parvum*.

The method adopted by the jurists who established the fame of the Bologna law school was that of the gloss (γλῶσσα, equivalent to *verbum*, *lingua*, *vox*), or textual interpretation. The jurists themselves thus came to be known as the Glossators; and it was they who gave to the school its earlier tendency and character. Glosses were not a new thing; within the field of law they had already been employed in the study of medieval Lombard and Roman Law. The new feature of the Bolognese school, the one which gives it its unique position, was the application of the glossatorial method for the first time to the texts of the law-books of Justinian. The adoption of this method at Bologna came about quite naturally, inasmuch as the law school was itself an outgrowth of the grammar school; and there was also the additional reason to be found in the persistent tradition of Justinian's order that his laws should not be altered in sense by a liberal as distinct from a literal interpretation. Literal interpretation, moreover, was particularly needful as a means of arriving at a correct text of the Justinianean codification. Although at first, therefore, the gloss was but a short explanation or interpretation of a difficult single word in terms of an equivalent, it soon became also,

---

[1] Constitutio *Omnem*, prefixed to the Digest. See Buckland, *Roman Law from Augustus to Justinian*, p. 49.

in the hands of the jurists, an explanation of a passage or of an entire
lex or even of a legal principle embodied in the text. These two forms
of the gloss became known respectively as the "interlinear" and the
"marginal." The explanation of a single word was placed above it,
between the lines ("interlinear"), while the explanation of a passage was
placed beside it on the margin of the text ("marginal"); and to each
gloss the glossator affixed his initials or some other mark or indication
of his identity. As the work of the school advanced, the gloss became
more and more elaborate and lost its original signification. It became,
in fact, the means of embodying the results of the master's legal researches. "It included," says Calisse[1], "critical notes on the variant
readings (*variantia*) of different manuscripts. It brought together *loci
paralleli*, which helped to elucidate the point. When these passages were
in conflict (*antinomia*), it sought to reconcile them or to decide on
the preferable one. Thus, finally, we find the gloss developing into a
genuine commentary, with all its proper appurtenances—the summary
(*summa*), the putting of illustrative cases (*casus*), the deduction of a
genuine maxim (*brocardus*), and the discussion of concrete legal problems
(*quaestiones*)."

The creative work of the Glossators falls within the period from the
early part of the twelfth to the middle of the thirteenth century. Pepo,
the Pisan jurist who migrated to Bologna, was the one who first taught
by the new method, but the real establisher of the glossatorial school,
the *lucerna iuris*, was Irnerius. His glosses covered the whole range of
the Justinianean texts, and, inasmuch as he had practised at the bar and
had close touch with the actualities of legal life, his teaching combined
in a striking manner both theory and practice. The work of Irnerius was
followed by that of the famous "Four Doctors"—Bulgarus, Martinus,
Jacobus, and Hugo—the activities of these four Glossators constituting
perhaps the most illustrious period in the whole history of the Bologna
school. Two pupils of Bulgarus—Johannes and Rogerus—were at the
same time the teachers of Azo and Hugolinus. Azo's greatest work was
his *Summa* of the Institutes and the Codex, a work which superseded,
within its field, all previous productions of the school. At the bar there
was a proverb that "who has not Azo, goes not to court (*chi non ha Azzo,
non vada a palazzo*)." In the study of Roman Law Azo's *Summa* was
regarded as essential as the very text of the *Corpus iuris civilis* itself;
and a knowledge of it was necessary to one who would enter the gild of
judges. To the school of Glossators belonged also other distinguished
jurists, among them being Placentinus, Vacarius, Burgundio, Carolus of
Tocco, and Roffredus of Benevento. Accursius, the last of the prominent Glossators, is also the most famous of them all. He was born near
Florence in 1182. After a period of study at Bologna, he taught there

---

[1] See *General Survey of Events, Sources, Persons and Movements in Continental
Legal History* (Continental Legal History Series, Vol. 1), p. 137.

for over forty years, retired in order to finish his gloss, and died about 1260. The gloss of Accursius was marked off from those of all the other Glossators as the *Accursiana* or *ordinaria*. Accursius and his gloss soon came to represent everything that the Bologna school meant in jurisprudence. His work embodied the results of all his predecessors; and, in a way, he supplanted all of them. The accumulated glossatorial learning of a century and a half was confusing, in the wealth of its details and in the variety of juridical opinions, to the practitioners in the courts. They found it difficult or even impossible to make their way through the maze which the Glossators had gradually erected. To the practitioners, therefore, the comprehensive and orderly collection of Accursius was the new, the up-to-date luminary of the law which the work of Irnerius had been at an earlier time. In the schools the *Accursiana* supplanted all the other glosses and even the Justinianean text itself. In the practice of the courts the saying, *Quidquid non agnoscit glossa nec agnoscit curia*, a variant of the proverb *chi non ha Azzo non vada a palazzo*, was prevalent[1]; the gloss of Accursius, that is, was held by the courts to be the law. This very saying in the courts shews us, however, that the school of the Glossators was already in rapid process of decay. For a time Accursius was followed by other Glossators, such as Odofred; but, on the whole, it is fair to say that the great gloss of Accursius virtually terminated the work of the school of Glossators. The *Accursiana* was itself the main symptom of decadence in the school. The original intent of the Glossators, in the days of Pepo and Irnerius, had been to focus attention upon the texts of Justinian's codification as the primary and pure sources of the law. To the early Glossators the revival of the Justinianean law meant that the texts themselves should be the basis of study and practice alike. The discarding of the text for the gloss, the mechanical following of the *Accursiana*, indicated that the science of the pure Roman Law had yielded place to practice; for it was the gloss which adapted and applied the sixth-century texts to the practical course of thirteenth-century judicature. What society in the fourteenth century needed, therefore, was a new juristic method in place of the stereotyped mechanism of the *Accursiana* represented by the maxim *Quidquid non agnoscit glossa nec agnoscit curia*. The time was ripe for the emergence of a method of jurisprudence which should base itself upon contemporary Roman Law, and not upon the Roman Law of the classical jurists and of Justinian in times gone by. The method which was developed to supply this social need of medieval Italy and Europe was the method of the Post-Glossators—the "Commentators."

The method of the Commentators—the one which had its rise in the latter part of the thirteenth century at a time when Accursius was still in his ascendency—represented a reaction against the gloss. The path

[1] On the history of this saying in Germany, see Dernburg, *Pandekten*, 6th edn, §§ 3, 4.

chosen by the jurists of the newer tendency was the well-worn path of scholasticism as distinct from the route marked out for them by the fourteenth-century literary writers of the Renaissance, such as Dante, Petrarch, and Boccaccio. To the claims of this great intellectual awakening the lawyers, bound as they were by tradition and narrowed by the practice of courts, did not respond until, at a much later period, they turned from the narrow path of scholasticism into the broader ways of the humanists. Calisse remarks that, when the system of the Commentators "after a formative period was finally developed, it stood forth as the apotheosis of a painstaking logic. The jurist's ideal now was to divide and subdivide; to state premises and then to draw the inferences; to test the conclusion by extreme cases sometimes insoluble and always sophistical; to raise objections and then to make a parade of over-throwing them—in short, to solve all problems by a fine-spun logic. He who nearest reached this ideal was accorded the highest fame in his science." Although already antiquated by the time of the Commentators, the dialectic method as followed by them no doubt put new life into juristic studies. But decay set in rapidly. Prolixity upon easy topics and silence upon difficult ones became the rule. Cujas justly passes this sentence upon the Commentators as a school: *Verbosi in re facili, in difficili muti, in angusta diffusi.* A copious mass of books, written in a crude harsh style, poured forth: a mass which, it is said, would have made *multorum camelorum onus.* Once more the original texts of the Justinianean law were lost to view in the intricacies of the dialectic exercises of the Commentators. The worship of authorities followed as a necessary consequence; it is said that lecturers, practitioners, and judges did hardly more than cite authorities by name and treatise. Ultimately came the doctrine of *communis opinio,* the doctrine that the juristic view which had the greater number of supporters in the books was the sound view; and thus, after the lapse of nearly ten centuries, there was practically a return to the famous Law of Citations of Theodosius II and Valentinian III (426). Judged by the standards of the classical jurists of Rome, or by those of the Glossators in their period of brilliance, the Commentators stand on a far lower plane in respect of originality and fruitfulness of juristic thought. One of the main reasons is that they stood aloof from the spirit and purpose of the Renaissance. It is, however, generally agreed by scholars that the school of the Commentators had merits as well as faults. Although their modes of thought and their methods were of the past, their gaze was upon the present. The Glossators sought only to know the Roman Law of Justinian's time; the Commentators endeavoured to know the Roman Law of their own day. The real achievement of the Commentators consisted in their adaptation of the older law of Justinian to the legal conditions of their time, their har-monising of the Justinianean texts with the other legal sources invoked by the courts, notably the city statutes, feudal and Germanic customs, the rules and principles of Canon Law. In the words of Calisse, "the old science was made over into a new one; and Roman law was transformed into an Italian law." The special talent of the Commentators created a literature—a body of commentaries on Romano-Italian Law—which acquired the force of binding law and played a rôle of great importance in legal life. Their method—known as the *mos Italicus* or Italian method—was itself destined to have a far-reaching influence; for it was adopted in other European countries, chiefly in France and Germany.

To the school of the Commentators belonged the poet Cino of Pistoia (1270–1336), Albericus of Rosate (*ob.* 1354), Bartolus of Sassoferrato (1314–1357), Baldus of the Ubaldi (1327–1400), Luke of Penna (lecturer in 1345), Bartholomew Salicetus (1330–1412), Raphael Fulgosius (1367–1471), Paul of Castro (*ob.* 1441), Marian and Bartholomew Socinus of Siena, Philip Decius, and Jason Mainus. Of all the Commentators, Bartolus of Sassoferrato, who died at the age of forty-three in his early prime, stands out as the greatest and most influential. He studied under Cino at Perugia and also under Raniero of Forlì; at the age of twenty he became a lecturer at Bologna, later moving to Pisa and finally to Perugia; and, among his public appointments, he held the post of councillor to the Emperor. His writings, which cover nearly the whole range of the law and are of a higher quality than those of the other Commentators, include lectures at Bologna, commentaries on all the titles of the Digest, legal opinions (*consilia*), and many treatises or essays on various branches of public and private law. The chief title of Bartolus to fame rests upon his great contribution to the work of his school in transforming the legal growths of the past into the law of the fourteenth century. The lawyers of his school came to be known simply as "Bartolists." The eminence of Bartolus is also strikingly manifest in the professional maxim that no one is a jurist who is not a Bartolist (*Nemo iurista nisi sit Bartolista*). In many parts of Europe the opinions of the great Commentator were held to be the law itself. The most distinguished of all the successors of Bartolus was his own pupil, Baldus of the Ubaldi, who was a Canonist as well as a Romanist; he taught not only at Bologna, but also at Pisa, Florence, Padua, and Pavia.

The school of the Commentators long held dominance in Italy. Even the attacks of Dante, Petrarch, and Boccaccio, and the great movement of humanism in the fifteenth century, did not turn the jurists to freer and more enlightened methods of legal science. Boccaccio's remark, that law had ceased to be a science at all, summarised the antipathy of the new scholarship to the *communis opinio*, the casuistry, the *mos Italicus*, of the Commentators. The attack of the fifteenth-century humanists resulted in a protest against the *Corpus iuris civilis* itself. Tribonian was reproached for mutilating the writings of the classical jurists; and even the fragments of those writings embodied in the Digest were now, declared the humanists, buried beneath a mass of crude medieval commentaries. These attacks, however, did not turn into new channels the main current of professional thought and activity. Even into the sixteenth and seventeenth centuries the lawyers proceeded on the lines marked out by Bartolus. The "practical jurists" continued the work of the Commentators by adapting the mass of Roman legal materials to the needs of daily practice in the courts. For them practice, as distinct from legal science or the theory and the history of the law, was the main thing. Despite the defects of the school of practical jurists, their work was nevertheless of real value; for it brought prominently to view the fact that the law was changing day by day, and that the Roman element in the law must be shaped and adapted to social needs. Only in modern times has this viewpoint of the Commentators and the practical jurists been fully recognised as a true contribution to the science of law.

Humanism was not without its effects upon Italian legal studies in the fifteenth century; but, on the whole, the new movement was represented, within the domain of law, by the work of classical scholars and poets and not by that of professionally-trained lawyers. Lorenzo Valla (*ob.* 1457), Pomponius Leto (1428–1498), and Angelo Politian (1454–1496), were among the leaders of the new humanist school of legal science; and to the enthusiastic study of the Roman legal texts—not only the Justinianean codification but more especially the earlier materials, such as the fragments of the classical jurists and the Theodosian Code—these scholars turned their learning and their skill. Their aim was to restore the Roman Law of the classical jurists as the basis of Justinian's law-books and of later legal growth; they sought to establish legal science on the broad foundations of history and philosophy. Legal research, both in textual criticism and in methods of dealing with the substantive law embodied in the texts, was thus given new and more advanced tendencies. While preserving contempt for the Commentators, these early Italian humanists in law always recognised the soundness of the methods of the Glossators. Their full sympathy with the general movement of humanism, however, enabled Valla, Leto, Politian, and their successors to disregard the limitations which bound the Glossators; and it is the general view of scholars that their work meant indeed a real advance in Romanist legal studies. The work of these earlier humanists was carried on by Andrew Alciat (1492–1552), whose legal writings and career have given him a deserved place of fame among Italian jurists and have caused him to stand out as the personification of the new school of legal thought. His main work, however, was done abroad; for, in 1518, he proceeded to Avignon and transplanted to France the methods of the science he had learned in Italy.

Let us for a moment retrace our steps to consider the study and teaching of Canon Law in the Italian Middle Age.

We have already seen that Gratian himself taught Canon Law in the convent of St Felix at Bologna, and that in many of the schools influenced by the great law school of Bologna the Canon Law, no less than the Civil Law, formed a part of the curriculum. The schools or universities made *doctores decretorum* as well as *doctores legum*. In the teaching of the Canon Law the *magistri* gave oral lessons (*lecturae*) based directly on the text; and it was the short remarks, originally written in the margin of the text, in explanation of its words, which became the glosses of the masters. The glosses, constantly increased by additions, took permanent form. They were reproduced in later copies of the manuscripts and finally included in the printed editions of the *Corpus iuris canonici*, notably in the official Roman edition of 1582 prepared by the *correctores romani* in the pontificate of Gregory XIII. The Italian school of Glossators was not, therefore, confined to the civilians, embracing as it did the *magistri* who glossed the canonical texts; and this is a feature of the revival of juristic studies, at Bologna and other Italian schools, of far more than ordinary interest.

Among the chief glossators of the *Decretum* were Paucapalea, Gratian's first disciple, Rufinus (1160–1170), John of Faenza (*c.* 1170), Joannes Teutonicus (*c.* 1210). The gloss of Teutonicus, as revised and completed by Bartholomeus Brixiensis (of Brescia), became the *glossa ordinaria decreti*. Vincent the Spaniard and Bernard of Botone (Bernardus Parmensis, who died in 1263) wrote glosses on the Decretals, that of the latter being the *glossa ordinaria*. The well-known Joannes Andreae (*c.* 1340) was the author of the *glossa ordinaria* on the *Liber Sextus*. That on the *Clementinae*, begun by Andreae, was finished by Cardinal Zabarella (*ob.* 1417).

Apart from the glosses, the writings of the canonists, like those of the civilians, fall into several groups. Thus, the canonistic literature consists chiefly of *Apparatus*, *Summae*, *Quaestiones*, and *Consilia*. But while, owing to differences in method, different schools of the civilians may be distinguished, the canonists are not in general divided into schools, except upon questions as to the relations of the Papacy to the national Churches and the secular powers. The systematic Canon Law of the Middle Age is embodied very largely in the *Summae*. Some of the early disciples of Gratian wrote *Summae*, including Paucapalea (1150), Roland Bandinelli (later Alexander III, *c.* 1150), Rufinus (*c.* 1165), Étienne of Tournai (Stephanus Tornacensis, *c.* 1168), John of Faenza (*c.* 1170), Sicard, Bishop of Cremona (*c.* 1180), and, perhaps more important than all, Huguccio or Hugucius (*c.* 1180). Writers of *Summae* of the Decretals include Bernard of Pavia (*c.* 1195), Sinibaldo Fieschi (Innocent IV, *c.* 1240), Wilhelmus Durantis (Durandus), Joannes Andreae, and Nicholas de Tudeschis. The *Summa Aurea* or *Summa Hostiensis*, written by Henry of Susa (*ob.* 1271), who was Cardinal-bishop of Ostia, is a work of the highest value. The numerous treatises dealing with canonical procedure, which form a special branch of canonistic literature, are called *Ordines Iudiciarii* and are to be compared with the similar treatises of the *legistae* or civilians. The *Ordo Iudiciarius* of Tancred (1214–1216) largely displaced the works of earlier canonists on this subject[1]. The fifteenth century, although it is identified with the Spaniard John of Torquemada and the Italian Panormitanus, is not as rich in canonistic literature as the earlier ones. In the period after the Council of Trent many distinguished canonists wrote commentaries on the *Corpus iuris canonici*.

VII.

It is time to glance at the history of the spread of Roman and Canon Law in medieval Spain.

The mixture of racial elements in the peninsula from the very beginning of its history gives to Spanish legal history a complexity which distinguishes it from the history of most of the other bodies of European Law. Even to-day Spanish Law reflects the historical movements and changes which finally produced the Spanish nation and gave it political unity and imperial dominion. Of all the factors which have created the Spanish legal system in a long process of evolution Roman influence has been predominant; back to the law of Rome, Spain, of all the nations of Western Europe, traces her law in most direct descent. Numerous legal sources survive to prove that Roman legal influence was profound and that it left an indelible imprint on the law of succeeding ages. In many ways the history of peninsular law under the domination of the Romans constitutes one of the most enlightening chapters in the history of the spread of Roman Law to the provinces before the disappearance of the Western Empire. Profound as was the Romanisation of law in Spain, it was nevertheless not absolute. In Spain, as in other provinces of the Empire, the Roman Law came into contact with native (here Ibero-Celtic) customs and possibly also with Phoenician and Greek Law introduced by the early colonists from the East. Native law persisted, at least in some regions, after the coming of the Romans; though there is no evidence that it still persisted in the latest period of the Western Empire. Apart from the place filled by pre-Roman Law in the Roman period, there was also the opportunity for the growth of indigenous legal institutions; and it is clear from the evidence that down to the last the *mos provincialis* was recognised. Hybrid legal institutions were created by the contact of native and Roman legal types, and indigenous variants were either juxtaposed or fused with the legal forms of the Roman province. Some of these indigenous legal growths survived the Roman period; thus, the betrothal custom of Cordova as to kisses—the penalty of lessened

---

[1] Pollock and Maitland, *History of English Law*, 2nd edn, Vol. I, p. 207: Bracton "levied contributions from the canonist Tancred."

inheritance for kissing the bride, before marriage, except in the presence of eight relatives or neighbours—was adopted as general law by a constitution of Constantine in 336, included in the *Lex Romana Visigothorum*, and embodied in Castilian codes of medieval and modern times. Indeed, at many points native peninsular law influenced the Roman Law; and this influence was one of the main factors in the growth of Roman provincial law in Spain. Roman Law, both public and private, was in fact introduced into the peninsula and there moulded, under the political and social influences of the time, into that Roman provincial law, partly customary and partly regional written law, which was revealed in some measure, a century after the fall of Rome, in the *Lex Romana Visigothorum* of the Germanic conquerors. The stages in the evolution of this provincial Roman Law in Spain follow in general the main lines of the development of provincial law throughout the Empire: two of these stages are marked by the growth of the *jus gentium* and the grant of citizenship to the inhabitants of the provinces. In divers ways, indeed, the introduction of Roman Law materially affected the growth of law in Spain. It meant, in the first place, that the legal institutions and doctrines of the Romans in respect to persons, things, and obligations were to serve as one of the fundamental bases of future legal development; and, in general, it led to the substitution of individualism for the communistic ideas which had formerly permeated the law of the peninsula. But the Germanic invasions and the fall of the Western Empire interrupted this evolution. The stream of Roman Law still continued to flow under Visigothic rule: it now flowed, however, partly in the old and partly in new channels.

In this period of the Germanic invasions and Visigothic dominion (400–700) the outstanding feature of Spanish legal history is the introduction of the Germanic Law of the Visigoths into regions long governed, in the main, by the peninsular system of Roman Law. The meeting of these two different bodies of law produced results of the highest importance and gave to the Spanish Law of later times some of its characteristic features. There was an influence of the Roman Law on the Visigothic and of the Visigothic Law on the Roman. One of the ultimate effects of these influences and counter-influences was the growth of hybrid legal institutions—a feature of legal evolution which was characteristic of the Romano-Germanic civilisation of Europe in general. A striking example of these hybrid growths is furnished by the *Formulas Visigoticas* (615–620), the formularies or models of public documents.

Until the time of Chindaswinth (642–653) the Spanish population—composed of the Hispano-Romans and the Visigoths—lived under a legal system based on the principle of the personality of law. The first king who gave law to the Visigoths was Euric (467–485), whose code, although largely a written statement of Germanic custom, displayed nevertheless some traces of Roman influence. Euric's code was applied to the Visigoths;

and such of its parts as embodied public in contrast with private law were also applied to the whole population generally. In respect of their own inter-relations the Hispano-Romans continued to live under Roman private law, modified somewhat by Germanic custom. Alaric's Breviary —the *Lex Romana Visigothorum* (506), based on the Gregorian, Hermogenian, and Theodosian Codes, as well as upon other imperial sources —solemnly confirmed to the Roman population their own code of personal law. Private relations between the Hispano-Romans and the Visigoths were governed, however, by the code of Euric.

With Chindaswinth (642–653) an important change took place. The *Lex Romana Visigothorum* was abrogated. A common code—the *Fuero Juzgo* (*Forum Judicum*)—was promulgated for both peoples, a code which harmonised and fused the Germanic and Roman legal rules and ideas. Some of these rules and ideas of the *Fuero Juzgo* shew a preponderance of Visigothic Law, as in the case of the law of marriage and of persons. Others are especially marked by Roman influence, as in matters of inheritance, prescription, and contract. On the whole, Chindaswinth's code represents the firm establishment of Germanic legal institutions within a region which had been highly Romanised in the pre-Visigothic period. The tide of Romanist influence was to flow more freely and with greater force in later times.

In the period of the Christian and Moorish kingdoms (700–1300) vast transforming processes were at work in the law of the several regions of Spain; but many of the details and even some of the main tendencies of this development are as yet but imperfectly understood. The history of the *Fuero Juzgo* in this period has not yet been written. But we know in a general way that this code, compounded of Germanic and Roman elements, remained as one of the principal bases of practice in the several kingdoms. Apart from the prevalence of the Romanic features of this code, a code which in some regions at least was a sort of common law, Roman influence—although it may be detected in the municipal *fueros*, the charters, the acts of councils and cortes, and the judgments of courts—appears to have been, on the whole, slight. The Church exerted an influence upon the growth of the law; but, in its general character, this was more a moral than a legal influence. Not until the period of the Christian reconquest were ecclesiastical legal tendencies marked. Certain features of Spanish Law, such as partnership, are said to be derived from Muslim legal culture. French Law was indubitably influential, not only in the Pyrenean regions but also in other parts of the peninsula.

One of the outstanding features of the legal history of Spain in this period, and especially from the early part of the eleventh century onwards, is the firm establishment of four distinct and different legal regions—the Castilian, the Aragonese, the Catalan (including in its influence Valentia and the Balearic Isles), and the Navarro-Basque, the latter of which was in large measure a mingling of Castilian and Aragonese origins. This fourfold differentiation, based on many social, economic, and legal causes, it is well for us to remember; for, when we come to the next period of Spanish legal history (1252–1511), we shall see that the Justinianean and Canon Laws were worked into the legal systems of these four regions in varying degrees of intensity and effect. The way for this renaissance of Romanism in the later Middle Age was partly prepared during our present period (700–1300) by the study of Roman and Canon Law in the several kingdoms, and by the establishment, notably in Aragon, of right reason and equity as supplementary sources of the law. But, although Romanism during the period from the middle of the thirteenth century to the end of the Middle Age came into Spain as a unifying force, it had in fact differing effects in the four several legal regions—effects which corresponded to the reaction opposed to Romanism on the part of each one of the indigenous legal systems.

We must remember, indeed, that the dominant characteristic of legal growth in this period of the Christian reconquest and the political unification of the peninsula (1252–1511) is the spread of the Justinianean and the Canon Laws in the several kingdoms. The whole period was rich in legal sources, more particularly in legislative acts; and one of the chief tasks of the legal historian is to describe the process by which this mass of legal materials was influenced by the legislation of Justinian and the Canon Law. In periods prior to the one now under review, Roman and Canonical institutions and principles of law had exerted a notable influence on the law of Spain. So far as Roman Law is concerned, indeed, this influence was in large measure an influence of the pre-Justinianean law. Even before the thirteenth century, however, the law of Justinian had not been without its influence in Spain; and it is possible that it was introduced into the Spanish territories ruled by the Byzantines. But from the end of the eleventh century onwards the western European re-birth of the codification of Justinian, due in large measure to the work of Italian and French jurists, produced clear and unmistakable effects in the peninsula. In the twelfth and thirteenth centuries Roman Law was studied by Spanish jurists. The texts of Justinian were diffused throughout the kingdoms. Works inspired by the legal system of Justinian were written in Spain by Spanish lawyers. Indeed, the thirteenth century may be taken as the time when the Roman Law, in the form given to it by the great legislator at Constantinople, acquired real importance in the Spanish kingdoms; and from that time onwards the influence of the Justinianean law upon Spanish Law steadily increased. Coincident with this Romanising process there was also a steady diffusion of the Canon Law. Not only was the Canon Law enforced in the ecclesiastical courts of the peninsula, it was also employed as an instrument for the modification of the secular law.

The details of this development in the several kingdoms—during the period from 1252 to 1511—are of absorbing interest. The temptation to sketch the main features of the Romanising process, as it penetrated into all parts of the peninsula, must, however, be resisted. We may but glance for a moment at Castile and Leon in the thirteenth century.

The *Fuero Real*, issued by Alfonso X in 1254, is the only legal work of a truly legislative character that was inspired by the Justinianean law during the thirteenth century in Castile. The elements which compose the *Fuero Real* are, however, predominantly indigenous. The code has as its basis the earlier *fueros*, including the *Fuero Juzgo*, but with additions; and it preserves, with some changes, the general character of the Visigothic, Castilian, and Leonese law evolved during the first centuries of the period of reconquest. While the Roman element in the *Fuero Real* is thus in part due to Roman influence upon the earlier sources taken up into it, it is also, in part, the result of direct borrowings by the compilers from the Roman and Canonical legal systems. Among the novelties introduced in this way into Castilian law from the Roman Law a considerable part of the theory of contracts, the accession of *insula nata*, certain of the rules of intestate succession and testamentary executors, may be mentioned. Likewise in the matter of adoption, the compilers of the *Fuero Real* adjusted the indigenous law to the system of Justinian.

In the history of Roman and Canon Law in Castile and Leon the reign of Alfonso X is also notable by reason of the compilation of the *Libro de las Leges*, a great legal encyclopedia, which, owing to its division into seven parts, came to be known in the fourteenth century as the *Leges de Partidas* or *Las Partidas*, names which are still used to designate it. The jurists who compiled the *Partidas* under the supervision of the king, between the years 1256 and 1265, drew upon three classes of sources: the customs and *fueros* of Castile and Leon, including the *Fuero Juzgo*, the *Fuero Real*, and the *fueros* of Cuenca and Cordova; the accepted Canon Law (the Decretals); and the writings of the Roman jurists included in the Digest, together with the works of Italian jurists dealing with the law of Justinian. The main materials drawn upon by the compilers were the sources of the Roman and Canon Laws. Indeed, *Las Partidas* may best be described as a systematic compendium of these two legal systems, modified in some particulars by Alfonso's jurists in order to adapt them to Spanish conditions. In the legal history of Castile the *Partidas* is of supreme importance; for it not only adds new elements to the law, but also modifies materially the earlier Visigothic and indigenous foundations of the Castilian system. In fact, it seems to have been the king's purpose to express in his compilation the new influences of Roman and Canon Law, to impose the code as a common law upon all his subjects, and thus to annul the municipal *fueros*, the *Fuero Juzgo*, and even the *Fuero Real* itself. Although this latter purpose was not effected, the *fueros* retaining their force, the *Partidas*—embodying many fundamental features of the Roman and Canon systems—steadily gained ground. Among lawyers and students Alfonso's work was used as a reference and text-book; and ultimately it was confirmed both in the practice of the courts and by act of the Cortes. The compilation of *Las Partidas* thus marks an important stage in the gradual adoption of Roman and ecclesiastical legal rules and principles, a process which by the close of the Middle Age had given a dominant stamp to the legal system of Castile.

The permeation of the legal systems of Spain by Roman and Canon Law in the later Middle Age furthered the growth of Spanish legal science. The Spanish jurists of the period include civilians and canonists of great ability. They were teachers in Spanish, Italian, and French schools of law; they were writers of legal treatises; they were editors of legal texts. Among them may be mentioned Juan Garcia el Hispano, who lectured on Civil and Canon Law at Bologna and wrote learned works; Cardinal Torquemada, who lectured at Paris and wrote commentaries on Gratian's *Decretum*; Raymond de Peñafort, professor at Bologna and compiler, by order of Pope Gregory IX, of the Decretals in the *Liber Extra*; and Antonio de Nebrija (1444–1522), who revised the glosses of Accursius and wrote *Observaciones sobre las Pandectas* and a *Lexicon Juris Civilis*.

By the close of the Middle Age Spanish Law, in its several regional growths, had assumed its main permanent features.

VIII.

The main characteristic of legal growth in France before the twelfth century, as it was also the central feature of the history of law in other parts of Europe during the same period, was the meeting and the mingling of Germanic law and the Roman and Canon Laws. Under the system of the personality of law the *leges romanae* and the *leges barbarorum* were both in force within their respective spheres. While under this system the Church as an institution lived by the Roman Law, the evolution of the Canon Law meant that in France, as elsewhere, the Church courts, within their own province, enforced this newer or secondary body of Roman legal doctrine. The process of feudalisation furthered the growth of the notion that law was territorial; and the Capitularies of the Frankish rulers introduced a body of imperial law, applicable to all subjects, which embodied Roman and Canonical principles and had territorial validity as law in contrast with the various systems of personal law.

In time, as Esmein has pointed out[1], the personal laws and the Capitularies fell into desuetude. In their place many territorial customs gradually developed. The Roman Law, in certain regions at least, ceased to be invoked as written law, its rules being regarded as a part of unwritten custom. This process—developing during the chaotic period of the tenth and eleventh centuries and coming to a definite result in

[1] *Histoire du Droit Français*, 7th edn, pp. 705–707.

the course of the twelfth century—determined in many ways the whole future history of law in France. In the second part of the eleventh century, however, the Roman written law emerged once more as with a re-birth; and during the next two centuries it played a highly important rôle. It either had validity alongside custom or it shaped and modified custom itself. Down to the very end of the *ancien régime* the Roman Law remained in force as binding law, but in a measure which varied with subject-matter and locality. In the course of the twelfth century a new and vigorous source of law appeared in the form of royal legislative power. From the fourteenth century onwards the *ordonnances* of the kings evolved a body of public and private law of very great importance; and during the course of the sixteenth century they transformed most of the important *coûtumes* into true *lois*.

Meanwhile, during the centuries when this long process of development was taking its course, the Canon Law, profoundly influenced by the renaissance of Roman Law, had slowly taken its place as a world-wide system of jurisprudence. In France the canonical system not only exerted on many parts of the secular law a remarkable influence, but, down to the close of the *ancien régime*, it also retained, up to a certain point, the character of a body of laws binding the State as well as the Church.

The period from 1100 to 1500 is of special interest. The gradual adoption of the principle that law was territorial and not personal, an evolution due in large measure, as we have seen, to the establishment of feudalism, led to the division of France into two parts, the regions of written law (*pays de droit écrit*) and the regions of customary law (*pays de coûtumes*). The *pays de droit écrit* is the southern part of France, about one-third of the entire country; while north of an irregular line of boundary, running from the Ile d'Oléron to the Lake of Geneva, lies the *pays de coûtumes*. The place of Roman Law in each one of these two distinct parts of France forms one of the most instructive chapters in the history of French medieval law.

In the south the Roman population greatly exceeded in numbers the Germanic population. Under the system of the personality of laws the Roman Law had been applied to the Romans, and when the principle of the territoriality of laws was established the Roman Law, being the law of the majority, was applied to all persons, Roman and Germanic, as the customary and common law of the southern regions. The point that Roman Law was applied as the Custom of the South is worthy of special note. The authority of the Roman Law in the *pays de droit écrit* was not derived from any official promulgation in the Roman or Germanic periods of French history; it was derived from its character as local custom, and as such it was recognised as binding by the rulers of the southern regions. The fact that the Roman Law was applied as custom helps us to understand why it varied, in respect of its scope and force, from province to province and from century to century, and why, from time to time, one set of Roman legal sources supplanted another as the guide to the nature of legal rules and principles. For the very reason that the Roman Law in those regions was treated as custom, the earlier sources of that law were easily abandoned for the later ones as repositories of custom; and we find indeed that the gradual spread of the Justinianean compilations displaced not only the Theodosian Code but also the Breviary of Alaric and the *Lex Romana Burgundionum*. For the same reason we find that the customary Roman Law was modified by local statutes.

In the north—the *pays de coûtumes*—the place of the Roman legal system was different. In these regions the customary law was composed of diverse elements: mixed remnants of Germanic and Roman Law, Canon Law, the Capitularies which had not fallen into desuetude, and local usages. From an early time the Roman Law—the common law of all Christian peoples—possessed, even in the *pays de coûtumes*, a very great authority as the embodiment of juristic theory. From the universities came the lawyers; and in the universities the Roman and Canon Laws were the only subjects of legal study. At an early period the texts of the Digest and the writings of the Bolognese jurists were translated into French. In the interpretation and application of the *coûtumes*, courts and legal writers alike employed the Roman Law as a kind of universal legal logic and as the fountain of supplementary rules, helpful analogies, and principles of interpretation. During the sixteenth century Roman Law played so important a rôle in legal education, in the practice of the courts, and in the literature of the law, that jurists raised the question whether the Roman Law was not, after all, the common law of the *pays de coûtumes*. The question thus raised has been the subject of learned dispute from that day to this; and French lawyers have never really reached full accord. The better view seems to be, however, that in the regions of the *coûtumes* the Roman Law did not become, as it did in the regions of the *droit écrit*, the common law. In the north, as distinct from the south, Roman Law possessed a theoretical or juristic authority. This authority, although it was not absolutely binding, had persuasive power, influencing judges, practitioners, and legislators. The authority exerted was the authority of legal reason; and as legal reason the Roman Law spread throughout the regions of the *coûtumes* and influenced them, ultimately colouring them when they were reduced to writing.

In the manner and with the effect thus briefly indicated the Roman Law established itself in both parts of medieval France—the *pays de droit écrit* and the *pays de coûtumes*. Transmitted in this form to later ages, the Roman Law was ultimately embodied, as one of its fundamental elements, in the codified Civil Law of modern France.

The influence of the Roman and Canon Laws on the development of medieval law in France is to be observed in the legal literature of the time. Thus, in his compilation of the customs and usages of Vermandois,

Pierre de Fontaines, one of the councillors of St Louis, translates passages from Justinian's Digest and Code. The private work known as the *Anciens Usages d'Artois* (1283–1302) has citations from Roman and Canonical legal sources; while the *Livre de Jostice et de Plet*, a work concerned with the usages of Orléans and probably written shortly after 1259, is for the most part a translation of Roman texts. Philip de Rémy, lord of Beaumanoir (1246 or 1247–1296), employs as the sources of his *Coûtumes de Beauvaisis* not only the settled usages and the judgments of courts, but also the Roman Law, "the law which is common to the whole of France." Jehan Boutillier, who died about 1395, gives us in his *Somme Rural*—which is a sort of encyclopedia of the whole of the French Law at the close of the fourteenth century—the picture of a confused mingling of Roman and Canon Law with the customary law. At an early time the writings of Bolognese jurists, including the *Summa* of Azo, were translated into French.

In the Middle Ages the Civil and Canon Laws were both taught in the French universities; but not until modern times was French Law added to the curriculum. A break in the continuity of teaching Roman Law occurred, however, in the thirteenth century. Honorius III in 1219, by the papal decretal *Super specula*, expressly forbade the teaching of Roman Law at Paris; and a century later, in 1312, Philip the Fair confirmed the decretal in a royal ordinance. Down to 1679, when it was brought back once more into the official curriculum, Roman Law could be taught at Paris only *privatim*; Cujas, the great Romanist of the sixteenth century, was obliged to secure the express authority of the Parlement in order that he might teach it. It is not difficult to see that the Church had an interest in strengthening the position of Canon Law, at the expense of Civil Law, in the very centre of European theological studies. Inasmuch as the Ile de France, with Paris as its capital, was a region of custom as distinct from written law, there was of course less practical need for the teaching of Roman Law at Paris than at other French universities. Nevertheless, the prohibition of the King of France seems at first sight surprising. The explanation may well lie, as Brissaud suggests, in a fear of the political influence of the civilians of Bologna, who were at that time teaching the doctrine that the King of France was a subject of the Holy Roman Emperor.

Instruction in Roman Law at medieval French universities other than Paris was encouraged by the Church. In the period of the personality of laws the Church had lived by the Roman Law (*ecclesia vivit lege Romana*); and the Roman Law had contributed much to the formation of the Church's system of Canon Law. These features of the legal history of the Church seem to have played a part in leading the ecclesiastics to take a favourable view of the teaching of Roman Law at all the French universities except theological Paris. Furthermore, many jurists of the Middle Age were canonists as well as civilians; and a considerable number of them seem to have supported the Papacy's ultramontane doctrines. This factor in the situation may also have influenced Church policy as to Roman Law teaching.

The medieval civilians and canonists of France were greatly influenced, as were civilians and canonists in all European countries, by the methods of the Italian jurists—the Glossators and the Commentators. A little later, humanistic learning spread from Italy to France: it was Alciat, the Milanese, who carried to France the new jurisprudential methods of the humanists in the early part of the sixteenth century. In France—at famous Bourges and also at other universities—a flourishing school of humanistic legal thought soon came into being, which included such great Romanists as Cujas, Baudouin, Doneau, Douaren, and Hotman. Pothier, in the middle of the eighteenth century, summed up the work of the school in his *Pandectae Justinianeae in novum ordinem redactae* (1748). It was the work of this school which prepared the way for the great *Code Civil* and the many codes of civil law in other countries that have drawn their inspiration and much of their form and substance from Napoleon's.

IX.

In the early periods of the history of law in the regions now mostly within the German Republic—the Germanic epoch and the age of Frankish ascendency—the basis of the law was a great variety of Germanic customs. In the course of time the customs had been some-what modified by the Roman and Canon Laws as they slowly penetrated, by direct or indirect channels, into the regions held by the various Germanic peoples; and in the days of the Frankish Empire these foreign influences were more marked than in the earlier centuries. But, looking at Germany as a whole at the close of the tenth century, we can see that, save for the natural modifications due to the progress of the several peoples in the scale of civilisation, their laws still retained, in most fundamental features, their original Germanic character.

From the eleventh to the fifteenth centuries the main characteristics of legal growth in Germany were particularism and diversity. The written laws of the earlier period—the laws of the Saxons, Franks, and other Germanic peoples, and the Capitularies of Charlemagne and his successors—had gradually fallen into a state of disuse in German territories; for in Germany, in contrast with Italy, Germanic legal sources had not been made constantly the subject of legal instruction, nor had they formed the basis of a legal literature. Political and social changes vitally affected legal development. The principle of the personality of law was displaced, largely as the result of the rise of feudalism, by the notion that law was territorial and that it applied to every inhabitant. The old tribal laws were transformed, therefore, into the unwritten customary laws of localities.

It is true that there were royal courts and even royal-enacted laws; but there was no coherent central judicial organisation of sufficient strength to combat particularistic tendencies. German territories were covered by a network of special courts, such as the courts of feudal lords and of towns, and in these courts German Law was enforced. In Germany as a whole there was no legal unity, no common law. Legal particularism and diversity split the law into many laws enforced by many courts.

When we remember these legal conditions, we need not be surprised to find that German jurists endeavoured to produce orderly and consistent treatises of German Law out of the complex and diverse materials which they collected. Nor need it be a source of surprise to discover that these juristic efforts failed to achieve their main purpose of German legal unity ere the rising tide of foreign legal influence submerged large portions of the native law by the introduction or reception of Roman, Canon, and Lombard feudal Law. One of these native juristic attempts to produce order out of the chaos of German legal conditions deserves special notice. At a time when the Italian Glossators were reaching the end of their labours and Gregory IX's collection of decretals (1234) was added to the *corpus* of Canon Law, Eike von Repkow, a German knight who had long served as a lay-judge, seems to have realised the danger to the native law of his race from the foreign and rival systems. In the *Sachsenspiegel*, composed between 1198 and 1235, and probably in the third decade of the thirteenth century, Eike brought together the principles of Saxon customary law and gave them coherence and systematic order; and upon Eike's famous work some of the most important of the later treatises on German Law were based. A comparison of the *Sachsenspiegel* with the contemporary treatise of Bracton on the law of England shews us that Eike's work is distinguished from Bracton's by its originality and its freedom from the influence of the Glossators[1]. Eike's book of Saxon native jurisprudence and the works of other German lawyers helped for a time indeed to stem in some fashion the rising influence of Roman Law in northern Germany. But the conflict between German Law and the foreign laws was an unequal one from the beginning. The *Sachsenspiegel* marks, in fact, the end of the creative period in the evolution of German national law. Most of the main factors which determine legal growth in a period of conflict between competing laws—the fact, for example, that the Roman law-books contained a systematic *corpus* of general principles suitable to an advancing civilisation—were on the side of the foreign laws. Their reception in Germany turned—and turned permanently— the whole current of legal evolution into new channels. Even to-day the law of Germany is still flowing in the channels cut deep down into the

---

[1] It is possible, however, that the *Sachsenspiegel* owes something to the writings of Italian canonists. See K. Zeumer's essays cited in the bibliography appended to this chapter.

soil of German life and civilisation by this vast process of adopting the extraneous laws. The *Bürgerliches Gesetzbuch* of 1900 is a code of German private law—but at the same time it is a code of German private law in which Romanistic legal traditions form a constituent element as pervasive and important as the Germanic.

The "Reception" of foreign laws in Germany means the adoption of three systems—Roman Law, Canon Law, and the Lombard feudal law. Of the reception of the Lombard feudal law nothing need here be said; and of the Reception of Roman and Canon Law only the barest sketch can be given. First of all, let two things be specially noted. The reception of these two bodies of foreign law formed a long historical process extending through several centuries; it was not accomplished by a single sovereign fiat. Furthermore, although the reception of the two Romanic systems constituted, in a sense, but one single process, yet this process embraced two movements which differed one from the other in respect of their causes and their course. Scholars still dispute in regard to the matter of chronological priority as between these two movements. Brunner regards the Reception of Roman Law as first in point of time and of influence, and treats the Reception of Canon Law as its consequence, while Stintzing holds that the Canon Law came first into Germany, and, preparing the way, drew the Roman Law after it. When Brunner and Stintzing have spoken and have disagreed, other *doctores iuris utriusque* may be tempted to exercise the scholar's prerogative of silence.

In the history of the Reception of Roman Law two stages are to be distinguished—the stage of the theoretical and the stage of the practical Reception. The one consists of the gradual rooting of the conviction in the minds of German rulers, statesmen, and jurists that Roman Law may rightfully claim to be the law of Germany; the other consists of the actual embodiment of Roman Law in German judge-made law.

The theoretical Reception has its beginnings in the notion that the Roman Empire of the German nation was a continuation of the Roman Empire of ancient times, and that, in consequence, the Roman Law of the ancient Empire possessed subsidiary force in the medieval Empire. This notion gained ground in proportion as the native German Law became more and more enmeshed in the complex web of particularism. The spread of the knowledge of Roman Law by the many German students who obtained their legal education in the Italian law schools also furthered the growth of the idea. German legal literature—for example, the *Schwabenspiegel*, probably written about 1275, the glosses on the *Sachsenspiegel*, and the works of Nikolaus Wurms and Johannes von Brünn—shewed an influence of the Roman Law. German kings interpolated certain of their own laws into the *Corpus iuris civilis*.

The practical Reception of Roman Law has its beginnings with the appointment of judges who were trained in the foreign law. In the first instance jurists learned in the Roman Law were appointed by the king to advise him as to the law in cases which he personally decided; later they were appointed to his *Kammergericht*. After the establishment of the *Reichskammergericht* in 1495 Roman Law gained entry into this highest imperial court of justice itself. One half its members were required to be men learned in the law, and all its members were obliged to swear that they would judge cases in accordance with the "common laws of the Empire," Roman Law being included within this formula. Courts of lower instance—the territorial and city courts—followed the example of the imperial tribunals; but the village courts long kept themselves free from Roman influence, preserving the native law of the people. The struggle between the native and the Roman laws thus centred in the tribunals of justice. Step by step, however, Roman Law was adopted by the courts in their decisions; and it was thus incorporated in the German Law as one of its most vital elements. By the first half of the sixteenth century the Roman Law was decisive in the practice of the courts.

By the beginning of the twelfth century ecclesiastical jurisdiction had acquired an importance in Germany at least equal to that of the civil tribunals, and in the ecclesiastical courts the Canon Law was of course enforced. From the twelfth century onwards many German clerics proceeded to Bologna, Padua, Paris, and other foreign universities to study the Roman and Canon Laws; and this was one of several main factors making for the spread or reception of the Canon Law in the homeland of the students. Not only was the Canon Law administered in the courts of the Church; it also permeated the secular law. In many ways Roman Law and Canon Law went hand in hand in the work of modifying and shaping the laws of the German medieval communities.

In Switzerland during the pre-Confederation period (up to 1300) the various Germanic racial branches who dwelt there lived under their own folk-laws, which included the *Leges Alemannorum* and the *Lex Burgundionum*. Small communities grew rapidly from the eleventh century onwards, and each one of them developed a special law based on the old Germanic folk-law, Germanic medieval law being thus preserved in Switzerland in purer form than elsewhere in the German Empire. In Switzerland there was no "Reception" of Roman Law in the sense in which there was a Reception of Roman Law in Germany. In the period of the Old Confederation (1300–1800) there was indeed a Reception of Roman Law in the cantons; but it stopped short of the wholesale adoption of Roman rules and principles which marked the usual course of events in Germany. In fact in 1499 was signed the treaty by which for practical purposes Switzerland was severed from the Empire. In Catholic Swiss regions the Canon Law—in cases of marriage, usury, unchastity, and, in some jurisdictions, in cases of testamentary dispositions—retained its validity down to modern times.

The Roman Law influenced the laws of the Netherlands from a very early time. This influence increased, as time went on; but it cannot be said that there was ever a formal practical Reception in the sense in which this term is applied elsewhere in Germany. The truth of the matter seems to be that, owing to the decentralised conditions of political and legal evolution, an opening was made for the entry of the Roman Law as one of the important *subsidiary* legal sources, and that this influence of the Roman system was not equally strong in all the provinces. At an early time the *Codex Theodosianus* (A.D. 438) left its mark on tribal customs; and, similarly, the Frankish Law, which had been in contact with the Roman Law, influenced the customary law. The renaissance of Roman Law in the Italian law schools had important results in the Netherlands as in the rest of Germany. What, too, has been said of the influence of the Canon Law in Germany generally, also holds true in the provinces of the Netherlands.

X.

Law travels by sea as well as by land. Separated from the Continent by the intervening narrow seas, the British Isles came nevertheless within the reach of the influences of Roman and Canon Law. Of these influences one may not speak in detail. Nor is it possible to describe the spread of the Romanic Laws to Scotland, Ireland, and Wales[1]. Our attention for the moment must be restricted to England.

The law of England before the Norman Conquest was fundamentally Germanic in character, even though Celtic custom may here and there have left its trace on the customs and written laws of the Angles, Saxons, and Danes. Roman legal institutions do not appear to have survived the abandonment of Britain by the Romans; at least they do not appear to have contributed materially to the formation of the laws of the pre-Norman period of English history. " We speak of law," declares Maitland, " and within the sphere of law everything that is Roman or Romanized can be accounted for by later importation....And, in point of fact, there is no trace of the laws and jurisprudence of imperial Rome, as distinct from the precepts and traditions of the Roman Church, in the earliest Anglo-Saxon documents. Whatever is Roman in them is ecclesiastical. ...This inroad of the Roman ecclesiastical tradition, in other words, of the system which in course of time was organized as the Canon Law, was the first and by no means the least important of the Roman invasions, if we may so call them, of our Germanic polity." The Franks

---

[1] "The canon law of Scotland before the 16th century was generally that of the continent of Europe. The usages of the church were similar to those in France, and had not the insular character of those in England and Ireland. The canon law regulating marriage, legitimacy and succession was taken over by the Scottish secular courts and survived as part of the common law of the land almost unimpaired." Lord Phillimore's article on "Canon Law in England and in the Anglican Communion" (*Encyclopaedia Britannica*, 11th edn, *s.v.* Canon Law).

had, however, taken over Roman legal materials and embodied them in their own system; and, through English intercourse with the Franks, some of these Roman materials were imported into England. Roman influence of this character seems to have played upon the form and content of the Latin charters or land-books of the Anglo-Saxons.

Roman legal elements assimilated by the Franks had been adopted by the Normans in Normandy as a part of the Frankish legal system which they made their own. The Norman Conquest brought many of these elements into England, where they were to exert an important influence upon the growth of English Law, more especially perhaps the law of procedure. Nor, when we consider the Frankish-Roman influence, must we forget that Lanfranc, the Pavese lawyer, was William the Norman's counsellor. The fashion thus set by the Conqueror was followed by later kings. Many of the Roman legal influences that affected the growth of the prerogative and other features of England's constitutional and legal system were due to the advice and the work of royal legal counsellors trained in Roman and Canon Law. Henry III had Henry of Susa by his side, Edward I had Franciscus Accursii, the son of the great Glossator. Archbishops no less than kings imported foreign jurists trained in the Civil and Canon Laws. Archbishop Theobald brought from Italy a jurist who left his mark on English legal education and English civilian literature. Vacarius not only taught Roman Law in England—almost certainly at Oxford, where a law school was just then developing—and gathered round him a group of disciples, but he also wrote both the *Liber Pauperum*, which was a book on Roman Law for poor students who had not the means to acquire the Roman texts, and a tract on the law of marriage. There are other evidences that the Roman and Canon Laws were being more and more studied in England. The disciples of Vacarius glossed his glosses. Manuscripts were copied. John of Salisbury gave a sketch of civil procedure in his *Policraticus*. A manual of procedure is attributed to William Longchamp, King Richard's chancellor. William of Drogheda, law teacher at Oxford, wrote a *Summa Aurea*. In the fourteenth century an English canonist, John de Athona, wrote a gloss on the legatine constitutions which displays knowledge of Justinian's law-books. William of Lyndwood, still one of the leading English authorities on Canon Law, finished in 1430 his commentary on the provincial constitutions of the Archbishops of Canterbury.

English students early proceeded to Bologna to acquire knowledge of the Civil and the Canon Laws at the fountain-head. Schools of the two laws grew up at both Oxford and Cambridge, where degrees in each one of the laws were conferred. Some English lawyers were trained in both laws; and in various ways it was an advantage to them to be versed in Civil and Canon Law alike. The civilian, if he knew little or no Canon Law, might be employed as a teacher or as a servant of the king in the council or the chancery or in diplomacy, and he might also engage in practice in the courts of admiralty and the courts of the universities. But, on the whole, the civilian found less to do than the canonist. Canonists were not only required for the work of the ecclesiastical courts; they were also given employment in the royal service as clerks, as justices in the courts, and as chancellors.

The great law school at Bologna, which spread its influence throughout Europe, left its permanent mark on English juridical thought and on English law and procedure. What one may call the Bolognese factor in English medieval legal history worked subtly in two ways; for it meant the importation into England of Canon no less than of Roman legal ideas, rules, and processes. Closely related upon the Continent, these two legal systems were also closely related in England. Their separate influences flowed through many channels, but oft-times the two streams of influence united and flowed in one and the same channel. Only by a detailed and penetrating survey would it be possible to perceive and distinguish all the currents that were Roman and all the currents that were canonical. The revival of the ancient Roman Law as embodied in Justinian's books was the work of the Bolognese Glossators, and that work fell within the period from the early part of the twelfth to the middle of the thirteenth century. Tidings of the legal revival were not slow in reaching England, and for a full century—from the middle of the twelfth to the middle of the thirteenth century—the new learning materially affected the evolution of the English Law. Italian influence is to be seen in Glanvill's law-book; but it is chiefly noticeable in Bracton's great treatise, the main part of which appears to have been written between 1250 and 1258. The names of Azo and Bracton will always be linked together in legal literature. In the writing of his treatise on English law and procedure, Bracton, the ecclesiastic and the royal justice, while depending chiefly on the cases in the plea rolls, also made use of various Roman and Canonical legal materials, and among them, first and foremost, the writings of the great Glossator Azo. From these sources of the Romano-canonical jurisprudence of the Middle Age, and chiefly from Azo, Bracton derived his general notions as to what a law-book should be and how it should be written; and from them he also obtained specific legal rules and maxims. His main indebtedness to the civilians and canonists is to be found, however, in the form and arrangement of his book, for in its substance the *De Legibus et Consuetudinibus Angliae*, the book which Pollock and Maitland describe as "the flower and crown of English medieval jurisprudence," is fundamentally English in character. In the matter of civil procedure, however, there was a noticeable influence of the canonical system, and this influence may be studied in Glanvill's and Bracton's books. English civil procedure was rationalised under canonical influence; and, in some instances, it became indebted to the foreign system for direct borrowings. It borrowed from the exceptions against witnesses in the ecclesiastical courts the "exceptions," or "challenges," that can be made against jurors; it borrowed much of the science of pleading from the civilians and canonists. The *actio spolii* of canonical legal procedure was suggestive to English lawyers in the framing of their own action of Novel Disseisin. But, even though the main substantive features of Bracton's book represent English as distinct from Romano-canonical jurisprudence, we may nevertheless agree with Sir Paul Vinogradoff when he says that "the most important English contribution to Romanesque jurisprudence" in the Middle Age was made by Bracton[1]. Down through the centuries this Romanesque learning of Bracton, even though it was not very profound, has continually influenced not only English juridical thought, but also English legal rules and principles. In its origin and its essential features the foreign influence handed down by Bracton has been the influence of Azo and the other Italian Glossators. Great schools of law always live through the ages and continuously radiate waves of thought to places near and remote in the ever-changing world. Such a school of law was founded by the Glossators at Bologna.

As Pollock and Maitland, in the *History of English Law*, have pointed out, "the rapid and, to a first glance, overwhelming flow of Romanic learning," from the middle of the twelfth to the middle of the thirteenth century, "was followed in this country by an equally rapid ebb." From Bracton's day onwards the English Common Law developed on its own lines as a system distinct and different from both of the foreign systems now the object of our study. Some of the foreign elements which the Common Law had already assimilated it preserved; but, on the whole, the Common Law of post-Bractonian centuries seems to have adopted but little from either the Civil or the Canon Law. In the age of the Renaissance there was, indeed, the danger of a "Reception" of the foreign laws. But, as Maitland has taught us in his brilliant essay on *English Law and the Renaissance*, although English Law did not form a part of university education until modern times, it was nevertheless academically taught in the Inns of Court during the later Middle Age; and it was this teaching of English Law to the profession which "saved English law in the age of the Renaissance." In the words of Lord Justice Scrutton, in his *Influence of the Roman Law on the Law of England*, "the working out of an Equitable Jurisdiction, and the decisions of the Ecclesiastical and Admiralty Courts were building up systems largely of Civilian origin, but in the Common Law, the influence of Roman Law has rather retrograded than advanced since the time of Bracton."

Equity, as a distinct system of justice supplementary to the Common Law, has its beginnings in the later Middle Age; although not until modern times does it acquire many of its present-day features. The chief moulders of medieval Equity were the king's council and chancery; and many of the men who sat in these tribunals were ecclesiastics. Some of the ideas and principles applied by these courts, and certain of the

---

[1] *Roman Law in Mediaeval Europe*, p. 88.

features of their procedure, were unquestionably borrowed from the civil and canonical systems. But the extent of this foreign influence, both in medieval and in modern times, has long been a matter of dispute. Spence maintains that Equity's debt to Civil and Canon Law is very great; Maitland and Mr Justice Holmes contend that the chancellors had no intent to Romanise English Law and that indeed Equity does not in any way consist of wholesale borrowings from the foreign systems. The recent investigations of scholars seem to confirm the latter view. So far as the medieval period is concerned, the chief indebtedness of the council and chancery seems to have been to ecclesiastical procedure. Various important features of the procedure of the Courts Christian were taken over and adapted to the purposes of procedure in Equity.

In the English ecclesiastical courts, from the time of William the Conqueror to the Reformation, canonical jurisprudence had a wide field of application. In accordance with the older view, the English Church was always an independent national church, and, although it was subject to the general principles of the *ius commune ecclesiasticum*, it was not bound by particular constitutions of the Councils or of the Pope unless such constitutions had been "received" in England as part of English ecclesiastical law. Contrary to this view, which has persisted down to our own day, and is still held by some scholars, Maitland holds—basing his view on a study of Lyndwood's *Provinciale* and other authoritative sources—that the law enforced in the English Church courts in the pre-Reformation period is none other than the Canon Law of the Western Church, of which the English Church forms an integral part; and that the papal decretals were, therefore, as binding on the English ecclesiastical courts as they were on any other courts of the Western Church as a whole. "Whereas the English State was an independent whole," declares Maitland, "the English Church was in the eyes of its own judges a dependent fragment whose laws had been imposed on it from without."[1]

Without pursuing this controversy further, and remarking only that Maitland's view has been adopted by many scholars of eminence, let us take note of the fact that in the medieval struggle between State and Church in England the delimitation of the respective spheres of lay and ecclesiastical jurisdiction, and hence of the respective spheres of Common Law and Canon Law, played a rôle of the greatest importance. This contest between lay courts and laws and ecclesiastical courts and laws was not peculiar to England; it was a contest waged in nearly every country of medieval Europe. But in each one of these countries the struggle possessed its own local features; and the struggle in England was no exception to this. The claims of the English Church courts to wide jurisdiction were growing at the very time when Henry II was bent on the centralisation of justice in his realm, the strengthening of his own royal courts, and the expansion of their jurisdiction. The struggle

[1] *English Historical Review*, July, 1896, p. 475.

reached its climax in the dispute between Henry and Becket. Out of that dispute the king emerged the victor, and also in future disputes between the champions of the two jurisdictions the champions of the lay courts and of the Common Law were generally the victors. The victory of Henry VIII and his Church settlement marked the end of the long medieval struggle and the beginning of a new epoch[1].

Much of the subject-matter of the jurisdiction claimed by English Church courts in the Middle Age was purely ecclesiastical and spiritual. These matters were not claimed by the State as matters which fell within the proper competence of the royal tribunals; they were left to the Courts Christian. Apart from such matters, however, there was a wide field of law which the courts of the Common Law, with the greatest propriety, might well have occupied exclusively. It is, indeed, a striking feature of English legal history that, from the middle of the twelfth century onwards, the ecclesiastical courts exercised jurisdiction over many matters which can hardly be termed ecclesiastical in any true sense[2]. Thus, the ecclesiastical courts claimed jurisdiction in matrimonial causes —marriage, divorce, and legitimacy; and these claims neither Henry II nor his successors disputed. The claim to exercise jurisdiction in testamentary causes was likewise successfully asserted by the Church courts; they pronounced on the validity of wills and interpreted them, they regulated the acts of the Church's own creature, the testamentary executor, they decided all cases of succession to moveable property *ab intestato*. Despite prohibitions issued by the royal courts, ecclesiastical tribunals long enforced contractual promises made by oath or by pledge of faith[3]. The jurisdiction of the ecclesiastical courts over most of these matters was retained by them down to 1857.

In one direction the Civil Law exerted an influence on the growth of English Law which is worthy of special notice. In the course of the fourteenth century the Court of Admiralty acquired a jurisdiction to punish crimes, including piracy, committed at sea, and it also assumed a civil jurisdiction over shipping and commercial matters. While the law administered by the Admiralty was embodied in the great maritime codes of the Middle Age, as a supplementary law the Civil Law was also enforced; and the procedure of the Court was modelled on that of the Civil Law system. In the Admiralty, therefore, civilians found the opportunity to practise and to sit as judges. Although the criminal jurisdiction of the Court of Admiralty was transferred to the Common Law courts over three hundred years ago, its civil jurisdiction was retained down to our own

---

[1] See Tanner, *Tudor Constitutional Documents*, 1922, pp. 13–98, 357–374.

[2] It is not to be forgotten, however, that medieval views as to the nature of some of these matters differed widely from modern views.

[3] Compare the scope of the jurisdiction of French ecclesiastical courts in the Middle Age. See Brissaud, *History of French Public Law* (in Continental Legal History Series, edited by J. H. Wigmore and others, Boston), 1915, pp. 182–191.

times. In the course of the centuries English maritime law lost much of its international character. But it still retains, even to-day, certain features which it derived from the Roman system.

XI.

Difficult as it is to sketch in outline the history of the general development, the spread, and the sources of Roman and Canon Laws in the Middle Age, it is more difficult still to give, in a short compass, any clear conception of the medieval history of the rules and principles embodied in those systems. This difficulty in sketching the "inner," as distinct from the "external," history of Roman and Canon Laws arises in part from the fact that the historian is concerned with the several branches of each one of two extensive bodies of public and private law, and that he must study the rules and principles of each system in their relation to those of the other system. Nor is it sufficient to study these two Romanic systems in isolation. Not only their relations to each other, but also their relations to other bodies of law, such as the Greek and Germanic systems, feudal custom, town laws, and territorial legislation, must be taken into account. There are legal influences and counter-influences, in all the many parts of Europe, which produce modifications of older rules and doctrines and which lead to the introduction of new ones, the general result being an almost infinite variety of legal types. The difficulty of sketching the history of the rules and principles of the Roman and Canon Laws is increased by the further fact that these laws are never at rest; at all times and in all places they are subject to change in response to the pressure of the many forces at work in society. The words of Mr G. W. Cable, the novelist, are not inappropriate as an expression of legal change: for law is constantly "shifting like the fragments of colored glass in the kaleidoscope." The true picture of the law in its development is not obtained by methods similar to those of the older photography; it is obtained only by using methods that produce the impression of life and movement—methods comparable to those which now create the living and moving picture shewn upon the screen.

To the student of the inner history of Roman and Canon Laws in the Middle Age the vast range of the subject, both in time and place, is forbidding. An evolution—or, rather, a whole complex of diverse but related evolutions—extending through many centuries is spread over the entire surface of the Eastern and Western parts of the European world; and everywhere, in all the regions of the world, this evolution is intertwined with the other features of the history of medieval civilisation. How enlightening this inner history of the two laws may be made is evident to any reader of Zachariä von Lingenthal's *Geschichte des griechisch-römischen Rechts* and of the writings of other modern scholars dealing with the rules and principles of Roman and Canon Laws in their medieval environments. The history of *patria potestas* in the East after the time of Justinian may be taken as an illustration. This distinctive feature of the older Roman Law, this power or bundle of powers so intensive in the period of its full vigour that it was sometimes referred to as *patria maiestas*, was slowly modified in the course of Roman legal history, especially in the time of the Empire. Shorn of many of its older and harsher features it was given a place in Justinian's system[1]: and as a part of his great codification it played a rôle in the development of Graeco-Roman Law. Zachariä von Lingenthal has shewn[2] how the fortunes of the Justinianean *patria potestas* fluctuated in later Eastern history, how the rules of Justinian in regard to it were displaced, modified, allowed to fall into disuse, or revised, in accordance with the varying fortunes of Justinian's codification as a whole, two of the important stages in this development being marked by the appearance of the Ἐκλογὴ τῶν νόμων and Τὰ βασιλικά[3].

Many illustrations of the importance of studying the inner history of the two laws in the Middle Age may be drawn from the *leges romanae* and the *leges barbarorum* of the West. Rules of the ancient Roman Law, either in their original form or in modifications adapted to the needs of Germanic societies, were incorporated in these codes. The *leges barbarorum* are even more interesting than the *leges romanae* as embodiments of Roman legal rules; they are more interesting because they shew us more clearly the inroads of Romanic rules upon Germanic custom. Thus, the laws of Euric, the most ancient of all the written laws of the Visigoths, contain rules of Roman Law, some of which run counter to Visigothic custom. Sir Paul Vinogradoff has drawn special attention[4] to the declaration in Euric's laws that donations extorted by force or intimidation (*vi aut metu*) are to be null and void; and he cites this as a rule which breaks through the purely formalistic treatment of obligations natural to barbaric law.

When the student of the inner history of the two laws reaches the period of the revival of juristic studies in the West, he is appalled at the mass of the materials which lie to his hand. The very bulk of the *Corpus iuris civilis* and the *Corpus iuris canonici* is forbidding. Each one of these bodies of law is an extensive and complicated system, in which many branches are included; each system has its constitutional law, its law of persons, property, inheritance, contracts, and delicts, its law of procedure. In addition, each one of these two huge bodies of law is enveloped by a vast medieval literature: there are the glosses, the

---

[1] See Buckland, *Roman Law from Augustus to Justinian*, pp. 103–105.

[2] *Geschichte des griechisch-römischen Rechts*, 2nd edn, §§ 17–24.

[3] An instructive comparison of *patria potestas* in Byzantine law with its influence on Western secular law may be made by reading the works of Brissaud, Brunner, and other historians of European legal systems.

[4] *Roman Law in Mediaeval Europe*, p. 20.

summae, and all the other writings of the medieval civilians and canonists. The writing of a history of the rules and principles of these two great legal systems involves the tracing of origins and development, the setting forth of the relations of the several parts of each system one to another, the statement and criticism of the doctrines elaborated by the civilians and canonists[1], the recounting of the part played by each system in the legal history of many countries of the world in later medieval and in modern times[2]. It is clear that no adequate picture of the inner history of these two cosmopolitan legal systems can be given in a few words; any attempt to give such a picture at the end of the present chapter would be a grandiose project destined to failure.

[1] Gierke's *Staats- und Korporationslehre des Alterthums und des Mittelalters und ihre Aufnahme in Deutschland (Das deutsche Genossenschaftsrecht,* Vol. III) is one of the most brilliant of all the modern studies of the doctrines of medieval civilians and canonists. See also Maitland's illuminating Introduction to his translation of a small part of Gierke's volume (*Political Theories of the Middle Age,* pp. vii–xlv).

[2] For the influence of Canon Law on the several branches of secular law, see Brissaud's *Histoire du Droit Français* and Hinschius' essay on the history and sources of Canon Law in Holtzendorff's *Encyklopädie der Rechtswissenschaft,* 5th edition, 1890.

CHAPTER XXII.

MEDIEVAL SCHOOLS TO *c.* 1300.

THE schools of medieval Europe owed their curriculum of secular studies to the imperial rhetoric schools of Rome. For some centuries after the barbarian invasions Christian bishops kept alight the lamp of learning in schools where much "chant" and "doctrine" and but a meagre fragment of the old Roman studies were afforded, but the whole curriculum was eventually reclaimed for Christian schools. The imperial schools were "public schools," in the sense that access to them was open to all who could pay the fees, often small through the subvention of the State, to the rhetor or grammarian; when the expression "scholae publicae" is found, rarely enough, in early medieval documents, it always looks back to a school of this type—either one largely maintained by the State, or the school of a private master teaching for fees—in distinction to episcopal schools, where the pupil might be maintained and taught without payment, but where the bishop or his deputy settled questions of admission.

The curriculum of the imperial schools, viewed by medieval scholars through the writings of Martianus Capella, consisted of the seven liberal arts: grammar, rhetoric, dialectic, geometry, arithmetic, astronomy, music. The classification was retained by Boethius (*ob.* 524), who was the first to divide the subjects into two groups, the "trivium" and "quadrivium." Cassiodorus noted the appropriateness of the sevenfold distinction and its connexion with the perfect number of scripture, and Isidore of Seville preserved it in his *Origines.* The seven liberal arts fell into line with the general predilection for "seven" divisions in the medieval world, with the seven grades of the clerical *militia,* the seven articles of the creed, and the seven deadly sins. Under grammar was included the study of the Latin classics, under rhetoric the schemata, tropes, and figures so useful for the interpretation of Christian scriptures, under dialectic the logic of Porphyry and, after the twelfth-century renaissance, of Aristotle. Geometry included geography and such slender conceptions of a Ptolemaic universe as survived; arithmetic was for long represented chiefly by the "computus," or tables for establishing the date of Easter and the moveable feasts; and the last two subjects found for some time few professors, the study of Greek music not being necessary for the chant.

The question of the persistence of the rhetoric schools is of great interest. In Britain they perished with the withdrawal of the legions, though the tradition of classical learning survived in the British monasteries of Wales, Armorica, and Ireland. In Gaul in the fourth century masters were still numerous and schools flourishing, to judge from the information about his colleagues given by the rhetor Ausonius, and from other evidence. The continuity of schools in particular towns depended on the presence of celebrated professors; but during the century the existence of schools of several masters is to be inferred at Autun, Marseilles (where Greek was taught as well as Latin), Lyons, Bordeaux, Besançon, Toulouse, Narbonne, Poitiers, Angoulême, Saintes, and Auch. The fifth century brought to Gaul the shock of the Burgundian, Visigothic, and Frankish invasions, and the raid of Attila; the public schools were no longer supported by the State, and Sidonius Apollinaris witnesses to the willingness of the Roman provincial nobles to settle down under barbarian rule. The schools were no longer assured of a clientèle preparing for an imperial career, and, except at Lyons, there were no longer groups of masters, though individual rhetors are known to have taught at Marseilles, Arles, Agen, Perigueux, Bordeaux, and possibly at Narbonne and Clermont. In the sixth century the ruin of the schools was completed; the liberal arts were no longer taught; Gregory of Tours wrote that "the culture of liberal letters is declining, or rather perishing, in the towns of Gaul...one would not know how to find a single man instructed in dialectic or grammar"; Fortunatus, the great man of letters of the period, had been brought up in Ravenna. When schools were again founded in Gaul, they were schools of a different type.

In Italy, however, the rhetoric schools never perished—a fact vital to the survival of European civilisation, law, and politics. The Ostrogoths Theodoric (*ob.* 526) and Athalaric (*ob.* 534) protected them, and the generation which included Ennodius, Boethius, and Cassiodorus profited by the brief spell of peace. Schools were numerous, treatises on grammar were multiplied, and Cassiodorus planned with Pope Agapetus the foundation of a Christian rhetoric school at Rome for the teaching of the liberal arts—a scheme narrowed later to the foundation of his learned monastery at Vivarium. The Lombard invasion proved far more dangerous to the schools than that of the Ostrogoths; but the strength of local tradition, the nearness of the vernacular language to Latin, the contact with Byzantine learning by means of the Greek cities of the South, prevented their disappearance, and produced important results. First, up to and during the Carolingian renaissance, Italy supplied Europe, if not with great scholars, at least with grammar masters trained on the old classical lines. Bethar (*ob.* 623), an early scholasticus and Bishop of Chartres, who was for some time in charge of the Merovingian palace school (where his teaching was no doubt more religious than literary) came from Italy; as did Hadrian and Theodore, Paulus Diaconus and Peter of Pisa, Lanfranc and Anselm, and many others. Secondly, the tradition of lay scholarship persisted in Italy. Whereas elsewhere in Europe schools were maintained by ecclesiastics, and masters and scholars were clerks, in Italy the rhetoric masters and their scholars were not clerks, though they irritated the bishops by claiming benefit of clergy. Thirdly, the lay character of the Italian rhetoric schools, and the ecclesiastical character of other European schools, account for the fact that when, later, groups of schools flowered into universities, Italy took the lead in the secular studies of law and medicine, while Paris was mistress of theology.

The connexion between the other type of early medieval school, the episcopal or monastic school, and the minor orders of the clergy, was so close that some reference must be made to it. Those who taught in such schools before 1300, and, with the few exceptions of the children of princes and nobles, those who attended them also, were either clerks or probationers for the "clericatus": they received the tonsure and wore the clerical dress. The shearing of the hair (not at first the shaving of the top of the head, leaving a corona or fringe of hair all round) was a sacred rite administered by the abbot to the postulant whom he received, and who did not necessarily proceed afterwards to any of the seven orders of the Church; or by the bishop[1] before the administration of the first minor order. The idea in each case was the same—adoption into the abbot's or bishop's *familia*. The non-monastic tonsure was not an order, but (according to John de Burgh in the *Pupilla Oculi* of 1385) "a disposition towards an order." The seven orders (ostiarius, exorcista, lector, acolita, sub- (or hypo-) diaconus, diaconus, presbyter) were all, at first, given separately, but by the sixth century the first and second, or the first, second, and third, were conferred on the same day, and the candidate was ordained exorcist, or, more usually, lector. In England in Archbishop Ecgbert's time candidates would still seem to have been ordained to each order separately; but Pecham allowed the first three minor orders to be conferred together, and the *Pupilla Oculi* states that all four might be so conferred. The non-monastic tonsure (it is inexact to call it the "clerical tonsure" since monks were clerks) has always, in the Greek Church, accompanied ordination to the first minor order. In the Latin Church it was first allowed to be given separately, to those who had no intention of proceeding to orders, by Gregory the Great, in the case of the Sicilian *actionarii* employed in administering the papal patrimony. It was also given separately, after the Carolingian renaissance, to children of seven or over who were received into bishops' households to be trained as their diocesan clergy; before this, such children appear to have been ordained lectors at once. In pre-Conquest England, evidence that the (non-monastic) tonsure was given separately from the conferment of a minor order is lacking. In any case, in Europe generally, the number of those who received the (non-monastic) tonsure without proceeding then or later to minor orders was not great before the rise of the universities in the late twelfth century; afterwards, it was considerable. The reception of the tonsure, like the admission to minor orders, did not entail celibacy, though those who received them usually practised it for a time

---

[1] Cardinal-priests and a few others had also the right to administer it.

as living a community life, either, in the earlier centuries, in some bishop's familia, or, later, in some college of the university or provincial hostel. Episcopal statutes frequently reiterated that none could claim benefit of clergy who scorned to wear the tonsure and the clerical dress. Clerkship was proved by the production of letters of clerkship granted by the bishop at the time of conferment, or failing this, in France, by the production of barbers to swear that the tonsure had been properly made. It was only later than 1300 that English law allowed clerkship to be proved by the reading of certain psalm verses; and even then the verses usually chosen were from the sixteenth psalm: "The Lord himself is the portion of mine inheritance...thou shalt maintain my lot. The lot is fallen unto me in a fair ground" (lot, κλῆρος, clerk), which the candidate would have recited in alternate verses with the bishop who was shearing him. Clerkship before 1300 implied a definite ecclesiastical status and duties, and not merely ability to read or write; nor should clerks be confounded with those who were, for various reasons, entitled to benefit of clergy—a larger number.

By far the most important pre-Carolingian schools were the bishops' schools—small groups of lectors living in their households. The bishops formed the "ordo doctorum," and in this conception the teaching of the diocesan clergy personally in their own household seems to have been an equally important element with the teaching of the laity by means of sermons. Throughout the middle ages, "cathedra," of course, meant equally a "cathedral" or a professor's "chair." In the early Middle Ages, except for periods of confusion due to the barbarian invasions, bishops were ideally supposed to live a communal life with the clergy of their familia. References to this familia, and the ecclesiastical training afforded in it, are frequent in papal letters and conciliar decrees, and shew that the adoption of children of seven into it preceded even the fall of the public rhetoric schools. It was the disappearance of these, however, which made such episcopal schools vital. As long as the rhetoric schools existed, the lives of the more learned bishops shew them to have been taught in such schools; but, after their disappearance, the biographies of even the most learned bishops shew them to have been received (usually as children) and trained in some bishop's household. Pope Siricius wrote in 385 to Bishop Himerius of Tarragona that "Whoever vows himself to the service of the Church from his infancy (*i.e.* seven years old) ought to be baptized ...and joined to the ministry of the lectors." Certain *Statuta Antiqua*[1] mentioned these child lectors, who read in church, and laid down interesting rules for the regulation of the bishop's familia of clerks, "widows," and pilgrims. Pope Zosimus wrote (*c.* 418) to Esychius of these lectors: "If he shall have given his name from infancy to ecclesiastical ministries, let him remain until his twentieth year with continual observance among the lectors." Leo I wrote to the African bishops about the choice of suitable candidates for the priesthood: "The venerable sanctions of the holy

[1] Used by Caesarius of Arles, *see* Hefele, II, i, 104.

fathers justly adjudged those to be suitable for sacred functions whose whole life, from childhood to more advanced (*provectior*) age, has been passed by means of the stipends of ecclesiastical discipline." A stipend, an allowance sufficient to support life, could hardly have been made to children otherwise than by maintenance in the bishop's familia: and this is actually stated by the Council of Toledo in 531.

The first conciliar decree expressly dealing with familial schools came from sixth century Gaul, where the rhetoric schools had just perished. The Council of Vaison in 529 enacted that "all priests (*presbyteri*) who are appointed to *parochiae* shall, according to the custom which we have learned is wisely observed throughout all Italy, receive to live with them, in their house where they themselves dwell, young lectors (as many as have taken no wife); and, spiritually nourishing them like good fathers, they shall strive to prepare psalms, to persist in readings of Scripture (*divinae lectiones*), and in teaching the law of the Lord; so that they may provide for themselves worthy successors, and receive from the Lord the reward of eternal life. But when they shall come to full age, if any of them through the frailty of the flesh wishes to marry, he shall not be denied power to marry[1]." The school of a "matrix ecclesia" in a "rural diocese" is clearly here indicated; no chaplain of a rural "oratorium" could have nourished an indefinite number of young lectors. The cost of the maintenance and education of these ordinands is clearly the cause of the frequent enactments that no bishop should ordain the scholar of another. The Council of Toledo in 531 said expressly that it was unfair to the bishop who had taken the child "from rustic and mean surroundings" that he should later, "when imbued with such an education," transfer himself to another church. This council also echoed the decree of Vaison, applying it to bishops' schools: "Of those whom the will of their parents sets free from the years of their first infancy for the clerical office, we decree that immediately they have received the tonsure they shall be handed over to the ministry of the lectors; they ought to be taught in

---

[1] This decree has sometimes been taken to refer to "parish schools" in the modern sense, though this "parochia" actually corresponded far more to a modern archdeaconry or rural deanery than to a modern parish: the bishop had usually no more than two or three in his "rus" or "territorium." "Parochia," till post-Carolingian times, meant the sphere of a "matrix ecclesia," metropolitan, episcopal, or collegiate. There were besides priests and clerks serving chapels or oratories, but these had no "parochia"; the Rule of Chrodegang of Metz, as revised by the Council of Aix-la-Chapelle in 817, enacted that both the laity and priests who served such oratories were to attend Sunday mass in the *matrix ecclesia*. The spheres of such rural, presbyteral-collegiate, churches as existed in Gaul between *c.* 450 and *c.* 600 are referred to as "dioceses," and rarely, as at this council of Vaison, as "parochiae." While these rural dioceses, or rural parishes, were few, and served by a comparatively large familia, councils provided that the presbyter in charge should nourish lectors like a bishop; but when they became more numerous, smaller, and poorer, the requirement was dropped as impossible: the maintenance of a single clerk only was required from the ninth century.

the house of the church, in the bishop's presence, by his deputy. But, when they shall have completed their eighteenth year, their wishes concerning the taking of a wife ought to be scrutinised by the bishop in the presence of clerks and laity." It was doubtless to this formal choice of the young lectors trained in the familia of Augustine at Christ Church, Canterbury, that Gregory the Great looked forward, when he advised Augustine to live the apostolic (communal) life with his clergy, allowing such lectors as wished at this stage to marry to do so, and to receive their stipends (maintenance) outside the community, while attending its offices. The training of the Canterbury (and Rochester) child lectors by "masters and pedagogues" is independently attested. Gregory the Great himself founded a "schola cantorum" at Rome of a similar nature: he built, that is, two new houses for the school in the papal household which had already existed. The functions of "lectors" and "cantors" run into one another in medieval documents; the cantor or psalmista was not necessarily episcopally "blessed," the cantorate not being one of the seven orders in the Western Church, although it was in the Eastern. In St Ambrose's church at Milan (and in other instances), we find that it was the lectors who did the singing ("Lectores ecclesiae pondus portantes, docti cantu, lectione...").

In these episcopal schools the teaching depended on the learning of the bishop, or after the seventh century his deputy, the magister scholarum, scholasticus, or capischola. Latin and the computus were taught as necessary for ecclesiastical equipment, but the seven liberal arts were not usually so taught before the Carolingian renaissance. Paganism was still too real a danger in Italy for ecclesiastics, even those who like Gregory the Great had been taught in rhetoric schools themselves, to wish that classical learning should be sought for its own sake by clerks; hence Ireland, where Roman paganism had never been a danger, became for a time the nursery of classical scholarship. The Irish schools, however, were rather monastic than episcopal. The teaching of Hadrian and Theodore at Canterbury included the liberal arts and the study of Roman Law; but this far surpassed the teaching given in an average episcopal household between 529 and 800. Grammar masters were hard to obtain, as is shewn by the story told of Bishop Aitherius of Lisieux by Gregory of Tours. Aitherius rescued from prison, he says, a clerk, from the city of Sens, of extremely bad character. But the clerk " professed himself to be a doctor of letters, and promised the priest that, if he would commend the children to him, he would make them perfect in letters." Aitherius already had a "praeceptor," presumably for his household lectors, but he at once "rejoiced, and collected the children of the city, and commended them to him to teach." The clerk was presented with a vineyard by way of salary, and invited to the homes of the boys he taught. He tried to seduce one of the mothers, and complaints were made; but the bishop could not believe evil of a man so learned, and dismissed them. The wicked clerk then tried to induce the archdeacon to conspire to murder the bishop, and, failing, crept after the bishop, who was walking in a wood, with an axe. The bishop, however, turned and saw him; whereat he explained that the archdeacon had hired him to murder his benefactor, but that he had never intended to do the deed. The good bishop believed him, wept, and made him promise silence. Aitherius then returned to his house for supper, and afterwards "he rested upon his couch, having around his bed the many little beds of his clerks." The clerk approached in the night and raised an alarm, saying that he had seen a woman coming from the bishop; but the slander was apparent to all, for the bishop was over seventy, and was sleeping surrounded by his clerks. Aitherius' eyes were opened, and he got rid of him.

The lives of pre-Carolingian bishops and abbots refer frequently to these household schools, and shew that pupils were also taken for training by other priests; though in some cases the priest was probably, though it is not directly stated, the scholasticus of a bishop. Thus St Lomer (*ob.* 590), born of noble parents near Chartres, was confided by them to live with a priest Chirmirus and be imbued with sacred letters. Chirmirus, who was also the master of another Chartrain priest, Lancegesil, lived within the city of Chartres, "Domino militans": a member, that is, of the "clerical militia" or bishop's household, and probably his deputy in training the young lectors. St Rigomer was thus "trained from infancy by a certain religious priest"; many others, like Gregory of Tours, were thus "nutriti" by some bishop. St Germain de Granval (*ob.* 667) was delivered as an "infantulus" to Bishop Modoald of Tours; St Leger, Bishop of Autun, was confided to the Bishop of Poitiers and was "strenue enutritus." Acca was "nutritus atque eruditus" by Archbishop Bosa, the predecessor of John of Beverley at York; Headda (*ob.* 790) left a bequest to the cathedral of Worcester, "quia alumnus sum illius familiae, et iuxta limites ecclesiae disciplinatus et nutritus fui."

Even when, after the Frankish settlements in Gaul and during the fighting of the early Merovingian kings, the practice of the communal life of bishops with their households was relaxed, the familia still lived normally near the cathedra, and in the society of the bishop. The Council of Tours in 567 wrote: "Let the bishop have his wife as his sister, and so let him govern all his house, both his ecclesiastical and his own house, in holy conversation, that no suspicion...arise. And although by God's help he shall live chastely by the testimony of his clerks, because they dwell with him both in his *cella* and wherever he is, and thus the priests and deacons, or at least the crowd of young clerks, keep him safe: yet nevertheless, for zeal to God, let them be divided and sufficiently distant from his *mansio*, that those who are being nourished in the hope of being received into the clerical servitude be not polluted by the near contagion of the women (*famulae*)." When the reform of the Frankish Church was in progress under the influence of Boniface, the chief instrument of reform was the rule drawn up by Chrodegang, Bishop of Metz, in 754, to ensure a return to communal life on the part of the bishop and his familia. His own edition of the rule has no reference to the cathedral school, though young clerks were no doubt in his day received for training.

Monastic schools before the Carolingian renaissance were internal schools, and dealt almost solely with the training of oblate children, who might be received from seven years old, or even younger, like the young lectors in bishops' households. The children of princes and nobles were received for training by abbots both Benedictine and Celtic, but naturally not in large numbers; they would seem to have been received rather as pages into the abbots' households than strictly into the monastic school, though they were no doubt taught letters. In addition, where missionary houses, Benedictine or Celtic, occupied the whole ground, two other needs seem to have been met: that of teaching the outside peasantry the Creed, the Lord's Prayer, and the Ten Commandments by heart, and that of training internally boys for the clerical militia. The latter would only have been taught reading, writing, singing, and Latin. The monastic schools were intended for monks, and the great monastic schools, mainly post-Carolingian, were for adult monks; the practice of receiving monks from other monasteries, sent to complete their studies, was common. The greatest service to general education which the monks rendered was that of supplying learned monks who, as bishops, were competent to teach the young clerks of their household.

Educational activities which had been partial and sporadic before Charlemagne became normal or compulsory through the renaissance he inspired. The personal curiosity for learning, which made him attract learned clerks to his court, had immediate effects on the palace school, and on episcopal and monastic schools. He collected from Italy, at one time and another, Peter of Pisa, Paul the Deacon, Leidrad, probably Theodulf the Visigoth, and cantors from the Roman school, to teach the cathedral schools of Metz and Soissons; from England and Ireland he obtained Alcuin, the pupil of Aethelbert and the school of York, and some of his English students, and later Clement the Scot. The court became an "academia," where Charles himself learned classics from Peter of Pisa and the liberal arts from Alcuin—by way of question and answer. In this scholarly circle, Frankish names were too dull; Charles became "king David," Alcuin "Flaccus" (Horace), Theodulf "Pindar," Angilbert "Homer," Arno of Salzburg "Aquila," Eppin the cup-bearer "Nehemiah," and Charles' daughters "Lucia" and "Columba."

The palace school, to be distinguished from this "academia" of courtiers, had dated back to the days of St Leger (*ob.* 678), but not as a school where the liberal arts were taught. It had consisted of the young clerks under the archchaplain, and the sons of the nobility in training as pages and squires; young children do not seem to have been received, for the school was, like the court, ambulatory, and there are references to several "adolescentuli" who attended it after receiving training elsewhere. It is significant that Pepin the Short, by whom so many of the Carolingian reforms were begun, was educated, not in the palace school, but in the monastery of St Denis. In Charles' own time, when Peter of Pisa and Alcuin taught the school, the majority of boys and youths who attended it would seem to have been clerks, the future bishops and abbots of the kingdom, and to these the old classical education of the liberal arts was again afforded; but the point of great interest about the school is that some young lay nobles, like Einhard the historian, also received similar instruction, and this was a new departure. Bishop Wilfrid of York had received young nobles to train either as clerks or squires, according to their own wish when they were old enough to decide; but it was the greatness and magnificence of his household, his "innumerus sodalium exercitus," which procured his banishment. His successor, John of Beverley, also had young laymen in his train when travelling, and apparently living with him "in clero"; but if the tonsure was not yet given separately from a minor order in England, they may have been probationers for such orders. Certainly, the Carolingian palace school was the first to give classical (as distinct from religious) teaching to lay boys in any number, a feature in which it was copied by Alfred's palace school later. The account of Charlemagne's visit to his scholars, after they had been left behind for a time in Gaul under Clement the Scot, during one of his campaigns, would seem to shew that even his scholars were mainly clerks; for he rebuked the idle, and promised to the industrious "bishoprics and abbeys"—not lay offices. The sort of instruction conferred on the lay boys may have been of the nature of the "propositio" found in a manuscript contemporary with Alcuin and headed "Ad acuendos iuvenes." A certain man had a herd of 100 pigs, it begins; he wished to have them slaughtered in equal numbers on three days; how many should he have slaughtered each day? When time has been given for meditation, the "magister" should say, "quasi increpando iuvenes," "Now this is a fable and it can be solved by nobody."

From the accession of Charlemagne till *c.* 1170 episcopal schools were the most important organ of education, and were frequent subjects of legislation; after *c.* 1170 the universities, which grew out of them, replaced them as centres of the teaching of the liberal arts; though they, with the grammar schools of the diocese, continued to teach grammar and rhetoric to schoolboys, and theology to the greater part of the diocesan clergy. Monastic schools from about 800 to 1000 probably produced greater scholars, but these were monks who gave their whole lives to scholarship. From *c.* 1000 to *c.* 1170 the cathedral schools—Tours, Orleans, Utrecht, Liège, Rheims, Chartres, Paris—eclipsed the monastic schools even in the production of scholars; during this period they were the international centres of adult scholarship, as well as training-schools for the diocesan clergy.

Charlemagne's capitulary of 787, addressed to the Abbot of Fulda, ordered that in all the monasteries and bishops' houses under his rule there should be study, "litterarum meditationes," and "those who can shall teach," for grammar and rhetoric were indispensable for understanding the figures of scripture. In 789 he issued another more precise: "Let the ministers of God's altar...collect and associate with themselves (*i.e.* maintain in their houses) children, not only of servile condition but also free-born (ingenui)." Some bishops are known to have redeemed slaves for this purpose. "And that there may be schools of reading-boys (*i.e.* lectors), let them learn psalms, notes, chants, the computus, and grammar in each monastery and bishop's house." In these internal schools bishops were to train young clerks, and abbots were to train monks. The capitulary of 805 referred to such schools and ordered that all should learn truly about the computus, that children should be sent to learn the art of medicine (presumably, boarded in some school in South Italy), and that the Roman chant, as used at Metz, should be followed. Alcuin, exhausted with the perambulations of the court, retired in 796 to teach the liberal arts to the canons of the cathedral monastery of St Martin of Tours, and to such scholars as resorted to him[1]. He wrote in that year to Eanbald of York about the conduct of his familia, advising that his clerks should be separated according to their occupation, reading, the chant, or writing, and that a master should be provided for each "order." Possibly the scholastic classes coincided with the reception of some minor order, as a comparison with the clerks of Milan[2] suggests; or perhaps the use of the word is merely accidental. Alcuin wrote to Arno, later Archbishop of Salzburg, in 799, advising that he and his suffragans should have scholars, and make them diligently learn psalms and church melodies, that the daily course of the praises of God might be performed in each (mother) church; and to another bishop in Germany, advising him to hasten home and set in order the boys' lessons: who should learn grammar, who read epistles and small books, and who Holy Scripture.

Bishop Theodulf of Orleans carried the provision for education within his diocese a stage further. "If any priest wishes to send his nephew or his relation to school in the (cathedral) church of Ste Croix, or in the monastery of St Aignan, or St Benoît, or St Liphard, or in other of the monastic communities which it is granted us to govern: we give him leave to do this." The concession is here financial: the cathedral school shall receive their relations for nothing (and board them, probably); and the bishop will see that abbots also receive, board, and teach them for

[1] Cf. for an apparent reference to the reception and boarding of such scholars "quantum possibilitas sinit" in the monastery of Murbach, Pez, B., *Thesaurus anecdotorum novissimus*, Augsburg, 1721, tom. II, pt. iii, col. 378.

[2] For an account of the Milanese episcopal household and schools, see Landulf Junior, *Historia Mediolanensis*, in MGH, *Script.* VIII, p. 40; pp. 70-71.

nothing, as oblates, or possibly as candidates for the secular clergy also. The next canon probably refers to the teaching of day scholars: " Let priests in towns and villages have schools, and if any of the faithful wishes to commend his little ones to them to learn letters, they ought to receive them...and teach them with the greatest affection....They shall demand nothing in this matter by way of price, nor shall they receive anything from them, except what the parents...shall bestow upon them voluntarily."[1] This canon shews the high-water mark of Carolingian advance, and shews the ideal of one of the greatest scholars of Charles' court—of one also acquainted with conditions in Italy, where grammar masters were fairly plentiful. The whole set of canons are rather counsels of perfection than ecclesiastical laws; the laity were equally canonically bound to say their prayers at least twice a day, and priests to confess their sins with groans and tears, reciting the fifty-first psalm, once or twice a day, or as much oftener as possible. Theodulf was at one time Abbot of St Benoît (Fleury), and energetic in the reform movement connected with St Benedict of Aniane, and hence his capitulary was read and copied by monastic reformers. Dunstan and the English reformers were closely in touch with Fleury, and this probably explains the presence of different parts of the capitulary in two English manuscripts, both in Latin with English translations. The part of the capitulary dealing with schools occurs in a manuscript following some "statuta" collected by Abbot Aelfric of Eynsham; but there is no evidence that it was ever " lecta et publicata " in any English synod, or even that the translator was Aelfric. Another copy in a monastery at Ghent attributed it explicitly, but certainly wrongly, to the Council of Constantinople, 680, causing confusion to later writers. The canon about schools is not drawn from any Eastern council, but was Theodulf's own work.

Charlemagne's capitularies were not universally obeyed. In 813 the Council of Chalon reiterated that schools must be set up; and in 817 the Council of Aix-la-Chapelle dealt with both monastic and cathedral schools. In monasteries there were to be schools only of oblates; a few, like Fulda and St Gall, continued for a time to have " scholae exteriores seu canonicae " for training secular clerks. Chrodegang's rule, revised and enlarged by some chapters, was to be observed, as the " regula Aquisgranensis," by all the cathedrals of the Empire. A chapter of the rule regulated the provisions for the cathedral school. As earlier, it was to be an internal school, in which the young clerks were maintained by the chapter; the boys slept and worked together, in charge of an aged and discreet canon, though they might have a younger one to teach them. The rule was influential in reforms carried out by Dunstan in England,

---

[1] The teaching may have been intended to include Latin: it was certainly different from the learning by heart of the Creed and Lord's Prayer, in Latin or German, by the newly-converted Saxons, as ordered by the Council of Mayence. (Mansi, xiv, col. 74, cap. xlv.)

and was formally adopted by Leofric of Exeter *c.* 1050. The chapter describing the school must be taken as descriptive of the normal cathedral school in the Carolingian Empire from this time forward, apart from evidence to the contrary in particular cases, and till the communal life of chapters lapsed. Alcuin's teaching at Tours made the school so famous that conditions were perhaps abnormal there in his day. External scholars, boarding in the town, may have been taught by him; certainly in 843 Amalric, canon and scholasticus, left a bequest to the future preceptors in the school, to prevent the abominable custom, which had sprung up in his predecessors' day, of taking a price for instruction, "as from any other worldly business." Whether the endowment was to recompense the preceptors for renouncing the fees of external scholars, or to enable them to board these scholars gratis in their house, is not clear. There was certainly an internal and an external school at Rheims later; and, from about 900 onwards, the general practice of the cathedrals seems to have been for the chapter to maintain a number of "clericuli," while others were taken into the school as a private bargain with their relatives, and yet others were boarded by individual canons, who made a special bargain with relatives for "introducing them into the clerical order." Generally speaking, and theoretically, no fees, or very small fees, were charged for teaching only in the cathedral grammar or theology school, the masters being maintained by the chapter; but unless they had a prebend the maintenance was sometimes insufficient, and practice varied.

The ninth century brought difficulties to the schools. Louis the Pious, in 822, desired that schools should be amended: the parents or lords of scholars (no longer, significantly, the bishop) must help to provide for them; if the diocese (parochia) were very large, two or three places of study must be founded. The Council of Paris, in 824, ordered each bishop to shew more zeal to have a school to educate the *militia* of Christ; to encourage this, let each bishop bring his scholasticus to the provincial council. In 824 Lothar, as co-regent with his father, ordered that, since instruction was lacking in Italy, schools of "doctrina" should be maintained in certain towns, which he specified. In 826 Pope Eugenius II enacted that, since in some places there were neither masters nor care for the study of letters, each bishopric, and other places where there was need, should have masters and doctors to teach letters and the "dogmas of the liberal arts." The Council of Paris, in 829, repeated the provisions of 822, and the bishops petitioned the Emperor Louis that, lest his father's work should be lost, three "public schools" should be set up in his Empire; which three schools of Charlemagne they referred to is not clear, though a subsequent canon shews that they were including Italy in the Empire. The Council of Meaux, in 845, declared all the capitularies of Charles and Louis the Pious to be still in force, and ordered all bishops to build a cloister near their church for the regular training of their clerks (as Eugenius II had also ordered in 826). In 852 Archbishop

Hincmar of Rheims enjoined in a synod that answers should be made to certain questions, to be propounded by the magister and the dean " in each mother-church, and in each chapel of our parochia (archbishopric)" ; among others : " Had the priest a clerk who could keep school, or read the epistle and sing, according as was necessary"—the one, probably, in a mother-church (*ecclesia*), the other in a chapel (*capella*). This provision was perhaps due to a clause in the homilies of the contemporary Pope Leo IV that "each priest should have a scholar clerk, who could read the epistle or lesson[1] and respond at mass, and with whom he could sing psalms." The same Pope, in 853, practically repealed Eugenius' canon about the schools of liberal arts, by acknowledging that grammar masters were scarce, and ordering that, in lack of them, masters of divine scriptures and teachers of the office should be provided.

The ravages of the Northmen and internecine wars had half consumed learning by the mid-century, and the Council of Valence, summoned in 855 for the provinces of Lyons, Vienne, and Arles, could only order that " something should be discussed, and if possible decreed and ordained, about schools both of divine and secular literature and church chant, since, from the long intermission of this study, ignorance of the faith and of all knowledge has overtaken many bishoprics." Archbishop Herard of Tours, in 858, ordered that " priests should have schools as much as they can, and corrected books"; and Bishop Walter of Orleans in the same year interpreted this by enacting that "every priest must have a clerk, whom he must have religiously educated ; and, if it is possible for him, he must have a school in his church, and wisely take heed that those whom he receives to teach he may chastely and sincerely nourish." This seems an interesting attempt to extend the system of training lectors from episcopal and collegiate churches to those of single priests ; each priest must train or have trained (procuret educare) one clerk (the ancestor, of course, of the later parish clerk), and, if it be possible, let him nourish more. In 859 the Council of Savonnières urged that "scholae publicae" (apparently implying, at the date, royally-endowed schools) should be set up, so that fruit both of divine and human learning might accrue to the Church.

After these enactments, however, the schools gradually recovered and became flourishing ; the records of individual cathedrals indicate greater prosperity and scholarship. Bishop Ratherius of Verona in 966 decreed that he would in future promote no ordinands who had not lived in his own city, or in some monastery, or " apud quemlibet sapientem," and to some extent learned letters. The clause about private teaching is characteristic of Italian conditions ; north of the Alps ordinands would have attached themselves to some cathedral school (unless ordained without preparation in deference to the wish of some layman). Gregory VII in 1078 ordered that " all bishops were to have the arts of letters taught

---

[1] The Old Testament passage sometimes read in place of the Epistle.

in their churches," *i.e.* not merely "divine learning" but secular. The growth of the schools is marked by increase of masters. Fulbert (*ob.* 1028), the scholar-Bishop of Chartres, who raised the schools to the pitch of fame, gave Hildegaire both the birch of the grammaticus and the tablets of the chancellor as symbols of authority; in addition, Hildegaire held the position of sub-dean. Fluctuations still occurred at Chartres between the work and functions of the chancellor, vice-chancellor, and grammaticus; but by *c.* 1150 the chancellor as such had a prebend, taught only theology, and had under him a scholasticus now usually termed the "magister scholarum." The latter had no prebend as such, but was sometimes a canon; in any case, he received the usual distributions of food and money for attendance at offices. Development at other cathedrals was roughly parallel, the magister scholarum of the earlier centuries becoming the chancellor in the twelfth century, and teaching only theology, with a grammar master under him. In all dioceses other grammar schools were now fairly frequent, the right of teaching, however, remaining a strict monopoly, guarded by the chancellor of the diocese. After the rise of the universities (*c.* 1170), the best scholars were drawn away from the cathedral schools as such, and the teaching of the liberal arts in these dwindled to the teaching of grammar and rhetoric.

The decline of diocesan teaching roused the anxiety of the Church. In the lesser cathedrals there was difficulty even in obtaining a grammar master, since no benefice was provided for him, and there was more lucrative employment elsewhere. The Third Lateran Council, in 1179, ordered that a competent benefice should be given in every cathedral to a master, who should teach the clerks of the church and poor scholars for nothing; nor was the ecclesiastical authority to charge for the license to teach, nor deny it to any suitable candidate. The Fourth Lateran Council, in 1215, asserted that this provision had remained widely unfulfilled; it ordered each cathedral church, and other (collegiate) churches which had the means, to provide a prebend for a grammar master, and each metropolitan church one for a theology master. The provisions still remained largely unfulfilled, the difficulty being to get the chapter to give up a prebend for the purpose, especially as so many prebends were anticipated by papal provision. The friars, however, set up in this century their own hierarchy of schools, in some of which the presence of seculars was allowed. St Thomas Aquinas wrote in 1257 that the decree for the provision of a theology master in each metropolitan church had not been observed "through lack of letters," but now it had been more than fulfilled by the religious.

The monastic schools saw their two most flourishing centuries after the Carolingian renaissance. The external schools about which most is known were those of Fulda, St Gall, and Bec. Raban Maur of Fulda was sent by his abbot to study under Alcuin at Tours, and was afterwards given the direction of the monks' school at Fulda, with orders to preserve

Alcuin's method of teaching. He then ruled both schools (for oblates and clerks) "with piety and doctrine," and appointed two masters to teach under him. The schools of St Gall were famous in the ninth century, when Notker the Stammerer and other scholars were trained there. "The cloister school with blessed Notker and other children of the monastic habit was handed over to Marcellus, and the external school, that is the canonical school, to Iso." In 937 one of the scholars of this school started a serious fire in the monastery, to save himself a beating. The external school started at Bec by Lanfranc was somewhat of a new departure; it was not maintained to fill the place of a non-existent canonical, or cathedral, school, but to aid the poverty of the newly-founded house with fees; it was, in fact, a continuation of Lanfranc's work as a private rhetoric teacher in Italy. On the other hand, when St William of Dijon (*ob.* 1031) was called by Duke Richard to Normandy to introduce the Cluniac reforms, he substituted monks for clerks in the abbey of Fécamps, and started an external school there of the old, canonical type. "For when he saw that knowledge of singing and reading among the rural clerks was...almost perished, not only in that place but throughout the whole province,...he founded a school of the sacred ministry where the brothers skilled in this office taught freely, for the love of God."

The teaching of laymen in this period has been passed over, for there were no schools for laymen as such, even the little A.B.C. schools being mainly intended to teach "song" to little clerks. The sons of the nobility were more frequently taught reading, writing, and such Latin as they were considered to need, by their father's chaplain, or the chaplain of the lay noble, bishop, or abbot to whom they were sent for "nurture." Learned laywomen were similarly taught, though the nunneries, being poorer than the men's houses, more often received little "perhendinants" (boarders), boys as well as girls, for education. But as a rule the teaching of laymen and laywomen before 1300 was individual[1].

---

[1] No description of grammar schools, other than those attached to cathedral or collegiate churches, has been here attempted, for reasons of space. Between the rise of the universities, *c.* 1170, when grammar masters became more plentiful, and the end of the thirteenth century, such schools existed, and even in some numbers; but they were the same in character and method as they were in the next two centuries, when they became still more numerous. A full description of such grammar schools will be given in Vol. VIII.

CHAPTER XXIII.

PHILOSOPHY IN THE MIDDLE AGES.

NOT even the briefest sketch of medieval philosophy can dispense with a preface. Superfluous as it may seem to enquire what is meant by the "Middle Ages," and again by "philosophy," neglect of these elementary questions has often led to misunderstanding of those still shadowy centuries which lie between antiquity and ourselves. Precisely when and why the Middle Ages were first so designated it might be hard to decide. The presumption of some affinity between the ancient and modern world is tolerably clear, but when this vague resemblance is tried by a variety of tests, the grounds for affirming it become more and more obscure. And since our business here is only with philosophy, it may be well to assert at once that the ancient status of philosophy has never been reproduced. To the Greeks, from the days of the half-legendary Pythagoras, philosophy meant the adoption of a considered way of life which was not the common way of the world, and did not coincide with observance of the law. On the one side were the authority of custom and the religion of the State; on the other curiosity and criticism, the impulse to search for the hidden meaning of things and to establish a link between knowledge and life. The original freedom of Greek philosophy must indeed be largely attributed to the inseparable alliance between the Pagan State and the Pagan religion. For the official religion of the Greeks (as of the Romans) was founded on no articulate theology and embodied in no visible Church. The only theologians of early days were the poets. They at least gave an account of the gods, in the form of scandalous stories; and with them, therefore, rather than with popular piety, the philosophers were moved to quarrel when they too began to examine the cosmos and to meditate upon the agency of the gods. Then it was that "theology," in the predestined sense of that ominous word, cast its first deep shadow across the life of man. In answer to poetic travesties of the divine nature, Plato lightly sketches his "outlines of theology," with their innocent appearance and their promise of unending dispute. Aristotle in his turn, for all his reticence on the subject of the gods, gives "theology" as an alternative name for the "first philosophy," which posterity was to know as "metaphysics." Whatever name be preferred, the momentous fact is that monotheism, as an intellectual and moral doctrine, arose in philosophical circles beyond the range of civic religion, and without reference to the authority of the State.

The original stamp of philosophy was preserved with some difficulty in the respectable circumstances of the Academy and the Lyceum. The danger now was that a brotherhood of seekers after truth would degenerate into a school of dialecticians. Philosophy languishes sadly as the trade of professors and the sport of impertinent boys. From this fate it was partly delivered in Greece by the march of political events. When the career of Alexander put an end to the reality of the city-state, without providing a substitute, less attraction was found henceforward in the political life and more, therefore, in the theoretic. At the same time, philosophy began to be Hellenistic rather than Hellenic. Zeno of Citium was a portent of many things, and the tenets of Stoicism, though they rang a little hollow at times, sounded further abroad than the voice of the town-crier in Aristotle's diminutive metropolis. Philosophy grew daily more like a religion, a refuge for the disconsolate and a guide for the perplexed. Now when there is one religion derived from a philosophical valuation of life, and another bound up with the State but unsupported by theology, we have before us all the elements of a revolution which sooner or later will overturn the world. What delayed the catastrophe in the ancient world was the scorn of philosophers for the vulgar and the indifference of the State to theological speculation. It remains to consider briefly the causes which brought this mutual disregard to an end.

The single object of this hasty glance at the ancient world being to secure the right line of approach to the medieval period, the story of philosophy at Rome must be passed over, until the age when the old Latin elements of culture are well nigh lost in a medley of Greek and Oriental ideas. Never, perhaps, would the fortunes of philosophy have been united with those of the imperial city but for the advent of Plotinus in the third century and the eventual adoption of Neo-Platonism as the forlorn hope of pagan civilisation against the onset of the Christian Church. The story of the Church in its early generations has been related many times and with many objects. Seldom has it been presented in one of its most genuine aspects, as a struggle with rival philosophies at a time when the call to a spiritual life was audible to all serious men. When the Christian society escaped from the circle of Judaism and began to grasp the full nature of its mission, there existed only two forces sufficiently universal to compete with it for mastery of the world, Greek philosophy and Roman Law. The Pagan cults cannot rank as a third and equal competitor. Neither singly nor collectively did they embody an idea capable of welding mankind into social coherence. The *imperium*, on the other hand, the whole majestic apparatus of law and sovereignty, was a visible bond of union, and behind it lay, to all appearance, irresistible force. Yet in the end it was to prove easier for a Christian to mount the throne of the Caesars than for the new doctrine of the Logos to prevail against its philosophical rivals. The last and greatest victory of the Church was over

Neo-Platonism, when the spoils of the vanquished passed to the camp of the victor, to be handed down as part of the armour of faith.

To set Christianity among the philosophies is not fanciful, so long as we bear in mind that philosophy meant to the Greeks a way of life belonging to a particular society. When we read in the Acts of the Apostles how Paul had once persecuted "this way," or how the convert was taken to be further instructed in "the way," we hear a language long familiar to Hellenes and easily intelligible to educated Romans. Where the Christian way differed patently from the others was in making its first appeal to the simple and in its frank abhorrence of popular religion. For these reasons it figures in Roman authors as a kind of *odium humani generis* long before it was counted worthy of intellectual opposition. But by the age of Plotinus and Porphyry that phase was concluded. Christianity had now taken its place as one of the proffered ways of salvation, just as Gnosticism of a kind was a second, and Neo-Platonism a third. In the school of Plotinus we see the climax of the tendency to theologise philosophy, and thus to fashion an exalted religion far removed from the superstitions of the vulgar. To this conclusion ancient philosophy had grown steadily nearer, and this was its final legacy to the Church. No greater fiction, then, can well be alleged as history than the assertion that the Middle Ages corrupted the nature of philosophy by confusing it with theological doctrine. On the contrary, the attempted distinction between theology and philosophy was a characteristic medieval invention. For not until the last days of Paganism did the occasion for such discrimination arise.

For philosophy, as for political history, the arresting figure of Julian is full of significance. Sagacious enough to learn from the Church the secret of victory, he sought to create a bond between the religion of the many and the lofty speculations of the few. He failed because Neo-Platonism, however refined as theology, possessed no means of translating itself into a rule for the humble. Its solitary implement, already dull and rusty, was the allegorising of fable and myth. But the multitude, as Plato had foreseen, could not be saved by hidden meanings. When we read the last book of the last *Ennead*, we understand how the new faith may have failed to touch Plotinus; but when we set the unvarnished story of the Gospel side by side with any Pagan allegory, the contrast is almost painfully absurd. Nevertheless, we may learn from the story of Julian that, as Pagan philosophy had grown ever more theological, so the Pagan State, under a Neo-Platonist Emperor, might almost have assumed the character of an authoritative Church. To look at the same facts from the Christian point of view, we see how the Church, by her double victory over the *imperium* of Rome and the philosophy of Greece, committed herself to the two great enterprises of the Middle Ages, the search for a distinction between philosophy and theology, and the search for a way of reconciling the temporal with the spiritual power. As soon as those two problems are in being, we may know, in fact, that the Middle Ages have begun. To the Middle Ages, also, it fell to discover, through much toil and tribulation, that fundamentally the two problems are one.

For the student of philosophy the result of the successive blows which shattered the Roman Empire is almost wholly comprised in the division of civilisation into eastern and western halves. A prophet in the age of Marcus Aurelius, or even of Trajan, might well have foretold a time when Hellenism would have completely submerged the Latin elements of culture carried westward by victorious generals as far as the British Isles. Whether such a prophecy would ever have been fulfilled it is idle to speculate. The fact remains that it was not. For the various reasons narrated by historians there came the great reaction, when the tide of Hellenism rolled back eastwards, bearing with it the treasures of culture as well as the imperial throne. Even the greatest of Roman products, jurisprudence, appeared to forsake its proper home; and while the great codification was being accomplished at Byzantium, Roman Law in the West was becoming an adjunct of persons rather than the voice of an independent and sovereign society. In this cleavage of East and West there was, nevertheless, a kind of historical justice. For between the Greek and the Latin there was, and is, a deep and abiding antagonism. The enthusiasm of Roman authors for Hellenic models disguised that truth for antiquity, as the ambiguity of the term "classical" has often obscured it for ourselves. Yet the fact persisted, and one clear function of the Middle Ages was to make a new revelation of *latinitas*, barely possible until the superior light of Hellas was at least partially eclipsed. The contrast, perpetually recurring in medieval authors, between *Graeci* and *Latini* does not rest upon differences of nationality or race. The true line of demarcation was always the grammatical or literary language. The *Latini* were simply the miscellaneous assemblage of peoples who used Latin as their vehicle of literary expression; a similar interpretation must be given to *Graeci*; and for the same reason, when we arrive in due course at the philosophers of Islām, the single and sufficient excuse for calling them "Arabs" will be that their works were composed in the Arabic tongue. These divisions must not, however, be interpreted too narrowly. They stood less for the interruption of colloquial intercourse than for wide intellectual schisms and radical diversities of mind. Nothing proves this better than a scrutiny of the several occasions, from the ninth to the thirteenth century, when some Greek author was newly translated into Latin. We then learn that the famous *Graecia capta ferum*..., however true in antiquity, became conspicuously false in the medieval centuries. The truth was rather that each translated Greek became in his turn the captive of *latinitas*. He entered a world where the very terminology was steeped in Latin associations, and where there flourished a spirit of *auctoritas* as alien from the traditions of Hellas as the *Summa* of Aquinas from the dialogues of Plato. To mark the stages in medieval philosophy as a series of Greek invasions is not unscientific; but we have always to add that the result was rather to enlarge a Latin structure than to remodel it on pure Hellenic lines.

After two or three of the darkest centuries in European history the Carolingian renaissance offers a glimmer of daylight. With Charles the Great we see Europe awaking to the consciousness of ignorance and to the need of regaining touch with the past. When Alcuin (*ob.* 804) was summoned from England to reform the methods of school instruction, he revived the old curriculum of the seven liberal arts, the famous Trivium and Quadrivium, and thus incidentally renewed the study of dialectic, the most durable element in European education. By his own writings, and still more by his pupils, his educational influence was spread widely abroad. An attempt has been made to claim more for him. He has been hailed as the father of Scholasticism (most ambiguous of titles), or at least as the progenitor of philosophy in France. It is more than doubtful, however, if the claim can be upheld. The circle of Charles the Great caught eagerly at the threads of tradition and found novelty enough in ideas far from original. *Philosophia* itself was a name that stood for the general culture of the liberal arts, or sometimes for dialectic in particular, rather than for the apprehension of grave intellectual problems. In spite, therefore, of the noble work of Alcuin, and in spite of the encyclopedic learning of his pupil Rabanus Maurus, Archbishop of Mayence, and, as he has well been styled, *primus praeceptor Germaniae*, it is not unfair to judge that no figure of high import for philosophy emerges before the astonishing Johannes Scottus Eriugena, court-philosopher and even, if tales be true, court-jester to Charles the Bald.

The entrance and exit of this mysterious Irishman are swift and histrionic. Appearing suddenly from one wing, he remains on the stage of France just long enough to derange the plot and bewilder the actors, before he vanishes on the other side and is lost in "confused noise without." Long afterwards we learn from William of Malmesbury that the noise was caused by his English scholars, who were busy murdering their master with the points of their pens. Doubtless they took the hint from John's own observation: *stilus ferreus alia parte qua scribamus, alia qua deleamus a fabro factus est*[1]. Uncertainty about his origin and end is, however, of small consequence. His works are with us, and the occasion of his first and last appearance in the ecclesiastical drama is notorious. Gottschalk, a man of noble birth and a reluctant follower of St Benedict, had extracted from the study of St Augustine a doctrine of "double predestination," which ensured the damnation of the wicked no less firmly than the salvation of the good. Whatever the logical difficulty of evading that conclusion, the moral danger of fatalism was so plainly threatened by it that Hincmar, the powerful and restless Archbishop of Rheims (*ob.* 882), was roused to vigorous action. The unhappy monk was indicted, condemned, imprisoned, and finally harried into his grave. But Gottschalk

[1] MPL, cxxii, 422.

or his opinions, did not lack supporters. Assailed from many sides by weighty rebukes, Hincmar judged it expedient to add reason to force, and in a rash moment entrusted to John the Scot the task of demolishing Gottschalk's position. The result was (in the year 851) the treatise on Predestination, which defeated not only Gottschalk but Hincmar and all parties concerned.

The knowledge of Greek, now a rare accomplishment, which John brought with him from Ireland, stood for more than linguistic proficiency. His philosophy is a genuine derivation from Greek sources, Pagan and Christian, and must be interpreted rather by the ideas of the fifth century than by later developments of medieval thought. In the *De Praedestinatione*, it is true, he affects to rely solely on Latin authors; whence it has been doubtfully inferred that he had not yet acknowledged the sway of the Pseudo-Dionysius. A more likely explanation is found in the controversial character of the work. John's business was to turn against Gottschalk the authorities, especially Augustine, to whom he had appealed. With an ingenuity almost too subtle he carries out this programme, yet only on the surface. The force and substance of his argument belong to Neo-Platonism. Either, therefore, he was already familiar with the Areopagite, or he must in some other way have mastered a body of doctrine akin to the philosophy of Proclus. In any case, the refutation of Gottschalk depends entirely on an account of the Divine Nature developed by Plotinus and his school out of elements originally supplied by Plato. The essence of God, His will, and His intellect, are one pure and indivisible substance identical with goodness. From his eternal perfection no effects but what are good can proceed. If the will of the Creator is the necessity of the creature, yet that will is the pure expression of liberty, and man's necessity is but the appetite for goodness, in which human liberty essentially consists. How, then, shall we distinguish the good from the bad? And how leave room for the freedom of decision upon which moral responsibility depends? John firmly maintains the reality of *liberum arbitrium*, and denies that God compels any man to be either good or bad; but the critical question evidently is whether the existence of evil in any real sense can be allowed. Boldly and variously as John wrestles with his problem, he never wavers in his belief that evil is pure negation. Sin, death, and eternal punishment he sees as indivisible links in a chain, but God neither knows nor wills them. What God foreknows he predestinates; whence, if he is said to foreknow evils without predestinating them, this can only be a *modus locutionis*, designed to stimulate us to deeper understanding of the truth. Foreknowledge itself is but a metaphor; for priority in time has no meaning in relation to God, in whose life is neither past nor future, but only the eternal now.

To do justice to the argument in a few lines is impossible, but its two-edged character and its threat to the orthodox view of sin and punishment will easily be detected. The whole tone of the reasoning, too, must have been foreign to John's contemporaries, who can hardly have failed to see how little he trusted to familiar authorities, and how much to arguments derived from none knew where. It is a mistake, however, to lay as much emphasis as some modern writers have done on John's identification (in the first chapter) of *vera philosophia* with *vera religio*. In itself this was no startling novelty, nor was it a mere ruse of debate for John to quote the precedent of Augustine. *Verus philosophus est amator Dei*[1] was Augustine's summary of the aim of philosophy: the test by which he had tried Socrates and Plato, and found them not far from the Kingdom of Heaven. Thus far, in fact, John was expressing a sound historical judgment on the meaning of philosophy in the past. It is further to be observed that the word is *religio*, not *theologia*. A simple identification of philosophy with theology is far from his intention. Broadly speaking, *theologia* always signifies for him some measure of the divine illumination not vouchsafed outside the Catholic Church. *Johannes theologus* is his title for the author of the Fourth Gospel, and all *theologi* belong to a privileged class, from which many *philosophi* would be excluded. Thus *philosophi saeculares* is a name for the Pagan sages, and *inanis philosophia* serves to describe the practice of Jews and heretics, who cling to the letter of the scriptures and pay no heed to the spirit. On the other hand, *philosophia* in its widest sense can cover the entire search for wisdom, of which theology is the highest but not the only part. No greater libel, certainly, can be fastened on John the Scot than to represent him as dressing up in the garb of Christianity some Pagan philosophy in which alone he believed. No vestige of such an intention can be traced in his pages. He is ardently, almost passionately, Christian. What his feelings would have been had he learned that "Dionysius" was an author never heard of before the sixth century, and, possibly, a pupil of Proclus (*ob.* 485), it is vain to conjecture. As it is, he had probably never heard of Proclus, nor ever read a word of Plotinus. Plato he counts the chief of philosophers —the merest commonplace in Christian writers down to the end of the twelfth century—but from the Platonic *secta* he more than once dissociates himself, and never would he have dreamed of making Plato the equal, in his theological knowledge, of the Greek Fathers, or Dionysius, or Augustine.

Some caution is needed, again, in describing his view of reason and authority. For while it is common to quote from him such sayings as *auctoritas ex vera ratione processit, ratio vero nequaquam ex auctoritate*[2], it is no less common to ignore the qualifications of the context, and to omit altogether many other passages of a very different colour. *Ratio* itself is a difficult and ambiguous term. Sometimes it comprehends all the operations of the mind; sometimes it means only the discursive, dialectical reason, which stands on a permanently lower level than *intellectus sive animus sive mens*. The last thing John would suggest is that reason, in this narrower sense, can find out and interpret the ways of God. His point is

---

[1] Augustine, *De Civitate Dei*, VIII, 1.   [2] MPL, CXXII, 513.

rather that *auctoritas* is valuable only in so far as it represents what the intellect of saintly *theologi* has revealed. Reason itself demands our reverence for what is above reason; it does not, however, demand blind subservience to patristic utterances, or to the bare letter of the Scriptures, any more than it encourages us to put our trust in petty dialectic. *Vera auctoritas*, says John the Scot, *rectae rationi non obsistit, neque recta ratio verae auctoritati*[1]. To force him into a rigid dilemma of reason and authority is likely to be an anachronism only less regrettable than the proposal to enlist him on the side of the Nominalists or the Realists. A mind like his refuses to be imprisoned in any such antithesis. What he believes in is the illumination of the mind with a heavenly radiance, as easily dimmed by *ratio* in one way as by *auctoritas* in another.

The traditional accusation against the *De Divisione Naturae*—surely one of the most remarkable books in the world—is that of Pantheism. The charge would be more convincing if its authors would sometimes go so far as to tell us what Pantheism means. Presumably, it implies at least some kind of identification or confusion of God with His creatures, some materialisation of the Divine Nature, with loss of transcendence and the Creator's prerogative. Now in the *De Divisione Naturae* there is a rich abundance of statements that seem to point in that direction. Nothing could be plainer, for example, than the words, *proinde non duo a seipsis distantia debemus intelligere Deum et creaturam, sed unum et id ipsum*[2]; and this is but one out of many such passages. Yet no one, it is reasonable to suggest, who has striven to master the book as a whole, with due appreciation of its earlier sources, will judge "Pantheism" to be other than an idle and empty description of the doctrines set forth by John the Scot. The universe, as he conceived of it, is one stupendous yet graded *theophania*. God is *in omnibus* and *supra omnia*, revealed in all His creatures, yet eternally transcending them all. They who declare that God is thus degraded below Himself must be prepared to deny that Jesus was God as well as man. For man is the *officina omnis creaturae*, the perfect microcosm; whence the Incarnation reveals, in a single flash, the whole relation of God to the universe, even as the resurrection of Christ displays in a moment the *reditus* or *reversio* of all things to God. John himself was well aware of the danger to which he exposed himself. Anticipating the charge of Pantheism, he strove by many illustrations and analogies to accommodate his high and difficult thoughts to men of ruder understanding. In this he did not succeed. When not wholly neglected, his book was usually suspect. After lying comparatively dormant for more than three centuries, it was brought into fresh notoriety by the heretical Amalric of Bene. A preliminary condemnation at Paris in 1210 was followed in 1225 by the sentence of Honorius III, who ordered all discoverable copies to be committed to the flames. Upon this, perhaps, the fairest comment is that, if Amalric and his friends had read John as carelessly

[1] MPL, cxxii, 511. [2] *Ib.* cxxii, 678.

as some of his modern critics, the action of Honorius may easily be excused.

The false dawn of the Carolingian renaissance faded all too soon into a second spell of darkness. Knowledge of Greek and the power of comparing eastern with western traditions John the Scot did not bequeath to the following generations. His translations of Dionysius and Maximus Confessor—sad examples of the *verbum de verbo* method—may well have been unintelligible, while his commentaries or glosses on Martianus Capella and Boethius would distinguish him less clearly from other men. Disordered and confused by the trend of political events, the Latin world relapsed into the confinement of a narrow circle of authors conned over and over again, yet often imperfectly known and understood. It is possible, however, to draw too wide an inference from the poverty of a philosophical library. Paucity of materials alone will not account for mental stagnation. To interpret the intellectual condition of the Middle Ages we must look rather to the vast transformation of the world, as the notion of a *civitas Dei* gradually supplanted the ideals of Pagan society. In the eyes of Augustine the secular power, no less than the heathen religion, still belongs to the *civitas impiorum*; to possess and wield it can never be the ambition of the Church. Philosophy again, the property of the Greeks, though far superior to an idolatrous religion, is only an imperfect alternative to the Christian life. But the course of history was too strong for these older partitions and antagonisms. Before the end of the fifth century Pope Gelasius I was making his memorable pronouncement: *duo quippe sunt quibus principaliter mundus hic regitur, auctoritas sacrata pontificum et regalis potestas.* This royal or imperial power was henceforward to be no Babylonish relic, but a necessary element in the life of a single, all-embracing society. However delegated or dispersed among princes, the temporal sovereignty must remain the sword of the spiritual, the instrument for extending and protecting the Kingdom of God upon earth. Authority of all kinds was gradually concentrated, until the thought of a philosophy unrelated to dogmatic propositions became as intolerable as the pretence of any secular power to stand outside the Church. The Creed and the Scriptures became the official source alike of law and of wisdom. The *vis coactiva* was now the appurtenance of knowledge, the knowledge divinely imparted to the Christian society. In such a society (no matter how much the papal theory was disputed) the weight of tradition could not fail to be overwhelming. From heresy to schism was now the briefest of steps, and novelty had always to justify itself. "Many men," says John the Scot, "are roused from slumber by heretics, that they may see the day of the Lord and rejoice."[1] No shrewder judgment could be passed on the history of medieval philosophy. For most of the greater changes were due less to original speculation, or even to the acquisition of new materials, than to the suspicion of heresy. Opinions denounced at

[1] MPL, cxxii, 359.

first were often enough accepted on second thoughts. The power of adapting and absorbing fresh ideas never wholly ceased to operate, but all was governed by the general assumption that unchanging truth was already revealed. Meanwhile, the habit of deference to tradition was extended, almost unwittingly, to such records of Pagan knowledge as fortune had preserved. None would have ranked a Greek philosopher with the Scriptures, but when reverence for the past was combined with lack of critical power, the result was to establish certain books or authors in a position not easy to shake.

Some of the medieval limitations we may briefly illustrate by glancing at the sources of their acquaintance with Aristotle and Plato. The first name to be honoured is Boethius. To his translations of the *Categories* (with the *Isagoge* of Porphyry) and the *De Interpretatione*, together with his own commentaries and logical treatises, was due virtually the whole knowledge of Aristotle accessible to medieval students from the sixth century to the middle of the twelfth. Boethius had intended to introduce the whole of Aristotle to the Latins, and some confusion has been caused by the more than doubtful ascription to him of translations of the rest of the *Organon*, the *De Anima*, and the *Metaphysics*. It is fairly certain, however, that before the age of John of Salisbury Aristotle was directly represented only by two of his minor logical works, supplemented by a few fragments of information gathered from various sources. An important consequence, too often overlooked, was the restriction of his authority to a very narrow sphere. In dialectic he was admittedly the master, but in philosophy as a whole the evidence is incontestable that Plato occupied the highest place in general esteem. And yet, when we turn to the medieval knowledge of Plato, we may well be surprised at his lofty position. For nothing of his actual writings could be studied in Latin but a fragment of a single dialogue, the *Timaeus*.

Between the cases of Plato and Aristotle there was, however, a very wide difference. When Aristotle arrived in translations he was almost a stranger; and even when the work of Boethius had raised him to unchallenged sovereignty in the province of logic, he still was enthroned in a certain isolation, with little historical background and with no evident affinity to the Christian way of life. Platonism, on the other hand, was almost inhaled with the air. Boethius himself was a Platonist, and so was Porphyry. Augustine, too, never forgot his debt to the philosophy which had delivered him from Manichaeism and carried him a long stage on the road to Christ. To indicate all the sources of Platonism would be almost impossible. It must suffice here to notice two from outside the Christian circle, the commentary of Chalcidius that accompanied his version of the *Timaeus*, and the dissertation of Macrobius on the *Somnium Scipionis*. To class Chalcidius as non-Christian is perhaps questionable, for he was more probably a Christian than a Pagan or a Jew. His work, however, embodies very little Christian material except an extract from Origen.

Dating, perhaps, from the early fourth century, it is neither independent nor critical. The substance of it, if we accept the result of Switalski's investigation, is derived from an earlier commentary, very possibly by the hand of the eminent Stoic, Posidonius. The outcome is an eclectic medley or muddle of divers authorities, gathered under the sway of the infallible Plato. The later Platonism, we must remember, was even more than eclectic. Its aim was to absorb and to reconcile, to appear as a summary of all previous Greek speculation. Much of the uncritical confusion of ideas that meets us everywhere in the Middle Ages was simply a legacy from Chalcidius and the less intelligent followers of Plotinus in the decline of the ancient world.

Roughly similar qualities appear in the work of Macrobius, a writer who, late in the fifth century, had contrived to remain untouched by the Christian influence. His detachment from the Church makes it all the more interesting to discover in him that medievalism of mind so often rated as a purely Christian product. In him we have already the medieval Virgil, and along with that strange invention all the baffling mixture of science and nonsense that was to float about Europe for more than a thousand years. How medieval, too, is the deference of Macrobius to the great names of the past. *Neque vero tam immemor mei*, he writes, *aut ita male animatus sum, ut ex ingenio meo vel Aristoteli resistam vel adsim Platoni*[1]. Yet Macrobius is far from contemptible, and the debt of the Middle Ages to him was immense. To him was due what little was known of Plotinus (*inter philosophiae professores cum Platone princeps*)[2], the fourfold classification of the virtues, the threefold gradation of *Deus, mens,* and *anima,* the illumination of all creatures as in an orderly series of mirrors by the *unus fulgor*, the descent of the soul to its material habitation, and its yearning for restoration to its eternal home. When Christians read in Macrobius of the soul's imprisonment in a vesture of clay (*indumentum testeum*), of its wandering on earth as a pilgrim, of heaven as the true *patria*, of philosophy as *meditatio mortis*, they caught the genuine accent of religion and welcomed Platonism as a natural ally. Actual knowledge of the original Plato Macrobius did not greatly increase. Behind the *Somnium Scipionis*, according to Schedler's recent enquiry, lies once more the *Timaeus*, as interpreted first by Porphyry and handed on by intermediate writers to Macrobius. If that be so, it helps to account for the frequent difficulty of deciding, when no names are mentioned, whether a medieval writer is using Chalcidius, or Macrobius, or sometimes the *De Consolatione* of Boethius. The same brand of Platonism, with the same tincture of new Pythagoreanism, is recognisable in all.

The lines of thought broadly indicated by Plato and Aristotle run through the Middle Ages. From Plato came the wider inspiration and the higher call; from Aristotle the perception of difficulties and contradictions, with the demand for dialectical skill. Nowhere, as it happens,

[1] *Comm. in Somnium Scipionis*, II, 15.   [2] *Ib.* I, 8.

were the defects of medieval knowledge of history more conspicuous than in this very matter of dialectic. The most learned doctors were unaware that dialectic had held in Plato's estimation a far higher place than Aristotle would allow. They did not know why Aristotle himself had sometimes preferred and sometimes rejected it, nor how far removed was his trivial use of it as an exercise for students from the profundity of his dialectical analysis of moral experience. They knew just enough to warrant the dispute whether dialectic was properly concerned with words or with things; and enough, unfortunately, to encourage a confusion of the *ars disserendi* with the total activity of reason. During the two dark centuries after the appearance of John the Scot dialectic was, however, the beacon. We can dimly trace the rise of factions, the growth of the contest between dialecticians and anti-dialecticians, which was to reach its climax in the age of Abelard. For the rest, the condition of Europe was unfriendly to speculation, and the flagrance of moral disorders left no leisure for adventures of the intellect.

The tenth century is singularly barren. Scarcely a name of distinction is recorded in the annals of philosophy, save that of Gerbert of Aurillac (*ob.* 1003), who was raised to the Papacy as Sylvester II. Even Gerbert was more remarkable for his skill in mathematics, and for his services to humane education, than for any direct contribution to philosophy. To his pupil and patron, Otto III, he dedicated a logical text-book with the title *Libellus de rationali et ratione uti*, and he may be the author (though the point is disputed) of a work *De Corpore et Sanguine Domini*. If so, we can credit him with a perception of the value of dialectic in harmonising discrepant utterances of the Fathers. Some have failed, however, to note that his most striking observation is taken directly from John the Scot. The art which divides *genera* into *species*, and resolves *species* into *genera*, is not (he says) the product of human machinations, but was discovered by the wise in the very nature of things, where the Author of all the arts had placed it. This is taken verbatim from the *De Divisione Naturae*[1], where it stands as a comment on the work of the Creator. Gerbert's influence, however, did not depend exclusively on his books. His distinction as a teacher is indisputable, and while his personal association was with the cathedral-school of Rheims, he became, through his pupil Fulbert (*ob.* 1028), the indirect founder of the more famous school of Chartres.

The attribution to Gerbert of a work on the Eucharist is, in any case, an indication of the subject which did more, perhaps, than any other in this unproductive period to stimulate curiosity and to awaken controversy about the use and abuse of dialectic. Already in the ninth century Paschasius Radbert and Ratramnus had earned some notoriety by their discussion of the Blessed Sacrament; and now a larger disturbance was created, some while after Gerbert, by the *De Caena Domini* of Berengar of Tours. Devout minds not unnaturally felt a strong distaste for the

[1] MPL, cxxii, 749.

analysis of a mystery, but Berengar was less sensitive. He magnified the function of dialectic, *quia confugere ad eam ad rationem est confugere*, and thus proved himself an imperfect scholar of John the Scot, by whom he is said to have been inspired. For if John had championed the liberty of reason, he had also taught that even the angelic intelligences *ab introitu mysteriorum suos theologicos pedes, hoc est, intellectuales ingressus retractant*[1]. The most eminent critic of Berengar's "theological feet" was Archbishop Lanfranc (1005–1089), himself well reputed in dialectic but disposed to restrict the art to a subordinate position. Augustine, he allows, had thought well of it; and, lest he should seem to be afraid of Berengar's weapons, he will waive his own preference for trusting to the traditions of the Church where mysteries of the faith are concerned. He accuses Berengar of parading his skill in disputation, and suggests that a confession of ignorance is sometimes better than arrogant obstinacy. The tone of his remonstrance is dignified and sensible. He does not look on dialectic as necessarily hostile to the faith, but thinks it a perilous exercise for shallow and contentious minds.

Another contemporary name, Peter Damian (*ob.* 1072), deserves to be mentioned. Justly famed for his saintly life, *Petrus peccator*, as he styled himself, stands in the main for the monastic tendency to think more highly of practical religion than of intellectual attempts to explain and justify the faith. He wrote, however, several works of theology, in one of which, the *De Divina Omnipotentia*, he discusses the use of philosophy in "sacred disputations." It is here that he introduces the celebrated phrase, *ancilla dominae*, to denote the proper relation of dialectic to theology. Less energy, perhaps, would have been spent in remonstrance against this apparent degradation of reason, if more attention had been paid to the current usage of terms. *Philosophia* often means no more than dialectic, and dialectic no more than a display of captious arguments. That the Christian position as a whole (the Christian philosophy, in fact) was irrational, Peter Damian and his contemporaries would never have admitted. The antithesis of *ratio* and *auctoritas* was then far less comprehensive than the final problem, scarcely realised before the age of Aquinas, whether the independence of philosophy could be reconciled with the Catholic position. To assign to dialectic a merely ancillary office is not necessarily obscurantism. It often meant no more than the logical commonplace, that *ratiocinatio* presupposes the concession of premises. In a deeper sense, it meant that experience must precede the attempt to explain it, and that the testimony of many generations cannot easily be overthrown by a talent for repartee.

With the illustrious name of Anselm a new chapter begins. As a pupil of Lanfranc he belongs chronologically (1033–1109) to the eleventh century, but in mind and spirit must rank as the herald of the sustained intellectual effort which culminated two centuries later in the systems of

---

[1] MPL, cxxii, 668.

Albertus Magnus and Aquinas. For this reason he has often been saluted as the true founder of Scholasticism, a title we should bestow with greater confidence, did any definition of Scholasticism command universal assent. Unfortunately it is not so. After much pedantic and even acrimonious discussion we are left uncertain whether "scholastic" and "medieval" philosophy should be identified or clearly distinguished, whether "scholasticism" is the name of a method or of a result, whether there was one pre-eminently scholastic problem, and whether one particular solution has a right to be called scholastic. Thus is medieval philosophy, so fertile in distinctions, pursued by the shadow of itself. The wisest course, perhaps, is to stand aside from the controversy. It is agreed that the term *scholasticus* (applicable either to master or to pupil) meant uncommonly little; it is agreed also that the great doctors of the thirteenth century may rightly be called schoolmen. For the rest, it is enough to interpret, as best one can, the course of events.

To call Anselm an original thinker is not to deny his obligations to others. In the preface to the *Monologium* he protests that nothing in his doctrine is out of harmony with the Catholic Fathers, especially the Blessed Augustine. The product of his mind is, however, original inasmuch as it is the outcome of personal experience, the fruit of profound meditation upon the nature of his faith. "Enter into the cubicle of thy mind; shut out all things but God and whatsoever may help thee to seek for Him; then close the door and seek." Thus he writes in the first chapter of the *Proslogion*, before expounding his proof of God's existence; and none, perhaps, who are deaf to the exhortation will feel any force in the proof. *Fides quaerens intellectum* and *nisi credideritis, non intelligetis* are the formulas that meet us everywhere on his pages. Still more clearly does he express his position in the words of the *De Fide Trinitatis: qui non crediderit, non experietur, et qui non expertus fuerit, non intelliget.* The Church, he means, had not invented new intellectual instruments, but rather had proclaimed the advent of a new spiritual experience, itself the condition of understanding the meaning of life. Mere rationalism, on the other hand, could originate nothing; for reason, as discursive and critical, depends for its materials on a higher mode of experience. On this point at least Christianity was at one with Platonism, and Anselm himself is, on the whole, a kind of Platonist. His Platonism, however, is derived from Augustine, not, as some have alleged, from John the Scot; for Anselm is by no means committed to the negative theology of Neo-Platonism, which is the very essence of the Irish philosopher's teaching. Well as he knows that the names we apply to the Divine Nature are but shadows and symbols, he is never possessed by that ecstasy of intellectual asceticism which glories in the denial of attributes, and pays its last tribute to omniscience by declaring that God Himself cannot know what He is.

Anselm's argument for the necessary existence of *id quo maius cogitari nequit* is no plea for a negative abstraction. Read in connexion with the

Monologium it is seen as an attempt to clothe the One, which alone participates in nothing, but is what it is, with the attributes of an individual spirit, unbounded by space and time, yet present everywhere and always, without parts and qualities, yet containing in very essence life, salvation, beatitude, and all possible perfections. Nearest to God, and best able to serve as a mirror of His image, is *mens* (another link with Neo-Platonism); and since *mens* is the innermost nature of man, to "enter into the cubicle of the mind," shutting out all lower manifestations of being, is the true way of access. The formal weakness of the argument was at once detected by the monk Gaunilo; whose objection, however, that the transition from what exists only *in intellectu* to what exists also *in re* cannot thus be effected, leaves Anselm quite unperturbed. The pretence that the same argument might prove the existence of the most perfect island he declares to be a misapprehension of the point. If his argument can be applied to anything but the Supreme Being, he is ready to make Gaunilo a present of the island, and to promise that it shall never vanish away.

The "ontological" argument, however, was always viewed with suspicion. In this, as in some other respects, Anselm did not precisely anticipate the position of later scholastics. Even his *fides quaerens intellectum* does not accurately express the method of those who afterwards made a more exact distinction between truths demonstrable by reason and truths revealed only to faith. Tentative steps in that direction were taken by Anselm, but he went farther than his successors in attempting, for example, to arrive by reasoning at the doctrine of the Trinity; an image of which, following an Augustinian tradition, he discovers in the human soul. Anselm, in fact, was not directly interested in the question whether it was possible to concede to philosophy a province where certain problems could be solved by reason alone. He perceived the distinction (as he shews in the *Cur Deus homo*) between seeking reasons because you do not believe, and seeking them because you do; but it was the latter case that chiefly inspired his arguments, and so made him, in a certain sense, more rationalistic than those who afterwards defined their concessions to reason.

A fuller account of Anselm would refer to his theories of sense-perception, judgment, the freedom of the will, and other psychological matters. But these are of less importance in the history of his own time than his controversy with Roscelin, about whose doctrines, as it happens, Anselm is our best source of information. To call the controversy important is not for a moment to allow that the single theme of Nominalism and Realism is the clue to medieval philosophy. On the contrary, Roscelin is important because he succeeded, perhaps for the first and last time, in disturbing the ecclesiastical arena by manufacturing a heresy out of this topic of the schools. In his famous *Isagoge*, or Introduction to the *Organon* of Aristotle, Porphyry prepared the medieval battleground by a brief and cautious statement which it may be worth while to quote in the Latin of Boethius. *Mox de generibus et speciebus illud quidem, sive subsistant sive*

in solis nudis intellectibus posita sint, sive subsistentia corporalia sint an incor-
poralia, et utrum separata a sensibilibus an in sensibilibus posita et circa haec
consistentia, dicere recusabo. The original difference between Aristotle and
Plato was not properly a controversy about *genera* and *species*, but in the
Middle Ages the extreme "realistic" doctrine of universals was identified
with the teaching of Plato. It is, in fact, one of the bewildering accidents
of history that the Platonic "idea" became the basis of medieval "realism,"
whereas the "idealism" of Berkeley and later philosophers has nothing to
do with either Plato or the medieval controversy. For in whatever sense we
attribute "conceptualism" to medieval logicians, it must certainly not be
in a sense that would bring them into line with an idealist philosophy
never clearly formulated before the seventeenth or eighteenth century.

Apart from the unabashed Platonists, the prevailing tendency of
medieval writers was to follow Aristotle or Boethius in holding that
universals could not "subsist" except in association with individual things.
At the same time it was freely allowed that the intellect had the power
of viewing them in abstraction from sensible things, and that the common
element in things, from which we derive the notions of genus and species,
was no mere fiction of the mind. What complicated the dispute between
Platonists and Aristotelians was the appearance of Nominalism; and what
has thrown the whole history of the subject into confusion is the belief,
originating mainly with some distinguished French scholars, that the war
of Nominalists and Realists began in the ninth century and persisted
until the close of the Middle Ages. Since it is impossible here to scrutinise
the evidence, nothing more can be offered than a dogmatic assertion that
this view is untenable. Nominalism was an intellectual firework of the
age of Roscelin and Abelard; for which reason, among others, it is also
an anachronism to talk of Realism in connexion with John the Scot or
other writers of that period. Even when the *nominalis secta* (as John of
Salisbury was perhaps the first to call it) has been rightly dated, it is no
easy task to define and explain its doctrine. The contention that only
individual things exist in their own right is no more Nominalist than
Aristotelian. Nothing characteristic of the new sect appears until the
whole stress is laid on *voces* or *nomina*. If universals are mere *flatus vocis*,
if their reality is only the physical reality belonging to a *percussio aeris*,
then indeed we have a doctrine inconsistent alike with the Platonic Realism
and with the tradition of Boethius. Absurd as the doctrine may sound
to modern ears, it was a not unnatural product of the long-established
opinion that logic, in company with grammar and rhetoric, was primarily
concerned with words. Meanwhile the importance of Nominalism for the
twelfth century was that it re-opened the whole question of universals, split
up the camp of the anti-nominalists into factions, and produced all the
varieties of doctrine enumerated by John of Salisbury and other writers.
The logical and metaphysical problems thus brought to light were perfectly genuine. Much the same difficulties may be found in modern books

of logic, and the solutions offered do not differ fundamentally from those current in medieval times.

According to Anselm, Roscelin presented the world with a dilemma. Either, he argued, the three Persons of the Trinity are one *res*; in which case the Father and the Spirit were incarnate together with the Son: or they are three, like three souls or three angels; in which case only convention forbids us to speak of three Gods. The second alternative, a kind of Tritheism, Roscelin felt himself driven to prefer by his denial of reality to universals and his reduction of them to mere *flatus vocis*. Much ingenuity has been wasted in arguing that Roscelin's doctrine was not genuine Nominalism (whatever that may happen to be), and that Anselm must have misrepresented the case. But where is the evidence? There is none of importance but Roscelin's letter to Abelard, which contributes nothing to the point, a few words by Abelard himself, who speaks of Roscelin's "insane opinion" that *voces* alone could have parts or species, and a statement by John of Salisbury, who makes Roscelin the author of the "exploded opinion," *voces ipsas genera esse et species*. What little we learn from these sources is at least consistent with the assertions of Anselm. Anselm was no fanatical heresy-hunter, and Roscelin was doubtless sincere in repudiating heretical intentions. But that is not the point. The question is whether there is any ground for regarding him as a distressed and persecuted champion of reason; and the answer, surely, must be that there is none.

The *flatus vocis* theory, whether invented by Roscelin or by one John the Sophist, was clearly a modernism, a heresy in dialectic, with no support from tradition. To translate it into Conceptualism appears to be wholly unwarrantable; Anselm treats it rather as a kind of stupid materialism, and gives not the slightest hint that he and Roscelin are ranged on opposite sides in an old and respectable controversy. He does not even trouble to define his own view of universals, but leaves us to gather what we may from scattered passages in his writings. Distressing as this may be to the historian of logic, the historian of philosophy will find in Anselm's very silences and omissions fresh reason for rejecting the once common opinion that medieval thinkers exhausted themselves for centuries in trying to define the nature of universals. It is scarcely too much to say that Anselm does not care what they are, so long as the function of reason is not simply confounded with sensuous perception. Neither things nor ideas are mere words and breath, but in what sense things and ideas are identical or distinct he is at no great pains to decide. The term "Nominalism" was not yet invented, nor the varieties of Realism yet arranged for classification. Nevertheless, we may still find reason to doubt whether Nominalism is exactly the right name for the doctrine propounded by Roscelin.

Among those who once called Roscelin master was he who called no man master for long. The stormy and romantic career of Peter Abelard has won for him a kind of immortality not conceded to philosophy alone. By his side, to claim a share in that immortality, stands the partner in his calamities and his joys:

Poeta, volentieri
Parlerei a quei due che insieme vanno.

With all his weakness, his vanity, his almost wanton pugnacity, there must have been in Abelard some quality of greatness, something that forbade men to gaze on him with indifference and pass by on the other side. He had at least the virtuosity of genius; he was born to fascinate or to repel. Wherever his tent was pitched, at Paris or on the borders of the wilderness, thither, as an old chronicler has it, *paene de tota Latinitate viri litterati confluebant.* In vain was he driven into exile; for where the master was there was the school.

Much the same gift of attraction and repulsion has been transmitted, it would seem, with Abelard's writings, to perplex the judgment of modern historians, and to fashion estimates of his worth *non solum diversa verum etiam adversa,* as once he said himself of the utterances of the saints. Unfair detraction is too apt to provoke extravagant eulogy; for to maintain that we have in Abelard the greatest mind of the Middle Ages is surely extravagant. A great teacher he certainly was, a shrewd and fearless critic, a mighty champion of dialectic, the mistress, as he declared, of all philosophical studies. But when we look for inspiration, for profundity of insight, for constructive power and masterly comprehension, we find but little to justify comparison of Abelard with John the Scot or Anselm or Thomas Aquinas. His passion for dialectic was even a sign of his limitations, the more conspicuous as we come to understand by closer scrutiny that he never wholly succeeded in raising dialectic to the level at which it ceases to be an ingenious art of words. His theory of universals, which agrees neither with Roscelin's nor with contemporary realism, it will be convenient to postpone until we have occasion to look at John of Salisbury's review of the subject. Even apart from that vexatious question, Abelard exhibits clearly the disadvantages of imperfect acquaintance with Aristotle, and also the restricted scope of Aristotle's reputation. The title of *Peripateticus Palatinus* (*i.e.* of Palais), bestowed by the common voice on Abelard himself, is fully interpreted by his own repeated identification of Peripatetics with dialecticians. *Peripateticorum, id est, dialecticorum princeps* is his description of Aristotle, and of Aristotle he knew no more than the labours of Boethius had conveyed to the Latins six hundred years ago. We find, accordingly, in Abelard (as in other medieval writers) a curious gap between his logical or dialectical opinions and the general character of his philosophy. It is not so much a question of positive inconsistency as of failure to see any reason why a professed Peripatetic should not also be an ardent follower of Plato. For, as Platonism was then understood, Abelard may certainly be called a Platonist. Immensely influenced by Macrobius, and by what he knew of the *Timaeus*, he carries Platonism freely into his Christian theology, and, when he styles Plato *maximus omnium philosophorum*, we cannot doubt that he speaks with conviction. Here, as always before the thirteenth century, the explanation is that Aristotle, the supreme dialectician, was virtually unknown as a physicist, a psychologist, or a metaphysician. Plato, on the other hand, was known, through his admiring reporters, to have scaled all the heights of speculation, and to have won the approval of many Catholic theologians.

What actually brought Abelard to trial and condemnation was neither his general advocacy of dialectic, nor his doctrine of universals, nor the particular method proposed in the *Sic et Non*. Despite the strong opposition, of which he tells us, to the free use of argument in the province of theology, he would never have furnished his enemies with adequate weapons, had he not been lured by Macrobius into such hazardous suggestions as the identification of the Holy Spirit with the *anima mundi*, and had he refrained from speculations on the Person of Christ which involved him in questions beyond the range of any ancient philosopher. How far the actual condemnations, at Soissons in 1121 and at Sens in 1140, were due to genuine concern for the faith, and how far to personal hostility, it is difficult to tell. A man who ridiculed his masters, such as William of Champeaux and Anselm of Laon, besides imperilling the reputation of other accredited teachers, such as Alberic of Rheims, could not hope to tread with impunity even on the borders of heresy. Yet the case of St Bernard of Clairvaux, the chief instigator of the second prosecution, is different. Bernard was a great man, a saint and a mystic, sharply touched, no doubt, with the defects of his qualities, but neither petty nor insincere. His own unique position could scarcely be shaken by Abelard; and just as it is fair to Abelard to believe in the sincerity of his faith, so is it fair to Bernard to allow that he had considerable reasons for regarding as a pestilent fellow one who caused trouble always and everywhere, and who apparently encouraged his pupils to think that the rudiments of philosophy were enough to reveal to them the secrets of heaven and earth. But the time has gone by for taking sides in this unhappy quarrel. Our business is only to enquire what Abelard did, or failed to do, for philosophy in an age when it was as hard to distinguish philosophy from theology as to disentangle the State from the Church.

On the whole he must stand or fall by his services to dialectic, the chosen object of his perpetual enthusiasm. To what lengths he went in magnifying its importance (even though he inveighs at times against its abuse) we may gather from his thirteenth epistle, where he argues that logic, as derived from *logos*, and thus connected with the *verbum Dei*, is pre-eminently the Christian science. Jesus Christ was the Logos incarnate, and logic was the wisdom promised to the disciples, the *os et sapientia* which their enemies would be unable to resist. Christ prepares for them, says Abelard, an armour of reasons, *qua in disputando summi efficiantur logici.* And who is ignorant, he adds, that Our Lord Himself convinced the Jews by frequent disputations? Rarely has the fundamental ambiguity of the word *logos* been better illustrated than by this passage, or indeed by the whole work of Abelard. Natural as it seems to suppose him to be upholding the sacred cause of reason and the mission of philosophy as a fearless search for the truth, he is never, at least in his eulogies of dialectic, more than half way towards that position. Dialectic remains for him the *ars disputandi*, by which you sharpen your wits to detect fallacies, and learn to know a good argument from a bad. Much service, indeed, may thus be rendered to the cause of truth; for how can truth and falsity be distinguished by one whom sophistical reasoning may deceive? Nevertheless, the gulf between the art of reasoning without fallacy and the real inquisition of truth is formidable and wide, too wide, one is forced to admit, for any bridge of Abelard's construction. A fairer criticism would be that he did not try to span it. He glorified dialectic and believed that all theological questions should be freely debated. Again, he believed that Gentile philosophers, if not actually inspired from heaven, should at least be allowed to bring their treasures of knowledge into the house of the Lord. But the plea for an unfettered use of dialectic and the plea for (let us roughly call it) a Platonised theology were very imperfectly unified in Abelard's mind.

The *Sic et Non*, Abelard's most famous exposition of method, is chiefly remarkable for its prologue. Dialectic being the proper solvent of contradictions, he proposes to apply it to a long list of apparent discrepancies, some of them found in the canonical books of Scripture, others in the teaching of the Fathers and the Saints. His rules of procedure are various. We must beware of apocryphal books and sayings; we must note that the Fathers (Augustine, for instance) sometimes retracted their earlier views, sometimes quoted opinions not endorsed by themselves, sometimes adapted or modified their precepts to suit special cases. Especially must we take into account the diverse meanings of words and their various usage by different authors. If, however, there remain, after all these precautions, certain contradictions beyond the help of dialectic, we must first balance and compare the authorities, and then firmly take our stand with the best. Not even prophets and apostles were infallible; much more, then, must errors be expected in the doctrines of ordinary men. Abelard does not, however, admit that the Scriptures can err. When we seem to detect absurdities on the sacred pages, we must attribute them to bad manuscripts, to faulty interpretations, or to deficiencies in our own intelligence. Outside the Old and New Testaments, on the other hand, we have perfect freedom of judgment, and when dialectic has done its best for the Fathers, we retain our right to dissent from their doctrine.

The sanity and good sense of these principles has not prevented much uncertainty as to their ultimate intention. But while it is possible to hold that Abelard's real aim was the destruction of authority, it is more reasonable to credit him with the true purpose of the dialectician, the removal of apparent contradictions and the establishment of truth on a critical basis. For all his love of contention, Abelard was no mere rebel or anarchist. In his own way he had a sincere respect for authority. He believed that truth was inherent in the tradition of the Church, but he did not believe in the promiscuous swallowing of contradictions. We should do injustice, therefore, to his dialectical acumen, if we supposed him to have piled up a mass of affirmations and negations with no other design but to discredit the testimony of the past. Even when his candour and the excellence of his intentions are freely admitted, it is easy enough, if we please, to disparage Abelard's performance. The application of his method to a long array of theological problems is strangely barren of result. Again and again he simply opposes the *sic* and the *non*, without attempting any critical solution. Here, too, and elsewhere in his writings, he fails to advance much beyond the verbal or linguistic aspect of the dialectical art. The presentation of opposite views, quite apart from verbal ambiguities, as complementary to one another, and hence as equally true or equally false, is somewhat beyond his range. And again, the originality of his method has been challenged. Bernold of Constance (*ob.* 1100), lately resuscitated by Grabmann, seems to have adopted much the same procedure; while the influence of Ivo of Chartres and the canonists has also to be considered. Equally doubtful is it how far the dialectical method of subsequent theologians was due to imitation of Abelard, and how far to the recovery of Aristotle's *Topics*. On no hypothesis, however, can the weight of Abelard's contribution to intellectual progress be fairly denied. His stimulus to slumbering dogmatists was invaluable; his courage in attacking difficulties was an example to the timorous; in the number and eminence of his pupils his high distinction of mind is loudly proclaimed.

From Abelard it will be convenient to pass to one of his contemporaries, whose influence, very different in quality, was perhaps equally great. Hugh of St Victor (*c.* 1096–1141), the most distinguished of a group of men attached to the same religious foundation at Paris, is seldom named without expressions of the deepest respect. So far as he allows himself to appear in his writings, we cannot fail to get a delightful impression of his character, if only because he has the rare gift of wearing humility without affectation, as a kind of natural charm. By temperament he was a genuine mystic. *Principium in lectione, consummatio in meditatione*[1] was his motto, and the nature of our subject perhaps forbids us to disturb his meditations. Nor will it be possible to examine his theological masterpiece, the *De Sacramentis Christianae Fidei*. But Hugh was not only a mystic, nor merely, in the restricted sense, a theologian. In him were united, says St Bonaventura, the gifts derived from Augustine, from

[1] MPL, CLXXVI, 772.

Gregory the Great, and from Dionysius the Areopagite. In reasoning, in preaching, in contemplation he was equally proficient; to which we may add that in his *Didascalicon* he has left us a valuable document on the nature of philosophy, its divisions and ultimate goal. This book betrays, in the first place, a wide and generous appetite for knowledge. *Omnia disce*, he urges; *videbis postea nihil esse superfluum. Coarctata scientia iucunda non est*[1]. His own diligence as a schoolboy he paints in pleasing colours; and already, perhaps, he was noting the weakness of teachers who would not stick to their subject, but wandered away into variations too weighty for their theme. *Non omnia dicenda sunt quae dicere possumus, ne minus utiliter dicantur ea quae dicere debemus*[2].

Classification and definition of subjects within the whole field of knowledge form the main purpose of the *Didascalicon*. The fourfold partition into *theorica, practica, mechanica*, and *logica* is remarkable for the inclusion of *mechanica* (divided into seven arts and crafts), but is not, in that respect, original. Grabmann has found the same division in an unpublished work by Radulphus Ardens, who is last heard of in 1101. So much, in fact, is common to the two writers that it is difficult to believe in their complete independence. An even greater debt to Boethius must be acknowledged. From him Hugh borrows the threefold division, anciently though wrongly ascribed to Plato, upon which *mechanica* is grafted; and from him, in the main, come the subdivisions of *theorica* and *practica*, with their reminiscences of Aristotle, as well as of other sources familiar to Boethius. Much of the detail we must be content to pass over, but it is worth while to look rather narrowly at Hugh's conception of logic, which is not the less interesting because here too the authority of Boethius is preponderant.

Hugh of St Victor remarks and lays bare the historic ambiguity which, after perplexing so many medieval logicians, has not yet ceased to haunt their modern successors. The Greek *logos*, he says, means either *sermo* or *ratio*; whence logic may be called *sermotionalis sive rationalis scientia*[3]. *Sermotionalis* is the wider term, because it includes grammar, as well as dialectic and rhetoric, among the species of the genus. Logic covers, in fact, the entire field of *sermones*, and by *sermones* is meant the *mutuae locutiones* of mankind, which existed long before they were governed by any science or art. Not only logic, but all sciences, as Hugh observes, existed in practice before they were reduced to rule. In the order of time logic arose later than the other parts of philosophy, but in the order of studies it should precede them. Just because it does not deal with *res*, it is indispensable to those who would enquire *de rerum natura*. Without its aid they will be likely to go astray, by assuming that results established *in sermonum decursu* must always hold good in the nature of things. Now all this is taken, often word for word, from Boethius[4]. It

[1] MPL, clxxvi, 801.   [2] *Ib.* clxxvi, 770.   [3] *Ib.* clxxvi, 749.
[4] Cf. Boethius, *In Isagogen Porphyrii Commenta.* Editio secunda, i, 2.

expresses, too, the most general and persistent conception of logic in the Middle Ages; and whenever we, with our modern ideas, are tempted to wander away in the direction of metaphysics and the wider theory of knowledge, we begin to lose touch with an age that thought of logic as *sermotionalis*, as a study rather of words and speech than of things.

How, then, does the logician deal with *sermones*? Not as the rhetorician, whose business is persuasion, nor as the grammarian, who is interested in the structure and inflexion of words. The object of his study is what Hugh calls *intellectus*, a term to be clearly distinguished from *voces*. Words as *voces* are only sounds of the particular kind produced in human speech and analysed by the grammarian. *Intellectus* are much more than this. The worst translation of the word would be "concepts"; the best, perhaps, is "meanings." Thus when Hugh is explaining the inter-relation of mathematics, logic, and physics, he remarks that only physics *de rebus agit, ceterae omnes de intellectibus rerum*[1]: a statement to be explained with reference to the power of abstraction possessed by the human mind, and illustrated, though not precisely in the same way, by both logic and mathematics. The mathematician can examine the line and the surface by ignoring one or two dimensions; the logician can attend only to the fact of likeness, neglecting the properties of things in their concreteness. And thus it is, says Hugh, that the logician comes to consider *genera* and *species*. No discussion of the familiar controversy is offered in this context; we can only assume that, if Hugh had chosen to proceed further, he would have continued to follow Boethius. In that case he would have paid no heed to Nominalism, a heresy unknown to Boethius, and probably would have declined to discuss the metaphysics of Plato. He would only have defended the right of the intellect to discern what he calls *intellectus*, and would have refused to condemn the mathematical line or the logical genus as figments, merely because they were not concrete things such as the physicist examines.

More personal, and perhaps more interesting, than the account of logic are Hugh's general appreciation of philosophy and his usage of the term *theologia*. Even here it is not easy to shake off Boethius; for in some passages of the *Didascalicon* "theology" bears only the meaning derived by Boethius from an assortment of Greek philosophers, without reference to Christian doctrine. There is also a strange and difficult allusion to John the Scot, whom Hugh describes as "theologian of our times" (*i.e.*, of the Christian era), but classes with Linus among the Greeks and with Varro among the Latins[2]. Nor, again, is *philosophia* a name without ambiguity. It may denote a complete and almost religious devotion to the pursuit of knowledge, involving renunciation of the world. *Omnis mundus philosophantibus exsilium est*, Hugh writes in one place, and adds that he himself had known this exile from his youth up[3]. At other times, however, he seems to disparage philosophy, as when he declares that, in comparison

---

[1] MPL, CLXXVI, 758.   [2] *Ib.* CLXXVII, 765.   [3] *Ib.* CLXXVII, 778.

with the Scriptures, the books of the philosophers are but a white-washed wall of mud, gay with the tinsel of eloquence and the specious pretence of truth. The superiority of Scripture is shewn by the richer and more numerous senses hidden under its surface. As an allegorist, Hugh of St Victor is not extravagant; for at least he insists on the need of understanding the literal or historical sense as the foundation of all other meanings. Yet by allegory he understands something more complicated than diversity of meanings in words. Not only words but things have an inner significance. The philosopher, he says, *solam vocum novit significationem, sed excellentior valde est rerum significatio quam vocum*[1]. The higher way, he proceeds to explain, lies through *vox* to *intellectus*, through *intellectus* to *res*, and thence through the inward and unspoken *ratio* or *verbum* to the knowledge of truth. Whether Hugh's various judgments can be reconciled is very questionable, but his constant advocacy of all human knowledge forbids us to suppose that he ever desires to condemn philosophy as verbal trifling. His point is that the meaning of the world disclosed by philosophy falls short of the mystical insight which pierces the veil of phenomena and passes through "history" to the revelation of God.

Hugh's praise of allegory is important, finally, as marking the point of his opposition to Abelard, and his reasons for rejecting the method of the *Sic et Non*. Though Abelard is never mentioned in the *Didascalicon*, there is one probable and one almost certain allusion to him. The first is the rebuke to those who "wrinkle up their nose" in scorn at the teachers of divinity, as though the subject were too simple to require the aid of instructed masters. The second and more important is the chapter in which allegorical interpretation is proposed as the true way of removing apparent contradictions in Scripture. The surface of the divine page offers many discrepancies; *spiritualis autem intelligentia nullam admittit repugnantiam, in qua diversa multa, adversa nulla esse possunt*[2]. The reference to Abelard in the last words can hardly be mistaken. Strange as it may seem to us now, the allegorising of Scripture was for many centuries the only kind of "higher criticism" known to the Church. Hugh of St Victor still believes in it, because he is a mystic; Abelard prefers to substitute dialectic, because he is a logician. Yet the contrast between the two men must not be exaggerated. Both believe in the infallibility of Scripture when rightly interpreted; and, as Hugh has a genuine enthusiasm for mundane philosophy, so Abelard in his turn is far from repudiating the principle that all other kinds of knowledge are subservient to the *scientia divina*.

The rapid convergence of the Peripatetic and Victorine streams is illustrated in the *Summa Sententiarum* long ascribed to Hugh of St Victor himself, and in the more famous *Libri Sententiarum IV* of Peter the Lombard, who came from Italy to Paris about 1139, was advanced to the

[1] MPL, CLXXVI, 790. [2] *Ib.* CLXXVI, 802.

bishopric of that city in 1159, and died not later than 1164. Literature of the *Sententia* type was by no means the invention of him who secured the title of *Magister Sententiarum*. Much the same meaning of *Sententia* can be traced back at least as far as Isidore of Seville, and more recently there had been great development of the method by Abelard's masters or opponents, Anselm of Laon, William of Champeaux, and Alberic of Rheims, as well as by the canonist Irnerius (or Guarnerius), who composed, early in the twelfth century, a book of Sentences compiled from Augustine and other authorities. Broadly speaking, the collections of *Sententiae* form a stage between the ancient *Florilegia* or *Catenae* and the systematic *Summae* of the thirteenth century. The massing of authoritative statements with a view to establishing truth by consensus of witnesses led gradually to two results, the formation of an orderly scheme for the exposition of theology and the emergence of antitheses demanding the skill of the dialectician. Peter the Lombard was no original genius; we cannot even be sure that he was a man of exceptional learning; for, after the manner of the Middle Ages, he borrowed freely and without acknowledgment from the *Decretum* of Gratian, from Abelard and Hugh of St Victor, and from any other convenient treasury of sources. Nevertheless, he outran all competitors in his own kind of compilation, and finally established himself as the very text of theological education, upon which innumerable masters and students were to furnish the commentary. For the development of philosophy his chief importance lies in his frank submission to the influence of Abelard, whose lectures he probably had heard. The result was that the pupil, rather than the master, was responsible for the triumph of the dialectical method in later theology.

The triumph was not achieved, however, without a struggle, prolonged for more than fifty years after Peter the Lombard's death. Certain propositions in his Christology were easily open to attack, and were, in fact, so questionable that regular exponents of his treatise afterwards made a practice of omitting them. But the main opposition sprang from antidialecticians of the Victorine School. Shortly before the Third Lateran Council of 1179 Walter of St Victor wrote a violent pamphlet *Contra quattuor labyrinthos Franciae*: the four offenders being Abelard, Peter the Lombard, Gilbert de la Porrée, and Peter of Poitiers, an ardent follower of the Lombard, who had published his own five books of *Sententiae* before 1175. Other sources of hostility to the Master were the unknown writer of the *Liber de vera Philosophia* and the celebrated mystic, Joachim of Flora (*ob.* 1202). But Joachim himself was too suspect to bring home a charge of heresy against another, and the end of the matter, so far as the Fourth Lateran Council of 1215 could end it, was the condemnation of Joachim and the official recognition of Peter the Lombard. A considerable step was thus taken towards the conciliation of *ratio* and *auctoritas*, even though *ratio* still meant little more than the free use of dialectic, and *auctoritas* was still but vaguely defined.

Incidentally we may note that Walter of St Victor's attack was directed also against the work of John of Damascus (*ob.* 750), known to the Latins as the *De Fide Orthodoxa*, and newly translated from the Greek (as the result of a visit to Constantinople) by Burgundio of Pisa. In the Lombard's *Sentences* only some twenty-six citations of the "St Thomas of the East" have been discovered, and these are all taken from a section of the third book, relating to the Incarnation. As it came to be more fully known, the vogue of the *De Fide Orthodoxa* steadily increased, not least because the author's sympathy with Aristotelianism recommended him to the great doctors of the thirteenth century and supported their practice.

The intellectual condition of the twelfth century is nowhere so perfectly reflected as in the writings of John of Salisbury, the *vir plebeius et indoctus* who rose to be secretary to three Archbishops of Canterbury (including Becket), the intimate friend of Hadrian IV, the associate and critic of all the great teachers of the age, before he died, as Bishop of Chartres, in 1180. Traveller, scholar, gentleman, good Christian, and good man of the world, he has left behind him in the agreeable latinity of the *Policraticus* and the *Metalogicus* an impression of medieval life more illuminating than fifty treatises on logic, and more significant of what philosophy then really meant. In particular we owe to John of Salisbury a large part of our acquaintance with the school of Chartres, the most brilliant example of the old cathedral-school, now about to be superseded by the *studium generale*, or University. To say that he personally belonged to this school would, however, be inaccurate. He spent some years there and venerated its masters, but he learned also of Abelard, Robert of Melun, Alberic of Rheims, and many others outside the precincts of Chartres; nor is there anything in his works to prove his formal adherence to the characteristic tenets of the school. What makes his testimony so invaluable is just his gift of intellectual detachment and his distaste for the fury of the partisan. In politics, that is to say, in his estimate of the spiritual and the temporal power, it is otherwise; for his hierarchical opinions are definite and strong. Nor is he ever restrained by love of compromise from expressing the frankest of judgments on controversies of the day, much less from lively denunciation of Philistines and fools. Yet, as he passes from one seat of learning to another, he combines an honest respect for the teachers with the privilege of smiling at the school. Thus, for example, does he return after many years to Mount St Geneviève, to see how his friends are faring, and finds them still, as he says, at the same old questions, with not one little *propositiuncula* annexed to the familiar stock in trade. With the same aloofness, he admires Abelard, but laughs at his theory of universals; he reveres Bernard, the *senex Carnotensis*, but keeps clear of the Platonised *ideas*, and is aware that the master's hope of reconciling Plato and Aristotle is vain.

With justice, then, did John of Salisbury profess himself an Academic;

by which, it is well to add, he did not mean a Platonist. He knew that the Sceptics had captured the Academy, and attributes the rise of Scepticism to the Aristotelian criticism of Plato. He did not understand the return of the Platonists to their ancient home, and when he names Plotinus, Iamblichus, and Porphyry as the most distinguished of the Academics, he betrays the gaps in his knowledge of history. About his own position, however, he is perfectly clear. What he professes is the "Academic or Sceptical Philosophy," as Hume called it, not the Platonism of Chalcidius and Macrobius, or of his own contemporaries and friends. His Academicism does not mean extravagant distrust of reason, but chiefly a spirit of tolerant criticism, distaste for dogmatic obstinacy, and disinclination to swear allegiance *in verba magistri*. Had his bent been for mathematics, he might almost have anticipated the great saying of Pascal, that a man should be three things, a good mathematician, a good sceptic, and a humble follower of Jesus Christ.

Thanks largely to his cool and sceptical temper, we can readily learn from John of Salisbury what an utter misconception of the Middle Ages it is to confound the history of philosophy with the history of logic, or to oppose philosophy to the life of religion. As is shewn by the very title of his longest work, *Policratici, sive de nugis Curialium et vestigiis Philosophorum Libri VIII*, the world is roughly divided for him into the foolish and the wise. On the one side is the life of the courtier, a life devoted to hunting and gambling, or to laughing at actors and buffoons; on the other is the call to the higher life of the mind. The alternatives are plain and mutually repellent; *qui curialium ineptias induit, et philosophi vel boni viri officium pollicetur, Hermaphroditus est*[1]. All who respond to the serious call are philosophers, and therefore John of Salisbury's friends. And what is philosophy? Not the product of *copia litterarum*, but the choice of an arduous way. In its ancient sense, philosophy, as he says, *pulsat ad ostium*; and when the door of wisdom is opened, the soul is illumined with the "light of things," and the name of philosophy vanishes away. But that illumination is for the future. Philosophy in this world is the *viaticum* of the few who content themselves with following a road that leads to no worldly advantage. As to where and how the true road is to be found, John himself is not doubtful. The philosopher, as Plato had taught, is *cultor Dei*, and the end of all philosophy is the enlargement of charity. But in this respect no Christian is inferior to Plato; the rule of Christ surpasses the wisdom of antiquity; the *vita claustralium* outdoes the practice of all the schools.

> Philosophia quid est nisi fons, via, duxque salutis,
> Lux animae, vitae regula, grata quies?

So he asks in the *Entheticus*, and adds in the sad doggerel of that discursive poem:

> Non valet absque fide sincere philosophari[2].

---

[1] *Policraticus*, v, 10.   [2] *Entheticus*, 277–278 and 319.

Armed with this firm conviction, John goes forth to the defence and criticism of logic. By logic he understands, in the first instance, very much what we found in Hugh of St Victor. He notes the same quality of *sermo* and *ratio* as translations of *logos*, and insists, like Hugh, on the close alliance of logic with eloquence and grammar; not indeed because he deems logic a science of words, but because he has learned from Bernard of Chartres and William of Conches to believe in humane education as the first safeguard against arid disputes. In his championship of logic he has, in fact, to steer a difficult course between the scurrilous mockers, personified under the pseudonym of Cornificius, and the so-called *puri philosophi*[1], who identify philosophy with logic and disdain every other branch of knowledge. No modern critic of the Middle Ages has exposed so remorselessly the ineptitude of wrangling about trifles, the emptiness of logic divorced from natural and moral science. As an introduction to further studies logic is excellent; in isolation it is *exsanguis et sterilis*[2]. The teachers grow old in the exercises of boys; the boys (*hesterni pueri, magistri hodierni*) escape to-day from the rod, and to-morrow assume the gown and mount the *cathedra*[3]. The world is crowded with half-educated wiseacres, the schools with Peripatetics whose Peripateticism consists only in walking about.

After these caustic criticisms it is no surprise to find that John of Salisbury puts the whole controversy about universals into its proper and subordinate place. Far from being the sum of philosophy, this fashionable topic of the schools serves chiefly to provoke the emulous ingenuity of lecturers, no one of whom is content to agree with his predecessors or to remain within the bounds proposed by Boethius. John's own solution and the many varieties of Realism we have no space to examine. His main anxiety is to prevent the reduction of any part of philosophy to a conflict of words. For this reason he dislikes any verbalist theory of universals, and speaks with some contempt of Roscelin and Abelard. His distinction between the two is that Roscelin had talked of *voces*, Abelard of *sermones*[4], a term not adequately explained in the *Metalogicus*, but further illustrated by a parallel passage in the *Policraticus*, where an evident allusion to Roscelin is followed by a mention of those *qui indifferenter nomina pro rebus vel res pro nominibus posuerunt*[5]. If, then, *sermones* are not simply *voces* but *nomina*, it would seem that Abelard rather than Roscelin was the true nominalist. Whatever the exact import of Abelard's view, John declines to take it seriously, but offers to excuse its author on the ground that an elementary book like the *Categories* had perhaps to be taught in an elementary manner[6]. In no case is there room for the opinion that Abelard was a conceptualist. That opinion (which arose partly from the wrong attribution to Abelard of a treatise *De Generibus et Speciebus*) is sufficiently refuted by John himself,

---

[1] *Metalogicus*, II, 6.   [2] *Ib.* II, 20.   [3] *Ib.* I, 25.
[4] *Ib.* II, 17.   [5] *Policraticus*, VII, 12.   [6] *Metalogicus*, III, 1.

when he passes immediately from Roscelin and Abelard to a third non-realist theory, in which the universal is called a *notio* or *intellectus et simplex animi conceptio*. Here, if anywhere, we must look for Conceptualism, and not in the doctine of Abelard.

From John of Salisbury, lastly, we receive our first clear impression of the "new logic," already known in some measure to his senior contemporaries, Otto of Freising, Thierry of Chartres, and Adam du Petit Pont. The translation of the *Organon* by James of Venice is assigned to the year 1128, some thirty years before the *Metalogicus* was written; but John himself used another version, probably by Henry Aristippus of Catania, distinguished also as a translator of Plato. The effect of recovering the *Analytics*, the *Topics*, and the *Sophistici Elenchi* may be considered in two relations, to the general conception of logic and to the reputation of Aristotle. Hitherto, as we have often had occasion to remark, logic, in the character of dialectic, had hovered on the borderland between reasoning and discourse, while Aristotle had been simply the great dialectician. But now it began to be understood that the traditional Aristotelian books were but elementary prefaces to the dialectical treatises, and that the whole of dialectic must fall into a minor position, as compared with the *ars demonstrandi* or method of science. "The philosopher," says John of Salisbury, "who uses demonstration has his business with truth, the dialectician with opinion, the sophist with the bare appearance of probability."[1] The *Posterior Analytics*, evidently, were found very difficult, and John speaks of them with the most cautious respect. The art of demonstration, he says, has fallen into almost complete disuse. It survives only in mathematics, especially in geometry; *sed et huius disciplinae non est celebris usus apud nos, nisi forte in tractu Ibero vel confinio Africae*[2]. Mathematics, in other words, were studied only by the Arabs or their neighbours.

The revolution in logic, we should gather from John of Salisbury, magnified the reputation of Aristotle without radically altering its character. As *urbs* stands for Rome and *poeta* for Virgil, so the name of *philosophus* is reserved by common consent for Aristotle[3]. On the authority of Burgundio of Pisa, John adds in another place that Aristotle's prescriptive right to the name was based on his skill in demonstration, the art most highly esteemed by the Peripatetics[4]. It would be wrong, however, to infer from this anticipation of the title so freely employed in the thirteenth century that Aristotle had already usurped the throne of Plato. John's personal estimate of "the philosopher" reflects his attitude towards logic in general. Refusing to treat any utterance of Aristotle's as *sacrosanctum*, he accuses him (with how much knowledge?) of many errors in natural and moral philosophy[5]. Even in logic he does not count him infallible, but notes his deficiencies, and believes it possible for modern teachers to improve on his handling of some parts of the subject. John,

[1] *Metalogicus*, II, 5   [2] *Ib.* IV, 6.   [3] *Policraticus*, VII, 6.
[4] *Metalogicus*, IV, 7.   [5] *Ib.* IV, 27.

indeed, is at all times a champion of the *moderni*. He sympathises with Abelard's difficulty in getting a hearing for any doctrine not sanctioned by antiquity, and insists that respect for old authors should not hamper the critical exercise of reason. On the other hand, he does maintain that Aristotle is peerless in logic, and defends the study of the *Categories* and the *Sophistici Elenchi* against unintelligent critics, among whom he mentions some followers of Robert of Melun[1]. On the whole, Aristotle remains where he was, the prince of logicians, without as yet any claim to wider dominion. Down to the end of the twelfth century or even later, none but the "pure philosophers" were disposed to exalt the pupil above the master. The rest of the world would have endorsed the verdict of the *Policraticus*, where John describes Plato, with all deference to the Aristotelians, as *totius philosophiae princeps*[2].

The Platonism for which the school of Chartres was conspicuous meant, apparently, not much more than the traditional Platonism of the *Timaeus*, with its sundry exponents. The *Phaedo* and the *Meno*, which had been translated by Henry Aristippus of Catania (*ob.* 1162), produced no immediate effect on the interpretation of Plato. The Chartres account of universals, for example, identified them with the Platonic *ideas*, and understood *idea* in the sense of *exemplar aeternum*, a sense traditional in the Latin interpretation of the *Timaeus*, but certainly not derived from the *Phaedo*. And again, when followers of Bernard of Chartres, such as William of Conches, strayed on to dangerous theological ground, they were inclined to imitate Abelard in Platonising the Trinity and in identifying the Holy Spirit with the *anima mundi*. Perhaps it was the reminiscence of Abelard, as well as the widespread influence of Chartres, that caused fresh anxiety to ecclesiastical authority. The most famous disturbance connected with any scholar of Chartres was the trial of Gilbert de la Porrée (*ob.* 1154), the learned and venerable Bishop of Poitiers, himself sufficiently distinguished to rank as the founder of a school. The story of the trial, which took place at Rheims in 1148, is related by Otto of Freising and by John of Salisbury in his *Historia Pontificalis*. John was present throughout the proceedings, as were also Peter the Lombard, Robert of Melun, and other prominent divines, some to support St Bernard (once more the chief prosecutor), others to aid in the defence of the bishop. On this occasion Bernard fell short of victory. His followers refused to confess the defeat, but Gilbert returned safely to his diocese and was immune from all further attacks.

Apart from this political incident, the fame of Gilbert rests chiefly on his exposition of the theology of Boethius, and on his *Liber de Sex Principiis*, a logical text-book more highly esteemed than any other composed in the Middle Ages. For the most part Gilbert sticks to the "old logic," though there is some evidence of his acquaintance with the "new." He refers in one place to the *Analytics*, and his commentary on the *De*

---

[1] *Metalogicus*, IV, 24.   [2] *Policraticus*, I, 6.

Trinitate of Boethius perhaps implies more knowledge of Aristotle than could well be derived from the more elementary treatises. His treatment of time and space has even been thought to involve some reference to the *Physics*, but that is improbable. So again, his theory of universals, which he called *formae nativae*, does not agree with the ordinary Platonism. A *forma nativa* is an *exemplum* inherent in created things, related to the *exemplar* in the Creator's mind as *eidos* to *idea*[1]. The origin of such a view might well be Aristotelian, but the evidence is not clear.

Passing over with regret many other names associated more or less closely with the teaching of Chartres, we have space only to raise the general question, whether in the course of the twelfth century much advance was made towards a wider conception of philosophical problems. A certain restlessness and a certain feeling of expansion, greatly assisted by the enlargement of logic, there undoubtedly is. At the beginning of the century Adelard of Bath was wandering from country to country and realising the advantage of visiting different schools. In Spain he learnt enough Arabic to make a translation of Euclid, and to acquire some notion of the uses of mathematics for the purposes of scientific measurement. His general outlook, however, is reminiscent of what John of Salisbury imputes to Bernard of Chartres. At the close of the same century, Alan of Lille (Alanus de Insulis), who survived till 1203, is far from suspecting the immediate advent of a great intellectual revolution. He deserves to be remembered, if only for his saying: *sed quia auctoritas cereum habet nasum, id est, in diversum potest flecti, rationibus roborandum est*[2]. In his own age he won the title of *doctor universalis* by his manifold learning; in modern times his taste for a rigid, quasi-mathematical method has suggested a comparison with Spinoza. Yet his appetite for novelty was not striking. The first of the Latins to cite the *Liber de Causis*, he is but little affected by the peculiar qualities of that work. The new logic, far from arousing his enthusiasm, seems rather to have persuaded him that Aristotle loved to wrap himself in majestic obscurity. Thus, without disparaging his work, which deserves a much fuller account, we may fairly infer from his case that in the last hours of the twelfth century it was possible for a man of the highest reputation to enjoy no premonition of the great movement of thought which the coming century was immediately to witness.

If only by weight of materials, the thirteenth century stands apart from those through which we have rapidly travelled. The briefest catalogue of names such as Alexander of Hales, Albertus Magnus, Thomas Aquinas, Bonaventura, Roger Bacon, Duns Scotus, is enough to banish the thought of any detailed analysis. The only practicable course will be to sketch the line of development and the general character of the problems with which these and other authors, only less famous, were engaged. Nearly eight centuries had passed since Boethius presented Aristotle to

---

[1] John of Salisbury, *Metalogicus*, II, 17.   [2] MPL, ccx, 333.

the Latins, but during the whole of that period less had happened to disturb the intellectual atmosphere than was now to be accomplished in a single generation by the Aristotelian invasion of Paris. Customary and right as it is to place the name of Aristotle in the foreground, it would be idle to pretend that the mere recovery of his writings was enough to account for all the subsequent events. Without the organisation of studies in the new universities, and without the intervention of the Friars in educational and ecclesiastical politics, the story of the thirteenth century must have been very different. And again, it is difficult to exaggerate the importance of another fact, the conjunction of the new Aristotle with an interpretation of him developed by a series of Muslim philosophers, whose object had not been to keep on terms with Christian orthodoxy, but to avoid open collision with the Koran. The fragments of Arabian mathematics and medicine which had drifted from time to time into the Latin world had brought no anticipation of the tumult immediately aroused by the commentaries of Avicenna and Averroes. The roughly established *modus vivendi* with Pagan philosophy was of no avail when there suddenly appeared a new Aristotle, the author of a vast and comprehensive system, in which were contained, if the Muslims could be trusted, many doctrines incompatible with the Christian position. And most of this was brought about by the enterprise of a Christian, Archbishop Raymond of Toledo, who had instituted, in the second quarter of the twelfth century, a college of translators under the supervision of Dominic Gundisalvi, himself the author of a *De Divisione Philosophiae* and other philosophical works.

The unparalleled importance of translations in the Middle Ages was not diminished by the prevalence of a single literary language among the peoples of the West. Absence of linguistic barriers between the scholars of different European countries may even have helped to strengthen the frontiers dividing the larger units of culture denoted as the Arabs, the Latins, and the Greeks. We cannot, however, pursue that complicated question, but must be content to glance at the golden age of translators, which began early in the twelfth century and lasted about a hundred and fifty years. Visits of Western scholars to Byzantium had produced the translations of the *Organon* and of John of Damascus; another centre was the court of Palermo, where Greek and Arabic learning were united; but the widest diffusion of Muslim knowledge came from Toledo, and it is necessary to enquire how far the Latin Aristotelianism was affected by the mediation of the Arabic language. The story, once lightly bandied about, that the medieval Aristotle was only a Latin parody of an Arabic version of a Syrian translation of a Greek original is little more than a fable. It is true that the Muslims were first introduced to Aristotle by Syrians, chiefly Nestorian Christians; it is true also that Arabic Aristotelianism was coloured to the last by the commentators, such as Alexander of Aphrodisias, who had influenced the Syrians. But long before there was any question of extensive Muslim influence on the Latins, direct translations of Aristotle from Greek into Arabic had been made in abundance. The name of "philosophers," in the Arabic transcription of the word, was especially applied to those who had studied Greek originals; and among these "philosophers" were the whole series of writers, beginning with Kindī in the ninth century, whose names we encounter in the works of the Latin schoolmen. Strange to say, the most famous of all (at least in Latin estimation), Ibn Rushd or Averroes (*ob.* 1198), was an exception to the rule. For it is said that he never thought it worth while to learn Greek. If that be so, we must suppose that he saw no reason, after three centuries of Aristotelian scholarship, to doubt the adequacy of the Arabic translations. It was left for his Latin critics to entertain that doubt.

While the relation of the Latins to the Arabs is, at first sight, analogous to that of the Arabs to the Syrians, further scrutiny of the facts does not strengthen the analogy. There never was a time when the Latins depended entirely on translations from the Arabic; there never was a time when the Muslim inferences from Aristotle were not disputed and opposed; least of all was there a time when Christians could imitate Muslims in taking Aristotle as an infallible authority. To adopt that attitude was, in fact, to be an Averroist; and Averroism, as we shall see, was a movement destructive of all that Christian philosophers were striving to establish.

Now that the earlier researches of Jourdain have been supplemented by Grabmann and other recent scholars, it is possible to speak with some confidence about the translations of Aristotle used by the Latins. No simple generalisation can be accurate, for the case of each of Aristotle's works has to be separately considered. Yet on the whole it is safe to maintain that translations from the Greek relieved the schoolmen of undue dependence on the Arabs, and enabled them, thus far at least, to form an independent judgment on the meaning of Aristotle. To illustrate the facts from a few of the more important works, we find that the earliest version of the *Metaphysics* (containing only Books I–III and a small part of IV) came to Paris from Byzantium before 1210. Next to arrive (apparently before 1217) was a translation from the Arabic ascribed to Gerard of Cremona. This, too, was imperfect, for it omitted altogether Books K, M, and N, and mixed up the first book with the second. With this, however, the Latins had to content themselves until after 1260, when a Graeco-Latin version of the first twelve books, probably by William of Moerbeke, was put into circulation. Upon these twelve books St Thomas wrote his commentary, the last two being still untranslated when he saw a Greek manuscript of the whole fourteen in 1270. The history of the *Nicomachean Ethics* is rather similar: first a Graeco-Latin version of three books, disguised as four; then, in 1240, a paraphrase from the Arabic by Herman the German; lastly a full translation from the Greek, often explicitly attributed to Robert Grosseteste (*ob.* 1253), but

more probably, in Grabmann's opinion, by William of Moerbeke. Both
the *Physics* and the *De Anima* were known first in Graeco-Latin versions,
while the *Politics*, a book neglected by the Arabs, was derived only from
the Greek. Evidently, then, it would be less than a half-truth to say that
the Latins depended on second-hand translations for access to those works
of Aristotle which most deeply affected their thought. It remains to ask
whether the quality of the translations was such as to debar them from
a sound understanding of the text.

To claim distinction of style for the medieval translations would
indeed be courageous. Their rudeness, however, was perfectly deliberate.
It was not due to inability to write Latin, but to a frank mistrust of
elegance where the sole object was to get an exact reproduction of the
original. This they imagined they would best secure by simply replacing,
so far as possible, every Greek word by its Latin equivalent. For reasons
then potent, but now no longer operative, they demanded the letter
rather than the spirit; not a transformation of idiom into idiom, but
a raw and formless text. The task of the translators may have been
wrongly conceived, but in its way it was faithfully done. The belief, still
extant in some quarters, that the medieval understanding of Aristotle
was hopelessly vitiated by faulty translations is unsupported by the facts.
The prime author of this libel was Roger Bacon, whose bitter denuncia-
tions, often repeated as oracles, were in truth the product of ignorance
and spleen. Bacon's judgments on the translation and study of Aristotle
range over a quarter of a century, from about 1266 to 1292. Starting
from the excellent principle that a translator requires both a knowledge
of the languages and an understanding of the sciences concerned, he repeatedly declares that only Boethius possessed the first qualification,
only Robert Grosseteste the second. And here at once we begin to suspect him. For Grosseteste's scientific attainments, as Bacon knew, were
in mathematics and optics, neither of which would have helped him in
the least to understand the greater part of Aristotle.

The rest of the translators, Bacon continues, were ignorant of science,
of Greek, and even of Latin. The result of their labours was erroneous
and unintelligible; so great, indeed, was the consequent misapprehension
of Aristotle that it would have been better for all his works to be burnt.
In the *Opus Tertium* (cap. 25), composed not later than 1268, Bacon had
not yet heard of William of Moerbeke, but in the later *Compendium Studii
Philosophiae* he attacks him, under the name of William the Fleming,
with peculiar venom, and thinks him no better than Gerard of Cremona,
Herman, or Michael the Scot (the three chief translators from the
Arabic), or than any of the pretended experts in Greek. William of
Moerbeke (*ob.* 1286), Archbishop of Corinth during the last years of his
life, was actually the most important of the translators, if only because
so much of his work was instigated by Thomas Aquinas, when both were
attached to the court of Urban IV. His dated works, which include

translations of Proclus, Simplicius, Galen, and Hippocrates, cover the period from 1260 to 1280. As it happens, only one of his Aristotelian translations (the *De Partibus Animalium*) is dated, and there is also some uncertainty how far he made use of earlier versions. We know, however, that he was the first translator in that age of the *Politics*, and we know that a scholar of Susemihl's rank thought it worth while to print this translation with his own edition of the text. Bacon's judgment on William of Moerbeke has, in fact, no more value than a spiteful review in a modern periodical of a book which the reviewer has omitted to read.

Not even on sheer questions of fact can Bacon be trusted. He invents, for example, an intimacy between Gerard of Cremona and Herman the German, though one of them was about eighty-five years senior to the other. It is more than doubtful, too, if he is accurate in his account of Robert Grosseteste, one of the very few among his contemporaries whom he deigned to admire. Depreciation of other men was a passion with him, almost a disease. He was out of sympathy with the whole Aristotelian movement, and out of humour with all the world. As to the contemporary interpretation of Aristotle, his verdict is yet more ludicrous than his contempt for the translations. With all the disadvantages from which they inevitably suffered, Albertus Magnus and his still more famous pupil were two of the greatest Aristotelians the world has yet seen. Bacon himself was incompetent to judge them, but he resented the intellectual dictatorship, as he thought it, of Albert, and attacked him with such animosity that the great Dominican was moved at last to administer a weighty rebuke. To Bacon, at least, he is thought to be referring, when he speaks of those who seek a solace for their own indolence by looking only for objects to attack; who resemble the *humor fellis* that spreads through a body, by provoking all other students to bitterness and forbidding them *in dulcedine societatis quaerere veritatem*[1]. As a critic of others Bacon well deserves the rebuke; it is fortunate that, as an original thinker, he still can deserve our respect.

The comparative freedom of the Latins in the matter of translations by no means released them from conflict with the Muslim interpretation of Aristotle. From the first, apparently, the trouble caused by the new material was aggravated by the use of certain *commenta*, which were included in the prohibition of Aristotle at Paris in 1210. Whether the reference was to Avicenna or to Averroes, it is certain that the entire history of Aristotelianism at Paris is bound up with the claim of the Arabs to be the authentic exponents. Some indication, therefore, however slight and meagre, must be given of the character and position of philosophy in Islām. Why there should ever have been room for intellectual complications in that system is much less obvious than in the case of the Christian Church. The unitarian God of Mahomet could have a Prophet but not a Son. He dwelt apart from His creatures, neither incarnate nor

[1] Cf. Mandonnet, *Siger de Brabant*, Part i, p. 246.

immanent, a lonely presence in the desert which no man could cross. Such a creed might have continued to satisfy the Arabs of the peninsula, and, if Islām had remained in that primitive condition, it would have made no impression on the world. As soon, however, as it came into contact with Syrian, Persian, and Byzantine civilisation, it had to choose between adapting itself to a higher order of ideas and perishing altogether. Educated minds, when they began to reflect on the message of the Prophet, were not slow to discover in the Koran and its contents sufficient material for philosophic doubt. Was the sacred book itself created, or co-eternal with the Creator? Did not the Word or Wisdom of God resemble the Nous of the philosophers or the Logos of the Christians? Had God eternal attributes, or would their existence be incompatible with His absolute unity? Could the freedom of man be maintained against the Divine Omniscience?

The first debates on these topics date from early times, even before John of Damascus, as an official at the court of the Umayyads, provided a curious link between Christian and Muslim thought. The great age, however, both of translations and of philosophy began with the Abbasids and the founding of Baghdad, where the patronage of Nestorian physicians by Manṣūr and Ma'mūn led to the institution of a school of medicine and philosophy. The sect of the Mu'tazilites (once fanatical defenders of the unity of God) now became prominent in speculation, and from their ranks arose Kindī (*ob. c.* 873), the father of a notable line of philosophers, and himself almost the only one of them who was an Arab by race. In him we observe already the main characteristics which persisted down to Averroes, the last of the line. The predominance of Aristotle had been established from the first. From the first, too, the interpretation of Aristotle had borne the stamp of Neo-Platonism. Perhaps the most surprising example of this is the general reception of the *Theology of Aristotle* as a genuine work. Actually an abridgment of *Enneads* iv–vi, it was accepted as Aristotelian by Kindī, Fārābī, and many others, who must, as it seems to us, have been blind to the enormous gulf between the minds of Aristotle and Plotinus. Or were they, after all, so blind as we think? Plotinus himself might have dissented. The interpretation of Aristotle has always been determined by the interests and the methods of criticism belonging to some particular age. It is a question of emphasis, of the relative appreciation of his various works, of the special points selected for discussion. All ages have recognised the great logician, but what a vast difference it makes whether you take Aristotle as primarily an astronomer, a theologian, a political thinker, or a biologist.

The Arabs, beginning with Kindī, fastened especially upon the theory of the intellect in the *De Anima*. There, in a few brief and difficult statements, they found the origin of all the disputes about the *intellectus agens* and the *intellectus possibilis*, with other complications too technical to mention. Here too was the most patent opportunity for fusing together

CH. XXIII.

Platonist and Aristotelian doctrines. For Aristotle had certainly hinted that mind or spirit in its highest manifestations might be independent of bodily organs, perpetually active, immortal. Its energy was not a form of motion, and therefore not inseparably linked with time. How, then, could such an activity belong, like other psychical functions, to the life of the individual? From this question it was but a short step to the identification of the *intellectus agens* with the *nous* of Plotinus, understood as the manifestation of God. The wisdom of man thus becomes a divine illumination, undefiled and imperishable, indifferent to the accident of death. Such, in roughest expression, was the line of thought along which the Arabs advanced towards the denial of personal immortality, and thus to conflict with the Catholic faith.

In the opinion of many Arabic writers and scholars, the most original of the Muslim thinkers was Fārābī (*ob.* 950), who in the course of his life is heard of in Egypt, at Damascus, and at Baghdad. Especially famous for his commentaries on the *Organon*, with which the Arabs associated (not without reason) the *Rhetoric* and the *Poetics*, he wrote also on almost every part of Aristotle's system, on the *Laws* of Plato, on mathematics and music. Though his view of the *intellectus agens* was similar in principle to Kindī's, he is said to have regarded Aristotle's doctrine as a proof of the immortality of the soul. And here we may note that, down to Fārābī's time, there was no perceptible breach between the philosophers and orthodox Islām. Plato and Aristotle were welcomed at first as a kind of second revelation, harmonious with the official revelation of the Koran. Yet the connexion of philosophy with sectarianism was early; the Shī'ites were more given to speculation than the Sunnīs, and from the time of Fārābī onwards there was a gradual tendency towards the conversion of philosophy into an esoteric wisdom, remote from the orthodox profession of faith.

The last of the Asiatic philosophers, and, next to Averroes, the most notorious among the Latins, was Ibn Sīnā or Avicenna (*ob.* 1036), who passed through law and medicine to metaphysics, where he is said to have owed his first understanding of Aristotle to Fārābī's books. Among other things, he interested himself in the theory of universals, and formulated distinctions between the genus *ante res, in rebus,* and *post res.* In the main, however, he resembled the other Muslims in affecting the Christians chiefly by his doctrine of the intellect. Before Avicenna's day the position of the philosophers, in the special sense of followers of the Greek tradition, had become decidedly ambiguous. Two other kinds of teachers had now to be reckoned with, first the Sufis or mystics, secondly the orthodox scholastics (as it is convenient to call them), who did not wholly contemn philosophy but proposed to subordinate it strictly to the teaching of the Koran. Upon the Sufis we can make only one observation, that they were certainly touched by Neo-Platonistic influence. The other school, whose aim might be loosely compared with Anselm's *fides quaerens intellectum,* was represented first by Ash'arī, a contemporary of Fārābī, afterwards, in the period between Avicenna and Averroes, by Ghazālī or Algazel (*ob.* 1111). While the relation of Algazel's teaching to Islāmic orthodoxy scarcely concerns us, there is a real significance for the later Western scholasticism in his determined opposition to the professional philosophers. As the author of the *Destruction of the Philosophers* (to which Averroes afterwards replied with the *Destruction of the Destruction*), he not only denounced as heretical certain specific doctrines, such as the eternity of the world, but flatly refused to allow the independent status of philosophy. Philosophy, he contended, could not be a mode of revelation; it could not enunciate first principles at once explanatory of the origin of things and compatible with orthodox beliefs. Reason could serve religion only in the way of exposition, just as it might be of use to any special science, or in the management of ordinary affairs.

Now this was the true battleground of philosophers and theologians at Paris in the thirteenth century; and the character of the struggle was predetermined much less by the old Latin antithesis of *ratio* and *auctoritas* than by the defined antagonism between the school of Algazel and the school of Averroes. Moreover, it was not the fear of Islām that worked so profoundly upon the reasoning of Albertus Magnus and Aquinas, but the fear of doctrines which Islām was on the verge of rejecting. For Averroes in the West marked the decline of Muslim philosophy, already long decadent in the East. He owes his fame, first to Jewish thinkers, who, like the Christians and the Muslims, had their own problem of reconciling philosophy with "the book"; secondly to Latin universities, which both accepted him as the supreme commentator on Aristotle and cherished, as the most alluring of heresies, doctrines invented or renewed for the confusion of Algazel's disciples. Averroes, therefore, is rightly studied in connexion with Latin Averroism, to which we shall shortly return. As to the Jews, by their active minds and roving habits they played an important part as carriers of learning from place to place, but as philosophers they hardly constitute a class distinct from the Arabs. The *Fons Vitae* of Avencebrol (*ob.* 1058), a Neo-Platonist work in the Arabic style, translated by John the Spaniard and Dominic Gundisalvi, was widely quoted by Christian authors, not least by Duns Scotus, who perhaps took Avencebrol to be a Christian, and openly adhered to his doctrine of matter. The other Jewish name of high repute among the Latins was Moses ben Maymun (Maimonides or Rabbi Moses), best known for his authorship of the *Guide of the Perplexed*. He was contemporary with Averroes (outliving him by only six years) and one of his warmest admirers. As may be seen in a treatise of doubtful origin, the *De Erroribus Philosophorum*, the Latins came to class his errors with those of Averroes, Algazel, and the rest of the Arabs[1].

The stages in the development of Aristotelianism at Paris are marked by some definite dates. Precisely when the new books were first read in

[1] Cf. Mandonnet, *Siger de Brabant*, Part II, pp. 21–24.

public we do not know, but in 1210 a provincial council formally inter-dicted public or private study of the *libri de naturali philosophia*, with commentaries thereon; and in 1215 the papal legate, Robert de Courçon, renewed the prohibition in the words, *non legantur libri Aristotelis de metaphysica et de naturali philosophia, nec summae de eisdem.* It is doubtful here whether the mention of metaphysics implies a difference between the first and the second decree. The term *metaphysica* would be unfamiliar before the diffusion of Aristotle's book, and the older usage of *physica* or *naturalis philosophia* would cover many questions afterwards called meta-physical. In 1231, after the dispersion of the university, Gregory IX repeated the prohibition, but at the same time entrusted William of Auxerre and two colleagues with the task of expurgating Aristotle for use in the schools. Nothing came of this impossible project, and the prohibition remained formally valid, to be renewed once more by Urban IV in 1263. Meanwhile practice moved more rapidly than law. Outside Paris, to judge from the example of Toulouse in 1229, free study of Aristotle had always been possible. At Paris itself some regulations of 1252 mention only the *De Anima* in addition to the Logic, but in March 1255 the Faculty of Arts laid down a course of study which boldly included the *Physics*, the *Metaphysics*, and practically all the translated works. This defiance of papal authority provoked no reply until 1263. Even then we may safely presume that the action of Urban IV was only pro-visional; for now he was reviving on a grander scale the attempt of Gregory IX to produce a critical version of Aristotle, invoking to his aid the greatest of Christian commentators, St Thomas Aquinas, who just at this time was encouraging William of Moerbeke to produce his new translations.

The history of Aristotelianism in the thirteenth century is, in one of its aspects, the history of a political struggle in the University of Paris, too intricate for analysis in this chapter. As a convenient simplification of the facts, we may concentrate our attention upon the Order of Preachers, a society which in its earlier phases was by no means inclined to champion the cause of any Pagan philosopher. *In libris gentilium et philosophorum non studeant fratres.* So says an ordinance of 1228, with the object of confining the studies of the brethren to theology. The author of the revolution which brought the Dominicans into the front rank of Aristo-telians was the illustrious Albert of Cologne (*ob.* 1280), who taught at Paris from 1245 to 1248, and was occupied for some forty years altogether in the production of his monumental works. Except during his lifetime, the fame of this great man has always been a little overshadowed by that of his pupil Aquinas (*ob.* 1274), whose greater command of expository method makes him easier of access. Rash indeed would it be to say that Albert was the more remarkable of the two, but in the direction of experimental science he went farther, and to him, as the pioneer, fell the enterprise of making all parts of Aristotle intelligible to the Latins.

Impatient of the "brute animals" who attacked the use of philosophy and blasphemed everything of which they were ignorant, he saw that the study of Aristotle could not be prohibited, and already, perhaps, while teaching at Paris, discerned the seeds of Averroism which he was afterwards (in 1256) invited by Alexander IV to refute.

Averroism it was again, not merely as a local phenomenon, but as the climax of the whole Arabian interpretation of Aristotle, that moved Aquinas to continue his master's work in his own deep and searching exposition of the principal books. The task before him was one of unparalleled complexity, such as only a man of boundless courage, unfailing candour, and exceptional powers of mind could have faced. Now for the first time in the history of the Middle Ages, or indeed in the history of the world, was it imperative to delimit the provinces of philosophy and theology, and at the same time to vindicate the unity of truth. On the one hand, St Thomas was perfectly convinced that no truth discoverable by reason could be inconsistent with the Christian revelation; on the other hand, he was equally assured that the truths of revelation were accessible only to a mode of experience not commonly described as reason, and inseparable from the history and authority of the Church. What he had primarily to combat was not atheism, nor even any avowed heresy in dogma, but the impudent sophism, borrowed by certain Christians from the Muslims, that there can or must be two kinds of truth; so that, when the voice of reason or philosophy conflicts with the voice of authority and faith, we may legitimately hearken to both. Or if few quite professed that absurdity, the alternative was to insinuate that reason would often oblige us to believe one thing, were not its opposite enjoined on us by faith.

Aquinas took a wide view of his problem. He did not restrict himself to the Latin Averroists, against whom he wrote the *De Unitate Intellectus* in 1270, but went back to the higher sources of the mischief. By one of the most amazing accidents in history it had fallen to Aristotle, some fifteen centuries after his death, to stand as the representative of human reason. By another accident it was given to the Arabs to work out a systematic interpretation, and then to hand it over to the Latins. Now Aquinas, no less than Albert, was deeply interested in Aristotle, and not in the least afraid of his opinions. He might even, in the peculiar circumstances of the time, have agreed with the Averroists that the general liberty of speculation was summed up in the free study of Aristotle. It is ludicrous, however, to suppose that he took Aristotle to be infallible. Except in the last decadence of scholasticism, the only people who ever did that were the Averroists and the Muslims. For the most part St Thomas was not occupied in proving the rightness or wrongness of Aristotle, but in criticising the Arabian interpretation of him, relatively to such questions as the eternity of the world, the individuality of the immortal intellect, and the alleged subjection of the human will to planetary influences. Like a good Aristotelian, he perceived that in arguing *contra Gentiles* he must conduct the discussion on a basis accepted by his opponents. There could be no question of "authority"; for, as he says, *mahumetistae et pagani non conveniunt nobiscum in auctoritate alicuius Scripturae...unde necesse est ad naturalem rationem recurrere, cui omnes assentire coguntur*[1]. Now by "natural reason" the Muslims understood primarily, if not solely, the philosophy of Aristotle; and from that philosophy they had extracted inferences damaging to the Christian position; not indeed to the doctrines of the Trinity and the Incarnation—for on these points Aristotle could have nothing to say—but to the belief in moral responsibility and the immortality of the soul. To St Thomas, therefore, the alternatives were to reject the Muslim interpretation, or to prove that Aristotle himself was wrong. He does not choose either course to the total exclusion of the other, but to a large extent he argues that Averroes and Avicenna had misrepresented the master of their allegiance.

Whether Aquinas proves his case to the satisfaction of modern critics may be disputable, but he certainly marshals an array of arguments that none of his contemporaries was likely to defeat. Along with his elucidation of Aristotle he examines the still wider problem of the whole relation of reason to faith; upholding in his own sense a *duplex veritatis modus*, which yet avoids the duplicity of believing contradictory propositions on different grounds, and is, in effect, a plea for the unity of truth. If, once more, we may doubt whether the conditions of the age permitted him to arrive at a final appreciation of all the difficulties, none can reasonably doubt the candour of his intention, the subtlety of his intuitions, or the astonishing range and lucidity of his mind. Similar merits and similar inevitable deficiencies are revealed in his general understanding of Aristotle. He was no biologist, no physicist, no astronomer. He could not discriminate between paths of science where Aristotle had gone hopelessly astray, and other paths where he had advanced almost to the verge of modern achievement. Like the commentators of all ages, not excluding our own, he was strongest within the bounds of his own experience, and weakest where his sympathy failed. To the last he was hampered by ignorance of history. Often as he contested Neo-Platonist interpretations, he was far from disengaging Aristotle from later accretions. He knew, for example (with the help of William of Moerbeke), that the *Liber de Causis*, widely received as Aristotelian, was in fact an excerpt from Proclus; and yet he could make the almost staggering assertion that "Dionysius," in contrast to Augustine and others, *fere ubique sequitur Aristotelem*[2]. This, it is true, he says in an early work, and perhaps in later life he might have hesitated to repeat it. But neither by Aquinas, nor by anyone else in that century, was Aristotle fully divested of the Neo-Platonist garments in which the

---

[1] *Summa contra Gentiles*, i, 2.
[2] Cf. Mandonnet, *Siger de Brabant*, Part i, p. 43, note 2

course of history had clothed him. Yet after all these criticisms, to which others might be added, it remains incontestable that every modern student of Aristotle has much to learn from the exposition of Aquinas.

Averroism proper, as distinct from the general influence of the Arabs, is not heard of before the second half of the century. Moreover, when Albert wrote his *De Unitate Intellectus contra Averroem* in 1256, he appears to be attacking a tendency rather than actual teachers at Paris. Siger of Brabant is first mentioned in 1266, and the first official condemnation of Averroism occurs in 1270. Before that date, either in the autumn of 1268 or in the spring of 1269, Aquinas returned from Italy to Paris, where he remained until 1272. The resumption of a professorial chair by a Dominican (for Aquinas had taught at Paris for some years before 1260) was so unusual that we must attribute it to the manifold difficulties in which the Order was involved. Among these were the constant hostility of the seculars to the regulars, differences with the Franciscans and the "Augustinian" theologians, and finally the emergence of Averroism, a movement complicated by the attempt to involve the general credit of Peripateticism with the errors of Siger of Brabant. St Thomas, accordingly, had both to publish his *De Unitate Intellectus* as an answer to Siger's *De Anima Intellectiva*, and to protect the freedom of Aristotelian study against critics who still, perhaps, might appeal to Urban's decree of 1263. Evidence to the same effect is furnished by a work discovered and printed by Mandonnet, the *De Quindecim Problematibus* of Albertus Magnus, composed in answer to a letter of enquiry by Giles of Lessines. Of these fifteen problems the first thirteen are identical with the propositions condemned at Paris (10 December 1270), while the last two suggest an attempt to involve Aquinas in the downfall of the Averroists.

From a survey of the thirteen condemned propositions we gather that four main questions were prominent, the unity of the intelligence in all men, the eternity of the world, the freedom of the will, the knowledge and providence of God. A more drastic reduction might leave only the first of the four as of primary importance in 1270; for it seems that this had spread beyond philosophical circles, in its practical bearing on moral responsibility and personal salvation. While it is impossible here to discuss so intricate a problem, or to compare the Averroist and Dominican readings of the *De Anima*, it is necessary to remark that Averroes had advanced beyond the position of Avicenna and his predecessors. The others had removed from human conditions only the *intellectus agens*, which might even be identified with God; but Averroes converted also the *intellectus possibilis* into a "separate substance," and declared it to be *unus in omnibus hominibus*[1]. Opposed as he was to both these interpretations of Aristotle, St Thomas was aware that even Catholic doctors had identified the *intellectus agens* with God, in which case it would rightly

---

[1] Aquinas, *Summa contra Gentiles*, II, 59 and 73.

be excluded from human personality. Averroes, however, was clearly beyond the pale; for, since nothing in God can be merely potential, to affirm the unity of the *intellectus possibilis* is to deny the individuality of man.

Averroism was defeated, and Siger of Brabant, condemned again by the Inquisition of France in October 1277, passed his last years in Italy, as the prisoner of the Roman curia. There he perished, as the story goes, by the hand of a half-insane assassin, and thereafter was honourably translated to Dante's *Paradiso*. The subsequent fortunes of Averroism we cannot pursue. More important for the moment was the renewed attack on Aristotelianism in general, which gained a passing triumph in 1277. The mighty efforts of Albert and Thomas, with the favour of one or two Popes, had checked but not destroyed the force of the opposition. The currents of philosophical thought, not to say political faction, were numerous. The secular clergy, always jealous of the friars, did not shine in the use of intellectual weapons. If Roger Bacon, writing in 1271, can be trusted, they had failed to produce a single theological or philosophical treatise for the space of forty years. They merely took doctrinal questions as a convenient pretext for attack. Against that kind of onslaught the two Orders were united, but in other respects they tended to drift apart. Bonaventura and Aquinas were so happily united by personal friendship that they might have stood as models to an earlier Fra Angelico for the meeting of Francis and Dominic. Yet it is Bonaventura who best expresses the difference of temper between the two societies, when he says that the Preachers *principaliter intendunt speculationi, et postea unctioni*, the Friars Minor *principaliter unctioni, et postea speculationi*[1]. Even St Thomas, who was far from devoid of sympathy with mysticism, would hardly have written the *Itinerarium mentis in Deum*.

Something more, or less, than "unction" is required, however, to account for the attitude of John Pecham, the Franciscan Archbishop of Canterbury, who, besides attempting to implicate Aquinas with the heresies of Siger, went to the length of protesting that nothing was common to the two Orders but the bare foundations of the faith. So wide a division could only be affirmed in so far as the Franciscans identified themselves with the party sometimes called Augustinian. On the whole, and with many reservations, it is true that the Franciscan doctors looked askance at the Aristotelian movement. Roger Bacon, no doubt, falls outside all generalisations. Much as he disliked the ascendency of Albert, he was too much of an individualist to act merely as the partisan of one society against another. But a general review of the most distinguished Franciscan writers, from Alexander of Hales (who was not, it seems, the author of the *Summa* which bears his name) to Duns Scotus, would justify the opinion that by their influence alone Aristotle would never have secured the supremacy among philosophers. That supremacy was claimed

[1] Mandonnet, *op. cit.* Part i, p. 98.

for him neither by the earlier Middle Ages, nor yet by the thirteenth century as a whole, but only by the great Dominican masters, assisted undoubtedly by the Averroists whom, on some vital points, they felt bound to oppose. The delayed but eventual triumph of Thomism (never perfectly accomplished, one might add, until the revival in the nineteenth century) has too often cast back a false light on the age of St Thomas himself. Opposition, not merely to him but to Aristotle, was then frequent and bitter. A casual but interesting example is found in the *Summa*, of unknown authorship, which Baur has printed in the same volume with the works of Grosseteste. The writer, a man of strong intelligence and far from ignorant of Aristotle, has some exceedingly sharp things to say about him. In particular, he dismisses as ineffective the whole Aristotelian criticism of the Platonic "ideas," and hints pretty strongly that Aristotle was often as much moved by prejudice as by rational judgment.

In England, and at Oxford, where this *Summa* may probably have been composed, the Franciscans were especially strong. Encouraged by Grosseteste (not himself a member of the Order) and by the example of his writings, they gave more attention to mathematics and optics than to the wider problems of philosophy that chiefly exercised the Dominicans of Paris. But there must also have been something in the English air inimical to Thomism. For not only the Franciscan Archbishop, John Peckham, but his Dominican predecessor, Robert Kilwardby (author of an interesting work on the Division of Philosophy), persuaded Oxford to condemn a number of propositions maintained by St Thomas. His action was a sequel to the larger affair at Paris in March 1277, when the various forces opposed to the Dominicans united under Étienne Tempier, the Chancellor of the University, to secure the condemnation of no less than 219 propositions, some of them imputable only to Siger and the Averroists, others common to Aquinas and all the Peripatetics.

What was the meaning of this undiscriminating violence? Behind the political struggle there was doubtless some genuine apprehension of a fatal schism between philosophy and the authority of the Church. The system of Catholicism, as it was slowly shaped and consolidated in the Middle Ages, pointed to the indivisible union of all Christians in a single society, ideally as wide as the world. To the realisation of such an ideal the existence of Jews, Muslims, and Pagans was the most patent obstacle, but also the most superficial. More serious was the breach between the Greeks and the Latins, for that touched the internal principles upon which the Christian society was founded. More vital even than doctrinal unity was the maintenance of the claim by which alone the Church had succeeded in absorbing into herself the finer essence of Graeco-Roman civilisation. The substance of that claim was the possession of first principles comprehensive enough to supersede Greek philosophy, and to serve as the ultimate source of morality and law. Once allow the possibility of explaining the world without reference to the propositions of the

Creed, or of governing mankind without reference to the *lex divina*, and the whole structure of the Church must be threatened with collapse. The liberty of the sciences, therefore, and the liberty of princes were on the same plane; they were liberties conceded by the Church—liberties to arrive at any conclusions and to take any administrative measures not incompatible with the Christian presuppositions.

Such being the remorseless logic of the situation, the search for means of avoiding it persistently continued. After many makeshifts and evasions of the issue, it became clear at last to the acuter minds of the thirteenth century that only one solution was possible. If it could be shewn that the work of reason in the whole field of science could be accomplished without possible collision with the faith; if, in other words, there was a *duplex veritatis modus* consistent with intellectual honesty, then intolerable tyranny and disastrous revolution could alike be avoided. To make good this solution was the policy of Aquinas. Sincerely convinced that human reason could neither prove nor disprove the doctrines peculiar to Christianity, he proceeded to infer that all arguments destructive of the faith were spurious products of reason, which genuine philosophy could refute without appeal to authority. At the same time he allotted a wide province to reason, and believed it possible to demonstrate the principles of Theism and of theistic morality by the arguments relative to God, freedom, and immortality which Kant afterwards declared to be invalid. In the age of Aquinas there was neither a Kant nor even a magnified Gaunilo, but there were conservatives who mistrusted these new lines of division, and who failed to see that a position tenable in the days of Augustine, or even of Anselm, might be far from impregnable to the onslaught of Averroes. With the conservatives were allied the alarmists, who held that Aquinas himself was betraying the citadel by inviting reason to occupy the outworks. In their eyes a Peripatetic was no better than an Averroist; both alike deserved the penalty of traitors within the camp. The cleavage of parties and the hardening of the distinction between theology and philosophy must have been assisted by the organising of Faculties within the University. The control of philosophy belonged to the Faculty of Arts; the theologians, therefore, were clearly not philosophers. Hence, when Albert the Great, as a friar, was attacked by the students of theology, it was the artists who rushed in crowds to his support. So anomalous a position could not long be maintained. Sooner or later the lines of intellectual division would follow pretty closely the division of Faculties, with results that, without returning to the Middle Ages, we can readily imagine.

Among those swept away, a little ironically, with the 219 propositions was the unfortunate Roger Bacon. If he was to be engulfed in the company of so many Peripatetics, it seems a pity that, instead of railing at Albert, he did not collaborate with him for the advancement of chemistry and physics. We must beware, however, of misinterpreting either the position

of Bacon or the causes of his downfall. It would be unhistorical to suppose
that advocacy of mathematics, or prophecies of flying-machines and other
marvels, would have brought him to captivity. Whatever the value of his
contributions to science (about which the specialists are a little frigid),
no school of thought then suspected that geometry or optics or the propagation of force by "multiplication of species" were going to undermine
the Church. Bacon, like Abelard, may have damaged himself by making
enemies, and by his monotonous dispraise of authority; but where he
seems definitely to have stumbled was in the field of astrology. The
state of astronomy at the time permitted it to be a quasi-scientific
question whether the fortunes and even the characters of men might not
be shaped by celestial impressions. Bacon himself agreed with Aquinas
and other educated men in denying that the freedom of the will could
thus be affected, and in avoiding the more childish superstitions. The
attack on him was probably no more intelligent than the refusal to
discriminate between Aquinas and the Averroists. In the hour of
triumphant faction a few rash or ambiguous expressions would be
evidence enough. Deplorable as the result was, we have no more right
to accuse the whole age of persecuting science than we have to argue from
Bacon's own effort to prove the utility of mathematics to theology that
he saw no intrinsic value in theoretical reasoning. In any case, it is an
anachronism either to look for a new philosophy of the world in the
scientific tastes of Bacon, or to interpret his overthrow as mere hostility
to the study of natural phenomena. A still greater absurdity would be
to suppose that Bacon's praise of experience and experiment brought
upon him the wrath of Aristotelians.

Rightly to estimate Bacon's worth as a philosopher is, however, a very
difficult task. The combative spirit which enraged his contemporaries
has endeared him, perhaps unduly, to modern readers with little
sympathy for the temper of the Middle Ages. Similarly, his references to
actual or possible devices of mechanics and chemistry have won for him
more credit as an inventor than he would have claimed for himself. Our
concern, however, is rather with his general estimate of knowledge, and
with his broader relations to the intellectual attitude of his times. And
here we find that, in some respects, his mind was provincial, or even reactionary, while in others he certainly had a vision of the future *sicut in
aenigmate, non facie ad faciem.* His provincialism appears in his failure
to appreciate the higher contemporary thought, or to perceive the direction
in which minds really more critical than his own were moving. Much of
his criticism, as for example in the *De Viciis contractis in studio Theologiae*,
is singularly barren, if we suppose it to refer to such men as Albert the
Great or Thomas Aquinas. They in their turn might well have objected
that Bacon's whole conception of philosophy was obsolete. They would not
formally have disputed his statement that the chief and final intention
of philosophers was *circa divinam et angelorum cognitionem...cum con-*

temptu bonorum istius vitae temporalis, ut pervenirent ad statum futurae beatitudinis, but they might fairly have replied that amiable commonplaces were no substitute for a real delineation of the provinces of theology and human reason. Bacon is, in fact, reactionary in his extravagant subordination of philosophy to theology. He reverts to a position barely tenable in the thirteenth century unless supported by fresh arguments, and he appears to be imperfectly acquainted with the greatest controversy of his age.

Again, his praise of "mathematics" as an aid to civil and religious government is so mixed up with the puerilities of astrology and alchemy that his pretence of superiority to his times in this respect is far from convincing. On the other hand, there are many glimpses of genuine insight in his enthusiasm for linguistic studies, in his anticipation of the manifold uses of geography, and in his constant emphasis on the importance of experimental method. Very often he speaks of *scientia experimentalis* as a separate science rather than as a general method employed by natural philosophy; and in the *Opus Tertium* he makes the significant statement: *naturalis enim philosophus narrat et arguit, sed non experitur.* He maintains, nevertheless, that experiment or experience is required to verify all the sciences; nor can we reasonably complain if he is not yet in a position to discriminate between the more and the less experimental departments of knowledge. What we clearly discern in Bacon, when we get behind his peevishness, his superstitions, and his arrogance, is a profound discontent with the existing state of knowledge, a conviction that no further advance is possible except by a kind of intellectual return to Nature. In this he was indubitably right, and in this, rather than in actual achievement, lies his title to fame. At all times, too, he was hampered by his conflict with authority. Many of his books have the character of an apologia. He is desperately anxious to refute the slanders of his enemies, and to persuade Pope Clement IV that his philosophy is orthodox and profitable. Had he worked in a calmer atmosphere, and in harmony with the chiefs of his Order, it is probable that he would have left us a higher impression of his powers.

The imprisonment of Bacon was a political incident, in the same sense that the trials of Gottschalk, Abelard, and Gilbert de la Porrée, or the prohibitions of Aristotle, Averroism, and Peripateticism were political incidents. For the Church was, in theory and in fact, a political society based on first principles, and pledged therefore to test every movement of thought by its probable effect on the faith and conduct of Christians. Liberty of opinion we now take to be the foundation of all other liberties; interference with it we stamp as an act of tyranny or, at best, as a dangerous experiment. But that is because we are governed by opinion and desire no other master. The medieval Church, on the other hand, claimed to be governed by knowledge, and that makes all the difference in the world. That, too, is why the significance of the proposed division between theology and philosophy was graver than even an Aquinas could suspect. The scope of this chapter has excluded political thought in the more restricted sense, but facts like the growth of Canon Law, the revival of Roman juris-prudence, the rise of nations and communes, the struggle of Empire and Papacy, and the appearance of such a book as Marsilius of Padua's *De-fensor Pacis* are intimately connected with medieval philosophy. In the last chapter of his *Monarchia* Dante supports his plea for an independent Empire by the analogous independence of philosophy. To the Pope belong revealed truths and the theological virtues; to the Emperor moral virtue and the inventions of reason. That Dante grasped the whole possibilities of his argument is improbable; for no such division could be effective before the rise of the modern State, nor even then until the State had renounced the care of theology, only to find that philosophy had likewise vanished from its counsels. The heroic attempt of Aquinas to define a sphere for philosophy without detriment to the sovereign rights of theology was simply one expression of the whole medieval struggle so to adjust the temporal power to the spiritual as to create a dominion of political freedom within the higher sovereignty of the Church. The project, we may hold, was impossible. It is certain, at least, that it failed.

Yet this failure was the last and greatest achievement of medieval philosophy. Later developments, such as the rivalry of Thomists and Scotists, with all their wrangles about matter and form, universals and individuals, have their interest for students, but small importance for the historical movement of the world. When we gaze on the solid line of folios attributed to Duns Scotus (*ob.* 1308) it seems almost incredible that his life can have lasted—according to a common estimate—no more than thirty-four years. Even if the correct figure be a little larger, his youth is perhaps a fact to be remembered in estimating the quality of his work. For in Duns Scotus we cannot but recognise something of that joy in destruction attributed by Plato to young men attacked by the first fever of dialectic. It was his distinguished fate to found a school strong enough for a time to divide the world with the Thomists. The Franciscans adopted him as their champion and magnified his prestige. Modern readers, however, who stand apart from medieval factions, will be slow to recognise in Duns Scotus a serious intellectual rival to Thomas Aquinas. In method, in perspicuity, in dignity and breadth of mind he is plainly inferior. To charge him with insincerity would be uncharitable, but he strikes us as a man determined at all hazards to take up original positions, and therefore to seek with all his notorious "subtlety" for points of dis-tinction between his own and other views. The result in most cases is that his divergence from Aquinas and other doctors turns out to be smaller than his statements would suggest.

On the fundamental question of the relation of philosophy to theology he proposes a much sharper division than was approved by St Thomas. When any truth is enunciated as an article of faith, it is inexpedient, he says, to attempt a demonstration of it. The effect of your demonstration on the faithful will be to deprive them of the merit of faith, while to the infidel you will provide an opportunity of declaring that Christians are driven by lack of faith to fall back on argument. It would thus be improper to prove by reason that God exists, that God is one, or that the soul is immortal. Duns Scotus fails, however, to work out the consequences of his own hypothesis. He is far from meaning that faith is irrational, but equally far from grasping the importance of philosophical monotheism as a preparation for Christian doctrine, or from perceiving the danger of sheer obscurantism involved in his own contention. Nor does he deal with Aquinas' point that, since few men have leisure, or inclination, or ability to be philosophers, the bulk of mankind will be obliged to receive in the form of faith propositions which a few may be able to establish by reasoning. On the other hand, Duns Scotus goes quite as far as Aquinas in claiming for theology an interest in every branch of knowledge, not excluding geometry, and also in exalting the power of the intellect for the general purpose of arriving at truth. Theology, he maintains, is practical rather than speculative, but the practical consequences of Christian dogmas, as he explains them, would never have been questioned by Aquinas. In a word, Duns Scotus proposes a new division of provinces but does not adequately defend it. He tends to exalt will above intellect, but with the difficulties of their inter-relation he does not grapple half so closely as Aquinas.

Perhaps the most conspicuous point of difference between Duns Scotus and his contemporaries was his doctrine of matter. Entirely free from materialism in any sense that would make matter independent of the Creator, he insists, nevertheless, that all created beings, the spiritual no less than the corporeal, have matter as well as form in their composition. To support this doctrine he makes an important distinction between metaphysical and physical matter. He supposed that Pythagoras and some of the early Greek philosophers had thought of matter metaphysically, but he assigned to physics and natural philosophy, not the *materia prima*, but only the *secundo prima*, which is the substratum of generation and corruption. In its metaphysical sense matter need not be localised, and he excused himself from answering the question *ubi est?* Thus even the angelic nature contains matter in its being, and since Aquinas had allowed to the angels a kind of *potentia*, Duns Scotus is obliged to deny that the existence of matter is merely potential. How it can exist *actu*, without being *actus alicuius*, he finds it difficult to explain, but such is his doctrine. And further, since the whole universe of creatures has been developed out of this metaphysical substratum by progressive differentiation, the Thomist doctrine of matter as the *causa individuationis* must be rejected. Incidentally the angels thus recover the privilege of being individuals without constituting a species apiece. What individuality is, and how it arises, Duns Scotus exhausts his ingenuity to explain. He was doubtless right in suspecting that the puzzle could not be solved through the simple alternatives of matter and form. He perceived also that an individual could not be defined by negatives, and that there must be some positive quality involved in numerical distinction. If in the end his own doctrine only led to the thesis that *hoc est hoc* on account of *haecceitas*, we must still hesitate before we throw stones at him. For in the monstrous jargon of some modern philosophies a word like "thisness" has an air of almost classical refinement.

Impossible as it is to do justice in a page or two to the comprehensive knowledge of Duns Scotus or to his intellectual acumen, it is not unjust to deny that he is author of any momentous reform in philosophy. Rather does he testify, like Roger Bacon, though in very different style, to the approaching exhaustion of medieval thought. The air of finality that hangs over the weighty pages of Aquinas has a prophetic significance. For the work of Aquinas, consummate in its kind, had exhausted the materials then existing for the edifice of philosophy, though not the ingenious art of arranging them in new patterns. The great age of dialectic had vanished with the rebirth of Aristotle; the age of Aristotelianism was to perish in still greater revolutions. Alike in politics and in science more portentous questions were soon to be uttered: whether a society founded on an immutable gospel could find room for the modern State, and whether a *scientia experimentalis* beyond the dreams of Roger Bacon could be reconciled with an infallible Church.

LIST OF ABBREVIATIONS OF TITLES
OF PERIODICALS, SOCIETIES, ETC.

(1) The following abbreviations are used for titles of periodicals :

AB.	Analecta Bollandiana. Paris and Brussels. 1882 ff.
AHR.	American Historical Review. New York and London.
AKKR.	Archiv für katholisches Kirchenrecht. Innsbruck. 1857–61. Mayence. 1862 ff.
Arch. Ven. (and N. Arch. Ven.; Arch. Ven.-Tri.).	Archivio veneto. Venice. 40 vols. 1871–90; *continued as* Nuovo archivio veneto. 1st series. 20 vols. 1891–1900. New series. 42 vols. 1901–21. And Archivio veneto-tridentino. 10 vols. 1922–26. And Archivio veneto, 5th series. 1927 ff., in progress.
ASAK.	Anzeiger für schweizerische Alterthumskunde. Zurich.
ASI	Archivio storico italiano. Florence. Ser. I. 20 vols. and App. 9 vols. 1842–53. Index. 1857. Ser. nuova. 18 vols. 1855–63. Ser. III. 26 vols. 1865–77. Indexes to II and III. 1874. Supplt. 1877. Ser. IV. 20 vols. 1878–87. Index. 1891. Ser. v. 50 vols. 1888–1912. Index. 1900. Ser. VI. Anni 71–81. 20 vols. 1913–23. (Index up to 1917 in Catalogue of The London Library. Vol. I. 1913, and Supplt. 1920.) Ser. VII. Anni 82 etc. 1924 ff., in progress.
ASL.	Archivio storico lombardo. Milan.
ASPN.	Archivio storico per le province napoletane. Naples. 1876 ff.
ASRSP.	Archivio della Società romana di storia patria. Rome. 1878 ff.
BEC.	Bibliothèque de l'École des Chartes. Paris. 1839 ff.
BISI.	Bullettino dell' Istituto storico italiano. Rome. 1886 ff.
BRAH.	Boletin de la R. Academia de la historia. Madrid.
BZ.	Byzantinische Zeitschrift. Leipsic. 1892 ff.
CQR.	Church Quarterly Review. London. 1875 ff.
DZG.	Deutsche Zeitschrift für Geschichtswissenschaft. Freiburg-im-Breisgau.
DZKR.	Deutsche Zeitschrift für Kirchenrecht. Freiburg-im-Breisgau. 1891 ff.
EHR.	English Historical Review. London. 1886 ff.
FDG.	Forschungen zur deutschen Geschichte. Göttingen.
HJ.	Historisches Jahrbuch. Munich.
HVJS.	Historische Vierteljahrsschrift. Leipsic.
HZ.	Historische Zeitschrift (von Sybel). Munich and Berlin.
JA.	Journal Asiatique. Paris.
JB.	Jahresberichte der Geschichtswissenschaft im Auftrage der historischen Gesellschaft zu Berlin. Berlin. 1878 ff.
JRAS.	Journal of the Royal Asiatic Society of Great Britain. London.
JTS.	Journal of Theological Studies. London.
MA	Le moyen âge. Paris.
MIOGF.	Mittheilungen des Instituts für österreichische Geschichtsforschung. Innsbruck.
Neu. Arch.	Neues Archiv der Gesellschaft für ältere deutsche Geschichtskunde. Hanover and Leipsic.
NRDF (and RDF).	Nouvelle Revue hist. de droit français et étranger. Paris. 1877–1921; *continued as* Revue hist. de droit français et étranger. Paris. 1922 ff.
QFIA.	Quellen und Forschungen aus italienischen Archiven und Bibliotheken. Rome.
RA.	Revue archéologique. Paris.
RBén.	Revue bénédictine. Maredsous.
RCHL.	Revue critique d'histoire et de littérature. Paris.
RDF.	*See above*, NRDF.
RH.	Revue historique. Paris.
RHD.	Revue d'histoire diplomatique. Paris.

RHE.	Revue d'histoire ecclésiastique. Louvain.
Rhein. Mus.	Rheinisches Museum für Philologie. Frankfort-on-Main.
RN.	Revue de numismatique. Paris.
RQH.	Revue des questions historiques. Paris.
RSH.	Revue de synthèse historique. Paris.
RSI.	Rivista storica italiana. Turin. *See Gen. Bibl.* I.
SKAW.	Sitzungsberichte der Kaiserlichen Akademie der Wissenschaften. Vienna. [Philos.-hist. Classe.]
SPAW.	Sitzungsberichte der kön. preussischen Akademie der Wissenschaften. Berlin.
TRHS.	Transactions of the Royal Historical Society. London.
ZCK.	Zeitschrift für christliche Kunst. Düsseldorf.
ZDMG.	Zeitschrift der deutschen morgenländischen Gesellschaft. Leipsic.
ZKG.	Zeitschrift für Kirchengeschichte. Gotha.
ZKT.	Zeitschrift für katholische Theologie. Gotha.
ZR.	Zeitschrift für Rechtsgeschichte. Weimar. 1861–78. *Continued as*
ZSR.	Zeitschrift der Savigny-Stiftung für Rechtswissenschaft. Weimar. 1880 ff. [Each vol. contains a Romanistische, a Germanistische, and, after 1911, a Kanonistische Abteilung.]
ZWT.	Zeitschrift für wissenschaftliche Theologie. Frankfort-on-Main.

(2) Other abbreviations used are:

AcadIBL.	Académie des Inscriptions et Belles-Lettres.
AcadIP.	Académie Impériale de Pétersbourg.
AllgDB.	Allgemeine deutsche Biographie. *See Gen. Bibl.* I.
ASBen.	*See* Mabillon and Achery *in Gen. Bibl.* IV.
ASBoll.	Acta Sanctorum Bollandiana. *See Gen. Bibl.* IV.
BGén.	Nouvelle Biographie générale. *See Gen. Bibl.* IV.
BHE.	Bibliothèque de l'École des hautes études. *See Gen. Bibl.* V.
Bouquet.	*See* Rerum Gallicarum...scriptores *in Gen. Bibl.* IV.
BUniv.	Biographie universelle. *See Gen. Bibl.* I.
Class. hist.	Classiques de l'histoire de France au moyen âge. *See Gen. Bibl.* IV.
Coll. doc.	Collection de documents inédits sur l'histoire de France. *See Gen. Bibl.* IV.
Coll.textes.	Collection de textes pour servir à l'étude et à l'enseignement de l'histoire *See Gen. Bibl.* IV.
CSCO.	Corpus scriptorum christianorum orientalium. *See Gen. Bibl.* IV.
CSEL.	Corpus scriptorum ecclesiasticorum latinorum. *See Gen. Bibl.* IV.
CSHB.	Corpus scriptorum historiae Byzantinae. *See Gen. Bibl.* IV.
DNB.	Dictionary of National Biography. *See Gen. Bibl.* I.
EcfrAR.	Écoles françaises d'Athènes et de Rome. Paris.
EETS.	Early English Text Society. *See Gen. Bibl.* IV.
EncBr.	Encyclopaedia Britannica. *See Gen. Bibl.* I.
Fonti.	Fonti per la storia d'Italia. *See Gen. Bibl.* IV.
KAW.	Kaiserliche Akademie der Wissenschaften. Vienna.
Mansi.	*See Gen. Bibl.* IV.
MGH.	Monumenta Germaniae Historica. *See Gen. Bibl.* IV.
MHP.	Monumenta historiae patriae. Turin. *See Gen. Bibl.* IV.
MPG.	Migne's Patrologiae cursus completus. Ser. graeco-latina. [Greek texts with Latin translations in parallel columns.] *See Gen. Bibl.* IV.
MPL.	Migne's Patrologiae cursus completus. Ser. latina. *See Gen. Bibl.* IV.
PAW.	Königliche preussische Akademie d. Wissenschaften. Berlin.
RAH.	Real Academia de la Historia. Madrid.
RC.	Record Commissioners. *See Gen. Bibl.* IV.
Rec. hist. Cr.	Recueil des historiens des Croisades. *See Gen. Bibl.* IV.
Rolls.	Rerum Britannicarum medii aevi scriptores. *See Gen. Bibl.* IV.
RR.II.SS.	*See* Muratori *in Gen. Bibl.* IV.
SGUS.	Scriptores rerum Germanicarum in usum scholarum. *See* Monumenta Germaniae Historica *in Gen. Bibl.* IV.
SHF.	Société de l'histoire de France. *See Gen. Bibl.* IV.
SRD.	Scriptores rerum Danicarum medii aevi. *See Gen. Bibl.* IV.

Abh.	Abhandlungen.	mém.	mémoire.
antiq.	antiquarian, antiquaire.	n.s.	new series.
app.	appendix.	progr.	programme.
coll.	collection.	publ.	published, publié.
diss.	dissertation.	R. ⎱	real, reale.
enl.	enlarged.	r. ⎰	
hist.	history, histoire, historical, historique, historisch.	repr.	reprinted.
		rev.	revised.
Jahrb.	Jahrbuch.	roy.	royal, royale.
	⎧ kaiserlich.	ser.	series.
k.	⎨ königlich.	soc.	society, société, società.
	⎩ koninklijk.	stor.	storico, storica.
mem.	memoir.	Viert.	Vierteljahrschrift.

834

GENERAL BIBLIOGRAPHY.

I. DICTIONARIES, BIBLIOGRAPHIES, AND GENERAL WORKS OF REFERENCE.

For modern historical works, co-operate or in series, see Section V.

Allgemeine deutsche Biographie. (Historische Commission bei d. kön. Akademie der Wissenschaften zu München.) Ed. Liliencron, R. von, and Wegele, F. X. Munich and Leipsic. 56 vols. 1875–1912. (AllgDB.)

Annuario bibliografico della storia d' Italia. 1902 ff.

Balzani, U. Le cronache italiane nel Medio Evo. 3rd edn. Milan. 1909.

Below, G. von, and Meinecke, F. *edd.* Handbuch der mittelalterlichen und neueren Geschichte. Munich. 1903 ff., in progress. *Cited sub nom. auct.* (Below-Meinecke.)

Bernheim, E. Lehrbuch der historischen Methode und der Geschichtsphilosophie. 5th and 6th enl. edn. Leipsic. 1908.

Biographie nationale de Belgique. Brussels. 1866 ff., in progress. (Acad. Roy. des sciences, des lettres, et des beaux arts.)

Biographie universelle, ancienne et moderne. (Michaud.) 45 vols. Paris. 1854–65. [Greatly improved edn. of earlier work, 1811–28, and supplt., 1832–62.] (BUniv.)

Bresslau, H. Handbuch der Urkundenlehre für Deutschland und Italien. Leipsic. 1889. 2nd edn. enl. 2 vols. 1912–31.

Cabrol, F. and Leclercq, H. Dictionnaire d'archéologie chrétienne et de liturgie. Vols. i–xiv. Paris. 1907 ff., in progress.

Calvi, E. Bibliografia generale di Roma medioevale e moderna. Pt. i. Medio Evo. Rome. 1906. Supplt. 1908.

Capasso, B. Le fonti della storia delle provincie napolitane dal 568 al 1500. Ed. Mastrojanni, E. O. Naples. 1902.

Ceillier, R. Histoire générale des auteurs sacrés et ecclésiastiques. 23 vols. Paris. 1729–63. New edn. 14 vols. in 15. Paris. 1858–69.

Chevalier, C. U. J. Répertoire des sources historiques du moyen âge. Bio-bibliographie. Paris. 1883–8. Rev. edn. 2 vols. 1905–7. Topo-bibliographie. Montbéliard. 1894–1903.

Dahlmann, F. C. and Waitz, G. Quellenkunde der deutschen Geschichte. 9th edn. Heering, H. Leipsic. 1931. Index. 1932.

Dictionary of National Biography. Ed. Stephen, L. and Lee, S. 63 vols. London. 1885–1900. 1st supplt. 3 vols. 1901. Errata vol. 1904. Re-issue. 22 vols. 1908–9. 2nd supplt. 3 vols. 1912. (DNB.)

Dictionnaire de biographie française. Ed. Balteau, J. and others. Paris. 1933 ff., in progress.

Du Cange, C. du Fresne. Glossarium ad scriptores mediae et infimae Latinitatis. Edns. of Henschel, 7 vols., Paris, 1840–50, and Favre, 10 vols., Niort, 1883–7.
—— Glossarium ad scriptores mediae et infimae Graecitatis. 2 vols. Lyons. 1688.

Encyclopaedia Britannica. 11th and 12th edn. 32 vols. Cambridge. London and New York. 1910–22. (EncBr.)

Encyclopaedia of Islam. A dictionary of the geography, ethnography, and biography of the Muhammadan peoples. Ed. Houtsma, M. T., Arnold, T. W., and Basset, R. Leiden and London. 1913 ff., in progress.

Ersch, J. S. and Gruber, J. G. Allgemeine Encyklopädie der Wissenschaften und Künste. Berlin. 1818–90. (Ersch-Gruber.) [Incomplete.]

Giry, A. Manuel de diplomatique. 2nd edn. Paris. 1925.

Giuseppi, M. S. Guide to the Manuscripts preserved in the Public Record Office. 2 vols. London. 1923–4.

Grässe, J. G. T. Lehrbuch einer allgemeinen Litterärgeschichte aller bekannten Völker der Welt von der ältesten bis auf die neueste Zeit. 4 vols. Leipsic. 1837–59.

Gröber, G. *ed.* Grundriss der romanischen Philologie. 2 vols. Strasbourg. 1888–1902. 2nd edn. Vol. I. 1904–6.

Gross, C. Sources and Literature of English History from the earliest times to about 1485. 2nd edn. enl. London. 1915.

Hardy, T. D. Descriptive catalogue of materials relating to the history of Great Britain and Ireland to the end of the reign of Henry VII. 3 vols. in 4. (Rolls.) 1862–71.

Hastings, J. and Selbie, J. A. Encyclopaedia of Religion and Ethics. 12 vols. Edinburgh and New York. 1908–21.

Herre, P., Hofmeister, A., and Stübe, R. Quellenkunde zur Weltgeschichte. Leipsic. 1910.

Herzog, J. J. and Hauck, A. Real-Encyklopädie für protestantische Theologie und Kirche. 3rd edn. 24 vols. Leipsic. 1896–1913.

Holtzendorff, F. von. Encyklopädie der Rechtswissenschaft. 5th edn. Leipsic. 1890. 6th edn. Kohler, J. 2 vols. Leipsic. 1904. Vol. I. 7th edn. 1913.

Jansen, M. and Schmitz-Kallenberg, L. Historiographie und Quellen der deutschen Geschichte bis 1500. 2nd edn. (Grundriss der Geschichtswissenschaft. Ed. Meister, A. I, 7.) Leipsic and Berlin. 1914.

Keene, H. G. An Oriental Biographical Dictionary, founded on materials collected by Beale, T. W. New and revised edn. London. 1894.

Krumbacher, K. Geschichte der byzantinischen Literatur. *See below*, V.

Lees, B. A. Bibliography of Mediaeval History. (400–1500.) (Historical Assoc. Leaflet 44.) London. 1917.

Lichtenberger, F. Encyclopédie des Sciences religieuses. 13 vols. Paris. 1877–82.

Maigne d'Arnis, W. H. Lexicon manuale ad scriptores mediae et infimae Latinitatis. (Publ. by Migne.) Paris. 1858. Repr. 1866 and 1890.

Manzoni, L. Bibliografia statutaria e storica italiana. 2 vols. in 3. Bologna. 1876–92. I. Bibl. d. statuti, ordini, e legge dei municipii. 2 pts. II. Bibl. storica municipale, etc. A–E. [No more publ.]

Meister, A. *ed.* Grundriss der Geschichtswissenschaft zur Einführung in das Studium der deutschen Geschichte des Mittelalters und der Neuzeit. Leipsic. 1906 ff. 2nd edn. 1912 ff., in progress.

Molinier, A. Les Sources de l'histoire de France des origines aux guerres d'Italie (1494). 6 vols. Paris. 1901–6.

Monod, G. Bibliographie de l'hist. de France depuis les origines jusqu'en 1789. Paris. 1888.

Nouvelle Biographie générale, depuis les temps les plus reculés jusqu'à nos jours, avec les renseignements bibliographiques. Sous la direction de J. C. F. Höfer. 46 vols. Paris. 1854–66. (BGén.)

Oudin, Casimir. Commentarius de scriptoribus ecclesiae antiquae illorumque scriptis tam impressis quam manuscriptis adhuc extantibus in celebrioribus Europe bibliothecis a Bellarmino etc. omissis ad annum MCCCCLX. 3 vols. Frankfort-on-M. and Leipsic. 1722.

Paetow, L. J. Guide to the study of Medieval History. Revd. edn. New York and London. 1931.

Paul, H. *ed.* Grundriss der germanischen Philologie. 2nd edn. 3 vols. Strasbourg. 1896 ff.

Pauly, A. F. von. Real-Encyclopädie der classischen Alterthumswissenschaft. Vienna. 1837–52. New edn. Wissowa, G. Stuttgart. 1894 ff., in progr es (Pauly-Wissowa.)

Pirenne, H. Bibliographie de l'hist. de Belgique. Brussels and Ghent. 1893. 2nd edn. 1902.

Potthast, A. Bibliotheca historica medii aevi. Wegweiser durch die Geschichtswerke des europäischen Mittelalters bis 1500. 2nd edn. 2 vols. Berlin. 1896.

Redlich, O. and Erben, W. Urkundenlehre. Pts. I and III. (Below-Meinecke. *See above*.) Munich. 1907, 11.

Rivista storica italiana. Turin. 1884 ff., in progress. [Up to 1921 contained quarterly classified bibliography of books and articles on Italian history.] (RSI.)

Thompson, E. M. Introduction to Greek and Latin Palaeography. London. 1912.

Vacant, A. and Mangenot, E. Dictionnaire de théologie catholique. Paris. 1899 ff.

Victoria History of the Counties of England. London. 1900 ff., in progress. (Vict. Co. Hist.)

Vildhaut, H. Handbuch der Quellenkunde zur deutschen Geschichte bis zum Ausgange der Staufer. 2nd edn. Werl. 1906.

Villien, A. and Magnin, E. Dictionnaire de droit canonique. Paris. 1924 ff., in progress.

Waitz. *See above*, Dahlmann.

Wattenbach, W. Deutschlands Geschichtsquellen im Mittelalter bis zur Mitte des 13 Jahrhunderts. 6th edn. 2 vols. Berlin. 1893–4. Vol. I. 7th edn. Dümmler, E. Stuttgart and Berlin. 1904.

Wetzer, H. J. and Welte, B. Kirchenlexikon oder Encyklopädie der katholischen Theologie. 1847–60. 2nd edn. Kaulen, F. Freiburg-i.-B. 1882–1903. Index. 1903. (Wetzer-Kaulen.) French transl. Goschler, I. 26 vols. Paris. 1869–70.

Whitney, J. P. Bibliography of Church History. (Historical Assoc. Leaflet 55.) London. 1923.

II. ATLASES AND GEOGRAPHY.

Baudrillart-Vogt-Rouziès. Dictionnaire d'histoire et de géographie ecclésiastique. Paris. 1911 ff., in progress.

Droysen, G. Allgemeiner historischer Handatlas. Bielefeld. 1886.

Freeman, E. A. Historical Geography of Europe (with Atlas). London. 1881. 3rd edn. revised and ed. Bury, J. B. 1903.

Kretschmer, K. Historische Geographie von Mitteleuropa. (Below-Meinecke. *See above*, I.) Munich. 1904.

Le Strange, G. The lands of the Eastern Caliphate. Cambridge. 1905.

Longnon, A. Atlas historique de France depuis César jusqu'à nos jours. (Text separate.) Paris. 1912.

Muir, R. Philips' New Historical Atlas for students. 6th edn. London. 1927.

Poole, R. L. *ed*. Historical Atlas of Modern Europe. Oxford. 1902. [With valuable introductions.]

Putzger, F. W. Historischer Schul-Atlas. Ed. Baldamus, A. and others. 43rd edn. Bielefeld and Leipsic. 1922.

Saint-Martin, V. de, and others. Nouveau dictionnaire de Géographie Universelle. 7 vols. Paris. 1879–95. Supplt. by Rousselet, L. 2 vols. 1895, 97. [Contains short bibliographies.]

Schrader, F. Atlas de géographie historique. New edn. Paris. 1907.

Spruner-Menke. Hand-Atlas für die Geschichte des Mittelalters und der neueren Zeit. Gotha. 1880. (3rd edn. of Spruner's Hand-Atlas etc. Ed. Menke, Th.)

(FOR PLACE-NAMES :—)

Bischoff, H. T. and Möller, J. H. Vergleichendes Wörterbuch der alten, mittleren, und neuen Geographie. Gotha. 1892.

Deschamps, P. Dictionnaire de Géographie. (Supplt. to Brunet, J. C. Manuel du Libraire.) Paris. 1870. 2nd edn. 2 vols. 1878, 80.

Grässe, J. G. T. Orbis Latinus. Dresden. 1861. Ed. Benedict, F. Berlin. 1909. [Part I only.]

Martin, C. T. The Record Interpreter. London. 1892. 2nd edn. 1910. [For the British Isles.]

See also above, I. Chevalier, Répertoire etc., Topo-bibliographie.

III. CHRONOLOGY, NUMISMATICS, AND GENEALOGY.

(CHRONOLOGY :—)

L'Art de vérifier les dates et les faits historiques. 2ᵉ partie. Depuis la naiss. de J.-C. 3rd edn. Paris. 3 vols. 1783 ff., and other edns. and reprints. Also 4th edn. by Saint-Allais. 18 vols. 1818–19.

Belviglieri, C. Tavole sincrone e genealogiche di storia italiana dal 306 al 1870. Florence. 1875. Repr. 1885.

Bond, J. J. Handybook of rules and tables for verifying dates. London. Last edn. 1875.

Calvi, E. Tavole storiche dei comuni italiani. Pts. i–iii. Rome. 1903–7. i. Liguria e Piemonte. ii. Marche. iii. Romagna. [Also useful bibliographies.]

Gams, P. B. Series episcoporum ecclesiae Catholicae. (With supplt.) Ratisbon. 1873, 86.

Ginzel, F. K. Handbuch der mathematischen und technischen Chronologie. 3 vols. Leipsic. 1906–14.

Grotefend, H. Taschenbuch der Zeitrechnung des deutschen Mittelalters und der Neuzeit. 3rd enl. edn. Hanover. 1910.

—— Zeitrechnung des deutschen Mittelalters und d. Neuzeit. 2 vols. Hanover. 1891, 98.

Ideler, C. L. Handbuch der mathematischen und technischen Chronologie. 2 vols. Berlin. 1825. New edn. Breslau. 1883.

Lane-Poole, S. The Mohammadan Dynasties. London. 1894.

Mas Latrie, J. M. J. L. de. Trésor de chronologie, d'histoire, et de géographie pour l'étude des documents du moyen âge. Paris. 1889.

Nicolas, Sir H. N. The chronology of history. Revised edn. London. 1838.

Poole, R. L. Medieval reckonings of time. (Helps for Students of History.) S.P.C.K. London. 1918.

Ritter, C. Geographisch-statistisches Lexicon. 8th edn. Penzler, J. 2 vols. Leipsic. 1894–5.

Rühl, F. Chronologie des Mittelalters und der Neuzeit. Berlin. 1897.

Savio, F. Gli antichi vescovi d' Italia dalle origini al 1300. Il Piemonte. Turin 1899. La Lombardia. 3 vols. Florence. 1913–32.

Schram, R. Hilfstafeln für Chronologie. Vienna. 1883. New edn. Kalendariographische und chronologische Tafeln. Leipsic. 1908.

Stokvis, A. M. H. J. Manuel d'histoire, de généalogie, et de chronologie de tous le États du globe etc. 3 vols. Leiden. 1888–93.

Stubbs, W. Registrum sacrum Anglicanum. 2nd edn. Oxford. 1897.

Wallis, J. E. W. English regnal years and titles, hand-lists, Easter dates, etc (English Time-books. Vol. i. Helps for Students of History.) S.P.C.K, London. 1921.

Wislicenus, W. F. Astronomische Chronologie. Leipsic. 1895.

(*Note:*—Much information in such works as Gallia Christiana; Ughelli, Italia Sacra for which see iv.)

(Numismatics:—)

Blanchet, A. and Dieudonné, A. Manuel de numismatique française. Vols. i, ii Paris. 1912, 16, in progress.

Codrington, O. Manual of Musalman numismatics. (Royal Asiatic Soc.) London 1904.

Corpus nummorum italicorum. Vols. i–xvii. Rome. 1910 ff., in progress.

Engel, A. and Serrure, R. Traité de numismatique du moyen âge. 2 vols. Paris. 1891, 94.

Grueber, H. A. Handbook of the Coins of Great Britain and Ireland in the British Museum. London. 1899.

Hill, G. F. Coins and Medals. (Helps for Students of History.) S.P.C.K. London. 1920. [Bibliographical guide.]

Luschin von Ebengreuth, A. Allgemeine Münzkunde und Geldgeschichte des Mittelalters und der neueren Zeit. (Below-Meinecke. *See above*, i.) Munich. 1904. 2nd edn. 1926.

Macdonald, G. The Evolution of Coinage. Cambridge. 1916.

Martinori, E. La Moneta. Rome. 1915. [Dictionary of names of coins.]

Schlumberger, G. Numismatique de l'Orient Latin. (Société de l'Orient Latin.) 2 vols. Paris. 1878, 82.

(GENEALOGY:—)

Cokayne, G. E. Complete Peerage of England, Scotland, Ireland, Great Britain, and the United Kingdom. 8 vols. Exeter. 1887–98. New enl. edn. Gibbs, V. and others. London. 1910 ff., in progress.

Du Cange, C. du Fresne. Les familles d'outre-mer. Ed. Rey, E. (Coll. doc.) Paris. 1869.

Fernandez de Bethencourt, F. Historia genealógica y heráldica de la Monarquía Española, Casa Real, y Grandes de España. Madrid. 1897 ff., in progress.

Foras, E. A. de, and Maréschal de Luciane. Armorial et Nobiliaire de l'ancien duché de Savoie. Vols. I–IV. Grenoble. 1863–1902.

George, H. B. Genealogical Tables illustrative of Modern History. Oxford. 1873. 5th edn., Weaver, J. R. H., rev. and enl. 1916.

Grote, H. Stammtafeln mit Anhang calendarium medii aevi. (Münzstudien. Vol. IX.) Leipsic. 1877.

Guasco di Bisio, F. Dizionario feudale degli antichi stati sardi e della Lombardia dall' epoca carolingica ai nostri tempi (774–1909). 5 vols. (Biblioteca della soc. storica subalpina. Vols. 54–58.) Pinerolo. 1911.

Institut héraldique de France. Le Nobiliaire universel. 24 vols. Paris. 1854–1900.

Litta, P. (and continuators). Famiglie celebri italiane. 11 vols. Milan and Turin. 1819–99. 2nd series. Naples. 1902 ff., in progress.

Moreri, L. Le grand dictionnaire historique. Latest edn. 10 vols. Paris. 1759. English version, Collier, J., with App. London. 1721.

Voigtel, T. G. and Cohn, L. A. Stammtafeln zur Geschichte d. europäischen Staaten. Vol. I. Die deutschen Staaten u. d. Niederlande. Brunswick. 1871.

See also L'Art de vérifier les dates (*above*), Lane-Poole, Mohammadan Dynasties (*above*), and Stokvis (*above*).

IV. SOURCES AND COLLECTIONS OF SOURCES.

Achery, L. d'. Spicilegium sive collectio veterum aliquot scriptorum. 13 vols. Paris. 1655 (1665)–77. New edn. Barre, L. F. J. de la. 3 vols. Paris. 1723.

Acta Sanctorum Bollandiana. Jan.–Oct. VI. Antwerp, Brussels, and Tongerloo. 1643–1794. Oct. VII–XIII. Brussels, Paris and Rome, Paris. 1845–83. Nov. Paris and Rome, Brussels. 1887 ff., in progress. [The reprint of Jan.–Oct. X. published by Palmé at Paris and Rome, 1863 ff., among other variations, has 3 instead of 2 vols. of Jan., and re-arranges the contents of the 7 vols. of June.] (ASBoll.) [Supplemented by Analecta Bollandiana. 1882 ff. (AB.)]

Altnordische Saga Bibliothek. Ed. Cederschiöld, G., Gering, H., and Mogk, E. 7 vols. Halle. 1892–8.

Amari, M. *See under* Muratori.

Archivio storico italiano. (ASI.) *See List of Abbreviations* (1).

Biblioteca Arabico-Hispana. Ed. Codera and Ribera. 10 vols. Madrid and Saragossa. 1883–95.

Biblioteca della società storica subalpina. Ed. Gabotto, F. and Tallone, A. Pinerolo, etc. 1899 ff., in progress. [Contains charters and monographs.]

Bibliotheca rerum Germanicarum. Ed. Jaffé, P. 6 vols. Berlin. 1864–73. (Bibl. rer. German.)

Böhmer, J. P. Regesta imperii. (New edn. in several parts by various editors.) Innsbruck. 1877 ff.

    I. Regesten d. Kaiserreichs unter den Karolingern, 751–918. Ed. Mühlbacher, E. 2nd edn. Lechner, J. 1908 ff.

    II. Regesten d. Kaiserreichs...919–1024. Ed. Ottenthal, E. von. Liefg. I. 1893, in progress.

    V. Regesten d. Kaiserreichs...1198–1272. Ed. Ficker, J. and Winkelmann, E. 3 vols. 1881–1901.

    VI. Regesten d. Kaiserreichs...1273–1313. Ed. Redlich, O. Abtlg. 1. 1898, in progress.

    VIII. Regesten d. Kaiserreichs unter Karl IV, 1346–78. Ed. Huber, A. 1877. Additamentum I. 1889.

    XI. Urkunden Kaiser Sigmunds, 1410–37. Ed. Altmann, W. 2 vols. 1896–1900.

Bouquet. *See* Rerum Gallicarum...scriptores.

Brackmann, A. Germania Pontificia. *See under* Kehr, P. F.

Camden Society, Publications of the. London. 1838 ff., in progress. (Now publ. by the Roy. Hist. Soc.)

Chartes et diplômes relatifs à l'histoire de France. AcadIBL. Paris. 1908 ff., in progress.

Classiques de l'histoire de France au moyen âge. General editor: Halphen, L. Paris. 1924 ff., in progress. (Class. hist.) [Texts and French translations.]

Collection de chroniques Belges inédites. Brussels. 1836 ff., in progress.

Collection de documents inédits sur l'histoire de France. Paris. 1835 ff., in progress. (Coll. doc.)

Collection de textes pour servir à l'étude et à l'enseignement de l'histoire. Paris. 1886–1913. (Coll. textes.)

Corpus Iuris Canonici. Ed. Friedberg, E. 2 vols. Leipsic. 1879, 81. [Also 3 vols. Lyons. 1584 for the medieval Glosses.]

Corpus Iuris Civilis. 3 vols. Berlin. 1884–95.
> Vol. I. Institutiones. Ed. Krueger, P. Digesta. Ed. Mommsen, T. 13th edn. 1920.
> Vol. II. Codex Iustinianus. Ed. Krueger, P. 9th edn. 1915.
> Vol. III. Novellae. Ed. Schoell, R. and Kroll, W. 4th edn. 1912.
> [The medieval additions to the Corpus, as well as the Gloss, are to be found in, e.g., ed. Gothofredus, D. Cologne. 1612.]

Corpus scriptorum christianorum orientalium. Ed. Chabot, J. B. and others. Paris, Rome, and Leipsic. 1903 ff. (CSCO.)

Corpus scriptorum ecclesiasticorum latinorum. Vienna. 1866 ff., in progress. (CSEL.)

Corpus scriptorum historiae Byzantinae. Bonn. 1828–97. (CSHB.)

Domesday Book. Ed. Farley, A. and Ellis, H. 4 vols. (RC.) London. 1783–1816. Vols. I, II, contain text; Vol. III, introdn. and indices; Vol. IV, Exon. Domesday and Inquisitio Eliensis. Facsimile edn. publ. by the Ordnance Survey Office. 35 pts. Southampton. 1861–4.

Duchesne, L. Fastes épiscopaux de l'ancienne Gaule. Paris. 2nd edn. 3 vols. Paris. 1907–15.

Dugdale, W. Monasticon Anglicanum. 3 vols. London. 1655–73. New edn. by Caley, J. and others. 6 vols. in 8. London. 1817–30. Repr. 1846.

Early English Text Society, Publications of the. London. 1864 ff., in progress. (EETS.)

España Sagrada. Ed. Florez, H. and others. 51 vols. Madrid. 1747–1879.

Fejér, G. Codex diplomaticus Hungariae ecclesiasticus et civilis. (Chronological table by Knauz, F. Index by Czinár, M.) 45 vols. Buda-Pest. 1829–66.

Fonti per la storia d'Italia. Publ. by Istituto storico italiano. Rome. 1887 ff., in progress. (Chronicles, 36 vols. Letters, 6 vols. Diplomas, 7 vols. Statutes, 7 vols. Law, 1 vol. Antiquities, 3 vols.) (Fonti.)

Gallia Christiana. 16 vols. Paris. 1715–1865. [*See* Bibl. to ch. xx, sect. III (*b*).]

Gallia Christiana novissima. Albanès, J. H. and Chevalier, C. U. J. 3 vols. Montbéliard and Valence. 1895–1900. [*See* Bibl. to ch. xx, sect. III (*b*).]

Geschichtschreiber der deutschen Vorzeit etc. Ed. Pertz, Wattenbach, and others. New series. Leipsic. 1884, in progress. [German translations.]

Graevius, J. G. and Burmannus, P. Thesaurus antiquitatum et historiarum Italiae etc. 30 vols. Leiden. 1704–23.

—— —— Thesaurus antiq. et histor. Siciliae, Sardiniae, Corsicae, etc. 15 vols. Leiden. 1723–5. [Forms a continuation of the preceding.]

Guizot, F. P. C. Collection des mém. relatifs à l'hist. de France...jusqu'au 13e siècle. Paris. 1823–35. [French translations.]

Haddan, A. W. and Stubbs, W. Councils and ecclesiastical documents relating to Great Britain and Ireland. Ed. after Spelman and Wilkins. 3 vols. Oxford. 1869–78.

Haller, J. Die Quellen zur Gesch. der Entstehung des Kirchenstaates. (Quellensammlung zur deutschen Geschichte. Ed. Brandenburger, E. and Seeliger, G.) Leipsic and Berlin. 1907.

Hinschius, P. Decretales pseudo-Isidorianae et capitula Angilramni. Leipsic. 1863.

Historiae patriae monumenta. *See* Monumenta historiae patriae.

Jaffé, P. Regesta Pontificum Romanorum ab condita ecclesia ad annum post Christum natum 1198. Berlin. 1851. 2nd edn. Wattenbach, W., Loewenfeld, S., Kaltenbrunner, F., Ewald, P. 2 vols. Leipsic. 1885, 88. (Jaffé-Loewenfeld.)

—— *See under* Bibliotheca rerum Germanicarum.

Kehr, P. F. Regesta Pontificum Romanorum. Italia Pontificia. Ed. Kehr, P. F. Vol. i. Rome. ii. Latium. iii. Etruria. iv. Umbria etc. v. Aemilia. vi. Liguria (Lombardy, Piedmont, Genoa). vii. Venetiae et Histria. viii. Regnum Normann. Campania. Berlin. 1906–35, in progress.
> Germania Pontificia. Ed. Brackmann, A. Vol. i, i, ii. Salzburg. ii, i, ii. Mayence. Berlin. 1910–27, in progress.

Le Quien, M. Oriens Christianus. 3 vols. Paris. 1740.

Liber Censuum de l'église romaine. Ed. Fabre, P. and Duchesne, L. Vol. i. EcfrAR. Paris. 1889–1910. Vol. ii in progress.

Liber Pontificalis. 3 vols. Rome. 1724–55. Ed. Duchesne, L. 2 vols. EcfrAR. Paris. 1886, 92. *Also* ed. Mommsen, T. Gesta Pontif. Romanorum. Vol. i (to 715). MGH. 1898.

Liebermann, F. Die Gesetze der Angelsachsen. 3 vols. Halle-a.-S. 1903–16.

Mabillon, J. Annales Ordinis S. Benedicti. 6 vols. Paris. 1703–39. 2nd edn. Lucca. 1739–45.

Mabillon, J. and Achery, L. d'. Acta Sanctorum ord. S. Benedicti [A.D. 500–1100]. 9 vols. Paris. 1668–1701. Repr. Venice. 1733–40. (ASBen.)

Mansi, J. D. Sacrorum conciliorum collectio. 31 vols. Florence and Venice. 1759–98. Repr. Martin, J. B. and Petit, L. (With continuation, vols. 32–50.) Paris. 1901 ff., in progress. (Mansi.)

Marrier, M. and Quercetanus (Duchesne), A. Bibliotheca Cluniacensis. Paris. 1614.

Martène, E. and Durand, U. Thesaurus novus anecdotorum. 5 vols. Paris. 1717.

Mémoires et documents publiés par l'École des Chartes. Paris. 1896 ff.

Migne, J. P. Patrologiae cursus completus. Series graeco-latina. Paris. 1857–66. 161 vols. in 166. (MPG.) Indices, Cavallera, F. Paris. 1912. [This is the series containing Greek texts with Latin translations in parallel columns. The so-called Series graeca (81 vols. in 85. 1856–67) contains the Latin translations only.]

—— —— Series latina. 221 vols. Paris. 1844–55. Index, 4 vols. 1862–4. (MPL.)

Mirbt, C. Quellen zur Geschichte des Papsttums und des römischen Katholizismus. 2nd edn. Freiburg, Tübingen, and Leipsic. 1901. 4th edn. 1924. (Mirbt. Quellen.)

Monumenta Germaniae Historica. Ed. Pertz, G. H., Mommsen, T., and others. Hanover. 1826 ff. New edns. in progress. Hanover and Berlin. (MGH.) Index. 1890.
> Auctores Antiquissimi. 15 vols. in many pts. 1876 ff. (Auct. ant.) Vols. ix, xi, xiii form Chronica minora (saec. iv, v, vi).
>
> Deutsche Chroniken (Scriptores qui vernac. lingua usi sunt). i–vi. 1892 ff., in progress.
>
> Diplomata imperii. i. 1872. Fol. [No more publ.; contains Merovingian diplomas.]
>
> Diplomata Karolinorum. Die Urkunden d. Karolinger. i. 1906 ff., in progress.
>
> Diplomata regum et imperatorum Germaniae. Urkunden d. deutschen Könige und Kaiser. Vols. i–v, viii. 1879 ff., in progress.
>
> Epistolae. i–vii. 1887 ff., in progress. (iii–vii are Epist. Karolini aevi, i– v.)
>
> Epistolae saec. xiii e regestis pontificum Romanorum. i–iii. 1883–94.
>
> Epistolae selectae. i–iv. 1916 ff., in progress. 8°. (Epp. select.)
>
> Gesta pontificum Romanorum. In progress. [*See above*, Liber Pontificalis.]
>
> Leges. i–v. 1835–89. Fol.
>
> Legum sectiones quinque. 4°.
>> Sect. i. Legum nationum Germanicarum. i, ii 1, v 1. 1902 ff., in progress.
>>
>> Sect. ii. Capitularia regum Francorum. 2 vols. 1883, 97. Complete.
>>
>> Sect. iii. Concilia. 2 vols. in 4. 1893–1924.
>>
>> Sect. iv. Constitutiones etc. i–v, vi 1, viii. 1893 ff.
>>
>> Sect. v. Formulae Merovingici et Karolini aevi. 1886. Complete.

Libelli de lite imperatorum et pontificum (saec. xi, xii). i–iii. 1891 ff.

Libri confraternitatum. 1884.

Necrologia Germaniae. i–iv, v 2. 1884 ff., in progress.

Poetae Latini medii aevi (Carolini). 5 vols. in 6. 1831–1929, in progress.

Scriptores. 30 vols. in 32. Fol. 1826–1933. And 4°. Vols. xxxi, xxxii. 1903, 1913. In progress. (Script.)

Scriptores rerum Germanicarum in usum scholarum. Hanover. 1839 ff. Fresh series. 1890–1920. 8°. (SGUS.) [Contains revised editions of many of Scriptores in Fol. edition.]

Scriptores rerum Germanicarum. Nova Series. i–iv 1, v–ix. Berlin. 1922 ff., in progress. (Script. N.S.)

Scriptores rerum Langobardicarum et Italicarum. 1878.

Scriptores rerum Merovingicarum. i–vii. 1885 ff., in progress.

Monumenta historiae patriae. 19 vols. Fol. 2 vols. 4°. Turin. 1836 ff., in progress. (MHP.)

Monumenta historica Britannica. Ed. Petrie, H., Sharpe, T., and Hardy, T. D. Vol. i. (RC.) London. 1848. [No more publ.]

Monumenta Hungariae historica. (Published by the Hungarian Academy.) In four series. i. Diplomataria. ii. Scriptores. [Vols. xxi and xxii never published. *See* Krumbacher, K. Geschichte d. byzant. Lit. pp. 310–12. (*Sect.* v *below.*)] iii. Monumenta comitialia. iv. Acta extera. Buda-Pest. 1857 ff.

Muratori, L. A. Rerum Italicarum scriptores. 25 vols. Milan. 1723–51. Supplements: Tartini, J. M., 2 vols., Florence, 1748, 70; and Mittarelli, J. B., Venice, 1771; and Amari, M., Biblioteca arabo-sicula, versione italiana, and Appendix. Turin and Rome. 1880–1, 1889. Indices chronolog. Turin. 1885 New enlarged edn. with the chronicles printed as separate parts. Carducci, G., Fiorini, V., and Fedele, P. Città di Castello and Bologna. 1900 ff., in progress. (RR.II.SS.)

—— Antiquitates italicae medii aevi. 6 vols. Milan. 1738–42. Indices chronolog. Turin. 1885.

Papsturkunden in England. Ed. Holtzmann, W. i, ii. Berlin. 1930–6, in progress.

Papsturkunden in Frankreich. Ed. Meinert, H. i. Berlin. 1932–3, in progress.

Papsturkunden in den Niederlanden. Ed. Ramaakers, J. i, ii. Berlin. 1933–4.

Papsturkunden in Portugal. Ed. Erdmann, C. Berlin. 1927.

Papsturkunden in Spanien. Ed. Kehr, P. F. i, ii. Berlin. 1926–8.

Potthast, A. Regesta Pontificum Romanorum inde ab anno 1198 ad annum 1304. 2 vols. Berlin. 1874, 75.

Record Commissioners, Publications of the. London. 1802–69. (RC.)

Récueil des historiens des croisades. AcadIBL. Paris. 1841 ff. (Rec. hist. Cr.)

Regesta chartarum Italiae. Publ. by K. Preuss. Histor. Instit. and Istituto storico italiano. Rome. 1907 ff., in progress.

Regesta Pontificum Romanorum. *See above under* Jaffé, P., Kehr, P. F., and Potthast, A.

Rerum Britannicarum medii aevi scriptores. (Chronicles and Memorials of Great Britain and Ireland during the Middle Ages.) Published under direction of the Master of the Rolls. (Various editors.) London. 1858 ff. (Rolls.) [For convenient list see Gross (*Sect.* i, *above*), App. C.]

Rerum Gallicarum et Francicarum scriptores. (Recueil des hist. des Gaules et de la France.) Ed. Bouquet, M. and others. 23 vols. 1738–1876. Vols. i–xix re-ed. by Delisle, L. 1868–80, and vol. xxiv, 1894. New series. 4°. 1899, in progress. (Bouquet.)

Scriptores rerum Danicarum medii aevi. Ed. Langebek, I. 9 vols. Copenhagen. 1772–1878. (SRD.)

Scriptores rerum Germanicarum in usum scholarum. (SGUS.) *See above*, Monumenta Germaniae Historica.

Selden Society, Publications of the. London. 1888 ff., in progress.

Société de l'histoire de France, Ouvrages publiés par la. Paris. 1834 ff., in progress. (SHF.)

Stevenson, J. Church Historians of England. 8 vols. London. 1853–8. [Translations.]

Stubbs, W. Select Charters and other illustrations of English Constitutional History to the reign of Edward I. Oxford. 1870. 9th edn. rev. Davis, H. W. C. Oxford. 1913.

Stumpf-Brentano, K. F. Die Reichskanzler vornehmlich des x, xi, und xii Jahrhunderts. 3 vols. Innsbruck. 1865–83.

Theiner, A. Codex diplomaticus dominii temporalis S. Sedis. 3 vols. Rome. 1861–2.

Ughelli, F. Italia sacra. 2nd edn. Coleti, N. 10 vols. Venice. 1717–22.

Vic, C. de, and Vaissete, J. J. Histoire générale de Languedoc. New edn. Dulaurier, E. 16 vols. Toulouse. 1872–1904.

Watterich, J. M. Pontificum Romanorum qui fuerunt inde ab exeunte saeculo ix usque ad finem saeculi xii, vitae. 2 vols. Leipsic. 1862.

V. MODERN WORKS.

Altamira, R. Historia de España y de la civilización española. 3rd edn. 4 vols. Barcelona. 1913–14.

Alzog, J. Universalgeschichte der Kirche. Mayence. 1841. Best edn. 10th by Kraus, F. X. 1882. Transl. (from 9th German edn.). Pabisch, F. J. and Byrne, T. S. Manual of Church History. 4 vols. Dublin. 1895–1900.

Baronius, C. Annales Ecclesiastici una cum critica historico-chronologica P. A. Pagii, contin. Raynaldus, O. Ed. Mansi, J. D. Lucca. 34 vols. 1738–46. Apparatus, 1 vol. Index, 4 vols. 1740, 1757–9. New edn. Bar-le-duc. 1864–83.

Bédier, J. and Hazard, P. *edd.* Histoire de la littérature française illustrée. 2 vols. Paris. 1923–4.

Bibliothèque de l'École des Hautes Études. Paris. 1869 ff., in progress. (BHE.)

Bréhier, L'Eglise et l'Orient au moyen âge. Les Croisades. 5th edn. Paris. 1928. (Bibliothèque de l'enseignement de l'histoire ecclésiastique.) [With bibliography.]

Brown, G. Baldwin. The Arts in Early England. 6 vols. London. 1903–37.

Browne, P. Hume. History of Scotland to the present time. (Library edn.) 3 vols. Cambridge. 1911.

Brunner, H. Deutsche Rechtsgeschichte. 2 vols. Leipsic. 1887, 92. Vol. i. 2nd edn. 1906. Vol. ii. ed. Schwerin, C. von. 1928.

—— Grundzüge der deutschen Rechtsgeschichte. 7th edn. Heymann, E. Munich. 1919. [Bibliographies.]

Bryce, J. The Holy Roman Empire. New edn., corrected. London. 1906.

Caetani, L. C. (Duca di Sermoneta). Annali dell' Islam. Vols. i–x. Milan. 1905 ff.

Cambridge Economic History of Europe. Ed. Clapham, J. H. and Power, E. Vol. i. Cambridge. 1941, in progress.

Cambridge History of English Literature. Ed. Ward, A. W. and Waller, A. R. 15 vols. Cambridge. 1907–27.

Cánovas del Castillo, A. *ed.* Historia general de la España. (By members of R. Acad. de la Hist.) Madrid. 1892 ff., in progress.

Carlyle, R. W. and A. J. A history of Mediaeval Political Theory in the West. 6 vols. Edinburgh and London. 1903–36.

Coulton, G. G. Five Centuries of Religion. Vols. i–iii. Cambridge. 1923 ff., in progress.

Cunningham, W. The growth of English Industry and Commerce. [Vol. i.] Early and Middle Ages. 5th edn. Cambridge. 1910.

Denifle, H. Die Universitäten des Mittelalters bis 1400. Vol. i. Die Entstehung der Universitäten. Berlin. 1885. [No more publ.]

Diehl, C. Byzance: grandeur et décadence. Paris. 1919.

Dozy, R. P. A. Hist. des Mussulmans d'Espagne de 711–1110. 4 vols. Leiden. 1861. Transl. Stokes, F. G. Spanish Islam: a hist. of the Moslems in Spain. London. 1913.

Ebert, A. Allgemeine Geschichte der Litteratur des Mittelalters im Abendland. 3 vols. Leipsic. 1874–87. 2nd edn. of vols. i and ii. 1889.

England, A History of, in seven volumes. Ed. Oman, C. 7 vols. London. 1905–13.

—— The Political History of. Ed. Hunt, W. and Poole, R. L. 12 vols. London. 1905–10.

Ficker, G. and Hermelink, H. Das Mittelalter. (Handbuch d. Kirchengesch. für Studierende. Ed. Krüger, G. Vol. I, ii.) Tübingen. 1912.

Flach, J. Les origines de l'ancienne France. x^e et xie siècles. Vols. I–IV. Paris. 1886–1917.

Fleury, C. Histoire ecclésiastique. 20 vols. Paris. 1691–1720. Continued to end of 18th century under Vidal, O. Many editions. (Orig. edn. to 1414. 4 add. vols. by Fleury to 1517, publ. Paris. 1836–7.)

Gebhardt, B. Handbuch d. deutschen Geschichte. 2 vols. Stuttgart. 1891–2.

Gibbon, E. The History of the Decline and Fall of the Roman Empire. 1776–81. Ed. in 7 vols. by Bury, J. B. London. 1896–1900. Latest edn. London. 1909–14. [Notes essential, especially for bibliography.]

Gierke, O. Das deutsche Genossenschaftsrecht. 4 vols. Berlin. 1868–1913.
—— Political Theories of the Middle Age. Trans. and ed. Maitland, F. W. Cambridge. 1900. [Translation of a section of the preceding.]

Giesebrecht, W. von. Geschichte der deutschen Kaiserzeit. Vols. I–V. Brunswick and Leipsic. 1855–88. I–III. 5th edn. Leipsic. 1881–90. IV. 2nd. edn. Brunswick. 1899. VI. Ed. Simson, B. von. Leipsic. 1895.

Gieseler, J. C. L. Lehrbuch der Kirchengeschichte. Bonn. 3 vols. 1824 ff., and 6 vols. in 5, 1828–57. Transl. Davidson, S. 5 vols. Edinburgh, 1854.

Gilson, E. La philosophie au moyen âge. 2 vols. Paris. 1922. [Bibliographies.]

Glotz, G. ed. Histoire générale. Section II. Histoire du moyen âge. [To be 10 vols.] Paris. 1928 ff. in progress.

Gregorovius, F. Geschichte der Stadt Rom im Mittelalter. 8 vols. Stuttgart. 1859–72. (Engl. transl. from 4th edn. by Mrs A. Hamilton. 8 vols. in 13. London. 1894–1902.)

Halphen, L. and Sagnac, P. edd. Peuples et civilisations. Histoire générale. Vol. VI. L'essor de l'Europe. Paris. 1932.

Hampe, K. Deutsche Kaisergeschichte in der Zeit der Salier und Staufer. 5th edn. Leipsic. 1923.

Hanotaux, G. ed. Histoire de la nation française. Paris. 1920 ff., in progress.

Harnack, G. C. A. Lehrbuch der Dogmengeschichte. 4th edn. 3 vols. Tübingen. 1905–10. Engl. transl. Buchanan, N., etc. 7 vols. London. 1894–9.

Hartmann, L. M. Geschichte Italiens im Mittelalter. I–IV 1. (Heeren. *See below.*) Gotha. 1897–1915. Vol. I. 2nd edn. 1923.
—— ed. Weltgeschichte in gemeinverständlicher Darstellung.
Vol. IV. Hellmann, S. Das Mittelalter bis zum Ausgang der Kreuzzüge. 2nd edn. Gotha. 1924.
Vol. V. Kaser, K. Das späte Mittelalter. Gotha. 1921.

Haskins, C. H. Studies in the history of Medieval Science. Cambridge, Mass. 1924.

Hauck, A. Kirchengeschichte Deutschlands. 5 vols. Leipsic. 1887–1920. Vols. I–IV. 4th edn. 1906–13. Vol. V. 2nd edn. 2 pts. 1911, 20.

Heeren, A. H. L. and others, edd. Geschichte der europäischen Staaten. Hamburg and Gotha. 1829 ff. Continued as section I of Allgemeine Staatengeschichte. Ed. Lamprecht, K. and Oncken, H.

Hefele, C. J., contin. Hergenröther, J. A. G. Conciliengeschichte. 9 vols. Freiburg-i.-B. 1855 ff. 2nd edn. 1873 ff. New rev. Fr. transl. Leclercq, H. I–VIII 2. Paris. 1907 ff., in progress. (Hefele-Leclercq.)

Heyd, W. Histoire du Commerce du Levant au moyen-âge. 2nd edn. (in French transl. by Raynaud, F.). 2 vols. Leipsic. 1885–6. Reprinted. 2 vols. Leipsic. 1923.

Hinojosa, E. de. Historia general del derecho español. Vol. I. Madrid. 1887. [No more publ.]

Hinschius, P. Das Kirchenrecht der Katholiken und Protestanten in Deutschland. Pt. I. System des kathol. Kirchenrechts, mit besonderer Rücksicht auf Deutschland. Vols. I–VI, 1. Berlin. 1869–97.

Historische Studien. Ed. Ebering, E. Berlin. 1896 ff., in progress.

Holdsworth, W. S. History of English Law. 3rd edn. Vols. I–III. London. 1922–3.

Jahrbücher der deutschen Geschichte bis 1250. Kön. Akad. d. Wissenschaften (Munich). Berlin and Leipsic. 1862 ff., in progress.

Kirchenrechtliche Abhandlungen. Ed. Stutz, U. Stuttgart, 1902 ff., in progress.

Köhler, G. Die Entwicklung des Kriegswesen und der Kriegsführung in der Ritterzeit von der Mitte des 11 Jahrhunderts bis zu den Hussitenkriegen. 3 vols. Breslau. 1886–90.

Kraus, F. X. Geschichte der christlichen Kunst. 2 vols. in 4. Freiburg-i.-B. 1896–1908.

Kretschmayr, H. Geschichte von Venedig. 3 vols. (Heeren. *See above.*) Gotha. 1905 ff.

Krumbacher, K. Geschichte der byzantinischen Literatur. (527–1453.) 2nd edn. (Handbuch d. klass. Altertums-Wissenschaft. Ed. Müller, I. von. Vol. ix, i.) Munich. 1897.

Lamprecht, K. Deutsche Geschichte. 12 vols. in 16. Berlin. 1891–1909. Vols. i–v. 3rd edn. 1902–6. Supplts. 2 vols. in 3. 1902–4.

Langen, J. Geschichte der römischen Kirche. 4 vols. Bonn. 1881.

Lavisse, E. *ed.* Histoire de France jusqu'à la Révolution. 9 vols. in 18. Paris. 1900–11. Vols. i–iv.

Lavisse, E. and Rambaud, A. *edd.* Histoire générale du iv⁰ siècle jusqu'à nos jours. 12 vols. Paris. 1893–1900. Vols. i–iii.

Lea, H. C. History of Sacerdotal Celibacy in the Christian Church. 3rd edn. 2 vols. London. 1907.

Lloyd, J. E. History of Wales from the earliest times to the Edwardian Conquest. 2nd edn. 2 vols. London. 1912.

Luchaire, A. Histoire des institutions monarchiques de la France sous les premiers Capétiens (987–1180). 2nd edn. 2 vols. Paris. 1891.

—— Manuel des institutions françaises; période des Capétiens directs. Paris. 1892.

Manitius, M. Geschichte der lateinischen Literatur des Mittelalters. Vols. i–iii. (Handbuch d. klass. Altertums-Wissenschaft. Ed. Müller, I. von. Vol. ix, ii 1–3.) Munich. 1911 ff.

Merriman, R. B. The rise of the Spanish empire in the old world and the new. Vols. i and ii. New York. 1918.

Miller, W. The Latins in the Levant: a history of Frankish Greece (1204–1566). London. 1908. Enlarged Greek transl. Lampros (Lambros), S. P. Ἱστορία τῆς φραγκοκρατίας ἐν Ἑλλάδι. Athens. 1909–10.

—— The Latin Orient. (Helps for Students of History.) S.P.C.K. London. 1920. [Contains a Bibliography.]

Moeller, W. Hist. of the Christian Church (A.D. 1–1648). Transl. Rutherfurd and Freese. 3 vols. London. 1892–1900.

Mosheim, J. L. von. Institutionum historiae ecclesiasticae antiquae et recentioris libri iv. 4 vols. Helmstedt. 1755. Transl. Murdock, J., ed. Soames, H. 4 vols. London. 1841. 2nd rev. edn. 1850.

Muir, W. The Caliphate: its rise, decline, and fall. Revised edn. Weir, T. H. Edinburgh. 1915.

Müller, K. Kirchengeschichte. Vols. i, ii. Freiburg-i.-B. 1892.

Muratori, L. A. Annali d' Italia. 12 vols. Milan. 1744–9. Also other editions and reprints.

Norden, W. Das Papsttum und Byzanz. Berlin. 1903.

Oman, C. W. C. History of the Art of War in the Middle Ages. 2nd edn. enl. 2 vols. London. 1924.

Oncken, W. *ed.* Allgemeine Geschichte in Einzeldarstellungen. 45 vols. Berlin. 1879–93. *Cited sub nom. auct.* (Oncken.)

Orpen, G. H. Ireland under the Normans (1169–1333). 4 vols. Oxford. 1911–20.

Pertile, A. Storia del diritto italiano dalla caduta dell' impero Romano alla codificazione. 2nd edn. Del Giudice, P. 6 vols. Turin. 1892–1902. Index. Eusebio, L. Turin. 1893.

Petit de Julleville, L. *ed.* Histoire de la langue et de la littérature française. 8 vols. Paris. 1896–1900.

Pirenne, H. Histoire de Belgique. 5 vols. Brussels. Vol. i. 3rd edn. 1909. Vol. ii. 2nd edn. 1903.

Pollock, F. and Maitland, F. W. The history of English Law before Edward I. 2nd edn. 2 vols. Cambridge. 1898.

Poole, R. L. Illustrations of the history of Medieval Thought and Learning 2nd edn. London. 1920.

Previté-Orton, C. W. Outlines of Medieval History. 2nd edn. Cambridge. 1924.

Ranke, L. von. Weltgeschichte. 9 vols. Leipsic. 1831–8. And later edns.

Rashdall, H. The Universities of Europe in the Middle Ages. New edn. Powicke, F. M. and Emden, A. B. 3 vols. Oxford.

Reichel, O. J. The elements of Canon Law. London. 1887.

Richter, G. and Kohl, H. Annalen d. deutschen Geschichte im Mittelalter. 3 pts. in 5. Halle-a.-S. 1873–93.

Savigny, F. C. von. Geschichte des Römischen Rechts im Mittelalter. 2nd edn. 7 vols. Heidelberg. 1834–51. French transl. Guenoux, C. 4 vols. Paris. 1839.

Schaube, A. Handelsgeschichte der romanischen Völker des Mittelmeergebiets bis zum Ende der Kreuzzüge. (Below-Meinecke. *See above*, I.) Munich. 1906.

Schröder, R. Lehrbuch der deutschen Rechtsgeschichte. 6th edn. Ed. Künnsberg, E. von. Berlin and Leipsic. 1922.

Schupfer, F. Manuale di storia del diritto italiano. 3rd edn. Città di Castello. 1904.

Sismondi, J. C. L. S. de. Hist. des républiques italiennes du moyen âge. 16 vols. Paris. 1809–18. New edn. 10 vols. 1840.

Storia letteraria d' Italia scritta da una società di professori. Milan. 1900 ff.

Storia politica d' Italia scritta da una società d' amici. Ed. Villari, P. 8 vols. Milan. 1875–82.

Storia politica d' Italia scritta da una società di professori. Vols. I–VIII. Milan, in progress.

Stubbs, W. Constitutional History of England. 3 vols. Oxford. 1873–8. (Frequently reprinted.) French transl. Lefebvre, G., with notes and studies by Petit-Dutaillis, C. Vols. I, II. Paris. 1907, 13. English transl. of notes, etc. Ed. Tait, J. Studies and notes supplementary to Stubbs' Constitutional History. Vol. I. Transl. Rhodes, W. E. Vol. II. Transl. Waugh, W. T. Manchester. 1908, 14.

Tiraboschi, G. Storia della letteratura italiana. New edn. 9 vols. in 16. Florence. 1805–13. Milan. 1822–6.

Überweg, F. Grundriss der Geschichte der Philosophie. 10th edn. Ed. Heinze, M and Prächter, K. 4 vols. Berlin. 1904–9. [Bibliography.]

Vinogradoff, P. Roman Law in Mediaeval Europe. London and New York. 1909. [Bibliographies.]

Viollet, P. Histoire du droit civil français. 3rd edn. Paris. 1905.

—— Histoire des institutions politiques et administratives de la France. 3 vols. Paris. 1890–1903.

Waitz, G. Deutsche Verfassungsgeschichte. Vols. V–VIII. Vol. V. 2nd edn. Zeumer, K. Berlin. 1893; Vol. VI. 2nd edn. Seeliger, G. Berlin. 1896; Vol. VIII. Kiel. 1878.

Weil, G. Geschichte der Chalifen. 3 vols. Mannheim. 1846–51.

—— Geschichte der islamitischen Völker von Mohammed bis zur Zeit des Sultans Selim. Stuttgart. 1866.

Werminghoff, A. Geschichte der Kirchenverfassung Deutschlands im Mittelalter. Vol. I. Hanover and Leipsic. 1905.

Young, G. F. East and West through fifteen centuries. Vols. I, II. London. 1916.

Zachariae von Lingenthal, K. E. Geschichte des griechisch-römischen Rechts. 3rd edn. Berlin. 1892.

Zeller, J. Histoire d'Allemagne. Vols. I–IX. Paris. 1872–91. [No more publ.]

CHAPTER I.

THE REFORM OF THE CHURCH.

[Only the chief works are given, as the literature is so voluminous.]

I. BIBLIOGRAPHIES.

(*a*) Useful bibliographies will be found in:

Berlière, L'Ordre monastique, etc. (*see below*, III).
Cauchie, La Querelle des Investitures, etc. (*see below*, III).
Dresdner, Kultur- u. Sittengeschichte, etc. [short] (*see below*, III);

also in special notes in:

Hefele-Leclercq, Les Conciles (*see Gen. Bibl.* v).
Meyer von Knonau, Jahrbücher, etc. (*see below*, III).

(*b*) Very useful special bibliographies:

For Leo IX. Hefele-Leclercq, *op. cit.* IV, p. 995, note 1 (*see Gen. Bibl.* v).
For Peter Damian. *Ibid.* IV, p. 1231, note 3.
For Berengar of Tours. *Ibid.* IV, p. 1041, note 3.
For the Election Decree of 1059. Meyer v. Knonau, *op. cit.* I, Excursus VII, p. 678, and Hefele-Leclercq, *op. cit.* IV, p. 1139, note 2.

II. SOURCES.

(*a*) SEPARATE SOURCES.

See the Bibliographies (*Section*, Sources) of the following chapters of Vol. III: v (specially for Fulbert and Gerbert); VII (specially for Atto of Vercelli and Hugo abbas Farfensis); XII (specially for Anonymus Haserensis, Anselmus Leodensis, Lampertus Hersfeldensis, Leo episcopus Ostiensis); and XVII. Other specially important sources are:

Arnulf. Gesta archiepiscoporum Mediolanensium. Ed. Bethmann, L. C. and Wattenbach, W. MGH. Script. VIII. pp. 1–31. Repr. *in* MPL. CXLVII. coll. 279 sqq.

Bonitho. Liber ad amicum. Ed. Dümmler, E. *in* MGH. Libelli de Lite. I. pp. 568 sqq. 1891; *also* ed. Jaffé, P. *in* Monumenta Gregoriana. 1865. (Bibl. rer. German. II. *See Gen. Bibl.* IV.) *Also in* MPL. CL. coll. 803 sqq.

Desiderius, Abbot of Monte Cassino (Pope Victor III). Dialogi de miraculis S. Benedicti. *In* ASBen. Saec. IV, 2 pp. 425–61, *and* MPL. CXLIX. coll. 963 sqq.

Gesta Episcoporum Virdunensium. Ed. Waitz, G. MGH. Script. IV. pp. 36–51, and x. pp. 486–516. Repr. *in* MPL. CXXXII. coll. 501 sqq., and CCIV. coll. 915 sqq.

Hugo Flaviniacensis. Chronicon. Ed. Pertz, G. H. MGH. Script. VIII. pp. 368–404. *Also in* MPL. CLIV. coll. 1 sqq.

Humbert of Silva Candida, Cardinal. Tres libri contra simoniacos. Ed. Thaner, F. *in* MGH. Libelli de Lite. I. pp. 95–253. *Also* ed. Martène and Durand *in* Thesaurus Novus. v. pp. 629 sqq. Repr. *in* MPL. CXLIII.

Landulf Senior. Historia Mediolanensis. Ed. Bethmann, L. C. and Wattenbach, W. MGH. Script. VIII. pp. 32–100. *Also in* MPL. CXLVII. coll. 803 sqq.

Landulf Junior (de S. Paulo). Historia Mediolanensis. Ed. Bethmann, L. C. and Jaffé, P. MGH. Script. XX. pp. 21–49. *Also in* MPL. CLXXIII. coll. 1429 sqq.

Liber Pontificalis. *See Gen. Bibl.* IV.

Peter Damian. Opera. Ed. Caietanus, C. 3 vols. Rome. 1606–15. Repr. *in* MPL. CXLIV, CXLV.

—— Disceptatio synodalis. Ed. Heinemann, L. v. *in* MGH. Libelli de Lite. I. pp. 76–94. *Also in* MPL. CXLV.

[Extracts in English in Greenwood, Cathedra Petri. IV. pp. 423–7. (*See below*, III.)]

Peter Damian. Liber gratissimus. Ed. Heinemann, L. v. *in* MGH. Libelli de Lite. ɪ. pp. 15–75. *Also in* MPL. cxlv.
—— De Legatione Mediolanensi relatio. Ed. Watterich, J. M. *in* Pontif. Roman.... vitae. *See Gen. Bibl.* ɪv. *Also in* MPL. cxlv. coll. 89 sqq.
Ratherius of Verona. Opera. Ed. Ballerini, P. and H. Verona. 1765. *Also in* MPL. cxxxvi. coll. 1 sqq.
Vita S. Arialdi auct. Andrea. ASBoll. Iunii (die 27) vɪɪ. pp. 252–72. (Paris and Rome. 1867.) *Also in* MPL. cxlɪɪɪ. coll. 1457 sqq.
Vita Popponis abbatis Stabulensis. Ed. Wattenbach, W. MGH. Script. xɪ. pp. 291 sqq.
Vita Richardi abbatis S. Vitoni Virdunensis. Ed. Wattenbach, W. MGH. Script. xɪ. pp. 280 sqq. *Also in* ASBen. Saec. vɪ, 1. pp. 519 sqq.
Vita Wilhelmi auct. Rodulfo Glabro. MPL. cxlɪɪ. coll. 697 sqq.

(*b*) Collections of Sources, etc.

Jaffé, P. Monumenta Bambergensia. 1869. (Bibl. rer. German. v. *See Gen. Bibl.* ɪv.)
Jaffé-Loewenfeld. Regesta Pontif. Roman. *See Gen. Bibl.* ɪv.
Kehr and Brackmann. Regesta Pontif. Roman. *See Gen. Bibl.* ɪv.
Libelli de Lite. Vol. ɪ. MGH. 1891.
Liebermann, F. Die Gesetze der Angelsachsen. *See Gen. Bibl.* ɪv.
Mabillon and d'Achery. ASBen. *See Gen. Bibl.* ɪv.
Mansi. Sacrorum Conciliorum collectio. *See Gen. Bibl.* ɪv.
Martène and Durand. Thesaurus novus anecdotorum. *See Gen. Bibl.* ɪv.
Mirbt. Quellen zur Gesch. d. Papsttums, etc. *See Gen. Bibl.* ɪv.
Watterich. Pontif. Roman....vitae. *See Gen. Bibl.* ɪv. [Very useful collection; later editions of the texts should be consulted.]

III. MODERN WORKS.

Balzani, U. Le Cronache italiane, etc. *See Gen. Bibl.* ɪ. Engl. transl. of first edn. Early Chroniclers of Europe: Italy. London. 1883. [Short sketch, excellent on rise of historical writing in Italian monasteries in the xɪ century.]
Berlière, U. L'Ordre monastique des origines au xɪɪ^e siècle. 3rd edn. Lille, Paris, Maredsous. 1924.
Biron, R. Saint Pierre Damien. 2nd edn. Paris. 1908. [Very useful; a good appreciation.]
Borino, G. B. Per la storia della riforma della Chiesa nel secolo x. ASRSP. xxxɪx. 1916.
Butler, E. C. Benedictine monachism. London. 1919.
Cauchie, A. La Querelle des Investitures dans les diocèses de Liège et de Cambrai. Vol. ɪ. Louvain. 1890. [Most useful.]
Delarc, O. Le Pontificat de Nicolas II. RQH. xɪ. 1886. pp. 401 sqq.
Drehmann, J. Papst Leo IX und die Simonie. Leipsic and Berlin. 1908.
Dresdner, A. Kultur- und Sittengeschichte der italienischen Geistlichkeit im 10 und 11 Jahrhundert. Breslau. 1890.
Duchesne, L. Études sur le Liber Pontificalis. Paris. 1877.
—— Les Premiers temps de l'État Pontificale. 3rd edn. 1911. Engl. transl. Mathew, A. H. The beginnings of the temporal sovereignty of the Popes. London. 1908.
Fleury, C. Histoire ecclésiastique. *See Gen. Bibl.* v. [Still most useful; written with command of the literature and with insight.]
Fliche, A. Études sur la polémique religieuse à l'époque de Grégoire VII: les prégrégoriens. Paris. 1916. [Useful; but lays too much stress on Cluniac influence.]
Fournier, P. Études sur les fausses décrétales. RHE. vɪɪ (1906). pp. 33–51, 301–316, 543–64, 761–84, and vɪɪɪ (1907). pp. 19–56.
—— Le Décret de Burchard de Worms. RHE. xɪɪ (1911). pp. 451–73, 670–701.
Giesebrecht, W. von. Geschichte d. deutschen Kaiserzeit. *See Gen. Bibl.* v.
—— Die Gesetzgebung der römischen Kirche zur Zeit Gregors VII. *In* Münchner histor. Jahrbuch. ɪɪ. Munich. 1866.

Gieseler, J. C. L. Lehrbuch der Kirchengeschichte. *See Gen. Bibl.* v.

Gigalski, B. Bruno, Bischof von Segni, Abt von Monte-Cassino (1049–1123). Münster. 1898.

Greenwood, T. Cathedra Petri. A political history of the great Latin Patriarchate. 6 vols. 1856–72. [Anti-papal; much use of original authorities, and long extracts translated.]

Halfmann, H. Cardinal Humbert: sein Leben und seine Werke. Göttingen. 1882. [diss.]

Hartmann, L. M. Geschichte Italiens. *See Gen. Bibl.* v.

Hauck, A. Kirchengeschichte Deutschlands. Vol. III. *See Gen. Bibl.* v. [Indispensable.]

Heurtevent, R. Durand de Troarn et les origines de l'hérésie bérengarienne. Paris. 1912. [Useful, especially for studies of the day.]

Imbart de la Tour, P. Les Élections épiscopales dans l'église de France du IXe au XIIe siècle. Paris. 1891.

—— Les Paroisses rurales dans l'ancienne France du IVe au XIe siècle. RH. LX, LXI, LXIII, and LXVII. *Also* separately. Paris. 1900.

Jordan, K. Zur päpstlichen Finanzgeschichte im 11. und 12. Jahrh. *In* Quellen und Forschungen aus ital. Archiven und Bibliotheken. XXV. 1933–4.

Kleinermanns, J. Der heilige Petrus Damiani, Mönch, Bischof, Cardinal, Kirchenvater. Steyl. 1882. [Good and detailed.]

Krüger, A. Die Pataria in Mailand. Breslau. 1903–4. [progr.]

Kühn, L. Petrus Damiani und seine Anschauungen über Staat und Kirchen. Karlsruhe. 1913.

Langen, J. Geschichte d. römischen Kirche. *See Gen. Bibl.* v.

Lea, H. C. History of Sacerdotal Celibacy. *See Gen. Bibl.* v.

Lehmann, R. Forschungen zur Geschichte des Abtes Hugo I von Cluny (1049–1109). Göttingen. 1869. [diss.]

Ley, K. A. Die kölnische Kirchengeschichte im Anschlusse an die Geschichte der kölnischen Bischöfe und Erzbischöfe. Cologne. 1883.

Lindner, T. Anno II der Heilige, Erzbischof von Köln. Leipsic. 1869.

Lorenz, O. Papstwahl und Kirchenrecht. Berlin. 1874.

Lübberstedt, W. Die Stellung des deutschen Klerus auf päpstlichen Generalkonzilien von Leo IX bis Gregor VII. Cöthen-Anhalt. 1911. [Greifswald diss.]

Luchaire, A. Les Premiers Capétiens. (Lavisse, Histoire de France, II. 2. *See Gen. Bibl.* v.)

—— La Société française au temps de Philippe-Auguste. 2nd edn. Paris. 1909. Engl. transl. Krehbiel, E. B. Social France at the time of Philip Augustus. London. 1912. [Good sketches of clerical and monastic life a little later.]

Ludewig, P. Poppo von Stablo und die Klosterreformen unter den ersten Salier Breslau. 1883.

Meyer von Knonau, G. Jahrbücher des Deutschen Reiches unter Heinrich IV und Heinrich V. 7 vols. Leipsic. 1890–1909.

Mirbt, C. Die Publizistik im Zeitalter Gregors VII. Leipsic. 1894.

Neander, A. Allgemeine Geschichte d. christl. Religion u. Kirche. 6 vols. Hamburg. 1826–52. Engl. transl. Torrey, J., rev. by Morrison, A. J. W. 9 vols. London. 1850–8. [Still most useful; written with command of the literature and with insight.]

Neukirch, F. Das Leben des Petrus Damiani. Pt. I. Bis zur Ostersynode 1059. Göttingen. 1875. [diss.] [No more publ. A critical appendix on the letters, with chronology and notes. Excellent.]

Päch, H. Die Pataria in Mailand. Sondershausen. 1893.

Panvinius, O. De episcopatibus, titulis, et diaconiis cardinalium. Paris. 1609.

Pellegrini, C. I santi Arialdo ed Erlembaldo. Milan. 1897.

Pflugk-Harttung, J. v. Die Papstwahlen und die Kaisertum. ZKG. XXVII (1906). pp. 276–95; XXVIII (1907). pp. 14–36, 159–87, 299–369.

Polzin, H. Die Abtswahlen in den Reichsabteien von 1024–1056. Greifswald. 1908. [diss.]

Poole, R. L. Benedict IX and Gregory VI. *In* Proc. British Acad. VIII. London. 1917–18.

—— Illustrations of...Medieval Thought and Learning. *See Gen. Bibl.* v.

Poole, R. L.   Lectures on the history of the Papal Chancery down to the time of Innocent III. Cambridge. 1915.
—— The names and numbers of Medieval Popes. EHR. xxxii (1917), pp. 465–78.
—— Studies in chronology and history. Oxford. 1934.
Sackur, E. Die Cluniacenser. 2 vols. Halle. 1892, 94.
—— Richard von St Vannes. Breslau. 1886. [diss.]
Saltet, L. Les Réordinations. Paris. 1907.
Scharnagl, A. Der Begriff der Investitur in den Quellen und der Literatur des Investiturstreites. (Kirchenrechtliche Abhandlungen. Ed. Stutz, U. No. 86.) Stuttgart. 1908.
Schnitzer, J. Berengar von Tours. Stuttgart. 1892. [Most useful, full.]
Solmi, A. Stato e chiesa secondo gli scritti politici da Carlomagno fino al Concordato di Worms. Modena. 1901. [See review by Cauchie, A. *in* RHE. v (1904). pp. 573–88.]
Stutz, U. Die Eigenkirche als Element des mittelalterlich-germanischen Kirchenrechts. Berlin. 1895.
—— Geschichte des kirchlichen Benefizialwesens von seinen Anfängen bis auf die Zeit Alexanders III. Vol. i. Pt. i. Berlin. 1895.
—— Die kirchliche Rechtsgeschichte. Stuttgart. 1905.
Sudendorf, H. Berengar Turonensis oder eine Sammlung ihn betreffenden Briefe. Hamburg and Gotha. [Useful for Popes as well as for Berengar.]
Thomas, P. Le Droit de propriété des laïques sur les églises et le patronage laïque au moyen âge. Paris. 1906.
Vacandard, E. Études de critique et d'histoire religieuse. 1ʳᵉ série. Les origines du célibat ecclésiastique. 5th edn. Paris. 1913. pp. 71–120. [A clear historical sketch.]
Vogel, A. Ratherius von Verona und das 10 Jahrhundert. 2 pts. Jena. 1854.
Wattenbach, W. Deutschlands Geschichtsquellen im Mittelalter bis zur Mitte des 13 Jahrhunderts. *See Gen. Bibl.* i.
Wedemann, M. Gottfried der Bärtige. Leipsic. 1875. [diss.]
Werminghoff, A. Verfassungsgeschichte der deutschen Kirche im Mittelalter. 2nd edn. (Grundriss d. Geschichtswissenschaft. Ed. Meister, A. ii, 6.) Leipsic and Berlin. 1913.
Whitney, J. P. Pope Gregory VII and the Hildebrandine ideal. CQR. lxx (1910). pp. 414–46.
—— Gregory VII. EHR. xxxiv (1919). pp. 134 sqq [Both these for earlier movements.]
—— Peter Damiani. *In* Cambridge Historical Journal. October, 1925.
—— Hildebrandine Essays. Cambridge. 1932. [Reprints the above revised with additions.]
Will, C. Die Anfänge der Restauration der Kirche im 11. Jahrhundert. Pts i, ii. Marburg. 1859, 64.
Zoepffel, R. Die Papstwahlen und die mit ihnen im nächsten Zusammenhange stehenden Ceremonien in ihrer Entwickelung von 11. bis zum 14. Jahrhundert. Göttingen. 1871.

CHAPTERS II and III.

GREGORY VII: HENRY IV AND HENRY V.

[On the relations of the Papacy with France, England, and the Normans in South Italy, *see* Bibliographies to chapters IV, XV, XVIII, and Vol. III, chapter V.]

I. BIBLIOGRAPHIES.

Detailed in Dahlmann-Waitz, and critical treatment of original authorities in Potthast, Wattenbach, and Vildhaut (*see Gen. Bibl.* I). An excellent annual survey of new literature in Jahresberichte der deutschen Geschichte (Breslau); also bibliographies in Revue d'histoire ecclésiastique (Louvain) and other journals.

II. SOURCES.

A. Collections of Documents, etc.

(a) Papal letters and bulls.
Calendared in Jaffé-Loewenfeld. Regesta Pontificum Romanorum. *See Gen. Bibl.* IV. Kehr, P. Regesta Pontificum Romanorum. *See Gen. Bibl.* IV.
Gregorii VII Registrum. Ed. Caspar, E. MGH. Epp. select. II. 1920, 23. [*Cf.* Peitz, W. M. Das Originalregister Gregors VII. Vienna. 1911.]
Monumenta Gregoriana. Ed. Jaffé, P. (Bibl. rer. German. Vol. II. *See Gen. Bibl.* IV.) [Contains letters collected from various sources as well as the Registrum.]
Bullaire du pape Calixte II, 1119–24. Ed. Robert, U. 2 vols. Paris. 1891
Letters of other Popes in MPL.

(b) Church Councils.
Mansi, J. D. Sacrorum conciliorum collectio. *See Gen. Bibl.* IV.

(c) Lives of Popes.
Le Liber Pontificalis. Ed. Duchesne, L. *See Gen. Bibl.* IV.
Watterich, J. M. Pontificum Romanorum vitae. *See Gen. Bibl.* IV.

(d) Controversial literature.
Collected in MGH. Libelli de lite. 3 vols. 1891–7.

(e) Imperial acts and diplomas.
MGH. Constitutiones. Legum Sect. IV, I. Ed. Weiland, L. 1893.
Stumpf-Brentano, K. F. Die Reichskanzler. *See Gen. Bibl.* IV.

(f) Other letters and documents in:
Giesebrecht, W. von. Geschichte der deutschen Kaiserzeit. Vol. III. *See Gen. Bibl.* V.
Jaffé, P. Monumenta Bambergensia (Bibl. rer. German. Vol. V. *See Gen. Bibl.* IV).
Sudendorf, H. Registrum oder merkwürdige Urkunden für die deutsche Geschichte. 3 pts. Pt. I, Jena. 1849. Pts. II, III, Berlin. 1851, 54.

(g) Selected documents.
Altmann, W. and Bernheim, E. Ausgewählte Urkunden zur Erläuterung der Verfassungsgeschichte Deutschlands im Mittelalter. 4th edn. Berlin. 1909.
Bernheim, E. Quellen zur Geschichte des Investiturstreites. 2 pts. Leipsic and Berlin. 1907.
Keutgen, F. Urkunden zur städtischen Verfassungsgeschichte. Berlin. 1901.

B. Narrative Sources.

[The most important are marked *. Authorities quoted in SGUS. are improved editions of texts previously edited in MGH. Script.]

*Adam Bremensis, Gesta pontificum Hammaburgensium. Ed. Schmeidler, B. SGUS. 3rd edn.

Annales Altahenses maiores. Ed. Oefele, E. L. B. ab. SGUS. 1891.

Annales Augustani. Ed. Pertz, G. H. MGH. Script. III.

Annales Hildesheimenses. Ed. Waitz, G. SGUS. 1878.

*Annales Patherbrunnenses. Ed. Scheffer-Boichorst, P. Innsbruck. 1870.

*Arnulfi Gesta Archiepiscoporum Mediolanensium. Ed. Bethmann, L. and Wattenbach, W. MGH. Script. VIII.

Benzonis episcopi Albensis ad Heinricum IV imperatorem libri VII. Ed. Pertz K. MGH. Script. XI.

*Bernoldi Chronicon. Ed. Pertz, G. H. MGH. Script. V.

*Bertholdi Annales. Ed. Pertz, G. H. MGH. Script. V. [Begins as a continuation of Herman of Reichenau. From 1075 onwards, owing to the change in style and the violent anti-imperial bias, a new author has been conjectured, usually referred to as the Swabian Annalist. *Cf.* Meyer von Knonau, Jahrbücher. Vol. II. Excurs 8. *See below*, III A.]

*Bonizonis episcopi Sutrensis liber ad amicum. Ed. Dümmler, G. MGH. Libelli de lite. Vol. II. Also in Jaffé, P., Monumenta Gregoriana. *See above*, II A (a).

*Bruno, De bello Saxonico. Ed. Wattenbach, W. SGUS. 1880.

*Carmen de bello Saxonico. Ed. Holder-Egger, O. SGUS. 1889.

Chronicon Sancti Huberti Andaginensis. Ed. Bethmann, L. and Wattenbach, W. MGH. Script. VIII.

Cosmae Pragensis, Chronica Boemorum. Ed. Bretholz, B. MGH. Script. N.S. II. 1923.

*Donizonis vita Mathildis. Ed. Bethmann, L. MGH. Script. XII.

*Ekkehardi Chronicon Universale. Ed. Waitz, G. MGH. Script. VI. [H. Bresslau, *in* Neu. Arch. XXI, pp. 197 sqq., shews that the original chronicle up to 1101 was written by Frutolf of Bamberg.]

Gesta episcoporum Cameracensium. Ed. Bethmann, L. MGH. Script. VII.

Gesta Treverorum. Ed. Waitz, G. MGH. Script. VIII.

Herimanni Augiensis Chronicon (Herman of Reichenau). Ed. Pertz, G. H. MGH. Script. V.

*Hugonis abbatis Flaviniacensis Chronicon. Ed. Pertz, G. H. MGH. Script. VIII.

*Lamperti Hersfeldensis Annales. Ed. Holder-Egger, O. SGUS. 1894.

Landulfi Historia Mediolanensis. Ed. Bethmann, L. and Wattenbach, W. MGH. Script. VIII.

Mariani Scotti Chronicon. Ed. Waitz, G. MGH. Script. V.

Nortberti Vita Bennonis II episcopi Osnabrugensis. Ed. Bresslau, H. SGUS. 1902.

Sächsische Weltchronik (Eike von Repgow). Ed. Weiland, L. MGH. Deutsche Chroniken. II. 1877.

Sigeberti Gemblacensis monachi Chronica; Anselmi Gemblacensis continuatio. Ed. Bethmann, L. MGH. Script. VI.

Vita Altmanni episcopi Pataviensis. Ed. Wattenbach, W. MGH. Script. XII.

Vita Annonis archiepiscopi Coloniensis. Ed. Köpke, R. MGH. Script. XI.

Vita Anselmi episcopi Lucensis. Ed. Wilmans, R. MGH. Script. XII.

*Vita Heinrici IV imperatoris. Ed. Eberhard, W. SGUS. 1899.

Vita Ottonis episcopi Bambergensis. Ed. Köpke, R. MGH. Script. XII. Also in Jaffé, P., Monumenta Bambergensia. *See above*, II A (f).

III. MODERN LITERATURE.

[A complete bibliography would cover several pages. It seems better, therefore, to give a list only of the most useful books, especially in Section D. Besides the general bibliographies, such as Dahlmann-Waitz (*see Gen. Bibl.* I), most of the books mentioned below contain bibliographies.]

A. General Histories of the Period.

Gerdes, H. Geschichte des deutschen Volkes und seiner Kultur im Mittelalter Vol. II. Leipsic. 1898.

Giesebrecht, W. von. Geschichte der deutschen Kaiserzeit. Vol. III. *See Gen. Bibl.* v.
Hampe, K. Deutsche Kaisergeschichte in der Zeit der Salier und Staufer. 5th edn. *See Gen. Bibl.* v.
Lamprecht, K. Deutsche Geschichte. Vol. II. *See Gen. Bibl.* v.
Manitius, M. Deutsche Geschichte unter den sächsischen und salischen Kaisern (911–1125). Stuttgart. 1889.
Meister, A. Grundriss der Geschichtswissenschaft. Vol. II. *See Gen. Bibl.* I.
Meyer von Knonau, G. Jahrbücher des Deutschen Reiches unter Heinrich IV und Heinrich V. 7 vols. Leipsic. 1890–1909. [Valuable collection of all the evidence, and good bibliographies.]
Nitzsch, K. W. Geschichte des deutschen Volkes. Ed. Matthäi, G. Vol. II. Leipsic. 1883.
Richter, G. and Kohl, H. Annalen der deutschen Geschichte im Mittelalter. Vol. III, 2. Halle. 1898.
Schäfer, D. Deutsche Geschichte. Vol. I. Jena. 1910.

B. Church History and Institutions.

Bernheim, E. Politische Begriffe der Mittelalter im Lichte der Anschauungen Augustins. DZG. Neue Folge, I. 1896–7.
—— Mittelalterliche Zeitanschauungen in ihrem Einfluss auf Politik und Geschichtschreibung. Pt. I. Die Zeitanschauungen. Tübingen. 1918.
Fournier, P. Les collections canoniques romaines de l'époque de Grégoire VII. *In* Mém. AcadIBL. XLI. Paris. 1918.
Halphen, L. Études sur l'administration de Rome au moyen âge (751–1252). (BHE.) Paris. 1907.
Hauck, A. Kirchengeschichte Deutschlands. Vol. III. *See Gen. Bibl.* v.
Hefele, C. J. Conciliengeschichte. French edn. by Leclercq, H. (Histoire des Conciles.) *See Gen. Bibl.* v.
Hinschius, P. Das Kirchenrecht. *See Gen. Bibl.* v.
Imbart de la Tour, P. Les élections épiscopales dans l'église de France du IXe au XIIe siècle. (Étude sur la décadence du principe électif, 814–1150.) Paris. 1891.
Poole, R. L. Lectures on the history of the Papal Chancery down to the time of Innocent III. Cambridge. 1915.
Saltet, L. Les Réordinations: étude sur le sacrement de l'ordre. Paris. 1907.
Scharnagl, A. Der Begriff der Investitur in den Quellen nach der Litteratur des Investiturstreits. (Kirchenrechtliche Abhandlungen. Ed. Stutz, U. No. 56.) Stuttgart. 1908.
Schreiber, G. Kurie und Kloster im 12 Jahrhundert. 2 vols. (Kirchenrechtliche Abhandlungen. Ed. Stutz, U. Nos. 65–68.) Stuttgart. 1910.
Stutz, U. Die Eigenkirche als Element des mittelalterlich-germanischen Kirchenrechts. Berlin. 1895.
—— Geschichte des kirchlichen Benefizialwesens bis auf Alexander III. Vol. I. Berlin. 1895.
Werminghoff, A. Geschichte der Kirchenverfassung Deutschlands im Mittelalter. Vol. I. Hanover and Leipsic. 1905.

C. German History and Institutions.

Below, G. von. Der deutsche Staat des Mittelalters. Vol. I. Die allgemeinen Fragen. Leipsic. 1914.
Bretholz, B. Geschichte Böhmens und Mährens bis zum Aussterben der Premysliden (1306). Munich and Leipsic. 1912.
Brunner, H. Deutsche Rechtsgeschichte. *See Gen. Bibl.* v.
—— Grundzüge der deutschen Rechtsgeschichte. 7th edn. *See Gen. Bibl.* v.
Fisher, H. A. L. The Medieval Empire. 2 vols. London. 1898.
Heusinger, B. Servitium regis in der deutschen Kaiserzeit. Berlin and Leipsic. 1922. *Also in* Archiv für Urkundenforschung. Vol. VIII. Leipsic.
Inama-Sternegg, K. T. von. Deutsche Wirtschaftsgeschichte. Vol. II. Leipsic. 1891.
Lamprecht, K. Deutsches Wirtschaftsleben im Mittelalter. 3 vols. Leipsic. 1885–6.

Mayer, E. Deutsche und französische Verfassungsgeschichte vom 9 bis zum 14 Jahrhundert. 2 vols. Leipsic. 1899.

Nitzsch, K. W. Ministerialität und Bürgertum im 11 und 12 Jahrhundert. Leipsic. 1859.

Pirenne, H. Histoire de Belgique. Vol. I. *See Gen. Bibl.* v.

Schröder, R. Lehrbuch der deutschen Rechtsgeschichte. 6th edn. Ed. Künnsberg, E. von. Berlin and Leipsic. 1922.

Schulte, A. Der Adel und die deutsche Kirche im Mittelalter. (Kirchenrechtliche Abhandlungen. Ed. Stutz, U. Nos. 63 and 64.) Stuttgart. 1910.

Stimming, M. Das deutsche Königsgut im 11 und 12 Jahrhundert. Pt. I. Die Salierzeit. (Ebering's Historische Studien, No. 149.) Berlin. 1922.

Waitz, G. Deutsche Verfassungsgeschichte. Vols. v–viii. *See Gen. Bibl.* v.

For bibliography of the history of the towns in Germany, *see above*, Schröder, Lehrbuch, § 51.

D. Special Works.

Böhmer, H. Kirche und Staat in England und in der Normandie im xi und xii Jahrhundert. Leipsic. 1899.

Cauchie, A. La querelle des investitures dans les diocèses de Liège et de Cambrai. 2 vols. Louvain. 1890–1.

Chalandon, F. Histoire de la domination normande en Italie et en Sicile. Vol. I. Paris. 1907.

Delarc, O. Saint Grégoire VII et la réforme de l'église au xie siècle. 3 vols. Paris. 1889–90.

Fliche, A. Études sur la polémique religieuse à l'époque de Grégoire VII. Les Prégrégoriens. Paris. 1916.

Friedrich, R. Studien zur Vorgeschichte von Canossa. 2 pts. Hamburg. 1905, 8.

Giesebrecht, W. von. Die Gesetzgebung der römischen Kirche zur Zeit Gregors VII. *In* Münchner Historisches Jahrbuch. Vol. II. Munich. 1866.

Guleke, H. Deutschlands innere Kirchenpolitik von 1105–11. Dorpat. 1882. [diss.]

Gundlach, W. Ein Diktator aus der Kanzlei Kaiser Heinrichs IV. Innsbruck. 1884.

Kilian, E. Itinerar Kaiser Heinrichs IV. Karlsruhe. 1886.

Kolbe, F. Erzbischof Adalbert I von Mainz und Heinrich V. Heidelberg. 1872.

Martens, W. Gregor VII, sein Leben und Wirken. Leipsic. 1894.

Mirbt, C. Die Stellung Augustins in der Publizistik des gregorianischen Kirchenstreites. Leipsic. 1888.

—— Die Publizistik im Zeitalter Gregors VII. Leipsic. 1894.

Monod, B. Essai sur les rapports de Pascal II avec Philippe I, 1099–1108. (BHE. 164.) Paris. 1907.

Overmann, A. Gräfin Mathilde von Tuscien, ihre Besitzungen, Geschichte ihres Guts, 1115–1230, und ihre Regesten. Innsbruck. 1895.

Peiser, G. Der deutsche Investiturstreit unter König Heinrich V bis zu dem päpstlichen Privileg vom 13 April 1111. Berlin. 1883.

Previté-Orton, C. W. The early history of the House of Savoy, 1000–1233. Cambridge. 1912.

Robert, U. Histoire du pape Calixte II. Paris. 1891.

Sägmüller, J. B. Die Idee Gregors VII vom Primate in der päpstlichen Kanzlei. *In* Theologische Quartalschrift. Vol. LXXVIII. Tübingen. 1896.

Sander, P. Der Kampf Heinrichs IV und Gregors VII von der zweiten Exkommunikation des Königs bis zu seiner Kaiserkrönung (März 1080 bis März 1084). Strasbourg. 1893.

Whitney, J. P. Gregory VII. EHR. Vol. xxxiv. 1919. [Excellent account of the literature on the subject.]

—— Pope Gregory VII and the Hildebrandine ideal. CQR. LXX. 1910.

On the Concordat of Worms:

Bernheim, E. Zur Geschichte des Wormser Konkordats. Göttingen. 1878.

—— Das Wormser Konkordat und seine Vorurkunden hinsichtlich Entstehung, Formulierung, Rechtsgültigkeit. (Gierke's Untersuchungen zur deutschen Staats- und Rechtsgeschichte, No. 81.) Breslau. 1906.

Hofmeister, A. Das Wormser Konkordat. Zum Streit um seine Bedeutung. (Forschungen und Versuche zur Geschichte des Mittelalters und der Neuzeit. Festschrift Dietrich Schäfer zum 70 Geburtstag dargebracht von seinen Schülern, IV.) Jena. 1915.

Rudorff, H. Zur Erklärung des Wormser Konkordats. (Zeumer's Quellen und Studien zur Verfassungsgeschichte des Deutschen Reiches in Mittelalter und Neuzeit, I, 4.) Weimar. 1906.

Schäfer, D. Zur Beurteilung des Wormser Konkordats. *In* Abh. d. Kön. Preuss. Akad. d. Wissenschaften. Phil.-hist. Kl. I. Berlin. 1905.

Addenda.

The three following articles appeared too late for inclusion above or to be made use of in the text:

Caspar, E. Gregor VII in seinen Briefen. HZ. 3rd ser. Vol. XXXIV. 1924.

Danckelman, E. von.   Der kriegerische Geist in den rheinischen Bischofsstädten und die Ministerialität zu Zeiten Heinrichs IV. *In* Viert. f. Sozial- und Wirtschafts-geschichte. Vol. XVIII. Leipsic. 1924.

Stephenson, C. La taille dans les villes d'Allemagne. MA. 2nd ser. Vol. XXVI. 1924.

CHAPTER IV.

THE NORMANS IN SOUTH ITALY AND SICILY.

I. SPECIAL BIBLIOGRAPHIES.

Chalandon, F. Histoire de la domination normande en Italie et en Sicile. Vol. I.
pp. xciii sqq. *See below*, III (1).
Paetow, L. J. Guide to the study of Medieval History. pp. 224–8. *See Gen. Bibl.* I.
Cf. also Capasso, B. Le fonti della storia delle provincie napolitane. *See Gen. Bibl.* I.

II. SOURCES.

A. NARRATIVE SOURCES.

(1) *Latin and French.*

Aimé of Monte Cassino. L'ystoire de li Normant. Ed. Delarc, O. Rouen. 1892.
Also ed. Bartholomaeis, V. de. (Fonti.) Rome. 1935.
Alexander Telesinus abbas. Libri IV de rebus gestis Rogerii Siciliae regis (1127–35).
Ed. Del Re, G. *in* Cronisti e scrittori sincroni napoletani. Vol. I. Dominazione
normanna nel Regno di Puglia e di Sicilia. Naples. 1845. pp. 85–148.
Annales Barenses. Ed. Pertz, G. H. MGH. Script. V. pp. 51 sqq.
Annales Beneventani. BISI. 42 (1923). pp. 101–59. *Also in* MGH. Script. III.
pp. 173 sqq.
Annales Casinenses. MGH. Script. XIX. pp. 305 sqq.
Annales Cavenses. *Ibid.* III. pp. 185 sqq.
Annales Ceccanenses. *Ibid.* XIX. pp. 276 sqq.
Anonymi Vaticani Historia sicula. RR.II.SS. 1st edn. Vol. VIII. pp. 745 sqq.
Anonymus Barensis. *Ibid.* Vol. V. pp. 147 sqq.
Chronicon Amalfitanum. Ed. Muratori, L. A. *in* Antiquitates Italicae. Vol. I.
pp. 207 sqq. *See Gen. Bibl.* IV.
Chronicon Casauriense. RR.II.SS. 1st edn. Vol. II, pt. 2. pp. 775 sqq.
Chronicon S. Bartholomaei de Carpineto. Ed. Ughelli, F. *in* Italia sacra. 2nd edn.
Vol. X. pp. 349 sqq. *See Gen. Bibl.* IV.
Chronicon Vulturnense. Ed. Federici, V. 3 vols. (Fonti.) 1925 ff.
Falcandus, Hugo. Historia de rebus gestis in Siciliae regno. Ed. Siragusa, G. B.
as La Historia o liber de regno Sicilie e la epistola ad Petrum Panormitane
ecclesie thesaurarium. (Fonti.) Rome. 1897.
Falco Beneventanus. Chronicon. Ed. Del Re, G. *in* Cronisti e scrittori sincroni
napoletani. Vol. I. Dominazione normanna (*see above*). pp. 253 sqq.
Gaufredus Malaterra. Historia sicula. Ed. Pontieri, E. RR.II.SS. New edn.
Vol. V, pt. 1.
Guillermus Apuliensis. Gesta Roberti Wiscardi. Ed. Wilmans, R. MGH. Script.
IX. pp. 239 sqq.
Ignoti monachi Cisterciensis S. Mariae de Ferraria chronica. Ed. Gaudenzi, A.
(Soc. napol. di storia patria. Mon. stor., Ser. I. Cronache.) Naples. 1888.
Leo Marsicanus (Diaconus). Chronica monasterii Casinensis. Ed. Wattenbach, W.
MGH. Script. VII. pp. 574 sqq.
Lupus Protospatarius. Chronicon. Ed. Pertz, G. H. MGH. Script. V. pp. 52 sqq.
Peter of Eboli. Carmen de rebus siculis. Ed. Rota, E. RR.II.SS. New edn.
Vol. XXXI, pt. 1. 1904–10.
Peter the Deacon. (Continuator of Leo Marsicanus from book III, ch. XXXV.)
Chronica. Ed. Wattenbach, W. MGH. Script. VII. pp. 727 sqq.
Romuald of Salerno. Chronicon sive annales. Ed. Arndt, W. MGH. Script. XIX.
pp. 398 sqq. Also ed. Garufi, C. A. RR.II.SS. New edn. Vol. VII, pt. 1. 1914 ff.

(2) *Greek.*

Choniates, Nicetas (Acominatus). Historia. Ed. Bekker, I. CSHB. 1835.

Cinnamus, John. Ἐπιτομή. Ed. Meineke, A. CSHB. 1836.

Comnena, Anna. Ἀλεξίας. Ed. Reifferscheid, A. 2 vols. (Teubner.) Leipsic. 1884.

Eustathius. De Thessalonica a Latinis capta anno 1185 liber. Ed. Bekker, I. CSHB. 1842.

Scylitzes, John. A part of his chronicle is inserted in that of Cedrenus. The second part of his work is edited by Bekker, I., at the end of the work of Cedrenus. 2 vols. CSHB. 1838-9.

Zonaras, John. Ἐπιτομὴ ἱστοριῶν. Vol. III. Ed. Büttner-Wobst, T. CSHB. 1897.

(3) *Arabic.*

The extracts from Arabic works which concern the history of the Normans in Italy are collected and translated into Italian by Amari, M. *in* Biblioteca Arabo-Sicula, vers. ital. 2 vols. and App. 8vo edn. Turin, Florence, and Rome. 1880, 89.

B. DOCUMENTS.

In the period of the Norman Monarchy an incomplete register has been published by Behring, W. Sicilianische Studien. II. Regesten des normannischen Königshauses (1130-97). Programm d. Gymn. zu Elbing. 1882. There is also Heinemann, L. v. Normannische Herzogs- und Königsurkunden. Univ. Progr. Tübingen. 1899, but its use cannot be recommended, for the greater number of the acta have been partly re-worded by the editor. *Cf.* Chalandon, *op. cit.* Vol. I, p. v, note 2. *See below*, III (1).

Documents for the Norman period are printed in numerous publications of which only the principal are here given.

Battaglia, G. Diplomi inediti relativi all' ordinamento della proprietà fondiaria in Sicilia sotto i Normanni e gli Svevi. (Soc. siciliana per la storia patria. Documenti per servire alla storia di Sicilia. Ser. I. Diplomatica. Vol. XVI.) Palermo. 1898.

Beltrani, G. Documenti Longobardi e Greci per la storia dell' Italia meridionale nel medio-evo. Rome. 1877.

Catalogus baronum neapolitano in regno versantium qui sub auspiciis Gulielmi cognomento boni ad terram sanctam sibi vindicandam crucem susceperunt. Ed. Del Re, G. *in* Cronisti e scrittori sincroni napoletani. Vol. I. Dominazione normanna (*see above*, A (1)). pp. 571 sqq.

Chartularium Cupersanense. Ed. Morea, D. Vol. I. Monte Cassino. 1893.

Codex diplomaticus Caietanus. 2 vols. Monte Cassino. 1888, 91.

Codex diplomaticus Cavensis 8 vols. Naples, Milan, and Pisa. 1873-93.

Codice diplomatico Barese. Publ. by Comm. prov. di archeol. e storia patria di Bari. Vols. I-XV. Trani. 1896 ff., in progress.

Codice diplomatico Sulmonense. Ed. Faraglia, F. Lanciano. 1888.

Cusa, S. I Diplomi greci e arabi di Sicilia. 2 vols. in 1. Palermo. 1860, 82.

Del Giudice, G. Codice diplomatico del regno di Carlo I e II d' Angiò. 2 vols. Naples. 1863, 69. [Contains a certain number of acta of the Norman period.]

Di Meo, A. Annali critico-diplomatici del regno di Napoli della mezzana età. 12 vols. Naples. 1795-1819.

Filippi, G. Patto di pace tra Ruggiero II normanno e la città di Savona. ASPN. XXIV. 1899.

Garofalo, A. Tabularium regiae ac imperialis capellae collegiatae divi Petri in regio Panormitano palatio. Palermo. 1835.

Garufi, C. A. Catalogo illustrato del tabulario di S. Maria Nuova in Monreale. (Soc. siciliana per la storia patria. Documenti per servire alla storia di Sicilia. Ser. I. Diplomatica. Vol. XIX.) Palermo.

—— I Documenti inediti dell' epoca normanna in Sicilia. Pt. I. (*Ibid.* Vol. XVIII.) 1899.

—— Le Donazioni del Conte Enrico di Paternò al monastero di S. Maria di Valle Giosafat. *In* Revue de l'Orient Latin. IX. 1902.

Kohler, C. Chartes de l'abbaye de Notre Dame de la Vallée de Josaphat. *In* Revue de l'Orient Latin. vii. 1900.

Lello, G. L. and Del Giudice, M. Descrizione del real templo e monasterio di S. Maria Nuova di Monreale. Palermo. 1702. [Contains certain acta of the Norman period in an appendix.]

Minieri-Riccio, C. Saggio di codice diplomatico formato sulle antiche scritture dell' archivio di stato di Napoli. 2 vols. and supplt. Naples. 1878–83.

Mongitore, A. Bullae, privilegia, et instrumenta Panormitanae metropolitanae ecclesiae regni Siciliae primariae. Palermo. 1734.

Prologo, A. G. Le Carte che si conservano nello archivio del capitolo metropolitano della città di Trani. Barletta. 1877.

Starrabba, R. I Diplomi della cattedrale di Messina. Vol. i. (Soc. siciliana per la storia patria. Documenti per servire alla storia di Sicilia. Ser. i. Diplomatica. Vol. i.) Palermo. 1876.

Trinchera, F. Syllabus Graecarum membranarum. Naples. 1865.

Numerous acta are reproduced either completely or partially in the following works: Gattola, E. Historia abbatiae Cassinensis. 2 vols. in 1. Venice. 1733; Gregorio, R. Considerazioni sopra la storia di Sicilia. 2nd edn. Vol. i. Palermo. 1831; Ughelli, F. Italia sacra. 2nd edn. (*see Gen. Bibl.* iv); Pirro, R. Sicilia sacra. 3rd edn. 2 vols. in 1. Palermo. 1733; Kehr, K. A. Die Urkunden der normannisch-sicilischen Könige. Innsbruck. 1902 (Appendix, pp. 409 sqq.), and Jamison, E. The Norman administration. (*See below*, iii (2).)

C. Legislation.

The text of the Assises is to be found in: Merkel, J. Commentatio qua juris siculi sive Assisarum regum Siciliae fragmenta ex codicibus manuscriptis proponuntur. Halle. 1856; and also in Brandileone, F. Il diritto romano nelle leggi normanne e sveve del regno di Sicilia. Turin. 1884. pp. 92 sqq. For certain assises (not in the above works), which are reproduced in the Constitutions of Frederick II, *see* Historia diplomatica Friderici II. Ed. Huillard-Bréholles, A. 6 vols. in 12. Paris. 1852–61. Vol. iv, pt. 1. Constitutiones regni Siciliae.

III. MODERN WORKS.

(1) General.

Chalandon, F. Histoire de la domination normande en Italie et en Sicile (1009–1194). 2 vols. Paris. 1907.

Delarc, O. Les Normands en Italie. Paris. 1883. [Till 1073.]

Haskins, C. H. The Normans in European History. Boston and New York. 1915.

Heinemann, L. v. Geschichte der Normannen in Unteritalien und Sicilien. Vol. i [no more publ.]. Leipsic. 1894. [Till 1085.]

Schack, A. F. v. Geschichte der Normannen in Sicilien. 2 vols. Stuttgart. 1889.

(2) Special.

Amari, M. Storia dei Musulmani di Sicilia. 2nd edn. Nallino, C. A. 3 vols. in 5 pts. Catania. 1933–7.

Bertaux, E. L'Art dans l'Italie méridionale. Vol. i. Paris. 1904.

Besta, E. La Cattura dei Veneziani in Oriente per ordine dell' imperatore Emmanuele Comneno. Feltre. 1900.

Blasiis, G. de. La Insurrezione pugliese e la conquista normanna. 3 vols. Naples. 1869.

Bloch, H. Forschungen zur Politik Kaiser Heinrichs VI in den Jahren 1191–4. Berlin. 1892.

Brandileone, F. Il diritto greco-romano nell' Italia meridionale sotto la dominazione normanna. *In* Archivio Giuridico. Vol. xxxvi. 1886.

Caspar, E. Die Legatengewalt der normannisch-sicilischen Herrscher im 12 Jahrhundert. (Extract from Quellen und Forschungen aus italienischen Archiven und Bibliotheken. Vol. vi.) Rome. 1904.

Caspar, E. Roger II (1101–54) und die Gründung der normannisch-sicilischen Monarchie. Innsbruck. 1904.

Chalandon, F. Les Comnènes. Vol. i. Essai sur le règne d'Alexis Comnène (1081–1118). Vol. ii. Jean II Comnène et Manuel I Comnène (1118–80). Paris. 1900, 12.

—— La Diplomatique des Normands de Sicile et de l'Italie méridionale. *In* Mélanges d'archéol. et d'histoire. (École franç. de Rome.) Vol. xx. Rome. 1900.

—— Histoire de la première croisade. Paris. 1925.

Cohn, W. Die Geschichte der normannisch-sicilischen Flotte. Breslau. 1910.

Curtis, E. Roger of Sicily, and the Normans in Lower Italy, 1016–1154. New York. 1912.

Dentzer, B. Topographie der Feldzüge Robert Guiscards gegen das byzantinische Reich. *In* Festschrift des geographischen Seminars der Universität. Breslau. 1901.

Diehl, C. L'Art byzantin dans l'Italie méridionale. Paris. 1894.

—— Palerme et Syracuse. Paris. 1907.

Di Giovanni, V. La Topographia antica di Palermo dal secolo 10 al 15. 2 vols. Palermo. 1889, 90.

Gabrieli, A. Un grande statista barese del secolo xii vittima dell' odio feudale. Trani. 1899.

Garufi, C. A. Adelaïde, nipote di Bonifazio del Vasto e Goffredo figliuolo del gran conte Ruggiero. Palermo. 1903.

—— Sull' ordinamento amministrativo normanno in Sicilia, Exhiquier o diwan? ASI. Ser. v. Vol. xxvii. 1901.

Gay, J. L'Italie méridionale et l'empire byzantin (867–1071). EcfrAR. Paris. 1904.

Guillaume, P. Essai historique sur l'abbaye de la Cava. Naples. 1897.

Haskins, C. H. England and Sicily in the twelfth century. EHR. Vol. xxvi (1911). pp. 433 sqq. and pp. 641 sqq.

—— The Sicilian translators of the twelfth century and the first Latin version of Ptolemy's Almagest. Extract from Harvard Studies in Classical Philology. Vol. xxi. Boston, Mass. 1910.

—— Further notes on Sicilian translations of the twelfth century. *Ibid.* xxiii. 1912. [The last two revised *in* Studies in the history of Mediaeval Science. pp. 155 sqq. *See Gen. Bibl.* v.]

Hoffmann, M. Die Stellung des Königs von Sicilien nach den Assisen von Ariano (1140). Münster. 1910.

Holzach, F. Die auswärtige Politik des Königreichs Sicilien vom Tode Rogers II bis zum Frieden von Venedig. Basle. 1892.

Jamison, E. M. The Norman administration of Apulia and Capua, more especially under Roger I and William I (1127–66). *In* Papers of the British School at Rome. Vol. vi. London. 1913.

—— The administration of the county of Molise in the twelfth and thirteenth centuries. EHR. xliv, xlv. 1929, 30.

—— I conti di Molise e Marsia nei secoli xii e xiii. *In* Atti del Convegno Storico Abruzzese-Molisano, 1931. Casalbordino. 1932.

Jungfer, H. Untersuchung der Nachrichten über Friedrichs I griechische und normannische Politik bis zum Wormser Reichstag (1157). Berlin. 1874.

Kap-Herr, H. v. Die abendländische Politik Kaiser Manuels. Strasbourg. 1881.

Kehr, K. A. Die Urkunden der normannisch-sicilischen Könige. Innsbruck. 1902.

La Lumia, S. Storia della Sicilia sotto Guglielmo il buono. Florence. 1867.

Niese, H. Die Gesetzgebung der normannischen Dynastie im Regnum Siciliae. Halle. 1910.

Norden, W. Das Papsttum und Byzanz. *See Gen. Bibl.* v.

Ottendorf, H. Die Regierung der beiden letzten Normannenkönige Tancreds und Wilhelm III von Sicilien und ihre Kämpfe gegen Heinrich VI. Bonn. 1899.

Rinaldi, H. Dei primi feudi nell' Italia meridionale. Naples. 1886.

Salomon, R. Studien zur normannisch-italischen Diplomatik. Teil i. Die Herzogs-urkunden für Bari. Berlin. 1907.

Salvioli, G. Le decime di Sicilia e specialmente quelle di Girgenti. Palermo. 1901.

Savio, F. Il marchese Bonifazio del Vasto e Adelasia contessa di Sicilia. *In* Atti d. Accad. d. scienze di Torino. Vol. xxii. Turin. 1886–7.

Scaduto, F. Stato e chiesa nelle Due Sicilie dai Normanni ai giorni nostri, sec. xi–xix. Palermo. 1887.

Schlumberger, G. Deux chefs normands des armées byzantines. RH. xvi. 1881.

—— L'épopée byzantine à la fin du xe siècle. Vol. iii. Les Porphyrogénètes, Zoé et Théodora (1025–57). Paris. 1905.

Schwartz, C. Die Feldzüge Robert Guiscards gegen das byzantinische Reich. Fulda. 1854. [progr.]

Siragusa, G. B. Il regno di Guglielmo I in Sicilia. 2 vols. Palermo. 1885–6. 2nd edn. 1929.

Tafel, G. L. F. Komnenen und Normannen. Stuttgart. 1870.

Wagner, A. Die unteritalischen Normannen und das Papsttum (1086–1154). Breslau. 1885.

(3) Criticism of Sources.

Baitz, G. Zur Kritik der Normannengeschichte des Amatus von Monte Cassino. FDG. Vol. xxiv. 1884.

Balzani, U. Le Cronache italiane nel medio evo. *See Gen. Bibl.* i.

Bertolini, O. Gli Annales Beneventani. BISI. 42 (1923). pp. 1 sqq.

Block, P. Zur Kritik des Petrus de Ebulo. 2 vols. Breslau. 1883 ff.

Capasso, B. Le fonti della storia delle provincie napolitane. *See Gen. Bibl.* i.

—— Sul catalogo dei feudi e dei feudatarii delle provincie napoletane sotto la dominazione normanna. (Atti della r. Accad. di archeologia, lettere, e belle arti. Vol. iv.) Naples. 1869.

Heskel, A. Die Historia sicula des Anonymus Vaticanus und des Gaufredus Malaterra. Ein Beitrag zur Quellenkunde für die Geschichte Unteritaliens und Siziliens. Kiel. 1881. [diss.]

Hillger, F. Das Verhältniss des Hugo Falcandus zu Romuald von Salerno. Halle. 1888.

Hirsch, F. Amatus von Monte Cassino und seine Geschichte der Normannen. FDG. Vol. viii. 1868.

Longo, N. Ricerche su i diplomi normanni della chiesa di Troina. Catania. 1899.

Schroetter, F. Ueber die Heimath des Hugo Falcandus. Eisleben. 1880. [diss.]

Wilmans, R. Ueber die Quellen der Gesta Roberti Wiscardi des Guillermus Apuliensis. (Archiv d. Gesellschaft für ältere deutsche Geschichtskunde. Vol. x.) Hanover. 1874.

Winkelmann, E. Des magisters Petrus de Ebulo liber ad honorem Augusti. Leipsic. 1874.

CHAPTER V.

THE ITALIAN CITIES TILL *c.* 1200.

I. SPECIAL BIBLIOGRAPHIES.

Manzoni, L. Bibliografia statutaria e storica italiana. *See Gen. Bibl.* I.

For the towns of Piedmont, Liguria, Romagna, and the Marches:

Calvi, E. Tavole storiche dei Comuni italiani. *See Gen. Bibl.* III.

For the towns A to Mond. (vol. VI, Genoa):

Manno, A. Bibliografia storica degli stati della monarchia di Savoia. Vols. I–IX. Turin. 1884 ff.

For Florence:

Davidsohn, R. Geschichte von Florenz. Vol. I. *See below,* III B.

For Venice:

Kretschmayr, H. Geschichte von Venedig. Vol. I. *See below,* III B.

II. SOURCES.

A. CHRONICLES, ETC.

[Only Chronicles of special importance for the development of the communes, and those from which quotations are made in the chapter, are here given.]

Adalboldus. Vita Heinrici II imperatoris. MGH. Script. IV.

Annales Beneventani. Ed. Bertolini, O. BISI. 42 (1923). pp. 101 sqq.

Annales Ianuenses Cafari et continuatorum. Ed. Belgrano, L. T. and Imperiale di Sant' Angelo, C. *In* Fonti. Vols. I, II. 1890 ff.

Annales Mediolanenses maiores (Gesta Federici I imperatoris in Lombardia). Ed. Holder-Egger. O. SGUS. 1892.

Anonymus Ticinensis. Liber de laudibus civitatis Ticinensis. Ed. Maiocchi, R. and Quintavalle, F. RR.II.SS. New edn. XI. Pt. 1. [Opicino de Canistris.]

Arnulfus Mediolanensis. Gesta archiepiscoporum Mediolanensium. Ed. Bethmann, L. C. and Wattenbach, W. MGH. Script. VIII.

Carmina Mutinensia. Ed. Winterfeld, P. v. MGH. Poetae Carolini aevi. III.

Codagnellus. Annales Placentini. Ed. Holder-Egger, O. SGUS. 1901.

Instituta regalia regum Longobardorum (Honorancie civitatis Papie). Ed. Hofmeister, A. MGH. Script. XXX. Pt. 2. 1933.

Johannes de Viterbo. Liber de regimine civitatum. Ed. Gaudenzi, A. *in* Bibliotheca Iuridica Medii Aevi. III. Bologna. 1901.

Landulfus Junior de S. Paulo. Historia Mediolanensis. Ed. Bethmann, L. C. and Jaffé, P. MGH. Script. XX. *Also* ed. Castiglioni, C. RR.II.SS. New edn. Vol. V. Pt. 3.

Landulfus Senior. Historia Mediolanensis. Ed. Bethmann, L. C. and Wattenbach, W. MGH. Script. VIII.

Marago. Annales Pisani. Ed. Gentile, M. L. RR.II.SS. New edn. Vol. VI. Pt. 2. *Also* MGH. Script. XIX. [*See* Botteghi, L. A. Archivio Muratoriano. 22. (1922.)]

Oculus pastoralis. Ed. Muratori, L. A. *in* Antiquitates Italiae. IV.

Otto Frisingensis et Rahewinus. Gesta Friderici I imperatoris. Ed. Waitz, G. and Simson, B. v. SGUS. 1912.

Rangerius. Vita S. Anselmi Lucensis episcopi. Ed. Fuente, V. de la. Madrid. 1870. *Also* ed. Schmeidler, B. etc. MGH. Script. XXX. Pt. 2. 1933.

Wipo. Gesta Chuonradi II. Ed. Bresslau, H. SGUS. 1878.

B. CHARTERS, ETC.

[Only the more important collections of charters are here given. Many documents are printed in appendices to the histories, etc. in III.]

Gli Atti del comune di Milano fino all' anno MCCXVI. Ed. Manaresi, C. Milan. 1919. [Introduction.]

Berlan, F. Statuti di Pistoja del secolo XII. Bologna. 1882.

Biblioteca della società storica subalpina. Founded by Gabotto, F., directed by Tallone, A. Pinerolo, Turin. 1899 ff., in progress (see also *sub nom.*).

Bonaini, F. Diplomi Pisani. ASI. VI, 2. Suppl. 1848, 89.

—— Statuti inediti della città di Pisa. 3 vols. Florence. 1854–7.

Il "Chartarium dertonense" e altri documenti del Comune di Tortona. Ed. Gabotto, E. (Bibl. soc. stor. subalpina. xxxi.) Pinerolo. 1909.
Chartarum tomi i et ii. MHP. 1836, 53. [Mostly of Piedmont.]
Codex Astensis...de Malabayla. Ed. Sella, G. *In* Atti della r. Accad. dei Lincei. Ser. ii. Scienze morali, storiche ecc. Vols. ii, v, vi, vii. 1880–7.
Codex diplomaticus civitatis et ecclesiae Bergomatis. Ed. Lupi, M. Bergamo. 1784–9.
Codex diplomaticus Cremonae. Ed. Astigiano, L. MHP. 4°. 1896–9.
Codice diplomatico Barese. Publ. by Comm. prov. di archeol. e storia patria di Bari. Vols. i–xv. Trani. 1896 ff., in progress.
Codice diplomatico Brindisino. Ed. Monti, G. M. Vol. i. (R. Dep. di Storia Patria per le Puglie.) Trani. 1940.
Codice diplomatico Laudense. Ed. Vignati, C. 3 vols. (Bibl. hist. italica.) Milan. 1879–85.
Codice diplomatico Padovano del secolo vi a tutto l' xi. Ed. Gloria, A. (R. Dep. Ven. Monumenti storici. Documenti. ii.) Venice. 1877. [Introduction.]
Codice diplomatico Padovano dall' anno 1101 all' anno 1183. Ed. Gloria, A. (*Ibid.* iv, vi.) Venice. 1879, 81. [Introduction.]
Constitutiones et acta publica imperatorum et regum. Vol. i. Ed. Weiland, L. MGH. Legum Sect. iv. 1893.
Diplomata:
    I Diplomi di Guido e di Lamberto. Ed. Schiaparelli, P. *In* Fonti. 1906.
    I Diplomi di Berengario I. Ed. Schiaparelli, L. *Ibid.* 1903.
    I Diplomi italiani di Lodovico III e di Rodolfo II. Ed. Schiaparelli, L. *Ibid.* 1910.
    I Diplomi di Ugo e di Lotario, di Berengario II e di Adalberto. Ed. Schiaparelli, L. *Ibid.* 1924.
    Die Urkunden Konrad I, Heinrich I, und Otto I. Ed. Sickel, T. v. MGH. Diplomata regum et imperatorum. i.
    Die Urkunden Otto des II und Otto des III. Ed. Sickel, T. v. *Ibid.* ii.
    Die Urkunden Heinrich des II und Arduins. Ed. Bresslau, H. *Ibid.* iii.
    Die Urkunden Konrads II. Ed. Bresslau, H. *Ibid.* iv.
    Die Urkunden Heinrichs III. Ed. Bresslau, H. *Ibid.* v 1.
    Die Urkunden Lothars III. Ed. Ottenthal, E. v. and Hirsch, H. *Ibid.* viii.
    Stumpf-Brentano, K. F. Die Reichskanzler. *See Gen. Bibl.* iv.
Fantuzzi, M. Monumenti ravennati de' secoli di mezzo. 6 vols. Venice. 1801–4.
Lami, G. S. Ecclesiae Florentinae monumenta. Florence. 1758.
Leges municipales. Vol. ii. (MHP. xvi.) 1876.
Liber Consuetudinum Mediolani anni 1216. Ed. Berlan, F. Milan. 1868–9. Rev. edn. Berlan, F. Le due edizioni milanese e torinese delle consuetudini di Milano. Venice. 1872.
Liber Iurium Reipublicae Genuensis. Ed. Ricotti, E. (MHP. vii, ix.) 1854, 57.
Liber Potheris communis civitatis Brixiae. (MHP. xix.) 1899.
Il "Libro Rosso" del comune d' Ivrea. Ed. Assandria, G. (Bibl. soc. stor. subalpina. lxxiv.) Pinerolo. 1914.
Memorie e documenti per servire all' istoria della città e stato di Lucca. 11 vols. in 14. Lucca. 1813–84.
Pasqui, U. Documenti per la storia della città d' Arezzo. (Doc. di storia ital. xi.) Florence. 1899.
Regesta chartarum Italiae. Publ. by K. Preuss. Hist. Institut and Instituto storico italiano. 18 vols. Rome. 1907 ff., in progress.
Il Registrum Magnum del comune di Piacenza. Ed. Corna, A., Ercole, F., and Tallone, A. Vol. i. (Bibl. soc. stor. subalpina. xcv.) Turin. 1921. In progress.
Il "Rigestum Comunis Albe." Ed. Milano, E. and others. 3 vols. (Bibl. soc. stor. subalpina. xx–xxii.) Pinerolo. 1903–12.
Santini, P. Documenti dell' antica costituzione del comune di Firenze. (Doc. di storia ital. x.) Florence. 1895.
—— Nuovi documenti. ASI. Ser. v. Vol. xix. 1897.
Zdekauer, L. Il constituto del comune di Siena dell' anno 1262. Milan. 1897 [Introduction.]

III. MODERN WORKS.

A. General.

Caggese, R. Classi e comuni rurali nel medio evo italiano. 2 vols. Florence. 1907, 9.

Davidsohn, R. Entstehung des Consulats. DZG. vi. 1891.

—— Consules und boni homines. *Ibid.*

—— Origine del consolato. ASI. Ser. v. Vol. ix. 1892.

—— Ueber die Entstehung des Konsulats in Toscana. HVJS. iii. 1900.

—— Geschichte von Florenz. *See below,* iii b.

Doren, A. Italienische Wirtschaftsgeschichte. Jena. 1934. Ital. transl. Luzzatto, G. Padua. 1937.

Ficker, J. Forschungen zur Reichs- und Rechtsgeschichte Italiens. 4 vols. Innsbruck. 1868–74.

Handloike, M. Die lombardischen Städte unter der Herrschaft der Bischöfe und die Entstehung der Communen. Berlin. 1883.

Hartmann, L. M. Analekten. Zur Wirthschaftsgesch. Italiens im frühen Mittelalter. Gotha. 1904.

Hegel, C. Geschichte der Städteverfassung von Italien seit der Zeit der römischen Herrschaft bis zum Ausgang des 12. Jahrhunderts. 2 vols. Leipsic. 1847.

Heinemann, L. v. Zur Entstehung der Stadtverfassung in Italien. Leipsic. 1896.

Hertter, F. Die Potestàliteratur Italiens im 12. und 13. Jahrhundert. Leipsic. 1910.

Heyd, W. Histoire du Commerce du Levant au moyen-âge. *See Gen. Bibl.* v.

Lanzani, F. Storia dei comuni italiani dalle origini al 1313. (Storia d' Italia scritta da una società d' amici.) Milan. 1882.

Leicht, P. La curtis e il feudo nell' Italia superiore fino al secolo xiii. Verona, Padua. 1903.

Luchaire, J. Les démocraties italiennes. Paris. 1915.

Manfroni, C. Storia della marina italiana dalle invasioni barbariche al trattato di Ninfeo (400–1261). Leghorn. 1899.

Mayer, E. Italienische Verfassungsgeschichte von der Gothenzeit bis zur Zunftherrschaft. 2 vols. Leipsic. 1909.

Mengozzi, G. La città italiana nell' alto medio evo. Il periodo langobardo-franco. Rome. 1914.

Muratori, L. A. Antiquitates italicae medii aevi. *See Gen. Bibl.* iv. [Especially the dissertations in Vols. i and iv.]

Pawinski, A. Zur Entstehungsgeschichte des Konsulats in den Kommunen Nord- und Mittel-Italiens. Berlin. 1867.

Pivano, S. I contratti agrari in Italia nell' alto medioevo. Turin. 1904.

—— Sistema curtense. BISI. 30. (1909.)

—— Stato e Chiesa da Berengario I ad Arduino (888–1015). Turin. 1908.

Salvioli, G. L' immunità e le giustizie delle chiese in Italia. (Atti e memorie delle rr. deputazioni di storia patria per le provincie modenesi e parmensi. Ser. iii. Vols. v and vi.) Modena. 1888, 90.

—— Le nostre origini. Studi sulle condizioni fisiche, economiche, e sociali prima del mille. (Storia economica d' Italia nell' alto medio evo.) Naples. 1913.

Schaube, A. Handelsgeschichte der romanischen Völker des Mittelmeergebiets bis zum Ende der Kreuzzüge. *See Gen. Bibl.* v.

Schneider, F. Die Entstehung von Burg und Landgemeinde in Italien. (Abh. zur Mittleren u. Neueren Geschichte, 68.) Berlin-Grünewald. 1924.

Solmi, A. Le associazioni in Italia avanti le origini del comune. Modena. 1898.

Tamassia, N. Chiesa e popolo. Note per la storia dell' Italia precomunale. *In* Archivio Giuridico. lxvii (n.s. vii). Modena. 1901.

Volpe, G. Lombardi e Romani nelle campagne e nella città. *In* Studi Storici. Ed. Crivellucci, A. Vols. xiii, xiv. Pisa. 1904–5.

—— Medio Evo italiano. 2nd edn. Florence. 1928.

B. Single Communes.

[Certain Introductions to collections of charters, etc. are also important, *v. sub nom.* ii b.]

Anemüller, E. Gesch. d. Verfassung Mailands in d. Jahre 1075–1117. Halle. 1881.

Bonardi, A. Le origini del comune di Padova. Padua. 1898.

Buzzi, G. La Curia arcivescovile e la Curia cittadina di Ravenna dall' 850 al 1118. BISI. 35. (1915.)

Caggese, R. Storia di Firenze. 3 vols. Florence. 1912–21.

—— Un comune libero alle porte di Firenze nel secolo XIII. Florence. 1905.

Carabellese, F. L' Apulia e il suo comune nell' alto medio evo. (Documenti e monografie del Comm. prov. di archeol. e storia patria, VII.) Bari. 1905.

Caro, G. Die Verfassung Genuas zur Zeit des Podestats. Strasbourg. 1891. [diss.]

Chiappelli, A. L' età longobarda a Pistoia. ASI. Anno LXXIX. (1921.) Vol. II.

Ciccaglione, F. Le istituzioni politiche e sociali dei ducati napoletani. Naples. 1892.

Cipolla, C. Compendio della storia politica di Verona. Verona. 1900.

D' Amia, A. Studi sull' ordinamento giudiziario e sulla procedura delle curie pisane nel secolo XII. ASI. Anno LXXVII. (1919.) Vol. II.

Davidsohn, R. Geschichte von Florenz. Vol. I. Berlin. 1896. Ital. transl. Storia di Firenze. Le Origini. Florence. 1907–12.

—— Forschungen zur Gesch. von Florenz. I, II, III. Berlin. 1896-1901.

Del Giudice, P. Di un recente opuscolo intorno la prima costituzione comunale di Milano. *In* Rendiconti dell' Istituto Lombardo. Ser. II. Vol. XV (1832). p. 424.

Dina, A. L' ultimo periodo del principato longobardo e l' origine del dominio pontificio in Benevento. Benevento. 1899.

Fiastri, G. L' Assemblea del popolo a Venezia come organo costituzionale dello Stato. N. Arch. Ven. n.s. XXV. 1913.

Gallo, A. I curiali napoletani del medioevo. ASPN. XLIV–XLVI. (n.s. V–VII.) 1919–21.

Giulini, G. Memorie spettanti alla storia, al governo, e alla descrizione della città e della campagna di Milano nei secoli bassi. 2nd edn. 7 vols. Milan. 1854-7.

Gregorovius, F. Geschichte der Stadt Rom im Mittelalter. *See Gen. Bibl.* V.

Halphen, L. Études sur l'administration de Rome au moyen-âge (751–1252). (BHE.) Paris. 1907.

Hessel, A. Geschichte der Stadt Bologna von 1116 bis 1280. (Ebering's Historische Studien. No. 76.) Berlin. 1910.

Heywood, W. History of Pisa. Cambridge. 1921.

Imperiale di Sant' Angelo, C. Caffaro e i suoi tempi. Turin. 1894.

Kretschmayr, H. Geschichte von Venedig. Vol. I. *See Gen. Bibl.* V.

Mazzi, A. Studii bergomensi. Bergamo. 1888.

—— Le vicinie di Bergamo. Bergamo.

Merores, M. Gaeta im frühen Mittelalter. Gotha. 1911.

Plesner, J. L'émigration de la campagne à la ville libre de Florence au xiiie siècle. Copenhagen. 1934.

Salvemini, G. La dignità cavalleresca nel comune di Firenze. Florence. 1896.

—— Studi storici. Florence. 1901.

Santini, P. Società delle torri in Firenze. ASI. Series IV. Vol. XX. 1887.

—— Studi sull' antica costituzione del comune di Firenze. ASI. Ser. V. Vol. XVI. 1895.

—— Studi sull' antica costituzione del comune di Firenze. Contado e politica esteriore del secolo XII. ASI. Ser. V. Vols. XXV–XXVI. 1900.

—— Studi sull' antica costituzione del com. di Firenze. La città e le classi sociali in Firenze. ASI. Ser. V. Vols. XXXI–XXXII. 1903.

Schevill, F. Siena. London. 1909.

Simeoni, L. Le origini del Comune di Verona. N. Arch. Ven. n.s. XXV. 1913.

Solmi, A. Le leggi più antiche del comune di Piacenza. ASI. Anno LXXIII. (1915.) Vol. II.

—— Sul più antico documento consolare pisano scritto in lingua sarda. Arch. stor. sardo. II. 1906.

Villari, P. I primi due secoli della storia di Firenze. 2nd edn. Florence. 1905.

Volpe, G. Lunigiana medievale. (Biblioteca storica toscana.) Florence. 1923.

—— Pisa e i Longobardi. *In* Studi Storici. Ed. Crivellucci, A. Vol. X. Pisa. 1901.

—— Studi sulle istituzioni comunali a Pisa. Sec. XII–XIII. (Annali della r. Scuola Normale superiore di Pisa, filosofia e filologia. Vol. XV.) Pisa. 1902.

—— Volterra. (Biblioteca storica toscana.) Florence. 1923.

Zdekauer, L. Studi pistoiesi. Siena. 1889.

CHAPTER VI.

ISLĀM IN SYRIA AND EGYPT, 750–1100.

I. SPECIAL BIBLIOGRAPHIES.

Becker, C. H. Zur Geschichtsschreibung unter den Fatimiden. *In* Beiträge. Heft 1. *See below*, III (*b*). [Gives critical estimate of writers and their sources of information.]

Blochet, E. Liste des ouvrages qui traitent de l'histoire de l'Égypte à l'époque des Fatimites.... *In* Revue de l'Orient latin. Vol. VI. Paris. 1898.

II. (*a*) ORIENTAL SOURCES.

Abu'l-Fidā Ismā'īl ibn 'Alī. Annales muslemici, arabice et latine. Ed. Reiske, J. J. and Adler, J. G. C. 5 vols. Copenhagen. 1789–94. [In Vols. II and III are brief annals of the whole period covered by this chapter.]

Abu-Ya'là Ḥamzah ibn al-Qalānisī. Dhail tārīkh Dimashq. Ed. Amedroz, H. F. Leiden. 1908. [Valuable history of Damascus from A.D. 969 onwards. Important supplementary material from other unpublished sources is also printed by the editor.]

Aḥmad ibn 'Alī al-Maqrīzī. Kitāb itti'āz al-ḥunafā bi-akhbār al-khulafā. Ed. Bunz, H. Leipsic. 1909. [History of the Fāṭimites to the year A.H. 363; discusses the origin of the dynasty, with extracts from previous writers, giving their views; traces fully the history of the Qarmatians.]

'Alī ibn Muḥammad ibn al-Athīr. Kitāb al-kāmil fi't-tārīkh (Chronicon quod perfectissimum inscribitur). Ed. Tornberg, C. J. 14 vols. Leiden. 1851–76. (Vol. VI, A.H. 155–227; VII, A.H. 228–294; VIII, A.H. 295–369; IX, A.H. 370–450; X, A.H. 451–527.)

'Alī ibn Mūsā ibn Sa'īd. Kitāb al-mughrib. (1) Fragmenta. Ed. Vollers, K. Berlin. 1894. [Life of Ibn Ṭūlūn.] (2) Book IV. Ed. Tallquist, K. L. Leiden. 1899. [With German transl.; includes biographies of the Ikhshīds and others of the same period.]

'Arīb ibn Sa'd al-Qurṭubī. (1) Ṣillat tārīkh aṭ-ṭabarī. Ed. Goeje, J. de. Leiden. 1897. [History of the years A.H. 290–320 = A.D. 903–932.] (2) An account of the establishment of the Fatemite Dynasty in Africa. Tübingen and Bristol. 1840. [Transl. of extract from above, A.H. 290–301, by J. Nicholson; often entered in catalogues under the name of Mas'ūdī.]

Excerpta ex historiis Arabum de expeditionibus Syriacis Nicephori Phocae et Ioannis Tzimiscis. *With* Leo Diaconus. CSHB. 1828. [Latin transl. by C. Lassen of extracts from Abu'l-Faraj, Abu'l-Fidā, and Kamāl-ad-Dīn.]

Gregory Barhebraeus (Abu'l-Faraj). Chronicon Syriacum. (1) [Ed. Bedjan, P.] Paris. 1890. (2) Ed. Bruns, P. J. and Kirsch, G. G. Leipsic. 1789. [With Latin transl.]

Jamāl-ad-Dīn Abu'l-Maḥāsin Yūsuf ibn Taghrī Birdī. An-nujūm az-zāhirah. Vol. II, pt. 2. Ed. Popper, W. Berkeley, California. 1909–12. [Sequel to the Leiden edition of 1852–61; a history of Egypt during A.H. 366–523 = A.D. 976–1128.]

Jamāl-ad-Dīn 'Alī ibn Ẓāfir al-Halabī. Kitāb ad-duwal al-munqati'ah. [Important source not yet printed in full; extracts relating to Ibn Ṭūlūn and the Ikhshīds are given by Wüstenfeld, F. in Statthalter (Vol. XXI. *See below*, III (*b*)), and, referring to later events, by Rosen, V. R. *See* Yaḥyà *below*.]

Jirjīs (or 'Abdallāh) ibn Abu'l-Yāsir al-Makīn. Historia Saracenica. Latin transl. Erpenius, T. Leiden. 1625.

Kamāl-ad-Dīn 'Umar ibn Aḥmad ibn al-'Adīm. (1) Selecta ex historia Halebi. Text, with Latin transl., ed. Freytag, G. W. Paris. 1819. [K.'s Zubdat al-ḥalab, history of Aleppo, to the year A.H. 336.] (2) Regierung des Saahd-aldaula zu Aleppo. Arabic text, with German transl., ed. Freytag, G. W. Bonn. 1820. [Extract from the Zubdat al-ḥalab, covering the years A.H. 356–381.] (3) Dhikr mulk Sa'īd-ad-Daulah bi-madīnat Ḥalab. *In* Freytag, G. W. Locmani fabulae et...selecta. Bonn. 1823. pp. 41–46. [Extract from the Zubdat al-ḥalab, covering A.H. 381–392.] (4) Historia Merdasidarum ex Halebensibus Cemaleddini annalibus excerpta. Ed. Müller, J. J. Bonn. [1829.] [Latin transl. of extract from the Zubdat al-ḥalab, A.H. 392–472.]

Muḥammad ibn Yūsuf al-Kindī. The governors and judges of Egypt. Arabic texts ed. Rhuvon Guest. Beyrout. 1908. Leiden and London. 1912. [Includes kitāb al-'umarā to A.H. 335, with continuation to 362, and kitāb al-quḍāt to A.H. 246, with continuation to 424.]

Yaḥyà ibn Sa'īd al-Anṭākī. Tārīkh adh-dhail. (1) Ed. Cheikho, L., Carra de Vaux, B., and Zayyat, H. CSCO. Series III. Vol. VII. Beyrout. 1909. [Very important for the history of Aleppo, during A.H. 326–425, i.e. A.D. 933–1034.] (2) "Extracts from the chronicles of Yachya of Antioch, edited, translated, and explained by V. R. Rosen." *In* Mém. AcadIP. Vol. XLIV. 1833. [The extracts illustrate the life of the Emperor Basil, the commentary gives valuable extracts from other Arabic authors in the original, with Russian translation.]

These sources may be supplemented by reference to Muḥammad ibn Jarīr aṭ-Ṭabarī, Ibn al-'Adhārī, Ibn Khaldūn, Ibn Khallikān, etc.

(*b*) GREEK HISTORIANS. See Vol. IV, p. 837.

III. MODERN HISTORIES.

(*a*) GENERAL.

Huart, C. Histoire des Arabes. Vol. I. Paris. 1912. [With bibliography.]

Lane-Poole, S. History of Egypt in the Middle Ages. London. 1901. [Gives prominently the social conditions.]

Müller, A. Der Islam im Morgen- und Abendland. 2 vols. (Oncken. *See Gen. Bibl.* v.) Berlin. 1885, 87.

Weil, G. Geschichte der Chalifen. Vols. II and III. *See Gen. Bibl.* v.

(*b*) SPECIAL MONOGRAPHS.

Becker, C. H. Beiträge zur Geschichte Ägyptens unter dem Islam. 2 Hefte. Strasbourg. 1902–3. [Essays on the Ṭūlūnites, Fāṭimites, etc.]

Corbet, E. K. The life and works of Aḥmad ibn Ṭūlūn. JRAS. 1891. pp. 527–62.

Defrémery, C. L'histoire des Ismaéliens ou Batiniens de la Perse. JA. 1856, 60.

Freytag, G. W. Geschichte der Dynastien der Hamdaniden in Mosul und Aleppo. ZDMG. Vols. X and XI. 1856–7. [Gives detailed history from the Arabic sources.]

Goeje, M. J. de. Mémoire sur les Carmathes du Bahraïn et les Fatimides. 2nd edn. Leiden. 1886.

Quatremère, É. Mémoire historique sur la vie du khalife Fatimite Mostanser-Billah. *In* Mém. géog. et histor. Vol. II. Paris. 1811. [Largely transl. of extracts from the Arabic historians.]

—— Mémoires historiques sur la dynastie des khalifes fatimites. JA. 1836. [Incomplete; discusses origin of the family.]

—— Vie du khalife fatimite Moezz-li-din-Allah. JA. 1836–7.

Roorda, T. Abul Abbasi Amedis, Tulonidarum primi, vita et res gestae. Leiden. 1825.

Sacy, S. de. Exposé de la religion des Druzes. 2 vols. Paris. 1838. [With introduction explaining the origin and doctrines of the Ismailians and giving a detailed life of the caliph Ḥākim.]

Schlumberger, G. Un empereur Byzantin au xᵉ siècle: Nicéphore Phocas. Paris. 1890. [Includes the wars of Aleppo with the Greeks till A.D. 969; with bibliography.]
—— L'Épopée Byzantine à la fin du xᵉ siècle. 3 vols. Paris. 1896–1905. [Continues preceding work; makes particular use of Yaḥyà, as published by Rosen, V. R.]
Wüstenfeld, F. Die Statthalter von Aegypten zur Zeit der Chalifen. *In* Abh. d. k. Gesell. d. Wiss. zu Göttingen. Vols. xx, xxi. 1875–6. [Ends with the Fāṭimite occupation, A.D. 969; includes history of the Ṭūlūnites and Ikhshīds.]
—— Geschichte der Fatimiden Chalifen nach den Arabischen Quellen. *Ibid.* Vols. xxvi, xxvii. 1880–1.

IV. CHRONOLOGY.

Burnaby, S. B. The Jewish and Muhammadan Calendars. London. 1901. [Chronological table gives the Christian date corresponding to the first day of every Muslim year.]
Lane-Poole, S. The Mohammadan Dynasties. *See Gen. Bibl.* iii.
Stevenson, W. B. The chronology of the Arabic historians. Appendix to The Crusaders in the East. Cambridge. 1907. [Exposition of critical principles as applied to the chronological data of the Arabic historians.]
Wüstenfeld, F. Vergleichungs-Tabellen der Muhammedanischen und Christlichen Zeitrechnung. Leipsic. 1854. [Gives Christian dates corresponding to the first day of every month in each Muslim year.]

CHAPTER VII.

THE FIRST CRUSADE.

I. PRIMARY AUTHORITIES.

(a) HISTORIANS WHO ACCOMPANIED THE CRUSADE.

Albertus Aquensis. Historia Hierosolymitanae expeditionis. MPL. CLXVI. *Also in* Rec. Hist. Cr., Hist. occid. Vol. IV. 1879. [The work of a Lorraine crusader, joined to material from unreliable chansons.]

Anonymi Gesta Francorum et aliorum Hierosolymitanorum. Ed. Hagenmeyer, H. Heidelberg. 1890. *Also in* Rec. Hist. Cr., Hist. occid. Vol. III. 1866. *Also* ed. and transl. Bréhier, L. Histoire anonyme de la Première Croisade. (Classiques de l'histoire de France au moyen âge. Ed. Halphen, L. No. 4.) Paris. 1924. [The author was a follower of Bohemond; perhaps influenced by the chansons; generally assumed to be a source of Albert, Fulcher, Raymond, Ekkehard, and Guibert.]

Fulcherius Carnotensis. Historia Hierosolymitana. Ed. Hagenmeyer, H. Heidelberg. 1913. *Also* MPL. CLV; *and in* Rec. Hist. Cr., Hist. occid. Vol. III. 1866. [Author accompanied Robert of Normandy to Nicaea; then joined Baldwin of Edessa.]

Raimundus de Agiles. Historia Francorum qui ceperunt Ierusalem. MPL. CLV; *and in* Rec. Hist. Cr., Hist. occid. Vol. III. 1866. [Chaplain of Raymond of Toulouse; *see supra*, ch. VI, pp. 297 sq.]

(b) CONTEMPORARY WRITERS.

Anna Comnena. Alexias. Ed. Reifferscheid, A. 2 vols. Leipsic. 1884. *Also* ed. Schopen, J. CSHB. 1839. [Born 1083; gives the Greek point of view.]

Ekkehardus. Hierosolymita. Ed. Hagenmeyer, H. Tübingen. 1877.

Guibertus Abbas. Gesta Dei per Francos, sive Historia Hierosolymitana. MPL. CLVI; *and in* Rec. Hist. Cr., Hist. occid. Vol. IV. 1879. [*Floruit* 1053–1121; uses the *Gesta* and Fulcher, and gives independent information.]

(c) CONTEMPORARY LETTERS.

Epistulae et Chartae ad historiam primi belli sacri spectantes (A.D. 1088–1100). Eine Quellensammlung zur Geschichte des ersten Kreuzzuges. Ed. Hagenmeyer, H. Innsbruck. 1901.

S. Gregorius VII. [Epistolae.] MPL. CXLVIII; *and* ed. Jaffé, P. *in* Bibl. rer. German. Vol. II. *See Gen. Bibl.* IV.

(d) CONTEMPORARY ANONYMOUS NARRATIVES.

[Chronique de Zimmern.] Étude sur la Chronique de Zimmern; renseignements qu'elle fournit sur la première croisade. Par H. Hagenmeyer. *In* Archives de l'Orient Latin. Vol. II. Paris. 1884. [Gives German text with French transl. One of the sources is a contemporary narrative.]

Hebräische Berichte über die Judenverfolgungen während der Kreuzzüge. Ed. Neubauer, A. and Stein, M. *in* Quellen zur Geschichte der Juden in Deutschland. Vol. II. Berlin. 1892. [Hebrew, with German transl.]

II. CHANSONS.

(a) TEXTS.

La Chanson d'Antioche, composée par le pélerin Richard, renouvelée par Graindor de Douay. Ed. Paris, P. 2 vols. Paris. 1848.

Fragment d'une Chanson d'Antioche en provençal. Ed. Meyer, P. *in* Archives de l'Orient Latin. Vol. II. Paris. 1884.

(*b*) MODERN WORKS.

Gautier, L. Bibliographie des chansons de geste. Paris. 1897.
Pigeonneau, H. Le cycle de la croisade et de la famille de Bouillon. Saint Cloud.
1877. [Critical discussion of the chansons.]
See also Vercruysse. *See below,* III (*b*).

III. CRITICISM OF SOURCES.

(*a*) LETTERS.

Hagenmeyer, H. Der Brief des Kaisers Alexios I Komnenos an den Grafen
Robert I von Flandern. BZ. Vol. VI (1897). pp. 1–32.
Lair, J. Études critiques. Vol. I (Bulle du Pape Sergius IV; lettres de Gerbert).
Paris. 1899.
Riant, P. Alexii Comneni ad Robertum I Flandriae comitem epistola spuria.
Geneva. 1879. [With Latin text.]
—— Inventaire critique des lettres historiques des croisades. *In* Archives de
l'Orient Latin. Vol. I. Paris. 1881. [Covers period of A.D. 768–1100.]
See also Chalandon. *See below,* IV (*b*).

(*b*) ALBERT AQUENSIS.

Krebs, F. Zur Kritik Alberts von Aachen. Münster. 1881. pp. 1–64. [On Books
I and II.]
Kühn, F. Zur Kritik Alberts von Aachen. *In* Neu. Arch. Vol. XII. 1887. [Dis-
cusses chiefly narrative of events posterior to First Crusade.]
Kugler, B. Albert von Aachen. Stuttgart. 1885. [Important.]
—— Kaiser Alexius und Albert von Aachen. FDG. Vol. XXIII. 1882.
—— Peter der Eremite und Albert von Aachen. HZ. Vol. XLIV. 1880.
Vercruysse, F. Essai critique sur la chronique d'Albert d'Aix. *In* Annales de la
faculté de Philosophie, Université de Bruxelles. Vol. I. Brussels. 1889.
[Discusses relation of Albert to the *Chanson d'Antioche*.]

(*c*) OTHER SOURCES.

Klein, C. Raimund von Aguilers, Quellenstudie zur Geschichte des ersten Kreuz-
zuges. Berlin. 1892. pp. 1–146. [Important.]
See also von Sybel (*see below,* IV (*a*), Anonymi Gesta, ed. Hagenmeyer (*see above,*
I (*a*)), Fulcherius, ed. Hagenmeyer (*see above,* I (*a*)), and Wolff (*see below,* IV (*b*)).

IV. MODERN HISTORIES.

(*a*) GENERAL.

Röhricht, R. Geschichte des ersten Kreuzzuges. Innsbruck. 1901.
Sybel, H. v. Geschichte des ersten Kreuzzuges. Düsseldorf. 1841. 2nd edn. Leipsic.
1881. [Begins modern treatment; second edition differs little from first; discussion of sources still important.]

(*b*) MONOGRAPHS.

Chalandon, F. Les Comnènes. Vol. I. Essai sur le règne d'Alexis Ier Comnène.
Paris. 1900. [With critical appendix "La lettre d'Alexis au comte de Flandre."]
Hagenmeyer, H. Chronologie de la première croisade (1094–1100). *In* Revue de
l'Orient Latin. Vols. VI–VIII. Paris. 1898–1901. Also publ. separately. Paris.
1902.
—— Peter der Eremite, ein kritischer Beitrag zur Geschichte des ersten Kreuz-
zuges. Leipsic. 1879.
Norden, W. Das Papsttum und Byzanz. *See Gen. Bibl.* V. [Summary in French by
Chalandon, F. *in* Revue de l'Orient Latin. Vol. X. Paris. 1905.]
Paulot, L. Un pape français, Urbain II. Paris. 1903.
Wolff, T. Die Bauernkreuzzüge des Jahres 1096. Ein Beitrag zur Geschichte des
ersten Kreuzzuges. Tübingen. 1891. [Gives 119 pp. out of 194 to discussion
of sources.]

(c) Introductory to the Period—Byzantine and Muslim History.

Amari, M. Storia dei Musulmani di Sicilia. 3 vols. in 4 pts. Florence. 1854–72.
Herzberg, G. F. Geschichte der Byzantiner und des Osmanischen Reiches. (Oncken. *See Gen. Bibl.* v.) Berlin. 1883.
Mercier, E. Histoire de l'Afrique septentrionale (Berbérie). 3 vols. Paris. 1888–91. Vol. I.
Müller, A. Der Islam im Morgen- und Abendland. 2 vols. (Oncken. *See Gen. Bibl.* v.) Berlin. 1885, 87.
Neumann, C. Die Weltstellung des Byzantinischen Reiches vor den Kreuzzügen. Leipsic. 1894. French transl. Renauld and Kozlowski *in* Revue de l'Orient Latin. Vol. x. Paris. 1905. Also publ. separately. Paris. 1905.

(d) Introductory to the Period—Western History.

Bréhier, L. L'église et l'orient au moyen âge. Les croisades. [With bibliography.] *See Gen. Bibl.* v.
Chalandon, F. Histoire de la domination normande en Italie et en Sicile. 2 vols. Paris. 1907. [With bibliography.]
Gabriel, C. N. Verdun au xime siècle. Verdun. 1891–2. [Contains the history of Godfrey of Bouillon before the crusade.]
Manfroni, C. Storia della marina italiana (400–1261). Leghorn. 1899.

V. GEOGRAPHY.

Jireček, C. J. Die Heerstrasse von Belgrad nach Constantinopel und die Balkanpässe. Prague. 1877.
Le Strange, G. The lands of the Eastern Caliphate. *See Gen. Bibl.* II.
Matkovič, P. Reisen durch die Balkanhalbinsel während des Mittelalters. German transl. Knapp, J. A. *in* Mittheilungen der geographischen Gesellschaft zu Wien. Vol. xxiii. Vienna. 1880. [Describes the routes of the First Crusade.]
Ramsay, W. M. Historical geography of Asia Minor. (RGS. Suppl. papers, 4.) London. 1890.
Tomaschek, W. Zur historischen Topographie von Kleinasien im Mittelalter. SKAW. cxxiv. 1891.

VI. MILITARY HISTORY.

Delbrück, H. Geschichte der Kriegskunst im Rahmen der politischen Geschichte. Vol. iii. Berlin. 1907.
Delpech, H. Tactique au xe siècle. 2 vols. Paris. 1886.
Heermann, O. Gefechtsführung abendländischer Heere im Orient in der Epoche des ersten Kreuzzugs. Marburg. 1888.
Ludwig, F. Reise und Marschgeschwindigkeit im 12ten und 13ten Jahrhundert. Berlin. 1897.
Oman, C. History of the art of war in the Middle Ages. *See Gen. Bibl.* v.

CHAPTER VIII.

THE KINGDOM OF JERUSALEM, 1099–1292.

I. SPECIAL BIBLIOGRAPHIES.

A compendious and critical account of the sources and authorities will be found in the article on the Crusades by Barker, E. in EncBr. (*see Gen. Bibl.* I). There is a valuable critical account of the sources in Molinier, A. Les Sources de l'histoire de France (*see Gen. Bibl.* I). Vol. II. pp. 266–304. Vol. III. pp. 25–54, pp. 104–113, pp. 237–244. Useful bibliographies and criticism are also contained in the works of Bréhier, L. and Dodu, G. *cited below* (III). For the First Crusade see the Bibliography to ch. VII *above*. For sources and literature on the Crusades the reader may also consult the Bibliographies to Vol. IV, chapters VI, XI, XII, XIII, XIV, XV, and XIX; for the Military Orders see also the Bibliography of ch. XX *below*.

II. SOURCES.

Les Assises d'Antioche. (Armenian text with French transl. Alishanian, G.) Venice. 1876.

Cartulaire de l'Eglise du St Sépulcre. Ed. Rozière, E. de. Paris, 1849.

Cartulaire général de l'ordre des Hospitaliers de St Jean de Jérusalem. Ed. Delaville le Roulx, J. 4 vols. Paris. 1894–1906.

Eudes of Deuil. De Ludovici VII profectione in orientem. MPL. CLXXXV. Coll. 1205 sqq.

Gesta Francorum et aliorum Hierosolimitanorum (Histoire anonyme de la première croisade). Ed. and French transl. Bréhier, L. (Class. hist.) Paris. 1924.

Ibn-al-Qalānisī. The Damascus Chronicle of the Crusades. Ed. and transl. Gibb, H. A. R. London. 1932.

Itinerarium peregrinorum et gesta regis Ricardi. Ed. Stubbs, W. (Rolls.) 1864. [For the Third Crusade.]

Quellen zur Geschichte des Kreuzzuges Kaiser Friedrichs I. Ed. Chroust, A. MGH. Script. N.S. v. Berlin. 1930.

Recueil des historiens des croisades. (Rec. hist. Cr.) In progress. *See Gen. Bibl.* IV.
  Documents arméniens. 2 vols. 1869, 1906. [Contents given in Bibl. to Vol. IV, ch. VI, sect. 1.]
  Historiens grecs. 2 vols. 1875, 81.
  Historiens occidentaux.
    Vols. I and II. 1844, 59. [William of Tyre and his French continuators.]
    Vol. III. 1866. [Raymond of Aguilers; Fulcher of Chartres; Ralph of Caen; Robert the Monk (of Rheims); Stephen, Count of Blois and Anselm of Ribemont (Letters of); Peter Tudebodus (Hist. de Hierosolymitano itinere); Gesta Francorum et aliorum Hierosolymitanorum (Tudebodus abbreviatus).]
    Vol. IV. 1879. [Albert of Aix; Baldric of Bourgueil (Bp. of Dol); Guibert, Abbot of Nogent.]
    Vol. V. 1895. [Accolti, B.; Aegidius (Gilo), cardinal; Baldwin III, Hist. Nicaena vel Antiochena; Caffarus; Documenta Lipsanographica; Ekkehard, Abbot of Aura; Éstoire de Jerusalem et d'Antioche; Exordium Hospitalariorum; Fulco; Gualterius Cancellarius; Henry of Breitenau; Historia ducis Gotfridi; Itinerario di la gran militia; Primi belli sacri narrationes minores; Theodore of Poehlde.]
  Historiens orientaux. 5 vols. 1872–1906.
  Lois. 2 vols. 1841, 43. [Les Assises de Jérusalem.]

Röhricht, R. Regesta regni Hierosolymitani. (*With* Additamentum.) Innsbruck. 1893, 1904.

Société de l'Orient Latin. Publications. Geneva and Paris. 1877 ff.
Archives. 2 vols. 1881, 84.
Revue de l'Orient Latin. 1893 ff.
Schlumberger, G. Numismatique de l'Orient Latin. *See Gen. Bibl.* III.
Série géographique. 5 vols. 1877 ff. Série historique. 6 vols. 1877 ff.

III. MODERN WORKS.

Archer, T. A. and Kingsford, C. L. The Crusades. The story of the Latin Kingdom of Jerusalem. London. 1895.
Barker, E. The Crusades. London. 1923.
Bréhier, L. L'Église et l'Orient au moyen âge. Les Croisades. *See Gen. Bibl.* v.
Chalandon, F. Les Comnènes. Études sur l'empire byzantin aux xiᵉ et xiiᵉ siècles. 2 vols. Paris. 1900, 12.
Coulton, G. G. Crusades, commerce, and adventure. London. 1930.
Dodu, G. Histoire des institutions monarchiques dans le royaume latin de Jérusalem. Paris. 1894.
Grousset, R. Histoire des Croisades et du Royaume Franc de Jerusalem. 3 vols. Paris. 1934 ff.
Heyd, W. Histoire du commerce du Levant au moyen-âge. *See Gen. Bibl.* v.
Kugler, B. Geschichte der Kreuzzüge. 2nd edn. (Oncken. *See Gen. Bibl.* v.) Berlin. 1891.
La Monte, J. L. Feudal Monarchy in the Latin Kingdom of Jerusalem, 1100 to 1291. Cambridge, Mass. 1932.
Lane-Poole, S. History of Egypt in the Middle Ages. (History of Egypt. Ed. Flinders-Petrie, W. M. Vol. vi.) London. 1901.
—— The Mohammadan Dynasties. *See Gen. Bibl.* III.
—— Saladin and the fall of the Kingdom of Jerusalem. London and New York. 1898.
Le Strange, G. Palestine under the Moslems. (Palestine Exploration Fund.) London. 1890.
Miller, W. Essays on the Latin Orient. Cambridge. 1921.
Prutz, H. G. Kulturgeschichte der Kreuzzüge. Berlin. 1883. [Includes an account of the Latin East.]
Rey, E. G. Les Colonies franques de Syrie aux xiiᵉ et xiiiᵉ siècles. Paris. 1883.
Röhricht, R. Beiträge zur Geschichte der Kreuzzüge. 2 vols. Berlin. 1874–8.
—— Geschichte des Königreichs Jerusalem. Innsbruck. 1898.
—— Kleine Studien zur Geschichte der Kreuzzüge. Berlin. 1890.
Schaube, A. Handelsgeschichte der romanischen Völker des Mittelmeergebiets bis zum Ende der Kreuzzüge. *See Gen. Bibl.* v.
Stevenson, W. B. The Crusaders in the East. Cambridge. 1907.

CHAPTER IX.

THE EFFECTS OF THE CRUSADES UPON WESTERN EUROPE.

The nature of the subject precludes a separate Bibliography; all those of Vol. v and Vol. vi may be consulted. In Vol. v special reference may be made to the Bibliographies of chapters viii (The Kingdom of Jerusalem), iv (The Normans in South Italy), v (The Italian Cities), xi (Italy 1125–1152), xix (The Communal Movement, especially in France), xx (The Monastic Orders), xxiii (Philosophy in the Middle Ages).

CHAPTER X.

GERMANY, 1125–1152.

I. SPECIAL BIBLIOGRAPHIES.

In addition to the standard bibliographies (Dahlmann-Waitz, Quellenkunde; Potthast, Bibliotheca Historica Medii Aevi; Wattenbach, Deutschlands Geschichtsquellen; Jansen and Schmitz-Kallenberg, Historiographie und Quellen der deutschen Geschichte bis 1500, 2nd edn.; for all which *see Gen. Bibl.* i), a very useful list and description of the sources will be found in vols. iv and vi of Giesebrecht, W. v., Geschichte der deutschen Kaiserzeit (*see Gen. Bibl.* v); a shorter but a useful one in Hampe, K., Deutsche Kaisergeschichte (*see Gen. Bibl.* v); and by the same author an excellent bibliography and review of recent works (1914–20) will be found in Wissenschaftliche Forschungsberichte: Mittelalterliche Geschichte. Gotha. 1922.

II. ORIGINAL DOCUMENTS.

Constitutiones et Acta publica imperatorum et regum. i. Ed. Weiland, L. MGH. Legum Sect. iv. 1893.
Monumenta Germaniae Selecta. Ed. Doeberl, M. Vol. iv. Munich. 1890.
Origines Guelficae. Ed. Scheidt, C. L. Hanover. 5 vols. 1750–80.
Udalrici Codex. Ed. Jaffé, P. Monumenta Bambergensia. 1869. (Bibl. rer. German. v. *See Gen. Bibl.* iv.)
Wibaldi epistolae. Ed. Jaffé, P. Monumenta Corbeiensia. 1864. (Bibl. rer. German. i. *See Gen. Bibl.* iv.)

Stumpf-Brentano, K. F. Die Reichskanzler. *See Gen. Bibl.* iv.
Bresslau, H. Handbuch der Urkundenlehre für Deutschland und Italien. *See Gen. Bibl.* i.

III. AUTHORITIES.

Annales Cameracenses. MGH. Script. xvi.
Annales Egmundani. *Ibid.*
Annales Herbipolenses. *Ibid.*
Annales Magdeburgenses. *Ibid.*
Annales Palidenses. *Ibid.*
Annales Patherbrunenses. Ed. Scheffer-Boichorst, P. Innsbruck. 1870.
Annales Pegavienses. MGH. Script. xvi.
Annales Ratisponenses. *Ibid.* xvii.
Annales Reicherspergenses. *Ibid.*
Annales Rodenses. *Ibid.* xvi.
Annales Rosenfeldenses. *Ibid.*
Annales S. Disibodi. *Ibid.* xvii.
Annales S. Jacobi Leodiensis. *Ibid.* xvi.
Annales Stadenses. *Ibid.*
Annales Stederburgenses. *Ibid.*
Annalista Saxo. *Ibid.* vi.
Anselmi Havelbergensis Vita Adalberti II Moguntini. Ed. Jaffé, P. Monumenta Moguntina. 1866. (Bibl. rer. German. iii. *See Gen. Bibl.* iv.)
Chronica Regia Coloniensis. Ed. Waitz, G. SGUS. 1880.
Chronicon Montis Sereni. MGH. Script. xxiii.
Cosmae Pragensis Chronica Bohemorum (Continuationes). *Ibid.* ix.

Gerhohi praepositi Reichersbergensis libelli selecti. Ed. Sackur, E. MGH. Libelli de Lite. III.
Gesta Alberonis metrica. MGH. Script. VIII.
Gesta Alberonis. Auctore Balderico. *Ibid.*
Gesta Episcoporum Halberstadensium. *Ibid.* XXIII.
Gesta Treverorum (Continuationes). *Ibid.* VIII and XXIV.
Helmoldi Presbyteri Bozoviensis Cronica Slavorum. Ed. Schmeidler, B. SGUS. 1909.
Henricus de Antwerpe. Tractatus de Urbe Brandenburg. MGH. Script. XXV.
Herbordi Dialogus de Vita Ottonis Episcopi Bambergensis. *Ibid.* XX; and in Jaffé, P. Monumenta Bambergensia. 1869. (Bibl. rer. German. v. *See Gen. Bibl.* IV.)
Historia Welforum Weingartensis. MGH. Script. XXI; and ed. Weiland, L. SGUS. 1869.
Kaiserchronik. Ed. Schröder, E. MGH. Deutsche Chroniken. I, 1. 1892.
Monumenta Erphesfurtensia. Ed. Holder-Egger, O. SGUS. 1899.
Narratio de electione Lotharii. MGH. Script. XII.
Orderici Vitalis Historia ecclesiastica. Ed. Le Prévost, A. and Delisle, L. 5 vols. (SHF.) Paris. 1838–55.
Ottonis Frisingensis Chronicon. Ed. Hofmeister, A. SGUS. 2nd edn. 1912.
Radulfi de Diceto, decani Lundoniensis, Opera historica. Ed. Stubbs, W. 2 vols. (Rolls.) 1876.
Sigeberti Gemblacensis Chronica (Continuationes). MGH. Script. VI.
Vincentii Pragensis chronicon Boemorum. *Ibid.* XVII.
Vita Conradi archiepiscopi Salisburgensis. *Ibid.* XI.
Vita Eberhardi archiepiscopi Salisburgensis. *Ibid.* XI.
Vita S. Norberti archiepiscopi Magdeburgensis. *Ibid.* XII.
Vitae Ottonis Episcopi Bambergensis. *Ibid.* XII; and in Jaffé, P. Monumenta Bambergensia. 1869. (Bibl. rer. German. v. *See Gen. Bibl.* IV.)

IV. MODERN WORKS.

(a) GENERAL.

Bernhardi, W. Konrad III. (Jahrbücher d. deutsch. Geschichte.) Leipsic. 1883.
—— Lothar von Supplinburg. (Jahrbücher d. deutsch. Geschichte.) Leipsic. 1879.
Giesebrecht, L. Wendische Geschichte aus den Jahren 780–1182. Leipsic. 1843.
Giesebrecht, W. v. Geschichte d. deutschen Kaiserzeit. Vol. IV. *See Gen. Bibl.* V.
Hampe, K. Deutsche Kaisergeschichte in der Zeit der Salier und Staufer. 5th edn. *See Gen. Bibl.* V.
Hauck, A. Kirchengeschichte Deutschlands. Vol. IV. *See Gen. Bibl.* V.
Jaffé, P. Geschichte des Deutschen Reichs unter Lothar dem Sachsen. Berlin. 1843.
—— Geschichte des Deutschen Reichs unter Konrad III. Hanover. 1845.
Jastrow, J. and Winter, G. Deutsche Geschichte im Zeitalter der Hohenstaufen. 2 vols. Stuttgart. 1897.
Meister, A. Deutsche Verfassungsgeschichte. 3rd edn. (Grundriss der Geschichtswissenschaft. Ed. Meister, A. II, 3.) Leipsic and Berlin. 1922.
Philippson, M. Heinrich der Löwe. Sein Leben und seine Zeit. 2nd edn. 2 vols. Leipsic. 1918.
Poole, A. L. Henry the Lion. London. 1912.
Prutz, H. Heinrich der Löwe. Leipsic. 1865.
Ranke, L. v. Weltgeschichte. *See Gen. Bibl.* V.
Raumer, F. v. Geschichte der Hohenstaufen und ihrer Zeit. 6 vols. Leipsic. 1823–5. 5th edn. 6 vols. Leipsic. 1878.
Richter, G. and Kohl, H. Annalen des deutschen Geschichte. Abt. III. Vol. II. *See Gen. Bibl.* V.
Waitz, G. Deutsche Verfassungsgeschichte. *See Gen. Bibl.* V.
Werminghoff, A. Verfassungsgeschichte der deutschen Kirche im Mittelalter. 2nd edn. (Grundriss der Geschichtswissenschaft. Ed. Meister, A. II, 6.) Leipsic and Berlin. 1913.

(b) SPECIAL.

Bernheim, E. Lothar III und das Wormser Konkordat. Strasbourg. 1874.

Böhmer, A. Vicilin. Rostock. 1887. [diss.]

Graber, E. Die Urkunden König Konrads III. Innsbruck. 1908.

Hampe, K. Kritische Bemerkungen zur Kirchenpolitik der Stauferzeit. HZ. xcIII. 1904.

Heinemann, O. v. Albrecht der Bär. Darmstadt. 1864.

Jastrow, J. Die Welfenprozesse und die ersten Regierungsjahre Friedrich Barbarossas (1138–56). DZG. x. 1893.

Kalbfuss, H. Zur Entstehung der "Narratio de electione Lotharii." MIOGF. xxxi. 1910.

Kap-herr, H. v. Die abendländische Politik Manuels mit besonderer Rücksicht auf Deutschland. Strasbourg. 1881.

Krabbo, H. Albrecht der Bär. (Forsch. zur brandenburgischen und preussischen Geschichte. xix.) Leipsic. 1906.

Lampel, J. Studien zur Reichsgeschichte unter Konrad III. MIOGF. xxxii. 1911.

Mann, W. Wibald Abt von Stablo und Corvei nach seiner politischen Tätigkeit. Halle. 1875. [diss.]

Meister, A. Die Hohenstaufen im Elsass. Mayence. 1890. [diss.]

Schäfer, D. Zur Beurteilung des Wormser Konkordats. SPAW. 1905.

—— Lothars Heereszug nach Böhmen, 1126. *In* Historische Aufsätze, Karl Zeumer…dargebracht. Weimar. 1910.

Scheffer-Boichorst, P. Zur Geschichte des xII und xIII Jahrhunderts. Berlin. 1897.

Schneiderreit, F. Die Wahl Lothars III zum Deutschen König. Halle. 1892. [diss.]

Scholz, R. Beiträge zur Geschichte der Hoheitsrechte der Deutschen Königs zur Zeit der ersten Staufer (1138–97). Leipsic. 1896.

Schultze, J. Die Urkunden Lothars III. Innsbruck. 1905.

Schulze, E. O. Die Kolonisierung und Germanisierung der Gebiete zwischen Saale und Elbe. Leipsic. 1896.

Simson, B. v. Analecten zur Geschichte der deutschen Königswahlen. Freiburg. 1895. [progr.]

Ulich, P. Die deutsche Kirche unter Lothar von Sachsen. Leipsic. 1885. [diss.]

Vacandard, E. Saint Bernard et la seconde Croisade. RQH. xxxvIII. 1885.

Volkmar, C. Das Verhältnis Lothars III zur Investiturfrage. FDG. xxvI. 1886.

Weiland, L. Das Sächsische Herzogtum unter Lothar und Heinrich dem Löwen. Greifswald. 1866.

Wichert, T. F. A. Die Wahl Lothars III zum Deutschen König. FDG. xII. 1872.

CHAPTERS XI AND XIII.

ITALY AND THE LOMBARD LEAGUE, 1125–1185.

I. SPECIAL BIBLIOGRAPHIES AND CRITICISM OF THE SOURCES.

Balzani, U. Le cronache italiane etc. *See Gen. Bibl.* I. (Engl. transl. of first edn. Early Chroniclers of Europe: Italy. London. 1883.)

Chevalier, C. U. J. Répertoire des sources historiques du moyen âge. *See Gen. Bibl.* I.

Dahlmann-Waitz. Quellenkunde der deutschen Geschichte. *See Gen. Bibl.* I.

Giesebrecht, W. v. Zur mailändischen Geschichtsschreibung im 12 und 13 Jahrhundert. FDG. XXI.

—— Uebersicht der Quellen und Hülfsmittel. (Appendix to Geschichte der deutschen Kaiserzeit. Vol. IV. *See Gen. Bibl.* v.) [Important.]

Lorenz, O. Deutschlands Geschichtsquellen seit der Mitte des 13 Jahrhunderts. 3rd edn. 2 vols. Berlin. 1886–7.

Paetow, L. J. Guide to the study of Medieval History. *See Gen. Bibl.* I.

Schmeidler, B. Italienische Geschichtsschreiber des 12 und 13 Jahrhunderts. Leipsic. 1909.

Wattenbach, W. Deutschlands Geschichtsquellen im Mittelalter. *See Gen. Bibl.* I.

II. COLLECTIONS OF AUTHORITIES.

Del Re, G. Cronisti e scrittori sincroni Napoletani. 2 vols. Naples. 1845, 68.

Fonti per la storia d'Italia. *See Gen. Bibl.* IV.

Jaffé-Loewenfeld. Regesta Pontificum Romanorum. *See Gen. Bibl.* IV.

Liber Pontificalis. *See Gen. Bibl.* IV.

Manaresi, C. Gli Atti del comune di Milano fino all' anno MCCXVI. Milan. 1919.

MGH. Legum Sect. IV. Constitutiones. I. Ed. Weiland, L. 1893.

—— Libelli de lite. III. 1897.

—— Script. XII, XVIII, XIX, XX, XXII.

Muratori, L. A. Rerum Italicarum Scriptores. *See Gen. Bibl.* IV.

Watterich, J. M. Pontificum Romanorum...vitae. *See Gen. Bibl.* IV.

III. CONTEMPORARY AUTHORITIES.

The principal contemporary authorities for these chapters are to be found in the collections mentioned above. Wattenbach's Geschichtsquellen and Balzani's Cronache italiane (*see above*, I) give a detailed account of them. It would be impossible to mention them all here. Of great value are: the letters of Wibald, Abbot of Corvey (ed. Jaffé, P. *in* Monumenta Corbeiensia. 1864. *In* Bibl. rer. German. I. *See Gen. Bibl.* IV); the correspondence of St Bernard, of John of Salisbury, and of the various contemporary Popes; all reprinted in MPL. Among the chroniclers the more important are:

Anonymus. Poema de bello et excidio urbis Comensis. Muratori. RR.II.SS. 1st edn. Vol. v.

Boncompagnus magister Florentinus. De obsidione Anconae. Ed. Gaudenzi, A. BISI. 15 (1895). *Also* ed. Zimolo, C. G. RR.II.SS. New edn. Vol. VI, pt. 3.

Cafarus (and continuators). Annales Ianuenses. Vols. I. and II. Ed. Belgrano, L. T. and Imperiale di S. Angelo, C. (Fonti.) 1891, 1901. *Also* ed. Pertz, G. H. MGH. Script. XVIII.

De pace Veneta relatio. Ed. Balzani, U. BISI. 10 (1891). *Also* ed. Arndt, W. MGH. Script. XIX.

Falco Beneventanus. Chronicon. Muratori. RR.II.SS. 1st edn. Vol. v.

Gesta di Federico I in Italia. Ed. Monaci, E. (Fonti.) 1887.

Gesta Federici I imperatoris in Lombardia auctore cive Mediolanensi. (Annales Mediolanenses maiores.) Ed. Holder-Egger, O. SGUS. 1892.

Gotifredus Viterbiensis. Opera. Ed. Waitz, G. MGH. Script. XXII. Gesta Friderici et Heinrici Imperatorum. Ed. Waitz, G. SGUS. 1870.

Johannes Saresberiensis. Historia Pontificalis. Ed. Poole, R. L. Oxford. 1927.
Landulfus Junior de S. Paulo. Historia Mediolanensis. Ed. Bethmann, L. C. and Jaffé, P. MGH. xx. *Also* ed. Castiglione, C. RR.II.SS. New ed. Vol. v, pt. 3.
Leo Marsicanus and Petrus Diaconus. Chronica monasterii Casinensis. Ed. Wattenbach, W. MGH. Script. vii.
Marago. Annales Pisani. Ed. Gentile, M. L. RR.II.SS. New edn. Vol. vi, pt. 2.
Otto Frisingensis. Chronica. Ed. Hofmeister, A. SGUS. 2nd edn. 1912.
Otto Frisingensis and Rahewinus. Gesta Friderici I imperatoris. Ed. Waitz, G. and Simson, B. v. SGUS. 3rd edn. 1912.
Otto Morena, Acerbus Morena, and Anonymus. De rebus laudensibus. Ed. Güterbock, F. (*as* Historia Frederici I). MGH. Script. rer. Germ. vii. 1930. *Also in* Muratori. RR.II.SS. 1st edn. Vol. vi.
Otto de S. Blasio. Chronica. Ed. Hofmeister, A. SGUS. 1912.
Romualdus Salernitanus. Annales. Ed. Arndt, W. MGH. Script. xix. *Also* ed. Garufi, C. A. RR.II.SS. New edn. Vol. vii, pt. 1. 1914 ff.
Vincentius Pragensis. Chronicon Boemorum. Ed. Wattenbach, W. MGH. Script. xvii.

IV. MODERN WORKS.

(a) General.

Balzani, U. The Popes and the Hohenstaufen. London. 1889. [General sketch.]
Butler, W. F. The Lombard communes. London. 1906.
Caggese, R. Storia di Firenze. 3 vols. Florence. 1912–21.
Chalandon, F. Histoire de la domination normande en Italie et en Sicile. 2 vols. Paris. 1907.
Davidsohn, R. Geschichte von Florenz. Vol. i. Berlin. 1896. Italian transl. Storia di Firenze. Le origini. Florence. 1907–12.
Emiliani-Giudici, P. Storia politica dei municipj italiani. 3 vols. Firenze. 1851–4.
Ficker, J. Forschungen zur Reichs- und Rechtsgeschichte Italiens. 4 vols. Innsbruck. 1868–74.
Fisher, H. The Medieval Empire. 2 vols. London. 1898.
Gianani, F. I comuni (1000–1300). (Storia politica d' Italia scritta da una società di professori.) Milan. [190–.]
Giesebrecht, W. v. Gesch. der deutschen Kaiserzeit. Vols. iv–vi. *See Gen. Bibl.* v.
Gregorovius, F. Geschichte der Stadt Rom im Mittelalter. *See Gen. Bibl.* v.
Hampe, K. Deutsche Kaisergeschichte in der Zeit der Salier und Staufer. 5th edn. *See Gen. Bibl.* v.
Hauck, A. Kirchengeschichte Deutschlands. Vol. iv. *See Gen. Bibl.* v.
Hefele, C. J. v. Conciliengeschichte. Vol. v. *See Gen. Bibl.* v.
Hegel, C. Geschichte der Städteverfassung von Italien. 2 vols. Leipsic. 1847.
Jastrow, J. and Winter, G. Deutsche Geschichte im Zeitalter der Hohenstaufen. Vol. i. Stuttgart. 1897.
Jordan, E. L'Allemagne et l'Italie aux xiie et xiiie siècles. (Glotz, Histoire Générale. *See Gen. Bibl.* v.)
Kretschmayr, H. Geschichte von Venedig. Vol. i. *See Gen. Bibl.* v.
Lanzani, F. Storia dei comuni italiani. (Storia d' Italia scritta da una società d' amici.) Milan. 1882.
Mayer, E. Italienische Verfassungsgeschichte von der Gothenzeit bis zur Zunftherrschaft. 2 vols. Leipsic. 1909.
Muratori, L. Annali d' Italia. *See Gen. Bibl.* v.
Paschini, P. Storia del Friuli. 3 vols. Udine. 1934–6.
Raumer, F. v. Geschichte der Hohenstaufen. 5th edn. 6 vols. Leipsic. 1878.
Reumont, A. v. Geschichte der Stadt Rom. 3 vols. Berlin. 1867–70.
Rocquain, F. La Cour de Rome et l'esprit de réforme avant Luther. Vol. i. Paris. 1893.
Villari, P. Italia da Carlo Magno alla morte di Arrigo VII. Milan. 1910. Engl. transl. Hulton, C. Mediaeval Italy from Charlemagne to Henry VII. London. 1910. [General sketch.]
Visconti, A. Storia de Milano. Milan. 1937.
Zeller, J. Histoire d'Allemagne. Vol. iv. L'Empire Germanique sous les Hohenstaufen. *See Gen. Bibl.* v.

(b) SPECIAL.

Arras, P. Die roncalischen Beschlüsse vom Jahre 1158 und ihre Durchführung. Leipsic. 1882. [diss.]

Bernhardi, W. Konrad III. 2 vols. (Jahrbücher d. deutsch. Geschichte.) Leipsic. 1883.

—— Lothar von Supplinburg. (Jahrbücher d. deutsch. Geschichte.) Leipsic. 1879.

Bonghi, R. Arnaldo da Brescia. Città di Castello. 1885.

Caspar, E. Roger II (1101–1154) und die Gründung der normannisch-sicilischen Monarchie. Innsbruck. 1904.

Curtis, E. Roger of Sicily, and the Normans in Lower Italy (1016–1154). New York and London. 1912.

De Castro, G. Arnaldo da Brescia. Leghorn. 1875.

Francke, H. Arnold von Brescia und seine Zeit. Zurich. 1825.

Fumagalli, A. Le Vicende di Milano durante la guerra con Federico I. 2nd edn. Milan. 1855.

Giesebrecht, W. v. Ueber Arnold von Brescia. *In* Sitzungsberichte d. k. bayer. Akad. d. Wissenschaft. Philos.-philol.-hist. Klasse. Munich. 1873.

Gräf, F. Die Gründung Alessandrias. Berlin. 1887. [diss.]

Guadagnini, G. B. Apologia e vita di Arnaldo da Brescia. Pavia. 1790.

Guibal, G. Arnaud de Brescia et les Hohenstaufen. Paris. 1868.

Güterbock, F. Alla vigilia della Lega Lombarda. Florence. 1938.

—— Der Friede von Montebello und die Weiterentwicklung des Lombardenbundes. Berlin. 1895. [diss.]

Halphen, L. Études sur l'administration de Rome au moyen âge (751–1252). (BHE.) Paris. 1907.

Hausrath, A. Arnold von Brescia. Leipsic. 1891.

Jaffé, P. Gesch. des Deutschen Reiches unter Lothar dem Sachsen. Berlin. 1843.

—— Geschichte des Deutschen Reiches unter Konrad III. Hanover. 1845.

Kauffmann, H. Die italienische Politik K. Friedrichs I. nach dem Frieden von Constanz. Greifswald. 1933.

Kehr, P. Der Vertrag von Anagni im Jahre 1176. Neu. Arch. XIII.

Krammer, M. Der Reichsgedanke des staufischen Kaiserhauses. (Untersuchungen zur deutschen Staats- und Rechtsgeschichte. Ed. Gierke, O. No. 95.) Breslau. 1908.

Laforge, F. de. Alexandre III, ou rapports de ce Pape avec la France aux débuts de la lutte du sacerdoce et de l'Empire. Sens. 1905.

La Lumia, I. Storia della Sicilia sotto Guglielmo il buono. Florence. 1867.

Luchaire, A. Louis VII, Philippe Auguste, Louis VIII. (Lavisse, E. Histoire de France. III, 1. *See Gen. Bibl.* v.)

Mackie, J. D. Pope Adrian IV. Oxford. 1907.

Mann, H. K. Nicholas Breakspear (Hadrian IV), the only English Pope (1154–9). London. 1914.

Morison, J. C. The life and times of St Bernard. 2nd edn. London. 1884.

Mühlbacher, E. Die streitige Papstwahl des Jahres 1130. Innsbruck. 1876.

Neander, A. Der heilige Bernhard. New edn. Gotha. 1889.

Prutz, H. Kaiser Friedrich I. 3 vols. Danzig. 1871–4.

Ratisbonne, M. T. Histoire de St Bernard et de son siècle. 6th edn. 2 vols. Paris. 1864.

Reuter, H. Geschichte Alexanders des Dritten und der Kirche seiner Zeit. Leipsic. 3 vols. 1860–4.

Ribbeck, W. Friedrich I und die römische Curie in den Jahren 1157–9. Leipsic. 1881. [diss.]

Sainati, G. Vita del B. Eugenio III. Monza. 1874.

Schneider, F. Die Reichsverwaltung in Toscana (568–1268). Rome. 1914.

Schrörs, H. Untersuchungen zu dem Streite Kaiser Friedrichs I mit Papst Hadrian IV (1157–8). Bonn, Univ. Progr. 1915. Also publ. Freiburg-i.-B. 1916.

Simonsfeld, H. Jahrbücher des Deutschen Reiches unter Friedrich I. Vol. I. (Jahrbücher d. deutsch. Geschichte.) Leipsic. 1908. [To be continued by Schneider, F.]

Testa, G. B. History of the war of Frederick I against the communes of Lombardy. Engl. transl. rev. by the author. London. 1877.

Tosti, L. Storia della Lega Lombarda. Monte Cassino. 1848.

Vignati, C. Storia diplomatica della Lega Lombarda. Milan. 1867.

Voigt, G. Storia della Lega Lombarda. Milan. 1848.

CHAPTER XII.

FREDERICK BARBAROSSA AND GERMANY.

I. SPECIAL BIBLIOGRAPHIES.

See Bibliography for Chapter x.

II. ORIGINAL DOCUMENTS.

See Bibliography for Chapter x.

III. AUTHORITIES.

Annales Cameracenses. MGH. Script. xvi.
Annales Egmundani. *Ibid.*
Annales Herbipolenses. *Ibid.*
Annales Magdeburgenses. *Ibid.*
Annales Marbacenses. Ed. Bloch, H. SGUS. 1907.
Annales Palidenses. MGH. Script. xvi.
Annales Pegavienses. *Ibid.*
Annales Ratisponenses. *Ibid.* xvii.
Annales Reicherspergenses. *Ibid.*
Annales Reinhardsbrunnenses. *Ibid.* xxx.
Annales Rosenfeldenses. *Ibid.* xvi.
Annales S. Disibodi. *Ibid.* xvii.
Annales S. Jacobi Leodiensis. *Ibid.* xvi.
Annales Stadenses. *Ibid.*
Annales Stederburgenses. *Ibid.*
Arnoldi Chronica Slavorum. Ed. Lappenberg, J. M. SGUS. 1868.
Braunschweigische Reimchronik. MGH. Deutsche Chroniken. ii.
Burchardi Praepositi Urspergensis Chronicon. Ed. Holder-Egger, O. and Simson, B. v. SGUS. 1916.
Christiani Chronicon Moguntinum. Ed. Jaffé, P. Monumenta Moguntina. 1866. (Bibl. rer. German. iii. *See Gen. Bibl.* iv.)
Chronica Magistri Rogeri de Houedene. Ed. Stubbs, W. 4 vols. (Rolls.) 1868–71.
Chronica Regia Coloniensis. Ed. Waitz, G. SGUS. 1880.
Chronica Roberti de Torigneio. Ed. Howlett, R. *in* Chronicles of the reigns of Stephen, Henry II, and Richard I. Vol. iv. (Rolls.) 1889.
Chronicon Montis Sereni. MGH. Script. xxiii.
Continuatio Zwetlensis altera a 1170 usque ad 1189. *Ibid.* ix.
Cosmae Pragensis Chronica Bohemorum (Continuationes). *Ibid.*
Epistola de morte Friderici imperatoris. *Ibid.* xx.
Gedichte des Mittelalters auf König Friedrich 1 den Staufer und aus seiner so wie der nächstfolgenden Zeit. Ed. Grimm, J. *in* Kleinere Schriften. Vol. iii. Berlin. 1866. Also ed. Manitius, M. *in* Die Gedichte des Archipoeta. (München Texte, 6.) Munich. 1913.
Gerhohi praepositi Reichersbergensis libelli selecti. Ed. Sackur, E. MGH. Libelli de Lite. iii.
Gesta Episcoporum Halberstadensium. MGH. Script. xxiii.
Gesta Federici I Imperatoris in Expeditione sacra. Ed. Holder-Egger, O. *in* Gesta Federici Imperatoris in Lombardia. SGUS. 1892.
Gesta Treverorum continuata. MGH. Script. xxiv.
Gisleberti Chronicon Hanoniense. Ed. Arndt, W. SGUS. 1869
Gotifredi Viterbiensis Gesta Friderici et Heinrici Imperatorum. Ed. Waitz, G. SGUS. 1870.

Günther of Pairis. Ligurinus sive de rebus gestis imp. caes. Friderici libri x. Ed. Rittershusius, C. Tübingen. 1598. Also ed. Dümge, C. G. *in* MPL. ccxii. coll. 255 sqq.

Helmoldi Presbyteri Bozoviensis Cronica Slavorum. Ed. Schmeidler, B. SGUS. 1909.

Historia de Expeditione Friderici Imperatoris edita a quodam Austriensi clerico, qui eidem interfuit, nomine Ansbertus. 1187–96. *In* Fontes rerum Austriacarum. Script. v. Vienna. 1863.

Historia de Peregrinorum (Anonymi expeditio Asiatica Friderici Barbarossae imperatoris). Ed. Canisius, H. *in* Lectiones antiquae. v, 2. Ingolstadt. 1604.

Historia Welforum Weingartensis. MGH. Script. xxi; and ed. Weiland, L. SGUS. 1869.

Itinerarium peregrinorum et gesta regis Ricardi. Ed. Stubbs, W. *in* Chronicles and Memorials of the reign of Richard I. Vol. i. (Rolls.) 1864.

Johannes de Piscina de Transfretatione Friderici I. MGH. Script. xxii.

Monumenta Erphesfurtensia. Ed. Holder-Egger, O. SGUS. 1899.

Ottonis Frisingensis Chronicon. Ed. Hofmeister, A. SGUS. 2nd edn. 1912.

Ottonis et Rahewini Gesta Friderici I Imperatoris. Ed. Simson, B. v. SGUS. 3rd edn. 1912.

Ottonis de Sancto Blasio Chronica. Ed. Hofmeister, A. SGUS. 1912.

Radulfi de Diceto, decani Lundoniensis, Opera historica. Ed. Stubbs, W. 2 vols. (Rolls.) 1876.

Sächsische Weltchronik (Eike von Repgow). MGH. Deutsche Chroniken. ii.

Saxonis Grammatici Gesta Danorum. MGH. Script. xxix.

Sigeberti Gemblacensis Chronica (Continuatio Aquicinctina). *Ibid.* vi.

Vincentii Pragensis Chronicon Boemorum. *Ibid.* xvii.

Vita Arnoldi archiepiscopi Moguntini. Ed. Jaffé, P. Monumenta Moguntina. 1866. (Bibl. rer. German. iii. *See Gen. Bibl.* iv.)

Vita Eberhardi archiepiscopi Salisburgensis. MGH. Script. xi.

IV. MODERN WORKS.

(a) General.

Cartellieri, A. Philipp II August, König von Frankreich. 4 vols. Leipsic. 1899–1922.

Fournier, P. Le Royaume d'Arles et de Vienne. Paris. 1891.

Giesebrecht, L. Wendische Geschichte aus den Jahren 780–1182. Leipsic. 1843.

Giesebrecht, W. v. Geschichte d. deutschen Kaiserzeit. Vol. v. *See Gen. Bibl.* v.

—— and Simson, B. v. Geschichte d. deutschen Kaiserzeit. Vol. vi. *See Gen. Bibl.* v.

Hampe, K. Deutsche Kaisergeschichte in der Zeit der Salier und Staufer. 5th edn. *See Gen. Bibl.* v.

Hauck, A. Kirchengeschichte Deutschlands. Vol. iv. *See Gen. Bibl.* v.

Jastrow, J. and Winter, G. Deutsche Geschichte im Zeitalter der Hohenstaufen. 2 vols. Stuttgart. 1897.

Meister, A. Deutsche Verfassungsgeschichte. 3rd edn. (Grundriss der Geschichtswissenschaft. Ed. Meister, A. ii, 3.) Leipsic and Berlin. 1922.

Philippson, M. Heinrich der Löwe. Sein Leben und seine Zeit. 2nd edn. 2 vols. Leipsic. 1918.

Poole, A. L. Henry the Lion. London. 1912.

Prutz, H. Heinrich der Löwe. Leipsic. 1865.

—— Kaiser Friedrich I. 3 vols. Danzig. 1871–4.

Ranke, L. v. Weltgeschichte. *See Gen. Bibl.* v.

Raumer, F. v. Geschichte der Hohenstaufen und ihrer Zeit. 6 vols. Leipsic. 1823–5. 5th edn. 6 vols. Leipsic. 1878.

Simonsfeld, H. Jahrbücher des Deutschen Reichs unter Friedrich I. Vol. i. (Jahrbücher d. deutsch. Geschichte.) Leipsic. 1908.

Waitz, G. Deutsche Verfassungsgeschichte. *See Gen. Bibl.* v.

Werminghoff, A. Verfassungsgeschichte der deutschen Kirche im Mittelalter. 2nd edn. (Grundriss der Geschichtswissenschaft. Ed. Meister, A. ii, 6.) Leipsic and Berlin. 1913.

(b) SPECIAL.

Adler, S. Herzog Welf VI und sein Sohn. Hanover. 1881.
Bloch, H. Die staufischen Kaiserwahlen und die Entstehung des Kurfürstentums.
    Leipsic. 1911. (Also in part in HVJS. XII. 1909.)
Chroust, A. Tageno, Ansbert, und die Historia Peregrinorum. Graz. 1892.
Dehio, G. Hartwich von Stade, Erzbischof von Hamburg-Bremen. Göttingen. 1872.
    [diss.]
Erben, W. Das Privilegium Friedrich I für das Herzogthum Oesterreich. Vienna.
    1902.
Ficker, J. Reinald von Dassel, Erzbischof von Köln. Cologne. 1850.
—— Vom Reichsfürstenstande. Innsbruck. 1861.
—— Ueber das Verfahren gegen Heinrich den Löwen nach dem Berichte der Geln-
    häuser Urkunde. FDG. XI. 1871.
Geselbracht, F. Das Verfahren bei den deutschen Bischofswahlen in der zweiten
    Hälfte des 12 Jahrhunderts. Leipsic. 1905. [diss.]
Gossmann, F. Heinrich von Herford und die angebliche Einnahme Hannovers durch
    die Gegner Heinrichs des Löwen. Neu. Arch. XLI. 1919.
Gronen, E. Die Machtpolitik Heinrichs des Löwen und sein Gegensatz gegen das
    Kaisertum. (Ebering's Hist. Studien, 139.) Berlin. 1919.
G'sell, P. Amandus, O.S.B. Die Vita des Erzbischofs Arnold von Mainz. Neu.
    Arch. XLIII. 1920–1.
Güterbock, F. Der Prozess Heinrichs des Löwen. Berlin. 1909.
—— Neuere Forschungen zur Geschichte Heinrichs des Löwen. In Deutsche
    Litteraturzeitung. 6 March. Berlin. 1920.
—— Die Neubildung des Reichsfürstenstandes und der Prozess Heinrichs des
    Löwen. In Historische Aufsätze, Karl Zeumer...dargebracht. Weimar. 1910.
Haller, J. Der Sturz Heinrichs des Löwen. Leipsic. 1911.
Hampe, K. Heinrichs des Löwen Sturz in politisch-histor. Beurteilung. HZ. CIX.
    1912.
—— Kritische Bemerkungen zur Kirchenpolitik der Stauferzeit. HZ. XCIII. 1904.
Hauck, A. Friedrich Barbarossa als Kirchenpolitiker. (Rectoratsrede.) Leipsic.
    1898.
Hausrath, H. Die Stellung Kaiser Friedrichs I zu den Einforstungen. HZ. CXIII.
    1914.
Hecker, G. Die territoriale Politik des Erzbischofs Philipp I von Köln. Leipsic.
    1882.
Heigel, K. Th. and Riezler, S. Das Herzogtum Bayern zur Zeit Heinrichs des
    Löwen und Ottos I von Wittelsbach. Munich. 1867.
Heinemann, O. v. Albrecht der Bär. Darmstadt. 1864.
Hofmeister, A. Zur Epistola de Morte Friderici imperatoris. Neu. Arch. XLI. 1919.
Holzmann, R. Die Wahl Friedrich I zum Deutschen König. HVJS. I. 1898.
Hüffer, G. Das Verhältniss des Königreiches Burgund zu Kaiser und Reich. Pader-
    born. 1874.
Jastrow, J. Die Welfenprozesse und die ersten Regierungsjahre Friedrich Barbarossas
    (1138–56). DZG. X. 1893.
Kap-Herr, H. v. Die abendländische Politik Kaiser Manuels mit besonderer Rück-
    sicht auf Deutschland. Strasbourg. 1881. [diss.]
Kleeman, G. Papst Gregor VIII. (Jenaer Historische Arbeiten, 4.) Bonn. 1912.
Kötzschke, R. Staat und Kultur im Zeitalter der ostdeutschen Kolonisation. Leipsic.
    1910.
Krabbo, H. Albrecht der Bär. (Forsch. zur brandenburgischen und preussischen
    Geschichte. XIX.) Leipsic. 1906.
Krammer, M. Der Reichsgedanke des staufischen Kaiserhauses. (Untersuchungen
    zur deutschen Staats- und Rechtsgeschichte. Ed. Gierke, O. No. 95.) Breslau.
    1908.
Kuch, F. Die Landfriedensbestrebungen Friedrichs I. Marburg. 1887. [diss.]
Lucas, F. Zwei kritische Untersuchungen zur Geschichte Friedrichs I. Berlin.
    1904. [diss.]
Mackie, J. D. Pope Adrian IV. Oxford. 1907.

Martini, R. Die Trierer Bischofswahlen vom Beginn des 10 bis zum Ausgang des 12 Jahrhunderts. Berlin. 1909.

Meister, A. Die Hohenstaufen im Elsass. Mayence. 1890. [diss.]

Niese, H. Der Sturz Heinrichs des Löwen. HZ. cxii. 1914.

Peters, A. Die Reichspolitik des Erzbischofs Philipp von Köln 1167–91. Marburg. 1899. [diss.]

Peters, U. Charakteristik der inneren Kirchenpolitik Friedrich Barbarossas. Greifswald. 1909. [diss.]

Pflugk-Harttung, J. v. Die Papstwahlen und das Kaisertum. Gotha. 1909.

Philippi, F. Heinrich der Löwe als Beförderer von Kunst und Wissenschaft. HZ. cxxvii. 1922.

Pomtow, M. Ueber den Einfluss der altrömischen Vorstellungen vom Staat auf die Politik Kaiser Friedrichs I und die Anschauungen seiner Zeit. Halle. 1885. [diss.]

Reese, R. Die staatsrechtliche Stellung der Bischöfe Burgunds und Italiens unter Kaiser Friedrich I. Göttingen. 1885. [diss.]

Reichel, H. Die Ereignisse an der Saone im Aug. und Sept. 1162. Halle. 1909. [diss.]

Ribbeck, W. Friedrich I und die römische Curie in den Jahren 1157–9. Leipsic. 1881. [diss.]

Rietschel, S. Die Stadtpolitik Heinrichs des Löwen. HZ. cii. 1908.

Schäfer, D. Die Verurteilung Heinrichs des Löwen. HZ. lxxvi. 1895.

—— Zur Beurteilung des Wormser Konkordats. SPAW. 1905.

Schambach, K. Friedrich Rotbart und Eskil von Lund. HVJS. xiii. 1910.

—— Zwei Bemerkungen zu dem päpstlichen Schreiben von 1157 (Besançon). HVJS. xiv. 1911.

Scheffer-Boichorst, P. Deutschland und Philipp II August von Frankreich in den Jahren 1180–1214. FDG. viii. 1868.

—— Kaiser Friedrichs I letzter Streit mit der Kurie. Berlin. 1866.

—— Zur Geschichte des xii und xiii Jahrhunderts. Diplomatische Forschungen. (Ebering's Hist. Studien, 8.) Berlin. 1897.

Scholz, R. Beiträge zur Geschichte der Hoheitsrechte der Deutschen Königs zur Zeit der ersten Staufer (1138–97). Leipsic. 1896.

Schrörs, H. Untersuchungen zum Streite Kaiser Friedrichs I mit Papst Hadrian IV (1157–8). Bonn, Univ. Progr. 1915.

Simonsfeld, H. Die Wahl Friedrichs I Rotbart. *In* Sitzungsberichte d. k. bayer. Akad. d. Wiss. zu München. Philos.-philol.-hist. Klasse. Munich. 1894. *Cf.* HVJS. ii. 1899.

—— Zur Geschichte Friedrich Rotbarts. *In* Sitzungsberichte d. k. bayer. Akad. d. Wiss. zu München. Philos.-philol.-hist. Klasse. Munich. 1909.

Tangl, M. Die Echtheit der österreichischen Privilegium minus. ZSR. xxv. 1904.

Waitz, G. Ueber den Bericht der Gelnhäuser Urkunde von der Verurtheilung Heinrich des Löwen. FDG. x. 1870.

Weiland, L. Der Prozess gegen Heinrich den Löwen. FDG. vii. 1867.

—— Das Sächsische Herzogtum unter Lothar und Heinrich dem Löwen. Greifswald. 1866.

Wolfram, G. Friedrich I und das Wormser Concordat. Marburg. 1883.

CHAPTER XIV.

THE EMPEROR HENRY VI.

I. SPECIAL BIBLIOGRAPHIES.

See Bibliography for chapter x.

II. ORIGINAL DOCUMENTS.

Constitutiones et Acta publica imperatorum et regum. I. Ed. Weiland, L. MGH. Legum Sect. IV. 1893.
Monumenta Germaniae Selecta. Ed. Doeberl, M. Vol. v. Munich. 1894.
Regesta Pontificum Romanorum. Ed. Jaffé, P. 2nd edn. Loewenfeld, Kaltenbrunner, and Ewald. *See Gen. Bibl.* IV *under* Jaffé.
Regesta Pontificum Romanorum. Ed. Kehr, P. F. *See Gen. Bibl.* IV *under* Kehr.
Epistolae Pontificum Romanorum ineditae. Ed. Loewenfeld, S. Leipsic. 1885.
Stumpf-Brentano, K. F. Die Reichskanzler. *See Gen. Bibl.* IV.
Bresslau, H. Handbuch der Urkundenlehre für Deutschland und Italien. *See Gen. Bibl.* I.

III. AUTHORITIES.

Aegidii Aureaevallensis Gesta Episcoporum Leodiensium. MGH. Script. XXV.
Annales Augustani minores. *Ibid.* X.
Annales Casinenses. *Ibid.* XIX.
Annales Ceccanenses. *Ibid.*
Annales Egmundani. *Ibid.* XVI.
Annales Marbacenses. Ed. Bloch, H. SGUS. 1907.
Annales Pegavienses. MGH. Script. XVI.
Annales Placentini Gibellini. *Ibid.* XVIII.
Annales Reicherspergenses. *Ibid.* XVII.
Annales Reinhardsbrunnenses. *Ibid.* XXX.
Annales Stadenses. *Ibid.* XVI.
Annales Stederburgenses. *Ibid.*
Anonymi Zwetlensis Historia Romanorum Pontificum. *In* Pez, B. Thesaurus Anecdotorum novissimus. Vol. I, pt. iii. Augsburg. 1721.
Arnoldi Chronica Slavorum. Ed. Lappenberg, J. M. SGUS. 1868.
Braunschweigische Reimchronik. MGH. Deutsche Chroniken. II.
Burchardi Praepositi Urspergensis Chronicon. Ed. Holder-Egger, O. and Simson, B. v. SGUS. 1916.
Chronica Magistri Rogeri de Houedene. Ed. Stubbs, W. 4 vols. (Rolls.) 1868–71.
Chronica Monasterii S. Bartholomaei de Carpineto. *In* Ughelli, Italia Sacra. X. *See Gen. Bibl.* IV.
Chronica Regia Coloniensis. Ed. Waitz, G. SGUS. 1880.
Chronicon anonymi Laudunensis canonici. MGH. Script. XXVI.
Chronicon Montis Sereni. *Ibid.* XXIII.
Chronicon Tolosani canoniciǀFaventini. *In* Documenti di Storia Italiana. VI. Florence. 1876.
Cosmae Pragensis, Chronica Bohemorum (Continuationes). MGH. Script. IX.
Gerlaci Abbatis Milovicensis Chronicon Bohemiae. *Ibid.* XVII.
Gervasii Tilleberiensis Otia Imperialia. *Ibid.* XXVII.
Gesta Episcoporum Halberstadensium. *Ibid.* XXIII.
Gesta regis Henrici II Benedicti Abbatis Petriburgensis. Ed. Stubbs, W. 2 vols. (Rolls.) 1867.
Gesta Treverorum continuata. MGH. Script. XXIV.
Gisleberti Chronicon Hanoniense. Ed. Arndt, W. SGUS. 1869. *Also* ed. Vanderkindere, L. (Recueil de textes pour servir à l'étude de l'histoire de Belgique.) Brussels. 1904.

Gotifredi Viterbiensis opera. MGH. Script. xxii. (Gesta Friderici I et Henrici VI *also in* SGUS. Ed. Waitz, G. 1870.)

Historia de Expeditione Friderici Imperatoris edita a quodam Austriensi clerico, qui eidem interfuit, nomine Ansbertus. 1187–96. *In* Fontes rerum Austriacarum. Script. **v.** Vienna. 1863.

Itinerarium peregrinorum et gesta regis Ricardi Ed. Stubbs, W. *in* Chronicles and Memorials of the reign of Richard I. Vol. i. (Rolls.) 1864.

Liber Pontificalis. Ed. Duchesne, L. *See Gen. Bibl.* iv.

Monumenta Erphesfurtensia. Ed. Holder-Egger, O. SGUS. 1899

Monumenta Welforum antiqua. Ed. Weiland, L. SGUS. 1869.

Nicetas Acominatus. Byzantina historia. Ed. Bekker, I. CSHB. 1835.

Ottoboni scribae Annales. MGH. Script. xviii.

Ottonis de Sancto Blasio Chronica. Ed. Hofmeister, A. SGUS. 1912.

Petri de Ebulo, Liber ad Honorem Augusti. Ed. Siragusa, G. B. (Fonti.) 1906.

Radulfi de Diceto, decani Lundoniensis, Opera Historica. Ed. Stubbs, W. 2 vols. (Rolls.) 1876.

Ryccardi de S. Germano Notarii Chronica. Ed. Pertz, G. H. SGUS. 1864.

Sächsische Weltchronik (Eike von Repgow). MGH. Deutsche Chroniken. ii.

Sigeberti Gemblacensis Chronica (Continuatio Aquicinctina). MGH. Script. vi.

Vita Alberti episcopi Leodiensis. *Ibid.* xxv.

Willelmi Parvi, Canonici de Novoburgo, Historia rerum Anglicarum. Ed. Howlett, R. *in* Chronicles of the Reigns of Stephen, Henry II, and Richard I. Vols. i and ii. (Rolls.) 1884.

IV. MODERN WORKS.

(a) GENERAL.

Cartellieri, A. Philipp II August, König von Frankreich. 4 vols. Leipsic. 1899–1922.

Chalandon, F. Histoire de la Domination Normande en Italie et en Sicile. Vol. ii. Paris. 1907.

Fournier, P. Le Royaume d'Arles et de Vienne. Paris. 1891.

Giesebrecht, W. v. and Simson, B. v. Geschichte d. deutschen Kaiserzeit. Vol. vi. *See Gen. Bibl.* v.

Hampe, K. Deutsche Kaisergeschichte in der Zeit der Salier und Staufer. 5th edn. *See Gen. Bibl.* v.

Hauck, A. Kirchengeschichte Deutschlands. Vol. iv. *See Gen. Bibl.* v.

Jastrow, J. and Winter, G. Deutsche Geschichte im Zeitalter der Hohenstaufen. 2 vols. Stuttgart. 1897.

Meister, A. Deutsche Verfassungsgeschichte. 3rd edn. (Grundriss der Geschichtswissenschaft. Ed. Meister, A. ii, 3.) Leipsic and Berlin. 1922.

Philippson, M. Heinrich der Löwe. Sein Leben und seine Zeit. 2nd edn. 2 vols. Leipsic. 1918.

Prutz, H. Heinrich der Löwe. Leipsic. 1865.

Ranke, L. v. Weltgeschichte. *See Gen. Bibl.* v.

Raumer, F. v. Geschichte der Hohenstaufen und ihrer Zeit. 6 vols. Leipsic. 1823–5. 5th edn. 1878.

Toeche, T. Kaiser Heinrich VI. (Jahrb. d. deutsch. Geschichte.) Leipsic. 1867.

Waitz, G. Deutsche Verfassungsgeschichte. *See Gen. Bibl.* v.

Werminghoff, A. Verfassungsgeschichte der deutschen Kirche im Mittelalter. 2nd edn. (Grundriss der Geschichtswissenschaft. Ed. Meister, A. ii, 6.) Leipsic and Berlin. 1913.

(b) SPECIAL.

Bloch, H. Forschungen zur Politik Kaiser Heinrichs VI in den Jahren 1191–4. Berlin. 1892.

—— Ueber die sogenannten "Marbacher" Annalen. Neu. Arch. xxxviii. 1913.

—— Die staufischen Kaiserwahlen und die Entstehung des Kurfürstentums. Leipsic. 1911. (Also in part in HVJS. xii. 1909.) *See also* review by G. Husak *in* Göttingische Gelehrte Anzeigen, 175. pp. 189–227. Berlin. 1913.

Bresslau, H. Kanzleigebühren unter Heinrich VI (1191). *In* Strassburger Festschrift zur xlvi Versammlung Deutscher Philologen und Schulmänner. Strasbourg. 1901.

Caro, J.　Die Beziehungen Heinrichs VI zur römischen Kurie während der Jahre 1190–7. Rostock. 1902. [diss.]

Cartellieri, A.　Heinrich VI und der Höhepunkt der staufischen Kaiserpolitik. Leipsic. 1914.

Ficker, J.　De Henrici VI imperatoris conatu electiciam regum in imperio Romano-Germanico successionem in hereditariam mutandi. Bonn. 1849. [diss.]

—— Über das Testament Kaiser Heinrichs VI. Vienna. 1871.

Geselbracht, F.　Das Verfahren bei den deutschen Bischofswahlen in der zweiten Hälfte des 12 Jahrhunderts. Leipsic. 1905. [diss.]

Geyer, J.　Papst Klemens III (1187–91). (Jenaer Hist. Arbeiten, 7.) Bonn. 1914.

Gronen, E.　Die Machtpolitik Heinrichs des Löwen und sein Gegensatz gegen das Kaisertum. (Ebering's Hist. Studien, 139.) Berlin. 1919.

Haller, J.　Die Marbacher Annalen. Berlin. 1912.

—— Kaiser Heinrich VI. HZ. cxiii. 1915.

—— Heinrich VI und die römische Kirche. MIOGF. xxxv. 1914.

—— Innozenz III und das Kaisertum Heinrichs VI. HVJS. xx. 1920.

Hampe, K.　Zum Erbkaiserplan Heinrichs VI. MIOGF. xxvii. 1906.

Hecker, H.　Die territoriale Politik des Erzbischof Philipp I von Köln. Leipsic. 1883.

Heinemann, L. v.　Heinrichs VI angeblicher Plan einer Säcularisation des Kirchenstaates. MIOGF. ix. 1888.

Kalbfuss, H.　Die staufischen Kaiserwahlen und ihre Vorgeschichte. MIOGF. xxxiv. 1913.

Kap-herr, H. v.　Die "unio regni ad imperium." Ein Beitrag zur Geschichte der staufischen Politik. DZG. i. 1889.

Kienast, W.　Die deutschen Fürsten im Dienste d. Westmächte. Vol. i. Utrecht. 1924.

Kleeman, G.　Papst Gregor VIII. (1187.) (Jenaer Hist. Arbeiten, 4.) Bonn. 1912.

Kneller, K. A.　Des Richard Löwenherz deutsche Gefangenschaft 1192–4. Freiburg-i.-B. 1893.

Köhler, H.　Die Ketzerpolitik der Deutschen Kaiser und Könige in den Jahren 1152–1254. (Jenaer Hist. Arbeiten, 6.) Bonn. 1913.

Krammer, M.　Der Reichsgedanke des staufischen Kaiserhauses. (Untersuchungen zur deutschen Staats- und Rechtsgeschichte. Ed. Gierke, O. No. 95.) Breslau. 1908. [*See also* review by Bloch, H. *in* Göttingische Gelehrte Anzeigen, 171. pp. 363–91. Berlin. 1909.]

Leineweber, J.　Studien zur Geschichte Papst Cölestins III. Jena. 1905. [diss.]

Leonhardt, W.　Der Kreuzzugsplan Kaiser Heinrichs VI. Giessen. 1913. [diss.]

Martini, R.　Die Trierer Bischofswahlen vom Beginn des 10 bis zum Ausgang des 12 Jahrhunderts. Berlin. 1909.

Ottendorf, H. J. W.　Die Regierung der beiden letzten Normannen Könige Tankreds und Wilhelms III von Sizilien und ihre Kämpfe gegen Kaiser Heinrich VI. Bonn. 1899. [diss.]

Peters, K. W. A.　Die Reichspolitik des Erzbischofs Philipp von Köln 1167–91. Marburg. 1899.

Philippi, F.　Heinrich der Löwe als Beförderer von Kunst und Wissenschaft. HZ. cxxvii. 1922.

Powicke, F. M.　The loss of Normandy (1189–1204). Manchester. 1913.

Prinz, P.　Markward von Anweiler. Emden. 1875.

Scheffer-Boichorst, P.　Kaiser Friedrichs I letzter Streit mit der Kurie. Berlin. 1866.

—— Deutschland und Philipp August von Frankreich in den Jahren 1180–1214. FDG. viii. 1868.

—— Zur Geschichte des xii und xiii Jahrhunderts. Diplomatische Forschungen. (Ebering's Hist. Studien, 8.) Berlin. 1897.

Scholz, R.　Beiträge zur Geschichte der Hoheitsrechte der Deutschen Königs zur Zeit der ersten Staufer (1138–97). Leipsic. 1896.

Schwartz, P.　Die Fürstenempörung von 1192–3. Berlin. 1879. [Rostock diss.]

Traub, E.　Der Kreuzzugsplan Kaiser Heinrichs VI in Zusammenhang mit der Politik der Jahre 1195–7. Jena. 1910. [diss.]

Trautmann, C.　Heinrich VI und der Lütticher Bischofsmord. Jena. 1912. [diss.]

Winter, A.　Der Erbfolgeplan und das Testament Kaiser Heinrichs VI. Erlangen. 1908. [diss.]

CHAPTERS XV AND XVI.

ENGLAND AND NORMANDY, UNDER THE NORMAN KINGS.

I. ORIGINAL SOURCES.

(a) CHRONICLES, ANNALS, BIOGRAPHIES, ETC.

Aelred, Abbot of Rievaulx. Opera omnia. MPL. CXLV.
—— Relatio de Standardo. Ed. Howlett, R. *in* Chronicles of Stephen, etc. Vol. III. (Rolls.) 1886.

Amiens, Guy of. De bello Hastingensi Carmen. Ed. Petrie, H. *in* Monumenta historica Britannica. pp. 856–72. *See Gen. Bibl.* IV.

Anglia Sacra. Ed. Wharton, H. London. 1691.

Anglo-Saxon Chronicle. Ed. Plummer, C. 2 vols. Oxford. 1892, 99. [Worcester Chronicle (D) to 1079. Peterborough Chronicle (E) to 1154.] Transl. Gomme, E. E. C. London. 1909. *Also* transl. Giles, J. A. 2nd edn. London. 1912.

Annales Cambriae. Ed. Williams ab Ithel, J. (Rolls.) 1860.

Annales Radingenses (1066–1189). Ed. Liebermann, F. *in* Ungedruckte anglo-normannische Geschichtsquellen. *See below,* I (b).

Annals of Lewes Priory, The. Ed. Liebermann, F. EHR. XVII (1902). 86.

Brevis Relatio de origine Willelmi. Ed. Giles, J. A. *in* Scriptores Rerum Gest. Willelmi Conquestoris. (Caxton Soc.) London. 1845.

Brut y Tywysogion (681–1282). Ed. Williams ab Ithel, J. (Rolls.) 1866.

Canterbury, Gervase of. Historical Works (1100–99). Ed. Stubbs, W. (Rolls.) 1879–80.

Dudo of Saint-Quentin. De moribus et actis primorum Normanniae ducum. Ed. Lair, J. Caen. 1865.

Durham, Simeon of. Opera omnia. Ed. Arnold, T. (Rolls.) 1882–5.

Eadmer. Historia Novorum (960–1122), and Vita Anselmi. Ed. Rule, M. (Rolls.) 1884.

Gaimar, Geffroi. L'estorie des Engles (495–1100). Ed. Hardy, T. D. and Martin, C. T. (Rolls.) 1888–9. [Vol. I, Text: Vol. II, Translation.]

Gesta Consulum Andegavorum. Ed. Halphen, L. and Poupardin, R. *in* Chroniques des Comtes d'Anjou et des Seigneurs d'Amboise. pp. 25–171. (Coll. textes.) 1913.

Gesta Herwardi. Ed. Hardy, T. D. and Martin, C. T. *in* Gaimar. Vol. I. *See above.* [A romance written *c.* 1150.]

Gesta Stephani (1135–47). Ed. Howlett, R. *in* Chronicles of Stephen, etc. Vol. III. (Rolls.) 1886.

Hexham, John of. Historia (1130–54). Ed. Arnold, T. *in* Symeon of Durham. Vol. II. (Rolls.) 1885.

Hexham, Richard of. Historia de Gestis Regis Stephani (1135–9). Ed. Howlett, R. *in* Chronicles of Stephen, etc. Vol. III. (Rolls.) 1886.

Historiae Normannorum Scriptores Antiqui. Ed. Duchesne, A. Paris. 1619.

Historians of the Church of York and its Archbishops; contains *inter alia* lives of Thomas I, Gerard, Thomas II, and Thurstan (1070–1127), with additions to 1153 by Hugo Sottovagina, Precentor of York. Ed. Raine, J. (Rolls.) 1879–94.

Huntingdon, Henry, Archdeacon of. Historia Anglorum (–1154). Ed. Arnold, T. (Rolls.) 1879. Engl. transl. Forester, T. (Bohn's Antiq. Library.) London. 1853.

Jumièges, Guillaume de. Gesta Normannorum Ducum (851–1137). Ed. Marx, J. Rouen. 1914.

Liber Eliensis. Ed. Stewart, D. J. London. 1848.

Liber Monasterii de Hyda. Ed. Edwards, E. (Rolls.) 1866.

Malmesbury, William of. De Gestis Regum (449–1127). Historia Novella (1125–42). Ed. Stubbs, W. 2 vols. (Rolls.) 1887, 89. Engl. transl. Giles, J. A. (Bohn's Antiq. Library.) London. 1847.
—— De Gestis Pontificum. Ed. Hamilton, N. E. S. (Rolls.) 1870.
—— Vita S. Wulstani, episcopi Wigorniensis. Ed. Darlington, R. R. (Camden Ser.) London. 1928.
Newburgh, William, Canon of. Ed. Howlett, R. *in* Chronicles of Stephen, etc. Vols. I and II. (Rolls.) 1884–5.
Poitiers, William of (Archdeacon of Lisieux). Gesta Guillelmi Ducis (–1067). Ed. Duchesne, A. *in* Hist. Normann. Scriptores. (*See above*.) pp. 178–213. *Also* in MPL. CXLIX. col. 1216.
Recueil d'annales Angevines et Vendômoises. Ed. Halphen, L. (Coll. textes.) 1903.
Suger. Historia Ludovici VII. Ed. Molinier, A. (Coll. textes.) 1887.
Torigni (*or* Monte), Robert de. Chronica (–1185). Ed. Howlett, R. *in* Chronicles of Stephen, etc. Vol. IV. (Rolls.) 1889.
Vitalis, Ordericus. Historia Ecclesiastica (–1141). Ed. Le Prévost, A. and Delisle, L. 5 vols. (SHF.) Paris. 1838–55. Engl. transl. Forester, T. The Ecclesiastical History of England and Normandy. 4 vols. (Bohn's Antiq. Library.) London. 1853–6.
Wace. Le Roman de Rou (from Rollo to 1106). Ed. Andresen, H. 2 vols. Heilbronn. 1877, 79. Engl. transl. Taylor, E. London. 1837. Transl. into English rhyme. Malet, A. London. 1860.
Worcester, Florence of. Chronica ex Chronicis (–1117). Continued by John of Worcester (–1141). Ed. Thorpe, B. 2 vols. (English Hist. Soc.) London. 1848–9. Engl. transl. Forester, T. (Bohn's Antiq. Library.) London. 1854.

(b) Diplomata, Letters, etc.

Acta archiepiscoporum Rotomagensium. MPL. CXLVII. col. 273.
Ancient Charters (1095–1200). Ed. Round, J. H. (Pipe Roll Soc.) London. 1888.
Anselmi Opera. MPL. CLVIII, CLIX.
Antiquus Cartularius Ecclesiae Baiocensis (Livre Noir). Ed. Bourrienne, V. Paris. 1902–3.
Bayeux Inquest, 1133. *In* Bouquet. XXIII. pp. 699–702. Also in a curtailed form *in* Liber Rubeus de Scaccario. Ed. Hall, H. pp. 624–45. (Rolls.) 1896.
Bayeux Tapestry, The. Reproduced in autotype, with historical notes, by Fowke, F. R. (Arundel Soc.) London. 1895.
Bedfordshire in 1086. An analysis and synthesis of Domesday Book. Fowler, G. H. Bedfordshire Hist. Rec. Soc. XXIII. p. 693. 1922.
Sancti Bernardi Opera. Ed. Mabillon, J. 2 vols. Paris. 1690.

Borough Charters, Writs, and Custumals:
Beverley. Henry I. Gross. Gild Merchant. Vol. II. p. 21. *See below*, II *b* (i).
—— Archbp. Thurstan. Beverley Town Documents. Ed. Leach, A. F. (Selden Soc. XIV.) London. 1900. p. 132.
Burford. R. fitz Hamon. Gross. Gild Merchant. Vol. II. p. 29.
Bury St Edmunds. Henry I. EHR. XXIV (1909). 425.
—— Stephen. EHR. XXIV (1909). 429.
—— Abbot Anselm. AHR. II. 689.
Cambridge. Henry I. Charters of...Cambridge. Ed. Maitland, F. W. and Bateson, M. Cambridge. 1901. p. 2.
Canterbury. Henry I. Brit. Mus. MSS. Julius, D. 2. p. 88 *b*.
Chichester. Stephen. Ballard, A. History of Chichester. Chichester. 1898. p. 92.
Colchester. Henry I. Cartularium Monast. S. Johannis de Colecestria. Vol. I. p. 28. *See below*.
—— Henry I (later). *Ibid*. p. 23.
Folkestone. Stephen. Boys, W. History of Sandwich. Canterbury. 1792. p. 816.
Fordwich. Odo of Bayeux. Brit. Mus. MSS. Julius, D. 2. p. 91.
—— William I. *Ibid*.

Guildford. Henry I. Journal British Archaeol. Assoc. xxix. 260.
Huntingdon. Henry I. Dugdale. Monasticon. Vol. vi. p. 80. *See Gen. Bibl.* iv.
Leicester. Robert of Meulan. Records of...Leicester. Ed. Bateson, M. Vol. i.
    London. 1899. p. 1.
—— Henry I. *Ibid.*
London. William I. Gesetze. Ed. Liebermann. Vol. i. p. 486. *See below.*
—— Henry I. *Ibid.* p. 524.
Newcastle. Henry I. Stubbs. Select Charters. Ed. Davis. p. 133. *See Gen. Bibl.* iv.
Rye. Abbot of Fécamp. Fécamp Chartal. In Public Library, Rouen. 34.
Salisbury. Henry I. Gross. Gild Merchant. Vol. ii. p. 209.
Sandwich. Odo of Bayeux. Bodleian Library. MS. Top. Kent. D. i. 44.
—— William I. Calendar...Patent Rolls...Public Record Office. 1429–36.
    London. 1907. p. 416.
Taunton. Stephen. Calendar...Charter Rolls...Public Record Office. Vol. iii.
    London. 1908. p. 354.
Wilton. Henry I. Journal British Archaeol. Assoc. xvii. 311.
British Borough Charters, 1042–1216. By Ballard, A. Cambridge. 1913.
Calendar of Documents preserved in France illustrative of the history of Great Britain
    and Ireland 918–1206. Ed. Round, J. H. (Rolls.) 1899.
Canons of the Council of Lillebonne (1080). *In* Teulet, A. Layettes du Trésor
    des Chartes. Vol. i. Paris. 1863. p. 25. *Also in* Vitalis, Ordericus. Vol. ii.
    pp. 316–23. *See above,* i (*a*).
Cartularium Monasterii de Rameseia. Ed. Hart, W. H. and Lyon, P. A. (Rolls.)
    1884–93.
Cartularium Monasterii Sancti Johannis Baptiste de Colecestria. Ed. Moore, S. A.
    2 vols. (Roxburghe Club.) London. 1897.
Cartularium S. Petri Gloucestriae. Ed. Hart, W. H. 3 vols. (Rolls.) 1863–7.
Charter of Enfeoffment under William the Conqueror, A. By Douglas, D. C. EHR.
    xlii (1927). 245.
Chartes des libertés anglaises 1100–1305. Ed. Bémont, C. Paris. 1892.
Chronicon Monasterii de Abingdon. Ed. Stevenson, J. (Rolls.) 1858.
Consuetudines et Justicia, quas habet dux Normannie in eadem provincia, as re-
    corded at an inquest held at Caen, July 18, 1091. *In* Haskins. Norman
    Institutions. pp. 281–4. *See below,* ii (*a*).
Coutumiers de Normandie, textes critiques publiés avec notes et éclaircissements
    par E. J. Tardif. 2 vols. Rouen. 1881, 1903.
Dialogus de Scaccario. Ed. Hughes, A., Crump, C. G., and Johnson, E. Oxford. 1902.
Documents illustrative of the Social and Economic History of the Danelaw. Ed.
    Stenton, F. M. (British Academy. Records of the Social and Economic History
    of England and Wales. Vol. v.) London. 1920.
Domesday Book. *See Gen. Bibl.* iv. [For translations and introductions to surveys
    of individual counties *see* Victoria History of the Counties of England. *See Gen.
    Bibl.* i.]
Domesday Studies by various writers. Ed. Dove, P. E. London. 1888–91.
Domesday Tables. Baring, F. H. London. 1909.
Exon Domesday. Ed. Ellis, H. *in* Domesday Book. Vol. iv. *See Gen. Bibl.* iv.
Foliot, Gilbert. Epistolae. MPL. cxc. col. 739–1068. *Also* ed. Giles, J. A. 2 vols.
    (Patres eccl. Angl.) Oxford. 1845.
Gallia Christiana. Vol. xi. (Normandy.) *See Gen. Bibl.* iv.
Gesetze der Angelsachsen, Die. Ed. Liebermann, F. 3 vols. Halle-a.-S. 1898–1916.
    Vol. i contains the texts; Vol. ii, pt. i, a dictionary and concordance; pt. ii,
    a glossary; Vol. iii, introductions to each text and notes.
Henry I; Coronation Charter. Ed. Liebermann, F. TRHS. n.s. viii (1894). 21–48.
Inquest of fiefs in Normandy in 1172. *In* Bouquet. xxiii. pp. 693–9. *Also in* Liber
    Rubeus de Scaccario. Ed. Hall, H. pp. 624–45. (Rolls.) 1896.
Inquisitio Comitatus Cantabrigiensis. Subjicitur Inquisitio Eliensis. Ed. Hamilton,
    N. E. S. A. London. 1876.
Inquisitio Eliensis. Ed. Ellis, H. *in* Domesday Book. Vol. iv. *See Gen. Bibl.* iv.
Inquisitio Geldi (1084). Ed. Ellis, H. *Ibid.*
Instituta Cnuti aliorumque Regum Anglorum. Ed. Liebermann, F. TRHS. n.s.
    vii (1893). 77–107.

Ivo, Bishop of Chartres. Epistolae. *In* Bouquet. xv. 1808.
Landboc de Winchelcumba. Ed. Royce, D. Exeter. 1892.
Lanfranc. Omnia Opera. Ed. Giles, J. A. Oxford. 1844.
Leges Henrici Primi, *see* Gesetze, ed. Liebermann, *above*.
Leicestershire Survey (1124–9). Ed. Round, J. H. *in* Feudal England. pp. 197–203. London. 1895.
Libelli de lite Imperatorum, etc. Vol. iii. Tractatus Eboracenses. [Probably by Gerard of York, criticising Papal claims.] MGH. 1897.
Liber Niger of Peterborough. Ed. Stapleton, T. *in* Chronica Petriburgense. (Camden Soc.) London. 1849.
Liber Niger Scaccarii. Ed. Hearne, T. 2nd edn. 2 vols. Oxford. 1771.
Liber Rubeus de Scaccario. Ed. Hall, H. 3 vols. (Rolls.) 1896.
Liber Winton. Surveys of Winchester, 1103–15 and 1148. Ed. Ellis, H. *in* Domesday Book. Vol. iv. *See Gen. Bibl.* iv.
Lincolnshire Domesday and the Lindsey Survey. Transl. and ed. by Foster, C. W. and Langley, T., with an introduction by Stenton, F. M. Horncastle. 1924.
Lincolnshire Survey (Lindsey). Temp. Henry I (*c.* 1115–18). Ed. Greenstreet, J. London. 1884. [Discussed by Round, J. H. *in* Feudal England. pp. 181–95. London. 1895.]
Losinga, Herbert de. Epistolae. Ed. Anstruther, R. Brussels. 1848.
—— Letters and Sermons. Transl. with notes. By Goulburn, E. M. and Symonds, H. London. 1878.
Map, Walter. De nugis curialium. Ed. James, M. R. (Anecdota Oxoniensia, Mediaeval Series, xiv.) Oxford. 1914.
Monasticon Anglicanum. Ed. Dugdale, W. Re-edited Caley, Ellis, and Bandinel. *See Gen. Bibl.* iv.
Neustria Pia, seu de omnibus et singulis Abbatiis et Prioratibus totius Normanniae. Ed. Du Monstier, A. Rouen. 1663.
Northamptonshire Geld Roll. Ed. Ellis, H. *in* Introduction to Domesday Book. Vol. i. pp. 184–7. London. 1833.
Northamptonshire, The Hidation of. Round, J. H. EHR. xv. (1900.) 78.
Northamptonshire Survey. Ed. Round, J. H. *in* Feudal England. pp. 215–24. London. 1895
Pipe Roll. 31 Henry I. Ed. Hunter, J. (RC.) 1833.
Placita Anglo-Normannica (1066–1199). Ed. Bigelow, M. M. Boston, Mass. 1879.
Quadripartitus, ein englisches Rechtsbuch von 1114, nachgewiesen und, soweit bisher ungedruckt, herausg. von Liebermann, F. Halle. 1892.
Regesta Regum Anglo-Normannorum. Vol. i (1066–1100). Ed. Davis, H. W. C. Oxford. 1913.
St Augustine's Abbey, Canterbury, The Register of, commonly called the Black Book. Ed. Turner, G. J. and Salter, H. E. London. 1915.
Saint Évroul. Henry I's confirmation charter a.d. 1128 describing the origin of the barony of St Évroul. *In* Gallia Christiana. xi. Instruments 204–10. *See Gen. Bibl.* iv.
Salisbury, John of, Bp. of Chartres. Opera omnia. MPL. cxcix.
—— Policratica sive de nugis curialium et vestigiis philosophorum, libri viii. Ed. Webb, C. C. I. 2 vols. Oxford. 1909.
Select Charters. *See Gen. Bibl.* iv *under* Stubbs.
Textus Roffensis (*c.* 1140–50). Ed. Hearne, T. Oxford. 1720.
—— Notes on. By Liebermann, F. (Kent Archaeol. Soc., Archaeol. Cantiana. xxiii.) London. 1898. pp. 107–12.
Très Ancien Coutumier. Ed. Tardif, E. J. *in* Coutumiers de Normandie. Vol. i. *See above*.
Ungedruckte anglo-normannische Geschichtsquellen. (Contains Annales Anglo-Saxonici a.d. 925–1202 and Eadmer, Miracles of St Anselm.) Ed. Liebermann, F. Strasbourg. 1879.
Vetus Registrum Sarisberiense. The register of St Osmund. Ed. Jones, W. H. R. (Rolls.) 1883–4.
William of St Carilef. De injusta vexatione Willelmi Episcopi. *In* Symeon of Durham. Ed. Arnold, T. Vol. i. pp. 170–95. (Rolls.) 1882.

II. MODERN WORKS.

(a) GENERAL: ENGLAND AND NORMANDY.

Adams, G. B. History of England (1066–1216). (Political History of England. Ed. Hunt, W. and Poole, R. L. Vol. II.) London. 1905.
—— Constitutional History of England. New York. 1921.
Barnard, F. P. Companion to English History. Rev. edn. Davis, H. W. C. Mediaeval England. Oxford. 1924.
Bateson, M. Mediaeval England (1066–1350). London. 1905.
Böhmer, H. Kirche und Staat in England und in der Normandie im 11 und 12 Jahrhundert. Pt. I, Kirche und Staat im Zeitalter Gregors VII. Pt. II, Die kirchenpolitische Litteratur bis zum Konkordate von 1107. Pt. III, Die Inception des Gregorianismus. Leipsic. 1899.
Brown, G. Baldwin. The Arts in Early England. *See Gen. Bibl.* v.
Brown, P. Hume. History of Scotland. Vol. I. Cambridge. 1899.
Brunner, H. Die Entstehung der Schwurgerichte. Berlin. 1872.
Cambridge History of English Literature. *See Gen. Bibl.* v.
Coulton, G. G. Medieval Studies. (First series.) 2nd rev. edn. London. 1915.
—— Social Life in Britain from the Conquest to the Reformation. Cambridge. 1918.
—— Five Centuries of Religion. Vol. I. *See Gen. Bibl.* v.
Cunningham, W. The Growth of English Industry and Commerce. *See Gen. Bibl.* v.
Davis, H. W. C. England under the Normans and Angevins. (History of England. Ed. Oman, C. Vol. II.) London. 1905.
Dictionary of National Biography. *See Gen. Bibl.* I.
Dictionary of Political Economy. Ed. Palgrave, R. H. I. 3 vols. and app. London. 1894–1908 New edn. by Higgs, H. London. 1923 ff., in progress.
Dugdale, W. Monasticon Anglicanum. *See Gen. Bibl.* IV.
Freeman, E. A. History of the Norman Conquest of England. 2nd and 3rd edns. 6 vols. Oxford. 1871–9.
—— The Reign of William Rufus. 2 vols. Oxford. 1882.
Gneist, R. Englische Verfassungsgeschichte. Engl. transl. Ashworth, P. A. London. 1886.
Green, J. R. History of the English People. London. 1895–6.
Haskins, C. H. The Normans in European History. Boston and New York. 1915.
—— Norman Institutions. (Harvard Hist. Studies, 24.) Cambridge, Mass. 1918. [Invaluable for every side of Norman development.]
Histoire de France. Ed. Lavisse, E. II. 2. Les Premiers Capétiens (987–1137), par A. Luchaire. III. 1. Louis VII, Philippe Auguste, Louis VIII, par A. Luchaire. Paris. 1901–2.
Jusserand, J. J. Histoire Littéraire du Peuple Anglais des origines à la Renaissance. Paris. 1894.
La Borderie, A. de. Histoire de Brétagne. Vols. I–III. Rennes. 1896–1900.
Lang, A. History of Scotland. Vol. I. Edinburgh. 1900.
Lipson, E. An introduction to the Economic History of England. Vol. I. The Middle Ages. London. 1915.
Lloyd, J. E. History of Wales. *See Gen. Bibl.* v.
Maitland, F. W. The Constitutional History of England. Cambridge. 1908.
Makower, F. Constitutional History and Constitution of the Church of England. (Transl. from the German.) London. 1895.
Medley, D. J. Student's Manual of English Constitutional History. 6th edn. Oxford. 1925.
Meredith, H. O. Outlines of the Economic History of England. Bk. I. 1066–1272. London. 1908.
Norgate, K. England under the Angevin Kings (1100–1206). London. 1887.
Oman, C. W. C. A History of the Art of War in the Middle Ages. *See Gen. Bibl.* v.
Palgrave, F. History of Normandy and of England. 4 vols. London. 1851–64. New edn. 4 vols. Cambridge. 1919–21.
Pollock, F. and Maitland, F. W. The History of English Law before Edward I. *See Gen. Bibl.* v.

Poole, R. L. Illustrations of the History of Medieval Thought and Learning. *See Gen. Bibl.* v.

Ramsay, Sir J. H. The Foundations of England. London. 1898.

Rhys, J. and Jones, D. B. The Welsh People. London. 1900.

Rössler, O. Kaiserin Mathilde, Mutter Heinrichs von Anjou, und das Zeitalter der Anarchie in England. Berlin. 1897.

Social England. Ed. Traill, H. D. and Mann, T. S. Illustrated edn. 6 vols. London. 1901–4.

Stenton, F. M. William the Conqueror. London. 1908.

Stephens, W. R. W. The English Church from the Norman Conquest to the accession of Edward I. (Hist. of the English Church. Ed. Stephens, W. R. W. and Hunt, W. Vol. II.) London. 1901.

Stubbs, W. Constitutional History of England. *See Gen. Bibl.* v.

Tanner, T. Notitia Monastica. London. 1744. Repr. with addns. by Nasmith, J. Cambridge. 1787.

Ten Brink, B. Geschichte der englischen Litteratur. Vol. I. Strasbourg. 1877. 2nd edn. 1899.

Victoria History of the Counties of England. [Contains translations of the Domesday Survey with explanatory introductions.] *See Gen. Bibl.* I.

Vinogradoff, P. English Society in the eleventh century. Oxford. 1908.

—— Roman Law in Mediaeval Europe. *See Gen. Bibl.* v.

(b) Special.

(i) *England.*

Andrew, W. J. A numismatic history of the reign of Henry I. (Repr. from Numismatic Chronicle. 4th Series. Vol. I. pp. 221–515.) London. 1901.

Armstrong, E. S. The Early Norman Castles of the British Isles. London. 1912.

Ashley, W. J. Introduction to English Economic History and Theory. Vol. I. Pt. I. 3rd edn. London. 1894.

Ballard, A. The Domesday Boroughs. Oxford. 1904. Review by Bateson, M. *in* EHR. xx (1905). 143.

—— The Domesday Inquest. London. 1906.

—— British Borough Charters, 1042–1216. Cambridge. 1913.

—— The Walls of Malmesbury. EHR. xxi (1906). 98.

—— The Burgesses of Domesday. EHR. xxi (1906). 699.

—— Castle Guard and Barons' Houses. EHR. xxv (1910). 712.

—— The Laws of Bréteuil. EHR. xxx (1915). 644.

Bateson, M. The Laws of Bréteuil. EHR. xv (1900). 73–8, 302–18, 496–523, 754–7. EHR. xvi (1901). 92–110, 332–45.

—— The Burgesses of Domesday and the Malmesbury Walls. EHR. xxi (1906). 709.

—— Borough Customs. 2 vols. (Selden Soc.) London. 1904, 6.

Bigelow, M. M. History of Procedure in England. London. 1880.

Brooke, Z. N. Pope Gregory VII's demand for fealty from William the Conqueror. EHR. xxvi (1911). 225 sqq.

—— The English Church and the Papacy from the Conquest to the reign of John. Cambridge. 1931.

Browne, E. A. Norman Architecture. 2nd edn. London. 1919.

Brunner, H. Das anglo-normannische Erbfolgesystem. Leipsic. 1869.

Cam, H. M. The Hundred and the Hundred Rolls. Cambridge. 1930.

Church, R. W. St Anselm. London. 1883.

Clark, G. T. Medieval military architecture in England. London. 1884. [Antiquated, but gives details of English castles.]

Cunningham, W. Alien Immigrants to England. London. 1897.

David, C. W. A tract [on William of S. Carilef] attributed to Simeon of Durham. EHR. xxxii (1917). 382.

Davis, H. W. C. The Anarchy in Stephen's Reign. EHR. xviii (1903). 630.

—— Cumberland before the Norman Conquest. EHR. xx (1905). 61.

—— The Liberties of Bury St Edmunds. EHR. xxiv (1909). 417.

—— A contemporary account of the battle of Tinchebrai. EHR. xxiv (1909). 729.

—— Henry of Blois and Brian Fitz Count. EHR. xxv (1910). 297.

—— Waldric, the chancellor of Henry I. EHR. xxvi (1911). 84.

Dugdale, W. The Baronage of England. London. 1675.

Eyton, R. W. The antiquities of Shropshire. 12 vols. London. 1854–60.

—— A key to Domesday exemplified by an analysis and digest of the Dorset Survey. London. 1878.

—— Domesday Studies, analysis etc. of the Somerset Survey (according to the Exon codex). London. 1880.

—— Domesday Studies, analysis etc. of the Staffordshire Survey. London. 1881.

Farrer, W. The Lancashire Pipe Roll of 31 Henry I and early Lancashire charters (1093–1216). *In* Lancashire Pipe Rolls. Liverpool. 1902.

—— Feudal Cambridgeshire. Cambridge. 1920.

—— Honors and Knights' Fees. An attempt to identify certain honors and trace the descent of the tenants...from the eleventh to the fourteenth century. London; and Manchester. 3 vols. 1923–5. [Eight honours have been dealt with, including Chester, Huntingdon, and Peverell of Nottingham.]

—— The Sheriffs of Lincolnshire and Yorkshire, 1066–1130. EHR. xxx (1915). 277.

—— An Outline Itinerary of King Henry I. EHR. xxxiv (1919). 303 and 505. Also publ. separately. Oxford. 1920.

Freeman, E. A. The Legend of Hereward. *In* Hist. of the Norman Conquest. 2nd edn. Vol. iv. Appendix OO. *See above*, ii (*a*).

Gasquet, F. A. English Monastic Life. London. 1904.

Gierke, O. Political Theories of the Middle Age. *See Gen. Bibl.* v.

Goldschmidt, S. Geschichte der Juden in England. Vol. i. Berlin. 1886.

Graham, R. The intellectual influence of English Monasteries between the tenth and twelfth centuries. TRHS. n.s. xvii (1903). 23.

—— St Gilbert of Sempringham. London. 1911.

Gray, H. L. English Field Systems. (Harvard Hist. Studies, 22.) Cambridge, Mass. 1915.

Greenwell, W. Durham Cathedral. Durham. 1881.

Gross, C. The Gild Merchant. 2 vols. Oxford. 1890.

Hall, H. Antiquities and curiosities of the Exchequer. London. 1891.

—— Studies in English Official Historical Documents. Cambridge. 1908.

—— A Formula Book of Diplomatic Documents. Cambridge. 1908.

Haskins, C. H. A Canterbury monk at Constantinople, *c.* 1090. EHR. xxv (1910). 293.

—— England and Sicily in the twelfth century. EHR. xxvi (1911). 433 and 641.

—— Adelard of Bath. EHR. xxvi (1911). 491.

—— The Abacus and the King's Curia. EHR. xxvii (1912). 101.

—— Adelard of Bath and Henry Plantagenet. EHR. xxviii (1913). 515.

—— The reception of Arabic Science in England. EHR. xxx (1915). 56.

—— King Harold's Books. EHR. xxxvii (1922). 398.

Hasse, F. R. Anselm von Canterbury. 2 pts. Leipsic. 1843, 52.

Hemmeon, M. de W. Burgage Tenure in Medieval England. (Harvard Hist. Studies, 20.) Cambridge, Mass. 1914.

Holdsworth, W. S. A history of English Law. *See Gen. Bibl.* v.

Hook, W. F. Lives of the Archbishops of Canterbury. 12 vols. London. 1860–76.

Hudson, W. How the City of Norwich grew into shape. Norwich. 1896.

Jackson, T. G. Byzantine and Romanesque Architecture. 2nd edn. 2 vols. Cambridge. 1920. Vol. ii, ch. xxiv. French Romanesque, Normandy. Chs. xxvii, xxviii. English Romanesque after the Norman Conquest to 1180.

Jensen, O. The Denarii S. Petri in England (1066–1103). TRHS. n.s. xix (1905). 209.

Jeudwine, J. W. Tort, Crime, and Police in Mediaeval England. London. 1917.

Jones, W. H. Roger of Salisbury. *In* Wilts. Archaeol. Magazine. xvii (1878). 174.

Keyser, C. E. Norman tympana and lintels in the churches of Great Britain. London. 1904.

Lapsley, G. T. The County Palatine of Durham. (Harvard Hist. Studies, 8.) New York. 1900.

—— Cornage and Drengage. (Repr. from AHR. ix. No. 4.) New York. 1904.

Laws, E. The history of little England beyond Wales and the non-Kymric colony settled in Pembrokeshire. London. 1888.

Leach, A. F. Schools of Medieval England. London. 1915.

Levison, W. A report on the Pinenden Trial. EHR. xxviii (1912). **717.**

Liebermann, F. Anselm von Canterbury und Hugo von Lyon. *In* Historische Aufsätze dem Andenken an G. Waitz gewidmet. Hanover. 1886. pp. 156–203.
—— Magister Vacarius. EHR. xi (1896). 305.
—— Lanfranc and the Antipope. EHR. xvi (1901). 328.
—— Ueber die Leges Edwardi Confessoris. Halle. 1896.
—— Die Abfassungszeit der Leges Henrici Primi. FDG. xvi (1876). 581–6.
—— Ueber Pseudo-Cnuts constitutiones de foresta. Halle. 1894.
Madox, T. The history and antiquities of the Exchequer of England (1066–1327). London. 1711.
—— Baronia Anglica. London. 1736.
Maitland, F. W. Domesday Book and Beyond. Cambridge. 1897.
—— Township and Borough. Cambridge. 1898.
—— Roman Canon Law in the Church of England. London. 1898.
—— Northumbrian Tenures. EHR. v (1890). 625.
—— The Origin of the Borough. EHR. xi (1896). 13.
—— The Laws of the Anglo-Saxons. Quarterly Review, July, 1904. *Also in* Collected Papers. Vol. iii. Cambridge. 1911. pp. 447–73.
Massingberd, W. O. The Lincolnshire Sokemen. EHR. xx (1905). 699.
Morris, W. A. The Frankpledge System. London. 1910.
—— The Office of Sheriff in the Early Norman Period. EHR. xxxiii (1918). 145.
—— A mention of Scutage in the Year 1100. EHR. xxxvi (1921). 45.
—— The Sheriffs and the Administrative System of Henry I. EHR. xxxvii (1922). 161.
—— Plenus Comitatus. EHR. xxxix (1924). 404.
Parker, F. H. M. The Forest Laws and the death of William Rufus. EHR. xxvii (1912). 26.
Petit-Dutaillis, C. Studies and notes supplementary to Stubbs' Constitutional History. *See Gen. Bibl.* v *under* Stubbs.
Pike, L. O. A constitutional history of the House of Lords. London. 1894.
Poole, R. L. The Exchequer in the twelfth century. Oxford. 1912.
—— The English Bishops at the Lateran Council of 1139. EHR. xxxviii (1923). 61.
—— John of Salisbury at the Papal Court (1147–53). *Ibid.* p. 321.
—— The early correspondence of John of Salisbury. (Proc. Brit. Acad. xi.) London. 1924.
Powicke, F. M. Maurice of Rievaulx. EHR. xxxvi (1921). 17.
Ramsay, Sir J. H. The origin of the name "Pipe Rolls." EHR. xxvi (1911). 329.
Reid, R. R. Barony and Thanage. EHR. xxxv (1920). 161.
Rigg, J. M. St Anselm of Canterbury. London. 1896.
Robinson, J. A. Gilbert Crispin, Abbot of Westminster. Cambridge. 1911.
Round, J. H. Geoffrey de Mandeville: a study of the Anarchy. London. 1892.
—— Feudal England; historical studies on the xith and xiith centuries. London. 1895.
—— The Commune of London and other Studies. London. 1899.
—— Studies in Peerage and Family History. London. 1901.
—— The King's Sergeants and Officers of State. London. 1911.
—— English Castles. Quarterly Review. clxxix (1894). 27.
—— The Battle of Hastings. Sussex Archaeol. Soc. Collections. xlii. 1899.
—— Bernard the King's Scribe. EHR. xiv (1899). 417.
—— The Domesday Manor. EHR. xv (1900). 293.
—— The Early Charters of St John's Abbey, Colchester. EHR. xvi (1901). 721.
—— Castle Guard. Archaeol. Journal. lix (1902). 144.
—— The Castles of the Conquest. Archaeologia. lviii (1902). 313.
—— The Colchester Mint in Norman Times. EHR. xviii (1903). 305.
—— The Burton Abbey Surveys (1116–33). EHR. xx (1905). 275.
—— The Origin of Belvoir Castle. EHR. xxii (1907). 508.
—— The Weigher of the Exchequer. EHR. xxvi (1911). 724.
—— The Tertius denarius of the Borough. EHR. xxxiv (1919). 62.
—— The Staff of a Castle in the Twelfth Century. EHR. xxxv (1920). 90.
—— Castle Watchmen. EHR. xxxv (1920). 400.
—— The Early Sheriffs of Norfolk. EHR. xxxv (1920). 481.

Round, J. H. The dating of the Early Pipe Rolls. EHR. xxxvi (1921). 321.
—— A Butler's Sergeanty. EHR. xxxvi (1921). 46.
—— The Legend of Eudo Dapifer. EHR. xxxvii (1922). 1.
—— "Domesday" and "Doomsday." EHR. xxxviii (1923). 240.
Rule, M. Life and times of St Anselm. London. 1883.
Salter, H. E. A dated charter of Henry I. EHR. xxv (1911). 487.
Sawyer, F. E. The Rapes and their origin. *In* Archaeol. Review. i. London. 1888. p. 54.
Schmitz, M. Der englische Investiturstreit. Innsbruck. 1884.
Seebohm, F. The English Village Community. London. 1884.
Spatz, W. Die Schlacht von Hastings. Berlin. 1896. Reviewed by Round, J. H. *in* RH. lxv (1897). 61–77.
Stenton, F. M. Types of Manorial Structure in the Northern Danelaw. *In* Oxford Studies in Social and Legal History. Ed. Vinogradoff, P. Vol. ii. Pt. i. Oxford. 1910.
—— Sokemen and the village waste. EHR. xxxiii (1918). 344.
—— St Benet of Holme and the Norman Conquest. EHR. xxxvii (1922). 225.
—— The Danes in England. *In* Proc. Brit. Acad. xiii. 1927.
—— The first century of English feudalism. Oxford. 1932.
—— The free peasantry of the Northern Danelaw. Bull. Soc. Roy. de Lettres de Lund. 1925–6.
Stenton, Mrs F. M. Roger of Salisbury, Regni Angliae Procurator. EHR. xxxix (1924). 79.
Stevenson, W. H. An inedited charter of Henry I. EHR. xxi (1906). 505.
—— A contemporary description of the Domesday Survey. EHR. xxii (1907). 72.
Stubbs, W. Registrum sacrum Anglicanum. *See Gen. Bibl.* iii.
Surtees, R. The history and antiquities of the county palatine of Durham. 4 vols. London. 1816–40.
Tamassia, N. Lanfranco arcivescovo di Canterbury e la Scuola Pavese. *In* Mélanges Fitting. ii. Montpellier. 1908.
Turner, G. J. The Sheriff's Farm. TRHS. n.s. xii (1898). 117.
Tyrrell-Green, E. Parish Church Architecture. London. 1924.
Varenbergh, E. Histoire des relations diplomatiques entre le Comté de Flandre et l'Angleterre au moyen âge. Brussels. 1874.
Vinogradoff, P. Villainage in England. Oxford. 1892.
—— The Growth of the Manor. 3rd edn. London. 1920.
Walker, C. H. Sheriffs in the Pipe Roll of Henry I. EHR. xxxvii (1922). 67.
—— The date of the Conqueror's Ordinance separating the Ecclesiastical and Lay Courts. EHR. xxxix (1924). 399.
Zachrisson, R. E. A contribution to the study of Anglo-Norman influence on English place names. Lund. 1909.

(ii) *Normandy.*

Böhmer, H. Serlo von Bayeux. *In* Neu. Arch. xxii. 701–38.
Cartellieri, O. Abt Suger von Saint Denis, 1081–1151. Berlin. 1898.
Chalandon, F. Histoire de la Domination Normande en Italie et en Sicile. 2 vols. Paris. 1907.
Chéruel, A. Hist. de Rouen pendant l'époque communale, 1150–1382. Rouen. 1843.
Chesnel, P. Le Cotentin et l'Avranchin sous les ducs de Normandie. Caen. 1912.
Chevreux, P. and Vernier, J. Les archives de Normandie et de la Seine-Inférieure. Rouen. 1911.
David, C. W. Robert Curthose, Duke of Normandy. (Harvard Hist. Studies, 25.) Cambridge, Mass. 1920.
Delisle, L. Études sur la condition de la classe agricole en Normandie. Évreux. 1851.
—— Histoire du château et des sires de Saint-Sauveur-le-Vicomte. Valognes. 1867.
—— Recueil des actes de Henri II, roi d'Angleterre et duc de Normandie. Introduction. (Chartes et diplômes. AcadIBL.) Paris. 1909.
—— Des revenus publics en Normandie au douzième siècle. BEC. x, 173–210, 257–89, xi, 400–51, xiii, 97–135.

Demay, G. Inventaire des scéaux de la Normandie. Paris. 1881.

Deville, E. Analyse d'un ancien cartulaire de Saint-Étienne de Caen. (Repr. from Revue Catholique de Normandie, xv.) Évreux. 1905.

Du Motet, le Vicomte de. Origines de la Normandie et du duché d'Alençon de l'an 850 à l'an 1085. Paris. 1920

Flach, J. Les origines de l'ancienne France. x^e et xie siècles. Vol. iii. *See Gen. Bibl.* v.

Fliche, A. Le règne de Philippe 1er, roi de France (1060–1108). Paris. 1912.

—— Saint Grégoire VII. Paris. 1920.

Genestal, R. Le tenure en bourgage. Paris. 1900.

—— Le parage normand. Caen. 1911.

Giry, A. Les Établissements de Rouen. 2 vols. (BHE.) Paris. 1883, 85.

Guilhiermoz, P. Essai sur l'origine de la noblesse en France au moyen âge. Paris. 1902.

Halphen, L. Le Comté d'Anjou au xie siècle. Paris. 1906.

Haskins, C. H. A charter of Canute for Fécamp. EHR. xxxiii (1918). 342.

—— The Greek Element in the Renaissance of the twelfth century. AHR. xxv (1920). No. 4. 603.

Körting, G. Ueber die Quellen des Roman de Rou. Leipsic. 1867.

Lair, J. Étude sur la vie et la mort de Guillaume Longue-Épée, duc de Normandie. Paris. 1893.

La Touche, R. Histoire du Comté du Maine pendant le xe et le xie siècle. (BHE. 183.) Paris. 1920.

Legras, H. Le Bourgage de Caen: tenure à cens et tenure à rente (xie–xve siècles). Paris. 1911.

Le Prévost, A. Mémoires et notes pour servir à l'histoire du département de l'Eure. 3 vols. Évreux. 1862–9.

Longnon, A. Pouillés de la Province de Rouen. Paris. 1903.

—— Pouillés de la Province de Tours. Paris. 1903.

Lot, F. Fidèles ou vassaux? Paris. 1904.

—— Études critiques sur l'abbaye de Saint Wandrille. Paris. 1913.

Luchaire, A. Louis le Gros. Paris. 1890.

—— Histoire des institutions monarchiques de la France sous les premiers Capétiens. *See Gen. Bibl.* v.

Pfister, C. Études sur le règne de Robert le Pieux (996–1031). (BHE. 64.) Paris. 1885.

Pigeon, E. H. Le diocèse d'Avranches. Coutances. 1888.

Porée, A. A. L'Abbaye de Bec et ses écoles. Évreux. 1892.

Porée, E. Histoire de l'abbaye du Bec. 2 vols. Évreux. 1913.

Prentout, H. Essai sur les origines et la fondation du duché de Normandie. Paris. 1911.

—— Étude critique sur Dudon de Saint-Quentin et son histoire des premiers ducs normands. Paris. 1916.

Round, J. H. Wace and his authorities. *In* Feudal England. pp. 409–18. London. 1895.

—— Bernard the King's Scribe. EHR. xiv (1899). 417.

Ruprich-Robert, V. L'Architecture normande en Normandie et en Angleterre. 2 vols. Paris. 1884, 89.

Sauvage, R. N. L'Abbaye de Saint Martin de Troarn. *In* Mémoires des Antiquaires de Normandie. xxxiv. Caen. 1911.

Stapleton, T. Introduction to "Magni Rotuli Scaccarii Normanniae." 2 vols. London. 1840, 44. [One of the chief authorities upon the Norman baronage of the 12th century.]

Tardif, E. J. Étude sur les sources de l'ancien droit normand. Rouen. 1911.

Teulet, A. Layettes du Trésor des Chartes. Paris. 1863.

Valin, L. Le duc de Normandie et sa cour (912–1204). Paris. 1910.

Vernier, J. J. Chartes de l'abbaye de Jumièges. Rouen. 1916.

Vogel, W. Die Normannen und das Fränkische Reich bis zur Gründung der Normandie (799–911). Heidelberg. 1906.

CHAPTER XVII.

ENGLAND: HENRY II.

I. BIBLIOGRAPHIES.

Adams, G. B. History of England, 1066–1216. pp. 448–58. *See below,* III A (i).
Davis, H. W. C. England under the Normans and Angevins. pp. 534–44. *See below,* III A (i).
Gross, C. Sources and Literature of English History. *See Gen. Bibl.* I.
Ramsay, Sir J. H. The Angevin Empire. pp. 516–24. *See below,* III A (i).

II. ORIGINAL AUTHORITIES.

A. CENTRAL RECORDS.

The Pipe Rolls or Great Rolls of the Exchequer. Great Rolls of the Pipe, 2, 3, 4 Henry II. Ed. Hunter, J. (RC.) London. 1844. The Pipe Roll Society has published the Pipe Rolls for 5–34 Henry II. London. 1884–1925.
Magni Rotuli Scaccarii Normanniae sub regibus Angliae. Ed. Stapleton, T. 2 vols. (Soc. of Antiq. of London.) London. 1840, 44.
Receipt Roll of the Exchequer for the Michaelmas term 1185. Ed. Hall, H. London. 1899.
Delisle, L. and Berger, E. Recueil des actes de Henri II, Roi d'Angleterre. 3 vols. and atlas publ. (Chartes et diplômes, AcadIBL.) Paris. 1909 ff., in progress. [Dealing primarily with documents relating to Henry II's continental dominions, this collection contains many documents relating to English lands. A collection of the charters and writs of Henry II relating to England is one of the chief desiderata of the administrative historian of this period.]
Salter, H. E. The Charters of Henry II at Lincoln Cathedral. EHR. XXIV (1909). 303–13.
Texts of the Constitutions of Clarendon and the Assizes issued by Henry II have been many times printed. For the Constitutions *see* Robertson, J. C., Materials for the History of Thomas Becket, vol. v, p. 71 (Rolls); Gervase of Canterbury, vol. I, p. 178 (Rolls). For the Assize of Clarendon *see* Roger of Hoveden, vol. II, p. 248 (Rolls). For the Inquest of Sheriffs *see* Gervase of Canterbury, vol. I, p. 217. For the Assize of Northampton *see* Benedictus Abbas, vol. I, p. 108 (Rolls) and Hoveden, vol. II, p. 89. For the Assize of Arms *see* Benedictus Abbas, vol. I, p. 228 and Hoveden, vol. II, p. 261. For the Assize of the Forest *see* Benedictus Abbas, vol. II, p. clxi, and Hoveden, vol. II, p. 245. For the Ordinance of the Saladin Tithe *see* Benedictus Abbas, vol. II, p. 31 and Hoveden, vol. II, p. 335. All these have been reprinted in Stubbs, W., Select Charters. Ed. Davis, H. W. C. pp. 161–89. *See Gen. Bibl.* IV.
Rotuli de dominabus et pueris et puellis de donatione regis in XII comitatibus 31 Henry II, 1185. Ed. Grimaldi, S. London. 1830. Best edn. Round, J. H. (Pipe Roll Soc. Vol. XXXV.) London. 1913. [Contains most valuable notes on feudal history.]
Fragments of the Inquest of Sheriffs are to be found in (*a*) The Red Book of the Exchequer. Ed. Hall, H. Vol. II. *See below.* (*b*) EHR. XXXIX (1924). 89–93.
Placita Anglo-Normannica: Law cases from William I to Richard I preserved in historical records. Ed. Bigelow, M. M. Boston. 1879. For accounts of other pleas *see* Palgrave, F., English Commonwealth, pt. II, 5–87 for the suit of Richard of Anesty, 1158–63, and for the suit of the Abbot of Battle against the Bishop of Chichester, 1148–57. For a full account of the pleas of the Abbot of Battle *see* Chronicon monasterii de Bello. Ed. Brewer, J. S. (Anglia Christiana Soc.) London. 1846.

Liber Niger de Scaccario. Ed. Hearne, T. 2 vols. Oxford. 1728. 2nd edn. London. 1771. [An Exchequer memoranda book of the earlier part of the thirteenth century, containing, among other things, copies of treaties between Henry I and Henry II and the Count of Flanders, and the earliest text of the *Cartae* of 1166.]

Liber Rubeus de Scaccario. The Red Book of the Exchequer. Ed. Hall, H. (Rolls.) 3 vols. London. 1896. [Another Exchequer memoranda book of the earlier part of the thirteenth century containing masses of material relating to the financial administration. This edition has been much criticised, *cf.* Round, J. H. Studies on the Red Book of the Exchequer. London. 1898; Hall, H. Red Book of the Exchequer, A reply to Mr J. H. Round. London. 1898; Hall, H. The English Historical Review and the Red Book of the Exchequer, A letter to S. R. Gardiner, dated 1 Feb. 1899.]

Jenkinson, H. and Stead, M. T. William Cade, a financier of the twelfth century. EHR. xxviii (1913). 209–27, 731–2. [The document was commented on by Round, J. H. *Ibid.* 522–7 and Haskins, C. H. *Ibid.* 730–1.]

B. Treatises.

Dialogus de Scaccario. First ed. Madox, T. in the Appendix to his History of the Exchequer. London. 1711. Authoritative edn. by Hughes, A., Crump, C. G., and Johnson, C. Oxford. 1902. Transl. by Henderson, E. F. *in* Select Historical Documents of the Middle Ages. London. 1892. pp. 20–134.

Glanville, Ranulf de. Tractatus de Legibus et consuetudinibus Angliae. London. 1554. The edition of 1604 and its reprints of 1673 and 1780 are most commonly seen. [A new edition is much needed.] Transl. by Beames, J. London. 1812. The Law Book known as the Regiam Majestatem is a Scotch version of Glanville compiled in the early thirteenth century.

C. Miscellaneous Collections of Documents.

Dugdale, W. Monasticon Anglicanum. *See Gen. Bibl.* iv.

Farrer, W. Early Yorkshire Charters. 3 vols. Edinburgh. 1914–16.

—— Lancashire Pipe Rolls and early Charters. Liverpool. 1902.

Gale, R. Registrum honoris de Richmond. London. 1722.

Madox, T. Formulare Anglicanum. London. 1702.

Round, J. H. Ancient Charters. (Pipe Roll Soc. Vol. x.) London. 1888.

Stenton, F. M. Documents illustrative of the social and economic history of the Danelaw. (British Academy.) London. 1920.

—— Transcripts of Charters relating to Gilbertine houses in Lincolnshire. (Lincoln Record Soc. Vol. xviii.) Horncastle. 1922.

Very many cartularies relating to this period survive from the Middle Ages. Most of them come from religious houses, but a few collections of the title deeds of important families are still extant. A certain number of these have been printed, but many more remain in manuscript. They provide the richest unexplored source of material for twelfth century administrative, social, and economic history. It is unfortunate that few of the cartularies of English cathedral foundations have hitherto been printed. The most convenient list of unpublished cartularies is contained in the Guide to the Victoria Histories of the Counties of England. London. 1903. Incomplete texts of many important northern cartularies have been printed by the Surtees Society.

The following cartularies containing documents relating to this period were published in the Rolls Series:

Historia Monasterii de Abingdon. Ed. Stevenson, J. 2 vols. 1858.

Sarum Charters and Documents. Ed. Macray, W. D. 1891.

Cartularium Monasterii de Rameseia. Ed. Hart, W. H. and Lyons, P. A. 3 vols. 1884–93.

Historia et Cartularium Monasterii Sancti Petri Gloucestriae. Ed. Hart, W. H. 3 vols. 1863–7.

Registrum Malmesburiense. Ed. Brewer, J. S. 2 vols. 1874, 80.

Among other important cartularies of which a complete Latin text has been printed may be mentioned:

Cartularium Monasterii Sancte Johannis Baptiste de Colecestria. Ed. Moore, S. A. 2 vols. (Roxburghe Club.) London. 1897.

Cartulary of Chester Abbey. Ed. Tait, J. 2 vols. (Chetham Soc.) Manchester. 1920, 23.

Eynsham Cartulary. Ed. Salter, H. E. 2 vols. (Oxford Hist. Soc.) Oxford. 1907–8.

Landboc sive Registrum Monasterii beatae Mariae virginis et sancti Cenelmi de Winchelcumba. Ed. Royce, D. 2 vols. Exeter. 1892, 1903.

Coucher Book of Selby. Ed. Fowler, J. T. 2 vols. (Yorks. Archaeol. and Topog. Assoc., Record Series. Vols. x and xiii.) Durham. 1891, 93.

Cartulary of St John of Pontefract. Ed. Holmes, R. 2 vols. (*Ibid.* Vols. xxv and xxx.) Leeds. 1899, 1902.

Register of the priory of Wetheral. Ed. Prescott, J. E. (Cumberland and West-morland Antiq. and Archaeol. Soc.) London. 1897.

Registrum Antiquissimum of the cathedral church of Lincoln. Ed. Foster, C. W. and Major, K. (Lincoln Record Soc.) Hereford. 1931 ff., in progress.

D. Letters.

Alexander III. Romani pontificis opera omnia, id est epistolae et privilegia. MPL. cc.

Arnulfi Lexoviensis episcopi Epistolae. Ed. Giles, J. A. (Patres eccl. Angl.) Oxford. 1844. *Also in* MPL. cci.

Gilleberti episcopi primum Herefordiensis deinde Londoniensis Epistolae. Ed. Giles, J. A. 2 vols. (Patres eccl. Angl.) Oxford. 1845. *Also in* MPL. cxc.

Herberti de Boseham S. Thomae Cantuariensis clerici a secretis opera omnia. Ed. Giles, J. A. 2 vols. (Patres eccl. Angl.) Oxford. 1845–6. *Also in* MPL. cxc.

Joannis Saresberiensis opera omnia. Ed. Giles, J. A. 5 vols. (Patres eccl. Angl.) Oxford. 1848. [Vols. i and ii contain letters.] *Also in* MPL. cxcix.

Letters to and by Becket or relating to him. *In* Materials for the history of Thomas Becket. Ed. Robertson, J. C. Vols. v–vii. (Rolls.) 1875–85.

E. Occasional Literature.

Map, Walter. De Nugis Curialium. Best edn. James, M. R. (Anecdota Oxoniensia, Mediaeval Series, xiv.) Oxford. 1914. First, and badly, ed. by Wright, T. (Camden Soc.) London. 1850. [Interesting small talk of the court of Henry II.]

Tilbury, Gervase of. Otia Imperialia. Ed. Leibnitz, G. G. *in* Scriptores Rerum Brunsvicensium. 2 vols. Hanover. 1707, 10. Extracts: ed. Stevenson, J. *in* Radulphi de Coggeshall Chronicon. pp. 419–49. (Rolls.) 1875.

F. Political Theory.

Joannis Saresberiensis opera omnia. Ed. Giles, J. A. 5 vols. (Patres eccl. Angl.) Oxford. 1848. [Vols. iii and iv. Polycraticus sive de Nugis Curialium et vestigiis philosophorum. Vol. v. Opuscula; Metalogicus, etc.] *Also in* MPL. cxcix.

G. Narrative Sources.

(i) *England.*

Agnellus, Thomas. De morte et sepultura Henrici regis junioris. Ed. Stevenson, J. *in* Radulphi de Coggeshall Chronicon Anglicanum. pp. 263–73. (Rolls.) 1875.

Annales de Margan. Ed. Luard, H. R. *in* Annales Monastici. Vol. i. pp. 1–40. (Rolls.) 1864.

Annales Monasterii de Waverleia. Ed. Luard, H. R. *Ibid.* Vol. ii. pp. 127–411. 1865.

Benedict of Peterborough. Gesta regis Henrici secundi. Ed. Stubbs, W. 2 vols. (Rolls.) 1867. [A most valuable chronicle from 1172, with almost the character of an official narrative.]

Canterbury, Gervase of. Ed. Stubbs, W. 2 vols. (Rolls.) 1879–80. [Vol. i is valuable for a summary of the Becket controversy, derived largely from the archbishop's biographers, but containing some original matter.]

Chronicon Anglo-Scoticum. Ed. Bouterwek, C. W. Elberfeld. 1863. Also ed.
    Pitcairn, R. *as* Chronicon coenobii Sanctae Crucis Edinburgensis. (Bannatyne
    Club.) Edinburgh. 1828.
Chronicon monasterii de Bello. Ed. Brewer, J. S. (Anglia Christiana Soc.) London.
    1846. [*Cf.* Davis, H. W. C. The Chronicle of Battle Abbey. EHR. xxix
    (1914). 426–34.]
Continuatio Beccensis. Ed. Howlett, R. *in* Chronicles of the reigns of Stephen,
    Henry II, etc. Vol. iv. pp. 317–27. (Rolls.) 1889.
Diceto, Radulfi de, Opera Historica. Ed. Stubbs, W. 2 vols. (Rolls.) 1876. [Less
    valuable for the reign of Henry II than for that of Richard I.]
Fantosme, Jordan. Chronique de la guerre entre les Anglois et les Ecossois en 1173
    et 1174. Ed. Howlett, R. *in* Chronicles of the reigns of Stephen, Henry II, etc.
    Vol. iii. pp. 202–377. (Rolls.) 1886.
Giraldus Cambrensis. Opera. Ed. Brewer, J. S., Dimock, J. F., and Warner, G. F.
    8 vols. (Rolls.) 1861–91.
Hoveden, or Howden, Roger of. Chronica Rogeri de Houedene. Ed. Stubbs, W.
    4 vols. (Rolls.) 1868–71.
Newburgh, William of. Historia Rerum Anglicarum. Ed. Howlett, R. *in* Chronicles
    of the reigns of Stephen, Henry II, etc. Vol. i. pp. 1–408. Vol. ii. pp. 409–
    583. (Rolls.) 1884–5.
Niger, Radulfus. Radulphi Nigri Chronica. Ed. Anstruther, R. (Caxton Soc.)
    London. 1851.
Rouen, Etienne de. Stephani Rothomagensis monachi Beccensis poema cui titulus
    "Draco Normannicus." Ed. Howlett, R. *in* Chronicles of the reigns of Stephen,
    Henry II, etc. Vol. ii. pp. 585–781. (Rolls.) 1885.
Torigni, Robert de, *alias* Robert de Monte. Chronique. Ed. Delisle, L. 2 vols.
    (Soc. de l'Hist. de Normandie.) Rouen. 1872–3. *Also* ed. Howlett, R. *in*
    Chronicles of the reigns of Stephen, Henry II, etc. Vol. iv. pp. 3–315. (Rolls.)
    1889.

(ii) *Ireland.*

Annales Hiberniae, 1162–1370. Ed. Gilbert, J. T. Chartularies of St Mary's Abbey,
    Dublin. Vol. ii. pp. 303–98. (Rolls.) 1884.
Annals of the kingdom of Ireland by the Four Masters, from the earliest period to
    1616. Irish text with transl. Ed. O'Donovan, J. 7 vols. Dublin. 1851.
Annals of Ulster. Irish text with transl. Ed. Hennessy, W. M. and MacCarthy, B.
    Dublin. Vols. i and ii. 1887 ff.
Giraldus Cambrensis. Topographia Hibernica. *In* Opera. Ed. Brewer, J. S.,
    Dimock, J. F., etc. Vol. v. pp. 1–204. (Rolls.) 1867.
—— —— Expugnatio Hibernica. *Ibid.* pp. 205–411.
Song of Dermot and the Earl. Ed. Orpen, G. H. Oxford. 1892.

(iii) *Wales.*

Annales Cambriae. Ed. Williams ab Ithel, J. (Rolls.) 1860.
Giraldus Cambrensis. Itinerarium Cambriae. *In* Opera. Vol. vi. pp. 1–152. (Rolls.)
    1868.
—— —— Descriptio Cambriae. *Ibid.* pp. 153–227.

(iv) *Becket.*

Materials for the history of Thomas Becket. Ed. Robertson, J. C. 7 vols. (Rolls.)
    1875–85.
        Vol. i. Vita S. Thomae auctore Willelmo monacho Cantuariensi.
        Vol. ii. Lives by Benedict of Peterborough, John of Salisbury, Alan of
            Tewkesbury, and Edward Grim.
        Vol. iii. Lives by William Fitz Stephen and Herbert of Bosham.
        Vol. iv. Two contemporary anonymous lives.
        Vols. v–vii. Letters. *See above,* ii D.
Thomas Saga Erkibyskups. Ed. Magnússon, E. 2 vols. (Rolls.) 1875, 83.
Vie de St Thomas. Par Garnier de Pont-Sainte-Maxence. Ed. Hippeau, C. Paris.
    1859.

III. MODERN WRITERS.

A. General Narrative.

(i) *England.*

Adams, G. B. History of England, 1066–1216. (Political History of England. Ed. Hunt, W. and Poole, R. L. Vol. II.) London. 1905.
Davis, H. W. C. England under the Normans and Angevins. (History of England. Ed. Oman, C. W. C. Vol. II.) London. 1905. 4th edn. 1915.
Green, Mrs J. R. Henry II. London. 1888. Repr. London. 1903.
Lyttelton, G. The history of the life of Henry II. 3rd edn. 4 vols. London. 1769–71.
Norgate, K. England under the Angevin kings. 2 vols. London. 1887.
Ramsay, Sir J. H. The Angevin Empire. London. 1903.
Salzmann, L. F. Henry II. London. 1914.

(ii) *Ireland.*

Orpen, G. H. Ireland under the Normans. Vols. I, II. *See Gen. Bibl.* v.

(iii) *Wales.*

Lloyd, J. E. History of Wales. *See Gen. Bibl.* v.

B. Studies on Special Subjects.

(i) *Administration.*

Delisle, L. Mémoire sur la chronologie des Chartes de Henri II. BEC. LXVII (1906). 361–401.
—— Notes sur les Chartes originales de Henri II. *Ibid.* LXVIII (1907). 272–314.
Fowler, G. H. Henry FitzHenry at Woodstock. EHR. XXXIX (1924). 240–1.
Hall, H. Introduction to the study of the Pipe Rolls. (Pipe Roll Soc. Vol. III.) London. 1884.
Lunt, W. E. The text of the Ordinance of 1184 concerning an aid for the Holy Land. EHR. XXXVII (1922). 235–42.
Maitland, F. W. The Constitutional History of England. Cambridge. 1908.
—— Henry II and the criminous clerks. *See below* (iv).
Parow, W. Compotus Vicecomitis. Berlin. 1906.
Pollock, F. and Maitland, F. W. The history of English Law before the time of Edward I. *See Gen. Bibl.* v.
Poole, R. L. The dates of Henry II's Charters. EHR. XXII (1908). 79–83.
—— The publication of Great Charters by English Kings. EHR. XXVIII (1913). 444–53.
Round, J. H. The chronology of Henry II's Charters. *In* Archeol. Journ. LXIV (1907). 63–79. London.
—— The dating of the early Pipe Rolls. EHR. XXXVI (1921). 321–33.
—— The introduction of Knight service into England. *In* Feudal England. London. 1895. Repr. 1909.
—— The alleged debate on Danegeld in 1163. Twelfth Century Notes, IV. EHR. v (1890). 750–3.
—— The Inquest of Sheriffs. *In* The Commune of London and other studies. London. 1899.
—— Geoffrey de Mandeville. London. 1892.
—— The King's serjeants and officers of state, with their coronation services. London. 1911.
—— A Charter of William, Earl of Essex (1170). EHR. VI (1891). 364–7.
—— The Saladin Tithe. EHR. XXXI (1916). 447–50.
Stenton, F. M. An early Inquest relating to St Peter's, Derby. EHR. XXXII (1917). 47–8.
Stephenson, C. The aids of the English Boroughs. EHR. XXXIV (1919). 457–75.

Stubbs, W. The Constitutional History of England. *See Gen. Bibl.* v.
Turner, G. J. The Exchequer at Westminster. EHR. xix (1904). 236–8.

(ii) *Law.*

Pollock, F. and Maitland, F. W. The history of English Law before the time of Edward I. *See Gen. Bibl.* v.
Round, J. H. The date of the Grand Assize. EHR. xxxi (1916). 268–9.
—— The earliest Fines. EHR. xii (1897). 293–302.
Salzmann, L. F. Early Fines. EHR. xxv (1910). 708–10.
Stenton, Doris M. The Lincoln Assize Rolls of the reign of John. Lincoln Record Soc. Vol. xxii. 1925. Introduction, pp. xviii–lxxix, [connects Glanville with the procedure revealed in the earliest Assize Rolls.]

(iii) *Society.*

Farrer, W. Honors and Knights' Fees. London; and Manchester. 1923 ff., in progress.
Gross, C. The Gild Merchant. 2 vols. Oxford. 1890.
Lapsley, G. T. The Flemings in Eastern England in the reign of Henry II. EHR. xxi (1906). 509–13.
—— Some Castle Officers in the twelfth century. EHR. xxxiii (1918). 348–59.
Round, J. H. The staff of a castle in the twelfth century. EHR. xxxv (1920). 90–7.
—— Castle Watchmen. *Ibid.* 400–1.
—— The knight service of Malmesbury Abbey. EHR. xxxii (1917). 249–52.
Stenton, F. M. Documents illustrative of the social and economic history of the Danelaw. (British Academy.) London. 1920. Introduction, pp. xiii–cxxxvii.
—— Sokemen and the Village Waste. EHR. xxvi (1911). 93–7.

(iv) *Becket.*

Abbott, E. A. St Thomas of Canterbury; his death and miracles. 2 vols. London. 1898.
Brooke, Z. N. The English Church and the Papacy from the Conquest to the reign of John. Cambridge. 1931.
Darboy, G. St Thomas Becket: sa vie et ses lettres. 2 vols. Paris. 1878.
L'Huiller, A. Saint Thomas de Cantorbéry. 2 vols. Paris, etc. 1891–2.
Maitland, F. W. Henry II and the criminous clerks. EHR. vii (1892). 224–34. Repr. *in* Roman Canon Law in the Church of England. London. 1898; *and* Collected Papers. Vol. ii. Cambridge. 1911.
Morris, J. The Life and Martyrdom of St Thomas Becket. London. 1859. 2nd edn. 1885.
Radford, L. B. Thomas of London before his consecration. Cambridge. 1894.
Robertson, J. C. Becket. London. 1859.
Round, J. H. The alleged debate on Danegeld in 1163. Twelfth Century Notes, IV. EHR. v (1890). 750–3.

(v) *Miscellaneous.*

Eyton, R. W. Court, Household, and Itinerary of Henry II. London. 1878.
Haskins, C. H. England and Sicily in the twelfth century. EHR. xxvi (1912). 433–47 and 641–65.
Norgate, K. The Bull Laudabiliter. EHR. viii (1893). 18–52.
Powicke, F. M. Ailred of Rievaulx. *In* Bulletin of the John Rylands Library. Vol. vi. pp. 310–51, 452–521.
—— Maurice of Rievaulx. EHR. xxxvi (1921). 17–29.
Round, J. H. The Conquest of Ireland. *In* The Commune of London and other studies. London. 1899.
Salter, H. E. The death of Henry of Winchester. EHR. xxxvii (1922). 79–80.

CHAPTER XVIII.

FRANCE: LOUIS VI AND LOUIS VII.

I. SPECIAL BIBLIOGRAPHY.

Halphen, L. La France sous les premiers Capétiens (987–1226). RSH. Vol. XIV (1907). pp. 62–88.

II. ORIGINAL DOCUMENTS.

1. The Acta of Louis VI and Louis VII, catalogued in the two following works:
  Luchaire, A. Louis VI le Gros. Annales de sa vie et de son règne (1081–1137), avec une introduction historique. Paris. 1890.
  —— Études sur les actes de Louis VII. Paris. 1885. [Additions and corrections in Halphen, L. Observations sur la chronologie des actes de Louis VII. RH. Vol. CVIII (1911). pp. 55–8.]
  The charters of these two kings are to appear in the Chartes et Diplômes, AcadIBL.
2. Delisle, L. and Berger, E. Recueil des actes de Henri II, roi d'Angleterre et duc de Normandie, concernant les provinces françaises et les affaires de France. 4 vols. and atlas. (Chartes et diplômes, AcadIBL.) Paris. 1909 ff., in progress.
3. Contemporary correspondence, of which some is to be found in Bouquet, vols. XII sqq.; and in Materials for the history of Thomas Becket. Ed. Robertson, J. C. and Sheppard, J.B. Vols. VI, VII. (Rolls.) 1882, 85.

III. NARRATIVE AUTHORITIES.

The principal authorities are named in the following work:

Molinier, A. Les sources de l'histoire de France des origines aux guerres d'Italie. (*See Gen. Bibl.* IV.) Vol. II. 1902. pp. 181–91, *et passim.*

Of special importance (in addition to the authorities given above in the Bibliographies of chapters XV–XVI and XVII for the history of England during the same period) are the following:

Chronique de Morigny (1095–1152). Ed. Mirot, L. (Coll. textes.) Paris. 1909.
Galbert de Bruges. Histoire du meurtre de Charles le Bon, comte de Flandre (1127–8). Ed. Pirenne, H. (Coll. textes.) Paris. 1891.
Gautier de Thérouanne. Vita Karoli comitis Flandriae. Ed. Köpke, R. MGH. Script. Vol. XII. pp. 537 sqq.
Guibert de Nogent. De vita sua monodiarum libri tres. Ed. Bourgin, G. (Coll. textes.) Paris. 1907. [A new edn., with French transl., by Halphen, L. will appear in Class. hist.]
Guillaume. Vita Sugerii abbatis. Ed. Lecoy de la Marche, A. *in* Oeuvres complètes de Suger. (SHF.) Paris. 1867.
Ordericus Vitalis. Historia ecclesiastica. Ed. Le Prévost, A. (and Delisle, L.). 5 vols. (SHF.) Paris. 1838–55. [A new edn., with French transl., by Omont, H. will appear in Class. hist.]
Robert de Torigny. Appendix ad Sigebertum. Ed. Delisle, L. 2 vols. Paris. 1872–3. *Also* ed. Howlett, R. *in* Chronicles of...Stephen, Henry II, and Richard I. Vol. IV. (Rolls.) 1889.
Suger. Gesta Ludovici regis cognomento Grossi. Ed. Molinier, A. (Coll. textes.) Paris. 1887. [A new edn. of this and the following, with French transl., by Waquet, H. will appear in Class. hist.]
—— Historia gloriosi regis Ludovici (VII). Ed. Molinier, A. (with the preceding). [This is only partly the work of Suger.]

IV. MODERN WORKS.

See the Bibliographies of chapters xv–xvi and xvii for the history of England at the same period. The following works are specially important :

(a) GENERAL WORKS.

Cartellieri, A. Philipp II August, König von Frankreich. Vol. i (1165–89). Leipsic. 1899–1900.

Hirsch, R. Studien zur Geschichte König Ludwigs VII von Frankreich (1119–60). Leipsic. 1892.

Luchaire, A. Les premiers Capétiens (987–1137). (*In* Lavisse, E. Histoire de France. ii, 2. 1901. *See Gen. Bibl.* v.)

—— Louis VII, Philippe-Auguste, Louis VIII (1137–1226). (*Ibid.* iii, 1. 1902.)

—— Louis VI le Gros. Annales de sa vie et de son règne (1081–1137), avec une introduction historique. Paris. 1890.

—— Histoire des institutions monarchiques de la France sous les premiers Capétiens (987–1180). 2nd edn. *See Gen. Bibl.* v.

—— Manuel des institutions françaises. Période des Capétiens directs. *See Gen. Bibl.* v.

Thompson, J. W. The development of the French Monarchy under Louis VI le Gros (1108–37). Chicago. 1895.

(b) SPECIAL WORKS.

Arbois de Jubainville, H. d'. Histoire des ducs et des comtes de Champagne. 7 vols. Paris. 1859–66.

Cartellieri, O. Abt Suger von Saint-Denis, 1081–1151. Berlin. 1898.

Halphen, L. Les entrevues des rois Louis VII et Henri II durant l'exil de Thomas Becket en France. *In* Mélanges d'histoire offerts à M. Charles Bémont. Paris. 1913. pp. 151–62.

Hodgson, C. E. Jung Heinrich, König von England, Sohn König Heinrichs II, 1155–83. Jena. 1906.

Johnen, J. Philipp von Elsass, Graf von Flandern 1157–91. (Extrait des Bulletins de la Commission royale d'histoire de Belgique. Vol. lxxix.) Brussels. 1910.

Perrichet, L. La grande chancellerie de France des origines à 1328. Paris. 1912.

Reichel, H. Die Ereignisse an der Saone im August und September des Jahres 1162. Halle. 1908.

Reuter, H. Geschichte Alexanders des Dritten und der Kirche seiner Zeit. 3 vols. Leipsic. 1860–4.

Vacandard, E. Vie de Saint Bernard, abbé de Clairvaux. 4th edn. 2 vols. Paris. 1910.

CHAPTER XIX.

THE COMMUNAL MOVEMENT, ESPECIALLY IN FRANCE.

I. SPECIAL BIBLIOGRAPHIES.

Bourgin, G. La Commune de Soissons et le groupe communal Soissonnais. Paris. 1908. [Very full bibliography for French municipal history.]

EncBr. 11th edn. Article: Communes (by Keutgen, F. W. E.). [Short critical bibliography.]

Gross, C. Bibliography of British Municipal History. (Harvard Hist. Studies.) New York. 1897.

Lavisse, E. and Rambaud, A. Histoire générale. Vol. II. pp. 476–9. Bibliography to Ch. VIII (by Giry, A. and Réville, A.). See Gen. Bibl. V.

Pirenne, H. Bibliographie de l'histoire de Belgique. See Gen. Bibl. I.

Schröder, R. Lehrbuch der deutschen Rechtsgeschichte. 5th edn. Leipsic. 1907. §§ 51 and 56. [Full bibliography for German municipal history.]

Stein, H. Bibliographie générale des Cartulaires Français ou relatifs à l'histoire de France. Paris. 1907. [Both published and unpublished cartularies.]

(Several of the books below contain either bibliographies or bibliographical notes.)

II. MSS. SOURCES.

The amount of published material has rendered recourse to unprinted documents very little necessary. A certain number of charters to *bastides* in the south-west of France have been studied in the Departmental Archives of the Gironde at Bordeaux and of the Basses Pyrénées at Pau. Information as to the rural communities of the Pyrenees is to be found scattered in various documents still unpublished, contained in these same Archives, especially at Pau, under the heading E, and in the Cartulaire de la Vallée d'Ossau, AA. 1. For fuller information, see the excellent Inventories of M. Paul Raymond for the Archives Départementales des Basses Pyrénées.

III. PRINTED SOURCES: COLLECTIONS OF DOCUMENTS.

(A great many documents are printed in most of the works given below in IV.)

Abbadie, F. Le Livre Noir et les établissements de Dax. (Soc. des Archives hist. de la Gironde. Vol. XXXVII.) Bordeaux. 1902.

Alart, J. B. Cartulaire Roussillonnais. Perpignan. 1880.

—— Chartes de Villefranche-de-Conflent. Lectoure. 1852.

—— Privilèges de Roussillon et de Cerdagne. Perpignan. 1874.

Archives de la ville de Bayonne. Livre des Établissements. Bayonne. 1892.

Archives Municipales de Bordeaux. Vol. I. Livre des Bouillons. Vol. II. Livre de Privilèges. Vol. V. Livre des Coutumes. Bordeaux. 1867–90.

Baillaud, E. and Verlaguet, P. A. Coutumes et privilèges du Rouergue. 2 vols. Toulouse. 1910.

Beaumanoir, Philippe de Remi, Sire de. Coutumes de Beauvaisis. Ed. Salmon, A. (Coll. textes.) 2 vols. Paris. 1899, 1900.

Bémont, C. Le Coutumier de l'Île d'Oléron. Paris. 1919.

Bladé, G. F. Coutumes du Gers. Paris. 1864.

Bonnin, T. Cartulaire de Louviers. 2 vols. Évreux. 1870, 83.

Bouthors, J. L. A. Coutumes locales du bailliage d'Amiens. (Mém. de la Soc. des Antiquaires de Picardie. Documents inédits concernant la province.) 2 vols. Amiens. 1845.

Brossard, J. P. and Jarrin, C. Cartulaire de Bourg-en-Bresse. Bourg. 1882.

Cabié, E. Chartes et coutumes de la Gascogne Toulousaine. (Archives historiques de la Gascogne. Vol. v.) Paris and Auch. 1884.

Constans, L. Livre de l'épervier. Montpellier. 1882. [A cartulary concerning Montpellier.]

Garnier, Joseph. Chartes Bourguignonnes. *In* Mém. AcadIBL. 2nd ser. ii. (1849.) 1–68.

—— Chartes de Communes en Bourgogne. 3 vols. Dijon. 1877.

Giry, A. Relations de la royauté avec les villes. Paris. 1885. [Documents from 1180–1314.]

Imbart de la Tour, P. Les Coutumes de la Réole. Bordeaux. 1893.

Isnard, M. Z. Cartulaire municipal de Manosque. Paris. 1894.

Lemaire, E. and Bouchot, H. Livre Rouge de Saint-Quentin. Saint-Quentin. 1881.

Lemaire, E. and Giry, A. Archives de Saint-Quentin. Saint-Quentin. 1888.

Lhomel, G. de. Cartulaire de Montreuil-sur-Mer. Abbeville. 1904.

—— Collection de documents. Abbeville. 1908.

Magen, A. and Tholin, G. Archives municipales d'Agen. Villeneuve-sur-Lot. 1876.

Mahul, M. Cartulaire de Carcassonne. 6 vols. Paris. 1857–82.

Marque, M. Cartulaire d'Oloron. Pau. 1900.

Marty, É. Cartulaire de Rabastens. Albi. 1902.

Mouynés, G. Inventaire des Archives Communales de Narbonne. 5 vols. Paris. 1871–7.

Prou, M. Les Coutumes de Lorris. NRDF. 1884.

Quantin, M. Cartulaire général de l'Yonne. (Société des Sciences historiques et naturelles.) Auxerre. 1854–60.

—— Recueil de pièces pour faire suite au Cartulaire de l'Yonne. Auxerre. 1873.

Recueil des ordonnances des rois de France de la troisième race. Especially vols. xi, xii. Paris. 1769, 77.

Stouff, L. Cartulaire d'Arbois. Dijon. 1893.

Thierry, J. N. A. Recueil des monuments inédits de l'histoire du Tiers État. 4 vols. Paris. 1850–70. [Only contains documents concerning Amiens and towns of Ponthieu.]

Villeneuve, É. de. Cartulaire municipal de la ville de Lyon. Ed. Guigue, M. C. Lyons. 1876.

Wauters, A. Les Libertés communales, etc. Vol. i, Preuves. *See below,* iv (*a*).

IV. MODERN WORKS.

(*a*) GENERAL (CHIEFLY ON FRANCE).

(Arranged in chronological order to shew the development of the subject.)

Thierry, J. N. A. Lettres sur l'histoire de France. Paris. 1827.

Leber, C. Histoire du pouvoir municipal. Paris. 1828.

Raynouard, F. J. M. Histoire du droit municipal en France. Paris. 1829. [Both this and the preceding book support the theory of Roman influence.]

Tailliar, E. F. J. Affranchissements des communes dans le Nord de la France. Cambrai. 1837.

Hegel, C. Geschichte der Städteverfassung von Italien. 2 vols. Leipsic. 1847. [Still the best general account of Italian towns. Against the theory of Roman origin.]

Thierry, J. N. A. Recueil des monuments inédits de l'histoire du Tiers État. *See above,* iii. [The introductions to vols. i and ii give a description and classification of the various French towns. These need supplementing and correcting with later authorities, but are still valuable.]

Haulleville, P. de. Histoire des communes Lombardes. 2 vols. Ghent. 1857–8.

Wauters, A. Les Libertés communales...en Belgique, dans le Nord de la France, et sur les bords du Rhin. 3 vols. Brussels. 1869–78. [According to Luchaire "un livre plein d'une érudition un peu confuse."]

Wauters, A. Les Gildes communales. *In* Bulletins de l'Acad. royale...de Belgique
    Brussels. 1874. [Emphasises the importance of gild influence.]
Fustel de Coulanges, N. D. Histoire des institutions politiques de l'ancienne
    France, Vols. I, II. *See Gen. Bibl.* v. [Supports the theory of Roman influence.]
Bonvalot, É. T. Le Tiers État d'après la charte de Beaumont. Paris. 1884.
Tholin, G. Villes libres et barons. Paris. 1886.
Pauffin, H. Essai sur l'organisation et la juridiction municipale au moyen âge dans
    l'Est et dans le Nord de la France. Paris. 1886. [Interesting and useful.]
Luchaire, A. Les Communes françaises à l'époque des Capétiens directs. Paris.
    1890. Ed. Halphen, L. Paris. 1911. [A very useful account of the *Commune
    jurée* of the North of France; and a general discussion of the theories pre-
    valent up to 1890; Halphen gives a further résumé up to 1911.]
Gross, C. The Gild Merchant. 2 vols. Oxford. 1890. [A very useful book on
    English towns; against the theory which would make the Merchant Gild and
    Borough identical.]
Hegel, C. Städte und Gilden der germanischen Völker im Mittelalter. 2 vols.
    Leipsic. 1891. [Very valuable for Northern Europe; opposes the theory con-
    necting the Gild and the Town. On this see a review by Keutgen, F. W. E.
    in EHR. VIII (1863), pp. 120 sqq.]
Luchaire, A. Manuel des Institutions françaises; période des Capétiens directs.
    See Gen. Bibl. v.
Giry, A. and Réville, A. Chapter VIII *in* Lavisse, E. and Rambaud, A. Histoire
    générale. Vol. II. pp. 411–76. *See Gen. Bibl.* v.
Flach, J. Les Origines de l'ancienne France. Vol. II. *See Gen. Bibl.* v. [Very
    useful; opposes the theory of Roman influence.]
Heinemann, L. v. Zur Entstehung der Stadtverfassung in Italien. Leipsic. 1896.
L'Éleu, A. Les Communautés rurales dans l'ancienne France. Paris. 1896.
Ashley, W. J. Beginnings of town life. Boston, Mass. 1896. [An excellent
    summary of different theories.]
Ramalho, A. L'Administration municipale au XIIIe siècle. Paris. 1896. [A clear
    and simple résumé.]
Gross, C. The affiliation of Mediaeval Boroughs. New York. 1897. [Appeared
    earlier in Gild Merchant, vol. I, app. E. *See above*.]
Flach, J. Origine de l'habitation en France. Paris. 1899. [Interesting on village
    growth and rural settlements.]
Hegel, C. Die Entstehung des deutschen Stadtteswesens. Leipsic. 1898. [A good
    clear account, with a brief enumeration of theories.]
Mayer, E. Deutsche und französische Verfassungsgeschichte. Leipsic. 1899.
Dubois, P. Les asseurements au XIIIe siècle. Paris. 1900. [Shews the very slight
    effect of the *Paix de Dieu* on the origin of the communes, a theory which had
    been urged by Sémichon. Other criticisms on this theory can be found in
    Luchaire, Les Communes françaises, p. 39.]
Viollet, P. Les Communes françaises au moyen âge. Paris. 1900. [Very clear
    and useful.]
Caggese, R. Classi e comuni rurali nel medio evo italiano. 2 vols. Florence.
    1907, 9.
Schröder, R. Lehrbuch der deutschen Rechtsgeschichte. 5th edn. Leipsic. 1907.
    §§ 51 and 56. [A useful short account for German towns: § 56 is especially on
    the affiliation of communes.]
Keutgen, F. W. E. Article: Communes *in* EncBr. 11th edn. [A useful summary:
    fullest on German towns.]
Mayer, E. Italienische Verfassungsgeschichte. Vol. II. Leipsic. 1909. [Gives
    arguments in favour of the continuity of Roman influence.]
Pirenne, H. Histoire de Belgique. Vol. I. *See Gen. Bibl.* v.
Mengozzi, G. La città italiana nell' alto medio evo. Rome. 1914. [Town institu-
    tions before 900.]
Pirenne, H. Les anciennes démocraties des Pays-Bas. Paris. 1910. Transl. Saunders,
    J. V. as: Belgian Democracy, its early history. Manchester. 1915. [A valuable
    and popular account, laying especial stress on economic development.]
Luchaire, J. Les Démocraties italiennes. Paris. 1915. [A good summary.]

(*b*) Books on Special Districts.

Alart, J. B. Notices historiques sur les communes de Roussillon. 2 vols. Perpignan. 1868, 78.

Bascle de Lagrèze, G. Histoire du droit dans les Pyrénées. Paris. 1867. [Valley communities.]

Benoit, L. Institutions communales de Westrich. Nancy. 1866. [Chiefly rural.]

Bernard, A. De la commune Lyonnaise. Lyons. 1843.

Bonvalot, E. Histoire du droit et des institutions de la Lorraine. Paris. 1895.

Bourdette, J. Les sept vallées du Labéda. Argelès. 1898. [Interesting for rural communities in Pyrenees.]

Bourgeois, A. Mouvement communal dans le Comté de Champagne. Paris. 1904. [Valuable; contains a great many documents.]

Brutails, J. A. Étude sur la condition des populations rurales du Roussillon au moyen âge. Paris. 1891. [A useful chapter on rural communities.]

Clos, L. Recherches sur le régime municipal dans le midi de la France au moyen âge. *In* Mém. AcadIBL. 2nd ser. III. 1854. [Supports the Roman theory.]

Compayré, C. Études historiques sur l'Albigeois. Albi. 1841. [Contains documents.]

Cros-Mayrevieille. Histoire du Comté et de la Vicomté de Carcassonne. 2 vols. Carcassonne. 1848, 96.

Curie-Seimbres, A. Essai sur les villes fondées dans le sud-ouest de la France. Toulouse. 1880. [Chiefly on *bastides*. *See* Giry's criticism in BEC (*below*, IV *d*); and A. Molinier's notes *in* Vic, C. de, and Vaissete, J. J. Hist. gén. de Languedoc. Vol. VIII. *See Gen. Bibl.* IV.

Delisle, L. La Classe agricole en Normandie au moyen âge. Évreux. 1851. [For rural communities.]

Dey, A. Communes dans la province de Reims. Paris. 1873.

—— Conditions de personnes et communes en Bourgogne. Paris. 1870–2

Dognon, P. Institutions politiques du pays de Languedoc. Toulouse. 1895. [Useful and interesting.]

Du Bourg, A. Études sur les coutumes communales du sud-ouest de la France. Paris. 1882.

Guibert, L. Les Communes en Limousin. Paris. 1891.

Hanauer, C. A. Constitutions des Campagnes de l'Alsace au moyen âge. Paris and Strasbourg. 1864.

—— Les Paysans d'Alsace au moyen âge. Les cours colongères. Paris and Strasbourg. 1865. [Very interesting on rural communities.]

Lambert, G. Essai sur le régime municipal et l'affranchissement des communes en Provence au moyen âge. Toulon. 1882.

Lepage, H. Les Communes de la Meurthe. 2 vols. Nancy. 1853.

Leymarie, A. Le Limousin historique. Limoges. 1837.

Melleville, M. Histoire de l'affranchissement communal dans les anciens diocèses de Laon, Soissons, et Noyon. Laon and Paris. 1858.

—— Histoire de la commune du Laonnais. Laon and Paris. 1853. [Useful for the history of rural communes.]

Praet, J. van. Origine des communes flamandes. Ghent. 1829. [Chiefly shewing their very peaceful development.]

Schmidt, C. G. A. Les Seigneurs, les paysans, et le propriété rurale en Alsace. Paris and Nancy. 1897.

Sée, H. Les Classes rurales et le régime domanial en France au moyen âge. Paris. 1906. [For rural communities.]

Vial, E. Institutions et coutumes Lyonnaises. Lyons. 1903–9. [Especially Coutumes consulaires, pp. 29 sqq.]

Webster, W. Le mot république dans les Pyrénées occidentales. Pau. 1888. [An interesting pamphlet on rural communities.]

(*c*) Monographs on Separate Places.

Balasque, J. and Dulaurens, E. Études historiques sur la ville de Bayonne. 3 vols. Bayonne. 1862–75.

Bardon, A. Histoire de la ville d'Alais. 2 vols. Nimes. 1894, 96.

Bonassieux, P. De la réunion de Lyon à France. Paris. 1873.

Bonnardot. Régime municipal à Orléans. Orleans. 1881. [pamphlet.]

Bourgin, G. La Commune de Soissons et le groupe communal Soissonnais. Paris. 1908. [Very valuable; lays especial stress on the economic side of communal development.]

Bourquelot, L. F. Histoire de Provins. 2 vols. Paris. 1837, 40.

Brémond, É. Marseille au XIIIᵉ siècle. Marseilles. 1905. [A specially interesting town; a republic in the early 13th century.]

Cassassoles, F. Notices historiques sur la ville de Lectoure. Auch. 1839.

Charléty, S. Histoire de Lyon. Lyons. 1903. [Interesting.]

Chéruel, P. A. Histoire de Rouen 1150–1382. 2 vols. Rouen. 1843–4.

Clos, L. Notice historique sur Castelnaudary. Castelnaudary. 1880.

Clouet, L. Histoire de Verdun. 3 vols. Verdun. 1867–70.

Damasc-Arbaud. Études historiques sur la ville de Manosque. Paris. 1847.

Dognon, P. and Le Palenc, C. Histoire de Lézat. Toulouse. 1899. [A very rural town.]

Ducom, A. La Commune d'Agen. Paris. 1892.

Dufour, É. La communauté de Cahors. Cahors. 1846.

Espinas, G. La Vie urbaine de Douai au moyen âge. 4 vols. Paris. 1913. [Plenty of material, but badly arranged. The origin of Douai is discussed in vol. II.]

Flammermont, J. Histoire des institutions municipales de Senlis. BHE. Paris. 1881.

Gauban, O. Histoire de la Réole. La Réole. 1873.

Germain, A. C. Histoire de la commune de Montpellier. 3 vols. Montpellier. 1851.

Giraudet, E. Histoire de Tours. 2 vols. Tours. 1873. [Not a well-arranged book; contains a few documents.]

Giry, A. Établissements de Rouen. 2 vols. Paris. 1883. [Very valuable. Vol. II consists of documents.]

—— Études sur les origines de la commune de Saint-Quentin. Paris. 1887. [Interesting and useful.]

—— Institutions municipales de St Omer. Paris. 1877. [Valuable; lays stress on the great importance of the merchant gild in this region.]

Huisman, G. La Juridiction de la municipalité Parisienne, de Saint Louis à Charles VII. Paris. 1912. [Shews how the municipality grew out of the Hanse merchants of the Water Corporation.]

Jullian, C. Histoire de Bordeaux. Bordeaux. 1895. [Interesting, but not especially detailed on the commune.]

Labande, L. H. Histoire de Beauvais et de ses institutions communales. Paris. 1892. [Valuable.]

Lambert, G. Histoire de Toulon. 4 vols. Toulon. 1886–92. [Here the communal organisation was acquired very late.]

Lefranc, A. Histoire de la ville de Noyon. BHE. Paris. 1887.

Le Glay, E. Notice sur le village d'Esne. Cambrai. 1835. [pamphlet.]

Marlot, Dom G. Histoire de Reims. 4 vols. Rheims. 1843–6. [Largely ecclesiastical history.]

Maugis, É. Recherches sur la ville d'Amiens. Paris. 1906.

Merlet, L. Origines de la Commune de Dreux. Chateaudun. 1887.

Pfister, C. Histoire de Nancy. Paris. 1902.

Pirenne, H. Histoire de la constitution de la ville de Dinant. (Université de Gand. Recueil de travaux.) Ghent. 1889.

Porée, C. Consulat de Mende. Paris. 1902.

Portal, C. La République Marseillaise du XIIIᵉ siècle. Marseilles. 1907. [Interesting; it points out differences between the towns of the North and those of the South, and prints a good many documents.]

Soyer, J. La Communauté des habitants de Blois. Paris. 1894.
Steyert, A. Nouvelle histoire de Lyon. Vol. II. (Moyen âge.) Lyons. 1897. [A very interesting town. Various points in its development are still subjects of dispute.]
Tholin, G. and Bellecombe, A. de. Histoire de Montpezat. Auch. 1898.

(*d*) PERIODICAL LITERATURE.

Bastard, L. de. Histoire de Vézelay. BEC. 1851.
Bémont, C. Les institutions municipales de Bordeaux au moyen âge. RH. CXXIII. 1916. [Very valuable.]
Beugnot, A. A. L'origine des municipalités rurales. *In* Revue Française. Vols. VIII and IX. Paris. 1838.
Bourgin, G. Origines urbaines. RSH. Vol. VII. 1903. [Extremely useful.]
Bourquelot, L. F. Notice sur le Cartulaire de Provins. BEC. 1855–6.
Castéran. Traités de lies et passeries. *In* Revue des Pyrénées. Vol. IX. Pau. 1897
Giry, A. Review of Curie-Seimbres, A. Essai sur les villes du sud-ouest. (*See above*, IV *b*.) BEC. 1881.
Molinier, A. La commune de Toulouse. *Ibid.* 1882.
Ottocar, N. Essays on the history of the French towns in the Middle Ages. (In Russian.) *See* Review *in* RH. CXL. 1922.
Petit-Dutaillis, C. La concession de commune en France. *In* Comptes rendus des séances de l'Acad. des Inscriptions et Belles-Lettres, 1936. Paris.
Pirenne, H. L'origine de constitutions urbaines. RH. 1893, 95. [Very valuable.]
—— Villes et marchés. *Ibid.* 1898.
Tauzin. Les bastides Landaises. RQH. 1901.
Valois. Régime municipal à Figeac. BEC. 1880.
Vidal, A Cartulaires d'Albi. *In* Revue des Langues Romanes. Vol. XLV. Montpellier. 1902.

CHAPTER XX.

THE MONASTIC ORDERS.

I. BIBLIOGRAPHIES.

For the chief general bibliographies see Vol. I, ch. xviii, bibliography (pp. 683 sqq.). In addition to those mentioned there, full bibliographies with reference to special orders are given in such volumes as Janauschek's Origines Cistercienses (*see below*, iv *b*) and Bibliotheca Cluniacensis (*see Gen. Bibl.* iv under Marrier). Of the numerous works of the sixteenth and seventeenth centuries upon the subject there is a bibliography, classified under the various orders and congregations, in Hélyot's Histoire des ordres monastiques. Vol. I. *See below*, ii.

II. GENERAL HISTORY.

Ammanus, J. *See below*, Modius, F.
Bonanni, F. Ordinum religiosorum in ecclesia militanti catalogus eorumque indumenta in iconibus expressa. 4 vols. Rome. 1706–10. Nuremberg. 1720 ff.
Bullot, M. *See* Hélyot, P.
Butler, E. C. Articles: Monasticism; Benedictines, etc. *in* EncBr. 11th edn. *See Gen. Bibl.* I.
Coulton, G. G. Five centuries of religion. Vols. I, II. *See Gen. Bibl.* v.
Crescenzio, G. P. Presidio Romano, ò vero della militia ecclesiastica e delle religioni cavaleresche come claustrali. Piacenza. 1648.
Gasquet, F. A. Monastic life in the middle ages. London. 1922. *See below*, Montalembert.
Hannay, J. O. Spirit and origin of Christian monasticism. London. 1903.
Harnack, A. Das Mönchtum. Giessen. 1881, etc. Reprinted in Reden u. Aufsätze. Giessen. 1903. Engl. transl. Kellett, E. E. London. 1901.
Heimbucher, M. Orden u. Kongregationen der kathol. Kirche. 2nd edn. 3 vols. Paderborn. 1907.
[Hélyot, P. (Le père Hippolyte) and Bullot, M.] Histoire des ordres monastiques, religieux et militaires. 8 vols. Paris. 1714–19 and later edns. German transl. Leipsic. 1753–6. Frankfort-on-Main. 1830. Ital. transl. Lucca. 1737, etc.
Henrion, M. R. A. Histoire des ordres religieux. 2nd edn. 2 vols. Paris. 1835. German transl. Fehr, M. Tübingen. 1845.
Hermant, G. Histoire de l'établissement des ordres religieux et des congrégations régulières et séculières de l'église. 2nd edn. enl. 4 vols. Rouen. 1710.
Histoire des ordres religieux. (Engravings by Schoonebeek, A.) 2nd edn. 2 vols. Amsterdam. 1695 and 1700.
Histoire des ordres religieux. [Compiled from Hélyot, etc.] 4 vols. Amsterdam.
Hospinianus, R. De origine et progressu monachatus ac ordinum monasticorum equitumque militarium. Zurich. 1588.
Kuen, M. *ed.* Scriptores rerum historico-monastico-ecclesiasticarum variorum religiosorum ordinum. 6 vols. Ulm. 1755–68.
Le Pelletier, L. Histoire des ordres de religion et congrégations ecclésiastiques. Angers. 1626.
Martène, E. De antiquis monachorum ritibus libri v. Lyons. 1690. Also printed in De antiquis ecclesiae ritibus. Vol. iv. Antwerp and Milan. 1738.
Maurolico (Maruli), S. Historia sagra intitolata Mare Oceano di tutte le religioni del mondo. Messina. 1613.
Modius, F. Libellus singularis in quo cuiusque ordinis ecclesiastici origo, etc. delineantur. [Supplement to Ammanus, J. Cleri totius Romanae ecclesiae subjecti ...habitus, etc., expressi.] Frankfort-on-Main. 1585.

Montalembert, C. F. R. de. Les moines d'occident depuis St-Benoît jusqu'à St-Bernard. 7 vols. Paris, 1860–77. Engl. transl. with introdn. by Gasquet, F. A. [Reprinted in Monastic life in the middle ages. *See above*, Gasquet.] 6 vols. London. 1896. German transl. Brandes, K., and Müller, J. 7 vols. Ratisbon. 1869–78. Ital. transl. Carraresi, A. 5 vols. Siena. 1894 ff.

Morigi, P. Historia dell' origine di tutte le religioni. Venice. 1569. (French transl. Lourdereau, J. Paris. 1578.) New edn. Venice. 1581.

Workman, H. B. The evolution of the monastic ideal from the earliest times to the coming of the friars. London. 1913.

Zöckler, O. Askese u. Mönchtum. 2 vols. Frankfort-on-Main. 1897.

III. EUROPEAN COUNTRIES: GENERAL.

(a) Great Britain and Ireland.

Alemand, L. A. Histoire monastique d'Irlande. Paris. 1690. English transl. Meres, W. London. 1722.

Archdall, M. Monasticon Hibernicum. Dublin. 1786. 2nd edn. Moran, P. F. Dublin. 1873.

Burton, J. Monasticon Eboracense. York. 1753.

Dugdale, W. [and Dodsworth, R.]. Monasticon Anglicanum. *See Gen. Bibl.* IV.

Fosbrooke, T. D. British monachism. 2 vols. London. 1802. 3rd edn. 1 vol. London. 1843.

Gasquet, F. A. English monastic life. London. 1904.

Graham, R. Essay on English monasteries (Historical Assoc. Leaflet 32). London. 1913.

Jessopp, A. *ed.* Visitations of the diocese of Norwich 1492–1532. (Camden Soc. n.s. XLIII.) London. 1888.

Moran, P. F. *See above*, Archdall, M.

Nasmith, J. *See below*, Tanner, T.

Oliver, G. Monasticon dioecesis Exoniensis. Exeter. 1846.

Tanner, T. Notitia Monastica. London. 1744. Reprinted with addns. by Nasmith, J. Cambridge. 1787.

Taylor, R. Index Monasticus, or the abbeys, etc., formerly established in the diocese of Norwich and the ancient kingdom of East Anglia. London, 1821.

Thompson, A. Hamilton. English monasteries. 2nd edn. Cambridge. 1922.

—— *ed.* Visitations of religious houses in the diocese of Lincoln. Vols. I, II. (Lincoln Record Soc. VII, XIV.) Horncastle. 1914, 18. (*Also issued by* Canterbury and York Soc. XVII, XXIV. London. 1915, 19.)

Walcott, M. E. C. Church work and life in English minsters. 2 vols. London. 1879.

—— Scoti-monasticon. London. 1874.

Willis, Browne. An history of the mitred parliamentary abbeys. 2 vols. London. 1718–19.

(b) France.

Albanès, J. H. *See below*, Gallia Christiana.

Beaunier, Dom. Recueil historique, etc., des archevêchez, evêchez, abbayes, et prieurez de France. 2 vols. Paris. 1726. 3rd edn. 1743.

—— and Besse, J. Les archives de la France monastique. Vol. I. Paris. 1905 ff.

Bonnin, T. *ed.* Regestum visitationum archiepiscopi Rothomagensis. Rouen. 1852.

Bourassé, J. J. Abbayes et monastères de France. Tours. 1900.

Denifle, H. La Désolation des églises, monastères, et hôpitaux en France pendant la guerre de cent ans. 2 vols. Paris. 1897, 99.

Gallia Christiana (Vetus). Ed. Sainte-Marthe, S. de, and others. 4 vols. Paris. 1656.

—— —— (Nova). Vols. I–XIII. Ed. Sainte-Marthe, D. de, and others. Vols. XIV–XVI. Ed. Hauréau, B. Paris. 1715–1865. 2nd edn. Revised by Piolin, P. Vols. I–V, XI, XIII. Paris. 1870–8. Provincia Tolosana. New edn. Vol. I. Toulouse. 1892.

Gallia Christiana (Novissima). Ed. Albanès, J. H. and Chevalier, C. U. J. 3 vols.
    Montbéliard and Valence. 1895–1900.
—— —— French transl. Clavel de St-Geniez. Vols. ɪ, ɪɪ. Paris. 1855–6.
    Fisquet, H. (La France pontificale.) 25 vols. Paris. 1864 ff.
Monstier, A. du. Neustria pia. Rouen. 1663.
Tresvaux, F. M. L'Église de Bretagne. Paris. 1839.

(c) Germany, Austria-Hungary, and Switzerland.

Brusch, G. Monasteriorum Germaniae praecipuorum...centuria prima. Ingolstadt.
    1551. 2nd edn. (Chronologia monasteriorum.) Sulzbach. 1682. Centuria se-
    cunda (Supplementum Bruschianum). Ed. Nessel, D. de. Vienna. 1692.
Duval, C. Die Klöster und Klosterruinen Deutschlands. 2 vols. Nordhausen.
    1844, 46.
Fidler, M. Austria sacra. Vols. ɪ–ɪx. Vienna. 1779–89.
Fuschoffer, D. Monasteriologia regni Hungariae. Veszprim. 1803. Ed. Czinár, M.
    2 vols. Pest. 1858, 60.
Grote, O. v. Lexicon deutscher Stifter, Klöster, und Ordenshäuser. 2 vols. Oster-
    wieck-a.-H. 1880.
Hansizius, M. Germania sacra. Vols. ɪ, ɪɪ. Augsburg. 1727, 29. Vol. ɪɪɪ. Vienna.
    1754.
Mülinen, E. F. v. Helvetia sacra. 2 vols. Bern. 1858, 61.
Petrus, F. Suevia ecclesiastica. Augsburg and Dillingen. 1699.
Rader, M. Bavaria sancta. 2 vols. Ingolstadt. 1581. (B. sacra.) 3 vols. Munich.
    1615–27. 4 vols. Dillingen. 1704. German transl. Rassler, M. 3 vols. Augs-
    burg. 1714–15.
Rein, W. Thuringia sacra. 2 vols. Weimar. 1863, 65.
Remling, F. X. Urkundliche Gesch. der ehemaligen Abteien u. Klöster im jetzigen
    Rheinbayern. Neustadt-an-der-Haardt. 1838.
Steinbrück, J. J. Gesch. der Klöster in Pommern u. den angränzenden Provinzen.
    Stettin. 1796.
Stelzhammer, J. C. Historische u. topogr. Darstellung der Pfarren, Stifte, Klöster,
    etc., im Erzherzogthume Oesterreich. 18 vols. Vienna. 1819–40.
Stredowski, J. G. Sacra Moraviae historia. Sulzbach. 1710.
Styriae collegia et monasteria praecipua. Graz. 1740.
Thuringia sacra sive historia monasteriorum quae olim in Thuringia floruerunt.
    Frankfort-on-Main. 1737.
Tibus, A. Gründungsgesch. der Stifter, Pfarrkirchen, Klöster, u. Kapellen im
    Bereiche des alten Bisthums Münster. 3 pts. Münster. 1869.

(d) Italy, Sicily, and Dalmatia.

Farlati, D. Illyricum sacrum. 8 vols. (Vol. vɪɪɪ by Coleti, J.) Venice. 1751–1819.
Giovanni, G. di. Storia ecclesiastica di Sicilia. 2 vols. (cont. by Lanza, S.). Palermo.
    1846–7.
Lubin, A. Abbatiarum Italiae brevis notitia. Rome. 1693.
Meyranesius, J. F. Pedemontium sacrum. Vol. ɪ. Turin. 1784. Ed. Bosio, A.
    2 vols. [Turin.] 1863.
Pirrus, R. Sicilia sacra. 5 vols. Palermo. 1630–49. Revised and cont. by Mongi-
    tore, A., with notes on abbeys, etc. by Amico, V. M. 2 vols. Venice. 1733.
Ughelli, F. Italia sacra. 9 vols. Rome. 1644–62. 2nd edn. *See Gen. Bibl.* ɪv.
    Revised edn. by Lucentius, J. A. Vol. ɪ. Rome. 1704.

(e) The Netherlands.

Berlière, U. Monasticon belge. 2 vols. Bruges. 1890, 97.
Brasseur, P. Origines omnium Hannoniae coenobiorum. Mons. 1650.
Castillion, J. B. L. de. Sacra Belgii chronologia. Ghent. 1719.
Gazet, G. L'histoire ecclésiastique des Pays-bas. Valenciennes and Arras. 1614.
Sanderus, A. Chorographia sacra Brabantiae. 2 vols. Brussels and Antwerp.
    1659, 63; 1664, 69. 3 vols. The Hague. 1726–7.

Suur, H. Gesch. der ehemaligen Klöster in der Provinz Ostfriesland. Emden. 1838.

(*f*) SCANDINAVIA.

Daugaard, J. B. Om de danske Klostre i middelalderen. Copenhagen. 1830.
Lange, C. C. A. De norske klostres historie i middelalderen. Christiania. 1856.
Sparmann, J. Antiqua collegia canonicorum et monasteria regni Sueciae. Lund. 1671.
Wieselgren, P. De claustris Svio-Gothicis disquisitio. Lund. 1832.

(*g*) SPAIN AND PORTUGAL.

Bernardes Branco, M. Historia das ordens monasticas em Portugal. 3 vols. Lisbon. 1888.
España sagrada. Ed. Florez, H. *See Gen. Bibl.* IV.
Fuente, V. de la. Historia ecclesiastica de España. 3 vols. Barcelona. 1855.
Thomas ab Incarnatione. Historia ecclesiae Lusitanae. 4 vols. Coimbra. 1759–63.

IV. VARIOUS RELIGIOUS ORDERS.

(*a*) BENEDICTINE.

Alliez, L. Histoire du monastère de Lérins. 2 vols. Draguignan and Paris. 1862.
Berlière, U. *ed.* Mélanges d'histoire bénédictine. Maredsous. 1897 ff.
Besse, J. Le Moine bénédictin. 2nd edn. Ligugé. 1898.
Blemur, J. B. de. L'Année bénédictine. 7 vols. Paris. 1667–73.
Bucelin, G. Annales benedictini. 2 vols. Augsburg. 1656.
—— Aquila imperii benedictina. Venice. 1651.
—— Chronologiae benedictinae compendium. Augsburg. 1679.
——— Menologium benedictinum. Pt. I. Feldkirch. 1655. Pt. II. Augsburg. 1656.
Bulteau, L. Abrégé de l'histoire de l'ordre de St-Benoît. 2 vols. Paris. 1684.
Butler, C. Benedictine monachism. London. 1918.
—— *ed.* Regulae S. Benedicti editio critico-practica. Freiburg-im-Breisgau. 1918.
Calmet, A. Commentaire sur la règle de St-Benoît. Paris. 1782.
Chomton, L. Histoire de l'église St-Bénigne de Dijon. Dijon. 1900.
Clausse, G. Les origines bénédictines. Paris. 1899.
Delatte, P. Commentaire sur la règle de St-Benoît. Paris. 1913. English transl. McCann, J. London. 1921.
Egger, F. Idea ordinis hierarcho-benedictina. 3 vols. Constance and Kempten. 1715–21.
Félibien, M. Histoire de l'abbaye royale de St-Denys. Paris. 1706.
Fowler, J. T. *ed.* Rites of Durham. (Surtees Soc.) Durham. 1907.
Gattola, E. Historia abbatiae Cassinensis (*with* Accessiones). 4 pts. in 2 vols. Venice. 1733–4.
Grützmacher, G. Die Bedeutung Benedikts v. Nursia u. seiner Regel in der Gesch. des Mönchtums. Berlin. 1892.
Haeften, B. S. Benedictus illustratus, sive disquisitiones monasticae. Antwerp. 1664.
Holstenius, L. *ed.* Codex regularum monasticarum et canonicarum...collectus olim a S. Benedicto Anianensi abbati. 3 vols. Rome. 1661. Paris. 1663. Ed. Brockier, M. 6 vols. Augsburg. 1759.
Hugo. Historiae Farfenses. MGH. Script. XI. 1854. *Also* ed. Balzani, U. (Fonti.)
Le Mire, A. Chronicon benedictinum. Cologne. 1614.
—— Origines coenobiorum Benedictinorum. Antwerp. 1608.
Leo [Diaconus], Cardinal-bishop of Ostia. Chronicon monasterii Cassinensis. Ed. Nuce, A. de. Paris. 1668.
Mabillon, J. [with d'Achery, L. and Ruinart, T.]. Acta sanctorum o. s. B. (ASBen.) *See Gen. Bibl.* IV.
—— Annales o. s. B. 6 vols. [Vol. v by Massuet, R. Vol. VI completed by Martène, E.] 1703–39. *See Gen. Bibl.* IV.
Martène, E. Commentarius in regulam s. p. Benedicti. Paris. 1690; 1695.

Martène, E. Histoire de l'abbaye de Marmoutiers. Ed. Chevalier, C. *in* Mém. Soc. Archéol. de Touraine. xxiv, xxv. Tours. 1874–5.

Mège, J. de. Commentaire sur la règle de St-Benoist. Paris. 1687.

—— Vie de St-Benoît et un abrégé de l'histoire de son ordre. Paris. 1690.

Ménard, H. *ed.* Concordia regularum. Paris. 1638.

Pantin, W. A. Documents illustrating the activities of the General and Provincial Chapters of the English Black Monks, 1215–1540. 3 vols. (Camden Ser.) London. 1931–7.

Pearce, E. H. The monks of Westminster. Cambridge. 1916.

Pez, B. Epistolae apologeticae pro o. s. B. Kempten. 1715.

Porée, A. A. Histoire de l'abbaye du Bec. 2 vols. Évreux. 1901.

Puteo, M. de, *ed.* Benedictina sive constitutiones Benedicti papae ad monachos nigros in pristinam lucem redacta. Paris. 1517.

Regulae monasticae ss. patrum...acc. J. Trithemii liber exhortationis ad monachos. Louvain. 1574.

Revue bénédictine de l'abbaye de Maredsous. Maredsous. 1884 ff., in progress (RBén.).

Rivista storica benedettina. Monte Cassino. 1906 ff., in progress.

S. Thomas, L. de. Benedictina Lusitana. 2 vols. Coimbra. 1644, 51.

Sandoval, P. de. Primera parte de las fundaciones de los monasteros del glorioso padre S. Benito, que los reyes de España fundaron y dotaron. Madrid. 1601.

Schannat, J. F. Historia monasterii Fuldensis et ejus abbatum. 2 vols. Frankfort-on-Main. 1729.

Schramm, A. Chronicon Mellicense. Vienna. 1702.

Schuster. L'abbaye de Farfa et sa restauration au xie siècle sous Hugues 1er. RBén. 1907.

Sczygielski, S. Aquila Polono-benedictina. Cracow. 1668.

Spicilegium benedictinum. Rome. 1896 ff., in progress.

Spicilegium Casinense. Monte Cassino. 1893 ff., in progress.

Staaff, P. De ordine Benedictino monachorum Svio-Gothiae. Upsala. 1727.

Stengel, C. Monasteriologia...monasteriorum S. Benedicti in Germania origines. 2 vols. Augsburg. 1619, 38.

Studien und Mittheilungen aus dem Benedictiner- und dem Cisterzienserorden. Würzburg, Brünn. 1880 ff., in progress.

Taunton, E. L. The English black monks of St Benedict. 2 vols. London. 1897.

Thompson, E. M. *ed.* Customary of the Benedictine monasteries of St Augustine, Canterbury and St Peter, Westminster. 2 vols. (Hen. Bradshaw Soc.) London. 1902, 4.

Tornamira, A. Historia monastica dell' ordine di San Benedetto. 1673.

Tosti, L. Storia della badia di Monte Cassino. 3 vols. Naples. 1842–3.

Traube, L. Textgesch. der Regula s. Benedicti. *In* Abh. d. k. bayer. Akad. d. Wiss. Hist. Klasse. xxi. Munich. 1898. 2nd edn. Plenkers, H. *Ibid.* Philos.-philol.-hist. Klasse. xxv. Munich. 1910.

Trithemius, J. Liber lugubris de ruina monastici ordinis. *In* Opera. Mayence. 1604.

—— *ed.* Annales monasterii Hirsaugiensis ad ann. 1514. 2 vols. St Gall. 1690.

—— *See also above*, Regulae monasticae.

Vita S. Benedicti Anianensis. MPL. ciii.

Vita S. Guilielmi abbatis S. Benigni Divionensis. MPL. cxlii.

Westlake, H. F. Westminster Abbey. 2 vols. London. 1923.

Williams, L. F. Rushbrook. History of the abbey of St Albans. London. 1917.

Willis, R. The architectural history of the conventual buildings of the monastery of Christchurch in Canterbury. London. 1869.

Wion, A. Lignum vitae, ornamentum et decus ecclesiae. 2 vols. Venice. 1595.

Wölfflin, E. Benedict v. Nursia u. seine Mönchsregel. Munich. 1895.

Yepez, A. Coronica general de la orden de San Benito. 7 vols. Pampeluna and Valladolid. 1609–21. Latin transl. Weiss, T. Vols. i, ii. Cologne. 1648, 50. French transl. Rethelois, M. 7 vols. Toul. 1674.

(b) Cistercians

Arbois de Jubainville, H. d', and Pigeotte, L. Études sur l'état intérieur des abbayes cisterciennes et principalement de Clairvaux au xiie et au xiiie siècle. Paris. 1858.

Bernard, St, of Clairvaux. Epistolae, etc. MPL. CLXXXII–CLXXXIV.

Brito, B. de. Primeira parte da chronica de Cister. Lisbon. 1602. 2nd edn. 1720.

Chalemot, C. Series et vitae sanctorum et beatorum ac illustrium virorum sacri ordinis Cisterciensis. Paris. 1670.

Cooke, A. M. The settlement of the Cistercians in England. EHR. VIII. 1893.

Exordia [magnum et minus] sacri ordinis Cisterciensis. MPL. CLXXXV.

Finestres y de Monsalvo, J. Historia de el real monasterio de Poblet. Vol. I. Barcelona. 1746.

Fowler, J. T. ed. Cistercian statutes, A.D. 1256–7, with supplementary statutes of the order, A.D. 1257–88. (Repr. from Yorkshire Archaeol. Journal.) London. 1890.

Girschner, W. Die vormalige Reichsabtei Walkenried am Harz. Nordhausen. 1870.

Grillnberger, O. Catalogi abbatiarum ord. Cist. Pt. I. Vienna. 1904.

Guignard, P. Les monuments primitifs de la règle Cistercienne. (Analecta Divionensia VI.) Dijon. 1878.

Henri, V. B. Histoire de l'abbaye de Pontigny. Auxerre and Avallon. 1839.

Henriquez, C. Fasciculus sanctorum ord. Cist. 2 vols. Brussels. 1623. 2nd edn. Cologne. 1631.

—— Menologium Cisterciense notationibus illustratum. Accedunt seorsim regula, constitutiones, et privilegia ejusdem ordinis ac congregationum monasticarum et militarium quae Cist. institutum observant. 2 vols. Antwerp. 1630. German transl. Prague. 1731.

Hope, W. H. St John. Fountains Abbey. *In* Yorkshire Archaeol. Journal. XV. 1900.

—— and Bilson, J. Architectural description of Kirkstall Abbey. (Thoresby Soc.) Leeds. 1907.

Janauschek, P. L. Der Cisterzienserorden historische Skizze. Brünn. 1884.

—— Origines Cistercienses. Vol. I. Vienna. 1877.

—— and Gsell, B. Xenia Bernardina. 6 vols. Vienna. 1891 ff.

Jongelin, G. Notitia abbatiarum ord. Cist. per orbem universum. Cologne. 1640.

—— Origines et progressus ord. Cist. abbatiarum et equestrium militarium de Calatrava, etc. Cologne. 1641.

—— Purpura divi Bernardi. Cologne. 1644.

Kierulf, A. C. A. Esrom Klosters historie. Copenhagen. 1833.

Le Mire, A. Chronicon Cist. ordinis. Cologne. 1614.

Le Nain, P. Essai de l'histoire de l'ordre de Cîteaux. 9 vols. Paris. 1696–7.

Linck, B. Annales Austrio-Claravallenses. 2 vols. Vienna. 1723, 25.

Manrique, A. Cisterciensium seu verius ecclesiasticorum annalium a condito Cistercio libri. 4 vols. Lyons. 1642–9. German transl. Hiltprand, B. 2 vols. Augsburg. 1739, 42.

Méchet, L. ed. Privilèges de l'ordre de Cisteaux. Paris. 1713.

Michels, F. Gesch. u. Beschreibung der ehemal. Abtei Kamp bei Rheinsberg. Crefeld. 1832.

Micklethwaite, J. T. The Cistercian order. *In* Yorkshire Archaeol. Journal. XV. 1900.

Montalvo, B. de. Primera parte de la coronica del orden de Cister. Madrid. 1602.

Morison, J. C. The life and times of St Bernard. 2nd edn. London. 1884.

Muñiz, R. Biblioteca Cisterciense Española. Burgos. 1793.

—— Medulla historica Cisterciensis. 7 vols. Valladolid. 1787.

Newman, J. H. ed. Life of St Stephen Harding. *In* The Cistercian Saints of England: Lives of the English Saints. London. 1844.

Palmer, B. A concise history of the Cistercian order. London. 1852.

Paris, J. ed. Nomasticon Cisterciense seu antiquiores ord. Cist. consuetudines. Paris. 1664. New edn. Séjalon, H. Solesmes. 1892.

Powicke, F. M. Ailred of Rievaulx and his biographer Walter Daniel. Manchester. 1922.

Ratisbonne, M. T. Histoire de St Bernard. 3rd edn. 2 vols. Paris. 1843. Engl. transl. Dublin. 1859.

Rusca, R. Origine del sacro ordine Cisterciense e suoi progressi. Milan. 1598.

Sainati, G. Vita del B. Eugenio III pontefice massimo. Pisa. 1868. Monza. 1874.

Santos, M. dos. Alcobaça illustrada. Pt. I. Coimbra. 1710.

São Bonaventura, F. de. Historia...da real abbadia de Alcobaça. Lisbon. 1827.
Sartorius, A. Cistercium bis-tertium seu historia elogialis ord. Cist. 2 vols. Prague. 1700. German transl. 2 vols. Prague. 1708.
Scheinpflug, B. Ausbreitung des Cist.-Ordens...in Böhmen. (Deutsch. Ober-Real-schule.) Prague. 1864.
Statuta Capitulorum Generalium ordinis Cisterciensis ab anno 1116 ad annum 1786. Ed. Canavaz, J. M. Vols. I–VI. Louvain. 1933–8.
Tissier, B. *ed.* Bibliotheca patrum Cisterciensium. Vols. I–VI. Bonnefont. 1660–4. Vols. VII, VIII. Paris. 1669.
Vacandard, E. Vie de St Bernard. 2 vols. Paris. 1895.
Visch, C. de, *ed.* Bibliotheca scriptorum sacri ord. Cist. 2nd edn. Cologne. 1656.
Vita sancti Roberti abbatis Molismensis. MPL. CLVII.
Vitae sancti Bernardi [by Guillaume de St Thierry, etc.]. MPL. CLXXXV.
Walbran, J. R. and Fowler, J. T. *edd.* Memorials of Fountains Abbey. 3 vols. (Surtees Soc.) Durham. 1863–1918.
Wegele, F. X. *ed.* Monumenta Eberacensia. Nördlingen, 1863.
Weigand, P. W. Gesch. der fränkischen Cist.-Abtei Ebrach. Landshut. 1834.
Winter, F. Die Cistercienser des nordöstlichen Deutschlands. 3 vols. Gotha. 1868–71.
Yberius, I. Exordia sacri ord. Cist. Pampeluna. 1621.
Zapater, M. R. Cister militante. Saragossa. 1662.

(c) CLUNY AND ALLIED REFORMS.

Aimoinus. Vita Abbonis. MPL. CXXXIX. col. 387 sqq.
Albers, B. *ed.* Consuetudines monasticae. I. Consuetudines Farfenses. Stuttgart. 1900.
Annales Blandinienses. MGH. Script. v. 1844.
Berlière, U. L'abbaye de St-Gérard [Brogne]. (Mess. des fidèles. v.) 1888.
—— Cluny, son action religieuse et sociale. RBén. IX. 1892.
Bernard, A. and Bruel, A. *edd.* Recueil des chartes de l'abbaye de Cluny. 6 vols. (Coll. doc.) Paris. 1876–1903.
Bosco (Dubois), J. à, *ed.* Floriacensis vetus bibliotheca. 3 pts. Lyons. 1605.
Bruel, A. Les chapitres généraux de l'ordre de Cluny. (BEC. XXXIV.) 1873. Nogent-le-Rotrou. 1874.
Chronicon Farfense. Ed. Balzani, U. (Fonti.) *Also* ed. Muratori. RR.II.SS. 1st edn. Vol. II. 2.
Cucherat, F. Cluny au XIᵉ siècle. 2nd edn. Autun. 1873.
Duckett, G. F. *ed.* Monasticon Cluniacense Anglicanum, or Charters and records among the archives of the abbey of Cluni, 1077–1534. 2 vols. [Lewes.] 1888.
—— *ed.* Visitations and chapters-general of the order of Cluni. London. 1893.
Graham, R. Life at Cluny in the eleventh century. CQR. April, 1916.
—— The relation of Cluny to some other movements of monastic reform. JTS. XV. 1914.
Hafner, O. Regesten zur Gesch. des schwäbischen Klosters Hirsau. *In* Studien und Mittheil. XII–XVI. 1891–5. *See above*, IV (a).
Hauviller, E. Ulrich v. Cluny. (Kirchengeschichtliche Studien. Ed. Knöpfler, A. 3.) Münster. 1896.
Herrgott, M. Vetus disciplina monastica. Paris. 1726.
Historiae Farfenses. MGH. Script. XI. 1854.
Jardet, P. St-Odilon, sa vie, son temps, ses oeuvres. Lyons. 1898.
Joannes. Vita Odonis. MPL. CXXXIII.
Jotsaldus. Vita S. Odilonis. MPL. CXLII.
Lager, J. C. Die Abtei Gorze in Lothringen. *In* Studien und Mittheil. VIII. 1887. *See above*, IV (a).
L'Huillier, A. Vie de Saint-Hugues, abbé de Cluny. Solesmes. 1888.
Lokeren, A. v. *ed.* Chartes et documents de l'abbaye de St-Pierre au Mont Blandin à Gand. Ghent. 1868.
Lorain, P. Essai historique sur l'abbaye de Cluny. Dijon. 1839.
—— Histoire de l'abbaye de Cluny. Paris. 1845.

Marchand, L. A. Souvenirs historiques sur l'ancienne abbaye de St-Benoît-s.-Loire. Orléans. 1838.

Marrier, M. and Duchesne, A. *edd.* Bibliotheca Cluniacensis. *See Gen. Bibl.* IV.

Millénaire de Cluny. 2 vols. Mâcon. 1910.

Nalgodus. Vita Odonis. MPL. CXXXIII.

Odilo. Vita Maioli. MPL. CXLII.

Penjon, A. Cluny, la ville et l'abbaye. Cluny. 1873.

Petrus Venerabilis. Epistolae, etc. MPL. CLXXXIX.

Pignot, J. H. Histoire de l'ordre de Cluny. 3 vols. (Soc. Éduenne.) Autun and Paris. 1868.

Putte, F. van de. Annales abbatiae sancti Petri Blandiniensis. Ghent. 1842.

Robinson, J. A. St Dunstan and his times. Oxford. 1923.

Rocher, J. N. M. Histoire de l'abbaye royale de St-Benoît-s.-Loire. Orléans. 1865.

Sackur, E. Die Cluniacenser in ihrer kirchlichen u. allgemeingeschichtlichen Wirksamkeit bis zur Mitte des XI[ten] Jahrh. 2 vols. Halle. 1892, 94.

Smith, L. M. The early history of the monastery of Cluny. Oxford. 1920.

Syrus. Vita Maioli. MPL. CXXXVII.

Udalricus (Ulrich). Antiquiores consuetudines Cluniacensis monasterii. MPL. CXLIX.

Vita Joannis Gorziensis. MPL. CXXXVII.

(d) Carthusians and other Hermit Orders.

(i) *Carthusians.*

Alfaura, J. Origines omnium domorum ord. Carthus. Valencia. 1670.

Corbin, J. L'histoire sacrée de l'ordre des Chartreux. Paris. 1653; 1659.

Dorland, P. Chronicon Cartus. Ed. Petraeus, T. Cologne. 1608. French transl. Driscart, A. Tournai. 1844.

Guigo. Liber de exercitio cellae. MPL. CLIII.

Hendriks, L. The London Charterhouse, its monks and its martyrs. London. 1889.

Hope, W. H. St John, and others. Mount Grace Priory. *In* Yorkshire Archaeol. Journal. Vol. XVIII.

Le Couteulx, C. Annales ord. Cartus. Vol. I. Correrie. 1687. Continued by Carthusian monks. 8 vols. Montreuil-sur-Mer. 1888–91.

Lefebvre, F. A. St-Bruno et l'ordre des Chartreux. 2 vols. Paris. 1883.

Le Masson, I. Annales ord. Carthus. Vol. I. Correrie. 1687. 2nd edn. with title De disciplina ord. Carthus. Paris. 1703.

Le Mire, A. Origines monasteriorum Carthus. per orbem universum. Cologne. 1609. [Appendix to Petreius, T. Bibl. Cartusiana. *See below.*]

Le Vasseur, L. Ephemerides ord. Cartus. 4 vols. Montreuil-sur-Mer. 1891–2.

Loebbel, H. Der Stifter des Carthäuser-Ordens, der h. Bruno aus Köln (Kirchengeschichtliche Studien. Ed. Knöpfler, A., 5). Münster. 1899.

Nova collectio statutorum ord. Cartus. 2nd edn. Correrie. 1681.

Petreius, T. Bibliotheca Cartusiana. Cologne. 1609.

Tromby, B. Storia...del patriarca S. Brunone e del suo ord. cartus. 10 vols. Naples. 1773–9.

Vallier, G. Sigillographie de l'ordre des Chartreux. Montreuil-sur-Mer. 1891.

(ii) *Camaldoli.*

Constitutiones eremitarum S. Romualdi ordinis Camaldulensis. Florence. 1595.

Florentinus [Fortunio], A. Historiarum Camald. libri tres. Florence. 1575. Pt. II. Venice. 1579.

Grandis, G. de. Dissertationes Camaldulenses. Lucca. 1707.

Hastivillius, A. Romualdina seu eremitica Camald. ord. historia. Paris. 1631.

Masetti, F. Teatro storico del sacro eremo di Camaldoli. Lucca. 1733.

Mittarelli, J. B. and Costadoni, A. Annales Camaldulenses. 9 vols. Venice. 1755–73.

Petrus Damianus. Vita sancti patriarchae Romualdi. MPL. CXLIV.

Razzi, S. Vite dei santi e beati dell' ordine di Camaldoli. Florence. 1600.

Ziegelbauer, M. Centifolium Camaldulense. Venice. 1750.

(iii) *Grandmont.*

Antiqua statuta ordinis Grandimontensis. *In* Martène, E. Thesaurus novus anecdotorum. IV. *See Gen. Bibl.* IV.
Geraldus. Vita S. Stephani Grandimontensis. MPL. CCIV.
Historiae [brevis et prolixior] priorum Grandimontensium. *In* Martène. E. Scriptorum veterum...ampl. collectio. VI. Paris. 1729.
Levesque, J. Annales ordinis Grandimontensis. Troyes. 1662.
Regula S. Stephani. Dijon. 1635. *Also* MPL. CCIV.

(iv) *Vallombrosa.*

Casari, G. A. Vallumbrosanae congregationis sancti, beati, ac venerabiles. Rome. 1695.
Franchi, D. de'. Historia del patriarcha S. Giovanni Gualberto. Florence. 1640.
Locatelli, E. Vita di S. Giovanni Gualberto insieme con le vite di tutti i generali, beati, e beate di questa religione. Florence. 1633.
Nardi, F. Abbatiae et monasteria...per monachos et moniales nostrae congregationis vel fundata vel...habitata. Florence. 1726.
—— *ed.* Bullarium Vallumbrosanum. Florence. 1729.
Simius, V. Catalogus sanctorum, etc. qui...effloruerunt in Valle Umbrosa. Rome. 1693.

(*e*) FONTEVRAULT, ETC.

Constitutions de l'ordre de Fontevrault. Paris. 1642. [Lat. and Fr.]
Cosnier, M. Fontis-Ebraldi exordium. La Flèche. 1641.
Édouard [Biron, A.]. Fontevrault et ses monuments. 2 vols. Paris. 1874–5.
Ganot, S. La vie de Robert d'Arbrissel. La Flèche. 1648.
Gaufridus Grossus. Vita b. Bernardi de Tironio. MPL. CLXXII.
La Mainferme, J. de. Clypeus nascentis Fontebraldensis ordinis. 3 vols. Paris. 1684.
Nicquet, H. Histoire de l'ordre de Font-Evraud. Paris. 1642.
Pavillon, B. Vie du bienh. Robert d'Arbrissel. Saumur. 1667.

(*f*) MISCELLANEOUS ORDERS OF MONKS.

[Becquet, A.] Gallicae Coelestinorum congregationis...monasteriorum fundationes. Paris. 1719.
Belforti, M. A. Chronologia brevis coenobiorum, etc. congregationis Montis Oliveti. Milan. 1720.
Constitutiones fratrum Coelestinorum. Paris. 1590 and 1670.
Constitutiones ordinis Olivetani. Venice. 1541. Rome. 1573 and 1602.
Constitutioni della congregatione di S. Benedetto di Montefano, hora detta di monachi Silvestrini. Camerino. 1610.
Constitutioni della congregatione Silvestrina. Rome. 1691.
Costo, T. Istoria dell' origine del sagratissimo luogo di Monte-Vergine.
Fabrini, S. Cronica della congregazione de' monachi Silvestrini. Camerino. 1618. Ed. Morosi, A. and Lucantovi, A. Rome. 1706.
Giordano, G. G. Chroniche di Monte-Vergine. Naples. 1649.
Lancellotti, S. Historiae Olivetanae...libri II. Venice. 1623.
Lombardelli, G. Vita b. Bernardi Tolomei. Lucca. 1659.
Marino, L. Vita e miracoli di S. Pietro del Morrone. Milan. [1637.]
Telera di Manfredonia, C. Historie sagre degli huomini illustri...della congregatione de Celestini. Bologna. 1648.

(*g*) ORDERS AND CONGREGATIONS OF REGULAR CANONS.

Amort, E. Vetus disciplina canonicorum regularium et saecularium. 2 vols. Venice. 1747.
Baro, B. Annales ordinis S. Trinitatis pro redemptione captivorum. Vol. I. Rome. 1684.
Bonnard, F. Histoire de l'abbaye royale de St-Victor de Paris. 2 vols. Paris. 1904, 8.
Busch, J. Chronicon Windeshemense und Liber de reformatione monasteriorum. Ed. Grube, K. Halle. 1887.

Clark, J. W. The observances in use at the Augustinian priory of Barnwell. Cambridge. 1897.

Crusenius, N. Monasticon Augustinianum omnium ordinum sub regula S. Augustini militantium. Munich. 1622.

Dupré, M. Annales breves ordinis Praemonstratensis. Namur. 1836.

Fasseau, A. T. Arbor genealogica ordinis Praemonstratensis. Augsburg. 1727.

Frere, W. H. The early history of canons regular. *In* Fasciculus J. W. Clark dicatus. Cambridge. 1907. pp. 186–216.

Gasquet, F. A. *ed.* Collectanea Anglo-Premonstratensia. 3 vols. (Camden 3rd series. Vols. VI, X, and XII. RHS.) London. 1904–6.

Gosse, E. Histoire de l'abbaye et de l'ancienne congrégation des chanoines réguliers d'Arrouaise. Lille. 1786.

Graham, R. St Gilbert of Sempringham and the Gilbertines. London. 1903.

Grube, K. Gerhard Groot u. seine Stiftungen. Cologne. 1883.

—— Johannes Busch, Augustinerpropst zu Hildesheim. Freiburg-im-Breisgau. 1881.

—— *See also above*, Busch, J.

Hermans. Annales canonicorum regularium S. Augustini ordinis S. Crucis. 3 vols. Bois-le-Duc. 1838.

Hugo, C. L. Vie de St-Norbert. Luxemburg. 1704.

Le Large. De canonicorum ordine disquisitiones. Paris. 1697.

Le Mire, A. Canonicorum regularium ordinis S. Augustini origines et progressus. Cologne. 1615.

—— Chronicon ordinis Praemonstratensis. Cologne. 1613.

—— De collegiis canonicorum regularium. Cologne. 1614.

—— De Windesimensi, Lateranensi, Aroasiensi, et congregationibus aliis canonicorum regularium ordinis S. Augustini. Brussels. 1622.

Le Paige, J. *ed.* Bibliotheca Praemonstratensis ordinis. 2 vols. Paris. 1633.

Leuckfeld, J. G. Antiquitates Praemonstratenses. Magdeburg and Leipsic. 1721. [Abbeys of Magdeburg and Calbe.]

Mozzagrugni, J. Narratio rerum gestarum canonicorum regularium. Venice. 1622.

Ossinger, J. F. Bibliotheca Augustiniana. Ingolstadt and Munich. 1776.

Paminius, O. Augustiniani ordinis chronicon. Rome. 1510.

Penotti, G. Generalis totius sacri ordinis clericorum canonicorum historia tripartita. Rome. 1624. Cologne. 1630 and 1645.

Salter, H. E. *ed.* Chapters of the Augustinian Canons. (Oxford Hist. Soc. LXXIV.) Oxford. 1922. (*Also issued by* Canterbury and York Soc. XXIX. London. 1922.)

S. Maria, F. de. Oceo aberto na terra: historia das sagradas congregaçáoes dos conegos seculares de S. Jorge em Alga de Veneta y de S. João Evangelista em Portugal. Lisbon. 1697.

—— N. de. Chronica del orden dos conegos regulares de S. Agostinho da congregação de S. Cruz de Coimbra. Lisbon. 1658.

Thomasini, J. P. Annales canonicorum secularium S. Georgii in Alga. Udine. 1642.

Torelli, L. Secoli Agostiniani ovvero istoria generale dell' ordine di S. Agostino. 8 vols. Bologna. 1659–86.

Trullus, J. Ordo canonicorum regularium IV libris elucidatus. Saragossa. 1571. Bologna. 1605.

Winter, F. Die Prämonstratenser des 12 Jahrhunderts u. ihre Bedeutung für das nordöstliche Deutschland. Berlin. 1865.

Zungg, J. A. Historiae generalis et specialis de ordine canonicorum regularium S. Augustini prodromus. 2 vols. Ratisbon. 1742, 45.

(*h*) ORDERS OF NUNS.

Accounts of orders of nuns and of individual nunneries will be found in many of the general histories of monasticism and religious orders cited in previous sections. See also:

Bateson, M. Origin and early history of double monasteries. TRHS. n.s. XIII (1899). pp. 137–98.

Eckenstein, L. Woman under monasticism. Cambridge. 1896.

Power, E. E. Medieval English nunneries. Cambridge. 1922. [With general biblio-
graphy.]
Thompson, A. Hamilton. Double monasteries and the male element in nunneries.
In Archbishops' report on the Ministry of women. London. 1919. App. VIII.

(*i*) MILITARY ORDERS.

Belloy, P. de. De l'origine et institution de divers ordres de chevalerie. Paris.
1613.
Bosio, G. Dell' istoria della sacra religione et illustrissima militia di S. Giovanni
Gierosolimitano. 3 vols. Rome. 1594–1602.
Delaville Le Roulx, J. *ed.* Cartulaire général de l'ordre des hospitaliers de St-Jean
de Jérusalem. 4 vols. Paris. 1894–1906.
Favyn, A. Le théâtre d'honneur et de chevalerie. 2 vols. Paris. 1620.
Funés, J. A. de. Coronica de la milicia y religion de S. Juan de Jerusalem. Pt. I.
Valencia. 1626. Pt. II. Saragossa. 1639.
Giustiniani, B. Historie chronologiche dell' origine degli ordini militari e di tutte le
religioni cavalleresche. 2 vols. Venice. 1692.
Goussaincourt, M. de. Martyrologe des chevaliers de S. Jean de Hiérusalem, dits de
Malte. Paris. 1643 [1654].
Gurter, N. Historia Templariorum. Amsterdam. 1691.
Hermant, G. Histoire des religions ou ordres militaires de l'église. Rouen. 1698.
Histoire des ordres militaires. [Compiled from Hélyot, etc.] 4 vols. Amsterdam.
Histoire de tous les ordres militaires. (Engravings by Schoonebeek, A.) 2 vols.
Amsterdam. 1699.
Larking, L. B. *ed.* The Knights Hospitallers in England. (Camden Soc. LXV.)
London. 1857.
Mendo, A. De ordinibus militaribus disquisitio canonica. Lyons. 1668.
Mennenius, F. Deliciae equestrium sive militarium ordinum et eorundem origines.
Cologne. 1613.
Montoya, G. de. Stabilimenta militum ordinis de S. Joanne Jerosolimitano. Sala-
manca. 1534.
Mota, D. de la. Del principio de la orden de la cavalleria de S. Jago del espada.
Valencia. 1599.
Rades y Andrada, F. de. Chronica de las tres ordenes y cavallerias de Sanctiago,
Calatrava, y Alcantara. Toledo. 1572.
Schurzfleisch, H. L. Historia ensiferorum ordinis Teutonici Livonorum. Wittem-
berg. 1701.
Vertot, R. A. de. Histoire des chevaliers hospitaliers de St-Jean de Jérusalem.
4 vols. Paris. 1726 ff. Revised and continued by Bussy, A. M. L. de. 3 vols.
Paris and Lyons. 1859.
Wai, baron de. Essai sur l'histoire de l'ordre teutonique. 8 vols. Paris and Rheims.
1784–90.
Wilcke, W. F. Geschichte des Tempelherrnordens. 3 vols. Leipsic. 1826–35.

See also the general works in section II above.

V. COLLECTIONS OF DOCUMENTS IN PRINT.

(*a*) Collections which throw special light upon the internal history and discipline
of monasteries, *e.g.* editions of visitation documents, have been included under one
or other of the special classes treated above.

(*b*) Editions of and excerpts from chartularies are numerous, and only specimens
of these need be mentioned. For French monasteries see especially, in the
Collection de documents inédits sur l'histoire de France (*See Gen. Bibl.* IV), Recueil
des chartes...de Cluny. Ed. Bernard, A. and Bruel, A. 6 vols. 1876–1903; and
the Chartularies of St Père, Chartres; St Bertin; St Victor, Marseilles, etc. Ed.
Guérard, B. and others. 1840 ff.

For chartularies of English monasteries see the index to Gross, C. Sources and Literature of English History. 2nd edn. (*See Gen. Bibl.* i) *s.v.* Chartularies, monastic.

(*c*) For monastic account-rolls see especially:

Chapman, F. R. *ed.* Sacrist Rolls of Ely. 2 vols. Cambridge. 1907.

Fowler, J. T. *ed.* Extracts from the Account rolls of the Abbey of Durham. 3 vols. (Surtees Soc.) Durham. 1898–1900.

Kitchin, G. W. *ed.* Compotus rolls of the obedientiaries of St Swithun's Priory, Winchester. (Hants Record Soc.) London and Winchester. 1892.

CHAPTER XXI.

ROMAN AND CANON LAW IN THE MIDDLE AGES.

I. BIBLIOGRAPHIES AND PERIODICALS.

A. BIBLIOGRAPHIES: ROMAN LAW.

(i) *Ancient Roman Law (to the death of Justinian).*

Buckland, W. W. Text-book of Roman Law from Augustus to Justinian. Cambridge. 1921. pp. xiii, xiv.

See also the works of Girard, P. F., Kipp, T., and Muirhead, J. H. cited in Vol. II, Bibl. to ch. III, p. 726. For Graeco-Roman Law see Vol. IV, Bibl. to ch. XXII, p. 890.

(ii) *Germano-Roman Law (Roman Law in Germanic Kingdoms).*

Brunner, H. Deutsche Rechtsgeschichte. Vol. I. 2nd edn. §§ 38–59. *See Gen. Bibl.* v. [Excellent for leges barbarorum, leges romanae, Frankish capitularies, documents, and formularies, and for modern works on them. *See also* Brunner, H. Grundzüge der deutschen Rechtsgeschichte. 7th edn. §§ 13–15. *See Gen. Bibl.* v.]

Savigny, F. C. v. Geschichte des Römischen Rechts im Mittelalter. *passim. See Gen. Bibl.* v. [Still most useful.]

Vinogradoff, P. Roman Law in Mediaeval Europe. pp. 1–2. *See Gen. Bibl.* v.

Viollet, P. Histoire du droit civil français. 3rd edn. pp. 1–262. *See Gen. Bibl.* [Valuable.]

(iii) *Separate Countries (as indicated in notes).*

Brunner, H. Deutsche Rechtsgeschichte. Vol. I. 2nd edn. §§ 38–59. *See Gen. Bibl.* v. [For Germany.]

—— Grundzüge der deutschen Rechtsgeschichte. 7th edn. *See Gen. Bibl.* v. [For Germany. § 61. Literature on the Reception.]

Carlyle, R. W. and A. J. A history of Mediaeval Political Theory in the West. Vol. II. pp. xvii–xix. *See Gen. Bibl.* v. [For Italy. Writings of civilians and canonists.]

Conrat (Cohn), M. Geschichte der Quellen und Literatur des Römischen Rechts im früheren Mittelalter. Vol. I. Leipsic. 1889. [For Italy. Detailed references to medieval sources and literature.]

Fockema-Andreae, S. J. Overzicht van Oud-Nederlandsche Rechtsbronnen. Haarlem 1881. [For sources of medieval Netherlands law.]

General Survey of events, sources, persons, and movements in continental legal history. Ed. Wigmore, J. H. (Continental Legal History Series. Vol. I.) Boston, Mass.; and London. 1912. [Valuable. For Italy, pp. 87–175. For the Netherlands, pp. 455–79. For Switzerland, pp. 483–530. For Spain, pp. 579–658.]

Gierke, O. Das deutsche Genossenschaftsrecht. Vol. III, pp. 186–9, 238–43, 351–3, 416–19. *See Gen. Bibl.* v. [For Italy. Useful lists of writings of medieval civilians and canonists.]

Lee, R. W. Introduction to Roman-Dutch law. Oxford. 1915. pp. xiii–xvii. [For the Netherlands.]

Pollock, F. and Maitland, F. W. History of English Law. 2nd edn. *See Gen. Bibl.* v. [Especially vol. I, pp. xix–xxii; and ch. v, Roman and Canon Law.]

Savigny, F. C. v. Geschichte des Römischen Rechts im Mittelalter. *passim. See Gen. Bibl.* v. [For Italy. Still indispensable.]

Schröder, R. Lehrbuch der deutschen Rechtsgeschichte. 4th edn. Leipsic. 1902.
　　[For Germany. §§ 30–34. (Legal sources of Frankish period.) §§ 52–60. (Legal
　　sources and literature of the Middle Ages.) § 66. (Literature on the Reception.)]
Vinogradoff, P. Roman Law in Mediaeval Europe. *See Gen. Bibl.* v. [For Italy,
　　p. 32; France, p. 59; England, p. 84; Germany, p. 106.]
Viollet, P. Histoire du droit civil français. 3rd edn. pp. 1–32, 145–262. *See Gen.
　　Bibl.* v. [For France. Valuable.]

B. Bibliographies: Canon Law.

(i) *Eastern Canon Law.*

(*See* Vol. iv, Bibl. to ch. xxii, p. 890.)

(ii) *Western Canon Law.*

Crouzet, L'Abbé, provides a bibliography of the sources and literature of Canon Law
　　in Phillips, G. Du Droit ecclésiastique dans ses sources. French translation.
　　See below, iii b (ii). [Very valuable on older sources.]
Friedberg, E. Lehrbuch des katholischen und evangelischen Kirchenrechts. 4th edn.
　　Leipsic. 1895. pp. 3–9, and *passim*. [Valuable. Contains, *inter alia*, biblio-
　　graphies of Canon Law in the various countries.]
Galante, A. Elementi di diritto ecclesiastico. Milan. 1909. pp. 1–13. [Very useful.]
Makower, F. The constitutional history and constitution of the Church of England.
　　(Transl. from the German.) London. 1895. pp. 504–34. [Valuable for England.]
Richter, A. L. Lehrbuch des kathol. und evangel. Kirchenrechts. 8th edn. Dove, R.
　　and Kahl, W. Leipsic. 1886. pp. 15–27, and *passim*. [Very useful.]
Stutz, U. Kirchenrecht. *In* Holtzendorff. Encykl. d. Rechtswiss. 6th edn. Vol. ii.
　　pp. 809–972. *See Gen. Bibl.* i. [Valuable.]
Viollet, P. Histoire du droit civil français accompagnée de notions de droit canonique.
　　3rd edn. pp. 33–100. *passim*. *See Gen. Bibl.* v. [Useful.]

C. Periodicals for Roman and Canon Law.

Archiv für katholisches Kirchenrecht. (AKKR.) *See Abbreviations,* p. 831.
Archivio giuridico. Bologna, Pisa. 1868 ff., in progress.
Deutsche Zeitschrift für Kirchenrecht. Freiburg-i.-B. 1891 ff., in progress. (DZKR.)
　　(*Continuation of* Zeitschrift für Kirchenrecht. Berlin, etc. 1861–89.)
Nouvelle Revue historique de droit français et étranger. (NRDF.) *And* Revue his-
　　torique de droit français et étranger. (RDF.) *See Abbreviations,* p. 831.
Zeitschrift für vergleichende Rechtswissenschaft. Stuttgart. 1878 ff., in progress.
Zeitschrift für Rechtsgeschichte. (ZR.) *And* Zeitschrift der Savigny-Stiftung für
　　Rechtswissenschaft. (ZSR.) *See Abbreviations,* p. 832.

II. ROMAN LAW.

A. Ancient and Medieval Authorities.

(i) (*a*) *Ancient Roman Law* (*to Justinian*).

(*See* Vol. ii, Bibl. to ch. iii, p. 726.)

(*b*) *Graeco-Roman Law.*

(*See* Vol. iv, Bibl. to ch. xxii, p. 890.)

(ii) *Germano-Roman Law.*

(*a*) *Leges Barbarorum.*

For a list of editions *see* Brunner, H. Deutsche Rechtsgeschichte. Vol. i. 2nd edn.
　　§§ 38–49 (*see Gen. Bibl.* v), and Brunner, H. Grundzüge der deutschen Rechts-
　　geschichte. 7th edn. §§ 13, 14 (*see Gen. Bibl.* v).

(b) Leges Romanae.

(In chronological order.)

Lex Romana Visigothorum. Ed. Hänel, G. Leipsic. 1847–9. [The "Breviarium Alaricianum."]

Lex Romana Burgundionum. Ed. Salis, L. R. v. MGH. Legum Sect. I. Vol. II, i. pp. 123 sqq. 1892.

Edictum Theoderici. Ed. Bluhme, F. MGH. Leges. v. pp. 145 sqq. 1875–89.

Lex Romana Raetica Curiensis. Ed. Zeumer, K. MGH. Leges. v. pp. 289 sqq. 1875–89. [Also called the Lex Romana Utinensis. Date disputed.]

Lex Romana Canonice compta. Ed. Conrat (Cohn), M. *in* Verhandelingen d. k. Akad. van Wetenschappen. Afdeeling letterkunde. n.s. VI, no. 1. Amsterdam. 1904. [*See* Maassen, F. Gesch. der Quellen...des Canon. Rechts. Vol. I. Graz. 1870. pp. 883–96.]

Full lists of editions of all the *leges romanae* in Brunner, H. Deutsche Rechtsgeschichte. Vol. I. 2nd edn. §§ 50–58. *See Gen. Bibl.* v.

(c) Frankish Capitularies.

Capitularia regum Francorum. MGH. Legum Sect. II. 2 vols. 1883, 97. [For older editions *see* MGH. Leges. I. 1835, and Brunner, H. Deutsche Rechtsgeschichte. *See Gen. Bibl.* v.]

(iii) Separate Countries.

(a) Italy: and the Revival of Jurisprudence.

Dissensiones dominorum. Ed. Hänel, G. Leipsic. 1834.

Petri Exceptiones Legum Romanorum. Ed. Savigny, F. C. v. *in* Geschichte des Römischen Rechts im Mittelalter. Vol. II, app. 1. *See Gen. Bibl.* v. Also ed. Fitting, H. *in* Juristische Schriften. Halle. 1876. p. 151. [Condensations or extracts for practitioners from Justinian's books; composed in the latter half of the eleventh century.]

Quaestiones de iuris subtilitatibus des Irnerius. Ed. Fitting, H. Berlin. 1894. [Of contested authorship.]

Summa Codicis des Irnerius. Ed. Fitting, H. Berlin. 1894. [Authorship disputed.]

(b) Spain.

Códigos antiguos de España. Ed. Alcubilla, M. M. Madrid. 1885.

Los Códigos Españoles concordados y anotados. Ed. Rivadeneyra, M. 12 vols. Madrid. 1847–51.

Leges Visigothorum. Ed. Zeumer, K. MGH. Legum Sect. I. Vol. I. 1902. [Contains all the Visigothic laws except Breviarium Alaricianum.]

(c) France.

Beaumanoir, Philippe de Remi, Sire de. Coutumes de Beauvaisis. Ed. Salmon, A. (Coll. textes.) 2 vols. Paris. 1899, 1900. [Is also a treatise on customary law.]

Lo Codi. Ed. Fitting, H. and Suchier, H. Halle. 1906. [Summary of Justinian's Code, for the use of judges in Provence; about 1149.]

Corpus Legum sive Brachylogus juris civilis. Ed. Böcking, E. Berlin. 1829. [Manual for teaching, probably from the early twelfth century.]

Les Établissements de St Louis. Ed. Viollet, P. 4 vols. Paris. 1881–6.

(d) Germany (with Switzerland and the Netherlands).

Constitutiones et acta publica imperatorum et regum. MGH. Legum Sect. IV Vols. I–V, VI 1, VIII. 1893 ff.

Sammlung schweizerischer Rechtsquellen. Publ. by Schweizerischer Juristenverein. Aarau. 1898 ff.

See Fockema-Andreae, S. J. Overzicht van Oud-Nederlandsche Rechtsbronnen. Haarlem. 1881.

See Stobbe, O. Geschichte der deutschen Rechtsquellen. *See below*, II B (iii) *d.*

(e) England.

Bracton, H. de. De legibus et consuetudinibus Angliae. Ed. Twiss, T. 6 vols. (Rolls.) 1878–83. Ed. Woodbine, G. E. New Haven, Connecticut. 2 vols. 1915, 22, in progress.

—— Bracton's Note Book. Ed. Maitland, F. W. 3 vols. London. 1887.

Britton. Ed. Nichols, F. M. 2 vols. Oxford. 1865.

Fleta, seu Commentarius Juris Anglicani. 2nd edn. London. 1685.

Glanvill, R. de. Tractatus de legibus et consuetudinibus regni Angliae. London. [1554] and later edns. Engl. transl. Beames, J. London. 1812. Ed. Beale, J. H. Washington. 1900.

Longchamp, W. Practica Legum et Decretorum. Ed. Caillemer, E. *in* Le Droit civil dans les provinces anglo-normandes. Caen. 1883. p. 50.

Placita Anglo-Normannica. Ed. Bigelow, M. M. London; and Boston, Mass. 1879.

Ricardus Anglicus. Ordo Judiciarius. Ed. Witte, C. Halle. 1853.

Vacarius. Liber Pauperum. [Large portions published by Wenck, C. F. C. Magister Vacarius. Leipsic. 1820. MS. at Worcester.]

William of Drogheda. Summa Aurea. [In MS.; extracts, ed. Maitland, F. W. *in* EHR. xii (1897). pp. 645 sqq.]

B. Modern Works.

(i) (a) Ancient Roman Law (to Justinian).

(See Vol. ii, Bibl. to ch. iii, p. 726, *to which add* Buckland. *See above*, i A (i).)

(b) Graeco-Roman Law.

(See Vol. iv, Bibl. to ch. xxii, p. 890.)

(ii) Germano-Roman Law (Roman Law in Germanic Kingdoms).

Brunner, H. Deutsche Rechtsgeschichte. *See Gen. Bibl.* v.

—— Grundzüge der deutschen Rechtsgeschichte. *See Gen. Bibl.* v.

—— Zur Rechtsgeschichte der römischen und germanischen Urkunde. Vol. i. Berlin. 1880. [No more publ.]

Bruns, C. G. and Pernice, A. Geschichte und Quellen des Römischen Rechts. §§ 73–78. *In* Holtzendorff. Encykl. d. Rechtswiss. 5th edn. *See Gen. Bibl.* i.

Conrat (Cohn), M. Das Breviarium Alaricianum. Leipsic. 1903.

—— Die Entstehung des westgothischen Gaius. *In* Verhandelingen d. k. Akad. van Wetenschappen. Afdeeling letterkunde. n.s. vi, no. 4. Amsterdam. 1905.

—— Der westgothische Paulus. *Ibid.* viii, no. 4. 1907.

—— Geschichte der Quellen und Literatur des Römischen Rechts im früheren Mittelalter. Vol. i. Leipsic. 1891.

Continental Legal History Series. Vol. i. General Survey. *See above*, i A (iii).

Eichhorn, K. F. Deutsche Staats- und Rechtsgeschichte. 4th edn. 4 vols. Göttingen. 1834–6. [Bibliographies.]

Ficker, J. Untersuchungen zur Rechtsgeschichte (zur Erbenfolge der ostgermanischen Rechte). Vols. i–v 1, vi 1. Innsbruck. 1891–1904.

Fitting, H. Die juristischen Schriften des früheren Mittelalters. 1876.

Flach, J. Études critiques sur l'histoire du droit romain au moyen âge. Paris. 1890.

Fustel de Coulanges, N. D. Histoire des institutions politiques de l'ancienne France. *See Gen. Bibl.* v. [Especially: Les origines du système féodal.]

Halban, A. v. Das Römische Recht in den germanischen Volksstaaten. 3 vols. Breslau. 1899–1907.

Holdsworth, W. S. The reception of Roman Law in the sixteenth century. *In* Law Quarterly Review. xxvii (1911). 387–98; xxviii (1912). 39–51, 131–47, 236–54. [First two articles on continental development, last two articles on English.]

Hugo, G. v. Lehrbuch eines zivilistischen Kursus. 7 vols. Berlin. 1792–1821. [By the founder of the historical school of jurisprudence; is still valuable for the history of Roman Law in the Middle Ages, though in large measure superseded.]

Karlowa, O. Römische Rechtsgeschichte. Vol. i. Leipsic. 1885. §§ 110–118.

Maassen, F. Geschichte der Quellen und der Literatur des Canonischen Rechts. Vol. I. [No more publ.] Graz. 1870. [*For* Sammlungen des Römischen Rechts für d. kirchlichen Gebrauch. pp. 887–900.]

Mommsen, T. Ostgothische Studien. Neu. Arch. xiv (1889). pp. 225–49; xv (1890). pp. 181–6. *Also in* Gesammelte Schriften. vi. Berlin. 1910. pp. 362–484.

Neumeyer, K. Die gemeinrechtliche Entwickelung des internationalen Privat- und Strafrechts bis Bartolus. Pts. I, II. Munich. 1901, 16.

Puchta, G. F. Gesch. d. Rechts bei dem römischen Volk. 10th edn. Krüger, P. (Vol. I of Cursus der Institutionen.) Leipsic. 1893. § 137.

Savigny, F. C. v. Geschichte des Römischen Rechts im Mittelalter. *See Gen. Bibl.* v. [Still the standard work.]

Vinogradoff, P. Roman Law in Mediaeval Europe. *See Gen. Bibl.* v.

Viollet, P. Histoire du droit civil français. 3rd edn. *See Gen. Bibl.* v. [Especially pp. 1–262. Sources of Roman, Canon, Germanic, and French Law.]

(iii) *Roman (and Canon) Law: Separate Countries.*

(a) *Italy: and the Revival of Jurisprudence.*

Besta, E. L' opera d' Irnerio. 2 vols. Turin. 1896.

Brie, S. Die Lehre vom Gewohnheitsrecht. Vol. I. Breslau. 1899.

Bruns, C. G., Pernice, A., and Lenel, O. Geschichte und Quellen des Römischen Rechts. *In* Holtzendorff. Encykl. d. Rechtswiss. 6th edn. Vol. I. *See Gen. Bibl.* I.

Calisse, C. Storia del diritto italiano. 4 vols. Florence. 1891. Vol. I. 2nd edn. 1902. [Translation of part of vol. I *in* Continental Legal History Series. Vol. I. General Survey. pp. 87–199. *See above*, I A (iii).]

Chiappelli, L. Lo Studio bolognese. Pistoia. 1888.

Conrat (Cohn), M. Geschichte der Quellen und Literatur des Römischen Rechts im früheren Mittelalter. Vol. I. Leipsic. 1889.

Ficker, J. Forschungen zur Reichs- und Rechtsgeschichte Italiens. 4 vols. Innsbruck. 1868–74.

Fitting, H. Die Anfänge der Rechtsschule zu Bologna. Berlin. 1888.

—— Juristische Schriften des früheren Mittelalters. Halle. 1876.

—— Pepo zu Bologna. ZSR. xxiii. Romanist. Abt. 1902. pp. 31–45.

—— Zur Gesch. der Rechtswissenschaft am Anfange des Mittelalters. Halle. 1875.

Gaudenzi, A. Appunti per servire alla storia della Università di Bologna e dei suoi maestri. *In* L' Università. Vol. III.

Krüger, P. Geschichte der Quellen und Litteratur des Römischen Rechts. Leipsic. 1888. [Especially §§ 50–53.]

Landsberg, E. Die Glosse des Accursius und ihre Lehre vom Eigenthum. Leipsic. 1883.

Meynial, E. Encore Irnerius. NRDF. xx. 1896.

Pertile, A. Storia del diritto italiano. *See Gen. Bibl.* v.

Pescatore, G. Die Glossen des Irnerius. Greifswald. 1888.

Phillipson, C. Andrea Alciati and his predecessors. *In* Great Jurists of the World. Ed. Macdonell, J. and Manson, E. (Continental Legal History Series.) Boston, Mass.; and London. 1914. pp. 58–82.

Puchta, G. F. Gesch. d. Rechts bei d. römischen Volk. pp. 406–20. *See above*, II B (ii).

Rattigan, W. Bartolus. *In* Great Jurists of the World. pp. 45–57. *See above*, Phillipson.

Rivalta, V. Dispute celebri di diritto civile. Bologna. 1895.

—— Il Rinnovamento della giurisprudenza filosofica secondo la scolastica. Bologna. 1888. [diss.]

Rivier. La science du droit dans la première moitié du moyen âge. NRDF. I. 1877.

Salvioli, G. L' Istruzione pubblica in Italia nei secoli viii, ix, x. Florence. 1898.

—— Storia del diritto italiano. 8th edn. Turin. 1921.

Savigny, F. C. v. Geschichte des Römischen Rechts im Mittelalter. *See Gen. Bibl.* v.

Seckel, E. Quellenfunde zum lombardischen Lehnrecht, insbesondere zu den Extravaganten-Sammlungen. *In* Festgabe der Berliner jurist. Fakult. für O. Gierke. Vol. I. Breslau. 1910. pp. 47–168.

Solmi, A. La scuola di Pavia nell' alto medio evo. *In* Nuova Antologia. 1 May, 1925.

Solmi, A. Sulla persistenza della scuola di Pavia nel medio evo fino alla fondazione dello studio generale. *In* Rendiconti del r. istituto lombardo di scienze e lettere. Vol. LVIII. 1925.

Stintzing, R. and Landsberg, E. Geschichte der deutschen Rechtswissenschaft. 3 vols. in 4. (III by Landsberg, E.) Munich. 1880–1910.

Tamassia, N. Lanfranco arcivescovo di Canterbury e la Scuola Pavese. *In* Mélanges Fitting. Vol. II. Montpellier. 1908.

Tourtoulon, P. de. Placentin. Paris. 1896.

Woolf, C. N. S. Bartolus of Sassoferrato. Cambridge. 1913.

(b) Spain.

Altamira, R. Historia de España. *See Gen. Bibl.* v.

—— Historia del derecho español. Cuestiones preliminares. Madrid. 1905.

—— Les lacunes de l'histoire du droit romain en Espagne. *In* Mélanges Fitting. Vol. I. Montpellier. 1907.

—— Magna Carta and Spanish Mediaeval Jurisprudence. *In* Magna Carta Commemoration Essays. Ed. Malden, H. E. (RHS) London. 1917. pp. 227–43.

—— Origen y desarrollo del derecho civil español. *In* Revista de Legislación Universal y de Jurisprudencia Española. August, 1908 ff. Engl. adaptation *in* Continental Legal History Series. Vol. I. General Survey. pp. 579 sqq. *See above*, I A (iii).

—— Sobre el estado actual de los estudios de historia jurídica y de la enseñanza de este orden en España. *In* Bulletin Hispanique. 1909.

Antequera, J. M. de. Historia de la legislación española. Madrid. 1849, and later edns.

Bové, S. Institucions de Catalunya. Barcelona. 1894.

Colmeiro, M. Curso de derecho político. Madrid. 1873.

Coroleu, J. Código de los Usajes de Barcelona. Estudio crítico. BRAH. IV. pp. 85–104.

—— and Pella y Forgas, J. Los Fueros de Cataluña. Barcelona. 1878.

Costa, J. Ensayo de un plan de historia del derecho español en la antiguedad. *In* Revista General de Legislación y Jurisprudencia. LXVIII–LXXV. Madrid. 1889.

Danvila y Collado, M. Estudios acerca de la legislación de Valencia. Madrid. 1905.

Fita y Colomé, F. Cortes y Usajes de Barcelona en 1064. BRAH. XVII. pp. 385–423.

Fuente, V. de la. Estudios críticos sobre la historia y el derecho de Aragón. 3 vols. Madrid. 1884–6.

Hinojosa, E. de. Estudios sobre la historia del derecho español. Madrid. 1903.

—— Das germanische Element im spanischen Rechte. ZSR. XXXI. German. Abt. pp. 282–359.

—— Historia general del derecho español. *See Gen. Bibl.* v.

Ladreda, M. F. Estudios históricos sobre los Códigos de Castilla. Corunna. 1896.

Marichalar, A. and Manrique, C. Historia de la legislación y recitaciones del derecho civil de España. 9 vols. Madrid. 1861–72.

Merriman, R. B. The rise of the Spanish Empire. *See Gen. Bibl.* v.

Oliver, B. Historia del derecho en Cataluña, Mallorca, y Valencia. 4 vols. Madrid. 1876–81.

Pérez Pujol, E. Historia de las instituciones sociales de la España Goda. 4 vols. Valencia. 1896.

Sánchez Roman, F. Estudios de derecho civil…é historia general de la legislación española. 2nd edn. 5 vols. in 6. Madrid. 1889–1900.

Taraçona, P. H. Institucions dels Furs de Valencia. Valencia. 1580.

Ureña y Smenjaud, R. de. Las Ediciones de los Fueros y Observancias del Reino de Aragón. Madrid. 1900.

—— La Legislación Gótico-Hispana. Madrid. 1905.

—— Historia de la literatura jurídica española. 2nd edn. Vol. I. Madrid. 1906.

(c) France.

Bordier, H. L. Philippe de Remi, sire de Beaumanoir. Paris. 1869.

Brissaud, J. Manuel d'histoire du droit français. 2 vols. Paris. 1898, 1904.

Brunner, H. Überblick über die Geschichte der französischen, normannischen... Rechtsquellen. *In* Holtzendorff. Encykl. 5th edn. (*not* 6th). *See Gen. Bibl.* i.

Caillemer, R. Les Idées coutumières et la Renaissance du droit romain dans le Sud-Est de la France. *In* Essays in Legal History. Ed. Vinogradoff, P. Oxford. 1913.

Esmein, A. Cours élémentaire d'histoire du droit français. 11th edn. Paris. 1912.

Flach, J. Cujas, les Glossateurs et les Bartholistes. Paris. 1883.

Fournier, M. Histoire de la science du droit en France. Vol. iii. Les universités françaises et l'enseignement du droit en France au moyen âge. Paris. 1892.

—— Les statuts et privilèges des Universités françaises. 4 vols. Paris. 1890-5.

Giraud, C. Essai sur l'histoire du droit français au moyen âge. Paris. 1846.

Glasson, E. Histoire du droit et des institutions de la France. 8 vols. Paris. 1887-1903.

Litten, E. Über lo Codi und seine Stellung in der Entwicklungs-Geschichte des Culpa-Problems. *In* Mélanges Fitting. Vol. ii. Montpellier. 1908.

Meynial, É. Des renonciations au moyen âge et dans notre ancien droit. NRDF. 1900-4.

Pollock, F. and Maitland, F. W. History of English Law. 2nd edn. *See Gen. Bibl.* v. [Vol. i, ch. iii. Norman Law.]

Pothier, R. J. Pandectae Justinianeae. 5 vols. Paris. 1818-20.

Tardif, A. Histoire des sources du droit français. Origines romaines. Paris. 1890.

Viollet, P. Histoire du droit civil français. 3rd edn. *See Gen. Bibl.* v.

Wetter, P. van. Le droit romain et Beaumanoir. *In* Mélanges Fitting. Vol. ii. Montpellier. 1908.

(d) Germany (with Switzerland and the Netherlands).

Below, G. v. Die Ursachen der Rezeption des Römischen Rechts in Deutschland. Munich. 1906.

Brie, S. Die Stellung der deutschen Rechtsgelehrten der Rezeptionszeit zum Gewohnheitsrecht. *In* Festgabe für F. Dahn. Vol. i. Breslau. 1905.

Brunner, H. Deutsche Rechtsgeschichte. *See Gen. Bibl.* v.

—— Grundzüge der deutschen Rechtsgeschichte. *See Gen. Bibl.* v.

—— Zur Rechtsgeschichte der römischen und germanischen Urkunde. Vol. i. Berlin. 1880. [No more publ.]

Eichhorn, K. F. Deutsche Staats- und Rechtsgeschichte. 4th edn. 4 vols. Göttingen. 1834-6.

Franken, A. Romanisten und Germanisten. Jena. 1882.

Franklin, O. Beiträge zur Geschichte der Rezeption des Römischen Rechts in Deutschland. Hanover. 1863.

Gierke, O. Das deutsche Genossenschaftsrecht. *See Gen. Bibl.* v.

—— Deutsches Privatrecht. 2 vols. Leipsic. 1895, 1905. [*See* Vol. i, ch. i. Geschichte des deutschen Privatrechts.]

Heusler, A. Institutionen des deutschen Privatrechts. 2 vols. Leipsic. 1885-6.

Hübner, R. A history of Germanic Private Law. (Continental Legal History Series.) Boston, Mass.; and London. 1918. [Transl. from German.]

Kohler, J. Beiträge zur Geschichte des Römischen Rechts in Deutschland. Stuttgart. 1896.

Landsberg, E. Über die Entstehung der Regel "Quicquid non agnoscit glossa, nec agnoscit forum." Bonn. 1880.

Modderman, W. De Receptie van het Romeinsche Regt. Groningen. 1874. German transl. Schulz, K. Jena. 1875.

Muther, J. G. T. Zur Geschichte der Rechtswissenschaft und der Universitäten in Deutschland. Jena. 1876.

Otto, C. E., Schilling, B., and Sintenis, C. F. F. Das Corpus Juris Civilis in's Deutsche übersetzt. 7 vols. Leipsic. 1830-3. Vol. i. 2nd edn. 1839.

Schmidt, C. A. Die Rezeption des Römischen Rechts in Deutschland. Rostock. 1868.

Schröder, R. Deutsche Rechtsgeschichte. 4th edn. Leipsic. 1902.

Seckel, E. Beiträge zur Geschichte beider Rechte im Mittelalter. Vol. i. Zur Gesch. d. populären Literatur d. römisch-kanonischen Rechts. Tübingen. 1898.

Stintzing, R. Geschichte der populären Literatur des römisch-kanonischen Rechts in Deutschland am Ende ... [des Mittelalters]. Leipsic. 1867.
—— Ulrich Zasius. Basle. 1857.
—— and Landsberg, E. Geschichte der deutschen Rechtswissenschaft. *See above*, II B (iii) *a*.
Stobbe, O. Geschichte der deutschen Rechtsquellen. 2 pts. Brunswick. 1860, 64.
Stölzel, A. Die Entwickelung des gelehrten Richterthums in deutschen Territorien. 2 vols. Stuttgart. 1872.
Zeumer, K. Die Sächsische Weltchronik, ein Werk Eikes von Repgow. *In* Festschrift H. Brunner...dargebracht. Weimar. 1910. pp. 135–74, 839–42.
—— Über den verlorenen lateinischen Urtext des Sachsenspiegels. *In* Festschrift O. Gierke...dargebracht. Weimar. 1911. pp. 455–74.

(For Switzerland.)

Huber, E. Switzerland. *In* Continental Legal History Series. Vol. I. General Survey. pp. 483–530. *See above*, I A (iii).
—— System und Geschichte des schweizerischen Privatrechts. 4 vols. Basle. 1886–93. [Reception of Roman Law in vol. IV.]
Matile, G. A. De l'autorité du droit romain et de la Caroline dans la principauté de Neuchâtel. 1838.
Orelli, A. V. Grundriss zu den Vorlesungen über schweizerische Rechtsgeschichte. 2nd edn. Zürich. 1884.

(For the Netherlands.)

Brissaud, J. Manuel d'histoire du droit français. 2 vols. Paris. 1898, 1904.
Colonial Laws and Courts. Ed. Renton, A. W. and Phillimore, G. G. London. 1907. [Contains historical sketch of Roman-Dutch law by W. R. Bischop, S. J. Fockema-Andreae, and J. E. Heeres.]
Fockema-Andreae, S. J. Bijdragen tot de nederlandsche Rechtsgeschiedenis. 4 vols. Haarlem. 1888–1900.
—— Overzicht van Oud-Nederlandsche Rechtsbronnen. Haarlem. 1881.
Hamel, J. A. van. Netherlands. *In* Continental Legal History Series. Vol. I. General Survey. pp. 455–79. *See above*, I A (iii).
Lee, R. W. Introduction to Roman-Dutch Law. Oxford. 1915.
Leeuwen, S. van. Commentaries on Roman-Dutch Law. Transl. and ed. by Kotzé, S. G. 2nd edn. 2 vols. London. 1921, 23. [Especially vol. I.]
Modderman, W. De Receptie van het Romeinsche Regt. *See above*, p. 927.
Morice, G. T. English and Roman-Dutch Law. 2nd edn. London. 1903.
Spiegel, L. P. van de. Oorsprong en historie der vaderlandsche Rechten. 1769.
Voet, P. De usu juris civilis et canonici in Belgio Unito. Utrecht. 1657.
Vries, G. de. Historia introducti in provincias quas deinceps respublica Belgii Uniti comprehendit Juris Romani. Leiden. 1839. [diss.]
Warnkönig, L. A. Flandrische Staats- und Rechtsgeschichte. 3 vols. Tübingen. 1835–42.
Wessels, J. W. History of the Roman-Dutch Law. Grahamstown. 1908.

(e) England.

Anglo-American Legal History, Select Essays in. Compiled and ed. by a committee of the Association of American Law Schools. (Wigmore, J. H. and others.) 3 vols. Boston, Mass.; and Cambridge. 1907–9. [Vol. I contains essays by Bryce, J., Holdsworth, W. S., Jenks, E., Maitland, F. W., Scrutton, T. E., and Stubbs, W. on the influence of Roman and Canon Law.]
Baldwin, J. F. The King's Council in England during the Middle Ages. Oxford. 1913. [For civilians and canonists in England.]
Brunner, H. The sources of English Law. *In* Select Essays in Anglo-American Legal History. Vol. II. *See above*. [Revised by author and transl. by Freund, E. from article in Holtzendorff. Encykl. 5th edn. (*not* 6th). *See Gen. Bibl.* I.]
Caillemer, E. Le Droit civil dans les provinces anglo-normandes au XIIᵉ siècle. Caen. 1883.
Clark, E. C. Cambridge legal studies. Cambridge. 1888.

Conrat (Cohn), M. Geschichte der Quellen des Römischen Rechts im früheren Mittelalter. Vol. I. Leipsic. 1889. Ch. VI.

Duck, A. De usu et authoritate Juris Civilis. London. 1653, and later edns.

Fournier, M. L'Église et le droit romain au XIIIᵉ siècle. NRDF. XIV. 1890.

Goudy, H. An inaugural lecture on the fate of the Roman Law north and south of the Tweed. London. 1894.

Güterbock, C. Heinricus de Bracton und sein Verhältniss zum Römischen Recht. Berlin. 1862. Engl. transl. Coxe, B. Philadelphia. 1866.

Hale, M. History of the Common Law of England. 2nd edn. London. 1716.

Holdsworth, W. S. History of English Law. *See Gen. Bibl.* v.

Holland, T. E. The origin of the University of Oxford. EHR. VI (1891). pp. 238–49.

—— The University of Oxford in the twelfth century. *In* Collectanea. Ser. II. (Oxford Hist. Soc. XVI.) Oxford. 1890. [On Vacarius.]

Holmes, O. W. The Common Law. London. 1911. [For influence of Roman Law.]

Leadam, I. S. and Baldwin, J. F. Select Cases before the King's Council 1243–1482. (Selden Soc. XXXV.) Cambridge, Massachusetts. 1918. [Introduction deals with influence of Civil and Canon Law on procedure of English courts.]

Liebermann, F. Magister Vacarius. EHR. XI (1896). pp. 305–14, 514–15. [Valuable. See also his note, *ibid.* XIII (1898). pp. 297–8.]

Maitland, F. W. English Law and the Renaissance. Cambridge. 1901.

—— Select passages from the works of Bracton and Azo. (Selden Soc. VIII.) London. 1895.

—— and Montague, F. C. A sketch of English Legal History. Ed. Colby, J. F. New York and London. 1915. [For influence of Roman and Canon Law.]

Pollock, F. The genius of the Common Law. New York. 1912. [For influence of Civil and Canon Law.]

—— History of the Law of Nature. *In* Essays in the Law. London. 1922. pp. 31–79.

—— and Maitland, F. W. History of English Law. 2nd edn. *See Gen. Bibl.* v. [Especially vol. I, pp. 1–225.]

Pound, R. The spirit of the Common Law. Boston. 1921. [For influence of Roman and Canon Law.]

Reeves, J. History of the English Law. 5 vols. (I–IV, 3rd edn.) London. 1814–29.

Savigny, F. C. v. Geschichte des Römischen Rechts im Mittelalter. Chapters X and XXXVI. (2nd edn. Vols. II and IV.) *See Gen. Bibl.* v.

Scrutton, T. E. The influence of the Roman Law on the Law of England. Cambridge. 1885.

Selden, J. Ad Fletam dissertatio. Ed. with transl., introdn., and notes. Ogg, D. (Cambridge Studies in English Legal History.) Cambridge. 1925.

—— Of the original of ecclesiastical jurisdiction of testaments. *In* Opera omnia. Ed. Wilkins, D. Vol. III, pt. 2. London. 1726.

—— Of the disposition or administration of intestates' goods. *Ibid.*

Stephen, J. F. History of the Criminal Law of England. 3 vols. London. 1883.

Stölzel, A. Über Vacarius. ZR. VI (1867). pp. 234–68.

Stubbs, W. Constitutional History of England. *See Gen. Bibl.* v.

Vinogradoff, P. Zur Geschichte der englischen Klassifikation der Vermögensarten. *In* Festschrift H. Brunner...dargebracht. Weimar. 1910. pp. 573–7.

—— Reason and conscience in sixteenth-century Jurisprudence. *In* Law Quarterly Review. October, 1908.

—— Romanistische Einflüsse im angelsachsischen Recht: das Buchland. *In* Mélanges Fitting. Vol. II. Montpellier. 1908.

—— Villainage in England. Oxford. 1892.

Wenck, C. F. C. Magister Vacarius. Leipsic. 1820. [Suppl. material by Wenck *in* Haubold, C. G. Opuscula Academica. Leipsic. 1825, 29.]

Williams, J. Latin maxims in English Law. *In* Law Magazine and Review. Aug. 1895.

Zulueta, F. de. The Avranches manuscript of Vacarius. EHR. XXXVI (1921). pp. 545–53.

(iv) *Roman (and Canon) Law: General Works and Special Subjects.*

Adams, G. B. Civilization during the Middle Ages. New York. 1894.

Bar, C. L. v. A history of Continental Criminal Law. Transl. from the German by Bell, T. S. (Continental Legal History Series.) Boston, Mass.; and London. 1916. [Influence of Roman and Canon Law.]

Bryce, J. Studies in History and Jurisprudence. 2 vols. Oxford. 1901. [Comparison of Roman and English legal development.]

Carlyle, R. W. and A. J. A history of Mediaeval Political Theory in the West. *See Gen. Bibl.* v. [Influence of civilians and canonists.]

Continental Legal History Series. Ed. Wigmore, J. H. and others. 8 vols. Boston, Mass.; and London. 1912–18. [Vol. I. General Survey of events, sources, persons, and movements in continental legal history. (*See under separate countries.*) Subsequent volumes deal with separate branches of law or with separate countries. Often translations from standard authorities.]

Dunning, W. A. A history of Political Theories, Ancient and Mediaeval. New York. 1902. [Influence of Roman and Canon Law.]

Gierke, O. Das deutsche Genossenschaftsrecht. *See Gen. Bibl.* v. [Vol. III. Die Staats- und Korporationslehre des Alterthums und des Mittelalters und ihre Aufnahme in Deutschland. Deals with the theories of medieval civilians and canonists. Engl. transl. of a section of a chapter, with introduction, by Maitland, F. W. Political theories of the Middle Age. Cambridge. 1900.]

—— Johannes Althusius und die Entwickelung der naturrechtlichen Staatstheorien. 2nd edn. Breslau. 1902.

Holdsworth, W. S. History of English Law. Vol. v. *See Gen. Bibl.* v. [Influence of civilians and canonists on medieval Law Merchant in Europe.]

Jenks, E. Law and Politics in the Middle Ages. 2nd edn. London. 1913.

Maine, H. S. Ancient Law. Ed. Pollock, F. London. 1906. [Pollock's notes important.]

Oppenheim, L. International Law. 3rd edn. by Roxburgh, R. F. Vol. I. London. 1920. [Ch. II. Influence of medieval civilians and canonists on the emergence of International Law.]

Pollock, F. and Maitland, F. W. History of English Law. 2nd edn. *See Gen. Bibl.* v. [Vol. I, ch. I. The Dark Age in Legal History.]

Rashdall, H. The Universities of Europe in the Middle Ages. *See Gen. Bibl.* v.

Stubbs, W. The historical origin of European Law. *In* Lectures on early English history. Ed. Hassall, A. London. 1906.

Taylor, H. O. The Medieval Mind. 2 vols. London. 1911. [Vol. II, ch. XXXIII. Medieval appropriation of the Roman Law. Deals also with Canon Law.]

Walker, T. A. A history of the Law of Nations. Vol. I (to 1648). Cambridge. 1899. [Valuable for the influence of Roman and Canon Law.]

III. CANON LAW.

A. Ancient and Medieval Authorities.

(i) *Eastern Canon Law.*

Bruns, H. T. Canones apostolorum et conciliorum veterum selecti. Berlin. 1839.

Mansi, J. D. Sacrorum conciliorum collectio. *See Gen. Bibl.* IV.

Pitra, J. B. Iuris ecclesiastici Graecorum historia et monumenta. 2 vols. Rome. 1864, 68.

Rhalles, G. A. and Potles, M. Σύνταγμα...κανόνων. 6 vols. Athens. 1852–9. [Contains sources of Byzantine Canon Law.]

Voellus, G. and Justel, H. Bibliotheca iuris canonici veteris. 2 vols. Paris. 1661.

(ii) *Western Canon Law.*

(a) *Before Gratian.*

Ballerini, P. and J. De antiquis...collectionibus et collectoribus canonum. Venice. 1757. Repr. in MPL. LVI.

Berardi, C. S. De variis sacrorum canonum collectionibus ante Gratianum. Turin. 1752.

Burchard of Worms. Decretum (=Collectarium=Brocardum). MPL CXL

Collectio canonum Ecclesiae Hispanae. Madrid. 1808. Repr. in MPL. LXXXIV. [The "Hispana."]

Coustant, P. De antiquis canonum collectionibus, deque variis epistolarum Romanorum Pontificum editionibus. Paris. 1721.

Dionysio-Hadriana. Collection. Printed in Voellus, G. and Justel, H. Bibl. iuris canonici veteris. Vol. I. *See above*, III A (i). Repr. in MPL. LXVII. coll. 135 sqq.

Dionysius Exiguus. Collection. Repr. in MPL. LXVII. coll. 139, 230 sqq.

Fulgentius Ferrandus. Breviatio canonum. Ed. Pithou, P. Paris. 1588. Also ed. Chifflet, P. F. *in* Fulgentii Ferrandi opera. Dijon. 1649. Repr. in MPL. LXVII.

Haddan, A. W. and Stubbs, W. Councils and ecclesiastical documents relating to Great Britain and Ireland. *See Gen. Bibl.* IV.

Hinschius, P. Decretales Pseudo-Isidorianae et capitula Angilramni. *See Gen. Bibl.* IV. [With critical introduction.]

Ivo, Bishop of Chartres. Decretum *and* Panormia. Repr. in MPL. CLXI. *See* Fournier, P. Les Collections canoniques attribuées à Yves de Chartres. BEC. LVII, LVIII. 1896–7. Also publ. separately. Paris. 1897.

Maassen, F. Glossen d. Canon. Rechts aus d. carolingischen Zeitalter. 1887.

Mansi, J. D. Sacrorum conciliorum collectio. *See Gen. Bibl.* IV.

Marca, P. de. De veteribus collectionibus canonum. Paris. 1681.

"Quesnel" Collection. Ed. with notes by Ballerini, P. and J. *in* Opera sancti Leonis. Vol. III. Venice. 1757. Repr. in MPL. LVI. coll. 899 sqq.

Schmitz, H. J. Die Bussbücher und die Bussdisciplin der Kirche. 2 vols. Mayence. 1883, 98.

Turner, C. H. Ecclesiae Occidentalis monumenta iuris antiquissima. 2 vols. in 3. Oxford. 1899 ff., in progress.

Wasserschleben, H. Beiträge zur Geschichte der vorgratian. Kirchenrechtsquellen. Leipsic. 1839.

—— Die Bussordnungen der abendländischen Kirche. Halle. 1851.

—— Die irische Kanonensammlung. Giessen. 1874.

(b) *From Gratian to the Council of Trent.*

Corpus Iuris Canonici. *See Gen. Bibl.* IV.

Gratian. Decretum. *See above*, Corpus Iuris Canonici.

Lyndwood, W. Provinciale, (seu Constitutiones Angliae). [Authoritative digest of English Medieval Canon Law. Completed in 1430. Best edn. 2 pts. in 3. Oxford. 1679. *Cf.* Gross, C. Sources...of English History. No. 622. *See Gen. Bibl.* I.]

Quinque compilationes. Ed. Friedberg, E. Leipsic. 1883. [Bernard of Pavia, John of Wales, Innocent III, Anon., and Honorius III.]

Schilling, B. and Sintenis, C. F. F. Das Corpus Juris Canonici in's Deutsche übersetzt und systematisch zusammengestellt. 2 vols. Leipsic. 1834, 37.

Summa Decretalium, Bernardi Papiensis. Ed. Laspeyres, E. A. T. Mayence. 1860.

Summa Hostiensis. Henricus de Segusia Cardinalis Ostiensis. Summa Aurea. Lyons. 1548. Basle. 1573.

Summa des Paucapalea. Ed. Schulte, J. F. v. Giessen. 1890.

Summa Magistri Rolandi (Pope Alexander III). Ed. Thaner, F. Innsbruck. 1874. Another edn. Die Sentenzen Rolands. Ed. Gietl, A. M. Freiburg-i.-B. 1891.

Summa Decretorum des Magister Rufinus. Ed. Singer, H. Paderborn. 1902.

Summa des Stephanus Tornacensis. Ed. Schulte, J. F. v. Giessen. 1891.

Vacarius. Summa de Matrimonio. *See below, under* Maitland, III B (ii).

—— Liber Pauperum. Ed. Zulueta, F. de. (Selden Soc.) London. 1927.

Wilkins, D. Concilia Magnae Britanniae et Hiberniae, A.D. 446–1718. 4 vols. London. 1737. [Earlier portions, to A.D. 870, superseded by Haddan and Stubbs. *See above*, III A (ii) a.]

B. MODERN WORKS.

(i) *Eastern Canon Law.*

Mortreuil, J. A. B. Histoire du droit byzantin. 3 vols. Paris. 1843–6.

Pitra, J. B. Juris eccl. Graecorum historia et monumenta. *See above*, III A (i).

Vering, F. H. Lehrbuch des kathol., orient., und protestant. Kirchenrechts. 3rd edn. Freiburg-im-Breisgau. 1893. §§ 14–183.

Zachariae von Lingenthal, K. E. Die griechischen Nomokanones. *In* Mem. AcadIP. XXIII. 1877. p. 47.

Many of the works cited below under ii, Western Canon Law, deal with aspects of the history of Canon Law in the East. See also works on Graeco-Roman Law cited in Vol. ɪv, Bibl. to ch. xxɪɪ, p. 892.

(ii) *Western Canon Law.*

Agustin, Antonio. De emendatione Gratiani. Tarragona. 1586.

Anglo-American Legal History, Select Essays in. Vol. ɪ. *See above*, ɪɪ в (iii) *e.*
[Contains essays on the influence of Canon Law.]

Barraclough, G. Papal Provisions. Oxford. 1935.

Bickell, J. W. Geschichte des Kirchenrechts. Vol. ɪ, pt. 1. Giessen. 1843. Vol. ɪ, pt. 2, ed. Röstell, F. W. Frankfort-on-Main. 1849. [No more publ.]

Böhmer, G. L. Principia iuris canonici, speciatim iuris ecclesiastici publici et privati quod per Germaniam obtinet. 7th edn. Schönemann, C. T. G. Göttingen. 1802.

Boudinhon, A. Articles: Canon Law; *and* False Decretals. *In* EncBr. 11th edn.

Boyd, W. K. The Ecclesiastical Edicts of the Theodosian Code. New York. 1905.

Conrat (Cohn), M. Geschichte der Quellen und Literatur des Römischen Rechts im früheren Mittelalter. Vol. ɪ. Leipsic. 1889.

Dodd, J. History of Canon Law. Oxford. 1884.

Doujat, J. Histoire du droit canonique. Paris. 1677.

Esmein, A. Le Mariage en droit canonique. 2 vols. Paris. 1891.

Florens, F. De methodo atque auctoritate collectionis Gratiani. Paris. 1679. Reprinted in Gallandius. *See below.*

Fournier, P. Deux controverses sur les origines du Décret de Gratien. *In* Revue d'histoire et de littérature religieuses. ɪɪɪ. Paris. 1898.

—— De l'influence de la collection irlandaise sur la formation des collections canoniques. NRDF. xxɪɪɪ, note 1.

—— Le premier Manuel canonique de la réforme du xɪᵉ siècle. *In* Mélanges d'archéologie et d'histoire. (École franç. de Rome.) xɪv. Rome. 1894.

Friedberg, E. Lehrbuch des katholischen und evangelischen Kirchenrechts. 4th edn. Leipsic. 1895. [History of sources, §§ 31–49.]

Galante, A. Elementi di diritto ecclesiastico. Milan. 1909.

—— The modern study of Canon Law. *In* Essays in Legal History. Ed. Vinogradoff, P. Oxford. 1913.

Gallandius, A. De vetustis canonum collectionibus dissertationum sylloge. Venice 1778. [Reprints.]

Gams, P. B. Die Kirchengeschichte von Spanien. 3 vols. in 5. Ratisbon. 1862–79

Gaudenzi, A. Lezioni di storia del diritto canonico. Bologna. 1896.

Gitzler, L. Geschichte der Quellen des Kirchenrechts. Breslau. 1855.

Hase, C. A. Commentarii historici de jure ecclesiastico. 2 pts. Leipsic. 1828, 32.

Hinschius, P. Geschichte und Quellen des Kanonischen Rechts. *In* Holtzendorff Encykl. d. Rechtswiss. 5th edn. (*not* 6th). *See Gen. Bibl.* ɪ.

—— Das Kirchenrecht. *In* Birkmeyer, K. Encyclopädie der Rechtswissenschaft. Berlin. 1901.

—— System des katholischen Kirchenrechts, mit besonderer Rücksicht auf Deutschland. *See Gen. Bibl.* v. [Invaluable for the history of Canon Law.]

Hüffer, H. Beiträge zur Geschichte der Quellen des Kirchenrechts und des Römischen Rechts im Mittelalter. Münster. 1862.

Kirchenrechtliche Abhandlungen. Ed. Stutz, U. *See Gen. Bibl.* v. [Valuable series of monographs.]

Lang, J. J. Geschichte und Institutionen des kathol. und protestant. Kirchenrechts. Pt. ɪ. Aeussere Kirchenrechts-Geschichte. Tübingen. 1827.

Laurin, F. Introductio in Corpus Juris Canonici. Freiburg-im-Breisgau. 1889.

Löning, E. Geschichte des deutschen Kirchenrechts. 2 vols. Strasbourg. 1878. [For the Merovingian period.]

Maassen, F. Geschichte der Quellen und der Literatur des Canonischen Rechts im Abendlande. Vol. ɪ. [No more publ.] Graz. 1870. [To the ninth century.]

Maitland, F. W. Collected papers. Ed. Fisher, H. A. L. 3 vols. Cambridge. 1911. [Contain several essays on the history of Canon Law.]

—— Summa de Matrimonio. *In* Law Quarterly Review. xɪɪɪ (1897). pp. 133–43, 270–87. Partly reprinted in Collected papers. Vol. ɪɪɪ. pp. 87–105. *See above.*

—— Roman Canon Law in the Church of England. London. 1898.

Maitland, F. W. and Montague, F. C. A sketch of English legal history. Ed. Colby, J. F. New York and London. 1915. [For influence of Roman and Canon Law.]

Makower, F. The constitutional history and constitution of the Church of England. (Transl. from the German.) London. 1895.

Mastricht, G. v. Historia iuris ecclesiastici. Doesburg. 1676. Halle. 1705, 19.

Mulzer, I. Historia legum ecclesiasticarum positivarum quibus in Germania utimur. Bamberg. 1772.

Ogle, A. The Canon Law in Mediaeval England. London. 1912. [A reply to F. W. Maitland.]

Pertsch, J. G. Kurze Historie des Kanon- und Kirchenrechts. Breslau. 1753.

Phillimore, R. The Ecclesiastical Law of the Church of England. 2nd edn. by Phillimore, W. G. F. and Jemmett, C. F. 2 vols. London. 1895.

Phillips, G. Du Droit ecclésiastique dans ses sources. French transl. with bibliography by l'Abbé Crouzet. Paris. 1852. [Very valuable bibl. of the older sources.]

Pound, R. The spirit of the Common Law. Boston. 1921. [For influence of Roman and Canon Law.]

Reichel, O. J. The Canon Law of Church Institutions. Vol. i. London. 1922.

Richter, A. L. Lehrbuch des kathol. und evangel. Kirchenrechts. 8th edn. Dove, R. and Kahl, W. Leipsic. 1886. [History of the sources, §§ 27–59.]

Rosshirt, J. C. É. F. Geschichte des Rechts im Mittelalter. Vol. i. Kanonisches Recht. Mayence. 1846.

Schneider, P. Die Lehre von d. Kirchenrechtsquellen. 2nd edn. Freiburg-i.-B. 1892.

Schulte, J. F. v. Die Geschichte der Quellen und Literatur des Canonischen Rechts von Gratian bis auf die Gegenwart. 3 vols. Stuttgart. 1875–80. [Indispensable.]

—— Die Paleae im Decret Gratians. [Off-print from SKAW.] Vienna. 1874.

—— Das katholische Kirchenrecht. 2 pts. Giessen. 1856, 60.

Seckel, E. Beiträge zur Geschichte beider Rechte im Mittelalter. Vol. i. Zur Gesch. d. populären Litteratur d. römisch-kanonischen Rechts. Tübingen. 1898.

Smith, A. L. Church and State in the Middle Ages. Oxford. 1913.

Sohm, R. Kirchenrecht. Vol. i. Die geschichtlichen Grundlagen. Leipsic. 1892.

Spittler, L. T. v. Geschichte des Kanonischen Rechts bis auf die Zeiten des falschen Isidor. Halle. 1778. [See Richter, A. L. op. cit. p. 16.]

Steck, J. C. W. De interpolationibus Raymundi de Pennaforte. Leipsic. 1754.

Stintzing, R. Geschichte der populären Literatur des römisch-kanonischen Rechts in Deutschland am Ende...[des Mittelalters]. Leipsic. 1867.

Stubbs, W. Seventeen lectures on...mediaeval and modern history. 3rd edn. Oxford. 1900. [Lectures xiii, xiv. The history of the Canon Law in England.]

Stutz, U. Geschichte des kirchlichen Benefizialwesens von seinen Anfängen bis auf Alexander III. Berlin. 1895.

—— Kirchenrecht. In Holtzendorff. Encykl. d. Rechtswiss. 6th edn. Vol. ii. pp. 809–972. See Gen. Bibl. i.

Tanon, L. Étude de littérature canonique. Paris. 1889.

Tardif, A. Histoire des sources du droit canonique. Paris. 1887.

Vering, F. H. Lehrbuch d. kathol., orient., u. protest. Kirchenrechts. 3rd edn. Freiburg-im-Breisgau. 1893.

Villien, A. and Magnin, E. Dictionnaire de droit canonique. See Gen. Bibl. i.

Viollet, P. Histoire du droit civil français, accompagnée de notions de droit canonique. 3rd edn. pp. 33–91. See Gen. Bibl. v.

Voet, P. De usu juris civilis et canonici in Belgio Unito. Utrecht. 1657.

Werminghoff, A. Zu den bayrischen Synoden am Ausgang des achten Jahrhunderts. In Festschrift H. Brünner...dargebracht. Weimar. 1910. pp. 39–55. [For Germany.]

Wetzer, H. J. and Welte, B. Kirchenlexicon. 2nd edn. See Gen. Bibl. i. [Articles on Canon Law.]

CHAPTER XXII.

MEDIEVAL SCHOOLS TO *c.* 1300.

I. SPECIAL BIBLIOGRAPHIES.

Catholic Encyclopedia. Ed. Herbermann, C. G. and others. 15 vols. New York. 1907 ff. Vol. XIII. p. 562. Article: Schools.

Herzog-Hauck. Real-Encyklopädie. (*See Gen. Bibl.* I.) Vol. XVII (1906). p. 789. Article: Schule und Kirche.

Roger, M. L'Enseignement des lettres classiques d'Ausone à Alcuin. Paris. 1905. pp. ix–xviii.

Schmid, K. A. Geschichte der Erziehung. 5 vols. in 10. Stuttgart. 1884–1902. [Before Charlemagne, Vol. II, Abth. I, p. 94; under Charlemagne, *ib.* p. 145; tenth and eleventh centuries, *ib.* p. 232; in period of Crusades and Scholasticism, *ib.* p. 258; town schools, *ib.* p. 309.]

Watson, Foster. Encyclopedia and Dictionary of Education. 4 vols. London. 1922. [Many bibliographies: and see especially IV, col. 1791, for bibliography and article by E. E. Power on "The Education of Women in the Middle Ages."]

Wattenbach, W. Deutschlands Geschichtsquellen im Mittelalter. *See Gen. Bibl.* I.

II. ORIGINAL AUTHORITIES.

For texts of conciliar decrees about schools, for royal or episcopal capitularies or statutes dealing with them, and for many monastic rules, the chief collections of texts are given below. For other editions of monastic rules, with their references, or absence of references, to schools in monasteries, nunneries, or friaries, see the Bibliography of ch. XX, *supra,* and that of the chapter on the Friars in Vol. VI.

Acta Sanctorum Bollandiana. *See Gen. Bibl.* IV. [For references to education in lives contemporary, or nearly contemporary, with the saints: later lives, from this collection and the A.SS. ord. S. Benedicti (*see below*), have afforded pitfalls by supplying detail as to studies, schools, etc. from the writer's own day.]

Capitularia regum Francorum. MGH. Legum Sect. II. 2 vols. 1883, 97. [For Carolingian capitularies.]

Chrodegang of Metz. Regula Canonicorum. MPL. LXXXIX. col. 1057. [For chapter XLVI, descriptive of cathedral school.]

Hugh of St Victor. De institutione novitiorum. MPL. CLXXVI. col. 925.

Leach, A. F. Educational Charters and Documents. Cambridge. 1911.

Mabillon, J. and Achery, L. d'. Acta Sanctorum ord. S. Benedicti. *See Gen. Bibl.* IV.

Mansi. III–XXV. *See Gen. Bibl.* IV.

Migne. Patrologiae cursus completus. Series latina. *See Gen. Bibl.* IV.

Napier, A. S. The Old English version of the enlarged rule of Chrodegang together with the Latin original. An Old English version of the Capitula of Theodulf together with the Latin original. EETS. Orig. ser. No. 150. 1916.

Raban Maur. De clericorum institutione. MPL. CVII. col. 197; and Liber de oblatione puerorum. *Ib.* col. 419.

III. MODERN WORKS.

(*a*) GENERAL OUTLINES.

Joly, C. Traité historique des écoles épiscopales et ecclésiastiques. Paris. 1678.

Leach, A. F. Article in EncBr. 11th edn.: Schools.

Masius, H. Die Erziehung im Mittelalter. *In* Schmid, K. A. Geschichte der Erziehung. Vol. II, Abth. I (1892). pp. 94–333. *See above,* I. [Fuller and better than any other single treatment of the subject.]

Migne. Dictionnaire de Discipline Ecclésiastique. Paris. 1856. Articles: Écolâtre, École, Tonsure cléricale, etc.

Watson, Foster. Encyclopedia and Dictionary of Education. *See above*, I. [Several articles on medieval schools, of unequal value.]

(b) Monographs, etc.

Adamson, J. W. A short History of Education. Cambridge. 1920. [Deals in chapter I only with medieval schools. There are many short histories of education, which deal very slightly with the medieval period, and frequently repeat the errors of out-of-date authorities.]

Berlière, U. Les Écoles abbatiales au moyen-âge: Écoles externes. RBén. VI (1889). p. 499.

Clerval, A. Les Écoles de Chartres au moyen-âge. Paris. 1895.

Coulton, G. G. Five centuries of religion. Vol. I. *See Gen. Bibl.* V.

—— Monastic schools in the Middle Ages. (Medieval Studies. No. 10.) London. 1913.

—— Religious education before the Reformation. (No. 7 of Medieval Studies. First series. [Nos. 1–7.] 2nd edn.) London. 1915.

Denifle, H. Die Entstehung der Universitäten des Mittelalters bis 1400. *See Gen. Bibl.* V. [For schools which preceded universities in various towns, and "Hochschulen" not of university rank.]

Giesebrecht, W. v. De litterarum studiis apud Italos primis medii aevi saeculis. Berlin. 1845. [Useful.]

Haarhoff, T. Schools of Gaul. Oxford. 1920. [With reserve for Christian schools.]

Haddan, A. W. and Stubbs, W. Councils. *See Gen. Bibl.* IV.

Hauck, A. Kirchengeschichte Deutschlands. *See Gen. Bibl.* V. [For schools, II, pp. 116, 555 sqq.; III, p. 275; IV, p. 475; V, p. 237; for early German parishes, IV, pp. 20–24.]

Hepple, R. B. The Monastery School of Jarrow. *In* History. July, 1922. pp. 92–102.

Kaufmann, G. Rhetorenschulen und Klosterschulen oder heidnische und christliche Cultur in Gallien während des V und VI Jahrhunderts. *In* Historisches Taschenbuch. Ed. Raumer, F. v. Leipsic. 1869. p. 1.

Leach, A. F. The Schools of Medieval England. London. 1915. [To be read with reserve for pre-Conquest schools: *see* A. G. Little's review in EHR. XXX (1915). p. 525.]

—— Some results of research in the History of Education in England. British Academy Proceedings. Vol. VI. London. 1914.

Little, A. G. Educational organisation of the friars. TRHS. n.s. VIII (1894). p. 49.

—— Studies in English Franciscan History. Manchester. 1917. [For friary schools.]

Mabillon, J. Traité des études monastiques. 2 vols. Paris. 1692; answered by Rancé, abbot of La Trappe, *in*: Réponse au Traité des études monastiques, Paris, 1692; and supported by Mabillon *in*: Réflexions sur la réponse de M. l'abbé de la Trappe au Traité des études monastiques. Paris. 1692.

Maître, L. Les Écoles épiscopales et monastiques en Occident avant les universités (768–1180). 2nd edn. (Archives de la France monastique. XXVI.) Ligugé and Paris. 1924.

Mandonnet, P. La Crise scolaire au début du XIIIᵉ Siècle. RHE. January. 1914. pp. 34–50.

Maskell, W. Monumenta Ritualia Ecclesiae Anglicanae. 3 vols. London. 1846. [For useful dissertation on tonsure and minor orders in England, see vol. III, pp. lxxvii–cxx; for the "Modus faciendi tonsuras," *id.* p. 144; and the "Celebratio Ordinum," *id.* p. 154.]

Mullinger, J. B. The Schools of Charles the Great. London. 1877. Repr. New York. 1904 and 1911.

Ozanam, A. F. La Civilisation chrétienne chez les Francs. *In* Oeuvres complètes. IV (Études Germaniques, II). Paris. 1872.

—— Des Écoles et de l'instruction publique en Italie aux temps barbares. *In* Oeuvres complètes. II. Paris. 1873. p. 401.

Pitra, J. B. Histoire de Saint Léger. Paris. 1846. [For palace school of Franks: relies too much on non-contemporary lives.]

Poole, R. L. The Masters of the Schools at Paris and Chartres in John of Salisbury's Time. EHR. xxxv (1920). p. 321.

Power, E. E. Medieval English Nunneries, *c.* 1250–1535. Cambridge. 1922. Ch. vi.

Rashdall, H. The Universities of Europe in the Middle Ages. *See Gen. Bibl.* v. [For introduction, pre-university schools at Paris, etc.]

Roger, M. L'Enseignement des lettres classiques d'Ausone à Alcuin. Paris. 1905. [Very useful.]

Rösler, M. Erziehung in England vor der normannischen Eroberung. *In* Englische Studien. Vol. xlviii. Heilbronn and Leipsic. 1914. pp. 1–114.

Sandys, J. E. A History of Classical Scholarship. Vol. i. 3rd edn. Cambridge. 1920. [For some references to medieval schools.]

Vacandard, E. La Scola du Palais Mérovingien. RQH. lxi, p. 490; lxii, p. 546; lxxvi, p. 549.

Vict. Co. Hist. *See Gen. Bibl.* i. [For useful articles on schools of different counties, especially those of A. F. Leach.]

CHAPTER XXIII.

PHILOSOPHY IN THE MIDDLE AGES.

I. SOURCES.

Abelard. Opera. Ed. Cousin, V. Paris. Vol. I. 1849. Vol. II. 1859.
—— Ouvrages Inédits. Ed. Cousin, V. Paris. 1836.
Adelard of Bath. Tractatus de eodem et diverso. Ed. Willner, H. Münster. 1903.
Alanus de Insulis. Opera. MPL. ccx.
Albertus Magnus. Opera. Ed. Borgnet, A. 36 vols. Paris. 1890–9.
Alcuin. Opera. MPL. c–ci.
Alexander of Hales. Universae Theologiae Summa. Cologne. 1622.
Anselm. Opera. Ed. Gerberon. Paris. 1675. MPL. clviii–clix.
Aquinas, Thomas. Opera. 25 vols. Parma. 1852–73.
—— Opera omnia iussu impensaque Leonis XIII edita. Rome. 1882 ff.
Avencebrol (Ibn Gabirol). Fons Vitae. Ed. Baeumker, C. 3 vols. Münster. 1892–5.
Bacon, Roger. Opus Maius. Ed. Bridges, J. H. 3 vols. Oxford. 1897–1900.
—— Opera hactenus inedita. Ed. Steele, R. etc. Fasc. i–ix. Oxford. 1909–28.
—— Compendium Studii Theologiae. Ed. Rashdall, H. Aberdeen. 1911.
—— Opus Tertium (Part). Ed. Little, A. G. Aberdeen. 1912.
Bernard of Clairvaux. Opera. Ed. Mabillon, J. 2 vols. Paris. 1690. 4th edn. 2 vols. Paris. 1839.
Bonaventura. Opera omnia. 10 vols. Quaracchi. 1882–1902.
Chalcidius. Platonis Timaeus interprete Chalcidio. Ed. Wrobel, J. Leipsic. 1876.
Dionysius Areopagita. Opera. Ed. Corderius. 2 vols. Venice. 1755–6.
Duns Scotus. Opera. Ed. Wadding, L. 12 vols. Lyons. 1639.
Eriugena, Johannes Scottus. Opera. MPL. cxxii.
Gerbert (Pope Sylvester II). Opera. MPL. cxxxix.
—— Lettres de Gerbert. Ed. Havet, J. (Coll. textes.) Paris. 1889.
Gilbert de la Porrée. De Sex Principiis. MPL. clxxxiv.
Grosseteste, Robert. Opera. Ed. Baur, L. Münster. 1903.
Hugh of St Victor. Opera. MPL. clxxv–clxxvii.
John of Damascus. Opera. 2 vols. Ed. Lequien, M. Venice. 1748.
—— De Fide Orthodoxa. Transl. Salmond, S. Oxford. 1899.
John of Salisbury. Opera. MPL. cxcix.
—— Opera. Ed. Giles, J. A. 5 vols. Oxford. 1848.
—— Policraticus. Ed. Webb, C. C. J. 2 vols. Oxford. 1909.
Lanfranc. Opera. MPL. cl.
Maximus Confessor. Opera. Ed. Combefis, R. 2 vols. Paris. 1675.
Peter the Lombard. Libri Sententiarum iv. A critical text in the Quaracchi edition of Bonaventura, vols. i–iv. *See above.*
Porphyrius. Isagoge. Ed. Busse, A. (Commentaria in Aristotelem Graeca. Vol. iv.) Berlin. 1887.
Rabanus Maurus. Opera. MPL. cvii–cxii.
Raimundus Lullus (Ramón Lull). Opera. Ed. Salzinger, I. 10 vols. Mayence. 1721–42.
Richard of St Victor. Opera. MPL. cxciv.
William of Champeaux. Fragments in MPL. clxiii.
William of Conches. De Philosophia Mundi. MPL. clxxii.
Witelo. *See below,* II (*b*) under Baeumker, C.

II. MODERN WORKS.

(a) Histories and Works of General Reference.

Beiträge zur Geschichte der Philosophie des Mittelalters. Texte und Untersuchungen. Edited by Baeumker, C. and others. Münster. 1891 ff. [More than 20 vols. have appeared in this valuable series. In this bibliography all works published at Münster belong to it.]

Boer, T. J. de. Geschichte der Philosophie im Islam. Stuttgart. 1901.

Denifle, H. Die Entstehung der Universitäten des Mittelalters bis 1400. *See Gen. Bibl.* v.

—— and Chatelain, E. Chartularium Universitatis Parisiensis. Vol. i. Paris. 1889.

Franciscan Studies, British Society of. Aberdeen. 1908 ff.

Gilson, E. La philosophie au moyen âge. *See Gen. Bibl.* v.

Grabmann, M. Die Geschichte der scholastischen Methode. Freiburg. Vol. i. 1909. Vol. ii. 1911. [Gives the best account of unpublished sources. Vol. iii is expected.]

Hauréau, J. B. Histoire de la philosophie scolastique. 3 vols. Paris. 1872–80.

O'Leary, De L. Arabic Thought and its place in History. London and New York. 1922.

Picavet, F. Esquisse d'une histoire générale et comparée des philosophies médiévales. 2nd edn. Paris. 1907.

Prantl, K. Geschichte der Logik im Abendlande. Vol. ii. 2nd edn. Leipsic. 1885.

Rashdall, H. The Universities of Europe in the Middle Ages. *See Gen. Bibl.* v.

Stöckl, A. Geschichte der Philosophie des Mittelalters. 3 vols. Mayence. 1864–6.

Ueberweg, F. Grundriss der Geschichte der Philosophie. (*See Gen. Bibl.* v.) Part ii. 10th edn. by Baumgartner, M. Berlin. 1915.

Wulf, M. de. Histoire de la philosophie scolastique dans les Pays-Bas et la principauté de Liège. Louvain and Paris. 1895.

—— Histoire de la philosophie médiévale. 5th edn. 2 vols. Louvain. 1924–5. English transl. Messenger, E. C. London. 1926.

(b) Monographs, etc.

Asin y Palacios, M. Algazel, dogmatica, moral, ascetica. Saragossa. 1901.

Baeumker, C. Witelo, ein Philosoph und Naturforscher des xiii Jahrhunderts. Münster. 1908.

Bardenhewer, O. Die pseudo-Aristotelische Schrift über das reine Gute, bekannt unter dem Namen Liber de Causis. Freiburg. 1882.

Caird, E. The Evolution of Theology in the Greek Philosophers. 2 vols. Glasgow. 1904.

Carra de Vaux, A. Avicenne. Paris. 1900.

—— Gazali. Paris. 1902.

Charles, É. Roger Bacon. Paris and Bordeaux. 1861.

Endres, J. A. Über den Ursprung und die Entwickelung der scholastischen Lehrmethode. *In* Philosophisches Jahrbuch. 1889. pp. 52 sqq.

Gebhart, E. L'Italie mystique. Paris. 1899.

Ghellinck, J. de. Le Mouvement Théologique du xiie siècle. Paris. 1914.

Gilson, E. Le Thomisme. 2nd edn. Paris. 1923. English transl. Bullough, E. Cambridge. 1924.

—— La philosophie de Saint Bonaventure. Paris. 1924.

Grabmann, M. Forschungen über die lateinischen Aristotelesübersetzungen des xiii Jahrhunderts. Münster. 1916.

Guttmann, D. Die Scholastik des xiii Jahrhunderts in ihren Beziehungen zu Judenthum und zu jüdischen Litteratur. Breslau. 1902.

—— Moses ben Maimon. Leipsic. 1908.

Inge, W. R. The Philosophy of Plotinus. 2 vols. London. 1918.

Jourdain, A. Recherches critiques sur l'âge et l'origine des traductions latines d'Aristote. 2nd edn. Paris. 1843.

Keicher, O. Raymundus Lullus und seine Stellung zur arabischen Philosophie. Münster. 1909. [Contains the Declaratio Raymundi per modum dialogi.]

Little, A. G. *ed.* Roger Bacon. Essays...by various writers. Oxford. 1914.

Macdonald, D. B. Development of Muslim theology, jurisprudence, and constitutional theory. London. 1915.

Mandonnet, P. F. Siger de Brabant et l'averroïsme latin au xiiime siècle. 2nd edn. Louvain. 1911. [Part ii contains the works of Siger.]

Minges, P. P. Ist Duns Scotus Indeterminist? Münster. 1905.

—— Der angebliche exzessive Realismus des Duns Scotus. Münster. 1908.

Munk, S. Mélanges de philosophie juive et arabe. Paris. 1859.

—— Le Guide des Égarés de Maimonide. 3 vols. Paris. 1856–66.

Pelster, F. Kritische Studien zum Leben und zu den Schriften Alberts des Grossen. Freiburg. 1920.

Poole, R. L. Illustrations of the History of Medieval Thought and Learning. *See Gen. Bibl.* v.

Reiners, J. Der Nominalismus in der Frühscholastik. Münster. 1910.

Remusat, C. de. Abélard. Paris. 1845.

Renan, É. Averroës et l'averroïsme. 3rd edn. Paris. 1866.

Schaarschmidt, C. Joannes Saresberiensis. Leipsic. 1862.

Schneider, A. Beiträge zur Psychologie Alberts des Grossen. 2 pts. Münster. 1903, 6.

Sikes, J. G. Peter Abailard. Cambridge. 1932.

Steinschneider, M. Die europäischen Übersetzungen aus dem Arabischen bis Mitte des 17 Jahrhunderts. Vienna. 1904–5.

Switalski, B. W. Des Chalcidicius Commentar zu Plato's Timaeus. Münster. 1902.

Tocco, F. L' Eresia nel medio evo. Florence. 1884.

Whittaker, T. The Neo-Platonists. 2nd edn. Cambridge. 1918. [Gives the best account of Proclus.]

Willmann, O. Geschichte des Idealismus. 2nd edn. Brunswick. 1908.

Wittmann, M. Zur Stellung Avencebrols im Entwicklungsgang der arabischen Philosophie. Münster. 1905.

Wulf, M. de. Scholasticism old and new. London and Dublin. 1907.

CHRONOLOGICAL TABLE

OF

LEADING EVENTS MENTIONED IN THIS VOLUME.

1058–1061 Nicholas II Pope.
1059 Submission of the see of Milan to the Papacy.
 The Papal Election Decree (14 Apr.).
 The Treaty of Melfi (Aug.). Robert Guiscard recognised as Duke of
  Apulia.
 Hildebrand appointed Archdeacon of the Roman Church.
1060–1108 Philip I King of France.
1061–1073 Pope Alexander II.
1061 The capture of Messina by the Normans.
c. 1063 First appearance of the Rule of St Augustine.
1064–1069 Promulgation of the *Usatges* of Raymond Berengar I, the earliest
 known feudal code.
1065 End of the minority of Henry IV of Germany (29 Mar.).
 The Seljūq Turks enter Syria.
1066 (5 Jan.) Death of Edward the Confessor.
 (6 Jan.) Earl Harold elected King of England.
 (14 Oct.) Battle of Hastings. William the Conqueror King of England.
1068 Rebellion of Edwin and Morkere. Harrying of the North.
1070–1089 Lanfranc Archbishop of Canterbury.
1071 Capture of Bari by Robert Guiscard (Apr.). End of the Byzantine
 power in Italy.
 Battle of Manzikert (26 Aug.).
 The Seljūq Turks occupy Jerusalem.
 Completion of the Conquest of England by the Normans.
1073 (22 Apr.) Election of Pope Gregory VII (Hildebrand).
 (Aug.) Outbreak of the Saxon revolt.
1074 (18 Jan.) Henry IV grants a charter to the citizens of Worms.
1075 Pope Gregory VII enunciates papal powers in the *Dictatus Papae.*
 The first Investiture decree.
 (9 June) Henry IV defeats the Saxons on the Unstrut.
1076 (24 Jan.) Council of Worms.
 Excommunication of Henry IV by Gregory VII.
 (16 Oct.) Diet of Tribur.
 The Order of Grandmont founded by St Stephen.
1077 (Jan.) King Henry IV goes to Canossa.
 Diet of Forchheim. Election of Rudolf of Swabia as anti-king (13 Mar.).
 First English Cluniac monastery founded at Lewes.
1079 The appointment of Frederick, Count of Staufen, as Duke of Swabia
 founds the fortunes of the Hohenstaufen family.
1080 Final excommunication and deposition of Henry IV by the Pope.
 The Council of Brixen deposes the Pope and elects Guibert of Ravenna
  as anti-Pope Clement III (25 June).
 William the Conqueror refuses to do fealty to Pope Gregory VII.
 Pope Gregory VII reconciled to Robert Guiscard at Ceprano.
 Death of the anti-king Rudolf.
 Robert Guiscard begins attack on the Eastern Empire.
c. 1080–1130 General establishment of communes in the North Italian cities.
1081–1088 Count Herman of Salm as anti-king.
1084 Henry IV crowned at Rome by the anti-Pope Clement III.
 (May) Sack of Rome by the Normans.
 The Carthusian Order founded by Bruno of Cologne.
1085 (25 May) Death of Pope Gregory VII.
 (17 July) Death of Robert Guiscard.
1086 Compilation of Domesday Book.
1086–1087 Victor III Pope.
1087 Genoa and Pisa capture Mahdīyah in Barbary.
1087–1100 William Rufus King of England.
1088 End of the Saxon revolt. Climax of the power of Henry IV in Germany
1088–1096 Conquest of South Wales.
1088–1099 Urban II Pope.

1090–1097 Henry IV's expedition to Italy.
1091 Completion of the Norman conquest of Sicily.
1092 Annexation of Cumberland and Westmorland to England.
    (Nov.) Death of Malik Shāh.
1093 Revolt of Conrad in Italy.
1093–1109 Anselm Archbishop of Canterbury.
1095 (Mar.) Council of Piacenza.
    (27 Nov.) Council of Clermont. Pope Urban II proclaims the First Crusade.
1097 (19 June) Surrender of Nicaea.
    (1 July) Battle of Dorylaeum.
1098 (21 Mar.) The Cistercian Order founded by Robert of Molesme.
    (3 June) Fall of Antioch.
    (28 June) Defeat of Karbōghā's army near Antioch, the turning-point in the history of the First Crusade.
1099 (15 July) Capture of Jerusalem.
    (22 July) Godfrey of Bouillon chosen Prince of Jerusalem.
    (12 Aug.) Defeat of the Egyptians near Ascalon; the last achievement of the First Crusade.
1099–1118 Paschal II Pope.
1100–1135 Henry I King of England.
1100–1118 Baldwin I King of Jerusalem.
1100 (Sept.) Death of the anti-Pope Clement III.
    Coronation Charter of Henry I of England.
c. 1100 Irnerius, founder of the Glossators, teaches Roman Law at Bologna.
1103 Accession of Roger II, Count of Sicily.
1104 Revolt of Henry V against his father the Emperor Henry IV.
1106 (7 Aug.) Death of the Emperor Henry IV. End of the schism between the Empire and the Papacy.
    (28 Sept.) Battle of Tinchebrai.
    The Order of Fontevrault approved by Pope Paschal II.
1107 (23 May) Council of Troyes.
    (Aug.) Henry I of England reconciled to Anselm; English Investiture compromise.
1108–1137 Reign of Louis VI of France.
c. 1108 Practice of lay-investiture by the King of France lapses.
1110–1111 Henry V's expedition to Italy.
1111 Imprisonment of Pope Paschal II, and his concession of investiture; Henry V crowned Emperor.
1115 Revolt of Saxony.
    (25 June) Foundation of Clairvaux.
    (24 July) Death of the Countess Matilda of Tuscany.
1115–1153 St Bernard Abbot of Clairvaux.
1118–1119 Gelasius II Pope.
1118 (April) Excommunication of Henry V by Pope Gelasius II, and renewal of the schism between the Empire and the Papacy.
1118–1131 Baldwin II King of Jerusalem.
1119–1124 Calixtus II Pope.
1119 (23 Dec.) Pope Calixtus II confirms the *Carta Caritatis* of the Cistercian Order.
c. 1120 Foundation of the Orders of Templars and Hospitallers.
1120 Foundation of the Premonstratensian Order.
1121 Condemnation of Abelard at Soissons.
1122 (23 Sept.) The Concordat of Worms reconciles the Empire and the Papacy.
1123 First Lateran Council.
1124–1130 Honorius II Pope.
1125 (23 May) Death of the Emperor Henry V.
1125 (30 Aug.) Lothar of Supplinburg elected to the German kingship as Lothar III.

1127 (2 Mar.) Charles the Good, Count of Flanders, murdered at Bruges.
    Death of William, Duke of Apulia.
    Conversion of the Wends recommenced.
    (Dec.) Conrad of Hohenstaufen elected anti-king at Spires.
1128 (June) Marriage of the Empress Matilda to Geoffrey Plantagenet.
    (Aug.) Roger II of Sicily invested with the duchy of Apulia by Pope
        Honorius II.
1130 Disputed election of Innocent II and Anacletus II as Pope.
    Count Roger II crowned King of Sicily at Palermo (25 Dec.).
1131 The Gilbertine Order founded at Sempringham in Lincolnshire.
1131–1144 Fulk King of Jerusalem.
1133 (4 June) Lothar III crowned as Emperor at Rome by Pope Innocent II.
1135 (Mar.) The Diet of Bamberg ends the conflict between the Emperor
        Lothar III and the Hohenstaufen.
    Death of Henry I of England (1 Dec.). Succession of Stephen.
1136 Lothar III's second expedition to Italy.
1137 (4 Dec.) Death of the Emperor Lothar III.
1137–1180 Reign of Louis VII of France.
1138 (25 Jan.) Death of the anti-Pope Anacletus II.
    (3 Mar.) Conrad III elected King of Germany.
    (Aug.) Battle of the Standard near Northallerton.
1139 Second Lateran Council.
    Innocent II makes the Augustinian Rule compulsory on Canons Regular.
    Matilda lands in England. Outbreak of civil war.
    (22 July) Pope Innocent II defeated and captured by the Normans at
        the battle of the Garigliano.
1140 Condemnation of Abelard at Sens at the instance of St Bernard.
1141 (2 Feb.) Stephen taken prisoner at the battle of Lincoln.
    (3 Mar.) The Empress Matilda proclaimed Queen of England.
    Death of Hugh of St Victor.
c. 1141 Compilation of Gratian's *Decretum.*
1143 Communal rising at Rome.
    Foundation of the new city of Lübeck.
1143–1144 Celestine II Pope.
1144 (25 Dec.) The Muslims capture Edessa.
1144–1145 Lucius II Pope.
1144–1163 Baldwin III King of Jerusalem.
1145–1153 Eugenius III Pope.
1146 (31 Mar.) St Bernard preaches the Second Crusade at the assembly at
        Vézelay.
1147 Wendish massacre at Lübeck. The Wendish Crusade.
    Disasters to the Crusaders in Asia Minor.
1148 Matilda leaves England.
    (July) Defeat of the Crusaders before Damascus.
    Trial of Gilbert de la Porrée before the Pope at Rheims.
c. 1148 The *De Consideratione* of St Bernard.
1150 Henry becomes Duke of Normandy.
1151 (13 Jan.) Death of Suger, Abbot of St Denis.
    (7 Sept.) Death of Geoffrey Plantagenet. Henry of Normandy succeeds
        to Anjou and Maine.
1152 (15 Feb.) Death of Conrad III.
    (4 Mar.) Election of Frederick Barbarossa as King of Germany at
        Frankfort.
    (May) Marriage of Eleanor of Aquitaine to Henry of Anjou.
1153 (Mar.) Treaty of Constance between Frederick Barbarossa and Pope
        Eugenius III.
    Occupation of Bona. Norman dominion in Africa reaches its greatest
        extent.
    (Nov.) Treaty of Wallingford between Stephen and Henry of Anjou.
1154–1155 (Oct.) Frederick Barbarossa's first expedition to Italy.

1154 (25 Oct.) Death of Stephen of England.
1154–1166 William I King of Sicily.
1154–1159 Hadrian IV (Nicholas Breakspear) Pope.
1154–1189 Henry II King of England.
1155 Execution of Arnold of Brescia.
    (18 June) Frederick Barbarossa crowned Emperor at Rome by Pope Hadrian IV.
1156 (28 May) The Normans defeat the Byzantines at Brindisi.
    Treaty of Benevento between the Kingdom of Sicily and the Papacy.
    (17 Sept.) Diet of Ratisbon establishes the power of Henry the Lion and creates the duchy of Austria.
1157 (Oct.) Diet of Besançon.
1158 Peace between the Emperor Manuel and William I, King of Sicily.
    (July) Second expedition of Frederick Barbarossa to Italy.
    Surrender of Milan.
    Diet of Roncaglia.
1159 Revolt of Milan.
    (7 Sept.) Disputed election of Alexander III and Victor IV as Pope.
1160 (Jan.) Capture of Mahdīyah. End of the Norman dominion in Africa.
    (Feb.) Synod of Pavia. Frederick Barbarossa recognises the anti-Pope Victor IV.
1160–1162 Final subjection of the Wends by Henry the Lion.
1162 (Mar.) Capture and destruction of Milan by Frederick Barbarossa.
    Becket appointed Archbishop of Canterbury.
1163–1174 Amaury I King of Jerusalem.
1164 (Jan.) Constitutions of Clarendon.
    (Apr.) Death of the anti-Pope Victor IV.
    The Order of the Knights of Calatrava approved by Pope Alexander III.
c. 1164 Death of Peter the Lombard.
1165 (23 Nov.) Pope Alexander III enters Rome supported by Norman troops.
1166 Assize of Clarendon.
    The *Carta* of Henry II of England.
1166–1168 Frederick Barbarossa's fourth expedition to Italy.
1166–1189 William II King of Sicily.
1167 Beginnings of the Lombard League. Milan rebuilt.
    (24 July) Frederick Barbarossa begins the siege of Rome.
    (Aug.) The German army driven from Rome by pestilence.
1169 Conquest of Egypt for Nūr-ad-Dīn of Damascus.
1170 The Inquest of Sheriffs.
    (Aug.) Strongbow lands in Ireland.
    (29 Dec.) Murder of Becket in Canterbury Cathedral.
c. 1170 Rise of the Universities.
1171 Foundation of the Order of the Knights of Santiago.
1171–1172 Henry II visits Ireland, and receives general submission.
c. 1172 Writing of the *Roman de Rou*.
1173–1174 Rebellion in England.
1174–1177 Frederick Barbarossa's fifth expedition to Italy.
1174–1185 Baldwin IV King of Jerusalem.
1174–1193 Reign of Saladin.
1176 (29 May) Defeat of Frederick Barbarossa at Legnano.
    Treaty of Anagni between the Emperor and the Pope. End of the Papal schism.
    Assize of Northampton.
1177 (23 July) Treaty of Venice.
1179 (Mar.) Third Lateran Council.
    The Grand Assize (of Windsor).
1180 (13 Apr.) Diet of Gelnhausen. Partition of the Duchy of Saxony.
    (24 June) Diet of Ratisbon. Partition of the Duchy of Bavaria.
    Death of John of Salisbury.
1181 Henry II's Assize of Arms.

1181 Submission and exile of Henry the Lion.
1181–1185 Lucius III Pope.
1183 (June) The Peace of Constance.
1184 Diet of Mayence.
 (Sept.) Frederick Barbarossa's sixth journey to Italy.
1185 Failure of William II of Sicily's invasion of the Eastern Empire.
1185–1187 Urban III Pope.
1185–1186 Baldwin V King of Jerusalem.
1186 (27 Jan.) Marriage of Henry VI of Germany to Constance of Sicily.
1187 (4 July) Defeat of the Christians in Syria at Ḥiṭṭīn.
 (3 Oct.) Jerusalem taken by Saladin.
1187 (Oct.–Dec.) Gregory VIII Pope.
1187–1191 Clement III Pope.
1188 The Saladin Tithe.
1189 The Third Crusade.
 (3 Apr.) Peace of Strasbourg between Pope and Emperor.
 (May) Frederick Barbarossa goes on the Crusade.
 (6 July) Death of Henry II of England.
 (18 Nov.) Death of William II of Sicily.
1190 (Jan.) Tancred of Lecce crowned King of Sicily.
 (10 June) Death of the Emperor Frederick Barbarossa.
 Foundation of the Teutonic Order.
1191 (15 Apr.) Imperial coronation of Henry VI.
 Third Crusade. The Crusaders recover Acre (12 July).
 (7 Sept.) Richard Coeur-de-Lion defeats Saladin at Arsūf.
1191–1198 Celestine III Pope.
1192 (June) Concordat of Gravina.
 Truce with Saladin.
1193 (14 Feb.) Richard Coeur-de-Lion surrendered to the Emperor by Duke Leopold of Austria.
 (Feb.) Death of Saladin.
 The Knights of St John initiate the movement for a new Crusade.
1194 (3 Feb.) Release of Richard Coeur-de-Lion.
 (20 Feb.) Death of Tancred, King of Sicily.
 (Mar.) Reconciliation between the Emperor Henry VI and the Welfs at Tilleda.
 (25 Dec.) Henry VI crowned King of Sicily. End of the Norman dominion.
1195 (6 Aug.) Death of Henry the Lion.
1196 (Apr.) Diet of Würzburg. Henry VI attempts to make the German kingship hereditary.
 (Dec.) His son Frederick chosen king at Frankfort.
1197 (28 Sept.) Death of the Emperor Henry VI.
1198 (12 Dec.) Death of Averroes.
1204 Capture of Constantinople by the Fourth Crusade.
c. 1210 Latin translations from Aristotle's *Metaphysics* in the West.
1210 The study of certain books of Aristotle forbidden to the University ot Paris.
1215 Fourth Lateran Council.
1219 The Fifth Crusade.
 (5 Nov.) The Crusaders capture Damietta.
 St Francis of Assisi in Egypt.
1221 Restoration of Damietta to the Saracens.
c. 1225 Composition of the *Sachsenspiegel*.
1226 The Teutonic Order undertakes the conquest of the heathen Prussians.
1228 Frederick II recovers Jerusalem.
1234 Gregory IX's Collection of Decretals.
1244 (23 Aug.) The Khwārazmian Turks capture Jerusalem.
 (17 Oct.) Defeat of the Franks at Gaza.
1248–54 St Louis' First Crusade.

1250–1258 Bracton writes his *De Legibus et Consuetudinibus Angliae.*
1252 William of Rubruquis sent on a mission to the Great Khan.
1253 Pope Innocent IV forms the first Missionary Society since the conversion of the West.
1254 Alfonso of Castile issues the *Fuero Real.*
1256–1265 Compilation of the *Partidas.*
c. 1260 Death of Accursius the Glossator.
1268 Capture of Jaffa and Antioch by the Mamlūk Sultan Baibars.
1270 St Louis IX of France starts on his Second Crusade.
1273–1314 Missionary activity of Raymond Lull.
1274 (7 Mar.) Death of St Thomas Aquinas.
1277 Siger of Brabant condemned by the Inquisition of France.
1280 Death of Albert of Cologne (Albertus Magnus).
1286 Death of William of Moerbeke, the translator from the Greek.
1289 Capture of Tripolis by the Mamlūk Sultan Qalā'ūn.
1291 (18 May) Storm of Acre by the Mamlūks. End of the Kingdom of Jerusalem.
1294 Death of Roger Bacon.
1298 Boniface VIII's Decretals (the Sext).
1308 Death of Duns Scotus.
1335 Pope Benedict XII issues new constitutions for White monks (Cistercians).
1336 New constitutions issued for Black monks (Benedictines and Cluniacs).
1339 New constitutions issued for the Austin canons.
1357 Death of Bartolus of Sassoferrato, the Commentator.
1395 The Congregation (reformed Canons) of Windesheim founded in Germany.
1421 The reformed Benedictine congregation of Santa Giustina founded in Italy.
1430 William of Lyndwood finishes his Commentary on the provincial constitutions of the Archbishops of Canterbury.
1495 Erection of the Reichskammergericht and final Reception of Roman Law in Germany.

INDEX

Map 48

Germany
under Frederick Barbarossa
c. 1190

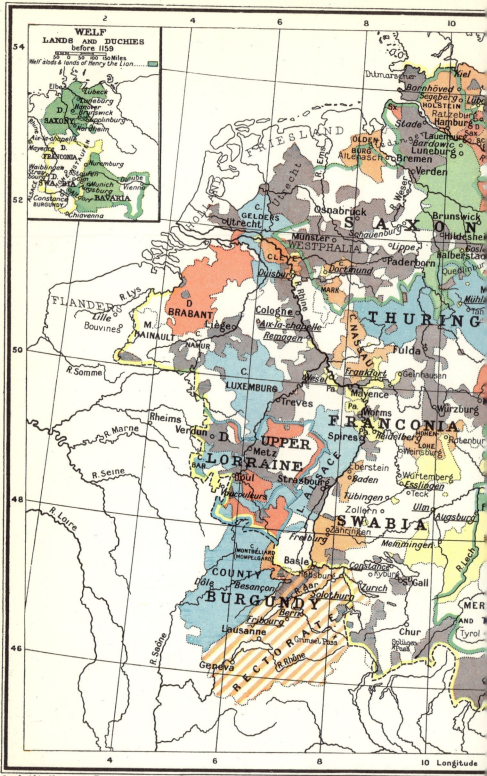

Cambridge University Press

Map 48

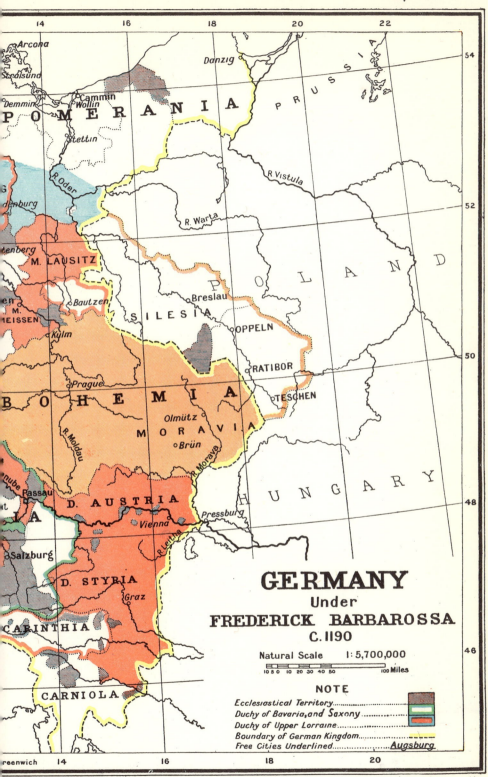

GERMANY
Under
FREDERICK BARBAROSSA
C. 1190

Natural Scale   1: 5,700,000

10 5 0   10   20 30 40 50   100 Miles

NOTE

Ecclesiastical Territory..........................

Duchy of Bavaria, and Saxony...................

Duchy of Upper Lorraine.......................

Boundary of German Kingdom....................

Free Cities Underlined..................*Augsburg*

Map 49

ITALY
UNDER THE HOHENSTAUFEN
Natural Scale 1:9,000,000
25   0   25   50   75   100 Miles
NOTE
Lands of the Countess Matilda
Papal lands under papal rule
Papal lands in the hands of secular rulers
I.F. Insula Fulcherii

N.B. The possessions of Matilda, here shown as
blocks of territory, were really scattered lands
and lordships lying within these regions

Longitude East 12 of Greenwich

Map 50

Duchy
of
Spoleto
Spoleto
R. Tronto
A B R U Z I Amiterno
Sabina
Marm
42
Rome Campania Molise CAPITANATA Fortore R. M. Gargano
Ponte Corvo Alife Loritello Civitate M. Sant'Angelo
Fondi TERRA DI LAVORO Lucera Andria Trani
Gaeta Troia Bisceglie Molfetta
Garigliano di Capua Ariano Canne Giovenazzo
Capua Benevento Corato Bari
Aversa Acerra Terra di Bari Conversano
Naples Avellino Melfi Gravina
Amalfi Salerno Principati Gravina Terra di Brindisi
M. Peloso Basilicata Oria Taranto Lecce
Montescaglioso di Taranto d'Otranto Otranto
40 Marsico Gallipoli 40
Scalea Val di Crati
S. Marco Crati
Bisignano
Ajello Cosenza
Martirano Jordana
Neocastro
Bivona Squillace
38 M. Leone Mileto Gerace 38
Lipari Is Bagnara
Messina Reggio
Trapani Monreale Palermo
Misilmeri Cefalù Etna Taormina
Ceramie di Demonio
Mazzara Val di Mazzara Troina
Caltabellotta Belice Castrogiovanni Catania
Girgenti Platani Val di Noto
Butera Syracuse
Noto
C. Passaro

SOUTHERN ITALY
AND SICILY
IN THE XIi CENTURY
Natural Scale 1:4,900,000
0 10 20 30 40 50   100 Mls.
Boundary of the
Norman Kingdom
Roads

Longitude East 16 of Greenwich

Cambridge University Press

W. & A. K. Johnston Ltd

Map 51
Latin States of Syria

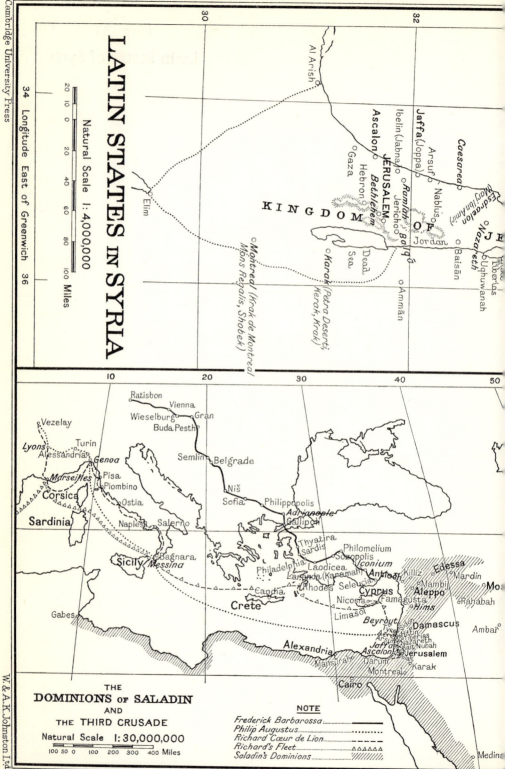

Cambridge University Press

LATIN STATES IN SYRIA

Natural Scale 1:4,000,000

20 10 0 20 40 60 80 100 Miles

Al Arish

Caesarea (Mersa ibn Hāmīl)

Ibelin (Jabna) Arsuf
Jaffa (Joppa) Nablus
Ascalon JERUSALEM Ramla Balqā
Jericho
Gaza Bethlehem Jordan
Hebron
Baisān Nazareth
Tiberias
Ughuwanah

KINGDOM OF JE

Dead Sea Amman

Elim

Montreal (Ḥrak de Montreal, Mōns Reyalis, Shobek)

Karak (Petra Deserti, Kerak, Krak)

30
32

Tiberias

Ratisbon
Vienna
Wieselburg Gran
Buda Pesth

Vezelay
Lyons
Turin
Alessandria Genoa
Marseilles Pisa
Piombino
Corsica Ostia
Sardinia Naples Salerno

Semlin Belgrade

Niš
Sofia
Philippopolis
Adrianople
Gallipoli

Bagnara
Sicily Messina
Thyatira
Sardis
Philomelium
Sozopolis Iconium
Philadelphia Laodicea
Larynda (Karaman) Antioch Killiz
Seleucia Edessa
Mambij Mardin
Candia Rhodes Cyprus Aleppo Mo
Nicosia Famagusta Rahabah
Limasol Hims

Crete
Beyrout Damascus
Tyre Ambar
Acre Hittin
Arsuf Tiberias
Nazareth
Jaffa Beit Nubah
Ascalon Jerusalem
Gabes
Darum Karak
Alexandria Montreal
Mansurah
Cairo

Medina

THE
DOMINIONS OF SALADIN
AND
THE THIRD CRUSADE

Natural Scale 1:30,000,000

100 50 0 100 200 300 400 Miles

<u>NOTE</u>

Frederick Barbarossa ....
Philip Augustus ....
Richard Cœur de Lion ....
Richard's Fleet ....△△△△△
Saladin's Dominions ....

10   20   30   40   50

W. & A. K. Johnston Ltd.

Map 51

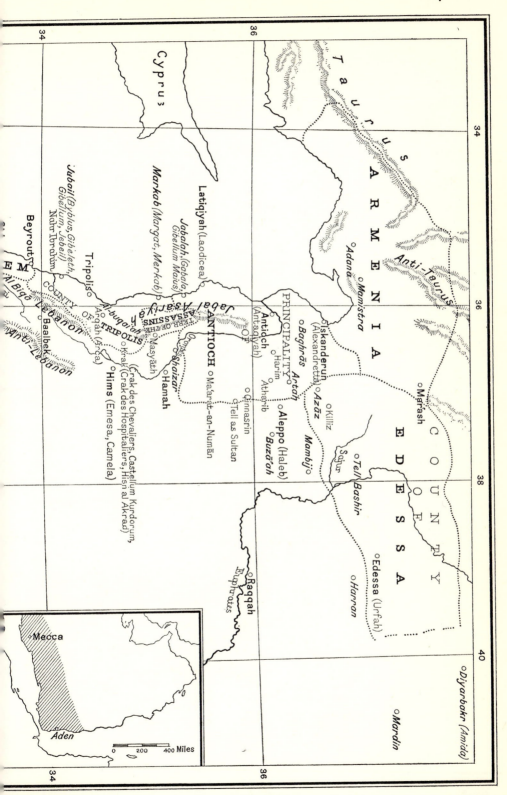

Cyprus

Taurus

A R M E N I A

Anti-Taurus

°*Adana*

°*Mamistra*

°*Marash*

C O U N T Y

°*Killiz*

°*Tell Bashir*

°*Sajur*

O F

E D E S S A

°*Harran*

°*Edessa* (Urfah)

°*Mardin*

°*Diyarbakr* (Amida)

°*Euphrates*

°*Raqqah*

Latiqiyah (Laodicea)

Jabalah (Gabala,
Gibellum Maius)

Markab (Margat, Merkab)

Jabal Aṣariyah

TERRA OF THE
ASSASSINS

°*Abugabaiš*

°*Masyāth*

°Slaiza

°*Hamah*

ANTIOCH

Antioch
(Antaqiyah)

°Harim

°Athārib

°*Buzā'ah*

°*Aleppo* (Haleb)

°*Mambij*

°*Baghrās Artah*

°*Azāz*

PRINCIPALITY

Iskanderun
(Alexandretta)

°Cinnasrin

°Tell as Sultan

°Ma'arat-an-Numān

Tripoliso

°Arqah (Arca)

TRIPOLIS

°Krak (Crak des Hospitaliers; Hisn al Akrad)

(Crak des Chevaliers, Castellum Kurdorum,
Crak des Hospitaliers, Hisn al Akrad)

COUNTY

Jubail (Byblus, Gibeleth,
Gibellum, Jebeil)
Nahr Ibrahim

Beyrout

E M

Al Biqā' Lebanon

Anti Lebanon

°Baalbek

°*Hims* (Emesa, Camela)

0   200   400 Miles

°*Mecca*

Aden

34

36

36

38

40

34

36

34

36

NORTHERN ITALY

IN THE

HOHENSTAUFEN PERIOD

Natural Scale 1 : 2,500,000

10 5 0   10   20   30   40   50 Miles

NOTE

Lombard League } At the truce of Venice 1177.
Imperialists

Districts mainly under feudal control
Roads

Map 52

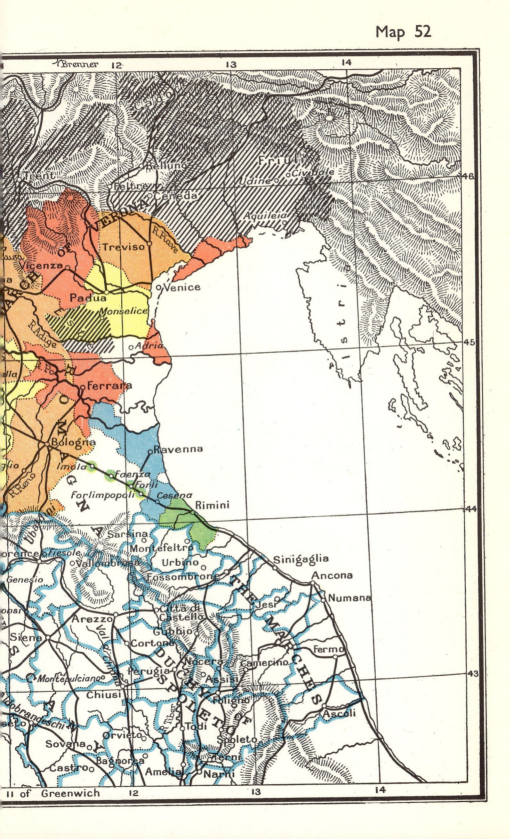

Friuli

Trent

Belluno

Feltre

Udine

Civdale

Ceneda

Aquileia

46

VERONA

R.Piave

Treviso

Vicenza

MARCH OF

Venice

Padua

Monselice

R.Adige

Istria

Adria

45

Ferrara

R.Po

ROMAGNA

Bologna

Ravenna

Imola

Faenza

Forli

Forlimpopoli

Cesena

Rimini

44

Sarsina

Montefeltro

orence

Fiesole

Vallombrosa

Urbino

Sinigaglia

Fossombrone

Ancona

Genesio

Arezzo

Città di Castello

Jesi

Numana

Siena

Gubbio

THE MARCHES

Cortona

Montepulciano

DUCHY

Nocera

Camerino

Fermo

Chiusi

Perugia

Assisi

43

OF

Foligno

SPOLETO

Ascoli

Orvieto

Todi

R.Tiber

Sovana

Spoleto

Terni

Bagnorea

Castro

Amelia

Narni

Map 53

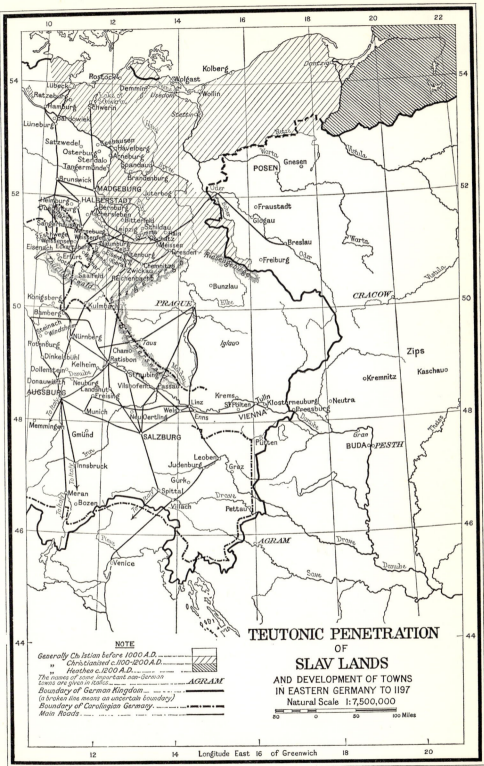

TEUTONIC PENETRATION
OF
SLAV LANDS
AND DEVELOPMENT OF TOWNS
IN EASTERN GERMANY TO 1197
Natural Scale 1:7,500,000

NOTE

Generally Christian before 1000 A.D.
„ Christianised c.1100-1200 A.D.
„ Heathen c.1200 A.D.
The names of some important non-German
towns are given in italics.   AGRAM
Boundary of German Kingdom
(a broken line means an uncertain boundary)
Boundary of Carolingian Germany.
Main Roads

50   0   50   100 Miles

Map 54

England and Normandy
circa A.D. 1070

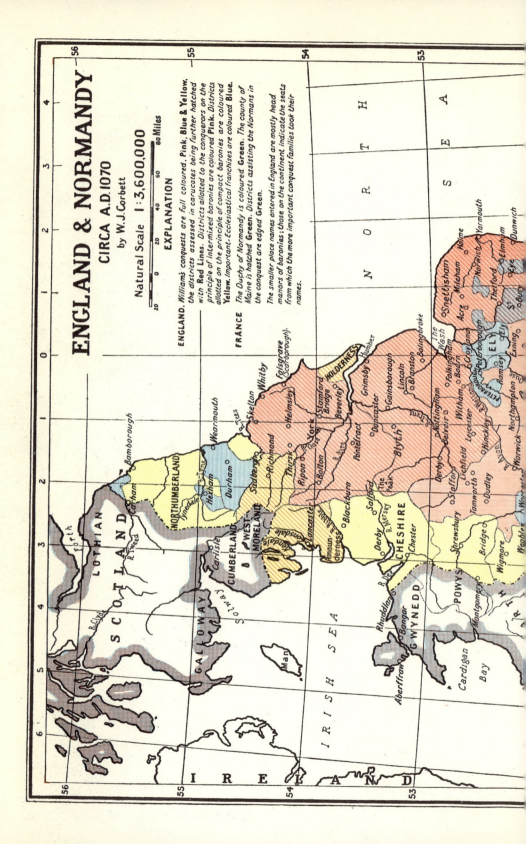

ENGLAND & NORMANDY

CIRCA A.D. 1070

by W. J. Corbett

Natural Scale 1:3,600,000

20 0 20 40 60 80 Miles

EXPLANATION

ENGLAND. William's conquests are full coloured. Pink, Blue & Yellow, the districts assessed in carucates being further hatched with Red Lines. Districts allotted to the conquerors on the principle of intermixed baronies are coloured Pink. Districts allotted on the principle of compact baronies are coloured Yellow. Important Ecclesiastical franchises are coloured Blue.

FRANCE The Duchy of Normandy is coloured Green. The county of Maine is hatched Green. Districts assisting the Normans in the conquest are edged Green.

The smaller place names entered in England are mostly head manors of baronies; those on the continent indicate the seats from which the more important conquest families took their names.

Map 54

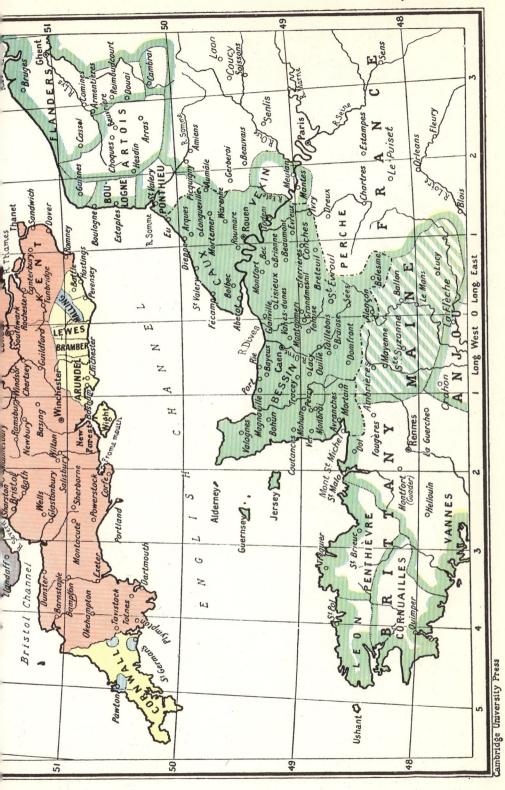

Map 55

The Dominions of Henry II,

Plantagenet

Map 55

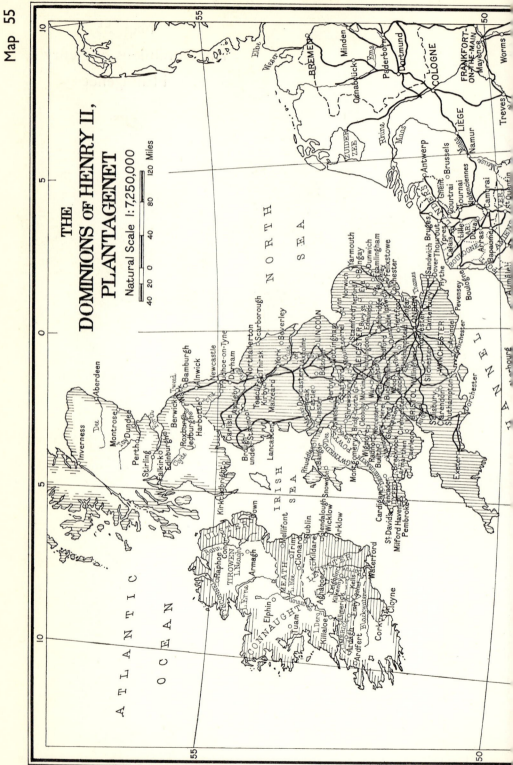

THE
DOMINIONS of HENRY II, PLANTAGENET

Natural Scale 1:7,250,000

40 20 0 40 80 120 Miles

ATLANTIC OCEAN

NORTH SEA

IRISH SEA

Inverness

Aberdeen
Montrose
Dundee
Perth
Stirling
Edinburgh
Falkirk
Roxburgh
Jedburgh
Harbottle
Berwick
Bamburgh
Alnwick
Newcastle
Tynemouth-on-Tyne
Durham
Northallerton
Scarborough
Thirsk
Beverley
York
Appleby
Kirby
Maizeand
Tepcliffe
Peak
Castleton
Carlisle
Brough under St. Amon
Lancaster
Chester
Rhuddlan
Bangor
Snowdon
Kirkcudbright

CONNAUGHT
Raphoe
Conu
L.Neagh
Armagh
TIROWEN
L.Erne
Elphin
Tuam
Killaloe
MEATH
Melifont
Trim
Kells
Dublin
LEINSTER
Kildare
Glendalough
Wicklow
Arklow
Waterford
Cork
Cloyne
Down
Mellifont

St Davids
Cardigan
Pembroke
Milford Haven
Exeter

LINCOLN
Lynn
Norwich
Yarmouth
Bungay
Eye
Dunwich
Framlingham
Ipswich
Felixstowe
Colchester
Harwich
LEICESTER
Stamford
Bury St Edmunds
Derby
Nottingham
Chester
Shrewsbury
Worcester
Gloucester
Hereford
BRISTOL
Salisbury
Clarendon
Southampton
WINCHESTER
Chichester
Arundel
Pevensey
Hastings
Canterbury
Sandwich
Dover
Hythe
Boulogne

NETHERLANDS
Bruges
Ghent
Brussels
Antwerp
Courtrai
Tournai
Valenciennes
Cambrai
Arras
Calais
BOULOGNE
Amiens

Elbe
Weser
BREMEN
Minden
Osnabrück
Ems
Paderborn
Dortmund
COLOGNE
Rhine
LIÈGE
Namur
FRANKFORT-ON-THE-MAIN
Mayence
Worms
Treves
ZUIDER ZEE

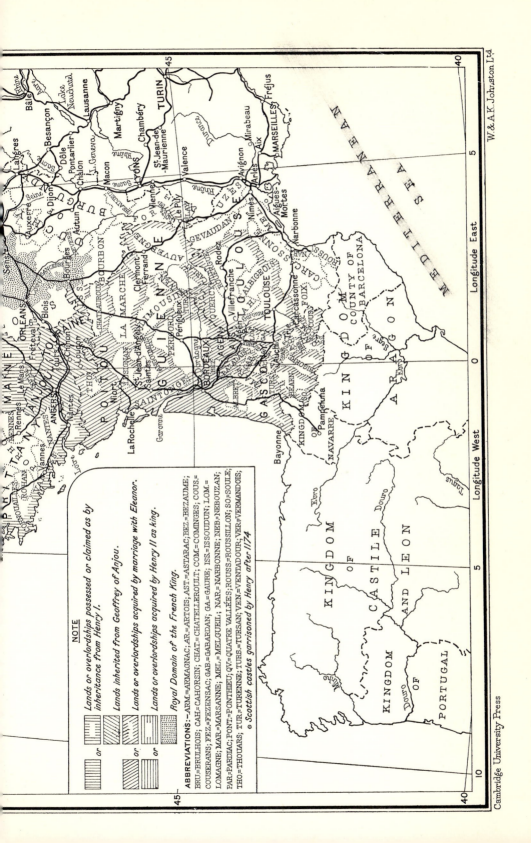

NOTE

Lands or overlordships possessed or claimed as by inheritance from Henry I.

Lands inherited from Geoffrey of Anjou.

Lands or overlordships acquired by marriage with Eleanor.

Lands or overlordships acquired by Henry II as king.

Royal Domain of the French King.

ABBREVIATIONS:—ARM=ARMAGNAC; AR=ARTOIS; AST=ASTARAC; BEZ=BEZAUME; BRU=BRULHOIS; CAH=CAHORSIN; CHAT=CHATELLEROULT; COM=COMINGES; COUS.=COUSERANS; FEZ=FEZENSAC; GAB=GABARDAN; GA=GAURE; ISS=ISSOUDUN; LOM=LOMAGNE; MAR=MARSANNE; MEL=MELGUEIL; NAR=NARBONNE; NEB=NEBOUZAN; PAR=PARDIAC; PONT=PONTHIEU; QV=QUATRE VALLÉES; ROUSS=ROUSSILLON; SO=SOULE; THO=THOUARS; TUR=TURENNE; TURS.=TURSAN; VEN=VENTADOUR; VER=VERMANDOIS; ⊙ *Scottish castles garrisoned by Henry after 1174*

Cambridge University Press

W.&A.K.Johnston Ltd